10	11	12	13	14	15	16	17	18
							1 H 1.008	2 He 4.003
			5 B 10.81	6 C 12.01	7 N 14.01	8 O 16.00	9 F 19.00	10 Ne 20.18
			13 Al 26.98	14 Si 28.09	15 P 30.97	16 S 32.07	17 Cl 35.45	18 Ar 39.95
28 Ni 58.69	29 Cu 63.55	30 Zn 65.39	31 Ga 69.72	32 Ge 72.61	33 As 74.92	34 Se 78.96	35 Br 79.90	36 Kr 83.80
46 Pd 106.4	47 Ag 107.9	48 Cd 112.4	49 In 114.8	50 Sn 118.7	51 Sb 121.8	52 Te 127.6	53 I 126.9	54 Xe 131.3
78 Pt 195.1	79 Au 197.0	80 Hg 200.6	81 Tl 204.4	82 Pb 207.2	83 Bi 209.0	84 Po (209.0)	85 At (210.0)	86 Rn (222.0)
110 Ds (271)	111 Rg (272)	112 Uub (285)	113 Uut (284)	114 Uuq (289)	115 Uup (288)			

62 Sm 150.4	63 Eu 152.0	64 Gd 157.2	65 Tb 158.9	66 Dy 162.5	67 Ho 164.9	68 Er 167.3	69 Tm 168.9	70 Yb 173.0
94 Pu (244.1)	95 Am (243.1)	96 Cm (247.1)	97 Bk (247.1)	98 Cf (251.1)	99 Es (252.1)	100 Fm (257.1)	101 Md (258.1)	102 No (259.1)

SIXTH EDITION

Chemistry

Principles and Reactions

William L. Masterton
University of Connecticut

Cecile N. Hurley
University of Connecticut

BROOKS/COLE
CENGAGE Learning™

Australia • Brazil • Japan • Korea • Mexico • Singapore • Spain • United Kingdom • United States

BROOKS/COLE
CENGAGE Learning™

Chemistry: Principles and Reactions, Sixth Edition
William L. Masterton and Cecile N. Hurley

Senior Acquisitions Editor: Lisa Lockwood
Senior Development Editor: Peter McGahey
Assistant Editor: Ashley Summers
Editorial Assistant: Liz Woods
Technology Project Manager: Lisa Weber
Marketing Manager: Amee Mosley
Marketing Assistant: Elizabeth Wong
Marketing Communications Manager: Talia Wise
Project Manager, Editorial Production: Teresa L. Trego
Creative Director: Rob Hugel
Art Director: John Walker
Print Buyer: Rebecca Cross
Permissions Editor: Mardell Glinski-Schultz
Production Service: Graphic World Publishing Services
Text Designer: Carolyn Deacy
Photo Researcher: Marcy Lunetta
Copy Editor: Graphic World Publishing Services
Illustrator: 2064 Design/Greg Gambino
OWL Producers: Stephen Battisti, Cindy Stein, David Hart (Center for Educational Software Development, University of Massachusetts, Amherst)
Cover Designer: Real Time Design/Dare Porter
Cover Image: © 2007 Chris Robinson, Department of Art/NanoCenter, University of South Carolina
Compositor: Graphic World Inc.

Library of Congress Control Number: 2007938694

ISBN-13: 978-0-495-12671-3

ISBN-10: 0-495-12671-3

Brooks/Cole Cengage Learning
10 Davis Drive
Belmont, CA 94002-3098
USA

Cengage Learning products are represented in Canada by Nelson Education, Ltd.

Printed in Canada
1 2 3 4 5 6 7 12 11 10 09 08

Dedication

To the memory of William Lewis Masterton

Teacher without peer
Expositor without parallel
Friend and mentor

You are missed.

Brief Contents

Contents

Charles D. Winters

S. Ruven Smith

George Semple

11 RATE OF REACTION 284

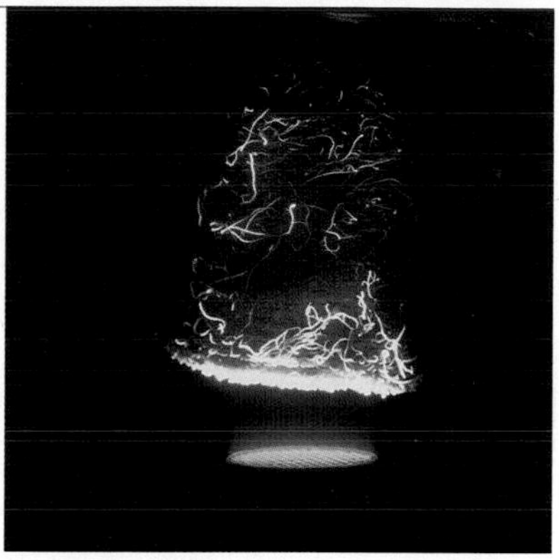

12 GASEOUS CHEMICAL EQUILIBRIUM 322

Charles D. Winters

Charles D. Winters

NASA

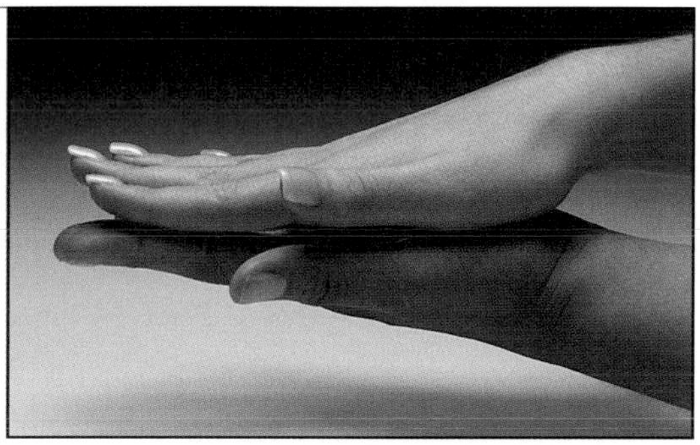

Charles D. Winters

Appendices

Preface

The Preface of a textbook is one of the most difficult sections to write. In the past five editions, Bill Masterton and I would go for a long lunch and talk about the items we wished to include in the Preface. Lunch (always a cheeseburger and fries for Bill, unless there was mackerel and fried okra on the menu) always ended with Bill saying, "You write your outline of the Preface, and I will flesh it out." For this edition, there was no long lunch, no one to talk to, and no one to flesh out my outline. But I will try to flesh out the ideas that Bill and I talked about in one long phone call. These are the questions we tried to answer.

Why Do We Continue to Write a Short Book?

With rising tuition costs, depleted forests, and students' aching backs, the answer is obvious. The cartoon on this page illustrates one of our reasons. We remained steadfast in our belief that it should be possible to cover a text completely (or at least *almost* completely) in a two-semester course. The students justifiably ask why they have to pay for 1000-page books with "stuff" that is never covered in the course. We still do not have a good reason, so a 600-plus-page book was the aim for the sixth edition.

With textbook loads ever increasing, many students are finding alternatives to backpacks.

How Will We Write This Edition of a Short Book?

After we bemoaned the common perception that a short book is a low-level book, we reiterated our commitment to the principle that in treating general concepts in a concise way we would not sacrifice depth, rigor, or clarity. Our criteria for including material continue to be its importance and relevance to the student, not its difficulty. To achieve this, we decided on a three-pronged approach.

1. Eliminate repetition and duplication wherever possible. Like its earlier editions, this text uses:
   - Only one method for balancing redox reactions, the half-equation method introduced in Chapter 4.
   - Only one way of working gas-law problems, using the ideal gas law in all cases (Chapter 5).
   - Only one way of calculating ΔH (Chapter 8), using enthalpies of formation.
   - Only one equilibrium constant for gas-phase reactions (Chapter 12), the thermodynamic constant K, often referred to as K_p. This simplifies not only the treatment of gaseous equilibrium, but also the discussion of reaction spontaneity (Chapter 17) and electrochemistry (Chapter 18).
2. Relegate to the appendices or "Chemistry: Beyond the Classroom" essays topics ordinarily covered in texts of 1000 or more pages. Items in this category include:
   - MO (molecular orbital) theory (Appendix 5). Our experience has been (and continues to be) that although this approach is important to chemical bonding, most general chemistry students do not understand it but only memorize the principles discussed in the classroom.

- Nomenclature of complex ions and organic compounds. We believe that this material is of little value in a beginning course. The students promptly forget how to name a complex ion, because they have little chance to use the rules. The naming of organic compounds seems better left to a course in organic chemistry.
- Qualitative analysis. This is summarized in a couple of pages in an essay in Chapter 16 in the "Chemistry: Beyond the Classroom" section. An extended discussion of the qual scheme and the chemistry behind it belongs in a lab manual, not a textbook.
- Biochemistry. This material is traditionally covered in the last chapter of general chemistry texts. While we have included several biochemical topics in the text (among them a discussion of heme in Chapter 15 and carotenoids in Chapter 6), we do not see the value of an entire chapter on biochemistry. Interesting as this material is, it requires a background in organic chemistry that first-year students lack.

3. Avoid superfluous asides, applications to the real-world, or stories about scientists in the exposition of principles. We have incorporated many applications in the context of problems and some of the exposition of general principles. In general, however, we have stayed with a bare-bones approach. Students can easily be distracted by such interesting tidbits while they are striving hard to understand the concepts. We have put some of our favorite real-world applications and personal stories about scientists in separate sections, "Chemistry: Beyond the Classroom" and "Chemistry: The Human Side." Our students tell us that they read these two sections first and that these sections are the parts of the book that they "really enjoy the most." (Talk about faint praise!) They do admit to enjoying the marginal notes too.

How Will the Sixth Edition Differ from the Fifth Edition?

Although the principles of general chemistry do not change, there are always many ways to make a text better, more user-friendly, more interesting. It was our hope that if a student compared the fifth edition to the sixth edition, he or she would say, "The revision was worth having. It let me understand better." (We doubted that students would be that forthcoming—but we hoped anyway!) The changes that we decided to make in pursuit of that hope are:

- Upgrading the in-text Examples. About 30% have been revised, to raise the rigor of the quantitative examples and deepen the conceptual understanding of the principles. Many students have admitted (because of the proverbial lack of time) that instead of solving problems at the end of the chapter, they did the Examples (because they had the solution right there to look at). They complained that some of those Examples were too simple to help them prepare for homework and exams.
- Adding new end-of-chapter questions and problems. There are almost 200 new end-of-chapter questions and problems, many of them conceptual.
- Continuing the process of updating static art to new balloon-caption art in which explanations previously presented in the text narrative or figure captions move into the art itself. We felt that today's students are more likely to see and understand it with such placement.
- Updating and modernizing photographs and molecular models.
- Revising the style for presenting graphs to make them clearer.
- Inviting contributing authors to write essays about their current or recent research. There are four new essays for the end-of-chapter sections called "Chemistry: Beyond the Classroom."
- Fully integrating, for the first time, *Chemistry: Principles and Reactions* with the OWL web-based chemistry learning system and assessment tool. Select end-of-chapter Questions and Problems from this edition are available in OWL with chemical and numeric parameterization, to provide students with a mastery learning environment and online graded homework. These problems are correlated to the Key Concepts summary list at the end of each chapter. OWL is described in more detail later in this Preface.

SUPPORT MATERIALS

A full complement of supporting materials to assist the instructor and student are available for use with this text.

For the Instructor

Supporting instructors' materials are available to qualified adopters. Please consult your local Cengage Learning, Brooks/Cole representative for details. Visit **academic.cengage.com/chemistry/masterton** to:

- See samples of materials.
- Request a desk copy.
- Locate your local representative.
- Download electronic files of the *Instructor's Manual,* the *Test Bank,* and other helpful materials for instructors and students.

Instructor's Manual by Cecile N. Hurley, University of Connecticut
ISBN-10: 0-495-38768-1; ISBN-13: 978-0-495-38768-8

This manual includes lecture outlines, lists of demonstrations for each chapter, and worked-out solutions for all of end-of-chapter Questions and Problems that do not have answers in Appendix 6 of the text (and the *Student Solutions Manual*). Electronic files of the *Instructor's Manual* are available on the PowerLecture CD-ROM and on the instructors' companion site at **academic.cengage.com/chemistry/masterton.**

Test Bank
ISBN-10: 0-495-38769-X; ISBN-13: 978-0-495-38769-5

This question bank features more than 1000 multiple-choice, five-part questions. Electronic files of the *Test Bank* are available on the PowerLecture CD-ROM. BlackBoard and WebCT formatted files for the *Test Bank* are also available on the instructor's companion site at **academic.cengage.com/chemistry/masterton.**

OWL: Online Web-based Learning by Roberta Day and Beatrice Botch of the University of Massachusetts, Amherst, and William Vining of the State University of New York at Oneonta

Used by more than 300 institutions and proven reliable for tens of thousands of students, OWL offers an online homework and quizzing system with unsurpassed ease of use, reliability, and dedicated training and service. OWL makes homework management a breeze and helps students improve their problem-solving skills and visualize concepts by providing instant analysis and feedback on a variety of homework problems, including tutors, simulations, and chemically and/or numerically parameterized short-answer questions. OWL is the only system specifically designed to support mastery learning, where students work as long as they need to master each chemical concept and skill. To view an OWL demo and for more information, visit **academic.cengage.com/owl** or contact your Brooks/Cole representative.

New to OWL!

For the sixth edition, approximately 20 end-of-chapter questions (marked in the text with ■) can be assigned in OWL.

The **e-book in OWL** is a complete electronic version of the text, fully assignable and linked to OWL homework. This exclusive option is available to students with instructor permission. Instructors can consult their Brooks/Cole representative to determine the best option: access to the e-book can be bundled with the text and/or ordered as a text replacement. Please consult your Brooks/Cole representative for details.

Learning Resources allow students to quickly access valuable help to master each homework question with integrated e-book readings, tutors, simulations, and exercises that accompany each question. Learning Resources are configurable by instructors.

More new OWL features:

- New student Learning Resources and Toolbars.
- New Answer Input tool for easy subscript and superscript formatting.
- Enhanced reports that give instant snapshots of your class progress.
- Easier grading access for quick report downloads.
- New Survey and Authoring features for creating your own content.
- Enhanced security to help you comply with FERPA regulations.

A fee-based access code is required for OWL. OWL is available only to North American adopters.

Instructor's PowerLecture CD-ROM with ExamView®
ISBN-10: 0-495-38770-3; ISBN-13: 978-0-495-38770-1
PowerLecture is a one-stop digital library and presentation tool that includes:

- Prepared Microsoft® PowerPoint® lecture slides covering all key points from the text in a convenient format that you can enhance with your own materials or with additional interactive video and animations on the CD-ROM for personalized, media-enhanced lectures.
- Image libraries in PowerPoint and in JPEG format that contain electronic files for all text art, most photographs, and all numbered tables in the text. These files can be used to print transparencies or to customize your lectures.
- Electronic files for the *Instructor's Manual, Test Bank,* and *Cooperative Learning Worksheets.*
- Sample chapters from the *Student Solutions Manual* and *Study Guide.*
- ExamView® testing software, with all the test items from the printed *Test Bank* in electronic format, that enables you to create customized tests of up to 250 items in print or online.

Cooperative Learning Worksheets by Cecile N. Hurley, University of Connecticut
Available for download from the Instructor's Companion Site and on the PowerLecture CD-ROM.

This collection of worksheets (about three per chapter) is for students to use in collaborative groups. Designed to stimulate group activity and discussion, the questions provided on each worksheet are equally conceptually and quantitatively oriented. Also included are instructions for use, information on how to guide student discussion, and supporting data on the success of cooperative learning at the University of Connecticut.

For the Student

Visit the student companion website at **academic.cengage.com/chemistry/masterton** to see sample materials of selected student supplements. You can purchase any Brooks/Cole product at your local college bookstore or at our preferred online store **www.ichapters.com.**

Student Solutions Manual by Richard L. Nafshun, Oregon State University
ISBN-10: 0-495-38767-3; ISBN-13: 978-0-495-38767-1
This manual includes complete solutions to all end-of-chapter Questions and Problems answered in Appendix 6, including the Challenge Problems. The author includes references to textbook sections and tables to help guide students to use the problem-solving techniques employed by the authors. Selected solutions from each chapter, identified by the WEB icon, are on the student companion site at **academic.cengage.com/chemistry/masterton.**

Study Guide/Workbook by Cecile N. Hurley, University of Connecticut
ISBN-10: 0-495-38766-5; ISBN-13: 978-0-495-38766-4
This study aid contains additional worked examples and problem-solving techniques that complement and expand on those presented in the textbook. Each chapter also includes

an outline with fill-in-the-blanks for students to complete, exercises, and self-tests to help gauge mastery of the chapter. Sample chapters are available for review on the student companion website at **academic.cengage.com/chemistry/masterton.**

CengageNOW

CengageNOW's online self-assessment tools give you the choices and resources you need to study smarter. You can explore a variety of tutorials, exercises, and simulations (cross-referenced throughout the text by margin annotations) or take chapter-specific Pre-Tests and get a Personalized Study plan that directs you to specific interactive materials that can help you master areas where you need additional work. Access to CengageNOW for two semesters may be included with your new textbook, or can be purchased at **www.ichapters.com** using ISBN 0-495-39431-9.

Go Chemistry for General Chemistry

27-Module Set ISBN-10: 0-495-38228-0; ISBN-13: 978-0-495-38228-7

These new mini video lectures, playable on video iPods, iPhones, and MP3 players as well as on iTunes, include animations and problems for a quick summary of key general chemistry concepts. e-Flashcards in selected modules briefly introduce a key concept and then test student understanding of the basics with a series of questions. Modules are also available separately. Go Chemistry is included in CengageNOW. To purchase, enter ISBN 0-495-38228-0 at **www.ichapters.com.**

OWL for General Chemistry

See description of this online homework and quizzing system under Instructor's Support Materials.

Essential Algebra for Chemistry Students, second edition, by David W. Ball, Cleveland State University

ISBN-10: 0-495-01327-7; ISBN-13: 978-0-495-01327-3

This short book is intended for students who lack confidence and/or competency in the essential mathematical skills necessary to survive in general chemistry. Each chapter focuses on a specific type of skill and has worked-out examples to show how these skills translate to chemical problem solving.

Survival Guide for General Chemistry with Math Review, second edition, by Charles H. Atwood, University of Georgia

ISBN-10: 0-495-38751-7; ISBN-13: 978-0-495-38751-0

Intended to help you practice for exams, this "survival guide" shows you how to solve difficult general chemistry problems by dissecting them into manageable chunks. The guide includes three levels of proficiency questions—A, B, and minimal—to quickly build confidence as you master the knowledge you need to succeed in your course.

For the Laboratory

Brooks/Cole Lab Manuals

Brooks/Cole offers a variety of printed manuals to meet all general chemistry laboratory needs. Visit the chemistry site at **academic.cengage.com/chemistry** for a full listing and description of these laboratory manuals and laboratory notebooks. All Brooks/Cole lab manuals can be customized for your specific needs.

Signature Labs—for the customized laboratory

Signature Labs (**www.signaturelabs.com**) combines the resources of Brooks/Cole, CER, and OuterNet Publishing to provide you unparalleled service in creating your ideal customized lab program. Select the experiments and artwork you need from our collection of content and imagery to find the perfect labs to match your course. Visit **www.signaturelabs.com** or contact your Brooks/Cole representative for more information.

ACKNOWLEDGMENTS

Many people who have used this book—instructors, teaching assistants, and students—have e-mailed, written, and called with suggestions on how to improve this book. Others just called to offer their condolences and encouragement on the loss of my co-author. I am grateful.

Reviewers who have helped in the preparation of this edition include:

Christopher Babb, Berry College
Kathleen Brunke, Christopher Newport University
Kevin Cantrell, University of Portland
S. Michael Condren, Christian Brothers University
Becky A. Gee, Long Island University
Richard L. Nafshun, Oregon State University
Edward J. Neth, University of Connecticut
James A. Phillips, University of Wisconsin, Eau Claire
David Treichel, Nebraska Wesleyan University
Will Wickun, Montana State University, Billings

I am particularly grateful to Professors Fatma Selampinar (University of Connecticut) and David Shinn (University of Hawaii, Manoa) for their accuracy reviews. Their thoroughness and absolute attention to detail are incredible.

Professors Harry Frank (University of Connecticut), Steven Shaw (Montana State University), Greg Sotzing (University of Connecticut), and Leslie Sperling (Lehigh University) graciously consented to write essays on their research interests. Their essays are interesting and understandable to freshmen (no mean feat!).

Many people worked on the editorial and production team for this text. They took pages of manuscript, rough ideas, crude sketches, and long wish lists and put them together to create this edition. They prodded, cajoled, and set impossible deadlines, all with incredible patience. I couldn't have done it without them. They are: Lisa Lockwood, chemistry editor; Ashley Summers, assistant editor; Lisa Weber, technology project manager; Teresa Trego, content project manager; Amee Mosely, marketing manager; and Dan Fitzgerald, production editor at the production service Graphic World Publishing Services.

Missing from this list is Peter McGahey, my developmental editor, who deserves special thanks. He soothed frayed nerves and lifted sagging spirits with his positive, optimistic personality. His good humor provided an extra dose of energy. It also helped to get off topic once in a while to chat about tulip bulbs in the spring and perennials in the summer. Thanks, Peter. You were an oasis of calm on many days.

Two people who do not belong to any team deserve special recognition. To Joseph Hurley, best proofreader bar none, thanks for giving up your weekends to lend an extra pair of eyes. To Jim Hurley, who typed manuscript, read drafts through a nonchemist's (read mathematician's) eye, and listened to endless complaints, thank you for taking this journey with me.

Cecile N. Hurley
University of Connecticut
Storrs, CT

November 2007

To the Student

You've probably already heard a lot about your general chemistry course. Many think it is more difficult than other courses. There may be some justification for that opinion. Besides having its very own specialized vocabulary, chemistry is a quantitative science, which means that you need mathematics as a tool to help you understand the concepts. As a result, you will probably receive a lot of advice from your instructor, teaching assistant, and fellow students about how to study chemistry. We hesitate to add our advice; experience as teachers and parents has taught us that students do surprisingly well without it. We would, however, like to acquaint you with some of the learning tools in this text. They are described in the pages that follow.

Learning Tools in *Chemistry: Principles and Reactions*, Sixth Edition

Examples

In a typical chapter, you will find ten or more Examples, each designed to illustrate a particular principle. These have answers, screened in color. Most of them contain a **Strategy** statement, which describes the reasoning behind the **Solution.** You should find it helpful to get into the habit of working all problems this way. First, spend a few moments deciding how the problem should be solved. Then, and only then, set up the mathematics to solve it.

Many of the examples end with a **Reality Check,** which encourages you to check whether the answer makes sense. We hope you will get into the habit of doing this when you work problems on your own in quizzes and examinations.

Graded Examples

Throughout the text, you will encounter special *Graded* Examples. A typical Graded Example looks as follows:

Example Graded

For the reaction

$$A + 2B \longrightarrow C$$

determine

*(a) the number of moles of A required to react with 5.0 mol of B.
**(b) the number of grams of A required to react with 5.0 g of B.
***(c) the volume of a 0.50 *M* solution of A required to react with 5.0 g of B.
****(d) the volume of a 0.50 *M* solution of A required to react with 25 mL of a solution that has a density of 1.2 g/mL and contains 32% by mass of B.

There are two advantages to working a Graded Example.

1. By working parts (a) through (d) of this sample in succession, you can see how many different ways there are to ask a question about mass relations in a reaction. That should cushion the shock should you see only part (d) in an exam.

2. The parts of the Graded Example do not just progress from an easy mass relations question to a more difficult one. The value of the Graded Example is that the last question *assumes the ability to answer the earlier ones.* You may be able to answer parts (a) and (b) with a limited understanding of the material, but to answer part (d) you need to have mastered the material.

Use the graded example as you review for exams. Try to skip the earlier parts—in this case (a), (b), and (c)—and go directly to the last part, (d). If you can solve (d), you do not need to try (a), (b), and (c); you know how to do them. If you can't, then try (c) to see where you may have a problem. If you can't do (c), then try (b). As a last resort, start at (a) and work your way back through (d).

Marginal Notes

Sprinkled throughout the text are a number of short notes in the margin. Many of these are of the "now, hear this" variety, others are mnemonics, and still others make points that we forgot to put in the text. (These were contributed by your fellow students.) Some—probably fewer than we think—are supposed to be humorous. See, for example, the reference to ice skating on page 239; through five editions WLM thought it was uproariously funny.

OWL and CengageNOW

Two web-based resources accompany the text to aid your understanding of the concepts presented in each chapter:

CENGAGENOW™

- CengageNOW annotations appear throughout the text, directing you to tutorials, exercises, and simulations available online to help learn and reinforce the concepts presented in the text and your lecture. Each chapter is also supported by a diagnostic Pre-Test that directs you to those modules most likely to help you understand the topics where you need further work. More information about accessing CengageNOW is available in the Preface.
- For those courses using OWL (Online Web-based Learning), tutorials and end-of-chapter Questions and Problems from this book are available online as assigned by your instructor. OWL is described in more detail in the Preface.

Chemistry: The Human Side

Throughout the text, short biographies of some of the pioneers of chemistry appear in sections with this heading. They emphasize not only the accomplishments of these individuals but also their personalities.

Chemistry: Beyond the Classroom

Each chapter contains a "Chemistry: Beyond the Classroom" feature. It is a self-contained essay that illustrates a current example either of chemistry in use in the world or an area of chemical research. It does not intrude into the explanation of the concepts, so it won't distract you. But we promise that those essays—if you read them—will make you more scientifically literate.

Chapter Highlights

At the end of each chapter, you will find a brief review of its contents. A review is always helpful not only to refresh your memory of past material but also to organize your time and notes when preparing for an examination. The "Chapter Highlights" include:

- The *Key Terms* in the chapter. If a particular term is unfamiliar, refer to the index at the back of the book. You will find the term in the glossary that is incorporated in the index and also the pages in the text where it appears (if you need more explanation).

- The *Key Concepts* and *Key Equations* introduced in the chapter. These are indexed to the corresponding Examples and end-of-chapter problems. End-of-chapter problems available in OWL are also cross-referenced. If you have trouble working a particular problem here, it may help to go back and reread the Example that covers the same concept.
- Each chapter is summarized by a multi-step *Summary Problem* that covers all or nearly all of the key concepts in the chapter. You can test your understanding of the chapter by working this problem. A major advantage of the Summary Problems is that they tie together many different ideas, showing how they correlate with one another. An experienced general chemistry professor who uses the book always tells his class, "If you can answer the Summary Problem without help, you are ready for a test on its chapter."

Questions and Problems

At the end of each chapter is a set of Questions and Problems that your instructor may assign for homework. They are also helpful in testing the depth of your knowledge about the chapter. These sets include:

- Questions that test your knowledge of the specialized vocabulary that chemists use (e.g., write the names of formulas, write the chemical equation for a reaction that is described).
- **Quantitative problems** that require a calculator and some algebraic manipulations.
- **Classified problems** that start the set and are grouped by type under a particular heading that indicates the topic from the chapter that they address. The classified problems occur in matched pairs, so the second member illustrates the same principle as the first. This allows you more than one opportunity to test yourself. The second problem (even-numbered) is numbered in color and answered in Appendix 6. If your instructor assigns the odd problems without answers for homework, wait until the problem solution is discussed and solve the even problem to satisfy yourself that you understand how to solve the problem of that type.
- Each chapter also contains a smaller number of **unclassified problems,** which may involve more than one concept, including, perhaps, topics from a preceding chapter.
- **Conceptual questions** test your understanding of principles. A calculator is not (or should not be) necessary to answer these questions.
- The section of **challenge problems** presents problems that may require extra skill and/or insight and effort. They are all answered in Appendix 6.

Blue-numbered questions answered in Appendix 6 have fully worked solutions available in the *Student Solution Manual.* The *Student Solution Manual* is described in more detail in the Preface. To further aid your study, selected worked solutions for problems from each chapter, identified by the WEB icon, are posted on the book's companion website at **academic.cengage.com/chemistry/masterton.**

Appendices

The appendices at the end of the book provide not only the answers to the even-numbered problems but also additional materials you may find useful. Among them are:

- Appendix 1 includes a review of SI base units as well as tables of thermodynamic data and equilibrium constants.
- Appendix 3 contains a mathematical review touching on just about all the mathematics you need for general chemistry. Exponential notation and logarithms (natural and base 10) are emphasized.

1 Matter and Measurements

I have measured out my life with coffee spoons.

—T. S. Eliot
"The Love Song of J. Alfred Prufrock"

Chapter Outline

"The Alchemist" by William F. Douglas/© Victoria & Albert Museum, London/Art Resource, NY

The flask shown in the painting is still part of glassware used in a modern chemist's laboratory.

Almost certainly, this is your first college course in chemistry; perhaps it is your first exposure to chemistry at any level. Unless you are a chemistry major, you may wonder why you are taking this course and what you can expect to gain from it. To address that question, it will be helpful to look at some of the ways in which chemistry contributes to other disciplines.

If you're planning to be an engineer, you can be sure that many of the materials you will work with have been synthesized by chemists. Some of these materials are organic (carbon-containing). They could be familiar plastics like polyethylene (Chapter 23) or the more esoteric plastics used in unbreakable windows and nonflammable clothing. Other materials, including metals (Chapter 20) and semiconductors, are inorganic in nature.

Perhaps you are a health science major, looking forward to a career in medicine or pharmacy. If so, you will want to become familiar with the properties of aqueous solutions (Chapters 4, 10, 14, and 16), which include blood and other body fluids. Chemists today are involved in the synthesis of a variety of life-saving products. These range from drugs used in chemotherapy (Chapter 15) to new antibiotics used against resistant microorganisms.

Beyond career preparation, an objective of a college education is to make you a better informed citizen. In this text, we'll look at some of the chemistry-related topics referred to on the evening news—

- depletion of the ozone layer (Chapter 11).
- alternative sources of fuel (Chapter 18).
- the pros and cons of nuclear power (Chapter 19).

Another goal of this text is to pique your intellectual curiosity by trying to explain the chemical principles behind such recent advances as

- "self-cleaning" windows (Chapter 1).
- "the ice that burns" (Chapter 3).
- "maintenance-free" storage batteries (Chapter 18).
- "chiral" drugs (Chapter 22).

We hope that when you complete this course you too will be convinced of the importance of chemistry in today's world. We should, however, caution you on one point. Although we will talk about many of the applications of chemistry, *our main concern will be with the principles that govern chemical reactions.* Only by mastering these principles will you understand the basis of the applications referred to in the preceding paragraphs.

This chapter begins the study of chemistry by—

- considering the different types of matter: pure substances versus mixtures, elements versus compounds (Section 1.1).
- looking at the kinds of measurements on which chemistry is founded, the uncertainties associated with these measurements, and a method used to convert measured quantities from one unit to another (Section 1.2).
- focusing on certain physical properties including color, density, and water solubility, which can be used to identify substances (Section 1.3). ■

Online homework for this chapter may be assigned in OWL.

CENGAGENOW™

This icon introduces an opportunity for self-study and to explore interactive modules by signing in at **academic.cengage.com/now.**

Chemistry deals with the properties and reactions of substances.

Figure 1.1
Classification of matter.

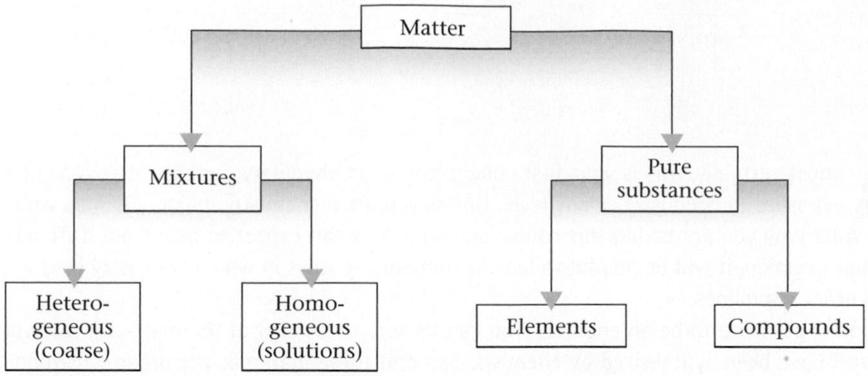

1.1 TYPES OF MATTER

Matter is anything that has mass and occupies space. It exists in three phases: solid, liquid, and gas. A solid has a fixed shape and volume. A liquid has a fixed volume but is not rigid in shape; it takes on the shape of the container. A gas has neither a fixed volume nor a rigid shape; it takes on both the volume and the shape of the container.

Matter can be classified into two categories—

Most materials you encounter are mixtures.

- pure substances, each of which has a fixed composition and a unique set of properties.
- mixtures, composed of two or more substances.

Pure substances are either elements or compounds (Figure 1.1), whereas mixtures can be either homogeneous or heterogeneous.

Elements

An **element** is a type of matter that cannot be broken down into two or more pure substances. There are 115 known elements, of which 91 occur naturally.

Many elements are familiar to all of us. The charcoal used in outdoor grills is nearly pure carbon. Electrical wiring, jewelry, and water pipes are often made from copper, a metallic element. Another such element, aluminum, is used in many household utensils.

Some elements come in and out of fashion, so to speak. Sixty years ago, elemental silicon was a chemical curiosity. Today, ultrapure silicon has become the basis for the multibillion-dollar semiconductor industry. Lead, on the other hand, is an element moving in the other direction. A generation ago it was widely used to make paint pigments, plumbing connections, and gasoline additives. Today, because of the toxicity of lead compounds, all of these applications have been banned in the United States.

In chemistry, an element is identified by its symbol. This consists of one or two letters, usually derived from the name of the element. Thus the symbol for carbon is C; that for aluminum is Al. Sometimes the symbol comes from the Latin name of the element or one of its compounds. The two elements copper and mercury, which were known in ancient times, have the symbols Cu *(cuprum)* and Hg *(hydrargyrum).*

Table 1.1 lists the names and symbols of several elements that are probably familiar to you. In either free or combined form, they are commonly found in the laboratory or in commercial products. The abundances listed measure the relative amount of each element in the earth's crust, the atmosphere, and the oceans.

Mercury thermometers, both for laboratory and clinical use, have been replaced by digital ones.

Curiously, several of the most familiar elements are really quite rare. An example is mercury, which has been known since at least 500 B.C., even though its abundance is only 0.00005%. It can easily be prepared by heating the red mineral cinnabar (Figure 1.2). Beyond that, its unique properties make it extremely useful. Because of its high density, mercury is the liquid used in barometers and manometers. Mercury dissolves many metals, forming solutions (amalgams). A silver-mercury-tin amalgam is used in filling teeth.

Table 1.1 Some Familiar Elements with Their Percentage Abundances

Element	Symbol	Percentage Abundance	Element	Symbol	Percentage Abundance
Aluminum	Al	7.5	Manganese	Mn	0.09
Bromine	Br	0.00025	Mercury	Hg	0.00005
Calcium	Ca	3.4	Nickel	Ni	0.010
Carbon	C	0.08	Nitrogen	N	0.03
Chlorine	Cl	0.2	Oxygen	O	49.4
Chromium	Cr	0.018	Phosphorus	P	0.12
Copper	Cu	0.007	Potassium	K	2.4
Gold	Au	0.0000005	Silicon	Si	25.8
Hydrogen	H	0.9	Silver	Ag	0.00001
Iodine	I	0.00003	Sodium	Na	2.6
Iron	Fe	4.7	Sulfur	S	0.06
Lead	Pb	0.0016	Titanium	Ti	0.56
Magnesium	Mg	1.9	Zinc	Zn	0.008

In contrast, aluminum (abundance = 7.5%), despite its usefulness, was little more than a chemical curiosity until about a century ago. It occurs in combined form in clays and rocks, from which it cannot be extracted. In 1886 two young chemists, Charles Hall in the United States and Paul Herroult in France, independently worked out a process for extracting aluminum from a relatively rare ore, bauxite. That process is still used today to produce the element. By an odd coincidence, Hall and Herroult were born in the same year (1863) and died in the same year (1914).

Compounds

A **compound** is a pure substance that contains more than one element. Water is a compound of hydrogen and oxygen. The compounds methane, acetylene, and naphthalene all contain the elements carbon and hydrogen, in different proportions.

Compounds have fixed compositions. That is, a given compound always contains the same elements in the same percentages by mass. A sample of pure water contains precisely 11.19% hydrogen and 88.81% oxygen. In contrast, mixtures can vary in composition. For example, a mixture of hydrogen and oxygen might contain 5, 10, 25, or 60% hydrogen, along with 95, 90, 75, or 40% oxygen.

The properties of compounds are very different from those of the elements they contain. Ordinary table salt, sodium chloride, is a white, unreactive solid. As you can guess from its name, it contains the two elements sodium and chlorine. Sodium (Na) is a shiny, extremely reactive metal. Chlorine (Cl) is a poisonous, greenish-yellow gas. Clearly, when these two elements combine to form sodium chloride, a profound change takes place (Figure 1.3, page 4).

Many different methods can be used to resolve compounds into their elements. Sometimes, but not often, heat alone is sufficient. Mercury(II) oxide, a compound of mercury and oxygen, decomposes to its elements when heated to 600°C. Joseph Priestley, an English

Charles D. Winters

(a) (b)

Figure 1.2
Cinnabar and mercury. (a) The mineral cinnabar, from which mercury is obtained. (b) Mercury, an element.

Charles D. Winters

(a) (b) (c)

Figure 1.3
Sodium, chlorine, and sodium chloride. (a) Sodium, a metallic element that is soft enough to be cut with a knife. (b) Chlorine, a nonmetallic element that is a gas. (c) Sodium chloride, the crystalline chemical compound formed when sodium combines with chlorine.

chemist, discovered oxygen more than 200 years ago when he carried out this reaction by exposing a sample of mercury(II) oxide to an intense beam of sunlight focused through a powerful lens. The mercury vapor formed is a deadly poison. Sir Isaac Newton, who distilled large quantities of mercury in his laboratory, suffered the effects in his later years.

Another method of resolving compounds into elements is electrolysis, which involves passing an electric current through a compound, usually in the liquid state. By electrolysis it is possible to separate water into the gaseous elements hydrogen and oxygen. Several decades ago it was proposed to use the hydrogen produced by electrolysis to raise the *Titanic* from its watery grave off the coast of Newfoundland. It didn't work.

Mixtures

All gaseous mixtures, including air, are solutions.

A **mixture** contains two or more substances combined in such a way that each substance retains its chemical identity. When you shake copper sulfate with sand (Figure 1.4), the two substances do not react with one another. In contrast, when sodium is exposed to chlorine gas, a new compound, sodium chloride, is formed.

There are two types of mixtures:

1. Homogeneous or uniform mixtures are ones in which the composition is the same throughout. Another name for a homogeneous mixture is a **solution,** which is made up of a solvent, usually taken to be the substance present in largest amount, and one or more solutes. Most commonly, the solvent is a liquid, whereas solutes may be solids, liquids, or gases. Soda water is a solution of carbon dioxide (solute) in water (solvent). Seawater is a more complex solution in which there are several solid solutes, including sodium chloride; the solvent is water. It is also possible to have solutions in the solid state. Brass (Figure 1.5) is a solid solution containing the two metals copper (67%–90%) and zinc (10%–33%).

2. Heterogeneous or nonuniform mixtures are those in which the composition varies throughout. Most rocks fall into this category. In a piece of granite (Figure 1.5), several components can be distinguished, differing from one another in color.

CENGAGENOW™
Click Coached Problems for a self-study module on **identifying pure substances and mixtures.**

Many different methods can be used to separate the components of a mixture from one another. A couple of methods that you may have carried out in the laboratory are—

- *filtration,* used to separate a heterogeneous solid-liquid mixture. The mixture is passed through a barrier with fine pores, such as filter paper. Copper sulfate, which is water-soluble, can be separated from sand by shaking with water. On filtration the sand remains on the paper and the copper sulfate solution passes through it.

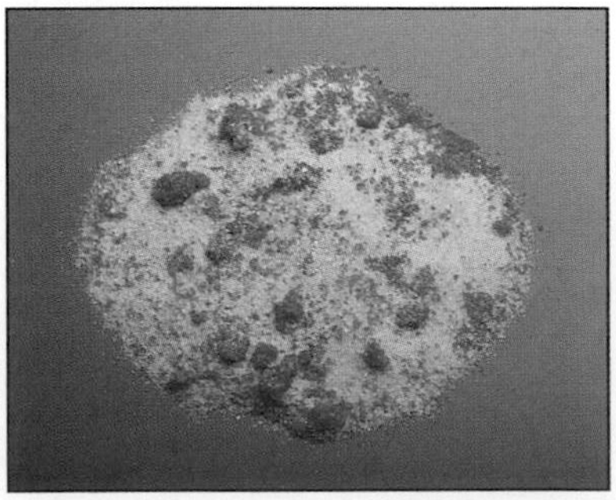

Charles D. Winters

Figure 1.4
A heterogeneous mixture of copper sulfate crystals (blue) and sand.

Figure 1.5
Two mixtures. On the left is brass, a *homogeneous* mixture of copper and zinc. On the right is a piece of granite, a *heterogeneous* mixture that contains discrete regions of different minerals (feldspar, mica, and quartz).

- *distillation,* used to resolve a homogeneous solid-liquid mixture. The liquid vaporizes, leaving a residue of the solid in the distilling flask. The liquid is obtained by condensing the vapor. Distillation can be used to separate the components of a water solution of copper sulfate (Figure 1.6).

CENGAGENOW™
Click Chemistry Interactive for a self-study module **separation of mixtures.**

A more complex but more versatile separation method is *chromatography,* a technique widely used in teaching, research, and industrial laboratories to separate all kinds of mixtures. This method takes advantage of differences in solubility and/or extent of adsorption on a solid surface. In *gas-liquid chromatography,* a mixture of volatile liquids and gases is introduced into one end of a heated glass tube. As little as one microliter (10^{-6} L) of sample may be used. The tube is packed with an inert solid whose surface is coated with a viscous

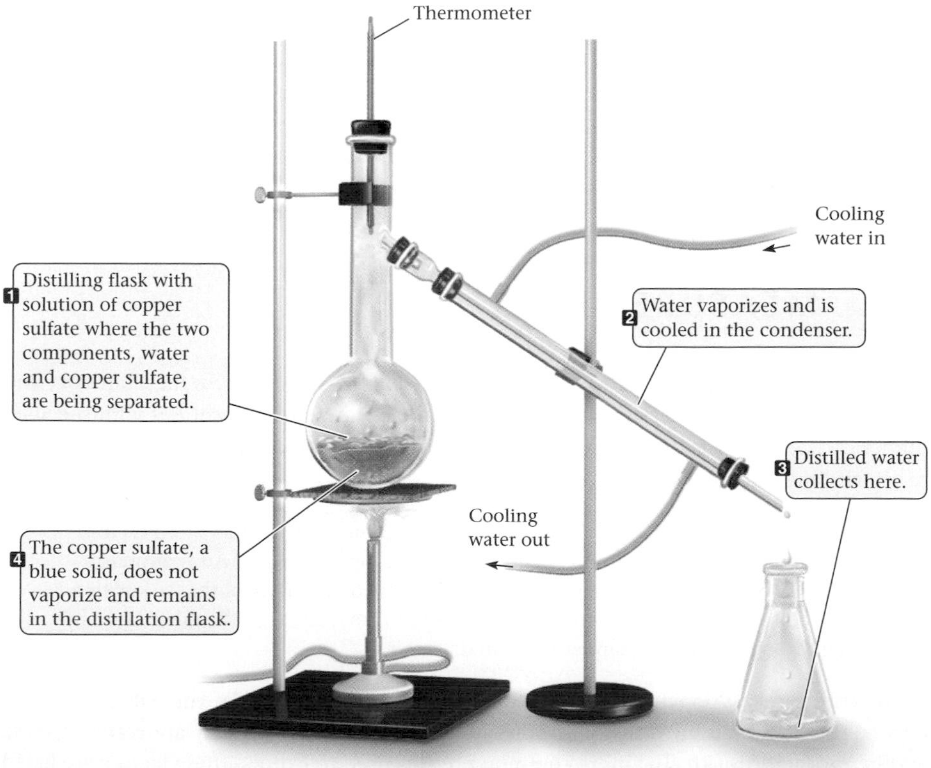

Figure 1.6
Apparatus for a simple distillation.

Figure 1.7
Result of gas-liquid chromatography of natural gas. With some volatile mixtures, the sample can be as small as 10^{-6} L.

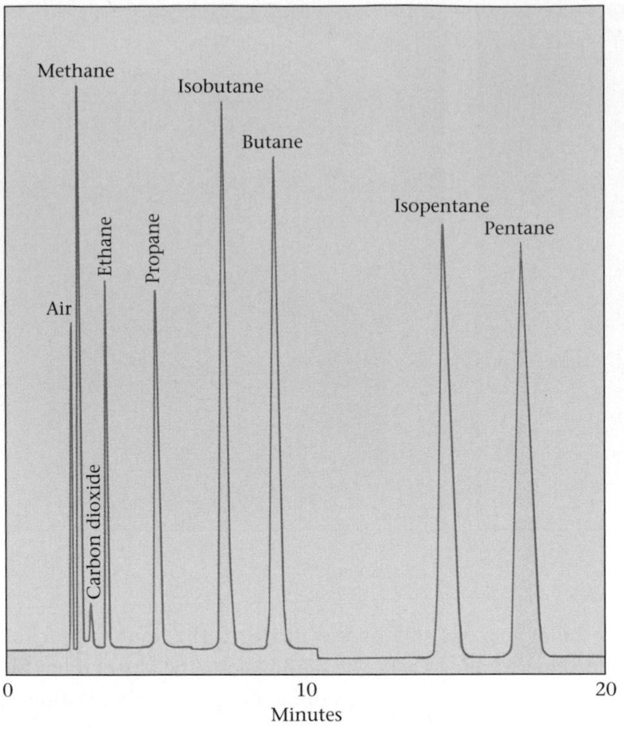

liquid. An unreactive "carrier gas," often helium, is passed through the tube. The components of the sample gradually separate as they vaporize into the helium or condense into the viscous liquid. Usually the more volatile fractions move faster and emerge first; successive fractions activate a detector and recorder. The end result is a plot such as that shown in Figure 1.7.

Gas-liquid chromatography (GLC) finds many applications outside the chemistry laboratory. If you've ever had an emissions test on the exhaust system of your car, GLC was almost certainly the analytical method used. Pollutants such as carbon monoxide and unburned hydrocarbons appear as peaks on a graph such as that shown in Figure 1.7. A computer determines the areas under these peaks, which are proportional to the concentrations of pollutants, and prints out a series of numbers that tells the inspector whether your car passed or failed the test. Many of the techniques used to test people for drugs (marijuana, cocaine, and others) or alcohol also make use of gas-liquid chromatography.

GLC is a favorite technique in the forensics labs of many TV shows.

1.2 MEASUREMENTS

Chemistry is a quantitative science. The experiments that you carry out in the laboratory and the calculations that you perform almost always involve measured quantities with specified numerical values. Consider, for example, the following set of directions for the preparation of aspirin (measured quantities are shown in italics).

> Add *2.0 g* of salicylic acid, *5.0 mL* of acetic anhydride, and *5 drops* of *85%* H_3PO_4 to a 50-mL Erlenmeyer flask. Heat in a water bath at *75°C* for *15 minutes.* Add cautiously *20 mL* of water and transfer to an ice bath at *0°C.* Scratch the inside of the flask with a stirring rod to initiate crystallization. Separate aspirin from the solid-liquid mixture by filtering through a Buchner funnel *10 cm* in diameter.

Scientific measurements are expressed in the *metric system.* As you know, this is a decimal-based system in which all of the units of a particular quantity are related to one another by factors of 10. The more common prefixes used to express these factors are listed in Table 1.2 (page 7).

Table 1.2 Metric Prefixes

Factor	Prefix	Abbreviation	Factor	Prefix	Abbreviation
10^6	mega	M	10^{-3}	**milli**	m
10^3	**kilo**	k	10^{-6}	micro	μ
10^{-1}	deci	d	10^{-9}	**nano**	n
10^{-2}	**centi**	c	10^{-12}	pico	p

In this section we will look at four familiar quantities that you will almost certainly measure in the laboratory: length, volume, mass, and temperature. Other quantities will be introduced in later chapters as they are needed.

Instruments and Units

The standard unit of ***length*** in the metric system is the meter, which is a little larger than a yard. The meter was originally intended to be 1/40,000,000 of the earth's meridian that passes through Paris. It is now defined as the distance light travels in 1/299,792,458 of a second.

Other units of length are expressed in terms of the meter, using the prefixes listed in Table 1.2. You are familiar with the centimeter, the millimeter, and the kilometer:

$$1\text{ cm} = 10^{-2}\text{ m} \qquad 1\text{ mm} = 10^{-3}\text{ m} \qquad 1\text{ km} = 10^3\text{ m}$$

The dimensions of very tiny particles are often expressed in nanometers:

$$1\text{ nm} = 10^{-9}\text{ m}$$

Volume is most commonly expressed in one of three units—

- cubic centimeters $1\text{ cm}^3 = (10^{-2}\text{ m})^3 = 10^{-6}\text{ m}^3$
- liters (L) $1\text{ L} = 10^{-3}\text{ m}^3 = 10^3\text{ cm}^3$
- milliliters (mL) $1\text{ mL} = 10^{-3}\text{ L} = 10^{-6}\text{ m}^3$

Notice that a milliliter is equal to one cubic centimeter:

$$1\text{ mL} = 1\text{ cm}^3$$

CENGAGENOW™
Click Coached Problems for a self-study module on **metric system prefixes.**

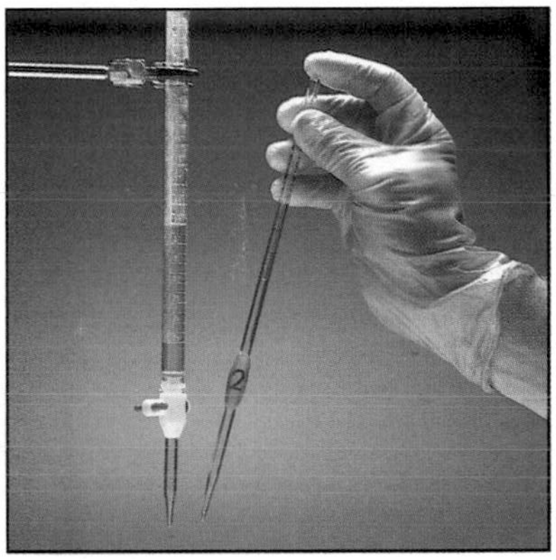

Figure 1.8
Measuring volume. A buret *(left)* delivers an accurately measured variable volume of liquid. A pipet *(right)* delivers a fixed volume (e.g., 25.00 mL) of liquid.

The device most commonly used to measure volume in general chemistry is the graduated cylinder. A pipet or buret (Figure 1.8) is used when greater accuracy is required. A pipet is calibrated to deliver a fixed volume of liquid—for example, 25.00 mL—when filled to the mark and allowed to drain. Variable volumes can be delivered accurately by a buret, perhaps to ±0.01 mL.

In the metric system, ***mass*** is most commonly expressed in grams, kilograms, or milligrams:

$$1\text{ g} = 10^{-3}\text{ kg} \qquad 1\text{ mg} = 10^{-3}\text{ g}$$

This book weighs about 1.5 kg. The megagram, more frequently called the *metric ton,* is

$$1\text{ Mg} = 10^6\text{ g} = 10^3\text{ kg}$$

Writing "m" in upper case or lower case makes a big difference.

Properly speaking, there is a distinction between mass and weight. *Mass* is a measure of the amount of matter in an object; *weight* is a measure of the gravitational force acting on the object. Chemists often use these terms interchangeably; we determine the mass of an object by "weighing" it on a balance (Figure 1.9, page 8).

Temperature is the factor that determines the direction of heat flow. When two objects at different temperatures are placed in contact with one another, heat flows from the one at the higher temperature to the one at the lower temperature.

Temperature is measured indirectly, by observing its effect on the properties of a substance. A mercury-in-glass thermometer takes advantage of the fact that mercury, like other substances, expands as temperature increases. When the temperature rises, the mercury in the thermometer expands up a narrow tube. The total volume of the tube is only about 2% of that of the bulb at the base. In this way, a rather small change in volume is made readily visible.

Charles D. Winters

Figure 1.9
Weighing a solid. The solid sample plus the paper on which it rests weighs 144.998 g. The pictured balance is a single-pan analytical balance.

Thermometers used in chemistry are marked in degrees *Celsius* (referred to as degrees centigrade until 1948). On this scale, named after the Swedish astronomer Anders Celsius (1701–1744), the freezing point of water is taken to be 0°C. The normal boiling point of water is 100°C. Household thermometers in the United States are commonly marked in *Fahrenheit* degrees. Daniel Fahrenheit (1686–1736) was a German instrument maker who was the first to use the mercury-in-glass thermometer. On this scale, the normal freezing and boiling points of water are taken to be 32° and 212°, respectively (Figure 1.10). It follows that (212°F − 32°F) = 180°F covers the same temperature interval as (100°C − 0°C) = 100°C. This leads to the general relation between the two scales:

Many countries still use degrees centigrade.

CENGAGENOW™
Click Coached Problems for a self-study module on **temperature.**

$$t_{°F} = 1.8\, t_{°C} + 32° \qquad \textbf{(1.1)}$$

Notice (Figure 1.10) that the two scales coincide at −40°; as can readily be seen from the equation just written:

$$\text{At } -40°\text{C:} \qquad t_{°F} = 1.8(-40°) + 32° = -72° + 32° = -40°$$

For many purposes in chemistry, the most convenient unit of temperature is the **kelvin (K);** note the absence of the degree sign. The kelvin is defined to be 1/273.16 of the difference between the lowest attainable temperature (0 K) and the triple point of water* (0.01°C). The relationship between temperature in K and in °C is

$$T_K = t_{°C} + 273.15 \qquad \textbf{(1.2)}$$

This scale is named after Lord Kelvin (1824–1907), a British scientist who showed in 1848, at the age of 24, that it is impossible to reach a temperature lower than 0 K.

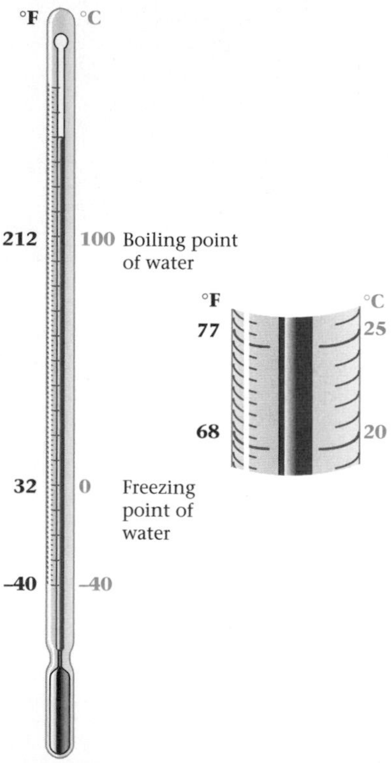

Figure 1.10
The Fahrenheit and Celsius temperature scales. The distance between the freezing and boiling points of water is 180° on the Fahrenheit scale and 100° on the Celsius scale. Thus the Celsius degree is 9/5 as large as the Fahrenheit degree, as is evident from the magnified section of the thermometer above.

Example 1.1 Mercury thermometers are being phased out because of the toxicity of mercury vapor. A common replacement for mercury is the organic liquid isoamyl benzoate, which boils at 262°C. What is its boiling point in °F? K?

Strategy Use Equations 1.1 and 1.2 above. Solve for the desired quantity, $t_{°F}$ in the first case, T_K in the second.

SOLUTION

$$t_{°F} = 1.8(262°) + 32° = 504°\text{F}$$

$$T_K = 262 + 273.15 = 535\text{ K}$$

*The triple point of water (Chapter 9) is the one unique temperature and pressure pair at which ice, liquid water, and water vapor can coexist in contact with one another.

As you can see from this discussion, a wide number of different units can be used to express measured quantities in the metric system. This proliferation of units has long been of concern to scientists. In 1960 a self-consistent set of metric units was proposed. This so-called International System of Units (SI) is discussed in Appendix 1. The SI units for the four quantities discussed are

Length:	meter (m)	*Mass:*	kilogram (kg)
Volume:	cubic meter (m^3)	*Temperature:*	kelvin (K)

Uncertainties in Measurements: Significant Figures

Every measurement carries with it a degree of uncertainty. Its magnitude depends on the nature of the measuring device and the skill with which it is used. Suppose, for example, you measure out 8 mL of liquid using the 100-mL graduated cylinder shown in Figure 1.11. Here the volume is uncertain to perhaps ± 1 mL. With such a crude measuring device, you would be lucky to obtain a volume between 7 and 9 mL. To obtain greater precision, you could use a narrow 10-mL cylinder, which has divisions in small increments. You might now measure a volume within 0.1 mL of the desired value, in the range of 7.9 to 8.1 mL. By using a buret, you could reduce the uncertainty to ± 0.01 mL.

Anyone making a measurement has a responsibility to indicate the uncertainty associated with it. Such information is vital to someone who wants to repeat the experiment or judge its precision. The three volume measurements referred to earlier could be reported as

8 ± 1 mL	(large graduated cylinder)
8.0 ± 0.1 mL	(small graduated cylinder)
8.00 ± 0.01 mL	(buret)

In this text, we will drop the $\pm$ notation and simply write

8 mL 8.0 mL 8.00 mL

When we do this, it is understood that there is an ***uncertainty of at least one unit in the last digit***—that is, 1 mL, 0.1 mL, 0.01 mL, respectively. This method of citing the degree of confidence in a measurement is often described in terms of **significant figures,** the meaningful digits obtained in a measurement. In 8.00 mL there are three significant figures; each of the three digits has experimental meaning. Similarly, there are two significant figures in 8.0 mL and one significant figure in 8 mL.

There's a big difference between 8 mL and 8.00 mL, perhaps as much as half a milliliter.

Frequently we need to know the number of significant figures in a measurement reported by someone else (Example 1.2).

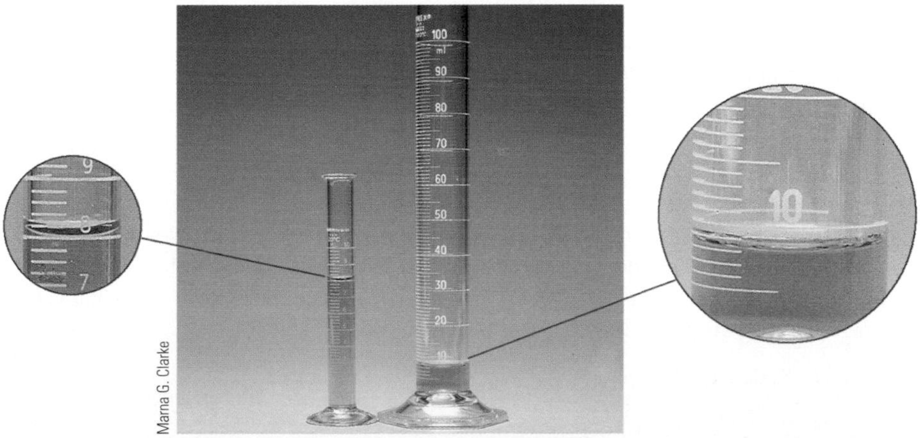

Figure 1.11
Uncertainty in measuring volume.
The uncertainty depends on the nature of the measuring device. Eight mL of liquid can be measured with less uncertainty in the 10-mL graduated cylinder than in the 100-mL graduated cylinder.

Example 1.2 Using different balances, three different students weigh the same object. They report the following masses:

(a) 1.611 g (b) 1.60 g (c) 0.001611 kg

How many significant figures does each value have?

Strategy Assume each student reported the mass in such a way as to indicate the uncertainty associated with the measurement. Then follow a common sense approach.

SOLUTION

(a) 4

(b) 3 The zero after the decimal point is significant. It indicates that the object was weighed to the nearest 0.01 g.

(c) 4 The zeros at the left are not significant. They are there only because the mass was expressed in kilograms rather than grams. Note that 1.611 g and 0.001611 kg represent the same mass.

Reality Check If you express these masses in exponential notation as 1.611×10^0 g, 1.60×10^0 g, and 1.611×10^{-3} kg, the number of significant figures becomes obvious: 4 in (a), 3 in (b), and 4 in (c).

Unfortunately, the uncertainty here is uncertain.

Sometimes the number of significant figures in a reported measurement is ambiguous. Suppose that a piece of metal is reported to weigh 500 g. You cannot be sure how many of these digits are meaningful. Perhaps the metal was weighed to the nearest gram (500 ± 1 g). If so, the 5 and the two zeros are significant; there are three significant figures. Then again, the metal might have been weighed only to the nearest 10 g (500 ± 10 g). In this case, only the 5 and one zero are known accurately; there are two significant figures. About all you can do in such cases is to wish the person who carried out the weighing had used exponential notation. The mass should have been reported as

The number of significant figures is the number of digits shown when a quantity is expressed in exponential notation.

$$5.00 \times 10^2 \text{ g} \qquad \text{(3 significant figures)}$$

or

$$5.0 \times 10^2 \text{ g} \qquad \text{(2 significant figures)}$$

or

$$5 \times 10^2 \text{ g} \qquad \text{(1 significant figure)}$$

In general, *any ambiguity concerning the number of significant figures in a measurement can be resolved by using exponential notation* (often referred to as "scientific notation"), discussed in Appendix 3.

Most measured quantities are not end results in themselves. Instead, they are used to calculate other quantities, often by multiplication or division. The precision of any such derived result is limited by that of the measurements on which it is based. ***When measured quantities are multiplied or divided, the number of significant figures in the result is the same as that in the quantity with the smallest number of significant figures.***

The rule is approximate, but sufficient for our purposes.

Example 1.3 A US Airways flight leaves Philadelphia in the early evening and arrives in Frankfurt 8.05 hours later. The airline distance from Philadelphia to Frankfurt is about 6.6×10^3 km, depending to some extent on the flight path followed. What is the average speed of the plane, in kilometers per hour?

Strategy Calculate the average speed by taking the quotient

$$\text{speed} = \frac{\text{distance traveled}}{\text{time elapsed}}$$

Count the number of significant figures in the numerator and in the denominator; the smaller of these two numbers is the number of significant figures in the quotient.

SOLUTION The average speed will appear on your calculator as

$$\frac{6.6 \times 10^3 \text{ km}}{8.05 \text{ h}} = 819.8757764 \text{ km/h}$$

It makes no sense to report all these numbers, so don't do it.

There are three significant figures in the denominator and two in the numerator. The answer should have two significant figures; round off the average speed to be

$$8.2 \times 10^2 \text{ km/h.}$$

The rules for "rounding off" a measurement, which were applied in Example 1.3, are as follows:

1. *If the digits to be discarded are less than - - 500 . . ., leave the last digit unchanged.* Masses of 23.315 g and 23.487 g both round off to 23 g if only two significant digits are required.
2. *If the digits to be discarded are greater than - - 500 . . ., add one to the last digit.* Masses of 23.692 g and 23.514 g round off to 24 g.
3. *If, perchance, the digits to be discarded are - - 500 . . . (or simply - - 5 by itself), round off so that the last digit is an even number.* Masses of 23.500 g and 24.5 g both round off to 24 g (two significant figures).

This way, you round up as often as you round down.

When measured quantities are added or subtracted, the uncertainty in the result is found in a quite different way than when they are multiplied and divided. It is determined by counting the number of decimal places, that is, the number of digits to the right of the decimal point for each measured quantity. ***When measured quantities are added or subtracted, the number of decimal places in the result is the same as that in the quantity with the greatest uncertainty and hence the smallest number of decimal places.***

To illustrate this rule, suppose you want to find the total mass of a solution made up of 10.21 g of instant coffee, 0.2 g of sugar, and 256 g of water.

	Mass	Uncertainty	
Instant coffee	10.21 g	± 0.01 g	2 decimal places
Sugar	0.2 g	± 0.1 g	1 decimal place
Water	256 g	± 1 g	0 decimal places
Total mass	266 g		

Because there are no digits after the decimal point in the mass of water, there are none in the total mass. Looking at it another way, we can say that the total mass, 266 g, has an uncertainty of ±1 g, as does the mass of water, the quantity with the greatest uncertainty.

In applying the rules governing the use of significant figures, you should keep in mind that certain numbers involved in calculations are exact rather than approximate. To illustrate this situation, consider the equation relating Fahrenheit and Celsius temperatures:

$$t_{°F} = 1.8t_{°C} + 32°$$

The numbers 1.8 and 32 are exact. Hence they do not limit the number of significant figures in a temperature conversion; that limit is determined only by the precision of the thermometer used to measure temperature.

A different type of exact number arises in certain calculations. Suppose you are asked to determine the amount of heat evolved when *one kilogram* of coal burns. The implication is that because "one" is spelled out, *exactly* one kilogram of coal burns. The uncertainty in the answer should be independent of the amount of coal.

A number that is spelled out (one, two, . . .) does not affect the number of significant figures.

CENGAGENOW™
Click Coached Problems for a self-study module on **unit conversion.**

Conversion of Units

It is often necessary to convert a measurement expressed in one unit (e.g., cubic centimeters) to another unit (liters). To do this we follow what is known as a **conversion factor** approach. For example, to convert a volume of 536 cm^3 to liters, the relation

$$1\text{ L} = 1000\text{ cm}^3$$

is used. Dividing both sides of this equation by 1000 cm^3 gives a quotient equal to 1:

$$\frac{1\text{ L}}{1000\text{ cm}^3} = \frac{1000\text{ cm}^3}{1000\text{ cm}^3} = 1$$

There are exactly 1000 cm^3 in exactly 1 L.

The quotient 1 L/1000 cm^3, which is called a conversion factor, is multiplied by 536 cm^3. Because the conversion factor equals 1, this does not change the actual volume. However, it does accomplish the desired conversion of units. The cm^3 in the numerator and denominator cancel to give the desired unit: liters.

$$536\text{ cm}^3 \times \frac{1\text{ L}}{1000\text{ cm}^3} = 0.536\text{ L}$$

The relation 1 L = 1000 cm^3 can be used equally well to convert a volume in liters, say, 1.28 L, to cubic centimeters. In this case, the necessary conversion factor is obtained by dividing both sides of the equation by 1 L:

$$\frac{1000\text{ cm}^3}{1\text{ L}} = \frac{1\text{ L}}{1\text{ L}} = 1$$

Multiplying 1.28 L by the quotient 1000 cm^3/1 L converts the volume from liters to cubic centimeters:

$$1.28\text{ L} \times \frac{1000\text{ cm}^3}{1\text{ L}} = 1280\text{ cm}^3 = 1.28 \times 10^3\text{ cm}^3$$

Notice that a single relation (1 L = 1000 cm^3) gives two conversion factors:

$$\frac{1\text{ L}}{1000\text{ cm}^3} \quad \text{and} \quad \frac{1000\text{ cm}^3}{1\text{ L}}$$

To go from cubic centimeters to liters, use the ratio 1 L/1000 cm^3; to go from liters to cubic centimeters, use the ratio 1000 cm^3/1 L. In general, when you make a conversion, ***choose the factor that cancels out the initial unit.***

$$\text{initial quantity} \times \text{conversion factor(s)} = \text{desired quantity}$$

Conversions between English and metric units can be made using Table 1.3.

Table 1.3 Relations Between Length, Volume, and Mass Units

Metric		English		Metric–English	
Length					
1 km	= 10^3 m	1 ft	= 12 in	1 in	= 2.54 cm*
1 cm	= 10^{-2} m	1 yd	= 3 ft	1 m	= 39.37 in
1 mm	= 10^{-3} m	1 mi	= 5280 ft	1 mi	= 1.609 km
1 nm	= 10^{-9} m = 10 Å				
Volume					
1 m^3	= 10^6 cm^3 = 10^3 L	1 gal	= 4 qt = 8 pt	1 ft^3	= 28.32 L
1 cm^3	= 1 mL = 10^{-3} L	1 qt (U.S. liq)	= 57.75 in^3	1 L	= 1.057 qt (U.S. liq)
Mass					
1 kg	= 10^3 g	1 lb	= 16 oz	1 lb	= 453.6 g
1 mg	= 10^{-3} g	1 short ton	= 2000 lb	1 g	= 0.03527 oz
1 metric ton	= 10^3 kg			1 metric ton	= 1.102 short ton

*This conversion factor is exact; the inch is defined to be exactly 2.54 cm. The other factors listed in this column are approximate, quoted to four significant figures. Additional digits are available if needed for very accurate calculations. For example, the pound is defined to be 453.59237 g.

Example 1.4 Graded

A gasoline station in Manila, Philippines, charges 37.57 pesos per liter for super unleaded gasoline at a time when one U.S. dollar (USD) buys 47.15 Philippine pesos (PHP). The car you are driving has a capacity of 14.00 U.S. gallons, and gets 24 miles per gallon.

*(a) What is the cost of super unleaded gasoline in Manila in U.S. dollars per gallon?
**(b) How much would a complete tankful of super unleaded for your car cost in dollars?
***(c) Suppose you have only 1255 pesos, and the car's tank is almost empty. How many kilometers can you expect to drive if you spend all your money on super unleaded gasoline?

SOLUTION

(a) Use Table 1.3 and the dollar-peso conversion rate. Start with 37.57 PHP/L

$$\frac{37.57\text{ PHP}}{\text{L}} \times \frac{1\text{ USD}}{47.15\text{ PHP}} \times \frac{1\text{ L}}{1.057\text{ qt}} \times \frac{4\text{ qt}}{1\text{ gal}} = 3.015\text{ USD/gal}$$

(b) With the price in dollars per gallon from (a), this is a simple conversion:

$$14.00\text{ gal} \times \frac{3.015\text{ USD}}{1\text{ gal}} = 42.22\text{ USD}$$

(c) First find how much gasoline (in gallons) you can buy. Then use the car's miles/gallon rating to find the number of miles you can travel. Finally, convert miles to kilometers (Table 1.3).

$$1255\text{ PHP} \times \frac{1\text{ USD}}{47.15\text{ PHP}} \times \frac{1\text{ gal}}{3.015\text{ USD}} \times \frac{24\text{ miles}}{1\text{ gal}} \times \frac{1.609\text{ km}}{1\text{ mile}} = 3.4 \times 10^2\text{ km}$$

Reality Check On the day of the above pricing in Manila, super unleaded gasoline in Storrs, Connecticut, sold for \$2.49 per gallon. However, 1255 PHP ($\approx$\$27) was about one day's wage for a teacher in the Philippines at that time.

Photo by J. Antonio Nespral

A gas station in the Philippines selling gasoline in pesos per liter.

Later (Chapters 3 and 4) we'll use conversion factors with chemical units.

CENGAGENOW™

Click Coached Problems for a self-study module on **physical properties of matter.**

1.3 PROPERTIES OF SUBSTANCES

Every pure substance has its own unique set of properties that serve to distinguish it from all other substances. A chemist most often identifies an unknown substance by measuring its properties and comparing them with the properties recorded in the chemical literature for known substances.

The properties used to identify a substance must be **intensive**; that is, they must be independent of amount. The fact that a sample weighs 4.02 g or has a volume of 229 mL tells us nothing about its identity; mass and volume are **extensive** properties; that is, they depend on amount. Beyond that, substances may be identified on the basis of their—

- **chemical properties,** observed when the substance takes part in a chemical reaction, a change that converts it to a new substance. For example, the fact that mercury(II) oxide decomposes to mercury and oxygen on heating to 600°C can be used to identify it. Again, the chemical inertness of helium helps to distinguish it from other, more reactive gases, such as hydrogen and oxygen.
- **physical properties,** observed without changing the chemical identity of a substance. Two such properties particularly useful for identifying a substance are
  –*melting point,* the temperature at which a substance changes from the solid to the liquid state.
  –*boiling point,* the temperature at which bubbles filled with vapor form within a liquid. If a substance melts at 0°C and boils at 100°C, we are inclined to suspect that it might just be water.

Taste is a physical property, but it is never measured in the lab.

Charles D. Winters

Properties of gold. The color of gold is an *intensive* property. The quantity of gold in a sample is an *extensive* property. The fact that gold can be stored in the air without undergoing any chemical reaction with oxygen in the air is a *chemical* property. The temperature at which gold melts (1063°C) is a *physical* property.

CHEMISTRY The Human Side

The discussion in Section 1.2 emphasizes the importance of making precise numerical measurements. Chemistry was not always so quantitative. The following recipe for finding the philosopher's stone was recorded more than 300 years ago.

> Take all the mineral salts there are, also all salts of animal and vegetable origin. Add all the metals and minerals, omitting none. Take two parts of the salts and grate in one part of the metals and minerals. Melt this in a crucible, forming a mass that reflects the essence of the world in all its colors. Pulverize this and pour vinegar over it. Pour off the red liquid into English wine bottles, filling them half-full. Seal them with the bladder of an ox (*not* that of a pig). Punch a hole in the top with a coarse needle. Put the bottles in hot sand for three months. Vapor will escape through the hole in the top, leaving a red powder. . . .

One man more than any other transformed chemistry from an art to a science. Antoine Lavoisier was born in Paris; he died on the guillotine during the French Revolution. Above all else, Lavoisier understood the importance of carefully controlled, quantitative experiments. These were described in his book *Elements of Chemistry.* Published in 1789, it is illustrated with diagrams by his wife.

Science Photo Library/Custom Medical Stock Photo

Antoine Lavoisier
(1743–1794)

Lavoisier was executed because he was a tax collector; chemistry had nothing to do with it.

The results of one of Lavoisier's quantitative experiments are shown in Table A; the data are taken directly from Lavoisier. If you add up the masses of reactants and products (expressed in arbitrary units), you find them to be the same, 510. As Lavoisier put it, "In all of the operations of men and nature, nothing is created. An equal quantity of matter exists before and after the experiment."

This was the first clear statement of the law of conservation of mass (Chapter 2), which was the cornerstone for the growth of chemistry in the nineteenth century. Again, to quote Lavoisier, "it is on this principle that the whole art of making experiments is founded."

E. I. DuPont (1772–1834) was a student of Lavoisier.

Table A Quantitative Experiment on the Fermentation of Wine (Lavoisier)

Reactants	Mass (Relative)	Products	Mass (Relative)
Water	400	Carbon dioxide	35
Sugar	100	Alcohol	58
Yeast	10	Acetic acid	3
		Water	409
		Sugar (unreacted)	4
		Yeast (unreacted)	1

In the remainder of this section we will consider a few other physical properties that can be measured without changing the identity of a substance.

Density

The **density** of a substance is the ratio of mass to volume:

$$\text{density} = \frac{\text{mass}}{\text{volume}} \qquad d = \frac{m}{V} \qquad (1.3)$$

CENGAGENOW™
Click Coached Problems for self-study modules on **density.**

Note that even though mass and volume are extensive properties, the ratio of mass to volume is intensive. Samples of copper weighing 1.00 g, 10.5 g, 264 g, . . . all have the same density, 8.94 g/mL at 25°C.

Density can be found in a straightforward way by measuring, independently, the mass and volume of a sample (Example 1.5).

Example 1.5 Palladium (Pd) is an element with properties similar to those of platinum. It is useful in eliminating harmful emissions produced by internal combustion engines. Two students were given identical cylindrical "palladium" bars with the following data:

$$\text{mass} = 96.03\text{ g, length} = 10.7\text{ cm, diameter} = 9.82\text{ mm, density} = 12.02\text{ g/cm}^3$$

(a) Student X was asked to determine whether her bar was made of pure palladium.
(b) Student Y was asked to determine how many grams of ethyl alcohol ($d = 0.789\text{ g/cm}^3$) his bar would displace.

Show the calculations that Students X and Y would do for the assigned tasks.

Strategy

(a) A pure bar of Pd should have density 12.02 g/cm^3. To determine the density of her bar, Student X would need its mass (given) and its volume. She could calculate the volume from the formula

$$\text{volume} = \pi(\text{radius})^2(\text{length})$$

(b) The bar will displace its volume of ethyl alcohol. So Student Y can use the density of alcohol to determine the mass of his bar.

SOLUTION

(a)
$$\text{mass of bar} = 96.03\text{ g}$$

$$\text{volume of bar} = \pi\left(\frac{9.82\text{ mm}}{2} \times \frac{1\text{ cm}}{10\text{ mm}}\right)^2 \times (10.7\text{ cm}) = 8.10\text{ cm}^3$$

$$\text{density of bar} = \frac{96.03\text{ g}}{8.10\text{ cm}^3} = 11.8\text{ g/cm}^3$$

Hence, the bar is not pure palladium.

(b) From (a), the volume of the bar is 8.10 cm^3. That is the volume of ethyl alcohol displaced by Student Y's bar. Thus,

$$\text{mass of ethyl alcohol displaced} = (\text{density of ethyl alcohol}) \times (\text{volume of ethyl alcohol displaced})$$

$$= \frac{0.789\text{ g}}{\text{cm}^3} \times 8.10\text{ cm}^3 = 6.39\text{ g}$$

Reality Check Since the density of palladium (12.02 g/cm^3) is larger than that of the metal bars, it would seem that they are slightly contaminated by a less dense metal.

Charles D. Winters

Density. The wood block has a lower density than water and floats. The ring has a higher density than water and sinks.

In a practical sense, density can be treated as a conversion factor to relate mass and volume. Knowing that mercury has a density of 13.6 g/mL, we can calculate the mass of 2.6 mL of mercury:

$$2.6\text{ mL} \times 13.6\frac{\text{g}}{\text{mL}} = 35\text{ g}$$

or the volume occupied by one kilogram of mercury:

$$1.000\text{ kg} \times \frac{10^3\text{g}}{1\text{ kg}} \times \frac{1\text{ mL}}{13.6\text{ g}} = 73.5\text{ mL}$$

Solubility

The process by which a solute dissolves in a solvent is ordinarily a physical rather than a chemical change. The extent to which it dissolves can be expressed in various ways. A common method is to state the number of grams of the substance that dissolves in 100 g of solvent at a given temperature.

Example 1.6 Graded

Sucrose is the chemical name for the sugar we consume. Its solubility at 20°C is 204 g/100 g water, and at 100°C is 487 g/100 g water. A solution is prepared by mixing 139 g of sugar in 33.0 g of water at 100°C.

The "100 g water" in this expression is an exact quantity.

*(a) What is the minimum amount of water required to dissolve the sugar at 100°C?

**(b) What is the maximum amount of sugar that can be dissolved in the water at 100°C?

***(c) The solution is cooled to 20°C. How much sugar (if any) will crystallize out?

****(d) How much more water is required to dissolve all the sugar at 20°C?

When the temperature changes, the amount of solute in solution changes, but the mass of water stays the same.

Strategy The solubility at a particular temperature gives a relationship between grams of sugar and grams of water. This in turn leads to a conversion factor to calculate either the mass of sugar or that of water.

SOLUTION

(a) $\text{mass of water required} = (139\text{ g sugar}) \times \dfrac{100\text{ g water}}{487\text{ g sugar}} = \boxed{28.5\text{ g water}}$

(b) $\text{mass of sugar} = (33.0\text{ g water}) \times \dfrac{487\text{ g sugar}}{100\text{ g water}} = \boxed{161\text{ g sugar}}$

(c) Since the amount of water will not change upon cooling, find the mass of sugar that will dissolve at 20°C:

$$\text{mass of sugar dissolved} = (33.0\text{ g water}) \times \frac{204\text{ g sugar}}{100\text{ g water}} = 67.3\text{ g}$$

$$\text{mass of sugar undissolved} = 139\text{ g} - 67.3\text{ g} = \boxed{72\text{ g}}$$

(d) The amount of sugar in the solution is 139 g. We find the mass of water that will dissolve that amount at 20°C:

$$\text{mass of water} = (139\text{ g sugar}) \times \frac{100\text{ g water}}{204\text{ g sugar}} = 68.1\text{ g}$$

The solution has only 33.0 g of water. Thus,

$$68.1\text{ g} - 33.0\text{ g} = \boxed{35.1\text{ g}}$$

is the minimum amount of water that needs to be added so that all the sugar will disslove at 20°C.

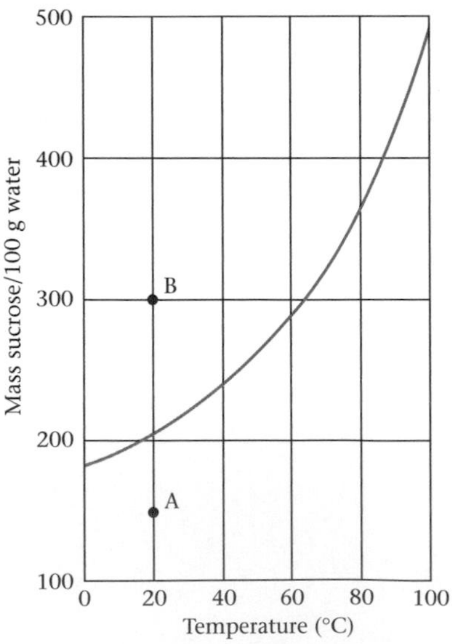

Figure 1.12
Solubility of table sugar (sucrose). The solubility of sugar, $C_{12}H_{22}O_{11}$, in water increases exponentially with temperature.

Figure 1.12 shows the solubility of sugar in water as a function of temperature. Alternatively, we can say that it gives the concentration of sugar in a **saturated** solution at various temperatures. For example, at 20°C, we could say that "the solubility of sugar is 204 g/100 g water" or that "a saturated solution of sugar contains 204 g/100 g water."

At any point in the area below the curve in Figure 1.12, we are dealing with an **unsaturated** solution. Consider, for example, point A (150 g sugar per 100 g water at 20°C). This solution is unsaturated; if we add more sugar, another 54 g will dissolve to give a saturated solution (204 g sugar per 100 g water at 20°C).

At any point in the area above the curve, the sugar solution is **supersaturated.** This is the case at point B (300 g sugar per 100 g water at 20°C). Such a solution could be formed by carefully cooling a saturated solution at 60°C to 20°C, where a saturated solution contains 204 g sugar per 100 g water. The excess sugar stays in solution until a small seed crystal of sugar is added, whereupon crystallization quickly takes place. At that point the excess sugar

$$300\text{ g} - 204\text{ g} = 96\text{ g}$$

comes out of solution.

The crystallization of excess solute is a common problem in the preparation of candies and in the storage of jam and honey. From these supersaturated solutions, sugar separates either as tiny crystals, causing the "graininess" in fudge, or as large crystals, which often appear in honey kept for a long time (Figure 1.13, page 17).

Table 1.4 Relation Between Color and Wavelength

Wavelength (nanometers)	Color Absorbed	Color Transmitted
<400 nm	Ultraviolet	Colorless
400–450 nm	Violet	Red, orange, yellow
450–500 nm	Blue	
500–550 nm	Green	Purple
550–580 nm	Yellow	
580–650 nm	Orange	Blue, green
650–700 nm	Red	
>700 nm	Infrared	Colorless

Figure 1.13
Rock candy. The candy is formed by crystallization of sugar from a saturated solution that is cooled slowly.

Color; Absorption Spectrum

Some of the substances you work with in general chemistry can be identified at least tentatively by their color. Gaseous nitrogen dioxide has a brown color; vapors of bromine and iodine are red and violet, respectively. A water solution of copper sulfate is blue, and a solution of potassium permanganate is purple (Figure 1.14).

The colors of gases and liquids are due to the selective absorption of certain components of visible light. Bromine, for example, absorbs in the violet and blue regions of the spectrum (Table 1.4). The subtraction of these components from visible light accounts for the red color of bromine liquid or vapor. The purple (blue-red) color of a potassium permanganate solution results from absorption in the green region (Figure 1.15).

The wavelengths of visible light range from 400 to 700 nm. For a substance to be colored, it must absorb somewhere within this region. However, many colorless substances absorb in the ultraviolet (<400 nm) or infrared (>700 nm) regions. Ozone in the upper atmosphere absorbs harmful, high-energy ultraviolet radiation from the sun. Carbon dioxide absorbs infrared radiation given off by the earth's surface, preventing it from escaping into outer space, and thereby contributing to global warming.

Figure 1.14
Crystals of potassium permanganate falling into water. The purple color of the solution results from absorption at approximately 550 nm.

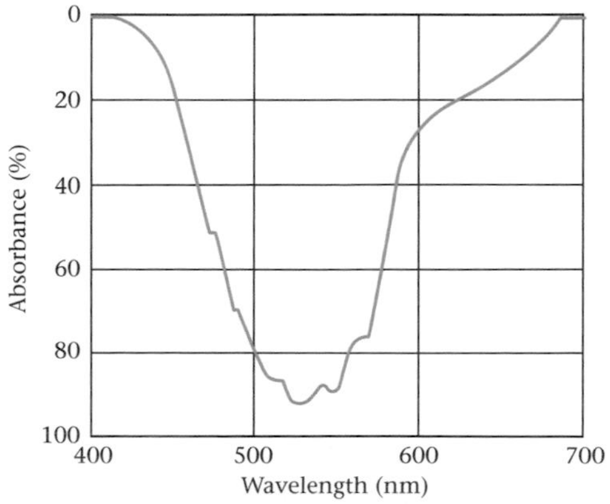

Figure 1.15
Absorption spectrum of potassium permanganate.

CHEMISTRY Beyond the Classroom

Titanium: A Space-Age Metal

The metallic element titanium (Ti) is relatively abundant in nature; it accounts for 0.56% of the earth's crust. This number may not seem very impressive until you realize that it exceeds the *combined* abundances of ten familiar elements: H, N, C, P, S, Cl, Cr, Ni, Cu, and Zn. The most important ore of titanium is ilmenite, a mineral commonly found as a deposit of black sand along beaches in the United States, Canada, Australia, and Norway. In ilmenite, titanium is chemically combined with iron and oxygen. The presence of iron makes the ore magnetic.

Erika Barahona Ede © FMGB Guggenheim Bilbao Museo

Figure A
The outside of this building is covered with half-millimeter-thick panels of titanium, guaranteed to last a hundred years.

Titanium has an unusually high ratio of strength to weight. It is considerably stronger than either aluminum or steel, two metals with which it competes (for special purposes). Its density (4.5 g/cm^3) is intermediate between that of Al (2.7 g/cm^3) and that of Fe (7.9 g/cm^3). Titanium is extremely resistant to corrosion by air, soil, seawater, and even such reactive chemicals as nitric acid and chlorine gas. Like aluminum, it forms a thin, tightly adherent oxide layer that protects the metal from further attack.

These properties of titanium make it useful in spacecraft of all types; it is widely used in jet engines and other components of modern airplanes. It has also found application in the exterior walls of large buildings such as the Guggenheim Museum in Bilbao, Spain (Figure A). On a smaller scale, articles such as golf club heads and eyeglass frames are now being made from titanium.

Titanium and its compounds are nontoxic and immune to attack by body fluids. These features account for the use of the metal in knee and hip replacements as well as dental implants.

Lest you suppose that titanium is a metal for all purposes, we should point out one of its limitations. It is far more expensive than aluminum or steel, selling for about $50 a kilogram in 2007. The high cost of extracting the metal from ilmenite ore makes it very, very unlikely that you will ever see lawnmowers or kitchen sinks made out of titanium.

By far the most important compound of titanium is the dioxide (TiO_2). About 94% of the ilmenite ore processed annually is converted to titanium dioxide as compared with only 4% for the metal itself. Putting it another way, the yearly production of titanium dioxide is about 2×10^6 metric tons as compared with only 10^5 metric tons of titanium.

The first major use of titanium dioxide was as a replacement for toxic lead compounds in paint. It combines a brilliant white color with very high covering power. Addition of certain compounds of nickel changes the white color to yellow; cobalt compounds give a green paint.

In the 1970s, textbook publishers (and other entrepreneurs) found that adding titanium dioxide to paper as a filler and whitener enormously increased its opacity (Figure B). This allowed for the use of thinner paper without having the type "bleed" from one side to the other. Perhaps this explains, at least in part, why most chemistry textbooks today (but not this one) run to a thousand pages or more.

Figure B
As you can see, paper treated with TiO_2 is more opaque than, let us say, bathroom tissue.

Quite recently (2001) titanium dioxide has been used to coat "self-cleaning" windows with a very thin film about 5×10^{-6} cm thick. The titanium dioxide acts as a catalyst for the decomposition of dust and grime by solar ultraviolet light. Probably more important, it lowers surface tension so that rain water "sheets down" the window, washing away dirt.

Lance Armstrong's very expensive racing bike is made of titanium.

Chapter Highlights

Key Concepts

1. Convert between °F, °C, and K.
   (Example 1.1; Problems 13–16) ■ Questions and Problems assignable in OWL: 14, 73
2. Determine the number of significant figures in a measured quantity.
   (Example 1.2; Problems 17, 18, 25, 26) ■ 18
3. Determine the number of significant figures in a calculated quantity.
   (Example 1.3; Problems 27–30) ■ 27
4. Use conversion factors to change the units of a measured quantity.
   (Example 1.4; Problems 31–44, 60) ■ 33, 36, 37, 40, 42, 65
5. Relate density to mass and volume.
   (Example 1.5; Problems 45–52, 61, 63) ■ 45, 47, 48, 50, 52, 62, 63
6. Given its solubility, relate mass of solute to that of solvent.
   (Example 1.6; Problems 53–56, 57) ■ 54

Select end of chapter Questions and Problems may be assigned in OWL and are cross-referenced in the Key Concepts list.

CENGAGENOW™

Sign in at **academic.cengage.com/now** to:

- Check your readiness for an exam by taking the Pre-Test and exploring the self-study modules recommended in your Personalized Study plan.
- For quick review, download Go Chemistry mini-lecture flashcard modules (or purchase them at **www.ichapters.com**)

Key Equations

Fahrenheit temperature	$t_{°F} = 1.8\, t_{°C} + 32°$ (Section 1.2)
Kelvin temperature	$T_K = t_{°C} + 273.15$ (Section 1.2)
Density	$d = m/V$ (Section 1.3)

Key Terms

centi-	mixture	—intensive
compound	—heterogeneous	—physical
conversion factor	—homogeneous	significant figure
density	nano-	solution
element	property	—saturated
kilo-	—chemical	—supersaturated
milli-	—extensive	—unsaturated

Summary Problem

Cane sugar is also known as sucrose. It is a white solid made up of three elements: carbon, hydrogen, and oxygen. At 20°C, it has a density of 1.588 g/cm^3; its melting point is 1.70×10^2 °C. At 20°C, its solubility is 203.9 g/100 g water; at 90°C, the solubility is 415.7 g/100 g water.

(a) What are the symbols of the three elements in cane sugar?

(b) List all the physical properties of sucrose given above.

(c) How many grams of sugar are in 155 mL of sugar?

(d) A cup of sugar weighs 2.00×10^2 g. How many cups of sugar are in a 5.0-lb bag of sugar?

(e) What is the melting point of sugar in °F?

(f) How many grams of sugar can be dissolved in 75.0 g of water at 20°C?

(g) A solution of sugar in water is prepared by dissolving 325 g of sugar in 100.0 g of water at 90°C. The solution is carefully cooled to 20°C. A homogeneous solution is obtained. State whether the solutions at 90°C and at 20°C are saturated, supersaturated, or unsaturated.

(h) At 20°C, a solution is prepared by dissolving 170.2 g of sucrose in 500.0 mL of water (d = 1.00 g/mL). The resulting solution has a volume of 531 mL. What is the density of the resulting solution? Is it saturated?

(i) A solution of sugar is prepared at 90°C by dissolving 237 g of sugar in 68 mL of water. Will all the sugar dissolve at 90°C? How many grams of sugar would you expect to crystallize out of solution when the solution is cooled to 20°C?

(j) A solution of sugar is colorless. What colors of visible light does the solution absorb? In what range of wavelengths of light does the solution absorb?

Express all your answers to the correct number of significant figures; use the conversion factor approach throughout.

Answers

(a) C, H, O
(b) color, density, melting point, solubility
(c) 246 g
(d) 11 cups
(e) 338°F
(f) 153 g
(g) At 90°C, solution is unsaturated.
At 20°C, solution is supersaturated.
(h) 1.26 g/mL; no
(i) yes; 98 g
(j) no color absorbed; < 400 nm (ultraviolet range) and > 700 nm (infrared range)

Questions and Problems

Blue-numbered questions have answers in Appendix 6 and fully-worked solutions in the *Student Solutions Manual.*

■ denotes questions assignable in OWL.

WEB indicates that the solution is available on this book's companion website.

The questions and problems listed here are typical of those at the end of each chapter. Some are conceptual. Most require calculations, writing equations, or other quantitative work. The headings identify the primary topic of each set of questions or problems, such as "Symbols and Formulas" or "Significant Figures." Those in the "Unclassified" category may involve more than one concept, including, perhaps, topics from a preceding chapter. "Challenge Problems," listed at the end of the set, require extra skill and/or effort. The "Classified" questions and problems (Problems 1–52 in this set) occur in matched pairs, one below the other, and illustrate the same concept. For example, Questions 1 and 2 are nearly identical in nature; the same is true of Questions 3 and 4, and so on.

Types of Matter

1. Classify each of the following as element, compound, or mixture.
(a) air **(b)** iron
(c) soy sauce **(d)** table salt

2. ■ Classify each of the following as element, compound, or mixture.
(a) gold
(b) milk
(c) sugar
(d) vinaigrette dressing with herbs

3. Classify the following as solution or heterogeneous mixture.
(a) maple syrup
(b) seawater passed through a sieve
(c) melted rocky road ice cream

4. Classify the following as solution or heterogeneous mixture.
(a) wine
(b) gasoline
(c) batter for chocolate chip cookies

5. How would you separate into its different components
(a) a solution of acetone and water?
(b) a mixture of aluminum powder and ethyl alcohol?

6. How would you separate into its different components
(a) a mixture of the volatile gases propane, butane, and isopropane?
(b) a solution of rubbing alcohol made up of isopropyl alcohol and water?

7. ■ Write the symbol for the following elements.
(a) titanium **(b)** phosphorus
(c) potassium **(d)** magnesium

8. Write the symbol for the following elements.
(a) manganese **(b)** lead
(c) gold **(d)** silver

9. Write the name of the element represented by the following symbols.
(a) Hg **(b)** Si **(c)** Na **(d)** I

10. Write the name of the element represented by the following symbols.
(a) Cr **(b)** Ca **(c)** Fe **(d)** Zn

Measurements

11. What instrument would you use to determine
(a) the mass of a head of lettuce?
(b) whether your refrigerator is cooling water to 10°C?
(c) the volume of a glass of orange juice?

12. What instrument would you use to determine
(a) the length of your bed?
(b) the amount of acid delivered to a beaker?
(c) whether you have a fever?

13. A glass of lukewarm milk is suggested for people who cannot sleep. Milk at 52°C can be characterized as lukewarm. What is the temperature of lukewarm milk in °F? In K?

14. ■ A recipe for apple pie calls for a preheated 350°F (three significant figures) oven. Express this temperature setting in °C and in K.

15. Liquid helium is extensively used in research on superconductivity. Liquid helium has a boiling point of 4.22 K. Express this boiling point in °C and °F.

16. Gallium is one of the few metals that can melt at room temperature. Its melting point is 29.76°C. If you leave solid gallium in your car on an early summer morning when the temperature is 75°F, in what physical state is the gallium when you return to your car and the interior car temperature is 85.0°F?

Significant Figures

17. How many significant figures are there in each of the following?
(a) 12.7040 g **(b)** 200.0 cm **(c)** 276.2 tons
(d) 4.00×10^3 mL **(e)** 100°C

18. ■ How many significant figures are there in each of the following?
(a) 0.136 m **(b)** 0.0001050 g
(c) 2.700×10^3 nm **(d)** 6×10^{-4} L **(e)** 56003 cm^3

19. Round off the following quantities to the indicated number of significant figures.
(a) 7.4855 g (three significant figures)
(b) 298.693 cm (five significant figures)
(c) 11.698 lb (one significant figure)
(d) 12.05 oz (three significant figures)

20. Round off the following quantities to the indicated number of significant figures.
(a) 132.505 g (four significant figures)
(b) 298.693 cm (five significant figures)
(c) 13.452 lb (two significant figures)
(d) 345 oz (two significant figures)

21. Express the following measurements in scientific notation.
(a) 4633.2 mg (b) 0.000473 L (c) 127,000.0 cm^3

22. **WEB** Express the following measurements in scientific notation.
(a) 4020.6 mL (b) 1.006 g (c) 100.1°C

23. Which of the following statements use exact numbers?
(a) You owe me $11.35 for 5.7 lb of tomatoes. They were $1.99 a pound.
(b) There are 16 oz in 1 lb.
(c) There are 7 cars in your driveway.

24. Which of the following statements use exact numbers?
(a) The little girl weighs 74.3 lb.
(b) The boiling point of ethyl alcohol is 78°C.
(c) The square root of 144 is 12.

25. A basketball game at the University of Connecticut's Gampel Pavilion attracted 10,000 people. The building's interior floor space has an area of 1.71×10^5 ft^2. Tickets to the game sold for $22.00. Senior citizens were given a 20% discount. How many significant figures are there in each quantity? (Your answer may include the words *ambiguous* and *exact*.)

26. A listing of a house for sale states that there are 5 bedrooms, 4000 ft^2 of living area, and a living room with dimensions 17 × 18.5 ft. How many significant figures are there in each quantity? (Your answer may include the words *ambiguous* and *exact*.)

27. ■ Calculate the following to the correct number of significant figures. Assume that all these numbers are measurements.
(a) $x = 17.2 + 65.18 - 2.4$
(b) $x = \dfrac{13.0217}{17.10}$
(c) $x = (0.0061020)(2.0092)(1200.00)$
(d) $x = 0.0034 + \dfrac{\sqrt{(0.0034)^2 + 4(1.000)(6.3 \times 10^{-4})}}{(2)(1.000)}$

28. Calculate the following to the correct number of significant figures.
(a) $x = 128.5 + 2116.44 - 2244.47$
(b) $x = 0.004010 \times 2.0000 \times 50054$
(c) $x = \dfrac{12.6 + 0.3 + 256.5}{1003.7}$
(d) $x = \dfrac{12.20 - \sqrt{1.60 + 4(0.36)}}{1.3409}$

29. The volume of a sphere is $4\pi r^3/3$, where r is the radius. One student measured the radius to be 4.30 cm. Another measured the radius to be 4.33 cm. What is the difference in volume between the two measurements?

30. A cylinder has a circular cross section with a radius of 2.500 cm. What is the volume of water in the cylinder with a measured height of 1.20 cm? (The volume of a cylinder is $\pi r^2 h$, where r is the radius and h is the height.)

Conversion Factors

31. Write the appropriate symbol in the blank (>, <, or =).
(a) 303 m ________ 303×10^3 km
(b) 500 g ________ 0.500 kg
(c) 1.50 cm^3 ________ 1.50×10^3 nm^3

32. **WEB** Write the appropriate symbol in the blank (>, <, or =).
(a) 37.12 g ________ 0.3712 kg
(b) 28 m^3 ________ 28×10^2 cm^3
(c) 525 mm ________ 525×10^6 nm

33. ■ Convert 22.3 mL to
(a) liters (b) in^3 (c) quarts

34. Convert 6743 nm to
(a) Å (b) inches (c) miles

35. The height of a horse is usually measured in hands. One hand is exactly 1/3 ft.
(a) How tall (in feet) is a horse of 19.2 hands?
(b) How tall (in meters) is a horse of 17.8 hands?
(c) A horse of 20.5 hands is to be transported in a trailer. The roof of the trailer needs to provide 3.0 ft of vertical clearance. What is the minimum height of the trailer in feet?

36. ■ At sea, distances are measured in nautical miles and speeds are expressed in knots.

$$1 \text{ nautical mile} = 6076.12 \text{ ft}$$

$$1 \text{ knot} = 1 \text{ nautical mi/h (exactly)}$$

(a) How many miles are in one nautical mile?
(b) How many meters are in one nautical mile?
(c) A ship is traveling at a rate of 22 knots. Express the ship's speed in miles per hour.

37. ■ The unit of land measure in the English system is the acre, while that in the metric system is the hectare. An acre is 4.356×10^4 ft^2. A hectare is ten thousand square meters. The town of Willington in Connecticut requires a minimum area of 2.0 acres of land for a single-family dwelling. How many hectares are required?

38. A lap in most tracks that use the English system is 0.25 mi (English lap). In countries that use the metric system, a metric lap is 0.50 km. A champion marathon runner covers a mile in about 5.0 min. How many minutes will the runner take to run an English lap at that speed? A metric lap?

39. An average adult has 6.0 L of blood. The Red Cross usually takes 1 pint of blood from each donor at a donation. What percentage (by volume) of a person's blood does a blood donor give in one donation?

40. ■ Cholesterol in blood is measured in milligrams of cholesterol per deciliter of blood. If the unit of measurement were changed to grams of cholesterol per milliliter of blood, what would a cholesterol reading of 185 mg/dL translate to?

41. Some states have reduced the legal limit for alcohol sobriety from 0.10% to 0.080% alcohol by volume in blood plasma.
(a) How many milliliters of alcohol are in 3.0 qt of blood plasma at the lower legal limit?
(b) How many milliliters of alcohol are in 3.0 qt of blood plasma at the higher legal limit?
(c) How much less alcohol is in 3.0 qt of blood plasma with the reduced sobriety level?

42. ■ The area of the 48 contiguous states is 3.02×10^6 mi^2. Assume that these states are completely flat (no mountains and no valleys). What volume of water, in liters, would cover these states with a rainfall of two inches?

43. In Europe, nutritional information is given in kilojoules (kJ) instead of nutritional calories (1 nutritional calorie = 1 kcal). A packet of soup has the following nutritional information:

$$250 \text{ mL of soup} = 235 \text{ kJ}$$

How would that same packet be labeled in the United States if the information has to be given in nutritional calories per cup? (There are 4.18 joules in one calorie and 2 cups to a pint.)

■ in OWL Blue-numbered questions answered in Appendix 6 **WEB** Solution is available on companion website

44. In the old pharmaceutical system of measurements, masses were expressed in grains. There are 5.760×10^3 grains in 1 lb. An old bottle of aspirin lists 5 grains of active ingredient per tablet. How many milligrams of active ingredient are there in the same tablet?

Physical and Chemical Properties

45. ■ The cup is a measure of volume widely used in cookbooks. One cup is equivalent to 225 mL. What is the density of clover honey (in grams per milliliter) if three quarters of a cup has a mass of 252 g?

46. The volume occupied by egg whites from four "large" eggs is 112 mL. The mass of the egg whites from these four eggs is 1.20×10^2 g. What is the average density of the egg white from one "large" egg?

47. ■ A metal slug weighing 25.17 g is added to a flask with a volume of 59.7 mL. It is found that 43.7 g of methanol ($d = 0.791$ g/mL) must be added to the metal to fill the flask. What is the density of the metal?

48. ■ **WEB** A solid with an irregular shape and a mass of 11.33 g is added to a graduated cylinder filled with water ($d = 1.00$ g/mL) to the 35.0-mL mark. After the solid sinks to the bottom, the water level is read to be at the 42.3-mL mark. What is the density of the solid?

49. A waterbed filled with water has the dimensions 8.0 ft $\times$ 7.0 ft $\times$ 0.75 ft. Taking the density of water to be 1.00 g/cm^3, how many kilograms of water are required to fill the waterbed?

50. ■ Wire is often sold in pound spools according to the wire gauge number. That number refers to the diameter of the wire. How many meters are in a 10-lb spool of 12-gauge aluminum wire? A 12-gauge wire has a diameter of 0.0808 in. Aluminum has a density of 2.70 g/cm^3. ($V = \pi r^2 \ell$)

51. Vinegar contains 5.00% acetic acid by mass and has a density of 1.01 g/mL. What mass (in grams) of acetic acid is present in 5.00 L of vinegar?

52. ■ Air is 21% oxygen by volume. Oxygen has a density of 1.31 g/L. What is the volume, in liters, of a room that holds enough air to contain 55 kg of oxygen?

53. The solubility of barium hydroxide in water at 20°C is 1.85 g/100 g water. A solution is made up of 256 mg in 35.0 g of water. Is the solution saturated? If not, how much more barium hydroxide needs to be added to make a saturated solution?

54. ■ Potassium sulfate has a solubility of 15 g/100 g water at 40°C. A solution is prepared by adding 39.0 g of potassium sulfate to 225 g of water, carefully heating the solution, and cooling it to 40°C. A homogeneous solution is obtained. Is this solution saturated, unsaturated, or supersaturated? The beaker is shaken, and precipitation occurs. How many grams of potassium sulfate would you expect to crystallize out?

55. Potassium chloride is widely used in the manufacture of fertilizers. Its solubility is 37.0 g/100 g water at 30°C. At 70°C its solubility is 48.3 g/100 g water.
   - **(a)** Calculate the mass of potassium chloride that dissolves in 44.5 g of water at 30°C.
   - **(b)** Calculate the mass of water required to dissolve 39.6 g of potassium chloride at 70°C.
   - **(c)** If 40.0 g of potassium chloride are added to 75.0 g of water at 30°C, will it all dissolve? If the temperature is increased to 70°C, will it all dissolve? How many grams (if any) are undissolved at 30°C? at 70°C?

56. Ammonium bromide can be used as a wood preservative. Its solubility in water at 20°C is 75.5 g/100 g water. At 50°C its solubility is 99.2 g/100 g water. Calculate
   - **(a)** the mass of ammonium bromide that dissolves in 82.5 g of water at 20°C.
   - **(b)** the mass of water required to dissolve 43.7 g of ammonium bromide at 50°C.
   - **(c)** the mass of ammonium bromide that would not remain in solution if a solution made up of 29.0 g of ammonium bromide in 35.0 g of water at 50°C is cooled to 20°C.

Unclassified

57. The solubility of lead nitrate at 100°C is 140.0 g/100 g water. A solution at 100°C consists of 57.0 g of lead nitrate in 64.0 g of water. When the solution is cooled to 10°C, 25.0 g of lead nitrate crystallize out. What is the solubility of lead nitrate in g/100 g water at 10°C?

58. The following data refer to the compound water. Classify each as a chemical or a physical property.
   - **(a)** It is a colorless liquid at 25°C and 1 atm.
   - **(b)** It reacts with sodium to form hydrogen gas as one of the products.
   - **(c)** Its melting point is 0°C.
   - **(d)** It is insoluble in carbon tetrachloride.

59. The following data refer to the element phosphorus. Classify each as a physical or a chemical property.
   - **(a)** It exists in several forms, for example, white, black, and red phosphorus.
   - **(b)** It is a solid at 25°C and 1 atm.
   - **(c)** It is insoluble in water.
   - **(d)** It burns in chlorine to form phosphorus trichloride.

60. A cup of brewed coffee is made with about 9.0 g of ground coffee beans. If a student brews three cups of gourmet coffee a day, how much does the student spend on a year's supply of gourmet coffee that sells at $8.99/lb?

61. Lead has a density of 11.34 g/cm^3 and oxygen has a density of 1.31×10^{-3} g/cm^3 at room temperature. How many cm^3 are occupied by 1 g of lead? By 1 g of oxygen? Comment on the difference in volume for the two elements.

62. ■ The dimensions of aluminum foil in a box for sale in supermarkets are 66⅔ yards by 12 inches. The mass of the foil is 0.83 kg. If its density is 2.70 g/cm^3, then what is the thickness of the foil in inches?

63. ■ The Kohinoor Diamond ($d = 3.51$ g/cm^3) is 108 carats. If one carat has a mass of 2.00×10^2 mg, what is the mass of the Kohinoor Diamond in pounds? What is the volume of the diamond in cubic inches?

64. A pycnometer is a device used to measure density. It weighs 20.455 g empty and 31.486 g when filled with water ($d = 1.00$ g/cm^3). Pieces of an alloy are put into the empty, dry pycnometer. The mass of the alloy and pycnometer is 28.695 g. Water is added to the alloy to exactly fill the pycnometer. The mass of the pycnometer, water, and alloy is 38.689 g. What is the density of the alloy?

65. ■ Titanium is used in airplane bodies because it is strong and light. It has a density of 4.55 g/cm^3. If a cylinder of titanium is 7.75 cm long and has a mass of 153.2 g, calculate the diameter of the cylinder. ($V = \pi r^2 h$, where V is the volume of the cylinder, r is its radius, and h is the height.)

Conceptual Questions

66. How do you distinguish
   - **(a)** density from solubility?
   - **(b)** an element from a compound?
   - **(c)** a solution from a heterogeneous mixture?

67. How do you distinguish
   - **(a)** chemical properties from physical properties?
   - **(b)** distillation from filtration?
   - **(c)** a solute from a solution?

68. Why is the density of a regular soft drink higher than that of a diet soft drink?

69. Mercury, ethyl alcohol, and lead are poured into a cylinder. Three distinct layers are formed. The densities of the three substances are

$$\text{mercury} = 13.55 \text{ g/cm}^3$$
$$\text{ethyl alcohol} = 0.78 \text{ g/cm}^3$$
$$\text{lead} = 11.4 \text{ g/cm}^3$$

Sketch the cylinder with the three layers. Identify the substance in each layer.

■ in OWL Blue-numbered questions answered in Appendix 6 **WEB** Solution is available on companion website

70. How many significant figures are there in the length of this line?

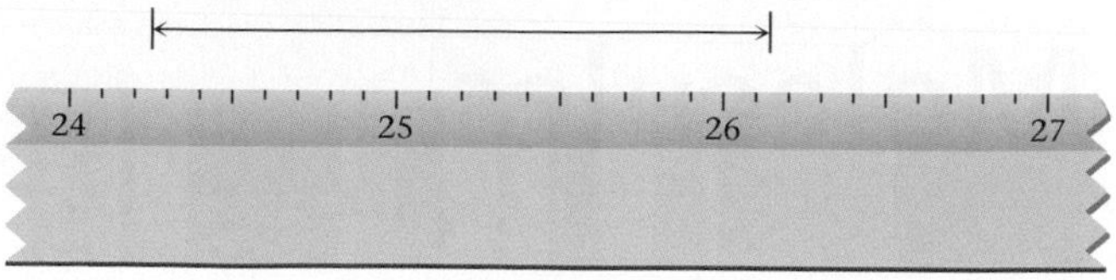

71. Consider the following solubility graph.

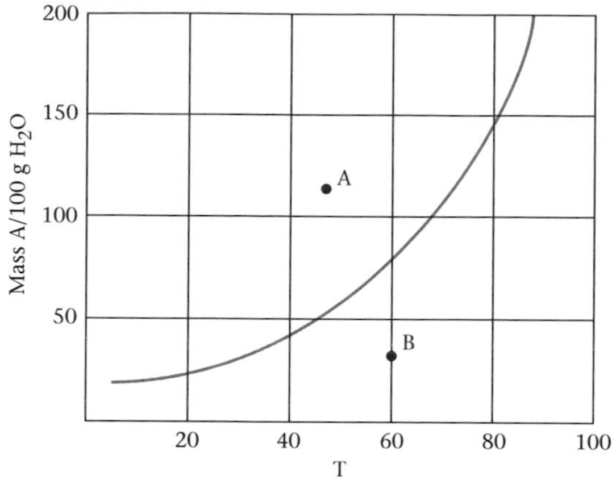

(a) At point *A*, how many grams of the compound are dissolved in 100 g of water? Is the solution saturated, unsaturated, or supersaturated?
(b) At point *B*, how many grams of the compound are dissolved in 100 g of water? Is the solution saturated, unsaturated, or supersaturated?
(c) How would you prepare a saturated solution at 30°C?

72. Given the following solubility curves, answer the following questions:
(a) In which of the two compounds can more solute be dissolved in the same amount of water when the temperature is decreased?
(b) At what temperature is the solubility of both compounds the same?
(c) Will an increase in temperature always increase solubility of a compound? Explain.

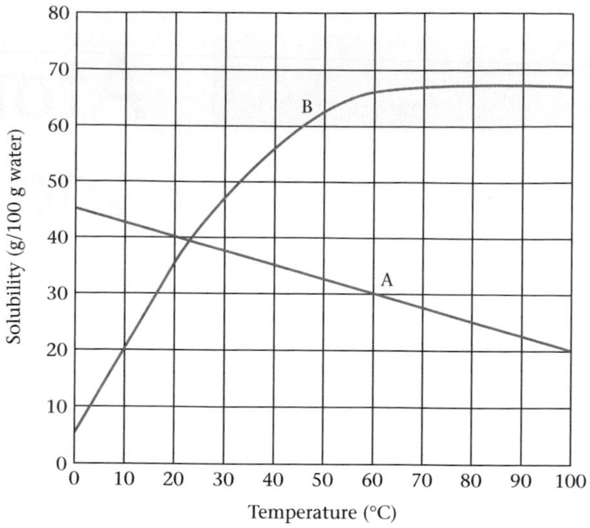

Challenge Problems

73. ■ At what point is the temperature in °F exactly twice that in °C?

74. Oil spreads on water to form a film about 100 nm thick (two significant figures). How many square kilometers of ocean will be covered by the slick formed when one barrel of oil is spilled (1 barrel = 31.5 U.S. gal)?

75. A laboratory experiment requires 12 g of aluminum wire (d = 2.70 g/cm^3). The diameter of the wire is 0.200 in. Determine the length of the wire, in centimeters, to be used for this experiment. The volume of a cylinder is $\pi r^2 \ell$, where r = radius and ℓ = length.

76. ■ An average adult breathes about 8.50×10^3 L of air per day. The concentration of lead in highly polluted urban air is 7.0×10^{-6} g of lead per one m^3 of air. Assume that 75% of the lead is present as particles less than 1.0×10^{-6} m in diameter, and that 50% of the particles below that size are retained in the lungs. Calculate the mass of lead absorbed in this manner in 1 year by an average adult living in this environment.

■ in OWL Blue-numbered questions answered in Appendix 6 **WEB** Solution is available on companion website

2 Atoms, Molecules, and Ions

The naming of cats is a different matter,
It isn't just one of your holiday games.
You may think at first I'm mad as a hatter
When I tell you, a cat must have THREE DIFFERENT NAMES.

—T. S. Eliot
"Old Possum's Book of Practical Cats"

Chapter Outline

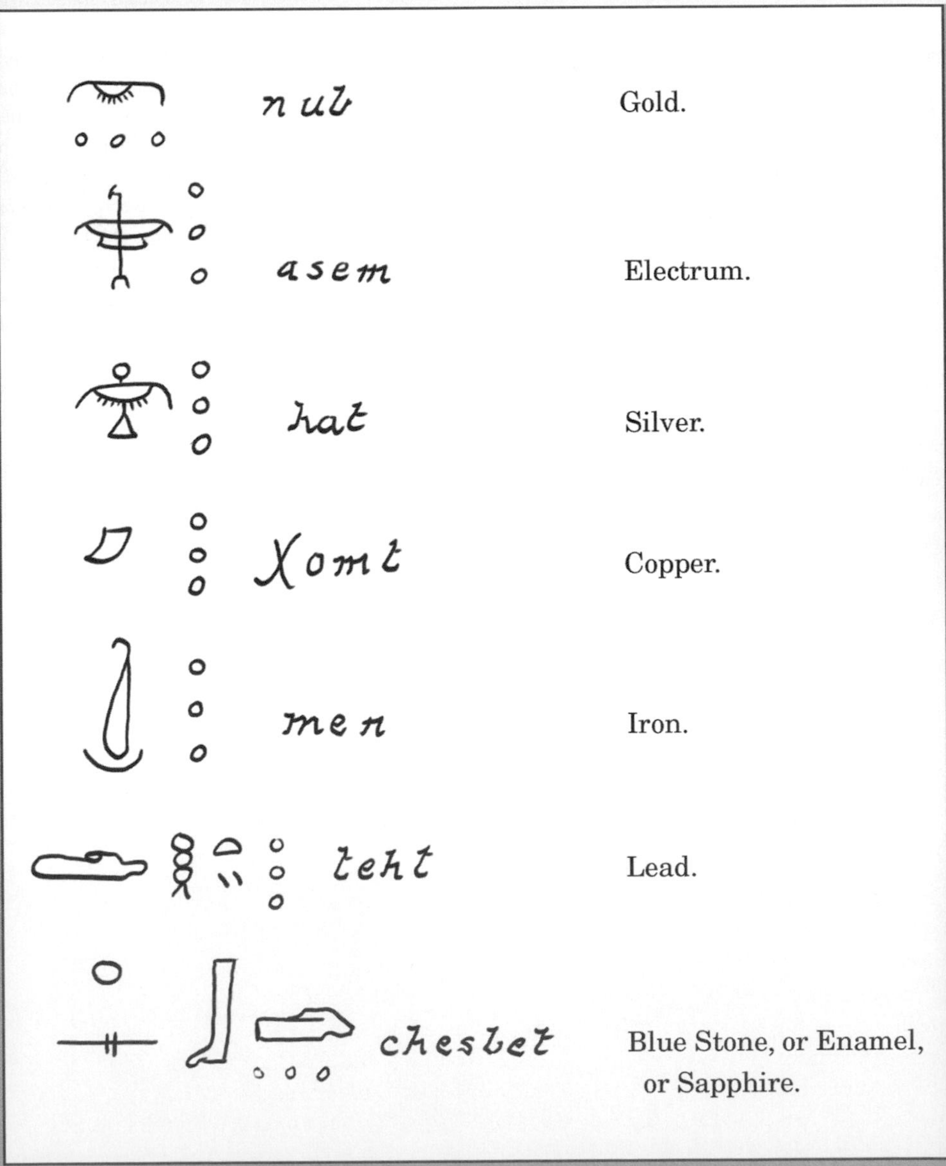

Redrawn from Lepsius, *Metals in Egyptian Inscriptions*, 1860

Just like chemists today, ancient Egyptians also used symbols as well as words to represent common elements and compounds. Electrum is an alloy of silver and gold.

To learn chemistry, you must become familiar with the building blocks that chemists use to describe the structure of matter. These include—

- *atoms* (Section 2.1), which in turn are composed of electrons, protons, and neutrons (Section 2.2).
- *molecules,* the building blocks of several elements and a great many compounds. Molecular substances can be identified by their formulas (Section 2.4) or their names (Section 2.6).
- *ions,* species of opposite charge found in all ionic compounds. Using relatively simple principles, it is possible to derive the formulas (Section 2.5) and names (Section 2.6) of ionic compounds.

Early in this chapter (Section 2.3) we will introduce a classification system for elements known as the *periodic table.* It will prove useful in this chapter and throughout the remainder of this text. ■

Online homework for this chapter may be assigned in OWL.

CENGAGENOW™
This icon introduces an opportunity for self-study and to explore interactive modules by signing in at **academic.cengage.com/now.**

2.1 ATOMS AND THE ATOMIC THEORY

In 1808, an English scientist and schoolteacher, John Dalton, developed the atomic model of matter that underlies modern chemistry. Three of the main postulates of modern atomic theory, all of which Dalton suggested in a somewhat different form, are stated below and illustrated in Figure 2.1.

1. *An element is composed of tiny particles called atoms.* All atoms of a given element show the same chemical properties. Atoms of different elements show different properties.
2. *In an ordinary chemical reaction, atoms move from one substance to another, but no atom of any element disappears or is changed into an atom of another element.*
3. *Compounds are formed when atoms of two or more elements combine.* In a given compound, the relative numbers of atoms of each kind are definite and constant. In general, these relative numbers can be expressed as integers or simple fractions.

On the basis of Dalton's theory, the **atom** can be defined as the smallest particle of an element that can enter into a chemical reaction.

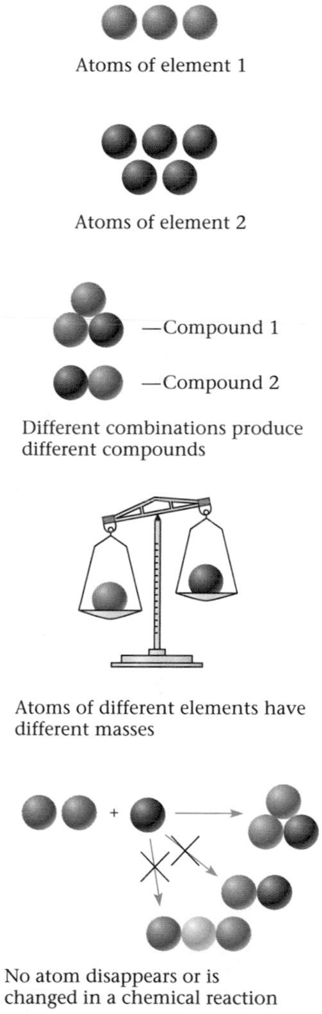

Figure 2.1
Some features of Dalton's atomic theory.

2.2 COMPONENTS OF THE ATOM

Like any useful scientific theory, the atomic theory raised more questions than it answered. Scientists wondered whether atoms, tiny as they are, could be broken down into still smaller particles. Nearly 100 years passed before the existence of subatomic particles was confirmed by experiment. Two future Nobel laureates did pioneer work in this area. J. J. Thomson was an English physicist working at the Cavendish Laboratory at Cambridge. Ernest Rutherford, at one time a student of Thomson's (Figure 2.2, page 26), was a native of New Zealand. Rutherford carried out his research at McGill University in Montreal and at Manchester and Cambridge in England. He was clearly the greatest experimental physicist of his time, and one of the greatest of all time.

Atoms are indeed tiny (they have diameters of about 10^{-10} m).

Figure 2.2
J. J. Thomson and Ernest Rutherford *(right).* They are talking, perhaps about nuclear physics, but more likely about yesterday's cricket match.

AIP Emilio Segre Visual Archives, Bainbridge Collections

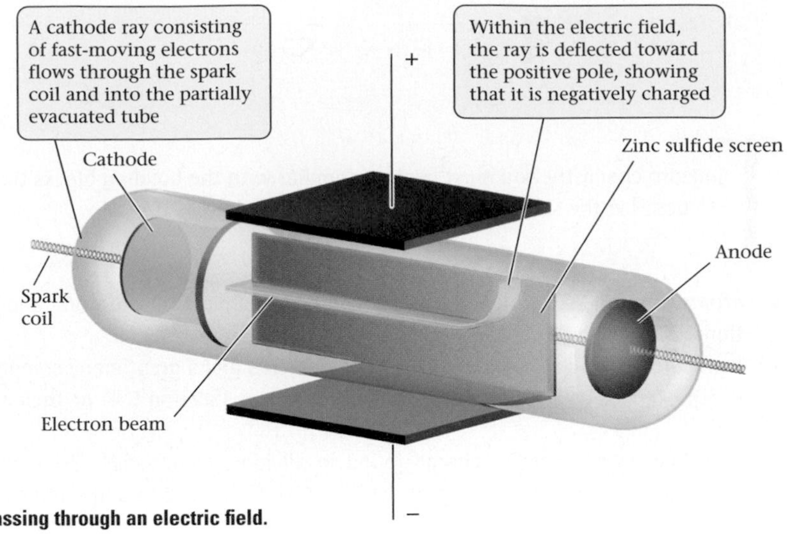

Figure 2.3
A cathode ray passing through an electric field.

Electrons

The first evidence for the existence of subatomic particles came from studies of the conduction of electricity through gases at low pressures. When the glass tube shown in Figure 2.3 is partially evacuated and connected to a spark coil, an electric current flows through it. Associated with this flow are colored rays of light called *cathode rays,* which are bent by both electric and magnetic fields. From a careful study of this deflection, J. J. Thomson showed in 1897 that the rays consist of a stream of negatively charged particles, which he called **electrons.** We now know that electrons are common to all atoms, carry a unit negative charge (−1), and have a very small mass, roughly 1/2000 that of the lightest atom.

Every atom contains a definite number of electrons. This number, which runs from 1 to more than 100, is characteristic of a neutral atom of a particular element. All atoms of hydrogen contain one electron; all atoms of the element uranium contain 92 electrons. We will have more to say in Chapter 6 about how these electrons are arranged relative to one another. Right now, you need only know that they are found in the outer regions of the atom, where they form what amounts to a cloud of negative charge.

CENGAGENOW™
Click Coached Problems for a self-study module on **the Rutherford experiment.**

Figure 2.4
Rutherford's α particle scattering experiment.

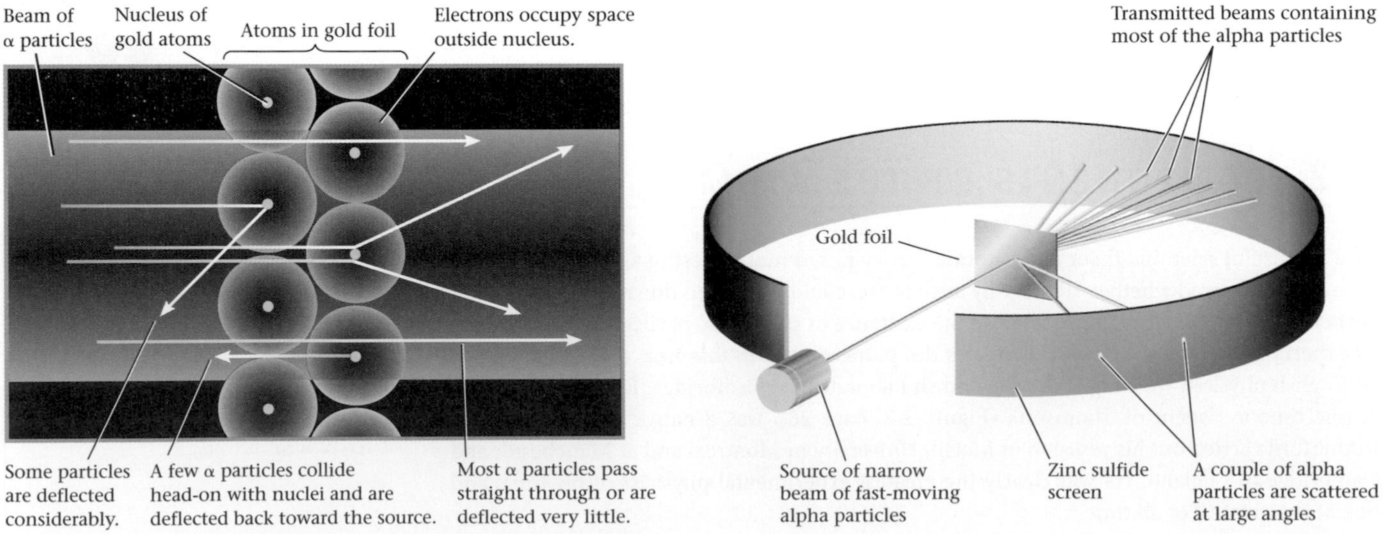

CHEMISTRY The Human Side

Dalton was a quiet, unassuming man and a devout Quaker. When presented to King William IV of England, Dalton refused to wear the colorful court robes because of his religion. His friends persuaded him to wear the scarlet robes of Oxford University, from which he had a doctor's degree. Dalton was color-blind, so he saw himself clothed in gray.

Dalton was a prolific scientist who made contributions to biology and physics as well as chemistry. At a college in Manchester, England, he did research and spent as many as 20 hours a week lecturing in mathematics and the physical sciences. Dalton never married; he said once, "My head is too full of triangles, chemical properties, and electrical experiments to think much of marriage."

The Edgar Fahs Smith Memorial Collection in the History of Chemistry, Department of Special Collections, Van Pelt-Dietrich Library, University of Pennsylvania

John Dalton
(1766–1844)

Dalton's atomic theory explained three of the basic laws of chemistry:

The **law of conservation of mass:** This states that *there is no detectable change in mass in an ordinary chemical reaction.* If atoms are conserved in a reaction (postulate 2 of the atomic theory), mass will also be conserved.

The **law of constant composition:** This tells us that *a compound always contains the same elements in the same proportions by mass.* If the atom ratio of the elements in a compound is fixed (postulate 3), their proportions by mass must also be fixed.

The **law of multiple proportions:** This law, formulated by Dalton himself, was crucial to establishing atomic theory. It applies to situations in which two elements form more than one compound. The law states that in these compounds, *the masses of one element that combine with a fixed mass of the second element are in a ratio of small whole numbers.*

The validity of this law depends on the fact that atoms combine in simple, whole-number ratios (postulate 3). Its relation to atomic theory is further illustrated in Figure A.

Marna G. Clarke

Figure A
Chromium-oxygen compounds and the law of multiple proportions. Chromium forms two different compounds with oxygen, as shown by their different colors. In the green compound on the left, there are two chromium atoms for every three oxygen atoms (2Cr : 3O) and 2.167 g of chromium per gram of oxygen. In the red compound on the right there is one chromium atom for every three oxygen atoms (1Cr : 3O) and 1.083 g of chromium per gram of oxygen. The ratio of the chromium masses, 2.167 : 1.083, is that of two small whole numbers, $2.167 : 1.083 = 2 : 1$, an illustration of the law of multiple proportions.

Protons and Neutrons; the Atomic Nucleus

A series of experiments carried out under the direction of Ernest Rutherford in 1911 shaped our ideas about the nature of the atom. He and his students bombarded a piece of thin gold foil (Figure 2.4, page 26) with α particles (helium atoms minus their electrons). With a fluorescent screen, they observed the extent to which the α particles were scattered. Most of the particles went through the foil unchanged in direction; a few, however, were reflected back at acute angles. This was a totally unexpected result, inconsistent with the model of the atom in vogue at that time. In Rutherford's words, "It was as though you had fired a 15-inch shell

Before this experiment, it was believed that positive and negative particles were more or less uniformly distributed throughout the atom.

Table 2.1 Properties of Subatomic Particles

Particle	Location	Relative Charge	Relative Mass*
Proton	Nucleus	+1	1.00728
Neutron	Nucleus	0	1.00867
Electron	Outside nucleus	−1	0.00055

*These are expressed in atomic mass units (Chapter 3).

at a piece of tissue paper and it had bounced back and hit you." By a mathematical analysis of the forces involved, Rutherford showed that the scattering was caused by a small, positively charged **nucleus** at the center of the gold atom. Most of the atom is empty space, which explains why most of the bombarding particles passed through the gold foil undeflected.

If the nucleus were the size of your head, the electron would be 5 miles away.

Since Rutherford's time scientists have learned a great deal about the properties of atomic nuclei. For our purposes in chemistry, the nucleus of an atom can be considered to consist of two different types of particles (Table 2.1):

1. The **proton,** which has a mass nearly equal to that of an ordinary hydrogen atom. The proton carries a unit positive charge (+1), equal in magnitude to that of the electron (−1).
2. The **neutron,** an uncharged particle with a mass slightly greater than that of a proton.

The diameter of an atom is 10,000 times that of its nucleus.

Because protons and neutrons are much heavier than electrons, most of the mass of an atom (>99.9%) is concentrated in the nucleus, even though the volume of the nucleus is much smaller than that of the atom.

Atomic Number

All the atoms of a particular element have the same number of protons in the nucleus. This number is a basic property of an element, called its **atomic number** and given the symbol Z:

$$Z = \text{number of protons}$$

In a neutral atom, the number of protons in the nucleus is exactly equal to the number of electrons outside the nucleus. Consider, for example, the elements hydrogen ($Z = 1$) and uranium ($Z = 92$). All hydrogen atoms have one proton in the nucleus; all uranium atoms have 92. In a neutral hydrogen atom there is one electron outside the nucleus; in a uranium atom there are 92.

CENGAGENOW™
Click Coached Problems for a self-study module on **summary of atomic composition.**

H atom:	1 proton, 1 electron	$Z = 1$
U atom:	92 protons, 92 electrons	$Z = 92$

Mass Numbers; Isotopes

The **mass number** of an atom, given the symbol A, is found by adding up the number of protons and neutrons in the nucleus:

$$A = \text{number of protons} + \text{number of neutrons}$$

Number of neutrons = $A - Z$

All atoms of a given element have the same number of protons, hence the same atomic number. They may, however, differ from one another in mass and therefore in mass number. This can happen because, although the number of protons in an atom of an element is fixed, the number of neutrons is not. It may vary and often does. Consider the element hydrogen ($Z = 1$). There are three different kinds of hydrogen atoms. They all have one proton in the nucleus. A light hydrogen atom (the most common type) has no neutrons in the nucleus ($A = 1$). Another type of hydrogen atom (deuterium) has one neutron ($A = 2$). Still a third type (tritium) has two neutrons ($A = 3$).

Atoms that contain the same number of protons but a different number of neutrons are called **isotopes.** The three kinds of hydrogen atoms just described are isotopes of that element. They have masses that are very nearly in the ratio 1:2:3. Among the isotopes of the element uranium are the following:

Isotope	*Z*	*A*	Number of Protons	Number of Neutrons
Uranium-235	92	235	92	143
Uranium-238	92	238	92	146

$^{2}_{1}H_2O$ ice and $^{1}_{1}H_2O$ ice. Solid deuterium oxide *(bottom)* is more dense than liquid water and sinks, whereas the ordinary water ice *(top)* is less dense than liquid water and floats.

The composition of a nucleus is shown by its **nuclear symbol.** Here, the atomic number appears as a subscript at the lower left of the symbol of the element. The mass number is written as a superscript at the upper left.

$$\begin{matrix}\text{Mass number} \longrightarrow \\ \text{Atomic number} \longrightarrow\end{matrix} {}^{A}_{Z}\text{X} \longleftarrow \text{element symbol}$$

The nuclear symbols for the isotopes of hydrogen and uranium referred to above are

$$^{1}_{1}\text{H}, {}^{2}_{1}\text{H}, {}^{3}_{1}\text{H} \qquad {}^{235}_{92}\text{U}, {}^{238}_{92}\text{U}$$

Quite often, isotopes of an element are distinguished from one another by writing the mass number after the symbol of the element. The isotopes of uranium are often referred to as U-235 and U-238.

Example 2.1

(a) An isotope of cobalt (Co, $Z = 27$) is used in radiation therapy for cancer. This isotope has 33 neutrons in its nucleus. What is its nuclear symbol?
(b) One of the most harmful components of nuclear waste is a radioactive isotope of strontium, $^{90}_{38}$Sr; it can be deposited in your bones, where it replaces calcium. How many protons are in the nucleus of Sr-90? How many neutrons?
(c) Write the nuclear symbol for the element used in diagnostic bone scans. It has 31 protons and 38 neutrons.

Strategy Remember the definitions of atomic number and mass number and where they appear in the nuclear symbol.

SOLUTION

(a) The mass number is $27 + 33 = 60$. The nuclear symbol is $^{60}_{27}$Co.
(b) The number of protons is given by the atomic number (left subscript) and is 38. The mass number (left superscript) is 90. The number of neutrons is $90 - 38 = 52$.
(c) The number of protons (31) identifies the element as gallium. Its mass number is 69 (31 protons + 38 neutrons). Its nuclear symbol is $^{69}_{31}$Ga.

Nuclear Stability; Radioactivity

There are eight known isotopes of carbon:

$$^{9}_{6}\text{C} \quad {}^{10}_{6}\text{C} \quad {}^{11}_{6}\text{C} \quad {}^{12}_{6}\text{C} \quad {}^{13}_{6}\text{C} \quad {}^{14}_{6}\text{C} \quad {}^{15}_{6}\text{C} \quad {}^{16}_{6}\text{C}$$

Of these, two ($^{12}_{6}$C, $^{13}_{6}$C) are stable in the sense that they do not decompose over time. In contrast, the three lighter nuclei ($^{9}_{6}$C, $^{10}_{6}$C, $^{11}_{6}$C) and the three heavier nuclei ($^{14}_{6}$C, $^{15}_{6}$C, $^{16}_{6}$C) are unstable; as time passes they decompose to other nuclei.

Whether or not a given nucleus will be stable depends on its neutron-to-proton ratio. The 264 known stable nuclei, shown as red dots in Figure 2.5 (page 30), fall within a relatively

Figure 2.5
Neutron-to-proton ratios of stable isotopes. The ratios of stable isotopes (red dots) fall within a narrow range, referred to as the "belt of stability." For light isotopes of small atomic number the stable ratio is 1:1. For heavier isotopes the ratio gradually increases to about 1.5:1. Isotopes outside the band of stability are unstable and radioactive. There are no stable isotopes for elements of atomic number greater than 83 (Bi).

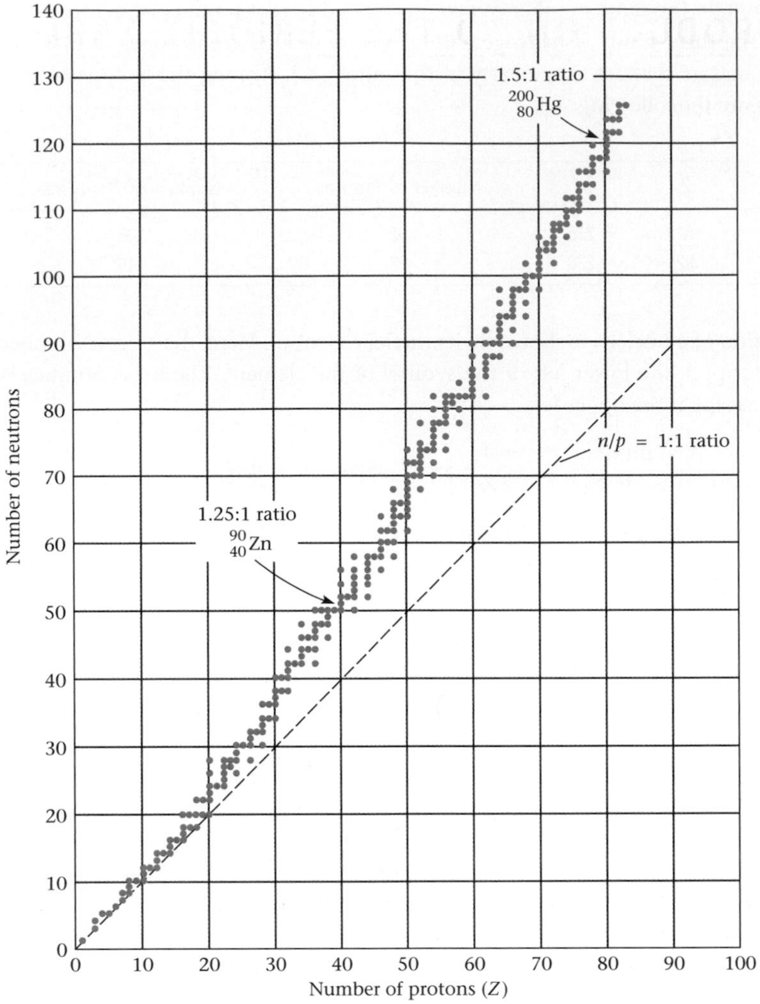

CENGAGENOW™
Click Coached Problems for a self-study module on **nuclear stability.**

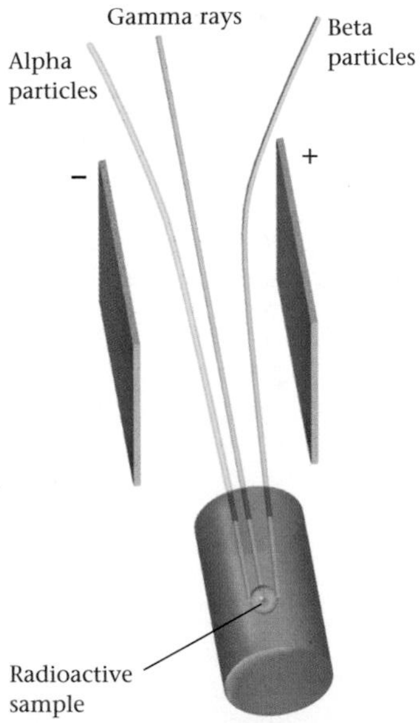

Figure 2.6
Nuclear radiation. In the presence of an electric field, alpha particles are deflected toward the negative pole, showing that they are positively charged, and beta particles are deflected toward the positive pole, showing that they are negatively charged. Because they are lighter, beta particles are deflected more than alpha particles. Gamma rays pass straight through the field and so must have no charge.

narrow "belt of stability"; $^{12}_{6}C$ and $^{13}_{6}C$ are in that category. Isotopes falling outside that belt because they have too few neutrons ($^{9}_{6}C$, $^{10}_{6}C$, $^{11}_{6}C$) or too many neutrons ($^{14}_{6}C$, $^{15}_{6}C$, $^{16}_{6}C$) are unstable.

As you can see from Figure 2.5, the neutron-to-proton ratio required for stability varies with atomic number. For light elements ($Z < 20$), this ratio is close to 1. For example, the isotopes $^{12}_{6}C$, $^{14}_{7}N$, and $^{16}_{8}O$ are stable. As atomic number increases, the ratio increases; the "belt of stability" shifts to higher numbers of neutrons. With very heavy isotopes such as $^{206}_{82}Pb$, the stable neutron-to-proton ratio is about 1.5:

$$(206 - 82)/82 = 124/82 = 1.51$$

Unstable isotopes decompose *(decay)* by a process referred to as *radioactivity.* Ordinarily the result is the *transmutation* of elements; the atomic number of the product nucleus differs from that of the reactant. For example, radioactive decay of $^{14}_{6}C$ produces a stable isotope of nitrogen, $^{14}_{7}N$. The radiation given off (Figure 2.6) may be in the form of—

- *beta (β)* particles identical in their properties to electrons.
- *alpha (α)* particles, which are $^{4}_{2}He$ nuclei, carrying a +2 charge because the two extranuclear electrons of the helium atom are missing.
- *gamma (γ)* rays, which consist of high-energy radiation.

2.3 INTRODUCTION TO THE PERIODIC TABLE

From a microscopic point of view, an element is a substance all of whose atoms have the same number of protons, that is, the same atomic number. The chemical properties of elements depend upon their atomic numbers, which can be read from the periodic table. A complete **periodic table** that lists symbols, atomic numbers, and atomic masses is given on the inside front cover of this text. For our purposes in this chapter, the abbreviated table shown in Figure 2.7 will suffice.

CENGAGENOW™
Click Coached Problems for a self-study module on **periodic table organization.**

Periods and Groups

The horizontal rows in the table are referred to as **periods.** The first period consists of the two elements hydrogen (H) and helium (He). The second period starts with lithium (Li) and ends with neon (Ne).

The vertical columns are known as **groups.** Historically, many different systems have been used to designate the different groups. Both Arabic and Roman numerals have been used in combination with the letters A and B. The system used in this text is the one recommended by the International Union of Pure and Applied Chemistry (IUPAC) in 1985. The groups are numbered from 1 to **18,** starting at the left.

Other periodic tables label the groups differently, but the elements have the same position.

Elements falling in Groups 1, 2, **13, 14, 15, 16, 17,** and **18*** are referred to as **main-group elements.** The ten elements in the center of periods 4 through 6 are called **transition metals;** they fall in Groups 3 through 12. The first transition series (period 4) starts with Sc (Group 3) and ends with Zn (Group 12).

The metals in Groups **13, 14,** and **15,** which lie to the right of the transition metals (Ga, In, Tl, Sn, Pb, Bi), are often referred to as *post-transition metals.*

You'll have to wait until Chapter 7 to learn why the second digit of some group numbers are in bold type.

Certain main groups are given special names. The elements in Group 1, at the far left of the periodic table, are called *alkali metals;* those in Group 2 are referred to as *alkaline earth metals.* As we move to the right, the elements in Group 17 are called *halogens;* at the far right, the *noble* (unreactive) *gases* constitute Group **18.**

Elements in the same main group show very similar chemical properties. For example—

- lithium (Li), sodium (Na), and potassium (K) in Group 1 all react vigorously with water to produce hydrogen gas.
- helium (He), neon (Ne), and argon (Ar) in Group **18** do not react with any other substances.

Figure 2.7
Periodic table. The group numbers stand above the columns. The numbers at the left of the rows are the period numbers. The black line separates the metals from the nonmetals. (*Note:* A complete periodic table is given inside the front cover.)

	1	2	3	4	5	6	7	8	9	10	11	12	13	14	15	16	17	18
1	1 H																1 H	2 He
2	3 Li	4 Be											5 B	6 C	7 N	8 O	9 F	10 Ne
3	11 Na	12 Mg											13 Al	14 Si	15 P	16 S	17 Cl	18 Ar
4	19 K	20 Ca	21 Sc	22 Ti	23 V	24 Cr	25 Mn	26 Fe	27 Co	28 Ni	29 Cu	30 Zn	31 Ga	32 Ge	33 As	34 Se	35 Br	36 Kr
5	37 Rb	38 Sr	39 Y	40 Zr	41 Nb	42 Mo	43 Tc	44 Ru	45 Rh	46 Pd	47 Ag	48 Cd	49 In	50 Sn	51 Sb	52 Te	53 I	54 Xe
6	55 Cs	56 Ba	71 Lu	72 Hf	73 Ta	74 W	75 Re	76 Os	77 Ir	78 Pt	79 Au	80 Hg	81 Tl	82 Pb	83 Bi	84 Po	85 At	86 Rn

Metals Metalloids Nonmetals

*Prior to 1985, Groups **13** to **18** were commonly numbered 3 to 8 or 3A to 8A in the United States.

Charles D. Winters

Inert gases. Neon is used in advertising signs. The gas in tubes adds both color and light. The test kit is used to detect radon in home basements.

On the basis of observations such as these, we can say that ***the periodic table is an arrangement of elements, in order of increasing atomic number, in horizontal rows of such a length that elements with similar chemical properties fall directly beneath one another in vertical groups.***

The person whose name is most closely associated with the periodic table is Dmitri Mendeleev (1836–1907), a Russian chemist. In writing a textbook of general chemistry, Mendeleev devoted separate chapters to families of elements with similar properties, including the alkali metals, the alkaline earth metals, and the halogens. Reflecting on the properties of these and other elements, he proposed in 1869 a primitive version of today's periodic table. Mendeleev shrewdly left empty spaces in his table for new elements yet to be discovered. Indeed, he predicted detailed properties for three such elements (scandium, gallium, and germanium). By 1886 all of these elements had been discovered and found to have properties very similar to those he had predicted.

Metals and Nonmetals

The diagonal line or stairway that starts to the left of boron in the periodic table (Figure 2.7, page 31) separates metals from nonmetals. The more than 80 elements to the left and below that line, shown in blue in the table, have the properties of **metals;** in particular, they have high electrical conductivities. Elements above and to the right of the stairway are **nonmetals** (yellow); about 18 elements fit in that category.

CHEMISTRY The Human Side

The Story of the Periodic Table

By Eric Scerri, University of California, Los Angeles

Dimitri Mendeleev is probably the greatest scientist that Russia has produced. He was the youngest of 14 children whose mother took him on a long journey, on foot, in order to enroll him into a university. However, several attempts initially proved futile because, as a Siberian, Mendeleev was barred from attending certain institutions. His mother did succeed in enrolling him in a teacher training college, thus giving Mendeleev a lasting interest in science education, which contributed to his eventually discovering the periodic system that is essentially a tool to simplify the subject of inorganic chemistry.

After completing a doctorate, he headed to Germany for a postdoctoral fellowship, then returned to Russia where he set about writing a book aimed at summarizing all of inorganic chemistry. It was while writing this book that he was forced to invent the organizing principle with which he is now invariably connected, namely the periodic system of the elements.

But more correctly, the periodic system was discovered by Mendeleev, as well as 5 other scientists, over a period of about 10 years, after the Italian chemist Cannizzaro had published a consistent set of atomic weights in 1860. It appears that Mendeleev was unaware of the work of several of his co-discoverers, however. In essence, the periodic table groups together sets of elements with similar properties into vertical columns. The underlying idea is that if the elements are arranged in order of increasing atomic weights, there are approximate repetitions in their chemical properties after certain intervals. As a result of the existence of the periodic table, students and even professors of chemistry were no longer obliged to learn the properties of all the elements in a disorganized fashion. Instead, they could concentrate on the properties of representative members of the eight columns or groups in the early short-form periodic table from which they could predict properties of other group members.

Mendeleev is justly regarded as the leading discoverer of the periodic table since he continued to champion the finding and drew out its consequences to a far greater extent than any of his contemporaries. First, he accommodated the sixty-five or so elements that were known at the time into a coherent scheme based on ascending order of atomic weight while also reflecting chemical and physical similarities. Next, he noticed gaps in his system, which he reasoned would eventually be filled by elements that had not yet been discovered. In addition, by judicious interpolation between the properties of known elements, Mendeleev predicted the nature of a number of completely new elements. Within a period of about 20 years, 3 of these elements, subsequently called gallium, scandium, and germanium were isolated and found to have almost exactly the properties that Mendeleev had predicted.

What is not well known is that about half of the elements that Mendeleev predicted were never found. But given the dramatic success of his early predictions these later lapses have largely been forgotten.

Eric Scerri is the author of *The Periodic Table: Its Story and Its Significance,* Oxford University Press, New York, 2007.

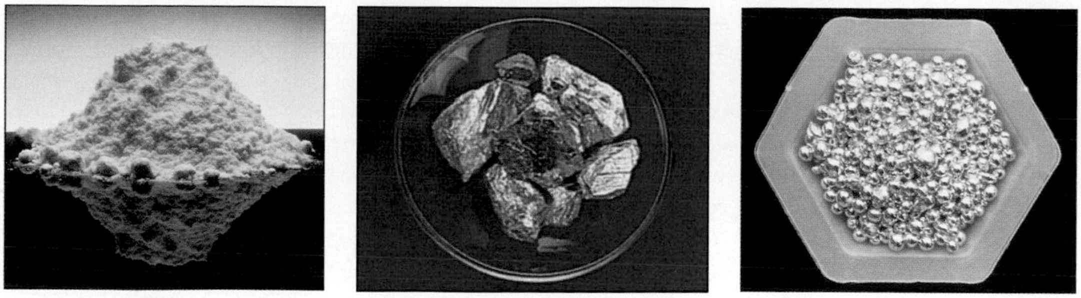

Charles D. Winters

Sulfur (a) — Antimony (b) — Silver (c)

Three elements. Sulfur (Group **16**) is a nonmetal. Antimony (Group **15**) is a metalloid; silver (Group 11) is a metal.

Along the stairway (zig-zag line) in the periodic table are several elements that are difficult to classify exclusively as metals or nonmetals. They have properties between those of elements in the two classes. In particular, their electrical conductivities are intermediate between those of metals and nonmetals. The six elements

B	Si	Ge	As	Sb	Te
boron	silicon	germanium	arsenic	antimony	tellurium

are often called **metalloids.**

These elements, particularly Si, are used in semiconductors.

Figure 2.8 shows the biologically important elements. The "good guys," essential to life, include the major elements (yellow), which account for 99.9% of total body mass, and the trace elements (green) required in very small quantities. In general, the abundances of elements in the body parallel those in the world around us, but there are some important exceptions. Aluminum and silicon, although widespread in nature, are missing in the human body. The reverse is true of carbon, which makes up only 0.08% of the earth's crust but 18% of the body, where it occurs in a variety of organic compounds including proteins, carbohydrates, and fats.

The "bad guys," shown in pink in Figure 2.8, are toxic, often lethal, even in relatively small quantities. Several of the essential trace elements *become* toxic if their concentrations in the body increase. Selenium is a case in point. You need about 0.00005 g/day to maintain good health, but 0.001 g/day can be deadly. That's a good thing to keep in mind if you're taking selenium supplements.

Figure 2.8
Biologically important elements and highly toxic elements. For the major elements in the body, their percent abundance in the body is given below the symbols.

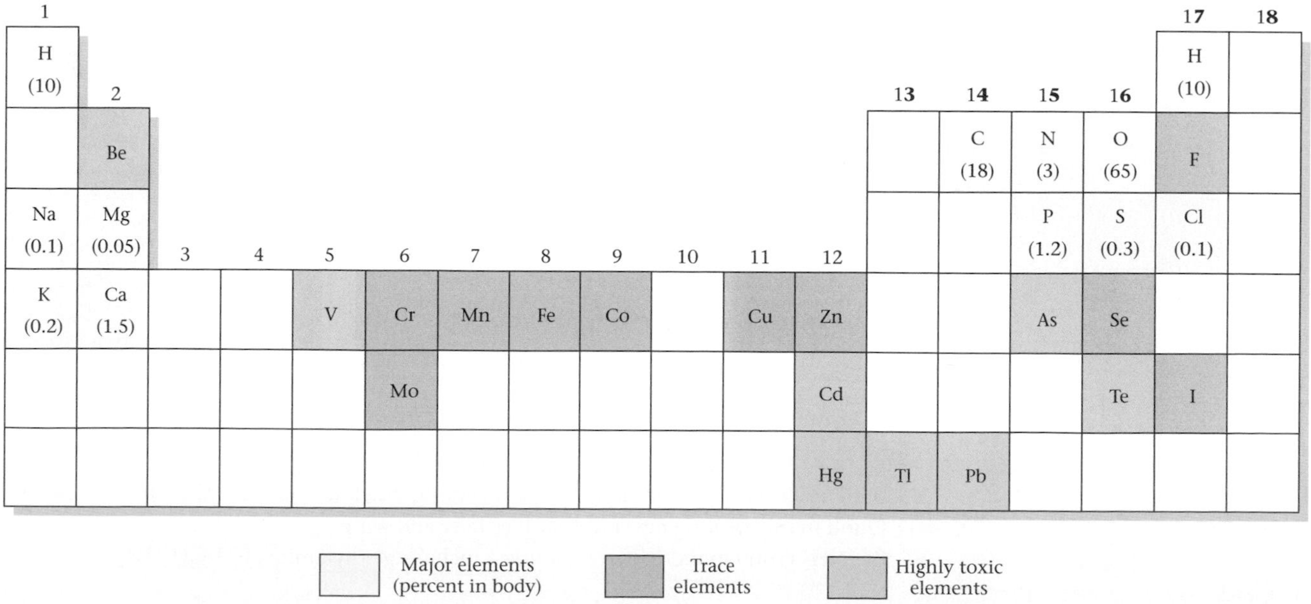

2.4 MOLECULES AND IONS

Isolated atoms rarely occur in nature; only the noble gases (He, Ne, Ar, . . .) consist of individual, nonreactive atoms. Atoms tend to combine with one another in various ways to form more complex structural units. Two such units, which serve as building blocks for a great many elements and compounds, are molecules and ions.

Molecules

Super Glue™ is weak compared with covalent bonds.

Two or more atoms may combine with one another to form an uncharged **molecule.** The atoms involved are usually those of nonmetallic elements. Within the molecule, atoms are held to one another by strong forces called *covalent bonds,* which consist of shared pairs of electrons (Chapter 7). Forces between neighboring molecules, in contrast, are quite weak.

CENGAGENOW™
Click Coached Problems for a self-study module on **representing compounds.**

Molecular substances most often are represented by **molecular formulas,** in which the number of atoms of each element is indicated by a subscript written after the symbol of the element. Thus we interpret the molecular formulas for water (H_2O), ammonia (NH_3), and methane (CH_4) to mean that in—

- the water molecule, there is one oxygen atom and two hydrogen atoms.
- the ammonia molecule, there is one nitrogen atom and three hydrogen atoms.
- the methane molecule, there is one carbon atom and four hydrogen atoms.

The structures of molecules are sometimes represented by **structural formulas,** which show the bonding pattern within the molecule. The structural formulas of water, ammonia, and methane are

Structural formulas help us predict chemical properties.

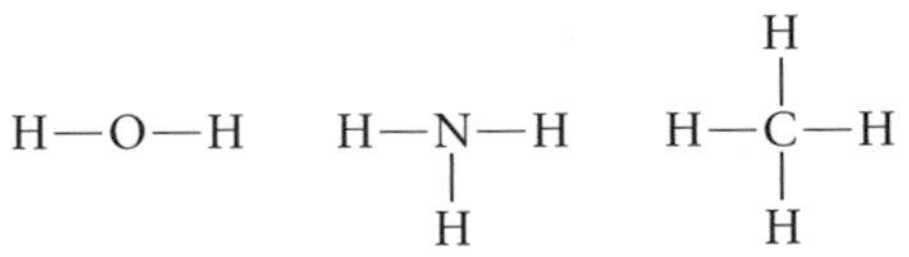

The dashes represent covalent bonds. The geometries of these molecules are shown in Figure 2.9 (page 35).

Sometimes we represent a molecular substance with a formula intermediate between a structural formula and a molecular formula. A **condensed structural formula** suggests the bonding pattern in the molecule and highlights the presence of a reactive group of atoms within the molecule. Consider, for example, the organic compounds commonly known as methyl alcohol and methylamine. Their structural formulas are

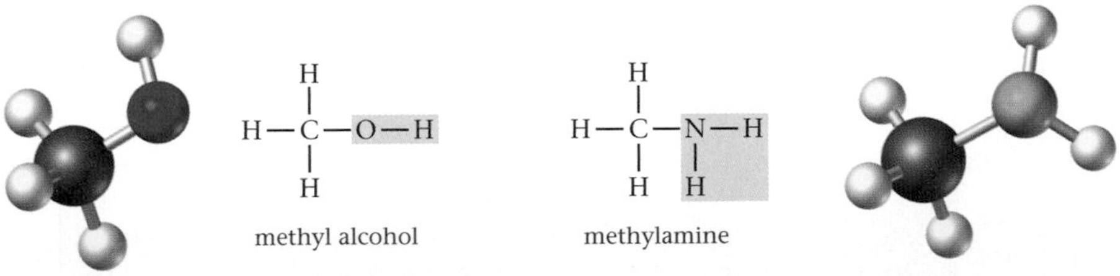

The condensed structural formulas of these compounds are written as

$$CH_3OH \qquad CH_3NH_2$$

These formulas take up considerably less space and emphasize the presence in the molecule of—

- the OH group found in all *alcohols,* including ethyl alcohol, CH_3CH_2OH, the alcohol found in intoxicating beverages such as beer and wine.
- the NH_2 group found in certain *amines,* including ethylamine, $CH_3CH_2NH_2$.

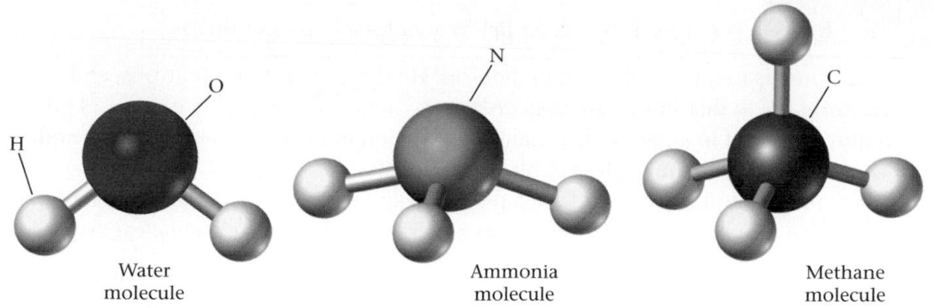

Figure 2.9
Ball-and-stick models of water (H_2O), ammonia (NH_3), and methane (CH_4). The "sticks" represent covalent bonds between H atoms and O, N, or C atoms. The models illustrate the geometry of the molecules (discussed in Chapter 7).

Example 2.2 Give the molecular formulas of (a) ethyl alcohol and (b) ethylamine.

Strategy To find the molecular formulas, simply add up the atoms of each type and use the sums as subscripts in the formulas.

SOLUTION

(a) C_2H_6O (b) C_2H_7N

Reality Check Note that although molecular formulas give the composition of the molecule, they reveal nothing about the way the atoms fit together. In that sense they are less useful than structural formulas.

Group 15	Group 16	Group 17
		H_2 (*g*)
N_2 (*g*)	O_2 (*g*)	F_2 (*g*)
P_4 (*s*)	S_8 (*s*)	Cl_2 (*g*)
		Br_2 (*l*)
		I_2 (*s*)

Figure 2.10
Molecular elements and their physical states at room temperature: gaseous *(g)*, liquid *(l)*, or solid *(s)*.

Elements as well as compounds can exist as discrete molecules. In hydrogen gas, the basic building block is a molecule consisting of two hydrogen atoms joined by a covalent bond:

$$H{-}H$$

Other molecular elements are shown in Figure 2.10.

Ions

When an atom loses or gains electrons, charged particles called **ions** are formed. Metal atoms typically tend to lose electrons to form positively charged ions called **cations** (pronounced CAT-i-ons). Examples include the Na^+ and Ca^{2+} ions, formed from atoms of the metals sodium and calcium:

$$\underset{(11p^+,\,11e^-)}{\text{Na atom}} \longrightarrow \underset{(11p^+,\,10e^-)}{\text{Na}^+ \text{ ion}} + e^-$$

$$\underset{(20p^+,\,20e^-)}{\text{Ca atom}} \longrightarrow \underset{(20p^+,\,18e^-)}{\text{Ca}^{2+} \text{ ion}} + 2e^-$$

CENGAGENOW
Click Coached Problems for self-study modules on **predicting ionic charge.**

(The arrows separate *reactants,* Na and Ca atoms, from *products,* cations and electrons.)

Nonmetal atoms form negative ions (**anions**—pronounced AN-i-ons) by gaining electrons. Consider, for example, what happens when atoms of the nonmetals chlorine and oxygen acquire electrons:

Metals form cations; nonmetals form anions; C, P, and the metalloids do not form monatomic ions.

$$\underset{(17p^+,\,17e^-)}{\text{Cl atom}} + e^- \longrightarrow \underset{(17p^+,\,18e^-)}{\text{Cl}^- \text{ ion}}$$

$$\underset{(8p^+,\,8e^-)}{\text{O atom}} + 2e^- \longrightarrow \underset{(8p^+,\,10e^-)}{\text{O}^{2-} \text{ ion}}$$

Notice that *when an ion is formed, the number of protons in the nucleus is unchanged.* It is the number of electrons that increases or decreases.

Aluminum oxide. Al^{3+} ions are present in corundum *(left)*, ruby *(top right)*, and sapphire *(bottom right)*. The anion in each case is O^{2-}.

We write +3 when describing the charge but 3+ when using it as a superscript in the formula of an ion.

Example 2.3 Answer the questions below about the ions described.

(a) Aluminum is found in rubies and sapphires. How many protons, neutrons, and electrons are in this aluminum ion: ${}^{27}_{13}Al^{3+}$?
(b) Sulfur is present in an ore called chalcocite. The ion in the ore has 16 neutrons and 18 electrons. Write the nuclear symbol for the ion.
(c) An element found more abundantly in the sun and meteorites than on earth has an ion with a +2 charge. It has 38 electrons and 51 neutrons. Write its nuclear symbol.

Strategy The atomic number gives directly the number of protons. The number of neutrons is found in the usual way by subtracting the atomic number from the mass number. The number of electrons can be deduced from the number of protons by taking into account the charge of the ion.

SOLUTION

(a) Number of protons = 13; number of neutrons = 27 − 13 = 14; number of electrons = 13 − 3 = 10.
(b) For sulfur, $Z = 16$, so there must be 16 protons. The mass number is 16 + 16 = 32. The charge on the ion is 16 − 18 (number of protons − number of electrons) = −2. The nuclear symbol is then ${}^{32}_{16}S^{2-}$.
(c) Since the element has a +2 charge and 38 electrons, it must have 40 protons. The element with that atomic number is zirconium. Its mass number is 40 + 51 = 91. Its nuclear symbol is ${}^{91}_{40}Zr^{2+}$.

Reality Check A cation always contains more protons than electrons; the reverse is true for an anion.

The ions dealt with to this point (e.g., Na^+, Cl^-) are *monatomic;* that is, they are derived from a single atom by the loss or gain of electrons. Many of the most important ions in chemistry are *polyatomic,* containing more than one atom. Examples include the hydroxide ion (OH^-) and the ammonium ion (NH_4^+). In these and other polyatomic ions, the atoms are held together by covalent bonds, for example,

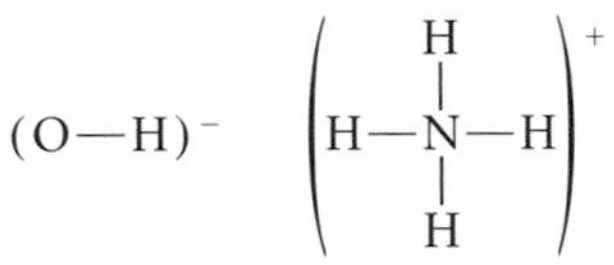

In a very real sense, you can think of a polyatomic ion as a "charged molecule."

Because a bulk sample of matter is electrically neutral, ionic compounds always contain both cations (positively charged particles) and anions (negatively charged particles). Ordinary table salt, sodium chloride, is made up of an equal number of Na^+ and Cl^- ions. The structure of sodium chloride is shown in Figure 2.11. Notice that—

You can't buy a bottle of Na^+ ions.

- there are two kinds of structural units in NaCl, the Na^+ and Cl^- ions.
- there are no discrete molecules; Na^+ and Cl^- ions are bonded together in a continuous network.

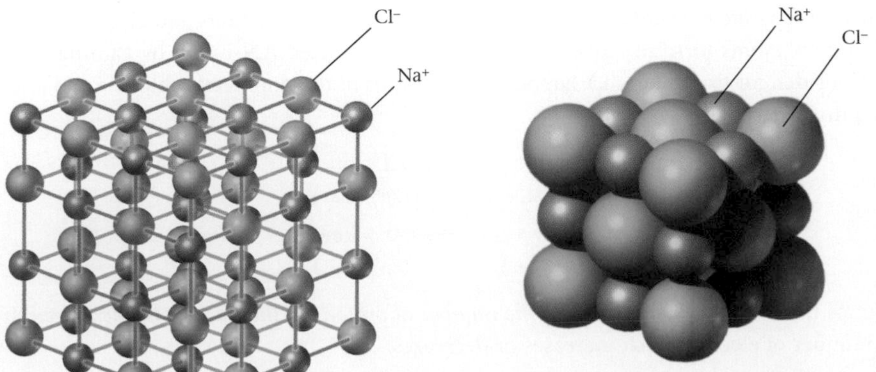

Figure 2.11
Sodium chloride structure. In these two ways of showing the structure, the small spheres represent Na^+ ions and the large spheres Cl^- ions. Note that in any sample of sodium chloride there are equal numbers of Na^+ and Cl^- ions, but no NaCl molecules.

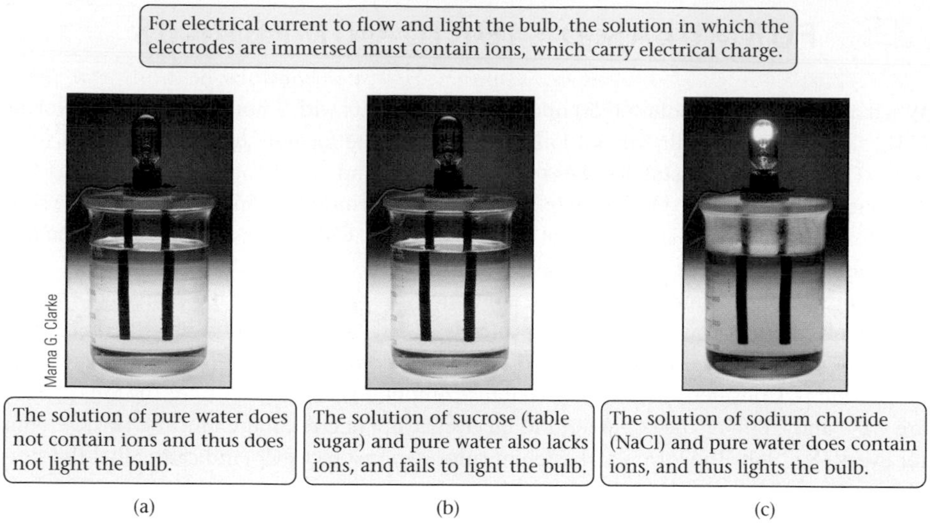

Figure 2.12
Electrical conductivity test.

Ionic compounds are held together by strong electrical forces between oppositely charged ions (e.g., Na^+, Cl^-). These forces are referred to as **ionic bonds.**

Typically, ionic compounds are solids at room temperature and have relatively high melting points (mp NaCl = 801°C, $CaCl_2$ = 772°C). To melt an ionic compound requires that oppositely charged ions be separated from one another, thereby breaking ionic bonds.

When an ionic solid such as NaCl dissolves in water, the solution formed contains Na^+ and Cl^- ions. Since ions are charged particles, the solution conducts an electric current (Figure 2.12) and we say that NaCl is a **strong electrolyte.** In contrast, a water solution of sugar, which is a molecular solid, does not conduct electricity. Sugar and other molecular solutes are **nonelectrolytes.**

Then there are **weak electrolytes,** which dissolve mostly as molecules with a few ions.

Example 2.4 Conceptual

The structure of a water solution of KNO_3, containing equal numbers of K^+ and NO_3^- ions, might be represented as

(H_2O molecules are not shown.) Construct a similar box to show the structure of a water solution of potassium sulfate. Use ● to represent a sulfur atom.

Strategy Once you deduce the formula of the ionic compound, it's all downhill. Remember, though, that you have to show the relative numbers of cations and anions.

SOLUTION

2.5 FORMULAS OF IONIC COMPOUNDS

When a metal such as sodium (Na) or calcium (Ca) reacts with a nonmetal such as chlorine (Cl_2), the product is ordinarily an ionic compound. The formula of that compound (e.g., NaCl, $CaCl_2$) shows the simplest ratio between cation and anion (one Na^+ ion for one Cl^- ion; one Ca^{2+} ion for two Cl^- ions). In that sense, the formulas of ionic compounds are simplest formulas. Notice that the symbol of the metal (Na, Ca) always appears first in the formula, followed by that of the nonmetal.

To predict the formula of an ionic compound, you need to know the charges of the two ions involved. Then you can apply the principle of electrical neutrality, which requires that ***the total positive charge of the cations in the formula must equal the total negative charge of the anions.*** Consider, for example, the ionic compound calcium chloride. The ions present are Ca^{2+} and Cl^-. For the compound to be electrically neutral, there must be two Cl^- ions for every Ca^{2+} ion. The formula of calcium chloride must be $CaCl_2$, indicating that the simplest ratio of Cl^- to Ca^{2+} ions is 2:1.

Cations and Anions with Noble-Gas Structures

The charges of ions formed by atoms of the main-group elements can be predicted by applying a simple principle:

> ***Atoms that are close to a noble gas*** (Group 18) ***in the periodic table form ions that contain the same number of electrons as the neighboring noble-gas atom.***

This is reasonable; noble-gas atoms must have an extremely stable electronic structure, because they are so unreactive. Other atoms might be expected to acquire noble-gas electronic structures by losing or gaining electrons.

Applying this principle, you can deduce the charges of ions formed by main-group atoms:

Group	No. of Electrons in Atom	Charge of Ion Formed	Examples
1	1 more than noble-gas atom	+1	Na^+, K^+
2	2 more than noble-gas atom	+2	Mg^{2+}, Ca^{2+}
16	2 less than noble-gas atom	−2	O^{2-}, S^{2-}
17	1 less than noble-gas atom	−1	F^-, Cl^-

Two other ions that have noble-gas structures are

Al^{3+} (Al has three more e^- than the preceding noble gas, Ne)

N^{3-} (N has three fewer e^- than the following noble gas, Ne)

Cations of the Transition and Post-Transition Metals

Several metals that are farther removed from the noble gases in the periodic table form positive ions. These include the transition metals in Groups 3 to 12 and the post-transition metals in Groups **13** to **15.** The cations formed by these metals typically have charges of +1, +2, or +3 and ordinarily do not have noble-gas structures. We will postpone to Chapter 4 a general discussion of the specific charges of cations formed by these metals.

Many of the transition and post-transition metals form more than one cation. Consider, for example, iron in Group 8. This metal forms two different series of compounds with nonmetals. In one series, iron is present as a +2 cation

$$Fe^{2+}:\quad FeCl_2, FeBr_2, \ldots$$

In the other series, iron exists as a +3 cation

$$Fe^{3+}:\quad FeCl_3, FeBr_3, \ldots$$

Charles D. Winters

Ionic compounds containing polyatomic ions. Potassium dichromate ($K_2Cr_2O_7$, orange), potassium permanganate ($KMnO_4$, very dark purple), and potassium nitrate (KNO_3, white).

Table 2.2 Some Common Polyatomic Ions

+1	−1	−2	−3
NH_4^+ (ammonium)	OH^- (hydroxide)	CO_3^{2-} (carbonate)	PO_4^{3-} (phosphate)
Hg_2^{2+} (mercury I)	NO_3^- (nitrate)	SO_4^{2-} (sulfate)	
	ClO_3^- (chlorate)	CrO_4^{2-} (chromate)	
	ClO_4^- (perchlorate)	$Cr_2O_7^{2-}$ (dichromate)	
	CN^- (cyanide)	HPO_4^{2-} (hydrogen phosphate)	
	$C_2H_3O_2^-$ (acetate)		
	MnO_4^- (permanganate)		
	HCO_3^- (hydrogen carbonate)		
	$H_2PO_4^-$ (dihydrogen phosphate)		

CENGAGENOW™

Click Coached Problems for a self-study module on **polyatomic ions.**

Polyatomic Ions

Table 2.2 lists some of the polyatomic ions that you will need to know, along with their names and charges. Notice that—

- there are only two common polyatomic cations, NH_4^+ and Hg_2^{2+}. ***All other cations considered in this text are derived from individual metal atoms*** (e.g., Na^+ from Na, Ca^{2+} from Ca, . . .).
- most of the polyatomic anions contain one or more oxygen atoms; collectively these species are called *oxoanions.*

Nearly all cations are monatomic; the majority of anions are polyatomic.

Example 2.5 Predict the formula of the ionic compound—

(a) formed by barium with iodine.
(b) containing a transition metal with a +1 charge in period 4 and Group 11 and oxide ions.
(c) containing an alkaline earth in period 5 and nitrogen.
(d) containing ammonium and phosphate ions.

Strategy First identify the elements. Then (using Table 2.2 as necessary) identify the charges of the cation and anion. Finally, balance positive and negative charges.

SOLUTION

(a) Barium is in Group 2, so it forms a +2 ion. Iodine in Group 17 forms the I^- ion. The formula is then BaI_2.
(b) The cation is Cu^+, the anion O^{2-}. Two cations are required to balance one anion. Hence, the formula is Cu_2O.
(c) The element is Sr (strontium), which is in Group 2 and so forms the Sr^{2+} ion. Nitrogen as an ion has a −3 charge. The formula thus is Sr_3N_2.
(d) From Table 2.2, the ions are NH_4^+ and PO_4^{3-}. The formula is therefore $(NH_4)_3PO_4$.

2.6 NAMES OF COMPOUNDS

A compound can be identified either by its formula (e.g., NaCl) or by its name (sodium chloride). In this section, you will learn the rules used to name ionic and simple molecular compounds. To start with, it will be helpful to show how individual ions within ionic compounds are named.

To name a compound, you have to decide whether it is molecular or ionic; the rules are different.

Ions

Monatomic cations take the name of the metal from which they are derived. Examples include

Na^+ sodium K^+ potassium

There is one complication. As mentioned earlier, certain metals in the transition and post-transition series form more than one cation, for example, Fe^{2+} and Fe^{3+}. To distinguish between these cations, the charge must be indicated in the name. This is done by putting the charge as a Roman numeral in parentheses after the name of the metal:

Fe^{2+} iron(II) Fe^{3+} iron(III)

(An older system used the suffixes *-ic* for the ion of higher charge and *-ous* for the ion of lower charge. These were added to the stem of the Latin name of the metal, so that the Fe^{3+} ion was referred to as ferric and the Fe^{2+} ion as ferrous.)

Monatomic anions are named by adding the suffix *-ide* to the stem of the name of the nonmetal from which they are derived.

						H^-	hydride
		N^{3-}	nitride	O^{2-}	oxide	F^-	fluoride
				S^{2-}	sulfide	Cl^-	chloride
				Se^{2-}	selenide	Br^-	bromide
				Te^{2-}	telluride	I^-	iodide

Polyatomic ions, as you have seen (Table 2.2), are given special names. Certain nonmetals in Groups 15 to 17 of the periodic table form more than one polyatomic ion containing oxygen (oxoanions). The names of several such oxoanions are shown in Table 2.3. From the entries in the table, you should be able to deduce the following rules:

1. When a nonmetal forms two oxoanions, the suffix *-ate* is used for the anion with the larger number of oxygen atoms. The suffix *-ite* is used for the anion containing fewer oxygen atoms.
2. When a nonmetal forms more than two oxoanions, the prefixes *per-* (largest number of oxygen atoms) and *hypo-* (fewest oxygen atoms) are used as well.

Cl, Br, and I form more than two oxoanions.

Ionic Compounds

CENGAGENOW™
Click Coached Problems for a self-study module on **naming ionic compounds.**

The name of an ionic compound consists of two words. The first word names the cation and the second names the anion. This is, of course, the same order in which the ions appear in the formula.

In naming the compounds of transition or post-transition metals, we ordinarily indicate the charge of the metal cation by a Roman numeral:

$Cr(NO_3)_3$ chromium(III) nitrate $SnCl_2$ tin(II) chloride

Table 2.3 Oxoanions of Nitrogen, Sulfur, and Chlorine

Nitrogen	Sulfur	Chlorine
		ClO_4^- *per*chlor*ate*
NO_3^- nitr*ate*	SO_4^{2-} sulf*ate*	ClO_3^- chlor*ate*
NO_2^- nitr*ite*	SO_3^{2-} sulf*ite*	ClO_2^- chlor*ite*
		ClO^- *hypo*chlor*ite*

The oxoanions of bromine and iodine are named like those of chlorine.

Example 2.6 Name the following ionic compounds:

(a) CaS (b) $Al(NO_3)_3$ (c) $FeCl_2$

Strategy To name an ionic compound, you must know the rules for naming individual ions, as discussed previously.

SOLUTION

(a) calcium sulfide (b) aluminum nitrate (c) iron(II) chloride

In contrast, we never use Roman numerals with compounds of the Group 1 or Group 2 metals; they always form cations with charges of +1 or +2, respectively.

Binary Molecular Compounds

When two nonmetals combine with each other, the product is most often a binary molecular compound. There is no simple way to deduce the formulas of such compounds. There is, however, a systematic way of naming molecular compounds that differs considerably from that used with ionic compounds.

The systematic name of a binary molecular compound, which contains two different nonmetals, consists of two words.

1. The first word gives the name of the element that appears first in the formula; a Greek prefix (Table 2.4) is used to show the number of atoms of that element in the formula.
2. The second word consists of—
   - the appropriate Greek prefix designating the number of atoms of the second element. (See Table 2.4.)
   - the stem of the name of the second element.
   - the suffix *-ide.*

To illustrate these rules, consider the names of the several oxides of nitrogen:

N_2O_5	*di*nitrogen *penta*ox*ide*	N_2O_3	*di*nitrogen *tri*ox*ide*
N_2O_4	*di*nitrogen *tetra*ox*ide*	NO	nitrogen ox*ide*
NO_2	nitrogen *di*ox*ide*	N_2O	*di*nitrogen ox*ide*

When the prefixes tetr*a*, pent*a*, hex*a*, . . . are followed by the letter "o," the *a* is often dropped. For example, N_2O_5 is often referred to as *dinitrogen pentoxide.*

Many of the best-known binary compounds of the nonmetals have acquired common names. These are widely—and in some cases exclusively—used. Examples include

H_2O	water	PH_3	phosphine
H_2O_2	hydrogen peroxide	AsH_3	arsine
NH_3	ammonia	NO	nitric oxide
N_2H_4	hydrazine	N_2O	nitrous oxide
C_2H_2	acetylene	CH_4	methane

CENGAGENOW™
Click Coached Problems for a self-study module on **naming compounds of the nonmetals.**

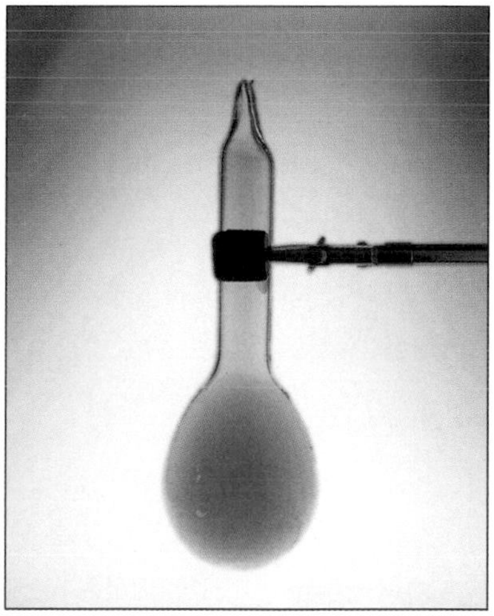

Charles D. Winters

Nitrogen dioxide (NO_2), a binary molecular compound. It is a reddish-brown gas at 25°C and 1 atm.

Table 2.4 Greek Prefixes Used in Nomenclature

Number*	Prefix	Number	Prefix	Number	Prefix
2	di	5	penta	8	octa
3	tri	6	hexa	9	nona
4	tetra	7	hepta	10	deca

*The prefix mono (1) is seldom used.

Example 2.7 Give the names of the following molecules:

(a) SO_2 (b) SO_3 (c) PCl_3 (d) Cl_2O_7

Strategy Start with the prefix denoting the number of atoms (if there is more than one) of the first element followed by the name of that element. Repeat for the second element, ending with the suffix *-ide.*

SOLUTION

(a) sulfur dioxide (b) sulfur trioxide
(c) phosphorus trichloride (d) dichlorine heptaoxide

Acids

A few binary molecular compounds containing H atoms ionize in water to form H^+ ions. These are called *acids.* One such compound is hydrogen chloride, HCl; in water solution it exists as aqueous H^+ and Cl^- ions. The water solution of hydrogen chloride is given a special name: It is referred to as *hydrochloric acid.* A similar situation applies with HBr and HI:

Pure Substance		Water Solution	
$HCl(g)$	Hydrogen chloride	$H^+(aq)$, $Cl^-(aq)$	Hydrochloric acid
$HBr(g)$	Hydrogen bromide	$H^+(aq)$, $Br^-(aq)$	Hydrobromic acid
$HI(g)$	Hydrogen iodide	$H^+(aq)$, $I^-(aq)$	Hydriodic acid

Most acids contain oxygen in addition to hydrogen atoms. Such species are referred to as *oxoacids.* Two oxoacids that you are likely to encounter in the general chemistry laboratory are

HNO_3 nitric acid H_2SO_4 sulfuric acid

The names of oxoacids are simply related to those of the corresponding oxoanions. The *-ate* suffix of the anion is replaced by *-ic* in the acid. In a similar way, the suffix *-ite* is replaced by the suffix *-ous.* The prefixes *per-* and *hypo-* found in the name of the anion are retained in the name of the acid.

ClO_4^-	*per*chlor*ate* ion	$HClO_4$	*per*chlor*ic* acid
ClO_3^-	chlor*ate* ion	$HClO_3$	chlor*ic* acid
ClO_2^-	chlor*ite* ion	$HClO_2$	chlor*ous* acid
ClO^-	*hypo*chlor*ite* ion	$HClO$	*hypo*chlor*ous* acid

Example 2.8 Give the names of

(a) $HCl(g)$ (b) $HNO_2(aq)$ (c) $H_2SO_3(aq)$ (d) $HIO(aq)$

Strategy In (a), note that the specie is a gas, not an acid. In (b) and (c), refer back to Table 2.3 for the name of the oxoanion. In (d), reason by analogy with chlorine oxoacids.

SOLUTION

(a) hydrogen chloride gas (b) nitrous acid
(c) sulfurous acid (d) hypoiodous acid

CHEMISTRY Beyond the Classroom

Ethyl Alcohol and the Law

There is a strong correlation between a driver's blood alcohol concentration (BAC) and the likelihood that he or she will be involved in an accident (Figure A). At a BAC of 0.08% his or her chance of colliding with another car is four times greater than that of a sober driver.

Blood alcohol concentration can be determined directly by gas chromatography (Chapter 1). However, this approach is impractical for testing a driver on the highway. It requires that the suspect be transported to a hospital, where trained medical personnel can take a blood sample, then preserve and analyze it.

It is simpler and quicker to measure a suspect's breath alcohol concentration (BrAc). This can be converted to BAC by multiplying by 2100; one volume of blood contains about 2100 times as much alcohol as the same volume of breath. In practice, this calculation is done automatically in the instrument used to measure BrAc; it reads directly the BAC of 0.05%, 0.08%, or whatever.

The first instruments used by police to determine BrAc were developed in the 1930s. Until about 1980, the standard method involved adding $K_2Cr_2O_7$, which reacts chemically with ethyl alcohol. Potassium dichromate has a bright orange-red color, whose intensity fades as reaction occurs. The extent of the color change is a measure of the amount of alcohol present.

The standard instrument used in police stations today (Intoxilizer 5000) measures infrared absorption at three wavelengths (3390, 3480, 3800 nm) where ethyl alcohol absorbs. At the scene of an accident, a police officer may use a less accurate handheld instrument about the size of a deck of cards, which estimates BAC by an electrochemical process (Chapter 18).

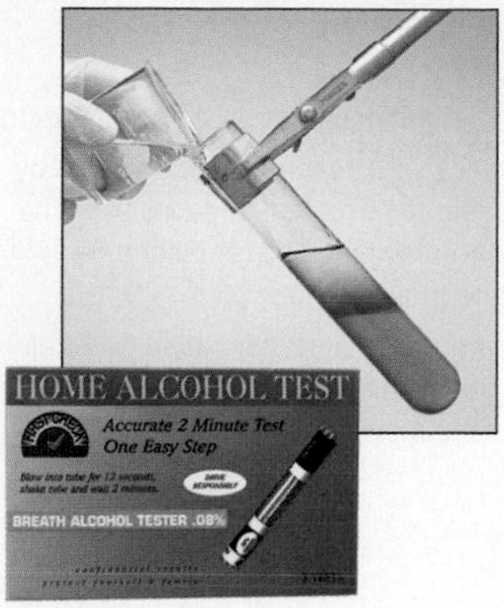

Charles D. Winters

An instrument used to determine BAC.

The greatest uncertainty in instruments such as the Intoxilizer lies in the conversion from BrAc to BAC values. The factor of 2100 referred to previously can vary considerably depending on the circumstances under which the sample is taken. Simultaneous measurements of BrAc and BAC values suggest that the factor can be anywhere between 1800 and 2400. This means that a calculated BAC value of 0.100% could be as low as 0.086% or as high as 0.114%.

After drinking an alcoholic beverage, a person's BAC rises to a maximum, typically in 30 to 90 minutes, and then drops steadily at the rate of about 0.02% per hour. The maximum BAC depends on the amount of alcohol consumed and the person's body weight. The data cited in Table A are for male subjects; females show maximum BACs about 20% higher. Thus a man weighing 60 kg who takes three drinks may be expected to reach a maximum BAC of 0.09%; a woman of the same weight consuming the same amount of alcohol may show a BAC of

$$0.09\% \times 1.2 = 0.11\%$$

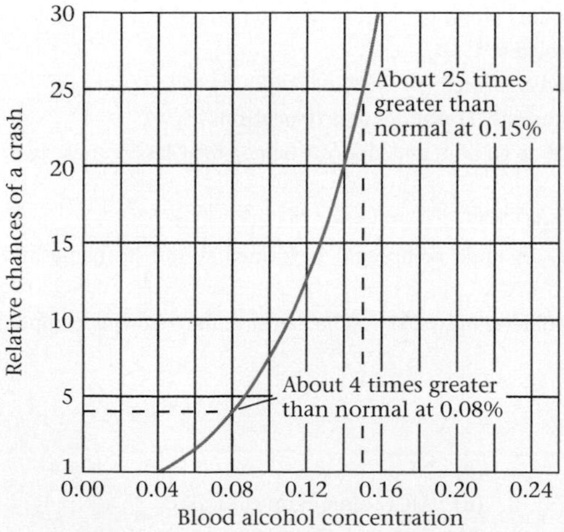

U.S. Department of Transportation, Washington, D.C.

Figure A

Blood alcohol concentration and risk of crash. With increasing alcohol concentration in the blood, the risk of an automobile crash rises rapidly to 25 times the normal risk of a crash (that is, the risk with no alcohol consumption).

Table A Maximum Blood Alcohol Concentrations (Percentages)*

	No. Drinks (1 drink = 1 oz 100-proof liquor or a 12-oz beer)					
Body Weight	1	2	3	4	5	6
50 kg = 110 lb	0.04	0.07	**0.10**	**0.14**	**0.17**	**0.21**
60 kg = 132 lb	0.03	0.06	0.09	**0.12**	**0.14**	**0.17**
70 kg = 154 lb	0.02	0.05	0.07	**0.10**	**0.12**	**0.15**
80 kg = 176 lb	0.02	0.04	0.06	0.09	**0.11**	**0.13**
90 kg = 198 lb	0.02	0.04	0.06	0.08	**0.10**	**0.11**

*Values are for men; values for women are about 20% higher; BAC values of 0.10% or higher are shown in boldface type.

Chapter Highlights

Key Concepts

Select end of chapter Questions and Problems may be assigned in OWL and are cross-referenced in the Key Concepts list.

CENGAGENOW™

Sign in at **academic.cengage.com/now** to:

- Check your readiness for an exam by taking the Pre-Test and exploring the self-study modules recommended in your Personalized Study plan.
- For quick review, download Go Chemistry mini-lecture flashcard modules (or purchase them at **www.ichapters.com**)

1. Relate a nuclear symbol to the number of protons and neutrons in the nucleus. **(Example 2.1; Problems 7–16)** ■ Questions and Problems assignable in OWL: 11, 13, 15, 65
2. Relate elements and the periodic table. **(Problems 17–24)** ■ 20, 24
3. Relate structural, condensed, and molecular formulas. **(Example 2.2; Problems 25, 26)** ■ 26
4. Relate the ionic charge to the number of electrons. **(Example 2.3; Problems 27–30)** ■ 27, 29
5. Predict formulas of ionic compounds from charges of ions. **(Example 2.5; Problems 37, 38)** ■ 37, 38
6. Relate names to formulas for
   - Ionic compounds **(Example 2.6; Problems 39–42)** ■ 40, 41
   - Binary molecular compounds **(Example 2.7; Problems 33–36)** ■ 33, 35
   - Oxoacids and oxoanions **(Example 2.8; Problems 43, 44)**

Key Terms

atom
atomic number
electron
formula
— condensed structural
— molecular
— structural
ion
— anion
— cation
ionic bond
isotope
main-group element
mass number
metal
metalloid
molecule
neutron
nonelectrolyte
nonmetal
nuclear symbol
nucleus
oxoacid
oxoanion
periodic table
— group
— period
proton
strong electrolyte
transition metal
weak electrolyte

Summary Problem

Sodium chloride is table salt. It is made up of sodium and chlorine atoms.

(a) Is sodium chloride an ionic or molecular compound? Is it an electrolyte?

(b) Write the formula for sodium chloride.

(c) If three chlorine atoms combine with an iodine atom, is the resulting compound ionic or molecular? What is its name and formula? Is it an electrolyte?

(d) What are the atomic numbers for sodium and chlorine?

(e) Write the nuclear symbol for the sodium atom with 11 protons and 10 neutrons.

(f) What group and period in the periodic table do sodium and chlorine belong to? Classify these two elements as metals, nonmetals, or metalloids.

(g) How many neutrons are in the chlorine isotope Cl-37?

(h) When aluminum combines with chlorine, an ionic compound is formed. Write its name and its formula.

(i) Chlorine can combine with oxygen in many different ways. Write the names of the following compounds and ions: ClO_2, ClO_2^-, $HClO_2$ *(aq)*, $NaClO_2$

Answers

(a) ionic; yes

(b) NaCl

(c) molecular; ICl_3; iodine trichloride; no

(d) Atomic number of Na is 11; atomic number of Cl is 17.

(e) $^{21}_{11}Na$

(f) Na: Group 1, period 3; metal
Cl: Group 17, period 3; nonmetal

(g) 20

(h) $AlCl_3$: aluminum chloride

(i) ClO_2: chlorine dioxide
ClO_2^-: chlorite ion
$HClO_2$: chlorous acid
$NaClO_2$: sodium chlorite

Questions and Problems

Blue-numbered questions have answers in Appendix 6 and fully-worked solutions in the *Student Solutions Manual.*

■ denotes questions assignable in OWL.

WEB indicates that the solution is available on this book's companion website.

Atomic Theory and Laws

1. State in your own words the law of conservation of mass. State the law in its modern form.

2. State in your own words the law of constant composition.

3. Two basic laws of chemistry are the law of conservation of mass and the law of constant composition. Which of these laws (if any) do the following statements illustrate?

(a) Lavoisier found that when mercury(II) oxide, HgO, decomposes, the total mass of mercury(Hg) and oxygen formed equals the mass of mercury(II) oxide decomposed.

(b) Analysis of the calcium carbonate found in the marble mined in Carrara, Italy, and in the stalactites of the Carlsbad Caverns in New Mexico gives the same value for the percentage of calcium in calcium carbonate.

(c) Hydrogen occurs as a mixture of two isotopes, one of which is twice as heavy as the other.

4. Which of the laws described in Question 3 do the following statements illustrate?

(a) The mass of phosphorus, P, combined with 1 g of hydrogen, H, in the highly toxic gas phosphene, PH_3, is a little more than twice the mass of nitrogen, N, combined with 1 g of hydrogen in ammonia gas, NH_3.

(b) A cold pack has the same mass before and after the seal between the two compartments is broken.

(c) It is highly improbable that the carbon monoxide gas found in Los Angeles is $C_{1.2}O_{2.2}$.

Nuclear Symbols and Isotopes

5. Who discovered the electron? Describe the experiment that led to the deduction that electrons are negatively charged particles.

6. Who discovered the nucleus? Describe the experiment that led to this discovery.

7. Selenium is widely sold as a dietary supplement. It is advertised to "protect" women from breast cancer. Write the nuclear symbol for naturally occurring selenium. It has 34 protons and 46 neutrons.

8. Radon is a radioactive gas that can cause lung cancer. It has been detected in the basements of some homes. How many protons are there in a Rn-220 atom? How many neutrons?

9. How do the isotopes of Cu-63 and Cu-65 differ from each other? Write nuclear symbols for both.

10. Consider two isotopes Fe-54 and Fe-56.

(a) Write the nuclear symbol for both isotopes.

(b) How do they differ from each other?

11. ■ Uranium-235 is the isotope of uranium commonly used in nuclear power plants. How many

(a) protons are in its nucleus?

(b) neutrons are in its nucleus?

(c) electrons are in a uranium atom?

12. Selenium-75 is used in the diagnosis of disorders related to the pancreas. How many

(a) protons are in its nucleus?

(b) neutrons are in its nucleus?

(c) electrons are in a selenium atom?

13. ■ Consider the following nuclear symbols. How many protons, neutrons, and electrons does each element have? What elements do R, T, and X represent?

(a) $^{30}_{14}R$ (b) $^{89}_{39}T$ (c) $^{133}_{55}X$

14. Consider the following nuclear symbols. How many protons, neutrons, and electrons does each element have? What elements do A, L, and Z represent?

(a) $^{75}_{33}A$ (b) $^{51}_{23}L$ (c) $^{131}_{54}Z$

15. ■ Nuclei with the same mass number but different atomic numbers are called *isobars*. Consider Ca-40, Ca-41, K-41 and Ar-41.

(a) Which of these are isobars? Which are isotopes?

(b) What do Ca-40 and Ca-41 have in common?

(c) Correct the statement (if it is incorrect): Atoms of Ca-41, K-41, and Ar-41 have the same number of neutrons.

16. **WEB** See the definition of isobars in Question 15. Consider Na-21 and write the nuclear symbol for

(a) an isotope of Na-21 that has one more neutron than Na-21.

(b) an isobar of Na-21 with atomic number 10.

(c) a nucleus with 11 protons and 12 neutrons. Is this nucleus an isotope of Na-21?

Elements and the Periodic Table

17. Give the symbols for

(a) potassium (b) cadmium (c) aluminum (d) antimony (e) phosphorus

18. Name the elements represented by the symbols

(a) Mn (b) Na (c) As (d) S (e) Pb

19. Classify the elements in Question 17 as metals (main group, transition, or post-transition), nonmetals, or metalloids.

20. ■ Classify the elements in Question 18 as metals (main group, transition, or post-transition), nonmetals, or metalloids.

21. How many metals are in the following groups?

(a) Group 1 (b) Group 13 (c) Group 17

22. How many nonmetals are in the following periods?

(a) period 2 (b) period 4 (c) period 6

23. Which group in the periodic table

(a) has one metalloid and no nonmetals?

(b) has no nonmetals or transition metals?

(c) has no metals or metalloids?

24. ■ Which period of the periodic table

(a) has no metals?

(b) has no nonmetals?

(c) has one post-transition metal and two metalloids?

Molecules and Ions

25. Given the following condensed formulas, write the molecular formulas for the following molecules.

(a) dimethylamine $(CH_3)_2NH$

(b) propyl alcohol $CH_3(CH_2)_2OH$

26. ■ Write the condensed structural formulas and molecular formulas for the following molecules. The reactive groups are shown in red.

(a) 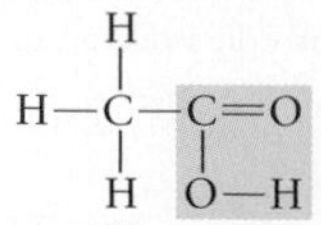 (acetic acid)

(b) 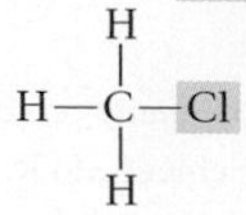 (methyl chloride)

27. ■ Give the number of protons and electrons in

(a) an N_2 molecule (identified in 1772).

(b) an N_3^- unit (synthesized in 1890).

(c) an N_5^+ unit (synthesized in 1999).

(d) an N_5N_5 salt (a U.S. Air Force research team's synthesis project).

28. Give the number of protons and electrons in

(a) a C_{60} molecule. (b) a CN^- ion.

(c) a CO_2 molecule. (d) an N^{3-} ion.

29. ■ Complete the table below. If necessary, use the periodic table.

Nuclear Symbol	Charge	Number of Protons	Number of Neutrons	Number of Electrons
______	0	9	10	______
^{31}P	0	______	16	______
______	+3	27	30	______
______	______	16	16	18

30. Complete the table below. Use the periodic table if necessary.

Nuclear Symbol	Charge	Number of Protons	Number of Neutrons	Number of Electrons
$^{79}_{35}Br$	0	______	______	______
______	−3	7	7	______
______	+5	33	42	______
$^{90}_{40}Zr^{4+}$	______	______	______	______

31. ■ Classify the following compounds as electrolytes or non-electrolytes.

(a) potassium chloride, KCl. (b) hydrogen peroxide, H_2O_2.

(c) methane, CH_4. (d) barium nitrate, $Ba(NO_3)_2$.

32. ■ Which (if any) of the following compounds are electrolytes?

(a) glucose, $C_6H_{12}O_6$. (b) ethanol, C_2H_5OH.

(c) magnesium sulfide, MgS. (d) sulfur hexafluoride, SF_6.

Names and Formulas of Ionic and Molecular Compounds

33. ■ Write the formulas for the following molecules.

(a) methane (b) carbon tetraiodide

(c) hydrogen peroxide (d) nitrogen oxide

(e) silicon dioxide

34. Write the formulas for the following molecules.

(a) water (b) ammonia

(c) hydrazine (d) sulfur hexafluoride

(e) phosphorus pentachloride

35. ■ Write the names of the following molecules.

(a) ICl_3 (b) N_2O_5 (c) PH_3 (d) CBr_4 (e) SO_3

36. Write the names of the following molecules.

(a) CO (b) SiC (c) XeF_6 (d) P_4O_{10} (e) C_2H_2

37. ■ Give the formulas of all the compounds containing no ions other than K^+, Ca^{2+}, Cl^-, and S^{2-}.

38. ■ **WEB** Give the formulas of compounds in which

(a) the cation is Ba^{2+}, the anion is I^- or N^{3-}.

(b) the anion is O^{2-}, the cation is Fe^{2+} or Fe^{3+}.

39. Write the formulas of the following ionic compounds.

(a) iron(III) carbonate (b) sodium azide (N_3^-)

(c) calcium sulfate (d) copper(I) sulfide

(e) lead(IV) oxide

40. ■ Write formulas for the following ionic compounds.

(a) cobalt(II) acetate (b) barium oxide

(c) aluminum sulfide (d) potassium permanganate

(e) sodium hydrogen carbonate

41. ■ Write the names of the following ionic compounds.

(a) $K_2Cr_2O_7$ (b) $Cu_3(PO_4)_2$ (c) $Ba(C_2H_3O_2)_2$

(d) AlN (e) $Co(NO_3)_2$

42. Write the names of the following ionic compounds.

(a) $ScCl_3$ (b) $Sr(OH)_2$ (c) $KMnO_4$

(d) Rb_2S (e) Na_2CO_3

43. Write the names of the following ionic compounds.

(a) $HCl(aq)$ (b) $HClO_3(aq)$ (c) $Fe_2(SO_3)_3$

(d) $Ba(NO_2)_2$ (e) NaClO

44. Write formulas for the following ionic compounds.

(a) hydrochloric acid

(b) sodium nitrite

(c) chromium(III) sulfite

(d) potassium chlorate

(e) iron(III) perbromate

45. Complete the following table.

Name	Formula
nitrous acid	______
______	$Ni(IO_3)_2$
gold(III) sulfide	______
______	$H_2SO_3(aq)$
nitrogen trifluoride	______

46. Complete the following table.

Name	Formula
sodium dichromate	______
______	BrI_3
copper(II) hypochlorite	______
______	S_2Cl_2
potassium nitride	______

■ in OWL Blue-numbered questions answered in Appendix 6 **WEB** Solution is available on companion website

Unclassified

47. Write the formulas and names of the following:

(a) An ionic compound whose cation is a transition metal with 25 protons and 22 electrons and whose anion is an oxoanion of nitrogen with two oxygen atoms.

(b) A molecule made up of a metalloid in Group 13 and three atoms of a halogen in period 2.

(c) An ionic compound made up of an alkaline earth with 20 protons, and an anion with one hydrogen atom, a carbon atom, and 3 oxygen atoms.

48. Identify the following elements:

(a) A member of the same period as tellurium with two fewer protons than tellurium.

(b) A transition metal in Group 5, period 4.

(c) An alkali with 55 protons.

(d) A metalloid in Group 15 with more than 40 protons.

49. Hydrogen-1 can take the form of a molecule, an anion (H^-), or a cation (H^+).

(a) How many protons, electrons, and neutrons are in each possible species?

(b) Write the name and formula for the compound formed between hydrogen and a metal in Group 2 with 12 protons.

(c) What is the general name of the aqueous compounds in which hydrogen is a cation?

50. A molecule of ethylamine is made up of two carbon atoms, seven hydrogen atoms, and one nitrogen atom.

(a) Write its molecular formula.

(b) The reactive group in ethylamine is NH_2. Write its condensed structural formula.

51. Criticize each of the following statements.

(a) In an ionic compound, the number of cations is always the same as the number of anions.

(b) The molecular formula for strontium bromide is $SrBr_2$.

(c) The mass number is always equal to the atomic number.

(d) For any ion, the number of electrons is always more than the number of protons.

52. **WEB** Which of the following statements is/are always true? Never true? Usually true?

(a) Compounds containing carbon atoms are molecular.

(b) A molecule is made up of nonmetal atoms.

(c) An ionic compound has at least one metal atom.

Conceptual Problems

53. Which statements are true?

(a) Neutrons have neither mass nor charge.

(b) Isotopes of an element have an identical number of protons.

(c) C-14 and N-14 have identical neutron/proton (n/p^+) ratios.

(d) The vertical columns in a periodic table are referred to as "groups."

(e) When an atom loses an electron, it becomes positively charged.

54. ■ A student saw the following nuclear symbol for an unknown element: $^{23}_{11}X$. Which of the following statements about X and $^{23}_{11}X$ are true?

(a) X is sodium.

(b) X is vanadium.

(c) X has 23 neutrons in its nucleus.

(d) X^{2+} has 13 electrons.

(e) $^{23}_{11}X$ has a proton/neutron ratio of about 1.1.

55. Using the laws of constant composition and the conservation of mass, complete the molecular picture of hydrogen molecules (○—○) reacting with chlorine molecules (□—□) to give hydrogen chloride (□—○) molecules.

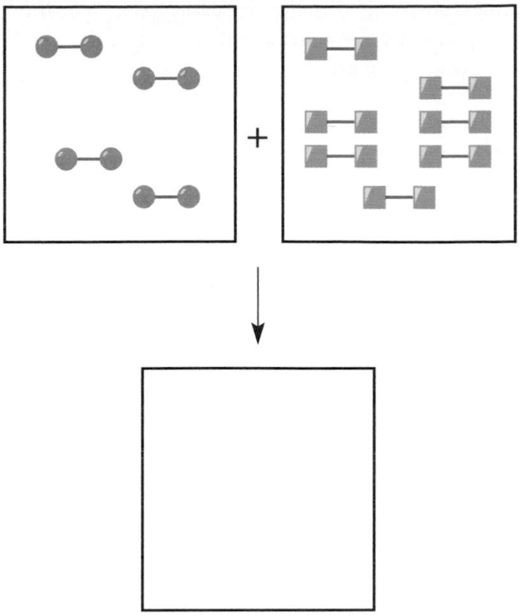

56. Use the law of conservation of mass to determine which numbered box(es) represent(s) the product mixture after the substances in the box at the top of the next column undergo a reaction.

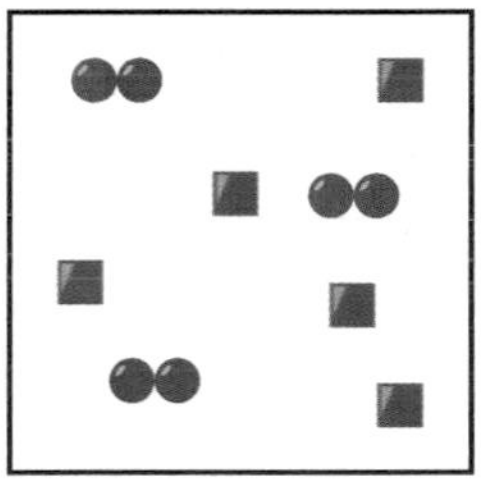

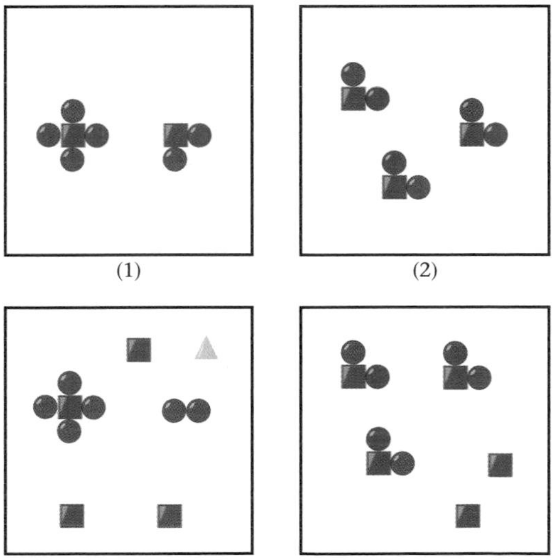

(1) (2) (3) (4)

■ in OWL Blue-numbered questions answered in Appendix 6 **WEB** Solution is available on companion website

57. If squares represent carbon and spheres represent chlorine, make a representation of liquid CCl_4.

58. If squares represent Cl atoms and spheres represent K atoms, make a representation of a KCl crystal.

59. Scientists are trying to synthesize elements with more than 114 protons. State the expected atomic number of

(a) the newest inert gas.

(b) the new element with properties similar to those of the alkaline earth metals.

(c) the new element that will behave like the halogens.

(d) the new (nontransition) metal whose ion will have a +2 charge.

(e) the new element that will start period 8.

60. ■ Write the atomic symbol for the element whose ion has a −2 charge, has 20 more neutrons than electrons, and has a mass number of 126.

61. Mercury(II) oxide, a red powder, can be decomposed by heating to produce liquid mercury and oxygen gas. When a sample of this compound is decomposed, 3.87 g of oxygen and 48.43 g of mercury are produced. In a second experiment, 15.68 g of mercury is allowed to react with an excess of oxygen and 16.93 g of red mercury(II) oxide is produced. Show that these results are consistent with the law of constant composition.

62. Consider the elements oxygen, fluorine, argon, sulfur, potassium, and strontium. From this group of elements, which ones fit the descriptions below?

(a) Two elements that are metals.

(b) Four elements that are nonmetals.

(c) Three elements that are solid at room temperature.

(d) An element that is found in nature as X_8.

(e) One pair of elements that may form a molecular compound.

(f) One pair of elements that may form an ionic compound with formula AX.

(g) One pair of elements that may form an ionic compound with formula AX_2.

(h) One pair of elements that may form an ionic compound with formula A_2X.

(i) An element that can form no compounds.

(j) Three elements that are gases at room temperature.

Challenge Problems

63. ■ Three compounds containing only carbon and hydrogen are analyzed. The results for the analysis of the first two compounds are given below:

Compound	Mass of Carbon (g)	Mass of Hydrogen (g)
A	28.5	2.39
B	34.7	11.6
C	16.2	—

Which, if any, of the following results for the mass of hydrogen in compound C follows the law of multiple proportions?

(a) 5.84 g (b) 3.47 g (c) 2.72 g

64. Ethane and ethylene are two gases containing only hydrogen and carbon atoms. In a certain sample of ethane, 4.53 g of hydrogen is combined with 18.0 g of carbon. In a sample of ethylene, 7.25 g of hydrogen is combined with 43.20 g of carbon.

(a) Show how the data illustrate the law of multiple proportions.

(b) Suggest reasonable formulas for the two compounds.

65. ■ Calculate the average density of a single Al-27 atom by assuming that it is a sphere with a radius of 0.143 nm. The masses of a proton, electron, and neutron are 1.6726×10^{-24} g, 9.1094×10^{-28} g, and 1.6749×10^{-24} g, respectively. The volume of a sphere is $4\pi r^3/3$, where r is its radius. Express the answer in grams per cubic centimeter. The density of aluminum is found experimentally to be 2.70 g/cm^3. What does that suggest about the packing of aluminum atoms in the metal?

66. The mass of a beryllium atom is 1.4965×10^{-23} g. Using that fact and other information in this chapter, find the mass of a Be^{2+} ion.

67. ■ Each time you inhale, you take in about 500 mL (two significant figures) of air, each milliliter of which contains 2.5×10^{19} molecules. In delivering the Gettysburg Address, Abraham Lincoln is estimated to have inhaled about 200 times.

(a) How many molecules did Lincoln take in?

(b) In the entire atmosphere, there are about 1.1×10^{44} molecules. What fraction of the molecules in the earth's atmosphere was inhaled by Lincoln at Gettysburg?

(c) In the next breath that you take, how many molecules were inhaled by Lincoln at Gettysburg?

■ in OWL Blue-numbered questions answered in Appendix 6 WEB Solution is available on companion website

3 Mass Relations in Chemistry; Stoichiometry

Ex umbris et imaginibus in veritatem!
(From shadows and symbols into the truth!)

—John Henry Cardinal Newman

Chapter Outline

Balanced chemical equations make it possible to relate masses of reactants and products. Scales are devices commonly used to measure mass.

"The Money-Lender (Banker) and His Wife" by Quentin Metsys/© Erich Lessing/Art Resource, NY

To this point, our study of chemistry has been largely qualitative, involving very few calculations. However, chemistry is a quantitative science. Atoms of elements differ from one another not only in composition (number of protons, electrons, neutrons), but also in mass. Chemical formulas of compounds tell us not only the atom ratios in which elements are present but also the mass ratios.

The general topic of this chapter is stoichiometry (stoy-key-OM-e-tree), the study of mass relations in chemistry. Whether dealing with atomic masses (Section 3.1), molar masses (Section 3.2), chemical formulas (Section 3.3), or chemical reactions (Section 3.4), you will be answering some very practical questions that ask "how much—" or "how many—." For example—

- how many atoms are in a gram of an element? (Section 3.1)
- how much iron can be obtained from a ton of iron ore? (Section 3.3)
- how much nitrogen gas is required to form a kilogram of ammonia? (Section 3.4) ■

Online homework for this chapter may be assigned in OWL.

CENGAGENOW™
This icon introduces an opportunity for self-study and to explore interactive modules by signing in at **academic.cengage.com/now.**

3.1 ATOMIC MASSES

Individual atoms are far too small to be weighed on a balance. However, as you will soon see, it is possible to determine quite accurately the relative masses of different atoms and molecules. Indeed, it is possible to go a step further and calculate the actual masses of these tiny building blocks of matter.

Atomic Masses; the Carbon-12 Scale

Relative masses of atoms of different elements are expressed in terms of their **atomic masses** (often referred to as atomic weights). The atomic mass of an element indicates how heavy, on the average, one atom of that element is compared with an atom of another element.

To set up a scale of atomic masses, it is necessary to establish a standard value for one particular species. The modern atomic mass scale is based on the most common isotope of carbon, $^{12}_{6}C$. This isotope is assigned a mass of exactly 12 **atomic mass units** (amu):

1 amu = 1/12 mass C atom ≈ mass H atom.

$$\text{mass of C-12 atom} = 12 \text{ amu (exactly)}$$

It follows that an atom half as heavy as a C-12 atom would weigh 6 amu, an atom twice as heavy as C-12 would have a mass of 24 amu, and so on.

In the periodic table, atomic masses are listed directly below the symbol of the element. In the table on the inside front cover of this text, atomic masses are cited to four significant figures. That ordinarily will be sufficient for our purposes, although more precise values are available (see the alphabetical list of elements on the inside back cover).

The average atomic mass shown in the periodic table is not equal to the mass number.

Notice that hydrogen has an atomic mass of 1.008 amu; helium has an atomic mass of 4.003 amu. This means that, on the average, a helium atom has a mass that is about one-third that of a C-12 atom:

$$\frac{4.003 \text{ amu}}{12.00 \text{ amu}} = 0.3336$$

or about four times that of a hydrogen atom:

$$\frac{4.003 \text{ amu}}{1.008 \text{ amu}} = 3.971$$

In general, for two elements X and Y:

Atomic masses give relative masses of different atoms.

$$\frac{\text{atomic mass X}}{\text{atomic mass Y}} = \frac{\text{mass of atom of X}}{\text{mass of atom of Y}}$$

Figure 3.1
The mass spectrometer.

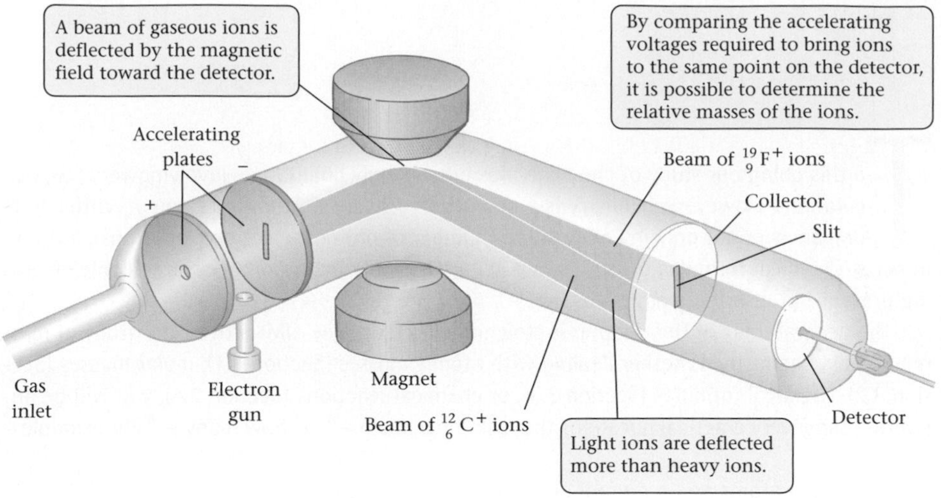

Atomic Masses and Isotopic Abundances

CENGAGENOW™
Click Coached Problems for a self-study module on **average atomic mass from isotopic abundance.**

Relative masses of individual atoms can be determined using a mass spectrometer (Figure 3.1). Gaseous atoms or molecules at very low pressures are ionized by removing one or more electrons. The cations formed are accelerated by a potential of 500 to 2000 V toward a magnetic field, which deflects the ions from their straight-line path. The extent of deflection is inversely related to the mass of the ion. By measuring the voltages required to bring two ions of different mass to the same point on the detector, it is possible to determine their relative masses. For example, using a mass spectrometer, it is found that a $^{19}_{9}F$ atom is 1.583 times as heavy as a $^{12}_{6}C$ atom and so has a mass of

$$1.583 \times 12.00 \text{ amu} = 19.00 \text{ amu}$$

As it happens, naturally occurring fluorine consists of a single isotope, $^{19}_{9}F$. It follows that the atomic mass of the element fluorine must be the same as that of F-19, 19.00 amu. The situation with most elements is more complex, because they occur in nature as a mixture of two or more isotopes. To determine the atomic mass of such an element, it is necessary to know not only the masses of the individual isotopes but also their atom percents **(isotopic abundances)** in nature.

Fortunately, isotopic abundances as well as isotopic masses can be determined by mass spectrometry. The situation with chlorine, which has two stable isotopes, Cl-35 and Cl-37, is shown in Figure 3.2. The atomic masses of the two isotopes are determined in the usual way. The relative abundances of these isotopes are proportional to the heights of the recorder peaks or, more accurately, to the areas under these peaks. For chlorine, the data obtained from the mass spectrometer are

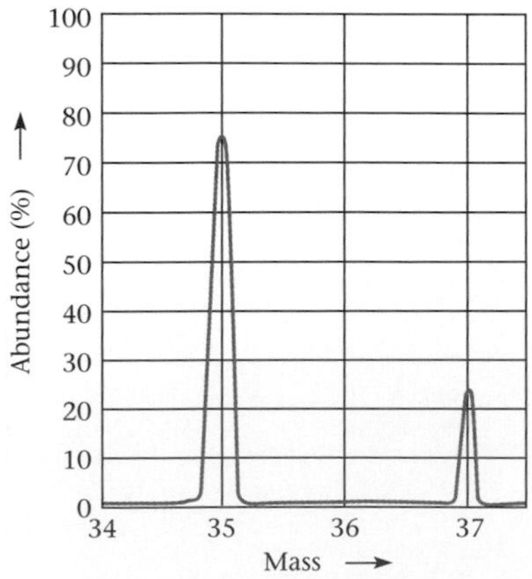

Figure 3.2
Mass spectrum of chlorine. Elemental chlorine (Cl_2) contains only two isotopes: 34.97 amu (75.53%) and 36.97 amu (24.47%).

	Atomic Mass	Abundance
Cl-35	34.97 amu	75.53%
Cl-37	36.97 amu	24.47%

We interpret this to mean that, in elemental chlorine, 75.53% of the atoms have a mass of 34.97 amu, and the remaining atoms, 24.47% of the total, have a mass of 36.97 amu. With this information we can readily calculate the atomic mass of chlorine using the general equation

atomic mass Y =

$$(\text{atomic mass } Y_1) \times \frac{\% \; Y_1}{100\%} + (\text{atomic mass } Y_2) \times \frac{\% \; Y_2}{100\%} + \cdots \qquad \textbf{(3.1)}$$

where $Y_1, Y_2, \ldots$ are isotopes of element Y.

$$\text{atomic mass Cl} = 34.97 \text{ amu} \times \frac{75.53}{100.0} + 36.97 \text{ amu} \times \frac{24.47}{100.0} = 35.46 \text{ amu}$$

Atomic masses calculated in this manner, using data obtained with a mass spectrometer, can in principle be precise to seven or eight significant figures. The accuracy of tabulated atomic masses is limited mostly by variations in natural abundances. Sulfur is an interesting case in point. It consists largely of two isotopes, $^{32}_{16}S$ and $^{34}_{16}S$. The abundance of sulfur-34 varies from about 4.18% in sulfur deposits in Texas and Louisiana to 4.34% in volcanic sulfur from Italy. This leads to an uncertainty of 0.006 amu in the atomic mass of sulfur.

If the atomic mass of an element is known *and* if it has only two stable isotopes, their abundances can be calculated from the general equation cited above.

Example 3.1 Bromine is a red-orange liquid with an average atomic mass of 79.90 amu. Its name is derived from the Greek word *bromos* ($\beta\rho o\mu o\varsigma$), which means stench. It has two naturally occurring isotopes: Br-79 (78.92 amu) and Br-81 (80.92 amu). What is the abundance of the heavier isotope?

Strategy The key to solving this problem is to realize that *the abundances of the isotopes have to add to 100%*. If we let x = abundance of Br-81, then the abundance of Br-79 must be $(100 - x)$.

SOLUTION Substituting in Equation 3.1,

$$79.90 \text{ amu} = 78.92 \text{ amu} \frac{(100 - x)}{100} + 80.92 \text{ amu} \frac{(x)}{100}$$

$$= 78.92 \text{ amu} + 2.00 \text{ amu} \frac{(x)}{100}$$

Solving: $$\frac{x}{100} = \frac{(79.90 - 78.92) \text{ amu}}{2.00 \text{ amu}} = 0.49; \quad x = 100(0.49) = 49\%$$

Reality Check The atomic mass of Br, 79.90, is just about halfway between the masses of the two isotopes, 78.92 and 80.92. So, it is reasonable that it should contain nearly equal amounts of the two isotopes.

Masses of Individual Atoms; Avogadro's Number

For most purposes in chemistry, it is sufficient to know the relative masses of different atoms. Sometimes, however, it is necessary to go one step further and calculate the mass in grams of individual atoms. Let us consider how this can be done.

If a nickel weighs twice as much as a dime, there are equal numbers of coins in 1000 g of nickels and 500 g of dimes.

To start with, consider the elements helium and hydrogen. A helium atom is about four times as heavy as a hydrogen atom (He = 4.003 amu, H = 1.008 amu). It follows that a sample containing 100 helium atoms weighs four times as much as a sample containing 100 hydrogen atoms. Again, comparing samples of the two elements containing a million atoms each, the masses will be in a 4 (helium) to 1 (hydrogen) ratio. Turning this argument around, it follows that a sample of helium weighing four grams must contain the same number of atoms as a sample of hydrogen weighing one gram. More exactly,

$$\text{no. of He atoms in 4.003 g helium} = \text{no. of H atoms in 1.008 g hydrogen}$$

This reasoning is readily extended to other elements. A sample of any element with a mass in grams equal to its atomic mass contains the same number of atoms, N_A, regardless of the identity of the element.

The question now arises as to the numerical value of N_A; that is, how many atoms are in 4.003 g of helium, 1.008 g of hydrogen, 32.07 g of sulfur, and so on? As it happens, this problem is one that has been studied for at least a century. Several ingenious experiments have been designed to determine this number, known as **Avogadro's number** and given the symbol N_A (see Problem 100, end of chapter). As you can imagine, it is huge. (Remember that atoms are tiny. There must be a lot of them in 4.003 g of He, 1.008 g of H, and so on.) To four significant figures,

$$N_A = 6.022 \times 10^{23}$$

Most people have better things to do.

To get some idea of how large this number is, suppose the entire population of the world were assigned to counting the atoms in 4.003 g of helium. If each person counted one atom per second and worked a 48-hour week, the task would take more than 10 million years.

The importance of Avogadro's number in chemistry should be clear. ***It represents the number of atoms of an element in a sample whose mass in grams is numerically equal to the atomic mass of the element.*** Thus there are

6.022×10^{23} H atoms in 1.008 g H	atomic mass H = 1.008 amu
6.022×10^{23} He atoms in 4.003 g He	atomic mass He = 4.003 amu
6.022×10^{23} S atoms in 32.07 g S	atomic mass S = 32.07 amu

Knowing Avogadro's number and the atomic mass of an element, it is possible to calculate the mass of an individual atom (Example 3.2a). You can also determine the number of atoms in a weighed sample of any element (Example 3.2b).

Example 3.2 Consider titanium (Ti), the "space-age" metal discussed at the end of Chapter 1. Taking Avogadro's number to be 6.022×10^{23}, calculate

(a) the mass of a titanium atom.
(b) the number of atoms in a ten-gram sample of the metal.
(c) the number of protons in 0.1500 lb of titanium.

Strategy From the periodic table, the atomic mass of titanium is 47.87 amu. It follows that

$$6.022 \times 10^{23} \text{ Ti atoms} = 47.87 \text{ g Ti}$$

The relation yields the required conversion factor for (a) and (b). Also from the periodic table, we see that the atomic number for titanium is 22, the number of protons in an atom of titanium.

SOLUTION

(a) $\text{mass of Ti atom} = 1 \text{ Ti atom} \times \dfrac{47.87 \text{ g Ti}}{6.022 \times 10^{23} \text{ Ti atoms}} = 7.949 \times 10^{-23} \text{ g}$

(b) $\text{no. of Ti atoms} = 10.00 \text{ g} \times \dfrac{6.022 \times 10^{23} \text{ Ti atoms}}{47.87 \text{ g Ti}} = 1.258 \times 10^{23} \text{ atoms}$

(c) First, change the given mass of Ti (0.1500 lb) to grams:

$$0.1500 \text{ lb} \times \frac{453.6 \text{ g}}{1 \text{ lb}} = 68.04 \text{ g}$$

$$\text{no. of protons} = 68.04 \text{ g} \times \frac{6.022 \times 10^{23} \text{ Ti atoms}}{47.87 \text{ g Ti}} \times \frac{22 \text{ protons}}{1 \text{ atom}}$$

$$= 1.883 \times 10^{25} \text{ protons}$$

Reality Check Because atoms are so tiny, we expect their mass to be very small: 7.949×10^{-23} g sounds reasonable. Conversely, it takes a lot of atoms, in this case 1.258×10^{23}, to weigh ten grams.

3.2 THE MOLE

The quantity represented by Avogadro's number is so important that it is given a special name, the **mole.** A mole represents 6.022×10^{23} items, whatever they may be (Figure 3.3).

$$1 \text{ mol H atoms} = 6.022 \times 10^{23} \text{ H atoms}$$
$$1 \text{ mol O atoms} = 6.022 \times 10^{23} \text{ O atoms}$$
$$1 \text{ mol } H_2 \text{ molecules} = 6.022 \times 10^{23}\ H_2 \text{ molecules}$$
$$1 \text{ mol } H_2O \text{ molecules} = 6.022 \times 10^{23}\ H_2O \text{ molecules}$$
$$1 \text{ mol electrons} = 6.022 \times 10^{23} \text{ electrons}$$
$$1 \text{ mol pennies} = 6.022 \times 10^{23} \text{ pennies}$$

(One mole of pennies is a lot of money. It's enough to pay all the expenses of the United States for the next billion years or so without accounting for inflation.)

A mole represents not only a specific number of particles but also a definite mass of a substance as represented by its formula (O, O_2, H_2O, NaCl, . . .). ***The molar mass, MM, in grams per mole, is numerically equal to the sum of the masses (in amu) of the atoms in the formula.***

Figure 3.3
One-mole amounts of sugar ($C_{12}H_{22}O_{11}$), baking soda ($NaHCO_3$), and copper nails (Cu).

The size of the mole was chosen to make this relation true.

Formula	Sum of Atomic Masses	Molar Mass, MM
O	16.00 amu	16.00 g/mol
O_2	2(16.00 amu) = 32.00 amu	32.00 g/mol
H_2O	2(1.008 amu) + 16.00 amu = 18.02 amu	18.02 g/mol
NaCl	22.99 amu + 35.45 amu = 58.44 amu	58.44 g/mol

CENGAGENOW™
Click Coached Problems for a self-study module on **determining molar mass.**

Notice that the formula of a substance must be known to find its molar mass. It would be ambiguous, to say the least, to refer to the "molar mass of hydrogen." One mole of hydrogen atoms, represented by the symbol H, weighs 1.008 g; the molar mass of H is 1.008 g/mol. One mole of hydrogen molecules, represented by the formula H_2, weighs 2.016 g; the molar mass of H_2 is 2.016 g/mol.

Mole–Gram Conversions

As you will see later in this chapter, it is often necessary to convert from moles of a substance to mass in grams or vice versa. Such conversions are readily made by using the general relation

$$\boxed{m = MM \times n} \qquad (3.2)$$

where m is the mass in grams, MM is the molar mass (g/mol), and n is the amount in moles. In effect, the molar mass, MM, is a conversion factor that allows you to calculate n from m or vice versa.

Example 3.3 Acetylsalicylic acid, $C_9H_8O_4$, is the active ingredient of aspirin.

(a) What is the mass in grams of 0.509 moles of acetylsalicylic acid?
(b) A one-gram sample of aspirin contains 75.2% by mass of $C_9H_8O_4$. How many moles of acetylsalicylic acid are in the sample?
(c) How many molecules of $C_9H_8O_4$ are there in 12.00 g of acetylsalicylic acid? How many carbon atoms?

Strategy Find the molar mass of $C_9H_8O_4$ and use it to convert moles to grams in (a), grams to moles in (b), and (with Avogadro's number) grams to molecules in (c).

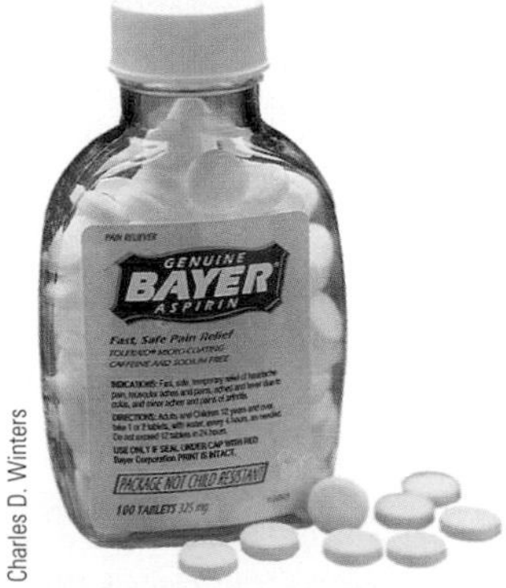

Aspirin (acetylsalicylic acid), $C_9H_8O_4$.

SOLUTION The molar mass of $C_9H_8O_4$ is

$$MM = [9(12.01) + 8(1.008) + 4(16.00)]\ g/mol = 180.15\ g/mol$$

(a) $0.509\ mol \times \frac{180.15\ g}{1\ mol} = 91.7\ g$

(b) $1.00\ g\ aspirin \times \frac{75.2\ g\ C_9H_8O_4}{100\ g\ aspirin} \times \frac{1\ mol}{180.15\ g} = 4.17 \times 10^{-3}\ mol$

(c) $12.00\ g\ C_9H_8O_4 \times \frac{1\ mol}{180.15\ g} \times \frac{6.022 \times 10^{23}\ molecules}{1\ mol} = 4.011 \times 10^{22}\ molecules$

Since there are 9 carbon atoms in one molecule of $C_9H_8O_4$,

$$\text{no. of C atoms} = 4.011 \times 10^{22}\ \text{molecules} \times \frac{9\ \text{C atoms}}{1\ \text{molecule}} = 3.610 \times 10^{23}$$

Reality Check Because every known substance has a molar mass greater than 1 g/mol, the mass of the sample in grams is always larger than the number of moles.

CENGAGENOW™
Click Coached Problems for a self-study module on **using molar mass.**

Almost every calculation that you will make in this chapter requires that you know precisely what is meant by a mole.

Conversions of the type we have just carried out come up over and over again in chemistry. They will be required in nearly every chapter of this text. Clearly, you must know what is meant by a mole. Remember, a mole always represents a certain number of items, 6.022×10^{23}. Its mass, however, differs with the substance involved: A mole of H_2O, 18.02 g, weighs considerably more than a mole of H_2, 2.016 g, even though they both contain the same number of molecules. In the same way, a dozen bowling balls weigh a lot more than a dozen eggs, even though the number of items is the same for both.

3.3 MASS RELATIONS IN CHEMICAL FORMULAS

As you will see shortly, the formula of a compound can be used to determine the mass percents of the elements present. Conversely, if the percentages of the elements are known, the simplest formula can be determined. Knowing the molar mass of a molecular compound, it is possible to go one step further and find the molecular formula. In this section we will consider how these three types of calculations are carried out.

Percent Composition from Formula

The **percent composition** of a compound is specified by citing the mass percents of the elements present. For example, in a 100-g sample of water there are 11.19 g of hydrogen and 88.81 g of oxygen. Hence the percentages of the two elements are

$$\frac{11.19\ g\ H}{100.00\ g} \times 100\% = 11.19\%\ H \qquad \frac{88.81\ g\ O}{100.00\ g} \times 100\% = 88.81\%\ O$$

We would say that the percent composition of water is 11.19% H, 88.81% O.

Knowing the formula of a compound, Fe_2O_3, you can readily calculate the mass percents of its constituent elements. It is convenient to start with one mole of compound (Example 3.4a). The formula of a compound can also be used in a straightforward way to find the mass of an element in a known mass of the compound (Example 3.4b).

CENGAGENOW™
Click Coached Problems for a self-study module on **percent composition.**

Example 3.4 Graded

Metallic iron is most often extracted from hematite ore, which consists of iron(III) oxide mixed with impurities such as silicon dioxide, SiO_2.

*(a) What are the mass percents of iron and oxygen in iron(III) oxide?

**(b) How many grams of iron can be extracted from one kilogram of Fe_2O_3?

***(c) How many metric tons of hematite ore, 66.4% Fe_2O_3, must be processed to produce one kilogram of iron?

SOLUTION

(a) In one mole of Fe_2O_3, there are two moles of iron and three moles of oxygen.

$$\text{mass Fe} = 2\text{ mol}(55.85\text{ g/mol}) = 111.7\text{ g}$$
$$\text{mass O} = 3\text{ mol}(16.00\text{ g/mol}) = \underline{48.00\text{ g}}$$
$$159.7\text{ g}$$

$$\%\text{ Fe} = \frac{111.7\text{ g}}{159.7\text{ g}} \times 100\% = 69.94;\ \%\text{ O} = 100.00 - 69.94 = 30.06$$

(b) $1.000 \times 10^3\text{ g Fe}_2\text{O}_3 \times \dfrac{111.7\text{ g Fe}}{159.7\text{ g Fe}_2\text{O}_3} = 699.4\text{ g Fe}$

(c) Perhaps the simplest way to proceed here is to start with one kilogram of Fe, convert that to kilograms of Fe_2O_3, then convert to kilograms of hematite and finally to metric tons.

$$\text{mass hematite} = 1.00\text{ kg Fe} \times \frac{159.7\text{ g Fe}_2\text{O}_3}{111.7\text{ g Fe}} \times \frac{100.0\text{ g hematite}}{66.4\text{ g Fe}_2\text{O}_3} \times \frac{1\text{ metric ton}}{10^3\text{ kg}}$$
$$= 2.15 \times 10^{-3}\text{ metric ton}$$

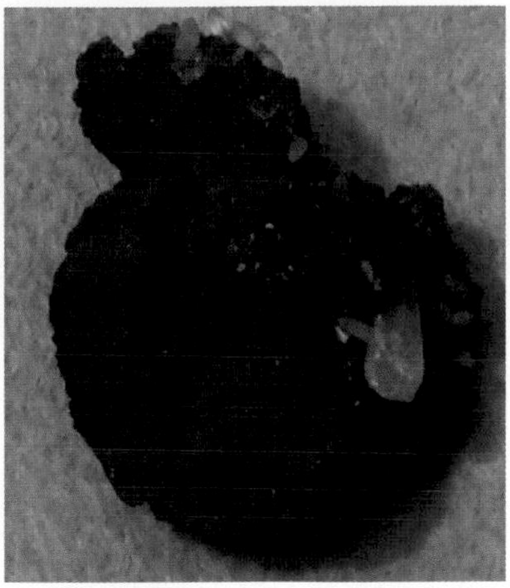

Jo Edkins, 2007. Used with permission.

Hematite ore.

The calculations in Example 3.4 illustrate an important characteristic of formulas. In one mole of Fe_2O_3 there are *two* moles of Fe (111.7 g) and *three* moles of O (48.00 g). This is the same as the atom ratio in Fe_2O_3, 2 atoms Fe : 3 atoms O. In general, ***the subscripts in a formula represent not only the atom ratio in which the different elements are combined but also the mole ratio.***

Can you explain why the mole ratio must equal the atom ratio?

Simplest Formula from Chemical Analysis

A major task of chemical analysis is to determine the formulas of compounds. The formula found by the approach described here is the **simplest formula,** which gives the simplest whole-number ratio of the atoms present. For an ionic compound, the simplest formula is ordinarily the only one that can be written (e.g., $CaCl_2$, Cr_2O_3). For a molecular compound, the molecular formula is a whole-number multiple of the simplest formula, where that number may be 1, 2, ...

CENGAGENOW™

Click Coached Problems for a self-study module on **empirical formulas.**

Compound	Simplest Formula	Molecular Formula	Multiple
Water	H_2O	H_2O	1
Hydrogen peroxide	HO	H_2O_2	2
Propylene	CH_2	C_3H_6	3

The analytical data leading to the simplest formula may be expressed in various ways. You may know—

- the masses of the elements in a weighed sample of the compound.
- the mass percents of the elements in the compound.
- the masses of products obtained by reaction of a weighed sample of the compound.

Mass data ⟶ mole ratio = atom ratio ⟶ simplest formula

The strategy used to calculate the simplest formula depends to some extent on which of these types of information is given. The basic objective in each case is to find the number of moles of each element, then the simplest mole ratio, and finally the simplest formula.

Example 3.5 A 25.00-g sample of an orange compound contains 6.64 g of potassium, 8.84 g of chromium, and 9.52 g of oxygen. Find the simplest formula.

Strategy First (1), convert the masses of the three elements to moles. Knowing the number of moles (n) of K, Cr, and O, you can then (2) calculate the mole ratios. Finally (3), equate the mole ratio to the atom ratio, which gives you the simplest formula.

SOLUTION

The mass of an *atom* of oxygen (O) is 16 g; the mass of a *molecule* of oxygen (O_2) is 32 g.

(1) $n_K = 6.64 \text{ g K} \times \dfrac{1 \text{ mol K}}{39.10 \text{ g K}} = 0.170 \text{ mol K}$

$n_{Cr} = 8.84 \text{ g Cr} \times \dfrac{1 \text{ mol Cr}}{52.00 \text{ g Cr}} = 0.170 \text{ mol Cr}$

$n_O = 9.52 \text{ g O} \times \dfrac{1 \text{ mol O}}{16.00 \text{ g O}} = 0.595 \text{ mol O}$

(2) To find the mole ratios, divide by the smallest number, 0.170 mol K:

$$\frac{0.170 \text{ mol Cr}}{0.170 \text{ mol K}} = \frac{1.00 \text{ mol Cr}}{1 \text{ mol K}} \qquad \frac{0.595 \text{ mol O}}{0.170 \text{ mol K}} = \frac{3.50 \text{ mol O}}{1 \text{ mol K}}$$

The mole ratio is 1 mol of K : 1 mol of Cr : 3.50 mol of O.

(3) As pointed out earlier, the mole ratio is the same as the atom ratio. To find the simplest whole-number atom ratio, multiply throughout by 2:

$$2 \text{ K} : 2 \text{ Cr} : 7 \text{ O}$$

The simplest formula of the orange compound is $K_2Cr_2O_7$.

Reality Check A mole ratio of 1.00 A : 1.00 B : 3.33 C would imply a formula $A_3B_3C_{10}$; if the mole ratio were 1.00 A : 2.50 B : 5.50 C, the formula would be $A_2B_5C_{11}$. In general, multiply through by the smallest whole number that will give integers for all the subscripts.

Sometimes you will be given the mass percents of the elements in a compound. If that is the case, one extra step is involved. ***Assume a 100-g sample and calculate the mass of each element in that sample.***

Suppose, for example, you are told that the percentages of K, Cr, and O in a compound are 26.6%, 35.4%, and 38.0%, respectively. It follows that in a 100.0-g sample there are

$$26.6 \text{ g K}, 35.4 \text{ g Cr}, 38.0 \text{ g O}$$

Working with these masses, you can go through the same procedure followed in Example 3.5 to arrive at the same answer. (Try it!)

The most complex problem of this type requires you to determine the simplest formula of a compound given only the raw data obtained from its analysis. Here, an additional step is involved; you have to determine the masses of the elements present in a fixed mass of the compound (Example 3.6).

Example 3.6 The compound that gives vinegar its sour taste is acetic acid, which contains the elements carbon, hydrogen, and oxygen. When 5.00 g of acetic acid are burned in air, 7.33 g of CO_2 and 3.00 g of water are obtained. What is the simplest formula of acetic acid?

Strategy The first step (1) is to calculate the masses of C, H, and O in the 5.00-g sample. To do this note that all of the carbon has been converted to carbon dioxide. One mole of C (12.01 g) forms one mole of CO_2 (44.01 g). Hence to find the mass of carbon in 7.33 g of CO_2, you use the conversion factor:

$$12.01 \text{ g C}/44.01 \text{ g CO}_2$$

By the same token, all the hydrogen ends up as water. Because there are two moles of H (2.016 g) in one mole of H_2O (18.02 g), the conversion factor is

$$2(1.008)\text{g H}/18.02 \text{ g H}_2\text{O}$$

The mass of oxygen in the sample cannot be found in a similar way because some of the oxygen in the products comes from the air required to burn the reactants. Instead we find the mass of oxygen by difference:

$$\text{mass O} = \text{mass of sample} - (\text{mass of C} + \text{mass of H})$$

Once the masses of the elements are obtained, it's all downhill; follow the same path as in Example 3.5.

Charles D. Winters

Vinegar. Vinegar gets its sour taste from acetic acid.

SOLUTION

(1) Find the mass of each element in the sample.

$$\text{mass C} = 7.33 \text{ g CO}_2 \times \frac{12.01 \text{ g C}}{44.01 \text{ g CO}_2} = 2.00 \text{ g C}$$

$$\text{mass H} = 3.00 \text{ g H}_2\text{O} \times \frac{2.016 \text{ g H}}{18.02 \text{ g H}_2\text{O}} = 0.336 \text{ g H}$$

$$\text{mass O} = 5.00 \text{ g sample} - 2.00 \text{ g C} - 0.336 \text{ g H} = 2.66 \text{ g O}$$

(2) Find the number of moles of each element.

$$n_C = 2.00 \text{ g C} \times \frac{1 \text{ mol C}}{12.01 \text{ g C}} = 0.167 \text{ mol C}$$

$$n_H = 0.336 \text{ g H} \times \frac{1 \text{ mol H}}{1.008 \text{ g H}} = 0.333 \text{ mol H}$$

$$n_O = 2.66 \text{ g O} \times \frac{1 \text{ mol O}}{16.00 \text{ g O}} = 0.166 \text{ mol O}$$

(3) Find the mole ratios and then the simplest formula.

$$\frac{0.167 \text{ mol C}}{0.166 \text{ mol O}} = \frac{1.01 \text{ mol C}}{1.00 \text{ mol O}} \qquad \frac{0.333 \text{ mol H}}{0.166 \text{ mol O}} = \frac{2.01 \text{ mol H}}{1.00 \text{ mol O}}$$

Rounding off to whole numbers, the mole ratios are

$$1 \text{ mol C} : 2 \text{ mol H} : 1 \text{ mol O}$$

The simplest formula of acetic acid is CH_2O.

Sometimes it's not so easy to convert the atom ratio to simplest formula (see Problem 47 at the end of the Chapter).

Molecular Formula from Simplest Formula

Chemical analysis always leads to the simplest formula of a compound because it gives only the simplest atom ratio of the elements. As pointed out earlier, the molecular formula is a whole-number multiple of the simplest formula. That multiple may be 1 as in H_2O, 2 as in H_2O_2, 3 as in C_3H_6, or some other integer. To find the multiple, one more piece of data is needed: the molar mass.

CENGAGENOW™
Click Coached Problems for a self-study module on **molecular formulas.**

Example 3.7 The molar mass of acetic acid, as determined with a mass spectrometer, is about 60 g/mol. Using that information along with the simplest formula found in Example 3.6, determine the molecular formula of acetic acid.

Strategy Calculate the molar mass corresponding to the simplest formula, CH_2O. Then find the multiple by dividing the actual molar mass, 60 g/mol, by the molar mass of CH_2O.

SOLUTION

In this case, you don't need to know the molar mass accurately. Why?

$$\text{MM } CH_2O = 12.01 \text{ g/mol} + 2(1.008 \text{ g/mol}) + 16.00 \text{ g/mol} = 30.03 \text{ g/mol}$$

The ratio of the actual molar mass, 60 g/mol, to that of CH_2O is

$$\frac{60 \text{ g/mol}}{30.03 \text{ g/mol}} = 2; \qquad \text{molecular formula} = C_2H_4O_2$$

3.4 MASS RELATIONS IN REACTIONS

CENGAGENOW™
Click Coached Problems for a self-study module on **balancing chemical equations.**

A chemist who carries out a reaction in the laboratory needs to know how much *product* can be obtained from a given amount of starting materials *(reactants)*. To do this, he or she starts by writing a balanced chemical equation.

Writing and Balancing Chemical Equations

Chemical reactions are represented by chemical equations, which identify reactants and products. Formulas of reactants appear on the left side of the equation; those of products are written on the right. In a balanced chemical equation, there are the same number of atoms of a given element on both sides. The same situation holds for a chemical reaction that you carry out in the laboratory; atoms are conserved. For that reason, ***any calculation involving a reaction must be based on the balanced equation for that reaction.***

Beginning students are sometimes led to believe that writing a chemical equation is a simple, mechanical process. Nothing could be further from the truth. One point that seems obvious is often overlooked. ***You cannot write an equation unless you know what happens in the reaction that it represents.*** All the reactants and all the products must be identified. Moreover, you must know their formulas and physical states.

NASA

Figure 3.4
A space shuttle taking off.

To illustrate how a relatively simple equation can be written and balanced, consider a reaction used to launch astronauts into space (Figure 3.4). The reactants are two liquids, hydrazine and dinitrogen tetraoxide, whose molecular formulas are N_2H_4 and N_2O_4, respectively. The products of the reaction are gaseous nitrogen, N_2, and water vapor. To write a balanced equation for this reaction, proceed as follows:

1. ***Write a "skeleton" equation in which the formulas of the reactants appear on the left and those of the products on the right.*** In this case,

$$N_2H_4 + N_2O_4 \longrightarrow N_2 + H_2O$$

2. ***Indicate the physical state of each reactant and product, after the formula, by writing***

Using the letters (*s*), (*l*), (*g*), (*aq*) lends a sense of physical reality to the equation.

(*g*) for a gaseous substance
(*l*) for a pure liquid
(*s*) for a solid
(*aq*) for an ion or molecule in water (aqueous) solution

In this case

$$N_2H_4(l) + N_2O_4(l) \longrightarrow N_2(g) + H_2O(g)$$

3. ***Balance the equation.*** To accomplish this, start by writing a coefficient of 4 for H_2O, thus obtaining 4 oxygen atoms on both sides:

$$N_2H_4(l) + N_2O_4(l) \longrightarrow N_2(g) + 4H_2O(g)$$

Now consider the hydrogen atoms. There are $4 \times 2 = 8$ H atoms on the right. To obtain 8 H atoms on the left, write a coefficient of 2 for N_2H_4:

$$2N_2H_4(l) + N_2O_4(l) \longrightarrow N_2(g) + 4H_2O(g)$$

Finally, consider nitrogen. There are a total of $(2 \times 2) + 2 = 6$ nitrogen atoms on the left. To balance nitrogen, write a coefficient of 3 for N_2:

6N is no good either.

$$2N_2H_4(l) + N_2O_4(l) \longrightarrow 3N_2(g) + 4H_2O(g)$$

This is the final balanced equation for the reaction of hydrazine with dinitrogen tetraoxide.

Three points concerning the balancing process are worth noting.

1. Equations are balanced by adjusting coefficients in front of formulas, never by changing subscripts within formulas. On paper, the equation discussed above could have been balanced by writing N_6 on the right, but that would have been absurd. Elemental nitrogen exists as diatomic molecules, N_2; there is no such thing as an N_6 molecule.

2. In balancing an equation, it is best to start with an element that appears in only one species on each side of the equation. In this case, either oxygen or hydrogen is a good starting point. Nitrogen would have been a poor choice, however, because there are nitrogen atoms in both reactant molecules, N_2H_4 and N_2O_4.

3. In principle, an infinite number of balanced equations can be written for any reaction. The equations

$$4N_2H_4(l) + 2N_2O_4(l) \longrightarrow 6N_2(g) + 8H_2O(g)$$
$$N_2H_4(l) + \tfrac{1}{2}N_2O_4(l) \longrightarrow \tfrac{3}{2}N_2(g) + 2H_2O(g)$$

are balanced in that there are the same number of atoms of each element on both sides. Ordinarily, the equation with the simplest whole-number coefficients

$$2N_2H_4(l) + N_2O_4(l) \longrightarrow 3N_2(g) + 4H_2O(g)$$

is preferred.

Frequently, when you are asked to balance an equation, the formulas of products and reactants are given. Sometimes, though, you will have to derive the formulas, given only the names (Example 3.8).

It's time to review Table 2.2 (page 39)!

Example 3.8 Crystals of sodium hydroxide (lye) react with carbon dioxide from air to form a colorless liquid, water, and a white powder, sodium carbonate, which is commonly added to detergents as a softening agent. Write a balanced equation for this chemical reaction.

Strategy To translate names into formulas, recall the discussion in Section 2.6, Chapter 2. The physical states are given or implied. To balance the equation, you could start with either sodium or hydrogen.

SOLUTION The skeleton equation is

$$NaOH(s) + CO_2(g) \longrightarrow Na_2CO_3(s) + H_2O(l)$$

Because there are two Na atoms on the right, a coefficient of 2 is written in front of NaOH:

$$2NaOH(s) + CO_2(g) \longrightarrow Na_2CO_3(s) + H_2O(l)$$

Careful inspection shows that all atoms are now balanced. There are two Na atoms, four O atoms, two H atoms, and one C atom on both sides of the equation.

Photo courtesy of Martin Walker

Sodium hydroxide pellets.

Mass Relations from Equations

The principal reason for writing balanced equations is to make it possible to relate the masses of reactants and products. Calculations of this sort are based on a very important principle:

> ***The coefficients of a balanced equation represent numbers of moles of reactants and products.***

To show that this statement is valid, recall the equation

$$2N_2H_4(l) + N_2O_4(l) \longrightarrow 3N_2(g) + 4H_2O(g)$$

The coefficients in this equation represent numbers of molecules, that is,

$$2 \text{ molecules } N_2H_4 + 1 \text{ molecule } N_2O_4 \longrightarrow 3 \text{ molecules } N_2 + 4 \text{ molecules } H_2O$$

A balanced equation remains valid if each coefficient is multiplied by the same number, including Avogadro's number, N_A:

$$2N_A \text{ molecules } N_2H_4 + 1N_A \text{ molecule } N_2O_4 \longrightarrow 3N_A \text{ molecules } N_2 + 4N_A \text{ molecules } H_2O$$

Recall from Section 3.2 that a mole represents Avogadro's number of items, N_A. Thus the equation above can be written

$$2 \text{ mol } N_2H_4 + 1 \text{ mol } N_2O_4 \longrightarrow 3 \text{ mol } N_2 + 4 \text{ mol } H_2O$$

The quantities 2 mol of N_2H_4, 1 mol of N_2O_4, 3 mol of N_2, and 4 mol of H_2O are chemically equivalent to each other in this reaction. Hence they can be used in conversion factors such as

$$\frac{2 \text{ mol } N_2H_4}{3 \text{ mol } N_2}, \frac{3 \text{ mol } N_2}{1 \text{ mol } N_2O_4}, \text{ or a variety of other combinations}$$

If you wanted to know how many moles of hydrazine were required to form 1.80 mol of elemental nitrogen, the conversion would be

$$n_{N_2H_4} = 1.80 \text{ mol } N_2 \times \frac{2 \text{ mol } N_2H_4}{3 \text{ mol } N_2} = 1.20 \text{ mol } N_2H_4$$

To find the number of moles of nitrogen produced from 2.60 mol of N_2O_4,

$$n_{N_2} = 2.60 \text{ mol } N_2O_4 \times \frac{3 \text{ mol } N_2}{1 \text{ mol } N_2O_4} = 7.80 \text{ mol } N_2$$

Simple mole relationships of this type are readily extended to relate moles of one substance to grams of another or grams of one substance to moles or molecules of another (Example 3.9).

Fertilizer. The label 5-10-5 on the bag means that the fertilizer has 5% nitrogen, 10% phosphorus, and 5% potassium.

Example 3.9 Graded

Ammonia is used to make fertilizers for lawns and gardens by reacting nitrogen gas with hydrogen gas.

- *(a) Write a balanced equation with smallest whole-number coefficients for this reaction.
- *(b) How many moles of ammonia are formed when 1.34 mol of nitrogen react?
- **(c) How many grams of hydrogen are required to produce 2.75×10^3 g of ammonia?
- **(d) How many molecules of ammonia are formed when 2.92 g of hydrogen react?
- ***(e) How many grams of ammonia are produced when 15.0 L of air (79% by volume nitrogen) react with an excess of hydrogen? The density of nitrogen at the conditions of the reaction is 1.25 g/L.

SOLUTION

(a) The equation for the reaction is

$$N_2(g) + 3H_2(g) \longrightarrow 2NH_3(g)$$

(b) The reaction gives you the stoichiometric mole ratio: 2 moles NH_3/1 mole N_2. Thus,

$$n_{NH_3} = 1.34 \text{ mol } N_2 \times \frac{2 \text{ mol } NH_3}{1 \text{ mol } N_2} = \boxed{2.68 \text{ mol } NH_3}$$

(c) Here we follow the scheme

$$m_{NH_3} \xrightarrow{MM} n_{NH_3} \xrightarrow{\text{ratio}} n_{H_2} \xrightarrow{MM} m_{H_2}$$

$$\text{mass } H_2 = 2.75 \times 10^3 \text{ g } NH_3 \times \frac{1 \text{ mol } NH_3}{17.03 \text{ g } NH_3} \times \frac{3 \text{ mol } H_2}{2 \text{ mol } NH_3} \times \frac{2.016 \text{ g } H_2}{1 \text{ mol } H_2} = \boxed{488 \text{ g } H_2}$$

(d) We add the Avogadro conversion factor N_A to the scheme:

$$m_{H_2} \xrightarrow{MM} n_{H_2} \xrightarrow{\text{ratio}} n_{NH_3} \xrightarrow{N_A} \text{molecules } NH_3$$

$$\text{molecules } NH_3 = 2.92 \text{ g } H_2 \times \frac{1 \text{ mol } H_2}{2.016 \text{ g } H_2} \times \frac{2 \text{ mol } NH_3}{3 \text{ mol } H_2} \times \frac{6.022 \times 10^{23} \text{ molecules}}{1 \text{ mol } NH_3}$$

$$= \boxed{5.81 \times 10^{23} \text{ molecules}}$$

(e) We first find the mass of nitrogen in air and then proceed using a scheme similar to those above.

$$m_{N_2} \xrightarrow{MM} n_{N_2} \xrightarrow{\text{ratio}} n_{NH_3} \xrightarrow{MM} m_{NH_3}$$

$$\text{mass } N_2 = 15.0 \text{ L air } \times \frac{79 \text{ L } N_2}{100 \text{ L air}} \times \frac{1.25 \text{ g } N_2}{1 \text{ L } N_2} = 14.8 \text{ g } N_2$$

$$m_{NH_3} = 14.8 \text{ g } N_2 \times \frac{1 \text{ mol } N_2}{28.02 \text{ g } N_2} \times \frac{2 \text{ mol } NH_3}{1 \text{ mol } N_2} \times \frac{17.03 \text{ g } NH_3}{1 \text{ mol } NH_3} = \boxed{18 \text{ g } NH_3}$$

Limiting Reactant and Theoretical Yield

When the two elements antimony and iodine are heated in contact with one another (Figure 3.5), they react to form antimony(III) iodide.

$$2Sb(s) + 3I_2(s) \longrightarrow 2SbI_3(s)$$

Figure 3.5
Reaction of antimony with iodine.

The coefficients in this equation show that two moles of Sb (243.6 g) react with exactly three moles of I_2 (761.4 g) to form two moles of SbI_3 (1005.0 g). Put another way, the maximum quantity of SbI_3 that can be obtained under these conditions, assuming the reaction goes to completion and no product is lost, is 1005.0 g. This quantity is referred to as the **theoretical yield** of SbI_3.

CENGAGENOW™
Click Coached Problems for a self-study module on **stoichiometry: theoretical yield.**

Ordinarily, in the laboratory, reactants are not mixed in exactly the ratio required for reaction. Instead, an excess of one reactant, usually the cheaper one, is used. For example, 3.00 mol of Sb could be mixed with 3.00 mol of I_2. In that case, after the reaction is over, 1.00 mol of Sb remains unreacted.

$$\begin{aligned}\text{excess Sb} &= 3.00 \text{ mol Sb originally} - 2.00 \text{ mol Sb consumed}\\ &= 1.00 \text{ mol Sb}\end{aligned}$$

The 3.00 mol of I_2 should be completely consumed in forming the 2.00 mol of SbI_3:

$$n_{SbI_3} \text{ formed} = 3.00 \text{ mol } I_2 \times \frac{2 \text{ mol } SbI_3}{3 \text{ mol } I_2} = 2.00 \text{ mol } SbI_3$$

After the reaction is over, the solid obtained would be a mixture of product, 2.00 mol of SbI_3, with 1.00 mol of unreacted Sb.

In situations such as this, a distinction is made between the *excess reactant* (Sb) and the **limiting reactant,** I_2. The amount of product formed is determined (limited) by the amount of limiting reactant. With 3.00 mol of I_2, only 2.00 mol of SbI_3 is obtained, regardless of how large an excess of Sb is used.

Under these conditions, the theoretical yield of product is the amount produced if the limiting reactant is completely consumed. In the case just cited, the theoretical yield of SbI_3 is 2.00 mol, the amount formed from the limiting reactant, I_2.

Often you will be given the amounts of two different reactants and asked to determine which is the limiting reactant, to calculate the theoretical yield of the product and to find how much of the excess reactant is unused. To do so, it helps to follow a systematic, four-step procedure.

1. ***Calculate the amount of product that would be formed if the first reactant were completely consumed.***
2. ***Repeat this calculation for the second reactant; that is, calculate how much product would be formed if all of that reactant were consumed.***
3. ***Choose the smaller of the two amounts calculated in (1) and (2). This is the theoretical yield of product; the reactant that produces the smaller amount is the limiting reactant.*** The other reactant is in excess; only part of it is consumed.
4. ***Take the theoretical yield of the product and determine how much of the reactant in excess is used up in the reaction. Subtract that from the starting amount to find the amount left.***

To illustrate how this procedure works, suppose you want to make grilled cheese sandwiches from 6 slices of cheese and 18 pieces of bread. The available cheese is enough for six grilled cheese sandwiches; the bread is enough for 9. Clearly, the cheese is the limiting reactant; there is an excess of bread. The theoretical yield is 6 sandwiches. Six grilled cheese sandwiches use up 12 slices of bread. Since there are 18 pieces available, 6 pieces of bread are left over.

Grilled cheese sandwiches are the favorite comfort food of WLM and CNH.

Example 3.10 Consider the reaction

$$2Sb(s) + 3I_2(s) \longrightarrow 2SbI_3(s)$$

Determine the limiting reactant and the theoretical yield when

(a) 1.20 mol of Sb and 2.40 mol of I_2 are mixed.
(b) 1.20 g of Sb and 2.40 g of I_2 are mixed. What mass of excess reactant is left when the reaction is complete?

You have 62 buns, 29 hamburgers, and 33 slices of cheese. How many cheeseburgers can you make?

Strategy Follow the four steps outlined above. In steps (1) and (2), follow the strategy described in Example 3.9 to calculate the amount of product formed. In (a), a simple one-step conversion is required; in (b), the path is longer because you have to go from mass of reactant to mass of product. To find the mass of reactant left over in (b), calculate how much is required to give the theoretical yield of product. Subtract that from the starting amount to find the amount left.

SOLUTION

(a) (1) n_{SbI_3} from Sb $= 1.20 \text{ mol Sb} \times \dfrac{2 \text{ mol SbI}_3}{2 \text{ mol Sb}} = 1.20 \text{ mol SbI}_3$

(2) n_{SbI_3} from I_2 $= 2.40 \text{ mol I}_2 \times \dfrac{2 \text{ mol SbI}_3}{3 \text{ mol I}_2} = 1.60 \text{ mol SbI}_3$

(3) Because 1.20 mol is the smaller amount of product, that is the theoretical yield of SbI_3. This amount of SbI_3 is produced by the antimony, so Sb is the limiting reactant.

(b) (1) mass of SbI_3 from Sb $= 1.20 \text{ g Sb} \times \dfrac{1 \text{ mol Sb}}{121.8 \text{ g Sb}} \times \dfrac{2 \text{ mol SbI}_3}{2 \text{ mol Sb}} \times \dfrac{502.5 \text{ g SbI}_3}{1 \text{ mol SbI}_3}$
$= 4.95 \text{ g SbI}_3$

(2) mass of SbI_3 from I_2 $= 2.40 \text{ g I}_2 \times \dfrac{1 \text{ mol I}_2}{253.8 \text{ g I}_2} \times \dfrac{2 \text{ mol SbI}_3}{3 \text{ mol I}_2} \times \dfrac{502.5 \text{ g SbI}_3}{1 \text{ mol SbI}_3}$
$= 3.17 \text{ g SbI}_3$

(3) The reactant that yields the smaller amount (3.17 g) of SbI_3 is I_2. Hence I_2 is the limiting reactant. The smaller amount, 3.17 g of SbI_3, is the theoretical yield.

(4) mass of Sb required $= 3.17 \text{ g SbI}_3 \times \dfrac{121.8 \text{ g Sb}}{502.5 \text{ g SbI}_3} = 0.768 \text{ g Sb}$

mass of Sb left $= 1.20 \text{ g} - 0.768 \text{ g} = 0.43 \text{ g}$

CENGAGENOW™
Click Coached Problems for a self-study module on **limiting reactants.**

Remember that in deciding on the theoretical yield of product, you ***choose the smaller of the two calculated amounts.*** To see why this must be the case, refer back to Example 3.10b. There 1.20 g of Sb was mixed with 2.40 g of I_2. Calculations show that the theoretical yield of SbI_3 is 3.17 g, and 0.43 g of Sb is left over. Thus

$$1.20 \text{ g Sb} + 2.40 \text{ g I}_2 \longrightarrow 3.17 \text{ g SbI}_3 + 0.43 \text{ g Sb}$$

This makes sense: 3.60 g of reactants yields a total of 3.60 g of products, including the unreacted antimony. Suppose, however, that 4.95 g of SbI_3 was chosen as the theoretical yield. The following nonsensical situation would arise.

$$1.20 \text{ g Sb} + 2.40 \text{ g I}_2 \longrightarrow 4.95 \text{ g SbI}_3$$

This violates the law of conservation of mass; 3.60 g of reactants cannot form 4.95 g of product.

Charles D. Winters

Percent yield. If you started with 20 popcorn kernels, but only 16 of them popped, the percent yield of popcorn from this "reaction" would be 16/20 × 100% = 80%.

Experimental Yield; Percent Yield

The theoretical yield is the maximum amount of product that can be obtained. In calculating the theoretical yield, it is assumed that the limiting reactant is 100% converted to product. In the real world, that is unlikely to happen. Some of the limiting reactant may be consumed in competing reactions. Some of the product may be lost in separating it from the reaction mixture. For these and other reasons, the experimental yield is ordinarily less than the theoretical yield. Put another way, the **percent yield** is expected to be less than 100%:

$$\text{percent yield} = \frac{\text{experimental yield}}{\text{theoretical yield}} \times 100\% \qquad (3.3)$$

You never do quite as well as you hoped, so you never get 100%.

CENGAGENOW™
Click Coached Problems for a self-study module on **percent yield.**

Example 3.11 Consider again the reaction discussed in Example 3.10:

$$2Sb(s) + 3I_2(s) \longrightarrow 2SbI_3(s)$$

Suppose that in part (a) the percent yield is 78.2%. How many grams of SbI_3 are formed?

Strategy Use Equation 3.3 to find the number of moles of SbI_3 and then the mass in grams (1 mol SbI_3 = 502.5 g SbI_3).

SOLUTION

$$\text{experimental yield } SbI_3 = 1.20 \text{ mol } SbI_3 \times \frac{78.2}{100} \times \frac{502.5 \text{ g } SbI_3}{1 \text{ mol } SbI_3} = 472 \text{ g } SbI_3$$

Remember the 6 grilled cheese sandwiches on page 64? If your dog ate one of them while you weren't looking, your yield would be 83%.

CHEMISTRY Beyond the Classroom

Hydrates

Ionic compounds often separate from water solution with molecules of water incorporated into the solid. Such compounds are referred to as **hydrates.** An example is hydrated copper sulfate, which contains five moles of H_2O for every mole of $CuSO_4$. Its formula is $CuSO_4 \cdot 5H_2O$; a dot is used to separate the formulas of the two compounds $CuSO_4$ and H_2O. A Greek prefix is used to show the number of moles of water; the systematic name of $CuSO_4 \cdot 5H_2O$ is copper(II) sulfate pentahydrate.

Certain hydrates, notably $Na_2CO_3 \cdot 10H_2O$ and $FeSO_4 \cdot 7H_2O$, lose all or part of their water of hydration when exposed to dry air. This process is referred to as *efflorescence;* the glassy (vitreous) hydrate crystals crumble to a powder. Frequently, dehydration is accompanied by a color change (Figure A). When $CoCl_2 \cdot 6H_2O$ is exposed to dry air or is heated, it loses water and changes color from red to purple or blue. Crystals of this compound are used as humidity indicators and as an ingredient of invisible ink. Writing becomes visible only when the paper is heated, driving off water and leaving a blue residue.

Marna G. Clarke

Figure A
Hydrates of copper(II) sulfate and cobalt(II) chloride. $CuSO_4 \cdot 5H_2O$ *(upper left)* is blue; the anhydrous solid—that is, copper sulfate without the water—is white *(lower left)*. $CoCl_2 \cdot 5H_2O$ *(upper right)* is reddish pink. Lower hydrates of cobalt such as $CoCl_2 \cdot 4H_2O$ are purple *(lower right)* or blue.

Molecular as well as ionic substances can form hydrates, but of an entirely different nature. In these crystals, sometimes referred to as *clathrates,* a molecule (such as CH_4, $CHCl_3$) is quite literally trapped in an ice-like cage of water molecules. Perhaps the best-known molecular hydrate is that of chlorine, which has the approximate composition $Cl_2 \cdot 7.3H_2O$. This compound was discovered by the great English physicist and electrochemist Michael Faraday in 1823. You can make it by bubbling chlorine gas through calcium chloride solution at 0°C; the hydrate comes down as feathery white crystals. In the winter of 1914, the German army used chlorine in chemical warfare on the Russian front against the soldiers of the Tsar. They were puzzled by its ineffectiveness; not until spring was deadly chlorine gas liberated from the hydrate, which is stable at cold temperatures.

In the 1930s when high-pressure natural gas (95% methane) pipelines were being built in the United States, it was found that the lines often became plugged in cold weather by a white, waxy solid that contained both water and methane (CH_4) molecules. Twenty years later, Walter Claussen at the University of Illinois deduced the structure of that solid, a hydrate of methane. Notice (Figure B) that CH_4 molecules are trapped within a three-dimensional cage of H_2O molecules.

In 1970 a huge deposit of methane hydrate was discovered at the bottom of the Atlantic Ocean, 330 km off the coast of North Carolina.

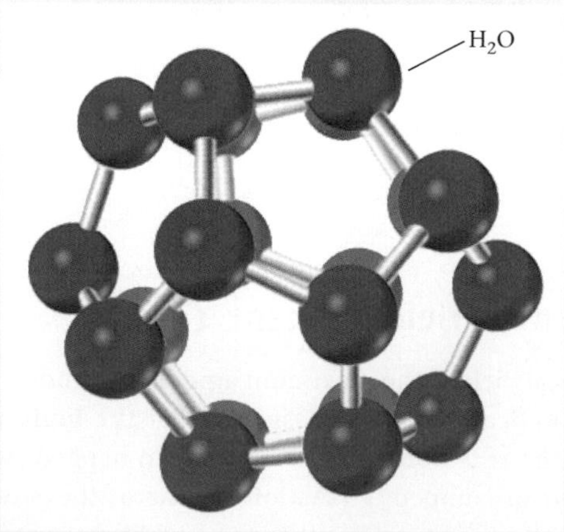

Figure B
In one of the cages within which gas molecules are trapped in methane hydrate, water molecules form a pentagonal dodecahedron, a three-dimensional figure in which each of the 12 sides is a regular pentagon.

The white solid was stable at the high pressure and low temperature (slightly above 0°C) that prevail at the ocean floor. When raised to the surface, the solid decomposed to give off copious amounts of methane gas (Figure C).

We now know that methane hydrate is widely distributed through the earth's oceans and the permafrost of Alaska and Siberia. The methane in these deposits could, upon combustion, produce twice as much energy as all the world's known resources of petroleum, natural gas, and coal. However, extracting the methane from undersea deposits has proved to be an engineering nightmare. Separating the hydrate from the mud, silt, and rocks with which it is mixed is almost as difficult as controlling its decomposition. Then there is the problem of transporting the methane to the shore, which may be 100 miles or more away.

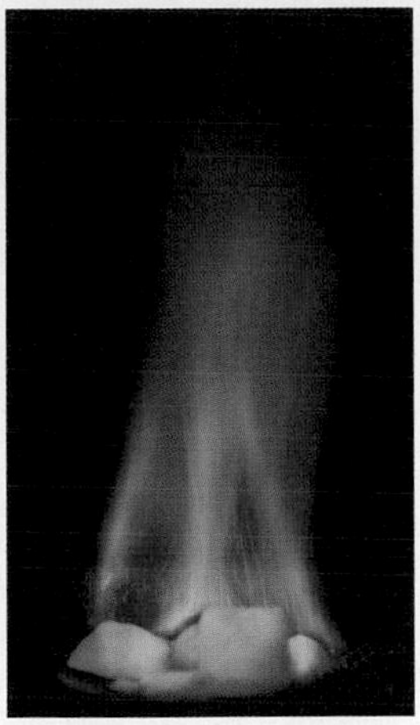

John Pinkston and Laura Stern/U.S. Geological Survey/Science News 11/9/96

Figure C
Methane hydrate is sometimes referred to as "the ice that burns."

Chapter Highlights

Key Concepts

1. Relate the atomic mass of an element to isotopic masses and abundances.
   (Example 3.1; Problems 3–12) ■ Questions and Problems assignable in OWL: 4, 7, 14
2. Use Avogadro's number to calculate the mass of an atom or molecule.
   (Example 3.2; Problems 17–24) ■ 17, 19, 21
3. Use molar mass to relate
   - moles to mass of a substance.
   (Example 3.3; Problems 25–32) ■ 25, 27, 30
   - molecular formula to simplest formula.
   (Example 3.7; Problems 51–52) ■ 52
4. Use the formula of a compound to find percent composition or its equivalent.
   (Example 3.4; Problems 33–42) ■ 34, 36
5. Find the simplest formula of a compound from chemical analysis.
   (Examples 3.5, 3.6; Problems 43–54) ■ 45, 99
6. Balance chemical equations by inspection.
   (Example 3.8; Problems 55–60) ■ 55, 57
7. Use a balanced equation to
   - relate masses of reactants and products.
   (Example 3.9; Problems 61–72) ■ 64, 65, 103
   - find the limiting reactant, theoretical yield, and percent yield.
   (Examples 3.10, 3.11; Problems 73–80) ■ 74, 76

Select end of chapter Questions and Problems may be assigned in OWL and are cross-referenced in the Key Concepts list.

CENGAGENOW™

Sign in at **academic.cengage.com/now** to:

- Check your readiness for an exam by taking the Pre-Test and exploring the self-study modules recommended in your Personalized Study plan.
- For quick review, download Go Chemistry mini-lecture flashcard modules (or purchase them at **www.ichapters.com**)

Key Equations

Atomic mass Y $= (\text{atomic mass } Y_1) \times \dfrac{\%\ Y_1}{100\%} + (\text{atomic mass } Y_2) \times \dfrac{\%\ Y_2}{100\%} + \cdots$ (Section 3.1)

Molar mass $\quad m = MM \times n$ (Section 3.2)

Percent yield $= \dfrac{\text{experimental yield}}{\text{theoretical yield}} \times 100\%$ (Section 3.4)

Key Terms

atomic mass	limiting reactant	simplest formula
atomic mass unit	molar mass	yield
Avogadro's number	mole	—percent
isotopic abundance	percent composition	—theoretical

Summary Problem

Consider titanium. It is a metal with the same strength as steel but it is 45% lighter. It is also resistant to corrosion by seawater and is used in the propeller shafts of boats.

(a) It consists of five isotopes with atomic masses 45.953 amu, 46.952 amu, 47.948 amu, 48.948 amu, and 49.945 amu. Their abundances are 8.01%, 7.31%, 73.8%, 5.51%, and 5.41%, respectively. What is the atomic mass of titanium?

(b) How many titanium atoms are in one nanogram (1×10^{-9} g) of titanium?

(c) How many grams of titanium are in 0.0217 mol?

(d) Write the formula for titanium(III) oxide. What is its molar mass?

(e) When titanium reacts with bromine gas, titanium(IV) bromide is obtained. Write a balanced equation for this reaction.

(f) How many grams of bromine are required to completely react with 22.1 g of titanium?

(g) Thirteen grams of titanium react with 60.0 g of bromine. How many grams of titanium(IV) bromide are produced, assuming 100% yield? How many grams of excess reactant are present after the reaction?

(h) The reaction in (g) is later found to have 79.3% yield. How many grams of titanium(IV) bromide are actually obtained?

(i) The mineral perovskite is an excellent source for titanium. It is made up of 29.4% Ca, 35.2% Ti, and 35.3% O. What is the simplest formula for perovskite?

(j) How many kilograms of the mineral are required to produce 5.00 kg of titanium?

Answers

(a) 47.90 g/mol **(b)** 1.258×10^{13} **(c)** 1.04 g **(d)** Ti_2O_3; 143.8 g/mol

(e) $Ti(s) + 2\,Br_2(g) \longrightarrow TiBr_4(s)$ **(f)** 148 g

(g) 69.0 g $TiBr_4$; 4.01 g of Ti left after reaction

(h) 54.7 g **(i)** $CaTiO_3$ **(j)** 14.2 kg

Questions and Problems

Blue-numbered questions have answers in Appendix 6 and fully-worked solutions in the *Student Solutions Manual.*

■ denotes questions assignable in OWL.

WEB indicates that the solution is available on this book's companion website.

Atomic Masses and Isotopic Abundances

1. Calculate the mass ratio of a bromine atom to an atom of
(a) neon (b) calcium (c) helium

2. Arrange the following in order of increasing mass.
(a) a sodium ion (b) a selenium atom
(c) a sulfur (S_8) molecule (d) a scandium atom

3. Cerium is the most abundant rare earth metal. Pure cerium ignites when scratched by even a soft object. It has four known isotopes: ^{136}Ce (atomic mass = 135.907 amu), ^{138}Ce (atomic mass = 137.905 amu), ^{140}Ce (atomic mass = 139.905 amu), and ^{142}Ce (atomic mass = 141.909 amu). Ce-140 and Ce-142 are fairly abundant. Which is the more abundant isotope?

4. ■ Silicon is widely used in the semi-conductor industry. Its isotopes and their atomic masses are: Si-28 (27.9769 amu), Si-29 (28.9765 amu), and Si-30 (29.9794 amu). Which is the most abundant?

5. Gallium has two naturally occurring isotopes: ^{69}Ga, with atomic mass 68.9257 amu, and ^{71}Ga, with atomic mass 70.9249 amu. The percent abundance of ^{69}Ga can be estimated to be which of the following?
(a) 0% (b) 25% (c) 50% (d) 75%

6. Rubidium has two naturally occurring isotopes: ^{85}Rb (atomic mass = 84.9118 amu) and ^{87}Rb (atomic mass = 86.9092 amu). The percent abundance of ^{87}Rb can be estimated to be which of the following?
(a) 0% (b) 25% (c) 50% (d) 75%

7. ■ Strontium has four isotopes with the following masses: 83.9134 amu (0.56%), 85.9094 amu (9.86%), 86.9089 amu (7.00%), and 87.9056 (82.58%). Calculate the atomic mass of strontium.

8. Oxygen consists of three isotopes with atomic masses 16.00, 17.00, and 18.00 amu. Their abundances are 99.76%, 0.04%, and 0.20%, respectively. What is the atomic mass of oxygen?

9. Naturally occurring silver (Ag) consists of two isotopes. One of the isotopes has a mass of 106.90509 amu and 51.84% abundance. What is the atomic mass of the other isotope?

10. Copper has two naturally occurring isotopes. Cu-63 has an atomic mass of 62.9296 amu and an abundance of 69.17%. What is the atomic mass of the second isotope? What is its nuclear symbol?

11. Chromium (atomic mass = 51.9961 amu) has four isotopes. Their masses are 49.94605 amu, 51.94051 amu, 52.94065 amu, and 53.93888 amu. The first two isotopes have a total abundance of 87.87%, and the last isotope has an abundance of 2.365%. What is the abundance of the third isotope? Estimate the abundances of the first two isotopes.

12. Potassium (atomic mass = 39.10 amu) has three isotopes with masses 38.9367 amu, 39.9640 amu, and 40.9618 amu. The abundance of the last isotope is 6.73%. Estimate the abundances of the other two isotopes.

13. Neon consists of three isotopes, Ne-20, Ne-21, and Ne-22. Their abundances are 90.48%, 0.27%, and 9.22%, respectively. Sketch the mass spectrum for neon.

14. ■ Chlorine has two isotopes, Cl-35 and Cl-37. Their abundances are 75.53% and 24.47%, respectively. Assume that the only hydrogen isotope present is H-1.
(a) How many different HCl molecules are possible?
(b) What is the sum of the mass numbers of the two atoms in each molecule?
(c) Sketch the mass spectrum for HCl if all the positive ions are obtained by removing a single electron from an HCl molecule.

The Mole, Molar Mass, and Mole-Gram Conversions

15. One chocolate chip used in making chocolate chip cookies has a mass of 0.324 g.
(a) How many chocolate chips are there in one mole of chocolate chips?

(b) If a cookie needs 15 chocolate chips, how many cookies can one make with a billionth (1×10^{-9}) of a mole of chocolate chips? (A billionth of a mole is scientifically known as a *nanomole*.)

16. The meat from one hazelnut has a mass of 0.985 g.

(a) What is the mass of a millionth of a mole (10^{-6}) of hazelnut meats? (A millionth of a mole is also called a *micromole*.)

(b) How many moles are in a pound of hazelnut meats?

17. ■ Lead is a heavy metal that remains in the bloodstream, causing mental retardation in children. It is believed that 3×10^{-7} g of Pb in 1.00 mL of blood is a health hazard. For this amount of lead

(a) how many atoms of lead are there in one mL of a child's blood?

(b) how many moles of lead are in 1.00 L of blood?

18. Silversmiths are warned to limit their exposure to silver in the air to 1×10^{-8} g Ag/L of air in a 40-hour week.

(a) What is the allowed exposure in terms of atoms of Ag/L/week?

(b) Translate the warning to moles of Ag/L of air.

19. ■ Determine

(a) the mass of 0.357 mol of gold.

(b) the number of atoms in 0.357 g of gold.

(c) the number of moles of electrons in 0.357 g of gold.

20. How many protons are in

(a) an atom of platinum? (b) one mole of platinum?

(c) one gram of platinum?

21. ■ The isotope Si-28 has a mass of 27.977 amu. For ten grams of Si-28, calculate

(a) the number of moles. (b) the number of atoms.

(c) the total number of protons, neutrons, and electrons.

22. Consider an isotope of yttrium, Y-90. This isotope is incorporated into cancer-seeking antibodies so that the cancer can be irradiated by the yttrium and destroyed. How many neutrons are in

(a) twenty-five atoms of yttrium?

(b) 0.250 mol of yttrium?

(c) one nanogram (10^{-9} g) of yttrium?

23. A cube of sodium has length 1.25 in. How many atoms are in that cube? (Note: $d_{Na} = 0.968$ g/cm^3.)

24. A cylindrical piece of pure copper ($d = 8.92$ g/cm^3) has diameter 1.15 cm and height 4.00 inches. How many atoms are in that cylinder? (Note: the volume of a right circular cylinder of radius r and height h is $V = \pi r^2 h$.)

25. ■ Calculate the molar masses (in grams per mole) of

(a) cane sugar, $C_{12}H_{22}O_{11}$.

(b) laughing gas, N_2O.

(c) vitamin A, $C_{20}H_{30}O$.

26. **WEB** Calculate the molar masses (in grams per mole) of

(a) gallium, Ga, a metal that literally melts in your hands.

(b) plaster of paris, $CaSO_4 \cdot \frac{1}{2}H_2O$, once used in making casts for broken bones.

(c) benzoyl peroxide, $C_{14}H_{10}O_4$, the active ingredient in many lotions used to treat acne.

27. ■ Convert the following to moles.

(a) 4.00×10^3 g of hydrazine, a rocket propellant

(b) 12.5 g of tin(II) fluoride, the active ingredient in fluoride toothpaste

(c) 13 g of caffeine, $C_4H_5N_2O$

28. Convert the following to moles.

(a) 35.00 g of CF_2Cl_2, a chlorofluorocarbon that destroys the ozone layer in the atmosphere

(b) 100.0 mg of iron(II) sulfate, an iron supplement prescribed for anemia

(c) 2.00 g of Valium ($C_{15}H_{13}ClN_2O$—diazepam)

29. Calculate the mass in grams of 2.688 mol of

(a) chlorophyll, $C_{55}H_{72}N_4O_5Mg$, responsible for the green color of leaves.

(b) sorbitol, $C_9H_{14}O_6$, an artificial sweetener.

(c) indigo, $C_{16}H_{10}N_2O_2$, a blue dye.

30. ■ Calculate the mass in grams of 13.5 mol of

(a) vinyl chloride, C_2H_3Cl, the starting material for a plastic.

(b) capsaicin, $C_{18}H_{27}NO_3$, the substance that makes red chili peppers "hot."

(c) stearic acid, $C_{18}H_{36}O_2$, used in soaps.

31. Complete the following table for TNT (trinitrotoluene), $C_7H_5(NO_2)_3$.

	Number of Grams	Number of Moles	Number of Molecules	Number of N Atoms
(a)	127.2	_____	_____	_____
(b)	_____	0.9254	_____	_____
(c)	_____	_____	1.24×10^{28}	_____
(d)	_____	_____	_____	7.5×10^{22}

32. Complete the following table for citric acid, $C_6H_8O_7$, the acid found in many citrus fruits.

	Number of Grams	Number of Moles	Number of Molecules	Number of O Atoms
(a)	0.1364	_____	_____	_____
(b)	_____	1.248	_____	_____
(c)	_____	_____	4.32×10^{22}	_____
(d)	_____	_____	_____	5.55×10^{19}

Mass Relations in Chemical Formulas

33. Turquoise has the following chemical formula: $CuAl_6(PO_4)_4(OH)_8 \cdot 4H_2O$. Calculate the mass percent of each element in turquoise.

34. ■ The active ingredient of some antiperspirants is $Al_2(OH)_5Cl$. Calculate the mass percent of each element in this ingredient.

35. Deer ticks are known to cause Lyme disease. The presence of DEET (diethyltoluamide) in insect repellents protects the user from the ticks. The molecular formula for DEET is $C_{12}H_{17}NO$. How many grams of carbon can be obtained from 127 g of DEET?

36. ■ Allicin is responsible for the distinctive taste and odor of garlic. Its simple formula is $C_6H_{10}O_2S$. How many grams of sulfur can be obtained from 25.0 g of allicin?

37. A tablet of Tylenol™ has a mass of 0.611 g. It contains 251 mg of its active ingredient, acetaminophen, $C_8H_9NO_2$.

(a) What is the mass percent of acetaminophen in a tablet of Tylenol?

(b) Assume that all the nitrogen in the tablet is in the acetaminophen. How many grams of nitrogen are present in a tablet of Tylenol?

38. **WEB** The active ingredient in Pepto-Bismol™ (an over-the-counter remedy for upset stomach) is bismuth subsalicylate, $C_7H_5BiO_4$. Analysis of a 1.500-g sample of Pepto-Bismol yields 346 mg of bismuth. What percent by mass is bismuth subsalicylate? (Assume that there is no other bismuth-containing compound in Pepto-Bismol.)

39. Combustion analysis of 1.00 g of the male sex hormone, testosterone, yields 2.90 g of CO_2 and 0.875 g H_2O. What are the mass percents of carbon, hydrogen, and oxygen in testosterone?

40. Hexachlorophene, a compound made up of atoms of carbon, hydrogen, chlorine, and oxygen, is an ingredient in germicidal soaps. Combustion of a 1.000-g sample yields 1.407 g of carbon dioxide, 0.134 g of water, and 0.523 g of chlorine gas. What are the mass percents of carbon, hydrogen, oxygen, and chlorine in hexachlorophene?

41. A compound XCl_3 is 70.3% (by mass) chlorine. What is the molar mass of the compound? What is the symbol and name of X?

42. A compound YO_2 is 50.0% (by mass) oxygen. What is the identity of Y? What is the molar mass of YO_2?

■ in OWL Blue-numbered questions answered in Appendix 6 **WEB** Solution is available on companion website

43. Phosphorus reacts with oxygen to produce different kinds of oxides. One of these oxides is formed when 1.347 g of phosphorus reacts with 1.744 g of oxygen. What is the simplest formula of this oxide? Name the oxide.

44. Nickel reacts with sulfur to form a sulfide. If 2.986 g of nickel reacts with enough sulfur to form 5.433 g of nickel sulfide, what is the simplest formula of the sulfide? Name the sulfide.

45. ■ Determine the simplest formulas of the following compounds:
(a) the food enhancer monosodium glutamate (MSG), which has the composition 35.51% C, 4.77% H, 37.85% O, 8.29% N, and 13.60% Na.
(b) zircon, a diamond-like mineral, which has the composition 34.91% O, 15.32% Si, and 49.76% Zr.
(c) nicotine, which has the composition 74.0% C, 8.65% H, and 17.4% N.

46. Determine the simplest formulas of the following compounds:
(a) saccharin, the artificial sweetener, which has the composition 45.90% C, 2.75% H, 26.20% O, 17.50% S, and 7.65% N.
(b) allicin, the compound that gives garlic its characteristic odor, which has the composition 6.21% H, 44.4% C, 9.86% O, and 39.51% S.
(c) sodium thiosulfate, the fixer used in developing photographic film, which has the composition 30.36% O, 29.08% Na, and 40.56% S.

47. Ibuprofen, the active ingredient in Advil™, is made up of carbon, hydrogen, and oxygen atoms. When a sample of ibuprofen, weighing 5.000 g, burns in oxygen, 13.86 g of CO_2 and 3.926 g of water are obtained. What is the simplest formula of ibuprofen?

48. Methyl salicylate is a common "active ingredient" in liniments such as Ben-Gay™. It is also known as oil of wintergreen. It is made up of carbon, hydrogen, and oxygen atoms. When a sample of methyl salicylate weighing 5.287 g is burned in excess oxygen, 12.24 g of carbon dioxide and 2.505 g of water are formed. What is the simplest formula for oil of wintergreen?

49. **WEB** DDT (dichlorodiphenyltrichloroethane) was the first chlorinated insecticide developed. It was used extensively in World War II to eradicate the mosquitoes that spread malaria. Its use was banned in the United States in 1978 because of environmental concerns. DDT is made up of carbon, hydrogen, and chlorine atoms. When a 5.000-g sample of DDT is burned in oxygen, 8.692 g of CO_2 and 1.142 g of H_2O are obtained. A second five-gram sample yields 2.571 g of HCl. What is the simplest formula for DDT?

50. Riboflavin is one of the B vitamins. It is also known as vitamin B_6 and is made up of carbon, hydrogen, nitrogen, and oxygen atoms. When 10.00 g of vitamin B_6 is burned in oxygen, 19.88 g of CO_2 and 4.79 g of H_2O are obtained. Another experiment shows that vitamin B_6 is made up of 14.89% N. What is the simplest formula for vitamin B_6?

51. Hexamethylenediamine (MM = 116.2 g/mol), a compound made up of carbon, hydrogen, and nitrogen atoms, is used in the production of nylon. When 6.315 g of hexamethylenediamine is burned in oxygen, 14.36 g of carbon dioxide and 7.832 g of water are obtained. What are the simplest and molecular formulas of this compound?

52. ■ Dimethylhydrazine, the fuel used in the Apollo lunar descent module, has a molar mass of 60.10 g/mol. It is made up of carbon, hydrogen, and nitrogen atoms. The combustion of 2.859 g of the fuel in excess oxygen yields 4.190 g of carbon dioxide and 3.428 g of water. What are the simplest and molecular formulas for dimethylhydrazine?

53. A certain hydrate of potassium aluminum sulfate (alum) has the formula $KAl(SO_4)_2 \cdot xH_2O$. When a hydrate sample weighing 5.459 g is heated to remove all the water, 2.583 g of $KAl(SO_4)_2$ remains. What is the mass percent of water in the hydrate? What is x?

54. Epsom salts are hydrates of magnesium sulfate. The formula for Epsom salts is $MgSO_4 \cdot 7H_2O$. A 7.834-g sample is heated until a constant mass is obtained indicating that all the water has been evaporated off. What is the mass of the anhydrous magnesium sulfate? What percentage of the hydrate is water?

Balancing Equations

55. ■ Balance the following equations:
(a) $CaC_2(s) + H_2O(l) \longrightarrow Ca(OH)_2(s) + C_2H_2(g)$
(b) $(NH_4)_2Cr_2O_7(s) \longrightarrow Cr_2O_3(s) + N_2(g) + H_2O(g)$
(c) $CH_3NH_2(g) + O_2(g) \longrightarrow CO_2(g) + N_2(g) + H_2O(g)$

56. Balance the following equations:
(a) $H_2S(g) + SO_2(g) \longrightarrow S(s) + H_2O(g)$
(b) $CH_4(g) + NH_3(g) + O_2(g) \longrightarrow HCN(g) + H_2O(g)$
(c) $Fe_2O_3(s) + H_2(g) \longrightarrow Fe(l) + H_2O(g)$

57. ■ Write balanced equations for the reaction of sulfur with the following metals to form solids that you can take to be ionic when the anion is S^{2-}.
(a) potassium (b) magnesium (c) aluminum
(d) calcium (e) iron (forming Fe^{2+} ions)

58. Write balanced equations for the reaction of aluminum metal with the following nonmetals:
(a) sulfur (b) bromine (c) nitrogen
(d) oxygen (forming O^{2-} ions)
(e) oxygen (forming O_2^{2-}, or peroxide ions)

59. Write a balanced equation for
(a) the combustion (reaction with oxygen gas) of glucose, $C_6H_{12}O_6$, to give carbon dioxide and water.
(b) the reaction between xenon tetrafluoride gas and water to give xenon, oxygen, and hydrogen fluoride gases.
(c) the reaction between aluminum and iron(III) oxide to give aluminum oxide and iron.
(d) the formation of ammonia gas from its elements.
(e) the reaction between sodium chloride, sulfur dioxide gas, steam, and oxygen to give sodium sulfate and hydrogen chloride gas.

60. Write a balanced equation for
(a) the reaction between fluorine gas and water to give oxygen difluoride and hydrogen fluoride gases.
(b) the reaction between oxygen and ammonia gases to give nitrogen dioxide gas and water.
(c) the burning of gold(III) sulfide in hydrogen to give gold metal and dihydrogen sulfide gas.
(d) the decomposition of sodium hydrogen carbonate to sodium carbonate, water, and carbon dioxide gas.
(e) the reaction between sulfur dioxide gas and liquid hydrogen fluoride to give sulfur tetrafluoride gas and water.

Mole-Mass Relations in Reactions

61. Cyanogen gas, C_2N_2, has been found in the gases of outer space. It can react with fluorine to form carbon tetrafluoride and nitrogen trifluoride.

$$C_2N_2(g) + 7F_2(g) \longrightarrow 2CF_4(g) + 2NF_3(g)$$

(a) How many moles of fluorine react with 1.37 mol of cyanogen?
(b) How many moles of CF_4 are obtained from 13.75 mol of fluorine?
(c) How many moles of cyanogen are required to produce 0.8974 mol of NF_3?
(d) How many moles of fluorine will yield 4.981 mol of nitrogen trifluoride?

62. Diborane, B_2H_6, can be prepared by the following reaction:

$$3NaBH_4(s) + 4BF_3(g) \longrightarrow 2B_2H_6(g) + 3NaBF_4(s)$$

(a) How many moles of $NaBH_4$ react with 1.299 mol of BF_3?
(b) How many moles of B_2H_6 can be obtained from 0.893 mol of $NaBH_4$?
(c) If 1.987 mol of B_2H_6 is obtained, how many moles of $NaBF_4$ are produced?
(d) How many moles of BF_3 are required to produce 4.992 mol of $NaBF_4$?

■ in OWL Blue-numbered questions answered in Appendix 6 **WEB** Solution is available on companion website

63. One way to remove nitrogen oxide (NO) from smoke stack emissions is to react it with ammonia.

$$4NH_3(g) + 6NO(g) \longrightarrow 5N_2(g) + 6H_2O(l)$$

Calculate

(a) the mass of water produced from 0.839 mol of ammonia.

(b) the mass of NO required to react with 3.402 mol of ammonia.

(c) the mass of ammonia required to produce 12.0 g of nitrogen gas.

(d) the mass of ammonia required to react with 115 g of NO.

64. ■ Phosphine gas reacts with oxygen according to the following equation:

$$4PH_3(g) + 8O_2(g) \longrightarrow P_4O_{10}(s) + 6H_2O(g)$$

Calculate

(a) the mass of tetraphosphorus decaoxide produced from 12.43 mol of phosphine.

(b) the mass of PH_3 required to form 0.739 mol of steam.

(c) the mass of oxygen gas that yields 1.000 g of steam.

(d) the mass of oxygen required to react with 20.50 g of phosphine.

65. ■ The combustion of liquid chloroethylene, C_2H_3Cl, yields carbon dioxide, steam, and hydrogen chloride gas.

(a) Write a balanced equation for the reaction.

(b) How many moles of oxygen are required to react with 35.00 g of chloroethylene?

(c) If 25.00 g of chloroethylene reacts with an excess of oxygen, how many grams of each product are formed?

66. Sand consists mainly of silicon dioxide. When sand is heated with an excess of coke (carbon), pure silicon and carbon monoxide are produced.

(a) Write a balanced equation for the reaction.

(b) How many moles of silicon dioxide are required to form 12.72 g of silicon?

(c) How many grams of carbon monoxide are formed when 44.99 g of silicon is produced?

67. Ethanol, C_2H_5OH, is responsible for the effects of intoxication felt after drinking alcoholic beverages. When ethanol burns in oxygen, carbon dioxide, and water are produced.

(a) Write a balanced equation for the reaction.

(b) How many liters of ethanol ($d = 0.789$ g/cm^3) will produce 1.25 L of water ($d = 1.00$ g/cm^3)?

(c) A wine cooler contains 4.5% ethanol by mass. Assuming that only the alcohol burns in oxygen, how many grams of wine cooler need to be burned to produce 3.12 L of CO_2 ($d = 1.80$ g/L at 25°C, 1 atm pressure) at the conditions given for the density?

68. **WEB** When tin comes in contact with the oxygen in the air, tin(IV) oxide, SnO_2, is formed.

$$Sn(s) + O_2(g) \longrightarrow SnO_2(s)$$

A piece of tin foil, 8.25 cm × 21.5 cm × 0.600 mm ($d = 7.28$ g/cm^3) is exposed to oxygen.

(a) Assuming that all the tin has reacted, what is the mass of the oxidized tin foil?

(b) Air is about 21% oxygen by volume ($d = 1.309$ g/L at 25°C, 1 atm). How many liters of air are required to completely react with the tin foil?

69. A crude oil burned in electrical generating plants contains about 1.2% sulfur by mass. When the oil burns, the sulfur forms sulfur dioxide gas:

$$S(s) + O_2(g) \longrightarrow SO_2(g)$$

How many liters of SO_2 ($d = 2.60$ g/L) are produced when 1.00×10^4 kg of oil burns at the same temperature and pressure?

70. Oxygen masks for producing O_2 in emergency situations contain potassium superoxide, KO_2. It reacts with CO_2 and H_2O in exhaled air to produce oxygen:

$$4KO_2(s) + 2H_2O(g) + 4CO_2(g) \longrightarrow 4KHCO_3(s) + 3O_2(g)$$

If a person wearing such a mask exhales 0.702 g CO_2/min, how many grams of KO_2 are consumed in 25 min?

71. Consider the hypothetical reaction

$$8A_2B_3(s) + 3X_4(g) \longrightarrow 4A_4X_3(s) + 12B_2(g)$$

When 10.0 g of A_2B_3 (MM = 255 g/mol) react with an excess of X_4, 4.00 g of A_4X_3 are produced.

(a) How many moles of A_4X_3 are produced?

(b) What is the molar mass of A_4X_3?

72. When three moles of a metal oxide, MO_2, react with ammonia gas, the metal (M), water, and nitrogen gas are formed.

(a) Write a balanced equation to represent the reaction.

(b) When 13.8 g of ammonia react with an excess of metal oxide, 126 g of M are formed. What is the molar mass for M? What is the identity of M?

73. A gaseous mixture containing 4.15 mol of hydrogen gas and 7.13 mol of oxygen gas reacts to form steam.

(a) Write a balanced equation for the reaction.

(b) What is the limiting reactant?

(c) What is the theoretical yield of steam in moles?

(d) How many moles of the excess reactant remain unreacted?

74. ■ Aluminum reacts with sulfur gas to form aluminum sulfide. Initially, 1.18 mol of aluminum and 2.25 mol of sulfur are combined.

(a) Write a balanced equation for the reaction.

(b) What is the limiting reactant?

(c) What is the theoretical yield of aluminum sulfide in moles?

(d) How many moles of excess reactant remain unreacted?

75. When potassium chlorate is burned, potassium chloride and oxygen are formed.

(a) Write a balanced equation for the reaction.

(b) How much potassium chlorate must be burned to produce 198.5 g of oxygen? The yield is found to be 83.2%.

76. ■ When iron and steam react at high temperatures, the following reaction takes place.

$$3Fe(s) + 4H_2O(g) \longrightarrow Fe_3O_4(s) + 4H_2(g)$$

How much iron must react with excess steam to form 897 g of Fe_3O_4 if the reaction yield is 69%?

77. Oxyacetylene torches used for welding reach temperatures near 2000°C. The reaction involved in the combustion of acetylene is

$$2C_2H_2(g) + 5O_2(g) \longrightarrow 4CO_2(g) + 2H_2O(g)$$

(a) Starting with 175 g of both acetylene and oxygen, what is the theoretical yield, in grams, of carbon dioxide?

(b) If 68.5 L ($d = 1.85$ g/L) of carbon dioxide is produced, what is the percent yield at the same conditions of temperature and pressure?

(c) How much of the reactant in excess is unused? (Assume 100% yield.)

78. The Space Shuttle uses aluminum metal and ammonium perchlorate in its reusable booster rockets. The products of the reaction are aluminum oxide, aluminum chloride, nitrogen oxide gas, and steam. The reaction mixture contains 7.00 g of aluminum and 9.32 g of ammonium perchlorate.

(a) Write a balanced equation for the reaction.

(b) What is the theoretical yield of aluminum oxide?

(c) If 1.56 g of aluminum oxide is formed, what is the percent yield?

(d) How many grams of excess reactant are unused? (Assume 100% yield.)

79. Aspirin, $C_9H_8O_4$, is prepared by reacting salicylic acid, $C_7H_6O_3$, with acetic anhydride, $C_4H_6O_3$, in the reaction

$$C_7H_6O_3(s) + C_4H_6O_3(l) \longrightarrow C_9H_8O_4(s) + C_2H_4O_2(l)$$

■ in OWL   Blue-numbered questions answered in Appendix 6   **WEB** Solution is available on companion website

A student is told to prepare 45.0 g of aspirin. She is also told to use a 55.0% excess of acetic anhydride and to expect to get an 85.0% yield in the reaction. How many grams of each reactant should she use?

80. A student prepares phosphorous acid, H_3PO_3, by reacting solid phosphorus triiodide with water.

$$PI_3(s) + 3H_2O(l) \longrightarrow H_3PO_3(s) + 3HI(g)$$

The student needs to obtain 0.250 L of H_3PO_3 ($d = 1.651$ g/cm^3). The procedure calls for a 45.0% excess of water and a yield of 75.0%. How much phosphorus triiodide should be weighed out? What volume of water ($d = 1.00$ g/cm^3) should be used?

Unclassified

81. Cisplatin, $Pt(NH_3)_2Cl_2$, is a chemotherapeutic agent that disrupts the growth of DNA. If the current cost of Pt is $1118.0/troy ounce (1 troy oz = 31.10 g), how many grams of cisplatin can you make with three thousand dollars worth of platinum? How many pounds?

82. Magnesium ribbon reacts with acid to produce hydrogen gas and magnesium ions. Different masses of magnesium ribbon are added to 10 mL of the acid. The volume of the hydrogen gas obtained is a measure of the number of moles of hydrogen produced by the reaction. Various measurements are given in the table below.

Experiment	Mass of Mg Ribbon (g)	Volume of Acid Used (mL)	Volume of H_2 Gas (mL)
1	0.020	10.0	21
2	0.040	10.0	42
3	0.080	10.0	82
4	0.120	10.0	122
5	0.160	10.0	122
6	0.200	10.0	122

(a) Draw a graph of the results by plotting the mass of Mg versus the volume of the hydrogen gas.

(b) What is the limiting reactant in experiment 1?

(c) What is the limiting reactant in experiment 3?

(d) What is the limiting reactant in experiment 6?

(e) Which experiment uses stoichiometric amounts of each reactant?

(f) What volume of gas would be obtained if 0.300 g of Mg ribbon were used? If 0.010 g were used?

83. Iron reacts with oxygen. Different masses of iron are burned in a constant amount of oxygen. The product, an oxide of iron, is weighed. The graph below is obtained when the mass of product used is plotted against the mass of iron used.

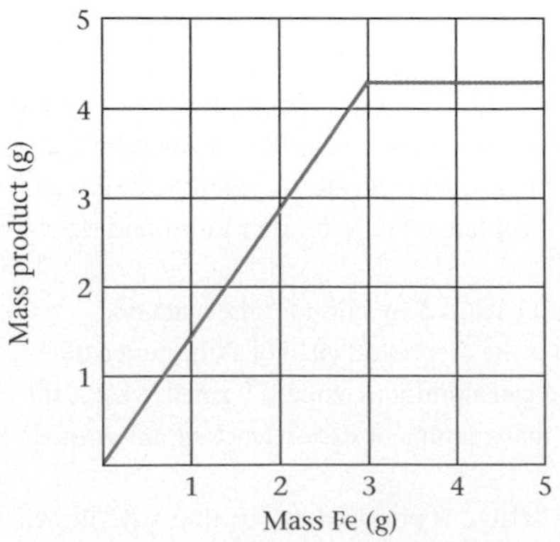

(a) How many grams of product are obtained when 0.50 g of iron is used?

(b) What is the limiting reactant when 2.00 g of iron is used?

(c) What is the limiting reactant when 5.00 g of iron is used?

(d) How many grams of iron react exactly with the amount of oxygen supplied?

(e) What is the simplest formula of the product?

84. Carbon tetrachloride, CCl_4, was a popular dry-cleaning agent until it was shown to be carcinogenic. It has a density of 1.589 g/cm^3. What volume of carbon tetrachloride will contain a total of 6.00×10^{25} molecules of CCl_4?

85. Some brands of salami contain 0.090% sodium benzoate ($NaC_7H_5O_2$) by mass as a preservative. If you eat 6.00 oz of this salami, how many atoms of sodium will you consume, assuming salami contains no other source of that element?

86. Most wine is prepared by the fermentation of the glucose in grape juice by yeast:

$$C_6H_{12}O_6(aq) \longrightarrow 2C_2H_5OH(aq) + 2CO_2(g)$$

How many grams of glucose should there be in grape juice to produce 725 mL of wine that is 11.0% ethyl alcohol, C_2H_5OH ($d = 0.789$ g/cm^3), by volume?

87. All the fertilizers listed below contribute nitrogen to the soil. If all these fertilizers are sold for the same price per gram of nitrogen, which will cost the least per 50-lb bag?

urea, $(NH_2)_2CO$
ammonia, NH_3
ammonium nitrate, NH_4NO_3
guanidine, $HNC(NH_2)_2$

88. Perhaps the simplest way to calculate Avogadro's number is to compare the charge on the electron, first determined by Robert Millikan in 1909, with the charge on a mole of electrons, determined electrochemically (Chapter 18). These charges, in coulombs (C), are given in Appendix 1. Use them to calculate Avogadro's number to five significant figures.

Conceptual Problems

89. Given a pair of elements and their mass relation, answer the following questions.

(a) The mass of 4 atoms of A = the mass of 6 atoms of B. Which element has the smaller molar mass?

(b) The mass of 6 atoms of C is less than the mass of 3 atoms of the element D. Which element has more atoms/gram?

(c) Six atoms of E have larger mass than six atoms of F. Which has more atoms/gram?

(d) Six atoms of F have the same mass as 8 atoms of G. Which has more atoms/mole?

90. The reaction between compounds made up of A (squares), B (circles), and C (triangles) is shown pictorially below. Using smallest whole-number coefficients, write a balanced equation to represent the picture shown.

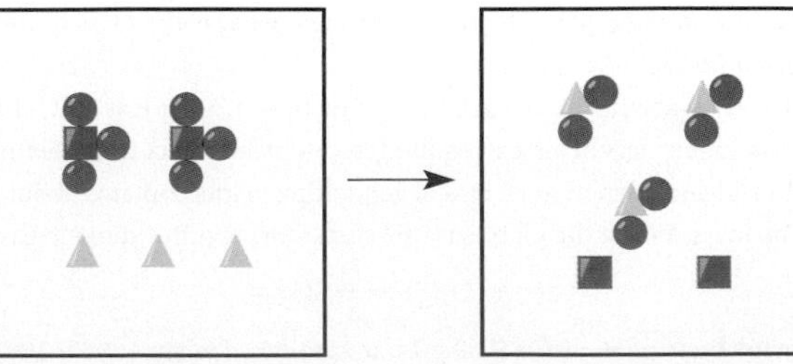

91. Represent the following equation pictorially (see Problem 90), using squares to represent A, circles to represent B, and triangles to represent C.

$$A_2B_3 + C_2 \longrightarrow C_2B_3 + A_2$$

After you have "drawn" the equation, use your drawing as a guide to balance it.

■ in OWL Blue-numbered questions answered in Appendix 6 WEB Solution is available on companion website

92. Nitrogen reacts with hydrogen to form ammonia. Represent each nitrogen atom by a square and each hydrogen atom with a circle. Starting with five molecules of both hydrogen and nitrogen, show pictorially what you have after the reaction is complete.

93. Consider the following diagram, where atom X is represented by a square and atom Y is represented by a circle.

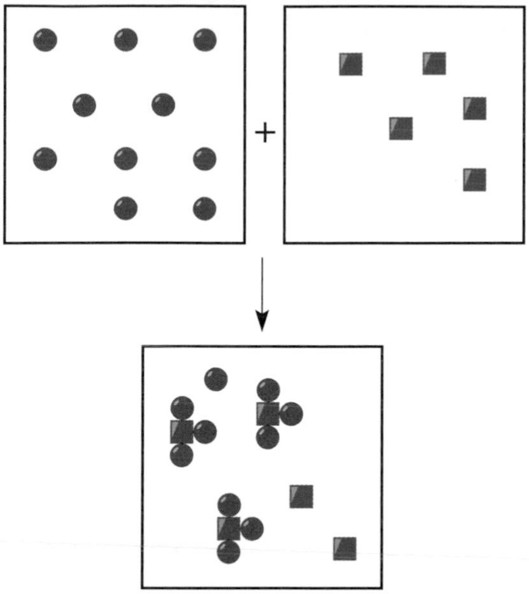

(a) Write the equation for the reaction represented by the diagram.

(b) If each circle stands for a mole of Y and each square a mole of X, how many moles of X did one start with? How many moles of Y?

(c) Using the same representation described in part (b), how many moles of product are formed? How many moles of X and Y are left unreacted?

94. When 4.0 mol of CCl_4 reacts with an excess of HF, 3.0 mol of CCl_2F_2 (Freon) is obtained. The equation for the reaction is

$$CCl_4(l) + 2HF(g) \longrightarrow CCl_2F_2(l) + 2HCl(g)$$

State which of the statements are true about the reaction and make the false statements true.

(a) The theoretical yield for CCl_2F_2 is 3.0 mol.

(b) The theoretical yield for HCl is 71 g.

(c) The percent yield for the reaction is 75%.

(d) The theoretical yield cannot be determined unless the exact amount of HF is given.

(e) From just the information given above, it is impossible to calculate how much HF is unreacted.

(f) For this reaction, as well as for any other reaction, the total number of moles of reactants is equal to the total number of moles of product.

(g) Half a mole of HF is consumed for every mole of CCl_4 used.

(h) At the end of the reaction, no CCl_4 is theoretically left unreacted.

95. Suppose that the atomic mass of C-12 is taken to be 5.000 amu and that a mole is defined as the number of atoms in 5.000 kg of carbon-12. How many atoms would there be in one mole under these conditions? (*Hint:* There are 6.022×10^{23} C atoms in 12.00 g of C-12.)

96. Suppose that Si-28 ($^{28}_{14}Si$) is taken as the standard for expressing atomic masses and assigned an atomic mass of 10.00 amu. Estimate the molar mass of lithium nitride.

97. Answer the questions below, using **LT** (for *is less than*), **GT** (for *is greater than*), **EQ** (for *is equal to*), or **MI** (for *more information required*) in the blanks provided.

(a) The mass (to three significant figures) of 6.022×10^{23} atoms of Na ________ 23.0 g.

(b) Boron has two isotopes, B-10 (10.01 amu) and B-11 (11.01 amu). The abundance of B-10 ________ the abundance of B-11.

(c) If S-32 were assigned as the standard for expressing relative atomic masses and assigned an atomic mass of 10.00 amu, the atomic mass for H would be ________ 1.00 amu.

(d) When phosphine gas, PH_3, is burned in oxygen, tetraphosphorus decaoxide and steam are formed. In the balanced equation (using smallest whole-number coefficients) for the reaction, the sum of the coefficients on the reactant side is ________ 7.

(e) The mass (in grams) of one mole of bromine molecules is ________ 79.90.

98. Determine whether the statements given below are true or false.

(a) The mass of an atom can have the unit mole.

(b) In N_2O_4, the mass of the oxygen is twice that of the nitrogen.

(c) One mole of chlorine atoms has a mass of 35.45 g.

(d) Boron has an average atomic mass of 10.81 amu. It has two isotopes, B-10 (10.01 amu) and B-11 (11.01 amu). There is more naturally occurring B-10 than B-11.

(e) The compound $C_6H_{12}O_2N$ has for its simplest formula $C_3H_6ON_{1/2}$.

(f) A 558.5-g sample of iron contains ten times as many atoms as 0.5200 g of chromium.

(g) If 1.00 mol of ammonia is mixed with 1.00 mol of oxygen the following reaction occurs,

$$4NH_3(g) + 5O_2(g) \longrightarrow 4NO(g) + 6H_2O(l)$$

All the oxygen is consumed.

(h) When balancing an equation, the total number of moles of reactant molecules must equal the total number of moles of product molecules.

Challenge Problems

99. ■ Chlorophyll, the substance responsible for the green color of leaves, has one magnesium atom per chlorophyll molecule and contains 2.72% magnesium by mass. What is the molar mass of chlorophyll?

100. By x-ray diffraction it is possible to determine the geometric pattern in which atoms are arranged in a crystal and the distances between atoms. In a crystal of silver, four atoms effectively occupy the volume of a cube 0.409 nm on an edge. Taking the density of silver to be 10.5 g/cm^3, calculate the number of atoms in one mole of silver.

101. A 5.025-g sample of calcium is burned in air to produce a mixture of two ionic compounds, calcium oxide and calcium nitride. Water is added to this mixture. It reacts with calcium oxide to form 4.832 g of calcium hydroxide. How many grams of calcium oxide are formed? How many grams of calcium nitride?

102. Consider the reaction between barium and sulfur:

$$Ba(s) + S(s) \longrightarrow BaS(s)$$

Both barium and sulfur also combine with oxygen to form barium oxide and sulfur dioxide. When 95.0 g of Ba react with 50.0 g of sulfur, only 65.15 g of BaS are obtained. Assuming 100% yield for the oxides, how many grams of BaO and SO_2 are formed?

103. ■ A mixture of potassium chloride and potassium bromide weighing 3.595 g is heated with chlorine, which converts the mixture completely to potassium chloride. The total mass of potassium chloride after the reaction is 3.129 g. What percentage of the original mixture was potassium bromide?

104. A sample of an oxide of vanadium weighing 4.589 g was heated with hydrogen gas to form water and another oxide of vanadium weighing 3.782 g. The second oxide was treated further with hydrogen until only 2.573 g of vanadium metal remained.

(a) What are the simplest formulas of the two oxides?

(b) What is the total mass of water formed in the successive reactions?

105. A sample of cocaine, $C_{17}H_{21}O_4N$, is diluted with sugar, $C_{12}H_{22}O_{11}$. When a 1.00-mg sample of this mixture is burned, 1.00 mL of carbon dioxide (d = 1.80 g/L) is formed. What is the percentage of cocaine in this mixture?

■ in OWL Blue-numbered questions answered in Appendix 6 **WEB** Solution is available on companion website

4 Reactions in Aqueous Solution

He takes up the waters of the sea in his
hand, leaving the salt;
He disperses it in mist through the skies;
He recollects and sprinkles it like grain in
six-rayed snowy stars over the earth,
There to lie till he dissolves the bonds again.

—Henry David Thoreau
"Journal" (January 5, 1856)

Chapter Outline

The three-phase firing process ancient Greek potters used to create this vase utilized both oxidation and reduction processes.

"Amphora with Four Men Holding Various Objects" by Kleophrades painter/Araldo de Luca/CORBIS

Most of the reactions considered in Chapter 3 involved pure substances reacting with each other. However, most of the reactions you will carry out in the laboratory or hear about in lecture take place in water (aqueous) solution. Beyond that, most of the reactions that occur in the world around you involve ions or molecules dissolved in water. For these reasons, among others, you need to become familiar with some of the more important types of aqueous reactions. These include—

- precipitation reactions (Section 4.2).
- acid-base reactions (Section 4.3).
- oxidation-reduction reactions (Section 4.4).

The emphasis is on writing and balancing chemical equations for these reactions. All of these reactions involve ions in solution. The corresponding equations are given a special name: net ionic equations. They can be used to do stoichiometric calculations similar to those discussed in Chapter 3.

To carry out these calculations for solution reactions, you need to be familiar with a concentration unit called molarity, which tells you how many moles of a species are in a given volume of solution. ■

Online homework for this chapter may be assigned in OWL.

CENGAGENOW™
This icon introduces an opportunity for self-study and to explore interactive modules by signing in at **academic.cengage.com/now.**

4.1 SOLUTE CONCENTRATIONS; MOLARITY

The concentration of a solute in solution can be expressed in terms of its **molarity:**

$$\text{molarity } (M) = \frac{\text{moles of solute}}{\text{liters of solution}} \qquad \textbf{(4.1)}$$

CENGAGENOW™
Click Coached Problems for a self-study module on **solution concentration.**

The symbol [ ] is commonly used to represent the molarity of a species in solution. For a solution containing 1.20 mol of substance A in 2.50 L of solution,

$[NH_3]$ means "concentration of ammonia in moles per liter."

$$[\text{A}] = \frac{1.20 \text{ mol}}{2.50 \text{ L}} = 0.480 \text{ mol/L} = 0.480\ M$$

One liter of such a solution would contain 0.480 mol of A; 100 mL of solution would contain 0.0480 mol of A, and so on.

The molarity of a soluble solute can vary over a wide range. With sodium hydroxide, for example, we can prepare a 6 *M* solution, a 1 *M* solution, a 0.1 *M* solution, and so on. The words "concentrated" and "dilute" are often used in a qualitative way to describe these solutions. We would describe a 6 *M* solution of NaOH as concentrated; it contains a relatively large amount of solute per liter. A 0.1 *M* NaOH solution is dilute, at least in comparison to 1 *M* or 6 *M*.

To prepare a solution to a desired molarity, you first calculate the amount of solute required. This is then dissolved in enough solvent to form the required volume of solution. Suppose, for example, you want to make one liter of 0.100 *M* K_2CrO_4 solution (Figure 4.1, p. 76). You first weigh out 19.4 g (0.100 mol) of K_2CrO_4 (MM = 194.20 g/mol). Then stir with enough water to form one liter (1000 mL) of solution.

The molarity of a solution can be used to calculate—

- the number of moles of solute in a given volume of solution.
- the volume of solution containing a given number of moles of solute.

Here, as in so many other cases, a conversion factor approach is used (Example 4.1).

Figure 4.1

Preparing one liter of 0.100 *M* potassium chromate. A 0.100 *M* potassium chromate solution is made by adding enough water to 19.4 g of K_2CrO_4 to make one liter of solution.

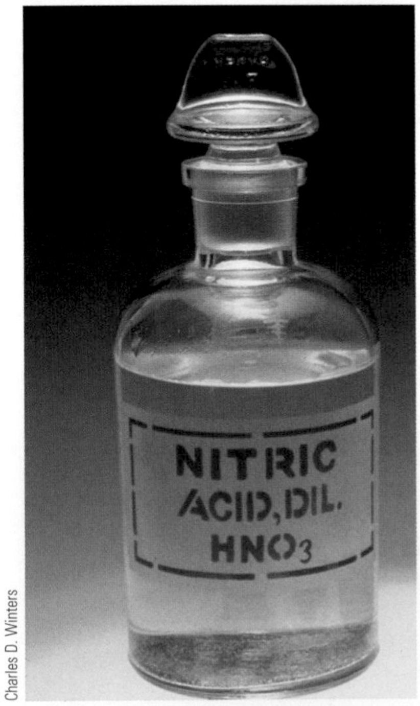

A dilute (≈ 6 *M*) solution of HNO_3.

Example 4.1 Nitric acid, HNO_3, is extensively used in the manufacture of fertilizer. A bottle containing 75.0 mL of nitric acid solution is labeled 6.0 *M* HNO_3.

(a) How many moles of HNO_3 are in the bottle?
(b) A reaction needs 5.00 g of HNO_3. How many mL of solution are required?
(c) Ten mL of water are added to the solution. What is the molarity of the resulting solution? (Assume volumes are additive.)

Strategy The required conversion factors are

$$\frac{6.0 \text{ mol } HNO_3}{1 \text{ L}} \text{ and } \frac{63.02 \text{ g } HNO_3}{1 \text{ mol}}$$

SOLUTION

(a) $n_{HNO_3} = 75.0 \text{ mL} \times \frac{6.0 \text{ mol } HNO_3}{1 \text{ L}} \times \frac{1 \text{ L}}{1000 \text{ mL}} = \boxed{0.45 \text{ mol}}$

(b) $V = 5.00 \text{ g} \times \frac{1 \text{ mol } HNO_3}{63.02 \text{ g}} \times \frac{1 \text{ L}}{6.0 \text{ mol } HNO_3} \times \frac{1000 \text{ mL}}{1 \text{ L}} = \boxed{13 \text{ mL}}$

(c) From (a) we see that there are 0.45 moles HNO_3 in the solution before addition of the water. That changes the volume (from 75 mL to 85 mL) but not the number of moles. Thus,

$$M = \frac{\text{moles } HNO_3}{V \text{ solution}} = \frac{0.45 \text{ moles}}{85.0 \text{ mL}} \times \frac{1000 \text{ mL}}{1 \text{ L}} = \boxed{5.3 \text{ mol/L}}$$

Reality Check The molarity decreases when water is added. The moles of solute stay the same, but the volume of the solution increases.

3	4	5	6	7	8	9	10	11	12
			Cr^{3+}	Mn^{2+}	Fe^{2+} Fe^{3+}	Co^{2+} Co^{3+}	Ni^{2+}	Cu^{2+}	Zn^{2+}
								Ag^{+}	Cd^{2+}
									Hg^{2+}

Figure 4.2
Charges of transition metal cations commonly found in aqueous solution.

As pointed out in Chapter 2, when an ionic solid dissolves in water, the cations and anions separate from each other. This process can be represented by a chemical equation in which the reactant is the solid and the products are the positive and negative ions in water (aqueous) solution. For the dissolving of $MgCl_2$, the equation is

CENGAGENOW™
Click Coached Problems for a self-study module on **direct addition method.**

$$MgCl_2(s) \longrightarrow Mg^{2+}(aq) + 2Cl^-(aq)$$

This equation tells us that one mole of $MgCl_2$ yields *one* mole of Mg^{2+} ions and *two* moles of Cl^- ions in solution. It follows that in any solution of magnesium chloride:

$$\text{molarity } Mg^{2+} = \text{molarity } MgCl_2 \qquad \text{molarity } Cl^- = 2 \times \text{molarity } MgCl_2$$

Similar relationships hold for ionic solids containing polyatomic ions (Table 2.2) or transition metal cations (Figure 4.2).

[ion] = ion subscript × [parent compound]

$$(NH_4)_3PO_4(s) \longrightarrow 3NH_4^+(aq) + PO_4^{3-}(aq)$$

$$\text{molarity } NH_4^+ = 3 \times \text{molarity } (NH_4)_3PO_4 \qquad \text{molarity } PO_4^{3-} = \text{molarity } (NH_4)_3PO_4$$

$$Cr_2(SO_4)_3(s) \longrightarrow 2Cr^{3+}(aq) + 3SO_4^{2-}(aq)$$

$$\text{molarity } Cr^{3+} = 2 \times \text{molarity } Cr_2(SO_4)_3 \qquad \text{molarity } SO_4^{2-} = 3 \times \text{molarity } Cr_2(SO_4)_3$$

Example 4.2 Potassium dichromate, $K_2Cr_2O_7$, is used in the tanning of leather. A flask containing 125 mL of solution is labeled 0.145 *M* $K_2Cr_2O_7$.

(a) What is the molarity of each ion in solution?
(b) A sample containing 0.200 moles of K^+ is added to the solution. Assuming no volume change, what is the molarity of the new solution?

Strategy To go from concentration of solute to concentration of an individual ion, you must know the conversion factor relating moles of ions to moles of solute. To find this conversion factor, it is helpful to write the equation for the solution process.

SOLUTION

(a) $K_2Cr_2O_7(s) \longrightarrow 2K^+(aq) + Cr_2O_7^{2-}(aq)$.
The conversion factors are 2 mol K^+/1 mol $K_2Cr_2O_7$ and 1 mol $Cr_2O_7^{2-}$/1 mol $K_2Cr_2O_7$. Thus,

For aluminum sulfate: $[Al^{3+}] = 2[Al_2(SO_4)_3]$, $[SO_4^{2-}] = 3[Al_2(SO_4)_3]$.

$$[K^+] = \frac{0.145 \text{ mol } K_2Cr_2O_7}{1 \text{ L}} \times \frac{2 \text{ mol } K^+}{1 \text{ mol } K_2Cr_2O_7} = 0.290\ M$$

$$[Cr_2O_7^{2-}] = \frac{0.145 \text{ mol } K_2Cr_2O_7}{1 \text{ L}} \times \frac{1 \text{ mol } Cr_2O_7^{2-}}{1 \text{ mol } K_2Cr_2O_7} = 0.145\ M$$

(b) First, find the moles of K^+ in the original solution:

$$(n_{K^+})_{\text{original}} = \frac{0.290 \text{ mol } K^+}{1 \text{ L}} \times 0.125 \text{ L} = 0.03625 \text{ mol}$$

Next, we find the molarity of K^+ after the addition of K^+ ions:

$$n_{K^+} = 0.03625 + 0.200 = 0.236$$

$$[K^+] = \frac{0.236 \text{ mol}}{0.125 \text{ L}} = 1.89\ M$$

Finally, we convert $[K^+]$ to $[K_2Cr_2O_7]$ using the ion-to-solute conversion factor.

$$[K_2Cr_2O_7] = \frac{1.89 \text{ mol } K^+}{1 \text{ L}} \times \frac{1 \text{ mol } K_2Cr_2O_7}{2 \text{ mol } K^+} = 0.945\ M$$

Reality Check The concentration of K^+ should be twice that of $Cr_2O_7^{2-}$ in either solution. It is!

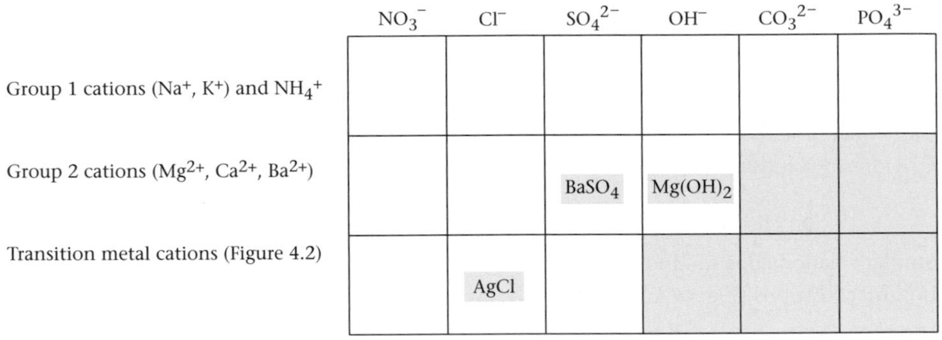

Figure 4.3
Precipitation diagram. Choose the cation row and read across to the anion column. If the block is blank, no precipitate will form. If the block is colored, a precipitate will form from dilute solution. Where a formula is given, that is the only cation-anion combination in that block that will precipitate.

4.2 PRECIPITATION REACTIONS

Sometimes when water solutions of two different ionic compounds are mixed, an insoluble solid separates out of solution. The **precipitate** that forms is itself ionic; the cation comes from one solution, the anion from the other. To predict the occurrence of reactions of this type, you must know which ionic substances are insoluble in water.

The precipitation diagram shown in Figure 4.3 enables you to determine whether or not a precipitate will form when dilute solutions of two ionic solutes are mixed. If a cation in solution 1 mixes with an anion in solution 2 to form an insoluble compound (colored squares), that compound will precipitate. Cation-anion combinations that lead to the formation of a soluble compound (white squares) will not give a precipitate. For example, if solutions of $NiCl_2$ (Ni^{2+}, Cl^- ions) and NaOH (Na^+, OH^- ions) are mixed (Figure 4.4)—

- a precipitate of $Ni(OH)_2$, an insoluble compound, will form.
- NaCl, a soluble compound, will not precipitate.

Charles D. Winters

Figure 4.4
Precipitation of nickel hydroxide ($Ni(OH)_2$). The precipitate forms when solutions of nickel chloride ($NiCl_2$) and sodium hydroxide (NaOH) are mixed.

Example 4.3 Using the precipitation diagram (Figure 4.3), predict what will happen when the following pairs of aqueous solutions are mixed.

(a) $Cu(NO_3)_2$ and $(NH_4)_2SO_4$ (b) $FeCl_3$ and $AgNO_3$

Strategy First decide what cation and anion are present in each solution. Then write the formulas of the two possible precipitates, combining a cation of one solution with the anion of the other solution. Check Figure 4.3 to see if one or both of these compounds are insoluble. If so, a precipitation reaction occurs.

SOLUTION

(a) Ions present in the first solution: Cu^{2+}, NO_3^-; the second solution: NH_4^+, SO_4^{2-}
Possible precipitates: $CuSO_4$, NH_4NO_3
From Figure 4.3, both of these compounds are soluble, so no precipitate forms.
(b) Ions present: Fe^{3+}, Cl^-; Ag^+, NO_3^-
Possible precipitates: AgCl, $Fe(NO_3)_3$
Iron(III) nitrate is soluble, but silver chloride is not. When these two solutions are mixed, silver chloride precipitates.

Charles D. Winters

Figure 4.5
Precipitation of calcium carbonate ($CaCO_3$). The precipitate forms when solutions of sodium carbonate (Na_2CO_3) and calcium chloride ($CaCl_2$) are mixed.

Net Ionic Equations

The precipitation reaction that occurs when solutions of Na_2CO_3 and $CaCl_2$ are mixed (Figure 4.5) can be represented by a simple equation. To obtain that equation, consider the identity of the reactants and products:

Reactants: Na^+, CO_3^{2-}, Ca^{2+}, and Cl^- ions in water solution:

$$2Na^+(aq) + CO_3^{2-}(aq) + Ca^{2+}(aq) + 2Cl^-(aq)$$

Products: solid $CaCO_3$, Na^+ and Cl^- ions remaining in solution:

$$2Na^+(aq) + 2Cl^-(aq) + CaCO_3(s)$$

The total ionic equation for the reaction is

$$2Na^+(aq) + CO_3^{2-}(aq) + Ca^{2+}(aq) + 2Cl^-(aq) \longrightarrow 2Na^+(aq) + 2Cl^-(aq) + CaCO_3(s)$$

Canceling out the ions that appear on both sides of the equation ($2Na^+$, $2Cl^-$), we obtain the final equation:

$$Ca^{2+}(aq) + CO_3^{2-}(aq) \longrightarrow CaCO_3(s)$$

Equations such as this that exclude "spectator ions," which take no part in the reaction, are referred to as **net ionic equations.** We will use net ionic equations throughout this chapter and indeed the entire text to represent a wide variety of reactions in water solution. Like all equations, net ionic equations must show—

Spectator ions are in solution before, during, and after reaction.

- ***atom balance.*** There must be the same number of atoms of each element on both sides. In the preceding equation, the atoms present on both sides are one calcium atom, one carbon atom, and three oxygen atoms.
- ***charge balance.*** There must be the same total charge on both sides. In this equation, the total charge is zero on both sides.

$$Ca^{2+}(aq) + CO_3^{2-}(aq) \longrightarrow CaCO_3(s)$$

Example 4.4 Write a net ionic equation for any precipitation reaction that occurs when solutions of the following ionic compounds are mixed.

(a) NaOH and $Cu(NO_3)_2$ (b) $BaCl_2$ and Ag_2SO_4 (c) $(NH_4)_3PO_4$ and K_2CO_3

CENGAGENOW™
Click Coached Problems for a self-study module on **net ionic equations.**

Strategy Follow the procedure of Example 4.3 to decide whether a precipitate will form. If it does, write its formula, followed by (*s*), on the right side of the equation. On the left (reactant) side, write the formulas of the ions (*aq*) required to produce the precipitate. Finally, balance the equation.

SOLUTION

(a) Ions present: Na^+, OH^-; Cu^{2+}, NO_3^-
Possible precipitates: $NaNO_3$, $Cu(OH)_2$
$NaNO_3$ is soluble, but $Cu(OH)_2$ is not.

To write a net ionic equation, you first have to identify the ions.

Equation: $Cu^{2+}(aq) + 2OH^-(aq) \longrightarrow Cu(OH)_2(s)$

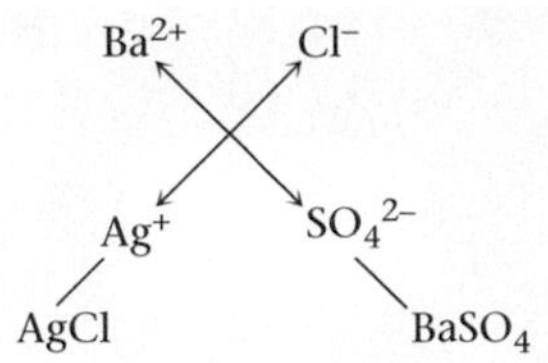

(b) Ions present: Ba^{2+}, Cl^-; Ag^+, SO_4^{2-}
Possible precipitates: $BaSO_4$, AgCl
Both compounds are insoluble, so two reactions occur.

Equations:
$$Ba^{2+}(aq) + SO_4^{2-}(aq) \longrightarrow BaSO_4(s)$$
$$Ag^+(aq) + Cl^-(aq) \longrightarrow AgCl(s)$$

(c) Ions present: NH_4^+, PO_4^{3-}, K^+, CO_3^{2-}
Both possible products are soluble, so there is no precipitation reaction and no equation.

For any reaction in water solution, always start with a balanced net ionic equation.

Although we have introduced net ionic equations to represent precipitation reactions, they have a much wider application. Indeed, we will use them for all kinds of reactions in water solution. In particular ***all of the chemical equations written throughout this chapter are net ionic equations.***

Stoichiometry

The approach followed in Chapter 3 to calculate mole-mass relations in reactions is readily applied to solution reactions represented by net ionic equations.

Example 4.5 Graded

When aqueous solutions of sodium hydroxide and iron(III) nitrate are mixed, a red precipitate forms.

*(a) Write a net ionic equation for the reaction.
**(b) What volume of 0.136 *M* iron(III) nitrate is required to produce 0.886 g of precipitate?
***(c) How many grams of precipitate are formed when 50.00 mL of 0.200 *M* NaOH and 30.00 mL of 0.125 *M* $Fe(NO_3)_3$ are mixed?

SOLUTION

(a) $Fe^{3+}(aq) + 3OH^-(aq) \longrightarrow Fe(OH)_3(s)$

(b) Determine the number of moles of precipitate. The molar mass of $Fe(OH)_3$ is 106.87 g/mol, so

$$n_{Fe(OH)_3} = 0.886\text{ g} \times \frac{1\text{ mol}}{106.87\text{ g}} = 8.29 \times 10^{-3}\text{ mol}$$

Note that in the reaction, one mole of Fe^{3+} produces one mole of $Fe(OH)_3$. Thus,

$$n_{Fe^{3+}} = 8.29 \times 10^{-3}\text{ mol}$$

You will need the molarity of $Fe(NO_3)_3$ to determine the volume required. Since there is one ion of Fe^{3+} in $Fe(NO_3)_3$,

$$n_{Fe(NO_3)_3} = 8.29 \times 10^{-3}\text{ mol}$$

To determine the volume, use the relation $n = V \times M$:

$$V = \frac{8.29 \times 10^{-3}\text{ mol}}{0.136\text{ mol/L}} = 0.0610\text{ L}$$

(c) This is a limiting-reactant problem. Specific amounts of both reactants are given. First, find the moles of $Fe(OH)_3$ produced if Fe^{3+} is limiting.

$$n_{Fe(OH)_3} = \frac{0.0300\text{ L} \times 0.125\text{ mol Fe(NO}_3)_3}{1\text{ L}} \times \frac{1\text{ mol Fe}^{3+}}{1\text{ mol Fe(NO}_3)_3} \times \frac{1\text{ mol Fe(OH)}_3}{1\text{ mol Fe}^{3+}}$$
$$= 0.00375\text{ mol}$$

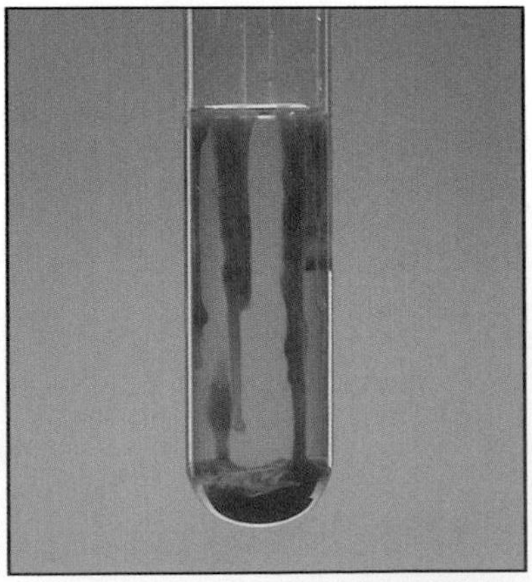

Charles D. Winters

Precipitation of iron(III) hydroxide ($Fe(OH)_3$). The red, gelatinous precipitate forms when aqueous solutions of sodium hydroxide (NaOH) and iron(III) nitrate ($Fe(NO_3)_3$) are mixed.

If OH^- is limiting,

$$n_{Fe(OH)_3} = \frac{0.0500\text{ L} \times 0.200\text{ mol NaOH}}{1\text{ L}} \times \frac{1\text{ mol OH}^-}{1\text{ mol NaOH}} \times \frac{1\text{ mol Fe(OH)}_3}{3\text{ mol OH}^-}$$

$$= 0.00333\text{ mol}$$

Because 0.00333 is less than 0.00375, OH^- is the limiting reactant. The theoretical yield of $Fe(OH)_3$ is 0.00333 mol. So, the mass produced is

$$0.00333\text{ mol Fe(OH)}_3 \times \frac{106.87\text{ g Fe(OH)}_3}{1\text{ mol Fe(OH)}_3} = 0.356\text{ g Fe(OH)}_3$$

4.3 ACID-BASE REACTIONS

Charles D. Winters

Figure 4.6

Acidic and basic household solutions. Many common household items, including vinegar, orange juice, and cola drinks, are acidic. In contrast, baking soda and most detergents and cleaning agents are basic.

You are probably familiar with a variety of aqueous solutions that are either acidic or basic (Figure 4.6). Acidic solutions have a sour taste and affect the color of certain organic dyes known as acid-base indicators. For example, litmus turns from blue to red in acidic solution. Basic solutions have a slippery feeling and change the colors of indicators (e.g., red to blue for litmus).

The species that give these solutions their characteristic properties are called acids and bases. In this chapter, we use the definitions first proposed by Svante Arrhenius more than a century ago.

An acid is a species that produces H^+ ions in water solution.
A base is a species that produces OH^- ions in water solution.

We will consider more general definitions of acids and bases in Chapter 13 (Brønsted-Lowry) and Chapter 15 (Lewis).

Charles D. Winters

Hydrochloric acid can be obtained from hardware stores, where it is called muriatic acid. This strong acid is used to clean metal and stone surfaces.

Strong and Weak Acids and Bases

There are two types of acids, strong and weak, which differ in the extent of their ionization in water. **Strong acids** ionize completely, forming H^+ ions and anions. A typical strong acid is HCl. It undergoes the following reaction on addition to water:

$$HCl(aq) \longrightarrow H^+(aq) + Cl^-(aq)$$

In a solution prepared by adding 0.1 mol of HCl to water, there is 0.1 mol of H^+ ions, 0.1 mol of Cl^- ions, and no HCl molecules. There are six common strong acids, whose names and formulas are listed in Table 4.1.

All acids other than those listed in Table 4.1 can be taken to be weak. A weak acid is only partially ionized to H^+ ions in water. All of the **weak acids** considered in this chapter are molecules containing an ionizable hydrogen atom. Their general formula can be represented as HB; the general ionization reaction in water is

$$HB(aq) \rightleftharpoons H^+(aq) + B^-(aq)$$

Table 4.1 Common Strong Acids and Bases

Acid	Name of Acid	Base	Name of Base
HCl	Hydrochloric acid	LiOH	Lithium hydroxide
HBr	Hydrobromic acid	NaOH	Sodium hydroxide
HI	Hydriodic acid	KOH	Potassium hydroxide
HNO_3	Nitric acid	$Ca(OH)_2$	Calcium hydroxide
$HClO_4$	Perchloric acid	$Sr(OH)_2$	Strontium hydroxide
H_2SO_4	Sulfuric acid	$Ba(OH)_2$	Barium hydroxide

You need to know the strong acids and bases to work with acid-base reactions.

Sulfuric acid ionization: $H_2SO_4(aq) \longrightarrow H^+(aq) + HSO_4^-(aq)$.

The double arrow implies that this reaction does not go to completion. Instead, a mixture is formed containing significant amounts of both products and reactants. With the weak acid hydrogen fluoride

$$HF(aq) \rightleftharpoons H^+(aq) + F^-(aq)$$

a solution prepared by adding 0.1 mol of HF to a liter of water contains about 0.01 mol of H^+ ions, 0.01 mol of F^- ions, and 0.09 mol of HF molecules.

CENGAGENOW™
Click Coached Problems for a self-study module on **acid ionization.**

Bases, like acids, are classified as strong or weak. A **strong base** in water solution is completely ionized to OH^- ions and cations. As you can see from Table 4.1, the strong bases are the hydroxides of the Group 1 and Group 2 metals. These are typical ionic solids, completely ionized both in the solid state and in water solution. The equations written to represent the processes by which NaOH and $Ca(OH)_2$ dissolve in water are

$$NaOH(s) \longrightarrow Na^+(aq) + OH^-(aq)$$
$$Ca(OH)_2(s) \longrightarrow Ca^{2+}(aq) + 2OH^-(aq)$$

In a solution prepared by adding 0.1 mol of NaOH to water, there is 0.1 mol of Na^+ ions, 0.1 mol of OH^- ions, and no NaOH molecules.

Weak bases produce OH^- ions in a quite different manner. They react with H_2O molecules, acquiring H^+ ions and leaving OH^- ions behind. The reaction of ammonia, NH_3, is typical:

$$NH_3(aq) + H_2O \rightleftharpoons NH_4^+(aq) + OH^-(aq)$$

As with all weak bases, this reaction does not go to completion. In a solution prepared by adding 0.1 mol of ammonia to a liter of water, there is about 0.001 mol of NH_4^+, 0.001 mol of OH^-, and nearly 0.099 mol of NH_3.

A hydrocarbon group has a string of C and H atoms.

A common class of weak bases consists of the organic molecules known as *amines.* An amine can be considered to be a derivative of ammonia in which one or more hydrogen atoms have been replaced by hydrocarbon groups.

In the simplest case, methylamine, a hydrogen atom is replaced by a $-CH_3$ group to give the CH_3NH_2 molecule, which reacts with water in a manner very similar to NH_3:

$$CH_3NH_2(aq) + H_2O \rightleftharpoons CH_3NH_3^+(aq) + OH^-(aq)$$

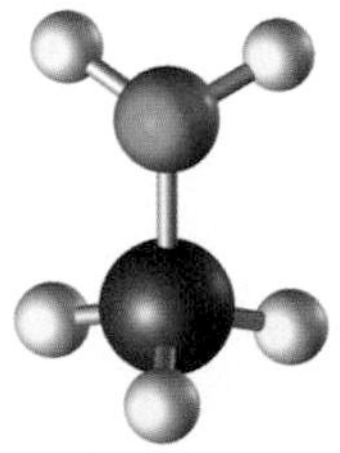

Methylamine, CH_3NH_2

As we have pointed out, strong acids and bases are completely ionized in water. As a result, compounds such as HCl and NaOH are strong electrolytes like NaCl. In contrast, molecular weak acids and weak bases are poor conductors because their water solutions contain relatively few ions. Hydrofluoric acid and ammonia are commonly described as *weak electrolytes.*

Equations for Acid-Base Reactions

When an acidic water solution is mixed with a basic water solution, an acid-base reaction takes place. The nature of the reaction and hence the equation written for it depend on whether the acid and base involved are strong or weak.

1. ***Strong acid–strong base.*** Consider what happens when a solution of a strong acid such as HNO_3 is added to a solution of a strong base such as NaOH. Because HNO_3 is a strong acid, it is completely converted to H^+ and NO_3^- ions in solution. Similarly, with the strong base NaOH, the solution species are the Na^+ and OH^- ions. When the solutions are mixed, the H^+ and OH^- ions react with each other to form H_2O molecules. This reaction, referred to as **neutralization,** is represented by the net ionic equation

$$H^+(aq) + OH^-(aq) \longrightarrow H_2O$$

The Na^+ and NO_3^- ions take no part in the reaction and so do not appear in the equation. Here again, we are dealing with "spectator ions."

When $HClO_4$ reacts with $Ca(OH)_2$, the equation is $H^+(aq) + OH^-(aq) \longrightarrow H_2O$.

There is considerable evidence to indicate that the neutralization reaction occurs when any strong base reacts with any strong acid in water solution. It follows that the neutralization equation written above applies to any strong acid–strong base reaction.

Table 4.2 Types of Acid-Base Reactions

Reactants	Reacting Species	Net Ionic Equation
Strong acid–strong base	H^+–OH^-	$H^+(aq) + OH^-(aq) \longrightarrow H_2O$
Weak acid–strong base	HB–OH^-	$HB(aq) + OH^-(aq) \longrightarrow H_2O + B^-(aq)$
Strong acid–weak base	H^+–B	$H^+(aq) + B(aq) \longrightarrow BH^+(aq)$

2. *Weak acid–strong base.* When a strong base such as NaOH is added to a solution of a weak acid, HB, a two-step reaction occurs. The first step is the ionization of the HB molecule to H^+ and B^- ions; the second is the neutralization of the H^+ ions produced in the first step by the OH^- ions of the NaOH solution.

$$(1)\ HB(aq) \rightleftharpoons H^+(aq) + B^-(aq)$$
$$(2)\ H^+(aq) + OH^-(aq) \longrightarrow H_2O$$

The equation for the overall reaction is obtained by adding the two equations just written and canceling H^+ ions:

$$HB(aq) + OH^-(aq) \longrightarrow B^-(aq) + H_2O$$

For the reaction between solutions of sodium hydroxide and hydrogen fluoride, the net ionic equation is

$$HF(aq) + OH^-(aq) \longrightarrow F^-(aq) + H_2O$$

When an acid is weak, like HF, its formula appears in the equation.

Here, as always, spectator ions such as Na^+ are not included in the net ionic equation.

3. *Strong acid–weak base.* As an example of a reaction of a strong acid with a weak base, consider what happens when an aqueous solution of a strong acid like HCl is added to an aqueous solution of ammonia, NH_3. Again, we consider the reaction to take place in two steps. The first step is the reaction of NH_3 with H_2O to form NH_4^+ and OH^- ions. Then, in the second step, the H^+ ions of the strong acid neutralize the OH^- ions formed in the first step.

$$(1)\ NH_3(aq) + H_2O \rightleftharpoons NH_4^+(aq) + OH^-(aq)$$
$$(2)\ H^+(aq) + OH^-(aq) \longrightarrow H_2O$$

The overall equation is obtained by summing those for the individual steps. Canceling species (OH^-, H_2O) that appear on both sides, we obtain the net ionic equation

$$H^+(aq) + NH_3(aq) \longrightarrow NH_4^+(aq)$$

When a base is weak, like NH_3, its formula appears in the equation.

In another case, for the reaction of a strong acid such as HNO_3 with methylamine, CH_3NH_2, the net ionic equation is

$$H^+(aq) + CH_3NH_2(aq) \longrightarrow CH_3NH_3^+(aq)$$

Table 4.2 summarizes the equations written for the three types of acid-base reactions just discussed. You should find it helpful in writing the equations called for in Example 4.6.

Example 4.6 Write a net ionic equation for each of the following reactions in dilute water solution.

(a) Hypochlorous acid (HClO) and calcium hydroxide.
(b) Ammonia with perchloric acid ($HClO_4$).
(c) Hydriodic acid (HI) with sodium hydroxide.

Strategy Decide whether the acid and base are strong or weak. Then decide which of the three types of acid-base reactions is involved. Finally, use Table 4.2 to derive the proper equation.

SOLUTION

(a) HClO is weak; $Ca(OH)_2$ is strong. This is a weak acid–strong base reaction:

$$HClO(aq) + OH^-(aq) \longrightarrow H_2O + ClO^-(aq)$$

(b) $HClO_4$ is strong (Table 4.1); ammonia is weak. This is a strong acid–weak base reaction:

$$H^+(aq) + NH_3(aq) \longrightarrow NH_4^+(aq)$$

(c) HI is strong, as is NaOH:

$$H^+(aq) + OH^-(aq) \longrightarrow H_2O$$

Acid-Base Titrations

CENGAGENOW™
Click Coached Problems for a self-study module on **Titration: mL Titrant Used.**

Acid-base reactions in water solution are commonly used to determine the concentration of a dissolved species or its percentage in a solid mixture. This is done by carrying out a **titration,** measuring the volume of a *standard solution* (a solution of known concentration) required to react with a measured amount of sample.

The experimental setup for a titration is shown in Figure 4.7. The flask contains vinegar, a water solution of a weak organic acid called acetic acid. A solution of sodium hydroxide of known concentration is added from a buret. The net ionic equation for the acid-base reaction that occurs is

$$HC_2H_3O_2(aq) + OH^-(aq) \longrightarrow C_2H_3O_2^-(aq) + H_2O$$

The objective of the titration is to determine the point at which reaction is complete, called the **equivalence point.** This is reached when the number of moles of OH^- added is exactly equal to the number of moles of acetic acid, $HC_2H_3O_2$, originally present. To determine this point, a single drop of an *acid-base indicator* such as phenolphthalein is used. It should change color (colorless to pink) at the equivalence point.

Figure 4.7
Titration of vinegar with sodium hydroxide (NaOH).

Example 4.7 Graded

Three beakers labeled A, B, and C contain the weak acid H_2X. The weak acid is titrated with 0.125 *M* NaOH. Assume the reaction to be

$$H_2X(aq) + 2\,OH^-(aq) \longrightarrow 2H_2O + X^{2-}(aq)$$

*(a) Beaker A contains 25.00 mL of 0.316 *M* H_2X. What volume of NaOH is required for complete neutralization?

**(b) Beaker B contains 25.00 mL of a solution of H_2X and requires 28.74 mL of NaOH for complete neutralization. What is the molarity of the H_2X solution?

***(c) Beaker C contains 0.124 g of H_2X and 25.00 mL of water. To reach the equivalence point, 22.04 mL of NaOH are required. What is the molar mass of H_2X?

Strategy Use the conversion factor obtained from the equation for the reaction:

$$\frac{2\text{ mol OH}^-}{1\text{ mol H}_2\text{X}}$$

Also, remember

$$n = V \times M \quad \text{and} \quad n = \frac{m}{\text{MM}}$$

SOLUTION

(a) Start by using data on H_2X. That will give you the moles of H_2X.

$$n_{H_2X} = 0.0250\text{ L} \times \frac{0.316\text{ mol H}_2\text{X}}{1\text{ L}} = 7.90 \times 10^{-3}\text{ mol}$$

$$n_{OH^-} = 7.90 \times 10^{-3}\text{ mol H}_2\text{X} \times \frac{2\text{ mol OH}^-}{1\text{ mol H}_2\text{X}} = 0.0158\text{ mol}$$

$$V_{OH^-} = \frac{n_{OH^-}}{M_{OH^-}} = \frac{0.0158\text{ mol}}{0.125\text{ mol/L}} = 0.126\text{ L}$$

(b) This time you have all the data (*V* and *M*) to determine the moles of OH^-.

$$n_{OH^-} = 0.02874\text{ L} \times \frac{0.125\text{ mol OH}^-}{1\text{ L}} = 3.59 \times 10^{-3}\text{ mol}$$

$$n_{H_2X} = 3.59 \times 10^{-3}\text{ mol OH}^- \times \frac{1\text{ mol H}_2\text{X}}{2\text{ mol OH}^-} = 1.80 \times 10^{-3}\text{ mol}$$

$$M_{H_2X} = \frac{n_{H_2X}}{V_{H_2X}} = \frac{1.80 \times 10^{-3}\text{ mol}}{0.02500\text{ L}} = 0.0720\ M$$

(c) We start by finding n_{OH^-}.

$$n_{OH^-} = 0.02204\text{ L} \times \frac{0.125\text{ mol OH}^-}{1\text{ L}} = 2.755 \times 10^{-3}\text{ mol}$$

$$n_{H_2X} = 2.755 \times 10^{-3}\text{ mol OH}^- \times \frac{1\text{ mol H}_2\text{X}}{2\text{ mol OH}^-} = 1.378 \times 10^{-3}\text{ mol}$$

$$\text{MM}_{H_2X} = \frac{m_{H_2X}}{n_{H_2X}} = \frac{0.124\text{ g}}{1.378 \times 10^{-3}\text{ mol}} = 90.0\text{ g/mol}$$

Reality Check In part (c), note that the amount of water added to the solid H_2X is irrelevant to the solution of the problem.

CHEMISTRY The Human Side

For reasons that are by no means obvious, Sweden produced a disproportionate number of outstanding chemists in the eighteenth and nineteenth centuries. Jöns Jakob Berzelius (1779–1848) determined with amazing accuracy the atomic masses of virtually all the elements known in his time. In his spare time, he invented such modern laboratory tools as the beaker, the flask, the pipet, and the ringstand.

Svante Arrhenius, like Berzelius, was born in Sweden and spent his entire professional career there. According to Arrhenius, the concept of strong and weak acids and bases came to him on May 13, 1883, when he was 24 years old. He added, "I could not sleep that night until I had worked through the entire problem."

Photo provided courtesy of the Nobel Foundation

Svante August Arrhenius
(1859–1927)

Almost exactly one year later, Arrhenius submitted his Ph.D. thesis at the University of Uppsala. He proposed that salts, strong acids, and strong bases are completely ionized in dilute water solution. Today, it seems quite reasonable that solutions of NaCl, HCl, and NaOH contain, respectively, Na^+ and Cl^- ions, H^+ and Cl^- ions, and Na^+ and OH^- ions. It did not seem nearly so obvious to the chemistry faculty at Uppsala in 1884. Arrhenius's dissertation received the lowest passing grade "approved not without praise."

Arrhenius sent copies of his Ph.D. thesis to several well-known chemists in Europe and America. Most ignored his ideas; a few were openly hostile. A pair of young chemists gave positive responses: Jacobus van't Hoff (1852–1911) (age 32) at Amsterdam (Holland) and Wilhelm Ostwald (1853–1932) (also 32) at Riga (Latvia). For some years, these three young men were referred to, somewhat disparagingly, as "ionists" or "ionians." As time passed, the situation changed. The first Nobel Prize in chemistry was awarded to van't Hoff in 1901. Two years later, in 1903, Arrhenius became a Nobel laureate; Ostwald followed in 1909.

Among other contributions of Arrhenius, the most important were probably in chemical kinetics (Chapter 11). In 1889 he derived the relation for the temperature dependence of reaction rate. In quite a different area in 1896 Arrhenius published an article, "On the Influence of Carbon Dioxide in the Air on the Temperature of the Ground." He presented the basic idea of the greenhouse effect, discussed in Chapter 17.

In his later years, Arrhenius turned his attention to popularizing chemistry. He wrote several different textbooks that were well received. In 1925, under pressure from his publisher to submit a manuscript, Arrhenius started getting up at 4 A.M. to write. As might be expected, rising at such an early hour had an adverse effect on his health. Arrhenius suffered a physical breakdown in 1925, from which he never really recovered, dying two years later.

Publishers are like that.

Charles D. Winters

Figure 4.8
Redox reaction of zinc with a strong acid.
The zinc atoms are oxidized to Zn^{2+} ions in solution; the H^+ ions are reduced to H_2 molecules.

4.4 OXIDATION-REDUCTION REACTIONS

Another common type of reaction in aqueous solution involves a transfer of electrons between two species. Such a reaction is called an oxidation-reduction or **redox reaction.** Many familiar reactions fit into this category, including the reaction of metals with acid.

In a redox reaction, one species *loses* (i.e., donates) electrons and is said to be *oxidized.* The other species, which *gains* (or receives) electrons, is *reduced.* To illustrate, consider the redox reaction that takes place when zinc pellets are added to hydrochloric acid (Figure 4.8). The net ionic equation for the reaction is

$$Zn(s) + 2H^+(aq) \longrightarrow Zn^{2+}(aq) + H_2(g)$$

This equation can be split into two half-equations, one of oxidation and the other of reduction. Zinc atoms are oxidized to Zn^{2+} ions by losing electrons. The oxidation half-equation is

$$\textit{oxidation:} \quad Zn(s) \longrightarrow Zn^{2+}(aq) + 2e^-$$

At the same time, H^+ ions are reduced to H_2 molecules by gaining electrons; the reduction half-equation is

$$\textit{reduction:} \quad 2H^+(aq) + 2e^- \longrightarrow H_2(g)$$

From this example, it should be clear that—

- ***oxidation and reduction occur together*** in the same reaction; you can't have one without the other.
- ***there is no net change in the number of electrons in a redox reaction.*** Those given off in the oxidation half-reaction are taken on by another species in the reduction half-reaction.

CENGAGENOW™
Click Coached Problems for a self-study module on **redox reactions.**

The two species that exchange electrons in a redox reaction are given special names. The ion or molecule that accepts electrons is called the **oxidizing agent;** by accepting electrons it brings about the oxidation of another species. Conversely, the species that donates electrons is called the **reducing agent;** when reaction occurs it reduces the other species.

The oxidizing agent is reduced; the reducing agent is oxidized.

To illustrate these concepts consider the reaction

$$Zn(s) + 2H^+(aq) \longrightarrow Zn^{2+}(aq) + H_2(g)$$

The H^+ ion is the oxidizing agent; it brings about the oxidation of zinc. By the same token, zinc acts as a reducing agent; it furnishes the electrons required to reduce H^+ ions.

Metallic elements taking part in redox reactions, such as zinc in the reaction above, commonly act as reducing agents; they are oxidized to cations such as Zn^{2+}. Other reducing agents include hydrogen gas, which can be oxidized to H^+ ions:

$$H_2(g) \longrightarrow 2H^+(aq) + 2e^-$$

and a few cations such as Fe^{2+} that can be oxidized to a higher state:

$$Fe^{2+}(aq) \longrightarrow Fe^{3+}(aq) + e^-$$

Nonmetallic elements frequently act as oxidizing agents, being reduced to the corresponding anions:

$$Cl_2(g) + 2e^- \longrightarrow 2Cl^-(aq)$$
$$S(s) + 2e^- \longrightarrow S^{2-}(aq)$$

In earlier sections of this chapter, we showed how to write and balance equations for precipitation reactions (Section 4.2) and acid-base reactions (Section 4.3). In this section we will concentrate on balancing redox equations, given the identity of reactants and products. To do that, it is convenient to introduce a new concept, oxidation number.

Oxidation Number

The concept of **oxidation number** is used to simplify the electron bookkeeping in redox reactions. For a monatomic ion (e.g., Na^+, S^{2-}), the oxidation number is, quite simply, the charge of the ion (+1, −2). In a molecule or polyatomic ion, the oxidation number of an element is a "pseudo-charge" obtained in a rather arbitrary way, assigning bonding electrons to the atom with the greater attraction for electrons.

Oxidation numbers are calculated, not determined experimentally.

In practice, oxidation numbers in all kinds of species are assigned according to a set of four arbitrary rules:

1. ***The oxidation number of an element in an elementary substance is 0.*** For example, the oxidation number of chlorine in Cl_2 or of phosphorus in P_4 is 0.
2. ***The oxidation number of an element in a monatomic ion is equal to the charge of that ion.*** In the ionic compound NaCl, sodium has an oxidation number of +1, chlorine an oxidation number of −1. The oxidation numbers of aluminum and oxygen in Al_2O_3 (Al^{3+}, O^{2-} ions) are +3 and −2, respectively.
3. ***Certain elements have the same oxidation number in all or almost all their compounds.*** The Group 1 metals always exist as +1 ions in their compounds and hence are assigned an oxidation number of +1. By the same token, Group 2 elements always have oxidation numbers of +2 in their compounds. Fluorine always has an oxidation number of −1.

Oxygen is ordinarily assigned an oxidation number of −2 in its compounds. (An exception arises in compounds containing the peroxide ion, O_2^{2-}, where the oxidation number of oxygen is −1.)

Charles D. Winters

Rusting and oxidation number. As iron rusts, its oxidation number changes from 0 in Fe(*s*) to +3 in Fe^{3+}.

Hydrogen in its compounds ordinarily has an oxidation number of +1. (The major exception is in metal hydrides such as NaH and CaH_2, where hydrogen is present as the H^- ion and hence is assigned an oxidation number of −1.)

4. *The sum of the oxidation numbers in a neutral species is 0; in a polyatomic ion, it is equal to the charge of that ion.* The application of this very useful principle is illustrated in Example 4.8.

CENGAGENOW™
Click Coached Problems for a self-study module on **assigning oxidation numbers.**

Example 4.8 What is the oxidation number of phosphorus in sodium phosphite, Na_3PO_3? In the dihydrogen phosphate ion?

Strategy First look for elements whose oxidation number is always or almost always the same (rule 3). Then solve for the oxidation number of phosphorus, applying rule 4.

SOLUTION In Na_3PO_3, the oxidation numbers of Na and O are +1 and −2, respectively. Since this compound, like all others, is neutral, the sum of the oxidation numbers must be zero. Letting x be the oxidation number of phosphorus then,

$$0 = 3(+1) + x + 3(-2) \qquad x = \text{oxidation number of P} = +3$$

In the $H_2PO_4^-$ ion, hydrogen and oxygen have oxidation numbers of +1 and −2, respectively. The ion has a charge of −1, so the sum of the oxidation numbers must be −1 (rule 4). Letting y be the oxidation number of phosphorus,

$$-1 = y + 2(+1) + 4(-2) \qquad y = \text{oxidation number of P} = +5$$

What is the oxidation number of phosphorus in PH_3? H_3PO_3?

The concept of oxidation number leads directly to a working definition of the terms oxidation and reduction. **Oxidation** is defined as ***an increase in oxidation number and* reduction *as a decrease in oxidation number.*** Consider once again the reaction of zinc with a strong acid:

$$Zn(s) + 2H^+(aq) \longrightarrow Zn^{2+}(aq) + H_2(g)$$

Zn is oxidized (oxid. no.: 0 ⟶ +2)
H^+ is reduced (oxid. no.: +1 ⟶ 0)

These definitions are of course compatible with the interpretation of oxidation and reduction in terms of loss and gain of electrons. An element that loses electrons must increase in oxidation number. The gain of electrons always results in a decrease in oxidation number.

An easy way to recognize a redox equation is to note changes in oxidation number of two different elements. The net ionic equation

$$2Al(s) + 3Cu^{2+}(aq) \longrightarrow 2Al^{3+}(aq) + 3Cu(s)$$

must represent a redox reaction because aluminum increases in oxidation number, from 0 to +3, and copper decreases from +2 to 0. In contrast, the reaction

$$CO_3^{2-}(aq) + 2H^+(aq) \longrightarrow CO_2(g) + H_2O$$

is not of the redox type because each element has the same oxidation number in both reactants and products: O = −2, H = +1, C = +4.

Balancing Half-Equations (Oxidation or Reduction)

Before you can balance an overall redox equation, you have to be able to balance two **half-equations,** one for oxidation (electron loss) and one for reduction (electron gain). Sometimes that's easy. Given the oxidation half-equation

$$Fe^{2+}(aq) \longrightarrow Fe^{3+}(aq) \qquad \text{(oxid. no. Fe: +2} \longrightarrow \text{+3)}$$

it is clear that mass and charge balance can be achieved by adding an electron to the right:

$$Fe^{2+}(aq) \longrightarrow Fe^{3+}(aq) + e^-$$

In another case, this time a reduction half-equation,

$$Cl_2(g) \longrightarrow Cl^-(aq) \qquad \text{(oxid. no. Cl: } 0 \longrightarrow -1)$$

mass balance is obtained by writing a coefficient of 2 for Cl^-; charge is then balanced by adding two electrons to the left. The balanced half-equation is

$$Cl_2(g) + 2e^- \longrightarrow 2Cl^-(aq)$$

(Throughout this discussion we will show balanced oxidation half-equations in yellow, balanced reduction half-equations in green.)

Sometimes, though, it is by no means obvious how a given half-equation is to be balanced. This commonly happens when elements other than those being oxidized or reduced take part in the reaction. Most often, these elements are oxygen (oxid. no. = −2) and hydrogen (oxid. no. = +1). Consider, for example, the half-equation for the reduction of the permanganate ion,

$$MnO_4^-(aq) \longrightarrow Mn^{2+}(aq) \qquad \text{(oxid. no. Mn: } +7 \longrightarrow +2)$$

or the oxidation of chromium(III) hydroxide,

$$Cr(OH)_3(s) \longrightarrow CrO_4^{2-}(aq) \qquad \text{(oxid. no. Cr: } +3 \longrightarrow +6)$$

To balance half-equations such as these, proceed as follows:

It's important to carry out these steps in the order indicated.

(a) ***Balance the atoms of the element being oxidized or reduced.***
(b) ***Balance oxidation number by adding electrons.*** For a reduction half-equation, add the appropriate number of electrons to the left; for an oxidation half-equation, add electrons to the right.
(c) ***Balance charge by adding H^+ ions in acidic solution, OH^- ions in basic solution.***
(d) ***Balance hydrogen by adding H_2O molecules.***
(e) ***Check to make sure that oxygen is balanced.*** If it is, the half-equation is almost certainly balanced correctly with respect to both mass and charge.

You have to assign oxidation numbers to decide how many electrons to use.

Example 4.9 shows how these rules are applied to balance half-equations.

Example 4.9

Balance the following half-equations:

(1) $MnO_4^-(aq) \longrightarrow Mn^{2+}(aq)$ (acidic solution)
(2) $Cr(OH)_3(s) \longrightarrow CrO_4^{2-}(aq)$ (basic solution)

Strategy Follow the rules outlined above, step by step in the proper order, and see what happens.

SOLUTION

(1) (a) Because there is one atom of Mn on both sides, no adjustment is required.

$$MnO_4^-(aq) \longrightarrow Mn^{2+}(aq)$$

(b) Because manganese is reduced from an oxidation number of +7 to +2, five electrons must be added to the left.

$$MnO_4^-(aq) + 5e^- \longrightarrow Mn^{2+}(aq)$$

(c) There is a total charge of −6 on the left versus +2 on the right. To balance, add eight H^+ to the left to give a charge of +2 on both sides.

$$MnO_4^-(aq) + 8H^+(aq) + 5e^- \longrightarrow Mn^{2+}(aq)$$

(d) To balance the eight H^+ ions on the left, add four H_2O molecules to the right.

$$MnO_4^-(aq) + 8H^+(aq) + 5e^- \longrightarrow Mn^{2+}(aq) + 4H_2O$$

(e) Note that there are the same number of oxygen atoms, four, on both sides, as there should be. The equation shown in green is the correctly balanced reduction half-equation.

(2) (a) Again, there is one chromium atom on both sides.

$$Cr(OH)_3(s) \longrightarrow CrO_4^{2-}(aq)$$

(b) Because the oxidation number of chromium increases from +3 to +6, add three electrons to the right.

$$Cr(OH)_3(s) \longrightarrow CrO_4^{2-}(aq) + 3e^-$$

(c) There is a charge of zero on the left, −5 on the right. To balance charge, add five OH^- ions to the left.

$$Cr(OH)_3(s) + 5OH^-(aq) \longrightarrow CrO_4^{2-}(aq) + 3e^-$$

(d) There are eight hydrogens on the left, none on the right. Add four H_2O molecules to the right.

$$Cr(OH)_3(s) + 5OH^-(aq) \longrightarrow CrO_4^{2-}(aq) + 4H_2O + 3e^-$$

(e) There are eight oxygen atoms on both sides; the oxidation half-equation is properly balanced.

Balancing Redox Equations

The process used to balance an overall redox equation is relatively straightforward, provided you know how to balance half-equations. Follow a systematic, four-step procedure:

(1) ***Split the equation into two half-equations,*** one for reduction, the other for oxidation.
(2) ***Balance one of the half-equations*** with respect to both atoms and charge as described above (steps a through e).
(3) ***Balance the other half-equation.***
(4) ***Combine the two half-equations in such a way as to eliminate electrons.***

Suppose, for example, the two balanced half-equations are

$$A(s) \longrightarrow A^{2+}(aq) + 2e^-$$
$$B^{3+}(aq) + 3e^- \longrightarrow B(s)$$

Multiplying the first half-equation by 3, the second by 2, and adding gives

$$3A(s) + 2B^{3+}(aq) \longrightarrow 3A^{2+}(aq) + 2B(s)$$

The electrons, six on both sides, cancel.

Example 4.10 Balance the following redox equations.

(a) $Fe^{2+}(aq) + MnO_4^-(aq) \longrightarrow Fe^{3+}(aq) + Mn^{2+}(aq)$ (acidic solution)
(b) $Cl_2(g) + Cr(OH)_3(s) \longrightarrow Cl^-(aq) + CrO_4^{2-}(aq)$ (basic solution)

Strategy Follow the four-step procedure described above. Actually, if you look carefully at the text preceding this example, you'll find that all the half-equations have already been balanced! The color coding should help you find them.

SOLUTION

(a) (1) oxidation: $Fe^{2+}(aq) \longrightarrow Fe^{3+}(aq)$
reduction: $MnO_4^-(aq) \longrightarrow Mn^{2+}(aq)$
(2), (3) The balanced half-equations, as obtained previously, are

$$Fe^{2+}(aq) \longrightarrow Fe^{3+}(aq) + e^-$$
$$MnO_4^-(aq) + 8H^+(aq) + 5e^- \longrightarrow Mn^{2+}(aq) + 4H_2O$$

(4) To eliminate electrons, multiply the oxidation half-equation by 5 and add to the reduction half-equation.

$$5[Fe^{2+}(aq) \longrightarrow Fe^{3+}(aq) + e^-]$$
$$MnO_4^-(aq) + 8H^+(aq) + 5e^- \longrightarrow Mn^{2+}(aq) + 4H_2O$$
$$\overline{5Fe^{2+}(aq) + MnO_4^-(aq) + 8H^+(aq) \longrightarrow 5Fe^{3+}(aq) + Mn^{2+}(aq) + 4H_2O}$$

Multiply the half-equations by coefficients (1,2, . . .) so that there are equal numbers of electrons on both sides.

(b) (1) reduction: $Cl_2(g) \longrightarrow Cl^-(aq)$
oxidation: $Cr(OH)_3(s) \longrightarrow CrO_4^{2-}(aq)$

(2), (3) Earlier, the balanced half-equations were found to be

$$Cl_2(g) + 2e^- \longrightarrow 2Cl^-(aq)$$
$$Cr(OH)_3(s) + 5OH^-(aq) \longrightarrow CrO_4^{2-}(aq) + 4H_2O + 3e^-$$

(4) Multiply the reduction half-equation by 3, the oxidation half-equation by 2, then add. This will produce $6e^-$ on both sides, so they will cancel.

$$3[Cl_2(g) + 2e^- \longrightarrow 2Cl^-(aq)]$$
$$2[Cr(OH)_3(s) + 5OH^-(aq) \longrightarrow CrO_4^{2-}(aq) + 4H_2O + 3e^-]$$
$$\overline{3Cl_2(g) + 2Cr(OH)_3(s) + 10OH^-(aq) \longrightarrow 6Cl^-(aq) + 2CrO_4^{2-}(aq) + 8H_2O}$$

Reality Check It's a good idea to check mass and charge balance in the final equation. In part (b), for example,

	Cl Atoms	Cr Atoms	O Atoms	H Atoms	Charge
Left	6	2	16	16	−10
Right	6	2	16	16	−10

Stoichiometric calculations for redox reactions in water solution are carried out in much the same way as those for precipitation reactions (Example 4.5) or acid-base reactions (Example 4.7).

Example 4.11

As you found in Example 4.10, the balanced equation for the reaction between MnO_4^- and Fe^{2+} in acidic solution is

$$MnO_4^-(aq) + 8H^+(aq) + 5Fe^{2+}(aq) \longrightarrow 5Fe^{3+}(aq) + Mn^{2+}(aq) + 4H_2O$$

What volume of 0.684 *M* $KMnO_4$ solution is required to react completely with 27.50 mL of 0.250 *M* $Fe(NO_3)_2$ (Figure 4.9, p. 92)?

Strategy (1) Start by calculating the number of moles of Fe^{2+}. Then (2) use the coefficients of the balanced equation to find the number of moles of MnO_4^-. Finally, (3), use molarity as a conversion factor to find the volume of $KMnO_4$ solution.

SOLUTION

(1) $n_{Fe^{2+}} = 0.02750 \text{ L} \times \dfrac{0.250 \text{ mol Fe(NO}_3)_2}{1 \text{ L}} \times \dfrac{1 \text{ mol Fe}^{2+}}{1 \text{ mol Fe(NO}_3)_2}$

$= 6.88 \times 10^{-3} \text{ mol Fe}^{2+}$

(2) $n_{MnO_4^-} = 0.00688 \text{ mol Fe}^{2+} \times \dfrac{1 \text{ mol MnO}_4^-}{5 \text{ mol Fe}^{2+}} = 0.00138 \text{ mol MnO}_4^-$

(3) $n_{KMnO_4} = n_{MnO_4^-} = 1.38 \times 10^{-3} \text{ mol KMnO}_4$

$V = 1.38 \times 10^{-3} \text{ mol KMnO}_4 \times \dfrac{1 \text{ L}}{0.684 \text{ mol KMnO}_4} = 2.02 \times 10^{-3} \text{ L (2.02 mL)}$

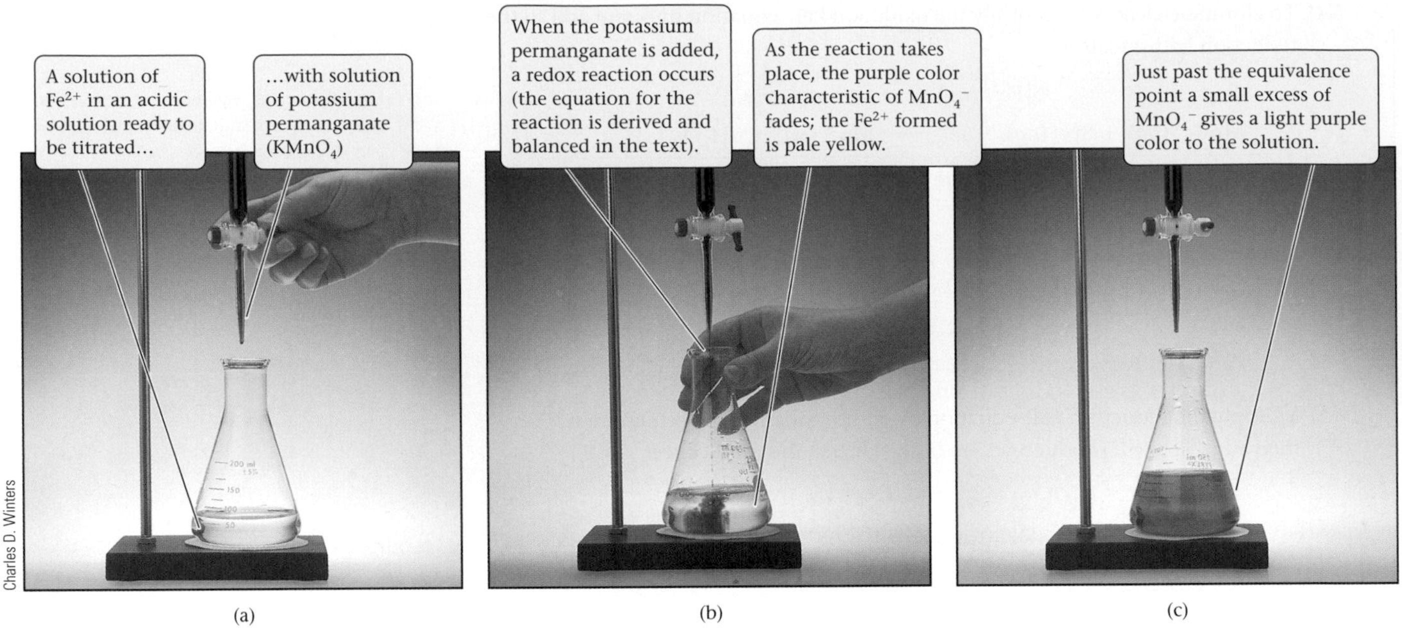

Figure 4.9
A redox titration.

CHEMISTRY Beyond the Classroom

Reversible Color Changes

Gregory Sotzing, University of Connecticut

Many compounds can change their color reversibly when subjected to some form of external stimulus. The phenomenon is called *chromism* and the materials are characterized as *chromogenic.* Photochromics (light stimulated) and thermochromics (temperature stimulated) are two of the most common chromogenic materials with practical applications. Optical lenses have photochromic film so they darken when exposed to sunlight. Thermochromics are used in the strips sold with alkaline batteries to test whether the battery is still usable.

Electrochromics are another form of chromogenic materials that undergo a color change when electrons are added or removed. Today, electrochromics are used in autodimming rearview mirrors to prevent headlights from blinding the driver, autoshading windows and skylights for privacy and energy conservation, and color changing transparent roofs for automobiles such as the Ferrari (Figure A) and other high-end vehicles.

Polymers, large molecules made up of smaller molecules in a repeating pattern, are used for many electrochromic materials. Conjugating polymers, which have alternating single and double bonds, are particularly suitable. Figure B shows the electrochemical oxidation of the conjugated polymer, polythiophene. Oxidation (in which electrons are removed) produces a semiconductive polymer. The neutral (unoxidized) polythiophene is red in color, whereas the semiconductive polythiophene (oxidized) is blue. In their neutral state, these polymers have a wavelength of maximum absorption in the visible region of the spectrum, which gives the polymer a specific color. When electrons are removed, "holes" are created, which act as charge carriers. These changes result in transition to a different color.

Different color transitions are obtained by simply changing the molecular structure of the polythiophene and then oxidizing or reducing it. Figure C, p. 93, shows the different colors obtained by taking the neutral form

Figure A
Revocromico color changing electrochromic rooftop on the Ferrari Superamerica.

(0), oxidizing it (+), reducing it (−), or reducing twice (− −).

The rigid chemical structure of a conjugated polymer helps in the movement of electrons. That stiff structure, however, has limited its use. They are like uncooked spaghetti and do not easily entangle themselves. Polymer chain entanglements are necessary to achieve high viscosities, which are required to create fibers out of these polymers.

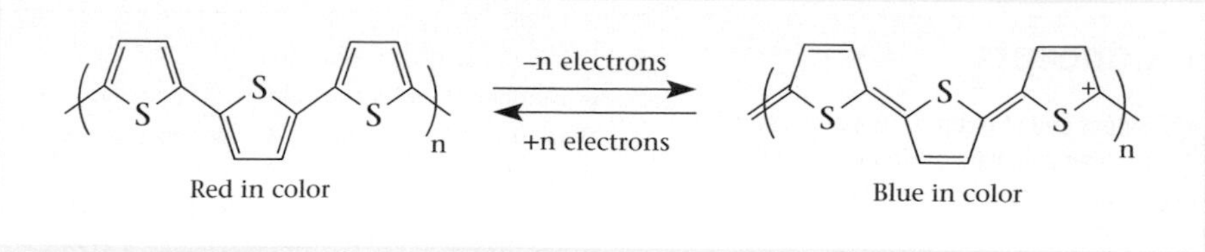

Figure B

Neutral polythiophene (left) is red in color and becomes blue and semiconductive when electrons are removed. The process can be reversed by adding electrons to the blue polymer to make it transition back to red.

Recent research in my group has devised a method to create long (about 3 feet) fibers. The fibers first appear white. When they are dipped into an oxidizing agent (to remove electrons), the fibers become conductive and turn a deep blue. When an electrical charge is applied (to add electrons), the color changes to bright orange.

There can be many uses for these fibers. Weaving them into fabric, for example, could create color-changing camouflage uniforms for soldiers. The colors could change to desert browns, or, when stimulated by a battery-produced electrical charge, the uniforms could have colors that resemble forest and jungle greens. Someday, you may have t-shirts that can change colors with the flip of a switch.

For more information on clothing incorporating these fibers, see *NewScientist* 07 April 2006 issue No. 2546.

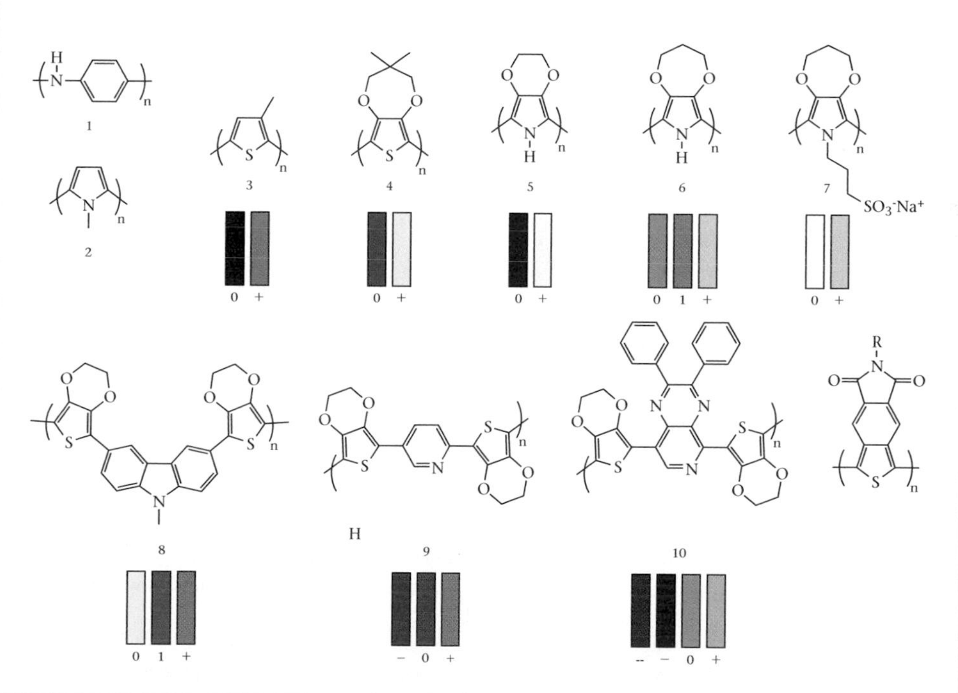

Figure C

Structures of different conjugated polymers including various thiophenes (3,4,8,9,10,11) and pyrroles (2,5,6,7) that show color variation. (From A. A. Argun, P. Aubert, B. Thompson, I. Schwendeman, C. L. Gaupp, J. Hwang, N. J. Pinto, D. B. Tanner, A. G. MacDiarmid, J. R. Reynolds "Multielectrochromism in Polymers: Structures and Devices" *Chem. Mater.* **2004,** *16,* 4401–4412).

Chapter Highlights

Key Concepts

Select end of chapter Questions and Problems may be assigned in OWL and are cross-referenced in the Key Concepts list.

CENGAGENOW™

Sign in at **academic.cengage.com/now** to:

- Check your readiness for an exam by taking the Pre-Test and exploring the self-study modules recommended in your Personalized Study plan.
- For quick review, download Go Chemistry mini-lecture flashcard modules (or purchase them at **www.ichapters.com**)

1. Relate molarity of a solute to
   - number of moles and volume.
   (Example 4.1; Problems 1, 2) ■ Questions and Problems assignable in OWL: 5, 10
   - molarities of ions.
   (Example 4.2; Problems 3, 4) ■ 3
2. Apply the precipitation diagram (Figure 4.3) to
   - predict precipitation reactions.
   (Example 4.3; Problems 11–20) ■ 14
   - write net ionic equations for precipitation reactions.
   (Examples 4.4, 4.5; Problems 15–20) ■ 17
3. Carry out stoichiometric calculations for reactions in solution.
   (Examples 4.5, 4.7, 4.11; Problems 21–26, 37–48, 69–80) ■ 21, 23, 25, 37, 42, 92, 95
4. With the aid of Tables 4.1 and 4.2, write net ionic equations for acid-base reactions.
   (Example 4.6; Problems 29–36) ■ 27, 33
5. Determine oxidation numbers.
   (Example 4.8; Problems 49–52) ■ 52, 53
6. Balance redox half-equations and overall equations.
   (Examples 4.9, 4.10; Problems 57–68) ■ 55, 63, 65

Key Equations

Molarity $M = \frac{\text{moles of solute}}{\text{liters of solution}}$ (Section 4.1)

Key Terms

acid	half-equation	precipitate
—strong	molarity	redox reaction
—weak	net ionic equation	reducing agent
base	neutralization	reduction
—strong	oxidation	titration
—weak	oxidation number	
equivalence point	oxidizing agent	

Summary Problem

An aqueous solution of hydrogen chloride is called hydrochloric acid. It is widely used for a host of industrial purposes. It reacts with a wide variety of compounds.

(a) Write net ionic equations for the reaction between aqueous solutions of hydrochloric acid with
  (1) an aqueous solution of strontium hydroxide.
  (2) an aqueous solution of silver nitrate.
  (3) an aqueous solution of methylamine (CH_3NH_2).
  (4) iron(II) hydroxide. (The chloride ions react with iron(II) hydroxide to form metallic iron. Chlorate ions are also formed.)

(b) How would you prepare 225.0 mL of 1.33 *M* HCl from a 6.00 *M* "stock solution"?

(c) When 25.00 mL of 0.695 *M* HCl reacts with an excess of silver nitrate, a precipitate forms. How many grams of precipitate can be theoretically obtained?

(d) What volume of 0.2500 *M* strontium hydroxide is required to completely react with 75.00 mL of 0.07942 *M* HCl?

(e) When 37.5 mL of 0.439 *M* HCl reacts with 22.0 mL of 0.573 *M* ammonia, ammonium ions are formed. What is the concentration of each species in solution after reaction is complete? (Assume that volumes are additive.)

(f) An alloy containing aluminum is analyzed. All the aluminum reacts with 212 mL of 0.493 *M* HCl in the 2.500-g sample of alloy. Calculate the mass percent of aluminum in the alloy. (Assume that the only component of the alloy that reacts with HCl is aluminum, and that the products of reaction are hydrogen gas and aluminum ions.)

Answers

(a) (1) $H^+(aq) + OH^-(aq) \longrightarrow H_2O$
(2) $Cl^-(aq) + Ag^+(aq) \longrightarrow AgCl(s)$
(3) $CH_3NH_2(aq) + H^+(aq) \longrightarrow CH_3NH_3^+(aq)$
(4) $3Fe(OH)_2(s) + Cl^-(aq) \longrightarrow 3Fe(s) + ClO_3^-(aq) + 3H_2O$

(b) Take 49.9 mL of stock solution and add enough water to form 225.0 mL.

(c) 2.49

(d) 11.91 mL

(e) NH_3: 0; $H^+ = 0.0655\ M$; $Cl^- = 0.277\ M$; $NH_4^+ = 0.212\ M$

(f) 37.6%

Questions and Problems

Blue-numbered questions have answers in Appendix 6 and fully-worked solutions in the *Student Solutions Manual.*

■ denotes questions assignable in OWL.

WEB indicates that the solution is available on this book's companion website.

Molarity

1. Household ammonia used for cleaning contains about 10 g (two significant figures) of NH_3 in 100 mL (two significant figures) of solution. What is the molarity of the NH_3 in solution?

2. The average adult has about 16 g of sodium ions in her blood. Assuming a total blood volume of 5.0 L, what is the molarity of Na^+ ions in blood?

3. ■ What is the molarity of each ion present in aqueous solutions prepared by dissolving 20.00 g of the following compounds in water to make 4.50 L of solution?

(a) cobalt(III) chloride
(b) nickel(III) sulfate
(c) sodium permanganate
(d) iron(II) bromide

4. **WEB** What is the molarity of each ion present in aqueous solutions prepared by dissolving 15.0 g of the following compounds in water to make 655 mL of solution?

(a) scandium(III) iodide
(b) sodium carbonate
(c) magnesium phosphate
(d) potassium oxide

5. ■ How would you prepare from the solid and pure water

(a) 0.400 L of 0.155 *M* $Sr(OH)_2$?
(b) 1.75 L of 0.333 *M* $(NH_4)_2CO_3$?

6. Starting with the solid and adding water, how would you prepare 2.00 L of 0.685 *M*

(a) $Ni(NO_3)_2$? (b) $CuCl_2$? (c) $C_6H_8O_6$ (vitamin C)?

7. You are asked to prepare a 0.8500 *M* solution of aluminum nitrate. You find that you have only 50.00 g of the solid.

(a) What is the maximum volume of solution that you can prepare?
(b) How many milliliters of this prepared solution are required to furnish 0.5000 mol of aluminum nitrate to a reaction?
(c) If 2.500 L of the prepared solution is required, how much more aluminum nitrate would you need?
(d) Fifty milliliters of a 0.450 *M* solution of aluminum nitrate is needed. How would you prepare the required solution from the solution prepared in (a)?

8. A reagent bottle is labeled 0.450 *M* K_2CO_3.

(a) How many moles of K_2CO_3 are present in 45.6 mL of this solution?
(b) How many milliliters of this solution are required to furnish 0.800 mol of K_2CO_3?
(c) Assuming no volume change, how many grams of K_2CO_3 do you need to add to 2.00 L of this solution to obtain a 1.000 *M* solution of K_2CO_3?
(d) If 50.0 mL of this solution is added to enough water to make 125 mL of solution, what is the molarity of the diluted solution?

9. A student combines two solutions of KOH and determines the molarity of the resulting solution. He records the following data:

Solution I:	30.00 mL of 0.125 *M* KOH
Solution II:	40.00 mL of KOH
Solution I + Solution II:	70.00 mL of 0.203 *M* KOH

What is the molarity of KOH in Solution II?

10. ■ Twenty-five mL of a 0.388 *M* solution of Na_2SO_4 is mixed with 35.3 mL of 0.229 *M* Na_2SO_4. What is the molarity of the resulting solution? Assume that the volumes are additive.

Precipitation Reactions

11. Write the formulas of the following compounds and decide which are soluble in water.

(a) sodium sulfate (b) iron(III) nitrate
(c) silver chloride (d) chromium(III) hydroxide

12. Follow the instructions for Question 11 for the following compounds:

(a) barium chloride
(b) magnesium hydroxide
(c) chromium(III) carbonate
(d) potassium phosphate

13. Describe how you would prepare

(a) cadmium(II) carbonate from a solution of cadmium(II) nitrate.
(b) copper(II) hydroxide from a solution of sodium hydroxide.
(c) magnesium carbonate from a solution of magnesium chloride.

14. ■ Name the reagent, if any, that you would add to a solution of cobalt(III) chloride to precipitate

(a) cobalt(III) phosphate.
(b) cobalt(III) carbonate.
(c) cobalt(III) hydroxide.

15. Write net ionic equations for the formation of

(a) a precipitate when solutions of magnesium nitrate and potassium hydroxide are mixed.
(b) two different precipitates when solutions of silver(I) sulfate and barium chloride are mixed.

16. Write net ionic equations to explain the formation of

(a) a white precipitate when solutions of calcium sulfate and sodium carbonate are mixed.
(b) two different precipitates formed when solutions of iron(III) sulfate and barium hydroxide are mixed.

17. ■ Decide whether a precipitate will form when the following solutions are mixed. If a precipitate forms, write a net ionic equation for the reaction.

(a) potassium nitrate and magnesium sulfate
(b) silver nitrate and potassium carbonate
(c) ammonium carbonate and cobalt(III) chloride
(d) sodium phosphate and barium hydroxide
(e) barium nitrate and potassium hydroxide

18. **WEB** Follow the directions of Question 17 for solutions of the following.

(a) copper(II) sulfate and sodium chloride
(b) manganese(II) nitrate and sodium hydroxide
(c) silver nitrate and hydrochloric acid
(d) cobalt(II) sulfate and barium hydroxide
(e) ammonium carbonate and potassium hydroxide

19. Write a net ionic equation for any precipitation reaction that occurs when 0.1 *M* solutions of the following are mixed.

(a) zinc nitrate and nickel(II) chloride
(b) potassium phosphate and calcium nitrate
(c) sodium hydroxide and zinc nitrate
(d) iron(III) nitrate and barium hydroxide

20. Follow the directions for Question 19 for the following pairs of solutions.

(a) sodium phosphate and barium chloride
(b) zinc sulfate and potassium hydroxide
(c) ammonium sulfate and sodium chloride
(d) cobalt(III) nitrate and sodium phosphate

21. ■ What volume of 0.2500 *M* cobalt(III) sulfate is required to react completely with

(a) 25.00 mL of 0.0315 *M* calcium hydroxide?
(b) 5.00 g of sodium carbonate?
(c) 12.50 mL of 0.1249 *M* potassium phosphate?

22. What volume of 0.4163 *M* barium chloride will react completely with

(a) 12.45 mL of 1.732 *M* sulfuric acid?
(b) 15.00 g of ammonium phosphate?
(c) 35.15 mL of 1.28 *M* potassium carbonate?

23. ■ A 50.00-mL sample of 0.0250 *M* silver nitrate is mixed with 0.0400 *M* chromium(III) chloride.

(a) What is the minimum volume of chromium(III) chloride required to completely precipitate silver chloride?
(b) How many grams of silver chloride are produced from (a)?

24. Aluminum ions react with carbonate ions to form an insoluble compound, aluminum carbonate.

(a) Write the net ionic equation for this reaction.
(b) What is the molarity of a solution of aluminum chloride if 30.0 mL is required to react with 35.5 mL of 0.137 *M* sodium carbonate?
(c) How many grams of aluminum carbonate are formed in (b)?

25. ■ When Na_3PO_4 and $Ca(NO_3)_2$ are combined, the following reaction occurs:

$$2PO_4^{3-}(aq) + 3Ca^{2+}(aq) \longrightarrow Ca_3(PO_4)_2(s)$$

How many grams of $Ca_3(PO_4)_2(s)$ (MM = 310.18 g/mol) are obtained when 15.00 mL of 0.1386 *M* Na_3PO_4 are mixed with 20.00 mL of 0.2118 *M* $Ca(NO_3)_2$?

26. When solutions of aluminum sulfate and sodium hydroxide are mixed, a white gelatinous precipitate forms.

(a) Write a balanced net ionic equation for the reaction.
(b) What is the mass of the precipitate when 2.76 g of aluminum sulfate in 125 mL of solution is combined with 85.0 mL of 0.2500 *M* NaOH?
(c) What is the molarity of the ion in excess? (Ignore spectator ions and assume that volumes are additive.)

Acid-Base Reactions

27. ■ Classify the following compounds as acids or bases, weak or strong.

(a) perchloric acid (b) cesium hydroxide
(c) carbonic acid, H_2CO_3 (d) ethylamine, $C_2H_5NH_2$

28. Follow the directions of Question 27 for

(a) sulfurous acid (b) ammonia
(c) barium hydroxide (d) hydriodic acid

29. For an acid-base reaction, what is the reacting species, that is, the ion or molecule that appears in the chemical equation, in the following acids?

(a) perchloric acid (b) hydriodic acid
(c) nitrous acid (d) nitric acid
(e) lactic acid ($HC_3H_5O_3$)

30. Follow the directions of Problem 29 for the following acids.

(a) sulfurous acid (b) chlorous acid
(c) perchloric acid (d) sulfuric acid
(e) formic acid ($HCHO_2$)

31. For an acid-base reaction, what is the reacting species (the ion or molecule that appears in the chemical equation) in the following bases?

(a) barium hydroxide (b) trimethylamine $(CH_3)_3N$
(c) aniline, $C_6H_5NH_2$ (d) sodium hydroxide

32. Follow the directions of Problem 31 for the following bases.

(a) indol, C_8H_6NH (b) potassium hydroxide
(c) aqueous ammonia (d) calcium hydroxide

33. ■ Write a balanced net ionic equation for each of the following acid-base reactions in water.

(a) nitrous acid and barium hydroxide
(b) potassium hydroxide and hydrofluoric acid
(c) aniline ($C_6H_5NH_2$) and perchloric acid

34. Write a balanced net ionic equation for each of the following acid-base reactions in water.

(a) acetic acid ($HC_2H_3O_2$) with strontium hydroxide
(b) diethylamine, $(C_2H_5)_2NH$, with sulfuric acid
(c) aqueous hydrogen cyanide (HCN) with sodium hydroxide

■ in OWL Blue-numbered questions answered in Appendix 6 **WEB** Solution is available on companion website

35. Consider the following generic equation:

$$H^+(aq) + B^-(aq) \longrightarrow HB(aq)$$

For which of the following pairs would this be the correct prototype equation for the acid-base reaction in solution? If it is not correct, write the proper equation for the acid-base reaction between the pair.

(a) nitric acid and calcium hydroxide
(b) hydrochloric acid and CH_3NH_2
(c) hydrobromic acid and aqueous ammonia
(d) perchloric acid and barium hydroxide
(e) sodium hydroxide and nitrous acid

36. **WEB** Consider the following generic equation

$$OH^-(aq) + HB(aq) \longrightarrow B^-(aq) + H_2O$$

For which of the following pairs would this be the correct prototype equation for the acid-base reaction in solution? If it is not correct, write the proper equation for the acid-base reaction between the pair.

(a) hydrochloric acid and pyridine, C_5H_5N
(b) sulfuric acid and rubidium hydroxide
(c) potassium hydroxide and hydrofluoric acid
(d) ammonia and hydriodic acid
(e) strontium hydroxide and hydrocyanic acid

37. ■ What is the molarity of a solution of nitric acid if 0.216 g of barium hydroxide is required to neutralize 20.00 mL of nitric acid?

38. What volume of 0.285 *M* strontium hydroxide is required to neutralize 25.00 mL of 0.275 *M* hydrofluoric acid (HF)?

39. What is the volume of 1.222 *M* sodium hydroxide required to react with

(a) 32.5 mL of 0.569 *M* sulfurous acid? (One mole of sulfurous acid reacts with two moles of hydroxide ion.)
(b) 5.00 g of oxalic acid ($H_2C_2O_4$)? (One mole of oxalic acid reacts with two moles of hydroxide ion.)
(c) 15.0 g of concentrated acetic acid ($HC_2H_3O_2$) that is 88% by mass pure?

40. What is the volume of 0.885 *M* hydrochloric acid required to react with

(a) 25.00 mL of 0.288 *M* aqueous ammonia?
(b) 10.00 g of sodium hydroxide?
(c) 25.0 mL of a solution (d = 0.928 g/cm³) containing 10.0% by mass of methylamine (CH_3NH_2)?

41. Analysis shows that a sample of H_2X (MM = 100.0 g/mol) reacts completely with 330.0 mL of 0.2000 *M* KOH.

$$H_2X(aq) + 2OH^-(aq) \longrightarrow X^-(aq) + 2H_2O$$

What is the volume of the sample? (Density of H_2X = 1.200 g/mL.)

42. ■ Analysis of an unknown acid shows that 24.55 mL of 0.128 *M* NaOH are required to react completely with 0.566 g of the acid. The equation for the reaction is

$$HB(aq) + OH^-(aq) \longrightarrow H_2O + B^-(aq)$$

What is the molar mass of the acid?

43. A lead storage battery needs sulfuric acid to function. The recommended minimum concentration of sulfuric acid for maximum effectivity is about 4.8 *M*. A 10.0-mL sample of battery acid requires 66.52 mL of 1.325 *M* KOH for its complete neutralization. Does the concentration of battery acid satisfy the minimum requirement? (*Note:* Two H^+ ions are produced for every mole of H_2SO_4.)

44. For a product to be called "vinegar," it must contain at least 5.0% acetic acid, $HC_2H_3O_2$, by mass. A 10.00-g sample of a "raspberry vinegar" is titrated with 0.1250 *M* $Ba(OH)_2$ and required 37.50 mL for complete neutralization. Can the product be called a "vinegar"?

45. The percentage of sodium hydrogen carbonate, $NaHCO_3$, in a powder for stomach upsets is found by titrating with 0.275 *M* hydrochloric acid. If 15.5 mL of hydrochloric acid is required to react with 0.500 g of the sample, what is the percentage of sodium hydrogen carbonate in the sample? The balanced equation for the reaction that takes place is

$$NaHCO_3(s) + H^+(aq) \longrightarrow Na^+(aq) + CO_2(g) + H_2O$$

46. A capsule of vitamin C, a weak acid, is analyzed by titrating it with 0.425 *M* sodium hydroxide. It is found that 6.20 mL of base is required to react with a capsule weighing 0.628 g. What is the percentage of vitamin C ($C_6H_8O_6$) in the capsule? (One mole of vitamin C reacts with one mole of hydroxide ion.)

47. An artificial fruit beverage contains 12.0 g of tartaric acid, $H_2C_4H_4O_6$, to achieve tartness. It is titrated with a basic solution that has a density of 1.045 g/cm³ and contains 5.00 mass percent KOH. What volume of the basic solution is required? (One mole of tartaric acid reacts with two moles of hydroxide ion.)

48. Lactic acid, $C_3H_6O_3$, is the acid present in sour milk. A 0.100-g sample of pure lactic acid requires 12.95 mL of 0.0857 *M* sodium hydroxide for complete reaction. How many moles of hydroxide ion are required to neutralize one mole of lactic acid?

Oxidation-Reduction Reactions

49. Assign oxidation numbers to each element in

(a) nitrogen oxide
(b) ammonia
(c) potassium peroxide
(d) chlorate ion (ClO_3^-)

50. Assign oxidation numbers to each element in

(a) methane
(b) sulfurous acid
(c) sodium oxide
(d) the dihydrogen phosphate ion ($H_2PO_4^-$)

51. Assign oxidation numbers to each element in

(a) P_2O_5 (b) NH_3 (c) CO_3^{2-}
(d) $S_2O_3^{2-}$ (e) N_2H_4

52. ■ Assign oxidation numbers to each element in

(a) HIO_3 (b) $NaMnO_4$ (c) SnO_2
(d) NOF (e) NaO_2

53. ■ Classify each of the following half-reactions as oxidation or reduction.

(a) $O_2(g) \longrightarrow O^{2-}(aq)$
(b) $MnO_4^-(aq) \longrightarrow MnO_2(s)$
(c) $Cr_2O_7^{2-}(aq) \longrightarrow Cr^{3+}(aq)$
(d) $Cl^-(aq) \longrightarrow Cl_2(g)$

54. Classify each of the following half-reactions as oxidation or reduction.

(a) $TiO_2(s) \longrightarrow Ti^{3+}(aq)$
(b) $Zn^{2+}(aq) \longrightarrow Zn(s)$
(c) $NH_4^+(aq) \longrightarrow N_2(g)$
(d) $CH_3OH(aq) \longrightarrow CH_2O(aq)$

■ in OWL Blue-numbered questions answered in Appendix 6 **WEB** Solution is available on companion website

55. ■ Classify each of the following half-equations as oxidation or reduction and balance.

(a) (acidic) $Mn^{2+}(aq) \longrightarrow MnO_4^-(aq)$
(b) (basic) $CrO_4^{2-}(aq) \longrightarrow Cr^{3+}(aq)$
(c) (basic) $PbO_2(s) \longrightarrow Pb^{2+}(aq)$
(d) (acidic) $ClO_2^-(aq) \longrightarrow ClO^-(aq)$

56. WEB Classify each of the following half-equations as oxidation or reduction and balance.

(a) (basic) $ClO^-(aq) \longrightarrow Cl^-(aq)$
(b) (acidic) $NO_3^-(aq) \longrightarrow NO(g)$
(c) (basic) $Ni^{2+}(aq) \longrightarrow Ni_2O_3(s)$
(d) (acidic) $Mn^{2+}(aq) \longrightarrow MnO_2(s)$

57. Balance the half-equations in Question 53. Balance (a) and (b) in basic medium, (c) and (d) in acidic medium.

58. Balance the half-equations in Question 54. Balance (a) and (b) in acidic medium, (c) and (d) in basic medium.

59. For each unbalanced equation given below—

- write unbalanced half-reactions.
- identify the species oxidized and the species reduced.
- identify the oxidizing and reducing agents.

(a) $Ag(s) + NO_3^-(aq) \longrightarrow Ag^+(aq) + NO(g)$
(b) $CO_2(g) + H_2O(l) \longrightarrow C_2H_4(g) + O_2(g)$

60. Follow the directions of Question 59 for the following unbalanced equations.

(a) $H_2O_2(aq) + Ni^{2+}(aq) \longrightarrow Ni^{3+}(aq) + H_2O$
(b) $Cr_2O_7^{2-}(aq) + Sn^{2+}(aq) \longrightarrow Cr^{3+}(aq) + Sn^{4+}(aq)$

61. Balance the equations in Question 59 in base.

62. Balance the equations in Question 60 in base.

63. ■ Write balanced equations for the following reactions in acid solution.

(a) $Ni^{2+}(aq) + IO_4^-(aq) \longrightarrow Ni^{3+}(aq) + I^-(aq)$
(b) $O_2(g) + Br^-(aq) \longrightarrow H_2O + Br_2(l)$
(c) $Ca(s) + Cr_2O_7^{2-}(aq) \longrightarrow Ca^{2+}(aq) + Cr^{3+}(aq)$
(d) $IO_3^-(aq) + Mn^{2+}(aq) \longrightarrow I^-(aq) + MnO_2(s)$

64. Write balanced equations for the following reactions in acid solution.

(a) $P_4(s) + Cl^-(aq) \longrightarrow PH_3(g) + Cl_2(g)$
(b) $MnO_4^-(aq) + NO_2^-(aq) \longrightarrow Mn^{2+}(aq) + NO_3^-(aq)$
(c) $HBrO_3(aq) + Bi(s) \longrightarrow HBrO_2(aq) + Bi_2O_3(s)$
(d) $CrO_4^{2-}(aq) + SO_3^{2-}(aq) \longrightarrow Cr^{3+}(aq) + SO_4^{2-}(aq)$

65. ■ Write balanced equations for the following reactions in basic solution.

(a) $SO_2(g) + I_2(aq) \longrightarrow SO_3(g) + I^-(aq)$
(b) $Zn(s) + NO_3^-(aq) \longrightarrow NH_3(aq) + Zn^{2+}(aq)$
(c) $ClO^-(aq) + CrO_2^-(aq) \longrightarrow Cl^-(aq) + CrO_4^{2-}(aq)$
(d) $K(s) + H_2O \longrightarrow K^+(aq) + H_2(g)$

66. Write balanced equations for the following reactions in basic solution.

(a) $Ni(OH)_2(s) + N_2H_4(aq) \longrightarrow Ni(s) + N_2(g)$
(b) $Fe(OH)_3(s) + Cr^{3+}(aq) \longrightarrow Fe(OH)_2(s) + CrO_4^{2-}(aq)$
(c) $MnO_4^-(aq) + BrO_3^-(aq) \longrightarrow MnO_2(s) + BrO_4^-(aq)$
(d) $H_2O_2(aq) + IO_4^-(aq) \longrightarrow IO_2^-(aq) + O_2(g)$

67. Write balanced net ionic equations for the following reactions in acid solution.

(a) Liquid hydrazine reacts with an aqueous solution of sodium bromate. Nitrogen gas and bromide ions are formed.
(b) Solid phosphorus (P_4) reacts with an aqueous solution of nitrate to form nitrogen oxide gas and dihydrogen phosphate ($H_2PO_4^-$) ions.
(c) Aqueous solutions of potassium sulfite and potassium permanganate react. Sulfate and manganese(II) ions are formed.

68. Write balanced net ionic equations for the following reactions in acid solution.

(a) Nitrogen oxide and hydrogen gases react to form ammonia gas and steam.
(b) Hydrogen peroxide reacts with an aqueous solution of sodium hypochlorite to form oxygen and chlorine gases.
(c) Zinc metal reduces the vanadyl ion (VO^{2+}) to vanadium(III) ions. Zinc ions are also formed.

69. A solution of potassium permanganate reacts with oxalic acid, $H_2C_2O_4$, to form carbon dioxide and solid manganese(IV) oxide (MnO_2).

(a) Write a balanced net ionic equation for the reaction.
(b) If 20.0 mL of 0.300 *M* potassium permanganate is required to react with 13.7 mL of oxalic acid, what is the molarity of the oxalic acid?
(c) What is the mass of manganese(IV) oxide formed?

70. Iodine reacts with thiosulfate ion, $S_2O_3^{2-}$, to give iodide ion and the tetrathionate ion, $S_4O_6^{2-}$.

(a) Write a balanced net ionic equation for the reaction.
(b) If 25.0 g of iodine is dissolved in enough water to make 1.50 L of solution, what volume of 0.244 *M* sodium thiosulfate will be needed for complete reaction?

71. Hydrogen gas is bubbled into a solution of barium hydroxide that has sulfur in it. The unbalanced equation for the reaction that takes place is

$$H_2(g) + S(s) + OH^-(aq) \longrightarrow S^{2-}(aq) + H_2O$$

(a) Balance the equation.
(b) What volume of 0.349 *M* $Ba(OH)_2$ is required to react completely with 3.00 g of sulfur?

72. Consider the reaction between silver and nitric acid for which the unbalanced equation is

$$Ag(s) + H^+(aq) + NO_3^-(aq) \longrightarrow Ag^+(aq) + NO_2(g) + H_2O$$

(a) Balance the equation.
(b) If 42.50 mL of 12.0 *M* nitric acid furnishes enough H^+ to react with silver, how many grams of silver react?

73. Limonite, an ore of iron, is brought into solution in acidic medium and titrated with $KMnO_4$. The unbalanced equation for the reaction is

$$MnO_4^-(aq) + Fe^{2+}(aq) \longrightarrow Fe^{3+}(aq) + Mn^{2+}(aq)$$

It is found that a 1.000-g sample of the ore requires 75.52 mL of 0.0205 *M* $KMnO_4$. What is the percent of Fe in the sample?

74. The molarity of iodine in solution can be determined by titration with H_3AsO_3. The unbalanced equation for the reaction is

$$H_3AsO_3(aq) + I_2(aq) \longrightarrow I^-(aq) + H_3AsO_4(aq)$$

Iodine crystals are dissolved in water to make 125 mL of solution. The resulting solution is titrated with 45.00 mL of 0.2317 *M* H_3AsO_3. What is the molarity of the solution? How many grams of iodine crystals were added?

75. Laundry bleach is a solution of sodium hypochlorite (NaClO). To determine the hypochlorite (ClO^-) content of bleach (which is responsible for its bleaching action), sulfide ion is added in basic solution. The balanced equation for the reaction is

$$ClO^-(aq) + S^{2-}(aq) + H_2O \longrightarrow Cl^-(aq) + S(s) + 2OH^-(aq)$$

The chloride ion resulting from the reduction of HClO is precipitated as AgCl. When 50.0 mL of laundry bleach ($d = 1.02$ g/cm^3) is treated as described above, 4.95 g of AgCl is obtained. What is the mass percent of NaClO in the bleach?

■ in OWL Blue-numbered questions answered in Appendix 6 WEB Solution is available on companion website

76. Laws passed in some states define a drunk driver as one who drives with a blood alcohol level of 0.10% by mass or higher. The level of alcohol can be determined by titrating blood plasma with potassium dichromate according to the unbalanced equation

$$H^+(aq) + Cr_2O_7^{2-}(aq) + C_2H_5OH(aq) \longrightarrow Cr^{3+}(aq) + CO_2(g) + H_2O$$

Assuming that the only substance that reacts with dichromate in blood plasma is alcohol, is a person legally drunk if 38.94 mL of 0.0723 *M* potassium dichromate is required to titrate a 50.0-g sample of blood plasma?

Unclassified

77. A sample of limestone weighing 1.005 g is dissolved in 75.00 mL of 0.2500 *M* hydrochloric acid. The following reaction occurs:

$$CaCO_3(s) + 2H^+(aq) \longrightarrow Ca^{2+}(aq) + CO_2(g) + H_2O$$

It is found that 19.26 mL of 0.150 *M* NaOH is required to titrate the excess HCl left after reaction with the limestone. What is the mass percent of $CaCO_3$ in the limestone?

78. The iron content of hemoglobin is determined by destroying the hemoglobin molecule and producing small water-soluble ions and molecules. The iron in the aqueous solution is reduced to iron(II) ion and then titrated against potassium permanganate. In the titration, iron(II) is oxidized to iron(III) and permanganate is reduced to manganese(II) ion. A 5.00-g sample of hemoglobin requires 32.3 mL of a 0.002100 *M* solution of potassium permanganate. What is the mass percent of iron in hemoglobin?

79. The standard set by OSHA for the maximum amount of ammonia permitted in the workplace is 5.00×10^{-3}% by mass. To determine a factory's compliance, 10.00 L of air ($d = 1.19$ g/L) is bubbled into 100.0 mL of 0.02500 *M* HCl at the same temperature and pressure. Ammonia in the air bubbled in reacts with H^+ as follows:

$$NH_3(aq) + H^+(aq) \longrightarrow NH_4^+(aq)$$

The unreacted hydrogen ions required 57.00 mL of 0.03500 *M* NaOH for complete neutralization. Is the factory compliant with the OSHA standards for ammonia in the workplace?

80. Gold metal will dissolve only in *aqua regia,* a mixture of concentrated hydrochloric acid and concentrated nitric acid in 3:1 volume ratio. The products of the reaction between gold and the concentrated acids are $AuCl_4^-(aq)$, $NO(g)$, and H_2O.

(a) Write a balanced net ionic equation for the redox reaction, treating HCl and HNO_3 as strong acids.

(b) What stoichiometric ratio of hydrochloric acid to nitric acid should be used?

(c) What volumes of 12 *M* HCl and 16 *M* HNO_3 are required to furnish the Cl^- and NO_3^- ions to react with 25.0 g of gold?

Conceptual Questions

81. Consider the following balanced redox reaction in basic medium.

$$3Sn^{2+}(aq) + Cr_2O_7^{2-}(aq) + 4H_2O \longrightarrow 3Sn^{4+}(aq) + Cr_2O_3(s) + 8OH^-(aq)$$

(a) What is the oxidizing agent?

(b) What species has the element that increases its oxidation number?

(c) What species contains the element with the highest oxidation number?

(d) If the reaction were to take place in acidic medium, what species would not be included in the reaction?

82. Identify the type of aqueous reaction using the symbols **PPT** for precipitation, **SA/SB** for strong acid–strong base, **SA/WB** for strong acid–weak base, **WA/SB** for weak acid–strong base, and **NR** for no reaction.

(a) $CH_3CH_2NH_2 + HCl$

(b) $Ca(OH)_2 + HF$

(c) $Ca(OH)_2 + Na_3PO_4$

(d) $Ag_2SO_4 + BaCl_2$

(e) $Mg(NO_3)_2 + NaCl$

83. Using circles to represent cations and squares to represent anions, show pictorially the reactions that occur between aqueous solutions of

(a) Ba^{2+} and OH^-

(b) Co^{3+} and PO_4^{3-}

84. Assuming that the circles represent cations and squares represent anions, match the incomplete net ionic equations to their pictorial representations

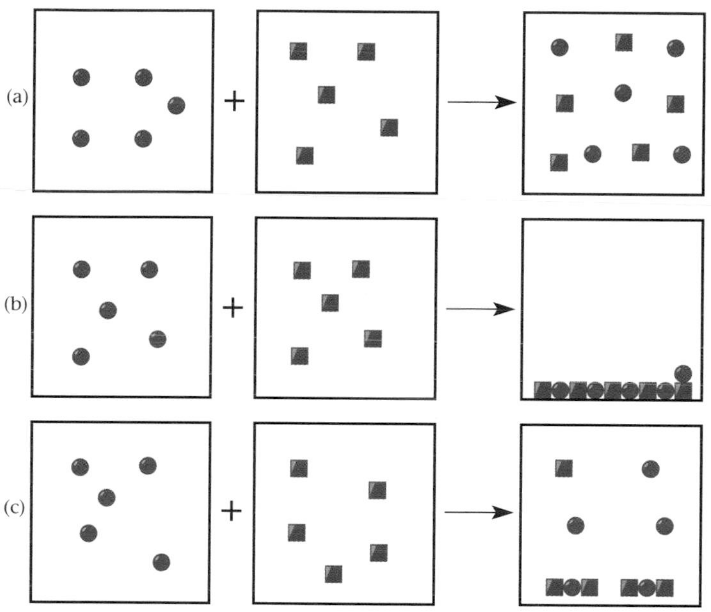

(1) $2Na^+ + SO_4^{2-} \longrightarrow$ ________

(2) $Mg^{2+} + 2OH^- \longrightarrow$ ________

(3) $Ba^{2+} + CO_3^{2-} \longrightarrow$ ________

85. Using squares to represent atoms of one element (or cations) and circles to represent the atoms of the other element (or anions), represent the principal species in the following pictorially. (You may represent the hydroxide anion as a single circle.)

(a) a solution of HCl

(b) a solution of HF

(c) a solution of KOH

(d) a solution of HNO_2

86. The following figures represent species before and after they are dissolved in water. Classify each species as weak electrolyte, strong electrolyte, or nonelectrolyte. You may assume that species that dissociate during solution break up as ions.

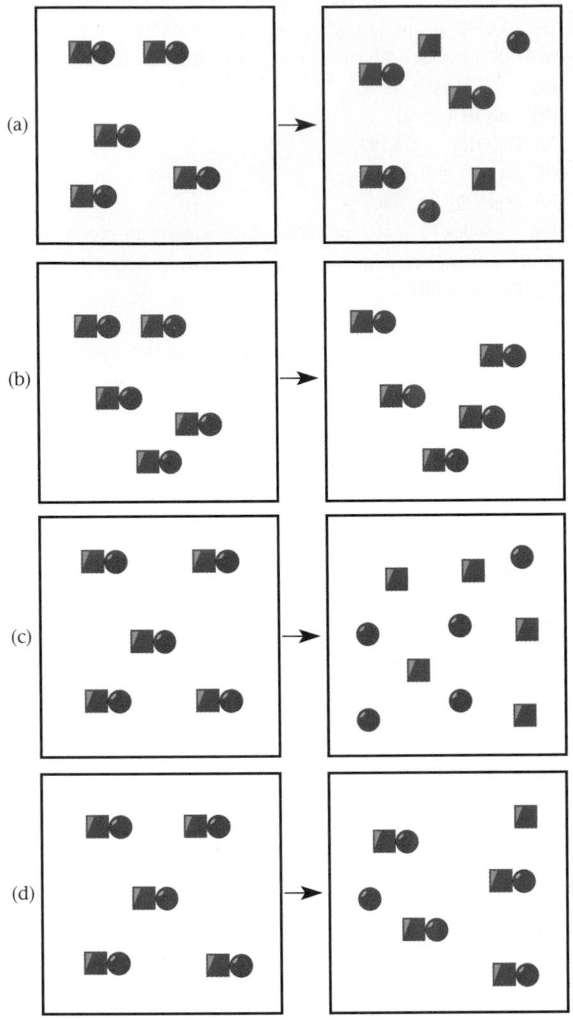

87. ■ A student is asked to identify the metal nitrate present in an aqueous solution. The cation in the solution can either be Na^+, Ba^{2+}, Ag^+, or Ni^{2+}. Results of solubility experiments are as follows:

unknown + chloride ions—no precipitate

unknown + carbonate ions—precipitate

unknown + sulfate ions—precipitate

What is the cation in the solution?

88. Use the following reactions to arrange the cations W^+, X^+, Y^+, and Z^+ in order of their increasing ability as oxidizing agents.

$$W^+ + Z \longrightarrow \text{no reaction}$$
$$X^+ + W \longrightarrow \text{no reaction}$$
$$Y^+ + X \longrightarrow X^+ + Y$$
$$Y^+ + Z \longrightarrow Z^+ + Y$$

89. Based on the relative oxidizing strengths of the cations obtained in Question 88, which of the following reactions would you expect to occur?

(a) $Y^+ + W \longrightarrow$ ________

(b) $Z^+ + X \longrightarrow$ ________

(c) $W^+ + X \longrightarrow$ ________

90. Three students titrate different samples of the same solution of HCl to obtain its molarity. Below are their data.

Student A:	20.00 mL HCl + 20.00 mL H_2O 0.100 *M* NaOH used to titrate to the equivalence point
Student B:	20.00 mL HCl + 40.00 mL H_2O 0.100 *M* NaOH used to titrate to the equivalence point
Student C:	20.00 mL HCl + 20.00 mL H_2O 0.100 *M* $Ba(OH)_2$ used to titrate to the equivalence point.

All the students calculated the molarities correctly. Which (if any) of the following statements are true?

(a) The molarity calculated by A is half that calculated by B.

(b) The molarity calculated by A is equal to that calculated by C.

(c) The molarity calculated by B is twice that calculated by C.

(d) The molarity calculated by A is twice that calculated by B.

(e) The molarity calculated by A is equal to that calculated by B.

Challenge Problems

91. Calcium in blood or urine can be determined by precipitation as calcium oxalate, CaC_2O_4. The precipitate is dissolved in strong acid and titrated with potassium permanganate. The products of the reaction are carbon dioxide and manganese(II) ion. A 24-hour urine sample is collected from an adult patient, reduced to a small volume, and titrated with 26.2 mL of 0.0946 *M* $KMnO_4$. How many grams of calcium oxalate are in the sample? Normal range for Ca^{2+} output for an adult is 100 to 300 mg per 24 hour. Is the sample within the normal range?

92. ■ Stomach acid is approximately 0.020 *M* HCl. What volume of this acid is neutralized by an antacid tablet that weighs 330 mg and contains 41.0% $Mg(OH)_2$, 36.2% $NaHCO_3$, and 22.8% NaCl? The reactions involved are

$$Mg(OH)_2(s) + 2H^+(aq) \longrightarrow Mg^{2+}(aq) + 2H_2O$$
$$HCO_3^-(aq) + H^+(aq) \longrightarrow CO_2(g) + H_2O$$

93. Copper metal can reduce silver ions to metallic silver. The copper is oxidized to copper ions according to the reaction

$$2Ag^+(aq) + Cu(s) \longrightarrow Cu^{2+}(aq) + 2Ag(s)$$

A copper strip with a mass of 2.00 g is dipped into a solution of $AgNO_3$. After some time has elapsed, the copper strip is coated with silver. The strip is removed from the solution, dried, and weighed. The coated strip has a mass of 4.18 g. What are the masses of copper and silver metals in the strip? (*Hint:* Remember that the copper metal is being used up as silver metal forms.)

94. A solution contains both iron(II) and iron(III) ions. A 50.00-mL sample of the solution is titrated with 35.0 mL of 0.0280 *M* $KMnO_4$, which oxidizes Fe^{2+} to Fe^{3+}. The permanganate ion is reduced to manganese(II) ion. Another 50.00-mL sample of the solution is treated with zinc, which reduces all the Fe^{3+} to Fe^{2+}. The resulting solution is again titrated with 0.0280 *M* $KMnO_4$; this time 48.0 mL is required. What are the concentrations of Fe^{2+} and Fe^{3+} in the solution?

95. ■ A student is given 0.930 g of an unknown acid, which can be either oxalic acid, $H_2C_2O_4$, or citric acid, $H_3C_6H_5O_7$. To determine which acid she has, she titrates the unknown acid with 0.615 *M* NaOH. The equivalence point is reached when 33.6 mL are added. What is the unknown acid?

96. Solid iron(III) hydroxide is added to 625 mL of 0.280 *M* HCl. The resulting solution is acidic and titrated with 238.2 mL of 0.113 *M* NaOH. What mass of iron(III) hydroxide was added to the HCl?

■ in OWL Blue-numbered questions answered in Appendix 6 **WEB** Solution is available on companion website

5 Gases

Religious faith is a most filling vapor.
It swirls occluded in us under tight
Compression to uplift us out of weight—
As in those buoyant bird bones thin as paper,
To give them still more buoyancy in flight.
Some gas like helium must be innate.

—Robert Frost
"Innate Helium"

Chapter Outline

The density of a gas decreases when the temperature of the gas is increased. The heated air in the balloon is lighter than the air around the balloon. This density difference causes the balloon to rise (after it is untethered).

By far the most familiar gas to all of us is the air we breathe. The Greeks considered air to be one of the four fundamental elements of nature, along with earth, water, and fire. Late in the eighteenth century, Cavendish, Priestley, and Lavoisier studied the composition of air, which is primarily a mixture of nitrogen and oxygen with smaller amounts of argon, carbon dioxide, and water vapor. Today it appears that the concentrations of some of the minor components of the atmosphere may be changing, with adverse effects on the environment. The depletion of the ozone layer and increases in the amounts of "greenhouse" gases are topics for the evening news, television dramas, and movies.

All gases resemble one another closely in their physical behavior. Their volumes respond in almost exactly the same way to changes in pressure, temperature, or amount of gas. In fact, it is possible to write a simple equation relating these four variables that is valid for all gases. This equation, known as the ideal gas law, is the central theme of this chapter; it is introduced in Section 5.2. The law is applied to—

- pure gases in Section 5.3.
- gases in chemical reactions in Section 5.4.
- gas mixtures in Section 5.5.

Section 5.6 considers the kinetic theory of gases, the molecular model on which the ideal gas law is based. Finally, in Section 5.7 we describe the extent to which real gases deviate from the law. ■

Online homework for this chapter may be assigned in OWL

CENGAGENOW™

This icon introduces an opportunity for self-study and to explore interactive modules by signing in at **academic.cengage.com/now.**

Ozone is a vital but minor component of the upper atmosphere (see Chapter 11).

5.1 MEASUREMENTS ON GASES

To completely describe the state of a gaseous substance, its volume, amount, temperature, and pressure are specified. The first three of these quantities were discussed in earlier chapters and will be reviewed briefly in this section. Pressure, a somewhat more abstract quantity, will be examined in more detail.

Volume, Amount, and Temperature

A gas expands uniformly to fill any container in which it is placed. This means that the volume of a gas is the volume of its container. Volumes of gases can be expressed in liters, cubic centimeters, or cubic meters:

$$1\text{ L} = 10^3\text{ cm}^3 = 10^{-3}\text{ m}^3$$

Most commonly, the amount of matter in a gaseous sample is expressed in terms of the number of moles (n). In some cases, the mass m in grams is given instead. These two quantities are related through the molar mass, MM:

$$n = \frac{m}{\text{MM}}$$

The temperature of a gas is ordinarily measured using a thermometer marked in degrees Celsius. However, as we will see in Section 5.2, ***in any calculation involving the physical behavior of gases, temperatures must be expressed on the Kelvin scale.*** To convert between °C and K, use the relation introduced in Chapter 1:

$$T_K = t_{°C} + 273.15$$

Typically, in gas law calculations, temperatures are expressed only to the nearest degree. In that case, the Kelvin temperature can be found by simply adding 273 to the Celsius temperature.

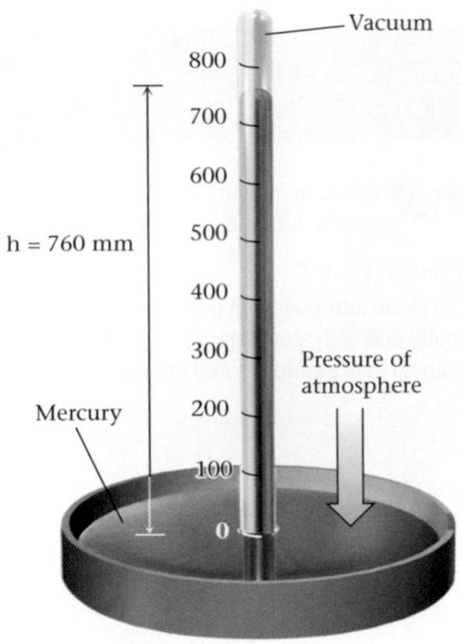

Figure 5.1

A mercury barometer. This is the type of barometer first constructed by Torricelli. The pressure of the atmosphere pushes the mercury in the dish to rise into the glass tube. The height of the column of mercury is a measure of the atmospheric pressure.

Pressure

Pressure is defined as force per unit area. You are probably familiar with the English unit "pounds per square inch," often abbreviated psi. When we say that a gas exerts a pressure of 15 psi, we mean that the pressure on the walls of the gas container is 15 pounds (of force) per square inch of wall area.

A device commonly used to measure atmospheric pressure is the mercury *barometer* (Figure 5.1), first constructed by Evangelista Torricelli in the seventeenth century. This consists of a closed gas tube filled with mercury inverted over a pool of mercury. The pressure exerted by the mercury column exactly equals that of the atmosphere. Hence the height of the column is a measure of the atmospheric pressure. At or near sea level, it typically varies from 740 to 760 mm, depending on weather conditions.

Most barometers contain mercury rather than some other liquid. Its high density allows the barometer to be a convenient size. A water barometer needs to be 10,340 mm (34 ft) high to register atmospheric pressure!

The pressure of a confined gas can be measured by a *manometer* of the type shown in Figure 5.2. Here again the fluid used is mercury. If the level in the inner tube (A) is lower than that in the outer tube (B), the pressure of the gas is greater than that of the atmosphere. If the reverse is true, the gas pressure is less than atmospheric pressure.

Because of the way in which gas pressure is measured, it is often expressed in **millimeters of mercury (mm Hg).** Thus we might say that the atmospheric pressure on a certain day is 772 mm Hg. This means that the pressure of the air is equal to that exerted by a column of mercury 772 mm (30.4 in) high.

The pressure exerted by a column of mercury depends on its density, which varies slightly with temperature. To get around this ambiguity, the *torr* was defined to be the pressure exerted by 1 mm of mercury at certain specified conditions, notably 0°C. Over time, the unit torr has become a synonym for millimeter of mercury. Throughout this text, we will use millimeter of mercury rather than torr because the former has a clearer physical meaning.

Another unit commonly used to express gas pressure is the standard atmosphere, or simply **atmosphere (atm).** This is the pressure exerted by a column of mercury 760 mm high with the mercury at 0°C. If we say that a gas has a pressure of 0.98 atm, we mean that the pressure is 98% of that exerted by a mercury column 760 mm high.

In the International System (Appendix 1), the standard unit of pressure is the *pascal* (Pa). A pascal is a very small unit; it is approximately the pressure exerted by a film of water 0.1 mm high on the surface beneath it. A related unit is the **bar** (10^5 Pa). A bar is nearly, but not quite, equal to an atmosphere:

$$1.013 \text{ bar} = 1 \text{ atm} = 760 \text{ mm Hg} = 14.7 \text{ psi} = 100 \text{ k Pa}$$

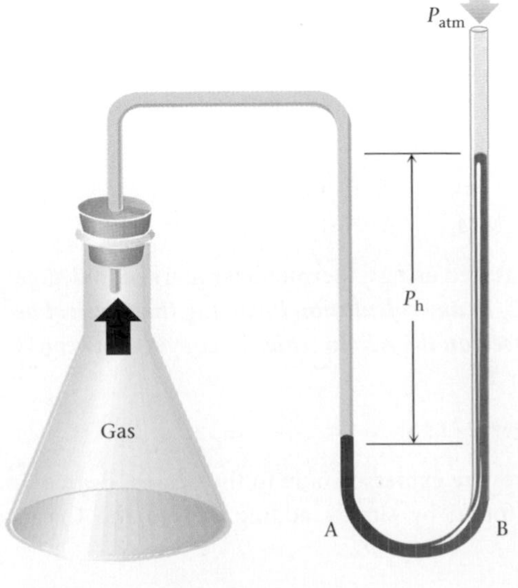

Figure 5.2

A manometer open to the atmosphere, used to measure gas pressure in a closed system. The pressure of the gas is given by $P_{gas} = P_{atm} + P_h$. In the figure, the gas pressure is greater than the atmospheric pressure.

Example 5.1 At room temperature, dry ice (solid CO_2) becomes a gas. At 77°F, 13.6 oz of dry ice are put into a steel tank with a volume of 10.00 ft³. The tank's pressure gauge registers 11.2 psi. Express the volume (V) of the tank in liters, the amount of CO_2 in grams and moles (n), the temperature (T) in °C and K and the pressure (P) in bars, mm Hg, and atmospheres.

Strategy Use the following conversion factors:

$$\frac{14.7\ \text{psi}}{1\ \text{atm}} \qquad \frac{760\ \text{mm Hg}}{1\ \text{atm}} \qquad \frac{1.013\ \text{bar}}{1\ \text{atm}}$$

$$\frac{44.0\ \text{g}\ CO_2}{1\ \text{mol}\ CO_2} \qquad \frac{28.32\ \text{L}}{1\ \text{ft}^3} \qquad \frac{0.03527\ \text{oz}}{1\ \text{g}}$$

In these relations, "760 mm Hg" and "1 atm" are exact; "1.013 bar" has four significant figures.

Most of these conversion factors can be found in Table 1.3. For the temperature conversion, use the relation:

$$t_{°F} = 1.8t_{°C} + 32$$

SOLUTION

$$V = 10.00\ \text{ft}^3 \times \frac{28.32\ \text{L}}{1\ \text{ft}^3} = 283.2\ \text{L}$$

$$m = 13.6\ \text{oz} \times \frac{1\ \text{g}}{0.03527\ \text{oz}} = 386\ \text{g}$$

$$n_{CO_2} = 386\ \text{g} \times \frac{1\ \text{mol}}{44.0\ \text{g}} = 8.77\ \text{mol}$$

$$t_{°C} = \frac{77 - 32}{1.8} = 25°\text{C}$$

$$T_K = 25 + 273 = 298\ \text{K}$$

$$P = 11.2\ \text{psi} \times \frac{1\ \text{atm}}{14.7\ \text{psi}} = 0.762\ \text{atm}$$

$$P = 0.762\ \text{atm} \times \frac{760\ \text{mm}}{1\ \text{atm}} = 579\ \text{mm Hg}$$

$$P = 0.762\ \text{atm} \times \frac{1.013\ \text{bar}}{1\ \text{atm}} = 0.772\ \text{bar}$$

5.2 THE IDEAL GAS LAW

All gases closely resemble each other in the dependence of volume on amount, temperature, and pressure.

CENGAGENOW™
Click Coached Problems for a self-study module and a simulation on **the ideal gas law.**

1. ***Volume is directly proportional to amount.*** Figure 5.3a (p. 106) shows a typical plot of volume (V) versus number of moles (n) for a gas. Notice that the graph is a straight line passing through the origin. The general equation for such a plot is

$$V = k_1n \qquad \text{(constant } T, P\text{)}$$

where k_1 is a constant; that is, it is independent of individual values of V and n and of the nature of the gas. This is the equation of a direct proportionality.

2. ***Volume is directly proportional to absolute temperature.*** The dependence of volume (V) on the Kelvin temperature (T) is shown in Figure 5.3b (p. 106). The graph is a straight line through the origin. The equation of the line is

$$V = k_2T \qquad \text{(constant } n, P\text{)}$$

Figure 5.3
Relation of gas volume (V) to number of moles (n) and temperature (T) at constant pressure (P). The volume of a gas at constant pressure is directly proportional to (a) the number of moles of gas and (b) the absolute temperature. The volume-temperature plot must be extrapolated to reach zero because most gases liquefy at low temperatures well above 0 K.

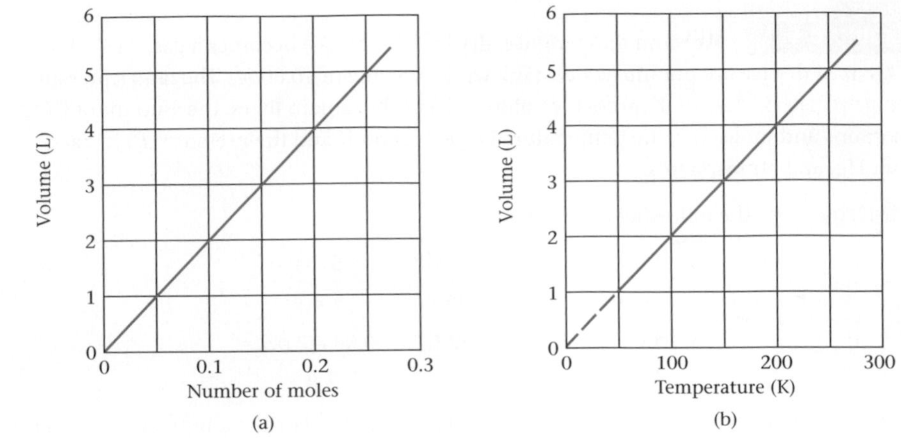

Gay-Lussac isolated boron and was the first to prepare HF.

where k_2 is a constant. This relationship was first suggested, in a different form, by two French scientists, Jacques Charles (1746–1823) and Joseph Gay-Lussac (1778–1850), both of whom were balloonists. Hence it is often referred to as the law of Charles and Gay-Lussac or, simply, as *Charles's law.*

3. ***Volume is inversely proportional to pressure.*** Figure 5.4 shows a typical plot of volume (V) versus pressure (P). Notice that V decreases as P increases. The graph is a hyperbola. The general relation between the two variables is

$$V = k_3/P \qquad \text{(constant } n, T\text{)}$$

The quantity k_3, like k_1 and k_2, is a constant. This is the equation of an inverse proportionality. The fact that volume is inversely proportional to pressure was first established in 1660 by Robert Boyle (1627–1691), an Irish experimental scientist. The equation above is one form of *Boyle's law.*

The three equations relating the volume, pressure, temperature, and amount of a gas can be combined into a single equation. Because V is directly proportional to both n and T,

$$V = k_1 n \qquad V = k_2 T$$

and inversely proportional to P,

$$V = \frac{k_3}{P}$$

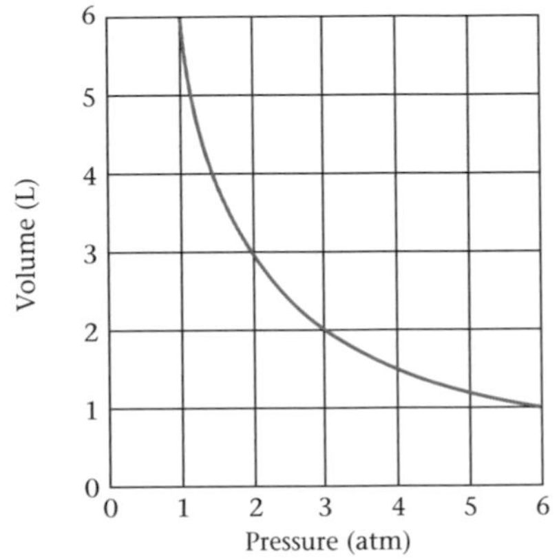

Figure 5.4
Relation of gas volume (V) to pressure (P) at constant temperature (T). The volume of a fixed quantity of gas at constant temperature is inversely proportional to the pressure. In this case, the volume decreases from 6 L to 1 L when the pressure increases from 1 atm to 6 atm.

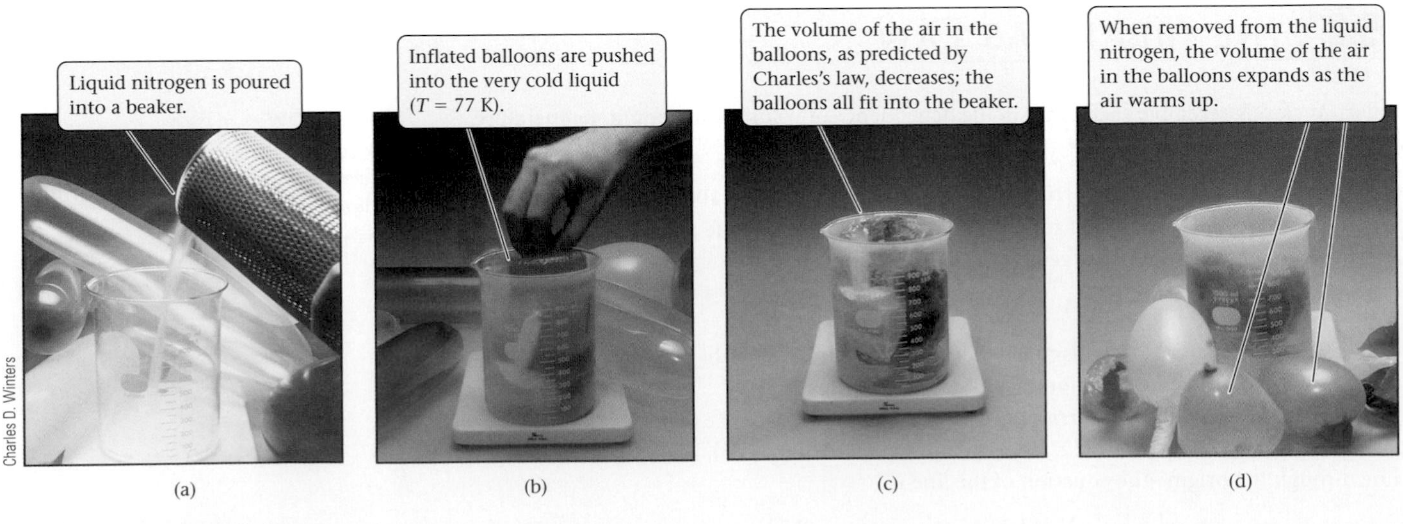

Charles D. Winters

An illustration of Charles's law.

Table 5.1 Values of *R* in Different Units

Value	Where Used	How Obtained
$0.0821 \frac{\text{L} \cdot \text{atm}}{\text{mol} \cdot \text{K}}$	Gas law problems with *V* in liters, *P* in atm	From known values of *P*, *V*, *T*, *n*
$8.31 \frac{\text{J}}{\text{mol} \cdot \text{K}}$	Equations involving energy in joules	$1\ \text{L} \cdot \text{atm} = 101.3\ \text{J}$
$8.31 \times 10^3 \frac{\text{g} \cdot \text{m}^2}{\text{s}^2 \cdot \text{mol} \cdot \text{K}}$	Calculation of molecular speed (page 119)	$1\ \text{J} = 10^3 \frac{\text{g} \cdot \text{m}^2}{\text{s}^2}$

R is a constant, independent of *P*, *V*, *n*, and *T*, but its numerical value depends on the units used.

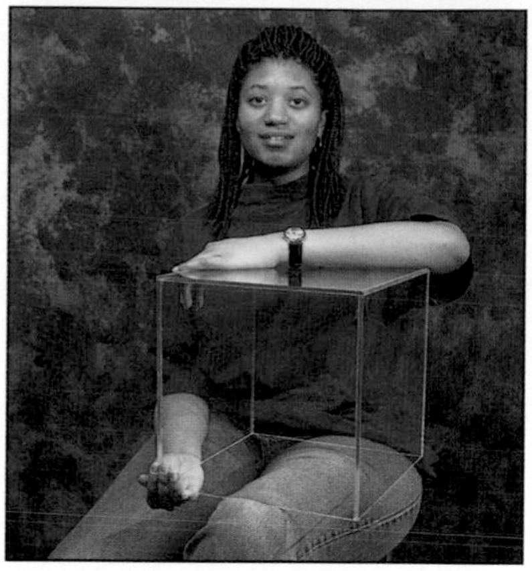

Molar volume. The cube has a volume of 22.4 L, which is the volume of one mole of gas at STP.

it follows that

$$V = \text{constant} \times \frac{n \times T}{P}$$

We can evaluate the constant ($k_1k_2k_3$) in this equation by taking advantage of *Avogadro's law,* which states that equal volumes of all gases at the same temperature and pressure contain the same number of moles. For this law to hold, the constant must be the same for all gases. Ordinarily it is represented by the symbol ***R.*** Both sides of the equation are multiplied by *P* to give the **ideal gas law**

$$PV = nRT \qquad \textbf{(5.1)}$$

where *P* is the pressure, *V* the volume, *n* the number of moles, and *T* the Kelvin temperature. Experimentally, it is found that the ideal gas law predicts remarkably well the experimental behavior of real gases (e.g., H_2, N_2, O_2 . . .) at ordinary temperatures and pressures.

The value of the gas constant *R* can be calculated from experimental values of *P*, *V*, *n*, and *T*. Consider, for example, the situation that applies at 0°C and 1 atm. These conditions are often referred to as ***standard temperature and pressure* (STP)** for a gas. At STP, one mole of any gas occupies a volume of 22.4 L. Solving the ideal gas law for *R*,

$$R = \frac{PV}{nT}$$

Substituting $P = 1.00$ atm, $V = 22.4$ L, $n = 1.00$ mol, and $T = 0 + 273 = 273$ K,

$$R = \frac{1.00\ \text{atm} \times 22.4\ \text{L}}{1.00\ \text{mol} \times 273\ \text{K}} = 0.0821\ \text{L} \cdot \text{atm/(mol} \cdot \text{K)}$$

Notice that *R* has the units of atmospheres, liters, moles, and K. These units must be used for pressure, volume, amount, and temperature in any problem in which this value of *R* is used.

Throughout most of this chapter, we will use 0.0821 L · atm/(mol · K) as the value of *R*. For certain purposes, however, *R* must be expressed in different units (Table 5.1).

5.3 GAS LAW CALCULATIONS

The ideal gas law can be used to solve a variety of problems. We will show how you can use it to find—

- the final state of a gas, knowing its initial state and the changes in *P*, *V*, *n*, or *T* that occur.
- one of the four variables, *P*, *V*, *n*, or *T*, given the values of the other three.
- the molar mass or density of a gas.

Final and Initial State Problems

A gas commonly undergoes a change from an initial to a final state. Typically, you are asked to determine the effect on V, P, n, or T of a change in one or more of these variables. For example, starting with a sample of gas at 25°C and 1.00 atm, you might be asked to calculate the pressure developed when the sample is heated to 95°C at constant volume.

The ideal gas law is readily applied to problems of this type. A relationship between the variables involved is derived from this law. In this case, pressure and temperature change, while n and V remain constant.

$$\text{initial state:} \quad P_1V = nRT_1$$
$$\text{final state:} \quad P_2V = nRT_2$$

To obtain a two-point equation, write the gas law twice and divide to eliminate constants.

Dividing the second equation by the first cancels V, n, and R, leaving the relation

$$P_2/P_1 = T_2/T_1 \qquad (\text{constant } n, V)$$

Applying this general relation to the problem just described,

$$P_2 = P_1 \times \frac{T_2}{T_1} = 1.00 \text{ atm} \times \frac{368 \text{ K}}{298 \text{ K}} = 1.23 \text{ atm}$$

Similar "two-point" equations can be derived from the ideal gas law to solve any problem of this type.

Example 5.2 A sealed 15.0-L steel tank is used to deliver propane (C_3H_8) gas. It is filled with 24.6 g of propane at 27°C. The pressure gauge registers 0.915 atm. (Assume that the expansion of steel from an increase in temperature is negligible.)

(a) If the tank is heated to 58°C, what is the pressure of propane in the tank?
(b) The tank is fitted with a valve to open and release propane to maintain the pressure at 1.200 atm. Will heating the tank to 58°C release propane?
(c) At 200°C, the pressure exceeds 1.200 atm. How much propane is released to maintain 1.200 atm pressure?

Strategy

(a) Read the problem carefully, and note that the volume of the tank and the number of moles of gas remain constant. (It is a *sealed, steel* tank.)
(b) Check both the calculated pressure at 58°C and the pressure at which propane is released.
(c) The problem now has three variables. Only volume remains constant.

SOLUTION

(a)

$$\text{initial state:} \quad \frac{P_1}{T_1} = \frac{nR}{V}$$
$$\text{final state:} \quad \frac{P_2}{T_2} = \frac{nR}{V}$$

It follows that

$$\frac{P_1}{T_1} = \frac{P_2}{T_2}$$

Because $P_1 = 0.915$ atm; $T_1 = 27 + 273 = 300$ K; and $T_2 = 58 + 273 = 331$ K,

$$P_2 = 0.915 \text{ atm} \times \frac{331 \text{ K}}{300 \text{ K}} = 1.01 \text{ atm}$$

(b) Since 1.01 atm < 1.200 atm, the valve will not open.

(c)

$$\text{initial state:} \quad \frac{P_1}{n_1T_1} = \frac{R}{V}$$
$$\text{final state:} \quad \frac{P_2}{n_2T_2} = \frac{R}{V}$$

Because $P_1 = 0.915$ atm; $T_1 = 300$ K; $n_1 = \frac{24.6 \text{ g}}{44.1 \text{ g/mol}} = 0.558$ mol; $P_2 = 1.200$ atm; and $T_2 = 473$ K,

$$n_2 = n_1 \times \frac{P_2}{P_1} \times \frac{T_1}{T_2}$$

$$= 0.558 \text{ mol} \times \frac{1.200 \text{ atm}}{0.915 \text{ atm}} \times \frac{300 \text{ K}}{473 \text{ K}}$$

$$= 0.464 \text{ mol}$$

The tank had 0.558 moles at the start and 0.464 moles after the release of propane. Hence, 0.094 mol of propane (MM = 44.1 g/mol) was released:

$$0.094 \text{ mol} \times \frac{44.1 \text{ g}}{1 \text{ mol}} = 4.15 \text{ g}$$

Reality Check The volume of the tank is never used in any of the calculations for the different parts of the problem. The mass of the propane is relevant only in part (c).

Calculation of *P, V, n,* or *T*

Frequently, values are known for three of these quantities (perhaps V, n, and T); the other one (P) must be calculated. This is readily done by direct substitution into the ideal gas law.

Example 5.3 Sulfur hexafluoride is a gas used as a long-term tamponade (plug) for a retinal hole to repair detached retinas in the eye. If 2.50 g of this compound is introduced into an evacuated 500.0-mL container at 83°C, what pressure in atmospheres is developed?

Strategy Substitute directly into the ideal gas law and solve for P. Note that V, n, and T have to be in units consistent with $R = 0.0821 \text{ L} \cdot \text{atm/mol} \cdot \text{K}$.

SOLUTION Converting to the appropriate units,

$$V = 500.0 \text{ mL} \times \frac{1 \text{ L}}{1000 \text{ mL}} = 0.5000 \text{ L}$$

$$T = 83 + 273 = 356 \text{ K}$$

The molar mass of sulfur hexafluoride, SF_6, is 146.07 g/mol.

$$n = 2.50 \text{ g} \times \frac{1 \text{ mol}}{146.07 \text{ g}} = 0.0171 \text{ mol}$$

Substituting into the ideal gas law,

$$P = \frac{nRT}{V} = \frac{0.0171 \text{ mol} \times 0.0821 \text{ L} \cdot \text{atm/(mol} \cdot \text{K)} \times 356 \text{ K}}{0.5000 \text{ L}} = 1.00 \text{ atm}$$

Molar Mass and Density

The ideal gas law offers a simple approach to the experimental determination of the molar mass of a gas. Indeed, this approach can be applied to volatile liquids like acetone (Example 5.4). All you need to know is the mass of a sample confined to a container of fixed volume at a particular temperature and pressure.

CENGAGENOW™
Click Coached Problems for a self-study module on **determining the molar mass of gases.**

Example 5.4 Graded

Acetone is widely used as a nail polish remover. A sample of liquid acetone is placed in a 3.00-L flask and vaporized by heating to 95°C at 1.02 atm. The vapor filling the flask at this temperature and pressure weighs 5.87 g.

*(a) What is the density of acetone vapor under these conditions?
**(b) Calculate the molar mass of acetone.
***(c) Acetone contains the three elements, C, H, and O. When 1.000 g of acetone is burned, 2.27 g of CO_2 and 0.932 g of H_2O are formed. What is the molecular formula of acetone?

SOLUTION

(a) $\text{density} = \frac{\text{mass}}{\text{volume}} = \frac{5.87\text{ g}}{3.00\text{ L}} = 1.96\text{ g/L}$

(b) Perhaps the simplest approach here is to use the ideal gas law to solve for n. When the number of moles and the mass in grams, m, are known, the molar mass, MM, is readily calculated from the relation

$$m = \text{MM} \times n$$

$$n = \frac{PV}{RT} = \frac{(1.02\text{ atm})\,(3.00\text{ L})}{(0.0821\text{ L}\cdot\text{atm/mol}\cdot\text{K})\,(368\text{ K})} = 0.101\text{ mol}$$

Substituting in the equation

$$m = \text{MM} \times n \qquad 5.87\text{ g} = \text{MM} \times 0.101\text{ mol}$$

Solving for MM

$$\text{MM} = 5.87\text{ g}/0.101\text{ mol} = 58.1\text{ g/mol}$$

(c) Recall from Chapter 3 that the simplest formula of a compound can be determined from combustion data (Example 3.6, page 58).

$$\text{mass C in 1.000-g sample} = 2.27\text{ g }CO_2 \times \frac{12.01\text{ g C}}{44.01\text{ g }CO_2} = 0.619\text{ g C}$$

$$\text{mass H in 1.000-g sample} = 0.932\text{ g }H_2O \times \frac{2.016\text{ g H}}{18.016\text{ g }H_2O} = 0.104\text{ g H}$$

$$\text{mass O} = 1.000\text{ g} - 0.619\text{ g} - 0.104\text{ g} = 0.277\text{ g O}$$

Converting these masses to moles, you should find that in this sample of acetone there are 0.0515 mol C, 0.103 mol H, and 0.0173 mol O.

It follows that the simplest formula is C_3H_6O, which has a molar mass of 58.1 g/mol. Clearly the molecular formula is also the simplest formula, C_3H_6O.

One way to calculate gas density is to use the ideal gas law where $\frac{m}{\text{MM}}$ is substituted for n.

$$PV = \frac{m}{\text{MM}}RT$$

Since $\text{density} = \frac{m}{V}$ the general relation

$$\text{density} = MM\left(\frac{P}{RT}\right) \qquad (5.2)$$

results.

From this equation we see that the density of a gas is dependent on—

- *pressure.* Compressing a gas increases its density.
- *temperature.* Hot air rises because a gas becomes less dense when its temperature is increased. Hot air balloons are filled with air at a temperature higher than that of the

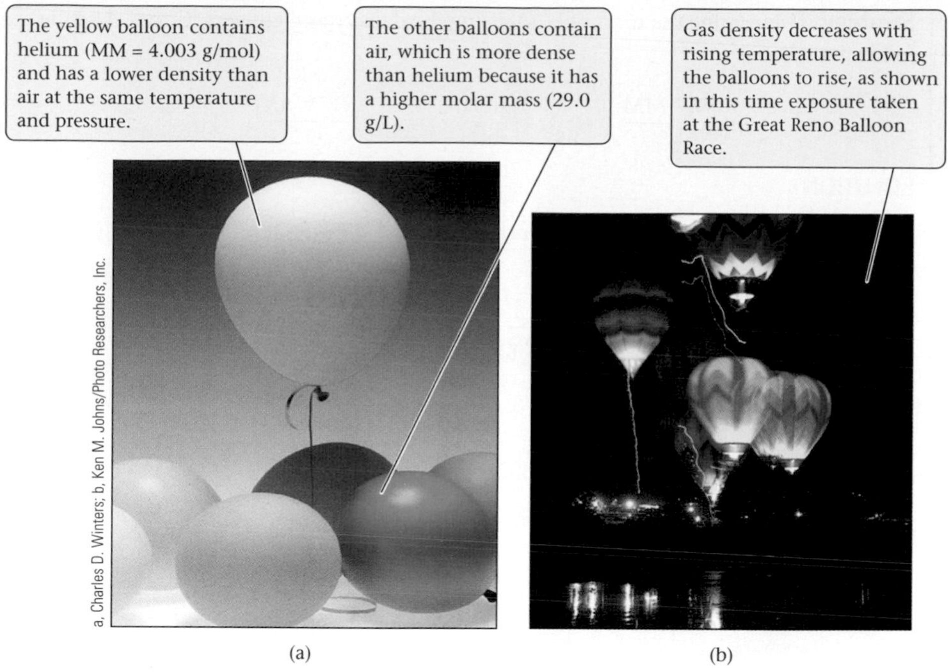

Gas density.

atmosphere, making the air inside less dense than that outside. First used in France in the eighteenth century, they are now seen in balloon races and other sporting events. Heat is supplied on demand by a propane burner.

- *molar mass.* Hydrogen (MM = 2.016 g/mol) has the lowest molar mass and the lowest density (at a given P and T) of all gases. Hence it has the greatest lifting power in "lighter-than-air" balloons. However, hydrogen has not been used in balloons carrying passengers since 1937, when the *Hindenburg*, a hydrogen-filled airship, exploded and burned. Helium (MM = 4.003 g/mol) is slightly less effective than hydrogen but a lot safer to work with because it is nonflammable. It is used in a variety of balloons, ranging from the small ones used at parties to meteorological balloons with volumes of a billion liters.

Very light gases, notably hydrogen and helium, tend to escape from the earth's atmosphere. The hydrogen you generate in the laboratory today is well on its way into outer space tomorrow. A similar situation holds with helium, which is found in very limited quantities mixed with natural gas in wells below the earth's surface. If helium is allowed to escape, it is gone forever, and our supply of this very useful gaseous element is depleted.

5.4 STOICHIOMETRY OF GASEOUS REACTIONS

As pointed out in Chapter 3, a balanced equation can be used to relate moles or grams of substances taking part in a reaction. Where gases are involved, these relations can be extended to include volumes. To do this, we use the ideal gas law and the conversion factor approach described in Chapter 3.

CENGAGENOW™
Click Coached Problems for a self-study module on **stoichiometry of gases.**

Example 5.5 Hydrogen peroxide, H_2O_2, is a common bleaching agent. It decomposes quickly to water and oxygen gas at high temperatures.

$$2H_2O_2(l) \longrightarrow 2H_2O(l) + O_2(g)$$

How many liters of oxygen are produced at 78°C and 0.934 atm when 1.27 L of H_2O_2 (d = 1.00 g/mL) decompose?

Strategy Determine the mass of H_2O_2 using the density and convert °C to K. Use the following scheme:

$$m_{H_2O_2} \xrightarrow{\text{MM}} n_{H_2O_2} \xrightarrow[\text{ratio}]{\text{molar}} n_{O_2} \xrightarrow{PV = nRT} V_{O_2}$$

SOLUTION

$$m_{H_2O_2} = 1.27\text{ L} \times \frac{1000\text{ mL}}{1\text{ L}} \times 1.00\frac{\text{g}}{\text{mL}} = 1270\text{ g}$$

$$n_{H_2O_2} = 1270\text{ g} \times \frac{1\text{ mol}}{34.02\text{ g}} = 37.3\text{ mol}$$

$$n_{O_2} = 37.3\text{ mol } H_2O_2 \times \frac{1\text{ mol } O_2}{2\text{ mol } H_2O_2} = 18.7\text{ mol } O_2$$

$$V_{O_2} = \frac{18.7\text{ mol} \times 0.0821\text{ L-atm/mol-K} \times (78 + 273)\text{ K}}{0.934\text{ atm}}$$

$$= 577\text{ L}$$

Example 5.6 Graded

Sodium bicarbonate (baking soda) is widely used to absorb odors inside refrigerators. When acid is added to baking soda, the following reaction occurs:

$$NaHCO_3(s) + H^+(aq) \longrightarrow Na^+(aq) + CO_2(g) + H_2O$$

All experiments here are performed with 2.45 *M* HCl and 12.75 g of $NaHCO_3$ at 732 mm Hg and 38°C.

*(a) If an excess of HCl is used, what volume of CO_2 is obtained?

**(b) If $NaHCO_3$ is in excess, what volume of HCl is required to produce 2.65 L of CO_2?

***(c) What volume of CO_2 is produced when all the $NaHCO_3$ is made to react with 50.0 mL of HCl?

Strategy Do not forget to convert temperature and pressure to the appropriate units.

(a) $$m_{NaHCO_3} \xrightarrow{\text{MM}} n_{NaHCO_3} \xrightarrow[\text{ratio}]{\text{molar}} n_{CO_2} \xrightarrow{PV = nRT} V_{CO_2}$$

(b) $$V_{CO_2} \xrightarrow{PV = nRT} n_{CO_2} \xrightarrow[\text{ratio}]{\text{molar}} n_{H^+} \xrightarrow{n = V \times M} V_{H^+}$$

(c) This is a limiting reactant problem.

$$n_{H^+} \longrightarrow n_{CO_2} \quad \text{compare to} \quad n_{NaHCO_3} \longrightarrow n_{CO_2}$$

Use the ideal gas law to convert the smaller number of moles of CO_2 to volume.

SOLUTION

(a) $$n_{NaHCO_3} = 12.75\text{ g} \times \frac{1\text{ mol}}{84.01\text{ g}} = 0.1518\text{ mol}$$

$$n_{CO_2} = 0.1518\text{ mol } NaHCO_3 \times \frac{1\text{ mol } CO_2}{1\text{ mol } NaHCO_2} = 0.1518\text{ mol}$$

$$V_{CO_2} = \frac{0.1518\text{ mol} \times 0.0821\text{ L-atm/mol-K} \times (38 + 273)\text{ K}}{732/760\text{ atm}} = 4.02\text{ L}$$

(b) $n_{CO_2} = \dfrac{2.65 \text{ L} \times 732/760 \text{ atm}}{0.0821 \text{ L-atm/mol-K} + (38 + 273) \text{ K}} = 0.100 \text{ mol}$

$n_{H^+} = 0.100 \text{ mol } CO_2 \times \dfrac{1 \text{ mol } H^+}{1 \text{ mol } CO_2} = 0.100 \text{ mol}$

$V_{H^+} = \dfrac{n}{M} = \dfrac{0.100 \text{ mol}}{2.45 \text{ mol/L}} = 0.0408 \text{ L} = \boxed{40.8 \text{ mL}}$

(c) $n_{CO_2} = n_{H^+} = V \times M = 0.0500 \text{ L} \times 2.45 \text{ mol/L} = 0.1225 \text{ mol}$

$n_{CO_2} = n_{NaHCO_3} = 0.152 \text{ mol (see (a))}$

The limiting reactant is H^+.

$V_{CO_2} = \dfrac{0.1225 \text{ mol} \times 0.0821 \text{ L-atm/mol-K} \times (38 + 273) \text{ K}}{732/760 \text{ atm}} = \boxed{3.25 \text{ L}}$

Perhaps the first stoichiometric relationship to be discovered was the *law of combining volumes,* proposed by Gay-Lussac in 1808: ***The volume ratio of any two gases in a reaction at constant temperature and pressure is the same as the reacting mole ratio.***

To illustrate the law, consider the reaction

$$2H_2O(l) \longrightarrow 2H_2(g) + O_2(g)$$

As you can see from Figure 5.5, the volume of hydrogen produced is twice that of the other gaseous product, oxygen.

The law of combining volumes, like so many relationships involving gases, is readily explained by the ideal gas law. At constant temperature and pressure, volume is directly proportional to number of moles ($V = k_1n$). It follows that for gaseous species involved in reactions, the volume ratio must be the same as the mole ratio given by the coefficients of the balanced equation.

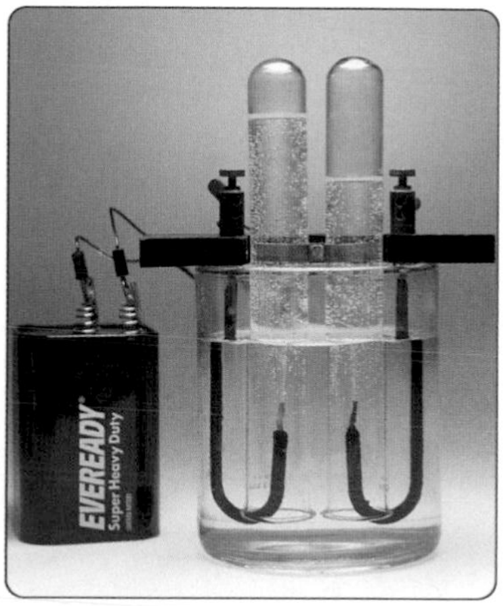

Charles D. Winters

Figure 5.5
Electrolysis of water (H_2O). The volume of hydrogen (H_2) formed in the tube at the right is twice the volume of oxygen (O_2) formed in the tube at the left, in accordance with the equation $2H_2O(l) \longrightarrow 2H_2(g) + O_2(g)$.

CHEMISTRY The Human Side

Avogadro's law, referred to on page 107, was proposed in 1811 by an Italian physicist at the University of Turin with the improbable name of Lorenzo Romano Amadeo Carlo Avogadro di Quarequa e di Cerreto (1776–1856).

Avogadro suggested this relationship to explain the law of combining volumes. Today it seems obvious. For example, in the reaction

$$2H_2O(l) \longrightarrow 2H_2(g) + O_2(g)$$

the volume of hydrogen, like the number of moles, is twice that of oxygen. Hence, equal volumes of these gases must contain the same number of moles or molecules. This was by no means obvious to Avogadro's contemporaries. Berzelius, among others, dismissed Avogadro's ideas because he did not believe diatomic molecules composed of identical atoms (H_2, O_2) could exist. Dalton went a step further; he refused to accept the law of combining volumes because he thought it implied splitting atoms.

Biblioteca civica centrale di Torino. Sezione Manoscritti e rari

Amadeo Avogadro
(1776–1856)

As a result of arguments like these, Avogadro's ideas lay dormant for nearly half a century. They were revived by another Italian scientist, Stanislao Cannizzaro, professor of chemistry at the University of Genoa. At a conference held in Karlsruhe in 1860, he persuaded the chemistry community of the validity of Avogadro's law and showed how it could be used to determine molar and atomic masses.

The quantity now called "Avogadro's number" (6.02×10^{23}/mol) was first estimated in 1865, nine years after Avogadro died. Not until well into the twentieth century did it acquire its present name. It seems appropriate to honor Avogadro in this way for the contributions he made to chemical theory.

Example 5.7 Graded

Consider the reaction

$$2H_2(g) + O_2(g) \longrightarrow 2H_2O(l)$$

*(a) What volume of $H_2(g)$ at 25°C and 1.00 atm is required to react with 1.00 L of $O_2(g)$ at the same temperature and pressure?

**(b) What volume of $H_2O(l)$ at 25°C and 1.00 atm ($d = 0.997$ g/mL) is formed from the reaction in (a)?

***(c) What mass of $H_2O(l)$ is formed from the reaction in (a), assuming a yield of 85.2%?

SOLUTION

(a) According to the law of combining volumes,

$$\text{volume } H_2 = 1.00 \text{ L } O_2 \times \frac{2 \text{ volumes } H_2}{1 \text{ volume } O_2} = \boxed{2.00 \text{ L } H_2}$$

(b) We cannot apply the law of combining volumes here, since water is a liquid. Instead we calculate the number of moles of $O_2(g)$, using the ideal gas law. Then we use the coefficients of the balanced equation to find the number of moles of $H_2O(l)$. Finally, we obtain first the mass of liquid water and then its volume.

$$n_{O_2} = \frac{PV}{RT} = \frac{(1.00 \text{ atm})(1.00 \text{ L})}{(0.0821 \text{ L} \cdot \text{atm/mol} \cdot \text{K})(298 \text{ K})} = 0.0409 \text{ mol } O_2$$

$$n_{H_2O} = 0.0409 \text{ mol } O_2 \times \frac{2 \text{ mol } H_2O}{1 \text{ mol } O_2(g)} = 0.0818 \text{ mol } H_2O$$

$$V_{H_2O} = 0.0818 \text{ mol } H_2O \times \frac{18.02 \text{ g } H_2O}{1 \text{ mol } H_2O} \times \frac{1.00 \text{ mL}}{0.997 \text{ g}} = \boxed{1.48 \text{ mL}}$$

(c) The theoretical yield of $H_2O(l)$, as calculated in (b), is 0.0818 mol. It follows that

$$\text{yield } H_2O = 0.0818 \text{ mol } H_2O \times \frac{18.02 \text{ g } H_2O}{1 \text{ mol } H_2O} \times 0.852 = \boxed{1.26 \text{ g } H_2O}$$

5.5 GAS MIXTURES: PARTIAL PRESSURES AND MOLE FRACTIONS

CENGAGENOW™
Click Coached Problems for a self-study module on **partial pressures.**

Because the ideal gas law applies to all gases, you might expect it to apply to gas mixtures. Indeed it does. For a mixture of two gases A and B, the total pressure is given by the expression

$$P_{tot} = n_{tot}\frac{RT}{V} = (n_A + n_B)\frac{RT}{V}$$

Separating the two terms on the right,

$$P_{tot} = n_A\frac{RT}{V} + n_B\frac{RT}{V}$$

Partial pressure is the pressure a gas would exert if it occupied the entire volume by itself.

The terms n_ART/V and n_BRT/V are, according to the ideal gas law, the pressures that gases A and B would exert if they were alone. These quantities are referred to as **partial pressures,** P_A and P_B.

$$P_A = \text{partial pressure A} = n_A\, RT/V$$
$$P_B = \text{partial pressure B} = n_B\, RT/V$$

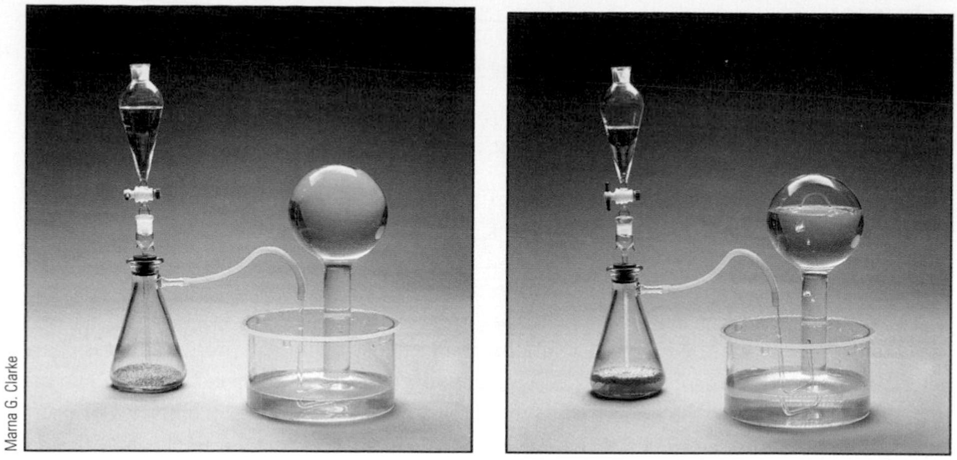

(a) (b)

Figure 5.6
Collecting a gas by water displacement.
(a) Hydrogen gas is being generated in the flask by an acidic solution dripping onto a metal.
(b) When a gas is collected by displacing water, it becomes saturated with water vapor. The partial pressure of $H_2O(g)$ in the collecting flask is equal to the vapor pressure of liquid water at the temperature of the system.

Substituting P_A and P_B for n_ART/V and n_BRT/V in the equation for P_{tot},

$$P_{tot} = P_A + P_B \tag{5.3}$$

The relation just derived was first proposed by John Dalton in 1801; it is often referred to as **Dalton's law** of partial pressures:

The total pressure of a gas mixture is the sum of the partial pressures of the components of the mixture.

To illustrate Dalton's law, consider a gaseous mixture of hydrogen and helium in which

$$P_{H_2} = 2.46 \text{ atm} \qquad P_{He} = 3.69 \text{ atm}$$

It follows from Dalton's law that

$$P_{tot} = 2.46 \text{ atm} + 3.69 \text{ atm} = 6.15 \text{ atm}$$

Wet Gases; Partial Pressure of Water

When a gas such as hydrogen is collected by bubbling through water (Fig. 5.6), it picks up water vapor; molecules of H_2O escape from the liquid and enter the gas phase. Dalton's law can be applied to the resulting gas mixture:

$$P_{tot} = P_{H_2O} + P_{H_2}$$

In this case, P_{tot} is the measured pressure. The partial pressure of water vapor, P_{H_2O}, is equal to the **vapor pressure** of liquid water. It has a fixed value at a given temperature (see Appendix 1). The partial pressure of hydrogen, P_{H_2}, can be calculated by subtraction. The number of moles of hydrogen in the wet gas, n_{H_2}, can then be determined using the ideal gas law.

Vapor pressure is further discussed in Chapter 9.

Example 5.8 A student prepares a sample of hydrogen gas by electrolyzing water at 25°C. She collects 152 mL of H_2 at a total pressure of 758 mm Hg. Using Appendix 1 to find the vapor pressure of water, calculate

(a) the partial pressure of hydrogen.
(b) the number of moles of hydrogen collected.

Strategy

(a) Use Dalton's law to find the partial pressure of hydrogen, P_{H_2}.
(b) Use the ideal gas law to calculate n_{H_2}, with P_{H_2} as the pressure.

SOLUTION

(a) From Appendix 1, $P_{H_2O} = 23.76$ mm Hg at 25°C. The total pressure, P_{tot}, is 758 mm Hg.

$$P_{H_2} = P_{tot} - P_{H_2O} = 758 \text{ mm Hg} - 23.76 \text{ mm Hg} = 734 \text{ mm Hg}$$

(b) $$n_{H_2} = \frac{(P_{H_2})V}{RT} = \frac{(734/760 \text{ atm})(0.152 \text{ L})}{(0.0821 \text{ L} \cdot \text{atm/mol} \cdot \text{K})(298 \text{ K})} = 0.00600 \text{ mol } H_2$$

Vapor pressure, like density and solubility, is an intensive physical property that is characteristic of a particular substance. The vapor pressure of water at 25°C is 23.76 mm Hg, independent of volume or the presence of another gas. Like density and solubility, vapor pressure varies with temperature; for water it is 55.3 mm Hg at 40°C, 233.7 mm Hg at 70°C, and 760.0 mm Hg at 100°C. We will have more to say in Chapter 9 about the temperature dependence of vapor pressure.

Partial Pressure and Mole Fraction

As pointed out earlier, the following relationship applies to a mixture containing gas A (and gas B):

$$P_A = \frac{n_A RT}{V} \qquad P_{tot} = \frac{n_{tot} RT}{V}$$

Dividing P_A by P_{tot} gives

$$\frac{P_A}{P_{tot}} = \frac{n_A}{n_{tot}}$$

The fraction n_A/n_{tot} is referred to as the **mole fraction** of A in the mixture. It is the fraction of the total number of moles that is accounted for by gas A. Using X_A to represent the mole fraction of A (i.e., $X_A = n_A/n_{tot}$),

$$P_A = X_A P_{tot} \qquad \textbf{(5.4)}$$

If a mixture contains equal numbers of A and B molecules, $X_A = X_B = 0.50$ and $P_A = P_B = \frac{1}{2}P_{tot}$.

In other words, ***the partial pressure of a gas in a mixture is equal to its mole fraction multiplied by the total pressure.*** This relation is commonly used to calculate partial pressures of gases in a mixture when the total pressure and the composition of the mixture are known (Example 5.9).

Example 5.9 When one mole of methane, CH_4, is heated with four moles of oxygen, the following reaction occurs:

$$CH_4(g) + 2\,O_2(g) \longrightarrow CO_2(g) + 2H_2O(g)$$

Assuming all of the methane is converted to CO_2 and H_2O, what are the mole fractions of O_2, CO_2, and H_2O in the resulting mixture? If the total pressure of the mixture is 1.26 atm, what are the partial pressures?

Strategy First, calculate the number of moles of each gas (remember that oxygen is in excess). Then determine the mole fractions and finally the partial pressures.

SOLUTION Since all the methane is consumed,

$$n_{CH_4} = 0; \qquad n_{CO_2} = 1.00; \qquad n_{H_2O} = 2.00; \qquad n_{O_2} = 4.00 - 2.00 = 2.00$$

The total number of moles is 1.00 + 2.00 + 2.00 = 5.00.

$$X_{CO_2} = \frac{1.00}{5.00} = 0.200; \; X_{H_2O} = \frac{2.00}{5.00} = 0.400; \; X_{O_2} = \frac{2.00}{5.00} = 0.400$$

$$P_{CO_2} = 0.200 \times 1.26 \text{ atm} = 0.252 \text{ atm}$$
$$P_{H_2O} = 0.400 \times 1.26 \text{ atm} = 0.504 \text{ atm}$$
$$P_{O_2} = 0.400 \times 1.26 \text{ atm} = 0.504 \text{ atm}$$

Reality Check The partial pressures (0.252 atm, 0.504 atm, 0.504 atm) add up to the total pressure, 1.26 atm, as they should according to Dalton's law. They are also in the same ratio as the mole fractions (0.200, 0.400, 0.400).

5.6 KINETIC THEORY OF GASES

The fact that the ideal gas law applies to all gases indicates that the gaseous state is a relatively simple one from a molecular standpoint. Gases must have certain common properties that cause them to follow the same natural law. Between about 1850 and 1880, James Maxwell (1831–1879), Rudolf Clausius (1822–1888), Ludwig Boltzmann (1844–1906), and others developed the **kinetic theory** of gases. They based it on the idea that all gases behave similarly as far as particle motion is concerned.

CENGAGENOW™
Click Coached Problems for a self-study module on **kinetic theory.**

Molecular Model

By the use of the kinetic theory, it is possible to derive or explain the experimental behavior of gases. To do this we start with a simple molecular model which assumes that—

- ***gases are mostly empty space.*** The total volume of the molecules is negligibly small compared with that of the container to which they are confined.
- ***gas molecules are in constant, chaotic motion.*** They collide frequently with one another and with the container walls. As a result, their velocities are constantly changing.
- ***collisions are elastic.*** There are no attractive forces that would tend to make molecules "stick" to one another or to the container walls.
- ***gas pressure is caused by collisions of molecules with the walls of the container*** (Figure 5.7). As a result, pressure increases with the energy and frequency of these collisions.

In air, a molecule undergoes about 10 billion collisions per second.

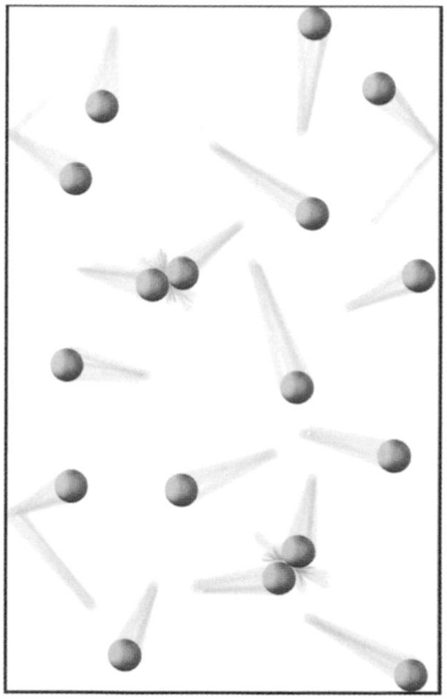

Figure 5.7
The kinetic molecular model of a gas. Gas molecules are in constant motion and their collisions are elastic. Collisions with the walls cause gas pressure.

Expression for Pressure, *P*

Applying the laws of physics to this simple model, it can be shown that the pressure (P) exerted by a gas in a container of volume V is

$$P = \frac{Nmu^2}{3V}$$

where N is the number of molecules, m is the mass of a molecule, and u is the average speed.* We will not attempt to derive this equation. However, it makes sense, at least qualitatively. In particular—

- the ratio N/V expresses the concentration of gas molecules in the container. The more molecules there are in a given volume, the greater the collision frequency and so the greater the pressure.
- the product mu^2 is a measure of the energy of collision. (When a Cadillac traveling at 100 mph collides with a brick wall, the energy transferred is much greater than would be obtained with a bicycle at 5 mph.) Hence, as this equation predicts, pressure is directly related to mu^2.

*More rigorously, u^2 is the average of the squares of the speeds of all molecules.

Average Kinetic Energy of Translational Motion, E_t

The kinetic energy, E_t, of a gas molecule of mass m moving at speed u is

$$E_t = \frac{mu^2}{2}$$

From the equation written above for P, we see that $mu^2 = 3PV/N$. Hence

$$E_t = \frac{3PV}{2N}$$

But the ideal gas law tells us that $PV = nRT$, so

$$E_t = \frac{3nRT}{2N}$$

This equation can be simplified by noting that the number of molecules, N, in a gas sample is equal to the number of moles, n, multiplied by Avogadro's number, N_A, that is, $N = n \times N_A$. Making this substitution in the above equation and simplifying, we obtain the final expression for the **average translational kinetic energy** of a gas molecule:

$$E_t = \frac{3RT}{2N_A} \qquad \textbf{(5.5)}$$

This equation contains three constants (3/2, R, N_A) and only one variable, the temperature T. It follows that—

A baseball in motion has translational energy.

- ***at a given temperature, molecules of different gases*** **(e.g., H_2, O_2, . . .)** ***must all have the same average kinetic energy of translational motion.***
- ***the average translational kinetic energy of a gas molecule is directly proportional to the Kelvin temperature, T.***

Average Speed, u

By equating the first and last expressions written above for E_t, we see that

$$\frac{mu^2}{2} = \frac{3RT}{2N_A}$$

E_t depends only on T; u depends on both T and MM.

Solving this equation for u^2:

$$u^2 = \frac{3RT}{mN_A}$$

But the product m (the mass of a molecule) times N_A (the number of molecules in a mole) is simply the molar mass MM, so we can write

$$u^2 = \frac{3RT}{\text{MM}}$$

Taking the square root of both sides of this equation, we arrive at the final expression for the **average speed, u,**

$$u = \left(\frac{3RT}{\text{MM}}\right)^{1/2} \qquad \textbf{(5.6)}$$

From this relation you can see that the average speed u is—

- ***directly proportional to the square root of the absolute temperature.*** For a given gas at two different temperatures, T_2 and T_1, the quantity MM is constant, and we can write

$$\frac{u_2}{u_1} = \left(\frac{T_2}{T_1}\right)^{1/2}$$

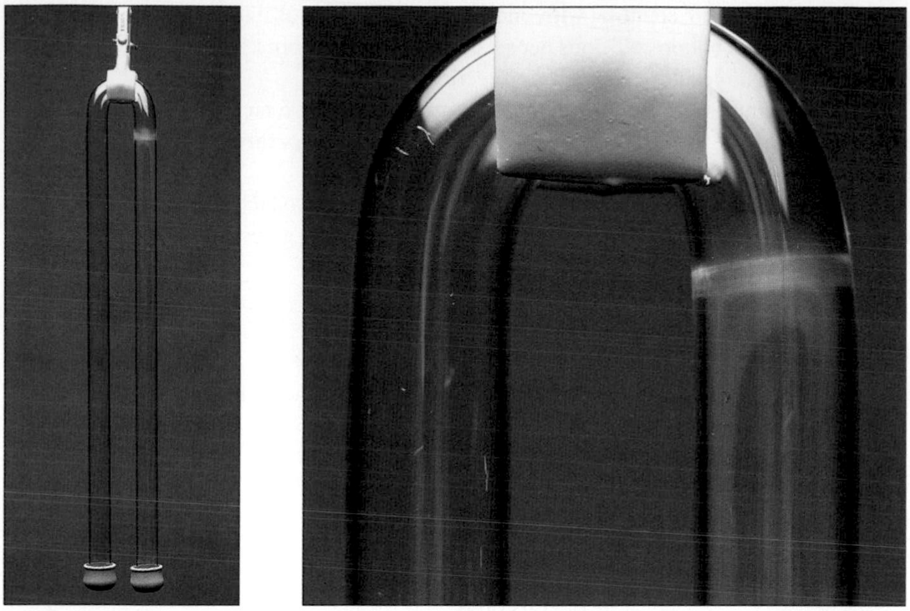

Marna G. Clarke

Figure 5.8
Relation of molecular speed to molar mass. When ammonia gas, which is injected into the left arm of the tube, comes in contact with hydrogen chloride, which is injected into the right arm of the tube, they react to form solid ammonium chloride: $NH_3(g) + HCl(g) \longrightarrow NH_4Cl(s)$. Because NH_3 (MM = 17 g/mol) moves faster than HCl (MM = 36.5 g/mol), the ammonium chloride forms closer to the HCl end of the tube.

- ***inversely proportional to the square root of molar mass* (MM)** (Figure 5.8). For two different gases A and B at the same temperature (T constant):

$$\frac{u_B}{u_A} = \left(\frac{MM_A}{MM_B}\right)^{1/2} \quad \textbf{(5.7)}$$

Example 5.10 Calculate the average speed, u, of an N_2 molecule at 25°C.

Strategy Use the equation $u = (3RT/MM)^{1/2}$; remember to use the proper value of $R = 8.31 \times 10^3\ g \cdot m^2/(s^2 \cdot mol \cdot K)$. Be careful about units!

SOLUTION

$$u = \left(\frac{3RT}{MM}\right)^{1/2} = \left[\frac{3 \times 8.31 \times 10^3 \frac{g \cdot m^2}{s^2 \cdot mol \cdot K} \times 298\ K}{28.02 \frac{g}{mol}}\right]^{1/2} = 515\ m/s$$

Reality Check Notice that the average speed is very high. In miles per hour it is

$$515 \frac{m}{s} \times \frac{1\ mi}{1.609 \times 10^3\ m} \times 3.600 \times 10^3 \frac{s}{h} = 1.15 \times 10^3\ mi/h$$

Effusion of Gases; Graham's Law

All of us are familiar with the process of gaseous diffusion, in which gas molecules move through space from a region of high concentration to one of low concentration. If your instructor momentarily opens a cylinder of chlorine gas at the lecture table, you will soon recognize the sharp odor of chlorine, particularly if you have a front-row seat in the classroom. On a more pleasant note, the odor associated with a freshly baked apple pie also reaches you via gaseous diffusion.

CENGAGENOW™
Click Coached Problems for a self-study module on **effusion.**

Diffusion is a relatively slow process; a sample of gas introduced at one location may take an hour or more to distribute itself uniformly throughout a room. At first glance this seems surprising, since as we saw in Example 5.10 gas molecules are moving very rapidly. However,

Diffusion is slower than effusion for the same reason that boarding a subway car is slower at 5 P.M. than at 5 A.M.

molecules are constantly colliding with one another; at 25°C and 1 atm, an N_2 molecule undergoes more than a billion collisions per second with its neighbors. This slows down the net movement of gas molecules in any given direction.

As we have implied, diffusion is a rather complex process so far as molecular motion is concerned. **Effusion,** the flow of gas molecules at low pressures through tiny pores or pinholes, is easier to analyze using kinetic theory.

The relative rates of effusion of different gases depend on two factors: the pressures of the gases and the relative speeds of their particles. If two different gases A and B are compared at the same pressure, only their speeds are of concern, and

$$\frac{\text{rate of effusion B}}{\text{rate of effusion A}} = \frac{u_B}{u_A}$$

where u_A and u_B are average speeds. As pointed out earlier, at a given temperature,

$$\frac{u_B}{u_A} = \left(\frac{MM_A}{MM_B}\right)^{1/2}$$

It follows that, at constant pressure and temperature,

$$\frac{\text{rate of effusion B}}{\text{rate of effusion A}} = \left(\frac{MM_A}{MM_B}\right)^{1/2}$$

This relation in a somewhat different form was discovered experimentally by the Scottish chemist Thomas Graham (1748–1843) in 1829. Graham was interested in a wide variety of chemical and physical problems, among them the separation of the components of air. **Graham's law** can be stated as

> ***At a given temperature and pressure, the rate of effusion of a gas, in moles per unit time, is inversely proportional to the square root of its molar mass.***

Graham's law tells us qualitatively that light molecules effuse more rapidly than heavier ones (Figure 5.8, p. 119). In quantitative form, it allows us to determine molar masses of gases (Example 5.11).

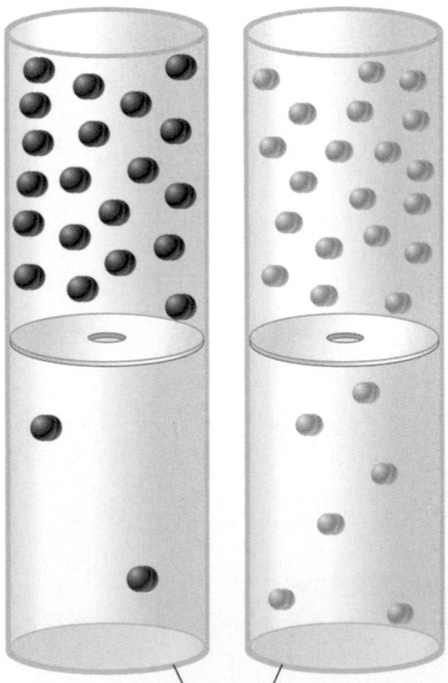

Effusion of gases. A gas with a higher molar mass (red molecules) effuses into a vacuum more slowly than a gas with a lower molar mass (gray molecules).

Example 5.11 In an effusion experiment, argon gas is allowed to expand through a tiny opening into an evacuated flask of volume 120 mL for 32.0 s, at which point the pressure in the flask is found to be 12.5 mm Hg. This experiment is repeated with a gas X of unknown molar mass at the same T and P. It is found that the pressure in the flask builds up to 12.5 mm Hg after 48.0 s. Calculate the molar mass of X.

Strategy The key to solving this problem is to realize that because P, T, and V are the same in the two experiments, *the number of moles of Ar and X effusing into the flask is the same:*

$$n_{Ar} = n_X = n$$

SOLUTION Comparing the two rates in moles per second

$$\frac{\text{rate Ar}}{\text{rate X}} = \frac{n/32.0\text{ s}}{n/48.0\text{ s}} = \frac{48.0}{32.0} = 1.50$$

Applying Graham's law

$$1.50 = \left(\frac{MM_X}{MM_{Ar}}\right)^{1/2}$$

Solving by squaring both sides and substituting $MM_{Ar} = 39.95$ g/mol

$$MM_X = (39.95\text{ g/mol}) \times (1.50)^2 = 89.9\text{ g/mol}$$

Reality Check Because it takes longer for gas X to effuse, it must have a larger molar mass than argon. It does!

A practical application of Graham's law arose during World War II, when scientists were studying the fission of uranium atoms as a source of energy. It became necessary to separate ${}^{235}_{92}U$, which is fissionable, from the more abundant isotope of uranium, ${}^{238}_{92}U$, which is not fissionable. Because the two isotopes have almost identical chemical properties, chemical separation was not feasible. Instead, an effusion process was worked out using uranium hexafluoride, UF_6. This compound is a gas at room temperature and low pressures. Preliminary experiments indicated that ${}^{235}_{92}UF_6$ could indeed be separated from ${}^{238}_{92}UF_6$ by effusion. The separation factor is very small, because the rates of effusion of these two species are nearly equal:

$$\frac{\text{rate of effusion of } {}^{235}_{92}UF_6}{\text{rate of effusion of } {}^{238}_{92}UF_6} = \left(\frac{352.0}{349.0}\right)^{1/2} = 1.004$$

so a great many repetitive separations are necessary. An enormous plant was built for this purpose in Oak Ridge, Tennessee. In this process, UF_6 effuses many thousands of times through porous barriers. The lighter fractions move on to the next stage, while heavier fractions are recycled through earlier stages. Eventually, a nearly complete separation of the two isotopes is achieved.

The time required for effusion is inversely related to rate.

Distribution of Molecular Speeds

As shown in Example 5.10, the average speed of an N_2 molecule at 25°C is 515 m/s; that of H_2 is even higher, 1920 m/s. However, not all molecules in these gases have these speeds. The motion of particles in a gas is utterly chaotic. In the course of a second, a particle undergoes millions of collisions with other particles. As a result, the speed and direction of motion of a particle are constantly changing. Over a period of time, the speed will vary from almost zero to some very high value, considerably above the average.

In 1860 James Clerk Maxwell, a Scottish physicist and one of the greatest theoreticians the world has ever known, showed that different possible speeds are distributed among particles in a definite way. Indeed, he developed a mathematical expression for this distribution. His results are shown graphically in Figure 5.9 for O_2 at 25°C and 1000°C. On the graph, the relative number of molecules having a certain speed is plotted against that speed. At 25°C, this number increases rapidly with the speed, up to a maximum of about 400 m/s. This is the most probable speed of an oxygen molecule at 25°C. Above about 400 m/s, the number of molecules moving at any particular speed decreases. For speeds in excess of about 1600 m/s, the fraction of molecules drops off to nearly zero. In general, most molecules have speeds rather close to the average value.

As temperature increases, the speed of the molecules increases. The distribution curve for molecular speeds (Figure 5.9) shifts to the right and becomes broader. The chance of a molecule having a very high speed is much greater at 1000°C than at 25°C. Note, for example,

CENGAGENOW™
Click Coached Problems for a self-study module on **distribution of molecular speeds.**

In a gas sample at any instant, gas molecules are moving at a variety of speeds.

Sort of like people—most of them go along with the crowd.

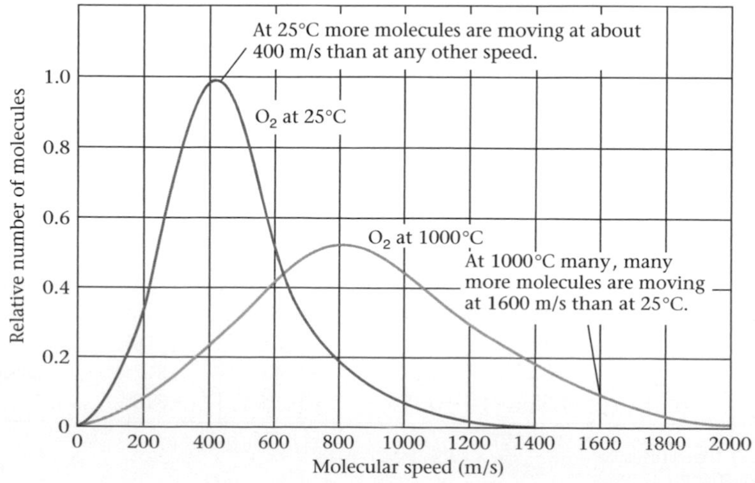

Figure 5.9
Distribution of molecular speeds of oxygen molecules at 25°C and 1000°C. At the higher temperature the fraction of molecules moving at very high speeds is greater.

that a large number of molecules have speeds greater than 1600 m/s at 1000°C; almost none have that speed at 25°C. The general principle here is one that we will find very useful when we look at the effect of temperature on reaction rate in Chapter 11.

Example 5.12 Conceptual

Consider the two boxes A and B shown below. Box B has a volume exactly twice that of box A. The circles ○ and ● represent one mole of HCl and He, respectively. The two boxes are at the same temperature.

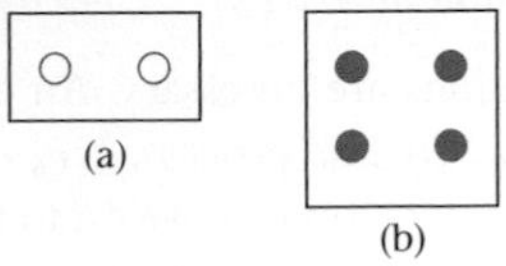

(a) Compare the pressures of the gases in the two containers.
(b) Compare the densities of the two gases.
(c) Compare the number of atoms in the two boxes.
(d) If the HCl in box A were transferred to box B, what would be the mole fraction of HCl in the mixture?
(e) Which of the two gases effuses faster?

SOLUTION

(a) Since n/V and T are the same in both cases, $P = nRT/V$ is the same for the two gases.
(b) The mass of HCl is 2(36.5 g) = 73.0 g; that of He is 4(4.00 g) = 16.0 g. Since $73.0\ g/V > 16.0\ g/2V$, HCl has the higher density.
(c) Two moles of diatomic HCl contain the same number of atoms as four moles of He.
(d) $X_{HCl} = 2/6 =$ 1/3
(e) Because HCl and He are at the same pressure, the lighter gas, He, effuses faster.

5.7 REAL GASES

In this chapter, the ideal gas law has been used in all calculations, with the assumption that it applies exactly. Under ordinary conditions, this assumption is a good one; however, all real gases deviate at least slightly from the ideal gas law. Table 5.2 shows the extent to which two gases, O_2 and CO_2, deviate from ideality at different temperatures and pressures. The data compare the experimentally observed molar volume, V_m

The molar volume is V when $n = 1$.

$$\text{molar volume} = V_m = V/n$$

Table 5.2 Real Versus Ideal Gases, Percent Deviation* in Molar Volume

	O_2			CO_2		
P(atm)	50°C	0°C	−50°C	50°C	0°C	−50°C
1	−0.0%	−0.1%	−0.2%	−0.4%	−0.7%	−1.4%
10	−0.4%	−1.0%	−2.1%	−4.0%	−7.1%	
40	−1.4%	−3.7%	−8.5%	−17.9%		
70	−2.2%	−6.0%	−14.4%	−34.2%	Condenses to liquid	
100	−2.8%	−7.7%	−19.1%	−59.0%		

*Percent deviation $= \dfrac{(V_m - V_m^\circ)}{V_m^\circ} \times 100\%$

with the molar volume calculated from the ideal gas law V_m°:

$$V_m^\circ = RT/P$$

It should be obvious from Table 5.2 that deviations from ideality become larger at *high pressures and low temperatures.* Moreover, the deviations are larger for CO_2 than for O_2. All of these effects can be correlated in terms of a simple, common-sense observation:

In general, the closer a gas is to the liquid state, the more it will deviate from the ideal gas law.

A gas is liquefied by going to low temperatures and/or high pressures. Moreover, as you can see from Table 5.2, carbon dioxide is much easier to liquefy than oxygen.

From a molecular standpoint, deviations from the ideal gas law arise because it neglects two factors:

1. attractive forces between gas particles.
2. the finite volume of gas particles.

We will now consider in turn the effect of these two factors on the molar volumes of real gases.

Attractive Forces

Notice that in Table 5.2 all the deviations are negative; the observed molar volume is less than that predicted by the ideal gas law. This effect can be attributed to attractive forces between gas particles. These forces tend to pull the particles toward one another, reducing the space between them. As a result, the particles are crowded into a smaller volume, just as if an additional external pressure were applied. The observed molar volume, V_m, becomes less than V_m°, and the deviation from ideality is *negative:*

Attractive forces make the molar volume smaller than expected.

$$\frac{V_m - V_m^\circ}{V_m^\circ} < 0$$

The magnitude of this effect depends on the strength of the attractive forces and hence on the nature of the gas. Intermolecular attractive forces are stronger in CO_2 than they are in O_2, which explains why the deviation from ideality of V_m is greater with carbon dioxide and why carbon dioxide is more readily condensed to a liquid than is oxygen.

Particle Volume

Figure 5.10 shows a plot of V_m/V_m° versus pressure for methane at 25°C. Up to about 150 atm, methane shows a steadily increasing negative deviation from ideality, as might be expected on the basis of attractive forces. At 150 atm, V_m is only about 70% of V_m°.

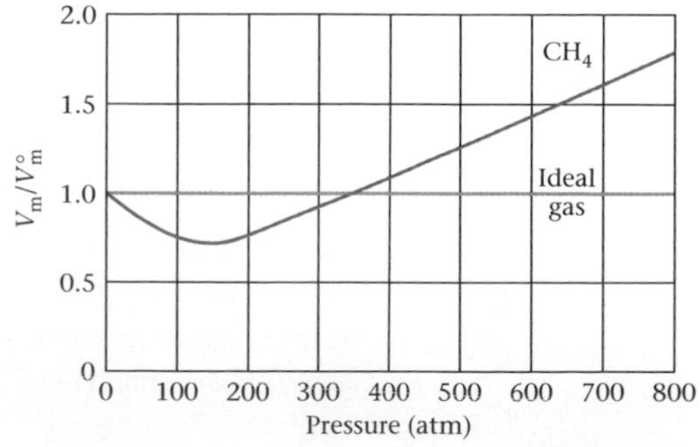

Figure 5.10
Deviation of methane gas from ideal gas behavior. Below about 350 atm, attractive forces between methane (CH_4) molecules cause the observed molar volume at 25°C to be less than that calculated from the ideal gas law. At 350 atm, the effect of the attractive forces is just balanced by that of the finite volume of CH_4 molecules, and the gas appears to behave ideally. Above 350 atm, the effect of finite molecular volume predominates and $V_m > V_m^\circ$.

At very high pressures, methane behaves quite differently. Above 150 atm, the ratio V_m/V_m° *increases,* becoming 1 at about 350 atm. Above that pressure, methane shows a *positive* deviation from the ideal gas law:

Particle volume makes the molar volume larger than expected.

$$\frac{V_m - V_m^\circ}{V_m^\circ} > 0$$

This effect is by no means unique to methane; it is observed with all gases. If the data in Table 5.2 are extended to very high pressures, oxygen and carbon dioxide behave like methane; V_m becomes larger than V_m°.

An increase in molar volume above that predicted by the ideal gas law is related to the finite volume of gas particles. These particles contribute to the observed volume, making V_m greater than V_m°. Ordinarily, this effect becomes evident only at high pressures, where the particles are quite close to one another.

CHEMISTRY Beyond the Classroom

Airbags

Since driver's-side airbags were made mandatory in 1984, it is estimated that they have saved thousands of lives (Figure A). The way they work is relatively simple. A mechanical sensor in the front of the vehicle is set off by any sudden impact equivalent to hitting a brick wall at 10 mph. The sensor sends an electrical signal to a gas generator attached to the airbag. The bag fills with gas in less than a tenth of a second, preventing the head or chest of the driver from striking the steering column.

Most airbags today are filled with nitrogen gas generated by a three-step reaction involving sodium azide (NaN_3), potassium nitrate (KNO_3), and silicon dioxide (SiO_2). In the first step, sodium azide decomposes to form nitrogen gas:

(1) $2NaN_3(s) \longrightarrow 2Na(s) + 3N_2(g)$

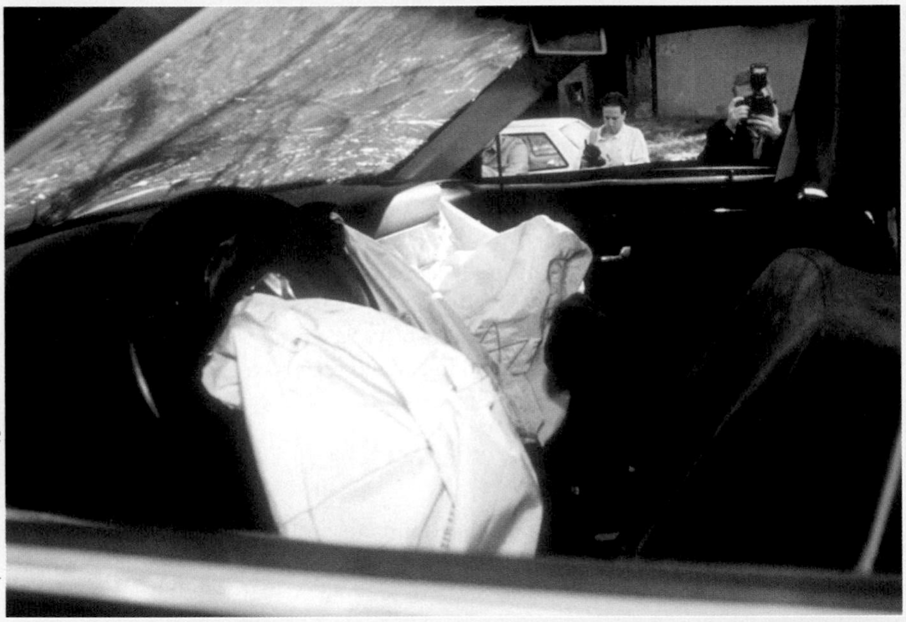

© Despotovic Dusko/Corbis Sygma

Figure A

Deployed airbags after a collision are filled with nitrogen gas. The gas is a byproduct of the decomposition of sodium azide, which is triggered by the collision.

The sodium metal formed as a by-product would react violently with any moisture present. The function of the potassium nitrate is to prevent this by reacting with the sodium:

(2) $2KNO_3(s) + 10Na(s) \longrightarrow K_2O(s) + 5Na_2O(s) + N_2(g)$

Finally, the strongly basic metal oxides react with silicon dioxide to form a glassy product:

(3) $K_2O(s) + Na_2O(s) + SiO_2(s) \longrightarrow$ glass

By applying the principles discussed in Section 5.4, you can calculate that for every liter of nitrogen (at 50°C and 1.25 atm) generated by Reaction 1, about 2.0 g of sodium azide and 0.63 g of potassium nitrate are required. This means that to inflate a 15-L airbag, the gas generator should contain at least 30 g of NaN_3 and 10 g of KNO_3.

Unfortunately, there are now more than 100 documented cases in which airbags have caused fatalities rather than preventing them. Many of the victims were infants or small children; it is now recommended that no child under the age of 12 should sit in the front seat of a vehicle equipped with a passenger-side airbag. Equally disturbing, adult drivers have been seriously injured or killed because they were sitting too close to the steering wheel when the airbag deployed; the minimum distance should be 25 cm (10 in.). That's easy to accomplish for a 6-ft 6-in. basketball player with long legs. It's not so easy for a short person who has trouble reaching the gas or brake pedal, let alone seeing over the steering wheel.

The solution to these problems is to develop "smart" airbag systems that can sense the severity of a collision, the size and weight of the driver, and how far his or her head is from the steering wheel. If desirable, the airbag can fill more slowly, perhaps in stages. Airbags of this type first became available in 2000 model cars, notably the Ford *Taurus*™.

Chapter Highlights

Key Concepts

1. Convert between units of *P*, *V*, *T*, and amount of gas.
   (Example 5.1; Problems 1–4) ■ Questions and Problems assignable in OWL: 3
2. Use the ideal gas law to
   - ■ solve initial and final state problems.
     (Example 5.2; Problems 5–14) ■ 8, 13
   - ■ calculate *P*, *V*, *T* or *n*.
     (Example 5.3; Problems 15–20) ■ 17
   - ■ calculate density or molar mass.
     (Example 5.4; Problems 21–30) ■ 22, 27
   - ■ relate amounts and volumes of gases in reactions.
     (Examples 5.5–5.7; Problems 31–40) ■ 31, 33, 35, 38, 90
3. Use Dalton's law.
   (Examples 5.8, 5.9; Problems 41–52) ■ 43, 46, 47
4. Calculate the speeds of gas molecules.
   (Example 5.10; Problems 53–56, 61, 62) ■ 53, 55, 61, 69
5. Use Graham's law to relate rate of effusion to molar mass.
   (Example 5.11; Problems 57–60) ■ 57

Select end of chapter Questions and Problems may be assigned in OWL and are cross-referenced in the Key Concepts list.

CENGAGENOW™

Sign in at **academic.cengage.com/now** to:

- ■ Check your readiness for an exam by taking the Pre-Test and exploring the self-study modules recommended in your Personalized Study plan.
- ■ For quick review, download Go Chemistry mini-lecture flashcard modules (or purchase them at **www.ichapters.com**)

Key Equations

Ideal gas law	$PV = nRT$ (Section 5.2)
Gas density	$d = (\text{MM}) \times P/RT$ (Section 5.3)
Dalton's law	$P_{\text{tot}} = P_A + P_B;\ P_A = X_A \times P_{\text{tot}}$ (Section 5.5)
Average translational energy	$E_t = 3RT/2N_A$ (Section 5.6)
Average speed	$u = (3RT/\text{MM})^{1/2}$ (Section 5.6)
Graham's law	$\text{rate}_B/\text{rate}_A = (\text{MM}_A/\text{MM}_B)^{1/2}$ (Section 5.6)

Key Terms

atmosphere (atm)
bar
effusion
kinetic theory
millimeter of mercury (mm Hg)
mole fraction
partial pressure
R (gas constant)
STP
vapor pressure

Summary Problem

Ammonia, NH_3, is the most important commercial compound of nitrogen. It can be produced by reacting nitrogen with hydrogen gas. This is the process used to produce ammonia commercially and is known as the Haber process.

$$N_2(g) + 3H_2(g) \longrightarrow 2NH_3(g)$$

(a) Ammonia is kept at 15°C in a 10.0-L flask with a pressure of 1.95 atm. What is the pressure in the flask if the temperature is increased to 25°C?

(b) Ammonia is kept in a cylinder with a movable piston at 25°C and 2.50 atm pressure. What is the pressure in the cylinder if the temperature is increased to 45°C and the piston is raised so that the volume occupied by the gas is doubled?

(c) How many grams of ammonia are produced if 7.85 L of ammonia is collected at −15°C and 5.93 atm pressure?

(d) What is the density of ammonia at 22°C and 745 mm Hg?

(e) If 5.0 L of nitrogen at 12°C and 1.30 atm pressure reacts with the same volume of hydrogen at the same temperature and pressure, what volume of ammonia is obtained at that temperature and pressure?

(f) What are the pressures of the gases in the flask after the reaction in (e) is complete? The total pressure in the flask is 1.75 atm.

(g) Ammonia can also be prepared by adding a strong base to an ammonium salt.

$$NH_4^+(aq) + OH^-(aq) \longrightarrow NH_3(g) + H_2O$$

What volume of ammonia gas at 25°C and 745 mm Hg is generated by mixing 25.00 mL of 6.50 *M* NH_4Cl and 45.00 mL of 0.432 *M* NaOH?

(h) Aqueous ammonia solutions are weak bases. They are obtained by bubbling ammonia gas in water. If 845 mL of gas at 1.00 atm pressure and 27°C is bubbled into 4.32 L of water, what is the molarity of the resulting solution? Assume the solution to have a final volume of 4.32 L.

(i) Compare the rate of effusion of NH_3 with that of N_2 at the same temperature and pressure. Compare the time required for equal numbers of moles of N_2 and NH_3 to effuse.

(j) The average speed of a nitrogen molecule at 25°C is 515 m/s. What is the average speed of an ammonia molecule at that temperature?

Answers

(a) 2.02 atm **(b)** 1.33 atm **(c)** 37.4 g **(d)** 0.689 g/L
(e) 3.3 L **(f)** 0.88 atm each **(g)** 0.485 L **(h)** 7.94×10^{-3}
(i) rate of NH_3 = 1.28 × rate of N_2; time of NH_3 = 0.780 × rate of N_2 **(j)** 659 m/s

Questions and Problems

Blue-numbered questions have answers in Appendix 6 and fully-worked solutions in the *Student Solutions Manual.*

■ denotes questions assignable in OWL.

WEB indicates that the solution is available on this book's companion website.

Measurements on Gases

1. A ten-gallon methane tank contains 1.243 mol of methane (CH_4) at 74°F. Express the volume of the tank in liters, the amount of methane in the tank in grams, and the temperature of the tank in Kelvin.

2. A 6.00-ft cylinder has a radius of 26 in. It contains 189 lb of helium at 25°C. Express the volume of the cylinder ($V = \pi r^2 h$) in liters, the amount of helium in moles, and the temperature in Kelvin.

3. ■ Complete the following table of pressure conversions.

mm Hg	atm	kPa	bar
396	______	______	______
______	1.15	______	______
______	______	97.1	______
______	______	______	1.00

4. Complete the following table of pressure conversions.

mm Hg	atm	kPa	bar
1215	______	______	______
______	0.714	______	______
______	______	143	______
______	______	______	0.904

Gas Law Calculations

5. A cylinder with a movable piston records a volume of 12.6 L when 3.0 mol of oxygen is added. The gas in the cylinder has a pressure of 5.83 atm. The cylinder develops a leak and the volume of the gas is now recorded to be 12.1 L at the same pressure. How many moles of oxygen are lost?

6. A tank is filled with a gas to a pressure of 977 mm Hg at 25°C. When the tank is heated, the pressure increases to 1.50 atm. To what temperature was the gas heated?

7. A sample of CO_2 gas at 22°C and 1.00 atm has a volume of 2.00 L. Determine the ratio of the original volume to the final volume when

(a) the pressure and amount of gas remain unchanged and the Celsius temperature is doubled.

(b) the pressure and amount of gas remain unchanged and the Kelvin temperature is doubled.

■ in OWL Blue-numbered questions answered in Appendix 6 **WEB** Solution is available on companion website

8. ■ A sample of air is originally at 32°C. If P and n are kept constant, to what temperature must the air be cooled to

(a) decrease its volume by 25%?

(b) decrease its volume to 25% of its original volume?

9. A basketball is inflated in a garage at 25°C to a gauge pressure of 8.0 psi. Gauge pressure is the pressure above atmospheric pressure, which is 14.7 psi. The ball is used on the driveway at a temperature of −7°C and feels flat. What is the actual pressure of the air in the ball? What is the gauge pressure?

10. A tire is inflated to a gauge pressure of 28.0 psi at 71°F. Gauge pressure is the pressure above atmospheric pressure, which is 14.7 psi. After several hours of driving, the air in the tire has a temperature of 115°F. What is the gauge pressure of the air in the tire? What is the actual pressure of the air in the tire? Assume that the tire volume changes are negligible.

11. A 38.0-L gas tank at 35°C has nitrogen at a pressure of 4.65 atm. The contents of the tank are transferred without loss to an evacuated 55.0-L tank in a cold room where the temperature is 4°C. What is the pressure in the tank?

12. **WEB** A sealed syringe has 25.0 mL of air at 23°C and 745 mm Hg pressure. The syringe is transferred to a water bath maintained at 82°C. The volume of the gas in the syringe increased by 8.0%. What is the pressure in the syringe? Did the pressure increase?

13. ■ A balloon filled with helium has a volume of 1.28×10^3 L at sea level where the pressure is 0.998 atm and the temperature is 31°C. The balloon is taken to the top of a mountain where the pressure is 0.753 atm and the temperature is −25°C. What is the volume of the balloon at the top of the mountain?

14. A flask has 1.35 mol of hydrogen gas at 25°C and a pressure of 1.05 atm. Nitrogen gas is added to the flask at the same temperature until the pressure rises to 1.64 atm. How many moles of nitrogen gas are added?

15. A two-liter plastic soft drink bottle can withstand a pressure of 5 atm. Half a cup (approximately 120 mL) of ethyl alcohol, C_2H_5OH (d = 0.789 g/mL), is poured into a soft drink bottle at room temperature. The bottle is then heated to 100°C (3 significant figures), changing the liquid alcohol to a gas. Will the soft drink bottle withstand the pressure, or will it explode?

16. Arterial blood contains about 0.25 mg of oxygen per milliliter. What is the pressure exerted by the oxygen in one liter of arterial blood at normal body temperature of 37°C?

17. ■ A piece of dry ice ($CO_2(s)$) has a mass of 22.50 g. It is dropped into an evacuated 2.50-L flask. What is the pressure in the flask at −4°C?

18. A 2.00-L tank, evacuated and empty, has a mass of 725.6 g. It is filled with butane gas (C_4H_{10}) at 22°C to a pressure of 1.78 atm. What is the mass of the tank after it is filled?

19. Complete the following table for dinitrogen tetroxide gas.

Pressure	Volume	Temperature	Moles	Grams
1.77 atm	4.98 L	43.1°C	______	______
673 mm Hg	488 mL	______	0.783	______
0.899 bar	______	912°C	______	6.25
______	1.15 L	39°F	0.166	______

20. **WEB** Use the ideal gas law to complete the following table for butane (C_4H_{10}) gas.

Pressure	Volume	Temperature	Moles	Grams
______	1.75 L	19°C	1.66	______
0.895 atm	______	6°C	______	14.0
433 mm Hg	92.4 mL	______	0.395	______
1.74 bar	8.66 L	98°F	______	______

21. Calculate the densities (in grams per liter) of the following gases at 75°F and 1.33 bar.

(a) argon (b) ammonia (c) acetylene (C_2H_2)

22. ■ Calculate the densities (in grams per liter) of the following gases at 97°C and 755 mm Hg.

(a) hydrogen chloride (b) sulfur dioxide

(c) butane (C_4H_{10})

23. Helium-filled balloons rise in the air because the density of helium is less than the density of air.

(a) If air has an average molar mass of 29.0 g/mol, what is the density of air at 25°C and 770 mm Hg?

(b) What is the density of helium at the same temperature and pressure?

(c) Would a balloon filled with carbon dioxide at the same temperature and pressure rise?

24. The air is said to be "thinner" in higher altitudes than at sea level. Compare the density of air at sea level where the barometric pressure is 755 mm Hg and the temperature is 0°C with the density of air on top of Mt. Everest at the same temperature. The barometric pressure at that altitude is 210 mm Hg (3 significant figures). Take the molar mass of air to be 29.0 g/mol.

25. Cyclopropane mixed in the proper ratio with oxygen can be used as an anesthetic. At 755 mm Hg and 25°C, it has a density of 1.71 g/L.

(a) What is the molar mass of cyclopropane?

(b) Cyclopropane is made up of 85.7% C and 14.3% H. What is the molecular formula of cyclopropane?

26. Phosgene is a highly toxic gas made up of carbon, oxygen, and chlorine atoms. Its density at 1.05 atm and 25°C is 4.24 g/L.

(a) What is the molar mass of phosgene?

(b) Phosgene is made up of 12.1% C, 16.2% O, and 71.7% Cl. What is the molecular formula of phosgene?

27. ■ The gas in the discharge cell of a laser contains (in mole percent) 11% CO_2, 5.3% N_2, and 84% He.

(a) What is the molar mass of this mixture?

(b) Calculate the density of this gas mixture at 32°C and 758 mm Hg.

(c) What is the ratio of the density of this gas to that of air (MM = 29.0 g/mol) at the same conditions?

28. Exhaled air contains 74.5% N_2, 15.7% O_2, 3.6% CO_2, and 6.2% H_2O (mole percent).

(a) Calculate the molar mass of exhaled air.

(b) Calculate the density of exhaled air at 37°C and 757 mm Hg, and compare the value obtained with that for ordinary air (MM = 29.0 g/mol).

29. A 1.58-g sample of $C_2H_3X_3(g)$ has a volume of 297 mL at 769 mm Hg and 35°C. Identify the element X.

30. A 2.00-g sample of $SX_6(g)$ has a volume of 329.5 cm^3 at 1.00 atm and 20°C. Identify the element X. Name the compound.

Stoichiometry of Gaseous Reactions

31. ■ Nitrogen oxide is a pollutant commonly found in smokestack emissions. One way to remove it is to react it with ammonia.

$$4NH_3(g) + 6NO(g) \longrightarrow 5N_2(g) + 6H_2O(l)$$

How many liters of ammonia are required to change 12.8 L of nitrogen oxide to nitrogen gas? Assume 100% yield and that all gases are measured at the same temperature and pressure.

32. Using the same reaction as in Question 31, and making the same assumptions, how many liters of nitrogen gas are formed when 297 L of NO are treated with ammonia?

33. ■ Dichlorine oxide is used as bactericide to purify water. It is produced by the chlorination of sulfur dioxide gas.

$$SO_2(g) + 2Cl_2(g) \longrightarrow SOCl_2(l) + Cl_2O(g)$$

■ in OWL Blue-numbered questions answered in Appendix 6 **WEB** Solution is available on companion website

How many liters of Cl_2O can be produced by mixing 5.85 L of SO_2 and 9.00 L of Cl_2? How many liters of the reactant in excess are present after reaction is complete? Assume 100% yield and that all the gases are measured at the same temperature and pressure.

34. Hydrogen sulfide gas (H_2S) is responsible for the foul odor of rotten eggs. When it reacts with oxygen, sulfur dioxide gas and steam are produced.

(a) Write a balanced equation for the reaction.

(b) How many liters of H_2S would be required to react with excess oxygen to produce 12.0 L of SO_2? The reaction yield is 88.5%. Assume constant temperature and pressure throughout the reaction.

35. ■ Nitric acid can be prepared by bubbling dinitrogen pentoxide into water.

$$N_2O_5(g) + H_2O \longrightarrow 2H^+(aq) + 2NO_3^-(aq)$$

(a) How many moles of H^+ are obtained when 1.50 L of N_2O_5 at 25°C and 1.00 atm pressure is bubbled into water?

(b) The solution obtained in (a) after reaction is complete has a volume of 437 mL. What is the molarity of the nitric acid obtained?

36. **WEB** Dinitrogen oxide, commonly called nitrous oxide, is used as a propellant gas for whipped-cream dispensers. It is prepared by heating ammonium nitrate to 250°C. Water vapor is also formed.

(a) Write a balanced equation for the decomposition of ammonium nitrate into nitrous oxide and steam.

(b) What volume of dinitrogen oxide gas is formed at 250°C and 1.0 atm when 5.00 g of NH_4NO_3 is heated? Assume 100% yield.

37. Hydrogen cyanide (HCN) is a poisonous gas that is used in gas chambers for the execution of those sentenced to death. It can be formed by the following reaction:

$$H^+(aq) + NaCN(s) \longrightarrow HCN(g) + Na^+(aq)$$

What volume of 6.00 *M* HCl is required to react with an excess of NaCN to produce enough HCN to fill a room 12 × 11 × 9 feet at a pressure of 0.987 atm and 72°F?

38. ■ When hydrogen peroxide decomposes, oxygen is produced:

$$2H_2O_2(aq) \longrightarrow 2H_2O + O_2(g)$$

What volume of oxygen gas at 25°C and 1.00 atm is produced from the decomposition of 25.00 mL of a 30.0% (by mass) solution of hydrogen peroxide (d = 1.05 g/mL)?

39. Nitroglycerine is an explosive used by the mining industry. It detonates according to the following equation:

$$4C_3H_5N_3O_9(l) \longrightarrow 12CO_2(g) + 6N_2(g) + 10H_2O(g) + O_2(g)$$

What volume is occupied by the gases produced when 10.00 g of nitroglycerine explodes? The total pressure is 1.45 atm at 523°C.

40. Ammonium nitrate can be used as an effective explosive because it decomposes into a large number of gaseous products. At a sufficiently high temperature, ammonium nitrate decomposes into nitrogen, oxygen, and steam.

(a) Write a balanced equation for the decomposition of ammonium nitrate.

(b) If 1.00 kg of ammonium nitrate is sealed into a 50.0-L steel drum and heated to 787°C, what is the pressure in the drum, assuming 100% decomposition?

Gas Mixtures

41. Some chambers used to grow bacteria that thrive on CO_2 have a gas mixture consisting of 95.0% CO_2 and 5.0% O_2 (mole percent). What is the partial pressure of each gas if the total pressure is 735 mm Hg?

42. A certain laser uses a gas mixture consisting of 9.00 g HCl, 2.00 g H_2, and 165.0 g of Ne. What pressure is exerted by the mixture in a 75.0-L tank at 22°C? Which gas has the smallest partial pressure?

43. ■ A sample of a smoke stack emission was collected into a 1.25-L tank at 752 mm Hg and analyzed. The analysis showed 92% CO_2, 3.6% NO, 1.2% SO_2, and 4.1% H_2O by mass. What is the partial pressure exerted by each gas?

44. The contents of a tank of natural gas at 1.20 atm is analyzed. The analysis showed the following mole percents: 88.6% CH_4, 8.9% C_2H_6, and 2.5% C_3H_8. What is the partial pressure of each gas in the tank?

45. A sample of gas collected over water at 42°C occupies a volume of one liter. The wet gas has a pressure of 0.986 atm. The gas is dried, and the dry gas occupies 1.04 L with a pressure of 1.00 atm at 90°C. Using this information, calculate the vapor pressure of water at 42°C.

46. ■ A sample of oxygen gas is collected over water at 25°C (vp $H_2O(l)$ = 23.8 mm Hg). The wet gas occupies a volume of 7.28 L at a total pressure of 1.25 bar. If all the water is removed, what volume will the dry oxygen occupy at a pressure of 1.07 atm and a temperature of 37°C?

47. ■ Consider two bulbs separated by a valve. Both bulbs are maintained at the same temperature. Assume that when the valve between the two bulbs is closed, the gases are sealed in their respective bulbs. When the valve is closed, the following data apply:

	Bulb A	Bulb B
Gas	Ne	CO
V	2.50 L	2.00 L
P	1.09 atm	0.773 atm

Assuming no temperature change, determine the final pressure inside the system after the valve connecting the two bulbs is opened. Ignore the volume of the tube connecting the two bulbs.

48. Follow the instructions of Problem 47 for the following set-up:

	Bulb A	Bulb B
Gas	Ar	Cl_2
V	4.00 L	1.00 L
P	2.50 atm	1.00 atm

49. When acetylene, C_2H_2, is burned in oxygen, carbon dioxide and steam are formed. A sample of acetylene with a volume of 7.50 L and a pressure of 1.00 atm is burned in excess oxygen at 225°C. The products are transferred without loss to a 10.0-L flask at the same temperature.

(a) Write a balanced equation for the reaction.

(b) What is the total pressure of the products in the 10.0-L flask?

(c) What is the partial pressure of each of the products in the flask?

50. Nitrogen can react with steam to form ammonia and nitrogen oxide gases. A 20.0-L sample of nitrogen at 173°C and 772 mm Hg is made to react with an excess of steam. The products are collected at room temperature (25°C) into an evacuated flask with a volume of 15.0 L.

(a) Write a balanced equation for the reaction.

(b) What is the total pressure of the products in the collecting flask after the reaction is complete?

(c) What is the partial pressure of each of the products in the flask?

51. A sample of oxygen is collected over water at 22°C and 752 mm Hg in a 125-mL flask. The vapor pressure of water at 22°C is 19.8 mm Hg.

(a) What is the partial pressure of oxygen?

(b) How many moles of dry gas are collected?

(c) How many moles of wet gas are in the flask?

(d) If 0.0250 g of $N_2(g)$ are added to the flask at the same temperature, what is the partial pressure of nitrogen in the flask?

(e) What is the total pressure in the flask after nitrogen is added?

■ in OWL Blue-numbered questions answered in Appendix 6 **WEB** Solution is available on companion website

52. **WEB** Hydrogen is collected over water at 25°C and 748 mm Hg in a 250-mL (3 significant figures) flask. The vapor pressure of water at 25°C is 23.8 mm Hg.

(a) What is the partial pressure of hydrogen?
(b) How many moles of water are in the flask?
(c) How many moles of dry gas are collected?
(d) If 0.0186 g of He are added to the flask at the same temperature, what is the partial pressure of helium in the flask?
(e) What is the total pressure in the flask after helium is added?

Kinetic Theory

53. ■ Rank the following gases

NO Ar N_2 N_2O_5

in order of

(a) increasing speed of effusion through a tiny opening.
(b) increasing time of effusion.

54. Rank the gases Xe, CH_4, F_2 and CH_2F_2 in order of

(a) increasing speed of effusion through a tiny opening.
(b) increasing time of effusion.

55. ■ What is the ratio of the rate of effusion of the most abundant gas, nitrogen, to the lightest gas, hydrogen?

56. A balloon filled with nitrogen gas has a small leak. Another balloon filled with hydrogen gas has an identical leak. How much faster will the hydrogen balloon deflate?

57. ■ A gas effuses 1.55 times faster than propane (C_3H_8) at the same temperature and pressure.

(a) Is the gas heavier or lighter than propane?
(b) What is the molar mass of the gas?

58. An unknown gas effuses through an opening at a rate one-fifth as fast as that of helium gas

(a) Is the gas heavier than helium?
(b) What is the molar mass of the gas?

59. If 0.0129 mol of N_2O_4 effuses through a pinhole in a certain amount of time, how much NO would effuse in that same amount of time under the same conditions?

60. It takes 12.6 s for 1.73×10^{-3} mol of CO to effuse through a pinhole. Under the same conditions, how long will it take for the same amount of CO_2 to effuse through the same pinhole?

61. ■ At what temperature will a molecule of uranium hexafluoride, the densest gas known, have the same average speed as a molecule of the lightest gas, hydrogen, at 37°C?

62. What is the average speed of

(a) a bromine molecule at 28°C?
(b) a krypton atom at −28°C?

Real Gases

63. The normal boiling points of CO and SO_2 are −192°C and −10°C, respectively.

(a) At 25°C and 1 atm, which gas would you expect to have a molar volume closest to the ideal value?
(b) If you wanted to reduce the deviation from ideal gas behavior, in what direction would you change the temperature? The pressure?

64. A sample of methane gas (CH_4) is at 50°C and 20 atm. Would you expect it to behave more or less ideally if

(a) the pressure were reduced to 1 atm?
(b) the temperature were reduced to −50°C?

65. Using Figure 5.10

(a) estimate the density of methane gas at 200 atm.
(b) compare the value obtained in (a) with that calculated from the ideal gas law.

66. Using Figure 5.10

(a) estimate the density of methane gas at 100 atm.
(b) compare the value obtained in (a) with that calculated from the ideal gas law.
(c) determine the pressure at which the calculated density and the actual density of methane will be the same.

Unclassified

67. When air pollution is high, ozone (O_3) contents can reach 0.60 ppm (i.e., 0.60 mol ozone per million mol air). How many molecules of ozone are present per liter of polluted air if the barometric pressure is 755 mm Hg and the temperature is 79°F?

68. The pressure exerted by a column of liquid is directly proportional to its density and height. If you wanted to make a barometer in which the liquid is a heavy oil instead of mercury, how long should the tube be? Take the density of the oil to be 2.73 g/mL (*d* Hg = 13.6 g/cm³).

69. ■ A mixture of 3.5 mol of Kr and 3.9 mol of He occupies a 10.00-L container at 300 K. Which gas has the larger

(a) average translational energy? (b) partial pressure?
(c) mole fraction? (d) effusion rate?

70. Given that 1.00 mol of neon and 1.00 mol of hydrogen chloride gas are in separate containers at the same temperature and pressure, calculate each of the following ratios.

(a) volume Ne/volume HCl (b) density Ne/density HCl
(c) average translational energy Ne/average translational energy HCl
(d) number of Ne atoms/number of HCl molecules

71. An intermediate reaction used in the production of nitrogen-containing fertilizers is that between ammonia and oxygen:

$$4NH_3(g) + 5O_2(g) \longrightarrow 4NO(g) + 6H_2O(g)$$

A 150.0-L reaction chamber is charged with reactants to the following partial pressures at 500°C: $P_{NH_3} = 1.3$ atm, $P_{O_2} = 1.5$ atm. What is the limiting reactant?

72. A Porsche 928 S4 engine has a cylinder volume of 618 cm³. The cylinder is full of air at 75°C and 1.00 atm.

(a) How many moles of oxygen are in the cylinder? (Mole percent of oxygen in air = 21.0.)
(b) Assume that the hydrocarbons in gasoline have an average molar mass of 1.0×10^2 g/mol and react with oxygen in a 1:12 mole ratio. How many grams of gasoline should be injected into the cylinder to react with the oxygen?

73. At 25°C and 380 mm Hg, the density of sulfur dioxide is 1.31 g/L. The rate of effusion of sulfur dioxide through an orifice is 4.48 mL/s. What is the density of a sample of gas that effuses through an identical orifice at the rate of 6.78 mL/s under the same conditions? What is the molar mass of the gas?

74. Glycine is an amino acid made up of carbon, hydrogen, oxygen, and nitrogen atoms. Combustion of a 0.2036-g sample gives 132.9 mL of CO_2 at 25°C and 1.00 atm and 0.122 g of water. What are the percentages of carbon and hydrogen in glycine? Another sample of glycine weighing 0.2500 g is treated in such a way that all the nitrogen atoms are converted to $N_2(g)$. This gas has a volume of 40.8 mL at 25°C and 1.00 atm. What is the percentage of nitrogen in glycine? What is the percentage of oxygen? What is the empirical formula of glycine?

Conceptual Questions

75. Consider a vessel with a movable piston. A reaction takes place in the vessel at constant pressure and a temperature of 200 K. When reaction is complete, the pressure remains the same and the volume and temperature double. Which of the following balanced equations best describes the reaction?

(a) $A + B_2 \longrightarrow AB_2$
(b) $A_2 + B_2 \longrightarrow 2AB$

■ in OWL Blue-numbered questions answered in Appendix 6 **WEB** Solution is available on companion website

(c) $2AB + B_2 \longrightarrow 2AB_2$

(d) $2AB_2 \longrightarrow A_2 + 2B_2$

76. Consider two flasks with the same volume, temperature, and pressure. One flask contains N_2, the other He. Which statements are true about the gases in the flasks?

(a) Both flasks have the same number of moles.

(b) The density of nitrogen in its flask is less than the density of helium in the other flask.

(c) Identical pinholes are made in both flasks. Nitrogen will effuse faster.

(d) The average translational energy of gas molecules in both flasks is the same.

(e) One mole of CO_2 is introduced to each flask. In the resulting mixture of gases, the mole fraction of He in one flask is equal to the mole fraction of N_2 in the other.

77. Consider three sealed tanks all at the same temperature, pressure, and volume.

Tank A contains SO_2 gas.
Tank B contains O_2 gas.
Tank C contains CH_4 gas.

Use **LT** (for "*is less than*"), **GT** (for "*is greater than*"), **EQ** (for "*is equal to*"), or **MI** (for "*more information required*") as answers to the blanks below.

(a) The mass of SO_2 in tank A ________ the mass of O_2 in tank B.

(b) The average translational energy of CH_4 in tank C ________ the average translational energy of SO_2 in tank A.

(c) It takes 20 s for all of the O_2 gas in tank B to effuse out of a pinhole in the tank. The time it takes for all of the SO_2 to effuse out of tank A from an identical pinhole ________ 40 s.

(d) The density of O_2 in tank B ________ the density of CH_4 in tank C.

(e) The temperature in tank A is increased from 150 K to 300 K. The temperature in tank B is kept at 150 K. The pressure in tank A is ________ half the pressure in tank B.

78. A rigid sealed cylinder has seven molecules of neon (Ne).

(a) Make a sketch of the cylinder with the neon molecules at 25°C. Make a similar sketch of the same seven molecules in the same cylinder at -80°C.

(b) Make the same sketches asked for in part (a), but this time attach a pressure gauge to the cylinder.

79. Sketch a cylinder with ten molecules of helium (He) gas. The cylinder has a movable piston. Label this sketch *before.* Make an *after* sketch to represent

(a) a decrease in temperature at constant pressure.

(b) a decrease in pressure from 1000 mm Hg to 500 mm Hg at constant temperature.

(c) five molecules of H_2 gas added at constant temperature and pressure.

80. Tank A has ammonia at 300 K. Tank B has nitrogen gas at 150 K. Tanks A and B have the same volume. Compare the pressures in tanks A and B if

(a) tank B has twice as many moles of nitrogen as tank A has of ammonia.

(b) tank A has the same number of moles of ammonia as tank B has of nitrogen. (Try to do this without a calculator!)

81. Two tanks have the same volume and are kept at the same temperature. Compare the pressure in both tanks if

(a) tank A has 2.00 mol of carbon dioxide and tank B has 2.00 mol of helium.

(b) tank A has 2.00 g of carbon dioxide and tank B has 2.00 g of helium. (Try to do this without a calculator!)

82. The graph below shows the distribution of molecular speeds for helium and carbon dioxide at the same temperature.

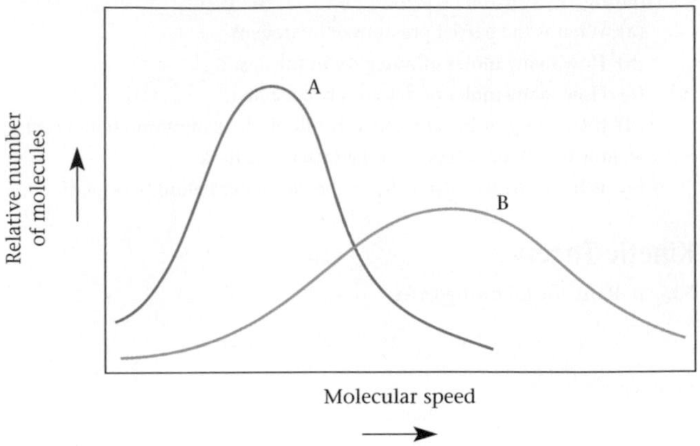

(a) Which curve could represent the behavior of carbon dioxide?

(b) Which curve represents the gas that would effuse more quickly?

(c) Which curve could represent the behavior of helium gas?

83. Consider the sketch below. Each square in bulb A represents a mole of atoms X. Each circle in bulb B represents a mole of atoms Y. The bulbs have the same volume, and the temperature is kept constant. When the valve is opened, atoms of X react with atoms of Y according to the following equation:

$$2X(g) + Y(g) \longrightarrow X_2Y(g)$$

The gaseous product is represented as □○□, and each □○□ represents one mole of product.

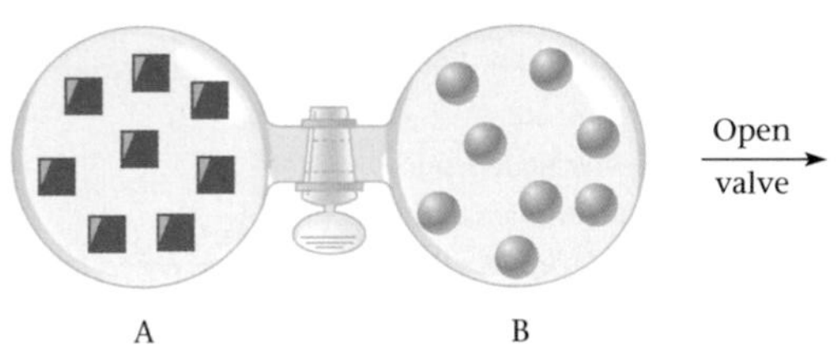

(a) If $P_A = 2.0$ atm, what is P_B before the valve is opened and the reaction is allowed to occur? What is $P_A + P_B$?

(b) Redraw the sketch above to represent what happens after the valve is opened.

(c) What is P_A? What is P_B? What is $P_A + P_B$? Compare your answer with the answer in part (a).

84. The following figure shows three 1.00-L bulbs connected by valves. Each bulb contains neon gas with amounts proportional to the number of atoms pictorially represented in each chamber. All three bulbs are maintained at the same temperature. Unless stated otherwise, assume that the valves connecting chambers are closed and seal the gases in their respective chambers. Assume also that the volume between chambers is negligible.

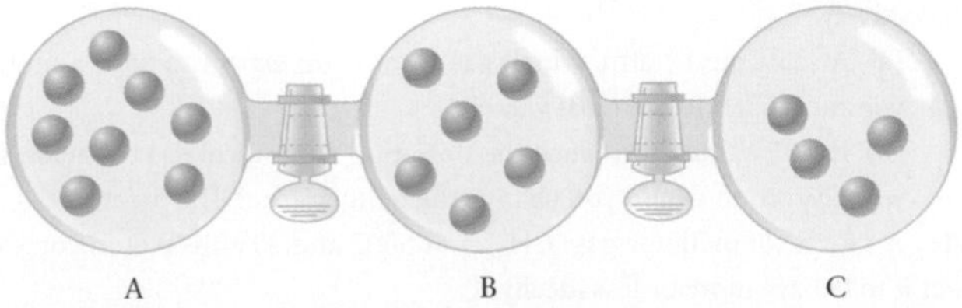

(a) Which bulb has the lowest pressure?

(b) If the pressure in bulb A is 2.00 atm, what is the pressure in bulb C?

(c) If the pressure in bulb A is 2.00 atm, what is the sum of $P_A + P_B + P_C$?

■ in OWL Blue-numbered questions answered in Appendix 6 **WEB** Solution is available on companion website

(d) If the pressure in bulb A is 2.00 atm and the valve between bulbs A and B is opened, redraw the above figure to accurately represent the gas atoms in all the bulbs. What is $P_A + P_B$? What is $P_A + P_B + P_C$? Compare your answer with your answer in part (c).

(e) Follow the same instructions as in (d) if all the valves are open.

85. Consider three sealed steel tanks, labeled X, Y, and Z. Each tank has the same volume and the same temperature. In each tank, one mole of CH_4 is represented by a circle, one mole of oxygen by a square, and one mole of SO_2 by a triangle. Assume that no reaction takes place between these molecules.

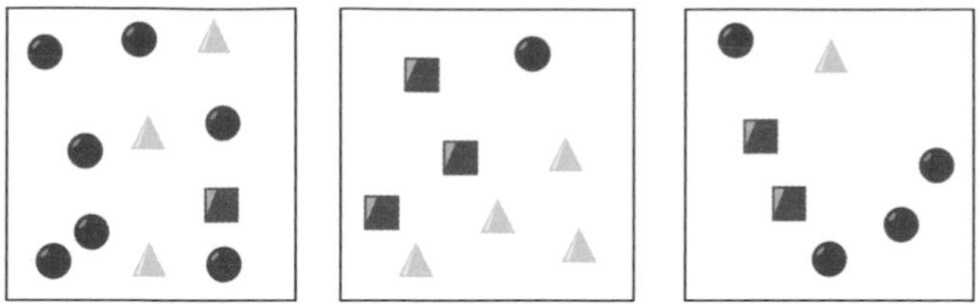

Tank X Tank Y Tank Z

(a) In which tank is the total pressure highest?

(b) In which tank is the partial pressure of SO_2 highest?

(c) In which tank is the mass of all three gases the same?

(d) Which tank has the heaviest contents?

Challenge Problems

86. ■ Consider an ideal gas that exerts a pressure of 23.76 mm Hg at 25°C. Assuming n and V are held constant, what would its pressure be at 40°C? 70°C? 100°C? Compare the numbers you have just calculated with the vapor pressures of water at these temperatures. Can you suggest a reason why the two sets of numbers are so different?

87. The escape velocity required for gas molecules to overcome the earth's gravity and go off to outer space is 1.12×10^3 m/s at 15°C. Calculate the molar mass of a species with that velocity. Would you expect to find He and H_2 molecules in the earth's atmosphere? How about argon atoms?

88. A tube 5.0 ft long is evacuated. Samples of NH_3 and HCl, at the same temperature and pressure, are introduced simultaneously through tiny openings at opposite ends of the tube. When the two gases meet, a white ring of $NH_4Cl(s)$ forms. How far from the end at which ammonia was introduced will the ring form?

89. The Rankine temperature scale resembles the Kelvin scale in that 0° is taken to be the lowest attainable temperature (0°R = 0 K). However, the Rankine degree is the same size as the Fahrenheit degree, whereas the Kelvin degree is the same size as the Celsius degree. What is the value of the gas constant in L-atm/(mol-°R)?

90. ■ A 0.2500-g sample of an Al-Zn alloy reacts with HCl to form hydrogen gas:

$$Al(s) + 3H^+(aq) \longrightarrow Al^{3+}(aq) + \tfrac{3}{2}H_2(g)$$

$$Zn(s) + 2H^+(aq) \longrightarrow Zn^{2+}(aq) + H_2(g)$$

The hydrogen produced has a volume of 0.147 L at 25°C and 755 mm Hg. What is the percentage of zinc in the alloy?

91. The buoyant force on a balloon is equal to the mass of air it displaces. The gravitational force on the balloon is equal to the sum of the masses of the balloon, the gas it contains, and the balloonist. If the balloon and the balloonist together weigh 168 kg, what would the diameter of a spherical hydrogen-filled balloon have to be in meters if the rig is to get off the ground at 22°C and 758 mm Hg? (Take $MM_{air} = 29.0$ g/mol.)

92. A mixture in which the mole ratio of hydrogen to oxygen is 2:1 is used to prepare water by the reaction

$$2H_2(g) + O_2(g) \longrightarrow 2H_2O(g)$$

The total pressure in the container is 0.950 atm at 25°C before the reaction. What is the final pressure in the container at 125°C after the reaction, assuming an 88.0% yield and no volume change?

93. The volume fraction of a gas A in a mixture is defined by the equation

$$\text{volume fraction A} = \frac{V_A}{V}$$

where V is the total volume and V_A is the volume that gas A would occupy alone at the same temperature and pressure. Assuming ideal gas behavior, show that the volume fraction is the same as the mole fraction. Explain why the volume fraction differs from the mass fraction.

■ in OWL Blue-numbered questions answered in Appendix 6 WEB Solution is available on companion website

6 Electronic Structure and the Periodic Table

Not chaos-like crush'd and bruis'd
But, as the world, harmoniously confus'd,
Where order in variety we see,
And where, though all things differ, all agree.
—Alexander Pope
"Windsor Forest"

Chapter Outline

A rainbow, usually seen when the sun comes out after a rainfall, is the result of the dispersion of visible light (from the sun) into its component colors. The water droplets act as prisms.

In Chapter 2 we briefly considered the structure of the atom. You will recall that every atom has a tiny, positively charged nucleus, made up of protons and neutrons. The nucleus is surrounded by negatively charged electrons. The number of protons in the nucleus is characteristic of the atoms of a particular element and is referred to as the atomic number. In a neutral atom, the number of electrons is equal to the number of protons and hence to the atomic number.

In this chapter, we focus on electron arrangements in atoms, paying particular attention to the relative energies of different electrons *(energy levels)* and their spatial locations *(orbitals)*. Specifically, we consider the nature of the energy levels and orbitals available to—

- the single electron in the hydrogen atom (Section 6.2).
- the several electrons in more complex atoms (Sections 6.3, 6.4).

With this background, we show how electron arrangements in multielectron atoms and the monatomic ions derived from them can be described in terms of—

- ***electron configurations,*** which show the number of electrons in each energy level (Sections 6.5, 6.7).
- ***orbital diagrams,*** which show the arrangement of electrons within orbitals (Sections 6.6, 6.7).

The electron configuration or orbital diagram of an atom of an element can be deduced from its position in the periodic table. Beyond that, position in the table can be used to predict (Section 6.8) the relative sizes of atoms and ions *(atomic radius, ionic radius)* and the relative tendencies of atoms to give up or acquire electrons *(ionization energy, electronegativity).*

Before dealing with electronic structures as such, it will be helpful to examine briefly the experimental evidence on which such structures are based (Section 6.1). In particular, we need to look at the phenomenon of *atomic spectra.* ■

Online homework for this chapter may be assigned in OWL

CENGAGENOW™

This icon introduces an opportunity for self-study and to explore interactive modules by signing in at **academic.cengage.com/now.**

Chemical properties of atoms and molecules depend on their electronic structures.

6.1 LIGHT, PHOTON ENERGIES, AND ATOMIC SPECTRA

Fireworks displays are fascinating to watch. Neon lights and sodium vapor lamps can transform the skyline of a city with their brilliant colors. The eerie phenomenon of the aurora borealis is an unforgettable experience when you see it for the first time. All of these events relate to the generation of light and its transmission through space.

Paul Silverman/Fundamental Photographs NYC

Fireworks. The different colors are created by the atomic spectra of different elements.

The Wave Nature of Light: Wavelength and Frequency

Light travels through space as a wave, which is made up of successive crests, which rise above the midline, and troughs, which sink below it. Waves have three primary characteristics (Fig. 6.1, p. 134), two of which are of particular interest at this point:

1. **Wavelength** (λ), the distance between two consecutive crests or troughs, most often measured in meters or nanometers (1 nm = 10^{-9} m).
2. **Frequency** (ν), the number of wave cycles (successive crests or troughs) that pass a given point in unit time. If 10^8 cycles pass a particular point in one second,

$$\nu = 10^8/\text{s} = 10^8 \text{ Hz}$$

The frequency unit *hertz* (Hz) represents one cycle per second.

λ is the Greek letter lambda; ν is the Greek letter nu.

CENGAGENOW™

Click Coached Problems for a self-study module on **determining frequency.**

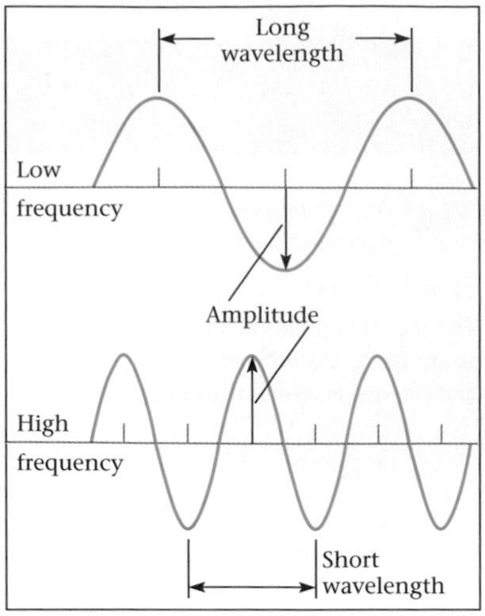

Figure 6.1
Characteristics of waves. The *amplitude* (Ψ) is the height of a crest or the depth of a trough. The *wavelength* (λ) is the distance between successive crests or troughs. The *frequency* (ν) is the number of wave cycles (successive crests or troughs) that pass a given point in a given time.

The speed at which a wave moves through space can be found by multiplying the length of a wave cycle (λ) by the number of cycles passing a point in unit time (ν). For light,

$$\lambda\nu = c \tag{6.1}$$

where c, the speed of light in a vacuum, is 2.998×10^8 m/s. To use this equation with this value of c—

- λ should be expressed in meters.
- ν should be expressed in reciprocal seconds (hertz).

Example 6.1 You sit in your back yard on a warm summer evening watching the red sky ($\lambda = 625$ nm) at sunset and listening to music from your CD player. The laser in the latter has frequency $3.84 \times 10^{14}\ \text{s}^{-1}$.

(a) What is the frequency of the radiation from the red sky?
(b) What is the wavelength of the laser in nm?

Strategy Use the equation: $\lambda\nu = c$, taking $c = 2.998 \times 10^8$ m/s. Note that λ must be expressed in meters.

SOLUTION

(a) $\lambda = 625\ \text{nm} \times \dfrac{1\ \text{m}}{10^9\ \text{nm}} = 6.25 \times 10^{-7}\ \text{m}$

$\nu = \dfrac{2.998 \times 10^8\ \text{m/s}}{6.25 \times 10^{-7}\ \text{m}} = 4.80 \times 10^{14}\ \text{s}^{-1} = 4.80 \times 10^{14}\ \text{Hz}$

(b) $\lambda = \dfrac{2.998 \times 10^8\ \text{m/s}}{3.84 \times 10^{14}\ \text{s}^{-1}} \times \dfrac{10^9\ \text{nm}}{1\ \text{m}} = 781\ \text{nm}$

Light visible to the eye is a tiny portion of the entire *electromagnetic spectrum* (Figure 6.2), covering only the narrow wavelength region 400 to 700 nm. You can see the red glow given off by charcoal on a barbecue grill, but the heat given off is largely in the infrared (IR) region, above 700 nm. Microwave ovens produce radiation at even longer wavelengths. At

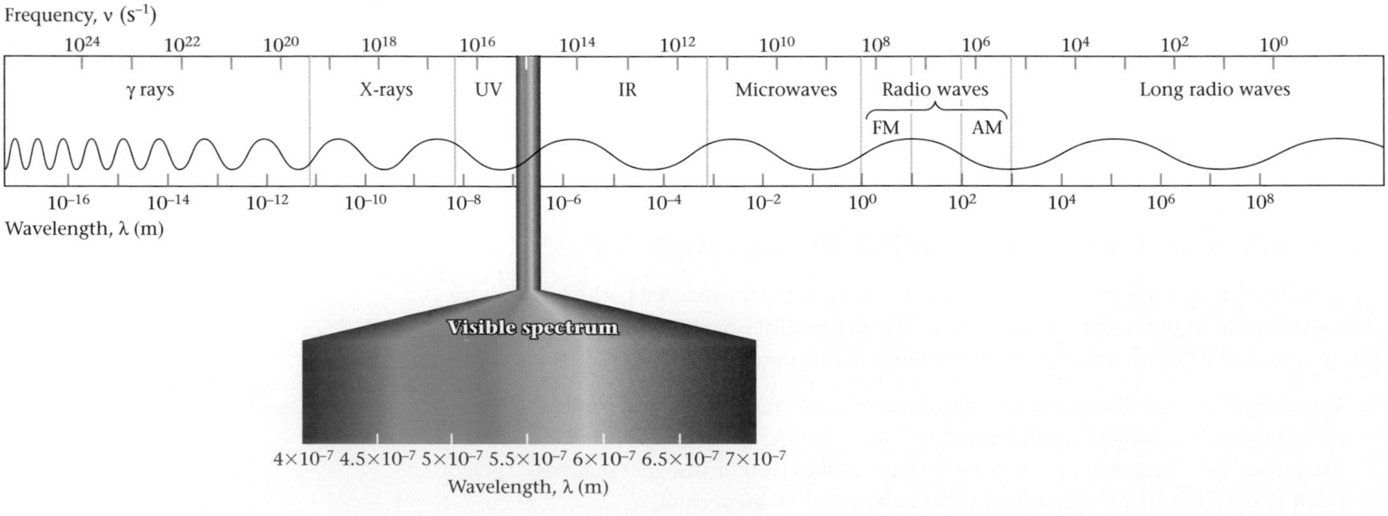

Figure 6.2
The electromagnetic spectrum. Note that only a small fraction is visible to the human eye.

the other end of the spectrum, below 400 nm, are ultraviolet (UV) radiation, responsible for sunburn, and x-rays, used for diagnostic purposes in medicine.

The Particle Nature of Light; Photon Energies

A hundred years ago it was generally supposed that all the properties of light could be explained in terms of its wave nature. A series of investigations carried out between 1900 and 1910 by Max Planck (1858–1947) (blackbody radiation) and Albert Einstein (1879–1955) (photoelectric effect) discredited that notion. Today we consider light to be generated as a stream of particles called **photons,** whose energy E is given by the equation

CENGAGENOW™
Click Coached Problems for a self-study module on **energy of light.**

$$E = h\nu = hc/\lambda \qquad \textbf{(6.2)}$$

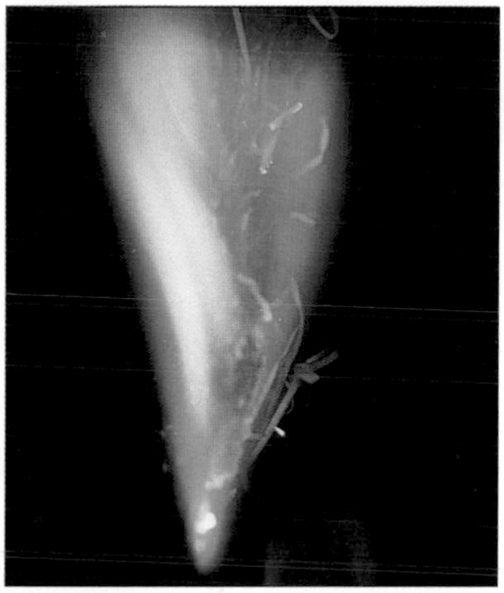
Charles D. Winters

Energy and wavelength. A copper wire held in a flame colors the flame green. The energy of the photons of this light can be calculated from its wavelength.

Throughout this text, we will use the SI unit ***joule*** (J), defined in Appendix 1, to express energy. A joule is a rather small quantity. One joule of electrical energy would keep a 10-W lightbulb burning for only a tenth of a second. For that reason, we will often express energies in ***kilojoules*** (1 kJ = 10^3 J). The quantity h appearing in Planck's equation is referred to as Planck's constant.

$$h = 6.626 \times 10^{-34}\ \text{J} \cdot \text{s}$$

Notice from this equation that energy is *inversely* related to wavelength. This explains why you put on sunscreen to protect yourself from UV solar radiation (<400 nm) and a "lead apron" when dental x-rays (<10 nm) are being taken. Conversely, IR (>700 nm) and microwave photons (>80,000 nm) are of relatively low energy (but don't try walking on hot coals).

Example 6.2 Graded

Sodium vapor lamps are commonly used to illuminate highways because of their intense yellow-orange emissions at 589 nm.

*(a) Calculate the energy, in joules, of one photon of this light.
**(b) Calculate the energy, in kilojoules, of one mole of such photons.
***(c) To sense visible light, the optic nerve needs at least 2.0×10^{-17} J of energy to trigger impulses that reach the brain. How many photons of the sodium lamp emissions are needed to "see" the yellow light?

Strategy Use the equation $E = hc/\lambda$. In part (b), remember to use Avogadro's number.

SOLUTION

(a) $$E = \frac{hc}{\lambda} = \frac{(6.626 \times 10^{-34}\ \text{J} \cdot \text{s})(2.998 \times 10^{8}\ \text{m/s})}{5.89 \times 10^{-7}\ \text{m}} = \boxed{3.37 \times 10^{-19}\ \text{J}}$$

This may seem like a tiny amount of energy, but bear in mind that it comes from a single photon.

(b) $$E = \frac{3.37 \times 10^{-19}\ \text{J}}{1\ \text{photon}} \times \frac{1\ \text{kJ}}{1000\ \text{J}} \times \frac{6.022 \times 10^{23}\ \text{photons}}{1\ \text{mol}} = \boxed{203\ \text{kJ}}$$

This is roughly comparable to the energy effects in chemical reactions; about 240 kJ of heat is evolved when a mole of H_2 burns, for instance.

(c) From (a) you obtain the conversion factor.

$$\frac{3.37 \times 10^{-19}\ \text{J}}{1\ \text{photon}}$$

Using that, we have

$$2.0 \times 10^{-17}\ \text{J} \times \frac{1\ \text{photon}}{3.37 \times 10^{-19}\ \text{J}} = \boxed{59\ \text{photons}}$$

Not too many photons are needed to sense the light.

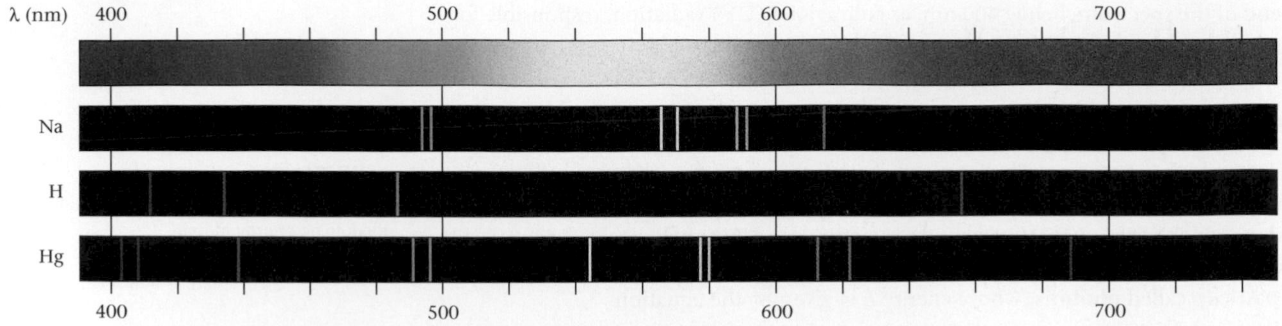

Figure 6.3
Continuous and line emission spectra. From the top down: The continuous visible spectrum; the line emission spectra for sodium (Na), hydrogen (H), and mercury (Hg).

Atomic Spectra

CENGAGENOW™
Click Coached Problems for a self-study module on **atomic line spectra.**

In the seventeenth century, Sir Isaac Newton showed that visible (white) light from the Sun can be broken down into its various color components by a prism. The **spectrum** obtained is continuous; it contains essentially all wavelengths between 400 and 700 nm.

The situation with high-energy atoms of gaseous elements is quite different (Figure 6.3). Here the spectrum consists of discrete lines given off at specific wavelengths. Each element has a characteristic spectrum that can be used to identify it. In the case of sodium, there are two strong lines in the yellow region at 589.0 nm and 589.6 nm. These lines account for the yellow color of sodium vapor lamps used to illuminate highways.

Atomic spectroscopy can identify metals at concentrations as low as 10^{-7} mol/L.

The fact that the photons making up atomic spectra have only certain discrete wavelengths implies that they can have only certain discrete energies, because

$$E = h\nu = hc/\lambda$$

Because these photons are produced when an electron moves from one energy level to another, the electronic energy levels in an atom must be *quantized,* that is, limited to particular values. Moreover, it would seem that by measuring the spectrum of an element it should be possible to unravel its electronic energy levels. This is indeed possible, but it isn't easy. Gaseous atoms typically give off hundreds, even thousands, of spectral lines.

One of the simplest of atomic spectra, and the most important from a theoretical standpoint, is that of hydrogen. When energized by a high-voltage discharge, gaseous hydrogen atoms emit radiation at wavelengths that can be grouped into several different series (Table 6.1). The first of these to be discovered, the Balmer series, lies partly in the visible region. It consists of a strong line at 656.28 nm followed by successively weaker lines, closer and closer together, at lower wavelengths.

Balmer was a Swiss high-school teacher.

Table 6.1 Wavelengths (nm) of Lines in the Atomic Spectrum of Hydrogen

Ultraviolet (Lyman Series)	Visible (Balmer Series)	Infrared (Paschen Series)
121.53	656.28	1875.09
102.54	486.13	1281.80
97.23	434.05	1093.80
94.95	410.18	1004.93
93.75	397.01	
93.05		

6.2 THE HYDROGEN ATOM

The hydrogen atom, containing a single electron, has played a major role in the development of models of electronic structure. In 1913 Niels Bohr (1885–1962), a Danish physicist, offered a theoretical explanation of the atomic spectrum of hydrogen. His model was based largely on classical mechanics. In 1922 this model earned him the Nobel Prize in physics. By that time, Bohr had become director of the Institute of Theoretical Physics at Copenhagen. There he helped develop the new discipline of quantum mechanics, used by other scientists to construct a more sophisticated model for the hydrogen atom.

Bohr, a giant of twentieth century physics, was respected by scientists and politicians alike.

Bohr, like all the other individuals mentioned in this chapter, was not a chemist. His only real contact with chemistry came as an undergraduate at the University of Copenhagen. His chemistry teacher, Niels Bjerrum, who later became his close friend and sailing companion, recalled that Bohr set a record for broken glassware that lasted half a century.

CENGAGENOW™
Click Coached Problems for a self-study module on **the hydrogen atom.**

Bohr Model

Bohr assumed that a hydrogen atom consists of a central proton about which an electron moves in a circular orbit. He related the electrostatic force of attraction of the proton for the electron to the centrifugal force due to the circular motion of the electron. In this way, Bohr was able to express the energy of the atom in terms of the radius of the electron's orbit. To this point, his analysis was purely classical, based on Coulomb's law of electrostatic attraction and Newton's laws of motion. To progress beyond this point, Bohr boldly and arbitrarily assumed, in effect, that the electron in the hydrogen atom can have only certain definite energies. Using arguments that we will not go into, Bohr obtained the following equation for the energy of the hydrogen electron:

$$E_{\mathbf{n}} = -R_H/\mathbf{n}^2 \qquad \textbf{(6.3)}$$

$E_{\mathbf{n}} = -2.180 \times 10^{-18}\ \mathrm{J}/\mathbf{n}^2$

where $E_{\mathbf{n}}$ is the energy of the electron, R_H is a quantity called the Rydberg constant (modern value = 2.180×10^{-18} J), and **n** is an integer called the principal quantum number. Depending on the state of the electron, **n** can have any positive, integral value, that is,

$$\mathbf{n} = 1, 2, 3, \ldots$$

Before proceeding with the Bohr model, let us make three points:

1. In setting up his model, Bohr designated zero energy as the point at which the proton and electron are completely separated. Energy has to be absorbed to reach that point. This means that the electron, in all its allowed energy states within the atom, must have an energy below zero; that is, it must be negative, hence the minus sign in the equation:

$$E_{\mathbf{n}} = -R_H/\mathbf{n}^2$$

2. Ordinarily the hydrogen electron is in its lowest energy state, referred to as the **ground state** or ground level, for which **n** = 1. When an electron absorbs enough energy, it moves to a higher, **excited state.** In a hydrogen atom, the first excited state has **n** = 2, the second **n** = 3, and so on.

3. When an excited electron gives off energy as a photon of light, it drops back to a lower energy state. The electron can return to the ground state (from **n** = 2 to **n** = 1, for example) or to a lower excited state (from **n** = 3 to **n** = 2). In every case, the energy of the photon ($h\nu$) evolved is equal to the difference in energy between the two states:

$$\Delta E = h\nu = E_{\mathrm{hi}} - E_{\mathrm{lo}}$$

where E_{hi} and E_{lo} are the energies of the higher and lower states, respectively.

Using this expression for ΔE and the equation $E_{\mathbf{n}} = -R_H/\mathbf{n}^2$, it is possible to relate the frequency of the light emitted to the quantum numbers, $\mathbf{n}_{\mathrm{hi}}$ and $\mathbf{n}_{\mathrm{lo}}$, of the two states:

$$h\nu = -R_H\left[\frac{1}{(\mathbf{n}_{\mathrm{hi}})^2} - \frac{1}{(\mathbf{n}_{\mathrm{lo}})^2}\right]$$

$$\nu = \frac{R_H}{h}\left[\frac{1}{(\mathbf{n}_{\mathrm{lo}})^2} - \frac{1}{(\mathbf{n}_{\mathrm{hi}})^2}\right] \qquad \textbf{(6.4)}$$

The last equation written is the one Bohr derived in applying his model to the hydrogen atom. Given

$$R_H = 2.180 \times 10^{-18}\,\text{J} \qquad h = 6.626 \times 10^{-34}\,\text{J} \cdot \text{s}$$

you can use the equation to find the frequency or wavelength of any of the lines in the hydrogen spectrum.

Example 6.3 Calculate the wavelength in nanometers of the line in the Balmer series that results from the transition **n** = 4 to **n** = 2.

Strategy Use Equation 6.4 to find the frequency; $\mathbf{n}_{lo} = 2$, $\mathbf{n}_{hi} = 4$. Then use the equation $\lambda = c/\nu$ to find the wavelength.

SOLUTION

$$\nu = \frac{2.180 \times 10^{-18}\,\text{J}}{6.626 \times 10^{-34}\,\text{J} \cdot \text{s}}\left[\frac{1}{4} - \frac{1}{16}\right] = 6.169 \times 10^{14}/\text{s}$$

$$\lambda = \frac{c}{\nu} = \frac{2.998 \times 10^{8}\,\text{m/s}}{6.169 \times 10^{14}/\text{s}} \times \frac{10^{9}\,\text{nm}}{1\,\text{m}} = 486.0\,\text{nm}$$

Reality Check Compare this value with that listed in Table 6.1 for the second line in the Balmer series.

All of the lines in the Balmer series (Table 6.1) come from transitions to the level **n** = 2 from higher levels (**n** = 3, 4, 5, . . .). Similarly, lines in the Lyman series arise when electrons fall to the **n** = 1 level from higher levels (**n** = 2, 3, 4, . . .). For the Paschen series, which lies in the infrared, the lower level is always **n** = 3.

Quantum Mechanical Model

Bohr's theory for the structure of the hydrogen atom was highly successful. Scientists of the day must have thought they were on the verge of being able to predict the allowed energy levels of all atoms. However, the extension of Bohr's ideas to atoms with two or more electrons gave, at best, only qualitative agreement with experiment. Consider, for example, what happens when Bohr's theory is applied to the helium atom. For helium, the errors in calculated energies and wavelengths are of the order of 5% instead of the 0.1% error with hydrogen. There appeared to be no way the theory could be modified to make it work well with helium or other atoms. Indeed, it soon became apparent that there was a fundamental problem with the Bohr model. The idea of an electron moving about the nucleus in a well-defined orbit at a fixed distance from the nucleus had to be abandoned.

Scientists in the 1920s, speculating on this problem, became convinced that an entirely new approach was required to treat electrons in atoms and molecules. In 1924 a young French scientist, Louis de Broglie (1892–1987), in his doctoral thesis at the Sorbonne made a revolutionary suggestion. He reasoned that if light could show the behavior of particles (photons) as well as waves, then perhaps an electron, which Bohr had treated as a particle, could behave like a wave. In a few years, de Broglie's postulate was confirmed experimentally. This led to the development of a whole new discipline, first called wave mechanics, more commonly known today as *quantum mechanics.*

The quantum mechanical atom differs from the Bohr model in several ways. In particular, according to quantum mechanics—

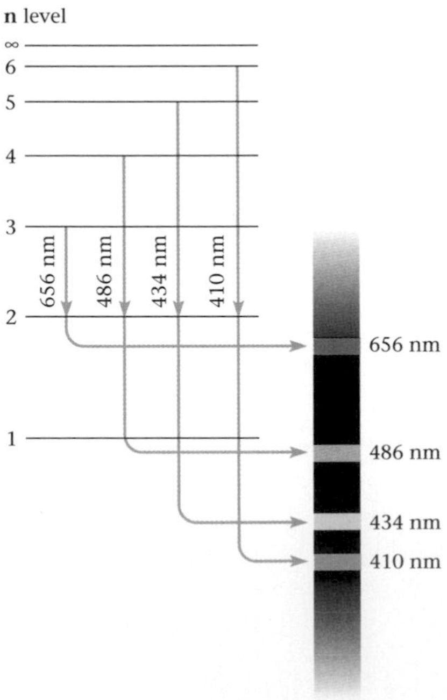

Some Balmer series lines for hydrogen. The lines in the visible region result from transitions from levels with values of **n** greater than 2 to the **n** = 2 level.

- ***the kinetic energy of an electron is inversely related to the volume of the region to which it is confined.*** This phenomenon has no analog in classical mechanics, but it helps to explain the stability of the hydrogen atom. Consider what happens when an electron moves closer and closer to the nucleus. The electrostatic energy decreases; that is, it becomes more negative. If this were the only factor, the electron should radiate energy and "fall" into the nucleus. However, the kinetic energy is increasing at the same time, because the electron is moving within a smaller and smaller volume. The two effects oppose each other; at some point a balance is reached and the atom is stable.

- ***it is impossible to specify the precise position of an electron in an atom at a given instant.*** Neither can we describe in detail the path that an electron takes about the nucleus. (After all, if we can't say where the electron is, we certainly don't know how it got there.) The best we can do is to estimate the *probability* of finding the electron within a particular region.

In 1926 Erwin Schrödinger (1887–1961), an Austrian physicist, made a major contribution to quantum mechanics. He wrote down a rather complex differential equation to express the wave properties of an electron in an atom. This equation can be solved, at least in principle, to find the amplitude (height) ψ of the electron wave at various points in space. The quantity ψ (psi) is known as the *wave function.* Although we will not use the Schrödinger wave equation in any calculations, you should realize that much of our discussion of electronic structure is based on solutions to that equation for the electron in the hydrogen atom.

In case you're curious, the equation is $\frac{d^2\Psi}{dx^2} + \frac{8\pi^2 m(E - V)}{h^2}\Psi = 0$ (and that's just in one dimension).

For the hydrogen electron, the square of the wave function, ψ^2, is directly proportional to the probability of finding the electron at a particular point. If ψ^2 at point A is twice as large as at point B, then we are twice as likely to find the electron at A as at B. Putting it another way, over time the electron will turn up at A twice as often as at B.

Figure 6.4a, an *electron cloud* diagram, shows how ψ^2 for the hydrogen electron in its ground state (**n** = 1) varies moving out from the nucleus. The depth of the color is supposed to be directly proportional to ψ^2 and hence to the probability of finding the electron at a point. As you can see, the color fades moving out from the nucleus in any direction; the value of ψ^2 drops accordingly.

Seems strange, but an electron is more likely to be found at the nucleus than at any other point.

Another, more common way of showing the electron distribution in the ground state of the hydrogen atom is to draw the *orbital* (Figure 6.4b) within which there is a 90% chance of finding the electron. Notice that the orbital is spherical, which means that the probability is independent of direction; the electron is equally likely to be found north, south, east, or west of the nucleus.

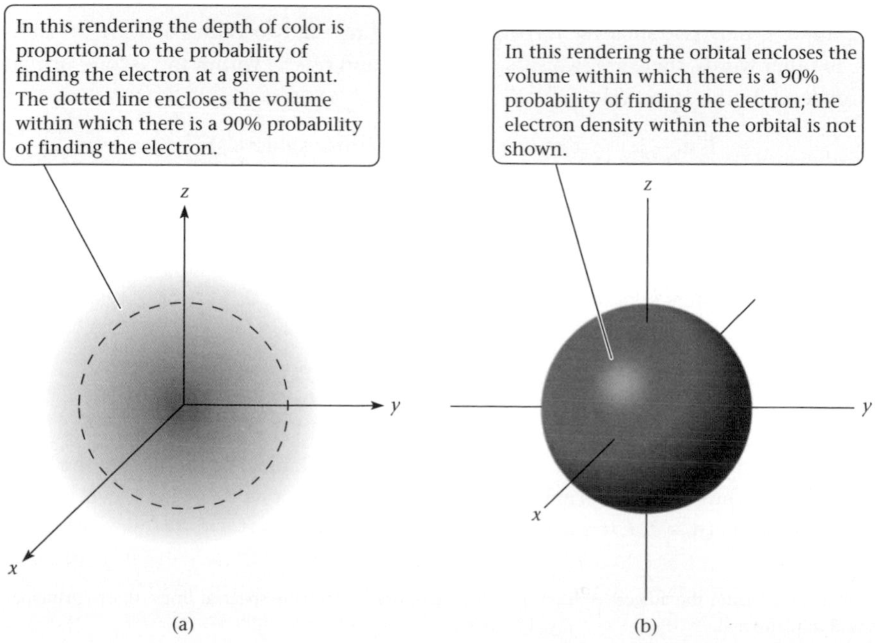

Figure 6.4
Two different ways of showing the electron distribution in the ground state of the hydrogen atom.

6.3 QUANTUM NUMBERS

CENGAGENOW™
Click Coached Problems for a self-study module on **quantum numbers.**

The Schrödinger equation can be solved approximately for atoms with two or more electrons. There are many solutions for the wave function, ψ, each associated with a set of numbers called quantum numbers. Three such numbers are given the symbols $\mathbf{n}$, ℓ, and $\mathbf{m}_\ell$. A wave function corresponding to a particular set of three quantum numbers (e.g., $\mathbf{n} = 2$, $\ell = 1$, $\mathbf{m}_\ell = 0$) is associated with an electron occupying an atomic orbital. From the expression for ψ, we can deduce the relative energy of that orbital, its shape, and its orientation in space.

For reasons we will discuss later, a fourth quantum number is required to completely describe a specific electron in a multielectron atom. The fourth quantum number is given the symbol $\mathbf{m}_s$. Each electron in an atom has a set of four quantum numbers: $\mathbf{n}$, ℓ, $\mathbf{m}_\ell$, and $\mathbf{m}_s$. We will now discuss the quantum numbers of electrons as they are used in atoms beyond hydrogen.

First Quantum Number, n; Principal Energy Levels

The first quantum number, given the symbol **n,** is of primary importance in determining the energy of an electron. For the hydrogen atom, the energy depends upon only **n** (recall Equation 6.3). In other atoms, the energy of each electron depends mainly, but not completely, upon the value of **n.** As **n** increases, the energy of the electron increases and, on the average, it is found farther out from the nucleus. The quantum number **n** can take on only integral values, starting with 1:

$$\mathbf{n} = 1, 2, 3, 4, \ldots \qquad (6.5)$$

An electron for which $\mathbf{n} = 1$ is said to be in the first **principal level.** If $\mathbf{n} = 2$, we are dealing with the second principal level, and so on.

Second Quantum Number, ℓ; Sublevels (s, p, d, f)

Each principal energy level includes one or more sublevels. The sublevels are denoted by the second quantum number, ℓ. As we will see later, the general shape of the electron cloud associated with an electron is determined by ℓ. Larger values of ℓ produce more complex shapes. The quantum numbers **n** and ℓ are related; ℓ can take on any integral value starting with 0 and going up to a maximum of $(\mathbf{n} - 1)$. That is,

$$\ell = 0, 1, 2, \ldots, (\mathbf{n} - 1) \qquad (6.6)$$

This relation between n and ℓ comes from the Schrödinger equation.

If $\mathbf{n} = 1$, there is only one possible value of ℓ—namely 0. This means that, in the first principal level, there is only one sublevel, for which $\ell = 0$. If $\mathbf{n} = 2$, two values of ℓ are possible, 0 and 1. In other words, there are two sublevels ($\ell = 0$ and $\ell = 1$) within the second principal energy level. In the same way,

if $\mathbf{n} = 3$:	$\ell = 0, 1, \text{or } 2$	(three sublevels)
if $\mathbf{n} = 4$:	$\ell = 0, 1, 2, \text{or } 3$	(four sublevels)

In general, ***in the* n*th principal level, there are* n *different sublevels.***

Another method is commonly used to designate sublevels. Instead of giving the quantum number ℓ, the letters s, p, d, or f* indicate the sublevels $\ell = 0, 1, 2,$ or 3, respectively. That is,

quantum number, ℓ	0	1	2	3
type of sublevel	s	p	d	f

Usually, in designating a sublevel, a number is included (Table 6.2) to indicate the principal level as well. Thus reference is made to a 1s sublevel ($\mathbf{n} = 1$, $\ell = 0$), a 2s sublevel ($\mathbf{n} = 2$, $\ell = 0$), a 2p sublevel ($\mathbf{n} = 2$, $\ell = 1$), and so on.

*These letters come from the adjectives used by spectroscopists to describe spectral lines: *s*harp, *p*rincipal, *d*iffuse, and *f*undamental.

Table 6.2	Sublevel Designations for the First Four Principal Levels									
n	1	2		3			4			
ℓ	0	0	1	0	1	2	0	1	2	3
Sublevel	1s	2s	2p	3s	3p	3d	4s	4p	4d	4f

For atoms containing more than one electron, the energy is dependent on ℓ as well as **n.** Within a given principal level (same value of **n**), sublevels increase in energy in the order

$$\mathbf{ns} < \mathbf{np} < \mathbf{nd} < \mathbf{nf}$$

Thus a 2p sublevel has a slightly higher energy than a 2s sublevel. By the same token, when $\mathbf{n} = 3$, the 3s sublevel has the lowest energy, the 3p is intermediate, and the 3d has the highest energy.

Which would have the higher energy, 4p or 3s?

Third Quantum Number, m_ℓ; Orbitals

An electron occupies an orbital within a sublevel of a principal energy level.

Each sublevel contains one or more orbitals, which differ from one another in the value assigned to the third quantum number, $\mathbf{m}_\ell$. This quantum number determines the direction in space of the electron cloud surrounding the nucleus. The value of $\mathbf{m}_\ell$ is related to that of ℓ. For a given value of ℓ, $\mathbf{m}_\ell$ can have any integral value, including 0, between ℓ and $-\ell$, that is

$$\mathbf{m}_\ell = \ell, \ldots, +1, 0, -1, \ldots, -\ell \qquad \mathbf{(6.7)}$$

To illustrate how this rule works, consider an s sublevel ($\ell = 0$). Here $\mathbf{m}_\ell$ can have only one value, 0. This means that an s sublevel contains only one orbital, referred to as an s orbital. For a p orbital ($\ell = 1$) $\mathbf{m}_\ell = 1, 0,$ or -1. Within a given p sublevel there are three different orbitals described by the quantum numbers $\mathbf{m}_\ell = 1,\ 0,$ and -1. All three of these orbitals have the same energy.

For the d and f sublevels

d sublevel:	$\ell = 2$	$\mathbf{m}_\ell = 2, 1, 0, -1, -2$	5 orbitals
f sublevel:	$\ell = 3$	$\mathbf{m}_\ell = 3, 2, 1, 0, -1, -2, -3$	7 orbitals

Here again all the orbitals in a given d or f sublevel have the same energy.

Fourth Quantum Number, m_s; Electron Spin

The fourth quantum number, $\mathbf{m}_s$, is associated with **electron spin.** An electron has magnetic properties that correspond to those of a charged particle spinning on its axis. Either of two spins is possible, clockwise or counterclockwise (Figure 6.5).

The quantum number $\mathbf{m}_s$ was introduced to make theory consistent with experiment. In that sense, it differs from the first three quantum numbers, which came from the solution to the Schrödinger wave equation for the hydrogen atom. This quantum number is not related to **n,** ℓ, or $\mathbf{m}_\ell$. It can have either of two possible values:

$$\mathbf{m}_s = +1/2 \quad \text{or} \quad -1/2 \qquad \mathbf{(6.8)}$$

Electrons that have the same value of $\mathbf{m}_s$ (i.e., both $+\frac{1}{2}$ or both $-\frac{1}{2}$) are said to have *parallel* spins. Electrons that have different $\mathbf{m}_s$ values (i.e., one $+\frac{1}{2}$ and the other $-\frac{1}{2}$) are said to have *opposed* spins.

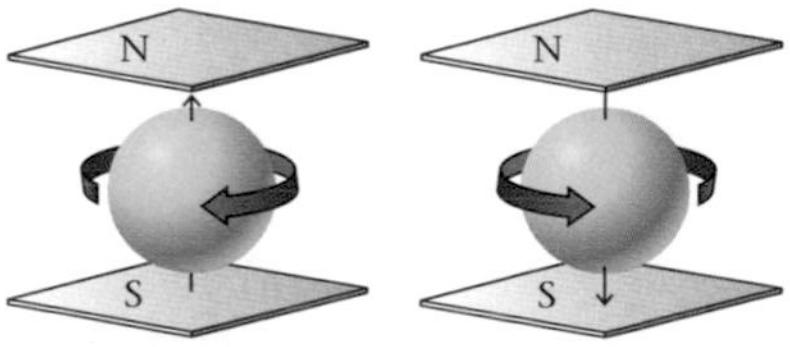

Figure 6.5
Electron spin. The spins can be represented as clockwise and counterclockwise, with the different values of $\mathbf{m}_s$ of $+\frac{1}{2}$ and $-\frac{1}{2}$.

Pauli Exclusion Principle

The four quantum numbers that characterize an electron in an atom have now been considered. There is an important rule, called the **Pauli exclusion principle,** that relates to these numbers. It requires that ***no two electrons in an atom can have the same set of four quan-***

Table 6.3 Permissible Values of the Quantum Numbers Through n = 4

n	ℓ	m_ℓ	m_s
1	0 (1s)	0	$+\frac{1}{2}, -\frac{1}{2}$
2	0 (2s)	0	$+\frac{1}{2}, -\frac{1}{2}$
	1 (2p)	−1, 0, +1	$\pm\frac{1}{2}$ for each value of $\mathbf{m}_\ell$
3	0 (3s)	0	$+\frac{1}{2}, -\frac{1}{2}$
	1 (3p)	−1, 0, +1	$\pm\frac{1}{2}$ for each value of $\mathbf{m}_\ell$
	2 (3d)	−2, −1, 0, +1, +2	$\pm\frac{1}{2}$ for each value of $\mathbf{m}_\ell$
4	0 (4s)	0	$+\frac{1}{2}, -\frac{1}{2}$
	1 (4p)	−1, 0, +1	$\pm\frac{1}{2}$ for each value of $\mathbf{m}_\ell$
	2 (4d)	−2, −1, 0, +1, +2	$\pm\frac{1}{2}$ for each value of $\mathbf{m}_\ell$
	3 (4f)	−3, −2, −1, 0, +1, +2, +3	$\pm\frac{1}{2}$ for each value of $\mathbf{m}_\ell$

Our model for electronic structure is a pragmatic blend of theory and experiment.

tum numbers. This principle was first stated in 1925 by Wolfgang Pauli (1900–1958), a colleague of Bohr, again to make theory consistent with the properties of atoms.

The Pauli exclusion principle has an implication that is not obvious at first glance. It requires that only two electrons can fit into an orbital, since there are only two possible values of $\mathbf{m}_s$. Moreover, if two electrons occupy the same orbital, they must have opposed spins. Otherwise they would have the same set of four quantum numbers.

The rules for assigning quantum numbers are summarized in Table 6.3 and applied in Examples 6.4 and 6.5.

Example 6.4 Consider the following sets of quantum numbers ($\mathbf{n}$, ℓ, $\mathbf{m}_\ell$, $\mathbf{m}_s$). Which ones could not occur? For the valid sets, identify the orbital involved.

(a) 3, 1, 0, $+\frac{1}{2}$ (b) 1, 1, 0, $-\frac{1}{2}$ (c) 2, 0, 0, $+\frac{1}{2}$
(d) 4, 3, 2, $+\frac{1}{2}$ (e) 2, 1, 0, 0

Strategy Use the selection rules for the four quantum numbers to find the sets that could not occur. For the valid sets, identify the principal level and sublevel.

SOLUTION

(a) valid; 3p (b) not valid; ℓ cannot equal $\mathbf{n}$ (c) valid; 2s
(d) valid; 4f (e) not valid; $\mathbf{m}_s$ cannot be zero

Example 6.5

(a) What is the capacity for electrons of an s sublevel? A p sublevel? A d sublevel? An f sublevel?
(b) What is the total capacity for electrons of the fourth principal level?

Strategy Since two electrons fill an orbital, multiply the number of orbitals in the sublevel by 2 to find its capacity. To find the total capacity of the principal level, add those of the individual sublevels.

SOLUTION

(a) s sublevel: 1 orbital $\times$ $2e^-$/orbital $= 2e^-$
p sublevel: 3 orbitals $\times$ $2e^-$/orbital $= 6e^-$
d sublevel: 5 orbitals $\times$ $2e^-$/orbital $= 10e^-$
f sublevel: 7 orbitals $\times$ $2e^-$/orbital $= 14e^-$
(b) $2e^-(4s) + 6e^-(4p) + 10e^-(4d) + 14e^-(4f) = 32e^-$

6.4 ATOMIC ORBITALS; SHAPES AND SIZES

You will recall (page 139) that an orbital occupied by an electron in an atom can be represented physically by showing the region of space in which there is a 90% probability of finding the electron. Orbitals are commonly designated by citing the corresponding sublevels. Thus we refer to 1s, 2s, 2p, 3s, 3p, 3d, . . . orbitals.

All s sublevels are spherical; they differ from one another only in size. As **n** increases, the radius of the orbital becomes larger (Figure 6.6). This means that an electron in a 2s orbital is more likely to be found far out from the nucleus than is a 1s electron.

The shapes and orientations of p orbitals are shown in Figure 6.7. Notice that—

- a p orbital consists of two lobes along an axis (*x, y,* or *z*). Among other things, this means that, in a p orbital, there is zero probability of finding an electron at the origin, that is, at the nucleus of the atom.
- the three p orbitals in a given sublevel are oriented at right angles to one another along *x*-, *y*-, and *z*-axis. For that reason, the three orbitals are often designated as p_x, p_y, and p_z.

Although it is not shown in Figure 6.7, p orbitals, like s orbitals, increase in size as the principal quantum number **n** increases. Also not shown are the shapes and sizes of d and f orbitals. We will say more about the nature of d orbitals in Chapter 15.

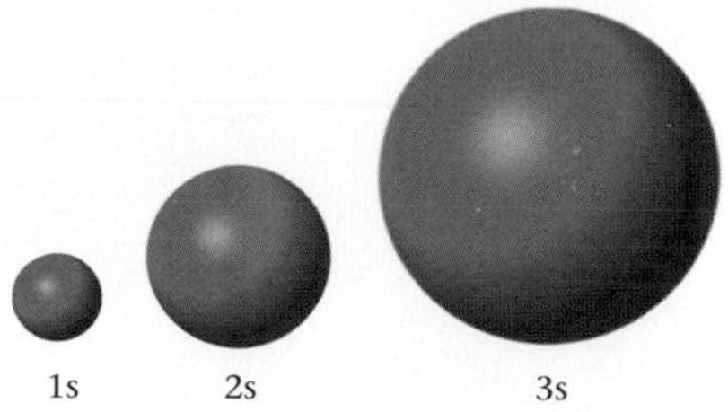

Figure 6.6
s orbitals. The relative sizes of the 90% contours (see Figure 6.4b) are shown for the 1s, 2s, and 3s orbitals.

CENGAGENOW™
Click Coached Problems for a self-study module on **shapes of atomic orbitals.**

6.5 ELECTRON CONFIGURATIONS IN ATOMS

Given the rules referred to in Section 6.3, it is possible to assign quantum numbers to each electron in an atom. Beyond that, electrons can be assigned to specific principal levels, sublevels, and orbitals. There are several ways to do this. Perhaps the simplest way to describe the arrangement of electrons in an atom is to give its **electron configuration,** which shows the number of electrons, indicated by a superscript, in each sublevel. For example, a species with the electron configuration

$$1s^22s^22p^5$$

has two electrons in the 1s sublevel, two electrons in the 2s sublevel, and five electrons in the 2p sublevel.

In this section, you will learn how to predict the electron configurations of atoms of elements. There are a couple of different ways of doing this, which we consider in turn. It should be emphasized that, throughout this discussion, we *refer to isolated gaseous atoms in the ground state.* (In *excited* states, one or more electrons are promoted to a higher energy level.)

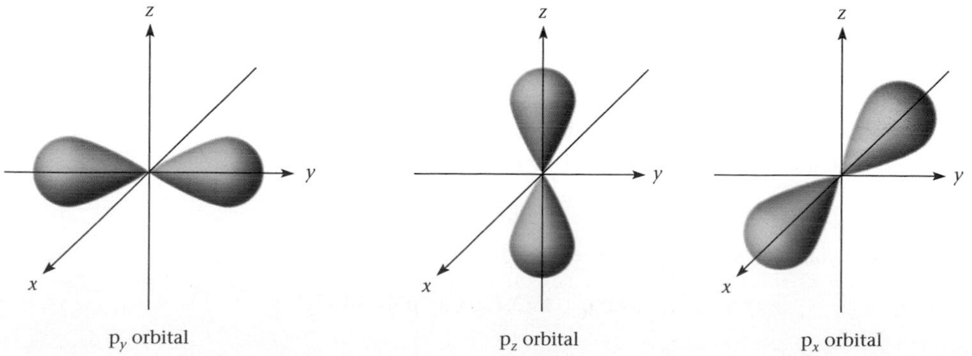

Figure 6.7
p orbitals. The electron density of the three p orbitals is directed along the *x*-, *y*-, or *z*-axes. The three p orbitals are located at 90° angles to each other.

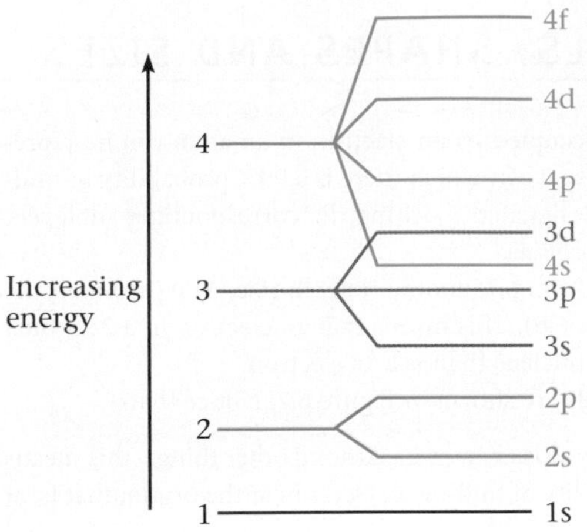

Figure 6.8
Electron energy sublevels in the order of increasing energy. The order shown is the order of sublevel filling as atomic number increases, starting at the bottom with 1s.

Electron Configuration from Sublevel Energies

CENGAGENOW™
Click Coached Problems for a self-study module on **electron configurations.**

Electron configurations are readily obtained if the order of filling sublevels is known. Electrons enter the available sublevels in order of increasing sublevel energy. Ordinarily, a sublevel is filled to capacity before the next one starts to fill. The relative energies of different sublevels can be obtained from experiment. Figure 6.8 is a plot of these energies for atoms through the **n** = 4 principal level.

From Figure 6.8 it is possible to predict the electron configurations of atoms of elements with atomic numbers 1 through 36. Because an s sublevel can hold only two electrons, the 1s is filled at helium ($1s^2$). With lithium ($Z = 3$), the third electron has to enter a new sublevel: This is the 2s, the lowest sublevel of the second principal energy level. Lithium has one electron in this sublevel ($1s^22s^1$). With beryllium ($Z = 4$), the 2s sublevel is filled ($1s^22s^2$). The next six elements fill the 2p sublevel. Their electron configurations are

These are ground-state configurations; $1s^22s^12p^2$ would be an excited state for boron.

$_5B$	$1s^22s^22p^1$	$_8O$	$1s^22s^22p^4$
$_6C$	$1s^22s^22p^2$	$_9F$	$1s^22s^22p^5$
$_7N$	$1s^22s^22p^3$	$_{10}Ne$	$1s^22s^22p^6$

Beyond neon, electrons enter the third principal level. The 3s sublevel is filled at magnesium:

$$_{12}Mg \quad 1s^22s^22p^63s^2$$

Six more electrons are required to fill the 3p sublevel with argon:

$$_{18}Ar \quad 1s^22s^22p^63s^23p^6$$

After argon, an "overlap" of principal energy levels occurs. The next electron enters the *lowest* sublevel of the fourth principal level (4s) instead of the *highest* sublevel of the third principal level (3d). Potassium ($Z = 19$) has one electron in the 4s sublevel; calcium ($Z = 20$) fills it with two electrons:

$$_{20}Ca \quad 1s^22s^22p^63s^23p^64s^2$$

Now the 3d sublevel starts to fill with scandium ($Z = 21$). Recall that a d sublevel has a capacity of ten electrons. Hence the 3d sublevel becomes filled at zinc ($Z = 30$):

$$_{30}Zn \quad 1s^22s^22p^63s^23p^64s^23d^{10}$$

The next sublevel, 4p, is filled at krypton ($Z = 36$):

The order of filling, through $Z = 36$, is 1s, 2s, 2p, 3s, 3p, 4s, 3d, 4p.

$$_{36}Kr \quad 1s^22s^22p^63s^23p^64s^23d^{10}4p^6$$

Example 6.6 Find the electron configurations of the sulfur and iron atoms.

Strategy Determine the number of electrons in the atom from its atomic number. Using the energy diagram in Figure 6.8, fill the appropriate sublevels.

SOLUTION The sulfur atom has atomic number 16, so there are $16e^-$. Two electrons go into the 1s sublevel, two into the 2s sublevel, and six into the 2p sublevel. Two more go into the 3s sublevel, and the remaining four go into the 3p sublevel. The electron configuration of the S atom is

$$1s^2 2s^2 2p^6 3s^2 3p^4$$

The iron atom has 26 electrons. Proceeding as above, the electron configuration must be

$$1s^2 2s^2 2p^6 3s^2 3p^6 4s^2 3d^6$$

The 4s sublevel fills before the 3d sublevel.

Reality Check You can use the periodic table to check your answer. See Figure 6.9 and the accompanying discussion.

Often, to save space, electron configurations are shortened; the **abbreviated electron configuration** starts with the preceding noble gas. For the elements sulfur and nickel,

	Electron Configuration	Abbreviated Electron Configuration
$_{16}S$	$1s^2 2s^2 2p^6 3s^2 3p^4$	[Ne] $3s^2 3p^4$
$_{28}Ni$	$1s^2 2s^2 2p^6 3s^2 3p^6 4s^2 3d^8$	[Ar]$4s^2 3d^8$

The symbol [Ne] indicates that the first 10 electrons in the sulfur atom have the neon configuration $1s^2 2s^2 2p^6$; similarly, [Ar] represents the first 18 electrons in the nickel atom.

Filling of Sublevels and the Periodic Table

In principle, a diagram such as Figure 6.8 can be extended to include all sublevels occupied by electrons in any element. As a matter of fact, that is a relatively simple thing to do; such a diagram is in effect incorporated into the periodic table introduced in Chapter 2.

To understand how position in the periodic table relates to the filling of sublevels, consider the metals in the first two groups. Atoms of the Group 1 elements all have one s electron in the outermost principal energy level (Table 6.4). In each Group 2 atom, there are two s electrons in the outermost level. A similar relationship applies to the elements in any group:

The periodic table works because an element's chemical properties depend on the number of outer electrons.

The atoms of elements in a group of the periodic table have the same distribution of electrons in the outermost principal energy level.

Table 6.4 Abbreviated Electron Configurations of Group 1 and 2 Elements

Group 1		Group 2	
$_{3}Li$	[He] **$2s^1$**	$_{4}Be$	[He] **$2s^2$**
$_{11}Na$	[Ne] **$3s^1$**	$_{12}Mg$	[Ne] **$3s^2$**
$_{19}K$	[Ar] **$4s^1$**	$_{20}Ca$	[Ar] **$4s^2$**
$_{37}Rb$	[Kr] **$5s^1$**	$_{38}Sr$	[Kr] **$5s^2$**
$_{55}Cs$	[Xe] **$6s^1$**	$_{56}Ba$	[Xe] **$6s^2$**

This means that the order in which electron sublevels are filled is determined by position in the periodic table. Figure 6.9 shows how this works. Notice the following points:

Mendeleev developed the periodic table before the discovery of protons and electrons. Amazing!

1. ***The elements in Groups 1 and 2 are filling an s sublevel.*** Thus Li and Be in the second period fill the 2s sublevel. Na and Mg in the third period fill the 3s sublevel, and so on.

2. ***The elements in Groups 13 through 18 (six elements in each period) fill p sublevels,*** which have a capacity of six electrons. In the second period, the 2p sublevel starts to fill with B ($Z = 5$) and is completed with Ne ($Z = 10$). In the third period, the elements Al ($Z = 13$) through Ar ($Z = 18$) fill the 3p sublevel.

3. ***The transition metals, in the center of the periodic table, fill d sublevels.*** Remember that a d sublevel can hold ten electrons. In the fourth period, the ten elements Sc ($Z = 21$) through Zn ($Z = 30$) fill the 3d sublevel. In the fifth period, the 4d sublevel is filled by the elements Y ($Z = 39$) through Cd ($Z = 48$). The ten transition metals in the sixth period fill the 5d sublevel. Elements 103 to 112 in the seventh period are believed to be filling the 6d sublevel.

4. ***The two sets of 14 elements listed separately at the bottom of the table are filling f sublevels with a principal quantum number two less than the period number.*** That is—

- 14 elements in the sixth period ($Z = 57$ to 70) are filling the 4f sublevel. These elements are sometimes called rare earths or, more commonly, **lanthanides,** after the name of the

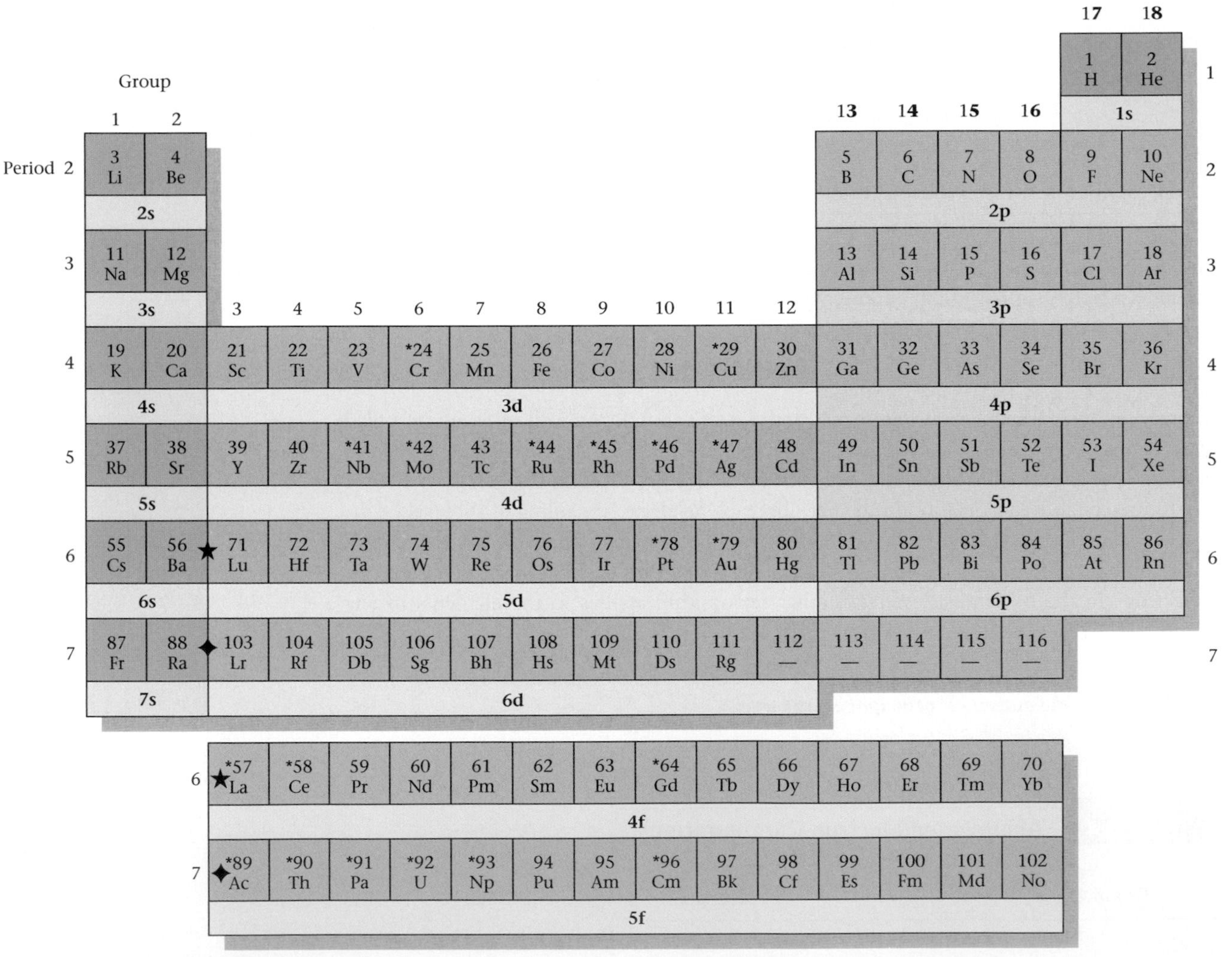

Figure 6.9
The periodic table and electron configurations. The periodic table can be used to deduce the electron configurations of atoms. The color code in the figure shows the energy sublevels being filled across each period. Elements marked with asterisks have electron configurations slightly different from those predicted by the table.

CHEMISTRY The Human Side

One name, more than any other, is associated with the actinide elements: Glenn Seaborg (1912–1999). Between 1940 and 1957, Seaborg and his team at the University of California, Berkeley, prepared nine of these elements (at. no. 94–102) for the first time. Moreover, in 1945 Seaborg made the revolutionary suggestion that the actinides, like the lanthanides, were filling an f sublevel. For these accomplishments, he received the 1951 Nobel Prize in chemistry.

Glenn Seaborg was born in a small town in middle America, Ishpeming, Michigan. After obtaining a bachelor's degree in chemistry from UCLA, he spent the rest of his scientific career at Berkeley, first as a Ph.D. student and then as a faculty member. During World War II, he worked on the Manhattan Project. Along with other scientists, Seaborg recommended that the devastating power of the atomic bomb be demonstrated by dropping it on a barren island before United Nations observers. Later he headed the U.S. Atomic Energy Commission under Presidents Kennedy, Johnson, and Nixon.

Glenn Theodore Seaborg
(1912–1999)

Sometimes referred to as the "gentle giant" (he was 6 ft 4 in. tall), Seaborg had a charming, self-deprecating sense of humor. He recalled that friends advised him *not* to publish his theory about the position of the actinides in the periodic table, lest it ruin his scientific reputation. Seaborg went on to say that, "I had a great advantage. I didn't have any scientific reputation, so I went ahead and published it." Late in his life there was considerable controversy as to whether a transuranium element should be named for him; that honor had always been bestowed posthumously. Seaborg commented wryly that, "They don't want to do it because I'm still alive and they can prove it." Element 106 was named seaborgium (Sg) in 1997; he considered this his greatest honor, even above the Nobel Prize.

first element in the series, lanthanum (La). Modern separation techniques, notably chromatography, have greatly increased the availability of compounds of these elements. A brilliant red phosphor used in color TV receivers contains a small amount of europium oxide, Eu_2O_3. This is added to yttrium oxide, Y_2O_3, or gadolinium oxide, Gd_2O_3. Cerium(IV) oxide is used to coat interior surfaces of "self-cleaning" ovens, where it prevents the build-up of tar deposits.

- 14 elements in the seventh period ($Z = 89$ to 102) are filling the 5f sublevel. The first element in this series is actinium (Ac); collectively, these elements are referred to as **actinides.** All these elements are radioactive; only thorium and uranium occur in nature. The other actinides have been synthesized in the laboratory by nuclear reactions. Their stability decreases rapidly with increasing atomic number. The longest lived isotope of nobelium ($_{102}No$) has a half-life of about 3 minutes; that is, in 3 minutes half of the sample decomposes. Nobelium and the preceding element, mendelevium ($_{101}Md$), were identified in samples containing one to three atoms of No or Md.

Electron Configuration from the Periodic Table

Figure 6.9 (or any periodic table) can be used to deduce the electron configuration of any element. It is particularly useful for heavier elements such as iodine (Example 6.7).

CENGAGENOW™
Click Coached Problems for a self-study module on **electron configurations.**

Example 6.7 For the iodine atom, write

(a) the electron configuration. (b) the abbreviated electron configuration.

Strategy To obtain the electron configuration, use Figure 6.9. Go across each period in succession, noting the sublevels occupied, until you get to iodine. To find the abbreviated configuration, start with the preceding noble gas, krypton.

SOLUTION

(a) Period 1: the 1s sublevel fills ($1s^2$)
Period 2: the 2s and 2p sublevels fill ($2s^22p^6$)

To obtain electron configurations from the periodic table, consider what sublevels are filled going across each period.

Period 3: the 3s and 3p sublevels fill ($3s^23p^6$)
Period 4: the 4s, 3d, and 4p sublevels fill ($4s^23d^{10}4p^6$)
Period 5: the 5s and 4d sublevels fill; five electrons enter the 5p ($5s^24d^{10}5p^5$)
Putting it all together, the electron configuration of iodine must be

$$1s^22s^22p^63s^23p^64s^23d^{10}4p^65s^24d^{10}5p^5$$

(b) [Kr] accounts for the first $36e^-$: [Kr] $5s^24d^{10}5p^5$

As you can see from Figure 6.9, the electron configurations of several elements (marked *) differ slightly from those predicted. In every case, the difference involves a shift of one or, at the most, two electrons from one sublevel to another of very similar energy. For example, in the first transition series, two elements, chromium and copper, have an extra electron in the 3d as compared with the 4s orbital.

	Predicted	Observed
$_{24}Cr$	[Ar] $4s^23d^4$	[Ar] $4s^13d^5$
$_{29}Cu$	[Ar] $4s^23d^9$	[Ar] $4s^13d^{10}$

These anomalies reflect the fact that the 3d and 4s orbitals have very similar energies. Beyond that, it has been suggested that there is a slight increase in stability with a half-filled (Cr) or completely filled (Cu) 3d sublevel.

6.6 ORBITAL DIAGRAMS OF ATOMS

For many purposes, electron configurations are sufficient to describe the arrangements of electrons in atoms. Sometimes, however, it is useful to go a step further and show how electrons are distributed among orbitals. In such cases, **orbital diagrams** are used. Each orbital is represented by parentheses ( ), and electrons are shown by arrows written ↑ or ↓, depending on spin.

To show how orbital diagrams are obtained from electron configurations, consider the boron atom ($Z = 5$). Its electron configuration is $1s^22s^22p^1$. The pair of electrons in the 1s orbital must have opposed spins ($+\frac{1}{2}$, $-\frac{1}{2}$, or ↑↓). The same is true of the two electrons in the 2s orbital. There are three orbitals in the 2p sublevel. The single 2p electron in boron could be in any one of these orbitals. Its spin could be either "up" or "down." The orbital diagram is ordinarily written

	1s	2s	2p
$_5B$	(↑↓)	(↑↓)	(↑)( )( )

with the first electron in an orbital arbitrarily designated by an up arrow, ↑.

With the next element, carbon, a complication arises. In which orbital should the sixth electron go? It could go in the same orbital as the other 2p electron, in which case it would have to have the opposite spin, ↓. It could go into one of the other two orbitals, either with a parallel spin, ↑, or an opposed spin, ↓. Experiment shows that there is an energy difference among these arrangements. The most stable is the one in which the two electrons are in different orbitals with parallel spins. The orbital diagram of the carbon atom is

	1s	2s	2p
$_6C$	(↑↓)	(↑↓)	(↑)(↑)( )

Similar situations arise frequently. There is a general principle that applies in all such cases; **Hund's rule** (Friedrich Hund, 1896–1997) predicts that, ordinarily,

when several orbitals of equal energy are available, as in a given sublevel, electrons enter singly with parallel spins.

Hund was still lecturing, colorfully and coherently, in his 90s. You and I should be so lucky. WLM was not.

Atom	Orbital diagram					Electron configuration
	1s	2s	2p			
B	(↑↓)	(↑↓)	(↑)	( )	( )	$1s^22s^22p^1$
C	(↑↓)	(↑↓)	(↑)	(↑)	( )	$1s^22s^22p^2$
N	(↑↓)	(↑↓)	(↑)	(↑)	(↑)	$1s^22s^22p^3$
O	(↑↓)	(↑↓)	(↑↓)	(↑)	(↑)	$1s^22s^22p^4$
F	(↑↓)	(↑↓)	(↑↓)	(↑↓)	(↑)	$1s^22s^22p^5$
Ne	(↑↓)	(↑↓)	(↑↓)	(↑↓)	(↑↓)	$1s^22s^22p^6$

Figure 6.10
Orbital diagrams for atoms with five to ten electrons. Orbitals of equal energy are all occupied by unpaired electrons before pairing begins.

Only after all the orbitals are half-filled do electrons pair up in orbitals.

Following this principle, the orbital diagrams for the elements boron through neon are shown in Figure 6.10. Notice that—

- ***in all filled orbitals, the two electrons have opposed spins.*** Such electrons are often referred to as being *paired.* There are four paired electrons in the B, C, and N atoms, six in the oxygen atom, eight in the fluorine atom, and ten in the neon atom.
- ***in accordance with Hund's rule, within a given sublevel there are as many half-filled orbitals as possible.*** Electrons in such orbitals are said to be *unpaired.* There is one unpaired electron in atoms of B and F, two unpaired electrons in C and O atoms, and three unpaired electrons in the N atom. When there are two or more unpaired electrons, as in C, N, and O, those electrons have parallel spins.

Hund's rule, like the Pauli exclusion principle, is based on experiment. It is possible to determine the number of unpaired electrons in an atom. With solids, this is done by studying their behavior in a magnetic field. If there are unpaired electrons present, the solid will be attracted into the field. Such a substance is said to be *paramagnetic.* If the atoms in the solid contain only paired electrons, it is slightly repelled by the field. Substances of this type are called *diamagnetic.* With gaseous atoms, the atomic spectrum can also be used to establish the presence and number of unpaired electrons.

Example 6.8 Construct orbital diagrams for atoms of sulfur and iron.

Strategy Start with the electron configuration, obtained as in Section 6.5. Then write the orbital diagram, recalling the number of orbitals per sublevel, putting two electrons of opposed spin in each orbital within a completed sublevel, and applying Hund's rule where sublevels are partially filled.

SOLUTION Recall from Example 6.6 that the electron configuration of sulfur is $1s^22s^22p^63s^23p^4$. Its orbital diagram is

	1s	2s	2p	3s	3p
$_{16}S$	(↑↓)	(↑↓)	(↑↓)(↑↓)(↑↓)	(↑↓)	(↑↓)(↑)(↑)

The atomic number of iron is 26; its electron configuration is $1s^22s^22p^63s^23p^64s^23d^6$. All the orbitals are filled except those in the 3d sublevel, which is populated according to Hund's rule to give four unpaired electrons.

	1s	2s	2p	3s	3p	4s	3d
$_{26}Fe$	(↑↓)	(↑↓)	(↑↓)(↑↓)(↑↓)	(↑↓)	(↑↓)(↑↓)(↑↓)	(↑↓)	(↑↓)(↑)(↑)(↑)(↑)

Reality Check To construct an orbital diagram, start with the electron configuration and apply Hund's rule.

6.7 ELECTRON ARRANGEMENTS IN MONATOMIC IONS

CENGAGENOW™
Click Coached Problems for a self-study module on **electron configurations of ions.**

The discussion so far in this chapter has focused on electron configurations and orbital diagrams of neutral atoms. It is also possible to assign electronic structures to monatomic ions, formed from atoms by gaining or losing electrons. In general, when a monatomic ion is formed from an atom, *electrons are added to or removed from sublevels in the highest principal energy level.*

Ions with Noble-Gas Structures

Important ideas are worth repeating.

As pointed out in Chapter 2, elements close to a noble gas in the periodic table form ions that have the same number of electrons as the noble-gas atom. This means that these ions have noble-gas electron configurations. Thus the three elements preceding neon (N, O, and F) and the three elements following neon (Na, Mg, and Al) all form ions with the neon configuration, $1s^22s^22p^6$. The three nonmetal atoms achieve this structure by gaining electrons to form anions:

$$_{7}N\ (1s^22s^22p^3) + 3e^- \longrightarrow {}_{7}N^{3-}\ (1s^22s^22p^6)$$
$$_{8}O\ (1s^22s^22p^4) + 2e^- \longrightarrow {}_{8}O^{2-}\ (1s^22s^22p^6)$$
$$_{9}F\ (1s^22s^22p^5) + e^- \longrightarrow {}_{9}F^-\ (1s^22s^22p^6)$$

The three metal atoms acquire the neon structure by losing electrons to form cations:

$$_{11}Na\ (1s^22s^22p^63s^1) \longrightarrow {}_{11}Na^+\ (1s^22s^22p^6) + e^-$$
$$_{12}Mg\ (1s^22s^22p^63s^2) \longrightarrow {}_{12}Mg^{2+}\ (1s^22s^22p^6) + 2e^-$$
$$_{13}Al\ (1s^22s^22p^63s^23p^1) \longrightarrow {}_{13}Al^{3+}\ (1s^22s^22p^6) + 3e^-$$

The species N^{3-}, O^{2-}, F^-, Ne, Na^+, Mg^{2+}, and Al^{3+} are said to be *isoelectronic;* that is, they have the same electron configuration.

There are a great many monatomic ions that have noble-gas configurations; Figure 6.11 shows 24 ions of this type. Note, once again, that ions in a given main group have the same charge (+1 for Group 1, +2 for Group 2, −2 for Group 16, −1 for Group 17). This explains, in part, the chemical similarity among elements in the same main group. In particular, ionic compounds formed by such elements have similar chemical formulas. For example,

- halides of the alkali metals have the general formula MX, where M = Li, Na, K, . . . and X = F, Cl, Br, ...
- halides of the alkaline earth metals have the general formula MX_2, where M = Mg, Ca, Sr, . . . and X = F, Cl, Br, ...
- oxides of the alkaline earth metals have the general formula MO, where M = Mg, Ca, Sr, ...

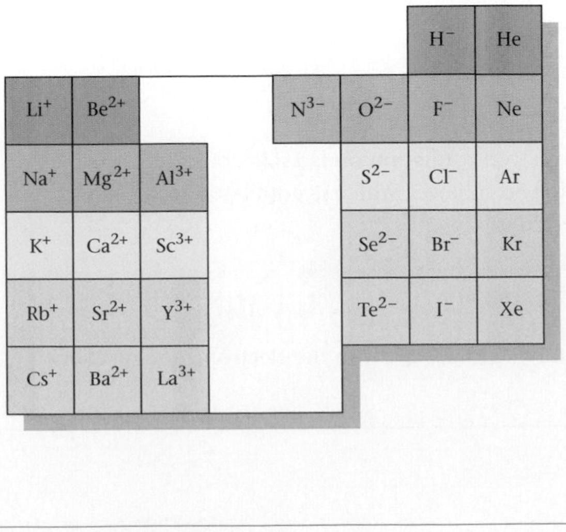

Figure 6.11
Cations, anions, and atoms with ground state noble-gas electron configurations. Atoms and ions shown in the same color are *isoelectronic;* that is, they have the same electron configurations.

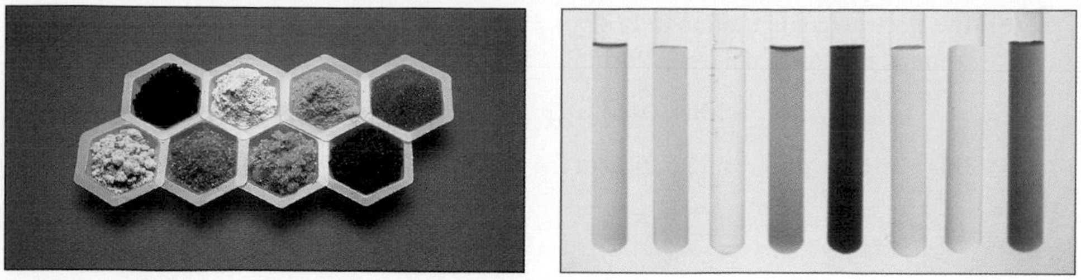
Charles D. Winters

(a) (b)

Transition metal ions. Transition metal ions impart color to many of their compounds and solutions. (a) Bottom row *(left to right):* iron(III) chloride, copper(II) sulfate, manganese(II) chloride, cobalt(II) chloride. Top row *(left to right):* chromium(III) nitrate, iron(II) sulfate, nickel(II) sulfate, potassium dichromate. (b) Solutions of the compounds in (a) in the order listed above.

Transition Metal Cations

The transition metals to the right of the scandium subgroup do not form ions with noble-gas configurations. To do so, they would have to lose four or more electrons. The energy requirement is too high for that to happen. However, as pointed out in Chapter 2, these metals do form cations with charges of $+1$, $+2$, or $+3$. Applying the principle that, in forming cations, electrons are removed from the sublevel of highest **n**, you can predict correctly that ***when transition metal atoms form positive ions, the outer s electrons are lost first.*** Consider, for example, the formation of the Mn^{2+} ion from the Mn atom:

$$_{25}\text{Mn} \qquad [\text{Ar}]\,4s^2 3d^5 \qquad _{25}\text{Mn}^{2+} \qquad [\text{Ar}]3d^5$$

Notice that it is the 4s electrons that are lost rather than the 3d electrons. This is known to be the case because the Mn^{2+} ion has been shown to have five unpaired electrons (the five 3d electrons). If two 3d electrons had been lost, the Mn^{2+} ion would have had only three unpaired electrons.

All the transition metals form cations by a similar process, that is, loss of outer s electrons. Only after those electrons are lost are electrons removed from the inner d sublevel. Consider, for example, what happens with iron, which, you will recall, forms two different cations. First the 4s electrons are lost to give the Fe^{2+} ion:

The s electrons are "first in" with the atoms and "first out" with the cations.

$$_{26}\text{Fe}(\text{Ar } 4s^2 3d^6) \longrightarrow {}_{26}\text{Fe}^{2+}(\text{Ar } 3d^6) + 2e^-$$

Then an electron is removed from the 3d level to form the Fe^{3+} ion:

$$_{26}\text{Fe}^{2+}(\text{Ar } 3d^6) \longrightarrow {}_{26}\text{Fe}^{3+}(\text{Ar } 3d^5) + e^-$$

In the Fe^{2+} and Fe^{3+} ions, as in all transition metal ions, there are no outer s electrons.

You will recall that for fourth period *atoms,* the 4s sublevel fills before the 3d. In the corresponding *ions,* the electrons come out of the 4s sublevel before the 3d. This is sometimes referred to as the "first in, first out" rule.

Seniority rules don't apply to electrons.

Example 6.9 Give the electron configuration of

(a) Fe^{2+} (b) Br^-

Strategy First obtain the electron configuration of the corresponding atom, as in Section 6.5. Then add or remove electrons from sublevels of highest **n.**

SOLUTION

(a) As pointed out in Example 6.6, the electron configuration of iron is $1s^2 2s^2 2p^6 3s^2 3p^6 4s^2 3d^6$. Two electrons are removed from the 4s sublevel to form Fe^{2+}:

$$\text{Fe}^{2+} \quad 1s^2 2s^2 2p^6 3s^2 3p^6 3d^6$$

(b) The electron configuration of Br ($Z = 35$) is $1s^22s^22p^63s^23p^64s^23d^{10}4p^5$. An electron is added to the 4p sublevel to form Br^-

$$Br^- \quad 1s^22s^22p^63s^23p^64s^23d^{10}4p^6$$

This is the electron configuration of the noble gas krypton, $Z = 36$.

6.8 PERIODIC TRENDS IN THE PROPERTIES OF ATOMS

CENGAGENOW™
Click Coached Problems for a self-study module on **orbital energies.**

One of the most fundamental principles of chemistry is the periodic law, which states that

> ***The chemical and physical properties of elements are a periodic function of atomic number.***

This is, of course, the principle behind the structure of the periodic table. Elements within a given vertical group resemble one another chemically because chemical properties repeat themselves at regular intervals of 2, 8, 18, or 32 elements.

In this section we will consider how the periodic table can be used to correlate properties on an atomic scale. In particular, we will see how atomic radius, ionic radius, ionization energy, and electronegativity vary horizontally and vertically in the periodic table.

Atomic Radius

CENGAGENOW™
Click Coached Problems for a self-study module on **atomic size.**

Strictly speaking, the "size" of an atom is a rather nebulous concept. The electron cloud surrounding the nucleus does not have a sharp boundary. However, a quantity called the **atomic radius** can be defined and measured, assuming a spherical atom. Ordinarily, the atomic radius is taken to be one half the distance of closest approach between atoms in an elemental substance (Figure 6.12).

The atomic radii of the main-group elements are shown at the top of Figure 6.13 (p. 153). Notice that, in general, atomic radii—

- decrease across a period from left to right in the periodic table.
- increase down a group in the periodic table.

It is possible to explain these trends in terms of the electron configurations of the corresponding atoms. Consider first the increase in radius observed as we move down the table, let us say among the alkali metals (Group 1). All these elements have a single s electron outside a filled level or filled p sublevel. Electrons in these inner levels are much closer to the nucleus than the outer s electron and hence effectively shield it from the positive charge of the nucleus. To a first approximation, each inner electron cancels the charge of one pro-

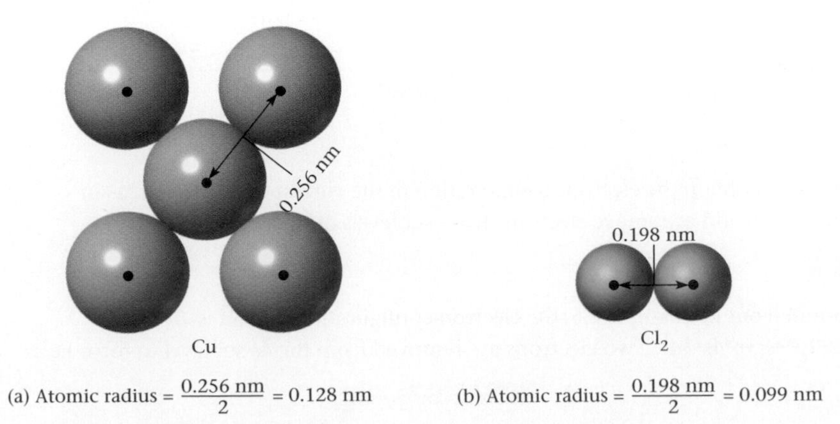

Figure 6.12
Atomic radii. The radii are determined by assuming that atoms in closest contact in an element touch one another. The atomic radius is taken to be one half of the closest internuclear distance. (a) Arrangement of copper atoms in metallic copper, giving an atomic radius of 0.128 nm for copper. (b) Chlorine atoms in a chlorine (Cl_2) molecule, giving an atomic radius of 0.099 nm for chlorine.

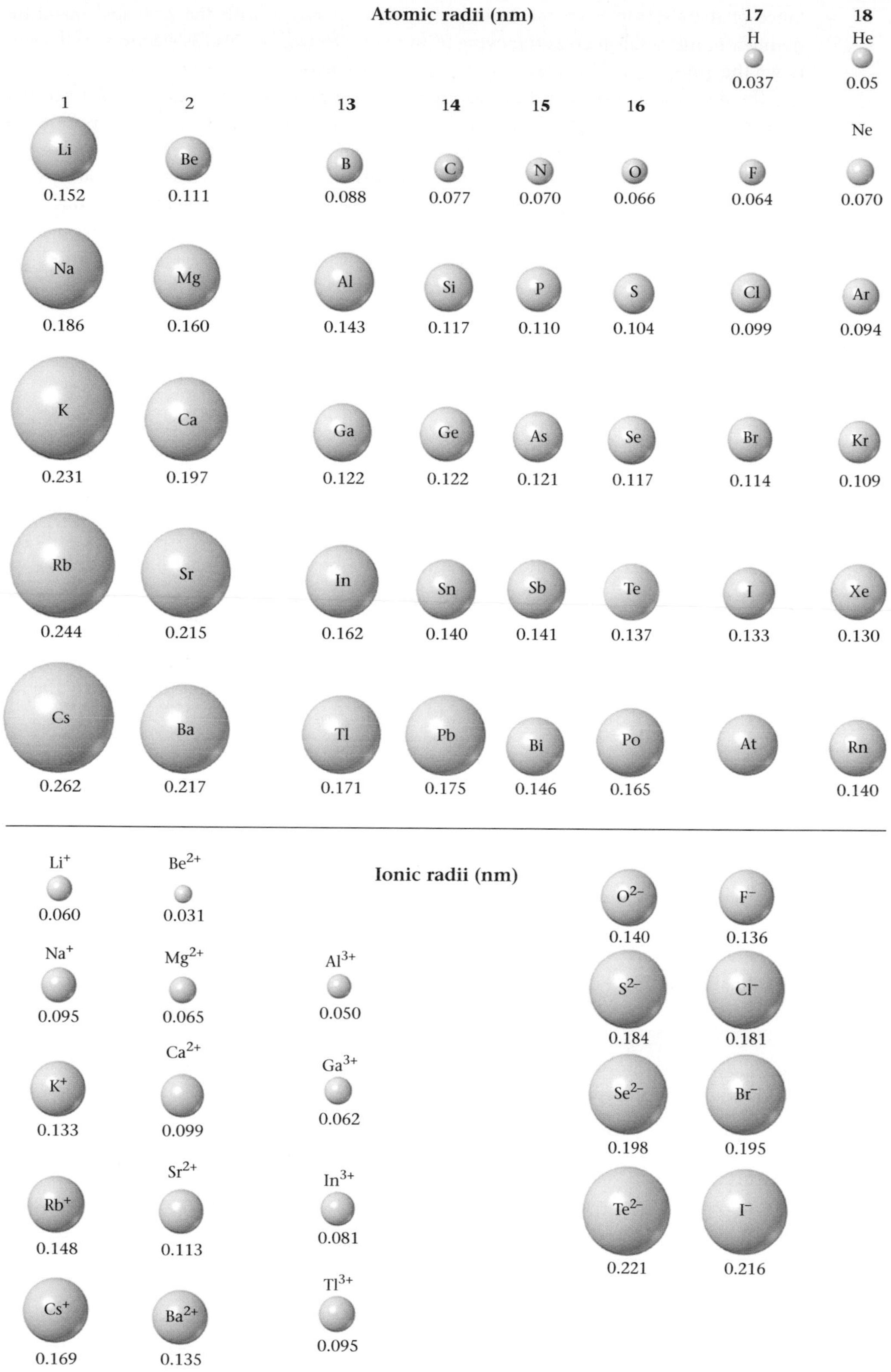

Figure 6.13

Atomic and ionic radii of the main-group elements. Negative ions are always larger than atoms of the same element, whereas positive ions are always smaller than atoms of the same element.

ton in the nucleus, so the outer s electron is attracted by a net positive charge of +1. In this sense, it has the properties of an electron in the hydrogen atom. Because the average distance of the electron from the hydrogen nucleus increases with the principal quantum number, **n,** the radius increases moving from Li (2s electron) to Na (3s electron) and so on down the group.

The decrease in atomic radius moving across the periodic table can be explained in a similar manner. Consider, for example, the third period, where electrons are being added to the third principal energy level. The added electrons should be relatively poor shields for each other because they are all at about the same distance from the nucleus. Only the ten core electrons in inner, filled levels (**n** = 1, **n** = 2) are expected to shield the outer electrons from the nucleus. This means that the charge felt by an outer electron, called the *effective nuclear charge,* should increase steadily with atomic number as we move across the period. As effective nuclear charge increases, the outermost electrons are pulled in more tightly, and atomic radius decreases.

Ionic Radius

The radii of cations and anions derived from atoms of the main-group elements are shown at the bottom of Figure 6.13. The trends referred to previously for atomic radii are clearly visible with ionic radius as well. Notice, for example, that **ionic radius** increases moving down a group in the periodic table. Moreover, the radii of both cations (left) and anions (right) decrease from left to right across a period.

Comparing the radii of cations and anions with those of the atoms from which they are derived—

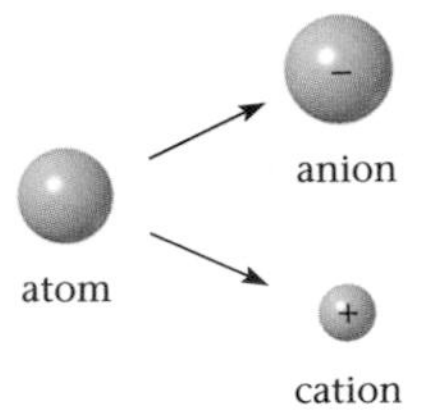

- ***positive ions are smaller than the metal atoms from which they are formed.*** The Na^+ ion has a radius, 0.095 nm, only a little more than half that of the Na atom, 0.186 nm.
- ***negative ions are larger than the nonmetal atoms from which they are formed.*** The radius of the Cl^- ion, 0.181 nm, is nearly twice that of the Cl atom, 0.099 nm.

As a result of these effects, anions in general are larger than cations. Compare, for example, the Cl^- ion (radius = 0.181 nm) with the Na^+ ion (radius = 0.095 nm). This means that in sodium chloride, and indeed in the vast majority of all ionic compounds, most of the space in the crystal lattice is taken up by anions.

The differences in radii between atoms and ions can be explained quite simply. A cation is smaller than the corresponding metal atom because the excess of protons in the ion draws the outer electrons in closer to the nucleus. In contrast, an extra electron in an anion adds to the repulsion between outer electrons, making a negative ion larger than the corresponding nonmetal atom.

Example 6.10 Using only the periodic table, arrange each of the following sets of atoms and ions in order of increasing size.

(a) Mg, Al, Ca (b) S, Cl, S^{2-} (c) Fe, Fe^{2+}, Fe^{3+}

Strategy Recall that radius decreases across a period and increases moving down a group. An atom is larger than the corresponding cation but smaller than the corresponding anion.

SOLUTION

(a) Compare the other atoms with Mg. Al, to the right, is smaller than Mg. Ca, below Mg, is larger. The predicted order is Al < Mg < Ca.
(b) Compare with the S atom. Cl, to the right, is smaller. The S^{2-} anion is larger than the S atom. The predicted order is Cl < S < S^{2-}.
(c) Compare with the Fe^{2+} ion. The Fe atom, with no charge, is larger. The Fe^{3+} ion, with a +3 charge, is smaller. The predicted order is $Fe^{3+} < Fe^{2+} <$ Fe (Figure 6.14).

Figure 6.14
Relative sizes of the iron atom and its ions.

1	2	13	14	15	16	17	18
						H 1312	He 2372
Li 520	Be 900	B 801	C 1086	N 1402	O 1314	F 1681	Ne 2081
Na 496	Mg 738	Al 578	Si 786	P 1012	S 1000	Cl 1251	Ar 1520
K 419	Ca 590	Ga 579	Ge 762	As 944	Se 941	Br 1140	Kr 1351
Rb 403	Sr 550	In 558	Sn 709	Sb 832	Te 869	I 1009	Xe 1170
Cs 376	Ba 503	Tl 589	Pb 716	Bi 703	Po 812	At	Rn 1037

Ionization energy decreases (down)

Ionization energy increases (left to right)

Figure 6.15
First ionization energies of the main-group elements, in kilojoules per mole. In general, ionization energy decreases moving down the periodic table groups and increases across the periods, although there are several exceptions.

Ionization Energy

Ionization energy is a measure of how difficult it is to remove an electron from a gaseous atom. Energy must always be *absorbed* to bring about ionization, so ionization energies are always *positive* quantities.

The (first) ionization energy is the energy change for the removal of the outermost electron from a gaseous atom to form a +1 ion:

$$M(g) \longrightarrow M^+(g) + e^- \qquad \Delta E_1 = \text{first ionization energy}$$

The more difficult it is to remove electrons, the larger the ionization energy.

Ionization energies of the main-group elements are listed in Figure 6.15. Notice that ionization energy—

- increases across the periodic table from left to right.
- decreases moving down the periodic table.

Comparing Figures 6.13 and 6.15 shows an inverse correlation between ionization energy and atomic radius. The smaller the atom, the more tightly its electrons are held to the positively charged nucleus and the more difficult they are to remove. Conversely, in a large atom such as that of a Group 1 metal, the electron is relatively far from the nucleus, so less energy has to be supplied to remove it from the atom.

Example 6.11 Consider the three elements C, N, and Si. Using only the periodic table, predict which of the three elements has

(a) the largest atomic radius; the smallest atomic radius.
(b) the largest ionization energy; the smallest ionization energy.

Strategy Because these three elements form a block,

C N
Si

in the periodic table, it is convenient to compare both nitrogen and silicon with carbon. Recall the trends for atomic radius and ionization energy.

SOLUTION

(a) C is larger than N but smaller than Si. Silicon must be the largest atom and nitrogen the smallest.

(b) C has a smaller ionization energy than N but a larger ionization energy than Si. Hence, Si has the smallest ionization energy and N the largest.

Reality Check Check these answers against Figure 6.13 and 6.15.

If you look carefully at Figure 6.15, you will note a few exceptions to the general trends referred to above and illustrated in Example 6.11. For example, the ionization energy of B (801 kJ/mol) is *less* than that of Be (900 kJ/mol). This happens because the electron removed from the boron atom comes from the 2p as opposed to the 2s sublevel for beryllium. Because 2p is higher in energy than 2s, it is not too surprising that less energy is required to remove an electron from that sublevel.

Electronegativity

Electronegativity is a positive quantity.

The ionization energy of an atom is a measure of its tendency to lose electrons; the larger the ionization energy, the more difficult it is to remove an electron. There are several different ways of comparing the tendencies of different atoms to gain electrons. The most useful of these for our purposes is the **electronegativity,** which measures the ability of an atom to attract to itself the electron pair forming a covalent bond.

The greater the electronegativity of an atom, the greater its attraction for electrons. Table 6.5 shows a scale of electronegativities first proposed by Linus Pauling. Each element is assigned a number, ranging from 4.0 for the most electronegative element, fluorine, to 0.8 for cesium, the least electronegative. Among the main-group elements, electronegativity increases moving from left to right in the periodic table. Ordinarily, it decreases moving down a group. You will find Table 6.5 very helpful when we discuss covalent bonding in Chapter 7.

Table 6.5 Electronegativity Values

H							—*
2.2							
Li	Be	B	C	N	O	F	—*
1.0	1.6	2.0	2.5	3.0	3.5	4.0	
Na	Mg	Al	Si	P	S	Cl	—*
0.9	1.3	1.6	1.9	2.2	2.6	3.2	
K	Ca	Sc	Ge	As	Se	Br	Kr
0.8	1.0	1.4	2.0	2.2	2.5	3.0	3.3
Rb	Sr	Y	Sn	Sb	Te	I	Xe
0.8	0.9	1.2	1.9	2.0	2.1	2.7	3.0
Cs	Ba						
0.8	0.9						

*The noble gases He, Ne, and Ar are not listed because they form no stable compounds.

CHEMISTRY Beyond the Classroom

Why Do Lobsters Turn Red When Cooked?

Harry A. Frank, University of Connecticut

Many biological organisms exhibit visible coloration. This occurs when specific molecules become bound in proteins or membranes of an organism and absorb light in the visible region of the electromagnetic spectrum. As described in this chapter, absorption occurs when an atom or molecule is excited by light from the ground electronic state to a higher excited state. Wavelengths of light not absorbed are either scattered or reflected. This may result in coloration or patterns that either blend with the environment or stand out from it. Why animal species select specific molecules for coloration has much to do with the pressures of survival in the wild. However, not all animals are able to synthesize what they need for this purpose. In many cases, dietary intake plays a role.

Animals ingest plant material in the course of their normal dietary intake, and the plant pigments then find their way into the outer covering of the organism, where they may be exhibited as coloration. Many complex biochemical and metabolic pathways are involved after ingestion in modifying and transporting the molecules that ultimately become pigments.

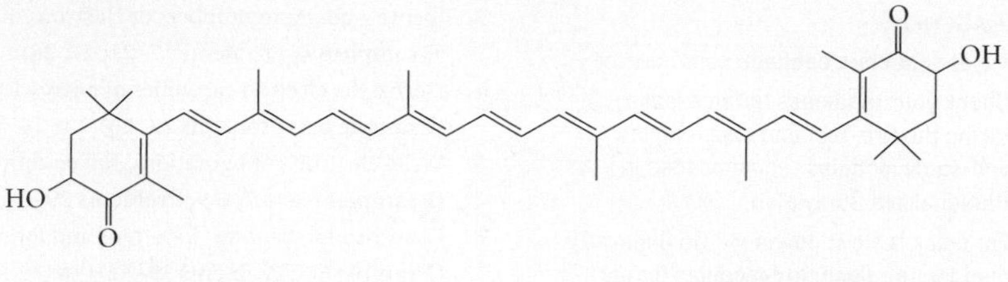

Figure A
The molecular structure of astaxanthin. β-carotene is the same molecule where the ═O and —OH groups are replaced with hydrogens.

Figure B
***Homarus americanus* before and after cooking.**

An excellent case in point is the coloration of the American lobster, *Homarus americanus*. The pigment associated with the typical greenish-brown outer layer of the lobster shell is the carotenoid, astaxanthin (Figure A), an oxygenated derivative of β-carotene, also known as the molecule that imparts the orange color to carrots.

Both astaxanthin and β-carotene belong to a class of pigments known as carotenoids. Carotenoids are not synthesized by any member of the animal kingdom, but are taken in through the diet. The lobster diet consists primarily of fish, mollusks, and other crustaceans. Therefore, the color of a live lobster can vary due to differences in available food sources and environmental conditions. This is why some lobsters may be orange, speckled, or even bright blue. Indeed, blue coloration is frequently observed in the joints of a live lobster's appendages (Figure B). When cooked, the color of the lobster turns red. How does this happen?

After being ingested, astaxanthin molecules are assembled in a large protein called crustacyanin, and then bound in the calcified outer layer of the lobster shell. When an astaxanthin molecule is bound in the crustacyanin protein, its structure becomes twisted and pairs up with another astaxanthin. This combination of twisting and pairing of astaxanthin molecules produces a pigment-protein complex that absorbs the long wavelengths of visible light (Figure C), and hence appears blue. Free astaxanthin dissolved in organic solvents such as methanol, absorbs the shorter wavelengths of blue-green light (Figure C), and therefore appears the complement of this color, which is red.

Because the lobster accumulates a combination of protein-bound (blue) and free (red) astaxanthin in its shell, the live animal appears greenish-brown, which apparently serves it well as a disguise against predators on the ocean floor. The color change upon cooking occurs because high temperatures denature the crustacyanin protein and release the bound astaxanthin. No longer constrained by the protein, but still intact, astaxanthin imparts the same red color to the shell that it exhibits as a free molecule in organic solvent. Our world is colored by an abundance of these carotenoid pigments in mammals, fish, reptiles, birds, and other living creatures.

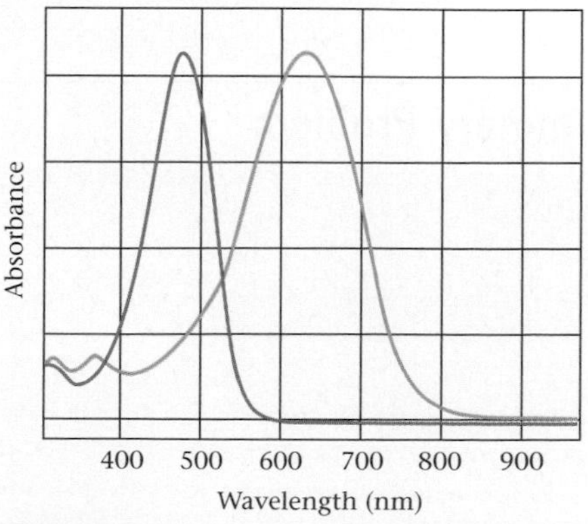

Figure C
Absorption spectra of astaxanthin (red line) in methanol and astaxanthin bound in crustacyanin protein (blue line).

Chapter Highlights

Key Concepts

Select end of chapter Questions and Problems may be assigned in OWL and are cross-referenced in the Key Concepts list.

CENGAGENOW™

Sign in at **academic.cengage.com/now** to:

- Check your readiness for an exam by taking the Pre-Test and exploring the self-study modules recommended in your Personalized Study plan.
- For quick review, download Go Chemistry mini-lecture flashcard modules (or purchase them at **www.ichapters.com**)

1. Relate wavelength, frequency, and energy.
   (Examples 6.1, 6.2; Problems 1–8, 61–63) ■ Questions and Problems assignable in OWL: 3, 80
2. Use the Bohr model to identify lines in the hydrogen spectrum.
   (Example 6.3; Problems 9–16) ■ 10, 71
3. Identify quantum numbers of electrons in atoms.
   (Example 6.4; Problems 17–22, 27, 28) ■ 18, 22, 28, 73
4. Derive the electron capacities of energy levels.
   (Example 6.5; Problems 23–26) ■ 24, 26
5. Write electron configurations, full or abbreviated, for atoms or ions.
   (Examples 6.6, 6.7, 6.9; Problems 29–38, 49, 50) ■ 30, 34, 50
6. Draw orbital diagrams for atoms and ions.
   (Example 6.8; Problems 39–52) ■ 40, 42, 46
7. Identify periodic trends in radii, ionization energy, and electronegativity.
   (Examples 6.10, 6.11; Problems 53–60) ■ 54, 56, 58, 67

Key Equations

Frequency-wavelength $\lambda\nu = c = 2.998 \times 10^8$ m/s (Section 6.1)

Energy-frequency $E = h\nu = hc/\lambda;\ h = 6.626 \times 10^{-34}$ J · s (Section 6.1)

Bohr model $E_\mathbf{n} = -R_H/\mathbf{n}^2;\ R_H = 2.180 \times 10^{-18}$ J (Section 6.2)

$$\nu = \frac{R_H}{h}\left[\frac{1}{(\mathbf{n}_{lo})^2} - \frac{1}{(\mathbf{n}_{hi})^2}\right] \text{ (Section 6.2)}$$

Quantum numbers $\mathbf{n} = 1, 2, 3, 4, \ldots$ (Section 6.3)

$\ell = 0, 1, 2, \ldots, (\mathbf{n} - 1)$ (Section 6.3)

$\mathbf{m}_\ell = \ell, \ldots, +1, 0, -1, \ldots, -\ell$ (Section 6.3)

$\mathbf{m}_s = +\frac{1}{2}, -\frac{1}{2}$ (Section 6.3)

Key Terms

actinide
atomic orbital
atomic radius
electron configuration
—abbreviated
electron spin
electronegativity
excited state
frequency
ground state
Hund's rule
ionic radius
ionization energy
lanthanide
orbital diagram
Pauli principle
photon
principal level
quantum number
spectrum
sublevel (s, p, d, f)
wavelength

Summary Problem

Consider the element vanadium ($Z = 23$).

(a) There is a line in the vanadium spectrum at 318.5 nm.

(1) In what region of the spectrum (ultraviolet, visible, or infrared) is this line found?

(2) What is the frequency of the line?

(3) What is the energy difference between the two levels responsible for this line in kilojoules per mole?

(4) The ionization energy of vanadium from the ground state is 650.2 kJ/mol. Assume that the transition in (3) is from the ground state to an excited state. If that is the case, calculate the ionization energy from the excited state.

(b) Give the electron configuration of the V atom; the V^{3+} ion.

(c) Give the orbital diagram (beyond argon) for V and V^{3+}.

(d) How many unpaired electrons are in the V atom? In the V^{3+} ion?

(e) How many electrons in V have $\ell = 1$ quantum number?

(f) How many electrons in V^{3+} have $\ell = 2$ quantum number?

(g) Rank V, V^{2+}, and V^{3+} in order of increasing size.

Summary Problem—cont'd

Answers

(a) (1) ultraviolet; (2) $9.413 \times 10^{14}\ s^{-1}$; (3) 376 kJ/mol; (4) 274 kJ/mol

(b) $1s^22s^22p^63s^23p^64s^23d^3$; $1s^22s^22p^63s^23p^63d^2$

(c)

	4s	3d
V:	(↑↓)	(↑)(↑)(↑)( )( )
V^{3+}:	( )	(↑)(↑)( )( )( )

(d) 3; 2

(e) 12

(f) 2

(g) $V^{3+} < V^{2+} < V$

Questions and Problems

Blue-numbered questions have answers in Appendix 6 and fully-worked solutions in the *Student Solutions Manual.*

■ denotes questions assignable in OWL.

WEB indicates that the solution is available on this book's companion website.

Light, Photon Energy and Atomic Spectra

1. A photon of violet light has a wavelength of 423 nm. Calculate
- **(a)** the frequency.
- **(b)** the energy in joules per photon.
- **(c)** the energy in kilojoules per mole.

2. Magnetic resonance imaging (MRI) is a powerful diagnostic tool used in medicine. The imagers used in hospitals operate at a frequency of 4.00×10^2 MHz (1 MHz = 10^6 Hz). Calculate
- **(a)** the wavelength.
- **(b)** the energy in joules per photon.
- **(c)** the energy in kilojoules per mole.

3. ■ A line in the spectrum of neon has a wavelength of 837.8 nm.
- **(a)** In what spectral range does the absorption occur?
- **(b)** Calculate the frequency of this absorption.
- **(c)** What is the energy in kilojoules per mole?

4. Carbon dioxide absorbs energy at a wavelength of 1498 nm.
- **(a)** In what spectral range does the absorption occur?
- **(b)** Calculate the frequency of this absorption.
- **(c)** What is the energy absorbed by one photon?

5. The ionization energy of rubidium is 403 kJ/mol. Do X-rays with a wavelength of 85 nm have sufficient energy to ionize rubidium?

6. Energy from radiation can cause chemical bonds to break. To break the nitrogen-nitrogen bond in N_2 gas, 941 kJ/mol is required.
- **(a)** Calculate the wavelength of the radiation that could break the bond.
- **(b)** In what spectral range does this radiation occur?

7. Microwave ovens heat food by the energy given off by microwaves. These microwaves have a wavelength of 5.00×10^6 nm.
- **(a)** How much energy in kilojoules per mole is given off by a microwave oven?
- **(b)** Compare the energy obtained in (a) with that given off by the ultraviolet rays ($\lambda \approx 100$ nm) of the Sun that you absorb when you try to get a tan.

8. **WEB** A bar code scanner in a grocery store is a He-Ne laser with a wavelength of 633 nm. If 12 kJ of energy is given off while the scanner is "reading" bar codes, how many photons are emitted?

The Hydrogen Atom

9. Consider the transition from the energy levels **n** = 4 to **n** = 2.
- **(a)** What is the frequency associated with this transition?
- **(b)** In what spectral region does this transition occur?
- **(c)** Is energy absorbed?

10. ■ Consider the transition from the energy levels **n** = 1 to **n** = 3.
- **(a)** What is the wavelength associated with this transition?
- **(b)** In what spectral region does this transition occur?
- **(c)** Is energy absorbed?

11. According to the Bohr model, the radius of a circular orbit is given by the equation

$$r(\text{in nm}) = 0.0529\ \mathbf{n}^2$$

Draw successive orbits for the hydrogen electron at **n** = 1, 2, 3, and 4. Indicate by arrows transitions between orbits that lead to lines in the
- **(a)** Lyman series ($\mathbf{n}_{lo} = 1$).
- **(b)** Balmer series ($\mathbf{n}_{lo} = 2$).

12. Calculate $E_\mathbf{n}$ for **n** = 1, 2, 3, and 4 ($R_H = 2.180 \times 10^{-18}$ J). Make a one-dimensional graph showing energy, at different values of **n**, increasing vertically. On this graph, indicate by vertical arrows transitions in the
- **(a)** Lyman series ($\mathbf{n}_{lo} = 1$).
- **(b)** Balmer series ($\mathbf{n}_{lo} = 2$).

13. For the Pfund series, $\mathbf{n}_{lo} = 5$.
- **(a)** Calculate the wavelength in nanometers of a transition from **n** = 7 to **n** = 5.
- **(b)** In what region of the spectrum are these lines formed?

14. The Brackett series lines in the atomic spectrum of hydrogen result from transitions from **n** > 4 to **n** = 4.
- **(a)** Calculate the wavelength, in nanometers, of a line in this series resulting from the **n** = 5 to **n** = 4 transition.
- **(b)** In what region of the spectrum are these lines formed?

15. A line in the Lyman series ($\mathbf{n}_{lo} = 1$) occurs at 97.23 nm. Calculate $\mathbf{n}_{hi}$ for the transition associated with this line.

16. In the Paschen series, $\mathbf{n}_{lo} = 3$. Calculate the longest wavelength possible for a transition in this series.

Quantum Numbers

17. What are the possible values for $\mathbf{m}_\ell$ for
- **(a)** the d sublevel?
- **(b)** the s sublevel?
- **(c)** all sublevels where **n** = 2?

18. ■ What are the possible values for m_ℓ for
(a) the p sublevel?
(b) the f sublevel?
(c) all sublevels where $n = 3$?

19. For the following pairs of orbitals, indicate which is lower in energy in a many-electron atom.
(a) 3d or 4s
(b) 4f or 3d
(c) 2s or 2p
(d) 4f or 4d

20. For the following pairs of orbitals, indicate which is higher in energy in a many-electron atom.
(a) 3s or 2p
(b) 4s or 4d
(c) 4f or 6s
(d) 1s or 2s

21. What type of electron orbital (i.e., s, p, d, or f) is designated by
(a) $n = 3, \ell = 2, m_\ell = -1$?
(b) $n = 6, \ell = 3, m_\ell = 2$?
(c) $n = 4, \ell = 3, m_\ell = 3$?

22. ■ WEB What type of electron orbital (i.e., s, p, d, or f) is designated by
(a) $n = 2, \ell = 1, m_\ell = -1$?
(b) $n = 1, \ell = 0, m_\ell = 0$?
(c) $n = 5, \ell = 2, m_\ell = 2$?

23. State the total capacity for electrons in
(a) $n = 4$.
(b) a 3s sublevel.
(c) a d sublevel.
(d) a p orbital.

24. ■ Give the number of orbitals in
(a) $n = 3$.
(b) a 4p sublevel.
(c) an f sublevel.
(d) a d sublevel.

25. How many electrons in an atom can have each of the following quantum number designations?
(a) $n = 2, \ell = 1, m_\ell = 0$
(b) $n = 2, \ell = 1, m_\ell = -1$
(c) $n = 3, \ell = 1, m_\ell = 0, m_s = +\frac{1}{2}$

26. ■ How many electrons in an atom can have each of the following quantum number designations?
(a) $n = 1, \ell = 0, m_\ell = 0$
(b) $n = 5, \ell = 3, m_\ell = +2$
(c) $n = 3, \ell = 2$

27. Given the following sets of electron quantum numbers, indicate those that could not occur, and explain your answer.
(a) $3, 0, 0, -\frac{1}{2}$
(b) $2, 2, 1, -\frac{1}{2}$
(c) $3, 2, 1, +\frac{1}{2}$
(d) $3, 1, 1, +\frac{1}{2}$
(e) $4, 2, -2, 0$

28. ■ Given the following sets of electron quantum numbers, indicate those that could not occur, and explain your answer.
(a) $1, 0, 0, -\frac{1}{2}$
(b) $1, 1, 0, +\frac{1}{2}$
(c) $3, 2, -2, +\frac{1}{2}$
(d) $2, 1, 2, +\frac{1}{2}$
(e) $4, 0, 2, +\frac{1}{2}$

29. Write the ground state electron configuration for
(a) N (b) Na (c) Ne (d) Ni (e) Si

30. ■ Write the ground state electron configuration for
(a) B (b) Ba (c) Be (d) Bi (e) Br

31. Write the abbreviated ground state electron configuration for
(a) P (b) As (c) Sn (d) Zr (e) Al

32. Write the abbreviated ground state electron configuration for
(a) Os (b) Mg (c) Ge (d) V (e) At

33. Give the symbol of the element of lowest atomic number whose ground state has
(a) a p electron.
(b) four f electrons.
(c) a completed d subshell.
(d) six s electrons.

34. ■ Give the symbol of the element of lowest atomic number whose ground state has
(a) a completed f subshell.
(b) 20 p electrons.
(c) two 4d electrons.
(d) five 5p electrons.

35. What fraction of the total number of electrons is in d sublevels in
(a) C (b) Cl (c) Co

36. What fraction of the total number of electrons is in p sublevels in
(a) Mg (b) Mn (c) Mo

37. Which of the following electron configurations are for atoms in the ground state? In the excited state? Which are impossible?
(a) $1s^22s^22p^1$
(b) $1s^21p^12s^1$
(c) $1s^22s^22p^33s^1$
(d) $1s^22s^22p^63d^{10}$
(e) $1s^22s^22p^53s^1$

38. Which of the following electron configurations (a–e) are for atoms in the ground state? In the excited state? Which are impossible?
(a) $1s^22p^1$
(b) $1s^22s^22p^4$
(c) $1s^22s^22p^53d^1$
(d) $1s^22s^22p^73s^2$
(e) $1s^22s^22p^64s^13d^{11}$

Orbital Diagrams; Hund's Rule

39. Give the orbital diagram of
(a) Li (b) P (c) F (d) Fe

40. ■ Give the orbital diagram for an atom of
(a) Na (b) O (c) Co (d) Cl

41. Give the symbol of the atom with the following orbital diagram beyond argon.

	4s	3d	4p
(a)	(↑↓)	(↑↓)(↑↓)(↑↓)(↑)(↑)	( )( )( )
(b)	(↑↓)	(↑↓)(↑↓)(↑)(↑)(↑)	( )( )( )
(c)	(↑↓)	(↑↓)(↑↓)(↑↓)(↑↓)(↑↓)	(↑)(↑)( )

42. ■ Give the symbol of the atom with the following orbital diagram

	1s	2s	2p	3s	3p
(a)	(↑↓)	(↑↓)	(↑↓)(↑↓)(↑↓)	(↑↓)	( )( )( )
(b)	(↑↓)	(↑↓)	(↑↓)(↑↓)(↑↓)	(↑↓)	(↑)(↑)(↑)
(c)	(↑↓)	(↑↓)	(↑↓)(↑)(↑)	( )	( )( )( )

43. Give the symbols of
(a) all the elements in period 2 whose atoms have empty 2p orbitals.
(b) all the metals in period 3 that have at least one unpaired electron.
(c) all the alkaline earth metals that have filled 3d sublevels.
(d) all the halogens that have unpaired 4p electrons.

■ in OWL Blue-numbered questions answered in Appendix 6 WEB Solution is available on companion website

44. Give the symbols of
(a) all the elements in period 5 that have at least two half-filled 5p orbitals.
(b) all the elements in Group 1 that have full 3p orbitals.
(c) all the metalloids that have paired 3p electrons.
(d) all the nonmetals that have full 3d orbitals and 3 half-filled 3p orbitals.

45. Give the number of unpaired electrons in an atom of
(a) phosphorus
(b) potassium
(c) plutonium (Pu)

46. ■ Give the number of unpaired electrons in an atom of
(a) mercury
(b) manganese
(c) magnesium

47. In what main group(s) of the periodic table do element(s) have the following number of filled p orbitals in the outermost principal level?
(a) 0 (b) 1 (c) 2 (d) 3

48. **WEB** Give the symbol of the main-group metals in period 4 with the following number of unpaired electrons per atom. (Transition metals are not included.)
(a) 0 (b) 1 (c) 2 (d) 3

Electron Arrangement in Monatomic Ions

49. Write the ground state electron configuration for
(a) Mg, Mg^{2+}
(b) N, N^{3-}
(c) Ti, Ti^{4+}
(d) Sn^{2+}, Sn^{4+}

50. ■ Write the ground state electron configuration for
(a) S, S^{2-}
(b) Al, Al^{3+}
(c) V, V^{4+}
(d) Cu^{+}, Cu^{2+}

51. How many unpaired electrons are in the following ions?
(a) Hg^{2+} (b) F^{-} (c) Sb^{3+} (d) Fe^{3+}

52. How many unpaired electrons are in the following ions?
(a) Al^{3+} (b) Cl^{-} (c) Sr^{2+} (d) Ag^{+}

Trends in the Periodic Table

53. Arrange the elements Sr, In, and Te in order of
(a) decreasing atomic radius.
(b) decreasing first ionization energy.
(c) increasing electronegativity.

54. ■ **WEB** Arrange the elements Na, Si, and S in order of
(a) increasing atomic radius.
(b) increasing first ionization energy.
(c) decreasing electronegativity.

55. Which of the four atoms Rb, Sr, Sb, or Cs
(a) has the smallest atomic radius?
(b) has the lowest ionization energy?
(c) is the least electronegative?

56. ■ Which of the four atoms Na, P, Cl, or K
(a) has the largest atomic radius?
(b) has the highest ionization energy?
(c) is the most electronegative?

57. Select the larger member of each pair.
(a) K and K^{+}
(b) O and O^{2-}
(c) Tl and Tl^{3+}
(d) Cu^{+} and Cu^{2+}

58. ■ Select the smaller member of each pair.
(a) N and N^{3-}
(b) Ba and Ba^{2+}
(c) Se and Se^{2-}
(d) Co^{2+} and Co^{3+}

59. List the following species in order of decreasing radius.
(a) C, Mg, Ca, Si
(b) Sr, Cl, Br, I

60. List the following species in order of increasing radius.
(a) Rb, K, Cs, Kr
(b) Ar, Cs, Si, Al

Unclassified

61. A lightbulb radiates 8.5% of the energy supplied to it as visible light. If the wavelength of the visible light is assumed to be 565 nm, how many photons per second are emitted by a 75-W lightbulb? (1 W = 1 J/s)

62. An argon-ion laser is used in some laser light shows. The argon ion has strong emissions at 485 nm and 512 nm.
(a) What is the color of these emissions?
(b) What is the energy associated with these emissions in kilojoules per mole?
(c) Write the ground state electron configuration and orbital diagram of Ar^{+}.

63. A carbon dioxide laser produces radiation of wavelength 10.6 micrometers (1 micrometer = 10^{-6} meter). If the laser produces about one joule of energy per pulse, how many photons are produced per pulse?

64. Name and give the symbol for the element with the characteristic given below:
(a) Its electron configuration is $1s^22s^22p^63s^23p^5$.
(b) Lowest ionization energy in Group 14.
(c) Its +2 ion has the configuration $[_{18}Ar]\ 3d^5$.
(d) It is the alkali metal with the smallest atomic radius.
(e) Largest ionization energy in the fourth period.

Conceptual Questions

65. Compare the energies and wavelengths of two photons, one with a low frequency, the other with a high frequency.

66. Consider the following transitions
1. **n** = 3 to **n** = 1
2. **n** = 2 to **n** = 3
3. **n** = 4 to **n** = 3
4. **n** = 3 to **n** = 5
(a) For which of the transitions is energy absorbed?
(b) For which of the transitions is energy emitted?
(c) Which transitions involve the ground state?
(d) Which transition absorbs the most energy?
(e) Which transition emits the most energy?

67. ■ Write the symbol of each element described below.
(a) largest atomic radius in Group 17
(b) smallest atomic radius in period 3
(c) largest first ionization energy in Group 2
(d) most electronegative in Group 16
(e) element(s) in period 2 with no unpaired p electron
(f) abbreviated electron configuration is $[Ar]\ 4s^23d^3$
(g) A +2 ion with abbreviated electron configuration $[Ar]\ 3d^5$
(h) A transition metal in period 4 forming a +2 ion with no unpaired electrons

68. Write the symbol and the abbreviated electron configuration of the element described.
(a) the metal in Group 1 whose atom is the smallest
(b) the alkaline earth metal with the heaviest atom

■ in OWL Blue-numbered questions answered in Appendix 6 **WEB** Solution is available on companion website

(c) the transition metal in period 4 whose atom contains the fewest protons

(d) the largest metalloid atom with the maximum number of unpaired p electrons

(e) an element in period 4 whose +2 ion is isoelectronic with argon

69. Explain in your own words what is meant by

(a) the Pauli exclusion principle.

(b) Hund's rule.

(c) a line in an atomic spectrum.

(d) the principal quantum number.

70. Explain the difference between

(a) the Bohr model of the atom and the quantum mechanical model.

(b) wavelength and frequency.

(c) the geometries of the three different p orbitals.

71. ■ Indicate whether each of the following statements is true or false. If false, correct the statement.

(a) An electron transition from **n** = 3 to **n** = 1 gives off energy.

(b) Light emitted by an **n** = 4 to **n** = 2 transition will have a longer wavelength than that from an **n** = 5 to **n** = 2 transition.

(c) A sublevel of $\ell = 3$ has a capacity of ten electrons.

(d) An atom of Group 13 has three unpaired electrons.

72. Criticize or comment on the following statements:

(a) The energy of a photon is inversely proportional to its wavelength.

(b) The energy of the hydrogen electron is inversely proportional to the quantum number ℓ.

(c) Electrons start to enter the fifth principal level as soon as the fourth is full.

73. ■ No currently known elements contain electrons in g ($\ell = 4$) orbitals in the ground state. If an element is discovered that has electrons in the g orbital, what is the lowest value for **n** in which these g orbitals could exist? What are the possible values of $\mathbf{m}_\ell$? How many electrons could a set of g orbitals hold?

74. Indicate whether each of the following is true or false.

(a) Effective nuclear charge stays about the same when one goes down a group.

(b) Group 17 elements have seven electrons in their outer level.

(c) Energy is given off when an electron is removed from an atom.

75. Explain why

(a) negative ions are larger than their corresponding atoms.

(b) scandium, a transition metal, forms an ion with a noble-gas structure.

(c) electronegativity decreases down a group in the periodic table.

Challenge Problems

76. The energy of any one-electron species in its **n**th state (**n** = principal quantum number) is given by $E = -BZ^2/\mathbf{n}^2$, where Z is the charge on the nucleus and B is 2.180×10^{-18} J. Find the ionization energy of the Li^{2+} ion in its first excited state in kilojoules per mole.

77. In 1885, Johann Balmer, a mathematician, derived the following relation for the wavelength of lines in the visible spectrum of hydrogen

$$\lambda = \frac{364.5\ \mathbf{n}^2}{(\mathbf{n}^2 - 4)}$$

where λ is in nanometers and **n** is an integer that can be 3, 4, 5, . . . Show that this relation follows from the Bohr equation and the equation using the Rydberg constant. Note that in the Balmer series, the electron is returning to the **n** = 2 level.

78. Suppose the rules for assigning quantum numbers were as follows

$$\mathbf{n} = 1, 2, 3, \ldots$$
$$\ell = 0, 1, 2, \ldots, \mathbf{n}$$
$$\mathbf{m}_\ell = 0, 1, 2, \ldots, \ell + 1$$
$$\mathbf{m}_s = +\tfrac{1}{2} \text{ or } -\tfrac{1}{2}$$

Prepare a table similar to Table 6.2 based on these rules for **n** = 1 and **n** = 2. Give the electron configuration for an atom with eight electrons.

79. Suppose that the spin quantum number could have the values $\frac{1}{2}$, 0, and $-\frac{1}{2}$. Assuming that the rules governing the values of the other quantum numbers and the order of filling sublevels were unchanged,

(a) what would be the electron capacity of an s sublevel? A p sublevel? A d sublevel?

(b) how many electrons could fit in the **n** = 3 level?

(c) what would be the electron configuration of the element with atomic number 8? 17?

80. ■ In the photoelectric effect, electrons are ejected from a metal surface when light strikes it. A certain minimum energy, E_{min}, is required to eject an electron. Any energy absorbed beyond that minimum gives kinetic energy to the electron. It is found that when light at a wavelength of 540 nm falls on a cesium surface, an electron is ejected with a kinetic energy of 2.60×10^{-20} J. When the wavelength is 400 nm, the kinetic energy is 1.54×10^{-19} J.

(a) Calculate E_{min} for cesium in joules.

(b) Calculate the longest wavelength, in nanometers, that will eject electrons from cesium.

■ in OWL Blue-numbered questions answered in Appendix 6 **WEB** Solution is available on companion website

7 Covalent Bonding

What immortal hand or eye
Could frame thy fearful symmetry?

—William Blake
"The Tiger"

Chapter Outline

The sculpture shows artistically stacked tetrahedra. The molecular geometry for the molecule CCl_4 is that of a tetrahedron.

Earlier we referred to the forces that hold nonmetal atoms to one another, covalent bonds. These bonds consist of an electron pair shared between two atoms. To represent the covalent bond in the H_2 molecule, two structures can be written:

$$H:H \qquad \text{or} \qquad H—H$$

These structures can be misleading if they are taken to mean that the two electrons are fixed in position between the two nuclei. A more accurate picture of the electron density in H_2 is shown in Figure 7.1. At a given instant, the two electrons may be located at any of various points about the two nuclei. However, they are more likely to be found between the nuclei than at the far ends of the molecule.

To understand the stability of the electron-pair bond, consider the graph shown in Figure 7.2 (p. 166), where we plot the energy of interaction between two hydrogen atoms as a function of distance. At large distances of separation (far right) the system consists of two isolated H atoms that do not interact with each other. As the atoms come closer together (moving to the left in Figure 7.2), they experience an attraction that leads gradually to an energy minimum. At an internuclear distance of 0.074 nm and an attractive energy of 436 kJ, the system is in its most stable state; we refer to that state as the H_2 molecule. If the atoms are brought closer together, forces of repulsion become increasingly important and the energy curve rises steeply.

The existence of the energy minimum shown in Figure 7.2 is directly responsible for the stability of the H_2 molecule. The attractive forces that bring about this minimum result from two factors:

1. Locating two electrons between the two protons of the H_2 molecule lowers the electrostatic energy of the system. Attractive energies between oppositely charged particles (electron-proton) slightly exceed the repulsive energies between particles of like charge (electron-electron, proton-proton).

2. When two hydrogen atoms come together to form a molecule, the electrons are spread over the entire volume of the molecule instead of being confined to a particular atom. As pointed out in Chapter 6, quantum mechanics tells us that increasing the volume available to an electron decreases its kinetic energy. We often describe this situation by saying that the two 1s orbitals of the hydrogen atom "overlap" to form a new bonding orbital. At any rate, calculations suggest that this is the principal factor accounting for the stability of the H_2 molecule.

This chapter is devoted to the covalent bond as it exists in molecules and polyatomic ions. We consider—

- the distribution of outer level *(valence)* electrons in species in which atoms are joined by covalent bonds. These distributions are most simply described by *Lewis structures* (Section 7.1).
- molecular geometries. The so-called *VSEPR model* can be used to predict the angles between covalent bonds formed by a central atom (Section 7.2).

Figure 7.1
Electron density in H_2. The depth of color is proportional to the probability of finding an electron in a particular region.

Online homework for this chapter may be assigned in OWL

CENGAGENOW™
This icon introduces an opportunity for self-study and to explore interactive modules by signing in at **academic.cengage.com/now.**

CENGAGENOW™
Click Chemistry Interactive for a self-study module **interatomic electrostatic interactions.**

Figure 7.2
Energy of two hydrogen atoms as a function of the distance between their nuclei.

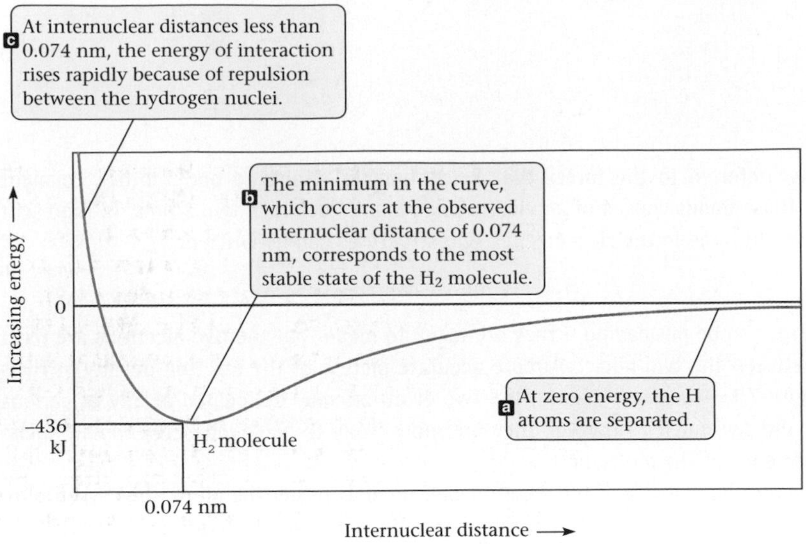

- the polarity of covalent bonds and the molecules they form (Section 7.3). Most bonds and many molecules are polar in the sense that they have a positive and a negative pole.
- the distribution of valence electrons among *atomic orbitals*, using the valence bond approach (Section 7.4). ■

7.1 LEWIS STRUCTURES; THE OCTET RULE

CENGAGENOW™
Click Coached Problems for a self-study module on **interpreting Lewis structures.**

The idea of the covalent bond was first suggested by the American physical chemist Gilbert Newton Lewis (1875–1946) in 1916. He pointed out that the electron configuration of the noble gases appears to be a particularly stable one. Noble-gas atoms are themselves extremely unreactive. Moreover, as pointed out in Chapter 6, a great many monatomic ions have noble-gas structures. Lewis suggested that ***nonmetal atoms, by sharing electrons to form an electron-pair bond, can acquire a stable noble-gas structure.*** Consider, for example, two hydrogen atoms, each with one electron. The process by which they combine to form an H_2 molecule can be shown as

Noble-gas structures are stable in molecules, as they are in atoms and ions.

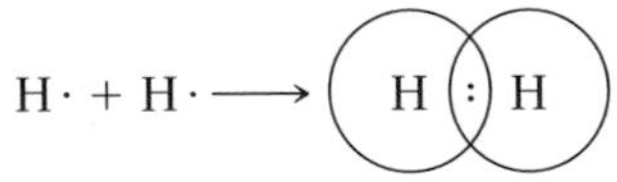

using dots to represent electrons; the circles emphasize that the pair of electrons in the covalent bond can be considered to occupy the 1s orbital of either hydrogen atom. In that sense, each atom in the H_2 molecule has the electronic structure of the noble gas helium, with the electron configuration $1s^2$.

This idea is readily extended to simple molecules of compounds formed by nonmetal atoms. An example is the HF molecule. You will recall that a fluorine atom has the electron configuration $1s^22s^22p^5$. It has seven electrons in its outermost principal energy level (**n** = 2). These are referred to as **valence electrons,** in contrast to the core electrons filling the principal level, **n** = 1. If the valence electrons are shown as dots around the symbol of the element, the fluorine atom can be represented as

Valence electrons are the ones involved in bonding.

$$:\ddot{\underset{\cdot\cdot}{F}}\cdot$$

The combination of a hydrogen with a fluorine atom leads to

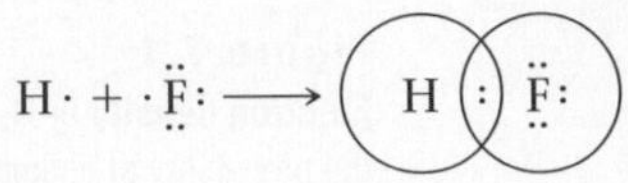

Table 7.1 Lewis Structures of Atoms Commonly Forming Covalent Bonds

Group:	1	2	13	14	15	16	17	18
No. of valence e^-:	1	2	3	4	5	6	7	8

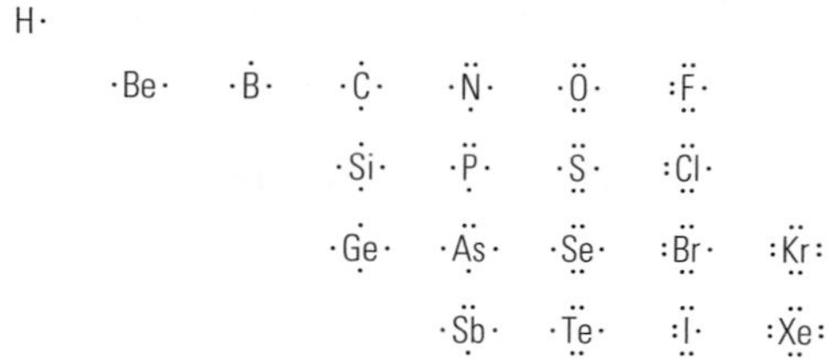

This is why we put the second digit of the group number in bold type.

As you can see, the fluorine atom "owns" six valence electrons outright and shares two others. Putting it another way, the F atom is surrounded by eight valence electrons; its electron configuration has become $1s^22s^22p^6$, which is that of the noble gas neon. This, according to Lewis, explains why the HF molecule is stable in contrast to species such as H_2F, H_3F, . . . none of which exist.

Shared electrons are counted for both atoms.

These structures (without the circles) are referred to as **Lewis structures.** In writing Lewis structures, only the valence electrons written above are shown, because they are the ones that participate in covalent bonding. For the main-group elements, the only ones dealt with here, the number of valence electrons is equal to the last digit of the group number in the periodic table (Table 7.1). Notice that elements in a given main group all have the same number of valence electrons. This explains why such elements behave similarly when they react to form covalently bonded species.

In the Lewis structure of a molecule or polyatomic ion, valence electrons ordinarily occur in pairs. There are two kinds of electron pairs.

1. A pair of electrons shared between two atoms is a **covalent bond,** ordinarily shown as a straight line between bonded atoms.
2. An **unshared pair** of electrons, owned entirely by one atom, is shown as a pair of dots on that atom. (An unshared pair is often referred to, more picturesquely, as a *lone pair.*)

The Lewis structures for the species OH^-, H_2O, NH_3, and NH_4^+ are

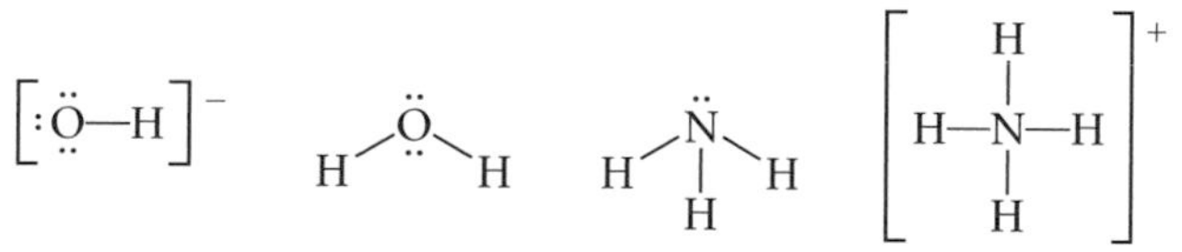

Notice that in each case the oxygen or nitrogen atom is surrounded by eight valence electrons. In each species, a single electron pair is shared between two bonded atoms. These bonds are called **single bonds.** There is one single bond in the OH^- ion, two in the H_2O molecule, three in NH_3, and four in NH_4^+. There are three unshared pairs in the hydroxide ion, two in the water molecule, one in the ammonia molecule, and none in the ammonium ion.

Forming a multiple bond "saves" electrons because bonding pairs are counted for both atoms.

Bonded atoms can share more than one electron pair. A **double bond** occurs when bonded atoms share two electron pairs; in a **triple bond,** three pairs of electrons are shared. In ethylene (C_2H_4) and acetylene (C_2H_2), the carbon atoms are linked by a double bond and triple bond, respectively. Using two parallel lines to represent a double bond and three for a triple bond, we write the structures of these molecules as

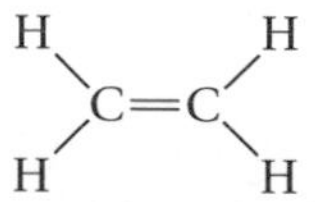

ethylene, C_2H_4

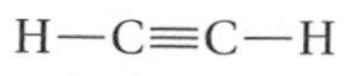

acetylene, C_2H_2

Note that each carbon is surrounded by eight valence electrons and each hydrogen by two.

Most molecules follow the octet rule.

These examples illustrate the principle that atoms in covalently bonded species tend to have noble-gas electronic structures. This generalization is often referred to as the **octet rule.** Nonmetals, except for hydrogen, achieve a noble-gas structure by sharing in an *octet* of electrons (eight). Hydrogen atoms, in molecules or polyatomic ions, are surrounded by a *duet* of electrons (two).

Writing Lewis Structures

CENGAGENOW™
Click Coached Problems for a self-study module on **drawing Lewis structures.**

For very simple species, Lewis structures can often be written by inspection. Usually, though, you will save time by following these steps:

1. ***Count the number of valence electrons.*** For a molecule, simply sum up the valence electrons of the atoms present. For a polyatomic anion, one electron is added for each unit of negative charge. For a polyatomic cation, a number of electrons equal to the positive charge must be subtracted.

2. ***Draw a skeleton structure for the species, joining atoms by single bonds.*** In some cases, only one arrangement of atoms is possible; in others, there are two or more alternative structures. Most of the molecules and polyatomic ions dealt with in this chapter consist of a *central atom* bonded to two or more *terminal atoms,* located at the outer edges of the molecule or ion. For such species (e.g., NH_4^+, SO_2, CCl_4), it is relatively easy to derive the skeleton structure. ***The central atom is usually the one written first in the formula*** (N in NH_4^+, S in SO_2, C in CCl_4); ***put this in the center of the molecule or ion. Terminal atoms are most often hydrogen, oxygen, or a halogen; bond these atoms to the central atom.***

3. ***Determine the number of valence electrons still available for distribution.*** To do this, deduct two valence electrons for each single bond written in step 2.

4. ***Determine the number of valence electrons required to fill out an octet for each atom*** (except H), ***in the skeleton.*** Remember that shared electrons are counted for both atoms.

(a) If the number of electrons available (step 3) is equal to the number required (step 4), distribute the available electrons as unshared pairs, satisfying the octet rule for each atom.

It would be nice if all shortages could be solved so simply.

(b) If the number of electrons available (step 3) is less than the number required (step 4), the skeleton structure must be modified by changing single to multiple bonds. If you are two electrons short, convert a single bond to a double bond; if there is a deficiency of four electrons, convert a single bond to a triple bond (or two single bonds to double bonds). Multiple bond formation is pretty much limited to the four atoms: C, N, O, and S. Hydrogen and halogen atoms never form double bonds.

The application of these steps and some further guiding principles are shown in Examples 7.1 and 7.2.

Charles D. Winters

Hypochlorite ions in action. The OCl^- ion is the active bleaching agent in Clorox™.

Example 7.1 Draw Lewis structures of

(a) the hypochlorite ion, OCl^- (b) ethane, C_2H_6

Strategy Follow the steps described above. For the OCl^- ion, only one skeleton is possible. For ethane keep in mind that the carbon atom ordinarily forms four bonds. Hydrogen must be a terminal atom because it forms only one bond.

SOLUTION

(a) (1) The number of valence electrons is 6 (from O) + 7 (from Cl) + 1 (from the −1 charge) = 14.

(2) The skeleton structure is $[O—Cl]^-$.

(3) The number of electrons available for distribution is 14 (originally) − 2 (used in skeleton) = 12.

(4) The number of electrons required to give each atom an octet is 6 (for O) + 6 (for Cl) = 12.

The number of available electrons is the same as the number required. This skeleton structure is correct; there are no multiple bonds. The Lewis structure is

$[:\ddot{\underset{..}{O}}-\ddot{\underset{..}{Cl}}:]^-$

(b) (1) the number of valence electrons is 8 (from the two carbon atoms) + 6 (from the six hydrogen atoms) for a total of 14.

(2) Because carbon forms four bonds and hydrogen must be a terminal atom, the only reasonable skeleton is

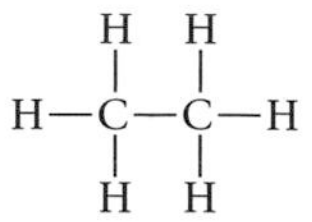

(3) The skeleton contains seven single bonds, using up $7 \times 2e^- = 14e^-$. This is exactly the number available, as shown in (1). It follows that the skeleton is also the Lewis structure:

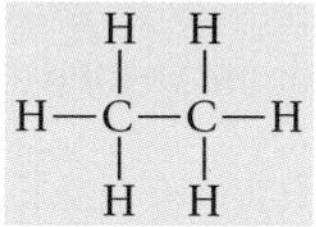

There are no unshared electron pairs.

Reality Check Whenever you write a Lewis structure, check to see if it follows the octet rule. The structures written for OCl^- and C_2H_6 do just that; each atom except H is surrounded by eight electrons.

Example 7.2 Draw Lewis structures for

(a) SO_2 (b) N_2

Strategy Follow the four steps for writing Lewis structures.

SOLUTION

(a) (1) There are 18 valence electrons. Both sulfur (two atoms) and oxygen (one atom) are in Group 16; $3 \times 6 = 18$.

(2) The skeleton structure, with sulfur as the central atom, is

$$O—S—O$$

The two single bonds account for four electrons.

(3) There are $18 - 4 = 14$ electrons available for distribution.

(4) Sixteen electrons are required to give each atom an octet (four for S and six for each O). There is a deficiency of two electrons. This means that a single bond in the skeleton must be converted to a double bond. The Lewis structure of SO_2 is

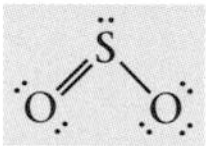

(b) (1) There are ten valence electrons; nitrogen is in Group 15.

(2) The skeleton structure is

$$N—N$$

(3) There are $10 - 2 = 8$ electrons available for distribution.

(4) Each N needs six electrons for an octet, so 12 electrons are needed. This means that there is a deficiency of $12 - 8 = 4$ electrons. Convert the single bond between the two N atoms to a triple bond. The Lewis structure is

$$:N\equiv N:$$

Resonance Forms

CENGAGENOW™
Click Coached Problems for a self-study module on **resonance structures.**

In certain cases, the Lewis structure does not adequately describe the properties of the ion or molecule that it represents. Consider, for example, the SO_2 structure derived in Example 7.2. This structure implies that there are two different kinds of sulfur-to-oxygen bonds in SO_2. One of these appears to be a single bond, the other a double bond. Yet experiment shows that there is only one kind of bond in the molecule.

One way to explain this situation is to assume that each of the bonds in SO_2 is intermediate between a single and a double bond. To express this concept, two structures, separated by a double-headed arrow, are written

The double-headed arrow is used to separate resonance structures.

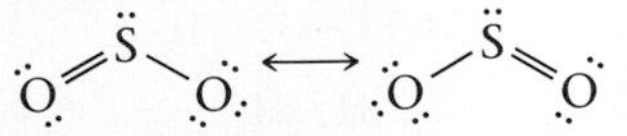

with the understanding that the true structure is intermediate between them. These are referred to as *resonance forms.* The concept of **resonance** is invoked whenever a single Lewis structure does not adequately reflect the properties of a substance.

Another species for which it is necessary to invoke the idea of resonance is the nitrate ion. Here three equivalent structures can be written

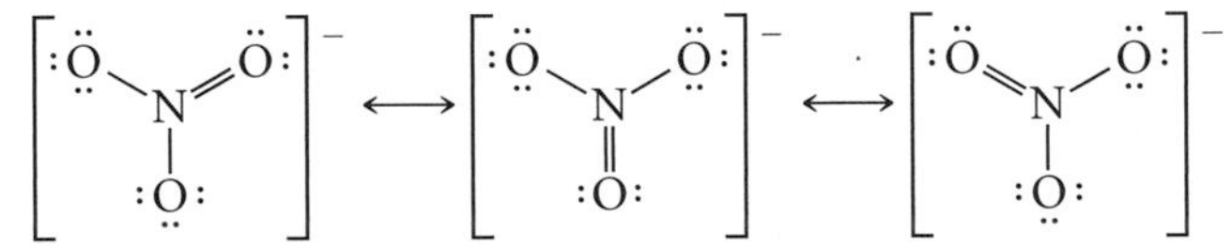

to explain the experimental observation that the three nitrogen-to-oxygen bonds in the NO_3^- ion are identical in all respects.

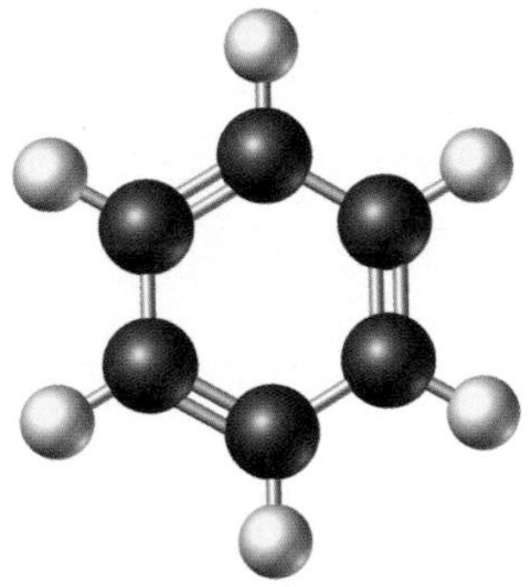

Benzene ball-and-stick model, showing double bonds.

Resonance can also occur with many organic molecules, including benzene, C_6H_6, which is known to have a hexagonal ring structure. Benzene can be considered a resonance hybrid of the two forms

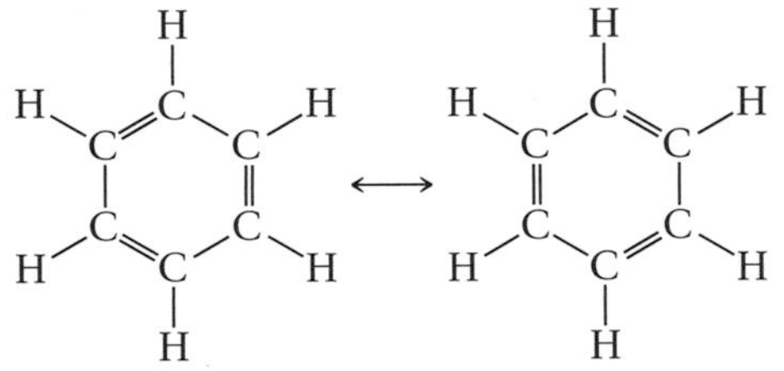

These structures are commonly abbreviated as

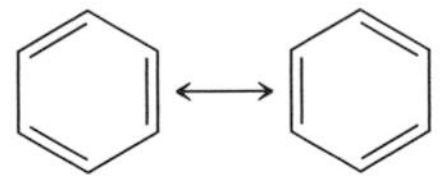

with the understanding that, at each corner of the hexagon, a carbon is attached to a hydrogen atom.

We will encounter other examples of molecules and ions whose properties can be interpreted in terms of resonance. In all such species,

1. Resonance forms do not imply different kinds of molecules with electrons shifting eternally between them. There is only one type of SO_2 molecule; its structure is intermediate between those of the two resonance forms drawn for sulfur dioxide.

2. Resonance can be anticipated when it is possible to write two or more Lewis structures that are about equally plausible. In the case of the nitrate ion, the three structures we have written are equivalent. One could, in principle, write many other structures, but none of them would put eight electrons around each atom.

3. Resonance forms differ only in the distribution of electrons, not in the arrangement of atoms. The molecule

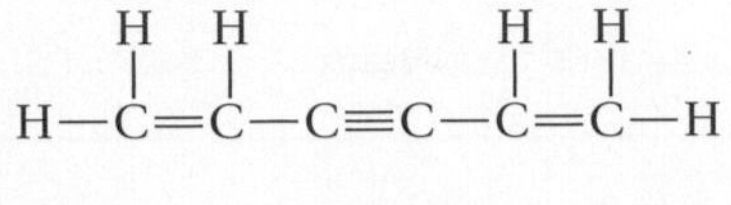

is not a resonance structure of benzene, even though it has the same molecular formula, C_6H_6. Indeed, it is an entirely different substance with different chemical and physical properties.

Example 7.3 Write two resonance structures for the NO_2^- ion.

Strategy Write a Lewis structure for the NO_2^- ion, following the usual steps. Then write the other resonance form by changing the position of the multiple bond. Do *not* change the skeleton structure.

SOLUTION The Lewis structures of the two resonance forms are

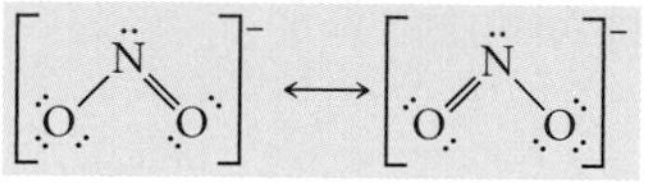

Formal Charge

CENGAGENOW™
Click Coached Problems for a self-study module on **calculating formal charge.**

Often it is possible to write two different Lewis structures for a molecule differing in the arrangement of atoms, that is,

A—A—B or A—B—A

Isomers have the same formula but different properties.

Sometimes both structures represent real compounds that are *isomers* of each other. More often, only one structure exists in nature. For example, methyl alcohol (CH_4O) has the structure

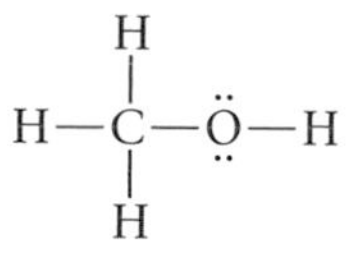

In contrast, the structure

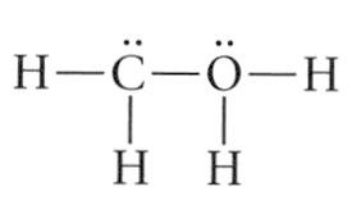

does not correspond to any real compound even though it obeys the octet rule.

There are several ways to choose the more plausible of two structures differing in their arrangement of atoms. As pointed out in Example 7.1, the fact that carbon almost always forms four bonds leads to the correct structure for ethane. Another approach involves a concept called **formal charge,** which can be applied to any atom within a Lewis structure. The formal charge is the difference between the number of valence electrons in the free atom and the number assigned to that atom in the Lewis structure. The assigned electrons include—

Formal charge is the charge an atom would have if valence electrons in bonds were distributed evenly.

- all the unshared electrons owned by that atom.
- one half of the bonding electrons shared by that atom.

This definition of formal charge, C_f, leads to the following equation

$$C_f = X - \left(Y + \frac{Z}{2}\right)$$

where X = the number of valence e^- in the free atom, which is equal to the last digit of the group number in the periodic table;
Y = the number of unshared e^- owned by the atom in the Lewis structure;
Z = the number of bonding e^- shared by the atom in the Lewis structure.

Table 7.2 Possible Structures for BeF_2 and BF_3

Structure I	C_f	Structure II	C_f
$:\ddot{F}{=}Be{=}\ddot{F}:$	Be = −2 F = +1	$:\ddot{F}{-}Be{-}\ddot{F}:$	Be = 0 F = 0
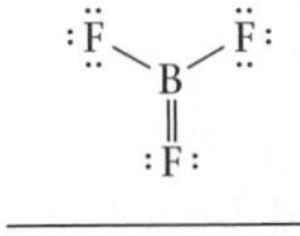	B = −1 F = +1,0,0	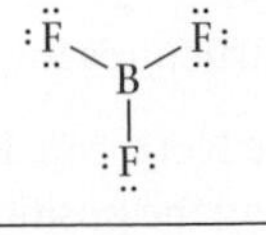	B = 0 F = 0

To show how this works, let's calculate the formal charges of carbon and oxygen in the two structures written above for methyl alcohol:

(1) 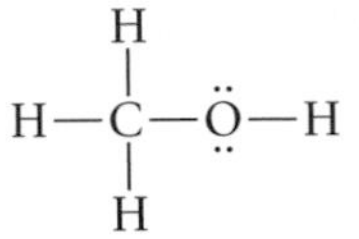

(2) 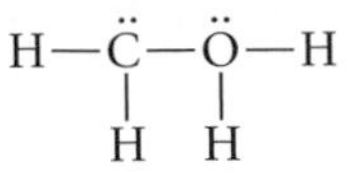

For C:	$X = 4, Y = 0, Z = 8$ $C_f = 4 - (0 + 8/2) = 0$	*For C:*	$X = 4, Y = 2, Z = 6$ $C_f = 4 - (2 + 6/2) = -1$
For O:	$X = 6, Y = 4, Z = 4$ $C_f = 6 - (4 + 4/2) = 0$	*For O:*	$X = 6, Y = 2, Z = 6$ $C_f = 6 - (2 + 6/2) = +1$

Ordinarily, the more likely Lewis structure is the one in which—

- the formal charges are as close to zero as possible.
- any negative formal charge is located on the most strongly electronegative atom.

Applying these rules, we can see that structure (1) for methyl alcohol is preferred over structure (2). In (1), both carbon and oxygen have formal charges of zero. In (2), a negative charge is assigned to carbon, which is actually less electronegative than oxygen (2.5 versus 3.5).

The concept of formal charge has a much wider applicability than this short discussion might imply. In particular, it can be used to predict situations in which conventional Lewis structures, written in accordance with the octet rule, may be incorrect (Table 7.2).

Formal charge is not an infallible guide to predicting Lewis structures.

CENGAGENOW™
Click Coached Problems for a self-study module on **electron-deficient compounds.**

Exceptions to the Octet Rule: Electron-Deficient Molecules

Although most of the molecules and polyatomic ions referred to in general chemistry follow the octet rule, there are some familiar species that do not. Among these are molecules containing an odd number of valence electrons. Nitric oxide, NO, and nitrogen dioxide, NO_2, fall in this category:

With an odd number of valence electrons, there's no way they could all be paired.

NO	no. of valence electrons = 5 + 6 = 11
NO_2	no. of valence electrons = 5 + 6(2) = 17

For such *odd electron* species (sometimes called free radicals) it is impossible to write Lewis structures in which each atom obeys the octet rule. In the NO molecule, the unpaired electron is put on the nitrogen atom, giving both atoms a formal charge of zero:

$$\cdot\ddot{N}{=}\ddot{O}:$$

In NO_2, the best structure one can write again puts the unpaired electron on the nitrogen atom:

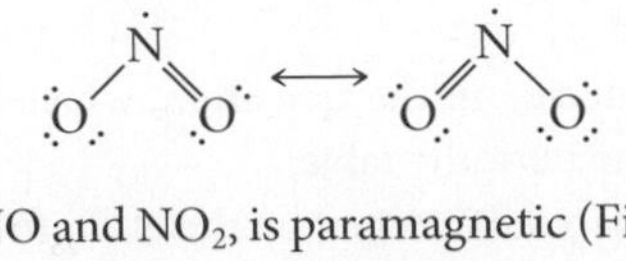

Charles D. Winters

Nitrogen dioxide. NO_2, a red-brown gas, has an unpaired electron on the N atom.

Elementary oxygen, like NO and NO_2, is paramagnetic (Figure 7.3, p. 173). Experimental evidence suggests that the O_2 molecule contains two unpaired electrons *and* a double bond.

S. Ruven Smith

Figure 7.3
Oxygen (O_2) in a magnetic field. The liquid oxygen, which is blue, is attracted into a magnetic field between the poles of an electromagnet. Both the paramagnetism and the blue color are due to the unpaired electrons in the O_2 molecule.

It is impossible to write a conventional Lewis structure for O_2 that has these two characteristics. A more sophisticated model of bonding, using molecular orbitals (Appendix 5), is required to explain the properties of oxygen.

There are a few species in which the central atom violates the octet rule in the sense that it is surrounded by two or three electron pairs rather than four. Examples include the fluorides of beryllium and boron, BeF_2 and BF_3. Although one could write multiple bonded structures for these molecules in accordance with the octet rule (Table 7.2), experimental evidence suggests the structures

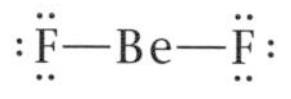

and

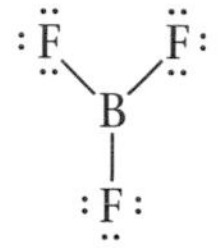

in which the central atom is surrounded by four and six valence electrons, respectively, rather than eight. Another familiar substance in which boron is surrounded by only three pairs of electrons rather than four is boric acid, H_3BO_3, used as an insecticide and fungicide.

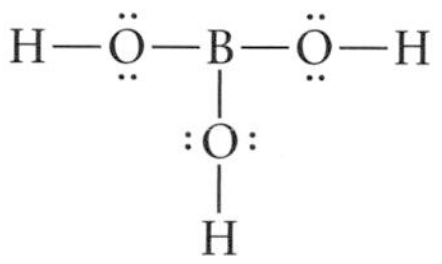

Exceptions to the Octet Rule: Expanded Octets

In most molecules, the central atom is surrounded by 8 electrons. Rarely, it is surrounded by 4 (BeF_2) or 6 (BF_3). Occasionally, the number is 10 (PCl_5) or 12 (SF_6).

The largest class of molecules to violate the octet rule consists of species in which the central atom is surrounded by more than four pairs of valence electrons. Typical molecules of this type are phosphorus pentachloride, PCl_5, and sulfur hexafluoride, SF_6. The Lewis structures of these molecules are

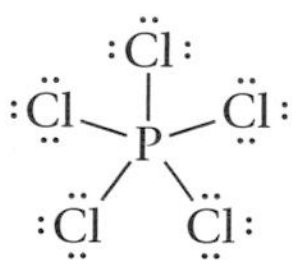

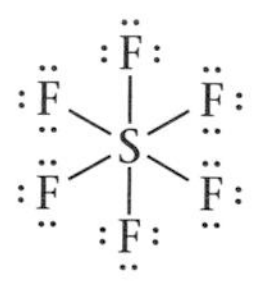

As you can see, the central atoms in these molecules have **expanded octets.** In PCl_5, the phosphorus atom is surrounded by 10 valence electrons (5 shared pairs); in SF_6, there are 12 valence electrons (6 shared pairs) around the sulfur atom.

In molecules of this type, the terminal atoms are most often halogens (F, Cl, Br, I); in a few molecules, oxygen is a terminal atom. The central atom is a nonmetal in the third, fourth, or fifth period of the periodic table. Most frequently, it is one of the following elements:

	Group 15	Group 16	Group 17	Group 18
3rd period	P	S	Cl	
4th period	As	Se	Br	Kr
5th period	Sb	Te	I	Xe

All these atoms have d orbitals available for bonding (3d, 4d, 5d). These are the orbitals in which the extra pairs of electrons are located in such species as PCl_5 and SF_6. Because there is no 2d sublevel, C, N, and O never form expanded octets.

Sometimes, as with PCl_5 and SF_6, it is clear from the formula that the central atom has an expanded octet. Often, however, it is by no means obvious that this is the case. At first glance, formulas such as ClF_3 or XeF_4 look completely straightforward. However, when you try to draw the Lewis structure it becomes clear that an expanded octet is involved. The number of electrons available after the skeleton is drawn is *greater* than the number required

CHEMISTRY The Human Side

Born in Massachusetts, G. N. Lewis grew up in Nebraska, then came back east to obtain his B.S. (1896) and Ph.D. (1899) at Harvard. Although he stayed on for a few years as an instructor, Lewis seems never to have been happy at Harvard. A precocious student and an intellectual rebel, he was repelled by the highly traditional atmosphere that prevailed in the chemistry department there in his time. Many years later, he refused an honorary degree from his alma mater.

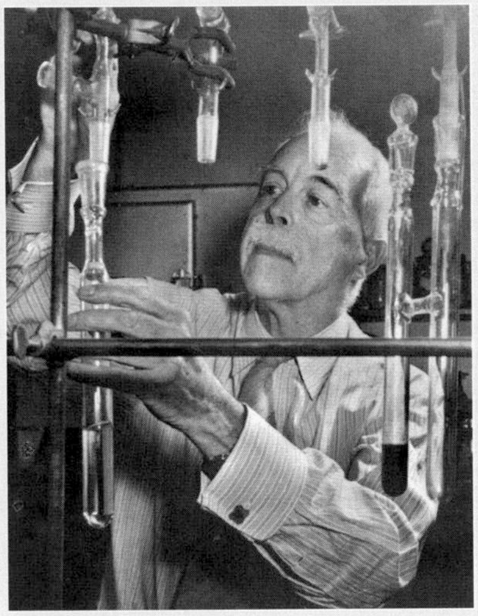

Dr. Glenn Seaborg, University of California, Lawrence Berkeley Laboratories

Gilbert Newton Lewis
(1875–1946)

After leaving Harvard, Lewis made his reputation at MIT, where he was promoted to full professor in only four years. In 1912, he moved across the country to the University of California, Berkeley, as dean of the College of Chemistry and department head. He remained there for the rest of his life. Under his guidance, the chemistry department at Berkeley became perhaps the most prestigious in the country. Among the faculty and graduate students that he attracted were five future Nobel Prize winners: Harold Urey in 1934, William Giauque in 1949, Glenn Seaborg in 1951, Willard Libby in 1960, and Melvin Calvin in 1961.

In administering the chemistry department at Berkeley, Lewis demanded excellence in both research and teaching. Virtually the entire staff was involved in the general chemistry program; at one time eight full professors carried freshman sections.

Lewis's interest in chemical bonding and structure dated from 1902. In attempting to explain "valence" to a class at Harvard, he devised an atomic model to rationalize the octet rule. His model was deficient in many respects; for one thing, Lewis visualized cubic atoms with electrons located at the corners. Perhaps this explains why his ideas of atomic structure were not published until 1916. In that year, Lewis conceived of the electron-pair bond, perhaps his greatest single contribution to chemistry. At that time, it was widely believed that all bonds were ionic; Lewis's ideas were rejected by many well-known organic chemists.

In 1923, Lewis published a classic book (later reprinted by Dover Publications) titled *Valence and the Structure of Atoms and Molecules.* Here, in Lewis's characteristically lucid style, we find many of the basic principles of covalent bonding discussed in this chapter. Included are electron-dot structures, the octet rule, and the concept of electronegativity. Here too is the Lewis definition of acids and bases (Chapter 15). That same year, Lewis published with Merle Randall a text called *Thermodynamics and the Free Energy of Chemical Substances.* Today, a revised edition of that text is still used in graduate courses in chemistry.

The years from 1923 to 1938 were relatively unproductive for G. N. Lewis insofar as his own research was concerned. The applications of the electron-pair bond came largely in the areas of organic and quantum chemistry; in neither of these fields did Lewis feel at home. In the early 1930s, he published a series of relatively minor papers dealing with the properties of deuterium. Then in 1939 he began to publish in the field of photochemistry. Of approximately 20 papers in this area, several were of fundamental importance, comparable in quality to the best work of his early years. Retired officially in 1945, Lewis died a year later while carrying out an experiment on fluorescence.

Lewis certainly deserved a Nobel Prize, but he never received one.

to give each atom an octet. When that happens, ***distribute the extra electrons (two or four) around the central atom as unshared pairs.***

Example 7.4 Draw the Lewis structure of XeF_4.

Strategy Follow the usual four-step sequence. If there is an electron surplus, add the extra electrons to the central xenon atom as unshared pairs.

SOLUTION

(1) The number of valence electrons is 8 (from Xe) + 28 (from four F atoms) = 36.
(2) The skeleton is

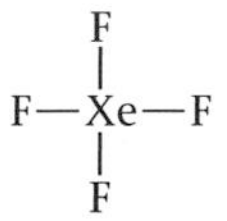

(3) The number of electrons available for distribution is 36 − 8 = 28.
(4) Each fluorine atom needs six electrons to complete its octet; the number of electrons required = 4(6) = 24.

There is a surplus of electrons; 28 are available and only 24 are required to fill out octets. The four extra electrons are added to the central Xe atom. The Lewis structure for XeF_4 is

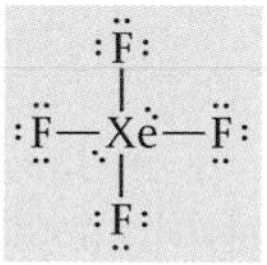

In this molecule there are six pairs of electrons around the xenon atom.

The extra electrons go to the central atom.

7.2 MOLECULAR GEOMETRY

The geometry of a diatomic molecule such as Cl_2 or HCl can be described very simply. Because two points define a straight line, the molecule must be linear.

Cl—Cl   H—Cl

With molecules containing three or more atoms, the geometry is not so obvious. Here, the angles between bonds, called **bond angles,** must be considered. For example, a molecule of the type YX_2, where Y represents the central atom and X an atom bonded to it, can be—

- *linear,* with a bond angle of 180°: X—Y—X
- *bent,* with a bond angle less than 180°: 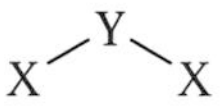

The major features of **molecular geometry** can be predicted on the basis of a quite simple principle—electron-pair repulsion. This principle is the essence of the *valence-shell electron-pair repulsion (VSEPR) model,* first suggested by N. V. Sidgwick and H. M. Powell in 1940. It was developed and expanded later by R. J. Gillespie and R. S. Nyholm. According to the **VSEPR model,** ***the valence electron pairs surrounding an atom repel one another. Consequently, the orbitals containing those electron pairs are oriented to be as far apart as possible.***

This is a very useful rule; to apply it you start with the Lewis structure.

In this section we apply this model to predict the geometry of some rather simple molecules and polyatomic ions. In all these species, a central atom is surrounded by from two to six pairs of electrons.

Charles D. Winters

Figure 7.4
VSEPR electron-pair geometries. The balloons, by staying as far apart as possible, illustrate the geometries *(left to right)* for two to six electron pairs.

Ideal Geometries with Two to Six Electron Pairs on the Central Atom

CENGAGENOW™
Click Coached Problems for a self-study module on **electron pair geometry.**

We begin by considering species in which a central atom, A, is surrounded by from two to six electron pairs, all of which are used to form single bonds with terminal atoms, X. These species have the general formulas AX_2, AX_3, . . . , AX_6. It is understood that there are no unshared pairs around atom A.

To see how the bonding orbitals surrounding the central atom are oriented with respect to one another, consider Figure 7.4, which shows the positions taken naturally by two to six balloons tied together at the center. The balloons, like the orbitals they represent, arrange themselves to be as far from one another as possible.

Figure 7.5 (page 177) shows the geometries predicted by the VSEPR model for molecules of the types AX_2 to AX_6. The geometries for two and three electron pairs are those associated with species in which the central atom has less than an octet of electrons. Molecules of this type include BeF_2 (in the gas state) and BF_3, which have the Lewis structures shown below:

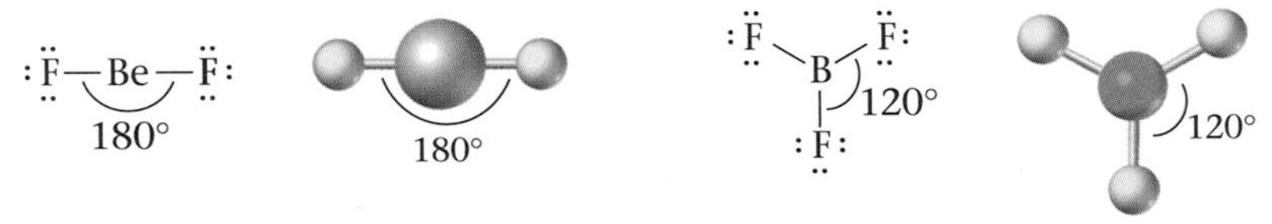

Two electron pairs are as far apart as possible when they are directed at 180° to one another. This gives BeF_2 a **linear** structure. The three electron pairs around the boron atom in BF_3 are directed toward the corners of an equilateral triangle; the bond angles are 120°. We describe this geometry as **trigonal planar.**

In species that follow the octet rule, the central atom is surrounded by four electron pairs. If each of these pairs forms a single bond with a terminal atom, a molecule of the type AX_4 results. The four bonds are directed toward the corners of a regular **tetrahedron.** All the bond angles are 109.5°, the tetrahedral angle. This geometry is found in many polyatomic ions such as NH_4^+ and SO_4^{2-} and in a wide variety of organic molecules, the simplest of which is methane, CH_4.

This puts the four electron pairs as far apart as possible.

Molecules of the type AX_5 and AX_6 require that the central atom have an expanded octet. The geometries of these molecules are shown at the bottom of Figure 7.5. In PF_5, the five bonding pairs are directed toward the corners of a **trigonal bipyramid,** a figure formed when two triangular pyramids are fused together, base to base. Three of the fluorine atoms are located at the corners of an equilateral triangle with the phosphorus atom at the center; the other two fluorine atoms are directly above and below the P atom. In SF_6, the six bonds are directed toward the corners of a regular **octahedron,** a figure with eight sides but *six* vertices. An octahedron can be formed by fusing two square pyramids base to base. Four of the fluorine atoms in SF_6 are located at the corners of a square with the S atom at the center; one fluorine atom is directly above the S atom, another directly below it.

Species type	Orientation of electron pairs	Predicted bond angles	Example	Ball and stick model
AX_2	Linear	180°	BeF_2	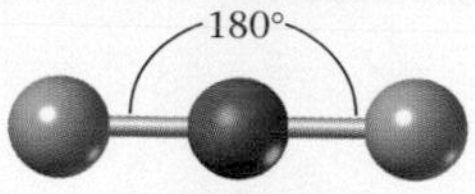
AX_3	Trigonal planar	120°	BF_3	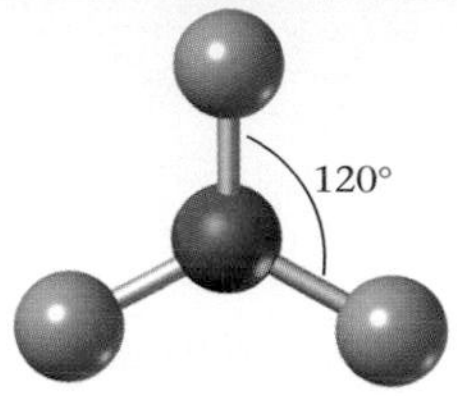
AX_4	Tetrahedron	109.5°	CH_4	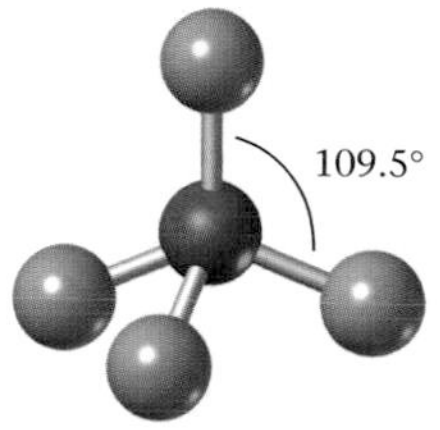
AX_5	Trigonal bipyramid	90° 120° 180°	PF_5	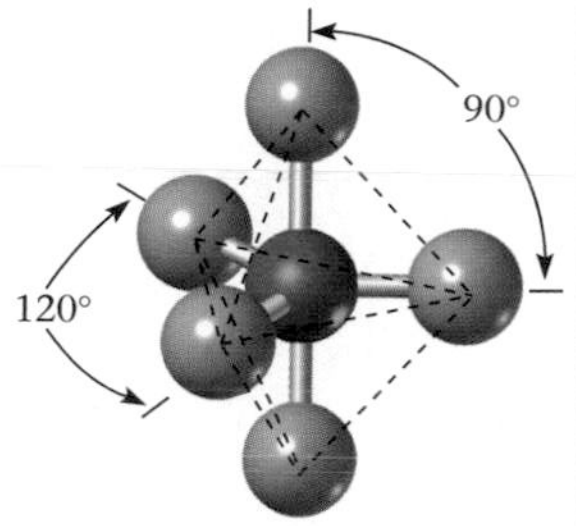
AX_6	Octahedron	90° 180°	SF_6	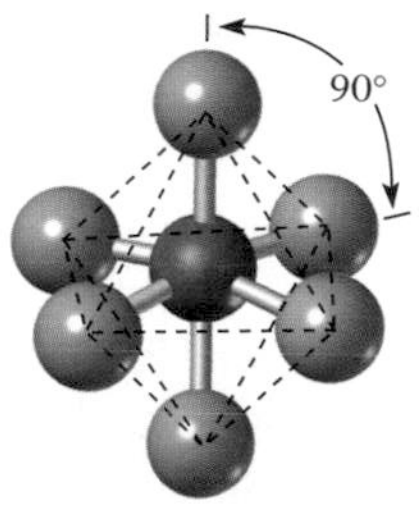

Figure 7.5
Molecular geometries for molecules with two to six electron-pair bonds around a central atom (A).

Effect of Unshared Pairs on Molecular Geometry

In many molecules and polyatomic ions, one or more of the electron pairs around the central atom are unshared. The VSEPR model is readily extended to predict the geometries of these species. In general—

1. The *electron-pair geometry* is approximately the same as that observed when only single bonds are involved. The bond angles are ordinarily a little smaller than the ideal values listed in Figure 7.5.

2. The *molecular geometry* is quite different when one or more unshared pairs are present. In describing molecular geometry, we refer only to the positions of the bonded atoms. These positions can be determined experimentally; positions of unshared pairs cannot be established by experiment. Hence, the locations of unshared pairs are not specified in describing molecular geometry.

Figure 7.6
Two ways of showing the geometry of the NH_3 molecule. The orientation of the electron pairs, including the unshared pair (black dots), is shown at left. The orientation of the atoms is shown at the right. The nitrogen atom is located directly above the center of the equilateral triangle formed by the three hydrogen atoms. The NH_3 molecule is described as a trigonal pyramid.

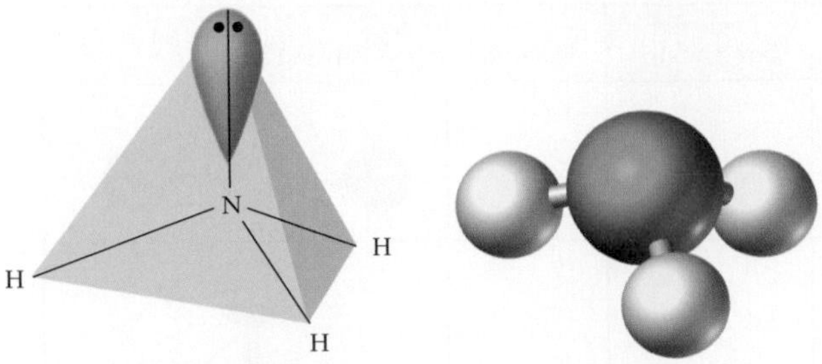

With these principles in mind, consider the NH_3 molecule:

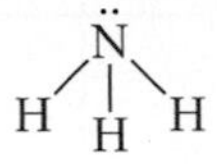

The apparent orientation of the four electron pairs around the N atom in NH_3 is shown at the left of Figure 7.6. Notice that, as in CH_4, the four pairs are directed toward the corners of a regular tetrahedron. The diagram at the right of Figure 7.6 shows the positions of the atoms in NH_3. The nitrogen atom is located above the center of an equilateral triangle formed by the three hydrogen atoms. The molecular geometry of the NH_3 molecule is described as a **trigonal pyramid.** The nitrogen atom is at the apex of the pyramid, and the three hydrogen atoms form its triangular base. The molecule is three-dimensional, as the word "pyramid" implies.

The development we have just gone through for NH_3 is readily extended to the water molecule, H_2O. Here the Lewis structure shows that the central oxygen atom is surrounded by two single bonds and two unshared pairs:

The diagram at the left of Figure 7.7 emphasizes that the four electron pairs are oriented tetrahedrally. At the right, the positions of the atoms are shown. Clearly they are not in a straight line; the H_2O molecule is **bent.**

Experiments show that the bond angles in NH_3 and H_2O are slightly less than the ideal value of 109.5°. In NH_3 (three single bonds, one unshared pair around N), the bond angle is 107°. In H_2O (two single bonds, two unshared pairs around O), the bond angle is about 105°.

Unshared pairs reduce bond angles below ideal values.

These effects can be explained in a rather simple way. An unshared pair is attracted by one nucleus, that of the atom to which it belongs. In contrast, a bonding pair is attracted by two nuclei, those of the two atoms it joins. Hence the electron cloud of an unshared pair is expected to spread out over a larger volume than that of a bonding pair. In NH_3, this tends to force the bonding pairs closer to one another, thereby reducing the bond angle. Where there are two unshared pairs, as in H_2O, this effect is more pronounced. In general, the VSEPR model predicts that unshared electron pairs will occupy slightly more space than bonding pairs.

Figure 7.7
Two ways of showing the geometry of the H_2O molecule. At the left, the two unshared pairs are shown. As you can see from the drawing at the right, H_2O is a bent molecule. The bond angle, 105°, is a little smaller than the tetrahedral angle, 109.5°. The unshared pairs spread out over a larger volume than that occupied by the bonding pairs.

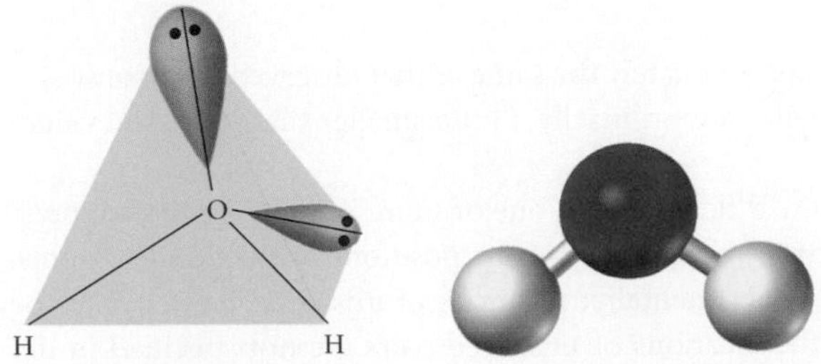

Table 7.3 Geometries with Two, Three, or Four Electron Pairs Around a Central Atom

No. of Terminal Atoms (X) + Unshared Pairs (E)	Species Type	Ideal Bond Angles*	Molecular Geometry	Examples
2	AX_2	180°	Linear	BeF_2, CO_2
3	AX_3	120°	Trigonal planar	BF_3, SO_3
	AX_2E	120°*	Bent	GeF_2, SO_2
4	AX_4	109.5°	Tetrahedron	CH_4
	AX_3E	109.5°*	Trigonal pyramid	NH_3
	AX_2E_2	109.5°*	Bent	H_2O

*In these species, the observed bond angle is ordinarily somewhat less than the ideal value.

Table 7.3 summarizes the molecular geometries of species in which a central atom is surrounded by two, three, or four electron pairs. The table is organized in terms of the number of terminal atoms, X, and unshared pairs, E, surrounding the central atom, A.

Example 7.5 Predict the geometry of

(a) NH_4^+ (b) GeF_2 (c) PF_3

Strategy Draw the Lewis structure as a first step. Then decide what type (AX_2, AX_3, and so on) the molecule is, focusing on the central atom. Remember, X represents a terminal atom, E an unshared pair of electrons.

CENGAGENOW™
Click Coached Problems for a self-study module on **determining molecular shapes.**

SOLUTION

(a) The Lewis structure for the ammonium ion is

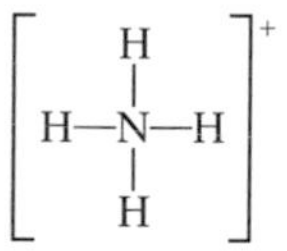

This is an AX_4 species. It is tetrahedral with 109.5° bond angles.

(b) The Lewis structure of GeF_2 (18 valence e^-) is

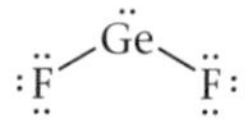

The way the Lewis structure is written does not necessarily imply geometry.

The central germanium atom has one unshared pair and two bonds.
This is a "bent" AX_2E species. The bond angle is expected to be a little less than 120°.

(c) The Lewis structure of PF_3 is

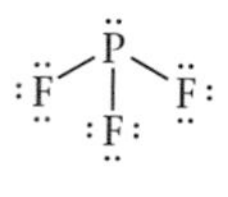

The central phosphorus atom has one unshared pair and three bonded atoms. The molecule is of type AX_3E; it should be a trigonal pyramid (like NH_3) with a bond angle somewhat less than 109.5° (actually, 104°).

Reality Check NH_4^+ is like CH_4, GeF_2 like SO_2, and PF_3 like NH_3.

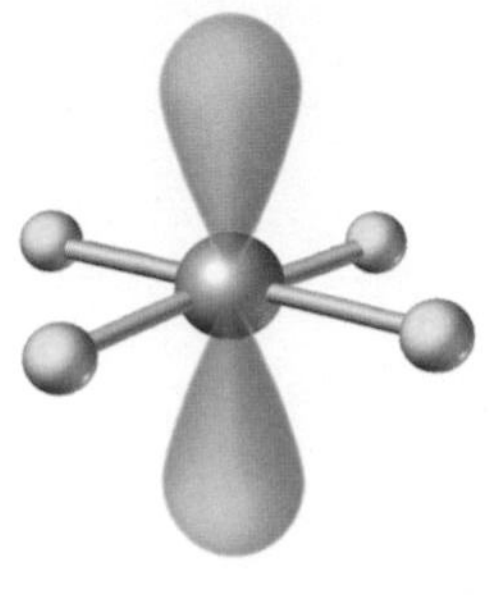

Xenon tetrafluoride, an AX_4E_2 molecule.

In many expanded-octet molecules, one or more of the electron pairs around the central atom are unshared. Recall, for example, the Lewis structure of xenon tetrafluoride, XeF_4 (Example 7.4).

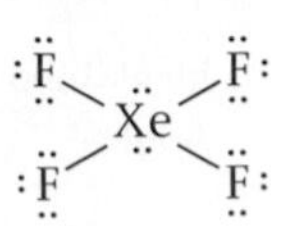

There are six electron pairs around the xenon atom; four of these are covalent bonds to fluorine and the other two pairs are unshared. This molecule is classified as AX_4E_2.

Geometries of molecules such as these can be predicted by the VSEPR model. The results are shown in Figure 7.8 (page 181). The structures listed include those of all types of molecules having five or six electron pairs around the central atom, one or more of which may be unshared. Note that—

- in molecules of the type AX_4E_2, the two lone pairs occupy opposite rather than adjacent vertices of the octahedron.
- in the molecules AX_4E, AX_3E_2, and AX_2E_3 the lone pairs occupy successive positions in the equilateral triangle at the center of the trigonal bipyramid.

Multiple Bonds

The VSEPR model is readily extended to species in which double or triple bonds are present. A simple principle applies: ***Insofar as molecular geometry is concerned, a multiple bond behaves like a single bond.*** This makes sense. The four electrons in a double bond, or the six electrons in a triple bond, must be located between the two atoms, as are the two electrons in a single bond. This means that the electron pairs in a multiple bond must occupy the same region of space as those in a single bond. Hence the "extra" electron pairs in a multiple bond have no effect on geometry.

To illustrate this principle, consider the CO_2 molecule. Its Lewis structure is

$$:\ddot{O}=C=\ddot{O}:$$

CO$_2$, like BeF$_2$, is an AX$_2$ molecule with no unshared pairs.

The central atom, carbon, has two double bonds and no unshared pairs. For purposes of determining molecular geometry, we pretend that the double bonds are single bonds, ignoring the extra bonding pairs. The bonds are directed to be as far apart as possible, giving a 180° O—C—O bond angle. The CO_2 molecule, like BeF_2, is linear:

F—Be—F (180°) O=C=O (180°)

This principle can be restated in a somewhat different way for molecules in which there is a single central atom. The geometry of such a molecule depends only on—

- ***the number of terminal atoms, X, bonded to the central atom, irrespective of whether the bonds are single, double, or triple.***
- ***the number of unshared pairs, E, around the central atom.***

This means that Table 7.3 can be used in the usual way to predict the geometry of a species containing multiple bonds.

Example 7.6 Predict the geometries of the ClO_3^- ion, the NO_3^- ion, and the N_2O molecule, which have the Lewis structures

(a) 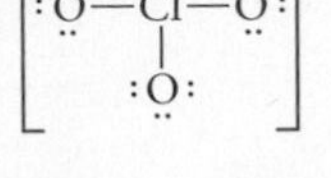 (b) 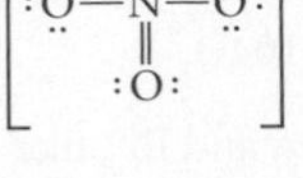 (c) $:\ddot{N}=N=\ddot{O}:$

AX_3E_2 means that the central atom A is bonded to three X atoms and has two unshared electron pairs.

Strategy Classify each species as AX_mE_n and use Table 7.3.

5 ELECTRON PAIRS

Species type	Structure	Description	Example	Bond angles
AX_5	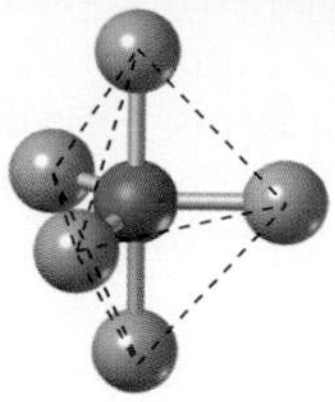	Trigonal bipyramidal	PF_5	90°, 120°, 180°
AX_4E	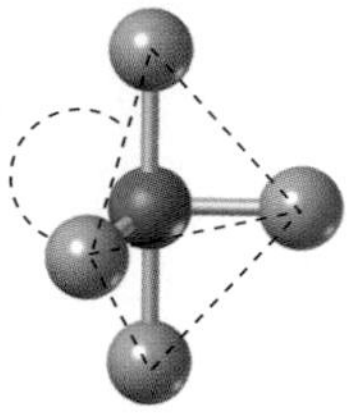	See-saw	SF_4	90°, 120°, 180°
AX_3E_2	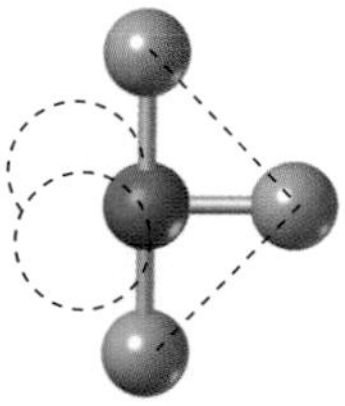	T-shaped	ClF_3	90°, 180°
AX_2E_3	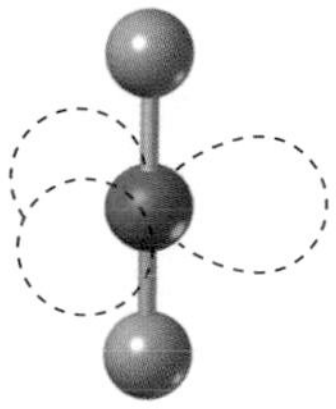	Linear	XeF_2	180°

6 ELECTRON PAIRS

AX_6	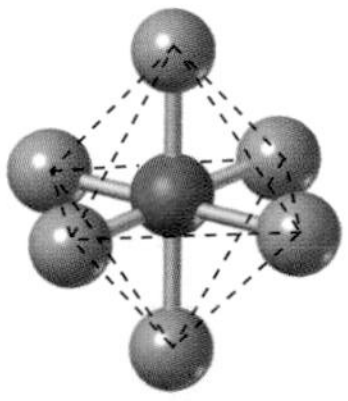	Octahedral	SF_6	90°, 180°
AX_5E	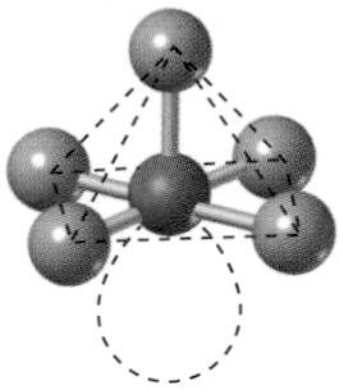	Square pyramidal	ClF_5	90°, 180°
AX_4E_2	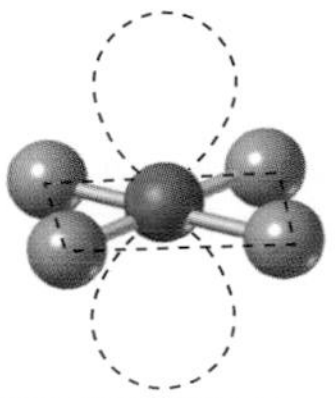	Square planar	XeF_4	90°, 180°

Figure 7.8
Molecular geometries for molecules with expanded octets and unshared electron pairs. The gray spheres represent terminal atoms (X), and the open ellipses represent unshared electron pairs (E). For example, AX_4E represents a molecule in which the central atom is surrounded by four covalent bonds and one unshared electron pair.

SOLUTION

(a) The central atom, chlorine, is bonded to three oxygen atoms; it has one unshared pair. The ClO_3^- ion is of the type AX_3E. It is a trigonal pyramid; ideal bond angle is 109.5°.

(b) The central atom, nitrogen, is bonded to three oxygen atoms; it has no unshared pairs. The NO_3^- ion is of the type AX_3. It has the geometry of an equilateral triangle, with the nitrogen atom at the center; the bond angle is 120°. The ion is trigonal planar.

(c) The central nitrogen atom is bonded to two other atoms with no unshared pairs. The molecule, type AX_2, is linear, with a bond angle of 180°.

The VSEPR model applies equally well to molecules in which there is no single central atom. Consider the acetylene molecule, C_2H_2. Recall that here the two carbon atoms are joined by a triple bond:

$$H—C\equiv C—H$$

Each carbon atom behaves as if it were surrounded by two electron pairs. Both of the bond angles ($H—C\equiv C$ and $C\equiv C—H$) are 180°. The molecule is linear; the four atoms are in a straight line. The two extra electron pairs in the triple bond do not affect the geometry of the molecule.

In ethylene, C_2H_4, there is a double bond between the two carbon atoms. The molecule has the geometry to be expected if each carbon atom had only three pairs of electrons around it.

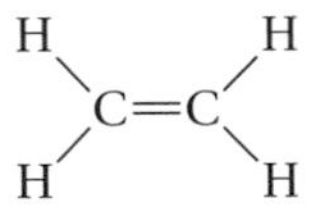

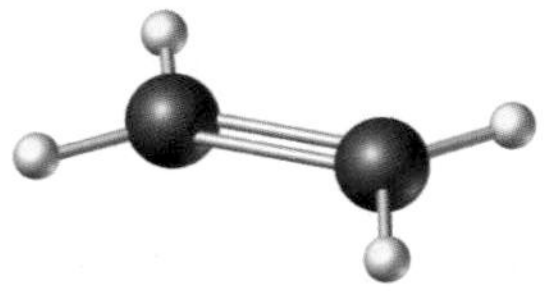

The six atoms are located in a plane with bond angles of approximately 120°. Actually, the double bond between the carbon atoms occupies slightly more space than a single bond joining carbon to hydrogen. As a result, the $H—C{=}C$ angles are slightly larger than 120°, and the $H—C—H$ angles are slightly less.

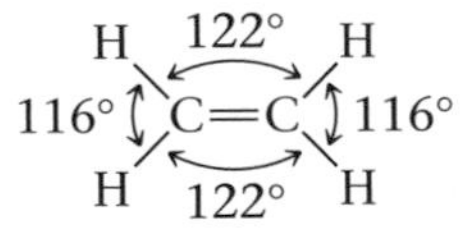

7.3 POLARITY OF MOLECULES

Covalent bonds and molecules held together by such bonds may be—

- *polar*. As a result of an unsymmetrical distribution of electrons, the bond or molecule contains a positive and a negative pole and is therefore a ***dipole.***
- ***nonpolar.*** A symmetrical distribution of electrons leads to a bond or molecule with no positive or negative poles.

Polar and Nonpolar Covalent Bonds

The two electrons in the H_2 molecule are shared equally by the two nuclei. Stated another way, a bonding electron is as likely to be found in the vicinity of one nucleus as another. Bonds of this type are described as nonpolar. **Nonpolar bonds** are formed whenever the two atoms joined are identical, as in H_2 and F_2.

In the HF molecule, the distribution of the bonding electrons is somewhat different from that found in H_2 or F_2. Here the density of the electron cloud is greater about the fluorine atom. The bonding electrons, on the average, are shifted toward fluorine and away from the hydrogen (atom Y in Figure 7.9). Bonds in which the electron density is unsymmetrical are referred to as **polar bonds.**

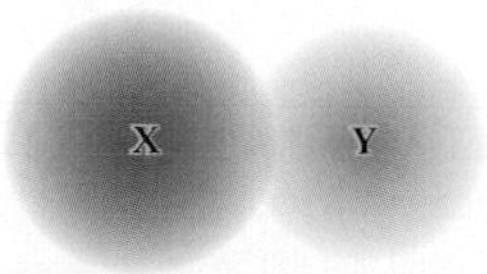

Figure 7.9
Bond polarity. If atom X is more electronegative than atom Y, the electron cloud of the bonding electrons will be concentrated around atom X. Thus the bond is polar.

Atoms of two different elements always differ at least slightly in their electronegativity (recall Table 6.5, page 156). Hence covalent bonds between unlike atoms are always polar. Consider, for example, the H—F bond. Because fluorine has a higher electronegativity (4.0) than does hydrogen (2.2), bonding electrons are displaced toward the fluorine atom. The H—F bond is polar, with a partial negative charge at the fluorine atom and a partial positive charge at the hydrogen atom.

The extent of polarity of a covalent bond is related to the difference in electronegativities of the bonded atoms. If this difference is large, as in HF ($\Delta EN = 1.8$), the bond is strongly polar. Where the difference is small, as in H—C ($\Delta EN = 0.3$), the bond is only slightly polar.

All molecules, except those of elements, have polar bonds.

Polar and Nonpolar Molecules

A **polar molecule** is one that contains positive and negative poles. There is a partial positive charge (positive pole) at one point in the molecule and a partial negative charge (negative pole) at a different point. As shown in Figure 7.10, polar molecules orient themselves in the presence of an electric field. The positive pole in the molecule tends to align with the external negative charge, and the negative pole with the external positive charge. In contrast, there are no positive and negative poles in a **nonpolar molecule.** In an electric field, nonpolar molecules, such as H_2, show no preferred orientation.

CENGAGENOW™
Click Coached Problems for a self-study module on **determining polarity.**

The extent to which molecules tend to orient themselves in an electrical field is a measure of their *dipole moment.* A polar molecule such as HF has a dipole moment; a nonpolar molecule such as H_2 or F_2 has a dipole moment of zero.

If a molecule is diatomic, it is easy to decide whether it is polar or nonpolar. A diatomic molecule has only one kind of bond; hence the polarity of the molecule is the same as the polarity of the bond. Hydrogen and fluorine (H_2, F_2) are nonpolar because the bonded atoms are identical and the bond is nonpolar. Hydrogen fluoride, HF, on the other hand, has a polar bond, so the molecule is polar. The bonding electrons spend more time near the fluorine atom so that there is a negative pole at that end and a positive pole at the hydrogen end. This is sometimes indicated by writing

$$\mathrm{H} \;{+}\!\!\!\longrightarrow \mathrm{F}$$

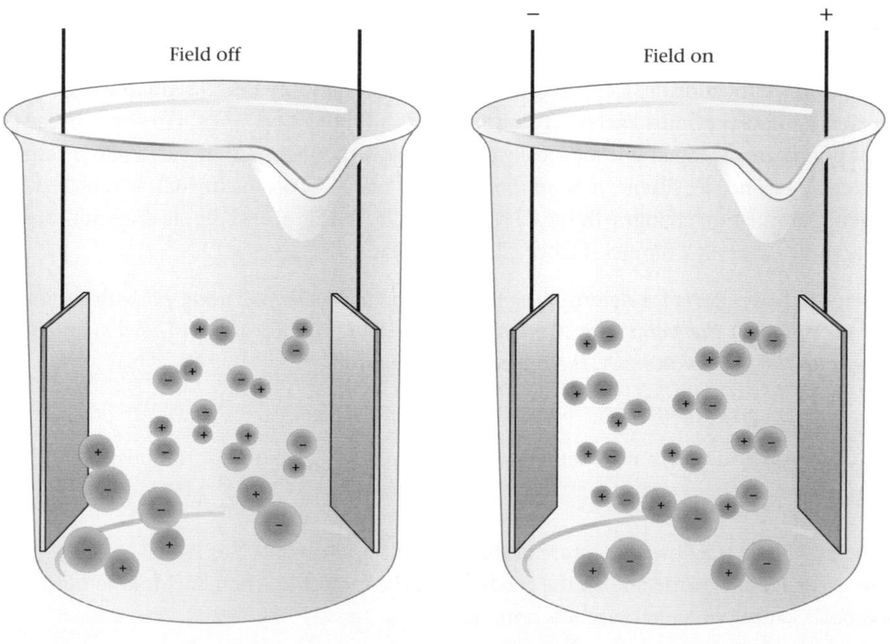

Figure 7.10
Orientation of polar molecules in an electric field. With the field off, polar molecules are randomly oriented. With the field on, polar molecules such as HF align their positive and negative ends toward the negative and positive poles of the field, respectively. Nonpolar molecules such as H_2 do not line up.

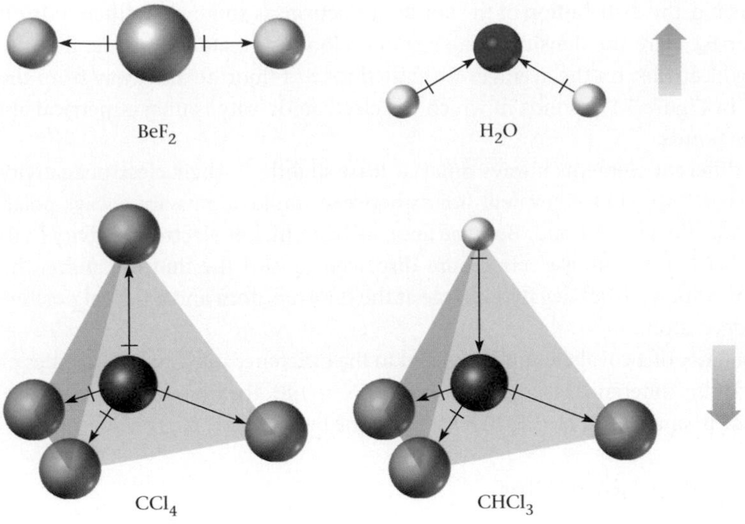

Figure 7.11
Polarity of molecules. All bonds in these molecules are polar, as shown by the $+\!\!\!\rightarrow$ symbol, in which the arrow points to the more negative end of the bond and the + indicates the more positive end. In BeF_2 and CCl_4 the bond dipoles cancel and the molecules are nonpolar. In H_2O and $CHCl_3$ the molecules are polar, with net dipoles shown by the broad arrows pointing toward the negative poles.

The arrow points toward the negative end of the polar bond (F atom); the plus sign is at the positive end (H atom). The HF molecule is called a **dipole;** it contains positive and negative poles.

If a molecule contains more than two atoms it is not so easy to decide whether it is polar or nonpolar. In this case, not only bond polarity but also molecular geometry determines the polarity of the molecule. To illustrate what is involved, consider the molecules shown in Figure 7.11.

1. In BeF_2 there are two polar Be—F bonds; in both bonds, the electron density is concentrated around the more electronegative fluorine atom. However, because the BeF_2 molecule is linear, the two Be $+\!\!\!\rightarrow$ F dipoles are in opposite directions and cancel one another. The molecule has no net dipole and hence is nonpolar. From a slightly different point of view, in BeF_2 the centers of positive and negative charge coincide with each other at the Be atom. There is no way that a BeF_2 molecule can line up in an electric field.

2. Because oxygen is more electronegative than hydrogen (3.5 versus 2.2) an O—H bond is polar, with the electron density higher around the oxygen atom. In the bent H_2O molecule, the two H $+\!\!\!\rightarrow$ O dipoles do not cancel each other. Instead, they add to give the H_2O molecule a net dipole. The center of negative charge is located at the O atom; this is the negative pole of the molecule. The center of positive charge is located midway between the two H atoms; the positive pole of the molecule is at that point. The H_2O molecule is polar. It tends to line up in an electric field with the oxygen atom oriented toward the positive electrode.

3. Carbon tetrachloride, CCl_4, is another molecule that, like BeF_2, is nonpolar despite the presence of polar bonds. Each of its four bonds is a dipole, C $+\!\!\!\rightarrow$ Cl. However, because the four bonds are arranged symmetrically around the carbon atom, they cancel. As a result, the molecule has no net dipole; it is nonpolar. If one of the Cl atoms in CCl_4 is replaced by hydrogen, the situation changes. In the $CHCl_3$ molecule, the H $+\!\!\!\rightarrow$ C dipole does not cancel with the three C $+\!\!\!\rightarrow$ Cl dipoles. Hence $CHCl_3$ is polar.

There are two criteria for determining the polarity of a molecule: bond polarity and molecular geometry. ***If the polar A—X bonds in a molecule AX_mE_n are arranged symmetrically around the central atom A, the molecule is nonpolar.***

Example 7.7 Determine whether each of the following is polar or nonpolar:

(a) SO_2 (b) BF_3 (c) CO_2

Strategy Write the Lewis structure of the molecule and classify it as AX_mE_n. Using Table 7.3 or Figure 7.5, decide on the geometry of the molecule. Then decide whether the dipoles cancel, in which case it is nonpolar.

SOLUTION

(a) The Lewis structure of SO_2 is shown on page 169; it is of the type AX_2E. The molecule is bent, so the dipoles do not cancel. The SO_2 molecule is polar.
(b) The Lewis structure of BF_3 is shown on page 173; it is of the type AX_3. The molecule is an equilateral triangle with the boron atom at the center. The three polar bonds cancel one another; BF_3 is nonpolar.
(c) The Lewis structure of CO_2 is shown on page 180; it is of the type AX_2. The molecule is linear, so the two C ⟶ O dipoles cancel each other; CO_2 is nonpolar.

Generalizing from Example 7.7 and the preceding discussion, we can establish the following rules—

- Molecules of the type AX_2 (linear), AX_3 (trigonal planar), and AX_4 (tetrahedral) are nonpolar. Examples: CO_2, BF_3, CCl_4
- Molecules of the type AX_2E (bent), AX_2E_2 (bent), and AX_3E (trigonal pyramid) are polar. Examples: SO_2, H_2O, NH_3

Example 7.8 Conceptual

For each of the species in column A, choose the description in column B that best applies.

A	B
(a) CO_2	(e) polar, bent
(b) CH_2Cl_2	(f) nonpolar, trigonal planar
(c) XeF_2	(g) nonpolar, linear
(d) BF_3	(h) nonpolar, trigonal pyramid
	(i) polar, tetrahedral
	(j) polar, trigonal pyramid

Strategy Start by drawing the Lewis structure. Beyond that, Table 7.3 and Figure 7.8 may be helpful.

SOLUTION

(a) The Lewis structure is given on page 180. Match with (g).
(b) The Lewis structure is similar to that of CH_4 or CCl_4, but it is polar. Match with (i).
(c) The Lewis structure is $:\ddot{\underset{..}{F}}-\ddot{\underset{..}{Xe}}-\ddot{\underset{..}{F}}:$ See Figure 7.8. Match with (g).
(d) The Lewis structure is given on page 173. Match with (f).

7.4 ATOMIC ORBITALS; HYBRIDIZATION

In the 1930s a theoretical treatment of the covalent bond was developed by, among others, Linus Pauling (1901–1994), then at the California Institute of Technology. The *atomic orbital* or **valence bond model** won him the Nobel Prize in chemistry in 1954. Eight years later, Pauling won the Nobel Peace Prize for his efforts to stop nuclear testing.

According to this model, a covalent bond consists of a pair of electrons of opposed spin within an orbital. For example, a hydrogen atom forms a covalent bond by accepting an electron from another atom to complete its 1s orbital. Using orbital diagrams, we could write

	1s
isolated H atom	(↑)
H atom in a stable molecule	(↑↓)

The second electron, shown in blue, is contributed by another atom. This could be another H atom in H_2, an F atom in HF, a C atom in CH_4, and so on.

This simple model is readily extended to other atoms. The fluorine atom (electron configuration $1s^2 2s^2 2p^5$) has a half-filled p orbital:

	1s	2s	2p
isolated F atom	(↑↓)	(↑↓)	(↑↓)(↑↓)(↑)

By accepting an electron from another atom, F can complete this 2p orbital:

	1s	2s	2p
F atom in HF, F_2, . . .	(↑↓)	(↑↓)	(↑↓)(↑↓)(↑↓)

According to this model, it would seem that for an atom to form a covalent bond, it must have an unpaired electron. Indeed, the number of bonds formed by an atom should be determined by its number of unpaired electrons. Because hydrogen has an unpaired electron, an H atom should form one covalent bond, as indeed it does. The same holds for the F atom, which forms only one bond. The noble-gas atoms He and Ne, which have no unpaired electrons, should not form bonds at all; they don't.

When this simple idea is extended beyond hydrogen, the halogens, and the noble gases, problems arise. Consider, for example, the three atoms Be ($Z = 4$), B ($Z = 5$), and C ($Z = 6$):

	1s	2s	2p
Be atom	(↑↓)	(↑↓)	( )( )( )
B atom	(↑↓)	(↑↓)	(↑)( )( )
C atom	(↑↓)	(↑↓)	(↑)(↑)( )

Notice that the beryllium atom has no unpaired electrons, the boron atom has one, and the carbon atom two. Simple valence bond theory would predict that Be, like He, should not form covalent bonds. A boron atom should form one bond, carbon two. Experience tells us that these predictions are wrong. Beryllium forms two bonds in BeF_2; boron forms three bonds in BF_3. Carbon ordinarily forms four bonds, not two.

To explain these and other discrepancies, simple valence bond theory must be modified. It is necessary to invoke a new kind of orbital, called a **hybrid orbital.**

The number of orbitals is shown by the superscript.

Hybrid Orbitals: sp, sp^2, sp^3, sp^{3}d, sp^{3}d^2

The formation of the BeF_2 molecule can be explained by assuming that, as two fluorine atoms approach Be, the atomic orbitals of the beryllium atom undergo a significant change. Specifically, the 2s orbital is mixed or *hybridized* with a 2p orbital to form two new **sp hybrid orbitals.** (Figure 7.12).

$$\text{one s atomic orbital} + \text{one p atomic orbital} \longrightarrow \text{two } \mathbf{sp\ hybrid\ orbitals}$$

In the BeF_2 molecule, there are two electron-pair bonds. These electron pairs are located in the two sp hybrid orbitals. In each orbital, one electron is a valence electron contributed by beryllium; the other electron comes from the fluorine atom.

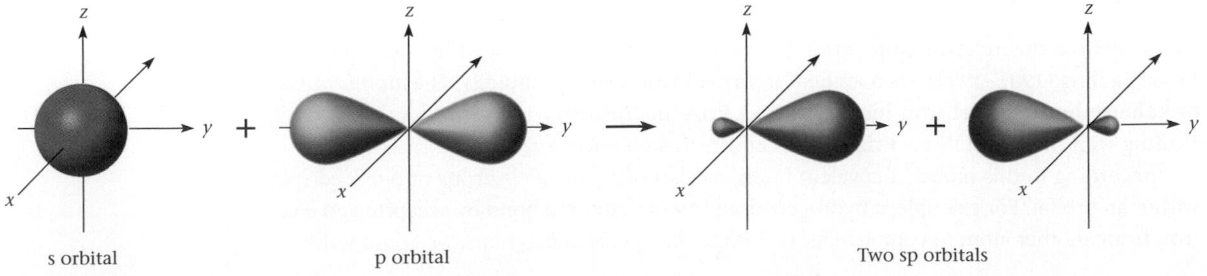

Figure 7.12
Formation of sp hybrid orbitals. The mixing of one s orbital and one p orbital gives two sp hybrid orbitals.

Table 7.4 Hybrid Orbitals and Their Geometries

Number of Electron Pairs	Atomic Orbitals	Hybrid Orbitals	Orientation	Examples
2	s, p	sp	Linear	BeF_2, CO_2
3	s, two p	sp^2	Trigonal planar	BF_3, SO_3
4	s, three p	sp^3	Tetrahedron	CH_4, NH_3, H_2O
5	s, three p, d	sp^3d	Trigonal bipyramid	PCl_5, SF_4, ClF_3
6	s, three p, two d	sp^3d^2	Octahedron	SF_6, ClF_5, XeF_4

A similar argument can be used to explain why boron forms three bonds and carbon forms four. In the case of boron:

one s atomic orbital + two p atomic orbitals ⟶ three **sp^2 hybrid orbitals**

With carbon:

one s atomic orbital + three p atomic orbitals ⟶ four **sp^3 hybrid orbitals**

Hybridization: sp (AX_2), sp^2 (AX_3, AX_2E), sp^3 (AX_4, AX_3E, AX_2E_2).

You will recall that the bond angles in NH_3 and H_2O are very close to that in CH_4. This suggests that the four electron pairs surrounding the central atom in NH_3 and H_2O, like those in CH_4, occupy sp^3 hybrid orbitals. In NH_3, three of these orbitals are filled by bonding electrons, the other by the unshared pair on the nitrogen atom. In H_2O, two of the sp^3 orbitals of the oxygen atom contain bonding electron pairs; the other two contain unshared pairs. The situation in NH_3 and H_2O is not unique. In general, we find that ***unshared as well as shared electron pairs can be located in hybrid orbitals.***

The extra electron pairs in an expanded octet are accommodated by using d orbitals. The phosphorus atom (five valence electrons) in PCl_5 and the sulfur atom (six valence electrons) in SF_6 make use of 3d as well as 3s and 3p orbitals:

With phosphorus:

one s orbital + three p orbitals + one d orbital ⟶ five **sp^3d hybrid orbitals**

With sulfur:

one s orbital + three p orbitals + two d orbitals ⟶ six **sp^3d^2 hybrid orbitals**

Table 7.4 summarizes all we have said about hybrid orbitals and also describes their geometry. Note that—

- *the number of hybrid orbitals formed is always equal to the number of atomic orbitals mixed.*
- the geometries, as found mathematically by quantum mechanics, are exactly as predicted by VSEPR theory. In each case, the hybrid orbitals are directed to be as far apart as possible.

Example 7.9 Give the hybridization of

(a) carbon in CH_3Cl (b) phosphorus in PH_3 (c) sulfur in SF_4

Strategy Draw the Lewis structure for the molecule and determine the number of electron pairs (single bonds or unshared pairs) around the central atom. The possible hybridizations are sp (two pairs), sp^2 (three pairs), sp^3 (four pairs), sp^3d (five pairs), and sp^3d^2 (six pairs).

SOLUTION

(a) The hybridization is similar to that of CH_4; sp^3

(b) The hybridization is similar to that of NH_3; sp^3

(c) Sulfur tetrafluoride has the Lewis structure

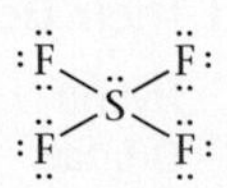

There are five electron pairs around sulfur: four bonds and one unshared pair. The hybridization is sp^3d.

Reality Check If you are asked to predict the hybridization, as you are here, the geometry as in Example 7.6, or the polarity as in Example 7.7, you have to start with Lewis structures; that is why they are so important.

Multiple Bonds

In Section 7.2, we saw that insofar as geometry is concerned, a multiple bond acts as if it were a single bond. In other words, the extra electron pairs in a double or triple bond have no effect on the geometry of the molecule. This behavior is related to hybridization. ***The extra electron pairs in a multiple bond (one pair in a double bond, two pairs in a triple bond) are not located in hybrid orbitals.***

To illustrate this rule, consider the ethylene (C_2H_4) and acetylene (C_2H_2) molecules. You will recall that the bond angles in these molecules are 120° for ethylene and 180° for acetylene. This implies sp^2 hybridization in C_2H_4 and sp hybridization in C_2H_2 (see Table 7.4). Using blue lines to represent hybridized electron pairs,

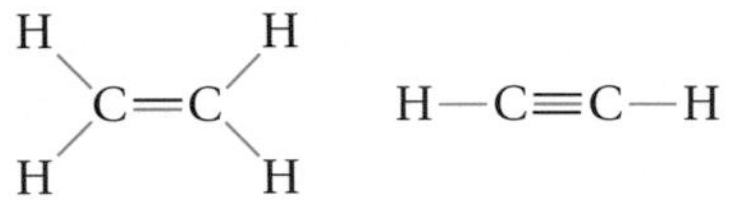

ethylene acetylene

In both cases, only one of the electron pairs in the multiple bond occupies a hybrid orbital.

Example 7.10 State the hybridization of nitrogen in

(a) NH_3 (b) NO_2^- (c) N_2

Strategy The first step is to draw Lewis structures. To find the hybridization of nitrogen, place in hybrid orbitals—

- unshared electron pairs.
- electron pairs forming single bonds.
- one and only one of the electron pairs in a multiple bond.

SOLUTION

(a) 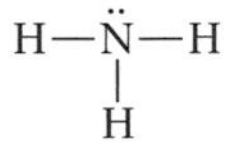 1 unshared electron pair, 3 single bonds; sp^3

(b) 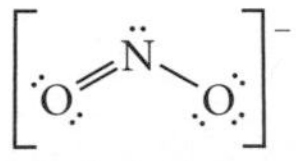 1 unshared electron pair, 1 single bond, 1 of the electron pairs in the double bond; sp^2

(c) :N≡N: 1 unshared electron pair, 1 of the electron pairs in the triple bond; sp

Sigma and Pi Bonds

We have noted that the extra electron pairs in a multiple bond are not hybridized and have no effect on molecular geometry. At this point, you may well wonder what happened to those electrons. Where are they in molecules like C_2H_4 and C_2H_2?

To answer this question, it is necessary to consider the shape or spatial distribution of the orbitals filled by bonding electrons in molecules. From this point of view, we can distinguish between two types of bonding orbitals. The first of these, and by far the more common, is called a *sigma* bonding orbital. It consists of a single lobe:

in which the electron density is concentrated in the region directly between the two bonded atoms, A and B. A **sigma** (σ) bond consists of an electron pair occupying a sigma bonding orbital.

The unhybridized electron pairs associated with multiple bonds occupy orbitals of a quite different shape, called **pi** (π) bonding orbitals. Such an orbital consists of two lobes, one above the bond axis, the other below it.

Sigma and pi orbitals, like s and p, differ in shape; each orbital can hold $2e^-$.

Along the bond axis itself, the electron density is zero. The electron pair of a pi (π) bond occupies a pi bonding orbital. There is one π bond in the C_2H_4 molecule, two in C_2H_2. The geometries of the bonding orbitals in ethylene and acetylene are shown in Figure 7.13.

In general, to find the number of σ and π bonds in a species, remember that—

- all single bonds are sigma bonds.
- one of the electron pairs in a multiple bond is a sigma bond; the others are pi bonds.

Example 7.11 Give the number of pi and sigma bonds in

(a) NH_3 (b) NO_2^- (c) N_2

Strategy Refer back to Example 7.10 for the Lewis structures and apply the rules just cited.

SOLUTION

(a) 3 sigma bonds
(b) 2 sigma bonds, 1 pi bond
(c) 1 sigma bond, 2 pi bonds

Reality Check There are two pi bonds in a triple bond, one in a double bond, and none in a single bond.

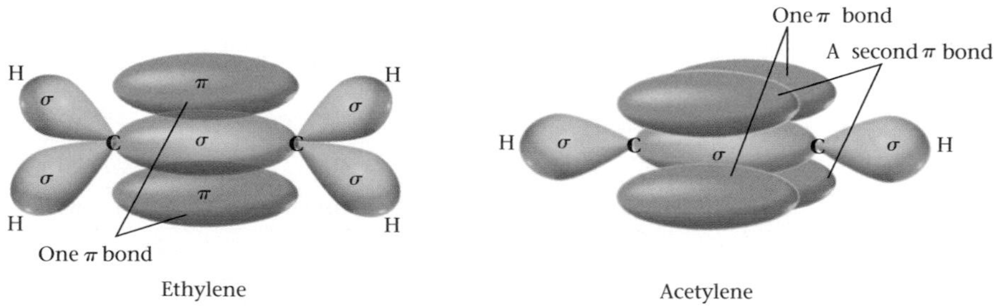

Figure 7.13
Bonding orbitals in ethylene ($CH_2{=}CH_2$) and acetylene ($CH{\equiv}CH$). The sigma bond backbones are shown in blue. The pi bonds (one in ethylene and two in acetylene) are shown in red. Note that a pi bonding orbital consists of two lobes.

CHEMISTRY **Beyond the Classroom**

The Noble Gases

The modern periodic table contains six relatively unreactive gases that were unknown to Mendeleev: the noble gases that make up Group 1**8** at the far right of the table. The first of these elements to be isolated was argon, which makes up about 0.9% of air. The physicist Lord Rayleigh found that the density of atmospheric nitrogen, obtained by removing O_2, CO_2, and H_2O from air, was slightly greater than that of chemically pure N_2 (MM = 28.02 g/mol). Following up on that observation, Sir William Ramsay (1852–1916) separated argon (MM = 39.95 g/mol) from air. Over a three-year period between 1895 and 1898, this remarkable Scotsman, who never took a formal course in chemistry, isolated three more noble gases: Ne, Kr, and Xe. In effect, Ramsay added a whole new group to the periodic table.

Helium, the first member of the group, was detected in the spectrum of the Sun in 1868. Because of its low density ($\frac{1}{7}$ that of air), helium is used in all kinds of balloons and in synthetic atmospheres to make breathing easier for people suffering from emphysema.

Research laboratories use helium as a liquid coolant to achieve very low temperatures (bp He = −269°C). Argon and, more recently, krypton are used to provide an inert atmosphere in lightbulbs, thereby extending the life of the tungsten filament. In neon signs, a high voltage is passed through a glass tube containing neon at very low pressures. The red glow emitted corresponds to an intense line at 640 nm in the neon spectrum.

Argonne National Laboratory

Figure A
Crystals of xenon tetrafluoride (XeF_4).

Until about 40 years ago, these elements were referred to as "inert gases"; they were believed to be entirely unreactive toward other substances. In 1962 Neil Bartlett, a 29-year-old chemist at the University of British Columbia, shook up the world of chemistry by preparing the first noble-gas compound. In the course of his research on platinum-fluorine compounds, he isolated a reddish solid that he showed to be $O_2^+(PtF_6^-)$. Bartlett realized that the ionization energy of Xe (1170 kJ/mol) is virtually identical to that of the O_2 molecule (1165 kJ/mol). This encouraged him to attempt to make the analogous compound $XePtF_6$. His success opened up a new era in noble-gas chemistry.

The most stable binary compounds of xenon are the three fluorides, XeF_2, XeF_4, and XeF_6. Xenon difluoride can be prepared quite simply by exposing a 1:1 mol mixture of xenon and fluorine to ultraviolet light; colorless crystals of XeF_2 (mp = 129°C) form slowly.

$$Xe(g) + F_2(g) \longrightarrow XeF_2(s)$$

The higher fluorides are prepared using excess fluorine (Figure A). All these compounds are stable in dry air at room temperature. However, they react with water to form compounds in which one or more of the fluorine atoms has been replaced by oxygen. Thus xenon hexafluoride reacts rapidly with water to give the trioxide

$$XeF_6(s) + 3H_2O(l) \longrightarrow XeO_3(s) + 6HF(g)$$

Xenon trioxide is highly unstable; it detonates if warmed above room temperature.

In the past 40 years, compounds have been isolated in which xenon is bonded to several nonmetals (N, C, and Cl) in addition to fluorine and oxygen. In the year 2000, it was reported (*Science,* Volume 290, page 117) that a compound had been isolated in which a metal atom was bonded to xenon. This compound is a dark red solid stable at temperatures below −40°C; it is believed to contain the $[AuXe_4]^{2+}$ cation.

The chemistry of xenon is much more extensive than that of any other noble gas. Only one binary compound of krypton, KrF_2, has been prepared. It is a colorless solid that decomposes at room temperature. The chemistry of radon is difficult to study because all its isotopes are radioactive. Indeed, the radiation given off is so intense that it decomposes any reagent added to radon in an attempt to bring about a reaction.

A group in Finland synthesized HArF, the first known compound of argon.

Chapter Highlights

Key Concepts

1. Draw Lewis structures for molecules and polyatomic ions.
   (Examples 7.1, 7.2, 7.4; Problems 1–20, 67, 68) ■ Questions and Problems assignable in OWL: 2, 4, 9, 17
2. Write resonance forms.
   (Example 7.3; Problems 21–26, 29, 30) ■ 22, 29
3. Use Table 7.3 and Figure 7.8, applying the VSEPR, to predict molecular geometry.
   (Examples 7.5, 7.6, 7.8; Problems 31–42) ■ 32, 34, 36, 39, 42, 74, 76
4. Knowing the geometry of a species, predict whether it will be polar.
   (Examples 7.7, 7.8; Problems 43–48) ■ 44, 47
5. State the hybridization of an atom in a bonded species.
   (Examples 7.9, 7.10; Problems 49–62) ■ 50, 54, 80
6. State the number of sigma and pi bonds in a species.
   (Example 7.11; Problems 63–66) ■ 64

Select end of chapter Questions and Problems may be assigned in OWL and are cross-referenced in the Key Concepts list.

CENGAGENOW™

Sign in at **academic.cengage.com/now** to:

- Check your readiness for an exam by taking the Pre-Test and exploring the self-study modules recommended in your Personalized Study plan.
- For quick review, download Go Chemistry mini-lecture flashcard modules (or purchase them at **www.ichapters.com**)

Key Terms

bond
—angle
—covalent
—double
—pi, sigma
—polar, nonpolar
—single
—triple
dipole
expanded octet

formal charge
geometry
—electron pair
—molecular
hybrid orbital
Lewis structure
molecule
—bent
—linear
—polar, nonpolar

octahedron
octet rule
resonance
tetrahedron
trigonal bipyramid
trigonal planar
trigonal pyramid
unshared (lone) pair
valence electron
VSEPR model

Summary Problem

Consider the species CO_2, SO_2, $COCl_2$, ICl_3, and $SeCl_6$.

(a) Draw the Lewis structures of these species.
(b) Draw the resonance structures for SO_2.
(c) Describe the geometries of these species, including bond angles.
(d) Which species are nonpolar?
(e) What is the hybridization of the central atom for each species?
(f) How many sigma and pi bonds are in each species?
(g) SO_2 can have two Lewis structures. One has an expanded octet and two double bonds. The other has an octet with one double bond. Draw both Lewis structures, calculate the formal charges, and state which is the more likely structure based on formal charge alone.

Answers

(a)
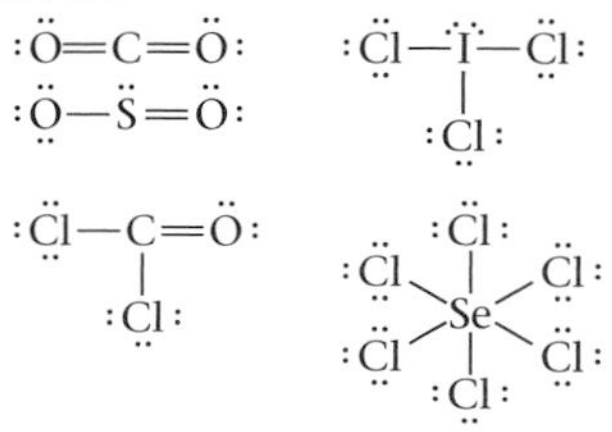

(b)
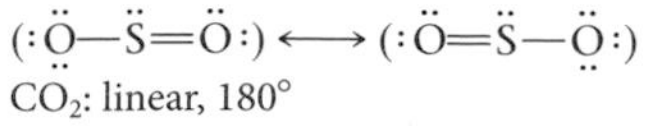

(c) CO_2: linear, 180°
SO_2: bent, 120°
$COCl_2$: trigonal planar, 120°
ICl_3: T-shaped, 90°, 180°
$SeCl_6$: octahedral, 90°, 180°

(d) CO_2, $SeCl_6$
(e) sp in CO_2; sp^2 in SO_2; sp^2 in $COCl_2$; sp^3d in ICl_3; sp^3d^2 in $SeCl_6$
(f) CO_2: $2\sigma, 2\pi$ SO_2: $2\sigma, 1\pi$ $COCl_2$: $3\sigma, 1\pi$
ICl_3: 3σ $SeCl_6$: 6σ
(g) :Ö=S̈=Ö: :Ö—S̈=Ö:
The structure on the left is more likely based on formal charge alone.

Questions and Problems

Blue-numbered questions have answers in Appendix 6 and fully-worked solutions in the *Student Solutions Manual.*

■ denotes questions assignable in OWL.

WEB indicates that the solution is available on this book's companion website.

Lewis Structures

1. Write the Lewis structures for the following molecules and polyatomic ions. In each case, the first atom is the central atom.
(a) CCl_4 (b) NCl_3 (c) $COCl_2$ (d) SO_3^{2-}

2. ■ Follow the directions of Question 1 for
(a) NH_3 (b) KrF_2 (c) NO^+ (d) BrO_2^-

3. Follow the directions of Question 1 for
(a) IO_2^- (b) SiF_4 (c) BrI_3 (d) CN^-

4. ■ Follow the directions of Question 1 for
(a) PCl_4^+ (b) BrF_2^+ (c) I_3^- (d) $SeBr_6$

5. Follow the directions of Question 1 for
(a) OCl_2 (b) PF_3 (c) $SbCl_6^-$ (d) ICl_4^-

6. Follow the directions of Question 1 for
(a) C_2^{2-} (b) NFO (c) BrF_4^+ (d) NI_3

7. Oxalic acid, $H_2C_2O_4$, is a poisonous compound found in rhubarb leaves. Draw the Lewis structure for oxalic acid. There is a single bond between the two carbon atoms, each hydrogen atom is bonded to an oxygen atom, and each carbon is bonded to two oxygen atoms.

8. Radioastronomers have detected the isoformyl ion, HCO^+, in outer space. Write the Lewis structure for this ion.

9. ■ Draw Lewis structures for the following species. (The skeleton is indicated by the way the molecule is written.)
(a) Cl_2CO (b) $H_3C—CN$ (c) $H_2C—CH_2$

10. Follow the directions of Question 9 for the following species.

(a) 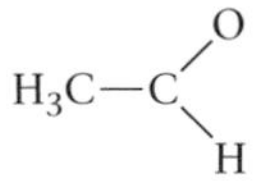 (b) $(HO)_2—S—O$ (c) $F_2C—CCl_2$

11. Dinitrogen pentoxide, N_2O_5, when bubbled into water can form nitric acid. Its skeleton structure has no N—N or O—O bonds. Write its Lewis structure.

12. **WEB** Glycine, an essential amino acid, has the formula NH_2CH_2COOH. Its skeleton structure has C—C and C—N bonds but no N—O bonds. Write its Lewis structure.

13. Two different molecules have the formula $C_2H_2Cl_2$. Draw a Lewis structure for each molecule. (All the H and Cl atoms are bonded to carbon. The two carbon atoms are bonded to each other.)

14. Several compounds have the formula C_3H_6O. Write Lewis structures for two of these compounds where the three carbon atoms are bonded to each other in a chain. The hydrogen and the oxygen atoms are bonded to the carbon atoms.

15. Give the formula of a polyatomic ion that you would expect to have the same Lewis structure as
(a) Cl_2 (b) H_2SO_4 (c) CH_4 (d) $GeCl_4$

16. Give the formula of a molecule that you would expect to have the same Lewis structure as
(a) OH^- (b) O_2^{2-} (c) CN^- (d) SO_4^{2-}

17. ■ Write a Lewis structure for
(a) XeF_3^+ (b) PCl_4^+
(c) BrF_5 (d) HPO_4^{2-} (no P—H or O—O bonds)

18. Write a Lewis structure for
(a) $P_2O_7^{4-}$ (no O—O or P—P bonds) (b) HOBr
(c) $NFBr_2$ (d) IF_4^-

19. Write reasonable Lewis structures for the following species, none of which follow the octet rule.
(a) BF_3 (b) NO (c) CO^+ (d) ClO_3

20. Write reasonable Lewis structures for the following species, none of which follow the octet rule.
(a) BeH_2 (b) CO^- (c) SO_2^- (d) CH_3

Resonance Forms and Formal Charge

21. Draw resonance structures for
(a) $Cl—NO_2$ (b) $H_2C—N—N$ (c) SO_3

22. ■ Draw resonance structures for
(a) NO_2^- (b) NNO (c) HCO_2^-

23. The Lewis structure for hydrazoic acid may be written as

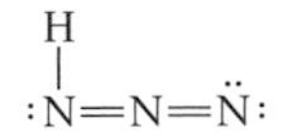

(a) Draw two other resonance forms for this molecule.
(b) Is

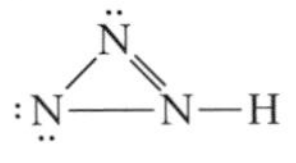

another form of hydrazoic acid? Explain.

24. The oxalate ion, $C_2O_4^{2-}$, has the skeleton structure

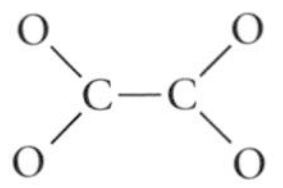

(a) Complete the Lewis structure of this ion.
(b) Draw three resonance forms for $C_2O_4^{2-}$, equivalent to the Lewis structure drawn in (a).
(c) Is

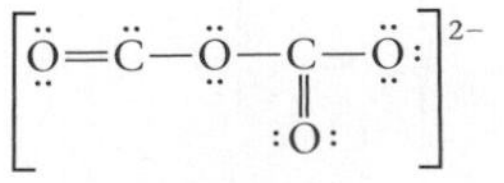

a resonance form of the oxalate ion?

25. The skeleton structure for disulfur dinitride, S_2N_2, is

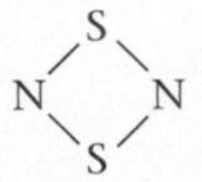

Draw the resonance forms of this molecule.

■ in OWL Blue-numbered questions answered in Appendix 6 **WEB** Solution is available on companion website

26. Borazine, $B_3N_3H_6$, has the skeleton

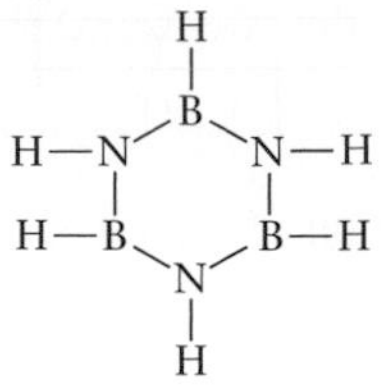

Draw the resonance forms of the molecule.

27. ■ What is the formal charge on the indicated atom in each of the following species?
   (a) sulfur in SO_2
   (b) nitrogen in N_2H_4
   (c) each oxygen atom in ozone, O_3

28. Follow the directions in Question 27 for
   (a) nitrogen in NH_2^-
   (b) bromine in BrF_3
   (c) oxygen in HOCl

29. ■ Below are two different Lewis structures for nitrous acid (HNO_2). Which is the better Lewis structure based only on formal charge?

Structure I Structure II

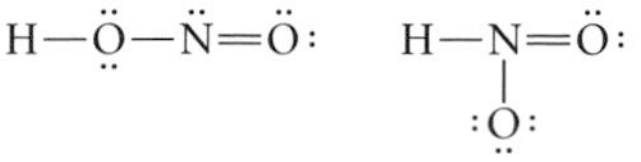

30. Below are two different Lewis structures for the thiosulfate ion ($S_2O_3^{2-}$). Which is the better Lewis structure based only on formal charge?

Structure I Structure II

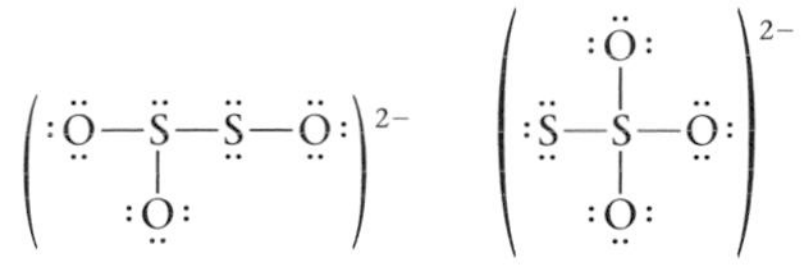

Molecular Geometry

31. Predict the geometry of the following species:
   (a) SCO (b) IBr_2^- (c) NO_3^- (d) RnF_4

32. ■ Predict the geometry of the following species:
   (a) SO_2 (b) $BeCl_2$ (c) $SeCl_4$ (d) PCl_5

33. Predict the geometry of the following species:
   (a) KrF_2 (b) NH_2Cl (c) CH_2Br_2 (d) SCN^-

34. ■ WEB Predict the geometry of the following species:
   (a) NNO (b) ONCl (c) NH_4^+ (d) O_3

35. Predict the geometry of the following species:
   (a) SF_6 (b) $BrCl_3$ (c) $SeCl_4$ (d) IO_4^-

36. ■ Predict the geometry of the following species:
   (a) ClF_2^- (b) SeF_5Br (c) SO_3^{2-} (d) BrO_2^-

37. Give all the ideal bond angles (109.5°, 120°, or 180°) in the following molecules and ions. (The skeleton does not imply geometry.)
   (a) Cl—S—Cl
   (b) F—Xe—F
   (c) 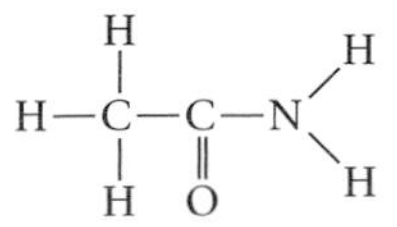
   (d) 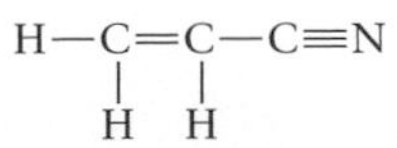

38. Follow the instructions for Question 37 for
   (a) O=C=O
   (b) 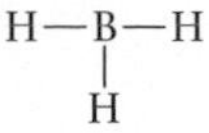
   (c) 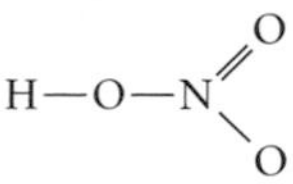
   (d) 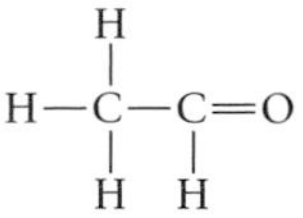

39. ■ Peroxypropionyl nitrate (PPN) is an eye irritant found in smog. Its skeleton structure is

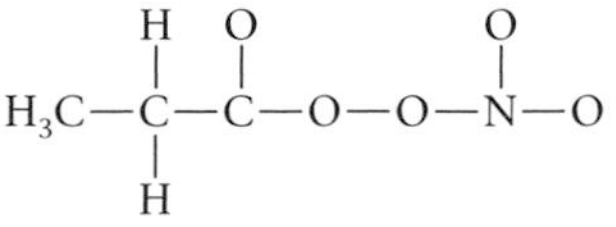

   (a) Draw the Lewis structure of PPN.
   (b) Indicate all the bond angles.

40. An objectionable component of smoggy air is acetylperoxide, which has the skeleton structure

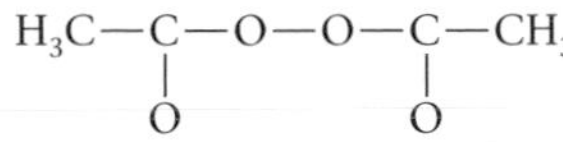

   (a) Draw the Lewis structure of this compound.
   (b) Indicate all the bond angles.

41. The uracil molecule is one of the bases in DNA. Estimate the approximate values of the indicated bond angles. Its skeleton (not its Lewis structure) is given below.

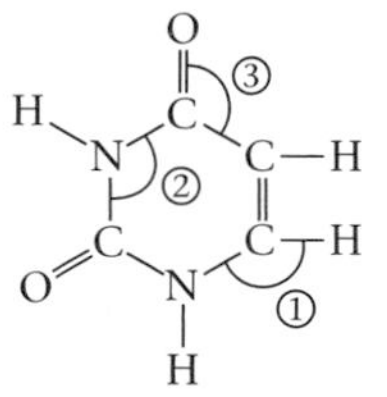

42. ■ Niacin is one of the vitamin B vitamins (B_3). Estimate the approximate values of the indicated bond angles. Its skeleton (not its Lewis structure) is given below.

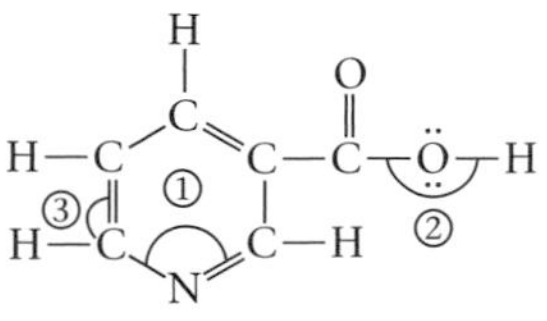

Molecular Polarity

43. Which of the species with octets in Question 31 are dipoles?

44. ■ Which of the species with octets in Question 32 are dipoles?

45. Which of the species with octets in Question 33 are dipoles?

46. Which of the species with octets in Question 34 are dipoles?

47. ■ There are three compounds with the formula $C_2H_2Cl_2$:

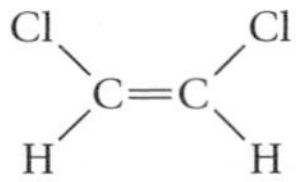 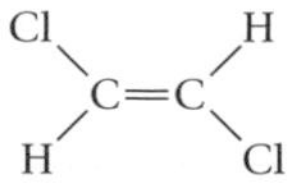 and 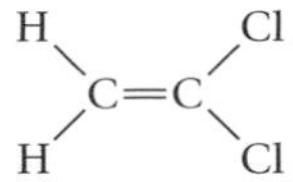

Which of these molecules are polar?

■ in OWL Blue-numbered questions answered in Appendix 6 WEB Solution is available on companion website

48. There are two different molecules with the formula N_2F_2:

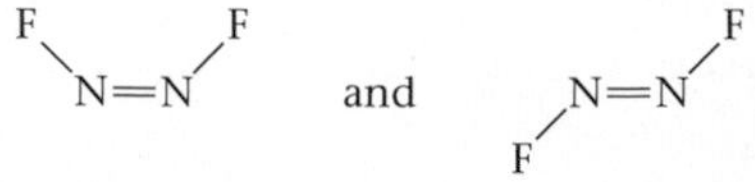

Is either molecule polar? Explain.

Hybridization

49. Give the hybridization of the central atom in each species in Question 31.

50. ■ Give the hybridization of the central atom in each species in Question 32.

51. Give the hybridization of the central atom in each species in Question 33.

52. WEB Give the hybridization of the central atom in each species in Question 34.

53. Give the hybridization of the central atom in each species in Question 35.

54. ■ Give the hybridization of the central atom in each species in Question 36.

55. In each of the following polyatomic ions, the central atom has an expanded octet. Determine the number of electron pairs around the central atom and the hybridization in

(a) SF_2^{2-} **(b)** $AsCl_6^-$ **(c)** SCl_4^{2-}

56. Follow the directions of Question 55 for the following polyatomic ions.

(a) ClF_4^- **(b)** $GeCl_6^{2-}$ **(c)** $SbCl_4^-$

57. Give the hybridization of each atom (except H) in the solvent dimethylsulfoxide. (Unshared electron pairs are not shown.)

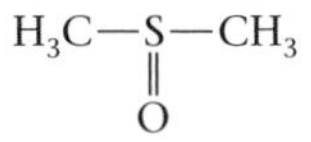

58. Give the hybridization of the B and N atoms in borazine.

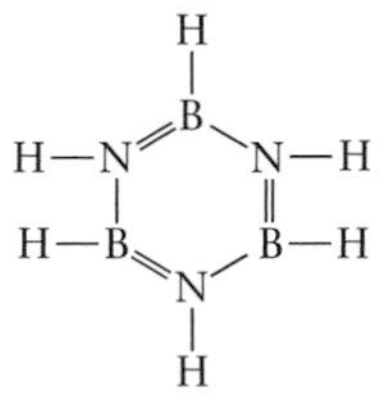

59. What is the hybridization of nitrogen in

(a)

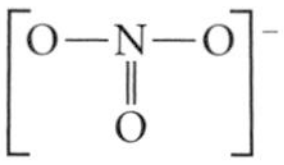

(b)

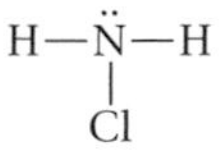

(c) $:N\equiv N:$ **(d)** $:N\equiv N—O$

60. What is the hybridization of carbon in

(a) CH_3Cl **(b)**

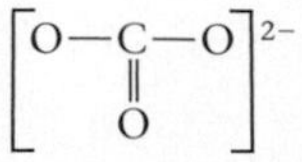

(c) O=C=O **(d)**

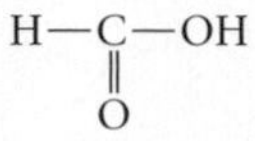

61. Give the hybridization of the central atom (underlined in red).
(a) $\underline{C}OCl_2$ **(b)** $H\underline{N}O_2$ **(c)** $(CH_3)_2\underline{C}HCH_3$

62. Give the hybridization of the central atom (underlined in red).
(a) $HO\underline{Br}O_3$ **(b)** $Cl_2\underline{O}$ **(c)** $O\underline{P}Br_3$

Sigma and Pi Bonds

63. Give the number of sigma and pi bonds in the molecule in Question 57.

64. ■ Give the number of sigma and pi bonds in the molecule in Question 58.

65. Give the number of sigma and pi bonds in each species in Question 59.

66. Give the number of sigma and pi bonds in each species in Question 60.

Unclassified

67. In which of the following molecules does the sulfur have an expanded octet? For those that do, write the Lewis structure.

(a) SO_2 **(b)** SF_4 **(c)** SO_2Cl_2 **(d)** SF_6

68. Consider the dichromate ion. It has no metal-metal nor oxygen-oxygen bonds. Write a Lewis structure for the dichromate ion. Consider chromium to have six valence electrons.

69. Consider vitamin C. Its skeleton structure is

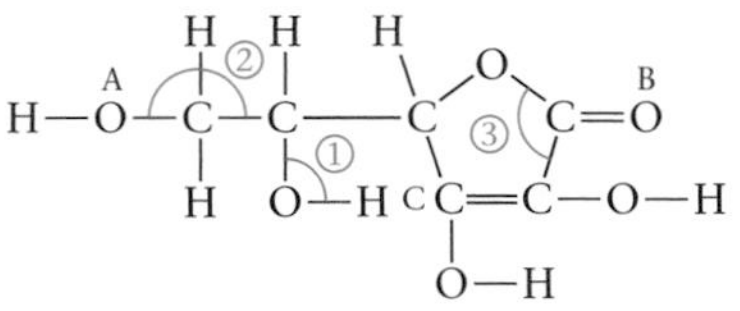

(a) How many sigma and pi bonds are there in vitamin C?
(b) How many unshared electron pairs are there?
(c) What are the approximate values of the angles marked (in blue) 1, 2, and 3?
(d) What is the hybridization of each atom marked (in red) A, B, and C?

70. Complete the table below.

Species	Atoms Around Central Atom A	Unshared Pairs Around A	Geometry	Hybridization	Polarity (Assume all X atoms the same)
AX_2E_2	______	______	______	______	______
______	3	0	______	______	______
AX_4E_2	______	______	______	______	______
______	______	______	trigonal bipyramid	______	______

■ in OWL Blue-numbered questions answered in Appendix 6 WEB Solution is available on companion website

Conceptual Questions

71. Given the following electronegativities

$$C = 2.5 \qquad N = 3.0 \qquad S = 2.6$$

what is the central atom in CNS^-?

72. Based on the concept of formal charge, what is the central atom in
   (a) HCN (do not include H as a possibility)?
   (b) NOCl (Cl is always a terminal atom)?

73. Describe the geometry of the species in which there are, around the central atom,
   (a) four single bonds, two unshared pairs of electrons.
   (b) five single bonds.
   (c) two single bonds, one unshared pair of electrons.
   (d) three single bonds, two unshared pairs of electrons.
   (e) two single bonds, two unshared pairs of electrons.
   (f) five single bonds, one unshared pair of electrons.

74. ■ Consider the following molecules: SiH_4, PH_3, H_2S. In each case, a central atom is surrounded by four electron pairs. In which of these molecules would you expect the bond angle to be less than 109.5°? Explain your reasoning.

75. Give the formula of an ion or molecule in which an atom of
   (a) N forms three bonds using sp^3 hybrid orbitals.
   (b) N forms two pi bonds and one sigma bond.
   (c) O forms one sigma and one pi bond.
   (d) C forms four bonds in three of which it uses sp^2 hybrid orbitals.
   (e) Xe forms two bonds using sp^3d^2 hybrid orbitals.

76. ■ In each of the following molecules, a central atom is surrounded by a total of three atoms or unshared electron pairs: $SnCl_2$, BCl_3, SO_2. In which of these molecules would you expect the bond angle to be less than 120°? Explain your reasoning.

77. Explain the meaning of the following terms.
   (a) expanded octet (b) resonance
   (c) unshared electron pair (d) odd-electron species

Challenge Problems

78. A compound of chlorine and fluorine, ClF_x, reacts at about 75°C with uranium to produce uranium hexafluoride and chlorine fluoride, ClF. A certain amount of uranium produced 5.63 g of uranium hexafluoride and 457 mL of chlorine fluoride at 75°C and 3.00 atm. What is *x*? Describe the geometry, polarity, and bond angles of the compound and the hybridization of chlorine. How many sigma and pi bonds are there?

79. Draw the Lewis structure and describe the geometry of the hydrazine molecule, N_2H_4. Would you expect this molecule to be polar?

80. ■ Consider the polyatomic ion IO_6^{5-}. How many pairs of electrons are around the central iodine atom? What is its hybridization? Describe the geometry of the ion.

81. It is possible to write a simple Lewis structure for the SO_4^{2-} ion, involving only single bonds, which follows the octet rule. However, Linus Pauling and others have suggested an alternative structure, involving double bonds, in which the sulfur atom is surrounded by six electron pairs.
   (a) Draw the two Lewis structures.
   (b) What geometries are predicted for the two structures?
   (c) What is the hybridization of sulfur in each case?
   (d) What are the formal charges of the atoms in the two structures?

82. Phosphoryl chloride, $POCl_3$, has the skeleton structure

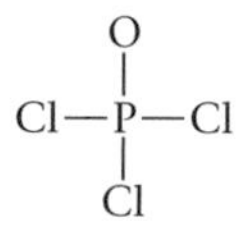

Write
   (a) a Lewis structure for $POCl_3$ following the octet rule. Calculate the formal charges in this structure.
   (b) a Lewis structure in which all the formal charges are zero. (The octet rule need not be followed.)

■ in OWL Blue-numbered questions answered in Appendix 6 WEB Solution is available on companion website

8 Thermochemistry

Some say the world will end in fire,
Some say in ice.
From what I've tasted of desire
I hold with those who favor fire.

—Robert Frost
"Fire and Ice"

Chapter Outline

The candle flame gives off heat, melting the candle wax. Wax melting is a phase change from solid to liquid and an endothermic reaction.

This chapter deals with energy and heat, two terms used widely by both the general public and scientists. Energy, in the vernacular, is equated with pep and vitality. Heat conjures images of blast furnaces and sweltering summer days. Scientifically, these terms have quite different meanings. *Energy* can be defined as the capacity to do work. *Heat* is a particular form of energy that is transferred from a body at a high temperature to one at a lower temperature when they are brought into contact with each other. Two centuries ago, heat was believed to be a material fluid (caloric); we still use the phrase "heat flow" to refer to heat transfer or to heat effects in general.

Thermochemistry refers to the study of the heat flow that accompanies chemical reactions. Our discussion of this subject will focus on—

- the basic principles of heat flow (Section 8.1).
- the experimental measurement of the magnitude and direction of heat flow, known as *calorimetry* (Section 8.2).
- the concept of enthalpy (heat content) and *enthalpy change*, ΔH (Section 8.3).
- the calculation of ΔH for reactions, using *thermochemical equations* (Section 8.4) and *enthalpies of formation* (Section 8.5).
- heat effects in the breaking and formation of covalent bonds (Section 8.6).
- the relation between heat and other forms of energy, as expressed by the first law of thermodynamics (Section 8.7). ■

Online homework for this chapter may be assigned in OWL

CENGAGENOW™

This icon introduces an opportunity for self-study and to explore interactive modules by signing in at **academic.cengage.com/now.**

8.1 PRINCIPLES OF HEAT FLOW

In any discussion of heat flow, it is important to distinguish between system and surroundings. The **system** is that part of the universe on which attention is focused. In a very simple case (Figure 8.1), it might be a sample of water in contact with a hot plate. The **surroundings,** which exchange energy with the system, make up in principle the rest of the universe. For all practical purposes, however, they include only those materials in close contact with the system. In Figure 8.1, the surroundings would consist of the hot plate, the beaker holding the water sample, and the air around it.

The universe is a big place.

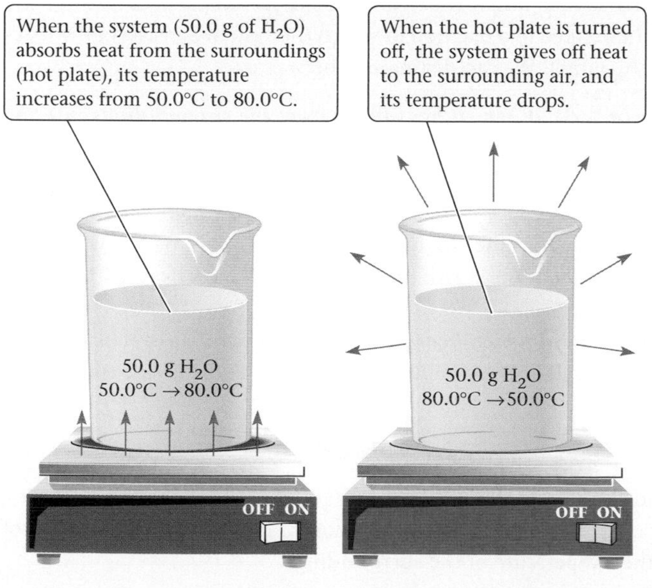

Figure 8.1
A system and its surroundings.

When a chemical reaction takes place, we consider the substances involved, reactants and products, to be the system. The surroundings include the vessel in which the reaction takes place (test tube, beaker, and so on) and the air or other material in thermal contact with the reaction system.

State Properties

The *state* of a system is described by giving its composition, temperature, and pressure. The system at the left of Figure 8.1 consists of

$$50.0 \text{ g of } H_2O(l) \text{ at } 50.0°C \text{ and } 1 \text{ atm}$$

When this system is heated, its state changes, perhaps to one described as

$$50.0 \text{ g of } H_2O(l) \text{ at } 80.0°C \text{ and } 1 \text{ atm}$$

Certain quantities, called **state properties,** depend only on the state of the system, not on the way the system reached that state. Putting it another way, if X is a state property, then

$$\Delta X = X_{\text{final}} - X_{\text{initial}}$$

The distance between two cities depends on path, so it isn't a state property.

That is, the change in X is the difference between its values in final and initial states. Most of the quantities that you are familiar with are state properties; volume is a common example. You may be surprised to learn, however, that heat flow is *not* a state property; its magnitude depends on how a process is carried out (Section 8.7).

Direction and Sign of Heat Flow

Consider again the setup in Figure 8.1. If the hot plate is turned on, there is a flow of heat from the surroundings into the system, 50.0 g of water. This situation is described by stating that the heat flow, q, for the system is a positive quantity.

q is positive when heat flows into the system from the surroundings.

Usually, when heat flows into a system, its temperature rises. In this case, the temperature of the 50.0-g water sample might increase from 50.0°C to 80.0°C. When the hot plate in Figure 8.1 is shut off, the hot water gives off heat to the surrounding air. In this case, q for the system is a negative quantity.

q is negative when heat flows out of the system into the surroundings.

As is usually the case, the temperature of the system drops when heat flows out of it into the surroundings. The 50.0-g water sample might cool from 80.0°C back to 50.0°C.

This same reasoning can be applied to a reaction in which the system consists of the reaction mixture (products and reactants). We can distinguish between—

- ***an* endothermic *process (q > 0), in which heat flows from the surroundings into the reaction system.*** An example is the melting of ice:

  $$H_2O(s) \longrightarrow H_2O(l) \qquad q > 0$$

  The melting of ice *absorbs* heat from the surroundings, which might be the water in a glass of iced tea. The temperature of the surroundings drops, perhaps from 25°C to 3°C, as they give up heat to the system.

endo = into system; exo = out of system.

- ***an* exothermic *process (q < 0), in which heat flows from the reaction system into the surroundings.*** A familiar example is the combustion of methane, the major component of natural gas.

  $$CH_4(g) + 2\,O_2(g) \longrightarrow CO_2(g) + 2H_2O(l) \qquad q < 0$$

This reaction *evolves* heat to the surroundings, which might be the air around a Bunsen burner in the laboratory or a potato being baked in a gas oven. In either case, the effect of the heat transfer is to raise the temperature of the surroundings.

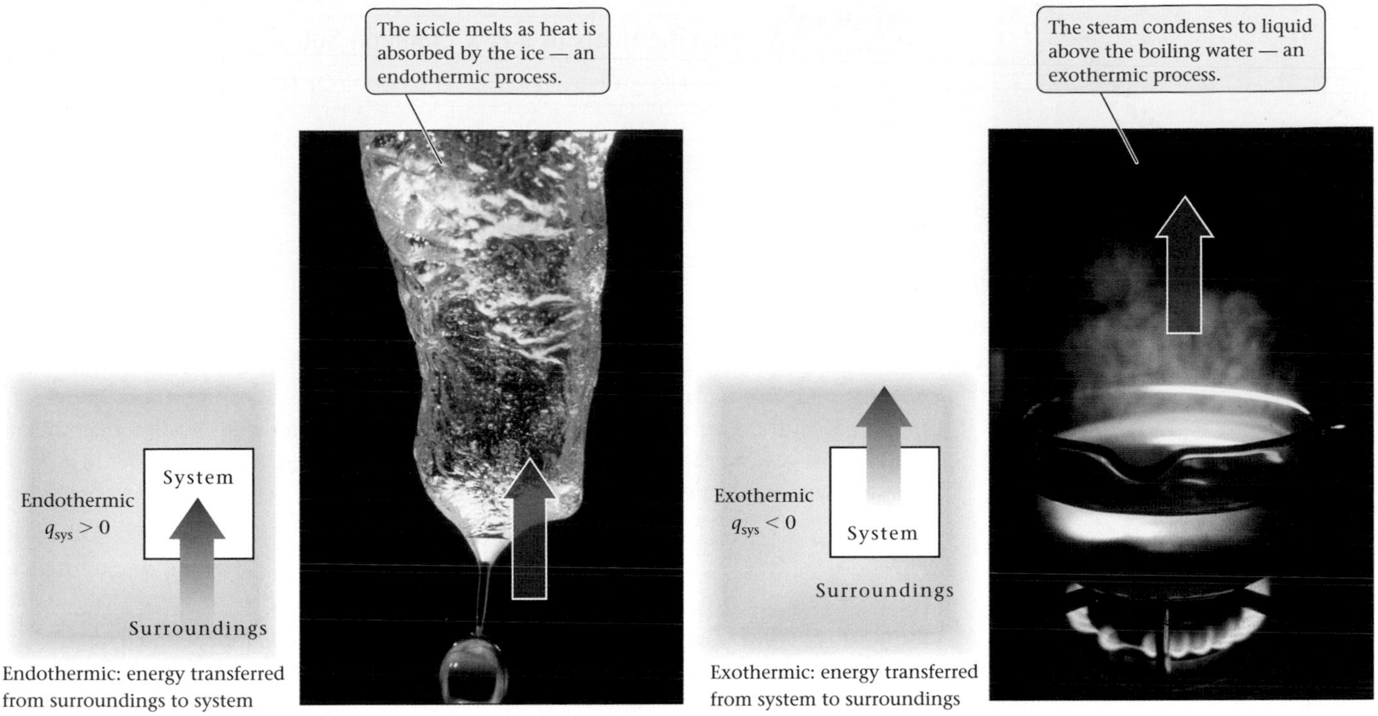

Endothermic and exothermic processes. On the left, the icicle melts as heat is absorbed by the ice, an endothermic process. On the right, steam rises from boiling water, an exothermic process.

left, Charles D. Winters; right, Jeff J. Daly/Fundamental Photographs NYC

Magnitude of Heat Flow

In any process, we are interested not only in the direction of heat flow but also in its magnitude. We will express q in the units introduced in Chapter 6, **joules** and **kilojoules.** The joule is named for James Joule (1818–1889), who carried out very precise thermometric measurements that established the first law of thermodynamics (Section 8.7).

1 J = 1 kg · m^2/s^2 in SI units

In the past, chemists used the calorie* as an energy unit. This is the amount of heat required to raise the temperature of one gram of water one degree Celsius. The calorie is a somewhat larger energy unit than the joule:

$$1 \text{ cal} = 4.184 \text{ J} \qquad 1 \text{ kcal} = 4.184 \text{ kJ}$$

Most of the remainder of this chapter is devoted to a discussion of the magnitude of the heat flow in chemical reactions or phase changes. However, we will focus on a simpler process in which the only effect of the heat flow is to change the temperature of a system. In general, the relationship between the magnitude of the heat flow, q, and the temperature change, Δt, is given by the equation

$$q = C \times \Delta t \qquad (\Delta t = t_{\text{final}} - t_{\text{initial}})$$

The quantity C appearing in this equation is known as the **heat capacity** of the system. It represents the amount of heat required to raise the temperature of the system 1°C and has the units J/°C.

For a pure substance of mass m, the expression for q can be written as

$$q = m \times c \times \Delta t \qquad \textbf{(8.1)}$$

The quantity c is known as the **specific heat;** it is defined as the amount of heat required to raise the temperature of one gram of a substance one degree Celsius.

CENGAGENOW™
Click Coached Problems for a self-study module on **specific heat capacity.**

Specific heat, like density or melting point, is an intensive property that can be used to identify a substance or determine its purity. Water has an unusually large specific heat,

*The "calorie" referred to by nutritionists is actually a kilocalorie (1 kcal = 10^3 cal). On a 2000-calorie per day diet, you eat food capable of producing 2000 kcal = 2×10^3 kcal = 2×10^6 cal of energy.

Charles D. Winters

Substances with varying specific heats. The metals shown (Cu, Al, and Fe) have specific heats ranging from 0.38 J/g · °C (Cu) to 0.90 J/g · °C (Al). This explains why water warms up and cools down more slowly than a container made of aluminum, copper, or iron.

Table 8.1 Specific Heats of a Few Common Substances

	c (J/g · °C)		c (J/g · °C)
$Br_2(l)$	0.474	$Cu(s)$	0.382
$Cl_2(g)$	0.478	$Fe(s)$	0.446
$C_2H_5OH(l)$	2.43	$H_2O(g)$	1.87
$C_6H_6(l)$	1.72	$H_2O(l)$	4.18
$CO_2(g)$	0.843	$NaCl(s)$	0.866

4.18 J/g · °C. This explains why swimming is not a popular pastime in northern Minnesota in May. Even if the air temperature rises to 90°F, the water temperature will remain below 60°F. Metals have a relatively low specific heat (Table 8.1). When you warm water in a stainless steel saucepan, for example, nearly all of the heat is absorbed by the water, very little by the steel.

Example 8.1 Compare the amount of heat given off by 1.40 mol of liquid water when it cools from 100.0°C to 10.0°C to that given off when 1.40 mol of steam cools from 200°C to 110°C.

Strategy You will need the change in temperature, Δt, and the mass in grams.

SOLUTION For liquid water,

$$\Delta t = 10.0°C - 100.0°C = -90.0°C$$

$$\text{mass of water} = 1.40 \text{ mol} \times 18.02 \text{ g/mol} = 25.2 \text{ g}$$

$$q = 25.2 \text{ g} \times 1.87 \frac{\text{J}}{\text{g} \cdot °\text{C}} \times (-90.0°C) = -9.48 \times 10^3 \text{ J}$$

For steam, Δt and m are the same as for liquid water. Only the specific heat c is different.

$$q = 25.2 \text{ g} \times \frac{1.87 \text{ J}}{\text{g} \cdot °\text{C}} \times (-90.0°C) = -4.24 \times 10^3 \text{ J}$$

Steam thus gives off less heat than liquid water when it cools.

Reality Check The negative sign indicates that heat flows from the water to its surroundings as it cools.

8.2 MEASUREMENT OF HEAT FLOW; CALORIMETRY

CENGAGENOW™
Click Coached Problems for a self-study module on **calorimetry.**

To measure the heat flow in a reaction, a device known as a **calorimeter** is used. The apparatus contains water and/or other materials of known heat capacity. The walls of the calorimeter are insulated so that there is no exchange of heat with the surrounding air. It follows that the only heat flow is between the reaction system and the calorimeter. The heat flow for the reaction system is equal in magnitude but opposite in sign to that of the calorimeter:

$$q_{reaction} = -q_{calorimeter}$$

The reaction mixture is the system; the calorimeter is the surroundings.

Notice that if the reaction is exothermic ($q_{reaction} < 0$), $q_{calorimeter}$ must be positive; that is, heat flows from the reaction mixture into the calorimeter. Conversely, if the reaction is endothermic, the calorimeter gives up heat to the reaction mixture.

The equation just written is basic to calorimetric measurements. It allows you to calculate the amount of heat absorbed or evolved in a reaction if you know the heat capacity, C_{cal}, and the temperature change, Δt, of the calorimeter.

$$q_{reaction} = -C_{cal} \times \Delta t \tag{8.2}$$

Coffee-Cup Calorimeter

Figure 8.2 shows a simple **coffee-cup calorimeter** used in the general chemistry laboratory. It consists of two nested polystyrene foam cups partially filled with water. The cups have a tightly fitting cover through which an accurate thermometer is inserted. Because polystyrene foam is a good insulator, there is very little heat flow through the walls of the cups. Essentially all the heat evolved by a reaction taking place within the calorimeter is absorbed by the water. This means that, to a good degree of approximation, the heat capacity of the coffee-cup calorimeter is that of the water:

$$C_{cal} = m_{water} \times c_{water} = m_{water} \times 4.18 \frac{\text{J}}{\text{g} \cdot {}^\circ\text{C}}$$

and hence

$$q_{reaction} = -m_{water} \times 4.18 \frac{\text{J}}{\text{g} \cdot {}^\circ\text{C}} \times \Delta t \tag{8.3}$$

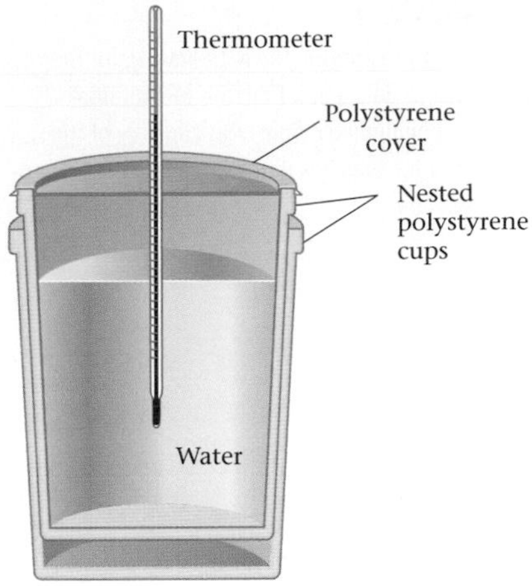

Figure 8.2
Coffee-cup calorimeter. The heat given off by a reaction is absorbed by the water. If you know the mass of the water, its specific heat (4.18 J/g · °C), and the temperature change as read on the thermometer, you can calculate the heat flow, *q*, for the reaction.

Example 8.2 Graded

Calcium chloride, $CaCl_2$, is added to canned vegetables to maintain the vegetables' firmness. When added to water, it dissolves:

$$CaCl_2(s) \longrightarrow Ca^{2+}(aq) + 2Cl^-(aq)$$

A calorimeter contains 50.0 g of water at 25.00°C. When 1.00 g of calcium chloride is added to the calorimeter, the temperature rises to 28.51°C. Assume that all the heat given off by the reaction is transferred to the water.

*(a) Calculate q for the reaction system.
**(b) How much $CaCl_2$ must be added to raise the temperature of the solution 9.00°C?

Strategy Apply Equation 8.1 to calculate q_{H_2O}. Remember that $q_{H_2O} = -q_{reaction}$.

SOLUTION

(a) $q_{H_2O} = 50.0 \text{ g} \times 4.18 \frac{\text{J}}{\text{g} \cdot {}^\circ\text{C}} \times (28.51^\circ\text{C} - 25.00^\circ\text{C}) = 734 \text{ J}.$

$q_{reaction} = -q_{H_2O} = -734 \text{ J}$

(b) $q_{H_2O} = 50.0 \text{ g} \times 4.18 \frac{\text{J}}{\text{g} \cdot {}^\circ\text{C}} \times 9.00^\circ\text{C} = 1.88 \times 10^3 \text{ J}.$

$q_{reaction} = -1.88 \times 10^3 \text{ J}$

We know from (a) that adding 1.00 g of $CaCl_2$ to the water gives off −734 J. Hence, we have the conversion factor

$$\frac{-734 \text{ J}}{1.00 \text{ g } CaCl_2}$$

Thus, to give off 1.88×10^3 J requires

$$-1.88 \times 10^3 \text{ J} \times \frac{1.00 \text{ g}}{-734 \text{ J}} = 2.56 \text{ g } CaCl_2$$

Reality Check Notice that $q_{reaction}$ is negative, so the solution process is exothermic. That is reasonable since the temperature of the water increases.

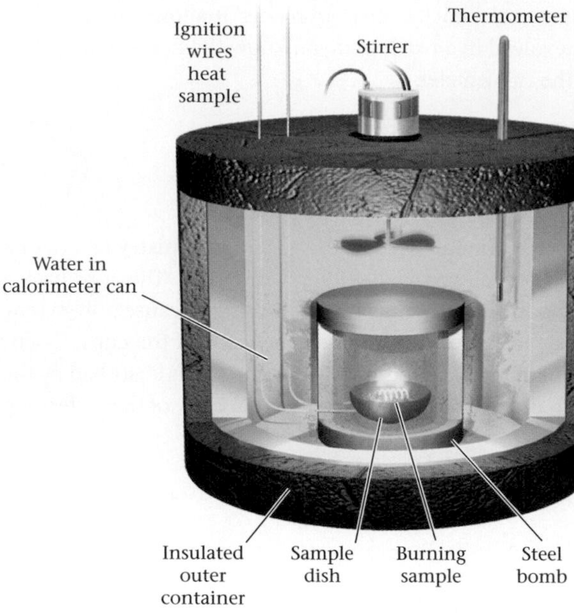

Figure 8.3
Bomb calorimeter. The heat flow, q, for the reaction is calculated from the temperature change multiplied by the heat capacity of the calorimeter, which is determined in a preliminary experiment.

Bomb Calorimeter

A coffee-cup calorimeter is suitable for measuring heat flow for reactions in solution. However, it cannot be used for reactions involving gases, which would escape from the cup. Neither would it be appropriate for reactions in which the products reach high temperatures. The **bomb calorimeter,** shown in Figure 8.3, is more versatile. To use it, a weighed sample of the reactant(s) is added to the heavy-walled metal vessel called a "bomb." This is then sealed and lowered into the insulated outer container. An amount of water sufficient to cover the bomb is added, and the entire apparatus is closed. The initial temperature is measured precisely. The reaction is then started, perhaps by electrical ignition. In an exothermic reaction, the hot products give off heat to the walls of the bomb and to the water. The final temperature is taken to be the highest value read on the thermometer.

All of the heat given off by the reaction is absorbed by the calorimeter, which consists of the metal bomb and the water that surrounds it. In other words,

$$q_{\text{reaction}} = -q_{\text{calorimeter}}$$

The heat absorbed by the calorimeter is equal to the product of its heat capacity, C_{cal}, and the temperature change, Δt. Hence

$$q_{\text{reaction}} = -C_{\text{cal}} \times \Delta t$$

C_{cal} depends upon the amount of water around the bomb.

To find the heat capacity, C_{cal}, the experiment is repeated using the same bomb and the same amount of water. This time, though, we carry out a reaction for which the amount of heat evolved is known; the temperature increase is again measured carefully. Suppose the reaction is known to evolve 93.3 kJ of heat and the temperature rises from 20.00°C to 30.00°C. It follows that

$$C_{\text{cal}} = \frac{93.3 \text{ kJ}}{10.00°\text{C}} = 9.33 \text{ kJ/°C}$$

Knowing the heat capacity of the calorimeter, the heat flow for any reaction taking place within the calorimeter can be calculated (Example 8.3).

Example 8.3 Hydrogen chloride is used in etching semiconductors. It can be prepared by reacting hydrogen and chlorine gases.

$$H_2(g) + Cl_2(g) \longrightarrow 2HCl(g)$$

It is found that when 1.00 g of H_2 is made to react completely with Cl_2 in a bomb calorimeter, the temperature in the bomb (heat capacity = 9.33 kJ/°C) rises from 20.00°C to 29.82°C. How much heat is evolved by the reaction?

Strategy Use the equation:

$$q_{reaction} = -C_{cal} \times \Delta t$$

SOLUTION

$$q_{reaction} = -9.33 \frac{kJ}{°C} \times (29.82°C - 20.00°C) = -91.6 \text{ kJ}$$

Charles D. Winters

An exothermic reaction. Hydrogen, a colorless gas, reacts with chlorine, a pale yellow gas, to form colorless hydrogen chloride gas.

8.3 ENTHALPY

We have referred several times to the "heat flow for the reaction system," symbolized as $q_{reaction}$. At this point, you may well find this concept a bit nebulous and wonder if it could be made more concrete by relating $q_{reaction}$ to some property of reactants and products. This can indeed be done; the situation is particularly simple for reactions taking place at constant pressure. Under that condition, the heat flow for the reaction system is equal to the difference in **enthalpy** (H) between products and reactants. That is,

$$q_{reaction} \text{ at constant pressure} = \Delta H = H_{products} - H_{reactants}$$

Enthalpy is a type of chemical energy, sometimes referred to as "heat content." Reactions that occur in the laboratory in an open container or in the world around us take place at a constant pressure, that of the atmosphere. For such reactions, the equation just written is valid, making enthalpy a very useful quantity.

Figure 8.4a (p. 204) shows the enthalpy relationship between reactants and products for an exothermic reaction such as

$$CH_4(g) + 2O_2(g) \longrightarrow CO_2(g) + 2H_2O(l) \qquad \Delta H < 0$$

Here, the products, 1 mol of $CO_2(g)$ and 2 mol of $H_2O(l)$, have a lower enthalpy than the reactants, 1 mol of $CH_4(g)$ and 2 mol of $O_2(g)$. The decrease in enthalpy is the source of the heat evolved to the surroundings. Figure 8.4b shows the situation for an endothermic process such as

$$H_2O(s) \longrightarrow H_2O(l) \qquad \Delta H > 0$$

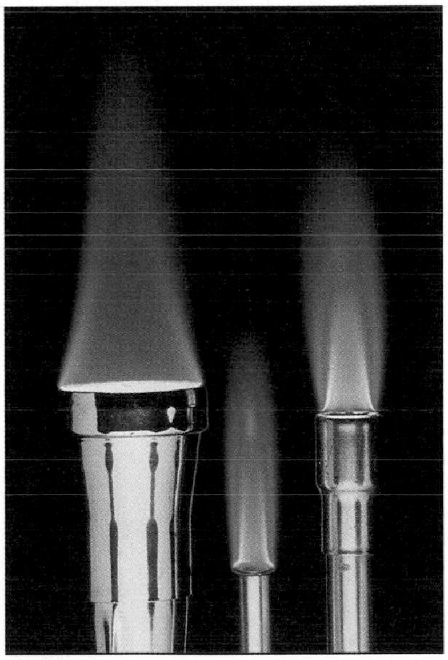

Charles D. Winters

Laboratory burners fueled by natural gas, which is mostly methane.

Liquid water has a higher enthalpy than ice, so heat must be transferred from the surroundings to melt the ice.

In general, the following relations apply for reactions taking place at constant pressure.

exothermic reaction:	$q = \Delta H < 0$	$H_{products} < H_{reactants}$
endothermic reaction:	$q = \Delta H > 0$	$H_{products} > H_{reactants}$

When CH_4 burns, ΔH is negative; when ice melts, ΔH is positive.

The enthalpy of a substance, like its volume, is a state property. A sample of one gram of liquid water at 25.00°C and 1 atm has a fixed enthalpy, H. In practice, no attempt is made to determine absolute values of enthalpy. Instead, scientists deal with changes in enthalpy, which are readily determined. For the process

$$1.00 \text{ g } H_2O\ (l, 25.00°C, 1 \text{ atm}) \longrightarrow 1.00 \text{ g } H_2O\ (l, 26.00°C, 1 \text{ atm})$$

ΔH is 4.18 J because the specific heat of water is 4.18 J/g · °C.

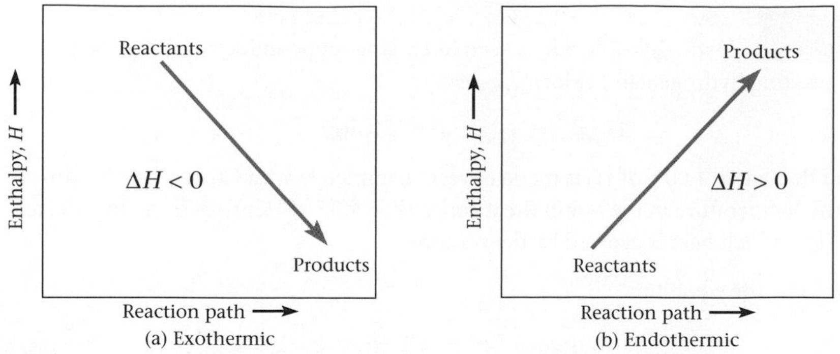

Figure 8.4
Energy diagram showing ΔH for a reaction. In an exothermic reaction (a), the products have a lower enthalpy than the reactants; thus ΔH is negative, and heat is given off to the surroundings. In an endothermic reaction (b), the products have a higher enthalpy than the reactants, so ΔH is positive and heat is absorbed from the surroundings.

8.4 THERMOCHEMICAL EQUATIONS

A chemical equation that shows the enthalpy relation between products and reactants is called a **thermochemical equation.** This type of equation contains, at the right of the balanced chemical equation, the appropriate value and sign for ΔH.

To see where a thermochemical equation comes from, consider the process by which ammonium nitrate dissolves in water:

$$NH_4NO_3(s) \longrightarrow NH_4^+(aq) + NO_3^-(aq)$$

A simple experiment with a coffee-cup calorimeter shows that when one gram of NH_4NO_3 dissolves, $q_{reaction} = 351$ J. The calorimeter is open to the atmosphere, the pressure is constant, and

$$\Delta H \text{ for dissolving } 1.00 \text{ g of } NH_4NO_3 = 351 \text{ J} = 0.351 \text{ kJ}$$

When one mole (80.05 g) of NH_4NO_3 dissolves, ΔH should be 80 times as great:

$$\Delta H \text{ for dissolving } 1.00 \text{ mol of } NH_4NO_3 = 0.351 \frac{\text{kJ}}{\text{g}} \times 80.05 \text{ g} = 28.1 \text{ kJ}$$

The thermochemical equation for this reaction (Figure 8.5) must then be

$$NH_4NO_3(s) \longrightarrow NH_4^+(aq) + NO_3^-(aq) \qquad \Delta H = +28.1 \text{ kJ}$$

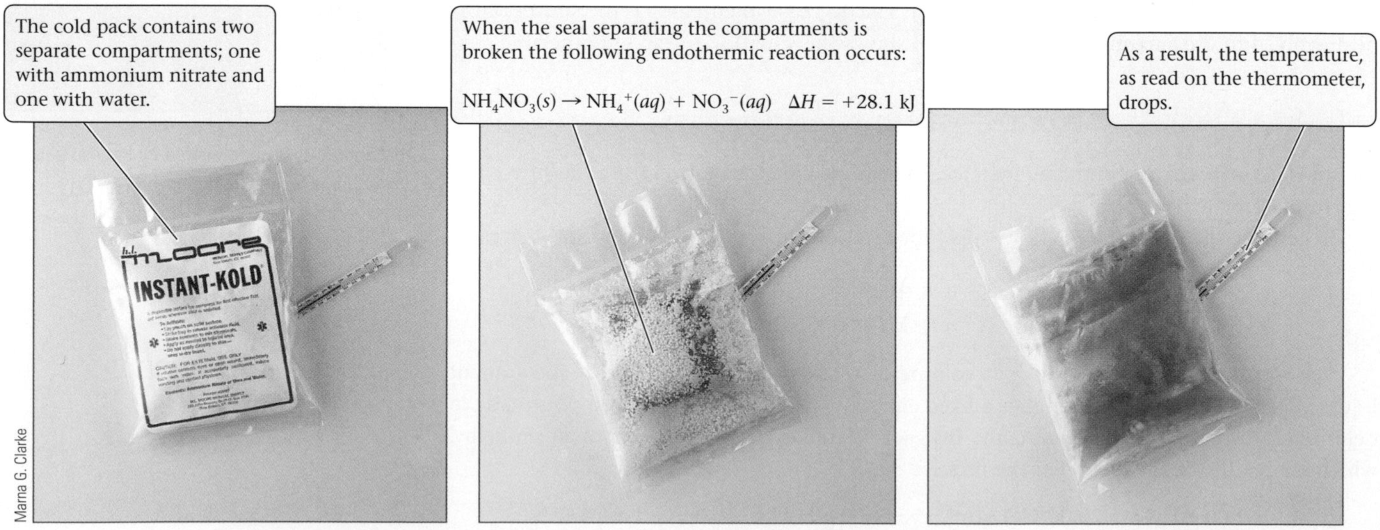

Figure 8.5
Endothermic reaction in a cold pack.

By an entirely analogous procedure, the thermochemical equation for the formation of HCl from the elements (Example 8.3) is found to be

$$H_2(g) + Cl_2(g) \longrightarrow 2HCl(g) \qquad \Delta H = -185\text{ kJ}$$

In other words, 185 kJ of heat is evolved when two moles of HCl are formed from H_2 and Cl_2.

These thermochemical equations are typical of those used throughout this text. It is important to realize that—

- the sign of ΔH indicates whether the reaction, when carried out at constant pressure, is endothermic (positive ΔH) or exothermic (negative ΔH).
- in interpreting a thermochemical equation, the coefficients represent numbers of moles (ΔH is -185 kJ when ***1 mol*** H_2 + ***1 mol*** $Cl_2 \rightarrow$ ***2 mol*** HCl).
- the phases (physical states) of all species must be specified, using the symbols (*s*), (*l*), (*g*), or (*aq*). The enthalpy of one mole of $H_2O(g)$ at 25°C is 44 kJ larger than that of one mole of $H_2O(l)$; the difference, which represents the heat of vaporization of water, is clearly significant.
- the value quoted for ΔH applies when products and reactants are at the same temperature, ordinarily taken to be 25°C unless specified otherwise.

This explains why burns from steam are more painful than those from boiling water.

Rules of Thermochemistry

To make effective use of thermochemical equations, three basic rules of thermochemistry are applied.

CENGAGENOW™
Click Coached Problems for a self-study module on **enthalpy changes.**

1. ***The magnitude of ΔH is directly proportional to the amount of reactant or product.*** This is a common-sense rule, consistent with experience. The amount of heat that must be absorbed to boil a sample of water is directly proportional to its mass. In another case, the more gasoline you burn in your car's engine, the more energy you produce.

This rule allows you to find ΔH corresponding to any desired amount of reactant or product. To do this, you follow the conversion-factor approach used in Chapter 3 with ordinary chemical equations. Consider, for example,

The magnitude of ΔH is dependent not only on the amount of the reactants and products but also on their physical states.

$$H_2(g) + Cl_2(g) \longrightarrow 2HCl(g) \qquad \Delta H = -185\text{ kJ}$$

The thermochemical equation allows us to relate the enthalpy change to amounts of reactants and products, leading to conversion factors such as

$$\frac{-185\text{ kJ}}{1\text{ mol } Cl_2} \qquad \frac{1\text{ mol } H_2}{-185\text{ kJ}} \qquad \frac{-185\text{ kJ}}{2\text{ mol HCl}}$$

Example 8.4 Graded

The Bunsen burners in your labs are fueled by natural gas, which is mostly methane, CH_4. The thermochemical equation for the combustion (burning in oxygen) of methane is

$$CH_4(g) + 2O_2(g) \longrightarrow CO_2(g) + 2H_2O(l) \qquad \Delta H = -890.3\text{ kJ}$$

CENGAGENOW™
Click Coached Problems for a self-study module on **phase changes from heat transfer.**

Calculate ΔH when

*(a) 5.00 g of CH_4 react with an excess of oxygen.
**(b) 2.00 L of O_2 at 49.0°C and 782 mm Hg react with an excess of methane.
***(c) 2.00 L of CH_4 react with 5.00 L of O_2 in a reaction vessel kept at 25°C and 1.00 atm.

SOLUTION

(a) Change 5.00 g of CH_4 to moles and use the conversion factor $\dfrac{-890.3\text{ kJ}}{1\text{ mol } CH_4}$:

$$\Delta H = 5.00\text{ g } CH_4 \times \frac{1\text{ mol } CH_4}{16.04\text{ g}} \times \frac{-890.3\text{ kJ}}{1\text{ mol } CH_4} = -278\text{ kJ}$$

(b) Use the ideal gas law to find the number of moles of O_2 and the conversion factor $\frac{-890.3\text{ kJ}}{2\text{ mol O}_2}$:

$$n = \frac{PV}{RT} = \frac{(782/760)\text{ atm} \times 2.00\text{ L}}{0.0821\text{ L}\cdot\text{atm/mol}\cdot\text{K} \times 322\text{ K}} = 0.0778\text{ mol}$$

$$\Delta H = 0.0778\text{ mol O}_2 \times \frac{-890.3\text{ kJ}}{2\text{ mol O}_2} = \boxed{-34.7\text{ kJ}}$$

(c) Use the law of combining volumes to find which reactant is limiting. Find the number of moles of limiting reactant and convert to ΔH.

$$2.00\text{ L CH}_4 \times \frac{1\text{ L CO}_2}{1\text{ L CH}_4} = 2.00\text{ L CO}_2$$

$$5.00\text{ L O}_2 \times \frac{1\text{ L CO}_2}{2\text{ L O}_2} = 2.50\text{ L CO}_2$$

CH_4 is the limiting reactant.

$$n_{CH_4} = \frac{PV}{RT} = \frac{1.00\text{ atm} \times 2.00\text{ L}}{0.0821\text{ L}\cdot\text{atm/mol}\cdot\text{K} \times 298\text{ K}} = 0.0817\text{ mol}$$

$$0.0817\text{ mol CH}_4 \times \frac{-890.3\text{ kJ}}{1\text{ mol CH}_4} = \boxed{-72.8\text{ kJ}}$$

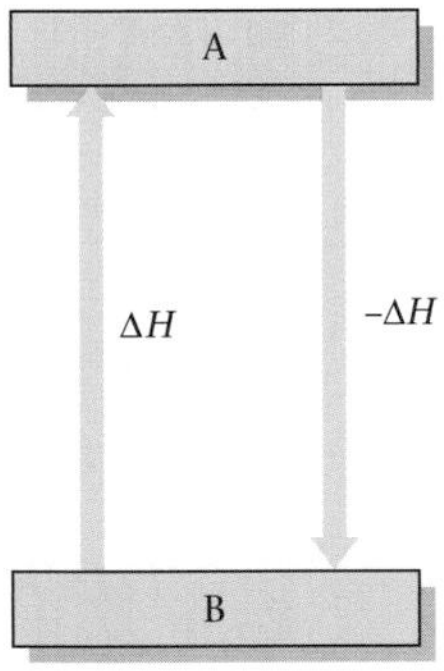

Thermochemistry rule 2.

The heat absorbed when a solid melts ($s \rightarrow l$) is referred to as the **heat of fusion;** that absorbed when a liquid vaporizes ($l \rightarrow g$) is called the **heat of vaporization.** Heats of fusion (ΔH_{fus}) and vaporization (ΔH_{vap}) are most often expressed in kilojoules per mole (kJ/mol). Values for several different substances are given in Table 8.2.

2. *ΔH for a reaction is equal in magnitude but opposite in sign to ΔH for the reverse reaction.* Another way to state this rule is to say that the amount of heat evolved in a reaction is exactly equal to the amount of heat absorbed in the reverse reaction. This again is a common-sense rule. If 6.00 kJ of heat is absorbed when a mole of ice melts,

$$H_2O(s) \longrightarrow H_2O(l) \qquad \Delta H = +6.00\text{ kJ}$$

then 6.00 kJ of heat should be evolved when a mole of liquid water freezes.

$$H_2O(l) \longrightarrow H_2O(s) \qquad \Delta H = -6.00\text{ kJ}$$

Table 8.2 ΔH (kJ/mol) for Phase Changes

Substance		mp (°C)	ΔH_{fus}*	bp (°C)	ΔH_{vap}*
Benzene	C_6H_6	5	9.84	80	30.8
Bromine	Br_2	−7	10.8	59	29.6
Mercury	Hg	−39	2.33	357	59.4
Naphthalene	$C_{10}H_8$	80	19.3	218	43.3
Water	H_2O	0	6.00	100	40.7

*Values of ΔH_{fus} are given at the melting point, values of ΔH_{vap} at the boiling point. The heat of vaporization of water decreases from 44.9 kJ/mol at 0°C to 44.0 kJ/mol at 25°C to 40.7 kJ/mol at 100°C.

Example 8.5 Given

$$2H_2(g) + O_2(g) \longrightarrow 2H_2O(l) \qquad \Delta H = -571.6\ \text{kJ}$$

calculate ΔH for the equation

$$H_2O(l) \longrightarrow H_2(g) + \tfrac{1}{2}O_2(g)$$

Strategy For the required equation, the coefficients are half as great as in the given equation; the equation is also reversed. Apply rules 1 and 2 in succession.

SOLUTION Applying rule 1

$$H_2(g) + \tfrac{1}{2}O_2(g) \longrightarrow H_2O(l) \qquad \Delta H = -571.6\ \text{kJ}/2 = -285.8\ \text{kJ}$$

Applying Rule 2:

$$H_2O(l) \longrightarrow H_2(g) + \tfrac{1}{2}O_2(g) \qquad \Delta H = +285.8\ \text{kJ}$$

3. ***The value of ΔH for a reaction is the same whether it occurs in one step or in a series of steps*** (Figure 8.6). If a thermochemical equation can be expressed as the sum of two or more equations,

$$\text{equation} = \text{equation (1)} + \text{equation (2)} + \ldots$$

then ΔH for the overall equation is the sum of the ΔH's for the individual equations:

$$\Delta H = \Delta H_1 + \Delta H_2 + \ldots$$

This relationship is referred to as **Hess's law,** after Germain Hess (1802–1850), professor of chemistry at the University of St. Petersburg, who deduced it in 1840. Hess's law is a direct consequence of the fact that enthalpy is a state property, dependent only on initial and final states. This means that, in Figure 8.6, ΔH *must* equal the sum of ΔH_1 and ΔH_2, because the final and initial states are the same for the two processes.

Hess's law is very convenient for obtaining values of ΔH for reactions that are difficult to carry out in a calorimeter. Consider, for example, the formation of the toxic gas carbon monoxide from the elements

$$C(s) + \tfrac{1}{2}O_2(g) \longrightarrow CO(g)$$

It is difficult, essentially impossible, to measure ΔH for this reaction because when carbon burns, the major product is always carbon dioxide, CO_2. It is possible, however, to calculate ΔH using thermochemical data for two other reactions that are readily carried out in the laboratory (Example 8.6).

CENGAGENOW™

Click Coached Problems for a simulation on **Hess's law.**

ΔH must be independent of path, since H is a state property.

Example 8.6 Carbon monoxide, CO, is a poisonous gas. It can be obtained by burning carbon in a limited amount of oxygen. Given

$$(1)\quad C(s) + O_2(g) \longrightarrow CO_2(g) \qquad \Delta H = -393.5\ \text{kJ}$$
$$(2)\quad 2CO(g) + O_2(g) \longrightarrow 2CO_2(g) \qquad \Delta H = -566.0\ \text{kJ}$$

calculate ΔH for the reaction

$$C(s) + \tfrac{1}{2}O_2(g) \longrightarrow CO(g) \qquad \Delta H = ?$$

Strategy The "trick" here is to work with the given information until you arrive at two equations that will add to give the equation you want ($C + \tfrac{1}{2}O_2 \rightarrow CO$). To do this, focus on CO, which, unlike CO_2 and O_2, appears in only one thermochemical equation. Notice that you want *one* mole (not two) of CO on the *right* side (not the left side) of the equation.

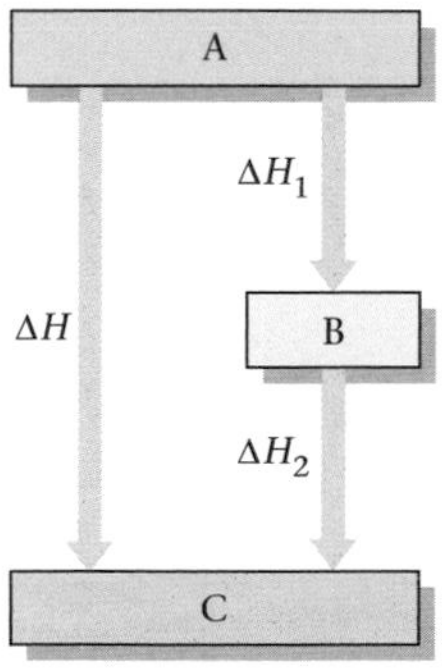

Figure 8.6
Thermochemistry rule 3, Hess's law, $\Delta H = \Delta H_1 + \Delta H_2$ because *H* is a state property.

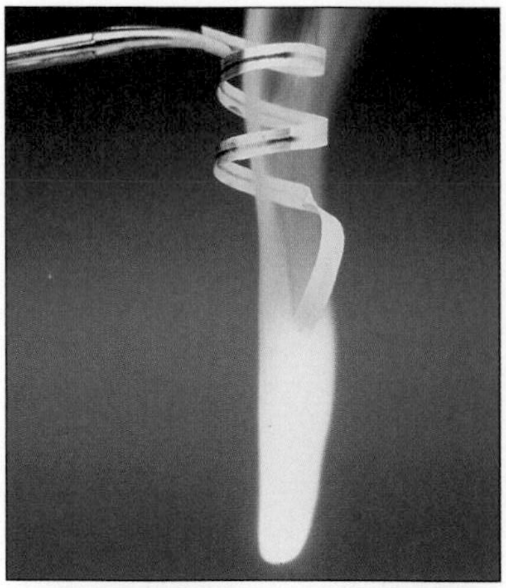

Charles D. Winters

Enthalpy of formation. Magnesium ribbon reacts with oxygen to give MgO, a white solid, and 601.7 kJ of heat per mole of MgO formed. Hence ΔH_f° MgO(*s*) = −601.7 kJ/mol.

SOLUTION To get one mole of CO on the right side, reverse equation (2) and divide the coefficients by 2. Applying rule 1 and rule 2 in succession,

$$CO_2(g) \longrightarrow CO(g) + \tfrac{1}{2}O_2(g) \qquad \Delta H = +566.0\ \text{kJ}/2 = +283.0\ \text{kJ}$$

Now, add equation (1) and simplify:

$$\begin{array}{lll} & CO_2(g) \longrightarrow CO(g) + \tfrac{1}{2}O_2(g) & \Delta H = +283.0\ \text{kJ} \\ (1) & C(s) + O_2(g) \longrightarrow CO_2(g) & \Delta H = -393.5\ \text{kJ} \\ \hline & C(s) + \tfrac{1}{2}O_2(g) \longrightarrow CO(g) & \Delta H = -110.5\ \text{kJ} \end{array}$$

Reality Check Notice that thermochemical equations can be added in exactly the same manner as algebraic equations; in this case $1CO_2$ and $\tfrac{1}{2}O_2$ canceled when the equations were added.

Summarizing the rules of thermochemistry:

1. ΔH is directly proportional to the amount of reactant or product.
2. ΔH changes sign when a reaction is reversed.
3. ΔH for a reaction has the same value regardless of the number of steps.

8.5 ENTHALPIES OF FORMATION

We have now written several thermochemical equations. In each case, we have cited the corresponding value of ΔH. Literally thousands of such equations would be needed to list the ΔH values for all the reactions that have been studied. Clearly, there has to be some more concise way of recording data of this sort. These data should be in a form that can easily be used to calculate ΔH for any reaction. It turns out that there is a simple way to do this, using quantities known as enthalpies of formation.

Meaning of ΔH_f°

Often called "heat of formation."

The standard molar **enthalpy of formation** of a compound, ΔH_f°, is equal to the enthalpy change when one mole of the compound is formed at a constant pressure of 1 atm and a fixed temperature, ordinarily 25°C, from the elements in their stable states at that pressure and temperature. From the equations

$$Ag(s, 25°C) + \tfrac{1}{2}Cl_2(g, 25°C, 1\ \text{atm}) \longrightarrow AgCl(s, 25°C) \qquad \Delta H = -127.1\ \text{kJ}$$

$$\tfrac{1}{2}N_2(g, 1\ \text{atm}, 25°C) + O_2(g, 1\ \text{atm}, 25°C) \longrightarrow NO_2(g, 1\ \text{atm}, 25°C) \qquad \Delta H = +33.2\ \text{kJ}$$

it follows that

$$\Delta H_f^\circ\ AgCl(s) = -127.1\ \text{kJ/mol} \qquad \Delta H_f^\circ\ NO_2(g) = +33.2\ \text{kJ/mol}$$

Enthalpies of formation for a variety of compounds are listed in Table 8.3. Notice that, with a few exceptions, enthalpies of formation are negative quantities. This means that the formation of a compound from the elements is ordinarily exothermic. Conversely, when a compound decomposes to the elements, heat usually must be absorbed.

You will note from Table 8.3 that there are no entries for elemental species such as $Br_2(l)$ and $O_2(g)$. This is a consequence of the way in which enthalpies of formation are defined. In effect, the enthalpy of formation of an element in its stable state at 25°C and 1 atm is taken to be zero. That is,

However, ΔH_f° $Br_2(g)$ is +29.6 kJ/mol. Explain.

$$\Delta H_f^\circ\ Br_2(l) = \Delta H_f^\circ\ O_2(g) = 0$$

Table 8.3 Standard Enthalpies of Formation at 25°C (kJ/mol) of Compounds at 1 atm, Aqueous Ions at 1 *M*

Compounds

$AgBr(s)$	−100.4	$CaCl_2(s)$	−795.8	$H_2O(g)$	−241.8	$NH_4NO_3(s)$	−365.6
$AgCl(s)$	−127.1	$CaCO_3(s)$	−1206.9	$H_2O(l)$	−285.8	$NO(g)$	+90.2
$AgI(s)$	−61.8	$CaO(s)$	−635.1	$H_2O_2(l)$	−187.8	$NO_2(g)$	+33.2
$AgNO_3(s)$	−124.4	$Ca(OH)_2(s)$	−986.1	$H_2S(g)$	−20.6	$N_2O_4(g)$	+9.2
$Ag_2O(s)$	−31.0	$CaSO_4(s)$	−1434.1	$H_2SO_4(l)$	−814.0	$NaCl(s)$	−411.2
$Al_2O_3(s)$	−1675.7	$CdCl_2(s)$	−391.5	$HgO(s)$	−90.8	$NaF(s)$	−573.6
$BaCl_2(s)$	−858.6	$CdO(s)$	−258.2	$KBr(s)$	−393.8	$NaOH(s)$	−425.6
$BaCO_3(s)$	−1216.3	$Cr_2O_3(s)$	−1139.7	$KCl(s)$	−436.7	$NiO(s)$	−239.7
$BaO(s)$	−553.5	$CuO(s)$	−157.3	$KClO_3(s)$	−397.7	$PbBr_2(s)$	−278.7
$BaSO_4(s)$	−1473.2	$Cu_2O(s)$	−168.6	$KClO_4(s)$	−432.8	$PbCl_2(s)$	−359.4
$CCl_4(l)$	−135.4	$CuS(s)$	−53.1	$KNO_3(s)$	−494.6	$PbO(s)$	−219.0
$CHCl_3(l)$	−134.5	$Cu_2S(s)$	−79.5	$MgCl_2(s)$	−641.3	$PbO_2(s)$	−277.4
$CH_4(g)$	−74.8	$CuSO_4(s)$	−771.4	$MgCO_3(s)$	−1095.8	$PCl_3(g)$	−287.0
$C_2H_2(g)$	+226.7	$Fe(OH)_3(s)$	−823.0	$MgO(s)$	−601.7	$PCl_5(g)$	−374.9
$C_2H_4(g)$	+52.3	$Fe_2O_3(s)$	−824.2	$Mg(OH)_2(s)$	−924.5	$SiO_2(s)$	−910.9
$C_2H_6(g)$	−84.7	$Fe_3O_4(s)$	−1118.4	$MgSO_4(s)$	−1284.9	$SnO_2(s)$	−580.7
$C_3H_8(g)$	−103.8	$HBr(g)$	−36.4	$MnO(s)$	−385.2	$SO_2(g)$	−296.8
$CH_3OH(l)$	−238.7	$HCl(g)$	−92.3	$MnO_2(s)$	−520.0	$SO_3(g)$	−395.7
$C_2H_5OH(l)$	−277.7	$HF(g)$	−271.1	$NH_3(g)$	−46.1	$ZnI_2(s)$	−208.0
$CO(g)$	−110.5	$HI(g)$	+26.5	$N_2H_4(l)$	+50.6	$ZnO(s)$	−348.3
$CO_2(g)$	−393.5	$HNO_3(l)$	−174.1	$NH_4Cl(s)$	−314.4	$ZnS(s)$	−206.0

Cations				Anions			
$Ag^+(aq)$	+105.6	$Hg^{2+}(aq)$	+171.1	$Br^-(aq)$	−121.6	$HPO_4^{2-}(aq)$	−1292.1
$Al^{3+}(aq)$	−531.0	$K^+(aq)$	−252.4	$CO_3^{2-}(aq)$	−677.1	$HSO_4^-(aq)$	−887.3
$Ba^{2+}(aq)$	−537.6	$Mg^{2+}(aq)$	−466.8	$Cl^-(aq)$	−167.2	$I^-(aq)$	−55.2
$Ca^{2+}(aq)$	−542.8	$Mn^{2+}(aq)$	−220.8	$ClO_3^-(aq)$	−104.0	$MnO_4^-(aq)$	−541.4
$Cd^{2+}(aq)$	−75.9	$Na^+(aq)$	−240.1	$ClO_4^-(aq)$	−129.3	$NO_2^-(aq)$	−104.6
$Cu^+(aq)$	+71.7	$NH_4^+(aq)$	−132.5	$CrO_4^{2-}(aq)$	−881.2	$NO_3^-(aq)$	−205.0
$Cu^{2+}(aq)$	+64.8	$Ni^{2+}(aq)$	−54.0	$Cr_2O_7^{2-}(aq)$	−1490.3	$OH^-(aq)$	−230.0
$Fe^{2+}(aq)$	−89.1	$Pb^{2+}(aq)$	−1.7	$F^-(aq)$	−332.6	$PO_4^{3-}(aq)$	−1277.4
$Fe^{3+}(aq)$	−48.5	$Sn^{2+}(aq)$	−8.8	$HCO_3^-(aq)$	−692.0	$S^{2-}(aq)$	+33.1
$H^+(aq)$	0.0	$Zn^{2+}(aq)$	−153.9	$H_2PO_4^-(aq)$	−1296.3	$SO_4^{2-}(aq)$	−909.3

The standard enthalpies of formation of ions in aqueous solution listed at the bottom of Table 8.3 are relative values, established by taking

$$\Delta H_f^\circ \, H^+(aq) = 0$$

From the values listed we see that the Cu^{2+} ion has a heat of formation *greater* than that of H^+ by about 65 kJ/mol, and Cd^{2+} has a heat of formation about 76 kJ/mol *less* than that of H^+.

Calculation of $\Delta H°$

Enthalpies of formation can be used to calculate $\Delta H°$ for a reaction. To do this, apply this general rule:

The standard enthalpy change, $\Delta H°$, for a given thermochemical equation is equal to the sum of the standard enthalpies of formation of the product compounds minus the sum of the standard enthalpies of formation of the reactant compounds.

Using the symbol Σ to represent "the sum of,"

$$\Delta H° = \Sigma\, \Delta H_f^\circ \text{ products} - \Sigma\, \Delta H_f^\circ \text{ reactants} \qquad (8.4)$$

This is a very useful equation, one we will use again and again.

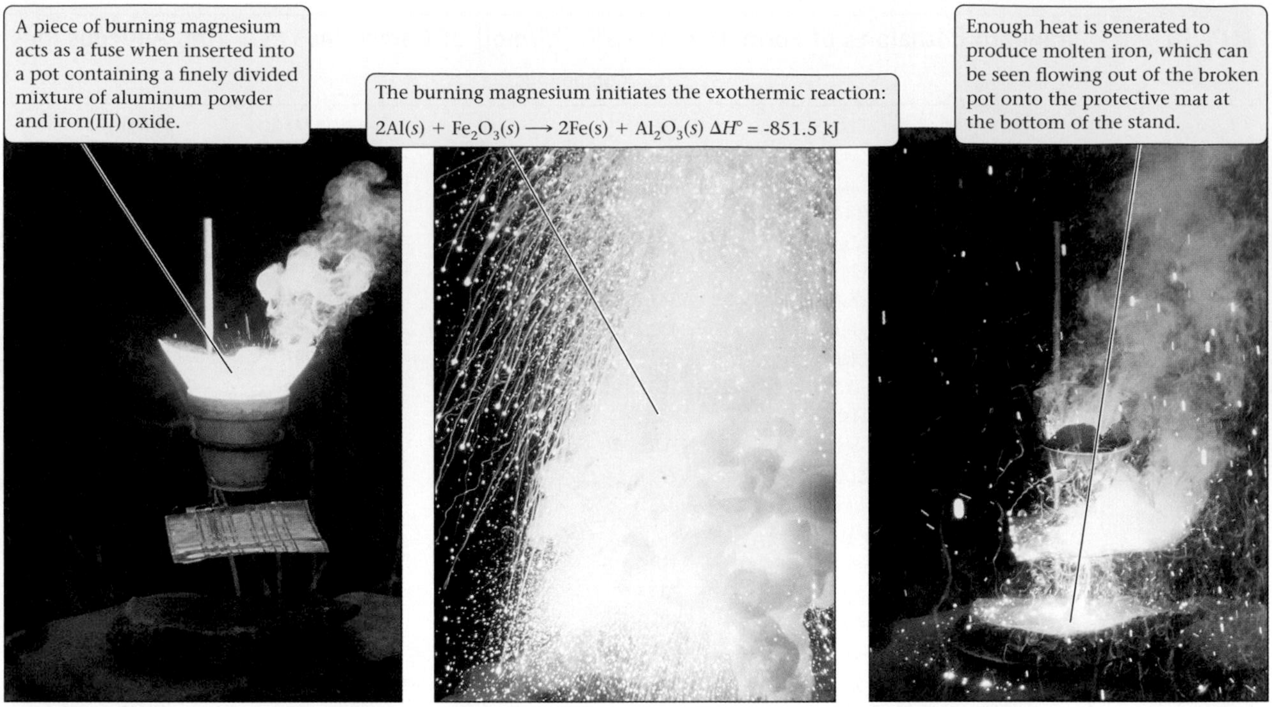

Figure 8.7
A thermite reaction.

In applying this equation—

- ***elements in their standard states can be omitted,*** because their heats of formation are zero. To illustrate, consider the thermite reaction once used to weld rails (Figure 8.7).

$$2Al(s) + Fe_2O_3(s) \longrightarrow 2Fe(s) + Al_2O_3(s)$$

We can write, quite simply,

$$\Delta H° = \Sigma\, \Delta H_f° \text{ products} - \Sigma\, \Delta H_f° \text{ reactants} = \Delta H_f°\, Al_2O_3(s) - \Delta H_f°\, Fe_2O_3(s)$$

- ***the coefficients of products and reactants in the thermochemical equation must be taken into account.*** For example, consider the reaction:

$$2Al(s) + 3Cu^{2+}(aq) \longrightarrow 2Al^{3+}(aq) + 3Cu(s)$$

for which:

$$\Delta H° = 2\Delta H_f°\, Al^{3+}(aq) - 3\Delta H_f°\, Cu^{2+}(aq)$$

Strictly speaking, $\Delta H°$ calculated from enthalpies of formation listed in Table 8.3 represents the enthalpy change at 25°C and 1 atm. Actually, ΔH is independent of pressure and varies relatively little with temperature, changing by perhaps 1 to 10 kJ per 100°C.

Example 8.7 Graded

Benzene, C_6H_6, used in the manufacture of plastics, is a carcinogen affecting the bone marrow. Long-term exposure has been shown to cause leukemia and other blood disorders. The combustion of benzene is given by the following equation:

$$C_6H_6(l) + \tfrac{15}{2}O_2(g) \longrightarrow 6CO_2(g) + 3H_2O(l) \qquad \Delta H° = -3267.4 \text{ kJ}$$

*(a) Calculate the heat of formation of benzene.

**(b) Calculate $\Delta H°$ for the reaction

$$12CO_2(g) + 6H_2O(l) \longrightarrow 2C_6H_6(l) + 15O_2(g)$$

***(c) Calculate $\Delta H°$ for the reaction

$$C_6H_6(g) + \frac{15}{2}O_2(g) \longrightarrow 6CO_2(g) + 3H_2O(g)$$

given that ΔH_{vap} for benzene at 25°C is 33.6 kJ/mol.

The unit for $\Delta H_f°$ is kJ/mol; that for ΔH is kJ.

SOLUTION

(a) Equation 8.4 takes the form

$$\Delta H° = 6\Delta H_f°\,CO_2(g) + 3\Delta H_f°\,H_2O(l) - \Delta H_f°\,C_6H_6(l)$$

Substituting values for all the variables except $\Delta H_f°\,C_6H_6(l)$, we have

$$-3267.4\text{ kJ} = 6\text{ mol} \times \left(\frac{-393.5\text{ kJ}}{1\text{ mol}}\right) + 3\text{ mol} \times \left(\frac{-285.8\text{ kJ}}{1\text{ mol}}\right) - \Delta H_f°\,C_6H_6(l)$$

Solving,

$$\Delta H_f°\,C_6H_6(l) = +49.0\text{ kJ/mol}$$

(b) Notice that the reaction is the reverse of the combustion reaction. Not only that, all coefficients have been doubled. Thus,

$$\Delta H° = -(-3267.4) \times 2 = +6534.8\text{ kJ}$$

(c) The reaction is similar to the combustion reaction. The difference is the physical states of both benzene and water. Remember that heat of vaporization is the amount of heat needed to change liquid to gas. We apply Hess's law:

$$C_6H_6(l) + \frac{15}{2}O_2(g) \longrightarrow 6CO_2(g) + 3H_2O(l) \qquad \Delta H = -3267.4\text{ kJ}$$

$$3H_2O(l) \longrightarrow 3H_2O(g) \qquad \Delta H° = 3(-241.8 - (-285.8)) = +132.0\text{ kJ}$$

$$C_6H_6(g) \longrightarrow C_6H_6(l) \qquad \Delta H° = -\Delta H_{vap} = -33.6\text{ kJ}$$

Adding the three chemical equations and the three $\Delta H°$ values, we get

$$\Delta H° = -3267.4\text{ kJ} + 132.0\text{ kJ} - 33.6\text{ kJ} = -3169.0\text{ kJ}$$

The relation between $\Delta H°$ and enthalpies of formation is perhaps used more often than any other in thermochemistry. Its validity depends on the fact that enthalpy is a state property. For any reaction, $\Delta H°$ can be obtained by imagining that the reaction takes place in two steps. First, the reactants (compounds or ions) are converted to the elements:

$$\text{reactants} \longrightarrow \text{elements} \qquad \Delta H_1° = -\Sigma\Delta H_f°\text{ reactants}$$

Then the elements are converted to products:

$$\text{elements} \longrightarrow \text{products} \qquad \Delta H_2° = \Sigma\Delta H_f°\text{ products}$$

Applying a basic rule of thermochemistry, Hess's law,

$$\Delta H° = \Delta H_1° + \Delta H_2° = \Sigma\,\Delta H_f°\text{ products} + (-\Sigma\,\Delta H_f°\text{ reactants})$$

Enthalpy changes for reactions in solution can be determined using standard enthalpies of formation of aqueous ions, applying the general relation

$$\Delta H° = \Sigma\,\Delta H_f°\text{ products} - \Sigma\,\Delta H_f°\text{ reactants}$$

and taking account of the fact that $\Delta H_f°\,H^+(aq) = 0$ (Example 8.8).

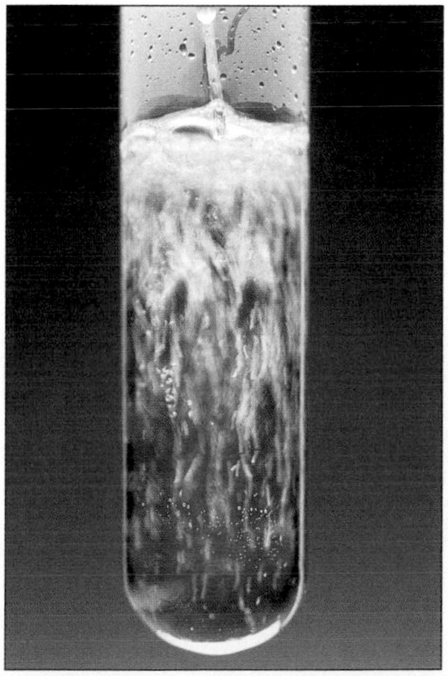

Charles D. Winters

Figure 8.8
Reaction of an acid with a carbonate.
Hydrochloric acid added to sodium carbonate solution produces CO_2 gas.

Example 8.8 Graded

Sodium carbonate is a white powder used in the manufacture of glass. When hydrochloric acid is added to a solution of sodium carbonate, carbon dioxide gas is formed (Figure 8.8). The equation for the reaction is

$$2H^+(aq) + CO_3^{2-}(aq) \longrightarrow CO_2(g) + H_2O(l)$$

*(a) Calculate $\Delta H°$ for the thermochemical equation.
**(b) Calculate $\Delta H°$ when 25.00 mL of 0.186 M HCl is added to sodium carbonate.

Strategy

(a) Use Table 8.3 to get enthalpies of formation. Remember that $\Delta H_f° \ H^+(aq) = 0$.
(b) $\Delta H°$ calculated in (a) is for two moles of $H^+(aq)$. How many moles of $H^+(aq)$ are used?

SOLUTION

(a) $$\Delta H° = \Delta H_f° \ CO_2(g) + \Delta H_f° \ H_2O(l) - [2(\Delta H_f° \ H^+(aq)) + \Delta H_f° \ CO_3^{2-}(aq)]$$

$$= 1 \text{ mol}\left(\frac{-393.5 \text{ kJ}}{1 \text{ mol}}\right) + 1 \text{ mol}\left(\frac{-285.8 \text{ kJ}}{1 \text{ mol}}\right) - 1 \text{ mol}\left(\frac{-677.1 \text{ kJ}}{1 \text{ mol}}\right)$$

$$= -2.2 \text{ kJ}$$

(b) HCl contributes all the H^+ ions in a 1:1 ratio. Thus

$$\text{moles HCl} = \text{moles } H^+ = V \times M = 0.02500 \text{ L} \times 0.186 \text{ mol/L}$$
$$= 0.00465$$

Using the conversion factor obtained in (a),

$$\frac{-2.2 \text{ kJ}}{2 \text{ mol } H^+}$$

we obtain

$$0.00465 \text{ mol } H^+ \times \frac{-2.2 \text{ kJ}}{2 \text{ mol } H^+} = -5.1 \times 10^{-3} \text{ kJ}$$

Reality Check Notice that the reaction is exothermic, but only slightly so. If you carry out the reaction in the laboratory, you find that the solution temperature increases slightly.

8.6 BOND ENTHALPY

CENGAGENOW™
Click Coached Problems for a self-study module on **enthalpy change.**

For many reactions, ΔH is a large negative number; the reaction gives off a lot of heat. In other cases, ΔH is positive; heat must be absorbed for the reaction to occur. You may well wonder why the enthalpy change should vary so widely from one reaction to another. Is there some basic property of the molecules involved in the reaction that determines the sign and magnitude of ΔH?

These questions can be answered on a molecular level in terms of a quantity known as bond enthalpy. (More commonly but less properly it is called bond energy.) The **bond enthalpy** is defined as ΔH when one mole of bonds is broken in the gaseous state. From the equations (see also Figure 8.9, p. 213)

What is $\Delta H_f°$ for $H(g)$? $Cl(g)$? Answer: 218 and 122 kJ/mol, respectively.

$$H_2(g) \longrightarrow 2H(g) \qquad \Delta H = +436 \text{ kJ}$$

$$Cl_2(g) \longrightarrow 2Cl(g) \qquad \Delta H = +243 \text{ kJ}$$

it follows that the H—H bond enthalpy is +436 kJ/mol, and that for Cl—Cl is 243 kJ/mol. In both reactions, one mole of bonds (H—H and Cl—Cl) is broken.

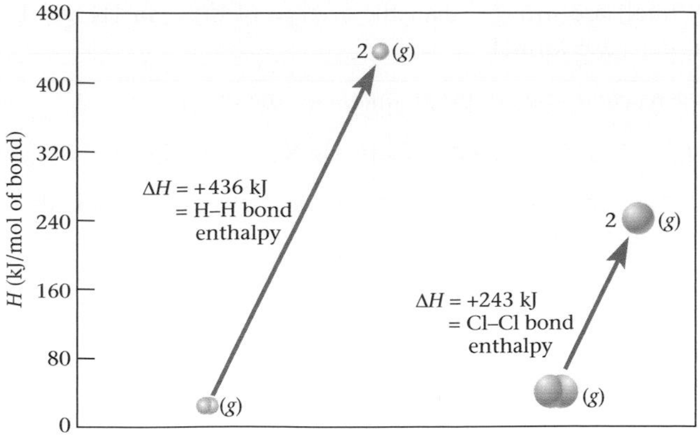

Figure 8.9
Bond enthalpies for H_2 and Cl_2. The H—H bond enthalpy is greater than the Cl—Cl bond enthalpy (+436 kJ/mol versus +243 kJ/mol). This means that the bond in H_2 is stronger than that in Cl_2.

Bond enthalpies for a variety of single and multiple bonds are listed in Table 8.4. Note that bond enthalpy is always a positive quantity; heat is always absorbed when chemical bonds are broken. Conversely, heat is given off when bonds are formed from gaseous atoms. Thus

$$H(g) + Cl(g) \longrightarrow HCl(g) \quad \Delta H = -431 \text{ kJ}$$

$$H(g) + F(g) \longrightarrow HF(g) \quad \Delta H = -565 \text{ kJ}$$

Using bond enthalpies, it is possible to explain why certain gas phase reactions are endothermic and others are exothermic. In general, a reaction is expected to be endothermic (i.e., heat must be absorbed) if—

- *the bonds in the reactants are stronger than those in the products.* Consider, for example, the decomposition of hydrogen fluoride to the elements, which can be shown to be endothermic from the data in Table 8.3.

$$2HF(g) \longrightarrow H_2(g) + F_2(g) \qquad \Delta H = -2\Delta H_f^\circ \text{HF} = +542.2 \text{ kJ}$$

The higher the bond enthalpy, the stronger the bond.

Table 8.4 Bond Enthalpies

Single Bond Enthalpy (kJ/mol)

	H	C	N	O	S	F	Cl	Br	I
H	436	414	389	464	339	565	431	368	297
C		347	293	351	259	485	331	276	218
N			159	222	—	272	201	243	—
O				138	—	184	205	201	201
S					226	285	255	213	—
F						153	255	255	277
Cl							243	218	209
Br								193	180
I									151

Multiple Bond Enthalpy (kJ/mol)

C=C	612	N=N	418	C≡C	820
C=N	615	N=O	607	C≡N	890
C=O	715	O=O	498	C≡O	1075
C=S	477	S=O	498	N≡N	941

The bonds in HF (565 kJ/mol) are stronger than the average of those in H_2 and F_2: (436 kJ/mol + 153 kJ/mol)/2 = 295 kJ/mol.

- *there are more bonds in the reactants than in the products.* For the reaction

$$2H_2O(g) \longrightarrow 2H_2(g) + O_2(g) \qquad \Delta H = -2\Delta H_f^\circ H_2O(g) = +483.6 \text{ kJ}$$

there are four moles of O—H bonds in two moles of H_2O as compared with only three moles of bonds in the products (two moles of H—H bonds, one mole of O=O bonds).

You will note from Table 8.4 that the bond enthalpy is larger for a multiple bond than for a single bond between the same two atoms. Thus

But, the double bond enthalpy is less than twice that for a single bond.

$$\text{bond enthalpy C—C} = 347 \text{ kJ/mol}$$
$$\text{bond enthalpy C=C} = 612 \text{ kJ/mol}$$
$$\text{bond enthalpy C}\equiv\text{C} = 820 \text{ kJ/mol}$$

This effect is a reasonable one; the greater the number of bonding electrons, the more difficult it should be to break the bond between two atoms.

We should point out a serious limitation of the bond enthalpies listed in Table 8.4. *Whenever the bond involves two different atoms* (e.g., O—H) *the value listed is approximate rather than exact,* because it represents an average taken over two or more different species. Consider, for example, the O—H bond where we find

$$\text{H—O—H}(g) \longrightarrow \text{H}(g) + \text{OH}(g) \qquad \Delta H = +499 \text{ kJ}$$
$$\text{H—O}(g) \longrightarrow \text{H}(g) + \text{O}(g) \qquad \Delta H = +428 \text{ kJ}$$

Both of these reactions involve breaking a mole of O—H bonds, yet the experimental values of ΔH are quite different. The bond enthalpy listed in Table 8.4, 464 kJ/mol, is an average of these two values.

This limitation explains why, whenever possible, we use enthalpies of formation (ΔH_f°) rather than bond enthalpies to calculate the value of ΔH for a reaction. Calculations involving enthalpies of formation are expected to be accurate within ±0.1 kJ; the use of bond enthalpies can result in an error of 10 kJ or more.

8.7 THE FIRST LAW OF THERMODYNAMICS

CENGAGENOW™
Click Chemistry Interactive for a self-study module on **heat and work.**

So far in this chapter our discussion has focused on thermochemistry, the study of the heat effects in chemical reactions. Thermochemistry is a branch of *thermodynamics,* which deals with all kinds of energy effects in all kinds of processes. Thermodynamics distinguishes between two types of energy. One of these is heat (q); the other is **work,** represented by the symbol w. The thermodynamic definition of work is quite different from its colloquial meaning. Quite simply, ***work includes all forms of energy except heat.***

The law of conservation of energy states that energy (E) can be neither created nor destroyed; it can only be transferred between system and surroundings. That is,

$$\Delta E_{\text{system}} = -\Delta E_{\text{surroundings}}$$

The first law of thermodynamics goes a step further. Taking account of the fact that there are two kinds of energy, heat and work, the first law states:

If work is done on the system or if heat is added to it, its energy increases.

In any process, the total change in energy of a system, ΔE, is equal to the sum of the heat, q, and the work, w, transferred between the system and the surroundings.

$$\Delta E = q + w \qquad \textbf{(8.5)}$$

In applying the first law, note (Figure 8.10, p. 215) that q and w are positive when heat or work enters the system from the surroundings. If the transfer is in the opposite direction, from system to surroundings, q and w are negative.

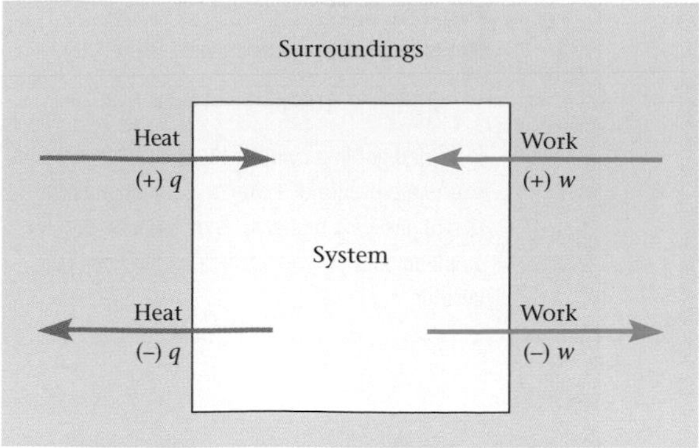

Figure 8.10
Heat and work. These quantities are positive when they enter a system and negative when they leave.

Example 8.9 Calculate ΔE of a gas for a process in which the gas

(a) absorbs 20 J of heat and does 12 J of work by expanding.
(b) evolves 30 J of heat and has 52 J of work done on it as it contracts.

Strategy First decide on the signs (+ or −) of q and w. Then substitute into the equation for ΔE.

SOLUTION

(a) $q = +20$ J; $w = -12$ J, because the gas does work on the surroundings.

$$\Delta E = +20\text{ J} - 12\text{ J} = +8\text{ J}$$

(b) $q = -30$ J; $w = +52$ J, because work is done on the gas by the surroundings.

$$\Delta E = -30\text{ J} + 52\text{ J} = +22\text{ J}$$

Ordinarily, when a chemical reaction is carried out in the laboratory, any energy evolved is in the form of heat. Consider, for example, the reaction of oxygen with methane, the principal constituent of natural gas.

$$CH_4(g) + 2\,O_2(g) \longrightarrow CO_2(g) + 2H_2O(l) \qquad \Delta E = -885\text{ kJ}$$

When you ignite methane in a Bunsen burner, the amount of heat evolved is very close to 885 kJ/mol. There is a small work effect, due to the decrease in volume that occurs when the reaction takes place (Fig. 8.11, p. 216), but this amounts to less than 1% of the energy change.

Dennis Bradbury Photos

(a) (b)

An automobile that runs on natural gas. (a) The vehicle pulled up to a CNG (compressed natural gas) pump. The gas is 90% methane, according to the label on the pump. (b) The car's gas tank (which occupies the dark space inside the back of the trunk) is being filled.

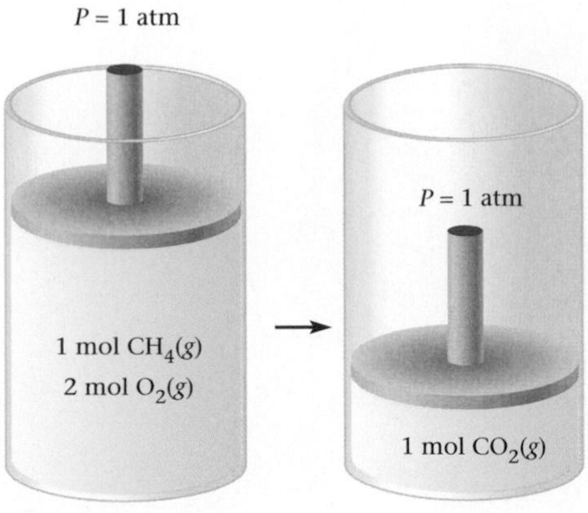

Figure 8.11
Pressure-volume work. When the reaction

$$CH_4(g) + 2O_2(g) \longrightarrow CO_2(g) + 2H_2O(l)$$

is carried out in a cylinder fitted with a piston that exerts a pressure of 1 atm, a contraction occurs (3 mol gas → 1 mol gas). The piston falls, and a small amount of work is done on the reaction system.

The situation changes if methane is used as a substitute for gasoline in an internal combustion engine. Here a significant fraction of the energy evolved in combustion is converted to useful work, propelling your car uphill, overcoming friction, charging the battery, or whatever. Depending on the efficiency of the engine, as much as 25% of the available energy might be converted to work; the amount of heat evolved through the tail pipe or radiator drops accordingly.

Finally, the energy available from the above reaction might be used to operate a fuel cell such as those involved in the space program. In that case, as much as 818 kJ/mol of useful electrical work could be obtained; relatively little heat is evolved. Summarizing this discussion in terms of an energy balance (per mole of methane reacting):

	ΔE	q	w
Bunsen burner	−885 kJ	−890 kJ	+5 kJ
Automobile engine	−885 kJ	−665 kJ	−220 kJ
Fuel cell	−885 kJ	−67 kJ	−818 kJ

Notice that ΔE, like ΔH, is a *state property;* it has the same value regardless of how or where or why the reaction is carried out. In contrast, q and w are path-dependent; their values vary depending on whether the reaction is carried out in the atmosphere, an engine, or an electrical cell.

ΔH Versus ΔE

As noted earlier, for a reaction at constant pressure, such as that taking place in an open coffee-cup calorimeter, the heat flow is equal to the change in enthalpy. If a reaction is carried out at constant volume (as is the case in a sealed bomb calorimeter) and there is no mechanical or electrical work involved, no work is done. Under these conditions, with $w = 0$, the heat flow is equal to the change in energy, ΔE. Hence we have

$$\Delta H = q_P \qquad \Delta E = q_v$$

(q_P = heat flow at constant pressure, q_v = heat flow at constant V).

Almost always, when you carry out a reaction in the laboratory, you do so at constant pressure, that of the atmosphere. That is why we devoted 90% of the space in this chapter to ΔH rather than ΔE.

We can obtain a relation between ΔH and ΔE for a chemical reaction at constant temperature by starting with the defining equation relating enthalpy, H, to energy, E:

$$H = E + PV$$

where V is the volume at pressure P. It follows that

$$\Delta H = \Delta E + \Delta(PV)$$

To evaluate $\Delta(PV)$ for a reaction note that—

- the PV product for a liquid or solid can be ignored, since their molar volume is typically only about 0.1% of that for a gas.
- gases taking part in the reaction can be assumed to obey the ideal gas law, $PV = nRT$.

It follows that

$$\Delta(PV) = \Delta n_g RT$$

where Δn_g is the change in the number of moles of gas when the reaction takes place. Finally, we obtain the relation

$$\Delta H = \Delta E + \Delta n_g RT \qquad \textbf{(8.6)}$$

For the reaction at 25°C

$$CH_4(g) + 2\,O_2(g) \longrightarrow CO_2(g) + 2H_2O(l)$$
$$\Delta n_g = n \text{ gaseous products} - n \text{ gaseous reactants}$$
$$= 1 \text{ mol} - 3 \text{ mol} = -2 \text{ mol}$$
$$R = 8.31 \text{ J/mol} \cdot \text{K} \qquad \text{(recall Table 5.1, page 107)}$$
$$T = (273 + 25) \text{ K} = 298 \text{ K}$$

Energy can also be expressed in liter-atmospheres: $1 \text{ L} \cdot \text{atm} = 0.1013$ kJ.

Hence:

$$\Delta H = \Delta E - 2 \text{ mol } (8.31 \text{ J/mol} \cdot \text{K})(298 \text{ K})$$
$$= \Delta E - 5.0 \times 10^3 \text{ J} = \Delta E - 5.0 \text{ kJ}$$

Recall that ΔE for this reaction is -885 kJ; it follows that ΔH is -890 kJ. The difference between ΔE and ΔH is less than 1%, which is typical for most reactions.

Example 8.10 Calculate ΔH and ΔE at 25°C for the reaction that takes place when an oxyacetylene torch is used.

$$C_2H_2(g) + \tfrac{5}{2}\,O_2(g) \longrightarrow 2CO_2(g) + H_2O(g)$$

Strategy First, calculate ΔH using heats of formation in Table 8.3. Then calculate ΔE using Equation 8.6.

SOLUTION

$$\Delta H = 2\Delta H_f^\circ\, CO_2(g) + \Delta H_f^\circ\, H_2O(g) - \Delta H_f^\circ\, C_2H_2(g)$$
$$= 2(-393.5 \text{ kJ}) - 241.8 \text{ kJ} - 226.7 \text{ kJ} = -1255.5 \text{ kJ}$$
$$\Delta n_g = 2 + 1 - (1 + 2\tfrac{1}{2}) = -0.5 \text{ mol}$$
$$\Delta E = \Delta H - \Delta n_g RT$$
$$= -1255.5 \text{ kJ} - (-0.5 \text{ mol} \times 8.31 \text{ J/mol} \cdot \text{K} \times 298 \text{ K})$$
$$= -1255.5 \text{ kJ} + 1.24 \times 10^3 \text{ J} = -1255.5 \text{ kJ} + 1.2 \text{ kJ} = -1254.3 \text{ kJ}$$

Reality Check Note that in this case ΔH and ΔE differ from one another by only about 0.1%, a very small difference indeed.

CHEMISTRY Beyond the Classroom

Energy Balance in the Human Body

All of us require energy to maintain life processes and do the muscular work associated with such activities as studying, writing, walking, or jogging. The fuel used to produce that energy is the food we eat. In this discussion, we focus on energy input or energy output and the balance between them.

Energy Input

Energy values of food can be estimated on the basis of the content of carbohydrate, protein, and fat:

carbohydrate:	17 kJ (4.0 kcal) of energy per gram*
protein:	17 kJ (4.0 kcal) of energy per gram
fat:	38 kJ (9.0 kcal) of energy per gram

Alcohol, which doesn't fit into any of these categories, furnishes about 29 kJ (7.0 kcal) per gram.

Using these guidelines, it is possible to come up with the data given in Table A, which lists approximate energy values for standard portions of different types of foods. With a little practice, you can use the table to estimate your energy input within ±10%.

*In most nutrition texts, energy is expressed in kilocalories rather than kilojoules, although that situation is changing. Remember that 1 kcal = 4.18 kJ; 1 kg = 2.20 lb.

Table A Energy Values of Food Portions*

		kJ	kcal
Skim milk	8-oz glass (250 g)	347	83
Whole milk	8-oz glass (250 g)	610	146
Beer	12-oz glass (375 g)	493	118
Mixed vegetables	1/2 cup (125 g)	247	59
Broccoli	1/2 cup (125 g)	63	15
Yellow corn	1 ear	447	107
Fruit cocktail	1/2 cup (125 g)	230	55
Whole wheat bread	1 slice	272	65
Baked potato	1 item	920	220
Black beans	1/2 cup (125 g)	477	114
Lean ground beef	3 oz (84 g)	966	231
Ground turkey	3 oz (84 g)	836	200
Butter	1 tablespoon (15 g)	451	108
Olive oil	1 tablespoon (15 g)	497	119
Canola oil	1 tablespoon (15 g)	502	120
Sugar	1 teaspoon (5 g)	63	15

*Adapted from Michelle McGuire and Kathy A. Beerman: *Table of Food Composition for Nutritional Sciences: From Fundamentals to Food,* Thomson Wadsworth, Belmont, CA, 2007.

Energy Output

Energy output can be divided, more or less arbitrarily, into two categories.

1. Metabolic energy. This is the largest item in most people's energy budget; it comprises the energy necessary to maintain life. Metabolic rates are ordinarily estimated based on a person's sex, weight, and age. For a young adult female, the metabolic rate is about 100 kJ per day per kilogram of body weight. For a 20-year-old woman weighing 120 lb

$$\text{metabolic rate} = 120\text{ lb} \times \frac{1\text{ kg}}{2.20\text{ lb}} \times 100\frac{\text{kJ}}{\text{d}\cdot\text{kg}}$$

$$= 5500\text{ kJ/d (1300 kcal/day)}$$

For a young adult male of the same weight, the figure is about 15% higher.

2. Muscular activity. Energy is consumed whenever your muscles contract, whether in writing, walking, playing tennis, or even sitting in class. Generally speaking, energy expenditure for muscular activity ranges from 50% to 100% of metabolic energy, depending on lifestyle. If the 20-year-old woman referred to earlier is a student who does nothing more strenuous than lift textbooks (and that not too often), the energy spent on muscular activity might be

$$0.50 \times 5500\text{ kJ} = 2800\frac{\text{kJ}}{\text{d}}$$

Her total energy output per day would be 5500 kJ + 2800 kJ = 8300 kJ (2000 kcal).

Energy Balance

To maintain constant weight, your daily energy input, as calculated from the foods you eat, should be about 700 kJ (170 kcal) greater than output. The difference allows for the fact that about 40 g of protein is required to maintain body tissues and fluids. If the excess of input over output is greater than 700 kJ/day, the unused food (carbohydrate, protein, or fat) is converted to fatty tissue and stored as such in the body.

Fatty tissue consists of about 85% fat and 15% water; its energy value is

$$0.85 \times 9.0\frac{\text{kcal}}{\text{g}} \times \frac{454\text{ g}}{1\text{ lb}} = 3500\text{ kcal/lb}$$

This means that to lose one pound of fat, energy input from foods must be decreased by about 3500 kcal. To lose weight at a sensible rate of one pound per week, it is necessary to cut down by 500 kcal (2100 kJ) per day.

It's also possible, of course, to lose weight by increasing muscular activity. Table B shows the amount of energy consumed per hour with various types of exercise. In principle, you can lose a pound a week by climbing mountains for an hour each day, provided you're not already doing that (most people aren't). Alternatively, you could spend $1\frac{1}{2}$ hours a day ice skating or water skiing, depending on the weather.

Table B Energy Consumed by Various Types of Exercise*

kJ/hour	kcal/hour	
1000–1250	240–300	Walking (3 mph), bowling, golf (pulling cart)
1250–1500	300–360	Volleyball, calisthenics, golf (carrying clubs)
1500–1750	360–420	Ice skating, roller skating
1750–2000	420–480	Tennis (singles), water skiing
2000–2500	480–600	Jogging (5 mph), downhill skiing, mountain climbing
>2500	>600	Running (6 mph), basketball, soccer

*Adapted from Jane Brody: *Jane Brody's Nutrition Book: A Lifetime Guide to Good Eating for Better Health and Weight Control by the Personal Health Columnist for the New York Times.* Norton, New York, 1981.

Chapter Highlights

Key Concepts

1. Relate heat flow to specific heat, m, and Δt.
   (Example 8.1; Problems 1–6) ■ Questions and Problems assignable in OWL: 2, 4, 84, 85
2. Calculate q for a reaction from calorimetric data.
   (Examples 8.2, 8.3; Problems 7–20) ■ 9, 10, 12, 15
3. Apply the rules of thermochemistry
   (Examples 8.4, 8.5; Problems 21–30) ■ 23, 26
4. Apply Hess's law to calculate ΔH.
   (Example 8.6; Problems 31–36) ■ 33, 35
5. Relate $\Delta H°$ to enthalpies of formation.
   (Examples 8.7, 8.8; Problems 37–52) ■ 37, 39, 42, 44, 46
6. Relate ΔE, q, and w.
   (Example 8.9; Problems 53–58) ■ 53, 56
7. Relate ΔH and ΔE.
   (Example 8.10; Problems 59–62) ■ 69

Select end of chapter Questions and Problems may be assigned in OWL and are cross-referenced in the Key Concepts list.

CENGAGENOW™

Sign in at **academic.cengage.com/now** to:

- Check your readiness for an exam by taking the Pre-Test and exploring the self-study modules recommended in your Personalized Study plan
- For quick review, download Go Chemistry mini-lecture flashcard modules (or purchase them at **www.ichapters.com**)

Key Equations

Heat flow	$q = m \times c \times \Delta t$ (Section 8.1)
Coffee-cup calorimeter	$q_{reaction} = -m_{water} \times 4.18\ J/g \cdot °C \times \Delta t$ (Section 8.2)
Bomb calorimeter	$q_{reaction} = -C_{cal} \times \Delta t$ (Section 8.2)
Standard enthalpy change	$\Delta H° = \Sigma\ \Delta H_f°\ \text{products} - \Sigma\ \Delta H_f°\ \text{reactants}$ (Section 8.5)
First law of thermodynamics	$\Delta E = q + w$ (Section 8.7)
ΔH versus ΔE	$\Delta H = \Delta E + \Delta n_g RT$ (Section 8.7)

Key Terms

bond enthalpy
calorimeter
—bomb
—coffee-cup
endothermic
exothermic
enthalpy
—of formation
heat
—capacity
—of fusion
Hess's law
joule
kilojoule
specific heat
state property
surroundings
system
thermochemical equation
work

Summary Problem

Carbon tetrachloride is a common commercial solvent. It can be prepared by the reaction of chlorine gas with carbon disulfide. The equation for the reaction is

$$CS_2(l) + 3Cl_2(g) \longrightarrow CCl_4(l) + S_2Cl_2(l)$$

(a) It is determined that when 2.500 g of CS_2 reacts with an excess of Cl_2 gas, 9.310 kJ of heat is evolved. Is the reaction exothermic? What is $\Delta H°$ for the reaction?
(b) Write the thermochemical equation for the reaction.
(c) What is $\Delta H°$ for the reaction

$$\tfrac{1}{3}CCl_4(l) + \tfrac{1}{3}S_2Cl_2(l) \longrightarrow \tfrac{1}{3}CS_2(l) + Cl_2(g)$$

(d) What volume of chlorine gas at 27°C, 812 mm Hg, is required to react with an excess of $CS_2(l)$ so that 5.00 kJ of heat is evolved?
(e) If $\Delta H_f°$ for $CS_2(l)$ = 89.9 kJ, what is $\Delta H_f°$ for S_2Cl_2?
(f) Ten milligrams of CS_2 reacts with an excess of chlorine gas. The heat evolved is transferred without loss to 6.450 g of water at 22.0°C. What is the final temperature of the water?
(g) How much heat is evolved when 50.0 mL of CS_2 (d = 1.263 g/mL) reacts with 5.00 L of chlorine gas at 2.78 atm and 27°C?

Answers

(a) yes; −283.5 kJ
(b) $CS_2(l) + 3\ Cl_2(g) \longrightarrow CCl_4(l) + S_2Cl_2(l) \qquad \Delta H° = -283.5$ kJ
(c) 94.50 kJ
(d) 1.22 L
(e) −58.2 kJ/mol
(f) 23.4°C
(g) 53.3 kJ

Questions and Problems

Blue-numbered questions have answers in Appendix 6 and fully-worked solutions in the *Student Solutions Manual.*

■ denotes questions assignable in OWL.

WEB indicates that the solution is available on this book's companion website.

Principles of Heat Flow

1. Titanium is a metal used in jet engines. Its specific heat is 0.523 J/g · °C. If 5.88 g of titanium absorbs 4.78 J, what is the change in temperature?

2. ■ Gold has a specific heat of 0.129 J/g · °C. When a 5.00-g piece of gold absorbs 1.33 J of heat, what is the change in temperature?

3. Stainless steel accessories in cars are usually plated with chromium to give them a shiny surface and to prevent rusting. When 5.00 g of chromium at 23.00°C absorbs 62.5 J of heat, the temperature increases to 50.8°C. What is the specific heat of chromium?

4. ■ Copper is used in building the integrated circuits, chips, and printed circuit boards for computers. When 228 J of heat are absorbed by 125 g of copper at 22.38°C, the temperature increases to 27.12°C. What is the specific heat of copper?

5. The specific heat of aluminum is 0.902 J/g · °C. How much heat is absorbed by an aluminum pie tin with a mass of 473 g to raise its temperature from room temperature (23.00°C) to oven temperature (375°F)?

6. Mercury has a specific heat of 0.140 J/g · °C. Assume that a thermometer has 20 (2 significant figures) grams of mercury. How much heat is absorbed by the mercury when the temperature in the thermometer increases from 98.6°F to 103.2°F? (Assume no heat loss to the glass of the thermometer.)

Calorimetry

7. Magnesium sulfate is often used in first-aid hot packs, giving off heat when dissolved in water. When 2.00 g of $MgSO_4$ dissolves in 15.0 mL of water (d = 1.00 g/mL) at 25°C in a coffee-cup calorimeter, 1.51 kJ of heat is evolved.
(a) Write a balanced equation for the solution process.
(b) Is the process exothermic?
(c) What is q_{H_2O}?
(d) What is the final temperature of the solution? (Specific heat of water is 4.18 J/g · °C.)
(e) What are the initial and final temperatures in °F?

8. **WEB** Urea, $(NH_2)_2CO$, is used in the manufacture of resins and glues. When 5.00 g of urea is dissolved in 250.0 mL of water (d = 1.00 g/mL) at 30.0°C in a coffee-cup calorimeter, 27.6 kJ of heat is absorbed.
(a) Is the solution process exothermic?
(b) What is q_{H_2O}?
(c) What is the final temperature of the solution? (Specific heat of water is 4.18 J/g · °C.)
(d) What are the initial and final temperatures in °F?

9. ■ When 225 mL of H_2O at 25°C are mixed with 85 mL of water at 89°C, what is the final temperature? (Assume that no heat is lost to the surroundings; d_{H_2O} = 1.00 g/mL.)

10. ■ How many mL of water at 10°C (2 significant figures) must be added to 75 mL of water at 35°C to obtain a final temperature of 19°C? (Make the same assumptions as in Question 9.)

11. When 35.0 mL of 1.43 M NaOH at 22.0°C is neutralized by 35.0 mL of HCl also at 22.0°C in a coffee-cup calorimeter, the temperature of the final solution rises to 31.29°C. Assume that the specific heat of all solutions is 4.18 J/g · °C, that the density of all solutions is 1.00 g/mL, and that volumes are additive.
(a) Calculate q for the reaction.
(b) Calculate q for the neutralization of one mole of NaOH.

12. ■ When one mole of KOH is neutralized by sulfuric acid, $q = -56$ kJ. At 22.8°C, 25.0 mL of 0.500 M H_2SO_4 is neutralized by 50.0 mL of 0.500 M KOH in a coffee-cup calorimeter. What is the final temperature of the solution? (Use the assumptions in Question 11.)

13. Fructose is a sugar commonly found in fruit. A sample of fructose, $C_6H_{12}O_6$, weighing 4.50 g is burned in a bomb calorimeter. The heat capacity of the calorimeter is 2.115×10^4 J/°C. The temperature in the calorimeter rises from 23.49°C to 27.71°C.

(a) What is q for the calorimeter?
(b) What is q when 4.50 g of fructose is burned?
(c) What is q for the combustion of one mole of fructose?

14. In earlier times, ethyl ether was commonly used as an anesthetic. It is, however, highly flammable. When five milliliters of ethyl ether, $C_4H_{10}O(l)$, ($d = 0.714$ g/mL) is burned in a bomb calorimeter, the temperature rises from 23.5°C to 39.7°C. The calorimeter heat capacity is 10.34 kJ/°C.

(a) What is q for the calorimeter?
(b) What is q when 5.00 mL of ethyl ether is burned?
(c) What is q for the combustion of one mole of ethyl ether?

15. ■ Isooctane is a primary component of gasoline and gives gasoline its octane rating. Burning 1.00 mL of isooctane ($d = 0.688$ g/mL) releases 33.0 kJ of heat. When 10.00 mL of isooctane is burned in a bomb calorimeter, the temperature in the bomb rises from 23.2°C to 66.5°C. What is the heat capacity of the bomb calorimeter?

16. **WEB** When one mole of caffeine ($C_8H_{10}N_4O_2$) is burned in air, 4.96×10^3 kJ of heat is evolved. Five grams of caffeine is burned in a bomb calorimeter. The temperature is observed to increase by 11.37°C. What is the heat capacity of the calorimeter in J/°C?

17. Isooctane, C_8H_{18}, is a component of gasoline. When 0.500 g of isooctane is burned, 24.06 kJ of heat is given off. If 10.00 mg of isooctane is burned in a bomb calorimeter (heat capacity = 5175 J/°C) initially at 23.6°C, what is the temperature of the calorimeter when reaction is complete?

18. Acetylene, C_2H_2, is used in welding torches. It releases a lot of energy when burned in oxygen. One gram of acetylene releases 48.2 kJ. When 0.750 g of acetylene is burned in a bomb calorimeter (heat capacity = 1.117 kJ/°C), the final temperature of the bomb is 54.5°C. What is the initial temperature of the calorimeter?

19. Salicylic acid, $C_7H_6O_3$, is one of the starting materials in the manufacture of aspirin. When 1.00 g of salicylic acid burns in a bomb calorimeter, the temperature rises from 23.11°C to 28.91°C. The temperature in the bomb calorimeter increases by 2.48°C when the calorimeter absorbs 9.37 kJ. How much heat is given off when one mole of salicylic acid is burned?

20. Naphthalene, $C_{10}H_8$, is the compound present in moth balls. When one mole of naphthalene is burned, 5.15×10^3 kJ of heat is evolved. A sample of naphthalene burned in a bomb calorimeter (heat capacity = 9832 J/°C) increases the temperature in the calorimeter from 25.1°C to 28.4°C. How many milligrams of naphthalene were burned?

Thermochemical Equations

21. Nitrogen oxide (NO) has been found to be a key component in many biological processes. It also can react with oxygen to give the brown gas NO_2. When one mole of NO reacts with oxygen, 57.0 kJ of heat is evolved.

(a) Write the thermochemical equation for the reaction between one mole of nitrogen oxide and oxygen.
(b) Is the reaction exothermic or endothermic?
(c) Draw an energy diagram showing the path of this reaction. (Figure 8.4 is an example of such an energy diagram.)
(d) What is ΔH when 5.00 g of nitrogen oxide reacts?
(e) How many grams of nitrogen oxide must react with an excess of oxygen to liberate ten kilojoules of heat?

22. Calcium carbide, CaC_2, is the raw material for the production of acetylene (used in welding torches). Calcium carbide is produced by reacting calcium oxide with carbon, producing carbon monoxide as a byproduct. When one mole of calcium carbide is formed, 464.8 kJ is absorbed.

(a) Write a thermochemical equation for this reaction.
(b) Is the reaction exothermic or endothermic?
(c) Draw an energy diagram showing the path of this reaction. (Figure 8.4 is an example of such an energy diagram.)
(d) What is ΔH when 1.00 g of $CaC_2(g)$ is formed?
(e) How many grams of carbon are used up when 20.00 kJ of heat is absorbed?

23. ■ In the late eighteenth century Priestley prepared ammonia by reacting $HNO_3(g)$ with hydrogen gas. The thermodynamic equation for the reaction is

$$HNO_3(g) + 4H_2(g) \longrightarrow NH_3(g) + 3H_2O(g) \qquad \Delta H = -637 \text{ kJ}$$

(a) Calculate ΔH when one mole of hydrogen gas reacts.
(b) What is ΔH when 10.00 g of $NH_3(g)$ is made to react with an excess of steam to form HNO_3 and H_2 gases?

24. In photosynthesis, the following reaction takes place:

$$6CO_2(g) + 6H_2O(l) \longrightarrow 6\,O_2(g) + C_6H_{12}O_6(s) \qquad \Delta H = 2801 \text{ kJ}$$

(a) Calculate ΔH when one mole of CO_2 reacts.
(b) How many kilojoules of energy are liberated when 15.00 g of glucose, $C_6H_{12}O_6$, is burned in oxygen?

25. Strontium metal is responsible for the red color in fireworks. Fireworks manufacturers use strontium carbonate, which can be produced by combining strontium metal, graphite (C), and oxygen gas. The formation of one mole of $SrCO_3$ releases 1.220×10^3 kJ of energy.

(a) Write a balanced thermochemical equation for the reaction.
(b) What is ΔH when 10.00 L of oxygen at 25°C and 1.00 atm is used by the reaction?

26. ■ Nitroglycerine, $C_3H_5(NO_3)_3(l)$, is an explosive most often used in mine or quarry blasting. It is a powerful explosive because four gases (N_2, O_2, CO_2, and steam) are formed when nitroglycerine is detonated. In addition, 6.26 kJ of heat is given off per gram of nitroglycerine detonated.

(a) Write a balanced thermochemical equation for the reaction.
(b) What is ΔH when 4.65 mol of products is formed?

27. A typical fat in the body is glyceryl trioleate, $C_{57}H_{104}O_6$. When it is metabolized in the body, it combines with oxygen to produce carbon dioxide, water, and 3.022×10^4 kJ of heat per mole of fat.

(a) Write a balanced thermochemical equation for the metabolism of fat.
(b) How many kilojoules of energy must be evolved in the form of heat if you want to get rid of five pounds of this fat by combustion?
(c) How many nutritional calories is this? (1 nutritional calorie = 1×10^3 calories)

28. **WEB** Using the same metabolism of fat equation from Question 27, how many grams of fat would have to be burned to heat 100.0 mL of water ($d = 1.00$ g/mL) from 22.00°C to 25.00°C? The specific heat of water is 4.18 J/g · °C.

29. Which requires the absorption of a greater amount of heat—vaporizing 100.0 g of benzene or boiling 20.0 g of water? (Use Table 8.2.)

30. Which evolves more heat—freezing 100.0 g of benzene or 100.0 g of bromine?

■ in OWL Blue-numbered questions answered in Appendix 6 **WEB** Solution is available on companion website

31. A student is asked to calculate the amount of heat involved in changing 10.0 g of liquid bromine at room temperature (22.5°C) to vapor at 59.0°C. To do this, one must use Tables 8.1 and 8.2 for information on the specific heat, boiling point, and heat of vaporization of bromine. In addition, the following step-wise process must be followed.

(a) Calculate ΔH for: $Br_2(l, 22.5°C) \longrightarrow Br_2(l, 59.0°C)$

(b) Calculate ΔH for: $Br_2(l, 59.0°C) \longrightarrow Br_2(g, 59.0°C)$

(c) Using Hess's law, calculate ΔH for: $Br_2(l, 22.5°C) \longrightarrow Br_2(g, 59.0°C)$

32. Follow the step-wise process outlined in Problem 31 to calculate the amount of heat involved in condensing 100.00 g of benzene gas (C_6H_6) at 80.00°C to liquid benzene at 25.00°C. Use Tables 8.1 and 8.2 for the specific heat, boiling point, and heat of vaporization of benzene.

33. ■ A lead ore, galena, consisting mainly of lead(II) sulfide, is the principal source of lead. To obtain the lead, the ore is first heated in the air to form lead oxide.

$$PbS(s) + \tfrac{3}{2}O_2(g) \longrightarrow PbO(s) + SO_2(g) \qquad \Delta H = -415.4 \text{ kJ}$$

The oxide is then reduced to metal with carbon.

$$PbO(s) + C(s) \longrightarrow Pb(s) + CO(g) \qquad \Delta H = +108.5 \text{ kJ}$$

Calculate ΔH for the reaction of one mole of lead(II) sulfide with oxygen and carbon, forming lead, sulfur dioxide, and carbon monoxide.

34. To produce silicon, used in semiconductors, from sand (SiO_2), a reaction is used that can be broken down into three steps:

$$SiO_2(s) + 2C(s) \longrightarrow Si(s) + 2CO(g) \qquad \Delta H = 689.9 \text{ kJ}$$
$$Si(s) + 2Cl_2(g) \longrightarrow SiCl_4(g) \qquad \Delta H = -657.0 \text{ kJ}$$
$$SiCl_4(g) + 2Mg(s) \longrightarrow 2MgCl_2(s) + Si(s) \qquad \Delta H = -625.6 \text{ kJ}$$

(a) Write the thermochemical equation for the overall reaction for the formation of silicon from silicon dioxide; CO and $MgCl_2$ are byproducts.

(b) What is ΔH for the formation of one mole of silicon?

(c) Is the overall reaction exothermic?

35. ■ Given the following thermochemical equations,

$$C_2H_2(g) + \tfrac{5}{2}O_2(g) \longrightarrow 2CO_2(g) + H_2O(l) \qquad \Delta H = -1299.5 \text{ kJ}$$
$$C(s) + O_2(g) \longrightarrow CO_2(g) \qquad \Delta H = -393.5 \text{ kJ}$$
$$H_2(g) + \tfrac{1}{2}O_2(g) \longrightarrow H_2O(l) \qquad \Delta H = -285.8 \text{ kJ}$$

calculate ΔH for the decomposition of one mole of acetylene, $C_2H_2(g)$, to its elements in their stable state at 25°C and 1 atm.

36. Given the following thermochemical equations

$$2H_2(g) + O_2(g) \longrightarrow 2H_2O(l) \qquad \Delta H = -571.6 \text{ kJ}$$
$$N_2O_5(g) + H_2O(l) \longrightarrow 2HNO_3(l) \qquad \Delta H = -73.7 \text{ kJ}$$
$$\tfrac{1}{2}N_2(g) + \tfrac{3}{2}O_2(g) + \tfrac{1}{2}H_2(g) \longrightarrow HNO_3(l) \qquad \Delta H = -174.1 \text{ kJ}$$

calculate ΔH for the formation of one mole of dinitrogen pentoxide from its elements in their stable state at 25°C and 1 atm.

$\Delta H°$ and Heats of Formation

37. ■ Write thermochemical equations for the decomposition of one mole of the following compounds into the elements in their stable states at 25°C and 1 atm.

(a) ethyl alcohol, C_2H_5OH (*l*) (b) sodium fluoride (*s*)
(c) magnesium sulfate (*s*) (d) ammonium nitrate (*s*)

38. Write thermochemical equations for the formation of one mole of the following compounds from the elements in their stable states at 25°C and 1 atm.

(a) acetylene, C_2H_2 (*g*) (b) nitrogen dioxide (*g*)
(c) lead(II) bromide (*s*) (d) phosphorus pentachloride (*g*)

39. ■ Given

$$2Al_2O_3(s) \longrightarrow 4Al(s) + 3O_2(g) \qquad \Delta H° = 3351.4 \text{ kJ}$$

(a) What is the heat of formation of aluminum oxide?

(b) What is $\Delta H°$ for the formation of 12.50 g of aluminum oxide?

40. Given

$$2CuO(s) \longrightarrow 2Cu(s) + O_2(g) \qquad \Delta H° = 314.6 \text{ kJ}$$

(a) Determine the heat of formation of CuO.

(b) Calculate $\Delta H°$ for the formation of 13.58 g of CuO.

41. Limestone, $CaCO_3$, when subjected to a temperature of 900°C in a kiln, decomposes to calcium oxide and carbon dioxide. How much heat is evolved or absorbed when one gram of limestone decomposes? (Use Table 8.3.)

42. ■ When ammonia reacts with oxygen, nitrogen oxide gas and steam are formed. How much heat is evolved or absorbed when one liter of ammonia gas at 23.0°C and at 765 mm Hg reacts?

43. Use Table 8.3 to obtain $\Delta H°$ for the following thermochemical equations:

(a) $Mg(OH)_2(s) + 2NH_4^+(aq) \rightarrow Mg^{2+}(aq) + 2NH_3(g) + 2H_2O(l)$

(b) $PbO(s) + C(s) \rightarrow CO(g) + Pb(s)$

(c) $Mn(s) + 4H^+(aq) + SO_4^{2-}(aq) \rightarrow Mn^{2+}(aq) + SO_2(g) + 2H_2O(l)$

44. ■ Use Table 8.3 to obtain $\Delta H°$ for the following thermochemical equations:

(a) $Zn(s) + 2H^+(aq) \rightarrow Zn^{2+}(aq) + H_2(g)$

(b) $2H_2S(g) + 3O_2(g) \rightarrow 2SO_2(g) + 2H_2O(g)$

(c) $3Ni(s) + 2NO_3^-(aq) + 8H^+(aq) \rightarrow 3Ni^{2+}(aq) + 2NO(g) + 4H_2O(l)$

45. Use the appropriate table to calculate $\Delta H°$ for

(a) the reaction between calcium hydroxide and carbon dioxide to form calcium carbonate and steam.

(b) the decomposition of one mole of liquid sulfuric acid to steam, oxygen, and sulfur dioxide gas.

46. ■ Use the appropriate table to calculate $\Delta H°$ for

(a) the reaction between copper(II) oxide and carbon monoxide to give copper metal and carbon dioxide.

(b) the decomposition of one mole of methyl alcohol (CH_3OH) to methane and oxygen gases.

47. Butane, C_4H_{10}, is widely used as a fuel for disposable lighters. When one mole of butane is burned in oxygen, carbon dioxide and steam are formed and 2658.3 kJ of heat is evolved.

(a) Write a thermochemical equation for the reaction.

(b) Using Table 8.3, calculate the standard heat of formation of butane.

48. When one mole of calcium carbonate reacts with ammonia, solid calcium cyanamide, $CaCN_2$, and liquid water are formed. The reaction absorbs 90.1 kJ of heat.

(a) Write a balanced thermochemical equation for the reaction.

(b) Using Table 8.3, calculate $\Delta H_f°$ for calcium cyanamide.

49. Chlorine trifluoride is a toxic, intensely reactive gas. It was used in World War II to make incendiary bombs. It reacts with ammonia and forms nitrogen, chlorine, and hydrogen fluoride gases. When two moles of chlorine trifluoride reacts, 1196 kJ of heat is evolved.

(a) Write a thermochemical equation for the reaction.

(b) What is $\Delta H_f°$ for ClF_3?

50. Nitroglycerine, $C_3H_5(NO_3)_3(l)$, is a powerful explosive used in rock blasting when roads are created. When ignited, it produces water, nitrogen, carbon dioxide, and oxygen. Detonation of one mole of nitroglycerine liberates 5725 kJ of heat.

(a) Write a balanced thermochemical equation for the reaction for the detonation of four moles of nitroglycerine.

(b) What is $\Delta H_f°$ for $C_3H_5(NO_3)_3(l)$?

■ in OWL Blue-numbered questions answered in Appendix 6 WEB Solution is available on companion website

51. Glucose, $C_6H_{12}O_6(s)$, ($\Delta H_f^\circ = -1275.2$ kJ/mol) is converted to ethyl alcohol, $C_2H_5OH(l)$, and carbon dioxide in the fermentation of grape juice. What quantity of heat is liberated when 750.0 mL of wine containing 12.0% ethyl alcohol by volume ($d = 0.789$ g/cm^3) is produced by the fermentation of grape juice?

52. When ammonia reacts with dinitrogen oxide gas ($\Delta H_f^\circ = 82.05$ kJ/mol), liquid water and nitrogen gas are formed. How much heat is liberated or absorbed by the reaction that produces 345 mL of nitrogen gas at 25°C and 717 mm Hg?

First Law of Thermodynamics

53. ■ How many kJ are equal to 3.27 L · atm of work?

54. How many L · atm are equal to 12.2 kJ of work?

55. Find

(a) ΔE when a gas absorbs 18 J of heat and has 13 J of work done on it.

(b) q when 72 J of work is done on a system and its energy is increased by 61 J.

56. ■ Calculate

(a) q when a system does 54 J of work and its energy decreases by 72 J.

(b) ΔE for a gas that releases 38 J of heat and has 102 J of work done on it.

57. Consider the following reaction in a vessel with a movable piston.

$$X(g) + Y(g) \longrightarrow Z(l)$$

As the reaction occurs, the system loses 1185 J of heat. The piston moves down and the surroundings do 623 J of work on the system. What is ΔE?

58. Consider the following reaction in the vessel of Question 57.

$$A(g) + B(g) \longrightarrow C(s)$$

For this reaction, $\Delta E = -329$ J, the piston moves down and the system loses 925 J of heat to the surroundings. Is work done by the system or by the surroundings? How much work?

59. Determine the difference between ΔH and ΔE at 25°C for

$$2CO(g) + O_2(g) \longrightarrow 2CO_2(g)$$

60. For the vaporization of one mole of water at 100°C determine

(a) ΔH (Table 8.3) (b) ΔPV (in kilojoules) (c) ΔE

61. Consider the combustion of propane, C_3H_8, the fuel that is commonly used in portable gas barbeque grills. The products of combustion are carbon dioxide and liquid water.

(a) Write a thermochemical equation for the combustion of one mole of propane.

(b) Calculate ΔE for the combustion of propane at 25°C.

62. Consider the combustion of one mole of acetylene, C_2H_2, which yields carbon dioxide and liquid water.

(a) Using Table 8.3, calculate ΔH.

(b) Calculate ΔE at 25°C.

Unclassified

63. Natural gas is almost entirely methane, CH_4. What volume of natural gas at 20°C and 1.00 atm pressure is required to heat one quart of water ($d = 1.00$ g/mL) from 20°C to 100°C? The density of methane at 20°C is 0.665 g/mL. The reaction for the combustion of methane is

$$CH_4(g) + 2O_2(g) \longrightarrow CO_2(g) + 2H_2O(g)$$

64. The BTU (British thermal unit) is the unit of energy most commonly used in the United States. One joule = 9.48×10^{-4} BTU. What is the specific heat of water in BTU/lb · °F? (Specific heat of water is 4.18 J/g · °C.)

65. Natural gas companies in the United States use the "therm" as a unit of energy. One therm is 1×10^5 BTU.

(a) How many joules are in one therm? (1 J = 9.48×10^{-4} BTU)

(b) When propane gas, C_3H_8, is burned in oxygen, CO_2 and steam are produced. How many therms of energy are given off by 1.00 mol of propane gas?

66. A 12-oz can of most colas has about 120 nutritional calories (1 nutritional calorie = 1 kilocalorie). Approximately how many minutes of walking are required to burn up as energy the calories taken in after drinking a can of cola? (Walking uses up about 250 kcal/h.)

67. Given the following reactions,

$$N_2H_4(l) + O_2(g) \longrightarrow N_2(g) + 2H_2O(g) \qquad \Delta H^\circ = -534.2 \text{ kJ}$$
$$H_2(g) + \tfrac{1}{2}O_2(g) \longrightarrow H_2O(g) \qquad \Delta H^\circ = -241.8 \text{ kJ}$$

calculate the heat of formation of hydrazine.

68. In World War II, the Germans made use of otherwise unusable airplane parts by grinding them up into powdered aluminum. This was made to react with ammonium nitrate to produce powerful bombs. The products of this reaction were nitrogen gas, steam, and aluminum oxide. If 10.00 kg of ammonium nitrate is mixed with 10.00 kg of powdered aluminum, how much heat is generated?

69. ■ One way to lose weight is to exercise. Playing tennis for half an hour consumes about 225 kcal of energy. How long would you have to play tennis to lose one pound of body fat? (One gram of body fat is equivalent to 32 kJ of energy.)

70. Consider the reaction of methane with oxygen. Suppose that the reaction is carried out in a furnace used to heat a house. If $q = -890$ kJ and $w = +5$ kJ, what is ΔE? ΔH at 25°C?

71. Brass has a density of 8.25 g/cm^3 and a specific heat of 0.362 J/g · °C. A cube of brass 22.00 mm on an edge is heated in a Bunsen burner flame to a temperature of 95.0°C. It is then immersed into 20.0 mL of water (d = 1.00 g/mL, c = 4.18 J/g · °C) at 22.0°C in an insulated container. Assuming no heat loss, what is the final temperature of the water?

72. On complete combustion at constant pressure, a 1.00-L sample of a gaseous mixture at 0°C and 1.00 atm (STP) evolves 75.65 kJ of heat. If the gas is a mixture of ethane (C_2H_6) and propane (C_3H_8), what is the mole fraction of ethane in the mixture?

73. Microwave ovens convert radiation to energy. A microwave oven uses radiation with a wavelength of 12.5 cm. Assuming that all the energy from the radiation is converted to heat without loss, how many moles of photons are required to raise the temperature of a cup of water (350.0 g, specific heat = 4.18 J/g · °C) from 23.0°C to 99.0°C?

74. Some solutes have large heats of solution, and care should be taken in preparing solutions of these substances. The heat evolved when sodium hydroxide dissolves is 44.5 kJ/mol. What is the final temperature of the water, originally at 20.0°C, used to prepare 1.25 L of 6.00 M NaOH solution? Assume that all the heat is absorbed by 1.25 L of water, specific heat = 4.18 J/g · °C.

75. Some solar-heated homes use large beds of rocks to store heat.

(a) How much heat is absorbed by 100.0 kg of rocks if their temperature increases by 12°C? (Assume that c = 0.82 J/g · °C.)

(b) Assume that the rock pile has total surface area 2 m^2. At maximum intensity near the earth's surface, solar power is about 170 watts/m^2. (1 watt = 1 J/s.) How many minutes will it take for solar power to produce the 12°C increase in part (a)?

■ in OWL Blue-numbered questions answered in Appendix 6 **WEB** Solution is available on companion website

Conceptual Questions

76. Using Table 8.2, write thermochemical equations for the following.
  (a) mercury thawing
  (b) bromine vaporizing
  (c) benzene freezing
  (d) mercury condensing
  (e) naphthalene subliming

77. Draw a cylinder with a movable piston containing six molecules of a liquid. A pressure of 1 atm is exerted on the piston. Next draw the same cylinder after the liquid has been vaporized. A pressure of one atmosphere is still exerted on the piston. Is work done *on* the system or *by* the system?

78. Redraw the cylinder in Question 77 after work has been done on the system.

79. Which statement(s) is/are true about bond enthalpy?
  (a) Energy is required to break a bond.
  (b) ΔH for the formation of a bond is always a negative number.
  (c) Bond enthalpy is defined only for bonds broken or formed in the gaseous state.
  (d) Because the presence of π bonds does not influence the geometry of a molecule, the presence of π bonds does not affect the value of the bond enthalpy between two atoms either.
  (e) The bond enthalpy for a double bond between atoms A and B is twice that for a single bond between atoms A and B.

80. Equal masses of liquid A, initially at 100°C, and liquid B, initially at 50°C, are combined in an insulated container. The final temperature of the mixture is 80°C. All the heat flow occurs between the two liquids. The two liquids do not react with each other. Is the specific heat of liquid A larger than, equal to, or smaller than the specific heat of liquid B?

81. Determine whether the statements given below are true or false. Consider an endothermic process taking place in a beaker at room temperature.
  (a) Heat flows from the surroundings to the system.
  (b) The beaker is cold to the touch.
  (c) The pressure of the system decreases.
  (d) The value of q for the system is positive.

82. Determine whether the statements given below are true or false. Consider specific heat.
  (a) Specific heat represents the amount of heat required to raise the temperature of one gram of a substance by 1°C.
  (b) Specific heat is the amount of heat flowing into the system.
  (c) When 20 J of heat is added to equal masses of different materials at 25°C, the final temperature for all these materials will be the same.
  (d) Heat is measured in °C.

83. Determine whether the statements given below are true or false. Consider enthalpy (H).
  (a) It is a state property.
  (b) $q_{reaction}$ (at constant P) $= \Delta H = H_{products} - H_{reactants}$
  (c) The magnitude of ΔH is independent of the amount of reactant.
  (d) In an exothermic process, the enthalpy of the system remains unchanged.

Challenge Problems

84. ■ Microwave ovens emit microwave radiation that is absorbed by water. The absorbed radiation is converted to heat that is transferred to other components of the food. Suppose the microwave radiation has wavelength 12.5 cm. How many photons are required to increase the temperature of 100 mL of water (d = 1 g/mL) from 20°C to 100°C if all the energy of the photons is converted to heat?

85. ■ On a hot day, you take a six-pack of soda on a picnic, cooling it with ice. Each empty (aluminum) can weighs 12.5 g and contains 12.0 oz of soda. The specific heat of aluminum is 0.902 J/g · °C; take that of soda to be 4.10 J/g · °C.
  (a) How much heat must be absorbed from the six-pack to lower the temperature from 25.0° to 5.0°C?
  (b) How much ice must be melted to absorb this amount of heat? (ΔH_{fus} of ice is given in Table 8.2.)

86. A cafeteria sets out glasses of tea at room temperature. The customer adds ice. Assuming that the customer wants to have some ice left when the tea cools to 0°C, what fraction of the total volume of the glass should be left empty for adding ice? Make any reasonable assumptions needed to work this problem.

87. The thermite reaction was once used to weld rails:

$$2Al(s) + Fe_2O_3(s) \longrightarrow Al_2O_3(s) + 2Fe(s)$$

  (a) Using heat of formation data, calculate ΔH for this reaction.
  (b) Take the specific heats of Al_2O_3 and Fe to be 0.77 and 0.45 J/g · °C, respectively. Calculate the temperature to which the products of this reaction will be raised, starting at room temperature, by the heat given off in the reaction.
  (c) Will the reaction produce molten iron (mp Fe = 1535°C, ΔH_{fus} = 270 J/g)?

88. A sample of sucrose, $C_{12}H_{22}O_{11}$, is contaminated by sodium chloride. When the contaminated sample is burned in a bomb calorimeter, sodium chloride does not burn. What is the percentage of sucrose in the sample if a temperature increase of 1.67°C is observed when 3.000 g of the sample is burned in the calorimeter? Sucrose gives off 5.64×10^3 kJ/mol when burned. The heat capacity of the calorimeter is 22.51 kJ/°C.

89. A wad of steel wool (specific heat = 0.45 J/g · °C) at 25°C is misplaced in a microwave oven, which later is accidentally turned on high. The oven generates microwaves of 13.5 cm wavelength at the rate of 925 moles of those photons per second. All of the photons are converted to high-heat energy, raising the temperature of the steel wool. Steel wool reacts explosively with the oxygen in the oven when the steel wool reaches 400.0°C. If the steel wool explodes after 1.55 seconds, how many grams of steel wool were accidentally put into the oven?

■ in OWL Blue-numbered questions answered in Appendix 6 WEB Solution is available on companion website

9 Liquids and Solids

See plastic Nature working to this end,
The single atoms each to other tend,
Attract, attracted to, the next in place
Form'd and impell'd its neighbour to embrace.

—Alexander Pope
From *"An Essay on Man: Epistle III"*

Chapter Outline

Ice, seen floating on the water in the painting, has its water molecules arranged in an open hexagonal pattern. This is a result of hydrogen bonding. The large portion of open space in the structure explains why ice floats on water.

In Chapter 5 we pointed out that at ordinary temperatures and pressures all gases follow the ideal gas law. Unfortunately, there is no simple "equation of state" that can be written to correlate the properties of liquids or solids. There are two reasons for this difference in behavior.

1. *Molecules are much closer to one another in liquids and solids.* In the gas state, particles are typically separated by ten molecular diameters or more; in liquids or solids, they touch one another. This explains why liquids and solids have densities so much larger than those of gases. At 100°C and 1 atm, $H_2O(l)$ has a density of 0.95 g/mL; that of $H_2O(g)$ under the same conditions is only 0.00059 g/mL. For the same reason, liquids and solids are much less compressible than gases. When the pressure on liquid water is increased from 1 to 2 atm, the volume decreases by 0.0045%; the same change in pressure reduces the volume of an ideal gas by 50%.

2. *Intermolecular forces, which are essentially negligible with gases, play a much more important role in liquids and solids.* Among the effects of these forces is the phenomenon of *surface tension,* shown by liquids. Molecules at the surface are attracted inward by unbalanced intermolecular forces; as a result, liquids tend to form spherical drops, for which the ratio of surface area to volume is as small as possible (Figure 9.1). Water, in which there are relatively strong intermolecular forces, has a high surface tension. That of most organic liquids is lower, which explains why they tend to "wet" or spread out on solid surfaces more readily than water. The wetting ability of water can be increased by adding a soap or detergent, which drastically lowers the surface tension.

Our discussion of liquids and solids will focus on—

- phase equilibria. Section 9.1 considers several different phenomena related to gas-liquid equilibria, including *vapor pressure, boiling point behavior,* and *critical properties.* Section 9.2 deals with phase diagrams, which describe all three types of phase equilibria (gas-liquid, gas-solid, and liquid-solid).
- the relationships among particle structure, interparticle forces, and physical properties. Section 9.3 explores these relationships for molecular substances; Section 9.4 extends the discussion to nonmolecular solids (network covalent, ionic, and metallic). Section 9.5 is devoted to the crystal structure of ionic and metallic solids. ■

9.1 LIQUID-VAPOR EQUILIBRIUM

All of us are familiar with the process of vaporization, in which a liquid is converted to a gas, commonly referred to as a *vapor.* In an open container, *evaporation* continues until all the liquid is gone. If the container is closed, the situation is quite different. At first, the movement of molecules is primarily in one direction, from liquid to vapor. Here, however, the vapor molecules cannot escape from the container. Some of them collide with the surface and reenter the liquid. As time passes and the concentration of molecules in the vapor increases, so does the rate of condensation. When the rate of condensation becomes equal to the rate of vaporization, the liquid and vapor are in a state of dynamic equilibrium:

$$\text{liquid} \rightleftharpoons \text{vapor}$$

The double arrow implies that the forward and reverse processes are occurring at the same rate, which is characteristic of a dynamic equilibrium. The vapor, like any gas, can be assumed to obey the ideal gas law.

Online homework for this chapter may be assigned in OWL

CENGAGENOW™
This icon introduces an opportunity for self-study and to explore interactive modules by signing in at **academic.cengage.com/now.**

Richard Megna/Fundamental Photographs NYC

Figure 9.1
Surface tension causes water to bead on the polished surface of a car.

Charles D. Winters

Liquid-vapor equilibrium. Under the conditions shown, the bromine liquid and vapor have established a dynamic equilibrium.

Vapor Pressure

CENGAGENOW™
Click Coached Problems for a self-study module on **vapor pressure.**

Once equilibrium between liquid and vapor is reached, the number of molecules per unit volume in the vapor does not change with time. This means that ***the pressure exerted by the vapor over the liquid remains constant.*** The pressure of vapor in equilibrium with a liquid is called the vapor pressure. This quantity is a characteristic property of a given liquid at a particular temperature. It varies from one liquid to another, depending on the strength of the intermolecular forces. At 25°C, the vapor pressure of water is 24 mm Hg; that of ether, in which intermolecular forces are weaker, is 537 mm Hg.

It is important to realize that ***so long as both liquid and vapor are present, the pressure exerted by the vapor is independent of the volume of the container.*** If a small amount of liquid is introduced into a closed container, some of it will vaporize, establishing its equilibrium vapor pressure. The greater the volume of the container, the greater will be the amount of liquid that vaporizes to establish that pressure. The ratio n/V stays constant, so $P = nRT/V$ does not change. Only if all the liquid vaporizes will the pressure drop below the equilibrium value.

Example 9.1 Graded

A "cool-mist" vaporizer with capacity 2.00 L is used to add moisture to dry air in a room at 25°C. The room has dimensions 12 ft by 12 ft by 8 ft. The vapor pressure of water at 25°C is 24 mm Hg. Take the density of water at 25°C to be 1.00 g/mL.

- *(a) If the vaporizer runs until it is empty, what is the vapor pressure of water in the room?
- **(b) How much water is required to completely saturate the air at 25°C?
- ***(c) A relative humidity of 33% is desirable in heated space on wintry days. What volume of water is left in the vaporizer when the room's relative humidity reaches that level? (Relative humidity $= 100 \times P/P^0$, where P is the actual pressure of water vapor and P^0 is the vapor pressure at saturation.)

SOLUTION

(a) Assume that all the water is vaporized and use the ideal gas law to calculate vapor pressure. To use the ideal gas law, you will need:

$$V = (12 \times 12 \times 8)\ \text{ft}^3 \times \frac{28.32\ \text{L}}{1\ \text{ft}^3} = 3.3 \times 10^4\ \text{L}$$

and

$$n_{H_2O} = 2.00\ \text{L} \times \frac{1000\ \text{mL}}{1\ \text{L}} \times \frac{1.00\ \text{g}}{1\ \text{mL}} \times \frac{1\ \text{mol}}{18.02\ \text{g}} = 111\ \text{mol}$$

Now substitute into the ideal gas law:

$$P = \frac{nRT}{V} = \frac{(111\ \text{mol})(0.0821\ \text{L}\cdot\text{atm/mol}\cdot\text{K})(298\text{K})}{3.3 \times 10^4\ \text{L}} = 0.082\ \text{atm} = 62\ \text{mm Hg}$$

It is impossible to have a vapor pressure larger than 24 mm Hg at 25°C. Thus, the assumption that all the water is vaporized is wrong. The pressure in the room is 24 mm Hg.

(b) The vapor pressure of water vapor in air that is saturated with water vapor is 24 mm Hg. We now need to find, with the help of the ideal gas law, the mass of water required.

$$n_{H_2O} = \frac{PV}{RT} = \frac{(24/760)\ \text{atm} \times 3.3 \times 10^4\ \text{L}}{(0.0821\ \text{L}\cdot\text{atm/mol}\cdot\text{K})(298\text{K})} = 43\ \text{mol}$$

$$\text{mass}_{H_2O} = 43\ \text{mol} \times 18.02\ \text{g/mol} = 7.7 \times 10^2\ \text{g}$$

(c) A relative humidity of 33% means that the actual pressure P of water vapor must be

$$P = \frac{\text{relative humidity}}{100} \times P^0 = \frac{33}{100} \times 24 \text{ mm Hg} = 7.9 \text{ mm Hg}$$

Again, use the ideal gas law to find the mass of water that must be vaporized to reach the calculated pressure (7.9 mm Hg). Subtract the mass of vaporized water from the mass of water in the vaporizer, and use density to calculate the volume of water in the vaporizer.

$$n_{H_2O} = \frac{PV}{RT} = \frac{(7.9/760) \text{ atm} \times 3.3 \times 10^4 \text{ L}}{(0.0821 \text{ L} \cdot \text{atm/mol} \cdot \text{K})(298\text{K})} = 14 \text{ mol}$$

The volume of water vaporized is thus

$$14 \text{ mol} \times \frac{18.02 \text{ g}}{1 \text{ mol}} = 2.5 \times 10^2 \text{ g} = 0.25 \text{ L}$$

The volume of water left in the vaporizer is therefore

$$2.00 \text{ L} - 0.25 \text{ L} = 1.75 \text{ L}$$

Reality Check The calculations in (b) show that about 770 grams are required for saturation (100% relative humidity). To get 33% relative humidity, you would expect to need about a third of that amount, which is what the calculations in (c) do give.

Vapor Pressure Versus Temperature

The vapor pressure of a liquid always increases as temperature rises. Water evaporates more readily on a hot, dry day. Stoppers in bottles of volatile liquids such as ether or gasoline pop out when the temperature rises.

The vapor pressure of water, which is 24 mm Hg at 25°C, becomes 92 mm Hg at 50°C and 1 atm (760 mm Hg) at 100°C. The data for water are plotted at the top of Figure 9.2. As you can see, the graph of vapor pressure versus temperature is not a straight line, as it would be if pressure were plotted versus temperature for an ideal gas. Instead, the slope increases steadily as temperature rises, reflecting the fact that more molecules vaporize at higher temperatures. At 100°C, the concentration of H_2O molecules in the vapor in equilibrium with liquid is 25 times as great as at 25°C.

In working with the relationship between two variables, such as vapor pressure and temperature, scientists prefer to deal with linear (straight-line) functions. Straight-line graphs are easier to construct and to interpret. In this case, it is possible to obtain a linear function by making a simple shift in variables. Instead of plotting vapor pressure (P) versus temperature (T), we plot the *natural logarithm** of the vapor pressure ($\ln P$) versus the reciprocal of the absolute temperature ($1/T$). Such a plot for water is shown at the bottom of Figure 9.2. As with all other liquids, a plot of $\ln P$ versus $1/T$ is a straight line.

The general equation of a straight line is

$$y = mx + b \qquad (m = \text{slope}, b = y\text{-intercept})$$

The y-coordinate in Figure 9.2b is $\ln P$, and the x-coordinate is $1/T$. The slope, which is a negative quantity, turns out to be $-\Delta H_{vap}/R$, where ΔH_{vap} is the molar heat of vaporization and R is the gas constant, in the proper units. Hence the equation of the straight line in Figure 9.2b is

$$\ln P = \frac{-\Delta H_{vap}}{RT} + b$$

*Many natural laws are most simply expressed in terms of natural logarithms, which are based on the number $e = 2.71828\ldots$ If $y = e^x$, then the natural logarithm of y, $\ln y$, is equal to x.

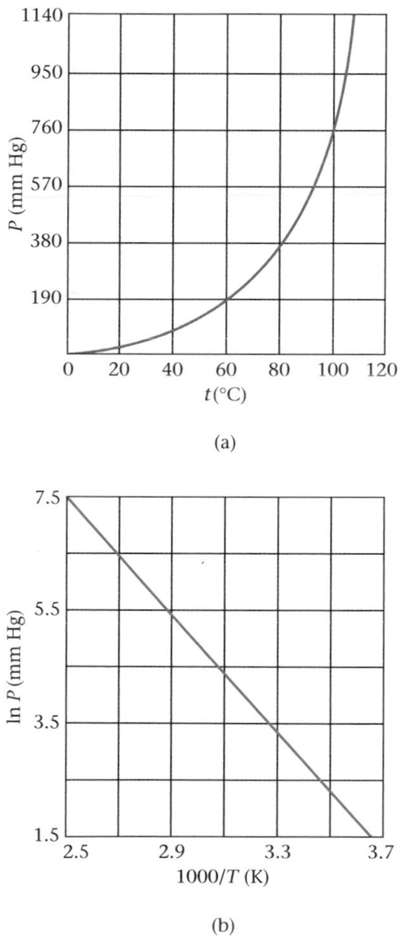

Figure 9.2
Vapor pressure versus temperature. (a) A plot of vapor pressure (P) versus temperature t(°C) for water (or any other liquid) is a curve with a steadily increasing slope. (b) A plot of the logarithm of the vapor pressure versus the reciprocal of the absolute temperature, $1/T$(K), is a straight line. (To provide larger numbers, we have plotted $1000 \times 1/T$).

For many purposes, it is convenient to have a two-point relation between the vapor pressures (P_2, P_1) at two different temperatures (T_2, T_1). Such a relation is obtained by first writing separate equations at each temperature:

$$\text{at } T_2: \qquad \ln P_2 = b - \frac{\Delta H_{vap}}{RT_2}$$

$$\text{at } T_1: \qquad \ln P_1 = b - \frac{\Delta H_{vap}}{RT_1}$$

On subtraction, the constant b is eliminated, and we obtain

$$\ln P_2 - \ln P_1 = \ln \frac{P_2}{P_1} = -\frac{\Delta H_{vap}}{R}\left[\frac{1}{T_2} - \frac{1}{T_1}\right] = \frac{\Delta H_{vap}}{R}\left[\frac{1}{T_1} - \frac{1}{T_2}\right] \qquad \textbf{(9.1)}$$

This equation is known as the *Clausius-Clapeyron equation.* Rudolph Clausius (1822–1888) was a prestigious nineteenth-century German scientist. B. P. E. Clapeyron (1799–1864), a French engineer, first proposed a modified version of the equation in 1834.

CENGAGENOW™
Click Coached Problems for a self-study module on **heat of vaporization: using the Clausius-Clapeyron equation.**

In using the Clausius-Clapeyron equation, the units of ΔH_{vap} and R must be consistent. If ΔH is expressed in joules, then R must be expressed in joules per mole per kelvin. Recall (Table 5.1, page 107) that

$$R = 8.31 \text{ J/mol} \cdot \text{K}$$

We'll use this value of R frequently in future chapters.

This equation can be used to calculate any one of the five variables (P_2, P_1, T_2, T_1, and ΔH_{vap}), knowing the values of the other four. For example, we can use it to find the vapor pressure (P_1) at temperature T_1, knowing P_2 at T_2 and the value of the heat of vaporization (Example 9.2).

Example 9.2 Benzene has a vapor pressure of 183 mm Hg at 40°C. Taking its heat of vaporization to be 30.8 kJ/mol, calculate its vapor pressure at 25°C.

Strategy It is convenient to use the subscript 2 for the higher temperature and pressure. Substitute into the Clausius-Clapeyron equation, solving for P_1. Remember to express temperature in K and take $R = 8.31$ J/mol · K.

SOLUTION

$$\ln \frac{183 \text{ mm Hg}}{P_1} = \frac{30.8 \times 10^3 \text{ J/mol}}{8.31 \text{ J/mol} \cdot \text{K}}\left[\frac{1}{298 \text{ K}} - \frac{1}{313 \text{ K}}\right] = 0.596$$

$$\text{Taking inverse logs:} \qquad \frac{183 \text{ mm Hg}}{P_1} = 1.81; P_1 = \boxed{101 \text{ mm Hg}}$$

Reality Check This value is reasonable in the sense that lowering the temperature should reduce the vapor pressure.

Boiling Point

CENGAGENOW™
Click Coached Problems for a self-study module on **vapor pressure and boiling point.**

When a liquid is heated in an open container, bubbles form, usually at the bottom, where heat is applied. The first small bubbles are air, driven out of solution by the increase in temperature. Eventually, at a certain temperature, large vapor bubbles form throughout the liquid. These vapor bubbles rise to the surface, where they break. When this happens, the liquid is said to be boiling. For a pure liquid, the temperature remains constant throughout the boiling process.

The temperature at which a liquid boils depends on the pressure above it. To understand why this is the case, consider Figure 9.3 (p. 231). This shows vapor bubbles rising in a boiling liquid. For a vapor bubble to form, the pressure within it, P_1, must be at least equal to the pressure above it, P_2. Because P_1 is simply the vapor pressure of the liquid, it follows that ***a liquid boils at a temperature at which its vapor pressure is equal to the pressure above its surface.*** If this pressure is 1 atm (760 mm Hg), the temperature is referred to as the **normal**

The vapor pressure of a substance at its normal bp is 760 mm Hg.

Figure 9.3
Boiling and vapor pressure. A liquid boils when it reaches the temperature at which the vapor pressure in its vapor bubbles (P_1) exceeds the pressure above the liquid (P_2).

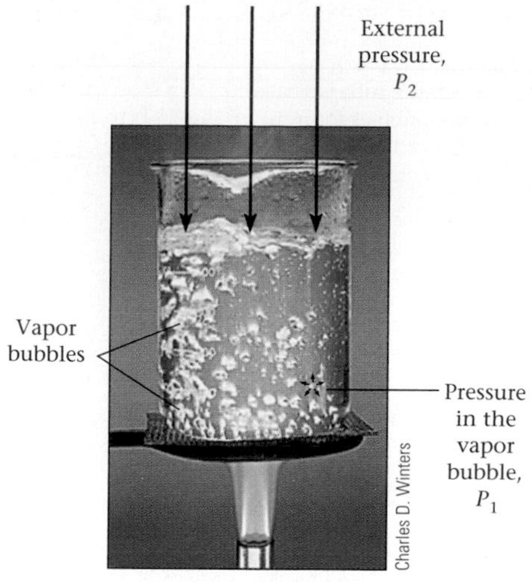

boiling point. (When the term "boiling point" is used without qualification, normal boiling point is implied.) The normal boiling point of water is 100°C; its vapor pressure is 760 mm Hg at that temperature.

As you might expect, the boiling point of a liquid can be reduced by lowering the pressure above it. Water can be made to boil at 25°C by evacuating the space above it. When a pressure of 24 mm Hg, the equilibrium vapor pressure at 25°C, is reached, the water starts to boil. Chemists often take advantage of this effect in purifying a high-boiling compound that might decompose or oxidize at its normal boiling point. They distill it at a reduced temperature under vacuum and condense the vapor.

If you have been fortunate enough to camp in the high Sierras or the Rockies, you may have noticed that it takes longer at high altitudes to cook foods in boiling water. The reduced pressure lowers the temperature at which water boils in an open container and thus slows down the physical and chemical changes that take place when foods like potatoes or eggs are cooked. In principle, this problem can be solved by using a pressure cooker. In that device, the pressure that develops is high enough to raise the boiling point of water above 100°C. Pressure cookers are indeed used in places like Salt Lake City, Utah (elevation 1340 m, bp $H_2O(l)$ = 95°C), but not by mountain climbers, who have to carry all their equipment on their backs.

Or in the Presidential Range of New Hampshire (WLM), or in the Swiss Alps (CNH)

Critical Temperature and Pressure

Consider an experiment in which liquid carbon dioxide is introduced into an otherwise evacuated glass tube, which is then sealed (Figure 9.4, p. 232). At 0°C, the pressure above the liquid is 34 atm, the equilibrium vapor pressure of $CO_2(l)$ at that temperature. As the tube is heated, some of the liquid is converted to vapor, and the pressure rises, to 44 atm at 10°C and 56 atm at 20°C. Nothing spectacular happens (unless there happens to be a weak spot in the tube) until 31°C is reached, where the vapor pressure is 73 atm. Suddenly, as the temperature goes above 31°C, the meniscus between the liquid and vapor disappears! The tube now contains only one phase.

It is impossible to have liquid carbon dioxide at temperatures above 31°C, no matter how much pressure is applied. Even at pressures as high as 1000 atm, carbon dioxide gas does not liquefy at 35 or 40°C. This behavior is typical of all substances. There is a temperature, called the **critical temperature,** above which the liquid phase of a pure substance cannot exist. The pressure that must be applied to cause condensation at that temperature is called the **critical pressure.** Quite simply, the critical pressure is the vapor pressure of the liquid at the critical temperature.

Table 9.1 lists the critical temperatures of several common substances. The species in the column at the left all have critical temperatures below 25°C. They are often referred to as "permanent gases." Applying pressure at room temperature will not condense a permanent

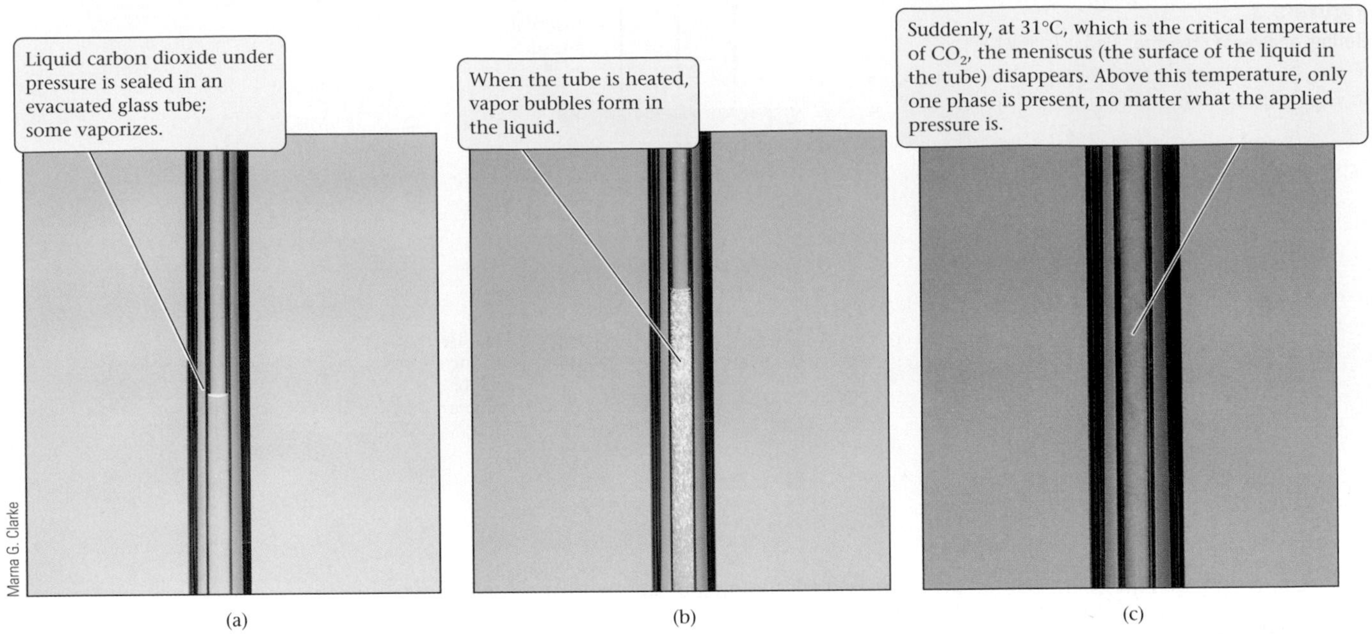

Figure 9.4
Critical temperature.

gas. It must be cooled as well. When you see a truck labeled "liquid nitrogen" on the highway, you can be sure that the cargo trailer is refrigerated to at least −147°C, the critical temperature of N_2.

"Permanent gases" are most often stored and sold in steel cylinders under high pressures, often 150 atm or greater. When the valve on a cylinder of N_2 or O_2 is opened, gas escapes, and the pressure drops accordingly. The substances listed in the center column of Table 9.1, all of which have critical temperatures above 25°C, are handled quite differently. They are available commercially as liquids in high-pressure cylinders. When the valve on a cylinder of propane is opened, the gas that escapes is replaced by vaporization of liquid. The pressure quickly returns to its original value. Only when the liquid is completely vaporized does the pressure drop as gas is withdrawn. This indicates that almost all of the propane is gone, and it is time to recharge the tank.

A pressure gauge on a propane tank doesn't indicate how much gas you have left.

Above the critical temperature and pressure, a substance is referred to as a *supercritical fluid*. Such fluids have unusual solvent properties that have led to many practical applications. Supercritical carbon dioxide is used most commonly because it is cheap, nontoxic, and relatively easy to liquefy (critical $T = 31°C$, $P = 73$ atm). It was first used more than 20 years ago to extract caffeine from coffee; dichloromethane, CH_2Cl_2, long used for this purpose, is both a narcotic and a potential carcinogen. Today more than 10^5 metric tons of decaf coffee are made annually using supercritical CO_2. It is also used on a large scale to extract nicotine from tobacco and various objectionable impurities from the hops used to make beer.

Table 9.1 Critical Temperatures (°C)

Permanent Gases		Condensable Gases		Liquids	
Helium	−268	Carbon dioxide	31	Ethyl ether	194
Hydrogen	−240	Ethane	32	Ethyl alcohol	243
Nitrogen	−147	Propane	97	Benzene	289
Argon	−122	Ammonia	132	Bromine	311
Oxygen	−119	Chlorine	144	Water	374
Methane	−82	Sulfur dioxide	158		

9.2 PHASE DIAGRAMS

In the preceding section, we discussed several features of the equilibrium between a liquid and its vapor. For a pure substance, at least two other types of phase equilibria need to be considered. One is the equilibrium between a solid and its vapor, the other between solid and liquid at the melting (freezing) point. Many of the important relations in all these equilibria can be shown in a **phase diagram.** A phase diagram is a graph that shows the pressures and temperatures at which different phases are in equilibrium with each other. The phase diagram of water is shown in Figure 9.5. This figure, which covers a wide range of temperatures and pressures, is not drawn to scale.

CENGAGENOW™
Click Coached Problems for a self-study module on **phase diagrams.**

To understand what a phase diagram implies, consider first the curves AB and AC, and the line AD in Figure 9.5. Each of these lines shows the pressures and temperatures at which two adjacent phases are at equilibrium.

1. Curve AB is a portion of the vapor pressure–temperature curve of liquid water. At any temperature and pressure along this line, liquid water is in equilibrium with water vapor. At point A on the curve, these two phases are in equilibrium at 0°C and about 5 mm Hg (more exactly, 0.01°C and 4.56 mm Hg). At B, corresponding to 100°C, the pressure exerted by the vapor in equilibrium with liquid water is 1 atm; this is the normal boiling point of water. The extension of line AB beyond point B gives the equilibrium vapor pressure of the liquid above the normal boiling point. The line ends at 374°C, the critical temperature of water, where the pressure is 218 atm.

2. Curve AC represents the vapor pressure curve of ice. At any point along this line, such as point A (0°C, 5 mm Hg) or point C, which might represent −3°C and 3 mm Hg, ice and vapor are in equilibrium with each other.

When *T* and *P* fall on a line, two phases are in equilibrium.

3. Line AD gives the temperatures and applied pressures at which liquid water is in equilibrium with ice.

Point A on a phase diagram is the only one at which all three phases, liquid, solid, and vapor, are in equilibrium with each other. It is called the **triple point.** For water, the triple-point temperature is 0.01°C. At this temperature, liquid water and ice have the same vapor pressure, 4.56 mm Hg.

In the three areas of the phase diagram labeled solid, liquid, and vapor, only one phase is present. To understand this, consider what happens to an equilibrium mixture of two phases when the pressure or temperature is changed. Suppose we start at the point on AB

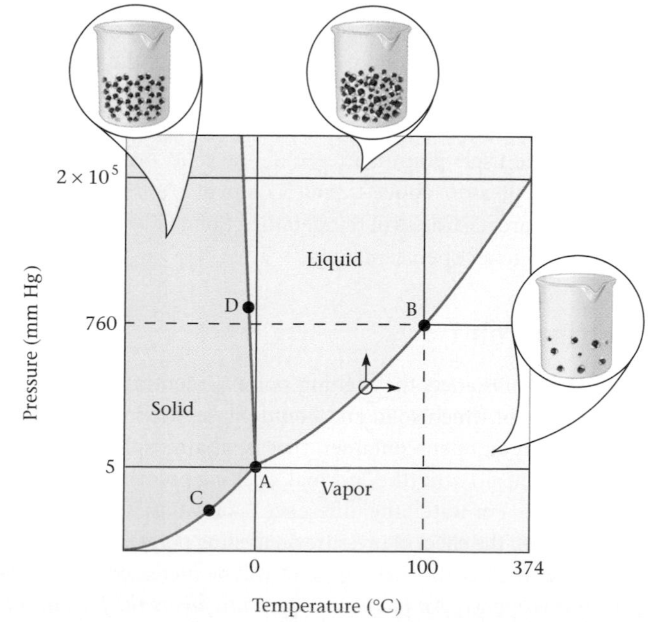

Figure 9.5
Phase diagram of water (not to scale). The curves and line represent the temperatures and pressures at which phases are in equilibrium. The triple point is at 0.01°C, 4.56 mm Hg; the critical point is at 374°C, 1.66×10^5 mm Hg (218 atm).

indicated by an open circle. Here liquid water and vapor are in equilibrium with each other, let us say at 70°C and 234 mm Hg. If the pressure on this mixture is increased, condensation occurs. The phase diagram confirms this; increasing the pressure at 70°C *(vertical arrow)* puts us in the liquid region. In another experiment, the temperature might be increased at a constant pressure. This should cause the liquid to vaporize. The phase diagram shows that this is indeed what happens. An increase in temperature *(horizontal arrow)* shifts us to the vapor region.

Example 9.3 Conceptual

Consider a sample of H_2O at point A in Figure 9.5.

(a) What phase(s) is (are) present?
(b) If the temperature of the sample were reduced at constant pressure, what would happen?
(c) How would you convert the sample to vapor without changing the temperature?

Strategy Use the phase diagram in Figure 9.5. Note that P increases moving up vertically; T increases moving to the right.

SOLUTION

(a) A is the triple point; ice, liquid water, and water vapor are present.
(b) Move to the left to reduce T. This penetrates the solid area, which implies that the sample freezes completely.
(c) Reduce the pressure to below the triple-point value, perhaps to 4 mm Hg.

Charles D. Winters

Figure 9.6
Sublimation. Solid iodine passes directly to the vapor at any temperature below the triple point, 114°C. The vapor condenses back to a solid on a cold surface like that of the upper flask, which is filled with ice.

Sublimation

The process by which a solid changes directly to vapor without passing through the liquid phase is called **sublimation.** A solid can sublime only at temperatures below the triple point; above that temperature it will melt to liquid (Figure 9.5, p. 233). At temperatures below the triple point, a solid can be made to sublime by reducing the pressure of the vapor above it to less than the equilibrium value. To illustrate what this means, consider the conditions under which ice sublimes. This happens on a cold, dry, winter day when the temperature is below 0°C and the pressure of water vapor in the air is less than the equilibrium value (4.5 mm Hg at 0°C). The rate of sublimation can be increased by evacuating the space above the ice. This is how foods are freeze-dried. The food is frozen, put into a vacuum chamber, and evacuated to a pressure of 1 mm Hg or less. The ice crystals formed on freezing sublime, which leaves a product whose mass is only a fraction of that of the original food.

Iodine sublimes more readily than ice because its triple-point pressure, 90 mm Hg, is much higher. Sublimation occurs on heating (Figure 9.6) below the triple-point temperature, 114°C. If the triple point is exceeded, the solid melts. Solid carbon dioxide (dry ice) has a triple-point pressure above 1 atm (5.2 atm at −57°C). Liquid carbon dioxide cannot exist at 1 atm pressure regardless of temperature. Solid CO_2 always passes directly to vapor if allowed to warm up in an open cantainer.

The white "smoke" around a piece of dry ice is $CO_2(g)$, formed by sublimation.

Melting Point

For a pure substance, the melting point is identical to the freezing point. It represents the temperature at which solid and liquid phases are in equilibrium. Melting points are usually measured in an open container, that is, at atmospheric pressure. For most substances, the melting point at 1 atm (the "normal" melting point) is virtually identical with the triple-point temperature. For water, the difference is only 0.01°C.

Although the effect of pressure on melting point is very small, its direction is still important. To decide whether the melting point will be increased or decreased by compression, a simple principle is applied. ***An increase in pressure favors the formation of the more dense phase.***

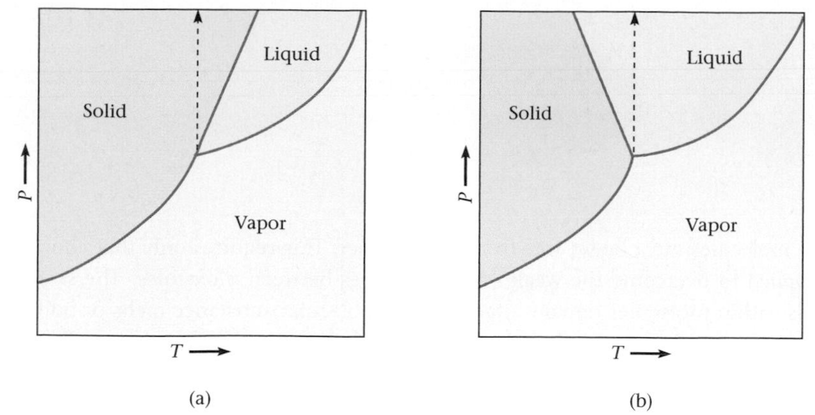

Figure 9.7
Effect of pressure on the melting point of a solid. (a) When the solid is the more dense phase, an increase in pressure converts liquid to solid; the melting point increases. (b) If the liquid is the more dense phase, an increase in pressure converts solid to liquid and the melting point decreases.

Two types of behavior are shown in Figure 9.7.

1. *The solid is the more dense phase* (Figure 9.7a). The solid-liquid equilibrium line is inclined to the right, shifting away from the y-axis as it rises. At higher pressures, the solid becomes stable at temperatures above the normal melting point. In other words, the melting point is raised by an increase in pressure. This behavior is shown by most substances.

2. *The liquid is the more dense phase* (Figure 9.7b). The liquid-solid line is inclined to the left, toward the y-axis. An increase in pressure favors the formation of liquid; that is, the melting point is decreased by raising the pressure. Water is one of the few substances that behave this way; ice is less dense than liquid water. The effect is exaggerated for emphasis in Figure 9.7b. Actually, an increase in pressure of 134 atm is required to lower the melting point of ice by 1°C.

9.3 MOLECULAR SUBSTANCES; INTERMOLECULAR FORCES

Molecules are the characteristic structural units of gases, most liquids, and many solids. As a class, molecular substances tend to have the following characteristics.

They are:

1. *Nonconductors of electricity when pure.* Molecules are uncharged, so they cannot carry an electric current. In most cases (e.g., iodine, I_2, and ethyl alcohol, C_2H_5OH), water solutions of molecular substances are also nonconductors. A few polar molecules, including HCl, react with water to form ions:

$$HCl(g) \longrightarrow H^+(aq) + Cl^-(aq)$$

and hence produce a conducting water solution.

2. *Insoluble in water but soluble in nonpolar solvents such as CCl_4 or benzene.* Iodine is typical of most molecular substances; it is only slightly soluble in water (0.0013 mol/L at 25°C), much more soluble in benzene (0.48 mol/L). A few molecular substances, including ethyl alcohol, are very soluble in water. As you will see later in this section, such substances have intermolecular forces similar to those in water.

3. *Low melting and boiling.* Many molecular substances are gases at 25°C and 1 atm (e.g., N_2, O_2, and CO_2), which means that they have boiling points below 25°C. Others (such as H_2O and CCl_4) are liquids with melting (freezing) points below room temperature. Of the molecular substances that are solids at ordinary temperatures, most are low-melting. For example, iodine melts at 114°C; the melting point of naphthalene, used in mothballs, is 80°C. The upper limit for melting and boiling points of most molecular substances is about 300°C.

Charles D. Winters

Molecular liquids. The bottom layer, carbon tetrachloride (CCl_4), and the top layer, octane (C_8H_{18}), are nonpolar molecular liquids that are not soluble in water. The middle layer is a water solution of blue copper sulfate.

It's much easier to separate two molecules than to separate two atoms within a molecule.

The generally low melting and boiling points of molecular substances reflect the fact that the forces between molecules **(intermolecular forces)** are weak. To melt or boil a molecular

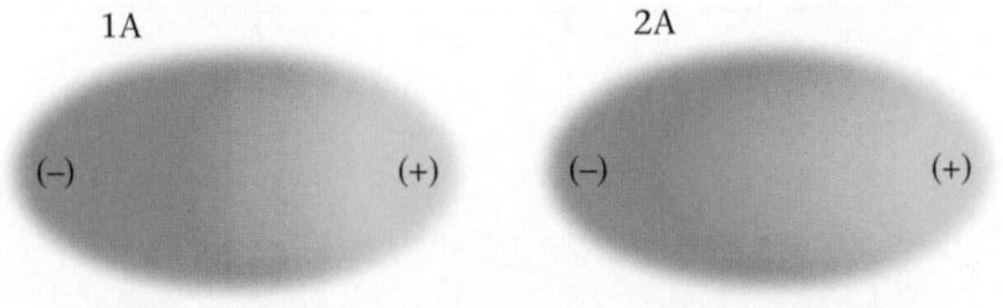

Figure 9.8
Dispersion force. Temporary dipoles in adjacent molecules line up to create an electrical attraction force known as the dispersion force. Deeply shaded areas indicate regions where the electron cloud is momentarily concentrated and creates partial charges, indicated by (+) and (−).

substance, the molecules must be set free from one another. This requires only that enough energy be supplied to overcome the weak attractive forces between molecules. The strong covalent bonds within molecules remain intact when a molecular substance melts or boils.

The boiling points of different molecular substances are directly related to the strength of the intermolecular forces involved. ***The stronger the intermolecular forces, the higher the boiling point of the substance.*** In the remainder of this section, we examine the nature of the three different types of intermolecular forces: *dispersion forces, dipole forces,* and *hydrogen bonds.*

Dispersion (London) Forces

It is time to review the material in Chapter 7.

The most common type of intermolecular force, found in all molecular substances, is referred to as a **dispersion force.** It is basically electrical in nature, involving an attraction between temporary or *induced* dipoles in adjacent molecules. To understand the origin of dispersion forces, consider Figure 9.8.

On the average, electrons in a nonpolar molecule, such as H_2, are as close to one nucleus as to the other. However, at a given instant, the electron cloud may be concentrated at one end of the molecule (position 1A in Figure 9.8). This momentary concentration of the electron cloud on one side of the molecule creates a temporary dipole in H_2. One side of the molecule, shown in deeper color in Figure 9.8, acquires a partial negative charge; the other side has a partial positive charge of equal magnitude.

This temporary dipole induces a similar dipole (an induced dipole) in an adjacent molecule. When the electron cloud in the first molecule is at 1A, the electrons in the second molecule are attracted to 2A. These temporary dipoles, both in the same direction, lead to an attractive force between the molecules. This is the dispersion force.

In nonpolar molecules, dispersion is the only intermolecular force.

All molecules have dispersion forces. The strength of these forces depends on two factors—

- the number of electrons in the atoms that make up the molecule.
- the ease with which electrons are *dispersed* to form temporary dipoles.

Dispersion forces are weak in H_2, much stronger in I_2.

Both these factors increase with increasing molecular size. Large molecules are made up of more and/or larger atoms. The outer electrons in larger atoms are relatively far from the nucleus and are easier to disperse than the electrons in small atoms. In general, molecular size and molar mass parallel one another. Thus within a given class of substances (Table 9.2) we can say that ***as molar mass increases, dispersion forces become stronger and the boiling point of nonpolar molecular substances increases.***

Table 9.2 Effect of Molar Mass on Boiling Points of Molecular Substances

Noble Gases*			Halogens			Hydrocarbons		
	MM (g/mol)	bp (°C)		MM (g/mol)	bp (°C)		MM (g/mol)	bp (°C)
He	4	−269	F_2	38	−188	CH_4	16	−161
Ne	20	−246	Cl_2	71	−34	C_2H_6	30	−88
Ar	40	−186	Br_2	160	59	C_3H_8	44	−42
Kr	84	−152	I_2	254	184	n-C_4H_{10}	58	0

*Strictly speaking, the noble gases are "atomic" rather than molecular. However, like molecules, the noble-gas atoms are attracted to one another by dispersion forces.

Figure 9.9
Dipole forces in the ICl crystal. The δ^+ and δ^- indicate partial charges on the I and Cl atoms in the polar molecules. The existence of these partial charges causes the molecules to line up in the pattern shown. Adjacent molecules are attracted to each other by the dipole forces between the δ^+ of one molecule and the δ^- of another molecule.

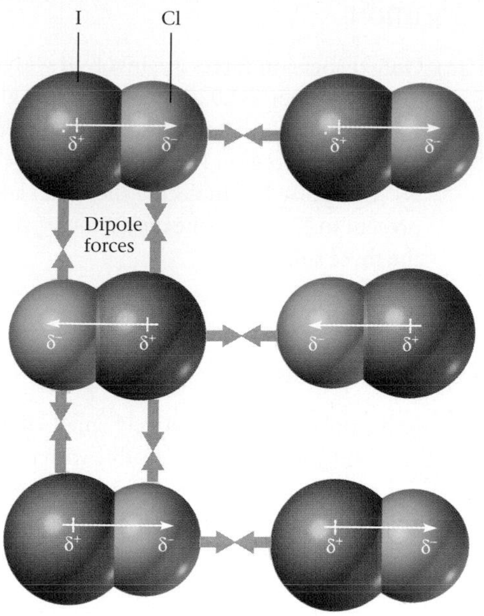

Table 9.3 Boiling Points of Nonpolar Versus Polar Substances

Nonpolar			Polar		
Formula	MM (g/mol)	bp (°C)	Formula	MM (g/mol)	bp (°C)
N_2	28	−196	CO	28	−192
SiH_4	32	−112	PH_3	34	−88
GeH_4	77	−90	AsH_3	78	−62
Br_2	160	59	ICl	162	97

Dipole Forces

Polar molecules, like nonpolar molecules, are attracted to one another by dispersion forces. In addition, they experience **dipole forces** as illustrated in Figure 9.9, which shows the orientation of polar molecules, such as ICl, in a crystal. Adjacent molecules line up so that the negative pole of one molecule (small Cl atom) is as close as possible to the positive pole (large I atom) of its neighbor. Under these conditions, there is an electrical attractive force, referred to as a dipole force, between adjacent polar molecules.

CENGAGENOW™
Click Chemistry Interactive for the self-study module **dipole-induced dipole forces.**

When iodine chloride is heated to 27°C, the weak intermolecular forces are unable to keep the molecules rigidly aligned, and the solid melts. Dipole forces are still important in the liquid state, because the polar molecules remain close to one another. Only in the gas, where the molecules are far apart, do the effects of dipole forces become negligible. Hence boiling points as well as melting points of polar compounds such as ICl are somewhat higher than those of nonpolar substances of comparable molar mass. This effect is shown in Table 9.3.

Example 9.4 Conceptual

Explain, in terms of intermolecular forces, why

(a) the boiling point of O_2 (−183°C) is higher than that of N_2 (−196°C).
(b) the boiling point of NO (−151°C) is higher than that of either O_2 or N_2.

Strategy Determine whether the molecule is polar or nonpolar and identify the intermolecular forces present. Remember, dispersion forces are always present and increase with molar mass.

In most molecules, dispersion forces are stronger than dipole forces.

SOLUTION

(a) Only dispersion forces are involved with these nonpolar molecules. The molar mass of O_2 is greater (32.0 g/mol versus 28.0 g/mol for N_2), so its dispersion forces are stronger, making its boiling point higher.

(b) Dispersion forces in NO (30 g/mol) are comparable in strength to those in O_2 and N_2. The polar NO molecule shows an additional type of intermolecular force not present in N_2 or O_2: the dipole force. As a result, its boiling point is the highest of the three substances.

Hydrogen Bonds

CENGAGENOW™
Click Coached Problems for a self-study module on **molecular structure and boiling point.**

Ordinarily, polarity has a relatively small effect on boiling point. In the series HCl → HBr → HI, boiling point increases steadily with molar mass, even though polarity decreases moving from HCl to HI. However, when hydrogen is bonded to a small, highly electronegative atom (N, O, F), polarity has a much greater effect on boiling point. Hydrogen fluoride, HF, despite its low molar mass (20 g/mol), has the highest boiling point of all the hydrogen halides. Water (MM = 18 g/mol) and ammonia (MM = 17 g/mol) also have abnormally high boiling points (Table 9.4). In these cases, the effect of polarity reverses the normal trend expected from molar mass alone.

The unusually high boiling points of HF, H_2O, and NH_3 result from an unusually strong type of dipole force called a **hydrogen bond.** The hydrogen bond is a force exerted between an H atom bonded to an F, O, or N atom in one molecule and an unshared pair on the F, O, or N atom of a neighboring molecule:

:X—H---:X—H   X=N, O, or F

↑ hydrogen bond

There are two reasons why hydrogen bonds are stronger than ordinary dipole forces:

1. The difference in electronegativity between hydrogen (2.2) and fluorine (4.0), oxygen (3.5), or nitrogen (3.0) is quite large. It causes the bonding electrons in molecules such as HF, H_2O, and NH_3 to be primarily associated with the more electronegative atom (F, O, or N). So the hydrogen atom, insofar as its interaction with a neighboring molecule is concerned, behaves almost like a bare proton.

2. The small size of the hydrogen atom allows the unshared pair of an F, O, or N atom of one molecule to approach the H atom in another very closely. It is significant that hydrogen bonding occurs only with these three nonmetals, all of which have small atomic radii.

Hydrogen bonding is important in biochemistry, particularly with proteins.

Hydrogen bonds can exist in many molecules other than HF, H_2O, and NH_3. The basic requirement is simply that hydrogen be bonded to a fluorine, oxygen, or nitrogen atom with at least one unshared pair. Consider, for example, the two compounds whose condensed structural formulas are

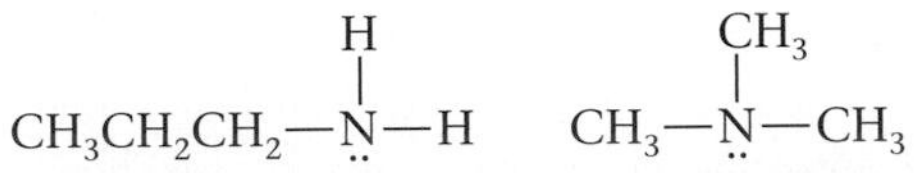

propylamine   trimethylamine

Table 9.4 Effect of Hydrogen Bonding on Boiling Point

	bp (°C)		bp (°C)		bp (°C)
NH_3	−33	H_2O	100	HF	19
PH_3	−88	H_2S	−60	HCl	−85
AsH_3	−63	H_2Se	−42	HBr	−67
SbH_3	−18	H_2Te	−2	HI	−35

Note: Molecules in blue show hydrogen bonding.

Propylamine, in which two hydrogen atoms are bonded to nitrogen, can show hydrogen bonding; it is a liquid with a normal boiling point of 49°C. Trimethylamine, which like propylamine has the molecular formula C_3H_9N, cannot hydrogen bond to itself; it boils at 3°C.

Example 9.5 Would you expect to find hydrogen bonds in

(a) acetic acid?

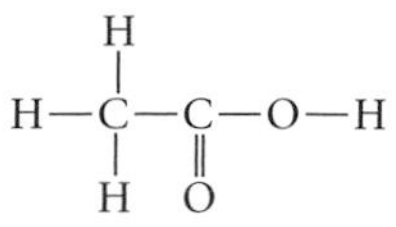

(b) diethyl ether?

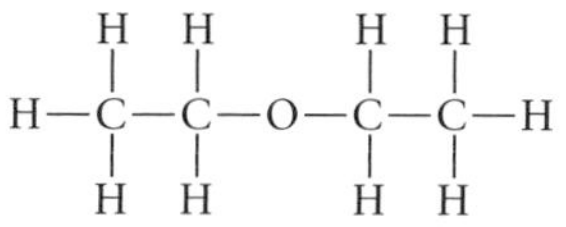

(c) hydrazine, N_2H_4?

Strategy For hydrogen bonding to occur, hydrogen must be bonded to F, O, or N. In (c), draw the Lewis structure first.

SOLUTION

(a) There should be hydrogen bonds in acetic acid because an H atom is bonded to oxygen.
(b) All the hydrogen atoms are bonded to carbon in diethyl ether, so there should be no hydrogen bonds.
(c) The Lewis structure of hydrazine is

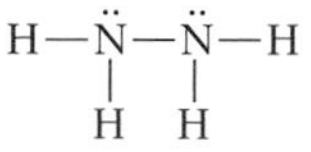

Because hydrogen is bonded to nitrogen, hydrogen bonding can occur between neighboring N_2H_4 molecules. The boiling point of hydrazine (114°C) is much higher than that of molecular O_2 (−183°C), which has the same molar mass.

Reality Check In acetic acid, the H atom bonded to oxygen in one molecule forms a hydrogen bond with an oxygen in an adjacent molecule. The same situation applies in hydrazine if you substitute nitrogen for oxygen.

Water has many unusual properties in addition to its high boiling point. As pointed out in Chapter 8, it has a very high specific heat, 4.18 J/g · °C. Its heat of vaporization per gram, 2.26 kJ/g, is the highest of all molecular substances. Both of these properties reflect the hydrogen-bonded structure of the liquid. Many of these bonds have to be broken when the liquid is heated; all of them disappear on boiling.

In contrast to most substances, water expands on freezing. Ice is one of the very few solids that has a density less than that of the liquid from which it is formed (d ice at 0°C = 0.917 g/cm^3; d water at 0°C = 1.000 g/cm^3). This behavior is an indirect result of hydrogen bonding. When water freezes to ice, an open hexagonal pattern of molecules results (Figure 9.10, p. 240). Each oxygen atom in an ice crystal is bonded to four hydrogens. Two of these are attached by ordinary covalent bonds at a distance of 0.099 nm. The other two form hydrogen bonds 0.177 nm in length. The large proportion of empty space in the ice structure explains why ice is less dense than water.

If ice were more dense than water, skating would be a lot less popular.

Figure 9.10
The structure of ice. In ice, the water molecules are arranged in an open pattern that gives ice its low density. Each oxygen atom (red) is bonded covalently to two hydrogen atoms (gray) and forms hydrogen bonds with two other hydrogen atoms.

Example 9.6 Conceptual

What types of intermolecular forces are present in nitrogen, N_2? Chloroform, $CHCl_3$? Carbon dioxide, CO_2? Ammonia, NH_3?

Strategy Determine whether the molecules are polar or nonpolar; only polar molecules show dipole forces. Check the Lewis structures for H atoms bonded to F, N, or O. All molecules have dispersion forces.

SOLUTION The N_2 and CO_2 molecules are nonpolar (Chapter 7), so only dispersion forces are present. Both $CHCl_3$ and NH_3 are polar molecules. Chloroform contains dipole forces as well as dispersion forces. Ammonia contains hydrogen bonds as well as dispersion forces.

We have now discussed three types of intermolecular forces: dispersion forces, dipole forces, and hydrogen bonds. You should bear in mind that **all these forces are relatively weak compared with ordinary covalent bonds.** Consider, for example, the situation in H_2O. The total intermolecular attractive energy in ice is about 50 kJ/mol. In contrast, to dissociate one mole of water vapor into atoms requires the absorption of 928 kJ of energy, that is, 2(OH bond energy). This explains why it is a lot easier to boil water than to decompose it into the elements. Even at a temperature of 1000°C and 1 atm, only about one H_2O molecule in a billion decomposes to hydrogen and oxygen atoms.

9.4 NETWORK COVALENT, IONIC, AND METALLIC SOLIDS

Virtually all substances that are gases or liquids at 25°C and 1 atm are molecular. In contrast, there are three types of nonmolecular solids (Figure 9.11, p. 241). These are—

- **network covalent solids,** in which atoms are joined by a continuous network of covalent bonds. The entire crystal, in effect, consists of one huge molecule.
- ***ionic solids,*** held together by strong electrical forces (ionic bonds) between oppositely charged ions adjacent to one another.
- ***metallic solids,*** in which the structural units are electrons (e^-) and cations, which may have charges of $+1$, $+2$, or $+3$.

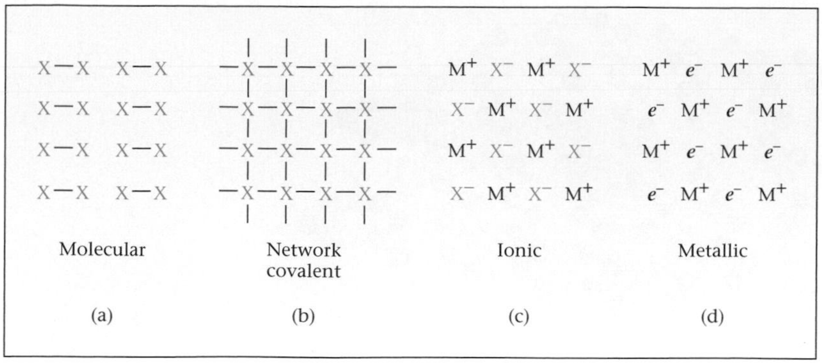

Figure 9.11
Diagrams of four types of substances (see text discussion). X represents a nonmetal atom, — represents a covalent bond, M^+ a cation, X^- an anion, and e^- an electron.

Network Covalent Solids

As a class, network covalent solids—

- ***have high melting points, often about 1000°C.*** To melt the solid, covalent bonds between atoms must be broken. In this respect, solids of this type differ markedly from molecular solids, which have much lower melting points.
- ***are insoluble in all common solvents.*** For solution to occur, covalent bonds throughout the solid would have to be broken.
- ***are poor electrical conductors.*** In most network covalent substances (graphite is an exception), there are no mobile electrons to carry a current.

Graphite and Diamond

Several nonmetallic elements and metalloids have a network covalent structure. The most important of these is carbon, which has two different crystalline forms of the network covalent type. Both graphite and diamond have high melting points, above 3500°C. However, the bonding patterns in the two solids are quite different.

In diamond, each carbon atom forms single bonds with four other carbon atoms arranged tetrahedrally around it. The hybridization in diamond is sp^3. The three-dimensional covalent bonding contributes to diamond's unusual hardness. Diamond is one of the hardest substances known; it is used in cutting tools and quality grindstones (Figure 9.12).

Hybridization is discussed in Section 7.4.

Graphite is planar, with the carbon atoms arranged in a hexagonal pattern. Each carbon atom is bonded to three others, two by single bonds, one by a double bond. The hybridization is sp^2. The forces between adjacent layers in graphite are of the dispersion type and are quite weak. A "lead" pencil really contains a graphite rod, thin layers of which rub off onto the paper as you write (Figure 9.13, p. 242).

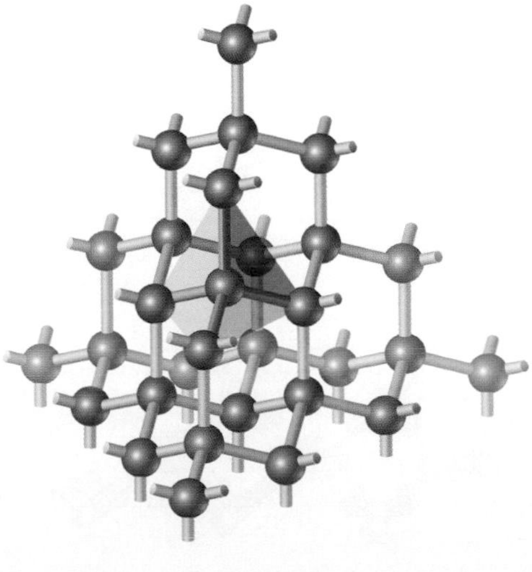

Figure 9.12
The structure of a diamond. Diamond has a three-dimensional structure in which each carbon atom is surrounded tetrahedrally by four other carbon atoms.

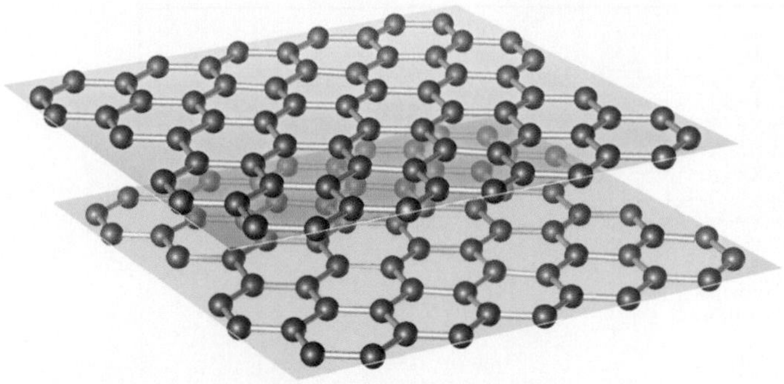

Figure 9.13
The structure of graphite. Graphite has a two-dimensional layer structure with weak dispersion forces between the layers.

At 25°C and 1 atm, graphite is the stable form of carbon. Diamond, in principle, should slowly transform to graphite under ordinary conditions. Fortunately for the owners of diamond rings, this transition occurs at zero rate unless the diamond is heated to about 1500°C, at which temperature the conversion occurs rapidly. For understandable reasons, no one has ever become very excited over the commercial possibilities of this process. The more difficult task of converting graphite to diamond has aroused much greater enthusiasm.

At high pressures, diamond is the stable form of carbon, since it has a higher density than graphite (3.51 vs 2.26 g/cm^3). The industrial synthesis of diamond from graphite or other forms of carbon is carried out at about 100,000 atm and 2000°C.

Compounds of Silicon

Perhaps the simplest compound with a network covalent structure is quartz, the most common form of SiO_2 and the major component of sand. In quartz, each silicon atom bonds tetrahedrally to four oxygen atoms. Each oxygen atom bonds to two silicons, thus linking adjacent tetrahedra to one another (Figure 9.14). Notice that the network of covalent bonds extends throughout the entire crystal. Unlike most pure solids, quartz does not melt sharply to a liquid. Instead, it turns to a viscous mass over a wide temperature range, first softening at about 1400°C. The viscous fluid probably contains long —Si—O—Si—O— chains, with enough bonds broken to allow flow.

More than 90% of the rocks and minerals found in the earth's crust are silicates, which are essentially ionic. Typically the anion has a network covalent structure in which SiO_4^{4-} tetrahedra are bonded to one another in one, two, or three dimensions. The structure shown at the left of Figure 9.15 (p. 243), where the anion is a one-dimensional infinite chain, is typical of fibrous minerals such as diopside, $CaSiO_3 \cdot MgSiO_3$. Asbestos has a related structure in which two chains are linked together to form a double strand.

The structure shown at the right of Figure 9.15 is typical of layer minerals such as talc, $Mg_3(OH)_2Si_4O_{10}$. Here SiO_4^{4-} tetrahedra are linked together to form an infinite sheet. The layers are held loosely together by weak dispersion forces, so they easily slide past one another. As a result, talcum powder, like graphite, has a slippery feeling.

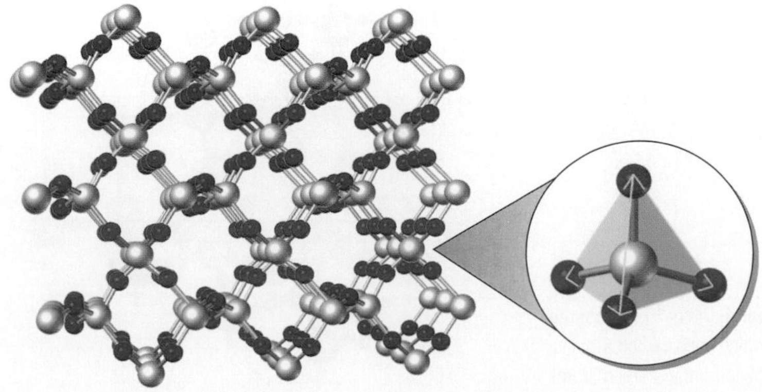

Figure 9.14
Crystal structure of quartz. The Si (gray) and O (red) atoms form six-membered rings. Each Si atom is bonded tetrahedrally to four O atoms.

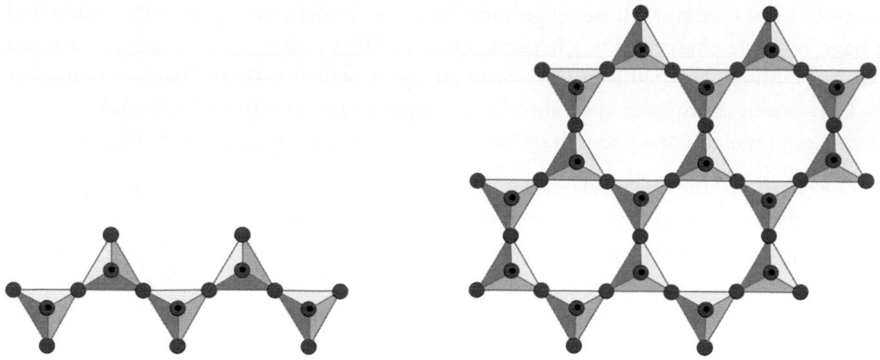

$(SiO_3^{2-})_n$ $(Si_4O_{10}^{4-})_n$

Figure 9.15
Silicate lattices. The red circles represent oxygen atoms. The black dot in the center of the red circle represents the Si atom, which is at the center of a tetrahedron. *(Left)* Diopside has a one-dimensional infinite chain. *(Right)* A portion of the talc structure, which is composed of infinite sheets.

Among the three-dimensional silicates are the *zeolites,* which contain cavities or tunnels in which Na^+ or Ca^{2+} ions may be trapped. Synthetic zeolites with made-to-order holes are used in home water softeners. When hard water containing Ca^{2+} ions flows through a zeolite column, an exchange reaction occurs. If we represent the formula of the zeolite as NaZ, where Z^- represents a complex, three-dimensional anion, the water-softening reaction can be represented by the equation

This type of water softener shouldn't be used if you're trying to reduce sodium intake.

$$Ca^{2+}(aq) + 2NaZ(s) \longrightarrow CaZ_2(s) + 2Na^+(aq)$$

Sodium ions migrate out of the cavities; Ca^{2+} ions from the hard water move in to replace them.

Ionic Solids

An ionic solid consists of cations and anions (e.g., Na^+, Cl^-). No simple, discrete molecules are present in NaCl or other ionic compounds; rather, the ions are held in a regular, repeating arrangement by strong ionic bonds, electrostatic interactions between oppositely charged ions. Because of this structure, shown in Figure 9.11 on page 241, ionic solids have the following properties:

CENGAGENOW™
Click Chemistry Interactive for the self-study module **formation of ionic compounds.**

1. ***Ionic solids are nonvolatile and have high-melting points*** (typically from 600°C to 2000°C). Ionic bonds must be broken to melt the solid, separating oppositely charged ions from each other. Only at high temperatures do the ions acquire enough kinetic energy for this to happen.

2. ***Ionic solids do not conduct electricity because the charged ions are fixed in position.*** They become good conductors, however, when melted or dissolved in water. In both cases, in the melt or solution, the ions (such as Na^+ and Cl^-) are free to move through the liquid and thus can conduct an electric current.

Charged particles must move to carry a current.

3. ***Many, but not all, ionic compounds*** (e.g., NaCl but not $CaCO_3$) ***are soluble in water, a polar solvent.*** In contrast, ionic compounds are insoluble in nonpolar solvents such as benzene (C_6H_6) or carbon tetrachloride (CCl_4).

The relative strengths of different ionic bonds can be estimated from Coulomb's law, which gives the electrical energy of interaction between a cation and anion in contact with one another:

$$E = \frac{k \times Q_1 \times Q_2}{d}$$

Here, Q_1 and Q_2 are the charges of anion and cation, and d, the distance between the centers of the two ions, is the sum of the ionic radii (Appendix 2):

$$d = r_{\text{cation}} + r_{\text{anion}}$$

The quantity k is a constant whose magnitude need not concern us. Because the cation and anion have opposite charges, E is a negative quantity. This makes sense; energy is evolved when two oppositely charged ions, originally far apart with $E = 0$, approach one another closely. Conversely, energy has to be absorbed to separate the ions from each other.

From Coulomb's law, the strength of the ionic bond should depend on two factors:

1. ***The charges of the ions.*** The bond in CaO (+2, −2 ions) is considerably stronger than that in NaCl (+1, −1 ions). This explains why the melting point of calcium oxide (2927°C) is so much higher than that of sodium chloride (801°C).
2. ***The size of the ions.*** The ionic bond in NaCl (mp = 801°C) is somewhat stronger than that in KBr (mp = 734°C) because the internuclear distance is smaller in NaCl:

$$d_{NaCl} = r_{Na^+} + r_{Cl^-} = 0.095 \text{ nm} + 0.181 \text{ nm} = 0.276 \text{ nm}$$

$$d_{KBr} = r_{K^+} + r_{Br^-} = 0.133 \text{ nm} + 0.195 \text{ nm} = 0.328 \text{ nm}$$

A more sophisticated model of metals is described in Appendix 5.

Metals

Figure 9.11d illustrates a simple model of bonding in metals known as the **electron-sea model.** The metallic crystal is pictured as an array of positive ions, for example, Na^+, Mg^{2+}. These are anchored in position, like buoys in a mobile "sea" of electrons. These electrons are not attached to any particular positive ion but rather can wander through the crystal. The electron-sea model explains many of the characteristic properties of metals:

1. ***High electrical conductivity.*** The presence of large numbers of relatively mobile electrons explains why metals have electrical conductivities several hundred times greater than those of typical nonmetals. Silver is the best electrical conductor but is too expensive for general use. Copper, with a conductivity close to that of silver, is the metal most commonly used for electrical wiring. Although a much poorer conductor than copper, mercury is used in many electrical devices, such as silent light switches, in which a liquid conductor is required.
2. ***High thermal conductivity.*** Heat is carried through metals by collisions between electrons, which occur frequently. Saucepans used for cooking commonly contain aluminum, copper, or stainless steel; their handles are made of a nonmetallic material that is a good thermal insulator.
3. ***Ductility and malleability.*** Most metals are ductile (capable of being drawn out into a wire) and malleable (capable of being hammered into thin sheets). In a metal, the electrons act like a flexible glue holding the atomic nuclei together. As a result, metal crystals can be deformed without shattering.
4. ***Luster.*** Polished metal surfaces reflect light. Most metals have a silvery white metallic color because they reflect light of all wavelengths. Because electrons are not restricted to a particular bond, they can absorb and re-emit light over a wide wavelength range. Gold and copper absorb some light in the blue region of the visible spectrum and so appear yellow (gold) or red (copper).

a, c, Charles D. Winters; b, Marna G. Clarke

(a) (b) (c)

Solids with different structures. (a) Diamond, a network covalent solid. (b) Potassium dichromate, $K_2Cr_2O_7$, an ionic solid. (c) Manganese, a metallic solid.

5. ***Insolubility in water and other common solvents.*** No metals dissolve in water; electrons cannot go into solution, and cations cannot dissolve by themselves. The only liquid metal, mercury, dissolves many metals, forming solutions called ***amalgams.*** An Ag-Sn-Hg amalgam is used in filling teeth.

In general, the melting points of metals cover a wide range, from $-39°C$ for mercury to 3410°C for tungsten. This variation in melting point corresponds to a similar variation in the strength of the metallic bond. Generally speaking, the lowest melting metals are those that form $+1$ cations, like sodium (mp = 98°C) and potassium (mp = 64°C).

Much of what has been said about the four structural types of solids in Sections 9.3 and 9.4 is summarized in Table 9.5.

Example 9.7 Conceptual

For each species in column A, choose the description in column B that best applies.

A	B
(a) CO_2	(e) ionic, high-melting
(b) $CuSO_4$	(f) liquid metal, good conductor
(c) SiO_2	(g) polar molecule, soluble in water
(d) Hg	(h) ionic, insoluble in water
	(i) network covalent, high-melting
	(j) nonpolar molecule, gas at 25°C

Strategy Refer to Table 9.5 and the preceding discussion.

SOLUTION

(a) matches (j)	(b) matches (e)
(c) matches (i)	(d) matches (f)

9.5 CRYSTAL STRUCTURES

Solids tend to crystallize in definite geometric forms that often can be seen by the naked eye. In ordinary table salt, cubic crystals of NaCl are clearly visible. Large, beautifully formed crystals of such minerals as fluorite, CaF_2, are found in nature. It is possible to observe distinct crystal forms of many metals under a microscope.

Table 9.5 Structures and Properties of Types of Substances

Type	Structural Particles	Forces Within Particles	Forces Between Particles	Properties	Examples
Molecular	Molecules				
	(a) nonpolar	Covalent bond	Dispersion	Low mp, bp; often gas or liquid at 25°C; nonconductors; insoluble in water, soluble in organic solvents	H_2 CCl_4
	(b) polar	Covalent bond	Dispersion, dipole, H bond	Similar to nonpolar but generally higher mp and bp, more likely to be water-soluble	HCl NH_3
Network covalent	Atoms	—	Covalent bond	Hard solids with very high melting points; nonconductors; insoluble in common solvents	C SiO_2
Ionic	Ions	—	Ionic bond	High mp; conductors in molten state or water solution; often soluble in water, insoluble in organic solvents	NaCl MgO $CaCO_3$
Metallic	Cations, mobile electrons	—	Metallic bond	Variable mp; good conductors in solid; insoluble in common solvents	Na Fe

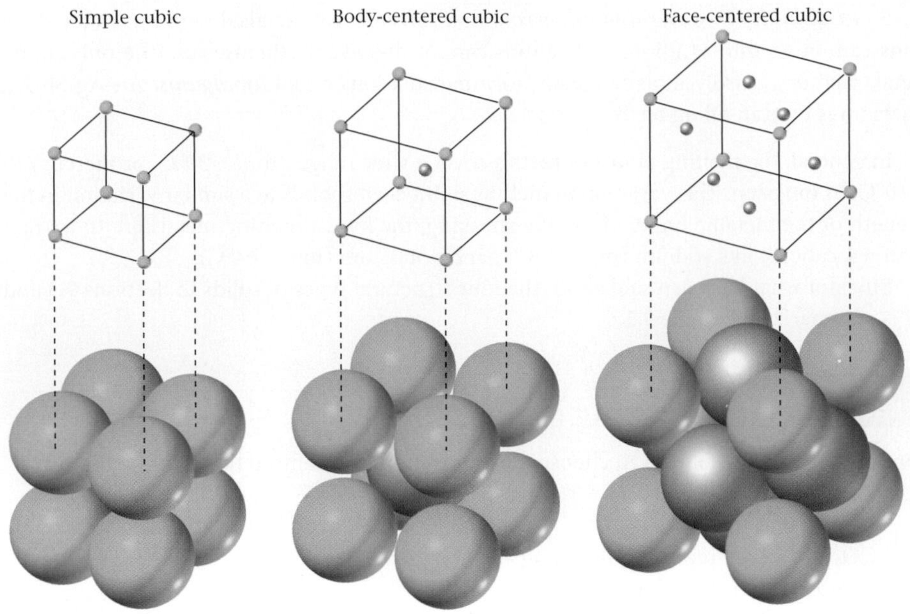

Figure 9.16
Three types of unit cells. In each case, there is an atom at each of the eight corners of the cube. In the body-centered cubic unit cell, there is an additional atom in the center of the cube. In the face-centered cubic unit cell, there is an atom in the center of each of the six faces.

Crystals have definite geometric forms because the atoms or ions present are arranged in a definite, three-dimensional pattern. The nature of this pattern can be deduced by a technique known as x-ray diffraction. The basic information that comes out of such studies has to do with the dimensions and geometric form of the **unit cell,** the smallest structural unit that, repeated over and over again in three dimensions, generates the crystal. In all, there are 14 different kinds of unit cells. Our discussion will be limited to a few of the simpler unit cells found in metals and ionic solids.

Metals

Three of the simpler unit cells found in metals, shown in Figure 9.16, are the following:

1. **Simple cubic cell (SC).** This is a cube that consists of eight atoms whose centers are located at the corners of the cell. Atoms at adjacent corners of the cube touch one another.

2. **Face-centered cubic cell (FCC).** Here there is an atom at each corner of the cube and one in the center of each of the six faces of the cube. In this structure, atoms at the corners of the cube do not touch one another; they are forced slightly apart. Instead, contact occurs along a face diagonal. The atom at the center of each face touches atoms at opposite corners of the face.

3. **Body-centered cubic cell (BCC).** This is a cube with atoms at each corner and one in the center of the cube. Here again, corner atoms do not touch each other. Instead, contact occurs along the body diagonal; the atom at the center of the cube touches atoms at opposite corners.

Table 9.6 lists three other ways in which these types of cubic cells differ from one another.

1. ***Number of atoms per unit cell.*** Keep in mind that a huge number of unit cells are in contact with each other, interlocking to form a three-dimensional crystal. This means that several of the atoms in a unit cell do not belong exclusively to that cell. Specifically—

- an atom at the corner of a cube forms a part of eight different cubes that touch at that point. (To convince yourself of this, look back at Figure 2.11 [page 36]; focus on the small sphere in the center.) In this sense, only $\frac{1}{8}$ of a corner atom belongs to a particular cell.
- an atom at the center of the face of a cube is shared by another cube that touches that face. In effect, only $\frac{1}{2}$ of that atom can be assigned to a given cell. This means, for example, that the number of atoms per FCC unit cell is

$$8 \text{ corner atoms} \times \tfrac{1}{8} + 6 \text{ face atoms} \times \tfrac{1}{2} = 4 \text{ atoms per cube}$$

Table 9.6 Properties of Cubic Unit Cells

	Simple	BCC	FCC
Number of atoms per unit cell	1	2	4
Relation between side of cell, *s*, and atomic radius, *r*	$2r = s$	$4r = s\sqrt{3}$	$4r = s\sqrt{2}$
% of empty space	47.6	32.0	26.0

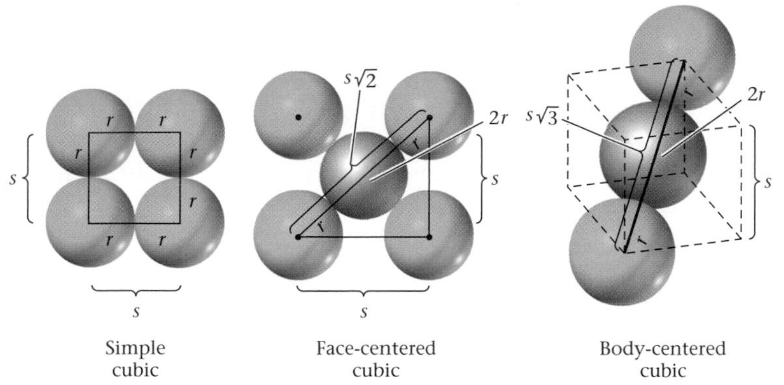

Figure 9.17
Relation between atomic radius (*r*) and length of edge (*s*) for cubic cells. In the simple cubic cell, $2r = s$. In the face-centered cubic cell, the face diagonal is equal to $s\sqrt{2}$ (hypotenuse of a right triangle) and to $4r$. Thus, $s\sqrt{2} = 4r$. In the body-centered cubic cell, the body diagonal is equal to $s\sqrt{3}$ (diagonal of a cube) and to $4r$. Thus $s\sqrt{3} = 4r$.

2. *Relation between side of cell (s) and atomic radius (r).* To see how these two quantities are related, consider an FCC cell in which atoms touch along a face diagonal. As you can see from Figure 9.17—

- the distance along the face diagonal, *d*, is equal to four atomic radii

$$d = 4r$$

- *d* can be related to the length of a side of the cell by the Pythagorean theorem, $d^2 = s^2 + s^2 = 2s^2$. Taking the square root of both sides,

$$d = s\sqrt{2}$$

Equating the two expressions for *d*, we have

$$4r = s\sqrt{2}$$

This relation offers an experimental way of determining the atomic radius of a metal, if the nature and dimensions of the unit cell are known.

Example 9.8 Graded

Silver is a metal commonly used in jewelry and photography. It crystallizes with a face-centered cubic (FCC) unit cell 0.407 nm on an edge.

*(a) What is the atomic radius of silver in cm? (1 nm = 10^{-7} cm)
**(b) What is the volume of a single silver atom? (The volume of a spherical ball of radius *r* is $V = \frac{4}{3}\pi r^3$.)
***(c) What is the density of a single silver atom?

SOLUTION

(a) The equation for the relation between the radius and the length of a side of an FCC cell is

$$4r = s\sqrt{2}$$

Substituting $s = 0.407$ nm and solving for *r*, we obtain

$$r = \frac{0.407 \text{ nm} \times \sqrt{2}}{4} = 0.144 \text{ nm} \times \frac{10^{-7} \text{ cm}}{1 \text{ nm}} = 1.44 \times 10^{-8} \text{ cm}$$

(b) Because an atom is spherical, the formula in parentheses applies. Using the value of r found in (a), that formula gives

$$V = \frac{4}{3}\pi(1.44 \times 10^{-8}\ \text{cm})^3 = \boxed{1.25 \times 10^{-23}\ \text{cm}^3}$$

(c) You will need the mass of a silver atom. To get it, use Avogadro's number and the molar mass of silver, 107.9 g/mol.

$$m_{\text{Ag atom}} = \frac{107.9\ \text{g}}{1\ \text{mol}} \times \frac{1\ \text{mol}}{6.022 \times 10^{23}\ \text{atoms}} = 1.792 \times 10^{-22}\ \text{g/atom}$$

$$\text{density}_{\text{Ag atom}} = \frac{1.792 \times 10^{-22}\ \text{g/atom}}{1.25 \times 10^{-23}\ \text{cm}^3} = \boxed{14.3\ \text{g/cm}^3 \cdot \text{atom}}$$

Reality Check In FCC unit cells, the fraction of empty space is 0.26. When this is factored into the above, the calculated density of silver becomes 14.3 − (0.26)(14.3) = 10.6 g/cm^3, which is almost the same as its experimentally determined value: 10.5 g/cm^3.

Golf balls and oranges pack naturally in an FCC structure.

3. *Percentage of empty space.* Metal atoms in a crystal, like marbles in a box, tend to pack closely together. As you can see from Table 9.6, nearly half of a simple cubic unit cell is empty space. This makes the SC structure very unstable; only one metal (polonium, $Z = 84$) has this type of unit cell. The body-centered cubic structure has less waste space; about 20 metals, including all those in Group 1, have a BCC unit cell. A still more efficient way of packing spheres of the same size is the face-centered cubic structure, where the fraction of empty space is only 0.26. About 40 different metals have a structure based on a face-centered cubic cell or a close relative in which the packing is equally efficient (hexagonal closest packed structure).

CHEMISTRY The Human Side

The crystal structures discussed in this section were determined by a powerful technique known as X-ray diffraction (Figure A). By studying the pattern produced when the scattered rays strike a target, it is possible to deduce the geometry of the unit cell. With molecular crystals, one can go a step further, identifying the geometry and composition of the molecule. A father and son team of two English physicists, William H. and William L. Bragg, won the Nobel Prize in 1915 for pioneer work in this area.

Dorothy Crowfoot Hodgkin
(1910–1994)

The Braggs and their successors strongly sought out talented women scientists to develop the new field of x-ray crystallography. Foremost among these women was Dorothy Crowfoot Hodgkin, who spent almost all of her professional career at Oxford University in England. As the years passed she unraveled the structures of successively more complex natural products. These included penicillin, which she studied between 1942 and 1949, vitamin B-12 (1948–1957), and her greatest triumph, insulin, which she worked on for more than 30 years. Among her students at Oxford was Margaret Thatcher, the future prime minister. In 1964, Dorothy Hodgkin became the third (and, so far, the last) woman to win the Nobel Prize in chemistry).* The other two women Noble laureates in Chemistry are Marie Curie and Irène Joliot-Curie.

Hodgkin's accomplishments were all the more remarkable when you consider some of the obstacles she had to overcome. At the age of 24, she developed rheumatoid arthritis, a crippling disease of the immune system. Gradually she lost the use of her hands; ultimately she was confined to a wheelchair. Dorothy Hodgkin succeeded because she combined a first-rate intellect with an almost infinite capacity for hard work. Beyond that, she was one of those rare individuals who inspire loyalty by taking genuine pleasure in the successes of other people. A colleague referred to her as "the gentle genius."

Dorothy's husband, Thomas Hodgkin, was a scholar in his own right with an interest in the history of Africa. Apparently realizing that hers was the greater talent, he acted as a "house-husband" for their three children so she would have more time to devote to research. One wonders how Dorothy and Thomas Hodgkin reacted to the 1964 headline in a London tabloid, "British Wife Wins Nobel Prize."

*To learn more about Dorothy Hodgkin and other women Nobel laureates, we recommend the book *Nobel Prize Women in Science* by Sharon Bertsch McGrayne, published in 1993.

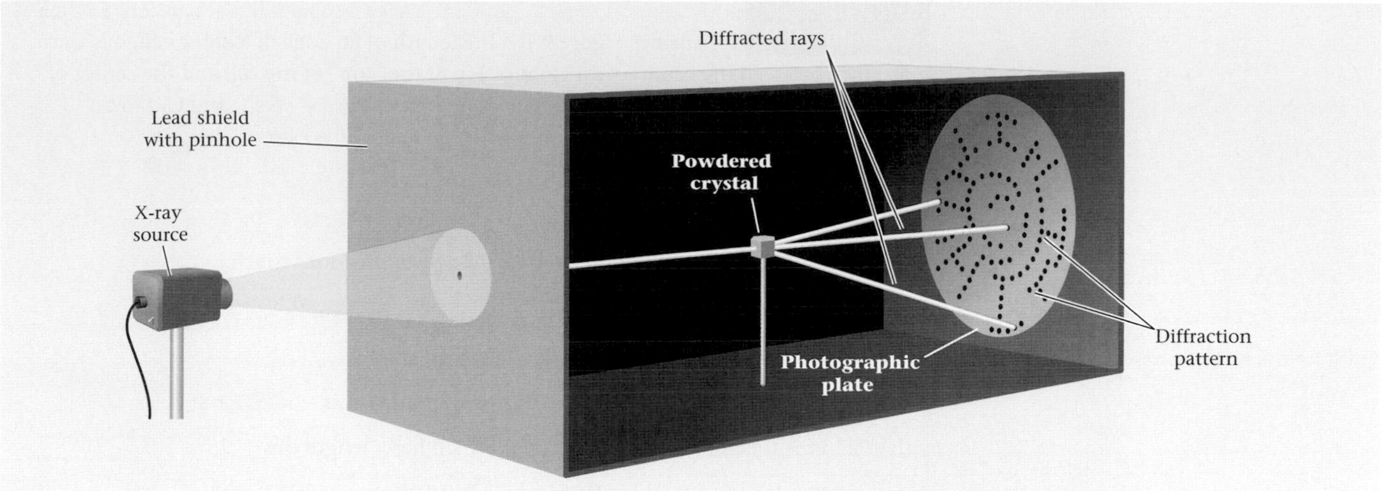

Figure A

X-ray diffraction. Knowing the angles and intensities at which X-rays are diffracted by a crystal, it is possible to calculate the distances between layers of atoms.

Ionic Crystals

The geometry of ionic crystals, in which there are two different kinds of ions, is more difficult to describe than that of metals. However, in many cases the packing can be visualized in terms of the unit cells described above. Lithium chloride, LiCl, is a case in point. Here, the larger Cl^- ions form a face-centered cubic lattice (Figure 9.18). The smaller Li^+ ions fit into "holes" between the Cl^- ions. This puts a Li^+ ion at the center of each edge of the cube.

In the sodium chloride crystal, the Na^+ ion is slightly too large to fit into holes in a face-centered lattice of Cl^- ions (Figure 9.18). As a result, the Cl^- ions are pushed slightly apart so that they are no longer touching, and only Na^+ ions are in contact with Cl^- ions. However, the relative positions of positive and negative ions remain the same as in LiCl: Each anion is surrounded by six cations and each cation by six anions.

NaCl is FCC in both Na^+ and Cl^- ions; CsCl is BCC in both Cs^+ and Cl^- ions.

The structures of LiCl and NaCl are typical of all the alkali halides (Group 1 cation, Group 17 anion) except those of cesium. Because of the large size of the Cs^+ ion, CsCl crystallizes in a quite different structure. Here, each Cs^+ ion is located at the center of a simple cube outlined by Cl^- ions. The Cs^+ ion at the center touches all the Cl^- ions at the corners; the Cl^- ions do not touch each other. As you can see, each Cs^+ ion is surrounded by eight Cl^- ions, and each Cl^- ion is surrounded by eight Cs^+ ions.

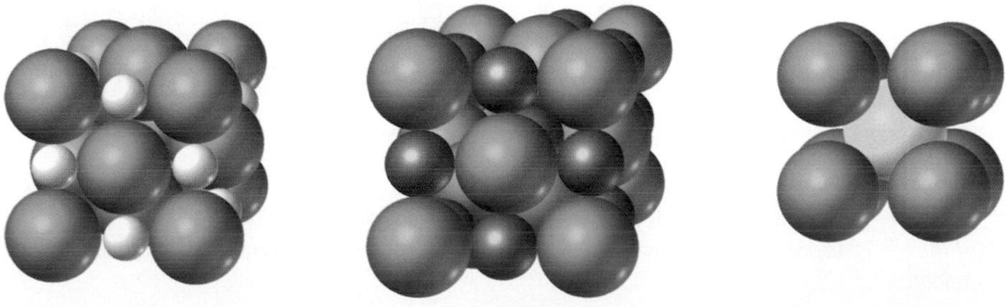

Figure 9.18

Three types of lattices in ionic crystals. In LiCl, the Cl^- ions are in contact with each other, forming a face-centered cubic lattice. In NaCl, the Cl^- ions are forced slightly apart by the larger Na^+ ions. In CsCl, the large Cs^+ ion at the center touches the Cl^- ions at each corner of the cube.

Example 9.9 Consider Figure 9.18. The length of an edge of a cubic cell, *s*, is the distance between the center of an atom or ion at the "top" of the cell and the center of the atom or ion at the "bottom." Taking the ionic radii of Li^+, Na^+, and Cl^- to be 0.060 nm, 0.095 nm, and 0.181 nm, respectively, determine *s* for

(a) NaCl (b) LiCl

Strategy Use Figure 9.18 to determine along what line ions touch.

SOLUTION

(a) Cl^- and Na^+ ions touch along an edge of the cell.

$$s = 0.181\text{ nm} + 2(0.095\text{ nm}) + 0.181\text{ nm} = \boxed{0.552\text{ nm}}$$

(b) Cl^- ions touch along a face diagonal, which has a length of $s \times 2^{1/2}$.

$$s \times 2^{1/2} = 0.181\text{ nm} + 2(0.181\text{ nm}) + 0.181\text{ nm}$$
$$s = 0.724\text{ nm}/2^{1/2} = \boxed{0.512\text{ nm}}$$

CHEMISTRY Beyond the Classroom

Allotropy

Two different forms of an element in the same physical state are called **allotropes.** Diamond and graphite, discussed in this chapter, satisfy this criterion. Indeed, there are several other allotropes of solid carbon. One of the most interesting was discovered in 1985 by Richard E. Smalley (1943–2005) and Robert F. Curl (1933–) at Rice University and Harold W. Kroto (1939–) at the University of Sussex, England. The structure of this allotrope is shown at the top of Figure A. Sixty carbon atoms are arranged in a nearly spherical cage. More exactly, the geometry of this molecule is that of a polygon with 32 faces; 12 of these are pentagons, and 20 are hexagons.

If you're a sports fan, you've almost certainly seen this structure before. It is that of a soccer ball with a carbon atom at each vertex. Smalley and his colleagues could have named this allotropic form of carbon "carbosoccer" or "soccerene," but they didn't. Instead they called it "buckminster fullerene" after the architect R. Buckminster Fuller, whose geodesic domes vaguely resembled truncated soccer balls. Less formally, the word "buckyball" is used.

Allotropy is a very common phenomenon shown by metals, metalloids, and nonmetals. In the gaseous or liquid state, allotropes most often differ from one another in molecular formula. Consider, for example, the two allotropes of gaseous oxygen, O_2, and ozone, O_3.

Solid allotropes may differ from one another in their bonding patterns (recall Figure 9.11, page 241). *White tin,* the stable form of solid tin at 25°C, shows metallic bonding and has the properties we associate with metals: luster, ductility, high electrical and thermal conductivity. When white tin is kept at low temperatures for long periods of time, it crumbles to powdery *grey tin,* which has the network covalent structure of diamond. The formation of grey tin seems to spread, like an infection, from a single point. This process was common in the cold cathedrals of northern Europe in the 1800s. Organ pipes made of tin were said to suffer from "tin disease."

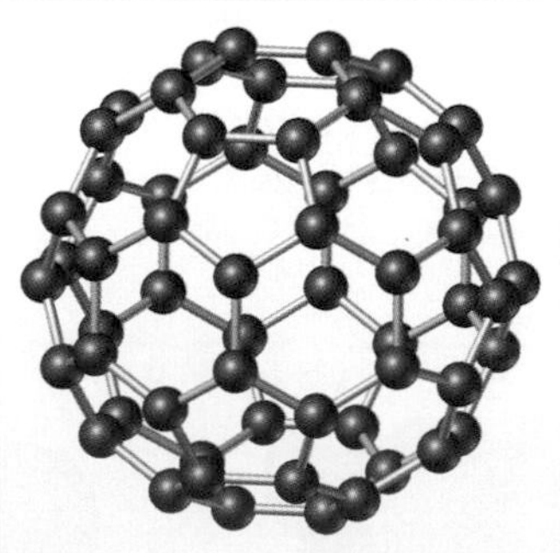
(a)

b, George Semple

(b)

Figure A
Buckminsterfullerene (buckyball). (a) The arrangement of the 60 carbon atoms in a buckyball. (b) The identical arrangement of the hexagons and pentagons on the surface of a soccer ball.

The element phosphorus forms a variety of allotropic forms in the solid state. In the chemistry stockroom, you are likely to find *red phosphorus* and possibly *white phosphorus* (Figure B). As you can see, white phosphorus has the molecular formula P_4, whereas red phosphorus might be represented as P_x, where x is a very large number. The difference in properties between the two allotropes reflects the difference in their bonding patterns, molecular versus network covalent:

White Phosphorus (P_4)	**Red Phosphorus (P_x)**
low melting point (44°C)	high melting point (590°C at 43 atm)
soluble in nonpolar solvents	insoluble
reactive; burns on exposure to air	less reactive; burns on heating to 250°C
extremely toxic; 0.1 g is fatal	much less toxic

Allotropy in the solid state can also arise because of differences in crystal structure. For example, solid iron has a body-centered cubic structure (recall Figure 9.16, page 246) at room temperature. This changes to a face-centered structure upon heating to 910°C.

The two most familiar allotropes of sulfur, rhombic and monoclinic, have the same molecular formula, S_8. However, they differ in crystal structure. Using the phase diagram shown in Figure C, you can deduce how to convert either of these allotropes to the other. Notice that rhombic sulfur is the stable allotrope at temperatures below about 95°C. If it is heated to that temperature at 1 (i.e., 10^0) atm, it very slowly converts to the monoclinic form. A more convenient way to accomplish this phase change is to melt sulfur, cool it to a temperature between 119°C and 95°C, and watch the formation of needle-like crystals of the monoclinic allotrope. If monoclinic sulfur is cooled quickly to 25°C, it stays around for a day or two. Gradually, it changes to the rhombic form, the more stable allotrope at room temperature.

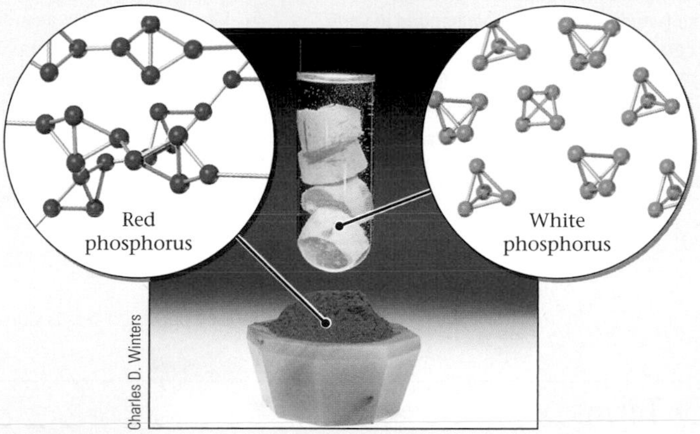

Figure B
Phosphorus allotropes. Because white phosphorus reacts with air at room temperature, it must be stored under water. Red phosphorus does not react with air at room temperature.

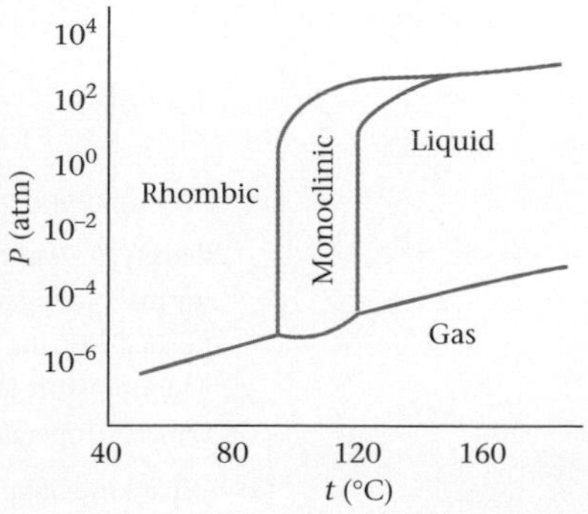

Figure C
Naturally occurring crystals of monoclinic sulfur *(top)* and rhombic sulfur *(below)*. The phase diagram of sulfur is shown on the right (see text discussion).

Chapter Highlights

Key Concepts

Select end of chapter Questions and Problems may be assigned in OWL and are cross-referenced in the Key Concepts list.

CENGAGENOW™

Sign in at **academic.cengage.com/now** to:

- Check your readiness for an exam by taking the Pre-Test and exploring the self-study modules recommended in your Personalized Study plan.
- For quick review, download Go Chemistry mini-lecture flashcard modules (or purchase them at **www.ichapters.com**)

1. Use the ideal gas law to determine whether a liquid will completely vaporize.
   (Example 9.1; Problems 1–6) ■ Questions and Problems assignable in OWL: 6, 59, 61
2. Use the Clausius-Clapeyron equation to relate vapor pressure to temperature.
   (Example 9.2; Problems 7–14) ■ 10, 13
3. Use a phase diagram to determine the phase(s) present at a given T and P.
   (Example 9.3; Problems 15–24) ■ 15, 18
4. Identify the type of intermolecular forces in different substances.
   (Examples 9.4–9.6; Problems 25–38) ■ 25, 27, 29, 33, 35, 37, 74
5. Classify substances as molecular, network covalent, ionic, or metallic.
   (Example 9.7; Problems 39–48) ■ 39, 41
6. Relate unit cell dimensions to atomic or ionic radii.
   (Examples 9.8, 9.9; Problems 49–58) ■ 51, 53, 56, 76

Key Equations

Clausius-Clapeyron $\ln \frac{P_2}{P_1} = \frac{\Delta H_{vap}}{R}\left[\frac{1}{T_1} - \frac{1}{T_2}\right]$ (Section 9.1)

Atomic radius (r) versus side of unit cell: SC: $2r = s$ FCC: $4r = s\sqrt{2}$ BCC: $4r = s\sqrt{3}$ (Section 9.5)

Key Terms

boiling point
—normal
critical
—pressure
—temperature
cubic cell
—body-centered (BCC)
—face-centered (FCC)
—simple (SC)
dipole force
dispersion force
electron-sea model
hydrogen bond
intermolecular forces
network covalent
phase diagram
sublimation
triple point
unit cell
vapor pressure

Summary Problem

Consider isopropyl alcohol, C_3H_8O. It is the component of rubbing alcohol and is also present in many household glass cleaners. Its structural formula is

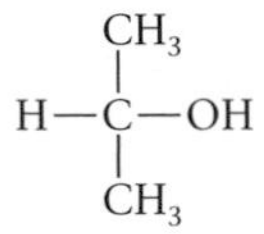

Some of its physical properties are

density: 0.79 g/mL
normal boiling point: 82.3°C
normal freezing point: −89°C
vapor pressure at 22°C: 44 mm Hg
critical temperature: 235°C

(a) What kind of intermolecular forces would you expect to find in isopropyl alcohol?

(b) Ethylmethyl ether, C_3H_8O, has the same molar mass as isopropyl alcohol but a different structural formula ($CH_3—O—C_2H_5$). Compare their normal boiling points and solubilities in water.

(c) Which is a better conductor: isopropyl alcohol or NaOH (*aq*)?

(d) Draw a rough sketch of the phase diagram for isopropyl alcohol. Assume that the solid phase is the densest phase.

(e) Approximate the highest temperature you could use to sublime isopropyl alcohol.

(f) A sample of isopropyl vapor at 230°C, 1 atm, is cooled. At what temperature will liquid first appear if the pressure is kept constant at 1 atm?

(g) Calculate ΔH_{vap} for isopropyl alcohol.

(h) What is the vapor pressure of isopropyl alcohol at 75°C? (Use the information obtained in the earlier parts of this problem.)

(i) Two liters of the alcohol is left in an open container at 22°C in a 12 × 12 × 8.0 ft room. After equilibrium is established, what is the pressure of isopropyl alcohol vapor in the room? Will there be any liquid left in the container? (1 ft^3 = 28.32 L)

Answers

(a) dispersion, dipole, H—bonds
(b) The boiling point of isopropyl alcohol is higher; isopropyl alcohol is more soluble in water.
(c) NaOH (*aq*)
(d) See Figure 9.7a for the general configuration. Put in the appropriate temperatures and pressures.
(e) below −89°C
(f) about 82°C
(g) 41.3 kJ/mol
(h) 566 mm Hg
(i) 15 mm Hg; no

Questions and Problems

Blue-numbered questions have answers in Appendix 6 and fully-worked solutions in the *Student Solutions Manual.*

■ denotes questions assignable in OWL.

WEB indicates that the solution is available on this book's companion website.

Vapor Pressure and Phase Equilibrium

1. Methyl alcohol can be used as a fuel instead of, or combined with, gasoline. A sample of methyl alcohol, CH_3OH, in a flask of constant volume exerts a pressure of 254 mm Hg at 57°C. The flask is slowly cooled.

(a) Assuming no condensation, use the ideal gas law to calculate the pressure of the vapor at 35°C; at 45°C.

(b) Compare your answers in (a) with the equilibrium vapor pressures of methyl alcohol: 203 mm Hg at 35°C; 325 mm Hg at 45°C.

(c) On the basis of your answers to (a) and (b), predict the pressure exerted by the methyl alcohol in the flask at 35°C; at 45°C.

(d) What physical states of methyl alcohol are present in the flask at 35°C? At 45°C?

2. Benzene, a known carcinogen, was once widely used as a solvent. A sample of benzene vapor in a flask of constant volume exerts a pressure of 325 mm Hg at 80°C. The flask is slowly cooled.

(a) Assuming no condensation, use the ideal gas law to calculate the pressure of the vapor at 50°C; at 60°C.

(b) Compare your answers in (a) to the equilibrium vapor pressures of benzene: 269 mm Hg at 50°C, 389 mm Hg at 60°C.

(c) On the basis of your answers to (a) and (b), predict the pressure exerted by the benzene at 50°C; at 60°C.

3. Naphthalene, $C_{10}H_8$, is the substance present in some moth balls. Its vapor pressure at 25°C is 0.300 mm Hg.

(a) How many milligrams of naphthalene will sublime into an evacuated 1.000-L flask?

(b) If 0.700 mg of naphthalene is used, what will the final pressure be? What physical state(s) of naphthalene is (are) in the flask?

(c) If 4.00 mg of naphthalene is used, what will the final pressure be? What physical state(s) of naphthalene is (are) in the flask?

4. The vapor pressure of $I_2(s)$ at 30°C is 0.466 mm Hg.

(a) How many milligrams of iodine will sublime into an evacuated 1.00-L flask?

(b) If 2.0 mg of I_2 is used, what will the final pressure be?

(c) If 10.0 mg of I_2 is used, what will the final pressure be?

5. The vapor pressure of bromine, $Br_2(l)$ at 25°C is 228 mm Hg.

(a) How many grams of bromine will be present as a gas if liquid bromine is poured into an evacuated 2.00-L flask at 25°C?

(b) If 2.00 g of bromine is used, what is the final pressure in the flask? Will there be liquid in the flask?

(c) If 2.00 g of bromine is put into an evacuated 750.0-mL flask at 25°C, what is the final pressure in the flask? Will there be any liquid in the flask?

6. ■ *p*-Dichlorobenzene, $C_6H_4Cl_2$, can be one of the ingredients in mothballs. Its vapor pressure at 20°C is 0.40 mm Hg.

(a) How many milligrams of $C_6H_4Cl_2$ will sublime into an evacuated 750-mL flask at 20°C?

(b) If 5.0 mg of *p*-dichlorobenzene were put into an evacuated 750-mL flask, how many milligrams would remain in the solid phase?

(c) What is the final pressure in an evacuated 500-mL flask at 20°C that contains 2.00 mg of *p*-dichlorobenzene? Will there be any solid in the flask?

7. Chloroform, $CHCl_3$, was once used as an anesthetic. In spy movies it is the liquid put in handkerchiefs to render victims unconscious. Its vapor pressure is 197 mm Hg at 23°C and 448 mm Hg at 45°C. Estimate its

(a) heat of vaporization.

(b) normal boiling point.

8. **WEB** Methyl alcohol, CH_3OH, has a normal boiling point of 64.7°C and has a vapor pressure of 203 mm Hg at 35°C. Estimate

(a) its heat of vaporization (ΔH_{vap}).

(b) its vapor pressure at 40.0°C.

9. Mt. McKinley in Alaska has an altitude of 20,320 ft. Water (ΔH_{vap} = 40.7 kJ/mol) boils at 77°C atop Mt. McKinley. What is the normal atmospheric pressure at the summit?

10. ■ Glacier National Park in Montana is a favorite vacation spot for backpackers. It is about 4100 ft above sea level with an atmospheric pressure of 681 mm Hg. At what temperature does water (ΔH_{vap} = 40.7 kJ/mol) boil at Glacier National Park?

11. At a resort in Sante Fe, New Mexico, the barometric pressure is 625 mm Hg. Water boils in an open pot at 94.5°C. A pressure cooker is set for 1.75 atm.

(a) At what temperature will water boil in that pressure cooker? (For water, ΔH_{vap} = 40.7 kJ/mol.)

(b) What is the difference between the boiling point in the open pot and in the pressure cooker?

12. At sea level, the barometric pressure is 760 mm Hg. Calculate the difference in the normal boiling point for water boiled in an open pot and water boiled in a pressure cooker set for 1.75 atm. (For water, ΔH_{vap} = 40.7 kJ/mol.)

13. ■ The data below give the vapor pressure of octane, a major component of gasoline.

vp (mm Hg)	10	40	100	400
t(°C)	19.2	45.1	65.7	104.0

Plot ln vp versus $1/T$. Use your graph to estimate the heat of vaporization of octane. ($\ln P = A - \frac{\Delta H_{vap}}{R}\left(\frac{1}{T}\right)$, where A is the y-intercept and ΔH_{vap} is the slope.)

14. Consider the following data for the vapor pressure of diethyl ether, a widely used anesthetic in the early days of surgery.

vp (mm Hg)	146	231	355	531
t(°C)	−5	5	15	25

Follow the instructions in Question 13 to estimate the heat of vaporization of diethyl ether.

Phase Diagrams

15. ■ Referring to Figure 9.5, state what phase(s) is (are) present at
(a) −30°C, 5 mm Hg (b) 25°C, 1 atm
(c) 70°C, 20 mm Hg

16. Referring to Figure 9.5, state what phase(s) is (are) present at
(a) 1 atm, 100°C (b) 0.5 atm, 100°C
(c) 0.8 atm, 50°C

17. Consider the phase diagram for CCl_4 below. Answer the questions about the diagram by writing your answers on the blanks provided.

_______ **(a)** What point (not including the triple point) represents an equilibrium between the solid and the vapor phase?
_______ **(b)** What is CCl_4 at point G called?
_______ **(c)** Does the boiling point increase as pressure above the liquid is decreased? (Yes or No)
_______ **(d)** What point represents CCl_4 only in the gas phase?
_______ **(e)** Does the melting point increase as pressure is applied to the solid? (Yes or No)
_______ **(f)** Is sublimation of CCl_4 impossible at any pressure? (Yes or No)
_______ **(g)** For a specific temperature above point E, is the density of the liquid phase larger than the density of the solid phase? (Yes or No)

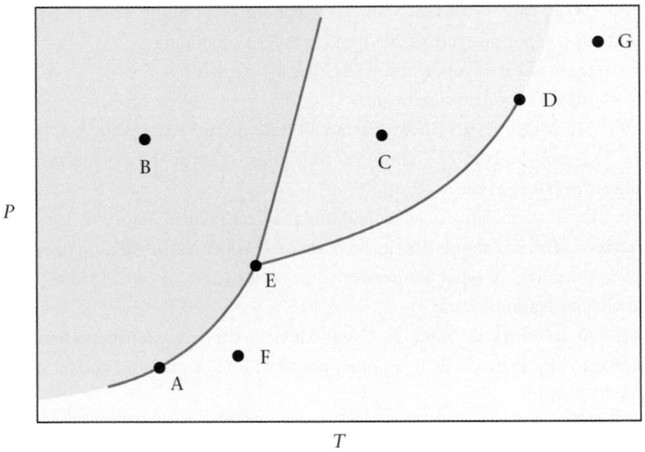

18. ■ Consider the phase diagram of the compound below to answer the following questions.

_______ **(a)** What is the physical state of the compound at 35 mm Hg and 120°C?
_______ **(b)** What is the normal freezing point of the compound?
_______ **(c)** What is the point A called?
_______ **(d)** What is the point B called?
_______ **(e)** What is the point C called?
_______ **(f)** What change occurs when at a constant pressure of 33 mm Hg, the temperature is decreased from 40°C to −20°C?
_______ **(g)** Will the solid float on the liquid?
_______ **(h)** Can the compound exist as a liquid at 180°C and 2 atm pressure?

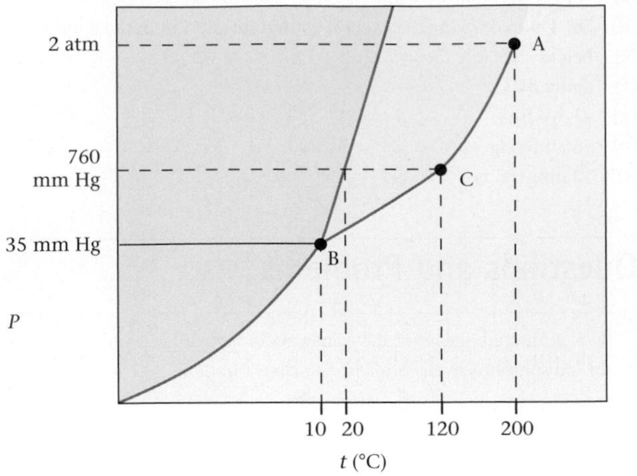

19. Argon gas has its triple point at −189.3°C and 516 mm Hg. It has a critical point at −122°C and 48 atm. The density of the solid is 1.65 g/cm^3, whereas that of the liquid is 1.40 g/cm^3. Sketch the phase diagram for argon and use it to fill in the blanks below with the words "boils," "melts," "sublimes," or "condenses."
(a) Solid argon at 500 mm Hg _______ when the temperature is increased.
(b) Solid argon at 2 atm _______ when the temperature is increased.
(c) Argon gas at −150°C _______ when the pressure is increased.
(d) Argon gas at −165°C _______ when the pressure is increased.

20. Iodine has a triple point at 114°C, 90 mm Hg. Its critical temperature is 535°C. The density of the solid is 4.93 g/cm^3, and that of the liquid is 4.00 g/cm^3. Sketch the phase diagram for iodine and use it to fill in the blanks using either "liquid" or "solid."
(a) Iodine vapor at 80 mm Hg condenses to the _______ when cooled sufficiently.
(b) Iodine vapor at 125°C condenses to the _______ when enough pressure is applied.
(c) Iodine vapor at 700 mm Hg condenses to the _______ when cooled above the triple point temperature.

21. Given the following data about xenon,

normal boiling point = −108°C
normal melting point = −112°C
triple point = −121°C at 281 mm Hg
critical point = 16.6°C at 58 atm

(a) Construct an approximate phase diagram for xenon.
(b) Estimate the vapor pressure of xenon at −115°C.
(c) Is the density of solid Xe larger than that for liquid Xe?

22. Given the following data about ammonia,

normal boiling point = −33°C
normal melting point = −78°C
triple point = −78°C at 46 mm Hg
critical point = 132°C at 112 atm

(a) Construct an approximate phase diagram for ammonia.
(b) Estimate the vapor pressure of ammonia at 40°C.

23. A pure substance X has the following properties: mp = 90°C, increasing slightly as pressure increases; normal bp = 120°C; liquid vp = 65 mm Hg at 100°C, 20 mm Hg at the triple point.

(a) Draw a phase diagram for X.
(b) Label solid, liquid, and vapor regions of the diagram.
(c) What changes occur if, at a constant pressure of 100 mm Hg, the temperature is raised from 100°C to 150°C?

24. A pure substance A has a liquid vapor pressure of 320 mm Hg at 125°C, 800 mm Hg at 150°C, and 60 mm Hg at the triple point, 85°C. The melting point of A decreases slightly as pressure increases.

(a) Sketch a phase diagram for A.
(b) From the phase diagram, estimate the boiling point.
(c) What changes occur when, at a constant pressure of 320 mm Hg, the temperature drops from 150°C to 100°C?

Intermolecular Forces

25. ■ Arrange the following in order of decreasing boiling point.

(a) I_2 (b) F_2 (c) Cl_2 (d) Br_2

26. Arrange the following in order of increasing boiling point.

(a) Ar (b) He (c) Ne (d) Xe

27. ■ Which of the following would you expect to show dispersion forces? Dipole forces?

(a) $GeBr_4$ (b) C_2H_2 (c) HF (*g*) (d) $TeCl_2$

28. **WEB** Which of the following would you expect to show dispersion forces? Dipole forces?

(a) PH_3 (b) N_2 (c) CH_4 (d) H_2O

29. ■ Which of the following would show hydrogen bonding?

(a) CH_3OH (b) $CH_3—N(H)—CH_3$
(c) CH_3NH_2 (d) HF

30. Which of the following would show hydrogen bonding?

(a) CH_3F (b) HO—OH
(c) NH_3 (d) $H_3C—O—CH_3$

31. Explain in terms of forces between structural units why

(a) HI has a higher boiling point than HBr.
(b) GeH_4 has a higher boiling point than SiH_4.
(c) H_2O_2 has a higher melting point than C_3H_8.
(d) NaCl has a higher boiling point than CH_3OH.

32. Explain in terms of forces between structural units why

(a) Br_2 has a lower melting point than NaBr.
(b) C_2H_5OH has a higher boiling point than butane, C_4H_{10}.
(c) H_2O has a higher boiling point than H_2Te.
(d) Acetic acid $CH_3—C(=O)—OH$ has a lower boiling point than benzoic acid, $C_6H_5—C(=O)—OH$

33. ■ In which of the following processes is it necessary to break covalent bonds as opposed to simply overcoming intermolecular forces?

(a) melting mothballs made of naphthalene
(b) dissolving HBr gas in water to form hydrobromic acid
(c) vaporizing ethyl alcohol, C_2H_5OH
(d) changing ozone, O_3, to oxygen gas, O_2

34. In which of the following processes is it necessary to break covalent bonds as opposed to simply overcoming intermolecular forces?

(a) subliming dry ice
(b) vaporizing chloroform ($CHCl_3$)
(c) decomposing water into H_2 and O_2
(d) changing chlorine molecules into chlorine atoms

35. ■ For each of the following pairs, choose the member with the lower boiling point. Explain your reason in each case.

(a) NaCl or PCl_3 (b) NH_3 or AsH_3
(c) C_3H_7OH or $C_2H_5OCH_3$ (d) HI (*g*) or HCl (*g*)

36. Follow the directions for Question 35 for the following substances.

(a) LiCl or CCl_4 (b) CH_3OH or CH_3F
(c) H_2O or SO_2 (d) N_2 or Cl_2

37. ■ What are the strongest attractive forces that must be overcome to

(a) boil silicon hydride SiH_4?
(b) vaporize calcium chloride?
(c) dissolve Cl_2 in carbon tetrachloride, CCl_4?
(d) melt iodine?

38. What are the strongest attractive forces that must be overcome to

(a) melt ice? (b) sublime bromine?
(c) boil chloroform ($CHCl_3$)?
(d) vaporize benzene (C_6H_6)?

Types of Substances

39. ■ Classify each of the following solids as metallic, network covalent, ionic, or molecular.

(a) It is insoluble in water, melts above 500°C, and does not conduct electricity either as a solid, dissolved in water, or molten.
(b) It dissolves in water but does not conduct electricity as an aqueous solution, as a solid, or when molten.
(c) It dissolves in water, melts above 100°C, and conducts electricity when present in an aqueous solution.

40. Classify each of the following solids as metallic, network covalent, ionic, or molecular.

(a) It melts below 100°C and is insoluble in water.
(b) It conducts electricity only when melted.
(c) It is insoluble in water and conducts electricity.

41. ■ Of the four general types of solids, which one(s)

(a) are generally low-boiling?
(b) are ductile and malleable?
(c) are generally soluble in nonpolar solvents?

42. Of the four general types of solids, which one(s)

(a) are generally insoluble in water?
(b) have very high melting points?
(c) conduct electricity as solids?

43. Classify each of the following species as molecular, network covalent, ionic, or metallic.

(a) Na (b) Na_2SO_4 (c) C_6H_6 (d) C_{60}
(e) HCl (*aq*)

44. Classify each of the following species as molecular, network covalent, ionic, or metallic.

(a) W (b) NO_2 (c) C (diamond)
(d) $(NH_4)_2CO_3$ (e) F_2 (*g*)

45. Give the formula of a solid containing carbon that is

(a) molecular (b) ionic
(c) network covalent (d) metallic

46. Give the formula of a solid containing oxygen that is

(a) a polar molecule (b) ionic
(c) network covalent (d) a nonpolar molecule

47. Describe the structural units in

(a) NaI (b) N_2 (c) KO_2 (d) Au

48. **WEB** Describe the structural units in

(a) C (graphite) (b) SiC (c) $FeCl_2$ (d) C_2H_2

■ in OWL Blue-numbered questions answered in Appendix 6 **WEB** Solution is available on companion website

Crystal Structure

49. Molybdenum has an atomic radius of 0.145 nm. The volume of its cubic unit cell is 0.0375 nm^3. What is the geometry of the molybdenum unit cell?

50. Nickel has an atomic radius of 0.162 nm. The edge of its cubic unit cell is 0.458 nm. What is the geometry of the nickel unit cell?

51. ■ Lead (atomic radius = 0.181 nm) crystallizes with a face-centered cubic unit cell. What is the length of a side of the cell?

52. Vanadium crystallizes with a body-centered cubic unit cell. The volume of the unit cell is 0.0278 nm^3. What is its atomic radius?

53. ■ In the LiCl structure shown in Figure 9.18, the chloride ions form a face-centered cubic unit cell 0.513 nm on an edge. The ionic radius of Cl^- is 0.181 nm.

(a) Along a cell edge, how much space is between the Cl^- ions?

(b) Would an Na^+ ion ($r = 0.095$ nm) fit into this space? A K^+ ion ($r = 0.133$ nm)?

54. Potassium iodide has a unit cell similar to that of sodium chloride (Figure 9.18). The ionic radii of K^+ and I^- are 0.133 nm and 0.216 nm, respectively. How long is

(a) one side of the cube?

(b) the face diagonal of the cube?

55. For a cell of the CsCl type (Figure 9.18), how is the length of one side of the cell, s, related to the sum of the radii of the ions, $r_{cation} + r_{anion}$?

56. ■ Consider the CsCl cell (Figure 9.18). The ionic radii of Cs^+ and Cl^- are 0.169 and 0.181 nm, respectively. What is the length of

(a) the body diagonal?

(b) the side of the cell?

57. Consider the sodium chloride unit cell shown in Figure 9.18. Looking only at the front face (five large Cl^- ions, four small Na^+ ions),

(a) how many cubes share each of the Na^+ ions in this face?

(b) how many cubes share each of the Cl^- ions in this face?

58. Consider the CsCl unit shown in Figure 9.18. How many Cs^+ ions are there per unit cell? How many Cl^- ions? (Note that each Cl^- ion is shared by eight cubes.)

Unclassified

59. ■ A 1.25-L clean and dry flask is sealed. The air in the flask is at 27°C and 38% relative humidity. The flask is put in a cooler at 5°C. How many grams of water will condense in the flask? (Use the table in the Appendix 1 for the vapor pressure of water at various temperatures.)

60. The density of liquid mercury at 20°C is 13.6 g/cm^3, its vapor pressure is 1.2×10^{-3} mm Hg.

(a) What volume (in cm^3) is occupied by one mole of Hg(l) at 20°C?

(b) What volume (in cm^3) is occupied by one mole of Hg(g) at 20°C and the equilibrium vapor pressure?

(c) The atomic radius of Hg is 0.155 nm. Calculate the volume (in cm^3) of one mole of Hg atoms ($V = 4\pi r^3/3$).

(d) From your answers to (a), (b), and (c), calculate the percentage of the total volume occupied by the atoms in Hg(l) and Hg(g) at 20°C and 1.2×10^{-3} mm Hg.

61. ■ Consider a sealed flask with a movable piston that contains 5.25 L of O_2 saturated with water vapor at 25°C. The piston is depressed at constant temperature so that the gas is compressed to a volume of 2.00 L. (Use the table in Appendix 1 for the vapor pressure of water at various temperatures.)

(a) What is the vapor pressure of water in the compressed gas mixture?

(b) How many grams of water condense when the gas mixture is compressed?

62. Packing efficiency is defined as the percent of the total volume of a solid occupied by (spherical) atoms. The formula is

$$\text{packing efficiency} = \frac{\text{volume of the atom(s) in the cell}}{\text{volume of the cell}} \times 100$$

The volume of one atom is $\frac{4}{3}\pi r^3$ and the volume of the cell is s^3. Calculate the packing efficiency of

(a) a simple cubic cell (1 atom/cell).

(b) a face-centered cubic cell (4 atoms/cell).

(c) a body-centered cubic cell (2 atoms/cell).

Use Table 9.6 to relate r to s.

63. Mercury is an extremely toxic substance. Inhalation of the vapor is just as dangerous as swallowing the liquid. How many milliliters of mercury will saturate a room that is 15 × 12 × 8.0 ft with mercury vapor at 25°C? The vapor pressure of Hg at 25°C is 0.00163 mm Hg and its density is 13 g/mL.

64. An experiment is performed to determine the vapor pressure of formic acid. A 30.0-L volume of helium gas at 20.0°C is passed through 10.00 g of liquid formic acid (HCOOH) at 20.0°C. After the experiment, 7.50 g of liquid formic acid remains. Assume that the helium gas becomes saturated with formic acid vapor and the total gas volume and temperature remain constant. What is the vapor pressure of formic acid at 20.0°C?

65. The normal boiling point for methyl hydrazine ($CH_3N_2H_3$) is 87°C. It has a vapor pressure of 37.0 mm Hg at 20°C. What is the concentration (in g/L) of methyl hydrazine if it saturates the air at 25°C?

Conceptual Problems

66. Which of the following statements are true?

(a) The critical temperature must be reached to change liquid to gas.

(b) To melt a solid at constant pressure, the temperature must be above the triple point.

(c) CHF_3 can be expected to have a higher boiling point than $CHCl_3$ because CHF_3 has hydrogen bonding.

(d) One metal crystallizes in a body-centered cubic cell and another in a face-centered cubic cell of the same volume. The two atomic radii are related by the factor $\sqrt{1.5}$.

67. Represent pictorially using ten molecules

(a) water freezing.

(b) water vaporizing.

(c) water being electrolyzed into hydrogen and oxygen.

68. In the blanks provided, answer the questions below, using **LT** (for *is less than*), **GT** (for *is greater than*), **EQ** (for *is equal to*), or **MI** (for *more information required*).

(a) The boiling point of C_3H_7OH (MM = 60.0 g/mol) ________ the boiling point of $C_2H_6C = O$ (MM = 58.0 g/mol).

(b) The vapor pressure of X is 250 mm Hg at 57°C. Given a sealed flask at 57°C that contains only gas, the pressure in the flask ________ 245 mm Hg.

(c) The melting-point curve for Y tilts to the right of a straight line. The density of Y(l) ________ the density of Y(s).

(d) The normal boiling point of A is 85°C, while the normal boiling point of B is 45°C. The vapor pressure of A at 85°C ________ the vapor pressure of B at 45°C.

(e) The triple point of A is 25 mm Hg and 5°C. The melting point of A ________ 5°C.

■ in OWL Blue-numbered questions answered in Appendix 6 WEB Solution is available on companion website

69. Answer the questions below, by filling in the blanks with **LT** for *is less than,* **GT** for *is greater than,* **EQ** for *is equal to,* or **MI** for *more information required.*

(a) At 50°C, benzene has a vapor pressure of 269 mm Hg. A flask that contains both benzene liquid and vapor at 50°C has a pressure ________ 269 mm Hg.

(b) Ether has a vapor pressure of 537 mm Hg at 25°C. A flask that contains only ether vapor at 37°C has a pressure ________ 537 mm Hg.

(c) The boiling point of H_2O ________ the boiling point of C_3H_8.

(d) The energy required to vaporize liquid bromine ________ the energy required to decompose Br_2 into Br atoms.

(e) The dispersion forces present in naphthalene, $C_{10}H_8$, ________ the dispersion forces present in butane, C_4H_{10}.

70. A liquid has a vapor pressure of 159 mm Hg at 20°C and 165 mm Hg at 30°C. Different amounts of the liquid are added to three identical evacuated steel tanks kept at 20°C. The tanks are all fitted with pressure gauges. For each part, write

L/G if both liquid and gas are present.
G if only gas is present.
I if the situation is impossible.

(a) The pressure gauge in Flask I registers a pressure of 256 mm Hg.

(b) The pressure gauge in Flask II registers a pressure of 135 mm Hg.

(c) The pressure gauge in Flask III registers a pressure of 165 mm Hg at 30°C. The temperature is lowered to 20°C, and the gauge registers a pressure of 159 mm Hg.

71. Criticize or comment on each of the following statements.

(a) Vapor pressure remains constant regardless of volume.

(b) The only forces that affect boiling point are dispersion forces.

(c) The strength of the covalent bonds within a molecule has no effect on the melting point of the molecular substance.

(d) A compound at its critical temperature is always a gas regardless of pressure.

72. Differentiate between

(a) a covalent bond and a hydrogen bond.

(b) normal boiling point and a boiling point.

(c) the triple point and the critical point.

(d) a phase diagram and a vapor pressure curve.

(e) volume effect and temperature effect on vapor pressure.

73. Four shiny solids are labeled A, B, C, and D. Given the following information about the solids, deduce the identity of A, B, C, and D.

(1) The solids are a graphite rod, a silver bar, a lump of "fool's gold" (iron sulfide), and iodine crystals.

(2) B, C, and D are insoluble in water. A is slightly soluble.

(3) Only C can be hammered into a sheet.

(4) C and D conduct electricity as solids; B conducts when melted; A does not conduct as a solid, melted, or dissolved in water.

74. ■ Consider the vapor pressure curves of molecules A, B, and C shown below.

(a) Which compound (A, B, or C) has the weakest forces between molecules?

(b) Which compound (A, B, or C) has a normal boiling point at about 15°C?

(c) At what temperature will B boil if the atmospheric pressure is 500 mm Hg?

(d) At 25°C and 400 mm Hg, what is the physical state of A?

(e) At what pressure will C boil at 40°C?

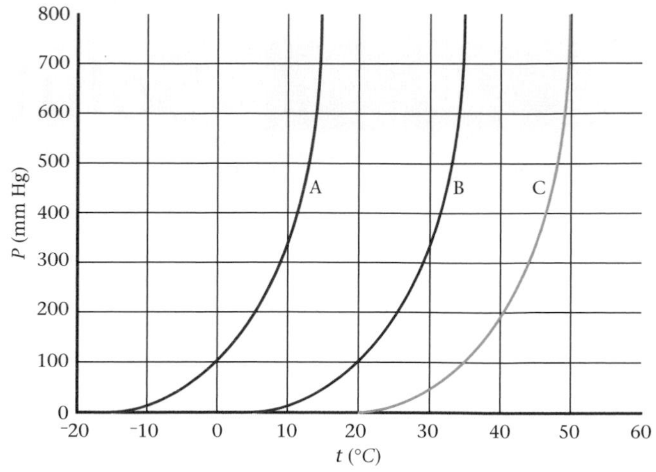

Challenge Problems

75. The following data are given for CCl_4:

normal melting point = −23°C
normal boiling point = 77°C
density of liquid = 1.59 g/mL
vapor pressure at 25°C = 110 mm Hg

How much heat is required to vaporize 20.0 L of CCl_4 at its normal boiling point?

76. ■ Iron crystallizes in a body-centered unit cell. Its atomic radius is 0.124 nm. Its density is 7.86 g/cm³. Using this information, estimate Avogadro's number.

77. A flask with a volume of 10.0 L contains 0.400 g of hydrogen gas and 3.20 g of oxygen gas. The mixture is ignited and the reaction

$$2H_2(g) + O_2(g) \longrightarrow 2H_2O$$

goes to completion. The mixture is cooled to 27°C. Assuming 100% yield,

(a) What physical state(s) of water is (are) present in the flask?

(b) What is the final pressure in the flask?

(c) What is the pressure in the flask if 3.2 g of each gas is used?

78. Trichloroethane, $C_2H_3Cl_3$, is the active ingredient in aerosols that claim to stain-proof men's ties. Trichloroethane has a vapor pressure of 100.0 mm Hg at 20.0°C and boils at 74.1°C. An uncovered cup ($\frac{1}{2}$ pint) of trichloroethane (d = 1.325 g/mL) is kept in an 18-ft³ refrigerator at 39°F. What percentage (by mass) of the trichloroethane is left as a liquid when equilibrium is established?

79. It has been suggested that the pressure exerted on a skate blade is sufficient to melt the ice beneath it and form a thin film of water, which makes it easier for the blade to slide over the ice. Assume that a skater weighs 120 lb and the blade has an area of 0.10 in². Calculate the pressure exerted on the blade (1 atm = 15 lb/in²). From information in the text, calculate the decrease in melting point at this pressure. Comment on the plausibility of this explanation and suggest another mechanism by which the water film might be formed.

80. As shown in Figure 9.18, Li^+ ions fit into a closely packed array of Cl^- ions, but Na^+ ions do not. What is the value of the r_{cation}/r_{anion} ratio at which a cation just fits into a structure of this type?

81. When the temperature drops from 20°C to 10°C, the pressure of a cylinder of compressed N_2 drops by 3.4%. The same temperature change decreases the pressure of a propane (C_3H_8) cylinder by 42%. Explain the difference in behavior.

10 Solutions

When water turns ice does it remember one time it was water?

When ice turns back into water does it remember it was ice?

—Carl Sandburg
"Metamorphosis"

Chapter Outline

Collecting maple sap and converting it to maple syrup utilize many of the chemical principles found in this chapter.

In the course of a day, you use or make solutions many times. Your morning cup of coffee is a solution of solids (sugar and coffee) in a liquid (water). The gasoline you fill your gas tank with is a solution of several different liquid hydrocarbons. The soda you drink at a study break is a solution containing a gas (carbon dioxide) in a liquid (water).

A solution is a homogeneous mixture of a *solute* (substance being dissolved) distributed through a *solvent* (substance doing the dissolving). Solutions exist in any of the three physical states: gas, liquid, or solid. Air, the most common gaseous solution, is a mixture of nitrogen, oxygen, and lesser amounts of other gases. Many metal alloys are solid solutions. An example is the U.S. "nickel" coin (25% Ni, 75% Cu). The most familiar solutions are those in the liquid state, especially ones in which water is the solvent. Aqueous solutions are most important for our purposes in chemistry and will be emphasized in this chapter.

This chapter covers several of the physical aspects of solutions, including—

- methods of expressing solution concentrations by specifying the relative amounts of solute and solvent (Section 10.1).
- factors affecting solubility, including the nature of the solute and the solvent, the temperature, and the pressure (Section 10.2).
- the effect of solutes on such solvent properties as vapor pressure, freezing point, and boiling point (Section 10.3, 10.4). ■

Online homework for this chapter may be assigned in OWL

CENGAGENOW™

This icon introduces an opportunity for self-study and to explore interactive modules by signing in at **academic.cengage.com/now.**

10.1 CONCENTRATION UNITS

Several different methods are used to express relative amounts of solute and solvent in a solution. Two concentration units, ***molarity*** and ***mole fraction,*** were referred to in previous chapters. Two others, ***mass percent*** and ***molality,*** are considered for the first time.

CENGAGENOW™

Click Coached Problems for a self-study module on **dilution.**

Molarity (*M*)

In Chapter 4, molarity was the concentration unit of choice in dealing with solution stoichiometry. You will recall that molarity is defined as

$$\text{molarity } (M) = \frac{\text{moles solute}}{\text{liters solution}}$$

A solution can be prepared to a specified molarity by weighing out the calculated mass of solute and dissolving in enough solvent to form the desired volume of solution. Alternatively, you can start with a more concentrated solution and dilute with water to give a solution of the desired molarity (Figure 10.1, p. 260). The calculations are straightforward if you keep a simple point in mind: Adding solvent cannot change the number of moles of solute. That is,

$$n_{\text{solute}} \text{ (concentrated solution)} = n_{\text{solute}} \text{ (dilute solution)}$$

In both solutions, n can be found by multiplying the molarity, M, by the volume in liters, V. Hence

$$M_cV_c = M_dV_d \qquad \textbf{(10.1)}$$

where the subscripts c and d stand for concentrated and dilute solutions, respectively.

The advantage of preparing solutions by the method illustrated in Figure 10.1 is that only volume measurements are necessary. If you wander into the general chemistry storeroom, you're likely to find concentrated "stock" solutions of various chemicals. Storeroom personnel prepare the more dilute solutions that you use in the laboratory on the basis of calculations like those in the following example.

It's easier to dilute a concentrated solution than to start from "scratch."

Figure 10.1
Preparation of one liter of 0.100 *M* $CuSO_4$ by dilution.

Example 10.1

Copper sulfate is widely used as a dietary supplement for animal feed. A lab technician prepares a "stock" solution of $CuSO_4$ by adding 79.80 g of $CuSO_4$ to enough water to make 500.0 mL of solution. An experiment requires a 0.1000 *M* solution of $CuSO_4$.

(a) What is the molarity of the $CuSO_4$ "stock" solution prepared by the technician?
(b) How would you prepare 1.500 L of 0.1000 *M* solution from the stock solution?

Strategy

(a) Review (from Chapter 4) the discussion on molarity of solutions.
(b) The question is equivalent to: What volume of $CuSO_4$ solution should be diluted to give 1.500 L of 0.1000 *M* $CuSO_4$? To answer this, use Equation 10.1 to calculate V_c, the volume of the more concentrated solution. M_c is the molarity from (a).

SOLUTION

(a) The given data are in the form g/mL. Convert that to *M* (mol/L) by using the molar mass, 159.6 g/mol, as the conversion factor.

$$\frac{79.80\text{ g CuSO}_4}{500.0\text{ mL}} \times \frac{1\text{ mol}}{159.6\text{ g CuSO}_4} \times \frac{1000\text{ mL}}{1\text{ L}} = 1.000\ M$$

(b) Using Equation 10.1 and solving for V_c, we get

$$V_c = \frac{M_d \times V_d}{M_c} = \frac{0.1000\ M \times 1.500\text{ L}}{1.000\ M} = 0.1500\text{ L}$$

Measure out 1.500×10^2 mL of the stock solution and dilute with enough water (about 1.35 L) to form 1.500 L of 0.1000 *M* solution.

Reality Check The molarity of $CuSO_4$ stock solution (1.000 *M*) is 10 times what you need (0.1000 *M*), so it is reasonable to use only one-tenth of the volume you want (1500 mL $\rightarrow$ 1.500 L).

Mole Fraction (X)

Recall from Chapter 5 the defining equation for mole fraction (X) of a component A:

$$X_A = \frac{\text{moles A}}{\text{total moles}} = \frac{n_A}{n_{tot}}$$

The mole fractions of all components of a solution (A, B, . . .) must add to unity:

$$X_A + X_B + \cdots = 1$$

Example 10.2 Hydrogen peroxide is used by some water treatment systems to remove the disagreeable odor of sulfides in drinking water. It is available commercially in a 20.0% by mass aqueous solution. What is the mole fraction of H_2O_2?

Strategy Start with a fixed mass of solution such as one hundred grams. First calculate the masses of H_2O and H_2O_2, then the number of moles, and finally the mole fraction of H_2O_2.

SOLUTION In 100.0 g of solution, there are 20.0 g of H_2O_2 and 80.0 g of H_2O.

$$n_{H_2O_2} = 20.0\text{ g} \times \frac{1\text{ mol }H_2O_2}{34.02\text{ g }H_2O_2} = 0.588\text{ mol }H_2O_2$$

$$n_{H_2O} = 80.0\text{ g} \times \frac{1\text{ mol }H_2O}{18.02\text{ g }H_2O} = 4.44\text{ mol }H_2O$$

$$X_{H_2O_2} = \frac{n_{H_2O_2}}{n_{tot}} = \frac{0.588}{0.588 + 4.44} = 0.117$$

Reality Check Notice that the mole fraction of H_2O_2 is considerably less than the "mass fraction" (0.200). That is reasonable because the molar mass of H_2O_2 is larger than that of H_2O.

Mass Percent; Parts per Million; Parts per Billion

The **mass percent** of solute in solution is expressed quite simply:

$$\text{mass percent of solute} = \frac{\text{mass solute}}{\text{total mass solution}} \times 100\%$$

In a solution prepared by dissolving 24 g of NaCl in 152 g of water,

$$\text{mass percent of NaCl} = \frac{24\text{ g}}{24\text{ g} + 152\text{ g}} \times 100\% = \frac{24}{176} \times 100\% = 14\%$$

When the amount of solute is very small, as with trace impurities in water, concentration is often expressed in **parts per million** (ppm) or **parts per billion** (ppb).

In the United States, drinking water cannot by law contain more than 5×10^{-8} g of arsenic per gram of water:

$$\text{ppm As} = \frac{5 \times 10^{-8}\text{ g}}{\text{g sample}} \times 10^6 = 0.05; \qquad \text{ppb As} = \frac{5 \times 10^{-8}\text{ g}}{\text{g sample}} \times 10^9 = 50$$

Molality (m)

The concentration unit **molality,** given the symbol m, is defined as the number of moles of solute per kilogram (1000 g) of *solvent.*

$$\text{molality } (m) = \frac{\text{moles solute}}{\text{kilograms solvent}}$$

Molality and molarity are concentration units; morality is something else.

The molality of a solution is readily calculated if the masses of solute and solvent are known (Example 10.3).

Example 10.3 Glucose, $C_6H_{12}O_6$, in water is often used for intravenous feeding. Sometimes sodium ions are added to the solution. A pharmacist prepares a solution by adding 2.0 mg of sodium ions (in the form of NaCl), 6.00 g of glucose, and 112 g of water.

(a) What is the molality of the glucose in solution?
(b) How many ppm of Na^+ does the solution contain?

Strategy

(a) Since molality is equal to the number of moles of solute (glucose) divided by the mass of the solvent (H_2O) in kg, find those two quantities and divide.
(b) To find ppm of Na^+, find the mass of Na^+ and the total mass of solution.

SOLUTION

(a) $$n_{\text{glucose}} = 6.00 \text{ g glucose} \times \frac{1 \text{ mol glucose}}{180.16 \text{ g glucose}} = 0.0333 \text{ mol glucose}$$

$$\text{kg } H_2O = 112 \text{ g} \times \frac{1 \text{ kg}}{1000 \text{ g}} = 0.112 \text{ kg}$$

$$\text{molality} = \frac{0.0333 \text{ mol glucose}}{0.112 \text{ kg } H_2O} = 0.297\ m$$

(b) $$\text{Mass } Na^+ = 2.0 \text{ mg} \times \frac{1 \text{ g}}{1000 \text{ mg}} = 2.0 \times 10^{-3} \text{ g}$$

$$\text{total mass of solution} = 2.0 \times 10^{-3}\ Na^+ + 6.00 \text{ g glucose} + 112 \text{ g water} = 118 \text{ g}$$

$$\text{ppm } Na^+ = \frac{2.0 \times 10^{-3} \text{ g } Na^+}{118 \text{ g solution}} \times 10^6 = 17 \text{ ppm}$$

Theoretically, you would also need to calculate the mass of Cl^- ions and add that to the masses of Na^+, glucose, and water. Practically, the mass of Cl^- ions (like the mass of Na^+ ions) is negligible when compared to the mass of the solution.

Conversions Between Concentration Units

It is frequently necessary to convert from one concentration unit to another. This problem arises, for example, in making up solutions of hydrochloric acid. Typically, the analysis or assay that appears on the label (Figure 10.2, p. 263) does not give the molarity or molality of the acid. Instead, it lists the mass percent of solute and the density of the solution.

Conversions between concentration units are relatively straightforward provided you *first decide on a fixed amount of solution.* The amount chosen depends on the unit in which concentration is originally expressed. Some suggested starting quantities are listed below.

Complex problems can usually be solved if you know where to start.

When the Original Concentration Is	Start With
Mass percent	100 g solution
Molarity (*M*)	1.00 L solution
Molality (*m*)	1000 g solvent
Mole fraction (*X*)	1 mol (solute + solvent)

Marna G. Clarke

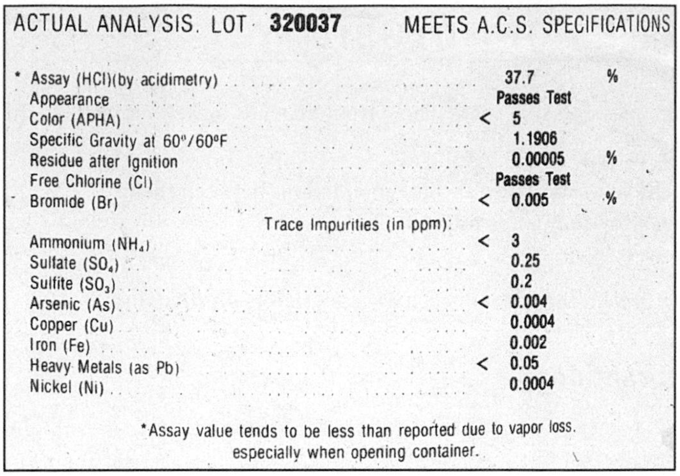

ACTUAL ANALYSIS. LOT 320037 MEETS A.C.S. SPECIFICATIONS

* Assay (HCl)(by acidimetry)	37.7	%
Appearance	Passes Test	
Color (APHA)	< 5	
Specific Gravity at 60°/60°F	1.1906	
Residue after Ignition	0.00005	%
Free Chlorine (Cl)	Passes Test	
Bromide (Br)	< 0.005	%
Trace Impurities (in ppm):		
Ammonium (NH_4)	< 3	
Sulfate (SO_4)	0.25	
Sulfite (SO_3)	0.2	
Arsenic (As)	< 0.004	
Copper (Cu)	0.0004	
Iron (Fe)	0.002	
Heavy Metals (as Pb)	< 0.05	
Nickel (Ni)	0.0004	

*Assay value tends to be less than reported due to vapor loss. especially when opening container.

Figure 10.2
The label on a bottle of concentrated hydrochloric acid. The label gives the mass percent of HCl in the solution (known as the *assay*) and the density (or *specific gravity*) of the solution. The molality, molarity, and mole fraction of HCl in the solution can be calculated from this information.

Example 10.4 Graded

Using the information in Figure 10.2, calculate

*(a) the mass percents of HCl and water in concentrated HCl.
**(b) the molality of HCl.
***(c) the molarity of HCl.

SOLUTION

(a) The mass percent of HCl (note the caption of Figure 10.2) is 37.7%. That of water must be 100.0 − 37.7 = 62.3%.

(b) Start with 100.0 g of solution, which contains 37.7 g of HCl and 62.3 g of water. Convert to moles of HCl (MM = 36.46 g/mol) and to kilograms of water. Finally, calculate the molality.

$$n_{HCl} = 37.7 \text{ g HCl} \times \frac{1 \text{ mol HCl}}{36.46 \text{ g HCl}} = 1.03 \text{ mol HCl}$$

$$\text{kg water} = 62.3 \text{ g} \times \frac{1 \text{ kg}}{1000 \text{ g}} = 0.0623 \text{ kg}$$

$$\text{molality} = \frac{1.03 \text{ mol}}{0.0623 \text{ kg}} = 16.5\ m$$

(c) Again, start with 100.0 g of solution. You have already calculated the number of moles of HCl. Find the volume of solution by using the density (1.19 g/mL). Finally, calculate the molarity.

$$n_{HCl} = 1.03 \text{ mol}$$

$$\text{volume of 100.0 g solution} = 100.0 \text{ g} \times \frac{1 \text{ mL}}{1.19 \text{ g}} \times \frac{1 \text{ L}}{1000 \text{ mL}} = 0.0840 \text{ L}$$

$$\text{molarity} = \frac{1.03 \text{ mol}}{0.0840 \text{ L}} = 12.3\ M$$

Charles D. Winters

Molarity and molality. On the left is a 0.10 *M* solution of potassium chromate. On the right is a 0.10 *m* solution that contains the same amount of potassium chromate (19.4 g, in dish). The 0.10 *M* solution was made by placing the solid in the flask and adding water to give 1 L of solution. The 0.10 *m* solution was prepared by placing the solid in the flask and adding 1000 g of water. You can see that the 0.10 *m* solution has a slightly larger volume.

10.2 PRINCIPLES OF SOLUBILITY

The extent to which a solute dissolves in a particular solvent depends on several factors. The most important of these are—

- the nature of solvent and solute particles and the interactions between them.
- the temperature at which the solution is formed.
- the pressure of a gaseous solute.

In this section we consider in turn the effect of each of these factors on solubility.

Solute-Solvent Interactions

In discussing solubility, it is sometimes stated that "like dissolves like." A more meaningful way to express this idea is to say that two substances with intermolecular forces of about the same type and magnitude are likely to be very soluble in one another. To illustrate, consider the hydrocarbons pentane, C_5H_{12}, and hexane, C_6H_{14}, which are completely soluble in each other. Molecules of these nonpolar substances are held together by dispersion forces of about the same magnitude. A pentane molecule experiences little or no change in intermolecular forces when it goes into solution in hexane.

Most nonpolar substances have very small water solubilities. Petroleum, a mixture of hydrocarbons, spreads out in a thin film on the surface of a body of water rather than dissolving. The mole fraction of pentane, C_5H_{12}, in a saturated water solution is only 0.0001. These low solubilities are readily understood in terms of the structure of liquid water, which you will recall (Chapter 9) is strongly hydrogen-bonded. Dissimilar intermolecular forces between C_5H_{12} (dispersion) and H_2O (H bonds) lead to low solubility.

Of the relatively few organic compounds that dissolve readily in water, many contain —OH groups. Three familiar examples are methyl alcohol, ethyl alcohol, and ethylene glycol, all of which are infinitely soluble in water.

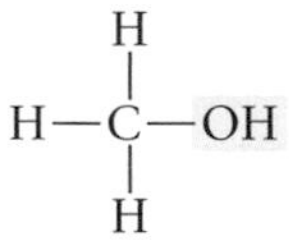
methyl alcohol

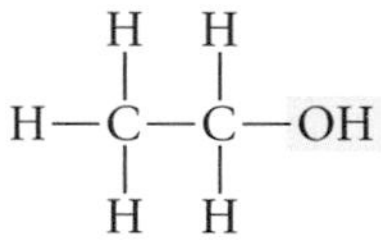
ethyl alcohol

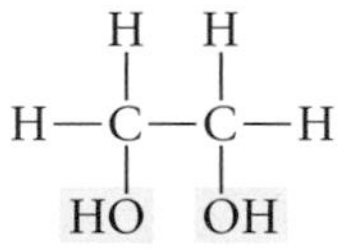
ethylene glycol

In these compounds, as in water, the principal intermolecular forces are hydrogen bonds. When a substance like methyl alcohol dissolves in water, it forms hydrogen bonds with H_2O molecules. These hydrogen bonds, joining a CH_3OH molecule to an H_2O molecule, are about as strong as those in the pure substances.

Not all organic compounds that contain —OH groups are soluble in water (Table 10.1). As molar mass increases, the polar —OH group represents an increasingly smaller portion of the molecule. At the same time, the nonpolar hydrocarbon portion becomes larger. As a result, solubility decreases with increasing molar mass. Butanol, $CH_3CH_2CH_2CH_2$ OH, is

Charles D. Winters

Solubility and intermolecular forces. Oil *(left)* is made up of nonpolar molecules. It does not mix well with water because water is polar. Ethylene glycol *(right)*, commonly used as antifreeze, mixes with water in all proportions because both form hydrogen bonds.

Table 10.1 Solubilities of Alcohols in Water

Substance	Formula	Solubility (g solute/L H_2O)
Methyl alcohol	CH_3OH	Completely soluble
Ethyl alcohol	CH_3CH_2OH	Completely soluble
Propanol	$CH_3CH_2CH_2OH$	Completely soluble
Butanol	$CH_3CH_2CH_2CH_2OH$	74
Pentanol	$CH_3CH_2CH_2CH_2CH_2OH$	27
Hexanol	$CH_3CH_2CH_2CH_2CH_2CH_2OH$	6.0
Heptanol	$CH_3CH_2CH_2CH_2CH_2CH_2CH_2OH$	1.7

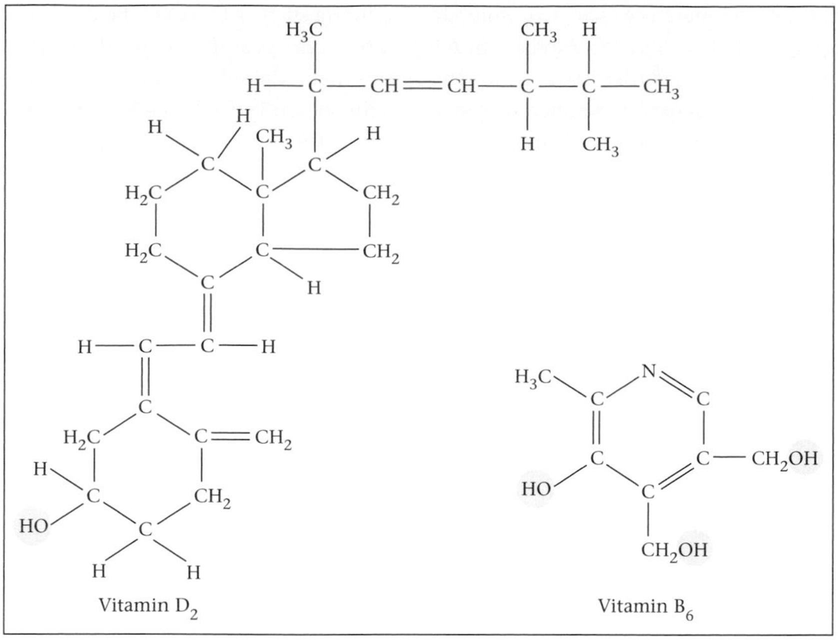

Figure 10.3
Molecular structures of vitamin D_2 and vitamin B_6. Polar groups are shown in color. Vitamin D_2 is water-insoluble and vitamin B_6 is water-soluble.

much less soluble in water than methyl alcohol, CH_3 OH. The hydrocarbon portion, shaded in green, is much larger in butanol.

The solubility (or insolubility) of different vitamins is of concern in nutrition. Molecules of vitamins B and C contain several —OH groups that can form hydrogen bonds with water (Figure 10.3). As a result, they are water-soluble, readily excreted by the body, and must be consumed daily. In contrast, vitamins A, D, E, and K, whose molecules are relatively nonpolar, are water-insoluble. These vitamins are not so readily excreted; they tend to stay behind in fatty tissues. This means that the body can draw on its reservoir of vitamins A, D, E, and K to deal with sporadic deficiencies. Conversely, megadoses of these vitamins can lead to very high, possibly toxic, concentrations in the body.

You can't remove the "hot" taste of chili peppers by drinking water because the compound responsible is nonpolar and water-insoluble.

As we noted in Chapter 4, the solubility of ionic compounds in water varies tremendously from one solid to another. The extent to which solution occurs depends on a balance between two forces, both electrical in nature:

1. The force of attraction between H_2O molecules and the ions, which tends to bring the solid into solution. If this factor predominates, the compound is very soluble in water, as is the case with NaCl, NaOH, and many other ionic solids.
2. The force of attraction between oppositely charged ions, which tends to keep them in the solid state. If this is the major factor, the water solubility is very low. The fact that $CaCO_3$ and $BaSO_4$ are almost insoluble in water implies that interionic attractive forces predominate with these ionic solids.

We can't predict which factor will predominate, so we can't predict solubility.

Effect of Temperature on Solubility

When an excess of a solid such as sodium nitrate, $NaNO_3$, is shaken with water, an equilibrium is established between ions in the solid state and in solution:

$$NaNO_3\,(s) \longrightarrow Na^+(aq) + NO_3^-(aq)$$

At 20°C, the saturated solution contains 87.6 g of $NaNO_3$ per one hundred grams of water.

A similar type of equilibrium is established when a gas such as oxygen is bubbled through water.

$$O_2(g) \rightleftharpoons O_2(aq)$$

At 20°C and 1 atm, 0.00138 mol of O_2 dissolves per liter of water.

CENGAGENOW™
Click Coached Problems for a self-study module on **effect of temperature change on solubility.**

Take a look back at Chapter 8.

The effect of a temperature change on solubility equilibria such as these can be predicted by applying a simple principle. ***An increase in temperature always shifts the position of an equilibrium to favor an endothermic process.*** This means that if the solution process absorbs heat ($\Delta H_{\text{soln.}} > 0$), an increase in temperature increases the solubility. Conversely, if the solution process is exothermic ($\Delta H < 0$), an increase in temperature decreases the solubility.

Dissolving a solid in a liquid is usually an endothermic process; heat must be absorbed to break down the crystal lattice.

CENGAGENOW™
Click Coached Problems for a self-study module on **factors affecting solubility.**

$$\text{solid} + \text{liquid} \rightleftharpoons \text{solution} \qquad \Delta H_{\text{soln.}} > 0$$

For example, for sodium nitrate,

$$\Delta H_{\text{soln.}} = \Delta H_f^\circ Na^+(aq) + \Delta H_f^\circ NO_3^-(aq) - \Delta H_f^\circ NaNO_3(s) = +22.8 \text{ kJ}$$

Consistent with this effect, the solubility of $NaNO_3$ and most (but not all) other solids increases with temperature (Figure 10.4).

Gases behave quite differently from solids. When a gas condenses to a liquid, heat is always evolved. By the same token, heat is usually evolved when a gas dissolves in a liquid:

$$\text{gas} + \text{liquid} \rightleftharpoons \text{solution} \qquad \Delta H_{\text{soln.}} < 0$$

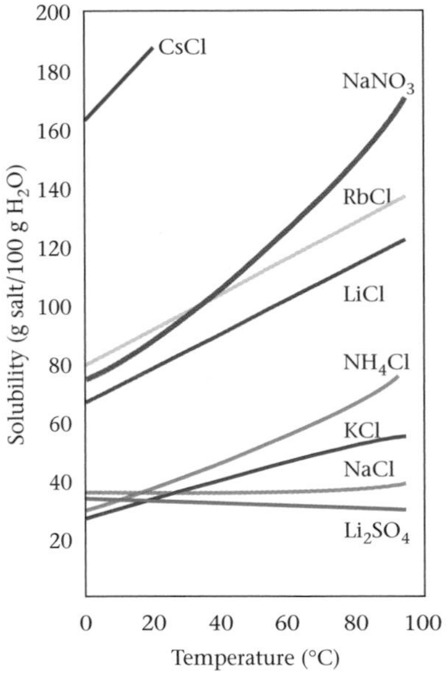

Figure 10.4
Solubility of ionic compounds vs. temperature.

This means that the reverse process (gas coming out of solution) is endothermic. Hence, it is favored by an increase in temperature; typically, gases become less soluble as the temperature rises. This rule is followed by all gases in water. You have probably noticed this effect when heating water in an open pan or beaker. Bubbles of air are driven out of the water by an increase in temperature. The reduced solubility of oxygen in water at high temperatures (Figure 10.5a, p. 267) may explain why trout congregate at the bottom of deep pools on hot summer days when the surface water is depleted of dissolved oxygen.

Effect of Pressure on Solubility

Pressure has a major effect on solubility only for gas-liquid systems. At a given temperature, raising the pressure increases the solubility of a gas. Indeed, at low to moderate pressures, gas solubility is directly proportional to pressure (Figure 10.5b).

$$C_g = kP_g \qquad \textbf{(10.2)}$$

where P_g is the partial pressure of the gas over the solution, C_g is its concentration in the solution, and k is a constant characteristic of the particular gas-liquid system. This relation is called **Henry's law** after its discoverer, William Henry (1775–1836), a friend of John Dalton.

Henry's law arises because increasing the pressure raises the concentration of molecules in the gas phase. To balance this change and maintain equilibrium, more gas molecules enter the solution, increasing their concentration in the liquid phase.

(a)

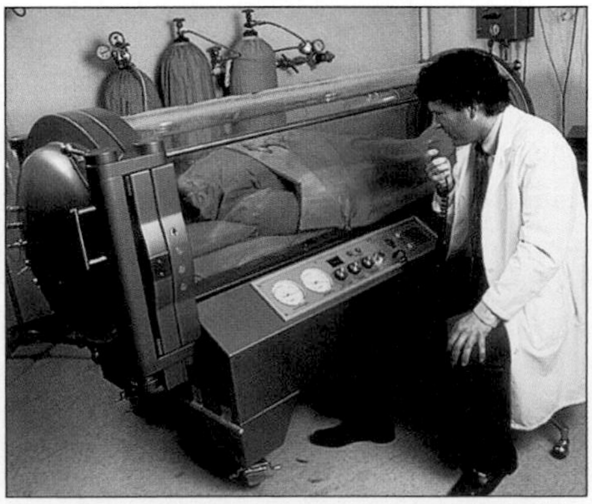

(b)

a, Taxi/Getty Images; b, Peter Arnold, Inc.

Solubility affected by pressure. (a) SCUBA divers must pay attention to the solubility of gases in the blood and the fact that solubility increases with pressure. (b) A hyperbaric chamber. People who have problems breathing can be placed in a hyperbaric chamber where they are exposed to a higher partial pressure of oxygen.

Example 10.5 The solubility of pure nitrogen in blood at body temperature, 37°C, and one atmosphere is 6.2×10^{-4} *M*. If a diver breathes air ($X\ N_2 = 0.78$) at a depth where the total pressure is 2.5 atm, calculate the concentration of nitrogen in his blood.

Strategy Use Henry's law in any problem involving gas solubility and pressure. Perhaps the simplest approach is to use the data at one atmosphere to calculate *k*. Then apply Henry's law to calculate C_g at the higher pressure. Note that it is the *partial* pressure of N_2 that is required; use the relation $P_{N_2} = X_{N_2} \times P_{tot}$ to find it.

SOLUTION At 1 atm:

$$k = \frac{\text{concentration of } N_2}{\text{pressure of } N_2} = \frac{6.2 \times 10^{-4}\ M}{1.00\ \text{atm}} = 6.2 \times 10^{-4}\ M/\text{atm}$$

At the higher pressure:

$$P_{N_2} = X_{N_2} \times P_{tot} = 0.78 \times 2.5\ \text{atm} = 2.0\ \text{atm}$$

$$[N_2] = kP_{N_2} = 6.2 \times 10^{-4} \frac{M}{\text{atm}} \times 2.0\ \text{atm} = 1.2 \times 10^{-3}\ M$$

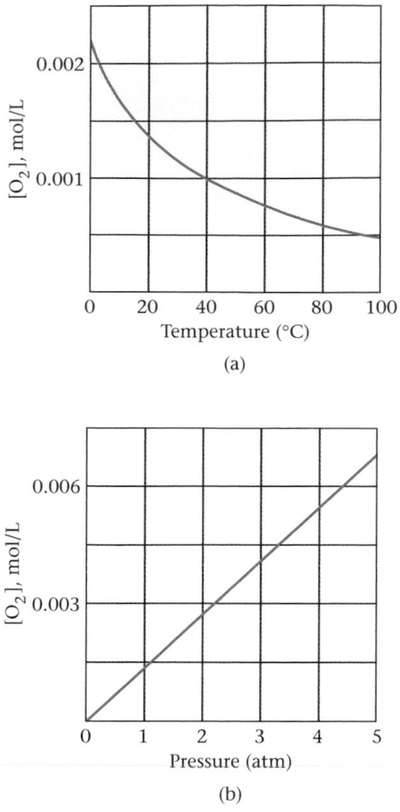

Figure 10.5
Oxygen solubility. The solubility of $O_2(g)$ in water decreases as temperature rises (a) and increases as pressure increases (b). In (a), the pressure is held constant at 1 atm; in (b), the temperature is held constant at 25°C.

The influence of partial pressure on gas solubility is used in making carbonated beverages such as beer, sparkling wines, and many soft drinks. These beverages are bottled under pressures of CO_2 as high as 4 atm. When the bottle or can is opened, the pressure above the liquid drops to 1 atm, and the carbon dioxide rapidly bubbles out of solution. Pressurized containers for shaving cream, whipped cream, and cheese spreads work on a similar principle. Pressing a valve reduces the pressure on the dissolved gas, causing it to rush from solution, carrying liquid with it as a foam.

Another consequence of the effect of pressure on gas solubility is the painful, sometimes fatal, affliction known as the "bends." This occurs when a person goes rapidly from deep water (high pressure) to the surface (lower pressure), where gases are less soluble. The rapid decompression causes air, dissolved in blood and other body fluids, to bubble out of solution. These bubbles impair blood circulation and affect nerve impulses. To minimize these effects, deep-sea divers and aquanauts breathe a helium-oxygen mixture rather than compressed air (nitrogen-oxygen). Helium is only about one-third as soluble as nitrogen, and hence much less gas comes out of solution on decompression.

Scuba divers have to worry about this.

10.3 COLLIGATIVE PROPERTIES OF NONELECTROLYTES

The properties of a solution differ considerably from those of the pure solvent. Those solution properties that depend primarily on the *concentration of solute particles* rather than their nature are called **colligative properties.** Such properties include vapor pressure lowering, osmotic pressure, boiling point elevation, and freezing point depression. This section considers the relations between colligative properties and solute concentration, with nonelectrolytes that exist in solution as molecules.

The relationships among colligative properties and solute concentration are best regarded as limiting laws. They are approached more closely as the solution becomes more dilute. In practice, the relationships discussed in this section are valid, for nonelectrolytes, to within a few percent at concentrations as high as 1 *M*. At higher concentrations, solute-solute interactions lead to larger deviations.

Charles D. Winters

Henry's law. As soon as the pressure is released, carbon dioxide begins to bubble out of solution in a carbonated beverage.

Vapor Pressure Lowering

You may have noticed that concentrated aqueous solutions evaporate more slowly than does pure water. This reflects the fact that the vapor pressure of water over the solution is less than that of pure water (Figure 10.6).

Vapor pressure lowering is a true colligative property; that is, it is independent of the nature of the solute but directly proportional to its concentration. For example, the vapor pressure of water above a 0.10 *M* solution of either glucose or sucrose at 0°C is the same, about 0.008 mm Hg less than that of pure water. In 0.30 *M* solution, the vapor pressure lowering is almost exactly three times as great, 0.025 mm Hg.

The relationship between solvent vapor pressure and concentration is ordinarily expressed as

$$P_1 = X_1 P_1^\circ \qquad \textbf{(10.3)}$$

In this equation, P_1 is the vapor pressure of solvent over the solution, P_1° is the vapor pressure of the pure solvent at the same temperature, and X_1 is the mole fraction of solvent. Note that because X_1 in a solution must be less than 1, P_1 must be less than P_1°. This relationship is called **Raoult's law;** François Raoult (1830–1901) carried out a large number of careful experiments on vapor pressures and freezing point lowering.

To obtain a direct expression for vapor pressure lowering, note that $X_1 = 1 - X_2$, where X_2 is the mole fraction of solute. Substituting $1 - X_2$ for X_1 in Raoult's law,

$$P_1 = (1 - X_2)\, P_1^\circ$$

Rearranging,

$$P_1^\circ - P_1 = X_2 P_1^\circ$$

The quantity $(P_1^\circ - P_1)$ is the vapor pressure lowering (ΔP). It is the difference between the solvent vapor pressure in the pure solvent and in solution.

$$\Delta P = X_2 P_1^\circ \qquad \textbf{(10.4)}$$

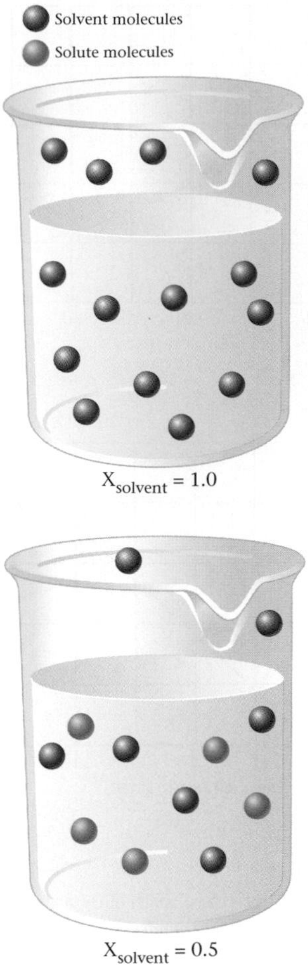

Figure 10.6
Raoult's law. Adding a solute lowers the concentration of solvent molecules in the liquid phase. To maintain equilibrium, the concentration of solvent molecules in the gas phase must decrease, thereby lowering the solvent vapor pressure.

CENGAGENOW™
Click Coached Problems for a self-study module on **vapor pressure changes and Raoult's law.**

Vapor pressure lowering is directly proportional to solute mole fraction.

Example 10.6 A solution contains 82.0 g of glucose, $C_6H_{12}O_6$, in 322 g of water. Calculate the vapor pressure lowering at 25°C (vapor pressure of pure water = 23.76 mm Hg).

Strategy First (1), calculate the number of moles of glucose (MM = 180.16 g/mol) and water (MM = 18.02 g/mol). That information allows you to find (2) the mole fraction of glucose. Finally (3), use Raoult's law to find the vapor pressure lowering.

SOLUTION

(1) $n_{\text{glucose}} = 82.0 \text{ g glucose} \times \dfrac{1 \text{ mol glucose}}{180.16 \text{ g glucose}} = 0.455 \text{ mol glucose}$

$n_{\text{water}} = 322 \text{ g water} \times \dfrac{1 \text{ mol water}}{18.02 \text{ g water}} = 17.9 \text{ mol water}$

(2) $X_{\text{glucose}} = \dfrac{0.455}{0.455 + 17.9} = 0.0248$

(3) $\Delta P = X_{\text{glucose}} \times P^\circ_{H_2O} = 0.0248 \times 23.76 \text{ mm Hg} = 0.589 \text{ mm Hg}$

Reality Check You expect the vapor pressure lowering to be small (0.589 mm Hg) because the mole fraction of solute is small (0.0248).

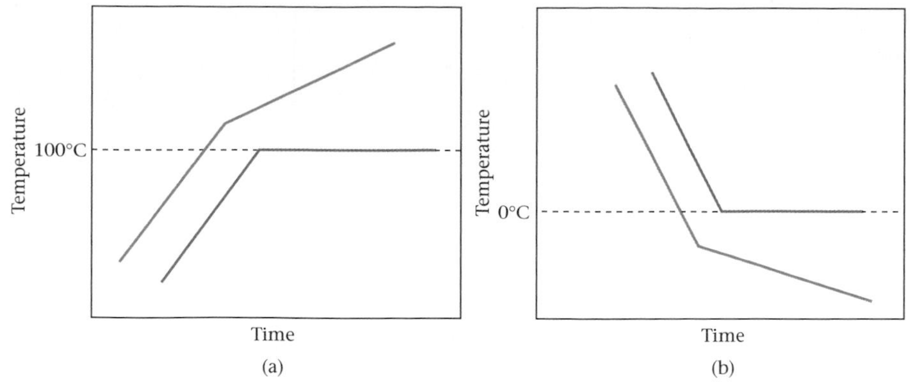

Figure 10.7
Boiling (a) and freezing (b) curves for pure water (red) and an aqueous solution (green). For pure water, the temperature remains constant during boiling or freezing. For the solution, the temperature changes steadily during the phase change because water is being removed, increasing the concentration of solute.

Boiling Point Elevation and Freezing Point Lowering

When a solution of a nonvolatile solute is heated, it does not begin to boil until the temperature exceeds the boiling point of the solvent. The difference in temperature is called the **boiling point elevation, ΔT_b.**

CENGAGENOW™
Click Coached Problems for a self-study module on **boiling point elevation.**

$$\Delta T_b = T_b - T_b^\circ$$

where T_b and T_b° are the boiling points of the solution and the pure solvent, respectively. As boiling continues, pure solvent distills off, the concentration of solute increases, and the boiling point continues to rise (Figure 10.7).

When a solution is cooled, it does not begin to freeze until a temperature below the freezing point of the pure solvent is reached. The **freezing point lowering, ΔT_f,** is defined to be a positive quantity:

$$\Delta T_f = T_f^\circ - T_f$$

where T_f°, the freezing point of the solvent, lies above T_f, the freezing point of the solution. As freezing takes place, pure solvent freezes out, the concentration of solute increases, and the freezing point continues to drop. This is what happens with "ice beer." When beer is cooled below 0°C, pure ice separates and the percentage of ethyl alcohol increases.

Boiling point elevation is a direct result of vapor pressure lowering. At any given temperature, a solution of a nonvolatile solute* has a vapor pressure *lower* than that of the pure solvent. Hence a *higher* temperature must be reached before the solution boils, that is, before its vapor pressure becomes equal to the external pressure. Figure 10.8 (p. 270) illustrates this reasoning graphically.

The freezing point lowering, like the boiling point elevation, is a direct result of the lowering of the solvent vapor pressure by the solute. Notice from Figure 10.8 that the freezing point of the solution is the temperature at which the solvent in solution has the same vapor pressure as the pure solid solvent. This implies that it is pure solvent (e.g., ice) that separates when the solution freezes.

Solutes raise the boiling point and lower the freezing point.

Boiling point elevation and freezing point lowering, like vapor pressure lowering, are colligative properties. They are directly proportional to solute concentration, generally expressed as molality, *m*. The relevant equations are

$$\Delta T_b = k_b \text{ (molality)}$$
$$\Delta T_f = k_f \text{ (molality)}$$

The proportionality constants in these equations, k_b and k_f, are called the *molal boiling point constant* and the *molal freezing point constant,* respectively. Their magnitudes depend on the nature of the solvent (Table 10.2). Note that when the solvent is water,

$$k_b = 0.52°\text{C}/m \qquad k_f = 1.86°\text{C}/m$$

*Volatile solutes ordinarily lower the boiling point because they contribute to the total vapor pressure of the solution.

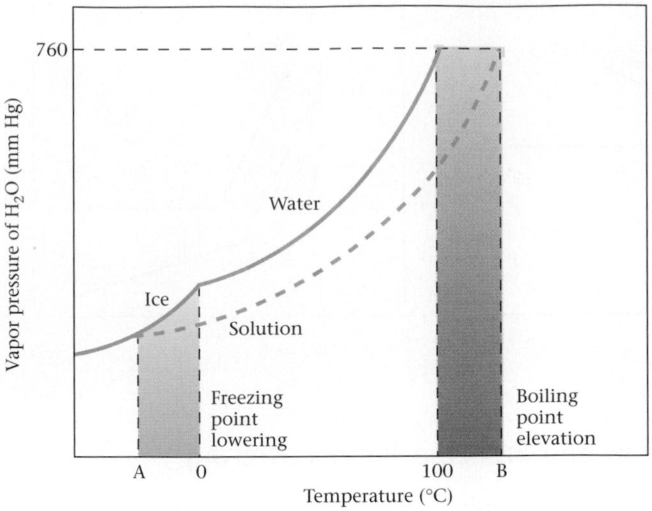

Figure 10.8
Effects of vapor pressure lowering. Because a nonvolatile solute lowers the vapor pressure of a solvent, the boiling point of a solution will be higher and the freezing point lower than the corresponding values for the pure solvent. Water solutions freeze *below* 0°C at point A and boil *above* 100°C at point B.

Example 10.7 An antifreeze solution is prepared containing 50.0 cm^3 of ethylene glycol, $C_2H_6O_2$ ($d = 1.12\ g/cm^3$), in 50.0 g of water. Calculate the freezing point of this 50-50 mixture.

Strategy First (1) calculate the number of moles of $C_2H_6O_2$ (MM = 62.07 g/mol). Then (2) apply the defining equation to calculate the molality. Finally (3), use the equation $\Delta T_f = (1.86°C/m) \times$ molality to find the freezing point lowering.

SOLUTION

$$(1)\ n_{C_2H_6O_2} = 50.0\ cm^3 \times \frac{1.12\ g}{1\ cm^3} \times \frac{1\ mol}{62.04\ g} = 0.903\ mol$$

$$(2)\ \text{molality} = \frac{\text{mol of } C_2H_6O_2}{\text{kg of water}} = \frac{0.903\ mol}{0.0500\ kg} = 18.1\ m$$

$$(3)\ \Delta\ T_f = k_f\,(\text{molality}) = 1.86°C/m \times 18.1\ m = 33.7°C$$

The freezing point of the solution is 33.7°C below that of pure water (0°C). Hence the solution should freeze at −33.7°C.

Reality Check Actually, the freezing point is somewhat lower, about −37°C (−35°F), which reminds us that the equation used, $\Delta T_f = k_f m$, is a limiting law, strictly valid only in very dilute solution.

Propylene glycol, HO—$(CH_2)_3$—OH, is much less toxic.

You take advantage of freezing point lowering when you add antifreeze to your automobile radiator in winter. Ethylene glycol, $HO(CH_2)_2OH$, is the solute commonly used. It has a

Table 10.2 Molal Freezing Point and Boiling Point Constants

Solvent	fp (°C)	k_f (°C/m)	bp (°C)	k_b (°C/m)
Water	0.00	1.86	100.00	0.52
Acetic acid	16.66	3.90	117.90	2.53
Benzene	5.50	5.10	80.10	2.53
Cyclohexane	6.50	20.2	80.72	2.75
Camphor	178.40	40.0	207.42	5.61
p-Dichlorobenzene	53.1	7.1	174.1	6.2
Naphthalene	80.29	6.94	217.96	5.80

high boiling point (197°C), is virtually nonvolatile at 100°C, and raises the boiling point of water. Hence antifreeze that contains ethylene glycol does not boil away in summer driving.

Osmotic Pressure

One interesting effect of vapor pressure lowering is shown at the left of Figure 10.9. We start with two beakers, one containing pure water and the other containing a sugar solution. These are placed next to each other under a bell jar (Figure 10.9a). As time passes, the liquid level in the beaker containing the solution rises. The level of pure water in the other beaker falls. Eventually, by evaporation and condensation, all the water is transferred to the solution (Figure 10.9b). At the end of the experiment, the beaker that contained pure water is empty. The driving force behind this process is the difference in vapor pressure of water in the two beakers. *Water moves from a region where its vapor pressure or mole fraction is high ($X_1 = 1$ in pure water) to one in which its vapor pressure or mole fraction is lower ($X_1 < 1$ in sugar solution).*

CENGAGENOW™
Click Coached Problems for a self-study module on **osmotic pressure.**

The apparatus shown in Figure 10.9c and d can be used to achieve a result similar to that found in the bell jar experiment. In this case, a sugar solution is separated from water by a semipermeable membrane. This may be an animal bladder, a slice of vegetable tissue, or a piece of parchment. The membrane, by a mechanism that is not well understood, allows water molecules to pass through it, but not sugar molecules. As before, water moves from a region where its mole fraction is high (pure water) to a region where it is lower (sugar solution). This process, taking place through a membrane permeable only to the solvent, is called **osmosis.** As a result of osmosis, the water level rises in the tube and drops in the beaker (Figure 10.9d).

The osmotic pressure, π, is equal to the external pressure, P, just sufficient to prevent osmosis (Figure 10.10, p. 272). If P is less than π, osmosis takes place in the normal way, and water moves through the membrane into the solution (Figure 10.10a). By making the external pressure large enough, it is possible to reverse this process (Figure 10.10b). When $P > \pi$, water molecules move through the membrane from the solution to pure water. This process, called ***reverse osmosis,*** is used to obtain fresh water from seawater in arid regions of the world, including Saudi Arabia. It is also used to concentrate the sap from which maple syrup is made (page 277).

Reverse osmosis absorbs energy, but there's plenty of that in Saudi Arabia.

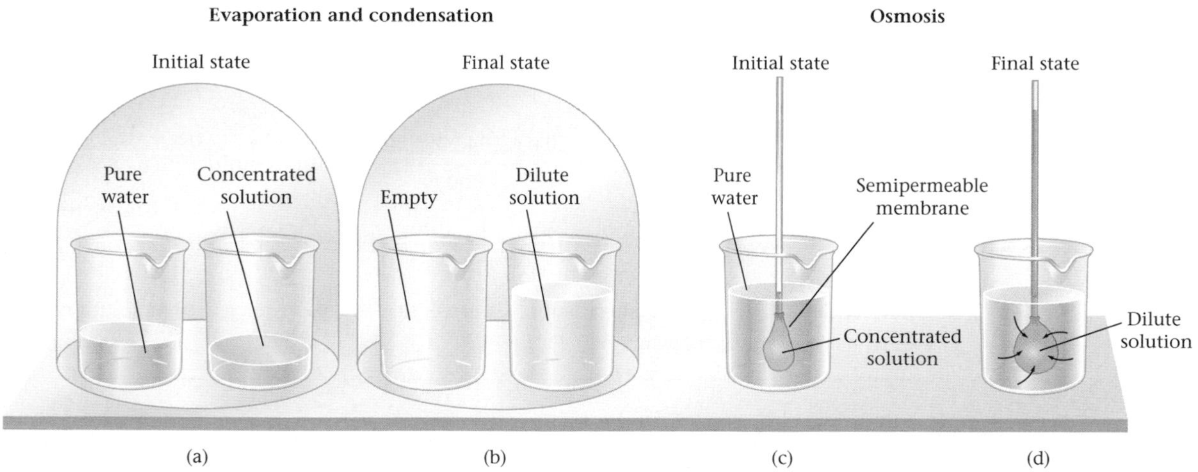

Figure 10.9
Evaporation and condensation (a and b); osmosis (c and d). Water tends to move spontaneously from a region where its vapor pressure is high to a region where it is low. In a → b, movement of water molecules occurs through the air trapped under the bell jar. In c → d, water molecules move by osmosis through a semipermeable membrane. The driving force is the same in the two cases, although the mechanism differs.

Figure 10.10
Reverse osmosis. (a) When the external pressure (P) is less than the osmotic pressure (π) ($P < \pi$), normal osmosis occurs. (b) When the external pressure exceeds the osmotic pressure, water flows in the opposite direction, producing reverse osmosis. Reverse osmosis can be used to obtain fresh water from seawater.

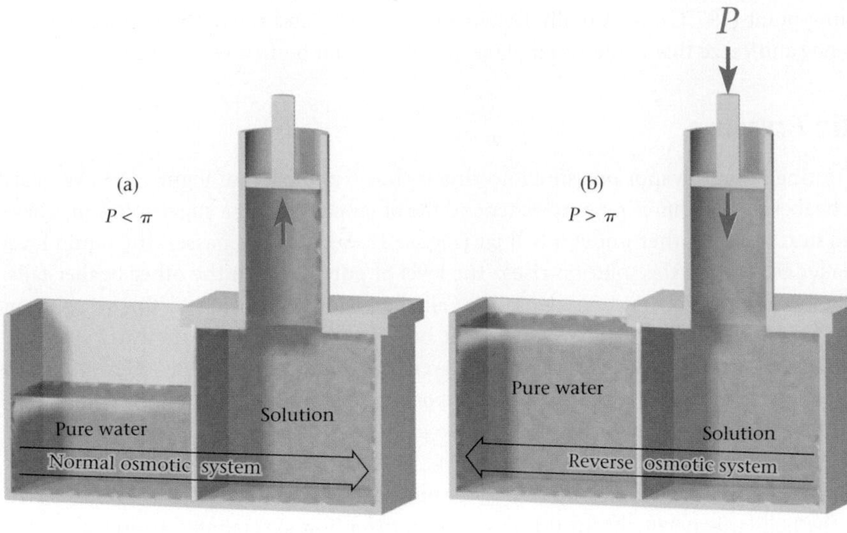

Osmotic pressure, like vapor pressure lowering, is a colligative property. For any non-electrolyte, π is directly proportional to molarity, M. The equation relating these two quantities is very similar to the ideal gas law:

$$\pi = \frac{nRT}{V} = MRT \qquad \textbf{(10.5)}$$

where R is the gas law constant, 0.0821 L · atm/mol · K, and T is the Kelvin temperature. Even in dilute solution, the osmotic pressure is quite large. Consider, for example, a 0.10 M solution at 25°C:

$$\pi = (0.10 \text{ mol/L})\left(0.0821 \frac{\text{L} \cdot \text{atm}}{\text{mol} \cdot \text{K}}\right)(298 \text{ K}) = 2.4 \text{ atm}$$

A pressure of 2.4 atm is equivalent to that of a column of water 25 m (more than 80 ft) high.

Example 10.8 Calculate the osmotic pressure at 15°C of a solution prepared by dissolving 50.0 g of sugar, $C_{12}H_{22}O_{11}$, in enough water to form one liter of solution.

Strategy Determine the molarity of the solution (MM $C_{12}H_{22}O_{11}$ = 342.3 g/mol). Then substitute into Equation 10.5 to obtain the osmotic pressure.

SOLUTION

$$\text{Molarity } (M) = \frac{50.0 \text{ g}/(342.3 \text{ g/mol})}{1.000 \text{ L}} = 0.146 \text{ mol/L}$$

$$\pi = 0.146 \frac{\text{mol}}{\text{L}} \times 0.0821 \frac{\text{L} \cdot \text{atm}}{\text{mol} \cdot \text{K}} \times 288 \text{ K} = \boxed{3.45 \text{ atm}}$$

Reality Check This is a quite reasonable answer; as shown earlier, a 0.10 M solution at 25°C has an osmotic pressure of 2.4 atm.

Dishwashers' hands get wrinkled too.

If a cucumber is placed in a concentrated brine solution, it shrinks and assumes the wrinkled skin of a pickle. The skin of the cucumber acts as a semipermeable membrane. The water solution inside the cucumber is more dilute than the solution surrounding it. As a result, water flows out of the cucumber into the brine (Figure 10.11, p. 273).

When a dried prune is placed in water, the skin also acts as a semipermeable membrane. This time the solution inside the prune is more concentrated than the water, so that water flows into the prune, making the prune less wrinkled.

Figure 10.11
Effect of osmosis on cucumbers and prunes. When a cucumber is pickled water moves out of the cucumber by osmosis into the concentrated brine solution. A prune placed in pure water swells as water moves into the prune, again by osmosis.

Nutrient solutions used in intravenous feeding must be *isotonic* with blood; that is, they must have the same osmotic pressure as blood. If the solution is too dilute, its osmotic pressure will be less than that of the fluids inside blood cells; in that case, water will flow into the cell until it bursts. Conversely, if the nutrient solution has too high a concentration of solutes, water will flow out of the cell until it shrivels and dies.

Determination of Molar Masses from Colligative Properties

Colligative properties, particularly freezing point depression, can be used to determine molar masses of a wide variety of nonelectrolytes. The approach used is illustrated in Example 10.9.

Example 10.9 A laboratory experiment on colligative properties directs students to determine the molar mass of an unknown solid. Each student receives 1.00 g of solute, 225 mL of solvent and information that may be pertinent to the unknown.

(a) Student A determines the freezing point of her solution to be 6.18°C. She is told that her solvent is cyclohexane, which has density 0.779 g/mL, freezing point 6.50°C and $k_f = 20.2°C/m$.
(b) Student B determines the osmotic pressure of his solution to be 0.846 atm at 25°C. He is told that his solvent is water (d = 1.00 g/mL) and that the density of the solution is also 1.00 g/mL.

Strategy To arrive at the molar mass, you must determine the concentration of the solution.

SOLUTION

(a) First, calculate the freezing point lowering, ΔT_f.

$$\Delta T_f = T_f^\circ - T_f = 6.50°C - 6.18°C = 0.32°C$$

Then obtain the molality by using the following equation:

$$\Delta T_f = m \times k_f$$

$$\text{molality} = \frac{0.32°C}{20.2°C/m} = 0.016\ m$$

To determine the number of moles of solute from the definition of molality, m = (moles solute)/(kg solvent), first find the mass of solvent using its density:

$$m_{\text{solvent}} = 225\text{ mL} \times \frac{0.779\text{ g}}{\text{mL}} = 175\text{ g} = 0.175\text{ kg}$$

Then the number of moles of solute is

$$n_{\text{solute}} = \text{molality} \times \text{mass of solvent} = \frac{0.016\text{ moles solute}}{\text{kg solvent}} \times 0.175\text{ kg solvent} = 2.8 \times 10^{-3}$$

Finally, the definition of molar mass ($MM = m/n$) gives

$$\text{MM of solute} = \frac{1.00\text{ g}}{2.8 \times 10^{-3}\text{ mol}} = 3.6 \times 10^2\text{ g/mol}$$

(b) The concentration unit in this case is molarity (M). We use the formula for osmotic pressure, $\pi = MRT$.

$$M = \frac{0.846\text{ atm}}{(0.0821\text{ L}\cdot\text{atm/mol}\cdot\text{K})(298\text{ K})} = 0.0346\text{ mol/L}$$

You then need the volume of the solution to get the moles of solute.

$$\text{mass of solution} = 1.00\text{ g solute} + 225\text{ g } H_2O = 226\text{ g}$$

$$\text{volume of solution} = 226\text{ g} \times \frac{1\text{ mL}}{1.00\text{ g}} \times \frac{1\text{ L}}{1000\text{ mL}} = 0.226\text{ L}$$

Again using the definition for the concentration unit M = (mol solute)/(L of solution), we arrive at the number of moles solute:

$$n_{\text{solute}} = \frac{0.0346\text{ mol solute}}{1\text{ L solution}} \times 0.226\text{ L solution} = 7.81 \times 10^{-3}\text{ moles solute}$$

The molar mass is therefore

$$\text{MM} = \frac{m}{n} = \frac{1.00\text{ g}}{7.81 \times 10^{-3}\text{ mol}} = 128\text{ g/mol}$$

In carrying out a molar mass determination by freezing point depression, we must choose a solvent in which the solute is readily soluble. Usually, several such solvents are available. Of these, we tend to pick one that has the largest k_f. This makes ΔT_f large and thus reduces the percent error in the freezing point measurement. From this point of view, cyclohexane or other organic solvents are better choices than water, because their k_f values are larger.

Molar masses can also be determined using other colligative properties. Osmotic pressure measurements are often used, particularly for solutes of high molar mass, where the concentration is likely to be quite low. The advantage of using osmotic pressure is that the effect is relatively large. Consider, for example, a 0.0010 M aqueous solution, for which

$$\pi \text{ at } 25°\text{C} = 0.024\text{ atm} = 18\text{ mm Hg}$$
$$\Delta T_f \approx 1.86 \times 10^{-3}\,°\text{C}$$
$$\Delta T_b \approx 5.2 \times 10^{-4}\,°\text{C}$$

A pressure of 18 mm Hg can be measured relatively accurately; temperature differences of the order of 0.001°C are essentially impossible to measure accurately.

10.4 COLLIGATIVE PROPERTIES OF ELECTROLYTES

As noted earlier, colligative properties of solutions are directly proportional to the concentration of solute *particles*. On this basis, it is reasonable to suppose that, at a given concentration, an electrolyte should have a greater effect on these properties than does a nonelectrolyte. When one mole of a nonelectrolyte such as glucose dissolves in water, one mole of solute molecules is obtained. On the other hand, one mole of the electrolyte NaCl yields two moles of ions (1 mol of Na^+, 1 mol of Cl^-). With $CaCl_2$, three moles of ions are produced per mole of solute (1 mol of Ca^{2+}, 2 mol of Cl^-).

This reasoning is confirmed experimentally. Compare, for example, the vapor pressure lowerings for 1.0 *M* solutions of glucose, sodium chloride, and calcium chloride at 25°C.

	Glucose	NaCl	$CaCl_2$
ΔP	0.42 mm Hg	0.77 mm Hg	1.3 mm Hg

With many electrolytes, ΔP is so large that the solid, when exposed to moist air, picks up water *(deliquesces)*. This occurs with calcium chloride, whose saturated solution has a vapor pressure only 30% that of pure water. If dry $CaCl_2$ is exposed to air in which the relative humidity is greater than 30%, it absorbs water and forms a saturated solution. Deliquescence continues until the vapor pressure of the solution becomes equal to that of the water in the air.

CENGAGENOW™
Click Coached Problems for a self-study module on **effect of ionic compounds on boiling point.**

The freezing points of electrolyte solutions, like their vapor pressures, are lower than those of nonelectrolytes at the same concentration. Sodium chloride and calcium chloride are used to lower the melting point of ice on highways; their aqueous solutions can have freezing points as low as −21 and −55°C, respectively.

Potassium chloride is sold for home use because it's kinder to the environment.

To calculate the freezing point lowering of an electrolyte in water, we use the general equation

$$\Delta T_f = i \times 1.86°C/m \times \text{molality} \qquad \textbf{(10.6)}$$

the multiplier *i* in this equation is known as the *Van't Hoff factor.* It tells us the number of moles of particles in solution (molecules or ions) per mole of solute. For sugar or other nonelectrolytes, *i* is 1:

$$C_{12}H_{22}O_{11}(s) \longrightarrow C_{12}H_{22}O_{11}(aq); \qquad 1\text{ mol sugar} \longrightarrow 1\text{ mol molecules}$$

For NaCl and $CaCl_2$, *i* should be 2 and 3, respectively.

$$NaCl(s) \longrightarrow Na^+(aq) + Cl^-(aq); \qquad 1\text{ mol NaCl} \longrightarrow 2\text{ mol ions}$$
$$CaCl_2(s) \longrightarrow Ca^{2+}(aq) + 2Cl^-(aq); \qquad 1\text{ mol } CaCl_2 \longrightarrow 3\text{ mol ions}$$

Charles D. Winters

Truck applying salt, NaCl, on a snow-packed road.

Similar equations apply for other colligative properties.

$$\Delta T_b = i \times 0.52°C/m \times \text{molality} \qquad \textbf{(10.7)}$$
$$\pi = i \times \text{molarity} \times RT$$

Example 10.10

Estimate the freezing points of 0.20 *m* solutions of

(a) KNO_3 (b) $Cr(NO_3)_3$

Assume that *i* is the number of moles of ions formed per mole of electrolyte.

Strategy Find *i* and apply Equation 10.6.

SOLUTION

(a) One mole of KNO_3 forms two moles of ions:

$$KNO_3(s) \longrightarrow K^+(aq) + NO_3^-(aq)$$

Hence *i* should be 2, and we have

$$\Delta T_f = (2)(1.86°C)(0.20) = 0.74°C; \qquad T_f = -0.74°C$$

(b) For $Cr(NO_3)_3$, $i = 4$:

$$Cr(NO_3)_3(s) \longrightarrow Cr^{3+}(aq) + 3NO_3^-(aq)$$
$$\Delta T_f = (4)(1.86°C)(0.20) = 1.5°C; \qquad T_f = -1.5°C$$

Table 10.3	Freezing Point Lowerings of Solutions			
	ΔT_f Observed (°C)		*i* (Calc from ΔT_f)	
Molality	NaCl	$MgSO_4$	NaCl	$MgSO_4$
0.00500	0.0182	0.0160	1.96	1.72
0.0100	0.0360	0.0285	1.94	1.53
0.0200	0.0714	0.0534	1.92	1.44
0.0500	0.176	0.121	1.89	1.30
0.100	0.348	0.225	1.87	1.21
0.200	0.685	0.418	1.84	1.12
0.500	1.68	0.995	1.81	1.07

The data in Table 10.3 suggest that the situation is not as simple as this discussion implies. The observed freezing point lowerings of NaCl and $MgSO_4$ are smaller than would be predicted with $i = 2$. For example, 0.50 *m* solutions of NaCl and $MgSO_4$ freeze at -1.68 and -0.995°C, respectively; the predicted freezing point is -1.86°C. Only in very dilute solution does the multiplier *i* approach the predicted value of 2.

This behavior is generally typical of electrolytes. Their colligative properties deviate considerably from ideal values, even at concentrations below 1 *m*. There are at least a couple of reasons for this effect.

1. Because of electrostatic attraction, an ion in solution tends to surround itself with more ions of opposite than of like charge (Figure 10.12). The existence of this *ionic atmosphere,* first proposed by Peter Debye (1884–1966), a Dutch physical chemist, in 1923, prevents ions from acting as completely independent solute particles. The result is to make an ion somewhat less effective than a nonelectrolyte molecule in its influence on colligative properties.

2. Oppositely charged ions may interact strongly enough to form a discrete species called an *ion pair.* This effect is essentially nonexistent with electrolytes such as NaCl, in which the ions have low charges ($+1$, -1). However, with $MgSO_4$ ($+2$, -2 ions), ion pairing plays a major role. Even at concentrations as low as 0.1 *m*, there are more $MgSO_4$ ion pairs than free Mg^{2+} and SO_4^{2-} ions.

Freezing point lowering (or other colligative properties) can be used to determine the extent of dissociation of a weak electrolyte in water. The procedure followed is illustrated in Example 10.11.

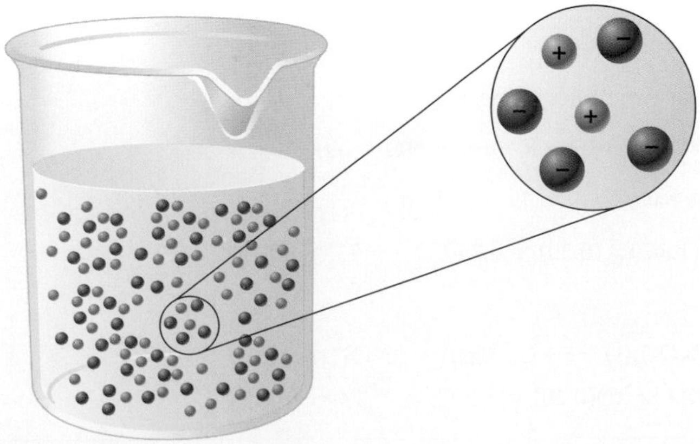

Figure 10.12
Ionic atmosphere. An ion, on the average, is surrounded by more ions of opposite charge than of like charge.

Example 10.11 Conceptual

The freezing point of a 0.50 *m* solution of oxalic acid, $H_2C_2O_4$, in water is −1.12°C. Which of the following equations best represents what happens when oxalic acid dissolves in water?

$$H_2C_2O_4(s) \longrightarrow H_2C_2O_4(aq)$$
$$H_2C_2O_4(s) \longrightarrow H^+(aq) + HC_2O_4^-(aq)$$
$$H_2C_2O_4(s) \longrightarrow 2H^+(aq) + C_2O_4^{2-}(aq)$$

Strategy Calculate *i* in Equation 10.6. For the three equations, *i* should be 1, 2, and 3, in that order.

SOLUTION

$$i = \frac{\Delta T_f}{(1.86°C)\,0.50} = \frac{1.12}{0.93} = 1.2$$

The first equation gives an *i* value closest to 1.2. Actually about 20% of the oxalic acid is ionized via the second equation.

CHEMISTRY Beyond the Classroom

Maple Syrup

The collection of maple sap and its conversion to syrup or sugar illustrate many of the principles covered in this chapter. Moreover, in northern New England, making maple syrup is an interesting way to spend the month of March (Figure A), which separates midwinter from "mud season."

The driving force behind the flow of maple sap is by no means obvious. The calculated osmotic pressure of sap, a 2% solution of sucrose (MM = 342 g/mol), is

$$\pi = \frac{20/342\ \text{mol}}{1\ \text{L}} \times 0.0821\,\frac{\text{L}\cdot\text{atm}}{\text{mol}\cdot\text{K}} \times 280\ \text{K} = 1.3\ \text{atm}$$

This is sufficient to push water to a height of about 45 ft; many maple trees are taller than that. Besides, a maple tree continues to bleed sap for several days after it has been cut down. An alternative theory suggests that sap is forced out of the tree by bubbles of $CO_2(g)$, produced by respiration. When the temperature drops at night, the carbon dioxide goes into solution, and the flow of sap ceases. This would explain the high sensitivity of sap flow to temperature; the aqueous solubility of carbon dioxide doubles when the temperature falls by 15°C.

From Masterton photo collection

Figure A
WLM collecting sap from red maple trees.

WLM made delicious maple syrup.—CNH

If you want to make your own maple syrup on a small scale, perhaps 10 to 20 L per season, there are a few principles to keep in mind.

1. Make sure the trees you tap are *maples;* hemlocks would be a particularly poor choice. Identify the trees to be tapped in the fall, before the leaves fall. If possible, select sugar maples, which produce about one liter of maple syrup per tree per season. Other types of maples are less productive.

2. It takes 20 to 40 L of sap to yield one liter of maple syrup. To remove the water, you could freeze the sap, as the Native Americans did 300 years ago. The ice that forms is pure water; by discarding it, you increase the concentration of sugar in the remaining solution. Large-scale operators today use reverse osmosis to remove about half of the water. The remainder must be boiled off. The characteristic flavor of maple syrup is caused by compounds formed on heating, such as

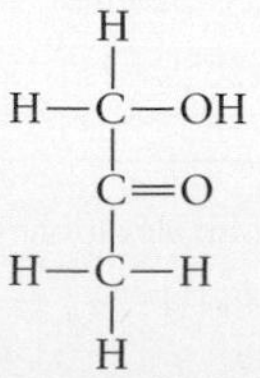

acetol

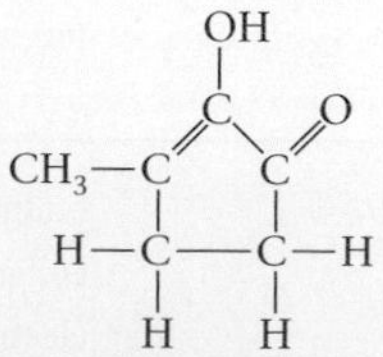

cyclotene

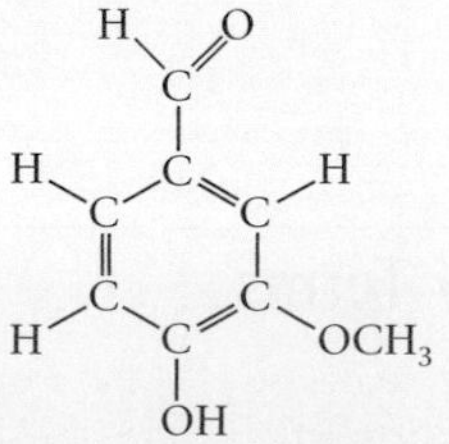

vanillin

(Continued)

It's best to boil off the water outdoors. If you do this in the kitchen, you may not be able to open the doors and windows for a couple of weeks. Wood tends to swell when it absorbs a few hundred liters of water.

3. When the concentration of sugar reaches 66%, you are at the maple syrup stage. The calculated boiling point elevation (660 g of sugar, 340 g of water)

$$\Delta T_b = 0.52°C \times \frac{660/342}{0.340} = 3.0°C$$

is somewhat less than the observed value, about 4°C. The temperature rises very rapidly around 104°C (Figure B), which makes thermometry the method of choice for detecting the end point. Shortly before that point, add a drop or two of vegetable oil to prevent foaming; perhaps this is the source of the phrase "spreading oil on troubled waters."

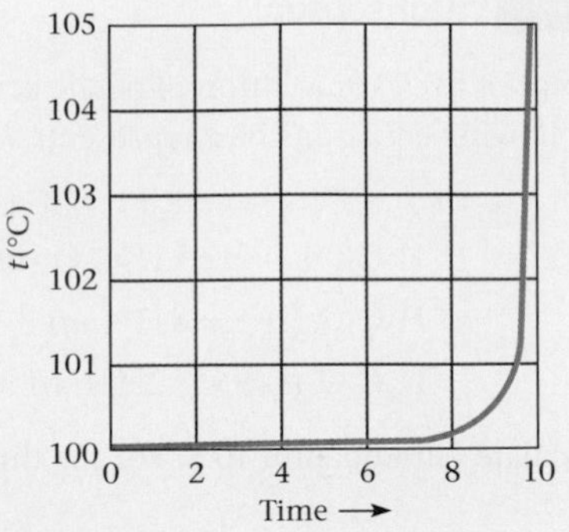

Figure B
Boiling maple sap. It seems to take forever to boil down maple sap until you reach 101°C. Then the temperature rises rapidly to the end point, 104°C. Further *careful* heating produces maple sugar.

Chapter Highlights

Key Concepts

Select end of chapter Questions and Problems may be assigned in OWL and are cross-referenced in the Key Concepts list.

CENGAGENOW™

Sign in at **academic.cengage.com/now** to:

- Check your readiness for an exam by taking the Pre-Test and exploring the self-study modules recommended in your Personalized Study plan
- For quick review, download Go Chemistry mini-lecture flashcard modules (or purchase them at **www.ichapters.com**)

1. Make dilution calculations.
   (Example 10.1; Problems 11–14, 16) ■ Questions and Problems assignable in OWL: 11a, 12b, 13, 86
2. Calculate a concentration (*M*, *X*, mass %, *m*, ppm)
   (Examples 10.2, 10.3; Problems 1–8) ■ 3, 5, 7
3. Convert from one concentration unit to another.
   (Example 10.4; Problems 9, 10, 15–20) ■ 15
4. Apply Henry's law to relate gas solubility to partial pressure.
   (Example 10.5; Problems 27–30) ■ 27, 66
5. Apply Raoult's law to calculate vapor pressure lowering.
   (Example 10.6; Problems 33–36) ■ 33, 35
6. Relate freezing point, boiling point, osmotic pressure to solute concentration.
   (Examples 10.7, 10.8, 10.10; Problems 31, 32, 37–44, 53–56) ■ 38, 41, 54
7. Use colligative properties to determine molar mass of a solute.
   (Example 10.9; Problems 45–52) ■ 50, 82
8. Use colligative properties to determine extent of ionization.
   (Example 10.11; Problems 57, 58) ■ 58

Key Equations

Dilution of solution	$M_cV_c = M_dV_d$ (Section 10.1)
Henry's law	$C_g = kP_g$ (Section 10.2)
Raoult's law	$P_1 = X_1P_1^\circ$; $\Delta P = X_2P_1^\circ$ (Section 10.3)
Osmotic pressure	$\pi = MRT \times i$ (Section 10.4)
Boiling point	$\Delta T_b = k_b \times m \times i$ (k_b = 0.52°C/m for water) (i = no. of moles of particles per mole of solute) (Section 10.4)
Freezing point	$\Delta T_f = k_f \times m \times i$ (k_f = 1.86°C/m for water) (Section 10.4)

Key Terms

boiling point elevation
colligative property
electrolyte
freezing point lowering
mass percent
molality
molarity
mole fraction
nonelectrolyte
osmosis
osmotic pressure
parts per billion
parts per million
vapor pressure lowering

Summary Problem

Consider palmitic acid, $C_{16}H_{32}O_2$, a common fatty acid used in the manufacture of soap. A solution of palmitic acid is prepared by mixing 112 g of palmitic acid with 725 mL of benzene, C_6H_6 ($d = 0.879$ g/mL). The density of the resulting solution is 0.902 g/mL.

(a) What is the mass percent of palmitic acid in the solution?
(b) What is the molarity of the solution?
(c) The vapor pressure of pure benzene at 26°C is 1.00×10^2 mm Hg. Assume that the vapor pressure exerted by palmitic acid at 26°C is negligible. What is the vapor pressure of the solution at this temperature?
(d) The normal boiling and freezing points of benzene and its boiling and freezing point constants can be found in Table 10.2. What is the normal boiling point and freezing point of this solution?
(e) Cholesterol is a soft waxy substance found in the bloodstream. Twelve grams of cholesterol is dissolved in benzene to make 525 mL of solution at 27°C. The osmotic pressure of this solution is determined to be 1.45 atm. What is the molar mass of cholesterol?

Answers

(a) 15.0%
(b) 0.527
(c) 95 mm Hg
(d) boiling point = 81.84°C; freezing point = 1.99°C
(e) 388 g/mol

Questions and Problems

Blue-numbered questions have answers in Appendix 6 and fully-worked solutions in the *Student Solutions Manual.*

■ denotes questions assignable in OWL.

WEB indicates that the solution is available on this book's companion website.

Concentrations of Solutions

1. A solution is prepared by dissolving 12.15 g of nickel(II) nitrate in 175 mL of water ($d = 1.00$ g/mL). Calculate

(a) the mass percent of nickel(II) nitrate in the solution.
(b) the mole fraction of nickel(II) ions in the solution.

2. Acetone, C_3H_6O, is the main ingredient of nail polish remover. A solution is made up by adding 35.0 mL of acetone ($d = 0.790$ g/mL) to 50.0 mL of ethyl alcohol, C_2H_6O ($d = 0.789$ g/mL). Assuming volumes are additive, calculate

(a) the mass percent of acetone in the solution.
(b) the volume percent of ethyl alcohol in the solution.
(c) the mole fraction of acetone in the solution.

3. ■ For a solution of acetic acid (CH_3COOH) to be called "vinegar," it must contain 5.00% acetic acid by mass. If a vinegar is made up only of acetic acid and water, what is the molarity of acetic acid in the vinegar? The density of vinegar is 1.006 g/mL.

4. Solutions introduced directly into the bloodstream have to be "isotonic" with blood; that is, they must have the same osmotic pressure as blood. An aqueous NaCl solution has to be 0.90% by mass to be isotonic with blood. What is the molarity of sodium ions in solution? Take the density of the solution to be 1.00 g/mL.

5. ■ Silver ions can be found in some of the city water piped into homes. The average concentration of silver ions in city water is 0.028 ppm.

(a) How many milligrams of silver ions would you ingest daily if you drank eight glasses (eight oz/glass) of city water daily?
(b) How many liters of city water are required to recover 1.00 g of silver chemically?

6. Lead is a poisonous metal that especially affects children because they retain a larger fraction of lead than adults do. Lead levels of 0.250 ppm in a child cause delayed cognitive development. How many moles of lead present in 1.00 g of a child's blood would 0.250 ppm represent?

7. ■ Complete the following table for aqueous solutions of copper(II) sulfate.

	Mass of Solute	Volume of Solution	Molarity
(a)	12.50 g	478 mL	______
(b)	______	283 mL	0.299 *M*
(c)	4.163 g	______	0.8415 *M*

8. Complete the following table for aqueous solutions of barium perchlorate.

	Mass of Solute	Volume of Solution	Molarity
(a)	______	1.370 L	0.08415 *M*
(b)	12.01 g	______	0.0579 *M*
(c)	26.44 g	2.750 L	______

9. Complete the following table for aqueous solutions of caffeine, $C_8H_{10}O_2N_4$.

	Molality	Mass Percent Solvent	Ppm Solute	Mole Fraction Solvent
(a)	______	______	______	0.900
(b)	______	______	1269	______
(c)	______	85.5	______	______
(d)	0.2560	______	______	______

10. WEB Complete the following table for aqueous solutions of urea, $CO(NH_2)_2$.

	Molality	Mass Percent Solvent	Ppm Solute	Mole Fraction Solvent
(a)	2.577	______	______	______
(b)	______	45.0	______	______
(c)	______	______	4768	______
(d)	______	______	______	0.815

11. Describe how you would prepare 465 mL of 0.3550 *M* potassium dichromate solution starting with

(a) ■ solid potassium dichromate.

(b) 0.750 *M* potassium dichromate solution.

12. Describe how you would prepare 1.00 L of 0.750 *M* barium hydroxide solution starting with

(a) solid barium hydroxide.

(b) ■ 6.00 *M* barium hydroxide solution.

13. ■ A solution is prepared by diluting 225 mL of 0.1885 *M* aluminum sulfate solution with water to a final volume of 1.450 L. Calculate

(a) the number of moles of aluminum sulfate before dilution.

(b) the molarities of the aluminum sulfate, aluminum ions, and sulfate ions in the diluted solution.

14. A solution is prepared by diluting 0.7850 L of 1.262 *M* potassium sulfide solution with water to a final volume of 2.000 L.

(a) How many grams of potassium sulfide were dissolved to give the original solution?

(b) What are the molarities of the potassium sulfide, potassium ions, and sulfide ions in the diluted solution?

15. ■ A bottle of phosphoric acid is labeled "85.0% H_3PO_4 by mass; density = 1.689 g/cm^3." Calculate the molarity, molality, and mole fraction of the phosphoric acid in solution.

16. A bottle of commercial concentrated aqueous ammonia is labeled "29.89% NH_3 by mass; density = 0.8960 g/mL."

(a) What is the molarity of the ammonia solution?

(b) If 250.0 mL of the commercial ammonia is diluted with water to make 3.00 L of solution, what is the molarity of the diluted solution?

17. Complete the following table for aqueous solutions of potassium hydroxide.

	Density (g/mL)	Molarity	Molality	Mass Percent of Solute
(a)	1.05	1.13	______	______
(b)	1.29	______	______	30.0
(c)	1.43	______	14.2	______

18. Complete the following table for aqueous solutions of ammonium sulfate.

	Density (g/mL)	Molarity	Molality	Mass Percent of Solute
(a)	1.06	0.886	______	______
(b)	1.15	______	______	26.0
(c)	1.23	______	3.11	______

19. Assume that 30 L of maple sap yields one kilogram of maple syrup (66% sucrose, $C_{12}H_{22}O_{11}$). What is the molality of the sucrose solution after one fourth of the water content of the sap has been removed?

20. In a sugar mill, sugar cane is shredded, mixed with water and crushed between rollers. The resulting juice contains 7–11% sucrose, $C_{12}H_{22}O_{11}$. Assume that 25 L of collected juice (of density 1.0 g/mL) yields 11% (by mass) sucrose. What is the molality of the sucrose solution after 33% (by mass) of the water content of the juice has been removed?

Solubilities

21. ■ Which of the following is more likely to be soluble in benzene (C_6H_6)? In each case, explain your answer.

(a) CCl_4 or NaCl

(b) hexane (C_6H_{14}) or glycerol ($CH_2OHCHOHCH_2OH$)

(c) acetic acid (CH_3COOH) or heptanoic acid ($C_6H_{13}COOH$)

(d) HCl or propylchloride ($CH_3CH_2CH_2Cl$)

22. Which of the following is more soluble in CCl_4? In each case, explain your answer.

(a) hexane (C_6H_{14}) or $CaCl_2$

(b) CBr_4 or HBr

(c) benzene (C_6H_6) or ethyl alcohol (C_2H_5OH)

(d) I_2 or NaI

23. Choose the member of each set that you would expect to be more soluble in water. Explain your answer.

(a) naphthalene, $C_{10}H_8$, or hydrogen peroxide, H—O—O—H

(b) silicon dioxide or sodium hydroxide

(c) chloroform, $CHCl_3$, or hydrogen chloride

(d) methyl alcohol, CH_3OH, or methyl ether, $H_3C—O—CH_3$

24. Choose the member of each set that you would expect to be more soluble in water. Explain your answer.

(a) chloromethane, CH_3Cl, or methanol, CH_3OH

(b) nitrogen triiodide or potassium iodide

(c) lithium chloride or ethyl chloride, C_2H_5Cl

(d) ammonia or methane

25. ■ Consider the process by which lead chloride dissolves in water:

$$PbCl_2(s) \longrightarrow Pb^{2+}(aq) + 2Cl^-(aq)$$

(a) Using data from tables in Chapter 8, calculate ΔH for this reaction.

(b) Based only on thermodynamic data, would you expect the solubility of $PbCl_2$ to increase if the temperature is increased?

26. WEB Consider the process by which sodium hydroxide dissolves in water:

$$NaOH(s) \longrightarrow Na^+(aq) + OH^-(aq)$$

(a) Using data from tables in Chapter 8, calculate ΔH for this reaction.

(b) Based only on thermodynamic data, would you expect the solubility of NaOH to increase if the temperature is increased?

27. ■ The Henry's law constant for the solubility of helium gas in water is 3.8×10^{-4} *M*/atm at 25°C.

(a) Express the constant for the solubility of helium gas in *M*/mm Hg.

(b) If the partial pressure of He at 25°C is 293 mm Hg, what is the concentration of dissolved He in mol/L at 25°C?

(c) What volume of helium gas can be dissolved in 10.00 L of water at 293 mm Hg and 25°C? (Ignore the partial pressure of water.)

28. The Henry's law constant for the solubility of argon gas in water is 1.0×10^{-3} *M*/atm at 30°C.

(a) Express the constant for the solubility of argon gas in *M*/mm Hg.

(b) If the partial pressure of argon gas at 30°C is 693 mm Hg, what is the concentration of dissolved argon in *M* at 30°C?

(c) How many grams of argon gas can be dissolved in 25 L of water at 693 mm Hg and 30°C? (Ignore the partial pressure of water.)

29. A carbonated beverage is made by saturating water with carbon dioxide at 0°C and a pressure of 3.0 atm. The bottle is then opened at room temperature (25°C), and comes to equilibrium with air in the room containing

■ in OWL Blue-numbered questions answered in Appendix 6 WEB Solution is available on companion website

CO_2 (P_{CO_2} = 3.4 × 10^{-4} atm). The Henry's law constant for the solubility of CO_2 in water is 0.0769 *M*/atm at 0°C and 0.0313 *M*/atm at 25°C.

(a) What is the concentration of carbon dioxide in the bottle before it is opened?

(b) What is the concentration of carbon dioxide in the bottle after it has been opened and come to equilibrium with the air?

30. The Henry's law constant for the solubility of oxygen in water is 3.30 × 10^{-4} *M*/atm at 12°C and 2.85 × 10^{-4} *M*/atm at 22°C. Air is 21 mol% oxygen.

(a) How many grams of oxygen can be dissolved in one liter of a trout stream at 12°C (54°F) at an air pressure of 1.00 atm?

(b) How many grams of oxygen can be dissolved per liter in the same trout stream at 22°C (72°F) at the same pressure as in (a)?

(c) A nuclear power plant is responsible for the stream's increase in temperature. What percentage of dissolved oxygen is lost by this increase in the stream's temperature?

Colligative Properties of Nonelectrolytes

31. Vodka is advertised to be *80 proof.* That means that the ethanol (C_2H_5OH) concentration is 40% (two significant figures) by volume. Assuming the density of the solution to be 1.0 g/mL, what is the freezing point of vodka? The density of ethanol is 0.789 g/mL.

32. What is the freezing point of maple syrup (66% sucrose)? Sucrose is $C_{12}H_{22}O_{11}$.

33. ■ Calculate the vapor pressure of water over each of the following ethylene glycol ($C_2H_6O_2$) solutions at 22°C (vp pure water = 19.83 mm Hg). Ethylene glycol can be assumed to be nonvolatile.

(a) $X_{\text{ethylene glycol}} = 0.288$

(b) % ethylene glycol by mass = 39.0%

(c) 2.42 *m* ethylene glycol

34. Repeat the calculations called for in Problem 33 at 96°C (vp pure water = 657.6 mm Hg).

35. ■ The vapor pressure of pure CCl_4 at 65°C is 504 mm Hg. How many grams of naphthalene ($C_{10}H_8$) must be added to 25.00 g of CCl_4 so that the vapor pressure of CCl_4 over the solution is 483 mm Hg? Assume the vapor pressure of naphthalene at 65°C is negligible.

36. How would you prepare 1.00 L of an aqueous oxalic acid ($H_2C_2O_4$) solution (*d* = 1.05 g/mL) with a vapor pressure of 21.97 mm Hg at 24°C (vp pure water = 22.38 mm Hg)?

37. Calculate the osmotic pressure of the following solutions of urea, $(NH_2)_2CO$, at 22°C.

(a) 0.217 *M* urea

(b) 25.0 g urea dissolved in enough water to make 685 mL of solution.

(c) 15.0% urea by mass (density of the solution = 1.12 g/mL)

38. ■ Pepsin is an enzyme involved in the process of digestion. Its molar mass is about 3.50 × 10^4 g/mol. What is the osmotic pressure in mm Hg at 30°C of a 0.250-g sample of pepsin in 55.0 mL of an aqueous solution?

39. Calculate the freezing point and normal boiling point of each of the following solutions:

(a) 25.0% by mass glycerine, $C_3H_8O_3$ in water

(b) 28.0 g of propylene glycol, $C_3H_8O_2$, in 325 mL of water (*d* = 1.00 g/cm³)

(c) 25.0 mL of ethanol, C_2H_5OH (*d* = 0.780 g/mL), in 735 g of water (*d* = 1.00 g/cm³)

40. How many grams of the following nonelectrolytes would have to be dissolved in 100.0 g of cyclohexane (see Table 10.2) to increase the boiling point by 2.0°C? To decrease the freezing point by 1.0°C?

(a) citric acid, $C_6H_8O_7$

(b) caffeine, $C_8H_{10}N_4O_2$

41. ■ What is the freezing point and normal boiling point of a solution made by adding 39 mL of acetone, C_3H_6O, to 225 mL of water? The densities of acetone and water are 0.790 g/cm³ and 1.00 g/cm³, respectively.

42. Antifreeze solutions are aqueous solutions of ethylene glycol, $C_2H_6O_2$ (*d* = 1.12 g/mL). In Connecticut, cars are "winterized" by filling radiators with an antifreeze solution that will protect the engine for temperatures as low as −20°F.

(a) What is the minimum molality of antifreeze solution required?

(b) How many milliliters of ethylene glycol need to be added to 250 mL of water to prepare the solution called for in (a)?

43. When 13.66 g of lactic acid, $C_3H_6O_3$, is mixed with 115 g of stearic acid, the mixture freezes at 62.7°C. The freezing point of pure stearic acid is 69.4°C. What is the freezing point constant of stearic acid?

44. A solution consisting of 4.50 g of propylene glycol, $C_3H_8O_2$, in 40.5 mL of t-butyl alcohol (*d* = 0.780 g/mL) freezes at 8.5°C. The freezing point of t-butyl alcohol is 25.5°C. What is its freezing-point constant?

45. Insulin is a hormone responsible for the regulation of glucose levels in the blood. An aqueous solution of insulin has an osmotic pressure of 2.5 mm Hg at 25°C. It is prepared by dissolving 0.100 g of insulin in enough water to make 125 mL of solution. What is the molar mass of insulin?

46. Lysozyme, extracted from egg whites, is an enzyme that cleaves bacterial cell walls. A 20.0-mg sample of this enzyme is dissolved in enough water to make 225 mL of solution. At 23°C the solution has an osmotic pressure of 0.118 mm Hg. Estimate the molar mass of lysozyme.

47. Lauryl alcohol is obtained from the coconut and is an ingredient in many hair shampoos. Its empirical formula is $C_{12}H_{26}O$. A solution of 5.00 g of lauryl alcohol in 100.0 g of benzene boils at 80.78°C. Using Table 10.2, find the molecular formula of lauryl alcohol.

48. The Rast method uses camphor ($C_{10}H_{16}O$) as a solvent for determining the molar mass of a compound. When 2.50 g of cortisone acetate is dissolved in 50.00 g of camphor (k_f = 40.0°C/*m*), the freezing point of the mixture is determined to be 173.44°C; that of pure camphor is 178.40°C. What is the molar mass of cortisone acetate?

49. Caffeine is made up of 49.5% C, 5.2% H, 16.5% O, and 28.9% N. A solution made up of 8.25 g of caffeine and 100.0 mL of benzene (*d* = 0.877 g/mL) freezes at 3.03°C. Pure benzene (k_f = 5.10°C/*m*) freezes at 5.50°C. What are the simplest and molecular formulas for caffeine?

50. ■ A compound contains 42.9% C, 2.4% H, 16.6% N, and 38.1% O. The addition of 3.16 g of this compound to 75.0 mL of cyclohexane (*d* = 0.779 g/cm³) gives a solution with a freezing point at 0.0°C. Using Table 10.2, determine the molecular formula of the compound.

51. A biochemist isolates a new protein and determines its molar mass by osmotic pressure measurements. A 50.0-mL solution is prepared by dissolving 225 mg of the protein in water. The solution has an osmotic pressure of 4.18 mm Hg at 25°C. What is the molar mass of the new protein?

52. **WEB** The molar mass of a type of hemoglobin was determined by osmotic pressure measurement. A student measured an osmotic pressure of 4.60 mm Hg for a solution at 20°C containing 3.27 g of hemoglobin in 0.200 L of solution. What is the molar mass of hemoglobin?

Colligative Properties of Electrolytes

53. Estimate the freezing and normal boiling points of 0.25 *m* aqueous solutions of

(a) NH_4NO_3 (b) $NiCl_3$ (c) $Al_2(SO_4)_3$

54. ■ Arrange 0.30 *m* solutions of the following solutes in order of increasing freezing point and boiling point.

(a) $Fe(NO_3)_3$ (b) C_2H_5OH
(c) $Ba(OH)_2$ (d) $CaCr_2O_7$

55. Aqueous solutions introduced into the bloodstream by injection must have the same osmotic pressure as blood; that is, they must be "isotonic" with blood. At 25°C, the average osmotic pressure of blood is 7.7 atm. What

■ in OWL Blue-numbered questions answered in Appendix 6 **WEB** Solution is available on companion website

is the molarity of an isotonic saline solution (NaCl in H_2O)? Recall that NaCl is an electrolyte; assume complete conversion to Na^+ and Cl^- ions.

56. What is the osmotic pressure of a 0.250 *M* solution of K_2CO_3 at 25°C? (Assume complete dissociation.)

57. The freezing point of a 0.20 *m* solution of aqueous HF is −0.38°C.
   (a) What is *i* for the solution?
   (b) Is the solution made of
      (i) HF molecules only?
      (ii) H^+ and F^- ions only?
      (iii) Primarily HF molecules with some H^+ and F^- ions?
      (iv) primarily H^+ and F^- ions with some HF molecules?

58. ■ The freezing point of a 0.21 *m* aqueous solution of H_2SO_4 is −0.796°C.
   (a) What is *i*?
   (b) Is the solution made up primarily of
      (i) H_2SO_4 molecules only?
      (ii) H^+ and HSO_4^- ions?
      (iii) 2 H^+ and 1 SO_4^{2-} ions?

59. An aqueous solution of LiX is prepared by dissolving 3.58 g of the electrolyte in 283 mL of H_2O (d = 1.00 g/mL). The solution freezes at −1.81°C. What is X^-? (Assume complete dissociation of LiX to Li^+ and X^-.)

60. An aqueous solution of M_2O is prepared by dissolving 10.91 g of the electrolyte in 435 mL of H_2O (d = 1.00 g/mL). The solution freezes at −4.68°C. What is M^+? (Assume complete dissociation of M_2O to M^+ and O^{2-}.)

Unclassified

61. A sucrose ($C_{12}H_{22}O_{11}$) solution that is 45.0% sucrose by mass has a density of 1.203 g/mL at 25°C. Calculate its
   (a) molarity.
   (b) molality.
   (c) vapor pressure (vp H_2O at 25°C = 23.76 mm Hg).
   (d) normal boiling point.

62. An aqueous solution made up of 32.47 g of iron(III) chloride in 100.0 mL of solution has a density of 1.249 g/mL at 25°C. Calculate its
   (a) molarity.
   (b) molality.
   (c) osmotic pressure at 25°C (assume i = 4).
   (d) freezing point.

63. Potassium permanganate can be used as a disinfectant. How would you prepare 25.0 L of a solution that is 15.0% $KMnO_4$ by mass if the resulting solution has a density of 1.08 g/mL? What is the molarity of the resulting solution?

64. Chloroform ($CHCl_3$) boils at 61.7°C and has a density of 1.49 g/mL.
   (a) A solution prepared by dissolving 0.146 mol of a nonelectrolyte in 132 mL of chloroform boils at 64.4°C. What is the boiling point constant (k_b) for chloroform?
   (b) Another solution is prepared by dissolving 45.2 g of an unknown electrolyte (MM = 154 g/mol) in 427.5 mL of chloroform. The resulting solution boils at 66.7°C. What is *i* for the electrolyte?

65. Twenty-five milliliters of a solution (d = 1.107 g/mL) containing 15.25% by mass of sulfuric acid is added to 50.0 mL of 2.45 *M* barium chloride.
   (a) What is the expected precipitate?
   (b) How many grams of precipitate are obtained?
   (c) What is the chloride concentration after precipitation is complete?

66. ■ The Henry's law constant for the solubility of radon in water at 30°C is 9.57×10^{-6} *M*/mm Hg. Radon is present with other gases in a sample taken from an aquifer at 30°C. Radon has a mole fraction of 2.7×10^{-6} in the gaseous mixture. The gaseous mixture is shaken with water at a total pressure of 28 atm. Calculate the concentration of radon in the water. Express your answers using the following concentration units.
   (a) molarity
   (b) ppm (Assume that the water sample has a density of 1.00 g/mL.)

67. Pure benzene boils at 80.10°C and has a boiling point constant, k_b, of 2.53°C/*m*. A sample of benzene is contaminated by naphthalene, $C_{10}H_8$. The boiling point of the contaminated sample is 81.20°C. How pure is the sample? (Express your answer as mass percent of benzene.)

68. Refer to Problem 55 and determine the concentration of a glucose solution isotonic with blood.

Conceptual Problems

69. A single-celled animal lives in a fresh-water lake. The cell is transferred into ocean water. Does it stay the same, shrink, or burst? Explain why.

70. One mole of $CaCl_2$ is represented as □8 where □ represents Ca and ○ represents Cl. Complete the picture showing only the calcium and chloride ions. The water molecules need not be shown.

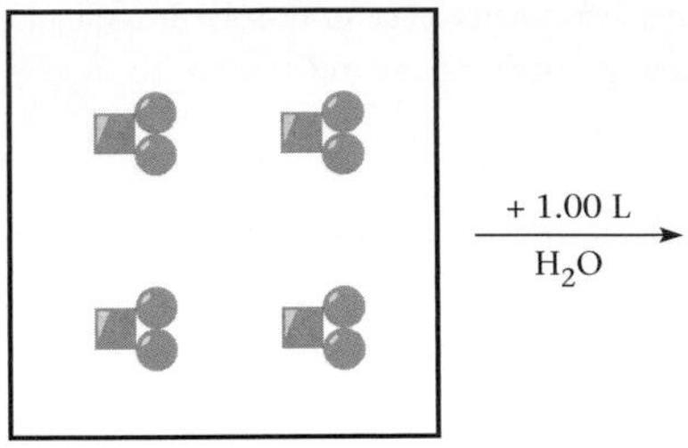

What is the molarity of Ca^{2+}? Of Cl^-?

71. One mole of Na_2S is represented as 8○ where □ represents Na and ○ represents S. Complete the picture showing only the sodium and sulfide ions. The water molecules need not be shown.

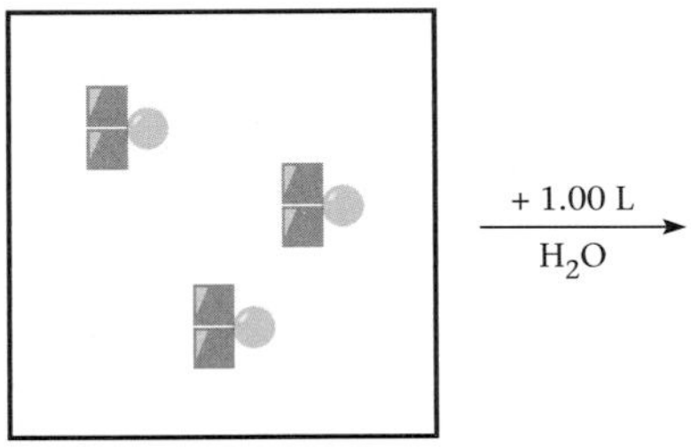

What is the molarity of Na^+? of S^{2-}?

72. Consider two nonelectrolytes X and Y. X has a higher molar mass than Y. Twenty-five grams of X is dissolved in 100 g of solvent C and labeled solution 1. Twenty-five grams of Y is dissolved in 100 g of solvent C and labeled solution 2. Both solutions have the same density. Which solution has
   (a) a higher molarity?
   (b) a higher mass percent?
   (c) a higher molality?
   (d) a larger multiplier *i*?
   (e) a larger mole fraction of solvent?

73. Show how 1 ppb (part per billion) is equivalent to 1 microgram/kg. One microgram = 10^{-6} g.

74. The freezing point of 0.20 *m* HF is −0.38°C. Is HF primarily nonionized in this solution (HF molecules), or is it dissociated to H^+ and F^- ions?

75. A certain gaseous solute dissolves in water, evolving 12.0 kJ of heat. Its solubility at 25°C and 4.00 atm is 0.0200 *M*. Would you expect the solubility to be greater or less than 0.0200 *M* at
   (a) 5°C and 6 atm? (b) 50°C and 2 atm?
   (c) 20°C and 4 atm? (d) 25°C and 1 atm?

76. The freezing point of 0.10 *M* $KHSO_3$ is −0.38°C. Which of the following equations best represents what happens when $KHSO_3$ dissolves in water?
   (a) $KHSO_3(s) \longrightarrow KHSO_3(aq)$
   (b) $KHSO_3(s) \longrightarrow K^+(aq) + HSO^{3-}(aq)$
   (c) $KHSO_3(s) \longrightarrow K^+(aq) + SO_3^{2-}(aq) + H^+(aq)$

■ in OWL Blue-numbered questions answered in Appendix 6 **WEB** Solution is available on companion website

77. Explain why
(a) the freezing point of 0.10 *m* $CaCl_2$ is lower than the freezing point of 0.10 *m* $CaSO_4$.
(b) the solubility of solids in water usually increases as the temperature increases.
(c) pressure must be applied to cause reverse osmosis to occur.
(d) 0.10 *M* $BaCl_2$ has a higher osmotic pressure than 0.10 *M* glucose.
(e) *molarity* and *molality* are nearly the same in dilute solutions.

78. Criticize the following statements.
(a) A saturated solution is always a concentrated solution.
(b) The water solubility of a solid always decreases with a drop in temperature.
(c) For all aqueous solutions, molarity and molality are equal.
(d) The freezing point depression of a 0.10 *m* $CaCl_2$ solution is twice that of a 0.10 *m* KCl solution.
(e) A 0.10 *M* sucrose solution and a 0.10 *M* NaCl solution have the same osmotic pressure.

79. In your own words, explain
(a) why seawater has a lower freezing point than fresh water.
(b) why one often obtains a "grainy" product when making fudge (a supersaturated sugar solution).
(c) why the concentrations of solutions used for intravenous feeding must be controlled carefully.
(d) why fish in a lake (and fishermen) seek deep, shaded places during summer afternoons.
(e) why champagne "fizzes" in a glass.

80. Explain, in your own words,
(a) how to determine experimentally whether a pure substance is an electrolyte or a nonelectrolyte.
(b) why a cold glass of beer goes "flat" upon warming.
(c) why the molality of a solute is ordinarily larger than its mole fraction.
(d) why the boiling point is raised by the presence of a solute.

81. Beaker A has 1.00 mol of chloroform, $CHCl_3$, at 27°C. Beaker B has 1.00 mol of carbon tetrachloride, CCl_4, also at 27°C. Equal masses of a nonvolatile, nonreactive solute are added to both beakers. In answering the questions below, the following data may be helpful.

	$CHCl_3$ (A)	CCl_4 (B)
Vapor pressure at 27°C	0.276 atm	0.164 atm
Boiling point	61.26°C	76.5°C
k_b (°C/*m*)	3.63	5.03

Write $<$, $>$, $=$, or *more information needed* in the blanks provided.
(a) Vapor pressure of solvent over beaker B ________ vapor pressure of solvent over beaker A.
(b) Boiling point of solution in beaker A ________ boiling point of solution in beaker B.
(c) Vapor pressure of pure $CHCl_3$ ________ vapor pressure of solvent over beaker A.
(d) Vapor pressure lowering of solvent in beaker A ________ vapor pressure lowering of solvent in beaker B.
(e) Mole fraction of solute in beaker A ________ mole fraction of solute in beaker B.

Challenge Problems

82. ■ What is the density of an aqueous solution of potassium nitrate that has a normal boiling point of 103.0°C and an osmotic pressure of 122 atm at 25°C?

83. A solution contains 158.2 g of KOH per liter; its density is 1.13 g/mL. A lab technician wants to prepare 0.250 *m* KOH, starting with 100.0 mL of this solution. How much water or solid KOH should be added to the 100.0-mL portion?

84. Show that the following relation is generally valid for all solutions:

$$\text{molality} = \frac{\text{molarity}}{d - \dfrac{\text{MM (molarity)}}{1000}}$$

where *d* is solution density (g/cm^3) and MM is the molar mass of the solute. Using this equation, explain why molality approaches molarity in dilute solution when water is the solvent, but not with other solvents.

85. The water-soluble nonelectrolyte X has a molar mass of 410 g/mol. A 0.100-g mixture containing this substance and sugar (MM = 342 g/mol) is added to 1.00 g of water to give a solution whose freezing point is −0.500°C. Estimate the mass percent of X in the mixture.

86. ■ A martini, weighing about 5.0 oz (142 g), contains 30.0% by mass of alcohol. About 15% of the alcohol in the martini passes directly into the bloodstream (7.0 L for an adult). Estimate the concentration of alcohol in the blood (g/cm^3) of a person who drinks two martinis before dinner. (A concentration of 0.0010 g/cm^3 or more is frequently considered indicative of intoxication in a "normal" adult.)

87. When water is added to a mixture of aluminum metal and sodium hydroxide, hydrogen gas is produced. This is the reaction used in commercial drain cleaners:

$$2Al(s) + 6H_2O(l) + 2OH^-(aq) \longrightarrow 2Al(OH)^{4-}(aq) + 3H_2(g)$$

A sufficient amount of water is added to 49.92 g of NaOH to make 0.600 L of solution; 41.28 g of Al is added to this solution and hydrogen gas is formed.
(a) Calculate the molarity of the initial NaOH solution.
(b) How many moles of hydrogen were formed?
(c) The hydrogen was collected over water at 25°C and 758.6 mm Hg. The vapor pressure of water at this temperature is 23.8 mm Hg. What volume of hydrogen was generated?

88. It is found experimentally that the volume of a gas that dissolves in a given amount of water is independent of the pressure of the gas; that is, if 5 cm^3 of a gas dissolves in 100 g of water at 1 atm pressure, 5 cm^3 will dissolve at a pressure of 2 atm, 5 atm, 10 atm, ... Show that this relationship follows logically from Henry's law and the ideal gas law.

11

Rate of Reaction

Not every collision,
not every punctilious trajectory
by which billiard-ball complexes
arrive at their calculable meeting
places leads to reaction.
Men (and women) are not
as different from molecules
as they think.

—Roald Hoffmann
"Men and Molecules"

Chapter Outline

The rate of reaction is often experimentally determined by relating the reactant (or product) concentration with time.

For a chemical reaction to be feasible, it must occur at a reasonable rate. Consequently, it is important to be able to control the rate of reaction. Most often, this means making it occur more rapidly. When you carry out a reaction in the general chemistry laboratory, you want it to take place quickly. A research chemist trying to synthesize a new drug has the same objective. Sometimes, though, it is desirable to reduce the rate of reaction. The aging process, a complex series of biological oxidations, believed to involve "free radicals" with unpaired electrons such as

$$\cdot\ddot{\underset{\cdot\cdot}{O}}—H \quad \text{and} \quad \cdot\ddot{\underset{\cdot\cdot}{O}}—\ddot{\underset{\cdot\cdot}{O}}:^-$$

is one we would all like to slow down.

This chapter sets forth the principles of *chemical kinetics*, the study of reaction rates. The main emphasis is on those factors that influence rate. These include—

- the concentrations of reactants (Sections 11.2, 11.3).
- the process by which the reaction takes place (Section 11.4).
- the temperature (Section 11.5).
- the presence of a catalyst (Section 11.6).
- the reaction mechanism (Section 11.7). ■

Online homework for this chapter may be assigned in OWL

CENGAGENOW™

This icon introduces an opportunity for self-study and to explore interactive modules by signing in at **academic.cengage.com/now.**

At least all of us who are over the age of 10.

11.1 MEANING OF REACTION RATE

To discuss **reaction rate** meaningfully, it must be defined precisely. ***The rate of reaction is a positive quantity that expresses how the concentration of a reactant or product changes with time.*** To illustrate what this means, consider the reaction

$$N_2O_5(g) \longrightarrow 2NO_2(g) + \tfrac{1}{2}O_2(g)$$

As you can see from Figure 11.1 (p. 286), the concentration of N_2O_5 decreases with time; the concentrations of NO_2 and O_2 increase. Because these species have different coefficients in the balanced equation, their concentrations do not change at the same rate. When *one* mole of N_2O_5 decomposes, *two* moles of NO_2 and *one-half* mole of O_2 are formed. This means that

$$-\Delta[N_2O_5] = \frac{\Delta[NO_2]}{2} = \frac{\Delta[O_2]}{\frac{1}{2}}$$

where Δ[ ] refers to the change in concentration in moles per liter. The minus sign in front of the N_2O_5 term is necessary because $[N_2O_5]$ decreases as the reaction takes place; the numbers in the denominator of the terms on the right (2, $\frac{1}{2}$) are the coefficients of these species in the balanced equation. The rate of reaction can now be defined by dividing by the change in time, Δt:

$$\text{rate} = \frac{-\Delta[N_2O_5]}{\Delta t} = \frac{\Delta[NO_2]}{2\Delta t} = \frac{\Delta[O_2]}{\frac{1}{2}\Delta t}$$

Δ [reactants] < 0.
Δ [products] > 0.

More generally, for the reaction

$$aA + bB \longrightarrow cC + dD$$

where A, B, C, and D represent substances in the gas phase (*g*) or in aqueous solution (*aq*), and *a*, *b*, *c*, *d* are their coefficients in the balanced equation,

$$\text{rate} = \frac{-\Delta[A]}{a\,\Delta t} = \frac{-\Delta[B]}{b\,\Delta t} = \frac{\Delta[C]}{c\,\Delta t} = \frac{\Delta[D]}{d\,\Delta t} \qquad \textbf{(11.1)}$$

This is the defining equation for rate.

Figure 11.1
Changes in reactant and product concentrations with time. For the reaction $N_2O_5(g) \longrightarrow 2NO_2(g) + \frac{1}{2}O_2(g)$, the concentrations of NO_2 and O_2 increase with time, whereas that of N_2O_5 decreases. The reaction rate is defined as $-\Delta[N_2O_5]/\Delta t = \Delta[NO_2]/2\ \Delta t = \Delta[O_2]/\frac{1}{2}\ \Delta t$.

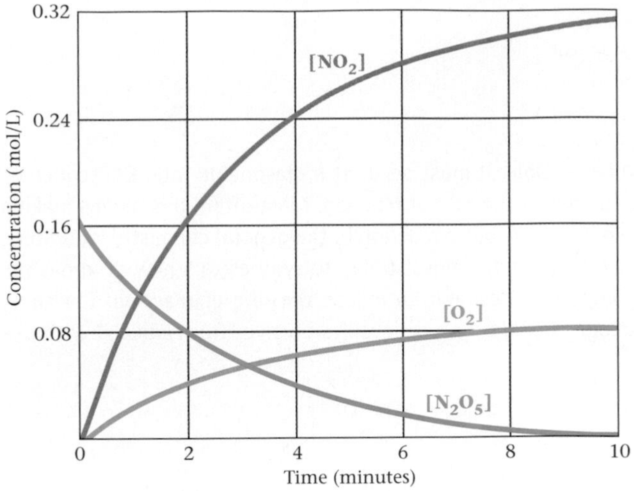

To illustrate the use of this expression, suppose that for the formation of ammonia,

$$N_2(g) + 3H_2(g) \longrightarrow 2NH_3(g)$$

molecular nitrogen is disappearing at the rate of 0.10 mol/L per minute, that is, $\Delta[N_2]/\Delta t = -0.10$ mol/L·min. From the coefficients of the balanced equation, we see that the concentration of H_2 must be decreasing three times as fast: $\Delta[H_2]/\Delta t = -0.30$ mol/L·min. By the same token, the concentration of NH_3 must be increasing at the rate of 2×0.10 mol/L·min: $\Delta[NH_3]/\Delta t = 0.20$ mol/L·min. It follows that

$$\text{rate} = \frac{-\Delta[N_2]}{\Delta t} = \frac{-\Delta[H_2]}{3\ \Delta t} = \frac{\Delta[NH_3]}{2\ \Delta t} = \frac{0.10\ \text{mol}}{\text{L} \cdot \text{min}}$$

By defining rate this way, it is independent of which species we focus on: N_2, H_2, or NH_3.

Notice that reaction rate has the units of concentration divided by time. We will always express concentration in moles per liter. Time, on the other hand, can be expressed in seconds, minutes, hours, ... A rate of 0.10 mol/L · min corresponds to

$$0.10 \frac{\text{mol}}{\text{L} \cdot \text{min}} \times \frac{1\ \text{min}}{60\ \text{s}} = 1.7 \times 10^{-3} \frac{\text{mol}}{\text{L} \cdot \text{s}}$$

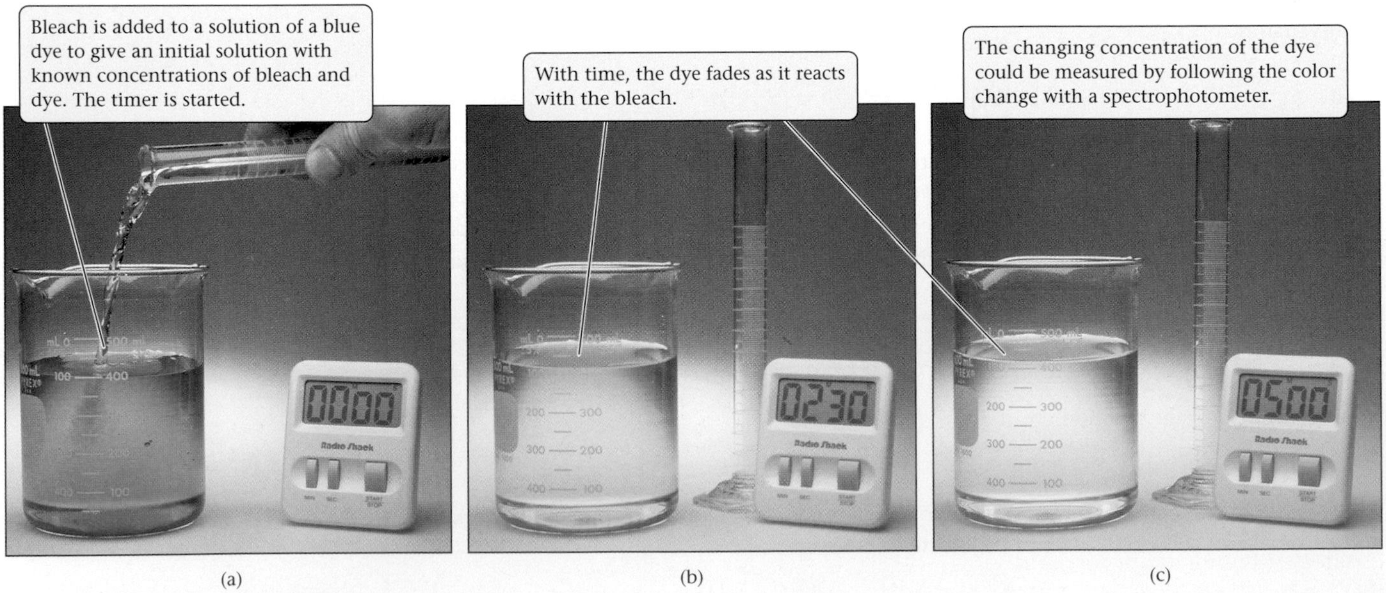

Measurement of reaction rate by observing color change.

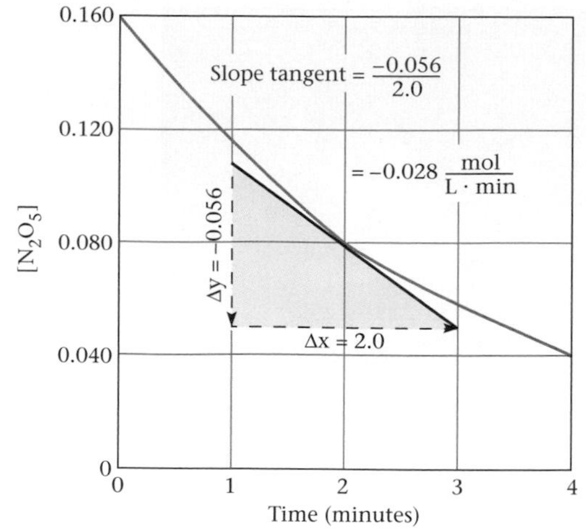

Figure 11.2
Determination of the instantaneous rate at a particular concentration. To determine the rate of reaction, plot concentration versus time and take the tangent to the curve at the desired point. For the reaction $N_2O_5(g) \longrightarrow 2NO_2(g) + \frac{1}{2}O_2(g)$, it appears that the reaction rate at $[N_2O_5] = 0.080\ M$ is 0.028 mol/L · min.

or

$$0.10 \frac{\text{mol}}{\text{L} \cdot \text{min}} \times \frac{60\ \text{min}}{1\ \text{h}} = 6.0 \frac{\text{mol}}{\text{L} \cdot \text{h}}$$

Measurement of Rate

For the reaction

$$N_2O_5(g) \longrightarrow 2NO_2(g) + \tfrac{1}{2}O_2(g)$$

the rate could be determined by measuring—

- the absorption of visible light by the NO_2 formed; this species has a reddish-brown color, whereas N_2O_5 and O_2 are colorless.
- the change in pressure that results from the increase in the number of moles of gas (1 mol reactant → $2\frac{1}{2}$ mol product).

The graphs shown in Figure 11.1 show plots of data from measurements of this type.

To find the rate of decomposition of N_2O_5, it is convenient to use Figure 11.2, which is a magnified version of a portion of Figure 11.1. If a tangent is drawn to the curve of concentration versus time, its slope at that point must equal $\Delta[N_2O_5]/\Delta t$. But because the reaction rate is $-\Delta[N_2O_5]/\Delta t$, it follows that

$$\text{rate} = -\text{slope of tangent}$$

From Figure 11.2 it appears that the slope of the tangent at $t = 2$ min is −0.028 mol/L · min. Hence

$$\text{rate at 2 min} = -(-0.028\ \text{mol/L} \cdot \text{min}) = 0.028\ \text{mol/L} \cdot \text{min}$$

11.2 REACTION RATE AND CONCENTRATION

Ordinarily, reaction rate is directly related to reactant concentration. The higher the concentration of starting materials, the more rapidly a reaction takes place. Pure hydrogen peroxide, in which the concentration of H_2O_2 molecules is about 40 mol/L, is an extremely dangerous substance. In the presence of trace impurities, it decomposes explosively

$$H_2O_2(l) \longrightarrow H_2O(g) + \tfrac{1}{2}O_2(g)$$

at a rate too rapid to measure. The hydrogen peroxide you buy in a drugstore is a dilute aqueous solution in which $[H_2O_2] \approx 1\ M$. At this relatively low concentration, decomposition is so slow that the solution is stable for several months.

CENGAGENOW™
Click Coached Problems for a self-study simulation module on **rate dependence on concentration.**

Effect of oxygen concentration on rate of combustion. (a) Steel wool in the flame reacts with atmospheric oxygen. (b) In a stream of pure oxygen, the steel wool burns much faster.

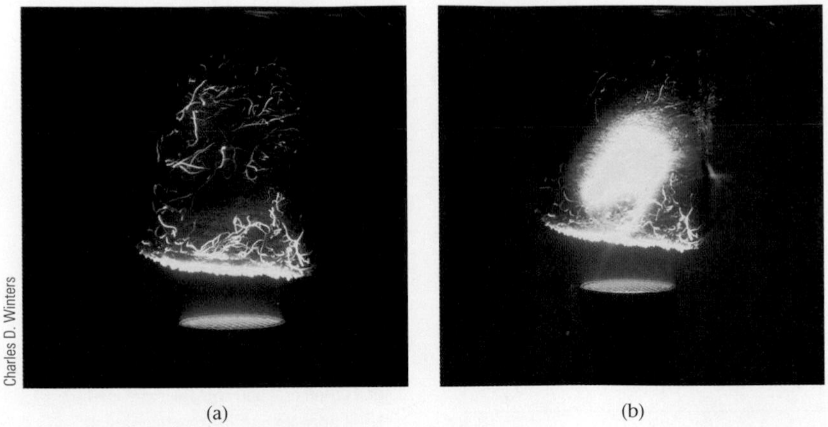

The dependence of reaction rate on concentration is readily explained. Ordinarily, ***reactions occur as the result of collisions between reactant molecules.*** The higher the concentration of molecules, the greater the number of collisions in unit time and hence the faster the reaction. As reactants are consumed, their concentrations drop, collisions occur less frequently, and reaction rate decreases. This explains the common observation that reaction rate drops off with time, eventually going to zero when the limiting reactant is consumed.

Rate Expression and Rate Constant

CENGAGENOW™
Click Coached Problems for a self-study module on **rate dependence on concentration.**

The dependence of reaction rate on concentration is readily determined for the decomposition of N_2O_5. Figure 11.3 shows what happens when reaction rate is plotted versus $[N_2O_5]$. As you would expect, rate increases as concentration increases, going from zero when $[N_2O_5] = 0$ to about 0.06 mol/L · min when $[N_2O_5] = 0.16\ M$. Moreover, as you can see from the figure, the plot of rate versus concentration is a straight line through the origin, which means that rate must be directly proportional to the concentration.

$$\text{rate} = k[N_2O_5]$$

This equation is referred to as the **rate expression** for the decomposition of N_2O_5. It tells how the rate of the reaction

$$N_2O_5(g) \longrightarrow 2NO_2(g) + \tfrac{1}{2}O_2(g)$$

Rate depends on concentration, but rate constant does not.

depends on the concentration of reactant. The proportionality constant k is called a **rate constant.** It is independent of the other quantities in the equation.

As we will see shortly, the rate expression can take various forms, depending on the nature of the reaction. It can be quite simple, as in the N_2O_5 decomposition, or exceedingly complex.

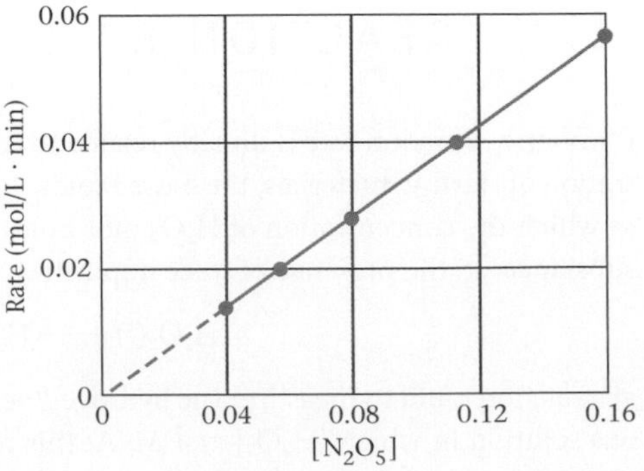

Figure 11.3
A plot of rate versus concentration for the decomposition of N_2O_5 is a straight line. The line, if extrapolated, passes through the origin. This means that rate is directionally proportional to concentration; that is, rate = $k[N_2O_5]$.

Order of Reaction Involving a Single Reactant

Rate expressions have been determined by experiment for a large number of reactions. For the process

$$A \longrightarrow \text{products}$$

the rate expression has the general form

$$\text{rate} = k[A]^m$$

Remember, [A] means the concentration of A in moles per liter.

The power to which the concentration of reactant A is raised in the rate expression is called the **order of the reaction,** *m*. If m is 0, the reaction is said to be "zero-order." If $m = 1$, the reaction is "first-order"; if $m = 2$, it is "second-order"; and so on. Ordinarily, the reaction order is integral (0, 1, 2, . . .), but fractional orders such as $\frac{3}{2}$ are possible.

The order of a reaction must be determined experimentally; ***it cannot be deduced from the coefficients in the balanced equation.*** This must be true because there is only one reaction order, but there are many different ways in which the equation for the reaction can be balanced. For example, although we wrote

$$N_2O_5(g) \longrightarrow 2NO_2(g) + \tfrac{1}{2}O_2(g)$$

to describe the decomposition of N_2O_5, it could have been written

$$2N_2O_5(g) \longrightarrow 4NO_2(g) + O_2(g)$$

The reaction is still first-order no matter how the equation is written.

One way to find the order of a reaction is to measure the initial rate (i.e., the rate at $t = 0$) as a function of the concentration of reactant. Suppose, for example, that we make up two different reaction mixtures differing only in the concentration of reactant A. We now measure the rates at the beginning of reaction, before the concentration of A has decreased appreciably. This gives two different initial rates (rate_1, rate_2) corresponding to two different starting concentrations of A, $[A]_1$ and $[A]_2$. From the rate expression,

Another approach is to measure concentration as a function of time (Section 11.3).

$$\text{rate}_2 = k[A]_2{}^m \qquad \text{rate}_1 = k[A]_1{}^m$$

Dividing the second rate by the first,

$$\frac{\text{rate}_2}{\text{rate}_1} = \frac{[A]_2{}^m}{[A]_1{}^m} = \left(\frac{[A]_2}{[A]_1}\right)^m$$

Because all the quantities in this equation are known except *m*, the reaction order can be calculated (Example 11.1).

Example 11.1 Acetaldehyle, CH_3CHO, occurs naturally in oak and tobacco leaves, and also is present in automobile and diesel exhaust. The initial rate of decomposition of acetaldehyde at 600°C

$$CH_3CHO(g) \longrightarrow CH_4(g) + CO(g)$$

was measured at a series of concentrations with the following results:

$[CH_3CHO]$	0.20 *M*	0.30 *M*	0.40 *M*	0.50 *M*
Rate (mol/L·s)	0.34	0.76	1.4	2.1

Using these data, determine the reaction order; that is, determine the value of *m* in the equation

$$\text{rate} = k[CH_3CHO]^m.$$

Strategy Choose the first two concentrations, 0.20 *M* and 0.30 *M*. Calculate the ratio of the rates, the ratio of the concentrations, and finally the order of the reaction, using the general relation derived above.

CENGAGENOW™

Click Coached Problems for a self-study module on **determining the rate equation: initial rates.**

SOLUTION

$$\frac{\text{rate}_2}{\text{rate}_1} = \frac{0.76}{0.34} = 2.2 \qquad \frac{[CH_3CHO]_2}{[CH_3CHO]_1} = \frac{0.30}{0.20} = 1.5$$

Hence the general relation becomes

$$2.2 = (1.5)^m$$

Clearly, $m = 2$; the reaction is second order.

Reality Check You would get the same result ($m = 2$) if you used any two points. Try it!

There are two variables in this equation, rate and concentration, and two constants, k and reaction order.

Once the order of the reaction is known, the rate constant is readily calculated. Consider, for example, the decomposition of acetaldehyde, where we have shown that the rate expression is

$$\text{rate} = k[CH_3CHO]^2$$

The data in Example 11.1 show that the rate at 600°C is 0.34 mol/L·s when the concentration is 0.20 mol/L. It follows that

$$k = \frac{\text{rate}}{[CH_3CHO]^2} = \frac{0.34 \text{ mol/L} \cdot \text{s}}{(0.20 \text{ mol/L})^2} = 8.5 \text{ L/mol} \cdot \text{s}$$

The same value of k would be obtained, within experimental error, using any other data pair.

Having established the value of k and the reaction order, the rate is readily calculated at any concentration. Again, using the decomposition of acetaldehyde as an example, we have established that

$$\text{rate} = 8.5 \frac{\text{L}}{\text{mol} \cdot \text{s}} [CH_3CHO]^2$$

If the concentration of acetaldehyde were 0.60 *M*,

$$\text{rate} = 8.5 \frac{\text{L}}{\text{mol} \cdot \text{s}} (0.60 \text{ mol/L})^2 = 3.1 \text{ mol/L} \cdot \text{s}$$

Order of Reaction with More Than One Reactant

Many reactions (indeed, most reactions) involve more than one reactant. For a reaction between two species A and B,

$$aA + bB \longrightarrow \text{products}$$

the general form of the rate expression is

$$\text{rate} = k[A]^m \times [B]^n$$

In this equation m is referred to as "the order of the reaction with respect to A." Similarly, n is "the order of the reaction with respect to B." The **overall order** of the reaction is the sum of the exponents, $m + n$. If $m = 1$, $n = 2$, then the reaction is first-order in A, second-order in B, and third-order overall.

This way, the concentration terms cancel for that reactant.

When more than one reactant is involved, the order can be determined by holding the initial concentration of one reactant constant while varying that of the other reactant. From rates measured under these conditions, it is possible to deduce the order of the reaction with respect to the reactant whose initial concentration is varied.

To see how this is done, consider the reaction between A and B referred to above. Suppose we run two different experiments in which the initial concentrations of A differ ($[A]_1$, $[A]_2$) but that of B is held constant at [B]. Then

$$\text{rate}_1 = k[A]_1{}^m \times [B]^n \qquad \text{rate}_2 = k[A]_2{}^m \times [B]^n$$

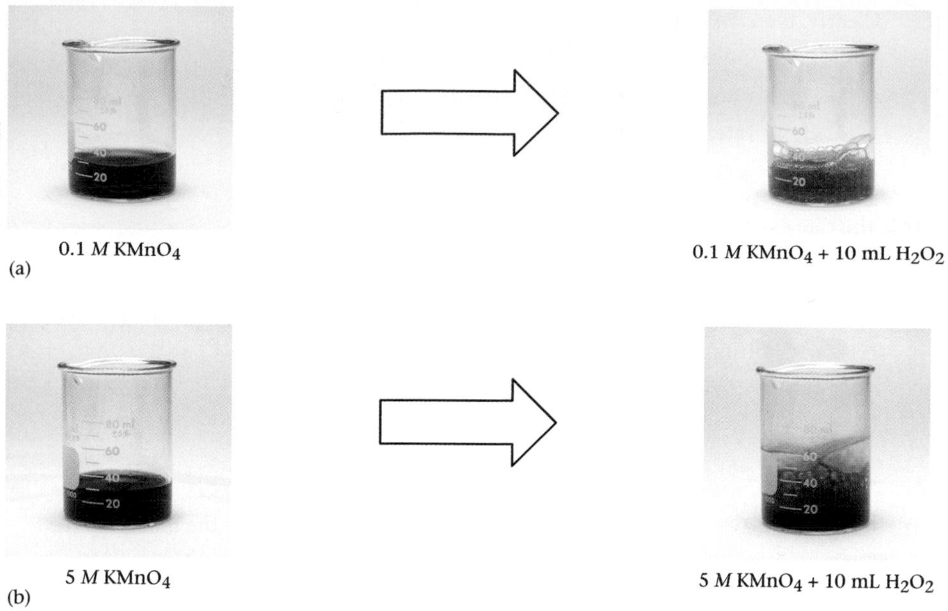

Charles D. Winters

Reaction rate and concentration. The rate of the reaction of potassium permanganate with hydrogen peroxide depends on the concentration of the permanganate. With dilute $KMnO_4$ the reaction is slow (a), but it is more rapid in more concentrated $KMnO_4$ (b).

Dividing the second equation by the first

$$\frac{\text{rate}_2}{\text{rate}_1} = \frac{k[A]_2{}^m \times [B]^n}{k[A]_1{}^m \times [B]^n} = \frac{[A]_2{}^m}{[A]_1{}^m} = \left(\frac{[A]_2}{[A]_1}\right)^m$$

Knowing the two rates and the ratio of the two concentrations, we can readily find the value of m.

Example 11.2 Consider the reaction between t-butylbromide and a base at 55°C:

$$(CH_3)_3CBr(aq) + OH^-(aq) \longrightarrow (CH_3)_3COH(aq) + Br^-(aq)$$

A series of experiments is carried out with the following results:

	Expt. 1	Expt. 2	Expt. 3	Expt. 4	Expt. 5
$[(CH_3)_3CBr]$	0.50	1.0	1.5	1.0	1.0
$[OH^-]$	0.050	0.050	0.050	0.10	0.20
Rate (mol/L · s)	0.0050	0.010	0.015	0.010	0.010

These are initial rates.

Find:

(a) the order of the reaction with respect to both $(CH_3)_3CBr$ and OH^-.
(b) Write the rate expression for the reaction.
(c) Calculate the rate constant at 55°C.
(d) What effect does doubling the concentration of OH^- have on the reaction if $[(CH_3)_3CBr]$ is kept at 1.0 M?

Strategy To find the order of the reaction with respect to $(CH_3)_3CBr$, choose two experiments, perhaps 1 and 3, where $[OH^-]$ is constant. A similar approach can be used to find n; compare experiments 2 and 5, where $[(CH_3)_3CBr]$ is constant. To write the rate expression, use the calculated reaction orders.

SOLUTION

(a) For the order of the reaction with respect to $(CH_3)_3CBr$,

$$\frac{\text{rate}_3}{\text{rate}_1} = \left(\frac{[(CH_3)_3CBr]_3}{[(CH_3)_3CBr]_1}\right)^m \qquad \frac{0.015}{0.0050} = \left(\frac{1.5}{0.50}\right)^m \qquad 3 = 3^m$$

Clearly, then, $m = 1$.

For the rate of the reaction with respect to OH^-,

$$\frac{\text{rate}_5}{\text{rate}_2} = \left(\frac{[OH^-]_5}{[OH^-]_2}\right)^n \qquad \frac{0.010}{0.010} = \left(\frac{0.20}{0.050}\right)^n \qquad 1 = 4^n$$

In this case, $n = 0$.

(b) The rate expression is

$$\text{rate} = k[(CH_3)_3CBr]^1[OH^-]^0 = k[(CH_3)_3CBr]$$

(c) You may choose any experiment to substitute a rate with its corresponding concentration. Choosing Experiment 3 gives

$$0.015\,\frac{\text{mol}}{\text{L}\cdot\text{s}} = k(1.5)\frac{\text{mol}}{\text{L}}$$

$$k = 0.010\ \text{s}^{-1}$$

Any number raised to the zero power equals 1.

(d) Changing the concentration of OH^- has no effect on the rate of the reaction. The reaction is zero-order with respect to $[OH^-]$, which means that the rate is independent of concentration.

11.3 REACTANT CONCENTRATION AND TIME

The rate expression

$$\text{rate} = k[N_2O_5]$$

shows how the rate of decomposition of N_2O_5 changes with concentration. From a practical standpoint, however, it is more important to know the relation between concentration and *time* rather than between concentration and rate. Suppose, for example, you are studying the decomposition of dinitrogen pentaoxide. Most likely, you would want to know how much N_2O_5 is left after 5 min, 1 h, or several days. An equation relating *rate* to concentration does not provide that information.

There are no speedometers for reactions, but every lab has a clock.

Using calculus, it is possible to develop integrated rate equations relating reactant concentration to time. We now examine several such equations, starting with first-order reactions.

First-Order Reactions

For the decomposition of N_2O_5 and other **first-order reactions** of the type

$$A \longrightarrow \text{products} \qquad \text{rate} = k[A]$$

it can be shown by using calculus that the relationship between concentration and time is*

$$\ln\frac{[A]_o}{[A]} = kt \qquad \textbf{(11.2)}$$

where $[A]_o$ is the original concentration of reactant, $[A]$ is its concentration at time t, k is the first-order rate constant, and the abbreviation "ln" refers to the natural logarithm.

Because $\ln a/b = \ln a - \ln b$, the first-order equation can be written in the form

$$\ln\,[A]_o - \ln\,[A] = kt$$

*Throughout Section 11.3, balanced chemical equations are written in such a way that the coefficient of the reactant is 1. In general, if the coefficient of the reactant is a, where a may be 2 or 3 or . . ., then k in each integrated rate equation must be replaced by the product ak. (See Problem 101.)

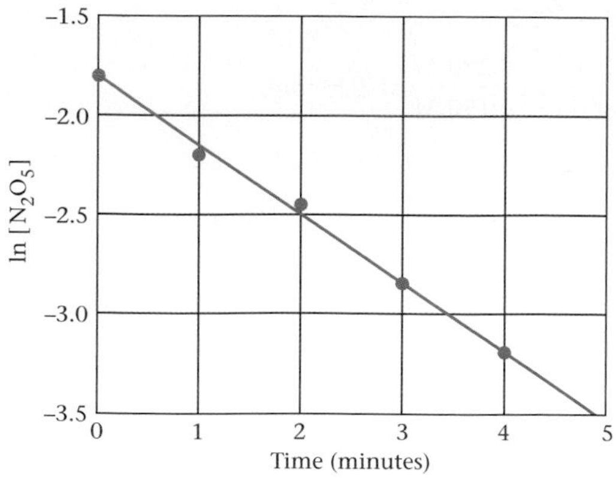

Figure 11.4
A first-order reaction plot. The rate constant for a first-order reaction can be determined from the slope of a plot of ln[A] versus time. The reaction illustrated, at 67°C, is $N_2O_5(g) \longrightarrow 2NO_2(g) + \frac{1}{2}O_2(g)$. Using two points on the line, one can find the slope of the line, which is the rate constant. In this case, k is found to be about 0.35/min.

Solving for ln [A],

$$\ln [A] = \ln [A]_o - kt$$

Comparing this equation with the general equation of a straight line,

$$y = b + mx \qquad (b = y\text{-intercept}, m = \text{slope})$$

it is clear that a plot of ln [A] versus t should be a straight line with a y-intercept of ln $[A]_o$ and a slope of $-k$. This is indeed the case, as you can see from Figure 11.4, in which we have plotted ln $[N_2O_5]$ versus t for the decomposition of N_2O_5. Drawing the best straight line through the points and taking the slope based on a point on the x-axis ($y_2 = -3.5$, $x_2 = 4.9$) and another on the y-axis ($y_1 = -1.8$, $x_1 = 0$)

$$\text{slope} = \frac{y_2 - y_1}{x_2 - x_1} = \frac{-3.5 + 1.8}{4.9 - 0} = \frac{-1.7}{4.9} = -0.35$$

It follows that the rate constant is 0.35/min; the integrated first-order equation for the decomposition of N_2O_5 is

The slope is negative but k is always positive.

$$\ln \frac{[N_2O_5]_o}{[N_2O_5]} = \frac{0.35}{\text{min}} t \qquad (\text{at } 67°\text{C})$$

Example 11.3 For the first-order decomposition of N_2O_5 at 67°C, where $k = 0.35/\text{min}$, calculate

(a) the concentration after six minutes, starting at 0.200 M.
(b) the time required for the concentration to drop to 0.150 M.
(c) the time required for half a sample of N_2O_5 to decompose.

Strategy In each case, the equation

$$\ln [N_2O_5]_o/[N_2O_5] = (0.35/\text{min})t$$

is used. In (a) and (b), two of the three variables, $[N_2O_5]_o$, $[N_2O_5]$, and t, are known; the other is readily calculated. In (c), you should be able to find the ratio $[N_2O_5]_o/[N_2O_5]$; knowing that ratio, the time can be calculated.

SOLUTION

(a) Substituting in the integrated first-order equation,

$$\ln \frac{0.200\ M}{[N_2O_5]} = \frac{0.35}{\text{min}}(6.0\ \text{min}) = 2.1$$

Taking inverse logarithms,

$$\frac{0.200\ M}{[N_2O_5]} = e^{2.1} = 8.2; \qquad [N_2O_5] = \frac{0.200\ M}{8.2} = 0.024\ M$$

If $\ln x = y$, then $x = e^y$.

(b) Solving the concentration-time relation for t,

$$t = \frac{1}{k}\ln\frac{[A]_o}{[A]} = \frac{1}{0.35/\text{min}}\ln\frac{0.200\ M}{0.150\ M} = 0.82\ \text{min}$$

(c) When half of the sample has decomposed,

$$[N_2O_5] = [N_2O_5]_o/2 \qquad [N_2O_5]_o = 2[N_2O_5] \qquad [N_2O_5]_o/[N_2O_5] = 2$$

Using the equation in (b),

$$t = \frac{1}{k}\ln 2 = \frac{0.693}{k}$$

With $k = 0.35$/min, we have

$$t = \frac{0.693}{0.35} = 2.0\ \text{min}$$

CENGAGENOW™
Click Coached Problems for a self-study module on **half-life and radiochemical dating.**

This relation holds only for a first-order reaction.

The analysis of Example 11.3c reveals an important feature of a first-order reaction: ***The time required for one half of a reactant to decompose via a first-order reaction has a fixed value, independent of concentration.*** This quantity, called the **half-life,** is given by the expression

$$t_{1/2} = \frac{\ln 2}{k} = \frac{0.693}{k} \qquad \text{first-order reaction} \qquad \textbf{(11.3)}$$

where k is the rate constant. For the decomposition of N_2O_5, where $k = 0.35$/min, $t_{1/2} =$ 2.0 min. Thus every two minutes, one half of a sample of N_2O_5 decomposes (Table 11.1).

Notice that for a first-order reaction the rate constant has the units of reciprocal time, for example, min^{-1}. This suggests a simple physical interpretation of k (at least where k is small); it is the fraction of reactant decomposing in unit time. For a first-order reaction in which

$$k = 0.010/\text{min} = 0.010\ \text{min}^{-1}$$

we can say that 0.010 (i.e., 1.0%) of the sample decomposes per minute.

Perhaps the most important first-order reaction is that of radioactive decay, in which an unstable nucleus decomposes (Chapter 2). Letting X be the amount of a radioactive isotope present at time t,

$$\text{rate} = kX$$

and

$$\ln\frac{X_o}{X} = kt$$

where X_o is the initial amount. The amount of a radioactive isotope can be expressed in terms of moles, grams, or number of atoms.

Table 11.1 Decomposition of N_2O_5 at 67°C ($t_{1/2} = 2.0$ min)

t(min)	0.0	2.0	4.0	6.0	8.0
$[N_2O_5]$	0.160	0.080	0.040	0.020	0.010
Fraction of N_2O_5 decomposed	0	$\frac{1}{2}$	$\frac{3}{4}$	$\frac{7}{8}$	$\frac{15}{16}$
Fraction of N_2O_5 left	1	$\frac{1}{2}$	$\frac{1}{4}$	$\frac{1}{8}$	$\frac{1}{16}$
Number of half-lives	0	1	2	3	4

Example 11.4 Graded

Plutonium-240 (Pu-240) is a byproduct of the nuclear reaction that takes place in a reactor. It takes one thousand years for 10.0% of a 4.60-g sample to decay.

*(a) What is the half-life of Pu-240?

**(b) How long will it take to reduce a 2.00-g sample to 15% of its original amount?

***(c) What is the rate of decay of a 5.00-g sample in g/year?

Strategy Nuclear decays are first-order reactions. Use the first-order rate calculation to find k. Part (b) differs from part (c) in that (b) relates concentration and time, while (c) relates concentration and rate. For nuclear decay, "concentration" can be expressed in moles, grams, or number of atoms.

SOLUTION

(a) When the 4.60-g sample decays, the amount lost is

$$0.100 \times 4.60 \text{ g} = 0.460 \text{ g}$$

Thus, $X_o = 4.60$ g and $X = 4.60 \text{ g} - 0.46 \text{ g} = 4.14$ g. To find the rate constant, substitute into

$$\ln X_o - \ln X = kt$$
$$\ln 4.60 - \ln 4.14 = k(1000 \text{ yr})$$
$$k = 1.05 \times 10^{-4} \text{ yr}^{-1}$$

The half-life ($t_{1/2}$) is therefore

$$t_{1/2} = \frac{0.693}{k} \qquad t_{1/2} = \frac{0.693}{1.05 \times 10^{-4} \text{ yr}^{-1}} = 6.60 \times 10^3 \text{ yr}$$

(b) Reducing the sample to 15% of its original mass means that $X = 0.15(2.00)$ remains. Thus

$$\ln 2.00 - \ln(0.15 \times 2.00) = 1.05 \times 10^{-4} \text{ yr}^{-1} \cdot t$$
$$t = 1.8 \times 10^4 \text{ yr}$$

(c) rate $= k\,(\text{mass of Pu-240})^1 = 1.05 \times 10^{-4} \text{ yr}^{-1} (5.00 \text{ g}) = 5.25 \times 10^{-4}$ g/yr

Reality Check In (b), reducing the amount present to 15% takes more time than two half-lives (i.e., more than the time to reduce to 25%). The answer is larger than $2(6.60 \times 10^3)$, as it should be. In (c), the rate is dependent on the initial concentration, unlike the half-life in (a)—which is independent of the initial amount.

Half-lives can be interpreted in terms of the level of radiation of the corresponding isotopes. Uranium has a very long half-life (4.5×10^9 yr), so it gives off radiation very slowly. At the opposite extreme is fermium-258, which decays with a half-life of 3.8×10^{-4} s. You would expect the rate of decay to be quite high. Within a second virtually all the radiation from fermium-258 is gone. Species such as this produce very high radiation during their brief existence.

Zero- and Second-Order Reactions

For a **zero-order reaction,**

$$\text{A} \longrightarrow \text{products} \qquad \text{rate} = k[\text{A}]^0 = k$$

because any non-zero quantity raised to the zero power, including [A], is equal to 1. In other words, the rate of a zero-order reaction is constant, independent of concentration. As you might expect from our earlier discussion, zero-order reactions are relatively rare. Most of

Table 11.2 Characteristics of Zero-, First-, and Second-Order Reactions of the Form A (g) $\longrightarrow$ products; [A], $[A]_o$ = conc. A at t and t = 0, respectively

Order	Rate Expression	Conc.-Time Relation	Half-Life	Linear Plot
0	rate = k	$[A]_o - [A] = kt$	$[A]_o/2k$	[A] vs. t
1	rate = $k[A]$	$\ln\frac{[A]_o}{[A]} = kt$	$0.693/k$	ln [A] vs. t
2	rate = $k[A]^2$	$\frac{1}{[A]} - \frac{1}{[A]_o} = kt$	$1/k[A]_o$	$\frac{1}{[A]}$ vs. t

them take place at solid surfaces, where the rate is independent of concentration in the gas phase. A typical example is the thermal decomposition of hydrogen iodide on gold:

$$HI(g) \xrightarrow{Au} \tfrac{1}{2}H_2(g) + \tfrac{1}{2}I_2(g)$$

When the gold surface is completely covered with HI molecules, increasing the concentration of HI(g) has no effect on reaction rate.

It can readily be shown (Problem 87) that the concentration-time relation for a zero-order reaction is

In a zero-order reaction, all the reactant is consumed in a finite time.

$$[A] = [A]_o - kt \qquad \textbf{(11.4)}$$

Comparing this equation with that for a straight line,

$$y = b + mx \qquad (b = y\text{-intercept}, m = \text{slope})$$

it should be clear that a plot of [A] versus t should be a straight line with a slope of $-k$. Putting it another way, if a plot of concentration versus time is linear, the reaction must be zero-order; the rate constant k is numerically equal to the slope of that line but has the opposite sign.

For a **second-order reaction** involving a single reactant, such as acetaldehyde (recall Example 11.1),

$$A \longrightarrow \text{products} \qquad \text{rate} = k[A]^2$$

it is again necessary to resort to calculus* to obtain the concentration-time relationship

$$\frac{1}{[A]} - \frac{1}{[A]_o} = kt \qquad \textbf{(11.5)}$$

where the symbols [A], $[A]_o$, t, and k have their usual meanings. For a second-order reaction, a plot of 1/[A] versus t should be linear.

The characteristics of zero-, first-, and second-order reactions are summarized in Table 11.2. To determine reaction order, the properties in either of the last two columns at the right of the table can be used (Example 11.5).

CENGAGENOW™
Click Coached Problems for a self-study module on **determining the rate law: graphical method.**

Example 11.5 The following data were obtained for the gas-phase decomposition of hydrogen iodide:

Time (h)	0	2	4	6
[HI]	1.00	0.50	0.33	0.25

Is this reaction zero-, first-, or second-order in HI?

*If you are taking a course in calculus, you may be surprised to learn how useful it can be in the real world (e.g., chemistry). The general rate expressions for zero-, first-, and second-order reactions are

$$-d[A]/dt = k \qquad -d[A]/dt = k[A] \qquad -d[A]/dt = k[A]^2$$

Integrating these equations from 0 to t and from $[A]_o$ to [A], you should be able to derive the equations for zero-, first-, and second-order reactions.

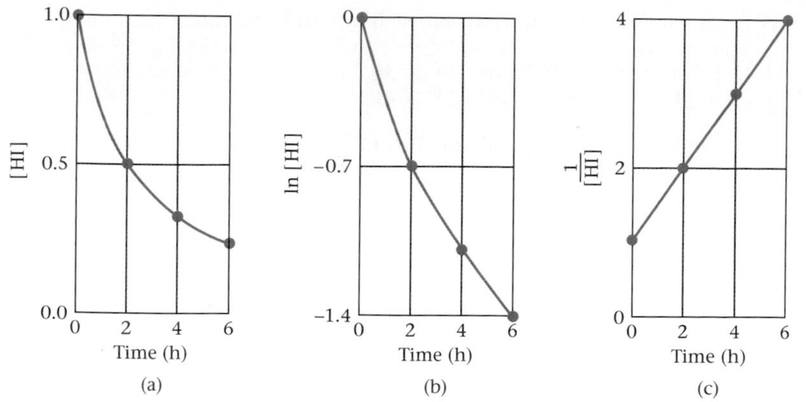

Figure 11.5
Determination of reaction order. One way to determine reaction order is to search for a linear relation between some function of concentration and time (Table 11.2). Because a plot of 1/[HI] versus *t* (plot c) is linear, the decomposition of HI must be second-order.

Strategy Note from the last column of Table 11.2 that—

- if the reaction is zero-order, a plot of [A] versus *t* should be linear.
- if the reaction is first-order, a plot of ln [A] versus *t* should be linear.
- if the reaction is second-order, a plot of 1/[A] versus *t* should be linear.

Using these data, prepare these plots and determine which one is a straight line.

SOLUTION It is useful to prepare a table listing [HI], ln [HI], and 1/[HI] as a function of time.

t(h)	[HI]	ln [HI]	1/[HI]
0	1.00	0	1.0
2	0.50	−0.69	2.0
4	0.33	−1.10	3.0
6	0.25	−1.39	4.0

If it is not obvious from this table that the only linear plot is that of 1/[HI] versus time, that point should be clear from Figure 11.5. This is a second-order reaction.

Reality Check Notice that the concentration drops from 1.00 *M* to 0.50 *M* in 2 h. If the reaction were zero-order, it would be all over after four hours. If it were first-order, the concentration would be 0.25 *M* after four hours.

Example 11.6 Conceptual

A certain reaction is first-order in A and second-order in B. In the box shown below, which is assumed to have a volume of one liter, a mole of A is represented by , a mole of B by .

(1)

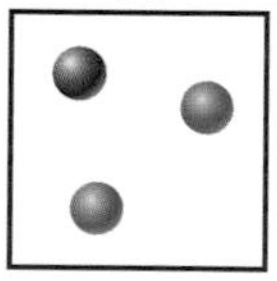

In which of the three boxes shown below is the rate of reaction the same as that in the box shown above?

(2) (3) (4)

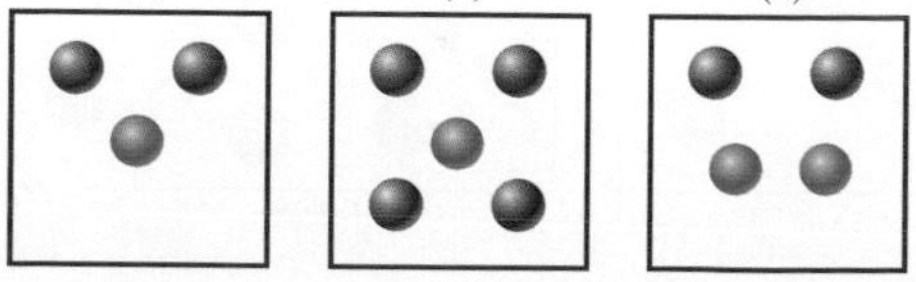

SOLUTION Write down the rate expressions for each box and compare.

(1) rate $= k(1)(2)^2 = 4k$ (3) rate $= k(4)(1)^2 = 4k$
(2) rate $= k(2)(1)^2 = 2k$ (4) rate $= k(2)(2)^2 = 8k$

Clearly, the rate in box (3) is the same as that in box (1).

11.4 MODELS FOR REACTION RATE

So far in this chapter we have approached reaction rate from an experimental point of view, describing what happens in the laboratory or the world around us. Now we change emphasis and try to explain why certain reactions occur rapidly while others take place slowly. To do this, we look at a couple of models that chemists have developed to predict rate constants for reactions.

Collision Model; Activation Energy

Consider the reaction

$$CO(g) + NO_2(g) \longrightarrow CO_2(g) + NO(g)$$

Above 600 K, this reaction takes place as a direct result of collisions between CO and NO_2 molecules. When the concentration of CO doubles (Figure 11.6), the number of these collisions in a given time increases by a factor of 2; doubling the concentration of NO_2 has the same effect. Assuming that reaction rate is directly proportional to the collision rate, the following relation should hold:

$$\text{reaction rate} = k[CO] \times [NO_2]$$

Experimentally, this prediction is confirmed; the reaction is first-order in both carbon monoxide and nitrogen dioxide.

There is a restriction on this simple model for the CO-NO_2 reaction. According to the kinetic theory of gases, for a reaction mixture at 700 K and concentrations of 0.10 *M*, every CO molecule should collide with about 10^9 NO_2 molecules in one second. If every collision were effective, the reaction should be over in a fraction of a second. In reality, this does not happen; under these conditions, the half-life is about 10 s. This implies that not every CO-NO_2 collision leads to reaction.

There would be an explosion.

There are a couple of reasons why collision between reactant molecules does not always lead to reaction. For one thing, the molecules have to be properly oriented with respect to one another when they collide. Suppose, for example, that the carbon atom of a CO molecule

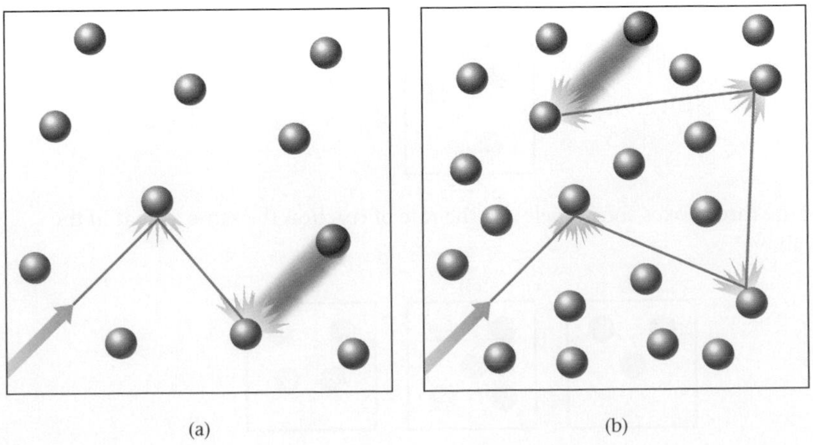

Figure 11.6
Concentration and molecular collisions. A red molecule must collide with a blue molecule for a reaction to take place. (a) A single red molecule moves among 10 blue molecules and collides with 2 of them per second. (b) With double the number of blue molecules, the number of collisions doubles to four per second.

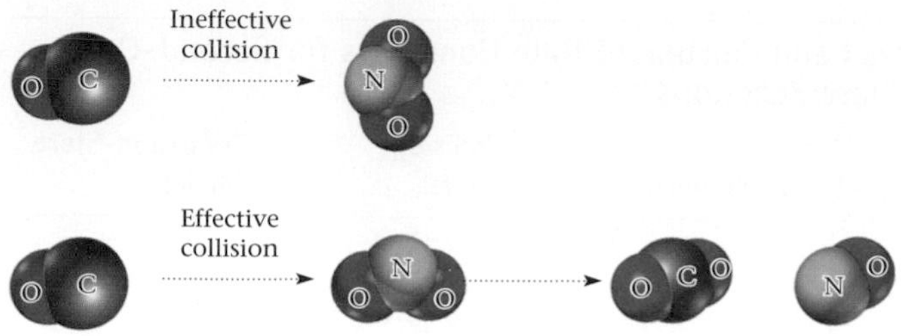

Figure 11.7
Effective and ineffective molecular collisions. For a collision to result in reaction, the molecules must be properly oriented. For the reaction $CO(g) + NO_2(g) \longrightarrow CO_2(g) + NO(g)$, the carbon atom of the CO molecule must strike an oxygen atom of the NO_2 molecule, forming CO_2 as one product, NO as the other.

strikes the nitrogen atom of an NO_2 molecule (Figure 11.7). This is very unlikely to result in the transfer of an oxygen atom from NO_2 to CO, which is required for reaction to occur.

A more important factor that reduces the number of effective collisions has to do with the kinetic energy of reactant molecules. These molecules are held together by strong chemical bonds. Only if the colliding molecules are moving very rapidly will the kinetic energy be large enough to supply the energy required to break these bonds. Molecules with small kinetic energies bounce off one another without reacting. As a result, only a small fraction of collisions are effective.

For every reaction, there is a certain minimum energy that molecules must possess for collision to be effective. This is referred to as the **activation energy.** It has the symbol E_a and is expressed in kilojoules/mol. For the reaction between one mole of CO and one mole of NO_2, E_a is 134 kJ/mol. The colliding molecules (CO and NO_2) must have a total kinetic energy of at least 134 kJ/mol if they are to react. The activation energy for a reaction is a positive quantity ($E_a > 0$) whose value depends on the nature of the reaction.

The collision model of reaction rates just developed can be made quantitative. We can say that the rate constant for a reaction, k, is a product of three factors:

$$k = p \times Z \times f$$

where—

- **p,** called a *steric factor,* takes into account the fact that only certain orientations of colliding molecules are likely to lead to reaction (recall Figure 11.7). Unfortunately, the collision model cannot predict the value of p; about all we can say is that it is less than 1, sometimes much less.
- **Z,** the *collision frequency,* which gives the number of molecular collisions occurring in unit time at unit concentrations of reactants. This quantity can be calculated quite accurately from the kinetic theory of gases, but we will not describe that calculation.
- **f,** the *fraction of collisions in which the energy of the colliding molecules is equal to or greater than E_a.* It can be shown that

$$f = e^{-E_a/RT}$$

where e is the base of natural logarithms, R is the gas constant, and T is the absolute temperature in K.

Substituting this expression for f into the equation written above for k, we obtain the basic equation for the collision model:

$$k = p \times Z \times e^{-E_a/RT}$$

This equation tells us, among other things, that *the larger the value of E_a, the smaller the rate constant.* Thus

$$\begin{aligned} \text{if } E_a &= 0, e^{-E_a/RT} = e^0 = 1 \\ E_a &= RT, e^{-E_a/RT} = e^{-1} = 0.37 \\ E_a &= 2RT, e^{-E_a/RT} = e^{-2} = 0.14 \end{aligned}$$

and so on. This makes sense; the larger the activation energy, the smaller the fraction of molecules having enough energy to react on collision, so the slower the rate of reaction.

High-energy molecules get the job done.

Table 11.3 Observed and Calculated Rate Constants for Second-Order Gas-Phase Reactions

Reaction	k Observed	Collision Model	Transition-State Model
$NO + O_3 \longrightarrow NO_2 + O_2$	6.3×10^{7}	4.0×10^{9}	3.2×10^{7}
$NO + Cl_2 \longrightarrow NOCl + Cl$	5.2	130	1.6
$NO_2 + CO \longrightarrow NO + CO_2$	1.2×10^{-4}	6.4×10^{-4}	1.0×10^{-4}
$2NO_2 \longrightarrow 2NO + O_2$	5.0×10^{-3}	1.0×10^{-1}	1.2×10^{-2}

Table 11.3 compares observed rate constants for several reactions with those predicted by collision theory, arbitrarily taking $p = 1$. As you might expect, the calculated k's are too high, suggesting that the steric factor is indeed less than 1.

Transition-State Model; Activation Energy Diagrams

CENGAGENOW™
Click Coached Problems for a self-study module on **reaction coordinate diagrams**.

Figure 11.8 is an energy diagram for the CO-NO_2 reaction. Reactants CO and NO_2 are shown at the left. Products CO_2 and NO are at the right; they have an energy 226 kJ less than that of the reactants. The enthalpy change, ΔH, for the reaction is -226 kJ. In the center of the figure is an intermediate called an *activated complex*. This is an unstable, high-energy species that must be formed before the reaction can occur. It has an energy 134 kJ greater than that of the reactants and 360 kJ greater than that of the products. The state of the system at this point is often referred to as a *transition state*, intermediate between reactants and products.

The exact nature of the activated complex is difficult to determine. For this reaction, the activated complex might be a "pseudomolecule" made up of CO and NO_2 molecules in close contact. The path of the reaction might be more or less as follows:

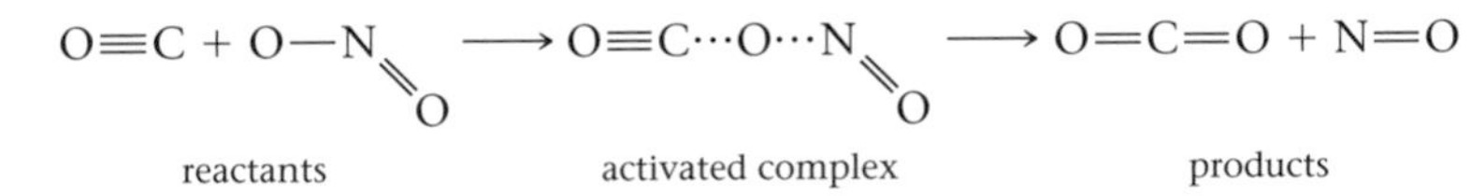

In the activated complex, electrons are often in excited states.

The dotted lines stand for "partial bonds" in the activated complex. The N—O bond in the NO_2 molecule has been partially broken. A new bond between carbon and oxygen has started to form.

The idea of the activated complex was developed by, among others, Henry Eyring at Princeton in the 1930s. It forms the basis of the *transition-state model* for reaction rate, which assumes that the activated complex—

- is in equilibrium, at low concentrations, with the reactants.
- may either decompose to products by "climbing" over the energy barrier or, alternatively, revert back to reactants.

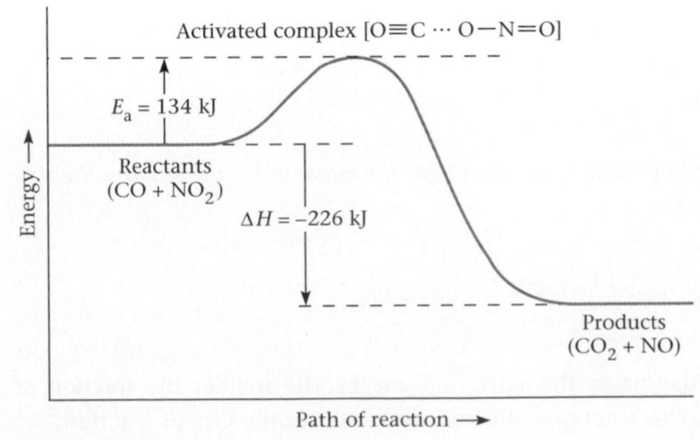

Figure 11.8
Reaction energy diagram. During the reaction initiation, 134 kJ—the activation energy E_a—must be furnished to the reactants for every mole of CO that reacts. This energy activates each CO—NO_2 complex to the point at which reaction can occur.

CHEMISTRY The Human Side

Chemical kinetics, the subject of this chapter, evolved from an art into a science in the first half of the twentieth century. One person more than any other was responsible for that change: Henry Eyring. Born in a Mormon settlement in Mexico, Henry emigrated to Arizona with his parents in 1912, when the Mexican revolution broke out. Many years later, he became a U.S. citizen, appearing before a judge who had just naturalized Albert Einstein.

AIP Emilio Segre Visual Archives

Henry Eyring
(1901–1981)

Eyring's first exposure to kinetics came as a young chemistry instructor at the University of Wisconsin in the 1920s. There he worked on the thermal decomposition of N_2O_5 (Section 11.2). In 1931 Eyring came to Princeton, where he developed the transition-state model of reaction rates. Using this model and making reasonable guesses about the nature of the activated complex, Eyring calculated rate constants that agreed well with experiment. After 15 productive years at Princeton, Eyring returned to his Mormon roots at the University of Utah in Salt Lake City. While serving as dean of the graduate school, he found time to do ground-breaking research on the kinetics of life processes, including the mechanism of aging.

Henry Eyring's approach to research is best described in his own words:

> I perceive myself as rather uninhibited, with a certain mathematical facility and more interest in the broad aspects of a problem than the delicate nuances. I am more interested in discovering what is over the next rise than in assiduously cultivating the beautiful garden close at hand.

Henry's enthusiasm for chemistry spilled over into just about every other aspect of his life. Each year he challenged his students to a 50-yard dash held at the stadium of the University of Utah. He continued these races until he was in his mid-70s. Henry never won, but on one occasion he did make the CBS evening news.

With these assumptions, it is possible to develop an expression for the rate constant k. Although the expression is too complex to discuss here, we show some of the results in Table 11.3.

The transition-state model is generally somewhat more accurate than the collision model (at least with $p = 1$). Another advantage is that it explains why the activation energy is ordinarily much smaller than the bond enthalpies in the reactant molecules. Consider, for example, the reaction

$$CO(g) + NO_2(g) \longrightarrow CO_2(g) + NO(g)$$

where $E_a = 134$ kJ/mol. This is considerably smaller than the amount of energy required to break any of the bonds in the reactants.

$$C{\equiv}O \quad 1075\text{ kJ} \qquad N{=}O \quad 607\text{ kJ} \qquad N{-}O \quad 222\text{ kJ}$$

Forming the activated complex shown in Figure 11.8 requires the absorption of relatively little energy, because it requires only the weakening of reactant bonds rather than their rupture.

11.5 REACTION RATE AND TEMPERATURE

The rates of most reactions increase as the temperature rises. A person in a hurry to prepare dinner applies this principle by turning the dial on the oven to the highest possible setting. By storing the leftovers in a refrigerator, the chemical reactions responsible for food spoilage are slowed down. As a general and very approximate rule, it is often stated that an increase in temperature of 10°C doubles the reaction rate. If this rule holds, foods should deteriorate four times as rapidly at room temperature (25°C) as they do in a refrigerator at 5°C.

Hibernating animals lower their body temperature, slowing down life processes.

The effect of temperature on reaction rate can be explained in terms of kinetic theory. Recall from Chapter 5 that raising the temperature greatly increases the fraction of molecules having very high speeds and hence high kinetic energies (kinetic energy $= mu^2/2$). These are the molecules that are most likely to react when they collide. The higher the temperature, the larger the fraction of molecules that can provide the activation energy required for reaction.

CENGAGENOW™
Click Coached Problems for a self-study module on **the Arrhenius equation.**

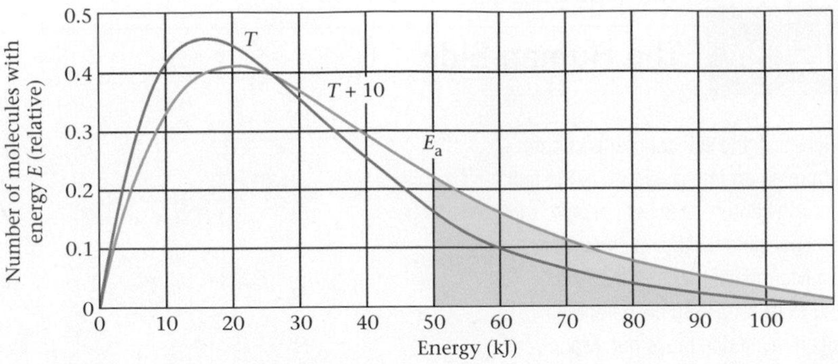

Figure 11.9
Temperature and activation energy. When T is increased to $T + 10$, the number of molecules with high energies increases. Hence many more molecules possess sufficient energy to react and the reaction occurs more rapidly. If E_a is 50 kJ/mol, any molecule with this or a higher energy can react. The number of molecules that react at T is represented by the orange area under the T curve, and the number that react at $T + 10$ is represented by the sum of the orange and green areas under the $T + 10$ curve.

$T\uparrow \rightarrow k\uparrow \rightarrow$ rate $\uparrow$

This effect is apparent from Figure 11.9, where the distribution of kinetic energies is shown at two different temperatures. Notice that the fraction of molecules having a kinetic energy equal to or greater than the activation energy E_a (shaded area) is considerably larger at the higher temperature. Hence the fraction of effective collisions increases; this is the major factor causing reaction rate to increase with temperature.

The Arrhenius Equation

You will recall from Section 11.4 that the collision model yields the following expression for the rate constant:

$$k = p \times Z \times e^{-E_a/RT} \qquad \textbf{(11.6)}$$

The steric factor, p, is presumably temperature-independent. The collision number, Z, is relatively insensitive to temperature. For example, when the temperature increases from 500 to 600 K, Z increases by less than 10%. Hence to a good degree of approximation we can write, as far as temperature dependence is concerned,

$$k = Ae^{-E_a/RT}$$

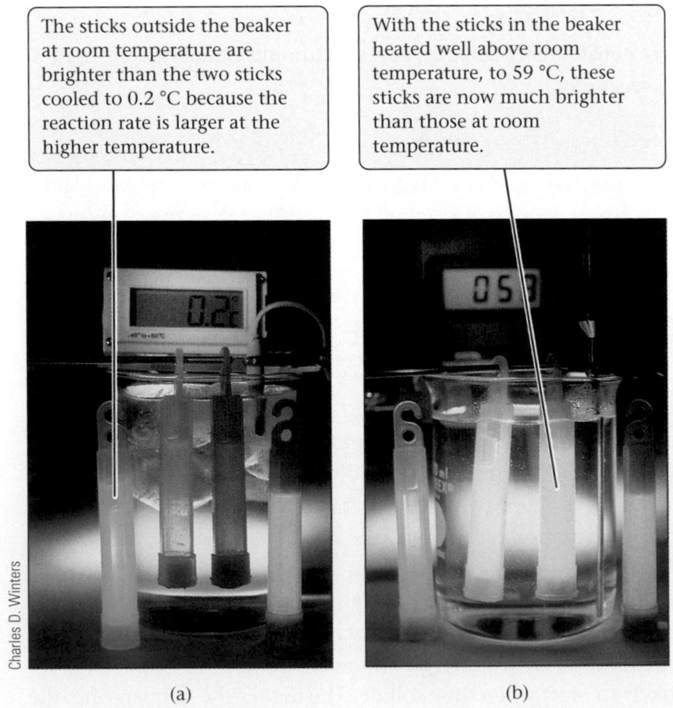

Temperature and reaction rate. A chemical reaction in the Cyalume® light sticks produces light as it takes place.

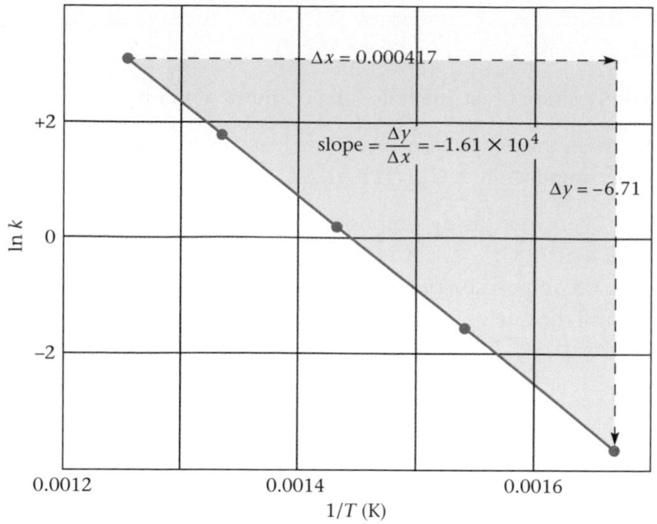

Figure 11.10
Arrhenius plot. A plot of ln k versus $1/T$ (k = rate constant, T = Kelvin temperature) is a straight line. From the slope of this line, the activation energy can be determined: $E_a = -R \times$ slope. For the CO—NO_2 reaction shown here,

$$E_a = -(8.31 \text{ J/mol} \cdot \text{K})(-1.61 \times 10^4 \text{ K})$$
$$= 1.34 \times 10^5 \text{ J/mol}$$
$$= 134 \text{ kJ/mol}$$

where A is a constant. Taking the natural logarithm of both sides of this equation,

$$\ln k = \ln A - E_a/RT$$

This equation was first shown to be valid by Svante Arrhenius (Chapter 4) in 1889. It is commonly referred to as the **Arrhenius equation.**

Comparing the Arrhenius equation with the general equation for a straight line,

$$y = b + mx$$

it should be clear that a plot of ln k ("y") versus $1/T$ ("x") should be linear. The slope of the straight line, m, is equal to $-E_a/R$. Figure 11.10 shows such a plot for the CO-NO_2 reaction. The slope appears to be about -1.61×10^4 K. Hence

$$\frac{-E_a}{R} = -1.61 \times 10^4 \text{ K}$$

$$E_a = 8.31 \frac{\text{J}}{\text{mol} \cdot \text{K}}(1.61 \times 10^4 \text{ K}) = 1.34 \times 10^5 \text{ J/mol} = 134 \text{ kJ/mol}$$

CENGAGENOW™
Click Coached Problems for a self-study simulation module on **temperature dependence.**

Two-Point Equation Relating k and T

The Arrhenius equation can be expressed in a different form by following the procedure used with the Clausius-Clapeyron equation in Chapter 9. At two different temperatures, T_2 and T_1,

$$\ln k_2 = \ln A - \frac{E_a}{RT_2}$$

$$\ln k_1 = \ln A - \frac{E_a}{RT_1}$$

Subtracting the second equation from the first eliminates ln A, and we obtain

$$\ln k_2 - \ln k_1 = \frac{-E_a}{R}\left[\frac{1}{T_2} - \frac{1}{T_1}\right]$$

$$\ln \frac{k_2}{k_1} = \frac{E_a}{R}\left[\frac{1}{T_1} - \frac{1}{T_2}\right] \quad \textbf{(11.7)}$$

Taking $R = 8.31$ J/mol·K, the activation energy is expressed in joules per mole.

CENGAGENOW™
Click Coached Problems for a self-study module on **temperature dependence.**

Example 11.7 Graded

Consider the first-order decomposition of A. The following is known about it—

- the rate constant doubles when the temperature increases from 15°C to 25°C.
- the rate constant for the decomposition at 40°C is 0.0125 s^{-1}.

*(a) What is the activation energy for the decomposition?
**(b) What is the half-life of *A* at 78°C?
***(c) What is the rate of the decomposition of a 0.200 M solution of *A* at 78°C?
***(d) At what temperature will the rate of the decomposition of 0.165 M be 0.124 mol/L · s?

SOLUTION

(a) $k_2/k_1 = 2.00 \qquad \ln k_2/k_1 = \ln 2.00 = 0.693 \qquad T_2 = 298\text{ K} \qquad T_1 = 288\text{ K}$
Substituting into the two-point form of the Arrhenius equation,

$$0.693 = \frac{E_a}{8.31\text{ J/mol}\cdot\text{K}}\left[\frac{1}{288\text{ K}} - \frac{1}{298\text{ K}}\right]$$

Solving

$$E_a = 4.9 \times 10^4\text{ J/mol} = 49\text{ kJ/mol}$$

(b) In order to calculate the half-life at 78°C, you must first find *k* at 78°C. Substituting into the Arrhenius equation, we get

$$\ln\frac{k_2}{k_1} = \frac{49{,}000\text{ J/mol}}{8.31\text{ J/mol}\cdot\text{K}}\left(\frac{1}{313\text{ K}} - \frac{1}{351\text{ K}}\right) = 2.04 \qquad \frac{k_2}{k_1} = 7.69$$

Taking $k_1 = 0.0125\text{ s}^{-1}$,

$$\frac{k_2}{k_1} = \frac{k_2}{0.0125} = 7.69$$

$$k_2 = 0.0961\text{ s}^{-1}$$

Then the half-life is

$$t_{1/2} = \frac{0.693}{0.0961\text{ s}^{-1}} = 7.21\text{ s.}$$

(c) The rate expression for this first-order reaction is

$$\text{rate} = k[A]$$

Substituting the value of the rate constant at 78°C, we get

$$\text{rate} = 0.0961\text{ s}^{-1}(0.200\text{ mol/L}) = 0.0192\text{ mol/L}\cdot\text{s}$$

(d) First, we find the rate constant for the decomposition at the unknown temperature.

$$0.165(\text{mol/L})(k) = 0.124\text{ mol/L}\cdot\text{s} \qquad k = 0.752\text{ s}^{-1}$$

Again we use the Arrhenius equation, where

$$T_1 = 313\text{ K}, \qquad k_1 = 0.0125\text{ s}^{-1} \qquad \text{and } k_2 = 0.752\text{ s}^{-1}$$

$$\ln\left(\frac{0.752}{0.0125}\right) = \frac{49{,}000\text{ J/mol}}{8.31\text{ J/mol}\cdot\text{K}}\left(\frac{1}{313\text{ K}} - \frac{1}{T_2}\right)$$

$$T_2 = 4.00 \times 10^2\text{ K} = 1.3 \times 10^2\text{°C}$$

11.6 CATALYSIS

A* catalyst *is a substance that increases the rate of a reaction without being consumed by it. It does this by changing the reaction path to one with a lower activation energy. Frequently the catalyzed path consists of two or more steps. In this case, the activation energy for the uncatalyzed reaction exceeds that for any of the steps in the catalyzed reaction (Figure 11.11).

CENGAGENOW™
Click Coached Problems for a self-study module on **identifying catalysts.**

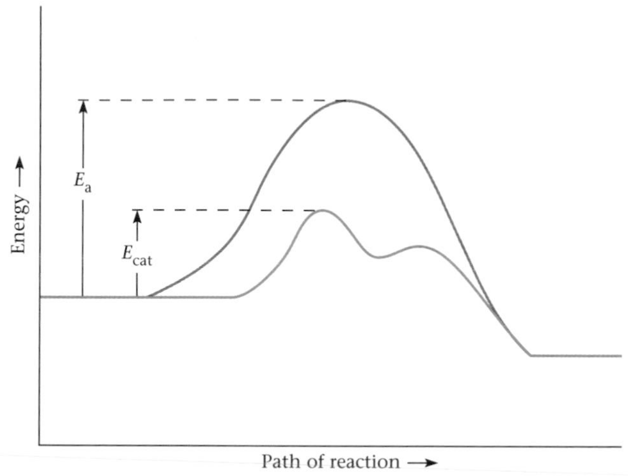

Figure 11.11
Catalysis and activation energy. By changing the path by which a reaction occurs, a catalyst can lower the activation energy that is required and so speed up a reaction.

Heterogeneous Catalysis

A *heterogeneous catalyst* is one that is in a different phase from the reaction mixture. Most commonly, the catalyst is a solid that increases the rate of a gas-phase or liquid-phase reaction. An example is the decomposition of N_2O on gold:

$$N_2O(g) \xrightarrow{\text{Au}} N_2(g) + \tfrac{1}{2}O_2(g)$$

In the catalyzed decomposition, N_2O is chemically adsorbed on the surface of the solid. A chemical bond is formed between the oxygen atom of an N_2O molecule and a gold atom on the surface. This weakens the bond joining nitrogen to oxygen, making it easier for the N_2O molecule to break apart. Symbolically, this process can be shown as

$$N{\equiv}N{-}O(g) \times Au(s) \longrightarrow N{\equiv}N{-}{-}{-}O{-}{-}{-}Au(s) \longrightarrow N{\equiv}N(g) + O(g) + Au(s)$$

where the broken lines represent weak covalent bonds.

Many industrial processes use heterogeneous catalysts.

Perhaps the most familiar example of heterogeneous catalysis is the series of reactions that occur in the catalytic converter of an automobile (Figure 11.12). Typically this device contains 1 to 3 g of platinum metal mixed with rhodium. The platinum catalyzes the oxidation of carbon monoxide and unburned hydrocarbons such as benzene, C_6H_6:

$$2CO(g) + O_2(g) \xrightarrow{\text{Pt}} 2CO_2(g)$$

$$C_6H_6(g) + \tfrac{15}{2}O_2(g) \xrightarrow{\text{Pt}} 6CO_2(g) + 3H_2O(g)$$

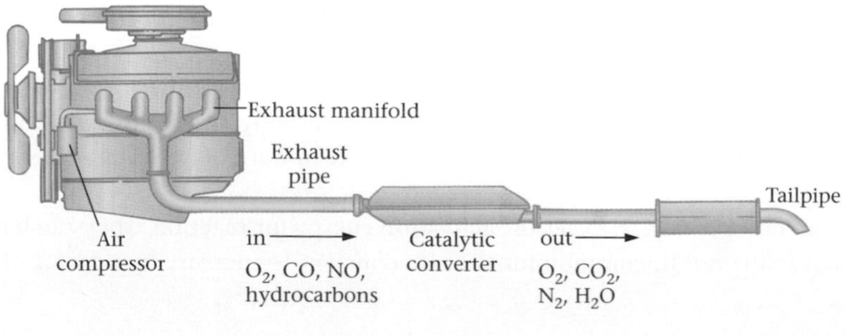

Figure 11.12
Automobile catalytic converter. Catalytic converters contain a "three-way" catalyst designed to convert CO to CO_2, unburned hydrocarbons to CO_2 and H_2O, and NO to N_2. The active components of the catalysts are the precious metals platinum and rhodium; palladium is sometimes used as well.

The rhodium acts as a catalyst to destroy nitrogen oxide by the reaction

$$2NO(g) \longrightarrow N_2(g) + O_2(g)$$

One problem with heterogeneous catalysis is that the solid catalyst is easily "poisoned." Foreign materials deposited on the catalytic surface during the reaction reduce or even destroy its effectiveness. A major reason for using unleaded gasoline is that lead metal poisons the Pt-Rh mixture in the catalytic converter.

Homogeneous Catalysis

A *homogeneous catalyst* is one that is present in the same phase as the reactants. It speeds up the reaction by forming a reactive intermediate that decomposes to give products. In this way, the catalyst provides an alternative process of lower activation energy.

An example of a reaction that is subject to homogeneous catalysis is the decomposition of hydrogen peroxide in aqueous solution:

$$2H_2O_2(aq) \longrightarrow 2H_2O + O_2(g)$$

Under ordinary conditions, this reaction occurs very slowly. However, if a solution of sodium iodide, NaI, is added, reaction occurs almost immediately; you can see the bubbles of oxygen forming.

The catalyzed decomposition of hydrogen peroxide is believed to take place by a two-step path:

$$\begin{array}{lll} \text{Step 1:} & H_2O_2(aq) + I^-(aq) & \longrightarrow H_2O + IO^-(aq) \\ \text{Step 2:} & H_2O_2(aq) + IO^-(aq) & \longrightarrow H_2O + O_2(g) + I^-(aq) \\ \hline & 2H_2O_2(aq) & \longrightarrow 2H_2O + O_2(g) \end{array}$$

Notice that the end result is the same as in the direct reaction.

The I^- ions are not consumed in the reaction. For every I^- ion used up in the first step, one is produced in the second step. The activation energy for this two-step process is much smaller than for the uncatalyzed reaction.

Figure 11.13
Enzyme catalysis. An enzyme in the potato is catalyzing the decomposition of a hydrogen peroxide solution, as shown by the bubbles of oxygen.

Enzymes

Many reactions that take place slowly under ordinary conditions occur readily in living organisms in the presence of catalysts called *enzymes.* Enzymes are protein molecules of high molar mass. An example of an enzyme-catalyzed reaction is the decomposition of hydrogen peroxide:

$$2H_2O_2(aq) \longrightarrow 2H_2O + O_2(g)$$

In blood or tissues, this reaction is catalyzed by an enzyme called catalase (Figure 11.13). When 3% hydrogen peroxide is used to treat a fresh cut or wound, oxygen gas is given off rapidly. The function of catalase in the body is to prevent the build-up of hydrogen peroxide, a powerful oxidizing agent.

Many enzymes are extremely specific. For example, the enzyme maltase catalyzes the hydrolysis of maltose:

$$\underset{\text{maltose}}{C_{12}H_{22}O_{11}(aq)} + H_2O \xrightarrow{\text{maltase}} \underset{\text{glucose}}{2C_6H_{12}O_6(aq)}$$

This is the only function of maltase, but it is one that no other enzyme can perform. Many such digestive enzymes are required for the metabolism of carbohydrates, proteins, and fats. It has been estimated that without enzymes, it would take upward of 50 years to digest a meal.

That would make dieting a lot easier.

Enzymes, like all other catalysts, lower the activation energy for reaction. They can be enormously effective; it is not uncommon for the rate constant to increase by a factor of

10^{12} or more. However, from a commercial standpoint, enzymes have some drawbacks. A particular enzyme operates best over a narrow range of temperature. An increase in temperature frequently deactivates an enzyme by causing the molecule to "unfold," changing its characteristic shape. Recently, chemists have discovered that this effect can be prevented if the enzyme is immobilized by bonding to a solid support. Among the solids that have been used are synthetic polymers, porous glass, and even stainless steel. The development of immobilized enzymes has led to a host of new products. The sweetener aspartame, used in many diet soft drinks, is made using the enzyme aspartase in immobilized form.

11.7 REACTION MECHANISMS

A **reaction mechanism** is a description of a path, or a sequence of steps, by which a reaction occurs at the molecular level. In the simplest case, only a single step is involved. This is a collision between two reactant molecules. This is the mechanism for the reaction of CO with NO_2 at high temperatures, above about 600 K:

$$CO(g) + NO_2(g) \longrightarrow NO(g) + CO_2(g)$$

At lower temperatures the reaction between carbon monoxide and nitrogen dioxide takes place by a quite different mechanism. Two steps are involved:

Reaction mechanisms frequently change with *T*, sometimes with *P*.

$$NO_2(g) + NO_2(g) \longrightarrow NO_3(g) + NO(g)$$
$$CO(g) + NO_3(g) \longrightarrow CO_2(g) + NO_2(g)$$
$$\overline{CO(g) + NO_2(g) \longrightarrow NO(g) + CO_2(g)}$$

Notice that the overall reaction, obtained by summing the individual steps, is identical with that for the one-step process. The rate expressions are quite different, however:

CENGAGENOW™
Click Coached Problems for a self-study module on **identification of reaction mechanisms.**

high temperatures: rate = $k[CO] \times [NO_2]$

low temperatures: rate = $k[NO_2]^2$

In general, the nature of the rate expression and hence ***the reaction order depend on the mechanism by which the reaction takes place.***

Elementary Steps

The individual steps that constitute a reaction mechanism are referred to as **elementary steps.** These steps may be *unimolecular*

$$A \longrightarrow B + C \qquad \text{rate} = k[A]$$

bimolecular

$$A + B \longrightarrow C + D \qquad \text{rate} = k[A] \times [B]$$

or, in rare cases, *termolecular*

$$A + B + C \longrightarrow D + E \qquad \text{rate} = k[A] \times [B] \times [C]$$

(A color screen is used to distinguish elementary steps from overall reactions.)

Notice from the rate expressions just written that ***the rate of an elementary step is equal to a rate constant k multiplied by the concentration of each reactant molecule.*** This rule is readily explained. Consider, for example, a step in which two molecules, A and B, collide effectively with each other to form C and D. As pointed out earlier, the rate of collision and hence the rate of reaction will be directly proportional to the concentration of each reactant.

Slow Steps

Often, one step in a mechanism is much slower than any other. If this is the case, ***the slow step is* rate-determining.** That is, the rate of the overall reaction can be taken to be that of the slow step. Consider, for example, a three-step reaction:

$$\begin{array}{lll} \text{Step 1:} & A \longrightarrow B & \text{(fast)} \\ \text{Step 2:} & B \longrightarrow C & \text{(slow)} \\ \text{Step 3:} & C \longrightarrow D & \text{(fast)} \\ \hline & A \longrightarrow D & \end{array}$$

The rate at which A is converted to D (the overall reaction) is approximately equal to the rate of conversion of B to C (the slow step).

To understand the rationale behind this rule, and its limitations, consider an analogous situation. Suppose three people (A, B, and C) are assigned to grade general chemistry examinations that contain three questions. On the average, A spends 10 s grading question 1 and B spends 15 s grading question 2. In contrast, C, the ultimate procrastinator, takes 5 min to grade question 3. The rate at which exams are graded is

Maybe questions 1 and 2 were multiple-choice.

$$\frac{1 \text{ exam}}{10 \text{ s} + 15 \text{ s} + 300 \text{ s}} = \frac{1 \text{ exam}}{325 \text{ s}} = 0.00308 \text{ exam/s}$$

This is approximately equal to the rate of the slower grader:

$$\frac{1 \text{ exam}}{300 \text{ s}} = 0.00333 \text{ exam/s}$$

Extrapolating from general chemistry exams to chemical reactions, we can say that—

- the overall rate of the reaction cannot exceed that of the slowest step.
- if that step is by far the slowest, its rate will be approximately equal to that of the overall reaction.
- the slowest step in a mechanism is ordinarily the one with the highest activation energy (Figure 11.14).

Deducing a Rate Expression from a Proposed Mechanism

As we have seen, rate expressions for reactions must be determined experimentally. Once this has been done, it is possible to derive a plausible mechanism compatible with the observed rate expression. This, however, is a rather complex process and we will not attempt it here. Instead, we will consider the reverse process, which is much more straightforward. *Given a mechanism for a several-step reaction, how can you deduce the rate expression corresponding to that mechanism?*

In principle, at least, all you have to do is to apply the rules just cited.

1. ***Find the slowest step and equate the rate of the overall reaction to the rate of that step.***
2. ***Find the rate expression for the slowest step.***

CENGAGENOW™
Click Coached Problems for a self-study module on **reaction mechanisms and rate equations.**

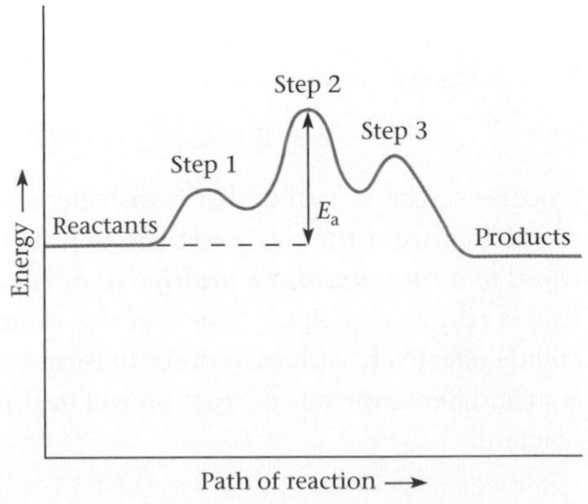

Figure 11.14
Reaction plot for a reaction with a three-step mechanism. The second of the three steps is rate-determining.

To illustrate this process, consider the two-step mechanism for the low-temperature reaction between CO and NO_2.

$$\begin{array}{ll} NO_2(g) + NO_2(g) \longrightarrow NO_3(g) + NO(g) & \text{(slow)} \\ CO(g) + NO_3(g) \longrightarrow CO_2(g) + NO_2(g) & \text{(fast)} \\ \hline CO(g) + NO_2(g) \longrightarrow CO_2(g) + NO(g) & \end{array}$$

Applying the above rules in order,

$$\text{rate of overall reaction} = \text{rate of first step} = k[NO_2]^2$$

This analysis explains why the rate expression for the two-step mechanism is different from that for the direct, one-step reaction.

Elimination of Intermediates

Sometimes the rate expression obtained by the process just described involves a reactive intermediate, that is, a species produced in one step of the mechanism and consumed in a later step. Ordinarily, concentrations of such species are too small to be determined experimentally. Hence they must be eliminated from the rate expression if it is to be compared with experiment. The final rate expression usually includes only those species that appear in the balanced equation for the reaction. Sometimes, the concentration of a catalyst is included, but never that of a reactive intermediate.

To illustrate this situation, consider the reaction between nitric oxide and chlorine, which is believed to proceed by a two-step mechanism:

$$\begin{array}{lll} \text{Step 1:} & NO(g) + Cl_2(g) \underset{k_{-1}}{\overset{k_1}{\rightleftharpoons}} NOCl_2(g) & \text{(fast)} \\ \text{Step 2:} & NOCl_2(g) + NO(g) \xrightarrow{k_2} 2NOCl(g) & \text{(slow)} \\ \hline & 2NO(g) + Cl_2(g) \longrightarrow 2NOCl(g) & \end{array}$$

The first step occurs rapidly and reversibly; a dynamic equilibrium is set up in which the rates of forward and reverse reactions are equal. Because the second step is slow and rate-determining, it follows that

$$\text{rate of overall reaction} = \text{rate of step 2} = k_2[NOCl_2] \times [NO]$$

The rate expression just written is unsatisfactory in that it cannot be checked against experiment. The species $NOCl_2$ is a reactive intermediate whose concentration is too small to be measured accurately, if at all. To eliminate the $[NOCl_2]$ term from the rate expression, recall that the rates of forward and reverse reactions in step 1 are equal, which means that

If the concentration of a species can't be measured, it better not appear in the rate expression.

$$k_1[NO] \times [Cl_2] = k_{-1}[NOCl_2]$$

Solving for $[NOCl_2]$ and substituting in this rate expression,

$$[NOCl_2] = \frac{k_1[NO] \times [Cl_2]}{k_{-1}}$$

$$\text{rate of overall reaction} = k_2[NOCl_2] \times [NO] = \frac{k_2k_1[NO]^2 \times [Cl_2]}{k_{-1}}$$

The quotient k_2k_1/k_{-1} is the experimentally observed rate constant for the reaction, which is found to be second-order in NO and first-order in Cl_2, as predicted by this mechanism.

Example 11.8 The decomposition of ozone, O_3, to diatomic oxygen, O_2, is believed to occur by a two-step mechanism:

$$\begin{array}{lll} \text{Step 1:} & O_3(g) \underset{k_{-1}}{\overset{k_1}{\rightleftharpoons}} O_2(g) + O(g) & \text{(fast)} \\ \text{Step 2:} & O_3(g) + O(g) \xrightarrow{k_2} 2O_2(g) & \text{(slow)} \\ \hline & 2O_3(g) \longrightarrow 3O_2(g) & \end{array}$$

Obtain the rate expression corresponding to this mechanism.

Strategy Write the rate expression for the rate-determining second step. This will involve the unstable intermediate, O. To get rid of [O], use the fact that reactants and products are in equilibrium in step 1, so forward and reverse reactions occur at the same rate.

SOLUTION

(1) Overall rate = rate step 2 = $k_2[O_3] \times [O]$

(2) $k_1[O_3] = k_{-1}[O_2] \times [O]$

$$[O] = \frac{k_1[O_3]}{k_{-1}[O_2]}$$

(3) Overall rate $= \dfrac{k_1k_2[O_3]^2}{k_{-1}[O_2]} = \dfrac{k[O_3]^2}{[O_2]}$

The quotient k_1k_2/k_{-1} is the observed rate constant, k.

Reality Check Notice that the concentration of O_2, a product in the reaction, appears in the denominator. The rate is inversely proportional to the concentration of molecular oxygen, a feature that you would never have predicted from the balanced equation for the reaction. As the concentration of O_2 builds up, the rate slows down.

It is important to point out one of the limitations of mechanism studies. Usually more than one mechanism is compatible with the same experimentally obtained rate expression. To make a choice between alternative mechanisms, other evidence must be considered. A classic example of this situation is the reaction between hydrogen and iodine

$$H_2(g) + I_2(g) \longrightarrow 2HI(g)$$

for which the observed rate expression is

$$\text{rate} = k[H_2] \times [I_2]$$

For many years, it was assumed that the H_2-I_2 reaction occurs in a single step, a collision between an H_2 molecule and an I_2 molecule. That would, of course, be compatible with the rate expression above. However, there is now evidence to indicate that a quite different and more complex mechanism is involved (see Problem 77).

CHEMISTRY Beyond the Classroom

The Ozone Story

In recent years, a minor component of the atmosphere, ozone, has received a great deal of attention. Ozone, molecular formula O_3, is a pale blue gas with a characteristic odor that can be detected after lightning activity, in the vicinity of electric motors, or near a subway train.

Depending on its location in the atmosphere, ozone can be a villain or a beleaguered hero. In the lower atmosphere (the *troposphere*), ozone is bad news; it is a major component of photochemical smog, formed by the reaction sequence

$$NO_2(g) \longrightarrow NO(g) + O(g)$$
$$O_2(g) + O(g) \longrightarrow O_3(g)$$
$$\overline{NO_2(g) + O_2(g) \longrightarrow NO(g) + O_3(g)}$$

Ozone is an extremely powerful oxidizing agent, which explains its toxicity to animals and humans. At partial pressures as low as 10^{-7} atm, it can cut in half the rate of photosynthesis by plants.

In the upper atmosphere (the *stratosphere*), the situation is quite different. There the partial pressure of ozone goes through a maximum of about 10^{-5} atm at an altitude of 30 km. From 95% to 99% of sunlight in the ultraviolet region between 200 and 300 nm is absorbed by ozone in this region, commonly referred to as the "ozone layer." The mechanism by which this occurs can be represented by the following pair of equations:

$$O_3(g) + \text{UV radiation} \longrightarrow O_2(g) + O(g)$$
$$O_2(g) + O(g) \longrightarrow O_3(g) + \text{heat}$$
$$\overline{\text{UV radiation} \longrightarrow \text{heat}}$$

The net effect is simply the conversion of ultraviolet to thermal energy.

If the UV radiation were to reach the surface of the earth, it could have several adverse effects. A 5% decrease in ozone concentration could increase the incidence of skin cancer by 10% to 20%. Ultraviolet radiation is also a factor in diseases of the eye, including cataract formation.

Ozone molecules in the stratosphere can decompose by the reaction

$$O_3(g) + O(g) \longrightarrow 2O_2(g)$$

This reaction takes place rather slowly by direct collision between an O_3 molecule and an O atom. It can occur more rapidly by a two-step process in which a chlorine atom acts as a catalyst:

$$O_3(g) + Cl(g) \longrightarrow O_2(g) + ClO(g) \qquad k = 5.2 \times 10^{9}\ \text{L/mol}\cdot\text{s at 220 K}$$
$$ClO(g) + O(g) \longrightarrow Cl(g) + O_2(g) \qquad k = 2.6 \times 10^{10}\ \text{L/mol}\cdot\text{s at 220 K}$$
$$\overline{O_3(g) + O(g) \longrightarrow 2O_2(g)}$$

A single chlorine atom can bring about the decomposition of tens of thousands of ozone molecules. Bromine atoms can substitute for chlorine; indeed the rate constant for the Br-catalyzed reaction is larger than that for the reaction just cited.

The chlorine atoms that catalyze the decomposition of ozone come from chlorofluorocarbons (CFCs) used in many refrigerators and air conditioners. A major culprit is CF_2Cl_2, Freon, which forms Cl atoms when exposed to ultraviolet radiation at 200 nm:

$$CF_2Cl_2(g) \longrightarrow CF_2Cl(g) + Cl(g)$$

The two scientists who first suggested (in 1974) that CFCs could deplete the ozone layer, F. Sherwood Rowland (1927–) and Mario Molina (1943–), won the 1995 Nobel Prize in chemistry, along with Paul Crutzen (1933–), who first suggested that oxides of nitrogen in the atmosphere could catalyze the decomposition of ozone.

The catalyzed decomposition of ozone is known to be responsible for the ozone hole (Figure A) that develops in Antarctica each year in September and October, at the end of winter in the Southern Hemisphere. No ozone is generated during the long, dark Antarctic winter. Meanwhile, a heterogeneous reaction occurring on clouds of ice crystals at −85°C produces species such as Cl_2, Br_2, and HOCl. When the Sun reappears in September, these molecules decompose photochemically to form Cl or Br atoms, which catalyze the decomposition of ozone, lowering its concentration.

Recent research suggests that ozone depletion has affected Antarctica's climate, cooling the interior and warming the extremities.

Ozone depletion is by no means restricted to the Southern Hemisphere. In the extremely cold winter of 1994–1995, a similar "ozone hole" was found in the Arctic. Beyond that, the concentration of ozone in the atmosphere over parts of Siberia dropped by 40%.

In 1987 an international treaty was signed in Montreal to cut back on the use of CFCs. Production of Freon in the United States ended in 1996. It has been replaced in automobile air conditioners by a related compound with no chlorine atoms, $C_2H_2F_4$:

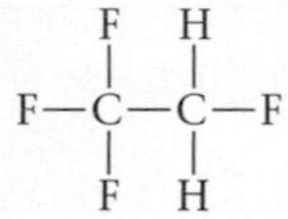

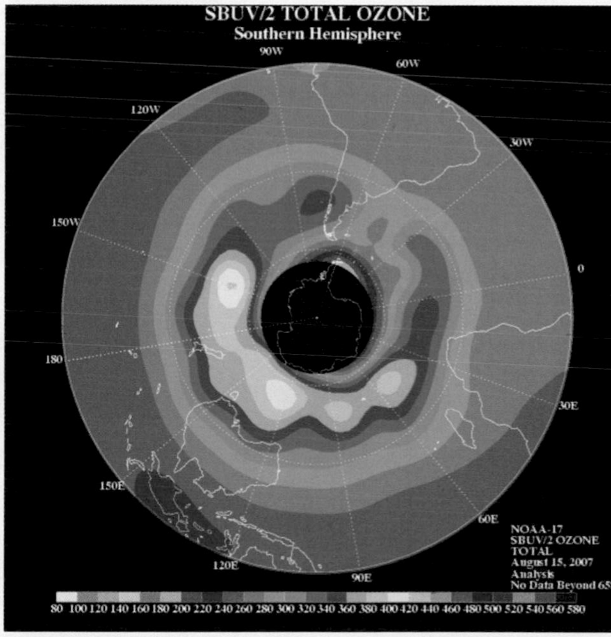

Courtesy of NOAA

Figure A

The ozone (O_3) layer over the southern hemisphere stratosphere in August, 2007. The bar at the bottom indicates the color-coding used to indicate the thickness of the layer. The thickness is measured in Dobsons (= 0.01 mm thick). The normal ozone layer for the stratosphere is 360 Dobsons (color coded as green). The ozone "hole" shown in pink is 200–220 Dobsons. The "hole" will increase when another reading is taken in September.

Chapter Highlights

Key Concepts

Select end of chapter Questions and Problems may be assigned in OWL and are cross-referenced in the Key Concepts list.

CENGAGENOW™

Sign in at **academic.cengage.com/now** to:

- Check your readiness for an exam by taking the Pre-Test and exploring the self-study modules recommended in your Personalized Study plan
- For quick review, download Go Chemistry mini-lecture flashcard modules (or purchase them at **www.ichapters.com**)

1. Determine the rate expression (reaction order) from—
   - initial rate data.
   (Examples 11.1, 11.2; Problems 19–28) ■ Questions and Problems assignable in OWL: 20, 22, 24, 26, 28
   - concentration-time data, using Table 11.2.
   (Example 11.5; Problems 29, 30) ■ 34
   - reaction mechanism.
   (Example 11.8; Problems 77, 78) ■ 79, 80
2. Relate concentration to time for a first-order reaction.
   (Examples 11.3, 11.4; Problems 35–48) ■ 37, 38, 55
3. Use the Arrhenius equation to relate rate constant to temperature.
   (Example 11.7; Problems 57–70) ■ 60, 66, 73

Key Equations

Rate of reaction	$a\text{A} + b\text{B} \longrightarrow c\text{C} + d\text{D}$ (Section 11.1)
	$\text{rate} = \dfrac{-\Delta[\text{A}]}{a\,\Delta t} = \dfrac{-\Delta[\text{B}]}{b\,\Delta t} = \dfrac{\Delta[\text{C}]}{c\,\Delta t} = \dfrac{\Delta[\text{D}]}{d\,\Delta t}$ (Section 11.1)
Zero-order reaction	$\text{rate} = k \quad [\text{A}] = [\text{A}]_o - kt$ (Section 11.3)
First-order reaction	$\text{rate} = k[\text{A}] \quad \ln[\text{A}]_o/[\text{A}] = kt \quad t_{1/2} = 0.693/k$ (Section 11.3)
Second-order reaction	$\text{rate} = k[\text{A}]^2 \quad 1/[\text{A}] - 1/[\text{A}]_o = kt$ (Section 11.3)
Rate constant	$\text{rate} = p \times Z \times e^{-E_a/RT}$ (Section 11.5)
Arrhenius equation	$\ln\dfrac{k_2}{k_1} = \dfrac{E_a}{R}\left[\dfrac{1}{T_1} - \dfrac{1}{T_2}\right]$ (Section 11.5)

Key Terms

activation energy
catalyst
elementary step
half-life
rate constant
rate-determining step
rate expression
reaction mechanism
reaction order
—first-order
—overall order
—second-order
—zero-order
reaction rate

Summary Problem

Dinitrogen pentaoxide, N_2O_5, decomposes to nitrogen dioxide and oxygen.

$$2N_2O_5(g) \longrightarrow 4NO_2(g) + O_2(g)$$

(a) At what rate is N_2O_5 decomposing if NO_2 is being formed at the rate of 0.0120 mol/L · s? At what rate is oxygen being produced?

(b) Initial rate determinations at 25°C for the decomposition give the following data:

$[N_2O_5]$	Initial rate (mol/L · min)
0.250	5.70×10^{-4}
0.350	7.98×10^{-4}
0.450	1.03×10^{-3}

(1) What is the order of the reaction?
(2) Write the rate equation for the decomposition.
(3) Calculate the rate constant and the half-life for the reaction at 25°C.

(c) How long will it take to decompose 40.0% of N_2O_5 at 25°C?

(d) At 40°C, the rate constant for the decomposition is 1.58×10^{-2} min^{-1}. Calculate the activation energy for this reaction.

(e) How much faster will 0.100 *M* N_2O_5 decompose at 40°C than at 25°C?

(f) How much longer will it take to decompose 65% of N_2O_5 at 25°C than at 40°C?

Answers

(a) N_2O_5 rate: 0.0060 mol/L · s; O_2 rate: 0.0030 mol/L · s
(b) (1) first-order
(2) rate = $k[N_2O_5]$
(3) $k = 2.28 \times 10^{-3}$ min^{-1}; $t_{1/2} = 304$ min
(c) 224 min
(d) 1.0×10^2 kJ/mol
(e) about seven times faster
(f) 394 min longer

Questions and Problems

Blue-numbered questions have answers in Appendix 6 and fully-worked solutions in the *Student Solutions Manual.*

■ denotes questions assignable in OWL.

WEB indicates that the solution is available on this book's companion website.

Meaning of Reaction Rate

1. Express the rate of the reaction

$$2C_2H_6(g) + 7\,O_2(g) \longrightarrow 4CO_2(g) + 6H_2O(g)$$

in terms of
(a) $\Delta[C_2H_6]$ (b) $\Delta[CO_2]$

2. ■ Express the rate of the reaction

$$2N_2H_4(l) + N_2O_4(l) \longrightarrow 3N_2(g) + 4H_2O(g)$$

in terms of
(a) $\Delta[N_2O_4]$ (b) $\Delta[N_2]$

3. Consider the following hypothetical reaction:

$$X(g) \longrightarrow Y(g)$$

A 200.0-mL flask is filled with 0.120 moles of X. The disappearance of X is monitored at timed intervals. Assume that temperature and volume are kept constant. The data obtained are shown in the table below.

Time (min)	0	20	40	60	80
moles of X	0.120	0.103	0.085	0.071	0.066

(a) Make a similar table for the appearance of Y.
(b) Calculate the average disappearance of X in *M*/s in the first two twenty-minute intervals.
(c) What is the average rate of appearance of Y between the 20- and 60-minute intervals?

4. Consider the following hypothetical reaction:

$$2\,AB_2(g) \longrightarrow A_2(g) + 2\,B_2(g)$$

A 500.0-mL flask is filled with 0.384 moles of AB_2. The appearance of A_2 is monitored at timed intervals. Assume that temperature and volume are kept constant. The data obtained are shown in the table below.

Time (min)	0	10	20	30	40	50
moles of A_2	0	0.0541	0.0833	0.1221	0.1432	0.1567

(a) Make a similar table for the disappearance of AB_2.
(b) What is the average rate of disappearance of AB_2 over the second and third 10-minute intervals?
(c) What is the average rate of appearance of A_2 between $t = 30$ and $t = 50$?

5. ■ Consider the combustion of ethane:

$$C_2H_6(g) + 7\,O_2(g) \longrightarrow 4CO_2(g) + 6H_2O(g)$$

If the ethane is burning at the rate of 0.20 mol/L · s, at what rates are CO_2 and H_2O being produced?

6. **WEB** For the reaction

$$5Br^-(aq) + BrO_3^-(aq) + 6H^+(aq) \longrightarrow 3Br_2(aq) + 3H_2O$$

it was found that at a particular instant bromine was being formed at the rate of 0.039 mol/L · s. At that instant, at what rate is
(a) water being formed?
(b) bromide ion being oxidized?
(c) H^+ being consumed?

7. Nitrosyl chloride (NOCl) decomposes to nitrogen oxide and chlorine gases.
(a) Write a balanced equation using smallest whole-number coefficients for the decomposition.
(b) Write an expression for the reaction rate in terms of $\Delta[NOCl]$.
(c) The concentration of NOCl drops from 0.580 *M* to 0.238 *M* in 8.00 min. Calculate the average rate of reaction over this time interval.

8. ■ Ammonia is produced by the reaction between nitrogen and hydrogen gases.
(a) Write a balanced equation using smallest whole-number coefficients for the reaction.
(b) Write an expression for the rate of reaction in terms of $\Delta[NH_3]$.
(c) The concentration of ammonia increases from 0.257 *M* to 0.815 *M* in 15.0 min. Calculate the average rate of reaction over this time interval.

9. Experimental data are listed for the hypothetical reaction

$$A + B \longrightarrow C + D$$

Time (s)	0	10	20	30	40	50
[A]	0.32	0.24	0.20	0.16	0.14	0.12

(a) Plot these data as in Figure 11.2.
(b) Draw a tangent to the curve to find the instantaneous rate at 30 s.
(c) Find the average rate over the 10 to 40 s interval.
(d) Compare the instantaneous rate at 30 s with the average rate over the thirty-second interval.

10. Experimental data are listed for the hypothetical reaction

$$X \longrightarrow Y + Z$$

Time (s)	0	10	20	30	40	50
[X]	0.0038	0.0028	0.0021	0.0016	0.0012	0.00087

(a) Plot these data as in Figure 11.2.
(b) Draw a tangent to the curve to find the instantaneous rate at 40 s.

(c) Find the average rate over the 10 to 50 s interval.

(d) Compare the instantaneous rate at 40 s with the average rate over the 40-s interval.

Reaction Rate and Concentration

11. A reaction has two reactants A and B. What is the order with respect to each reactant and the overall order of the reaction described by each of the following rate expressions?

(a) rate $= k_1[A]^3$ **(b)** rate $= k_2[A] \times [B]$

(c) rate $= k_3[A] \times [B]^2$ **(d)** rate $= k_4[B]$

12. ■ A reaction has two reactants X and Y. What is the order with respect to each reactant and the overall order of the reaction described by the following rate expressions?

(a) rate $= k_1[X]^2 \times [Y]$ **(b)** rate $= k_2[X]$

(c) rate $= k_3[X]^2 \times [Y]^2$ **(d)** rate $= k_4$

13. What will the units of the rate constants in Question 11 be if the rate is expressed in mol/L · min?

14. ■ What will the units of the rate constants in Question 12 be if the rate is expressed in mol/L · s?

15. Consider the reaction

$$X \longrightarrow \text{products}$$

The graph below plots the rate of the reaction versus the concentration of X.

(a) What is the order of the reaction with respect to X?

(b) Write the rate expression for the reaction.

(c) Estimate the value of *k*.

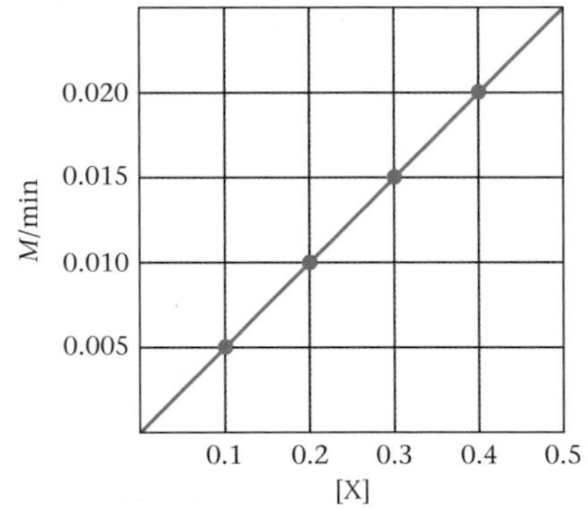

16. **WEB** Consider the reaction

$$Y \longrightarrow \text{products}$$

The graph below plots the rate of the reaction versus the concentration of Y.

(a) What is the order of the reaction with respect to Y?

(b) Write the rate expression for the reaction.

(c) Estimate the value of *k*.

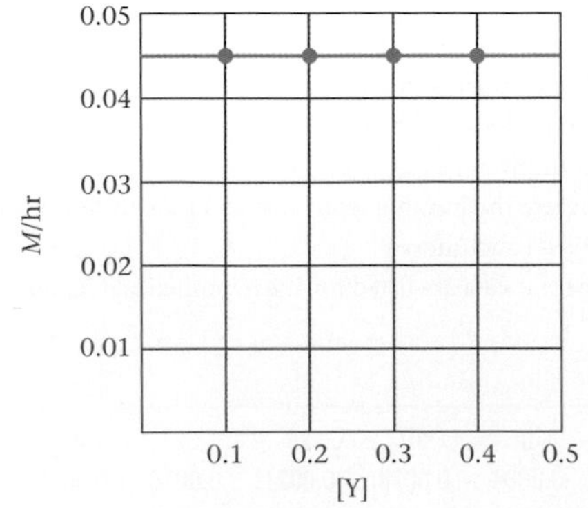

17. Complete the following table for the reaction

$$2R(g) + 3S(g) \longrightarrow \text{products}$$

that is first-order in R and second-order in S.

	[R]	[S]	k ($L^2/mol^2 \cdot min$)	Rate (mol/L · min)
(a)	0.200	0.200	1.49	______
(b)	______	0.633	0.42	0.833
(c)	0.100	______	0.298	0.162
(d)	0.0500	0.0911	______	0.00624

18. Complete the following table for the reaction

$$2X(g) + Y(g) \longrightarrow \text{products}$$

that is first-order in both X and Y.

	[X]	[Y]	k (L/mol · h)	Rate (mol/L · h)
(a)	0.100	0.400	1.89	______
(b)	0.600	______	0.884	0.159
(c)	______	0.025	13.4	0.0479
(d)	0.592	0.233	______	0.00112

19. The decomposition of nitrogen dioxide is a second-order reaction. At 550 K, a 0.250 *M* sample decomposes at the rate of 1.17 mol/L · min.

(a) Write the rate expression.

(b) What is the rate constant at 550 K?

(c) What is the rate of decomposition when $[NO_2] = 0.800$ *M*?

20. ■ The decomposition of ammonia on tungsten at 1100°C is zero-order with a rate constant of 2.5×10^{-4} mol/L · min.

(a) Write the rate expression.

(b) Calculate the rate when $[NH_3] = 0.075$ *M*.

(c) At what concentration of ammonia is the rate equal to the rate constant?

21. The reaction

$$NO(g) + \tfrac{1}{2}Br_2(g) \longrightarrow NOBr(g)$$

is second-order in nitrogen oxide and first-order in bromine. The rate of the reaction is 1.6×10^{-8} mol/L · min when the nitrogen oxide concentration is 0.020 *M* and the bromine concentration is 0.030 *M*.

(a) What is the value of *k*?

(b) At what concentration of bromine is the rate 3.5×10^{-7} mol/L · min and [NO] = 0.043 *M*?

(c) At what concentration of nitrogen oxide is the rate 2.0×10^{-6} mol/L · min and the bromine concentration one fourth of the nitrogen oxide concentration?

22. ■ The reaction

$$ICl(g) + \tfrac{1}{2}H_2(g) \longrightarrow \tfrac{1}{2}I_2(g) + HCl(g)$$

is first-order in both reactants. The rate of the reaction is 4.89×10^{-5} mol/L · s when the ICl concentration is 0.100 *M* and that of the hydrogen gas is 0.030 *M*.

(a) What is the value of *k*?

(b) At what concentration of hydrogen is the rate 5.00×10^{-4} mol/L · s and [ICl] = 0.233 *M*?

(c) At what concentration of iodine chloride is the rate 0.0934 mol/L · s if the hydrogen concentration is three times that of ICl?

■ in OWL Blue-numbered questions answered in Appendix 6 **WEB** Solution is available on companion website

Determination of Reaction Order

23. For the reaction

$$A \longrightarrow \text{products}$$

The following data are obtained.

Rate (mol/L · min)	0.0167	0.0107	0.00601	0.00267
[A]	0.100	0.0800	0.0600	0.0400

(a) Determine the order of the reaction.
(b) Write the rate expression for the reaction.
(c) Calculate k for the experiment above.

24. ■ For a reaction involving the decomposition of Y, the following data are obtained:

Rate (mol/L · min)	0.288	0.245	0.202	0.158
[Y]	0.200	0.170	0.140	0.110

(a) Determine the order of the reaction.
(b) Write the rate expression for the decomposition of Y.
(c) Calculate k for the experiment above.

25. The peroxysulfate ion reacts with the iodide ion in aqueous solution according to the following equation:

$$S_2O_8^{2-}(aq) + 3I^-(aq) \longrightarrow 2SO_4^{2-}(aq) + I_3^-(aq)$$

The following data are obtained at a certain temperature:

Expt.	$[S_2O_8^{2-}]$	$[I^-]$	Initial Rate (mol/L · min)
1	0.0200	0.0155	1.15×10^{-4}
2	0.0250	0.0200	1.85×10^{-4}
3	0.0300	0.0200	2.22×10^{-4}
4	0.0300	0.0275	3.06×10^{-4}

(a) What is the order of the reaction with respect to $[S_2O_8^{2-}]$, $[I^-]$, and overall?
(b) Write the rate expression for the reaction.
(c) Calculate k for the reaction.
(d) When $[S_2O_8^{2-}] = 0.105\ M$ and $[I^-] = 0.0875\ M$, what is the rate of the reaction at the temperature of the experiment?

26. ■ **WEB** When boron trifluoride reacts with ammonia, the following reaction occurs:

$$BF_3(g) + NH_3(g) \longrightarrow BF_3NH_3(g)$$

The following data are obtained at a particular temperature:

Expt.	$[BF_3]$	$[NH_3]$	Initial Rate (mol/L · s)
1	0.100	0.100	0.0341
2	0.200	0.233	0.159
3	0.200	0.0750	0.0512
4	0.300	0.100	0.102

(a) What is the order of the reaction with respect to BF_3, NH_3, and overall?
(b) Write the rate expression for the reaction.
(c) Calculate k for the reaction.
(d) When $[BF_3] = 0.553\ M$ and $[NH_3] = 0.300\ M$, what is the rate of the reaction at the temperature of the experiment?

27. Hydrogen bromide is a highly reactive and corrosive gas used mainly as a catalyst for organic reactions. It is produced by reacting hydrogen and bromine gases together.

$$H_2(g) + Br_2(g) \longrightarrow 2HBr(g)$$

The rate is followed by measuring the intensity of the orange color of the bromine gas. The following data are obtained:

Expt.	$[H_2]$	$[Br_2]$	Initial Rate (mol/L · s)
1	0.100	0.100	4.74×10^{-3}
2	0.100	0.200	6.71×10^{-3}
3	0.250	0.200	1.68×10^{-2}

(a) What is the order of the reaction with respect to hydrogen, bromine, and overall?
(b) Write the rate expression for the reaction.
(c) Calculate k for the reaction. What are the units for k?
(d) When $[H_2] = 0.455\ M$ and $[Br_2] = 0.215\ M$, what is the rate of the reaction?

28. ■ Diethylhydrazine reacts with iodine according to the following equation:

$$(C_2H_5)_2(NH)_2(l) + I_2(aq) \longrightarrow (C_2H_5)_2N_2(l) + 2HI(aq)$$

The rate of the reaction is followed by monitoring the disappearance of the purple color due to iodine. The following data are obtained at a certain temperature.

Expt.	$[(C_2H_5)_2(NH)_2]$	$[I_2]$	Initial Rate (mol/L · h)
1	0.150	0.250	1.08×10^{-4}
2	0.150	0.3620	1.56×10^{-4}
3	0.200	0.400	2.30×10^{-4}
4	0.300	0.400	3.44×10^{-4}

(a) What is the order of the reaction with respect to diethylhydrazine, iodine, and overall?
(b) Write the rate expression for the reaction.
(c) Calculate k for the reaction.
(d) What must $[(C_2H_5)_2(NH)_2]$ be so that the rate of the reaction is 5.00×10^{-4} mol/L · h when $[I_2] = 0.500$?

29. The equation for the reaction between iodide and bromate ions in acidic solution is

$$6I^-(aq) + BrO_3^-(aq) + 6H^+(aq) \longrightarrow 3I_2(aq) + Br^-(aq) + 3H_2O$$

The rate of the reaction is followed by measuring the appearance of I_2. The following data are obtained:

$[I^-]$	$[BrO_3^-]$	$[H^+]$	Initial Rate (mol/L · s)
0.0020	0.0080	0.020	8.89×10^{-5}
0.0040	0.0080	0.020	1.78×10^{-4}
0.0020	0.0160	0.020	1.78×10^{-4}
0.0020	0.0080	0.040	3.56×10^{-4}
0.0015	0.0040	0.030	7.51×10^{-5}

(a) What is the order of the reaction with respect to each reactant?
(b) Write the rate expression for the reaction.
(c) Calculate k.
(d) What is the hydrogen ion concentration when the rate is 5.00×10^{-4} mol/L · s and $[I^-] = [BrO_3^-] = 0.0075\ M$?

30. The equation for the iodination of acetone in acidic solution is

$$CH_3COCH_3(aq) + I_2(aq) \longrightarrow CH_3COCH_2I(aq) + H^+(aq) + I^-(aq)$$

The rate of the reaction is found to be dependent not only on the concentration of the reactants but also on the hydrogen ion concentration. Hence the rate expression of this reaction is

$$\text{rate} = k[CH_3COCH_3]^m[I_2]^n[H^+]^p$$

■ in OWL Blue-numbered questions answered in Appendix 6 **WEB** Solution is available on companion website

The rate is obtained by following the disappearance of iodine using starch as an indicator. The following data are obtained:

$[CH_3COCH_3]$	$[H^+]$	$[I_2]$	Initial Rate (mol/L · s)
0.80	0.20	0.001	4.2×10^{-6}
1.6	0.20	0.001	8.2×10^{-6}
0.80	0.40	0.001	8.7×10^{-6}
0.80	0.20	0.0005	4.3×10^{-6}

(a) What is the order of the reaction with respect to each reactant?
(b) Write the rate expression for the reaction.
(c) Calculate *k*.
(d) What is the rate of the reaction when $[H^+] = 0.933\ M$ and $[CH_3COCH_3] = 3[H^+] = 10[I^-]$?

31. In a solution at a constant H^+ concentration, iodide ions react with hydrogen peroxide to produce iodine.

$$H^+(aq) + I^-(aq) + \tfrac{1}{2}H_2O_2(aq) \longrightarrow \tfrac{1}{2}I_2(aq) + H_2O$$

The reaction rate can be followed by monitoring the appearance of I_2. The following data were obtained

$[I^-]$	$[H_2O_2]$	Initial Rate (mol/L · min)
0.015	0.030	0.0022
0.035	0.030	0.0052
0.055	0.030	0.0082
0.035	0.050	0.0087

(a) Write the rate expression for the reaction.
(b) Calculate *k*.
(c) What is the rate of the reaction when 25.0 mL of a 0.100 *M* solution of KI is added to 25.0 mL of a 10.0% by mass solution of $H_2O_2(d = 1.00\ g/mL)$? Assume volumes are additive.

32. Consider the reaction

$$Cr(H_2O)_6^{3+}(aq) + SCN^-(aq) \longrightarrow Cr(H_2O)_5SCN^{2+}(aq) + H_2O$$

The following data were obtained:

$[Cr(H_2O)_6^{3+}]$	$[SCN^-]$	Initial Rate (mol/L · min)
0.025	0.060	6.5×10^{-4}
0.025	0.077	8.4×10^{-4}
0.042	0.077	1.4×10^{-3}
0.042	0.100	1.8×10^{-3}

(a) Write the rate expression for the reaction.
(b) Calculate *k*.
(c) What is the rate of the reaction when 15 mg of KSCN is added to 1.50 L of a solution 0.0500 *M* in $Cr(H_2O)_6^{3+}$?

33. In dilute acidic solution, sucrose ($C_{12}H_{22}O_{11}$) decomposes to glucose and fructose, both with molecular formula $C_6H_{12}O_6$. The following data are obtained for the decomposition of sucrose.

Time (min)	$[C_{12}H_{22}O_{11}]$
0	0.368
20	0.333
60	0.287
120	0.235
160	0.208

Write the rate expression for the reaction.

34. ■ Nitrosyl bromide (NOBr) decomposes to nitrogen oxide and bromine. Use the following data to determine the order of the decomposition reaction of nitrosyl bromide.

Time (s)	0	6	12	18	24
[NOBr]	0.0286	0.0253	0.0229	0.0208	0.0190

First-Order Reactions

35. Azomethane decomposes into nitrogen and ethane at high temperatures according to the following equation:

$$(CH_3)_2N_2(g) \longrightarrow N_2(g) + C_2H_6(g)$$

The following data are obtained in an experiment:

Time (h)	$[(CH_3)_2N_2]$
1.00	0.905
2.00	0.741
3.00	0.607
4.00	0.497

(a) By plotting the data, show that the reaction is first-order.
(b) From the graph, determine *k*.
(c) Using *k*, find the time (in hours) that it takes to decrease the concentration to 0.100 *M*.
(d) Calculate the rate of the reaction when $[(CH_3)_2N_2] = 0.415\ M$.

36. Hypofluorous acid, HOF, is extremely unstable at room temperature. The following data apply to the decomposition of HOF to HF and O_2 gases at a certain temperature.

Time (min)	[HOF]
1.00	0.607
2.00	0.223
3.00	0.0821
4.00	0.0302
5.00	0.0111

(a) By plotting the data, show that the reaction is first-order.
(b) From the graph, determine *k*.
(c) Using *k*, find the time it takes to decrease the concentration to 0.100 *M*.
(d) Calculate the rate of the reaction when $[HOF] = 0.0500\ M$.

37. ■ The first-order rate constant for the decomposition of a certain hormone in water at 25°C is $3.42 \times 10^{-4}\ day^{-1}$.
(a) If a 0.0200 *M* solution of the hormone is stored at 25°C for two months, what will its concentration be at the end of that period?
(b) How long will it take for the concentration of the solution to drop from 0.0200 *M* to 0.00350 *M*?
(c) What is the half-life of the hormone?

38. ■ In the first-order decomposition of acetone at 500°C,

$$CH_3\text{—}CO\text{—}CH_3(g) \longrightarrow \text{products}$$

it is found that the concentration is 0.0300 *M* after 200 min and 0.0200 *M* after 400 min. Calculate the following.
(a) the rate constant
(b) the half-life
(c) the initial concentration

■ in OWL Blue-numbered questions answered in Appendix 6 **WEB** Solution is available on companion website

39. The decomposition of dimethyl ether (CH_3OCH_3) to methane, carbon monoxide, and hydrogen gases is found to be first-order. At 500°C, a 150.0-mg sample of dimethyl ether is reduced to 43.2 mg after three quarters of an hour. Calculate

(a) the rate constant.

(b) the half-life at 500°C.

(c) how long it will take to decompose 95% of the dimethyl ether.

40. The first-order rate constant for the decomposition of a certain drug at 25°C is 0.215 $month^{-1}$.

(a) If 10.0 g of the drug is stored at 25°C for one year, how many grams of the drug will remain at the end of the year?

(b) What is the half-life of the drug?

(c) How long will it take to decompose 65% of the drug?

41. The decomposition of phosphine, PH_3, to $P_4(g)$ and $H_2(g)$ is first-order. Its rate constant at a certain temperature is 1.1 min^{-1}.

(a) What is its half-life in seconds?

(b) What percentage of phosphine is decomposed after 1.25 min?

(c) How long will it take to decompose one fifth of the phosphine?

42. The decomposition of ethane, C_2H_6, is a first-order reaction. It is found that it takes 212 s to decompose 0.00839 *M* C_2H_6 to 0.00768 *M*.

(a) What is the rate constant for the reaction?

(b) What is the rate of decomposition (in mol/L · h) when $[C_2H_6]$ = 0.00422 *M*?

(c) How long (in minutes) will it take to decompose C_2H_6 so that 27% remains?

(d) What percentage of C_2H_6 is decomposed after 22 min?

43. Dinitrogen pentoxide gas decomposes to form nitrogen dioxide and oxygen. The reaction is first-order and has a rate constant of 0.247 h^{-1} at 25°C. If a 2.50-L flask originally contains N_2O_5 at a pressure of 756 mm Hg at 25°C, then how many moles of O_2 are formed after 135 minutes? (*Hint*: First write a balanced equation for the decomposition.)

44. Sucrose ($C_{12}H_{22}O_{11}$) hydrolyzes into glucose and fructose. The hydrolysis is a first-order reaction. The half-life for the hydrolysis of sucrose is 64.2 min at 25°C. How many grams of sucrose in 1.25 L of a 0.389 *M* solution are hydrolyzed in 1.73 hours?

45. Copper-64 is one of the metals used to study brain activity. Its decay constant is 0.0546 h^{-1}. If a solution containing 5.00 mg of Cu-64 is used, how many milligrams of Cu-64 remain after eight hours?

46. Iodine-131 is used to treat tumors in the thyroid. Its first-order half-life is 8.1 days. If a patient is given a sample containing 5.00 mg of I-131, how long will it take for 25% of the isotope to remain in her system?

47. Argon-41 is used to measure the rate of gas flow. It has a decay constant of 6.3×10^{-3} min^{-1}.

(a) What is its half-life?

(b) How long will it take before only 1.00% of the original amount of Ar-41 is left?

48. A sample of sodium-24 chloride contains 0.050 mg of Na-24 to study the sodium balance of an animal. After 24.9 h, 0.016 mg of Na-24 is left. What is the half-life of Na-24?

Zero- and Second-Order Reactions

49. The decomposition of Y is a zero-order reaction. Its half-life at 25°C and 0.188 *M* is 315 minutes.

(a) What is the rate constant for the decomposition of Y?

(b) How long will it take to decompose a 0.219 *M* solution of Y?

(c) What is the rate of the decomposition of 0.188 *M* at 25°C?

(d) Does the rate change when the concentration of Y is increased to 0.289 *M*? If so, what is the new rate?

50. ■ The decomposition of A at 85°C is a zero-order reaction. It takes 35 minutes to decompose 37% of an initial mass of 282 mg.

(a) What is *k* at 85°C?

(b) What is the half-life of 282 mg at 85°C?

(c) What is the rate of decomposition for 282 mg at 85°C?

(d) If one starts with 464 mg, what is the rate of its decomposition at 85°C?

51. For the zero-order decomposition of HI on a gold surface

$$HI(g) \xrightarrow{Au} \tfrac{1}{2}H_2(g) + \tfrac{1}{2}I_2(g)$$

it takes 16.0 s for the pressure of HI to drop from 1.00 atm to 0.200 atm.

(a) What is the rate constant for the reaction?

(b) How long will it take for the pressure to drop from 0.150 atm to 0.0432 atm?

(c) What is the half-life of HI at a pressure of 0.500 atm?

52. For the zero-order decomposition of ammonia on tungsten

$$NH_3(g) \xrightarrow{W} \tfrac{1}{2}N_2(g) + \tfrac{3}{2}H_2(g)$$

the rate constant is 2.08×10^{-4} mol/L · s.

(a) What is the half-life of a 0.250 *M* solution of ammonia?

(b) How long will it take for the concentration of ammonia to drop from 1.25 *M* to 0.388 *M*?

53. The following gas-phase reaction is second-order.

$$2C_2H_4(g) \longrightarrow C_4H_8(g)$$

Its half-life is 1.51 min when $[C_2H_4]$ is 0.250 *M*.

(a) What is *k* for the reaction?

(b) How long will it take to go from 0.187 *M* to 0.0915 *M*?

(c) What is the rate of the reaction when $[C_2H_4]$ is 0.335 *M*?

54. Ammonium cyanate, NH_4NCO, in water rearranges to produce urea, a common fertilizer, $(NH_2)_2CO$:

$$NH_4NCO(aq) \longrightarrow (NH_2)_2CO(aq)$$

The rearrangement is a second-order reaction. It takes 11.6 h for the concentration of NH_4NCO to go from 0.250 *M* to 0.0841 *M*.

(a) What is *k* for the reaction?

(b) What is the half-life of the reaction when NH_4NCO is 0.100 *M*?

(c) How long will it take to rearrange 39% of a 0.450 *M* solution?

(d) How fast is a 0.839 *M* solution being changed to urea?

55. ■ The rate constant for the second-order reaction

$$NOBr(g) \longrightarrow NO(g) + \tfrac{1}{2}Br_2(g)$$

is 48 L/mol · min at a certain temperature. How long will it take to decompose 90.0% of a 0.0200 *M* solution of nitrosyl bromide?

56. The decomposition of nitrosyl chloride

$$NOCl(g) \longrightarrow NO(g) + \tfrac{1}{2}Cl_2(g)$$

is a second-order reaction. If it takes 0.20 min to decompose 15% of a 0.300 *M* solution of nitrosyl chloride, what is *k* for the reaction?

Activation Energy, Reaction Rate, and Temperature

57. If a temperature increase from 20.0°C to 30.0°C doubles the rate constant of a reaction, then what is the activation energy for the reaction?

58. If the activation energy of a reaction is 4.86 kJ, then what is the percent increase in the rate constant of a reaction when the temperature is increased from 45° to 75°C?

■ in OWL Blue-numbered questions answered in Appendix 6 **WEB** Solution is available on companion website

59. The following data were obtained for the gas-phase decomposition of acetaldehyde:

k(L/mol · s)	0.0105	0.101	0.60	2.92
T(K)	700	750	800	850

Plot these data (ln k versus $1/T$) and find the activation energy for the reaction.

60. ■ The following data were obtained for the reaction

$$SiH_4(g) \longrightarrow Si(s) + 2H_2(g)$$

k(s^{-1})	0.048	2.3	49	590
t(°C)	500	600	700	800

Plot these data (ln k versus $1/T$) and find the activation energy for the reaction.

61. Consider the following hypothetical reaction:

$$A + B \longrightarrow C + D \qquad \Delta H = -125 \text{ kJ}$$

Draw a reaction-energy diagram for the reaction if its activation energy is 37 kJ.

62. For the reaction

$$X + Y \longrightarrow R + Z \qquad \Delta H = +295 \text{ kJ},$$

draw a reaction-energy diagram for the reaction if its activation energy is 378 kJ.

63. The uncoiling of deoxyribonucleic acid (DNA) is a first-order reaction. Its activation energy is 420 kJ. At 37°C, the rate constant is 4.90×10^{-4} min^{-1}.

(a) What is the half-life of the uncoiling at 37°C (normal body temperature)?

(b) What is the half-life of the uncoiling if the organism has a temperature of 40°C (≈104°F)?

(c) By what factor does the rate of uncoiling increase (per °C) over this temperature interval?

64. Cold-blooded animals decrease their body temperature in cold weather to match that of their environment. The activation energy of a certain reaction in a cold-blooded animal is 65 kJ/mol. By what percentage is the rate of the reaction decreased if the body temperature of the animal drops from 35°C to 22°C?

65. The activation energy for the reaction involved in the souring of raw milk is 75 kJ. Milk will sour in about eight hours at 21°C (70°F = room temperature). How long will raw milk last in a refrigerator maintained at 5°C? Assume the rate constant to be inversely related to souring time.

66. ■ The chirping rate of a cricket X, in chirps per minute near room temperature, is

$$X = 7.2t - 32$$

where t is the temperature in °C.

(a) Calculate the chirping rates at 25°C and 35°C.

(b) Use your answers in (a) to estimate the activation energy for the chirping.

(c) What is the percentage increase for a 10°C rise in temperature?

67. For the reaction

$$2N_2O(g) \longrightarrow 2N_2(g) + O_2(g)$$

the rate constant is 0.066 L/mol · min at 565°C and 22.8 L/mol · min at 728°C.

(a) What is the activation energy of the reaction?

(b) What is k at 485°C?

(c) At what temperature is k, the rate constant, equal to 11.6 L/mol · min?

68. For the decomposition of HI, the activation energy is 182 kJ/mol. The rate constant at 850°C is 0.0174 L/mol · h.

(a) What is the rate constant at 700°C?

(b) At what temperature will the rate constant be a fourth of what it is at 850°C?

69. At high temperatures, the decomposition of cyclobutane is a first-order reaction. Its activation energy is 262 kJ/mol. At 477°C, its half-life is 5.00 min. What is its half-life (in seconds) at 527°C?

70. The decomposition of N_2O_5 to NO_2 and NO_3 is a first-order gas-phase reaction. At 25°C, the reaction has a half-life of 2.81 s. At 45°C, the reaction has a half-life of 0.313 s. What is the activation energy of the reaction?

Catalysis

71. For a certain reaction, E_a is 135 kJ and $\Delta H = 45$ kJ. In the presence of a catalyst, the activation energy is 39% of that for the uncatalyzed reaction. Draw a diagram similar to Figure 11.11 but instead of showing two activated complexes (two humps) show only one activated complex (i.e., only one hump) for the reaction. What is the activation energy of the uncatalyzed reverse reaction?

72. Consider a reaction in which $E_a = 129$ kJ and $\Delta H = -29$ kJ. In the presence of a catalyst, the activation energy is 48% of the uncatalyzed reaction. Follow the directions in Question 71 in drawing an energy diagram.

73. ■ A catalyst lowers the activation energy of a reaction from 215 kJ to 206 kJ. By what factor would you expect the reaction-rate constant to increase at 25°C? Assume that the frequency factors (A) are the same for both reactions. (*Hint:* Use the formula $\ln k = \ln A - E_a/RT$.)

74. A reaction has an activation energy of 363 kJ at 25°C. If the rate constant has to increase ten-fold, what should the activation energy of the catalyzed reaction be? (See Question 73 for assumptions and a hint.)

Reaction Mechanisms

75. Write the rate expression for each of the following elementary steps:

(a) $NO_3 + CO \longrightarrow NO_2 + CO_2$

(b) $I_2 \longrightarrow 2I$

(c) $NO + O_2 \longrightarrow NO_3$

76. Write the rate expression for each of the following elementary steps:

(a) $NO + O_3 \longrightarrow NO_2 + O_2$

(b) $2NO_2 \longrightarrow 2NO + O_2$

(c) $K + HCl \longrightarrow KCl + H$

77. For the reaction between hydrogen and iodine,

$$H_2(g) + I_2(g) \longrightarrow 2HI(g)$$

the experimental rate expression is rate $= k[H_2] \times [I_2]$. Show that this expression is consistent with the mechanism

$$I_2(g) \rightleftharpoons 2I(g) \qquad \text{(fast)}$$

$$H_2(g) + I(g) + I(g) \longrightarrow 2HI(g) \qquad \text{(slow)}$$

78. For the reaction

$$2H_2(g) + 2NO(g) \longrightarrow N_2(g) + 2H_2O(g)$$

the experimental rate expression is rate $= k[NO]^2 \times [H_2]$. The following mechanism is proposed:

$$2NO \rightleftharpoons N_2O_2 \qquad \text{(fast)}$$

$$N_2O_2 + H_2 \longrightarrow H_2O + N_2O \qquad \text{(slow)}$$

$$N_2O + H_2 \longrightarrow N_2 + H_2O \qquad \text{(fast)}$$

Is this mechanism consistent with the rate expression?

79. ■ At low temperatures, the rate law for the reaction

$$CO(g) + NO_2(g) \longrightarrow CO_2(g) + NO(g)$$

■ in OWL Blue-numbered questions answered in Appendix 6 **WEB** Solution is available on companion website

is as follows: rate = constant × $[NO_2]^2$. Which of the following mechanisms is consistent with the rate law?

(a) $CO + NO_2 \longrightarrow CO_2 + NO$

(b) $2NO_2 \rightleftharpoons N_2O_4$ (fast)

$N_2O_4 + 2CO \longrightarrow 2CO_2 + 2NO$ (slow)

(c) $2NO_2 \longrightarrow NO_3 + NO$ (slow)

$NO_3 + CO \longrightarrow NO_2 + CO_2$ (fast)

(d) $2NO_2 \longrightarrow 2NO + O_2$ (slow)

$O_2 + 2CO \longrightarrow 2CO_2$ (fast)

80. ■ Two mechanisms are proposed for the reaction

$$2NO(g) + O_2(g) \longrightarrow 2NO_2(g)$$

Mechanism 1: $NO + O_2 \rightleftharpoons NO_3$ (fast)

$NO_3 + NO \longrightarrow 2NO_2$ (slow)

Mechanism 2: $NO + NO \rightleftharpoons N_2O_2$ (fast)

$N_2O_2 + O_2 \longrightarrow 2NO_2$ (slow)

Show that each of these mechanisms is consistent with the observed rate law: rate = $k[NO]^2 \times [O_2]$.

Unclassified

81. The decomposition of A_2B_2 to A_2 and B_2 at 38°C was monitored as a function of time. A plot of $1/[A_2B_2]$ vs. time is linear, with slope $0.137/M \cdot$min.

(a) Write the rate expression for the reaction.

(b) What is the rate constant for the decomposition at 38°C?

(c) What is the half-life of the decomposition when $[A_2B_2]$ is 0.631 *M*?

(d) What is the rate of the decomposition when $[A_2B_2]$ is 0.219 *M*?

(e) If the initial concentration of A_2B_2 is 0.822 *M* with no products present, then what is the concentration of A_2 after 8.6 minutes?

82. When a base is added to an aqueous solution of chlorine dioxide gas, the following reaction occurs:

$$2ClO_2(aq) + 2OH^-(aq) \longrightarrow ClO_3^-(aq) + ClO_2^-(aq) + H_2O$$

The reaction is first-order in OH^- and second-order for ClO_2. Initially, when $[ClO_2] = 0.010\ M$ and $[OH^-] = 0.030\ M$, the rate of the reaction is 6.00×10^{-4} mol/L · s. What is the rate of the reaction when 50.0 mL of 0.200 *M* ClO_2 and 95.0 mL of 0.155 *M* NaOH are added?

83. The decomposition of sulfuryl chloride, SO_2Cl_2, to sulfur dioxide and chlorine gases is a first-order reaction.

$$SO_2Cl_2(g) \longrightarrow SO_2(g) + Cl_2(g)$$

At a certain temperature, the half-life of SO_2Cl_2 is 7.5×10^2 min. Consider a sealed flask with 122.0 g of SO_2Cl_2.

(a) How long will it take to reduce the amount of SO_2Cl_2 in the sealed flask to 45.0 g?

(b) If the decomposition is stopped after 29.0 h, what volume of Cl_2 at 27°C and 1.00 atm is produced?

84. How much faster would a reaction proceed at 45°C than at 27°C if the activation energy of the reaction is 133 kJ/mol?

85. A reaction has an activation energy of 85 kJ. What percentage increase would one get for *k* for every 5°C increase in temperature around room temperature, 25°C?

86. For the first-order thermal decomposition of ozone

$$O_3(g) \longrightarrow O_2(g) + O(g)$$

$k = 3 \times 10^{-26}\ s^{-1}$ at 25°C. What is the half-life for this reaction in years? Comment on the likelihood that this reaction contributes to the depletion of the ozone layer.

87. Derive the integrated rate law, $[A] = [A]_o - kt$, for a zero-order reaction. (*Hint:* Start with the relation $-\Delta[A] = k\,\Delta t$.)

88. Page 303 has a two-point equation relating *k* (the rate constant) and *T* (temperature). Derive a two-point equation relating *k* and activation energy for a catalyzed and an uncatalyzed reaction at the same temperature. Assume that A is the same for both reactions.

Conceptual Problems

89. The greatest increase in the reaction rate for the reaction between A and C, where rate = $k[A]^{1/2}[C]$, is caused by

(a) doubling [A] (b) halving [C]

(c) halving [A] (d) doubling [A] and [C]

90. Consider the decomposition of B represented by squares, where each square represents a molecule of B.

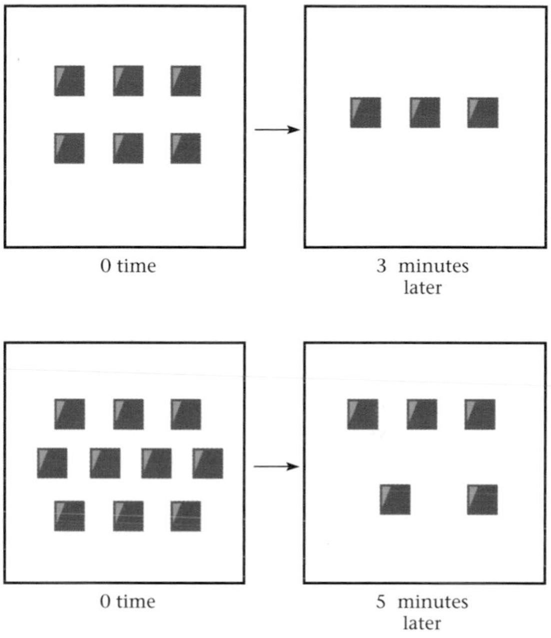

Is the reaction zero-order, first-order, or second-order?

91. Consider the decomposition of A represented by circles, where each circle represents a molecule of A.

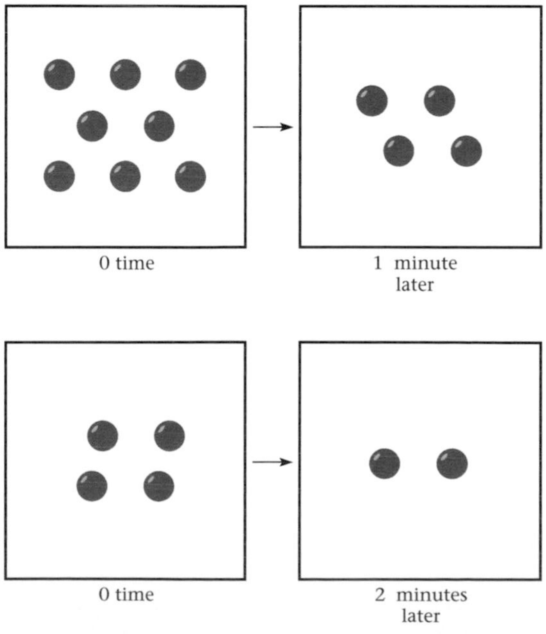

Is the reaction zero-order, first-order, or second-order?

■ in OWL Blue-numbered questions answered in Appendix 6 **WEB** Solution is available on companion website

92. Consider the decomposition reaction

$$2X \longrightarrow 2Y + Z$$

The following graph shows the change in concentration with respect to time for the reaction. What does each of the curves labeled 1, 2, and 3 represent?

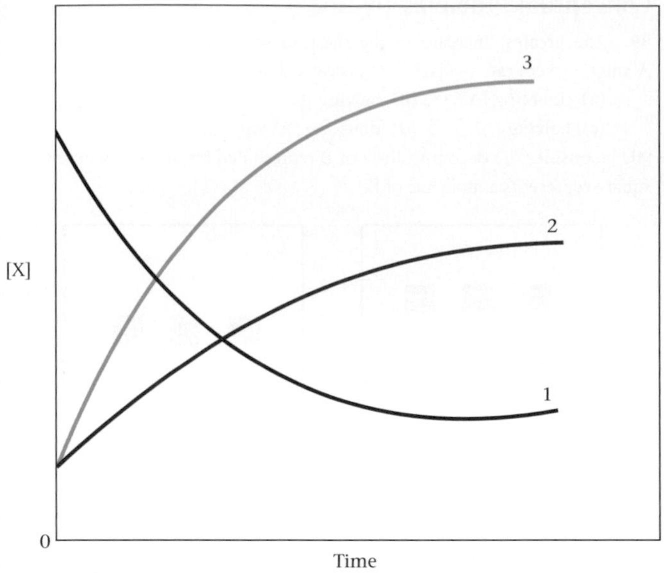

93. Consider the following activation energy diagram.

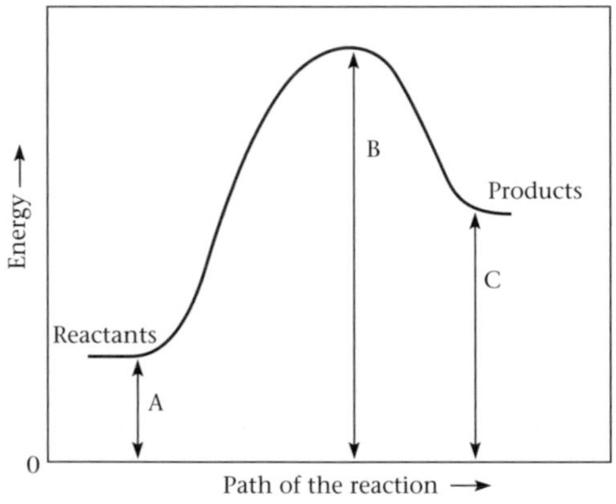

Which of the following statements about the diagram are true?

(a) E_a (forward) < E_a (reverse)

(b) A represents the energy of the reactants for the forward reaction.

(c) Energy (ΔH) for the reaction is A − C.

(d) E_a (forward) = B − A

(e) E_a (forward) = E_a (reverse) = B

(f) Energy (ΔH) for the reaction = B − C

94. Three first-order reactions have the following activation energies:

Reaction	A	B	C
E_a(kJ)	75	136	292

(a) Which reaction is the fastest?

(b) Which reaction has the largest half-life?

(c) Which reaction has the largest rate?

95. Consider the first-order decomposition reaction

$$A \longrightarrow B + C$$

where A (circles) decomposes to B (triangles) and C (squares). Given the following boxes representing the reaction at $t = 2$ minutes, fill in the boxes with products at the indicated time. Estimate the half-life of the reaction.

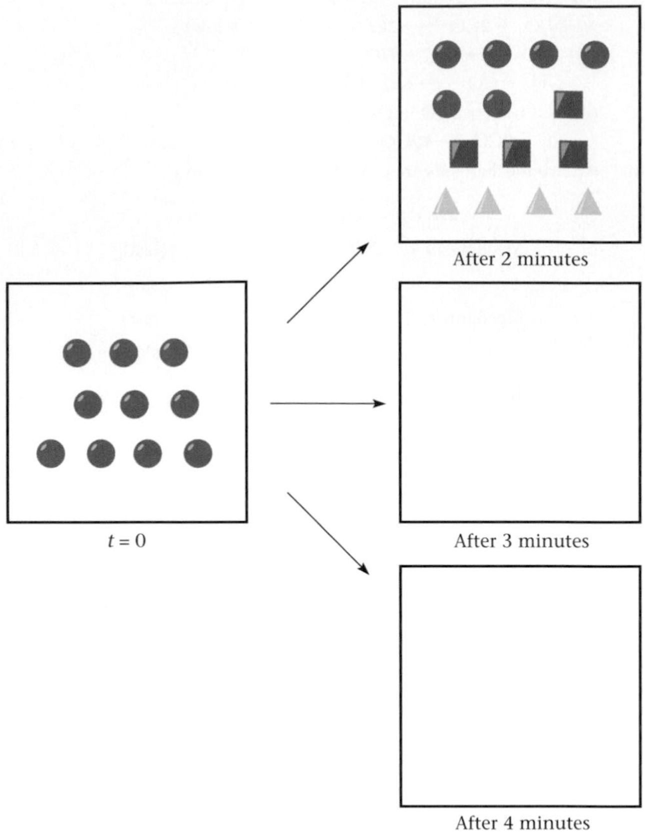

96. The following reaction is second-order in A and first-order in B.

$$A + B \longrightarrow \text{products}$$

(a) Write the rate expression.

(b) Consider the following one-liter vessel in which each square represents a mole of A and each circle represents a mole of B.

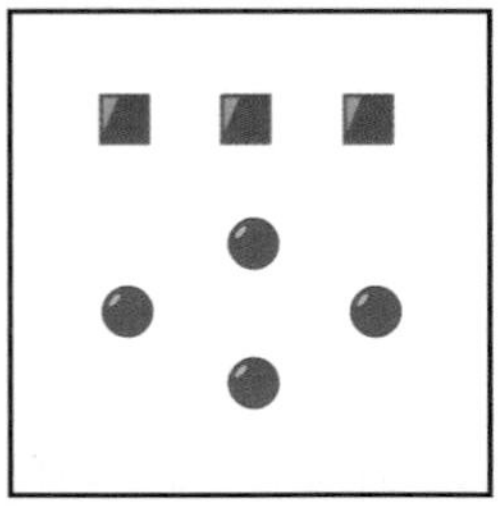

What is the rate of the reaction in terms of k?

(c) Assuming the same rate and k as (b), fill the similar one-liter vessel shown in the figure with an appropriate number of circles (representing B).

■ in OWL   Blue-numbered questions answered in Appendix 6   WEB Solution is available on companion website

97. For the reaction

$$A + B \longrightarrow C$$

the rate expression is rate $= k[A][B]$

(a) Given three test tubes, with different concentrations of A and B, which test tube has the smallest rate?

(1) 0.10 *M* A; 0.10 *M* B

(2) 0.15 *M* A; 0.15 *M* B

(3) 0.06 *M* A; 1.0 *M* B

(b) If the temperature is increased, describe (using the words *increases, decreases,* or *remains the same*) what happens to the rate, the value of *k*, and E_a.

98. The following experiments are performed for the first-order reaction:

$$A \longrightarrow \text{products}$$

Fill in the blanks. If the answer cannot be calculated with the given information, write NC on the blank(s) provided.

	Expt. 1	Expt. 2	Expt. 3	Expt. 4
[A]	0.100	0.200	0.100	0.100
Catalyst	No	No	Yes	No
Temperature	25°C	25°C	25°C	30°C
k (min^{-1})	0.5	______	1	0.6
Rate (mol/L · min)	______	______	______	______
E_a (kJ)	32	______	______	______

Challenge Problems

99. The gas-phase reaction between hydrogen and iodine

$$H_2(g) + I_2(g) \rightleftharpoons 2HI(g)$$

proceeds with a rate constant for the forward reaction at 700°C of 138 L/mol · s and an activation energy of 165 kJ/mol.

(a) Calculate the activation energy of the reverse reaction given that ΔH_f° for HI is 26.48 kJ/mol and ΔH_f° for $I_2(g)$ is 62.44 kJ/mol.

(b) Calculate the rate constant for the reverse reaction at 700°C. (Assume A in the equation $k = Ae^{-E_a/RT}$ is the same for both forward and reverse reactions.)

(c) Calculate the rate of the reverse reaction if the concentration of HI is 0.200 *M*. The reverse reaction is second-order in HI.

100. Consider the coagulation of a protein at 100°C. The first-order reaction has an activation energy of 69 kJ/mol. If the protein takes 5.4 minutes to coagulate in boiling water at 100°C, then how long will it take to coagulate the protein at an altitude where water boils at 87°C?

101. For a first-order reaction $aA \longrightarrow$ products, where $a \neq 1$, the rate is $-\Delta[A]/a\,\Delta t$, or in derivative notation, $-\frac{1}{a}\frac{d[A]}{dt}$. Derive the integrated rate law for the first-order decomposition of *a* moles of reactant.

102. The following data apply to the reaction

$$A(g) + 3B(g) + 2C(g) \longrightarrow \text{products}$$

[A]	[B]	[C]	Rate
0.20	0.40	0.10	*X*
0.40	0.40	0.20	8*X*
0.20	0.20	0.20	*X*
0.40	0.40	0.10	4*X*

Determine the rate law for the reaction.

103. Using calculus, derive the equation for

(a) the concentration-time relation for a second-order reaction (see Table 11.2).

(b) the concentration-time relation for a third-order reaction, A $\rightarrow$ product.

104. In a first-order reaction, suppose that a quantity *X* of a reactant is added at regular intervals of time, Δt. At first the amount of reactant in the system builds up; eventually, however, it levels off at a saturation value given by the expression

$$\text{saturation value} = \frac{X}{1 - 10^{-a}} \qquad \text{where } a = 0.30\frac{\Delta t}{t_{1/2}}$$

This analysis applies to prescription drugs, of which you take a certain amount each day. Suppose that you take 0.100 g of a drug three times a day and that the half-life for elimination is 2.0 days. Using this equation, calculate the mass of the drug in the body at saturation. Suppose further that side effects show up when 0.500 g of the drug accumulates in the body. As a pharmacist, what is the maximum dosage you could assign to a patient for an 8-h period without causing side effects?

■ in OWL Blue-numbered questions answered in Appendix 6 WEB Solution is available on companion website

12 Gaseous Chemical Equilibrium

Order is not pressure which is imposed on society from without, but an equilibrium which is set up from within.

—José Ortega y Gasset

Chapter Outline

The painting, "Equilibrium," shows arrows pointing in opposite directions. The same symbols are used to denote a chemical reaction in equilibrium.

Online homework for this chapter may be assigned in OWL

CENGAGENOW™

This icon introduces an opportunity for self-study and to explore interactive modules by signing in at **academic.cengage.com/now.**

Among the topics covered in Chapter 9 was the equilibrium between liquid and gaseous water:

$$H_2O(l) \rightleftharpoons H_2O(g)$$

The state of this equilibrium system at a given temperature can be described in a simple way by citing the equilibrium pressure of water vapor: 0.034 atm at 25°C, 1.00 atm at 100°C, and so on.

Chemical reactions involving gases carried out in closed containers resemble in many ways the $H_2O(l)$–$H_2O(g)$ system. The reactions are reversible; reactants are not completely consumed. Instead, an equilibrium mixture containing both products and reactants is obtained. At equilibrium, forward and reverse reactions take place at the same rate. As a result, the amounts of all species at equilibrium remain constant with time.

They can often be reversed by changing the temperature or pressure.

Ordinarily, where gaseous chemical equilibria are involved, more than one gaseous substance is present. We might, for example, have a system,

$$aA(g) + bB(g) \rightleftharpoons cC(g) + dD(g)$$

in which the equilibrium mixture contains two gaseous products (C and D) and two gaseous reactants (A and B). To describe the position of this equilibrium, we must cite the **partial pressure** of each species, that is, P_C, P_D, P_A, and P_B.

Recall from Chapter 5 that the partial pressure of gas, *i*, in a mixture is given by the expression

$$P_i = n_iRT/V$$

It follows that, for an equilibrium mixture confined in a closed container of volume V at temperature T, *the partial pressure,* P_i, *of each species is directly proportional to the number of moles,* n_i, *of that species.*

It turns out that there is a relatively simple relationship between the partial pressures of different gases present at equilibrium in a reaction system. This relationship is expressed in terms of a quantity called the *equilibrium constant,* symbol K.* In this chapter, you will learn how to—

- write the expression for K corresponding to any chemical equilibrium (Section 12.2).
- calculate the value for K from experimental data for the equilibrium system (Section 12.3).
- use the value of K to predict the extent to which a reaction will take place (Section 12.4).
- use K, along with Le Châtelier's principle, to predict the result of disturbing an equilibrium system (Section 12.5). ■

Don't confuse the *equilibrium* constant K with the *rate* constant k.

12.1 THE N_2O_4–NO_2 EQUILIBRIUM SYSTEM

Consider what happens when a sample of N_2O_4, a colorless gas, is placed in a closed, evacuated container at 100°C. Instantly, a reddish-brown color develops. This color is due to nitrogen dioxide, NO_2, formed by decomposition of part of the N_2O_4 (Figure 12.1, p. 324):

$$N_2O_4(g) \longrightarrow 2NO_2(g)$$

*Thermodynamically, the quantity that should appear for each species in the expression for K is the *activity* rather than the partial pressure. Activity is defined as the ratio of the equilibrium partial pressure to the standard pressure, 1 atm. This means that the activity and hence the equilibrium constant K are dimensionless, that is, a pure number without units.

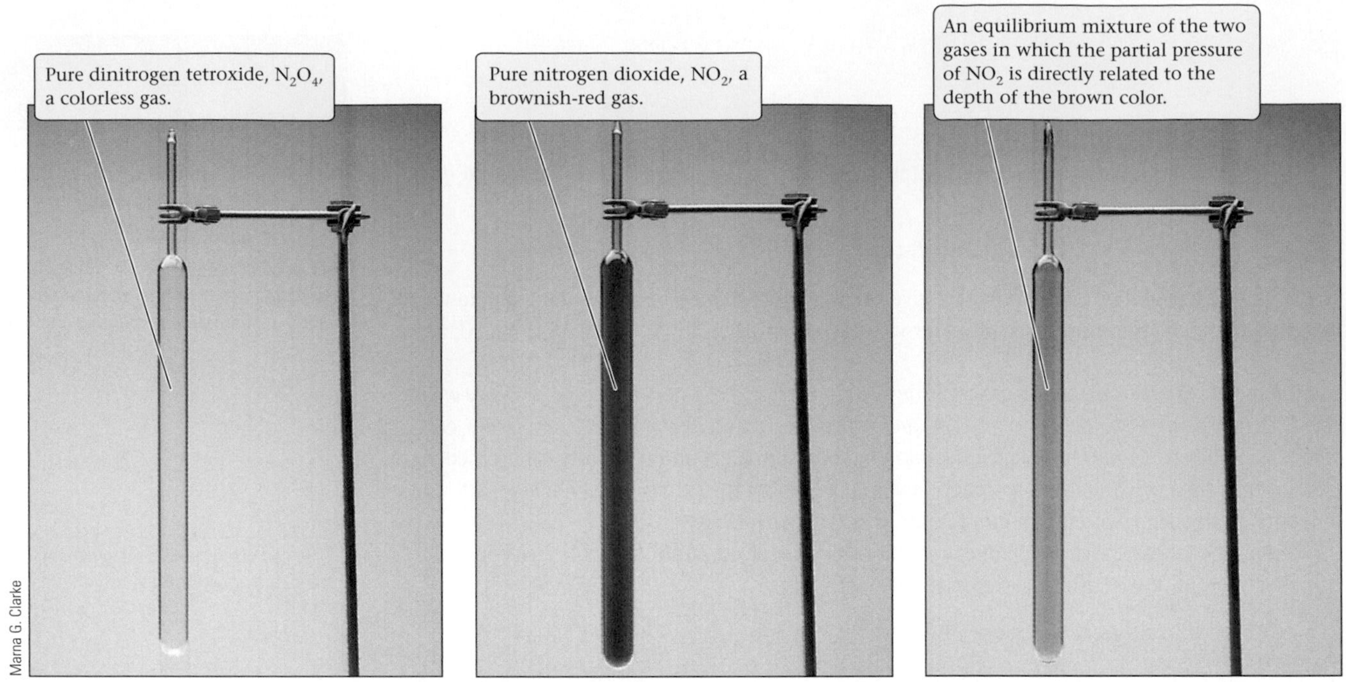

(a) (b) (c)

Figure 12.1
The N_2O_4–NO_2 system.

At first, this is the only reaction taking place. As soon as some NO_2 is formed, however, the reverse reaction can occur:

$$2NO_2(g) \longrightarrow N_2O_4(g)$$

Overall, the partial pressure of N_2O_4 drops, and the forward reaction slows down. Conversely, the partial pressure of NO_2 increases, so the rate of the reverse reaction increases. Soon these rates become equal. A dynamic equilibrium has been established.

$$N_2O_4(g) \rightleftharpoons 2NO_2(g)$$

At equilibrium, appreciable amounts of both gases are present. From that point on, the amounts of both NO_2 and N_2O_4 and their partial pressures remain constant, so long as the volume of the container and the temperature remain unchanged.

The characteristics just described are typical of all systems at equilibrium. First, *the forward and reverse reactions are taking place at the same rate.* This explains why *the concentrations of species present remain constant with time.* Moreover, these concentrations are independent of the direction from which equilibrium is approached.

The approach to equilibrium in the N_2O_4–NO_2 system is illustrated by the data in Table 12.1 and by Figure 12.2 (p. 325) (time is in arbitrary units). Originally, only N_2O_4 is present; its pressure is 1.00 atm. Because no NO_2 is around, its original pressure is zero. As equilibrium is approached, the overall reaction is

$$N_2O_4(g) \longrightarrow 2NO_2(g)$$

Table 12.1 Establishment of Equilibrium in the System $N_2O_4(g) \rightleftharpoons 2NO_2(g)$ (at 100°C)

Time	0	20	40	60	80	100
$P_{N_2O_4}$ (atm)	1.00	0.60	0.35	**0.22***	**0.22**	**0.22**
P_{NO_2} (atm)	0.00	0.80	1.30	**1.56**	**1.56**	**1.56**

*Boldface numbers are equilibrium pressures.

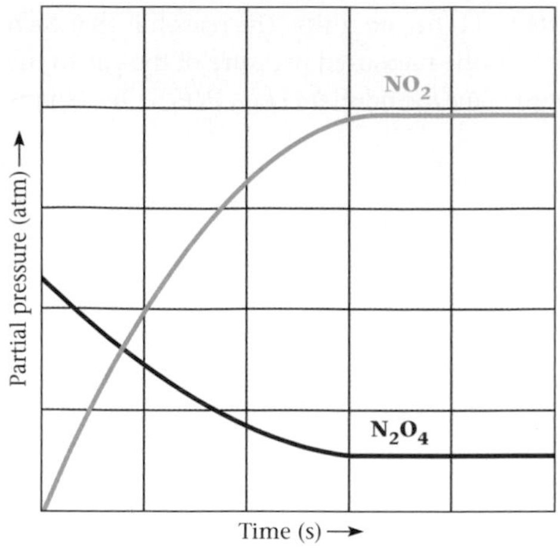

Figure 12.2
Approach to equilibrium in the N_2O_4–NO_2 system. The partial pressure of N_2O_4 starts off at 1.00 atm, drops sharply at first, and finally levels off at the equilibrium value of 0.22 atm. Meanwhile, the partial pressure of NO_2 rises from zero to its equilibrium value, 1.56 atm.

The amount and hence the partial pressure of N_2O_4 drop, rapidly at first, then more slowly. The partial pressure of NO_2 increases. Finally, both partial pressures level off and become constant. At equilibrium, at 100°C,

These pressures don't change, because forward and reverse reactions occur at the same rate.

$$P_{N_2O_4} = 0.22 \text{ atm} \qquad P_{NO_2} = 1.56 \text{ atm}$$

There are many ways to approach equilibrium in the N_2O_4–NO_2 system. Table 12.2 gives data for three experiments in which the original conditions are quite different. Experiment 1 is that just described, starting with pure N_2O_4. Experiment 2 starts with pure NO_2 at a partial pressure of 1.00 atm. As equilibrium is approached, some of the NO_2 reacts to form N_2O_4:

$$2NO_2(g) \longrightarrow N_2O_4(g)$$

Finally, in Experiment 3, both N_2O_4 and NO_2 are present originally, each at a partial pressure of 1.00 atm.

Looking at the data in Table 12.2, you might wonder whether these three experiments have anything in common. Specifically, is there any relationship between the equilibrium partial pressures of NO_2 and N_2O_4 that is valid for all the experiments? It turns out that there is, although it is not an obvious one. The value of the quotient $(P_{NO_2})^2/P_{N_2O_4}$ is the same, about 11, in each case:

$$\text{Expt. 1} \qquad \frac{(P_{NO_2})^2}{P_{N_2O_4}} = \frac{(1.56)^2}{0.22} = 11$$

$$\text{Expt. 2} \qquad \frac{(P_{NO_2})^2}{P_{N_2O_4}} = \frac{(0.86)^2}{0.07} = 11$$

$$\text{Expt. 3} \qquad \frac{(P_{NO_2})^2}{P_{N_2O_4}} = \frac{(2.16)^2}{0.42} = 11$$

Note that this relationship holds only at equilibrium; initial pressures can have any value.

Table 12.2 Equilibrium Measurements in the N_2O_4–NO_2 System at 100°C

		Original Pressure (atm)	Equilibrium Pressure (atm)
Expt. 1	N_2O_4	1.00	**0.22**
	NO_2	0.00	**1.56**
Expt. 2	N_2O_4	0.00	**0.07**
	NO_2	1.00	**0.86**
Expt. 3	N_2O_4	1.00	**0.42**
	NO_2	1.00	**2.16**

You may wonder why the equilibrium constant, 11, has no units. The reason is that each term in the reaction quotient represents the ratio of the measured pressure of the gas to the thermodynamic standard state of one atmosphere. Thus the quotient $(P_{NO_2})^2/P_{N_2O_4}$ in Experiment 1 becomes

$$K = \frac{\left(\dfrac{1.56 \text{ atm}}{1 \text{ atm}}\right)^2}{\left(\dfrac{0.22 \text{ atm}}{1 \text{ atm}}\right)} = 11$$

This relationship holds for any equilibrium mixture containing N_2O_4 and NO_2 at 100°C. More generally, it is found that, at any temperature, the quantity

$$\frac{(P_{NO_2})^2}{P_{N_2O_4}}$$

where P_{NO_2} and $P_{N_2O_4}$ are equilibrium partial pressures in atmospheres, is a constant, independent of the original composition, the volume of the container, or the total pressure. This constant is referred to as the **equilibrium constant *K*** for the system

$$N_2O_4(g) \rightleftharpoons 2NO_2(g)$$

The equilibrium constant for this system, like all equilibrium constants, changes with temperature. At 100°C, *K* for the N_2O_4–NO_2 system is 11; at 150°C, it has a different value, about 110. Any mixture of NO_2 and N_2O_4 at 100°C will react in such a way that the ratio $(P_{NO_2})^2/P_{N_2O_4}$ becomes equal to 11. At 150°C, reaction occurs until this ratio becomes 110.

12.2 THE EQUILIBRIUM CONSTANT EXPRESSION

CENGAGENOW™
Click Coached Problems for a self-study module on the **equilibrium constant.**

For every gaseous chemical system, an **equilibrium constant expression** can be written stating the condition that must be attained at equilibrium. For the general system involving only gases,

$$aA(g) + bB(g) \rightleftharpoons cC(g) + dD(g)$$

where A, B, C, and D represent different substances and *a, b, c,* and *d* are their coefficients in the balanced equation,

$$K = \frac{(P_C)^c \times (P_D)^d}{(P_A)^a \times (P_B)^b} \tag{12.1}$$

where P_C, P_D, P_A, and P_B are the partial pressures of the four gases at equilibrium.* ***These partial pressures must be expressed in atmospheres.*** Notice that in the expression for *K*—

- the equilibrium partial pressures of *products* (right side of equation) appear in the *numerator.*

*This equilibrium constant is often given the symbol K_p to emphasize that it involves partial pressures. Other equilibrium expressions for gases are sometimes used, including K_c:

$$K_c = \frac{[C]^c \times [D]^d}{[A]^a \times [B]^b}$$

where the brackets represent equilibrium concentrations in moles per liter. The two constants, K_c and K_p, are simply related (see Problem 78):

$$K_p = K_c(RT)^{\Delta n_g}$$

where Δn_g is the change in the number of moles of gas in the equation, *R* is the gas law constant, 0.0821 L · atm/mol · K, and *T* is the Kelvin temperature. Throughout this chapter, we deal only with K_p, referring to it simply as *K*.

- the equilibrium partial pressures of *reactants* (left side of equation) appear in the *denominator.*
- each partial pressure is raised to a *power* equal to its *coefficient* in the balanced equation.

Changing the Chemical Equation

K is meaningless unless accompanied by a chemical equation.

It is important to realize that ***the expression for K depends on the form of the chemical equation written to describe the equilibrium system.*** To illustrate what this statement means, consider the N_2O_4–NO_2 system:

$$N_2O_4(g) \rightleftharpoons 2NO_2(g) \qquad K = \frac{(P_{NO_2})^2}{P_{N_2O_4}}$$

Many other equations could be written for this system, for example,

$$\tfrac{1}{2}N_2O_4(g) \rightleftharpoons NO_2(g)$$

In this case, the expression for the equilibrium constant would be

$$K' = \frac{P_{NO_2}}{(P_{N_2O_4})^{1/2}}$$

Comparing the expressions for K and K', it is clear that K' is the square root of K. This illustrates a general rule, sometimes referred to as the **coefficient rule,** which states,

> ***If the coefficients in a balanced equation are multiplied by a factor n, the equilibrium constant is raised to the nth power:***

$$K' = K^n \qquad (12.2)$$

In this particular case, $n = \frac{1}{2}$ because the coefficients were divided by 2. Hence K' is the square root of K. If $K = 11$, then $K' = (11)^{1/2} = 3.3$.

Another equation that might be written to describe the N_2O_4–NO_2 system is

$$2NO_2(g) \rightleftharpoons N_2O_4(g)$$

for which the equilibrium constant expression is

$$K'' = \frac{P_{N_2O_4}}{(P_{NO_2})^2}$$

This chemical equation is simply the reverse of that written originally; N_2O_4 and NO_2 switch sides of the equation. Notice that K'' is the reciprocal of K; the numerator and denominator have been inverted. This illustrates the **reciprocal rule:**

> ***The equilibrium constants for forward and reverse reactions are the reciprocals of each other,***

$$K'' = 1/K \qquad (12.3)$$

If, for example, $K = 11$, then $K'' = 1/11 = 0.091$.

Adding Chemical Equations

A property of K that you will find very useful in this and succeeding chapters is expressed by the **rule of multiple equilibria,** which states

We will use this relationship frequently in later chapters.

> ***If a reaction can be expressed as the sum of two or more reactions, K for the overall reaction is the product of the equilibrium constants of the individual reactions.***

That is, if

$$\text{reaction 3} = \text{reaction 1} + \text{reaction 2}$$

then

$$K\,(\text{reaction 3}) = K\,(\text{reaction 1}) \times K\,(\text{reaction 2}) \qquad (12.4)$$

Table 12.3 Dependence of K on the Form of the Chemical Reaction

$$R(g) \rightleftharpoons Y(g) \qquad K = \frac{P_Y}{P_R}$$

Form of Equation	K Expression	Relation to K	Rule
$Y(g) \rightleftharpoons R(g)$	$K' = \frac{P_R}{P_Y}$	$K' = \frac{1}{K}$	Reciprocal Rule
$nR(g) \rightleftharpoons nY(g)$	$K'' = \frac{(P_Y)^n}{(P_R)^n}$	$K'' = K^n$	Coefficient Rule
$R(g) \rightleftharpoons A(g)$	$K_1 = \frac{P_A}{P_R}$		
$A(g) \rightleftharpoons Y(g)$	$K_2 = \frac{P_Y}{P_A}$		
$R(g) \rightleftharpoons Y(g)$		$K = K_1 \times K_2$	Rule of Multiple Equilibria

To illustrate the application of this rule, consider the following reactions at 700°C:

$$SO_2(g) + \tfrac{1}{2}O_2(g) \rightleftharpoons SO_3(g) \qquad K = 2.2$$

$$NO_2(g) \rightleftharpoons NO(g) + \tfrac{1}{2}O_2(g) \qquad K = 4.0$$

Adding these equations eliminates $\frac{1}{2}O_2$; the result is

$$SO_2(g) + NO_2(g) \rightleftharpoons SO_3(g) + NO(g)$$

For this overall reaction, $K = 2.2 \times 4.0 = 8.8$.

The validity of this rule can be demonstrated by writing the expression for K for the individual reactions and multiplying:

$$\frac{P_{SO_3}}{P_{SO_2} \times (P_{O_2})^{1/2}} \times \frac{P_{NO} \times (P_{O_2})^{1/2}}{P_{NO_2}} = \frac{P_{SO_3} \times P_{NO}}{P_{SO_2} \times P_{NO_2}}$$

The product expression, at the right, is clearly the equilibrium constant for the overall reaction, as it should be according to the rule of multiple equilibria.

Table 12.3 summarizes the rules for writing the expression for the equilibrium constant.

Example 12.1 Graded

Consider the air pollutants NO and NO_2, contributors to photochemical smog. Both can be formed by the reaction between atmospheric nitrogen and oxygen. At 25°C,

$$N_2(g) + O_2(g) \rightleftharpoons 2NO(g) \qquad K_1 = 4.2 \times 10^{-31} \qquad (1)$$

$$N_2(g) + 2O_2(g) \rightleftharpoons 2NO_2(g) \qquad K_2 = 1.0 \times 10^{-18} \qquad (2)$$

*(a) Write the equilibrium constant expression for the formation of two moles of NO at 25°C.

**(b) Calculate K for the formation of one mole of NO at 25°C.

***(c) Calculate K for the decomposition of one mole of NO_2 at 25°C.

****(d) Calculate K for the following reaction at 25°C:

$$2NO(g) + O_2(g) \rightleftharpoons 2NO_2(g)$$

SOLUTION

(a) Following the rules described on p. 327, we have

$$K_1 = \frac{(P_{NO})^2}{(P_{N_2})(P_{O_2})}$$

(b) The reaction for the formation of one mole of NO is

$$\tfrac{1}{2}N_2(g) + \tfrac{1}{2}O_2(g) \rightleftharpoons NO(g)$$

The coefficients for this equation are obtained by multiplying those in (1) by $\tfrac{1}{2}$. Using the coefficient rule,

$$K = (K_1)^{1/2} = (4.2 \times 10^{-31})^{1/2} = 6.5 \times 10^{-16}$$

(c) The reaction for the decomposition of one mole of NO_2 is

$$NO_2(g) \rightleftharpoons \tfrac{1}{2}N_2(g) + O_2(g)$$

To arrive at this equation, two changes are made:

1. The product (NO_2) and the reactants (N_2 and O_2) have switched sides (reciprocal rule).
2. The coefficients are multiplied by $\tfrac{1}{2}$ (coefficient rule).

Thus,

$$K = \frac{1}{(K_2)^{1/2}} = \frac{1}{(1.0 \times 10^{-18})^{1/2}} = 1.0 \times 10^{9}$$

(d) To obtain the equation asked for here, combine two other equations for which you can find equilibrium constants.

$$2NO(g) \rightleftharpoons N_2(g) + O_2(g) \qquad K_1 = 1/(4.2 \times 10^{-31})$$

$$N_2(g) + 2O_2(g) \rightleftharpoons 2NO_2(g) \qquad K_2 = 1.0 \times 10^{-18}$$

$$2NO(g) + O_2(g) \rightleftharpoons 2NO_2(g)$$

The rule of multiple equilibria gives

$$K_3 = K_1 \times K_2 = \frac{1.0 \times 10^{-18}}{4.2 \times 10^{-31}} = 2.4 \times 10^{12}$$

Heterogeneous Equilibria

In the reactions described so far, all the reactants and products have been gaseous; the equilibrium systems are *homogeneous.* In certain reactions, at least one of the substances involved is a pure liquid or solid; the others are gases. Such a system is *heterogeneous,* because more than one phase is present. Examples include

$$CO_2(g) + H_2(g) \rightleftharpoons CO(g) + H_2O(l)$$

$$I_2(s) \rightleftharpoons I_2(g)$$

Experimentally, it is found that for such systems—

- ***the position of the equilibrium is independent of the amount of solid or liquid, as long as some is present.***
- ***terms for pure liquids or solids need not appear in the expression for K.***

To see why this is the case, consider the data shown in Table 12.4 for the system

$$CO_2(g) + H_2(g) \rightleftharpoons CO(g) + H_2O(l)$$

at 25°C. In Experiments 1 through 4, liquid water is present, so the partial pressure of water in the gas phase, P_{H_2O}, is constant at 0.03 atm, the equilibrium vapor pressure of water at 25°C.

Notice that—

1. In all cases, the quantity

$$K_I = \frac{P_{CO} \times P_{H_2O}}{P_{CO_2} \times P_{H_2}}$$

is constant at 9×10^{-6}.

Table 12.4 Equilibrium Constant Expressions for $CO_2(g) + H_2(g) \rightleftharpoons CO(g) + H_2O(l)$

	Expt. 1	Expt. 2	Expt. 3	Expt. 4
Mass $H_2O(l)$	8 g	6 g	4 g	2 g
P_{H_2O} (atm)	3×10^{-2}	3×10^{-2}	3×10^{-2}	3×10^{-2}
K_I	9×10^{-6}	9×10^{-6}	9×10^{-6}	9×10^{-6}
K_{II}	3×10^{-4}	3×10^{-4}	3×10^{-4}	3×10^{-4}

$K_I = \frac{P_{CO} \times P_{H_2O}}{P_{CO_2} \times P_{H_2}}$ $\quad K_{II} = \frac{P_{CO}}{P_{CO_2} \times P_{H_2}}$

2. In all cases (Experiments 1 through 4), the quantity

$$K_{II} = \frac{P_{CO}}{P_{CO_2} \times P_{H_2}}$$

is constant at 3×10^{-4}. This must be true because

$$K_{II} = K_I/P_{H_2O}$$

and P_{H_2O} is constant at 3×10^{-2} atm. It follows that K_{II} is a valid equilibrium constant for the system

$$CO_2(g) + H_2(g) \rightleftharpoons CO(g) + H_2O(l)$$

Because the expression for K_{II} is simpler than that for K_I, it is the equilibrium constant of choice for the heterogeneous system.

A similar argument can be applied to the equilibrium involved in the sublimation of iodine:

$$I_2(s) \rightleftharpoons I_2(g)$$

At a given temperature, the pressure of iodine vapor is constant, independent of the amount of solid iodine or any other factor. The equilibrium constant expression is

$$K = P_{I_2}$$

Applying the reciprocal rule (page 327), we can deduce the equilibrium constant expression for the reverse reaction

$$I_2(g) \rightleftharpoons I_2(s) \qquad K = 1/P_{I_2}$$

Charles D. Winters

A heterogeneous equilibrium system: solid I_2–gaseous I_2.

Example 12.2 Write the expression for K for

(a) the reduction of black solid copper(II) oxide (1 mol) with hydrogen to form copper metal and steam.

(b) the reaction of 1 mol of steam with red-hot coke (carbon) to form a mixture of hydrogen and carbon monoxide, called water gas.

Strategy First write the chemical equation for the equilibrium system. Then write the expression for K, leaving out pure liquids and solids. Remember that gases are represented by their partial pressures.

SOLUTION

(a) The reaction is $CuO(s) + H_2(g) \rightleftharpoons Cu(s) + H_2O(g)$

The expression for K is $K = \frac{P_{H_2O}}{P_{H_2}}$

If the product were $H_2O(l)$, $K = 1/P_{H_2}$.

(b) The reaction is $C(s) + H_2O(g) \rightleftharpoons H_2(g) + CO(g)$

The expression for K is $K = \frac{P_{H_2} \times P_{CO}}{P_{H_2O}}$

In this and succeeding chapters, a wide variety of different types of equilibria will be covered. They may involve gases, pure liquids or solids, and species in aqueous solution. It will always be true that in the expression for the equilibrium constant—

To express K for any system, follow these rules.

- ***gases enter as their partial pressures in atmospheres.***
- ***pure liquids or solids do not appear; neither does the solvent for a reaction in dilute solution.***
- ***species (ions or molecules) in water solution enter as their molar concentrations.***

Thus for the equilibrium attained when zinc metal reacts with acid,

$$Zn(s) + 2H^+(aq) \rightleftharpoons Zn^{2+}(aq) + H_2(g)$$

$$K = \frac{P_{H_2} \times [Zn^{2+}]}{[H^+]^2}$$

We will have more to say in later chapters about equilibria involving species in aqueous solution.

12.3 DETERMINATION OF *K*

Numerical values of equilibrium constants can be calculated if the partial pressures of products and reactants at equilibrium are known. Sometimes you will be given equilibrium partial pressures directly (Example 12.3). At other times you will be given the original partial pressures and the equilibrium partial pressure of one species (Example 12.4). In that case, the calculation of K is a bit more difficult, because you have to calculate the equilibrium partial pressures of all the species.

CENGAGENOW™
Click Coached Problems for a self-study module on **determining the equilibrium constant.**

Example 12.3 Ammonium chloride is sometimes used as a flux in soldering because it decomposes on heating:

$$NH_4Cl(s) \rightleftharpoons NH_3(g) + HCl(g)$$

The HCl formed removes oxide films from metals to be soldered. In a certain equilibrium system at 400°C, 22.6 g of NH_4Cl is present; the partial pressures of NH_3 and HCl are 2.5 atm and 4.8 atm, respectively. Calculate K at 400°C.

Strategy First write the expression for K. Then substitute equilibrium partial pressures into that expression and solve.

SOLUTION

$$K = (P_{NH_3})(P_{HCl}) = 2.5 \times 4.8 = 12$$

Example 12.4 Consider the equilibrium system

$$2HI(g) \rightleftharpoons H_2(g) + I_2(g)$$

Originally, a system contains only HI at a pressure of 1.00 atm at 520°C. The equilibrium partial pressure of H_2 is found to be 0.10 atm. Calculate

(a) P_{I_2} and P_{HI} at equilibrium (b) K

Strategy To solve this problem, you must—

- carefully distinguish *original* from *equilibrium* partial pressures.
- learn how to relate the equilibrium partial pressures of H_2, I_2, and HI using the coefficients of the balanced equation.
- make a table to summarize your reasoning.

SOLUTION

(a) Start by creating the following table and enter the pertinent information obtained from the statement of the problem. (That will be the red entries in the following table.)

	$2HI(g)$	$\rightleftharpoons$	$H_2(g)$	+	$I_2(g)$
P_o (atm)	1.00		0		0
ΔP (atm)					
P_{eq} (atm)			0.10		

P_o = intial pressure, P_{eq} = equilibrium pressure, ΔP = change in pressure

Note that H_2 and I_2 are being made (pressure increases), and HI is being used up. Furthermore, ΔP for $H_2(g)$ must be 0.10 atm to get from an original pressure of zero to an equilibrium partial pressure of 0.10 atm. Your table should then look like:

	$2HI(g)$	$\rightleftharpoons$	$H_2(g)$	+	$I_2(g)$
P_o (atm)	1.00		0		0
ΔP (atm)	−		+0.10		+
P_{eq} (atm)			0.10		

Note from the balanced equation that one mole of I_2 is formed for every mole of H_2. Putting it another way, as the reaction proceeds from left to right, the increase in the number of moles of I_2 is the same as that for H_2:

$$\Delta n_{I_2} = \Delta n_{H_2}$$

Because $P = nRT/V$, it follows that for an equilibrium system at constant T and V, pressure is directly proportional to amount in moles, and the above relationship must hold for partial pressures as well:

$$\Delta P_{I_2} = \Delta P_{H_2}$$

If $\Delta P_{H_2} = x$, then $\Delta P_{I_2} = x$ and $\Delta P_{HI} = -2x$.

By similar reasoning, because two moles of HI are required to form one mole of H_2,

$$\Delta n_{HI} = -2\Delta n_{H_2}$$

and

$$\Delta P_{HI} = -2\Delta P_{H_2}.$$

The table now looks like:

	$2HI(g)$	$\rightleftharpoons$	$H_2(g)$	+	$I_2(g)$
P_o (atm)	1.00		0		0
ΔP (atm)	−2(0.10)		+0.10		+1(0.10)
P_{eq} (atm)	0.80		0.10		0.10

From this table, you see that $P_{HI} = 0.80$ atm and $P_{I_2} = 0.10$ atm.

(b) $K = \dfrac{P_{H_2} \times P_{I_2}}{P_{HI}} = \dfrac{(0.10)(0.10)}{(0.80)^2} = 0.016$

Reality Check

1. Note that the numbers for ΔP are related through the coefficients of the balanced equation (2HI, I_2, H_2)
2. You might expect that K would be rather small (0.016). Recall that at equilibrium, P_{I_2} is 0.100 atm, only one-tenth of the original pressure of HI (1.00 atm).

Example 12.4 illustrates a principle that you will find very useful in solving equilibrium problems throughout this (and later) chapters. ***As a system approaches equilibrium, changes in partial pressures of reactants and products—like changes in molar amounts—are related to one another through the coefficients of the balanced equation.***

12.4 APPLICATIONS OF THE EQUILIBRIUM CONSTANT

Sometimes, knowing only the magnitude of the equilibrium constant, it is possible to decide on the feasibility of a reaction. Consider, for example, a possible method for "fixing" atmospheric nitrogen—converting it to a compound—by reaction with oxygen:

$$N_2(g) + O_2(g) \rightleftharpoons 2NO(g)$$

$$K = \frac{(P_{NO})^2}{P_{N_2} \times P_{O_2}} = 1 \times 10^{-30} \text{ at } 25°C$$

Because K is so small, the partial pressure of NO in equilibrium with N_2 and O_2, and hence the amount of NO, must be extremely small, approaching zero. Clearly, this would not be a suitable way to fix nitrogen, at least at 25°C.

An alternative approach to nitrogen fixation involves reacting it with hydrogen:

$$N_2(g) + 3H_2(g) \rightleftharpoons 2NH_3(g)$$

$$K = \frac{(P_{NH_3})^2}{P_{N_2} \times (P_{H_2})^3} = 6 \times 10^5 \text{ at } 25°C$$

In this case, the equilibrium system must contain mostly ammonia. A mixture of N_2 and H_2 should be almost completely converted to NH_3 at equilibrium.

In general, if K is a very small number, the equilibrium mixture will contain mostly unreacted starting materials; for all practical purposes, the forward reaction does not go. Conversely, a large K implies a reaction that, at least in principle, is feasible; products should be formed in high yield. Frequently, K has an intermediate value, in which case you must make quantitative calculations concerning the *direction* or *extent* of reaction.

The concept of equilibrium is most useful when K is neither very large nor very small.

Direction of Reaction; the Reaction Quotient (Q)

Consider the general gas-phase reaction

$$aA(g) + bB(g) \rightleftharpoons cC(g) + dD(g)$$

for which

$$K = \frac{(P_C)^c \times (P_D)^d}{(P_A)^a \times (P_B)^b}$$

CENGAGENOW™
Click Coached Problems for a self-study module on **systems at equilibrium.**

As we have seen, for a given system at a particular temperature, the value of K is fixed.

In contrast, the actual pressure ratio, Q,

$$Q = \frac{(P_C)^c \times (P_D)^d}{(P_A)^a \times (P_B)^b}$$ (color is used to distinguish actual from equilibrium pressures)

can have any value at all. If you start with pure reactants (A and B), P_C and P_D are zero, and the value of Q is zero:

$$Q = \frac{0 \times 0}{(P_A)^a \times (P_B)^b} = 0$$

Q can have any value; K is fixed.

The direction of the reaction may change, but the expression for the equilibrium constant does not.

Table 12.5 Approach to Equilibrium in the System $A \rightleftharpoons B$ for which $K = 1.00$

	Experiment 1*				Experiment 2*			
t	0	20	40	60	0	20	40	60
conc. B	1.00	1.35	1.50	1.50	2.00	1.65	1.50	1.50
conc. A	2.00	1.65	1.50	1.50	1.00	1.35	1.50	1.50
$Q = [B]/[A]$	0.500	0.818	1.00	1.00	2.00	1.22	1.00	1.00
	$Q < K$		$Q = K$		$Q > K$		$Q = K$	

*In both experiments, systems to the right of the broken line have reached equilibrium.

Conversely, starting with only C and D, the value of Q is infinite as the values of P_A and P_B approach zero:

$$Q = \frac{(P_C)^c \times (P_D)^d}{(P_A)^a \times (P_B)^b \rightarrow 0} \longrightarrow \infty$$

If all four substances are present, Q can have any value between zero and infinity.

As equilibrium is approached, Q approaches K.

The form of the expression for Q, known as the **reaction quotient,** is the same as that for the equilibrium constant, K. The difference is that the partial pressures that appear in Q are those that apply at a particular moment, not necessarily when the system is at equilibrium. By comparing the numerical value of Q with that of K, it is possible to decide in which direction the system will move to achieve equilibrium.

$Q < K; \longrightarrow$

1. If $Q < K$ the reaction proceeds from left to right:

$$aA(g) + bB(g) \longrightarrow cC(g) + dD(g)$$

In this way, the partial pressures of products increase, while those of reactants decrease. As this happens, the reaction quotient Q increases and eventually at equilibrium becomes equal to K.

$Q > K; \longleftarrow$

2. If $Q > K$ the partial pressures of products are "too high" and those of the reactants "too low" to meet the equilibrium condition. Reaction proceeds in the reverse direction:

$$aA(g) + bB(g) \longleftarrow cC(g) + dD(g)$$

increasing the partial pressures of A and B while reducing those of C and D. This lowers Q to its equilibrium value, K.

3. If perchance $Q = K$, the system is already at equilibrium, so the amounts of products and reactants remain unchanged.

To illustrate these statements, consider the simple system shown in Table 12.5.

Example 12.5 Consider the following system at 100°C:

$$N_2O_4(g) \rightleftharpoons 2NO_2(g) \qquad K = 11$$

Predict the direction in which reaction will occur to reach equilibrium, starting with 0.10 mol of N_2O_4 and 0.20 mol of NO_2 in a 2.0-L container.

Strategy First calculate the partial pressures of N_2O_4 and NO_2, using the ideal gas law as applied to mixtures: $P_i = n_iRT/V$. Then calculate Q. Finally, compare Q and K to predict the direction of reaction.

SOLUTION

$$P_{N_2O_4} = \frac{nRT}{V} = \frac{(0.10\ \text{mol})\ (0.0821\ \text{L} \cdot \text{atm/mol} \cdot \text{K})\ (373\ \text{K})}{2.0\ \text{L}} = 1.5\ \text{atm}$$

Since there are twice as many moles of NO_2 at the same V and T,

$$P_{NO_2} = 2(1.5 \text{ atm}) = 3.0 \text{ atm}$$

$$Q = \frac{(P_{NO_2})^2}{P_{N_2O_4}} = \frac{(3.0)^2}{1.5} = 6.0$$

Because $Q < 11$, reaction must proceed in the forward direction.

Reality Check When reaction occurs in the forward direction, the partial pressure of NO_2 increases, that of N_2O_4 decreases, and Q becomes equal to K.

Extent of Reaction; Equilibrium Partial Pressures

The equilibrium constant for a chemical system can be used to calculate the partial pressures of the species present at equilibrium. In the simplest case, one equilibrium pressure can be calculated, knowing all the others. Consider, for example, the system

$$N_2(g) + O_2(g) \rightleftharpoons 2NO(g)$$

$$K = \frac{(P_{NO})^2}{P_{N_2} \times P_{O_2}} = 1 \times 10^{-30} \text{ at } 25°C$$

CENGAGENOW™
Click Coached Problems for a self-study module on **estimating equilibrium concentrations.**

In air, the partial pressures of N_2 and O_2 are about 0.78 and 0.21 atm, respectively. The expression for K can be used to calculate the equilibrium partial pressure of NO under these conditions:

$$(P_{NO})^2 = P_{N_2} \times P_{O_2} \times K$$
$$= (0.78)(0.21)(1 \times 10^{-30}) = 1.6 \times 10^{-31}$$
$$P_{NO} = (1.6 \times 10^{-31})^{1/2} = 4 \times 10^{-16} \text{ atm}$$

This is an extremely small pressure, as you might have guessed from the small magnitude of the equilibrium constant.

That's just as well; if N_2 and O_2 in the atmosphere were converted to NO, we'd be in big trouble.

More commonly K is used to determine the equilibrium partial pressures of all species, reactants, and products, knowing their original pressures. To do this, you follow what amounts to a four-step path.

1. ***Using the balanced equation for the reaction, write the expression for K.***
2. ***Express the equilibrium partial pressures of all species in terms of a single unknown, x.*** To do this, apply the principle mentioned earlier: ***The changes in partial pressures of reactants and products are related through the coefficients of the balanced equation.*** To keep track of these values, make an equilibrium table, like the one illustrated in Example 12.4.
3. ***Substitute the equilibrium terms into the expression for K. This gives an algebraic equation that must be solved for x.***
4. ***Having found x, refer back to the table and calculate the equilibrium partial pressures of all species.***

Example 12.6 Graded

For the system

$$CO_2(g) + H_2(g) \rightleftharpoons CO(g) + H_2O(g)$$

K is 0.64 at 900 K. Calculate the equilibrium partial pressures of all species, starting with

*(a) $P_{CO_2} = P_{H_2} = 1.00$ atm; $P_{CO} = P_{H_2O} = 0$
**(b) $P_{CO_2} = 2.00$ atm, $P_{H_2} = 1.00$ atm; $P_{CO} = P_{H_2O} = 0$

SOLUTION

(a) Follow the four steps described above.

(1) $K = \dfrac{P_{CO} \times P_{H_2O}}{P_{CO_2} \times P_{H_2}}$

(2) You must express all equilibrium partial pressures in terms of a single unknown, x. A reasonable choice for x is

$$x = \text{change in partial pressure of CO as the system goes to equilibrium} = \Delta P_{CO}$$

All the coefficients in the balanced equation are the same, 1. It follows that all the partial pressures change by the same amount, x.

$$\Delta P_{H_2O} = \Delta P_{CO} = x$$
$$\Delta P_{H_2} = \Delta P_{CO_2} = -x$$

You must distinguish carefully between initial pressures (P_o) and equilibrium pressures.

(The minus sign arises because H_2 and CO_2 are consumed, whereas CO and H_2O are formed.) The equilibrium table becomes

	$CO_2(g)$	+ $H_2(g)$ ⇌	$CO(g)$	+ $H_2O(g)$
P_o (atm)	1.00	1.00	0	0
ΔP (atm)	$-x$	$-x$	$+x$	$+x$
P_{eq} (atm)	$1.00 - x$	$1.00 - x$	x	x

(3) Substituting into the expression for K,

$$0.64 = \frac{(x)(x)}{(1.00 - x)(1.00 - x)}$$

Taking the square root of both sides,

$$(0.64)^{1/2} = 0.80 = \frac{x}{1.00 - x}$$

Solving for x,

$$x = 0.80 - 0.80x \qquad 1.80x = 0.80 \qquad x = 0.44$$

(4) Referring back to the equilibrium table,

$$P_{CO} = P_{H_2O} = x = 0.44 \text{ atm}$$
$$P_{CO_2} = P_{H_2} = 1.00 - x = 0.56 \text{ atm}$$

If you get a negative value for P_{eq}, something is wrong. Check your math and your reasoning.

(b) Proceeding in the same manner as in (a), the equilibrium table becomes

	$CO_2(g)$	+ $H_2(g)$ ⇌	$CO(g)$	+ $H_2O(g)$
P_o (atm)	2.00	1.00	0	0
ΔP (atm)	$-x$	$-x$	$+x$	$+x$
P_{eq} (atm)	$2.00 - x$	$1.00 - x$	x	x

Substituting into the expression for K,

$$0.64 = \frac{x^2}{(2.00 - x)(1.00 - x)}$$

This time, the equation is not as readily solved as in (a) because the right side is not a perfect square. Use the general method of solving a quadratic equation. This involves rearranging to the standard form

$$ax^2 + bx + c = 0$$

and applying the quadratic formula

$$x = \frac{-b \pm \sqrt{b^2 - 4ac}}{2a}$$

Putting the equilibrium constant expression in the desired standard form,

$$x^2 = 0.64(2.00 - x)(1.00 - x)$$
$$x^2 = 1.28 - 1.92x + 0.64x^2$$
$$0.36x^2 + 1.92x - 1.28 = 0$$

So

$$a = 0.36, b = 1.92, c = -1.28$$

Solving

$$x = \frac{-1.92 \pm \sqrt{3.69 + 1.84}}{0.72} = \frac{-1.92 \pm 2.35}{0.72}$$
$$x = 0.60, \text{ or } -5.93$$

For the most part, we'll avoid tedious calculations of this type.

Of the two answers, only 0.60 is plausible; a value of -5.93 would imply that CO and H_2 have *negative* partial pressures, which is ridiculous.

Substituting $x = 0.60$ back into the equilibrium table,

$$P_{CO} = P_{H_2O} = 0.60 \text{ atm}; \quad P_{CO_2} = 1.40 \text{ atm}; \quad P_{H_2} = 0.40 \text{ atm}$$

To check the arithmetic, substitute these values back into the expression for K:

$$\frac{(0.60)(0.60)}{(0.40)(1.40)} = 0.64 \quad \text{Voila!}$$

We should point out that the calculations involved in Example 12.6 assume ideal gas behavior. At the conditions specified (1 atm, relatively high temperatures), this assumption is a good one. However, many industrial gas-phase reactions are carried out at very high pressures. In that case, intermolecular forces become important, and calculated yields based on ideal gas behavior may be seriously in error.

12.5 EFFECT OF CHANGES IN CONDITIONS ON AN EQUILIBRIUM SYSTEM

Once a system has attained equilibrium, it is possible to change the ratio of products to reactants by changing the external conditions. We will consider three ways in which a chemical equilibrium can be disturbed:

CENGAGENOW™
Click Chemistry Interactive for the self-study module **Le Châtelier's principle: a water tank analogy.**

1. Adding or removing a gaseous reactant or product.
2. Compressing or expanding the system.
3. Changing the temperature.

You can deduce the direction in which an equilibrium will shift when one of these changes is made by applying the following principle:

If a system at equilibrium is disturbed by a change in concentration, pressure, or temperature, the system will, if possible, shift to partially counteract the change.

Equilibrium systems, like people, resist change.

This law was first stated, in a more complex form, in 1884 by Henri Le Châtelier (1850–1936), a French chemist who had studied a variety of industrial equilibria, including those involved in the production of iron in the blast furnace. The statement is commonly referred to as **Le Châtelier's principle.**

Adding or Removing a Gaseous Species

According to Le Châtelier's principle, ***if a chemical system at equilibrium is disturbed by adding a gaseous species (reactant or product), the reaction will proceed in such a direction as to consume part of the added species. Conversely, if a gaseous species is removed, the***

CENGAGENOW™
Click Coached Problems for a self-study module on **addition or removal of a reagent to a chemical equilibrium.**

system shifts to restore part of that species. In that way, the change in concentration brought about by adding or removing a gaseous species is partially counteracted when equilibrium is restored.

To apply this general rule, consider the reaction

$$N_2O_4(g) \rightleftharpoons 2NO_2(g)$$

Suppose this system has reached equilibrium at a certain temperature. This equilibrium could be disturbed by—

- *adding N_2O_4.* Reaction will occur in the forward direction (left to right). In this way, part of the N_2O_4 will be consumed.
- *adding NO_2,* which causes the reverse reaction (right to left) to occur, using up part of the NO_2 added.
- *removing N_2O_4.* Reaction occurs in the reverse direction to restore part of the N_2O_4.
- *removing NO_2,* which causes the forward reaction to occur, restoring part of the NO_2 removed.

It is possible to use K to calculate the extent to which reaction occurs when an equilibrium is disturbed by adding or removing a product or reactant. To show how this is done, consider the effect of adding hydrogen iodide to the HI–H_2–I_2 system (Example 12.7).

$$2HI(g) \rightleftharpoons H_2(g) + I_2(g)$$

Example 12.7 In Example 12.4 you found that the HI–H_2–I_2 system is in equilibrium at 520°C when $P_{HI} = 0.80$ atm and $P_{H_2} = P_{I_2} = 0.10$ atm. Suppose enough HI is added to raise its pressure temporarily to 1.00 atm. When equilibrium is restored, what are P_{HI}, P_{H_2}, and P_{I_2}?

Strategy This problem is entirely analogous to Example 12.6; the only real difference is that in this case the original pressures are those that prevail immediately after equilibrium is disturbed. Note that

$$Q = \frac{(0.10) \times (0.10)}{(1.00)^2} = 0.010 < K = 0.016$$

so some HI must dissociate to establish equilibrium.

SOLUTION

(1) Recall from Example 12.4 that

$$K = \frac{P_{H_2} \times P_{I_2}}{(P_{HI})^2} = 0.016 \text{ at } 520°C$$

(2) The partial pressure of HI must decrease; those of H_2 and I_2 must increase. Let x be the increase in partial pressure of H_2. Then

$$\Delta P_{I_2} = \Delta P_{H_2} = x \qquad \Delta P_{HI} = -2x$$

The equilibrium table becomes

	$2HI(g)$ $\rightleftharpoons$	$H_2(g)$ +	$I_2(g)$
P_o (atm)	1.00	0.10	0.10
ΔP (atm)	$-2x$	$+x$	$+x$
P_{eq} (atm)	$1.00 - 2x$	$0.10 + x$	$0.10 + x$

(3) Substituting into the expression for K,

$$0.016 = \frac{(0.10 + x)^2}{(1.00 - 2x)^2}$$

To solve this equation, take the square root of both sides:

$$0.13 = \frac{0.10 + x}{1.00 - 2x}$$

from which you should find that $x = 0.024$.

(4) $P_{H_2} = P_{I_2} = 0.10 + x =$ 0.12 atm

$P_{HI} = 1.00 - 2x =$ 0.95 atm

Reality Check Note that the equilibrium partial pressure of HI is intermediate between its value before equilibrium was established (0.80 atm) and that immediately afterward (1.00 atm). This is exactly what Le Châtelier's principle predicts; part of the added HI is consumed to re-establish equilibrium.

The system does *not* return to its original equilibrium state.

We should emphasize that adding a pure liquid or solid has no effect on a system at equilibrium. The rule is a simple one: *For a species to shift the position of an equilibrium, it must appear in the expression for K.*

Compression or Expansion

To understand how a change in pressure can change the position of an equilibrium, consider again the N_2O_4–NO_2 system:

$$N_2O_4(g) \rightleftharpoons 2NO_2(g)$$

CENGAGENOW™
Click Coached Problems for a self-study module on **equilibria and volume.**

Suppose the system is compressed by pushing down the piston shown in Figure 12.3. The immediate effect is to increase the gas pressure because the same number of molecules are crowded into a smaller volume ($P = nRT/V$). According to Le Châtelier's principle, the system will shift to partially counteract this change. There is a simple way in which the gas pressure can be reduced. Some of the NO_2 molecules combine with each other to form N_2O_4 (cylinder at right of Figure 12.3). That is, reaction occurs in the reverse direction:

When V decreases, NO_2 is converted to N_2O_4.

$$N_2O_4(g) \longleftarrow 2NO_2(g)$$

This reduces the number of moles, n, and hence the pressure, P.

It is possible (but not easy) to calculate from K the extent to which NO_2 is converted to N_2O_4 when the system is compressed. The results of such calculations are given in Table 12.6. As the pressure is increased from 1.0 to 10.0 atm, more and more of the NO_2 is converted to N_2O_4. Notice that the total number of moles of gas decreases steadily as a result of this conversion.

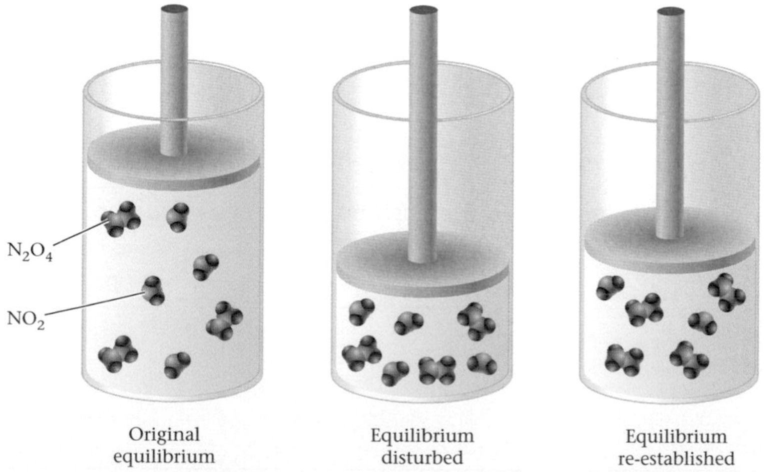

Figure 12.3
Effect of compression on the $N_2O_4(g) \rightleftharpoons 2NO_2(g)$ system at equilibrium. The immediate effect (middle cylinder) is to crowd the same number of moles of gas into a smaller volume and so increase the total pressure. This is partially compensated for by the conversion of some of the NO_2 to N_2O_4, thereby reducing the total number of moles of gas.

Table 12.6 Effect of Compression on the Equilibrium System $N_2O_4(g) \rightleftharpoons 2NO_2(g)$; $K = 11$ at 100°C

P_{tot} (atm)	n_{NO_2}	$n_{N_2O_4}$	n_{tot}
1.0	0.92	0.08	1.00
2.0	0.82	0.13	0.95
5.0	0.64	0.22	0.86
10.0	0.50	0.29	0.79

The analysis we have just gone through for the N_2O_4–NO_2 system can be applied to any equilibrium system involving gases—

- ***When the system is compressed, thereby increasing the total pressure, reaction takes place in the direction that decreases the total number of moles of gas.***
- ***When the system is expanded, thereby decreasing the total pressure, reaction takes place in the direction that increases the total number of moles of gas.***

The application of this principle to several different systems is shown in Table 12.7. In system 2, the number of moles of gas decreases from $\frac{3}{2}$ to 1 as the reaction goes to the right. Hence increasing the pressure causes the forward reaction to occur; a decrease in pressure has the reverse effect. Notice that it is the change in the number of moles of *gas* that determines which way the equilibrium shifts (system 4). When there is no change in the number of moles of gas (system 5), a change in pressure has no effect on the position of the equilibrium.

We should emphasize that in applying this principle it is important to realize that an "increase in pressure" means that the system is compressed; that is, the volume is decreased. Similarly, a "decrease in pressure" corresponds to expanding the system by increasing its volume. There are other ways in which pressure can be changed. One way is to add an unreactive gas such as helium at constant volume. This increases the total number of moles and hence the total pressure. It has no effect, however, on the position of the equilibrium, because it does not change the partial pressures of any of the gases taking part in the reaction. Remember that the partial pressure of a gas A is given by the expression

$$P_A = n_A RT/V \qquad (n_A = \text{no. of moles of A})$$

Adding a different gas at constant volume does not change any of the quantities on the right side of this equation, so P_A stays the same.

Change in Temperature

CENGAGENOW™
Click Coached Problems for a self-study module on the **effect of temperature on equilibrium.**

Le Châtelier's principle can be used to predict the effect of a change in temperature on the position of an equilibrium. In general, ***an increase in temperature causes the endothermic reaction to occur.*** This absorbs heat and so tends to reduce the temperature of the system, partially compensating for the original temperature increase.

Table 12.7 Effect of Pressure on the Position of Gaseous Equilibria

System	Δn_{gas}*	P_{tot} Increases	P_{tot} Decreases
1. $N_2O_4(g) \rightleftharpoons 2NO_2(g)$	+1	←	→
2. $SO_2(g) + \frac{1}{2}O_2(g) \rightleftharpoons SO_3(g)$	$-\frac{1}{2}$	→	←
3. $N_2(g) + 3H_2(g) \rightleftharpoons 2NH_3(g)$	−2	→	←
4. $C(s) + H_2O(g) \rightleftharpoons CO(g) + H_2(g)$	+1	←	→
5. $N_2(g) + O_2(g) \rightleftharpoons 2NO(g)$	0	0	0

*Δn_{gas} is the change in the number of moles of gas as the forward reaction occurs.

Applying this principle to the N_2O_4–NO_2 system,

$$N_2O_4(g) \rightleftharpoons 2NO_2(g) \qquad \Delta H° = +57.2 \text{ kJ}$$

it follows that raising the temperature causes the forward reaction to occur, because that reaction absorbs heat. This is confirmed by experiment (Figure 12.4). At higher temperatures, more NO_2 is produced, and the reddish-brown color of that gas becomes more intense.

For the synthesis of ammonia,

$$N_2(g) + 3H_2(g) \rightleftharpoons 2NH_3(g) \qquad \Delta H° = -92.2 \text{ kJ}$$

an increase in temperature shifts the equilibrium to the left; some ammonia decomposes to the elements. This reflects the fact that the reverse reaction is endothermic:

$$2NH_3(g) \longrightarrow N_2(g) + 3H_2(g) \qquad \Delta H° = +92.2 \text{ kJ}$$

As pointed out earlier, the equilibrium constant of a system changes with temperature. The form of the equation relating K to T is a familiar one, similar to the Clausius-Clapeyron equation (Chapter 9) and the Arrhenius equation (Chapter 11). This one is called the **van't Hoff equation,** honoring Jacobus van't Hoff (1852–1911), who was the first to use the equilibrium constant, K. Coincidentally, van't Hoff was a good friend of Arrhenius. The equation is

$$\ln \frac{K_2}{K_1} = \frac{\Delta H°}{R}\left[\frac{1}{T_1} - \frac{1}{T_2}\right] \qquad \textbf{(12.5)}$$

where K_2 and K_1 are the equilibrium constants at T_2 and T_1, respectively, $\Delta H°$ is the standard enthalpy change for the forward reaction, and R is the gas constant, 8.31 J/mol·K.

To illustrate how this equation is used, let us apply it to calculate the equilibrium constant at 100°C for the system

$$N_2(g) + 3H_2(g) \rightleftharpoons 2NH_3(g) \qquad \Delta H° = -92.2 \text{ kJ}$$

given that $K = 6 \times 10^5$ at 25°C. The relation is

$$\ln \frac{K \text{ at } 100°\text{C}}{6 \times 10^5} = \frac{-92{,}200 \text{ J/mol}}{8.31 \text{ J/mol} \cdot \text{K}}\left[\frac{1}{298 \text{ K}} - \frac{1}{373 \text{ K}}\right] = -7.5$$

Taking inverse logarithms,

$$\frac{K \text{ at } 100°\text{C}}{6 \times 10^5} = 6 \times 10^{-4}$$

$$K \text{ at } 100°\text{C} = 4 \times 10^2$$

Notice that the equilibrium constant becomes smaller as the temperature increases. In general—

- if the forward reaction is exothermic, as is the case here ($\Delta H° = -92.2$ kJ), K decreases as T increases.
- if the forward reaction is endothermic as in the decomposition of N_2O_4,

$$N_2O_4(g) \rightleftharpoons 2NO_2(g) \qquad \Delta H° = +57.2 \text{ kJ}$$

K increases as T increases. For this reaction K is 0.11 at 25°C and 11 at 100°C.

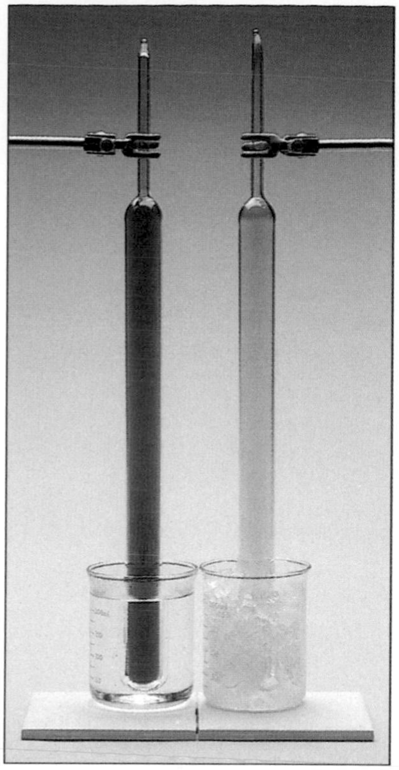

Marna G. Clarke

Figure 12.4
Effect of temperature on the N_2O_4–NO_2 system at equilibrium. At 0°C *(tube at right),* N_2O_4, which is colorless, predominates. At 50°C *(tube at left),* some of the N_2O_4 has disassociated to give the deep brown color of NO_2.

Example 12.8 Consider the following systems:

(a) $2CO(g) + O_2(g) \longrightarrow 2CO_2(g)$ $\quad \Delta H = -566$ kJ
(b) $H_2(g) + I_2(g) \longrightarrow 2HI(g)$ $\quad \Delta H = -2.7$ kJ
(c) $H_2(g) + I_2(s) \longrightarrow 2HI(g)$ $\quad \Delta H = +53.0$ kJ
(d) $I_2(g) \longrightarrow 2I(g)$ $\quad \Delta H = +36.2$ kJ

What will happen to the position of the equilibrium if the system is compressed (at constant temperature)? Heated at constant pressure?

Strategy An increase in pressure tends to drive the equilibrium in such a direction as to decrease the number of moles of *gas.* Endothermic reactions are favored by an increase in temperature.

SOLUTION

(a) increase in $P \longrightarrow$; increase in $T \longleftarrow$
(b) increase in P has no effect; increase in $T \longleftarrow$ (slightly!)
(c) increase in $P \longleftarrow$; increase in $T \longrightarrow$
(d) increase in $P \longleftarrow$; increase in $T \longrightarrow$

We should emphasize that of the three changes in conditions described in this section—

- adding or removing a gaseous species
- compressing or expanding the system
- changing the temperature

the only one that changes the value of the equilibrium constant is a change in temperature. In the other two cases, K remains constant.

CHEMISTRY Beyond the Classroom

An Industrial Application of Gaseous Equilibrium

A wide variety of materials, both pure substances and mixtures, are made by processes that involve one or more gas-phase reactions. Among these is one of the most important industrial chemicals, ammonia.

The process used to make this chemical applies many of the principles of chemical equilibrium, discussed in this chapter, and chemical kinetics (Chapter 11).

Haber Process for Ammonia

Combined ("fixed") nitrogen in the form of protein is essential to all forms of life. There is more than enough elementary nitrogen in the air, about 4×10^{18} kg, to meet all our needs. The problem is to convert the element to compounds that can be used by plants to make proteins. At room temperature and atmospheric pressure, N_2 does not react with any nonmetal. However, in 1908 in Germany, Fritz Haber (Figure A) showed that nitrogen does react with hydrogen at high temperatures and pressures to form ammonia in good yield:

$$N_2(g) + 3H_2(g) \rightleftharpoons 2NH_3(g) \qquad \Delta H° = -92.2 \text{ kJ}$$

The Haber process, represented by this equation, is now the main source of fixed nitrogen. Its feasibility depends on choosing conditions under which nitrogen and hydrogen react rapidly to give a high yield of ammonia. At 25°C and atmospheric pressure, the position of the equilibrium favors the formation of NH_3 ($K = 6 \times 10^5$). Unfortunately, however, the rate of reaction is virtually zero. Equilibrium is reached more rapidly by raising the temperature. However, because the synthesis of ammonia is exothermic, high temperatures reduce K and hence the yield of ammonia. High pressures, on the other hand, have a favorable effect on both the rate of the reaction and the position of the equilibrium (Table A).

Oesper Collection in the History of Chemistry/University of Cincinnati

Figure A
Fritz Haber (1868–1934).

The values of the equilibrium constant K listed in Table A are those obtained from data at low pressures, where the gases behave ideally. At higher pressures the mole percent of ammonia observed is generally larger than the calculated value. For example, at 400°C and 300 atm, the observed mole percent of NH_3 is 47; the calculated value is only 41.

The goal of Haber's research was to find a catalyst to synthesize ammonia at a reasonable rate without going to very high temperatures. These days two different catalysts are used. One consists of a mixture of iron, potassium oxide, K_2O, and aluminum oxide, Al_2O_3. The other, which uses finely divided ruthenium, Ru, metal on a graphite surface, is less susceptible to poisoning by impurities. Reaction takes place at 450°C and a pressure of 200 to 600 atm. The ammonia

Table A Effect of Temperature and Pressure on the Yield of Ammonia in the Haber Process ($P_{H_2} = 3P_{N_2}$)

		Mole Percent NH_3 in Equilibrium Mixture				
°C	K	10 atm	50 atm	100 atm	300 atm	1000 atm
200	0.30	51	74	82	90	98
300	3.7×10^{-3}	15	39	52	71	93
400	1.5×10^{-4}	4	15	25	47	80
500	1.4×10^{-5}	1	6	11	26	57
600	2.1×10^{-6}	0.5	2	5	14	31

formed is passed through a cooling chamber. Ammonia boils at −33°C, so it is condensed out as a liquid, separating it from unreacted nitrogen and hydrogen. The yield is typically less than 50%, so the reactants are recycled to produce more ammonia.

Fritz Haber

Haber had a distinguished scientific career. He received, among other honors, the 1918 Nobel Prize in chemistry. For more than 20 years, he was director of the prestigious Kaiser Wilhelm Institute for Physical Chemistry at Dahlem, Germany, a suburb of Berlin. He was forced to resign that position when Adolf Hitler came to power in 1933, presumably because of Haber's Jewish ancestry. A contributing factor may have been his comment after listening to a radio broadcast of one of Hitler's hysterical harangues. When asked what he thought of it, Haber replied, "Give me a gun so I can shoot him."

Haber, like all of us, suffered disappointment and tragedy in his life. In the years after World War I, he devised a scheme to pay Germany's war debts by extracting gold from seawater. The project, which occupied Haber for several years, was a total failure because the concentration of gold turned out to be only about one thousandth of the literature value.

During World War I, Haber was in charge of the German poison gas program. In April of 1915, the Germans used chlorine for the first time on the Western front, causing 5000 fatalities. Haber's wife, Clara, was aghast; she pleaded with her husband to forsake poison gas. When he adamantly refused to do so, she committed suicide.

On a lighter note, there is an amusing anecdote told by the author Morris Goran (*The Story of Fritz Haber,* 1967). It seems that in a PhD examination, Haber asked the candidate how iodine was prepared. The student made a wild guess that it was obtained from a tree (it isn't). Haber played along with him, asking where the iodine tree grew, what it looked like, and, finally, when it bloomed. "In the fall," was the answer. Haber smiled, put his arm around the student, and said, "Well, my friend, I'll see you again when the iodine blossoms appear once more."

Chapter Highlights

Key Concepts

1. Relate the expression for K to the corresponding chemical equation.
   (Examples 12.1, 12.2; Problems 5–14) ■ Questions and Problems assignable in OWL: 6, 8, 12, 14
2. Calculate K, knowing
   - appropriate K's for other reactions.
     (Example 12.1; Problems 15–20) ■ 16, 19
   - all the equilibrium partial pressures.
     (Example 12.3; Problems 21–24) ■ 23
   - all the original and one equilibrium partial pressure.
     (Example 12.4; Problems 25, 26) ■ 25, 62, 82
3. Use the value of K to determine
   - the direction of reaction.
     (Example 12.5; Problems 27–32) ■ 27
   - equilibrium partial pressures of all species.
     (Examples 12.6, 12.7; Problems 33–46) ■ 34, 38, 40, 44
4. Use Le Châtelier's principle to predict what will happen when the conditions on an equilibrium system are changed.
   (Examples 12.7, 12.8; Problems 47–60) ■ 48, 50, 52, 56, 74

Select end of chapter Questions and Problems may be assigned in OWL and are cross-referenced in the Key Concepts list.

CENGAGENOW™

Sign in at **academic.cengage.com/now** to:

- Check your readiness for an exam by taking the Pre-Test and exploring the self-study modules recommended in your Personalized Study plan
- For quick review, download Go Chemistry mini-lecture flashcard modules (or purchase them at **www.ichapters.com**)

Key Equations

Expression for K	$aA(g) + bB(g) \rightleftharpoons cC(g) + dD(g)$ (Section 12.2)
	$K = \dfrac{(P_C)^c \times (P_D)^d}{(P_A)^a \times (P_B)^b}$ (Section 12.2)
Coefficient rule	$K' = K^n$ (Section 12.2)
Reciprocal rule	$K'' = 1/K$ (Section 12.2)
Multiple equilibrium	$K_3 = K_1 \times K_2$ (Section 12.2)
van't Hoff equation	$\ln \dfrac{K_2}{K_1} = \dfrac{\Delta H^\circ}{R}\left[\dfrac{1}{T_1} - \dfrac{1}{T_2}\right]$ (Section 12.5)

Key Terms

equilibrium constant, K

Le Châtelier's principle

partial pressure

reaction quotient, Q

Summary Problem

Carbon monoxide and hydrogen can react under different conditions to give different products. One system produces methyl alcohol, $CH_3OH(g)$, when CO and H_2 react in the presence of a suitable catalyst.

(a) Write the equilibrium expression for the formation of methanol.

(b) At 227°C, after the reaction has reached equilibrium, the partial pressures of CO, H_2, and CH_3OH are 0.702 atm, 1.75 atm, and 0.0134 atm, respectively. Calculate K for the reaction at 227°C.

(c) What is K for the decomposition of a half mole of CH_3OH to CO and H_2 at the same temperature?

(d) Initially, a 10.00-L flask at 227°C contains only CH_3OH. After equilibrium is established, the partial pressure of CH_3OH is 0.0300 atm. What are the equilibrium partial pressures of hydrogen and carbon monoxide gases at that temperature?

(e) Calculate the equilibrium constant for the reaction at 50°C. (ΔH_f° for $CH_3OH(g) = -201.2$ kJ/mol)

(f) In which direction will this system shift if at equilibrium

- **(1)** the gas is compressed?
- **(2)** argon gas is added?
- **(3)** the temperature is increased?
- **(4)** CH_3OH is added?

(g) Under other conditions, carbon monoxide reacts with hydrogen gas to give methane and steam.

$$CO(g) + 3H_2(g) \rightleftharpoons CH_4(g) + H_2O(g)$$

At 654°C, K for this reaction is 2.57. At this temperature, a reaction flask has CH_4 and H_2O gases both at a partial pressure of 1.000 atm. What are the partial pressures of all the gases when equilibrium is established?

Answers

(a) $K = \dfrac{P_{CH_3OH}}{P_{CO} \times (P_{H_2})^2}$

(b) 6.23×10^{-3}

(c) 12.7

(d) $P_{CO} = 1.06$ atm; $P_{H_2} = 2.12$ atm

(e) 976

(f) (1) $\longrightarrow$; (2) no change; (3) $\longleftarrow$; (4) $\longleftarrow$

(g) $P_{CO} = 0.292$ atm; $P_{H_2} = 0.876$ atm; $P_{CH_4} = P_{H_2O} = 0.708$ atm

Questions and Problems

Blue-numbered questions have answers in Appendix 6 and fully-worked solutions in the *Student Solutions Manual.*

■ denotes questions assignable in OWL.

WEB indicates that the solution is available on this book's companion website.

Establishment of Equilibrium

1. The following data are for the system

$$A(g) \rightleftharpoons 2B(g)$$

Time (s)	0	20	40	60	80	100
P_A (atm)	1.00	0.83	0.72	0.65	0.62	0.62
P_B (atm)	0.00	0.34	0.56	0.70	0.76	0.76

(a) How long does it take the system to reach equilibrium?
(b) How does the rate of the forward reaction compare with the rate of the reverse reaction after 30 s? After 90 s?

2. The following data are for the system

$$A(g) \rightleftharpoons 2B(g)$$

Time (s)	0	30	45	60	75	90
P_A (atm)	0.500	0.390	0.360	0.340	0.325	0.325
P_B (atm)	0.000	0.220	0.280	0.320	0.350	0.350

(a) How long does it take the system to reach equilibrium?
(b) How does the rate of the forward reaction compare with the rate of the reverse reaction after 45 s? After 90 s?

3. Complete the table below for the reaction:

$$3A(g) + 2B(g) \rightleftharpoons C(g)$$

Time (s)	0	10	20	30	40	50	60
P_A (atm)	2.450	2.000	______	______	1.100	______	0.950
P_B (atm)	1.500	______	______	0.750	______	______	______
P_C (atm)	0.000	______	0.275	______	______	0.500	______

4. **WEB** Complete the table below for the reaction:

$$3A(g) + B(g) \rightleftharpoons 2C(g)$$

Time (min)	0	1	2	3	4	5	6
P_A (atm)	1.000	0.778	______	______	______	0.325	______
P_B (atm)	0.400	______	0.260	______	0.185	______	0.175
P_C (atm)	0.000	______	______	0.390	______	______	______

Equilibrium Constant Expression

5. Write equilibrium constant (*K*) expressions for the following reactions:
   (a) $I_2(g) + 5F_2(g) \rightleftharpoons 2IF_5(g)$
   (b) $CO(g) + 2H_2(g) \rightleftharpoons CH_3OH(l)$
   (c) $2H_2S + 3O_2(g) \rightleftharpoons 2H_2O(l) + 2SO_2(g)$
   (d) $SnO_2(s) + 2H_2(g) \rightleftharpoons Sn(s) + 2H_2O(l)$

6. ■ **WEB** Write equilibrium constant (*K*) expressions for the following reactions:
   (a) $CH_4(g) + H_2O(l) \rightleftharpoons CO(g) + 3H_2(g)$
   (b) $4NH_3(g) + 5O_2(g) \rightleftharpoons 4NO(g) + 6H_2O(g)$
   (c) $BaCO_3(s) \rightleftharpoons BaO(s) + CO_2(g)$
   (d) $NH_3(g) + HCl(g) \rightleftharpoons NH_4Cl(s)$

7. Write equilibrium constant expressions (*K*) for the following reactions:
   (a) $2NO_3^-(aq) + 8H^+(aq) + 3Cu(s) \rightleftharpoons 2NO(g) + 3Cu^{2+}(aq) + 4H_2O(l)$
   (b) $2PbS(s) + 3O_2(g) \rightleftharpoons 2PbO(s) + 2SO_2(g)$
   (c) $Ca^{2+}(aq) + CO_3^{2-}(aq) \rightleftharpoons CaCO_3(s)$

8. ■ Write equilibrium constant expressions (*K*) for the following reactions:
   (a) $Ni(s) + 4CO(g) \rightleftharpoons Ni(CO)_4(g)$
   (b) $HF(aq) \rightleftharpoons H^+(aq) + F^-(aq)$
   (c) $Cl_2(g) + 2Br^-(aq) \rightleftharpoons Br_2(l) + 2Cl^-(aq)$

9. Given the following descriptions of reversible reactions, write a balanced equation (simplest whole-number coefficients) and the equilibrium constant expression (*K*) for each.
   (a) Nitrogen gas reacts with solid sodium carbonate and solid carbon to produce carbon monoxide gas and solid sodium cyanide.
   (b) Solid magnesium nitride reacts with water vapor to form magnesium hydroxide solid and ammonia gas.
   (c) Ammonium ion in aqueous solution reacts with a strong base at 25°C, giving aqueous ammonia and water.

10. Given the following descriptions of reversible reactions, write a balanced net ionic equation (simplest whole-number coefficients) and the equilibrium constant expression (*K*) for each.
   (a) Liquid acetone (C_3H_6O) is in equilibrium with its vapor.
   (b) Hydrogen gas reduces nitrogen dioxide gas to form ammonia and steam.

■ in OWL Blue-numbered questions answered in Appendix 6 **WEB** Solution is available on companion website

(c) Hydrogen sulfide gas (H_2S) bubbled into an aqueous solution of lead(II) ions produces lead sulfide precipitate and hydrogen ions.

11. Write a chemical equation for an equilibrium system that would lead to the following expressions (a–d) for *K*.

(a) $K = \dfrac{(P_{CO_2})^3 (P_{H_2O})^4}{(P_{C_3H_8}) (P_{O_2})^5}$ (b) $K = \dfrac{P_{C_{10}H_{12}}}{(P_{C_5H_6})^2}$

(c) $K = \dfrac{[PO_4^{3-}][H^+]^3}{[H_3PO_4]}$ (d) $K = \dfrac{(P_{CO_2})(P_{H_2O})}{[CO_3^{2-}][H^+]^2}$

12. ■ Write a chemical equation for an equilibrium system that would lead to the following expressions (a–d) for *K*.

(a) $K = \dfrac{(P_{H_2S})^2 (P_{O_2})^3}{(P_{SO_2})^2 (P_{H_2O})^2}$ (b) $K = \dfrac{(P_{F_2})^{1/2} (P_{I_2})^{1/2}}{P_{IF}}$

(c) $K = \dfrac{[Cl^-]^2}{(P_{Cl_2})[Br^-]^2}$ (d) $K = \dfrac{(P_{NO})^2(P_{H_2O})^4[Cu^{2+}]^3}{[NO_3^-]^2[H^+]^8}$

13. Consider the following reaction at 250°C:

$$A(s) + 2B(g) \rightleftharpoons C(s) + 2D(g)$$

(a) Write an equilibrium constant expression for the reaction. Call the equilibrium constant K_1.

(b) Write an equilibrium constant expression for the formation of one mole of B(*g*) and call the equilibrium constant K_2.

(c) Relate K_1 and K_2.

14. ■ WEB Consider the following reaction at 122°C:

$$2SO_3(g) \rightleftharpoons 2SO_2(g) + O_2(g)$$

(a) Write an equilibrium constant expression for the reaction and call the constant K_1.

(b) Write an equilibrium constant expression for the decomposition of one mole of SO_3 to SO_2 and O_2 and call the constant K_2.

(c) Relate K_1 and K_2.

Determination of *K*

15. At 25°C, $K = 2.2 \times 10^{-3}$ for the reaction

$$ICl(g) \rightleftharpoons \tfrac{1}{2}I_2(g) + \tfrac{1}{2}Cl_2(g)$$

Calculate *K* at 25°C for

(a) the decomposition of ICl into one mole of iodine and chlorine.

(b) the formation of two moles of ICl(*g*).

16. ■ At 627°C, $K = 0.76$ for the reaction

$$2SO_2(g) + O_2(g) \rightleftharpoons 2SO_3(g)$$

Calculate *K* at 627°C for

(a) the synthesis of one mole of sulfur trioxide gas.

(b) the decomposition of two moles of SO_3.

17. Given the following reactions and their equilibrium constants,

$$H_2O(g) + CO(g) \rightleftharpoons H_2(g) + CO_2(g) \qquad K = 1.6$$

$$FeO(s) + CO(g) \rightleftharpoons Fe(s) + CO_2(g) \qquad K = 0.67$$

calculate *K* for the reaction

$$Fe(s) + H_2O(g) \rightleftharpoons FeO(s) + H_2(g)$$

18. Given the following reactions and their equilibrium constants,

$$C(s) + CO_2(g) \rightleftharpoons 2CO(g) \qquad K = 2.4 \times 10^{-9}$$

$$COCl_2(g) \rightleftharpoons CO(g) + Cl_2(g) \qquad K = 8.8 \times 10^{-13}$$

calculate *K* for the reaction

$$C(s) + CO_2(g) + 2Cl_2(g) \rightleftharpoons 2COCl_2(g)$$

19. ■ Given the following data at a certain temperature,

$$2N_2(g) + O_2(g) \rightleftharpoons 2N_2O(g) \qquad K = 1.2 \times 10^{-35}$$

$$N_2O_4(g) \rightleftharpoons 2NO_2(g) \qquad K = 4.6 \times 10^{-3}$$

$$\tfrac{1}{2}N_2(g) + O_2(g) \rightleftharpoons NO_2(g) \qquad K = 4.1 \times 10^{-9}$$

calculate *K* for the reaction between one mole of dinitrogen oxide gas and oxygen gas to give dinitrogen tetroxide gas.

20. Given the following data at 25°C,

$$2NO(g) \rightleftharpoons N_2(g) + O_2(g) \qquad K = 1 \times 10^{-30}$$

$$2NO(g) + Br_2(g) \rightleftharpoons 2NOBr(g) \qquad K = 8 \times 10^1$$

calculate *K* for the formation of one mole of NOBr from its elements in the gaseous state at 25°C.

21. When carbon monoxide reacts with hydrogen gas, methane and steam are formed.

$$CO(g) + 3H_2(g) \rightleftharpoons CH_4(g) + H_2O(g)$$

At 1127°C, analysis at equilibrium shows that $P_{CO} = 0.921$ atm, $P_{H_2} = 1.21$ atm, $P_{CH_4} = 0.0391$ atm, and $P_{H_2O} = 0.0124$ atm. What is the equilibrium constant, *K*, for the reaction at 1127°C?

22. Calculate *K* for the formation of methyl alcohol at 100°C:

$$CO(g) + 2H_2(g) \rightleftharpoons CH_3OH(g)$$

given that at equilibrium, the partial pressures of the gases are $P_{CO} = 0.814$ atm, $P_{H_2} = 0.274$ atm, and $P_{CH_3OH} = 0.0512$ atm.

23. ■ Ammonium carbamate solid ($NH_4CO_2NH_2$) decomposes at 313 K into ammonia and carbon dioxide gases. At equilibrium, analysis shows that there are 0.0451 atm of CO_2, 0.0961 atm of ammonia, and 0.159 g of ammonium carbamate.

(a) Write a balanced equation for the decomposition of one mole of $NH_4CO_2NH_2$.

(b) Calculate *K* at 313 K.

24. WEB At 1123 K, methane and hydrogen sulfide gases react to form carbon disulfide and hydrogen gases. At equilibrium the concentrations of methane, hydrogen sulfide, carbon disulfide, and hydrogen gas are 0.00142 *M*, 6.14×10^{-4} *M*, 0.00266 *M*, and 0.00943 *M*, respectively.

(a) Write a balanced equation for the formation of one mole of carbon disulfide gas.

(b) Calculate *K* for the reaction at 1123 K.

25. ■ Consider the decomposition of ammonium hydrogen sulfide:

$$NH_4HS(s) \rightleftharpoons NH_3(g) + H_2S(g)$$

In a sealed flask at 25°C are 10.0 g of NH_4HS, ammonia with a partial pressure of 0.692 atm, and H_2S with a partial pressure of 0.0532 atm. When equilibrium is established, it is found that the partial pressure of ammonia has increased by 12.4%. Calculate *K* for the decomposition of NH_4HS at 25°C.

26. A sealed flask has 0.541 atm of SO_3 at 1000 K. The following equilibrium is established.

$$2SO_3(g) \rightleftharpoons 2SO_2(g) + O_2(g)$$

At equilibrium, the partial pressure of oxygen is measured to be 0.216 atm. Calculate *K* for the decomposition of SO_3 at 1000 K.

K; Direction of the Reaction

27. ■ A gaseous reaction mixture contains 0.30 atm SO_2, 0.16 atm Cl_2, and 0.50 atm SO_2Cl_2 in a 2.0-L container. $K = 0.011$ for the equilibrium system

$$SO_2Cl_2(g) \rightleftharpoons SO_2(g) + Cl_2(g)$$

(a) Is the system at equilibrium? Explain.

(b) If it is not at equilibrium, in which direction will the system move to reach equilibrium?

■ in OWL Blue-numbered questions answered in Appendix 6 WEB Solution is available on companion website

28. For the system

$$PCl_5(g) \rightleftharpoons PCl_3(g) + Cl_2(g)$$

K is 26 at 300°C. In a 5.0-L flask, a gaseous mixture consists of all three gases with partial pressures as follows: $P_{PCl_5} = 0.012$ atm, $P_{Cl_2} = 0.45$ atm, $P_{PCl_3} = 0.90$ atm.

(a) Is the mixture at equilibrium? Explain.

(b) If it is not at equilibrium, which way will the system shift to establish equilibrium?

29. The reversible reaction between hydrogen chloride gas and one mole of oxygen gas produces steam and chlorine gas:

$$4HCl(g) + O_2(g) \rightleftharpoons 2Cl_2(g) + 2H_2O(g) \qquad K = 0.79$$

Predict the direction in which the system will move to reach equilibrium if one starts with

(a) $P_{H_2O} = P_{HCl} = P_{O_2} = 0.20$ atm

(b) $P_{HCl} = 0.30$ atm, $P_{H_2O} = 0.35$ atm, $P_{Cl_2} = 0.2$ atm, $P_{O_2} = 0.15$ atm

30. For the reaction

$$2NO_2(g) \rightleftharpoons 2NO(g) + O_2(g)$$

K at a certain temperature is 0.50. Predict the direction in which the system will move to reach equilibrium if one starts with

(a) $P_{O_2} = P_{NO} = P_{NO_2} = 0.10$ atm

(b) $P_{NO_2} = 0.0848$ atm, $P_{O_2} = 0.0116$ atm

(c) $P_{NO_2} = 0.20$ atm, $P_{O_2} = 0.010$ atm, $P_{NO} = 0.040$ atm

31. A compound, X, decomposes at 131°C according to the following equation:

$$2X(g) \rightleftharpoons A(g) + 3C(g) \qquad K = 1.1 \times 10^{-3}$$

If a flask initially contains X, A, and C, all at partial pressures of 0.250 atm, in which direction will the reaction proceed?

32. Consider the following reaction at 32°C:

$$2R(s) + 4B(g) \rightleftharpoons X(l) + 3Y(g) \qquad K = 39$$

A 25.0-L sample at 37°C initially contains 0.600 moles of R, B, X, and Y. In which direction will the reaction proceed?

K; Extent of the Reaction

33. Consider the reaction between ammonia and oxygen.

$$4NH_3(g) + 3O_2(g) \rightleftharpoons 2N_2(g) + 6H_2O(g)$$

At a certain temperature, $K = 0.0049$. Calculate the equilibrium partial pressure of ammonia if $P_{N_2} = 0.213$ atm, $P_{H_2O} = 0.883$ atm, and $P_{O_2} = 0.255$ atm at equilibrium.

34. ■ At 500°C, K for the formation of ammonia from nitrogen and hydrogen gases is 1.5×10^{-5}.

$$N_2(g) + 3H_2(g) \rightleftharpoons 2NH_3(g)$$

Calculate the equilibrium partial pressure of hydrogen if the equilibrium partial pressures of ammonia and nitrogen are 0.015 atm and 1.2 atm, respectively.

35. At a certain temperature, K is 1.3×10^5 for the reaction

$$2H_2(g) + S_2(g) \rightleftharpoons 2H_2S(g)$$

What is the equilibrium pressure of hydrogen sulfide if those of hydrogen and sulfur gases are 0.103 atm and 0.417 atm, respectively?

36. At a certain temperature, K is 0.040 for the decomposition of two moles of bromine chloride gas (BrCl) to its elements. An equilibrium mixture at this temperature contains bromine and chlorine gases at equal partial pressures of 0.0493 atm. What is the equilibrium partial pressure of bromine chloride?

37. For the reaction

$$N_2(g) + 2H_2O(g) \rightleftharpoons 2NO(g) + 2H_2(g)$$

K is 1.54×10^{-3}. When equilibrium is established, the partial pressure of nitrogen is 0.168 atm, and that of NO is 0.225 atm. The total pressure of the system at equilibrium is 1.87 atm. What are the equilibrium partial pressures of hydrogen and steam?

38. ■ **WEB** Nitrogen dioxide can decompose to nitrogen oxide and oxygen.

$$2NO_2(g) \rightleftharpoons 2NO(g) + O_2(g)$$

K is 0.87 at a certain temperature. A 5.0-L flask at equilibrium is determined to have a total pressure of 1.25 atm and oxygen to have a partial pressure of 0.515 atm. Calculate P_{NO} and P_{NO_2} at equilibrium.

39. Carbonyl fluoride, COF_2, is an important intermediate for organic fluorine compounds. It can be prepared by the following reaction:

$$CO_2(g) + CF_4(g) \rightleftharpoons 2COF_2(g)$$

At 1000°C, K for this reaction is 0.50. What are the partial pressures of all the gases at equilibrium when the initial partial pressures of CO_2 and CF_4 are 0.713 atm?

40. ■ Consider the equilibrium

$$N_2(g) + O_2(g) \rightleftharpoons 2NO(g)$$

At a certain temperature, the equilibrium constant for the reaction is 0.0255. What are the partial pressures of all gases at equilibrium if the initial partial pressure of the gases (both reactants and products) is 0.300 atm?

41. The reaction

$$CO(g) + H_2O(g) \rightleftharpoons H_2(g) + CO_2(g)$$

has an equilibrium constant of 1.30 at 650°C. Carbon monoxide and steam both have initial partial pressures of 0.485 atm, while hydrogen and carbon dioxide start with partial pressures of 0.159 atm.

(a) Calculate the partial pressure of each gas at equilibrium.

(b) Compare the total pressure initially with the total pressure at equilibrium. Would that relation be true of all gaseous systems?

42. At 460°C, the reaction

$$SO_2(g) + NO_2(g) \rightleftharpoons NO(g) + SO_3(g)$$

has $K = 84.7$. All gases are at an initial pressure of 1.25 atm.

(a) Calculate the partial pressure of each gas at equilibrium.

(b) Compare the total pressure initially with the total pressure at equilibrium. Would that relation be true of all gaseous systems?

43. Solid ammonium carbamate, $NH_4CO_2NH_2$, decomposes at 25°C to ammonia and carbon dioxide.

$$NH_4CO_2NH_2(s) \rightleftharpoons 2NH_3(g) + CO_2(g)$$

The equilibrium constant for the decomposition at 25°C is 2.3×10^{-4}. At 25°C, 7.50 g of $NH_4CO_2NH_2$ is sealed in a 10.0-L flask and allowed to decompose.

(a) What is the total pressure in the flask when equilibrium is established?

(b) What percentage of $NH_4CO_2NH_2$ decomposed?

(c) Can you state from the data calculated that the decomposition took place slowly?

44. ■ Solid ammonium iodide decomposes to ammonia and hydrogen iodide gases at sufficiently high temperatures.

$$NH_4I(s) \rightleftharpoons NH_3(g) + HI(g)$$

The equilibrium constant for the decomposition at 673 K is 0.215. Fifteen grams of ammonium iodide are sealed in a 5.0-L flask and heated to 673 K.

(a) What is the total pressure in the flask at equilibrium?

(b) How much ammonium iodide decomposes?

■ in OWL Blue-numbered questions answered in Appendix 6 **WEB** Solution is available on companion website

45. Hydrogen cyanide, a highly toxic gas, can decompose to cyanogen and hydrogen gases,

$$2HCN(g) \rightleftharpoons C_2N_2(g) + H_2(g)$$

At a certain temperature, K for this decomposition is 0.17. What are the partial pressures of all gases at equilibrium if initially the partial pressures are $P_{C_2N_2} = P_{H_2} = 0.32$ atm, $P_{HCN} = 0.45$ atm?

46. At 800 K, hydrogen iodide can decompose into hydrogen and iodine gases.

$$2HI(g) \rightleftharpoons I_2(g) + H_2(g)$$

At this temperature, $K = 0.0169$. What are the partial pressures at equilibrium of the hydrogen and iodine if initially a sealed flask at 800 K contains only HI at a pressure of 0.200 atm?

Changing Reaction Conditions; Le Châtelier's Principle

47. For the following reactions, predict whether the pressure of the reactants or products increases or remains the same when the volume of the reaction vessel is increased.

(a) $H_2O(l) \rightleftharpoons H_2O(g)$
(b) $N_2(g) + 3H_2(g) \rightleftharpoons 2NH_3(g)$
(c) $C_2H_4(g) + H_2O(g) \rightleftharpoons C_2H_5OH(g)$

48. ■ Follow the directions of Question 47 for the following reactions.

(a) $2H_2O_2(l) \rightleftharpoons O_2(g) + 2H_2O(l)$
(b) $2CH_4(g) \rightleftharpoons C_2H_2(g) + 3H_2(g)$
(c) $Br_2(g) + H_2(g) \rightleftharpoons 2HBr(g)$

49. Consider the system

$$SO_3(g) \rightleftharpoons SO_2(g) + \tfrac{1}{2}O_2(g) \qquad \Delta H = 98.9 \text{ kJ}$$

(a) Predict whether the forward or reverse reaction will occur when the equilibrium is disturbed by
(1) adding oxygen gas.
(2) compressing the system at constant temperature.
(3) adding argon gas.
(4) removing $SO_2(g)$.
(5) decreasing the temperature.

(b) Which of the above factors will increase the value of K? Which will decrease it?

50. ■ Consider the system

$$4NH_3(g) + 3O_2(g) \rightleftharpoons 2N_2(g) + 6H_2O(l) \qquad \Delta H = -1530.4 \text{ kJ}$$

(a) How will the amount of ammonia at equilibrium be affected by
(1) removing $O_2(g)$?
(2) adding $N_2(g)$?
(3) adding water?
(4) expanding the container at constant pressure?
(5) increasing the temperature?

(b) Which of the above factors will increase the value of K? Which will decrease it?

51. Predict the direction in which each of the following equilibria will shift if the pressure on the system is increased by compression.

(a) $H_2O(g) + C(s) \rightleftharpoons CO(g) + H_2(g)$
(b) $SbCl_5(g) \rightleftharpoons SbCl_3(g) + Cl_2(g)$
(c) $CO(g) + H_2O(g) \rightleftharpoons CO_2(g) + H_2(g)$

52. ■ Predict the direction in which each of the following equilibria will shift if the pressure on the system is decreased by expansion.

(a) $Ni(s) + 4CO(g) \rightleftharpoons Ni(CO)_4(g)$
(b) $ClF_5(g) \rightleftharpoons ClF_3(g) + F_2(g)$
(c) $HBr(g) \rightleftharpoons \tfrac{1}{2}H_2(g) + \tfrac{1}{2}Br_2(g)$

53. At a certain temperature, nitrogen and oxygen gases combine to form nitrogen oxide gas.

$$N_2(g) + O_2(g) \rightleftharpoons 2NO(g)$$

When equilibrium is established, the partial pressures of the gases are: $P_{N_2} =$ 1.2 atm, $P_{O_2} = 0.80$ atm, $P_{NO} = 0.022$ atm.

(a) Calculate K at the temperature of the reaction.
(b) After equilibrium is reached, more oxygen is added to make its partial pressure 1.2 atm. Calculate the partial pressure of all gases when equilibrium is reestablished.

54. A 1.0-L reaction vessel at 90°C contains 8.00 g of sulfur, hydrogen, and hydrogen sulfide gases with partial pressures of 6.0 atm and 0.40 atm, respectively, at equilibrium:

$$H_2(g) + S(s) \rightleftharpoons H_2S(g)$$

(a) Calculate K for the reaction at equilibrium.
(b) The mass of sulfur is increased to 10.0 grams. What are the partial pressures of H_2 and H_2S when equilibrium is reestablished?
(c) The pressure of H_2S is increased to 1.0 atm. What are the partial pressures of H_2 and H_2S when equilibrium is reestablished?

55. Iodine chloride decomposes at high temperatures to iodine and chlorine gases.

$$2ICl(g) \rightleftharpoons I_2(g) + Cl_2(g)$$

Equilibrium is established at a certain temperature when the partial pressures of ICl, I_2, and Cl_2 are (in atm) 0.43, 0.16, and 0.27, respectively.

(a) Calculate K.
(b) If enough iodine condenses to decrease its partial pressure to 0.10 atm, in which direction will the reaction proceed? What is the partial pressure of iodine when equilibrium is re-established?

56. ■ Carbonylbromide ($COBr_2$) can be formed by combining carbon monoxide and bromine gas.

$$CO(g) + Br_2(g) \rightleftharpoons COBr_2(g)$$

When equilibrium is established at 346 K, the partial pressures (in atm) of $COBr_2$, CO, and Br_2 are 0.12, 1.00, and 0.65, respectively.

(a) What is K at 346 K?
(b) Enough bromine condenses to decrease its partial pressure to 0.50 atm. What are the equilibrium partial pressures of all gases after equilibrium is re-established?

57. For the system

$$H_2(g) + I_2(g) \rightleftharpoons 2HI(g) \qquad \Delta H = -9.4 \text{ kJ}$$

$K = 62.5$ at 800 K. What is the equilibrium constant at 333°C?

58. For the system

$$2SO_3(g) \rightleftharpoons 2SO_2(g) + O_2(g)$$

$K = 1.32$ at 627°C. What is the equilibrium constant at 555°C?

59. For a certain reaction, $\Delta H°$ is +33 kJ. What is the ratio of the equilibrium constant at 400 K to that at 200 K?

60. What is the value of $\Delta H°$ for a reaction if K at 50°C is 40% of K at 37°C?

Unclassified

61. Hemoglobin (Hb) binds to both oxygen and carbon monoxide. When the carbon monoxide replaces the oxygen in an organism, the following reaction occurs:

$$HbO_2(aq) + CO(g) \rightleftharpoons HbCO(aq) + O_2(g)$$

At 37°C, K is about 200. When equal concentrations of HbO_2 and HbCO are present, the effect of CO inhalation is fatal. Assuming $P_{O_2} = 0.21$ atm, what is P_{CO} when $[HbO_2] = [HbCO]$?

■ in OWL Blue-numbered questions answered in Appendix 6 WEB Solution is available on companion website

62. ■ Mustard gas, used in chemical warfare in World War I, has been found to be an effective agent in the chemotherapy of Hodgkin's disease. It can be produced according to the following reaction:

$$SCl_2(g) + 2C_2H_4(g) \rightleftharpoons S(CH_2CH_2Cl)_2(g)$$

An evacuated five-liter flask at 20.0°C is filled with 0.258 mol SCl_2 and 0.592 mol C_2H_4. After equilibrium is established, 0.0349 mol mustard gas is present.

(a) What is the partial pressure of each gas at equilibrium?

(b) What is K at 20.0°C?

63. At 1800 K, oxygen dissociates into gaseous atoms:

$$O_2(g) \rightleftharpoons 2O(g)$$

K for the system is 1.7×10^{-8}. If one mole of oxygen molecules is placed in a 5.0-L flask and heated to 1800 K, what percentage by mass of the oxygen dissociates? How many O atoms are in the flask?

64. For the decomposition of $CaCO_3$ at 900°C, $K = 1.04$.

$$CaCO_3(s) \rightleftharpoons CaO(s) + O_2(g)$$

Find the smallest mass of $CaCO_3$ needed to reach equilibrium in a 5.00-L vessel at 900°C.

65. Isopropyl alcohol is the main ingredient in rubbing alcohol. It can decompose into acetone (the main ingredient in nail polish remover) and hydrogen gas according to the following reaction:

$$C_3H_7OH(g) \rightleftharpoons C_2H_6CO(g) + H_2(g)$$

At 180°C, the equilibrium constant for the decomposition is 0.45. If 20.0 mL ($d = 0.785$ g/mL) of isopropyl alcohol is placed in a 5.00-L vessel and heated to 180°C, what percentage remains undissociated at equilibrium?

66. Consider the equilibrium

$$C(s) + CO_2(g) \rightleftharpoons 2CO(g)$$

When this system is at equilibrium at 700°C in a 2.0-L container, 0.10 mol CO, 0.20 mol CO_2, and 0.40 mol C are present. When the system is cooled to 600°C, an additional 0.040 mol C(s) forms. Calculate K at 700°C and again at 600°C.

Conceptual Problems

67. Consider the following graph representing the progression of a reaction with time.

$$A(g) \rightleftharpoons 2B(g)$$

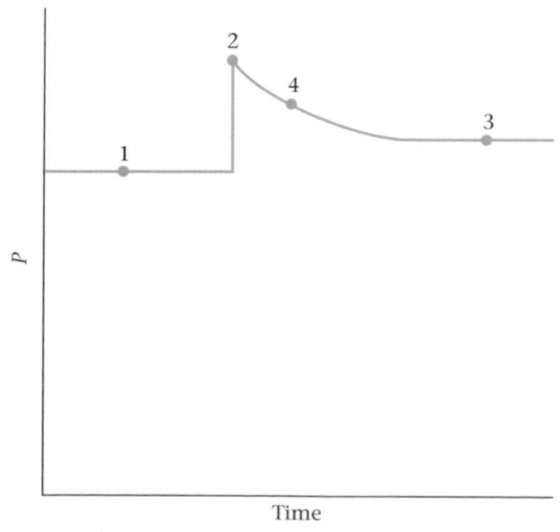

(a) What is the relationship between Q and K at Points 1, 3, and 4?

(b) What caused the disturbance at Point 2?

(c) Draw a similar graph for the same reaction, but increase the pressure in A.

68. The following data apply to the *unbalanced* equation

$$A(g) \rightleftharpoons B(g)$$

Time (s)	0	50	100	150	200	250
P_A (atm)	2.00	1.25	0.95	0.80	0.71	0.68
P_B (atm)	0.10	0.60	0.80	0.90	0.96	0.98

(a) On the basis of the data, balance the equation (simplest whole-number coefficients).

(b) Has the system reached equilibrium? Explain.

69. The following data are for the system

$$A(g) \rightleftharpoons 2B(g)$$

Time (s)	0	20	40	60	80	100
P_A (atm)	1.00	0.83	0.72	0.65	0.62	0.62
P_B (atm)	0.00	0.34	0.56	0.70	0.76	0.76

Prepare a graph of P_A and P_B versus time and use it to answer the following questions:

(a) Estimate P_A and P_B after 30 s.

(b) Estimate P_A after 150 s.

(c) Estimate P_B when $P_A = 0.700$ atm.

70. For the reaction

$$C(s) + CO_2(g) \rightleftharpoons 2CO(g)$$

$K = 168$ at 1273 K. If one starts with 0.3 atm of CO_2 and 12.0 g of C at 1273 K, will the equilibrium mixture contain

(a) mostly CO_2?

(b) mostly CO?

(c) roughly equal amounts of CO_2 and CO?

(d) only C?

71. Consider the system

$$A(g) + 2B(g) + C(s) \rightleftharpoons 2D(g)$$

at 25°C. At zero time, only A, B, and C are present. The reaction reaches equilibrium 10 min after the reaction is initiated. Partial pressures of A, B, and D are written as P_A, P_B, and P_D.

Answer the questions below, using **LT** (for *is less than*), **GT** (for *is greater than*), **EQ** (for *is equal to*), or **MI** (for *more information required*).

(a) P_D at 11 min ________ P_D at 12 min.

(b) P_A at 5 min ________ P_A at 7 min.

(c) K for the forward reaction ________ K for the reverse reaction.

(d) At equilibrium, K ________ Q.

(e) After the system is at equilibrium, more of gas B is added. After the system returns to equilibrium, K before the addition of B ________ K after the addition of B.

(f) The same reaction is initiated, this time with a catalyst. K for the system without a catalyst ________ K for the system with a catalyst.

(g) K for the formation of one mole of D ________ K for the formation of two moles of D.

(h) The temperature of the system is increased to 35°C. P_B at equilibrium at 25°C ________ P_B at equilibrium at 35°C.

(i) Ten more grams of C are added to the system. P_B before the addition of C ________ P_B after the addition of C.

72. ■ The graph below is similar to that of Figure 12.2.

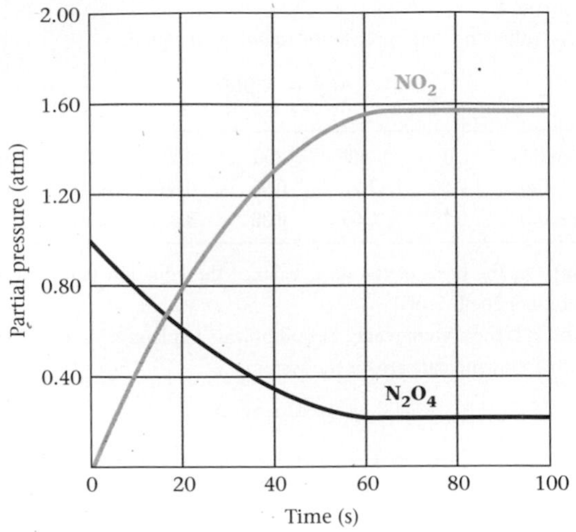

If after 100 s have elapsed the partial pressure of N_2O_4 is increased to 1.0 atm, what will the graph for N_2O_4 look like beyond 100 s?

73. The system

$$3Z(g) + Q(g) \rightleftharpoons 2R(g)$$

is at equilibrium when the partial pressure of Q is 0.44 atm. Sufficient R is added to increase the partial pressure of Q temporarily to 1.5 atm. When equilibrium is reestablished, the partial pressure of Q could be which of the following?

(a) 1.5 atm (b) 1.2 atm (c) 0.80 atm
(d) 0.44 atm (e) 0.40 atm

74. ■ The figures below represent the following reaction at equilibrium at different temperatures.

$$A_2(g) + 3B_2 \rightleftharpoons 2AB_3$$

where squares represent atom A and circles represent atom B. Is the reaction exothermic?

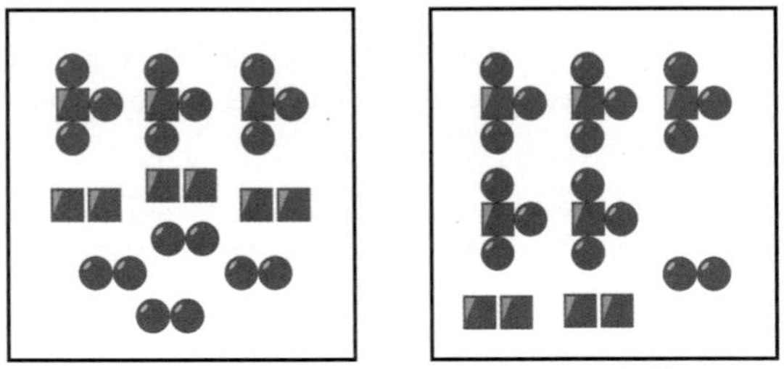

T = 300 K T = 400 K

75. Consider the statement "The equilibrium constant for a reaction at 400 K is 792. It must be a very fast reaction." What is wrong with the statement?

76. Consider the statement "The equilibrium constant for a mixture of hydrogen, nitrogen, and ammonia is 3.41." What information is missing from this statement?

Challenge Problems

77. Consider the following reaction at a certain temperature:

$$2NO(g) + O_2(g) \rightleftharpoons 2NO_2(g)$$

A reaction mixture contains 0.70 atm of O_2 and 0.81 atm of NO. When equilibrium is established, the total pressure in the reaction vessel is 1.20 atm. Find K.

78. Derive the relationship

$$K = K_c \times (RT)^{\Delta n_g}$$

where K_c is the equilibrium constant using molarities and Δn_g is the change in the number of moles of gas in the reaction (see page 326). (*Hint:* Recall that $P_A = n_ART/V$ and $n_A/V = [A]$.)

79. Ammonia can decompose into its constituent elements according to the reaction

$$2NH_3(g) \rightleftharpoons N_2(g) + 3H_2(g)$$

The equilibrium constant for the decomposition at a certain temperature is 2.5. Calculate the partial pressures of all the gases at equilibrium if ammonia with a pressure of 1.00 atm is sealed in a 3.0-L flask.

80. Hydrogen iodide gas decomposes to hydrogen gas and iodine gas:

$$2HI(g) \rightleftharpoons H_2(g) + I_2(g)$$

To determine the equilibrium constant of the system, identical one-liter glass bulbs are filled with 3.20 g of HI and maintained at a certain temperature. Each bulb is periodically opened and analyzed for iodine formation by titration with sodium thiosulfate, $Na_2S_2O_3$.

$$I_2(aq) + 2S_2O_3^{2-}(aq) \longrightarrow S_4O_6^{2-}(aq) + 2I^-(aq)$$

It is determined that when equilibrium is reached, 37.0 mL of 0.200 M $Na_2S_2O_3$ is required to titrate the iodine. What is K at the temperature of the experiment?

81. For the system

$$SO_3(g) \rightleftharpoons SO_2(g) + \tfrac{1}{2}O_2(g)$$

at 1000 K, $K = 0.45$. Sulfur trioxide, originally at 1.00 atm pressure, partially dissociates to SO_2 and O_2 at 1000 K. What is its partial pressure at equilibrium?

82. ■ A student studies the equilibrium

$$I_2(g) \rightleftharpoons 2I(g)$$

at a high temperature. She finds that the total pressure at equilibrium is 40% greater than it was originally, when only I_2 was present. What is K for this reaction at that temperature?

83. At a certain temperature, the reaction

$$Xe(g) + 2F_2(g) \rightleftharpoons XeF_4(g)$$

gives a 50.0% yield of XeF_4, starting with Xe (P_{Xe} = 0.20 atm) and F_2 (P_{F_2} = 0.40 atm). Calculate K at this temperature. What must the initial pressure of F_2 be to convert 75.0% of the xenon to XeF_4?

84. Benzaldehyde, a flavoring agent, is obtained by the dehydrogenation of benzyl alcohol.

$$C_6H_5CH_2OH(g) \rightleftharpoons C_6H_5CHO(g) + H_2(g)$$

K for the reaction at 250°C is 0.56. If 1.50 g of benzyl alcohol is placed in a 2.0-L flask and heated to 250°C,

(a) what is the partial pressure of the benzaldehyde when equilibrium is established?

(b) how many grams of benzyl alcohol remain at equilibrium?

■ in OWL Blue-numbered questions answered in Appendix 6 WEB Solution is available on companion website

13 Acids and Bases

There is nothing in the Universe but alkali and acid,
From which Nature composes all things.

—Otto Tachenius (1671)

Chapter Outline

Réunion des Musées Nationaux/Art Resource, NY

The intensity and color of the poppies in Monet's painting *The Poppyfield, near Giverny* are influenced by the acidity or basicity of the soil. Of course artistic license could also have something to do with the intensity and color of the poppies in this painting.

Among the solution reactions considered in Chapter 4 were those between acids and bases. In this chapter, we take a closer look at the properties of acidic and basic water solutions. In particular, we examine—

- the ionization of water and the equilibrium between hydrated H^+ ions (H_3O^+ ions) and OH^- ions in water solution (Section 13.2).
- the quantities pH and pOH, used to describe the acidity or basicity of water solutions (Section 13.3).
- the types of species that act as weak acids and weak bases and the equilibria that apply in their water solutions (Sections 13.4, 13.5).
- the acid-base properties of salt solutions (Section 13.6). ■

Online homework for this chapter may be assigned in OWL

CENGAGENOW™
This icon introduces an opportunity for self-study and to explore interactive modules by signing in at **academic.cengage.com/now.**

13.1 BRØNSTED-LOWRY ACID-BASE MODEL

In Chapter 4 we considered an acid to be a substance that produces an excess of H^+ ions in water. A base was similarly defined to be a substance that forms excess OH^- ions in water solution. This approach, first proposed by Svante Arrhenius in 1884, is a very practical one, but it has one disadvantage. It severely limits the number of reactions that qualify as acid-base.

CENGAGENOW™
Click Coached Problems for a self-study module on **Brønsted acids and bases.**

The model of acids and bases used in this chapter is a somewhat more general one developed independently by Johannes Brønsted (1879–1947) in Denmark and Thomas Lowry (1874–1936) in England in 1923. The **Brønsted-Lowry** model focuses on the nature of acids and bases and the reactions that take place between them. Specifically, it considers that—

Sometimes called the Lowry-Brønsted model, at least in England.

- ***an* acid *is a proton (H^+ ion) donor.***
- ***a* base *is a proton (H^+ ion) acceptor.***
- ***in an acid-base reaction, a proton is transferred from an acid to a base.***

A Brønsted-Lowry acid-base reaction might be represented as

$$HB(aq) + A^-(aq) \rightleftharpoons HA(aq) + B^-(aq)$$

The species shown in red, HB and HA, act as Brønsted-Lowry acids in the forward and reverse reactions, respectively; A^- and B^- (blue) act as Brønsted-Lowry bases. (We will use this color coding consistently throughout the chapter in writing Brønsted-Lowry acid-base equations.)

In connection with the Brønsted-Lowry model, there are some terms that are used frequently.

1. The species formed when a proton is removed from an acid is referred to as the **conjugate base** of that acid; B^- is the conjugate base of HB. The species formed when a proton is added to a base is called the **conjugate acid** of that base: HA is the conjugate acid of A^-. In other words, conjugate acid-base pairs differ only in the presence or absence of a proton, H^+. A conjugate acid has one more proton than its conjugate base. Thus we have

CENGAGENOW™
Click Chemistry Interactive for the self-study module **acid-base conjugate pairs.**

Conjugate Acid	Conjugate Base
HF	F^-
HSO_4^-	SO_4^{2-}
NH_4^+	NH_3

2. A species that can either accept or donate a proton is referred to as *amphiprotic*. An example is the H_2O molecule, which can gain a proton to form the hydronium ion, H_3O^+, or lose a proton, leaving the hydroxide ion, OH^-.

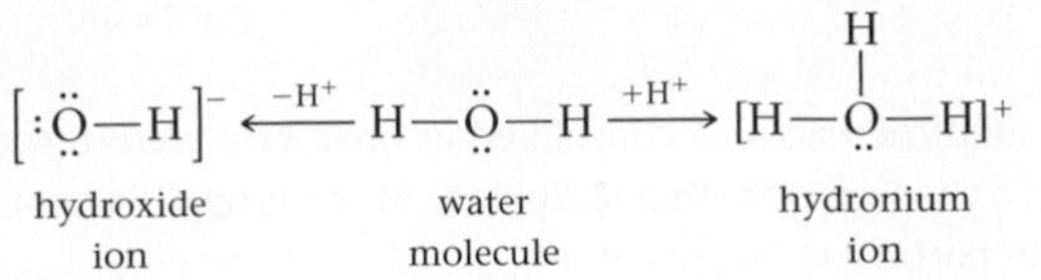

Example 13.1

(a) What is the conjugate base of HNO_2? The conjugate acid of F^-?

(b) The HCO_3^- ion, like the H_2O molecule, is amphiprotic. What is its conjugate base? Its conjugate acid?

Strategy To form a conjugate base, remove H^+; the effect is to lower the number of hydrogen atoms by one and lower the charge by one unit. Conversely, a conjugate acid is formed by adding H^+; this adds a H atom and increases the charge by one unit.

SOLUTION

(a) NO_2^-; HF (b) CO_3^{2-}; H_2CO_3

13.2 THE ION PRODUCT OF WATER

CENGAGENOW™
Click Coached Problems for a self-study module on **autoionization.**

The acidic and basic properties of aqueous solutions are dependent on an equilibrium that involves the solvent, water. The reaction involved can be regarded as a Brønsted-Lowry acid-base reaction in which the H_2O molecule shows its amphiprotic nature:

$$H_2O + H_2O \rightleftharpoons H_3O^+(aq) + OH^-(aq)$$

Alternatively, and somewhat more simply, the reaction can be viewed as the ionization of a single H_2O molecule:

$$H_2O \rightleftharpoons H^+(aq) + OH^-(aq)$$

Recall (page 331, Chapter 12) that in the equilibrium constant expression for reactions in solution—

- solutes enter as their molarity, [ ].
- the solvent, H_2O in this case, does not appear. Its concentration is essentially the same in all dilute solutions.

Hence for the ionization of water, the equilibrium constant expression can be written*

$$K_W = [H^+] \times [OH^-] \qquad (13.1)$$

where K_W, referred to as the **ion product constant of water,** has a very small value. At 25°C,

$$K_W = 1.0 \times 10^{-14} \qquad (13.2)$$

This equation applies to *any* water solution at 25°C.

The concentrations of H^+ ($[H^+] = [H_3O^+]$) ions and OH^- ions in *pure water* at 25°C are readily calculated from K_W. Notice from the equation for ionization that these two ions are formed in equal numbers. Hence in pure H_2O,

There are very few H^+ and OH^- ions in pure water.

$$[H^+] = [OH^-]$$

$$K_W = [H^+] \times [OH^-] = [H^+]^2 = 1.0 \times 10^{-14}$$

$$[H^+] = 1.0 \times 10^{-7}\,M = [OH^-]$$

*For simplicity, throughout this chapter, we will use H^+ rather than H_3O^+ in equilibrium constant expressions.

An aqueous solution in which $[H^+]$ *equals* $[OH^-]$ is called a **neutral solution.** It has a $[H^+]$ of $1.0 \times 10^{-7}\ M$ at 25°C.

In most water solutions, the concentrations of H^+ and OH^- are not equal. The equation $[H^+] \times [OH^-] = 1.0 \times 10^{-14}$ indicates that these two quantities are inversely proportional to one another (Figure 13.1). When $[H^+]$ is very high, $[OH^-]$ is very low, and vice versa.

An aqueous solution in which $[H^+]$ is greater than $[OH^-]$ is termed acidic. An aqueous solution in which $[OH^-]$ is greater than $[H^+]$ is basic (alkaline). Therefore,

if $[H^+] > 1.0 \times 10^{-7}\ M$, $[OH^-] < 1.0 \times 10^{-7}\ M$, solution is acidic

if $[OH^-] > 1.0 \times 10^{-7}\ M$, $[H^+] < 1.0 \times 10^{-7}\ M$, solution is basic

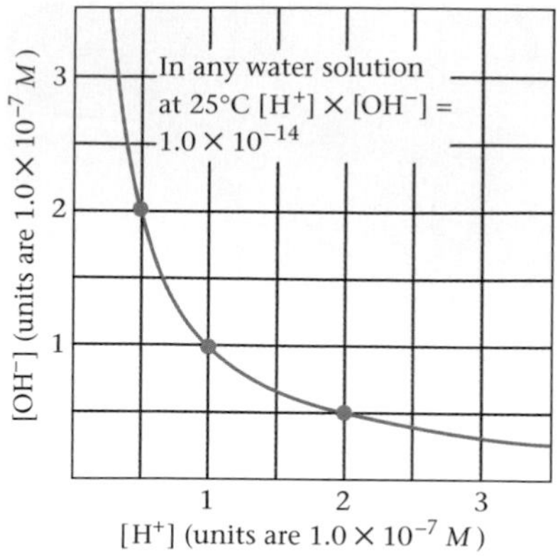

Figure 13.1
The $[H^+]$-$[OH^-]$ relationship. A graph of $[OH^-]$ versus $[H^+]$ looks very much like a graph of gas volume versus pressure. In both cases, the two variables are inversely proportional to one another. When $[H^+]$ gets larger, $[OH^-]$ gets smaller.

13.3 pH AND pOH

As just pointed out, the acidity or basicity of a solution can be described in terms of its H^+ concentration. In 1909, Søren Sørensen (1868–1939), a biochemist working at the Carlsberg Brewery in Copenhagen, proposed an alternative method of specifying the acidity of a solution. He defined a term called **pH** (for "power of the hydrogen ion"):

$$pH = -\log_{10}[H^+] = -\log_{10}[H_3O^+] \qquad \textbf{(13.3)}$$

or

$$[H^+] = [H_3O^+] = 10^{-pH}$$

Figure 13.2 shows the relationship between pH and $[H^+]$. Notice that, as the defining equation implies, pH increases by one unit when the concentration of H^+ decreases by a power of 10. Moreover, ***the higher the pH, the less acidic the solution.*** Most aqueous solutions have hydrogen ion concentrations between 1 and $10^{-14}\ M$ and hence have a pH between 0 and 14.

It is simpler to use numbers (pH = 4) than exponents ($[H^+] = 10^{-4}\ M$) to describe acidity.

The pH, like $[H^+]$ or $[OH^-]$, can be used to differentiate acidic, neutral, and basic solutions. At 25°C,

if pH < 7.0, solution is acidic

if pH $= 7.0$, solution is neutral

if pH > 7.0, solution is basic

CENGAGENOW™
Click Coached Problems for a self-study module on **the pH scale.**

Table 13.1 shows the pH of some common solutions.

A similar approach is used for the hydroxide ion concentration. The **pOH** of a solution is defined as

$$pOH = -\log_{10}[OH^-] \qquad \textbf{(13.4)}$$

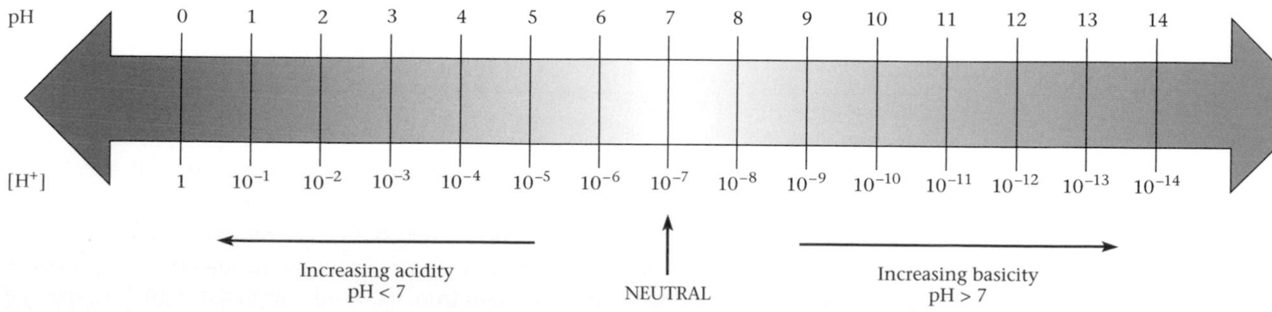

Figure 13.2
pH-$[H^+]$ relationship. Acidity is inversely related to pH; the higher the H^+ ion concentration, the lower the pH. In neutral solution, $[H^+] = [OH^-] = 1.0 \times 10^{-7}\ M$; pH = 7.00 at 25°C.

Art Brewer/Tony Stone Images

Seawater, a slightly basic solution. When these children emerge from the water, they may notice that their skin feels slippery, a result of the basic pH of the water (pH 8.3).

Table 13.1 pH of Some Common Materials

Lemon juice	2.2–2.4	Urine, human	4.8–8.4
Wine	2.8–3.8	Cow's milk	6.3–6.6
Vinegar	3.0	Saliva, human	6.5–7.5
Tomato juice	4.0	Drinking water	5.5–8.0
Beer	4–5	Blood, human	7.3–7.5
Cheese	4.8–6.4	Seawater	8.3

Because $[H^+] \times [OH^-] = 1.0 \times 10^{-14}$ at 25°C, it follows that at this temperature

$$pH + pOH = 14.00$$

Thus a solution that has a pH of 6.20 must have a pOH of 7.80, and vice versa.

Example 13.2 Graded

Knowing $[H^+]$, $[OH^-]$, pH, or pOH, you can calculate the other three quantities.

Calculate, at 25°C

*(a) the $[H^+]$ and pH of a tap-water sample in which $[OH^-] = 2.0 \times 10^{-7}$.

**(b) the $[H^+]$ and $[OH^-]$ of human blood at pH 7.40.

***(c) the pOH of a solution in which $[H^+] = 5.0[OH^-]$.

SOLUTION

(a) $$[H^+] = \frac{1.0 \times 10^{-14}}{2.0 \times 10^{-7}} = 5.0 \times 10^{-8}\ M$$

$$pH = -\log_{10}(5.0 \times 10^{-8})$$

You should find on your calculator that $\log_{10}(5.0 \times 10^{-8})$ is −7.30. Hence, pH = 7.30.

(b) Because the pH is 7.40, $[H^+] = 10^{-7.40}$. To find $[H^+]$, enter −7.40 on your calculator. Then either—

Remember to enter the minus sign first.

- punch the 10^x key, if you have one, or
- punch the INV and then the LOG key

Either way, you should find that $[H^+] = 4.0 \times 10^{-8}\ M$.

Knowing $[H^+]$, the concentration of OH^- is calculated from Equation 13.1.

$$[OH^-] = \frac{1.0 \times 10^{-14}}{4.0 \times 10^{-8}} = 2.5 \times 10^{-7}\ M.$$

(c) Substitute into the K_W expression to find $[OH^-]$ and then convert to pOH.

$$5.0[OH^-] \times [OH^-] = 1.0 \times 10^{-14}$$

$$[OH^-]^2 = \frac{1.0 \times 10^{-14}}{5.0}; \qquad [OH^-] = 4.5 \times 10^{-8}\ M$$

$$pOH = -\log_{10}(4.5 \times 10^{-8}) = 7.35$$

The number calculated in (b) for the concentration of H^+ in blood, $4.0 \times 10^{-8}\ M$, is very small. You may wonder what difference it makes whether $[H^+]$ is $4.0 \times 10^{-8}\ M$, $4.0 \times 10^{-7}\ M$, or some other such tiny quantity. In practice, it makes a great deal of difference because a large number of biological processes involve H^+ as a reactant, so the rates of these processes depend on its concentration. If $[H^+]$ increases from $4.0 \times 10^{-8}\ M$ to $4.0 \times 10^{-7}\ M$, the rate of a first-order reaction involving H^+ increases by a factor of 10. Indeed, if $[H^+]$ in blood increases by a much smaller amount, from $4.0 \times 10^{-8}\ M$ to $5.0 \times 10^{-8}\ M$ (pH 7.40 ⟶ 7.30),

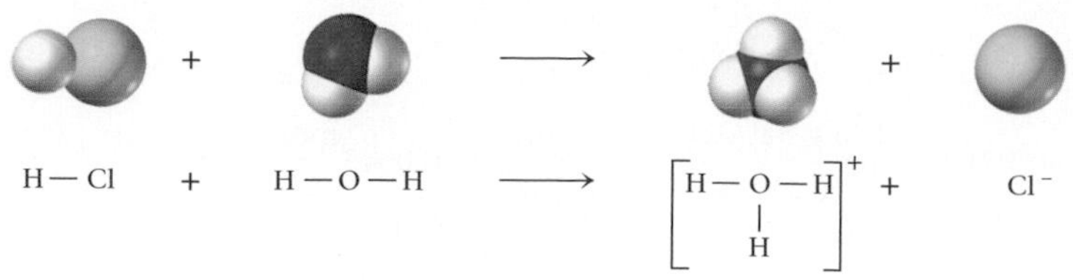

Figure 13.3
Ionization of a strong acid. When HCl is added to water, there is a proton transfer from HCl to an H_2O molecule, forming a Cl^- ion and an H_3O^+ ion. In the reaction, HCl acts as a Brønsted-Lowry acid, H_2O as a Brønsted-Lowry base.

a condition called *acidosis* develops. The nervous system is depressed; fainting and even coma can result.

pH of Strong Acids and Strong Bases

CENGAGENOW™
Click Coached Problems for a self-study module on **strong acids.**

As pointed out in Chapter 4, the following acids are strong

HCl	HBr	HI
$HClO_4$	HNO_3	H_2SO_4*

in the sense that they are completely ionized in water. The reaction of the strong acid HCl with water can be represented by the equation (Figure 13.3)

$$HCl(aq) + H_2O \longrightarrow H_3O^+(aq) + Cl^-(aq)$$

Because this reaction goes to completion, it follows that a 0.10 *M* solution of HCl is 0.10 *M* in both H_3O^+ (i.e., H^+) and Cl^- ions.

The strong bases

LiOH	NaOH	KOH
$Ca(OH)_2$	$Sr(OH)_2$	$Ba(OH)_2$

are completely ionized in dilute water solution. A 0.10 *M* solution of NaOH is 0.10 *M* in both Na^+ and OH^- ions.

The fact that strong acids and bases are completely ionized in water makes it relatively easy to calculate the pH and pOH of their solutions (Example 13.3).

1 *M* HCl has a pH of 0, 1 *M* NaOH a pH of 14.

Example 13.3 Graded

Consider barium hydroxide, $Ba(OH)_2$, a white, powdery substance. Student A prepares a solution of $Ba(OH)_2$ by dissolving 4.23 g of $Ba(OH)_2$ in enough water to make 455 mL of solution.

*(a) What is the pH of Student A's solution?

**(b) Student B was asked to prepare the same solution as Student A. Student B's solution had a pH of 13.51. Did Student B add more or less $Ba(OH)_2$ to his solution? How much more or less $Ba(OH)_2$ was added?

***(c) Student C was asked to add 0.60 g of NaOH to Student A's solution. What is the pH of Student C's solution? (Assume no volume change.)

Strategy

(a) $m_{Ba(OH)_2} \xrightarrow{MM} n_{Ba(OH)_2} \xrightarrow{V} [Ba(OH)_2] \longrightarrow [OH^-] \longrightarrow pH$

(b) $pH \longrightarrow [OH^-] \longrightarrow [Ba(OH)_2] \longrightarrow m_{Ba(OH)_2}$

(c) n_{OH^-} (from NaOH) + n_{OH^-} (from $Ba(OH)_2$) $\longrightarrow [OH^-] \longrightarrow pH$

*The *first* ionization of H_2SO_4 is complete:

$$H_2SO_4(aq) \longrightarrow H^+(aq) + HSO_4^-(aq)$$

The *second* ionization is reversible:

$$HSO_4^-(aq) \rightleftharpoons H^+(aq) + SO_4^{2-}(aq)$$

SOLUTION

(a)

$$[\text{Ba(OH)}_2] = \frac{4.23 \text{ g Ba(OH)}_2}{0.455 \text{ L}} \times \frac{1 \text{ mol}}{171.3 \text{ g}} = 0.0543 \frac{\text{mol}}{\text{L}}$$

$$[\text{OH}^-] = \frac{0.0543 \text{ mol Ba(OH)}_2}{1 \text{ L}} \times \frac{2 \text{ mol OH}^-}{1 \text{ mol Ba(OH)}_2} = 0.109 \frac{\text{mol}}{\text{L}}$$

$$\text{pOH} = -\log_{10}(0.109) = 0.96; \qquad \text{so pH} = 14.00 - 0.96 = 13.04$$

(b)

$$\text{pOH} = 14.00 - 13.51 = 0.49$$

$$-\log_{10}[\text{OH}^-] = 0.49; \qquad [\text{OH}^-] = 0.32 \frac{\text{mol}}{\text{L}}$$

$$[\text{Ba(OH)}_2] = \frac{0.32 \text{ mol OH}^-}{1 \text{ L}} \times \frac{1 \text{ mol Ba(OH)}_2}{2 \text{ mol OH}^-} = 0.16 \frac{\text{mol}}{\text{L}}$$

$$m_{\text{Ba(OH)}_2} = 0.16 \frac{\text{mol}}{\text{L}} \times 0.455 \text{ L} \times \frac{171.3 \text{ g Ba(OH)}_2}{1 \text{ mol}} = 12.5 \text{ g}$$

Since Student A added 4.23 g, Student B must have added an additional 8.2 g of $Ba(OH)_2$.

(c) moles OH^- contributed by NaOH =

$$0.60 \text{ g NaOH} \times \frac{1 \text{ mol}}{40.00 \text{ g}} \times \frac{1 \text{ mol OH}^-}{1 \text{ mol NaOH}} = 0.015$$

moles OH^- contributed by $Ba(OH)_2$ =

$$4.23 \text{ g Ba(OH)}_2 \times \frac{1 \text{ mol Ba(OH)}_2}{171.3 \text{ g}} \times \frac{2 \text{ mol OH}^-}{1 \text{ mol Ba(OH)}_2} = 0.0494$$

$$[\text{OH}^-] = \frac{(0.015 + 0.0494) \text{ mol}}{0.455 \text{ L}} = 0.14 \frac{\text{mol}}{\text{L}}$$

$$\text{pOH} = -\log_{10}(0.14) = 0.85; \qquad \text{pH} = 14.00 - 0.85 = 13.15$$

Measuring pH

The pH of a solution can be measured by an instrument called a pH meter. A pH meter translates the H^+ ion concentration of a solution into an electrical signal that is converted into either a digital display or a deflection on a meter that reads pH directly (Figure 13.4). Later, in Chapter 18, we will consider the principle on which the pH meter works.

A less accurate but more colorful way to measure pH uses a universal indicator, which is a mixture of acid-base indicators that shows changes in color at different pH values (Figure 13.5, p. 359). A similar principle is used with pH paper. Strips of this paper are coated with a mixture of pH-sensitive dyes; these strips are widely used to test the pH of biological fluids,

pH paper is also known as litmus paper.

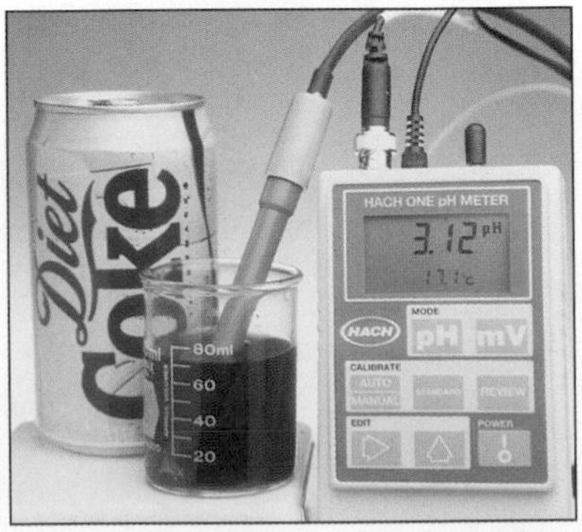

Charles D. Winters

Figure 13.4
A pH meter with a digital readout. With a pH of 3.12, cola drinks are quite acidic.

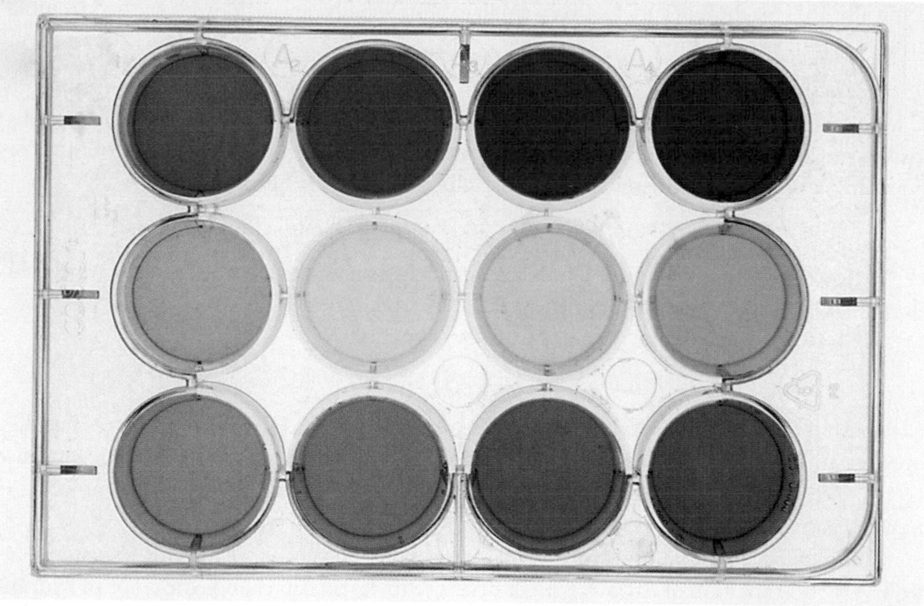

Charles D. Winters

Figure 13.5
pH as shown by a universal indicator. Universal indicator is deep red in strongly acidic solution *(upper left)*. It changes to yellow and green at pH 6 to 8, and then to deep violet in strongly basic solution *(lower right)*.

groundwater, and foods. Depending on the indicators used, a test strip can measure pH over a wide or narrow range.

Home gardeners frequently measure and adjust soil pH in an effort to improve the yield and quality of grass, vegetables, and flowers. Interestingly enough, the colors of many flowers depend on pH; among these are dahlias, delphiniums, and, in particular, hydrangeas (Figure 13.6). The first research in this area was carried out by Robert Boyle of gas-law fame, who published a paper on the relation between flower color and acidity in 1664.

The color change of hydrangeas is exactly the opposite of that for litmus.

13.4 WEAK ACIDS AND THEIR EQUILIBRIUM CONSTANTS

A wide variety of solutes behave as weak acids; that is, they react reversibly with water to form H_3O^+ ions. Using HB to represent a weak acid, its Brønsted-Lowry reaction with water is

$$HB(aq) + H_2O \longrightarrow H_3O^+(aq) + B^-(aq)$$

Michael Dalton/Fundamental Photographs NYC

Figure 13.6
Influence of acidic or basic soil. Hydrangeas grown in strongly acidic soil (below pH 5) are blue. When they are grown in neutral or basic soil, the flowers are rosy pink.

Typically, this reaction occurs to a very small extent; usually, fewer than 1% of the HB molecules are converted to ions.

Most weak acids fall into one of two categories:

You can assume that all acids other than HCl, HBr, HI, HNO_3, $HClO_4$, and H_2SO_4 are weak.

1. ***Molecules containing an ionizable hydrogen atom.*** This type of weak acid was discussed in Chapter 4. There are literally thousands of molecular weak acids, most of them organic in nature. Among the molecular inorganic weak acids is nitrous acid:

$$HNO_2(aq) + H_2O \rightleftharpoons H_3O^+(aq) + NO_2^-(aq)$$

2. ***Cations.*** The ammonium ion, NH_4^+, behaves as a weak acid in water; a 0.10 *M* solution of NH_4Cl has a pH of about 5. The process by which the NH_4^+ ion lowers the pH of water can be represented by the (Brønsted-Lowry) equation:

$$NH_4^+(aq) + H_2O \rightleftharpoons H_3O^+(aq) + NH_3(aq)$$

Comparing the equation just written with that cited above for HNO_2, you can see that they are very similar. In both cases, a weak acid (HNO_2, NH_4^+) is converted to its conjugate base (NO_2^-, NH_3). The fact that the NH_4^+ ion has a +1 charge, whereas the HNO_2 molecule is neutral, is really irrelevant here.

To get red hydrangeas, add lime (CaO).

You may be surprised to learn that many metal cations act as weak acids in water solution. A 0.10 *M* solution of $Al_2(SO_4)_3$ has a pH close to 3; you can change the color of hydrangeas from red to blue by adding aluminum salts to soil. At first glance it is not at all obvious how a cation such as Al^{3+} can make a water solution acidic. However, the aluminum cation in water solution is really a hydrated species, $Al(H_2O)_6^{3+}$, in which six water molecules are bonded to the central Al^{3+} ion. This species can transfer a proton to a solvent water molecule to form an H_3O^+ ion:

$$Al(H_2O)_6^{3+}(aq) + H_2O \rightleftharpoons H_3O^+(aq) + Al(H_2O)_5(OH)^{2+}(aq)$$

Figure 13.7 shows the structures of the $Al(H_2O)_6^{3+}$ cation and its conjugate base, $Al(H_2O)_5(OH)^{2+}$.

A very similar equation can be written to explain why solutions of zinc salts are acidic. Here it appears that the hydrated cation in water solution contains four H_2O molecules bonded to a central Zn^{2+} ion. The Brønsted-Lowry equation is

All transition metal cations behave this way.

$$Zn(H_2O)_4^{2+}(aq) + H_2O \rightleftharpoons H_3O^+(aq) + Zn(H_2O)_3(OH)^+(aq)$$

The Equilibrium Constant for a Weak Acid

In discussing the equilibrium involved when a weak acid is added to water, it is convenient to represent the proton transfer

$$HB(aq) + H_2O \rightleftharpoons H_3O^+(aq) + B^-(aq)$$

as a simple ionization

$$HB(aq) \rightleftharpoons H^+(aq) + B^-(aq)$$

in which case the expression for the equilibrium constant becomes

$$K_a = \frac{[H^+] \times [B^-]}{[HB]} \qquad \textbf{(13.5)}$$

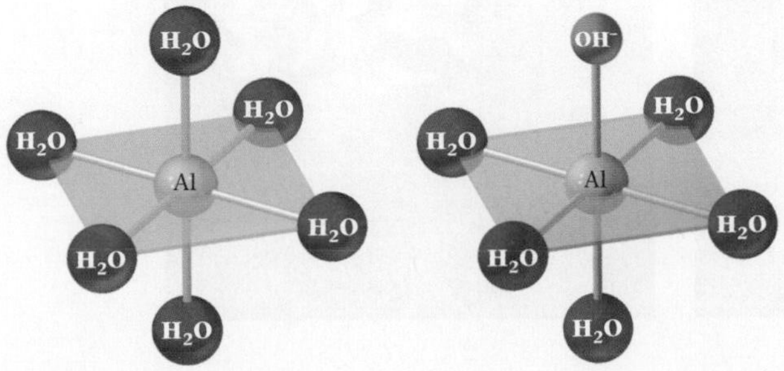

Figure 13.7
A weakly acidic cation. In water solution, the Al^{3+} ion is bonded to six water molecules in the $Al(H_2O)_6^{3+}$ ion *(left)*. In the $Al(H_2O)_5OH^{2+}$ ion *(right)*, one of the H_2O molecules has been replaced by an OH^- ion.

Table 13.2 Equilibrium Constants for Weak Acids and Their Conjugate Bases

	Acid	K_a	Base	K_b
Sulfurous acid	H_2SO_3	1.7×10^{-2}	HSO_3^-	5.9×10^{-13}
Hydrogen sulfate ion	HSO_4^-	1.0×10^{-2}	SO_4^{2-}	1.0×10^{-12}
Phosphoric acid	H_3PO_4	7.1×10^{-3}	$H_2PO_4^-$	1.4×10^{-12}
Hexaaquairon(III) ion	$Fe(H_2O)_6^{3+}$	6.7×10^{-3}	$Fe(H_2O)_5OH^{2+}$	1.5×10^{-12}
Hydrofluoric acid	HF	6.9×10^{-4}	F^-	1.4×10^{-11}
Nitrous acid	HNO_2	6.0×10^{-4}	NO_2^-	1.7×10^{-11}
Formic acid	$HCHO_2$	1.9×10^{-4}	CHO_2^-	5.3×10^{-11}
Lactic acid	$HC_3H_5O_3$	1.4×10^{-4}	$C_3H_5O_3^-$	7.1×10^{-11}
Benzoic acid	$HC_7H_5O_2$	6.6×10^{-5}	$C_7H_5O_2^-$	1.5×10^{-10}
Acetic acid	$HC_2H_3O_2$	1.8×10^{-5}	$C_2H_3O_2^-$	5.6×10^{-10}
Hexaaquaaluminum(III) ion	$Al(H_2O)_6^{3+}$	1.2×10^{-5}	$Al(H_2O)_5OH^{2+}$	8.3×10^{-10}
Carbonic acid	H_2CO_3	4.4×10^{-7}	HCO_3^-	2.3×10^{-8}
Dihydrogen phosphate ion	$H_2PO_4^-$	6.2×10^{-8}	HPO_4^{2-}	1.6×10^{-7}
Hydrogen sulfite ion	HSO_3^-	6.0×10^{-8}	SO_3^{2-}	1.7×10^{-7}
Hypochlorous acid	HClO	2.8×10^{-8}	ClO^-	3.6×10^{-7}
Hydrocyanic acid	HCN	5.8×10^{-10}	CN^-	1.7×10^{-5}
Ammonium ion	NH_4^+	5.6×10^{-10}	NH_3	1.8×10^{-5}
Tetraaquazinc(II) ion	$Zn(H_2O)_4^{2+}$	3.3×10^{-10}	$Zn(H_2O)_3OH^+$	3.0×10^{-5}
Hydrogen carbonate ion	HCO_3^-	4.7×10^{-11}	CO_3^{2-}	2.1×10^{-4}
Hydrogen phosphate ion	HPO_4^{2-}	4.5×10^{-13}	PO_4^{3-}	2.2×10^{-2}

$$HB(aq) \rightleftharpoons H^+(aq) + B^-(aq) \qquad K_a = \frac{[H^+] \times [B^-]}{[HB]}$$

$$B^-(aq) + H_2O \rightleftharpoons HB(aq) + OH^-(aq) \qquad K_b = \frac{[HB] \times [OH^-]}{[B^-]}$$

The equilibrium constant K_a is called, logically enough, the **acid equilibrium constant** of the weak acid HB. The K_a values of some weak acids (in order of decreasing strength) are listed in Table 13.2. The weaker the acid, the smaller the value of K_a. For example, HCN ($K_a = 5.8 \times 10^{-10}$) is a weaker acid than HNO_2, for which $K_a = 6.0 \times 10^{-4}$.

We sometimes refer to the **pK_a** value of a weak acid

$$pK_a = -\log_{10}K_a \qquad \textbf{(13.6)}$$

HNO_2	$K_a = 6.0 \times 10^{-4}$	$pK_a = 3.22$
HCN	$K_a = 5.8 \times 10^{-10}$	$pK_a = 9.24$

The formula of acetic acid is often written as CH_3COOH.

Example 13.4 Consider acetic acid, $HC_2H_3O_2$, and the hydrated zinc cation, $Zn(H_2O)_4^{2+}$.

(a) Write equations to show why these species are acidic.
(b) Which is the stronger acid?
(c) What is the pK_a of $Zn(H_2O)_4^{2+}$?

Strategy In (a), note that in both cases a proton is transferred to a water molecule. The products are an H_3O^+ ion and the conjugate base of the weak acid. In (b) use Table 13.2 to find which weak acid has the larger K_a. In (c) use the equation

$$pK_a = -\log_{10}K_a$$

SOLUTION

(a) $HC_2H_3O_2(aq) + H_2O \rightleftharpoons H_3O^+(aq) + C_2H_3O_2^-(aq)$
$Zn(H_2O)_4^{2+}(aq) + H_2O \rightleftharpoons H_3O^+(aq) + Zn(H_2O)_3(OH)^+(aq)$

(b) $HC_2H_3O_2$ ($K_a = 1.8 \times 10^{-5}$) is stronger than $Zn(H_2O)_4^{2+}$ ($K_a = 3.3 \times 10^{-10}$).

(c) $pK_a = -\log_{10}(3.3 \times 10^{-10}) = 9.48$

CENGAGENOW™

Click Coached Problems for a self-study module on **determining K_a and K_b values.**

There are several ways to determine K_a of a weak acid. A simple approach involves measuring $[H^+]$ or pH in a solution prepared by dissolving a known amount of the weak acid to form a given volume of solution.

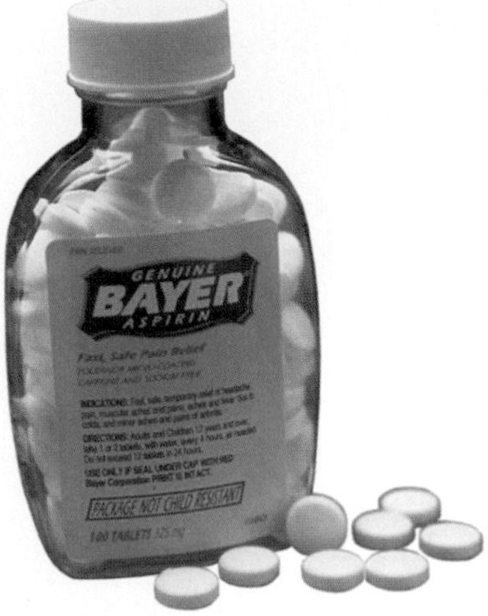

Charles D. Winters

Example 13.5 Aspirin, a commonly used pain reliever, is a weak organic acid whose molecular formula may be written as $HC_9H_7O_4$. An aqueous solution of aspirin has total volume 350.0 mL and contains 1.26 g of aspirin. The pH of the solution is found to be 2.60. Calculate K_a for aspirin.

Strategy The approach used is very similar to that of Chapter 12, except that concentrations in moles per liter replace partial pressures. Note that you readily calculate:

- the original concentration of $HC_9H_7O_4$ (MM = 180.15 g/mol)

$$[HC_9H_7O_4]_o = \frac{1.26\text{ g}}{0.3500\text{ L}} \times \frac{1\text{ mol}}{180.15\text{ g}} = 0.0200\ M$$

- the equilibrium concentration of H^+

$$[H^+]_{eq} = 10^{-2.60} = 2.5 \times 10^{-3}\ M$$

Your task is to calculate the acid equilibrium constant:

$$HC_9H_7O_4(aq) \rightleftharpoons H^+(aq) + C_9H_7O_4^-(aq) \qquad K_a = \frac{[H^+] \times [C_9H_7O_4^-]}{[HC_9H_7O_4]}$$

SOLUTION From the chemical equation for the ionization of the weak acid, it should be clear that *1 mol* of $C_9H_7O_4^-$ is *produced* and *1 mol* of $HC_9H_7O_4$ is *consumed* for every mole of H^+ produced. It follows that

$$\Delta[C_9H_7O_4^-] = \Delta[H^+] \qquad \Delta[HC_9H_7O_4] = -\Delta[H^+]$$

It is always true that $\Delta[H^+] = \Delta[B^-] = -\Delta[HB]$.

Originally, there is essentially no H^+ (ignoring the slight ionization of water). The same holds for the anion $C_9H_7O_4^-$; the only species present originally is the weak acid, $HC_9H_7O_4$, at a concentration of 0.0200 *M*.

Putting this information together in the form of a table,

	$HC_9H_7O_4(aq)$	$\rightleftharpoons H^+(aq)$	$+\ C_9H_7O_4^-(aq)$
$[\ ]_o$	0.0200	0.0000	0.0000
$\Delta[\ ]$	−0.0025	+0.0025	+0.0025
$[\ ]_{eq}$	0.0175	0.0025	0.0025

(Numbers in color are those given or implied in the statement of the problem; the other numbers are deduced using the ionization equation printed above the table. The symbols $[\ ]_o$ and $[\ ]_{eq}$ refer to original and equilibrium concentrations, respectively.)

All the information needed to calculate K_a is now available,

$$K_a = \frac{(2.5 \times 10^{-3})^2}{0.0175} = 3.6 \times 10^{-4}$$

Aspirin is more acidic than vinegar.

Reality Check Aspirin is a relatively *strong* weak acid; it would be located near the top of Table 13.2.

In discussing the ionization of a weak acid,

$$HB(aq) \rightleftharpoons H^+(aq) + B^-(aq)$$

we often refer to the **percent ionization:**

$$\%\text{ ionization} = \frac{[H^+]_{eq}}{[HB]_o} \times 100\% \qquad \textbf{(13.7)}$$

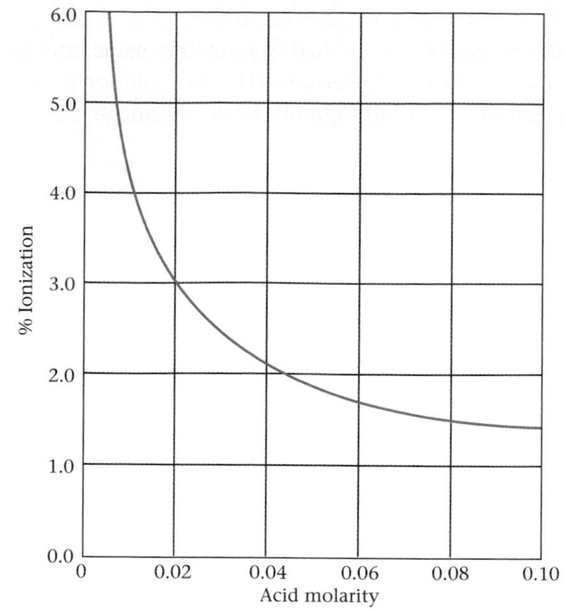

Figure 13.8
Percent ionization of acetic acid (K_a = 1.8 × 10^{-5}). Like any weak acid, the percent ionization of acetic acid is inversely related to its molar concentration.

For the aspirin solution referred to in Example 13.5,

$$\%\ \text{ionization} = \frac{2.5 \times 10^{-3}}{2.0 \times 10^{-2}} \times 100\% = 12\%$$

As you might expect, percent ionization at a given concentration is directly related to K_a. Ibuprofen ($K_a = 2.5 \times 10^{-5}$), a weaker acid than aspirin ($K_a = 3.6 \times 10^{-4}$), should be only 3.6% ionized at 0.020 *M* compared with 12% for aspirin.

Percent ionization also depends on the concentration of weak acid, increasing as the acid is diluted (Figure 13.8).

Example 13.6 Conceptual

In the box below, which has a volume of 0.50 L, the symbol ● represents 0.10 mol of a weak acid, HB. The symbol ● represents 0.10 mol of the conjugate base, B^-. Hydronium ions and water molecules are not shown. What is the percent ionization of the acid?

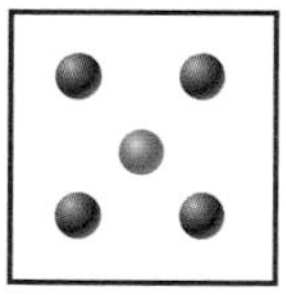

SOLUTION There must, originally, have been five red circles. So,

$$\%\ \text{ionization} = \tfrac{1}{5} \times 100 = 20\%$$

The other information given in the statement of the problem is irrelevant.

Calculation of $[H^+]$ in a Water Solution of a Weak Acid

Given the ionization constant of a weak acid and its original concentration, the H^+ concentration in solution is readily calculated. The approach used is the inverse of that followed in Example 13.5, where K_a was calculated knowing $[H^+]$; here, K_a is known and $[H^+]$ must be calculated.

CENGAGENOW™
Click Coached Problems for a self-study module on **estimating the pH of weak acid solutions.**

Example 13.7 Nicotinic acid, $HC_6H_4O_2N$ ($K_a = 1.4 \times 10^{-5}$) is another name for niacin, an important member of the vitamin B group. Determine $[H^+]$ in a solution prepared by dissolving 3.0 g of nicotinic acid (MM = 123.11 g/mol), HNic, in enough water to form 245 mL of solution.

Strategy First, determine the molarity of the prepared solution:

$$\frac{3.0\text{ g HNic}}{0.245\text{ L}} \times \frac{1\text{ mol}}{123.11\text{ g}} = 0.10\ M$$

Next, set up an equilibrium table similar to the one in the previous example. To accomplish that, note

- the original concentrations of HNic, H^+, and Nic^- are 0.10 *M*, 0.00 *M*, and 0.00 *M*, respectively, ignoring, tentatively at least, the H^+ ions from the ionization of water.
- the changes in concentration are related by the coefficients of the balanced equation, all of which are 1:

$$\Delta[\text{Nic}^-] = \Delta[\text{H}^+] \qquad \Delta[\text{HNic}] = -\Delta[\text{H}^+]$$

Letting $\Delta[H^+] = x$, it follows that $\Delta[Nic^-] = x$; $\Delta[HNic] = -x$. This information should enable you to express the equilibrium concentration of all species in terms of x. The rest is algebra; substitute into the expression for K_a and solve for $x = [H^+]$.

SOLUTION Setting up the table,

Equilibrium tables always help; be sure to include the equation.

	$HNic(aq) \rightleftharpoons$	$H^+(aq)$ +	$Nic^-(aq)$
$[\ ]_o$	0.10	0.00	0.00
$\Delta[\ ]$	$-x$	$+x$	$+x$
$[\ ]_{eq}$	$0.10 - x$	x	x

Substituting into the expression for K_a,

$$K_a = \frac{(x)(x)}{0.10 - x} = 1.4 \times 10^{-5}$$

This is a quadratic equation. It could be rearranged to the form $ax^2 + bx + c = 0$ and solved for x, using the quadratic formula. Such a procedure is time-consuming and, in this case, unnecessary. Nicotinic acid is a weak acid, only slightly ionized in water. The equilibrium concentration of HNic, $0.10 - x$, is probably only very slightly less than its original concentration, 0.10 *M*. So let's make the approximation $0.10 - x \approx 0.10$. This simplifies the equation written above:

$$\frac{x^2}{0.10} = 1.4 \times 10^{-5}$$

$$x^2 = 1.4 \times 10^{-6}$$

Taking square roots,

$$x = 1.2 \times 10^{-3}\ M = [H^+]$$

Reality Check Note that the concentration of H^+, 0.0012 *M*, is—

- much smaller than the original concentration of weak acid, 0.10 *M*. In this case, then, the approximation $0.10 - x \approx 0.10$ is justified. This will usually, but not always, be the case (see Example 13.8).
- much larger than $[H^+]$ in pure water, 1×10^{-7} *M*, justifying the assumption that the ionization of water can be neglected. *This will always be the case, provided $[H^+]$ from the weak acid is $\geq 10^{-6}$ M.*

In general, the value of K_a is seldom known more accurately than ±5%. Hence in the expression

$$K_a = \frac{x^2}{a - x}$$

where $x = [H^+]$ and $a =$ *original* concentration of weak acid, you can neglect the x in the denominator if doing so does not introduce an error of more than 5%. In other words,

$$\text{if } \frac{x}{a} \leq 0.05$$

This is known as the 5% rule.

then

$$a - x \approx a$$

Note that $x = [H^+]_{eq}$ and $a = [HB]_o$. Hence,

$$\frac{x}{a} = \frac{[H^+]_{eq}}{[HB]_o}$$

If we multiply by 100%, then

$$\frac{x}{a}(\%) = \frac{[H^+]_{eq}}{[HB]_o} \times 100\%,$$

which is the equation for determining percent ionization (13.7). In other words, the approximation $x - a \approx a$ is valid if the % ionization is less than 5%.

In most of the problems you will work, the approximation $a - x \approx a$ is valid, and you can solve for $[H^+]$ quite simply, as in Example 13.7, where $x = 0.012a$. Sometimes, though, you will find that the calculated $[H^+]$ is greater than 5% of the original concentration of weak acid. In that case, you can solve for x by using either the quadratic formula or the method of successive approximations.

Charles D. Winters

Some household weak acids. Vinegar contains acetic acid. Fruit juices and sodas contain citric acid. Baking powder contains the Al^{3+} ion.

Example 13.8 Calculate $[H^+]$ in a 0.100 *M* solution of nitrous acid, HNO_2, for which $K_a = 6.0 \times 10^{-4}$.

Strategy The setup is identical with that in Example 13.7. However, you will find, on solving for x, that $x > 0.050a$, so the approximation $a - x \approx a$ fails. The simplest way to proceed is to use the calculated value of x to obtain a better estimate of $[HNO_2]$, then solve again for $[H^+]$. An alternative is to use the quadratic formula. (This is a particularly shrewd choice if you have a calculator that can be programmed to solve quadratic equations.)

SOLUTION Proceeding as in Example 13.7, you arrive at the equation

$$K_a = \frac{x^2}{0.100 - x} = 6.0 \times 10^{-4}$$

Making the same approximation as before, $0.100 - x \approx 0.100$,

$$x^2 = 0.100 \times 6.0 \times 10^{-4} = 6.0 \times 10^{-5}$$

$$x = 7.7 \times 10^{-3} \approx [H^+]$$

To check the validity of the approximation, note that

$$\frac{x}{a} = \frac{7.7 \times 10^{-3}}{1.0 \times 10^{-1}} = 0.077 > 0.050$$

So the approximation is not valid.

To obtain a better value for x, you have a choice of two approaches.

(1) ***The method of successive approximations.*** In the first approximation, you ignored the x in the denominator of the equation. This time, you use the approximate value of x just calculated, 0.0077, to find a more exact value for the concentration of HNO_2:

$$[HNO_2] = 0.100 - 0.0077 = 0.092\ M$$

WLM liked this method; CNH leans toward the use of the quadratic formula.

Substituting in the expression for K_a,

$$K_a = \frac{x^2}{0.092} = 6.0 \times 10^{-4} \qquad x^2 = 5.5 \times 10^{-5}$$

$$x = 7.4 \times 10^{-3}\ M \approx [H^+]$$

This value is closer to the true $[H^+]$, because 0.092 M is a better approximation for $[HNO_2]$ than was 0.100 M. If you're still not satisfied, you can go one step further. Using 7.4×10^{-3} for x instead of 7.7×10^{-3}, you can recalculate $[HNO_2]$ and solve again for x. If you do, you will find that your answer does not change. In other words, you have gone about as far as you can go.

(2) ***The quadratic formula.*** This gives an exact solution for x but is more time-consuming. Rewrite the equation

$$\frac{x^2}{0.100 - x} = 6.0 \times 10^{-4}$$

in the form $ax^2 + bx + c = 0$. Doing this,

$$x^2 + (6.0 \times 10^{-4})x - (6.0 \times 10^{-5}) = 0$$

thus $a = 1$; $b = 6.0 \times 10^{-4}$; $c = -6.0 \times 10^{-5}$. Applying the quadratic formula,

$$x = \frac{-b \pm \sqrt{b^2 - 4ac}}{2a}$$

$$= \frac{-6.0 \times 10^{-4} \pm \sqrt{(6.0 \times 10^{-4})^2 + (24.0 \times 10^{-5})}}{2}$$

If you carry out the arithmetic properly, you should get two answers for x:

$$x = 7.4 \times 10^{-3}\ M \qquad \text{and} \qquad -8.0 \times 10^{-3}\ M$$

The second answer is physically ridiculous; the concentration of H^+ cannot be a negative quantity. The first answer is the same one obtained by the method of successive approximations.

Polyprotic Weak Acids

Certain weak acids are **polyprotic;** they contain more than one ionizable hydrogen atom. Such acids ionize in steps, with a separate equilibrium constant for each step. Oxalic acid, a weak organic acid sometimes used to remove bloodstains, is *diprotic:*

$$H_2C_2O_4(aq) \rightleftharpoons H^+(aq) + HC_2O_4^-(aq) \qquad K_{a1} = 5.9 \times 10^{-2}$$

$$HC_2O_4^-(aq) \rightleftharpoons H^+(aq) + C_2O_4^{2-}(aq) \qquad K_{a2} = 5.2 \times 10^{-5}$$

Phosphoric acid, a common ingredient of cola drinks, is *triprotic:*

$$H_3PO_4(aq) \rightleftharpoons H^+(aq) + H_2PO_4^-(aq) \qquad K_{a1} = 7.1 \times 10^{-3}$$

$$H_2PO_4^-(aq) \rightleftharpoons H^+(aq) + HPO_4^{2-}(aq) \qquad K_{a2} = 6.2 \times 10^{-8}$$

$$HPO_4^{2-}(aq) \rightleftharpoons H^+(aq) + PO_4^{3-}(aq) \qquad K_{a3} = 4.5 \times 10^{-13}$$

The behavior of these acids is typical of all polyprotic acids in that—

- ***the anion formed in one step*** (e.g., $HC_2O_4^-$, $H_2PO_4^-$) ***produces another*** H^+ ***ion in the next step.***
- ***the acid equilibrium constant becomes smaller with each successive step.***

$$K_{a1} > K_{a2} > K_{a3}$$

Table 13.3 Equilibrium Constants for Some Weak Polyprotic Acids at 25°C

Acid	Formula	K_{a1}	K_{a2}	K_{a3}
Carbonic acid*	H_2CO_3	4.4×10^{-7}	4.7×10^{-11}	
Oxalic acid	$H_2C_2O_4$	5.9×10^{-2}	5.2×10^{-5}	
Phosphoric acid	H_3PO_4	7.1×10^{-3}	6.2×10^{-8}	4.5×10^{-13}
Sulfurous acid	H_2SO_3	1.7×10^{-2}	6.0×10^{-8}	

*Carbonic acid is a water solution of carbon dioxide:

$$CO_2(g) + H_2O \rightleftharpoons H_2CO_3(aq)$$

The ionization constants listed are calculated assuming that all the carbon dioxide that dissolves is in the form of H_2CO_3.

Putting it another way, ***the acids in successive steps become progressively weaker.*** This is reasonable; it should be more difficult to remove a positively charged proton, H^+, from a negatively charged species like $H_2PO_4^-$ than from a neutral molecule like H_3PO_4.

Ordinarily, successive values of K_a for polyprotic acids decrease by a factor of at least 100 (Table 13.3). In that case, essentially all the H^+ ions in the solution come from the first step. This makes it relatively easy to calculate the pH of a solution of a polyprotic acid.

Example 13.9 The distilled water you use in the laboratory is slightly acidic because of dissolved CO_2, which reacts to form carbonic acid, H_2CO_3. Calculate the pH of a 0.0010 *M* solution of H_2CO_3.

Strategy In principle, there are two different sources of H^+ ions from H_2CO_3:

$$H_2CO_3(aq) \rightleftharpoons H^+(aq) + HCO_3^-(aq) \qquad K_{a1} = 4.4 \times 10^{-7}$$
$$HCO_3^-(aq) \rightleftharpoons H^+(aq) + CO_3^{2-}(aq) \qquad K_{a2} = 4.7 \times 10^{-11}$$

In practice, essentially all the H^+ ions come from the first reaction, because K_{a1} is so much larger than K_{a2}. In other words, H_2CO_3 can be treated as if it were a weak monoprotic acid.

SOLUTION For the first reaction, $H_2CO_3(aq) \rightleftharpoons H^+(aq) + HCO_3^-(aq)$

$$K_{a1} = \frac{x^2}{0.0010 - x} = 4.4 \times 10^{-7} \qquad (x = [H^+] = [HCO_3^-])$$

Making the approximation $0.0010 - x \approx 0.0010$ and solving gives

$$x = (4.4 \times 10^{-10})^{1/2} = 2.1 \times 10^{-5}$$
$$pH = -\log_{10}(2.1 \times 10^{-5}) = 4.68$$

Note that the solution is indeed acidic, with a pH considerably less than 7. Notice that since

$$[H^+] = [HCO_3^-] \qquad \text{and} \qquad \frac{[H^+] \times [CO_3^{2-}]}{[HCO_3^-]} = K_{a2} = 4.7 \times 10^{-11}$$

it follows that $[CO_3^{2-}] = K_{a2} = 4.7 \times 10^{-11}$.

In a water solution of CO_2, there are very, very few CO_3^{2-} ions.

The conclusions reached in Example 13.9 are ordinarily valid for any weak diprotic acid, H_2B.

$$[H^+] \text{ is calculated from } K_{a1}\text{: } [H^+] = (K_{a1} \times [H_2B])^{1/2}$$
$$[HB^-] = [H^+]$$
$$[B^{2-}] = K_{a2}$$

13.5 WEAK BASES AND THEIR EQUILIBRIUM CONSTANTS

Like the weak acids, a large number of solutes act as weak bases. It is convenient to classify weak bases into two groups, molecules and anions.

1. ***Molecules.*** As pointed out in Chapter 4, there are many molecular weak bases, including the organic compounds known as amines. The simplest weak base is ammonia, whose reversible Brønsted-Lowry reaction with water is represented by the equation

$$NH_3(aq) + H_2O \rightleftharpoons NH_4^+(aq) + OH^-(aq)$$

This reaction proceeds to only a very small extent. In 0.10 *M* NH_3, the concentrations of NH_4^+ and OH^- are only about 0.0013 M.

2. ***Anions. An anion derived from a weak acid is itself a weak base.*** A typical example is the fluoride ion, F^-, which is the conjugate base of the weak acid HF. The reaction of the F^- ion with water is

Only a few HF molecules ionize, so $[OH^-] >> [H^+]$.

$$F^-(aq) + H_2O \rightleftharpoons HF(aq) + OH^-(aq)$$

The OH^- ions formed make the solution basic. A 0.10 *M* solution of sodium fluoride, NaF, has a pH of about 8.1.

Notice the similarity between the equation just written and that for the NH_3 molecule cited above—

- both weak bases (NH_3, F^-) accept protons to form the conjugate acid (NH_4^+, HF).
- water acts as a Brønsted-Lowry acid in each case, donating a proton to form the OH^- ion.

Example 13.10 Write an equation to explain why each of the following produces a basic water solution.

(a) NO_2^- (b) Na_2CO_3 (c) $KHCO_3$

Strategy In each case, the anion reacts reversibly with a water molecule, picking up a proton from it. Two species are formed: the OH^- ion and the conjugate acid of the anion.

SOLUTION

(a) $NO_2^-(aq) + H_2O \rightleftharpoons HNO_2(aq) + OH^-(aq)$
(b) $CO_3^{2-}(aq) + H_2O \rightleftharpoons HCO_3^-(aq) + OH^-(aq)$
(c) $HCO_3^-(aq) + H_2O \rightleftharpoons H_2CO_3(aq) + OH^-(aq)$

The Equilibrium Constant for a Weak Base

For the weak base ammonia

$$NH_3(aq) + H_2O \rightleftharpoons NH_4^+(aq) + OH^-(aq)$$

the **base equilibrium constant** is written in the usual way, omitting the term for solvent water.

$$K_b = \frac{[NH_4^+] \times [OH^-]}{[NH_3]}$$

For an anion B^- that acts as a weak base,

$$B^-(aq) + H_2O \rightleftharpoons HB(aq) + OH^-(aq)$$

a very similar expression can be written:

$$K_b = \frac{[HB] \times [OH^-]}{[B^-]} \qquad \textbf{(13.8)}$$

Values of K_b are listed at the right of Table 13.2 (page 361). The larger the value of K_b, the stronger the base. Because K_b for NH_3 (1.8×10^{-5}) is larger than K_b for $C_2H_3O_2^-$ (5.6×10^{-10}), ammonia is a stronger base than the acetate ion.

The quantity **pK_b** is defined as

$$pK_b = -\log_{10}K_b \qquad \textbf{(13.9)}$$

The pK_b of ammonia ($K_b = 1.8 \times 10^{-5}$) is 4.74.

Calculation of $[OH^-]$ in a Water Solution of a Weak Base

We showed in Section 13.4 how K_a of a weak acid can be used to calculate $[H^+]$ in a solution of that acid. In a very similar way, K_b can be used to find $[OH^-]$ in a solution of a weak base.

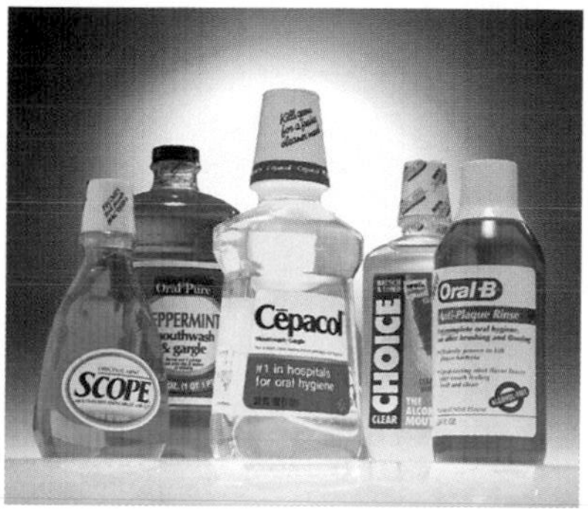

Charles D. Winters

Weak bases.

Example 13.11 Graded

Consider sodium hypochlorite, NaOCl, the main component in household bleach. The hypochlorite ion, OCl^-, has $K_b = 3.6 \times 10^{-7}$. A solution is prepared by dissolving 12.0 g of NaOCl (MM = 74.45 g/mol) in enough water to make 835 mL of solution.

*(a) What is the pH of the solution?

**(b) Household bleach is 5.25% NaOCl by mass. Assuming that its density is 1.00 g/mL, is household bleach more alkaline than the prepared solution?

Strategy

(a) The procedure is entirely analogous to that in Example 13.7. Take $[OH^-] = x$ and set up an equilibrium table, ignoring OH^- ions present in pure water. Solve for x, making the usual approximation. Then calculate pOH and finally the pH. You should obtain a pH greater than 7.

(b) Assume 100.0 g of solution, and determine [NaOCl], which is the same as $[OCl^-]$. Follow the strategy above for (a), and compare the two pH values obtained.

SOLUTION

(a) First, we obtain [NaOCl], which is equal to $[OCl^-]$:

$$[NaOCl] = \frac{12.0 \text{ g}}{0.835 \text{ L}} \times \frac{1 \text{ mol}}{74.45 \text{ g}} = 0.193\ M$$

The equilibrium table is

	$OCl^-(aq)$ + H_2O ⇌	$HOCl(aq)$ +	$OH^-(aq)$
$[\ ]_o$	0.193	0.00	0.00
$\Delta[\ ]$	$-x$	$+x$	$+x$
$[\ ]_{eq}$	$0.193 - x$	x	x

Substituting into the equilibrium-constant expression, we find

$$K_b = \frac{x^2}{0.193 - x} = 3.6 \times 10^{-7}$$

Assuming $0.193 - x \approx 0.193$ and solving for x,

$$x^2 = 6.9 \times 10^{-8} \qquad x = 2.6 \times 10^{-4}$$

CENGAGENOW™

Click Coached Problems for a self-study module on **estimating the pH of weak base solutions.**

Since the % ionization,

$$\left(\frac{2.6 \times 10^{-4}}{0.193}\right) \times 100 = 0.14\% < 5.00\%,$$

the approximation is justified.

HF is among the stronger of weak acids.

$$[OH^-] = 2.6 \times 10^{-4}$$

$$pOH = -\log_{10} 2.6 \times 10^{-4} = 3.59$$

$$pH = 14.00 - 3.59 = 10.41$$

(b) If we assume 100.0 g of solution, then we can say that there are 5.25 g NaOCl in 100.0 mL of solution (since density is assumed to be 1.00 g/mL). Thus,

$$[NaOCl] = [OCl^-] = \frac{5.25\text{ g}}{0.100\text{ L}} \times \frac{1\text{ mol}}{74.4\text{ g}} = 0.706\ M$$

Substituting into an equilibrium table (as in part (a)), we should get

$$K_b = \frac{x^2}{0.706 - x} = 3.6 \times 10^{-7}$$

Again assuming $0.706 - x \approx 0.706$ and solving for x, we obtain

$$x^2 = 2.5 \times 10^{-7} \qquad x = 5.0 \times 10^{-4}$$

The % ionization is

$$\frac{5.0 \times 10^{-4}}{0.706} \times 100 = 0.071\% << 5\%,$$

so the assumption is valid. Then

$$[OH^-] = 5.0 \times 10^{-4}$$

$$pOH = 3.30 \qquad pH = 10.70$$

The household bleach solution is more alkaline, since it has it has a higher pH.

Relation Between K_a and K_b

Equilibrium constants of weak bases can be measured in the laboratory by procedures very much like those used for weak acids. In practice, though, it is simpler to take advantage of a simple mathematical relationship between K_b for a weak base and K_a for its conjugate acid. This relationship can be derived by adding together the equations for the ionization of the weak acid HB and the reaction of the weak base B^- with water:

$$\begin{array}{lrl}
(1) & HB(aq) \rightleftharpoons H^+(aq) + B^-(aq) & K_I = K_a \text{ of HB} \\
(2) & B^-(aq) + H_2O(aq) \rightleftharpoons HB(aq) + OH^-(aq) & K_{II} = K_b \text{ of } B^- \\
\hline
(3) & H_2O \rightleftharpoons H^+(aq) + OH^-(aq) & K_{III} = K_W
\end{array}$$

Because Equation (1) + Equation (2) = Equation (3), we have, according to the rule of multiple equilibria (Chapter 12),

$$K_I \times K_{II} = K_{III}$$

or

$$(K_a \text{ of HB}) \times (K_b \text{ of } B^-) = K_W = 1.0 \times 10^{-14} \qquad \textbf{(13.10)}$$

Checking Table 13.2 (page 361), you can see that this relation holds in each case. For example,

$$K_aHNO_2 \times K_bNO_2^- = (6.0 \times 10^{-4})(1.7 \times 10^{-11})$$
$$= 10 \times 10^{-15} = 1.0 \times 10^{-14}$$

Table 13.4 Relative Strengths of Brønsted-Lowry Acids and Bases

K_a	Conjugate Acid	Conjugate Base	K_b
Very large	$HClO_4$	ClO_4^-	Very small
Very large	HCl	Cl^-	Very small
Very large	HNO_3	NO_3^-	Very small
	H_3O^+	**H_2O**	
6.9×10^{-4}	HF	F^-	1.4×10^{-11}
1.8×10^{-5}	$HC_2H_3O_2$	$C_2H_3O_2^-$	5.6×10^{-10}
1.2×10^{-5}	$Al(H_2O)_6^{3+}$	$Al(H_2O)_5(OH)^{2+}$	8.3×10^{-10}
4.4×10^{-7}	H_2CO_3	HCO_3^-	2.3×10^{-8}
2.8×10^{-8}	$HClO$	ClO^-	3.6×10^{-7}
5.6×10^{-10}	NH_4^+	NH_3	1.8×10^{-5}
4.7×10^{-11}	HCO_3^-	CO_3^{2-}	2.1×10^{-4}
	H_2O	**OH^-**	
Very small	C_2H_5OH	$C_2H_5O^-$	Very large
Very small	OH^-	O^{2-}	Very large
Very small	H_2	H^-	Very large

Species shown in deep color are unstable because they react with H_2O molecules.

The —OH group in C_2H_5OH does not act as an OH^- ion.

From the general relation between K_a of a weak acid and K_b of its conjugate weak base, it should be clear that these two quantities are inversely related to each other. *The larger the value of K_a, the smaller the value of K_b and vice versa.* Table 13.4 shows this effect and some other interesting features. In particular,

1. Brønsted-Lowry acids (left column) can be divided into three categories:
   (a) strong acids ($HClO_4$, . . .), which are stronger proton donors than the H_3O^+ ion.
   (b) weak acids (HF, . . .), which are weaker proton donors than the H_3O^+ ion, but stronger than the H_2O molecule.
   (c) species such as C_2H_5OH, which are weaker proton donors than the H_2O molecule and hence do not form acidic water solutions.
2. Brønsted-Lowry bases (right column) can be divided similarly:
   (a) strong bases (H^-, . . .), which are stronger proton acceptors than the OH^- ion.
   (b) weak bases (F^-, . . .), which are weaker proton acceptors than the OH^- ion, but stronger than the H_2O molecule.
   (c) the anions of strong acids (ClO_4^-, . . .), which are weaker proton acceptors than the H_2O molecule and hence do not form basic water solutions.

We should point out that, just as the three strong acids at the top of Table 13.4 are completely converted to H_3O^+ ions in aqueous solution:

$$HClO_4(aq) + H_2O \longrightarrow H_3O^+(aq) + ClO_4^-(aq)$$
$$HCl(aq) + H_2O \longrightarrow H_3O^+(aq) + Cl^-(aq)$$
$$HNO_3(aq) + H_2O \longrightarrow H_3O^+(aq) + NO_3^-(aq)$$

the three strong bases at the bottom of the table are completely converted to OH^- ions:

$$H^-(aq) + H_2O \longrightarrow OH^-(aq) + H_2(g)$$
$$O^{2-}(aq) + H_2O \longrightarrow OH^-(aq) + OH^-(aq)$$
$$C_2H_5O^-(aq) + H_2O \longrightarrow OH^-(aq) + C_2H_5OH(aq)$$

In other words, the species H^-, O^{2-}, and $C_2H_5O^-$ do not exist in water solution.

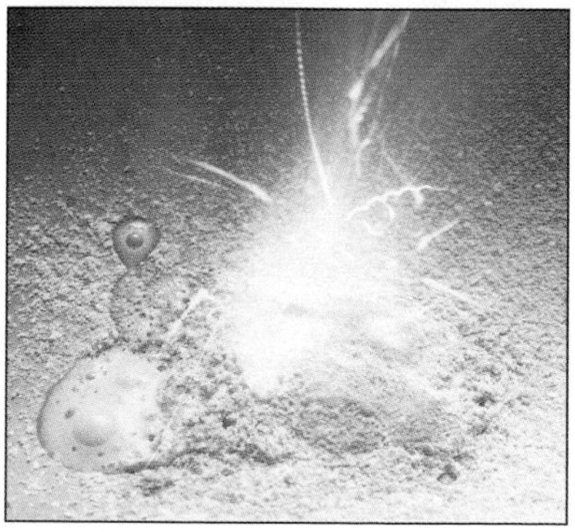

Charles D. Winters

Hydride ion–water reaction. As water is dropped onto solid calcium hydride, the hydride ion (H^-) reacts immediately and vigorously to form $H_2(g)$ (which is ignited by the heat of the reaction) and OH^-.

13.6 ACID-BASE PROPERTIES OF SALT SOLUTIONS

CENGAGENOW™
Click Coached Problems for a self-study module on **hydrolysis.**

A salt is an ionic solid containing a cation other than H^+ and an anion other than OH^- or O^{2-}. When a salt such as NaCl, K_2CO_3, or $Al(NO_3)_3$ dissolves in water, the cation and anion separate from one another.

$$NaCl(s) \longrightarrow Na^+(aq) + Cl^-(aq)$$
$$K_2CO_3(s) \longrightarrow 2K^+(aq) + CO_3^{2-}(aq)$$
$$Al(NO_3)_3(s) \longrightarrow Al^{3+}(aq) + 3NO_3^-(aq)$$

To predict whether a given salt solution will be acidic, basic, or neutral, you consider three factors in turn.

1. ***Decide what effect, if any, the cation has on the pH of water.***
2. ***Decide what effect, if any, the anion has on the pH of water.***
3. ***Combine the two effects to decide on the behavior of the salt.***

Cations: Weak Acids or Spectator Ions?

Learn the spectator ions, not the players.

As we pointed out in Section 13.4, certain cations act as weak acids in water solution because of reactions such as

$$NH_4^+(aq) + H_2O \rightleftharpoons H_3O^+(aq) + NH_3(aq)$$
$$Zn(H_2O)_4^{2+}(aq) + H_2O \rightleftharpoons H_3O^+(aq) + Zn(H_2O)_3(OH)^+(aq)$$

Essentially all transition metal ions behave like Zn^{2+}, forming a weakly acidic solution. Among the main-group cations, Al^{3+} and, to a lesser extent, Mg^{2+}, act as weak acids. In contrast the cations in Group 1 show little or no tendency to react with water.

If we say that *to classify an ion as acidic or basic in water solution, it must change the pH by more than 0.5 unit in 0.1 M solution,* then the cations derived from strong bases:

- the alkali metal cations (Li^+, Na^+, K^+ . . .)
- the heavier alkaline earth cations (Ca^{2+}, Sr^{2+}, Ba^{2+})

are spectator ions as far as pH is concerned (Table 13.5).

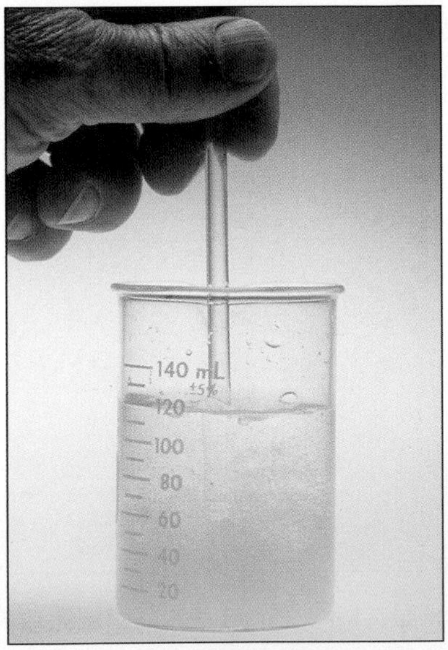

Charles D. Winters

Sodium chloride solution. When the NaCl is completely dissolved, the solution will contain only Na^+, Cl^-, and H_2O, and it will be neither acidic nor basic.

Anions: Weak Bases or Spectator Ions?

As pointed out in Section 13.5, anions that are the conjugate bases of weak acids act themselves as weak bases in water. They accept a proton from a water molecule, leaving an OH^- ion that makes the solution basic. The reactions of the fluoride and carbonate ions are typical:

$$F^-(aq) + H_2O \rightleftharpoons HF(aq) + OH^-(aq)$$
$$CO_3^{2-}(aq) + H_2O \rightleftharpoons HCO_3^-(aq) + OH^-(aq)$$

Table 13.5 Acid-Base Properties of Ions* in Water Solution

	Spectator		Basic		Acidic	
Anion	Cl^-	NO_3^-	$C_2H_3O_2^-$	CO_3^{2-}		
	Br^-	ClO_4^-	F^-	PO_4^{3-}		
	I^-		Many others			
Cation	Li^+	Ca^{2+}			NH_4^+	Al^{3+}
	Na^+	Sr^{2+}			Mg^{2+}	
	K^+	Ba^{2+}			Transition metal ions	

*For the acid-base properties of amphiprotic anions such as HCO_3^- or $H_2PO_4^-$, see the discussion at the end of this section.

Most anions behave this way, except those derived from strong acids (Cl^-, Br^-, I^-, NO_3^-, ClO_4^-), which show little or no tendency to react with water to form OH^- ions. Like the cations listed in the left column of Table 13.5, they act as spectator ions as far as pH is concerned.

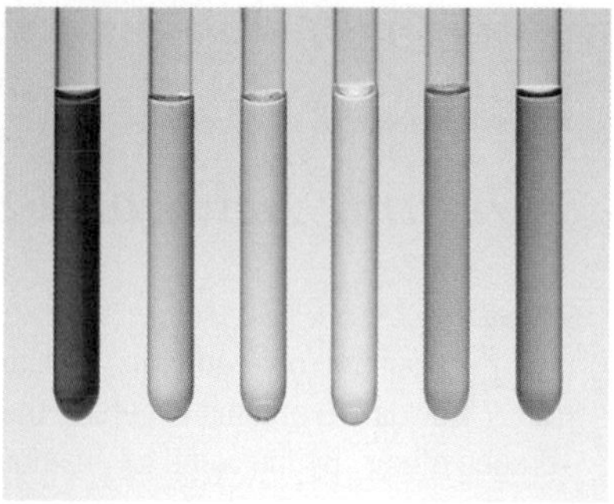

Charles D. Winters

Figure 13.9

pH of salt solutions. Universal indicator is red in strong acid *(far left)* and purple in strong base *(far right)*. Between these extremes, the dilute salt solutions are *(left to right)* weakly acidic NH_4I (pH about 4) and $Zn(NO_3)_2$ (pH about 5); neutral $KClO_4$; and basic Na_3PO_4 (pH about 12).

Salts: Acidic, Basic, or Neutral?

If you know how the cation and anion of a salt affect the pH of water, it is a relatively simple matter to decide what the net effect will be (Example 13.12).

Example 13.12 Consider water solutions of these four salts:

$$NH_4I,\ Zn(NO_3)_3,\ KClO_4,\ Na_3PO_4$$

Which of these solutions are acidic? Basic? Neutral?

Strategy First, decide what ions are present in the solution. Then classify each cation and anion as acidic, basic, or neutral, using Table 13.5. Finally, consider the combined effects of the two ions in each salt.

SOLUTION To implement this strategy, it is convenient to prepare a table.

Salt	Cation	Anion	Solution of Salt
NH_4I	NH_4^+ (acidic)	I^- (spectator)	acidic
$Zn(NO_3)_2$	Zn^{2+} (acidic)	NO_3^- (spectator)	acidic
$KClO_4$	K^+ (spectator)	ClO_4^- (spectator)	neutral
Na_3PO_4	Na^+ (spectator)	PO_4^{3-} (basic)	basic

These predictions are confirmed by experiment (Figure 13.9).

The procedure described in Example 13.12 does not cover one combination—an acidic cation (e.g., NH_4^+) and a basic anion (e.g., F^-). In that case K_a of the cation must be compared with K_b of the anion. In general,

1. ***If $K_a > K_b$, the salt is acidic.*** An example is NH_4F ($K_aNH_4^+ = 5.6 \times 10^{-10}$; $K_bF^- = 1.4 \times 10^{-11}$), where the pH is about 6.2.
2. ***If $K_b > K_a$, the salt is basic.*** An example is NH_4ClO ($K_aNH_4^+ = 5.6 \times 10^{-10}$; $K_bClO^- = 3.6 \times 10^{-7}$), where the pH is 8.4.

A similar argument can be used to decide whether an amphiprotic anion such as HCO_3^- or $H_2PO_4^-$ is acidic or basic. In principle, these ions can act as either weak acids or weak bases:

$$HCO_3^-(aq) + H_2O \rightleftharpoons H_3O^+(aq) + CO_3^{2-}(aq) \qquad K_a = 4.7 \times 10^{-11}$$

$$HCO_3^-(aq) + H_2O \rightleftharpoons H_2CO_3(aq) + OH^-(aq) \qquad K_b = 2.3 \times 10^{-8}$$

Because $K_b > K_a$, you would predict, correctly, that the HCO_3^- ion produces a basic water solution. Sodium hydrogen carbonate, $NaHCO_3$ ("bicarbonate of soda"), is used as an antacid because its water solution is basic, with a pH of about 8.3. The reverse situation applies with the $H_2PO_4^-$ ion ($K_a = 6.2 \times 10^{-8}$, $K_b = 1.4 \times 10^{-12}$). Because $K_a > K_b$, the $H_2PO_4^-$ ion gives an acidic solution. The compound NaH_2PO_4 is weakly acidic, with a solution pH of about 4.7.

Most ions of this type, like HCO_3^-, are basic.

CHEMISTRY Beyond the Classroom

Organic Acids and Bases

As pointed out earlier in this chapter, most molecular weak acids are organic in nature; they contain carbon as well as hydrogen atoms. By the same token, most molecular weak bases are organic compounds called amines, which were discussed briefly in Chapter 4.

Carboxylic Acids

Table A lists some of the organic acids found in foods. All of these compounds contain the carboxyl group

$$-\underset{\underset{\displaystyle O}{\|}}{C}-O-H$$

The general equation for the reversible dissociation of a carboxylic acid is

$$RCOOH(aq) \rightleftharpoons RCOO^-(aq) + H^+(aq)$$

where R is a hydrocarbon group such as CH_3, C_2H_5, ... The reaction of a carboxylic acid with a strong base can be represented by the equation

$$RCOOH(aq) + OH^-(aq) \longrightarrow RCOO^-(aq) + H_2O$$

This reaction, as is the case with all weak acids, goes essentially to completion.

Certain drugs, both prescription and over-the-counter, contain organic acids. Two of the most popular products of this type are the analgesics aspirin and ibuprofen (Advil, Nuprin, and so on).

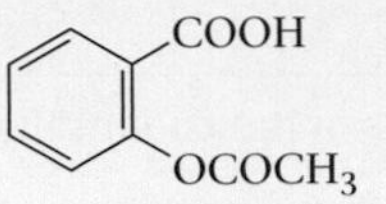

aspirin

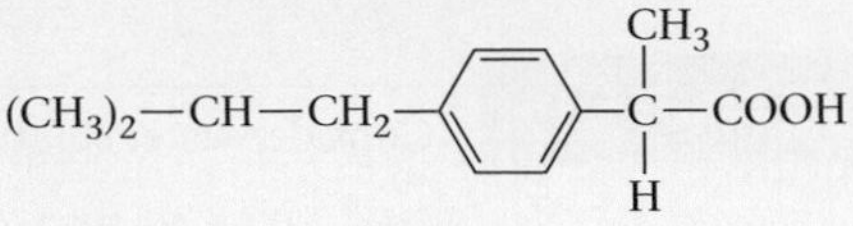

ibuprofen

Because these compounds are acidic, they can cause stomach irritation unless taken with food or water. Beyond that, aspirin inhibits blood clotting, which explains why it is often prescribed to reduce the likelihood of a stroke or heart attack. Indeed, it is now recommended for a person in the throes of a heart attack.

Amines

An amine is a derivative of ammonia, NH_3, in which one or more of the hydrogen atoms have been replaced by a hydrocarbon group (e.g., CH_3, C_2H_5). Amines can be classified according to the number

Table A Some Naturally Occurring Organic Acids

Name		Source
Acetic acid	CH_3-COOH	Vinegar
Citric acid	$HOOC-CH_2-C(OH)(COOH)-CH_2-COOH$	Citrus fruits
Lactic acid	$CH_3-CH(OH)-COOH$	Sour milk
Malic acid	$HOOC-CH_2-CH(OH)-COOH$	Apples, watermelons, grape juice, wine
Oxalic acid	$HOOC-COOH$	Rhubarb, spinach, tomatoes
Quinic acid	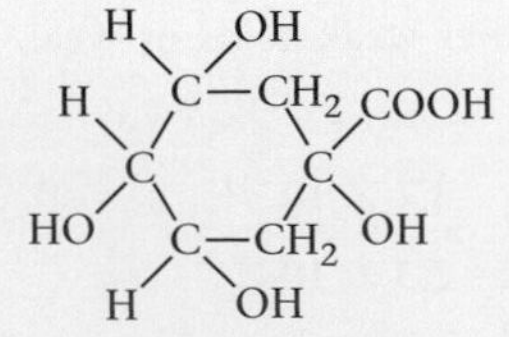	Cranberries
Tartaric acid	$HOOC-CH(OH)-CH(OH)-COOH$	Grape juice, wine

Table B Types of Amines

Type	General Formula	Example
Primary	RNH_2	$CH_3-N(H)-H$
Secondary	R_2NH	$CH_3-N(H)-CH_3$
Tertiary	R_3N	$CH_3-N(CH_3)-CH_3$
	where $R = CH_3, C_2H_5, \ldots$	

Scott Camazine/Photo Researchers, Inc.

Figure A

Flowers and unripe seed capsules of the opium poppy. Within the capsule is a milky, gummy substance that contains the alkaloid morphine.

(1, 2, or 3) of hydrocarbon groups bonded to nitrogen (Table B). Most amines of low molar mass are volatile with distinctly unpleasant odors. For example, $(CH_3)_3N$ is a gas at room temperature (bp = 3°C) with an odor somewhere between those of ammonia and spoiled fish.

The general equation for the reaction of a primary amine with water is

$$RNH_2(aq) + H_2O \rightleftharpoons RNH_3^+(aq) + OH^-(aq)$$

while its reaction with strong acid is

$$RNH_2(aq) + H^+(aq) \longrightarrow RNH_3^+(aq)$$

Secondary and tertiary amines react similarly, forming cations of general formula $R_2NH_2^+$ and R_3NH^+. In each case the added proton bonds to the unshared pair on the nitrogen atom. (Compare RNH_3^+, $R_2NH_2^+$ and R_3NH^+ with the ammonium ion, NH_4^+.)

The reaction of amines with H^+ ions has an interesting practical application. Amines of high molar mass, frequently used as drugs, have very low water solubilities. They can be converted to a water-soluble form by treatment with strong acid. For example,

$$\underset{\text{novocaine}}{C_9H_{10}NO_2-N(C_2H_5)-C_2H_5(s)} + HCl(aq) \longrightarrow$$

$$\underset{\text{novocaine hydrochloride}}{[C_9H_{10}NO_2-NH(C_2H_5)-C_2H_5]^+(aq)} + Cl^-(aq)$$

Novocaine hydrochloride is about 200 times as soluble as novocaine itself. When your dentist injects "Novocaine," the liquid in the syringe is a water solution of novocaine hydrochloride.

Alkaloids such as caffeine, coniine, and morphine (Figure A) are amines that are extracted from plants.

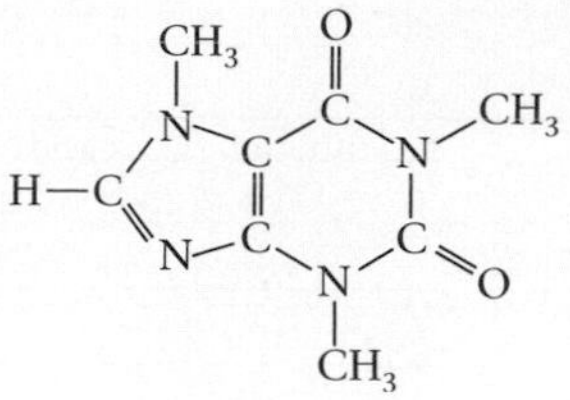

caffeine

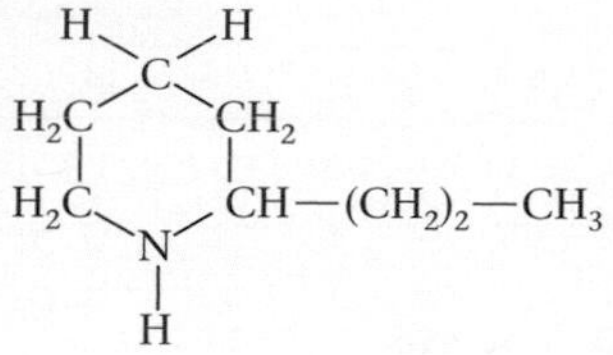

coniine

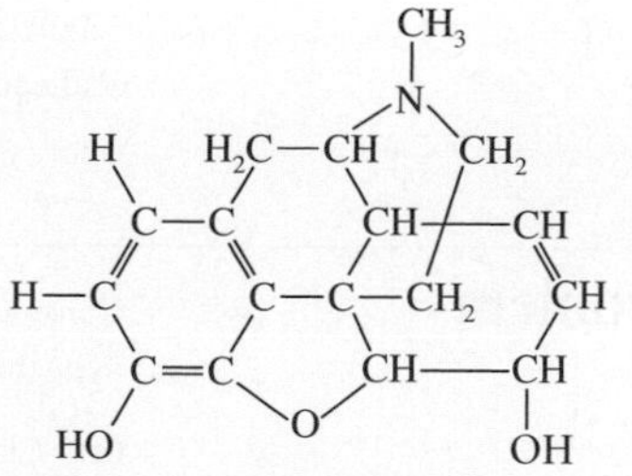

morphine

Caffeine occurs in tea leaves, coffee beans, and cola nuts. Morphine is obtained from unripe opium poppy seed pods. Coniine, extracted from hemlock, is the alkaloid that killed Socrates. He was sentenced to death because of unconventional teaching methods; teacher evaluations had teeth in them in ancient Greece.

Chapter Highlights

Key Concepts

Select end of chapter Questions and Problems may be assigned in OWL and are cross-referenced in the Key Concepts list.

CENGAGENOW™

Sign in at **academic.cengage.com/now** to:

- Check your readiness for an exam by taking the Pre-Test and exploring the self-study modules recommended in your Personalized Study plan
- For quick review, download Go Chemistry mini-lecture flashcard modules (or purchase them at **www.ichapters.com**)

1. Classify a species as a Brønsted-Lowry acid or base and explain by a net ionic equation. **(Examples 13.1, 13.4, 13.10; Problems 1–12)** ■ Questions and Problems assignable in OWL: 2, 4, 12, 34, 64
2. Given $[H^+]$, $[OH^-]$, pH, or pOH, calculate the other three quantities. **(Examples 13.2, 13.3; Problems 13–32)** ■ 14, 16, 25, 28, 90
3. Given the pH and original concentration of a weak acid solution, calculate K_a. **(Example 13.5; Problems 43–48)** ■ 43, 48
4. Given K_a of a weak acid and its original concentration, calculate $[H^+]$. **(Examples 13.7–13.9; Problems 49–56)** ■ 52, 60, 103
5. Given K_b of a weak base and its original concentration, calculate $[OH^-]$. **(Example 13.11; Problems 71–76)** ■ 74
6. Given K_a for a weak acid, calculate K_b for its conjugate base (or vice-versa). **(Problems 69, 70, 73, 74)** ■ 69
7. Predict whether a salt solution is acidic, basic, or neutral. **(Example 13.12; Problems 77–84)** ■ 80, 83

Key Equations

Ionization of water $$K_W = [H^+] \times [OH^-] = 1.0 \times 10^{-14} \text{ at } 25°C \quad \text{(Section 13.2)}$$

pH, pOH $$pH = -\log_{10}[H^+] \qquad pOH = -\log_{10}[OH^-] \quad \text{(Section 13.3)}$$

Expressions for K_a, K_b $$K_a = \frac{[H^+] \times [B^-]}{[HB]} \qquad pK_a = -\log_{10}K_a \quad \text{(Section 13.4)}$$

$$K_b = \frac{[HB] \times [OH^-]}{[B^-]} \qquad pK_b = -\log_{10}K_b \quad \text{(Section 13.5)}$$

$$K_a \times K_b = K_W \quad \text{(Section 13.5)}$$

% ionization (weak acid) $$\%\ \text{ionization} = \frac{[H^+]_{aq}}{[HB]_o} \times 100\% \quad \text{(Section 13.4)}$$

Key Terms

acid	base	pOH
—Brønsted-Lowry	—Brønsted-Lowry	pK_a
—conjugate	—conjugate	pK_b
—polyprotic	base equilibrium constant	salt
acid equilibrium constant	neutral solution	water
	pH	—ion product constant

Summary Problem

Consider aqueous solutions of potassium hydroxide, potassium formate ($KCHO_2$), hydrochloric acid, and hypochlorous acid.

(a) Classify each reactant as strong or weak, acid or base.
(b) Using the Brønsted-Lowry model, write equations to explain your answers in (a).
(c) Write the conjugate base of the weak acid and the conjugate acid of the weak base.
(d) What is the pH of 0.215 *M* solutions of KOH, $KCHO_2$, HCl, and HClO?
(e) What is K_b for the conjugate base of HClO? What is K_a for the conjugate acid of $KClO_2$?
(f) Classify the salts NH_4Cl and $KClO_4$ as acidic, basic, or neutral.
(g) Would NH_4ClO be acidic, basic, or neutral?

Answers

(a) HCl—strong acid; KOH—strong base; $KCHO_2$—weak base; HClO—weak acid
(b) $HCl(aq) + H_2O \longrightarrow H_3O^+(aq) + Cl^-(aq)$
$KOH(aq) \longrightarrow K^+(aq) + OH^-(aq)$
$CHO_2^-(aq) + H_2O \rightleftharpoons HCHO_2(aq) + OH^-(aq)$
$HClO(aq) + H_2O \rightleftharpoons H_3O^+(aq) + ClO^-(aq)$

(c) $HClO/ClO^-$; $CHO_2^-/HCHO_2$
(d) pH of HCl solution = 0.668; pH of KOH solution = 13.33
pH of HClO solution = 4.11; pH of $KCHO_2$ solution = 8.53
(e) K_b for ClO^- = 3.6×10^{-7}; K_a for $HCHO_2$ = 1.9×10^{-4}
(f) NH_4Cl is acidic; $KClO_4$ is neutral
(g) basic

Questions and Problems

Blue-numbered questions have answers in Appendix 6 and fully-worked solutions in the *Student Solutions Manual.*

■ denotes questions assignable in OWL.

WEB indicates that the solution is available on this book's companion website.

Brønsted-Lowry Acid-Base Model

1. For each of the following reactions, indicate the Brønsted-Lowry acids and bases. What are the conjugate acid/base pairs?

(a) $H_3O^+(aq) + CN^-(aq) \rightleftharpoons HCN(aq) + H_2O$
(b) $HNO_2(aq) + OH^-(aq) \rightleftharpoons NO_2^-(aq) + H_2O$
(c) $HCHO_2(aq) + H_2O \rightleftharpoons CHO_2^-(aq) + H_3O^+(aq)$

2. ■ Follow the directions for Question 1 for the following reactions.

(a) $CN^-(aq) + H_2O \rightleftharpoons HCN(aq) + OH^-(aq)$
(b) $HCO_3^-(aq) + H_3O^+(aq) \rightleftharpoons H_2CO_3(aq) + H_2O$
(c) $HC_2H_3O_2(aq) + HS^-(aq) \rightleftharpoons C_2H_3O_2^-(aq) + H_2S(aq)$

3. According to the Brønsted-Lowry theory, which of the following would you expect to act as an acid? Which as a base?

(a) $C_2H_5NH_3^+$ (b) HClO (c) CN^-

4. ■ According to the Brønsted-Lowry theory, which of the following would you expect to act as an acid? Which as a base?

(a) CHO_2^- (b) NH_4^+ (c) HSO_3^-

5. Give the formula of the conjugate acid of

(a) OH^- (b) HPO_4^{2-} (c) NH_3
(d) F^- (e) $Zn(H_2O)_2(OH)_2$

6. **WEB** Give the formula of the conjugate base of

(a) HCO_3^- (b) $Cu(H_2O)(OH)_3^-$ (c) HNO_2
(d) $(CH_3)_2NH_2$ (e) H_2SO_3

7. Write a balanced equation showing how the $H_2PO_4^-$ ion can be either a Brønsted-Lowry acid or a Brønsted-Lowry base.

8. Follow the instructions of Question 7 for the bicarbonate ion, HCO_3^-.

9. Using the Brønsted-Lowry model, write equations to show why the following species behave as weak acids in water.

(a) $Ni(H_2O)_5OH^+$ (b) $Al(H_2O)_6^{3+}$
(c) H_2S (d) HPO_4^{2-}
(e) $HClO_2$ (f) $Cr(H_2O)_5(OH)^+$

10. Follow the directions of Question 9 for the following species.

(a) $Zn(H_2O)_3OH^+$ (b) HSO_4^- (c) HNO_2
(d) $Fe(H_2O)_6^{2+}$ (e) $HC_2H_3O_2$ (f) $H_2PO_4^-$

11. Using the Brønsted-Lowry model, write an equation to show why each of the following species produces a basic aqueous solution.

(a) NH_3 (b) NO_2^- (c) $C_6H_5NH_2$
(d) CO_3^{2-} (e) F^- (f) HCO_3^-

12. ■ Follow the directions of Question 11 for the following species.

(a) $(CH_3)_3N$ (b) PO_4^{3-} (c) HPO_4^{2-}
(d) $H_2PO_4^-$ (e) HS^- (f) $C_2H_5NH_2$

[H+], [OH−], pH, and pOH

13. Find the pH and pOH of solutions with the following [H+]. Classify each as acidic or basic.

(a) 6.0 *M* (b) 0.33 *M*
(c) 4.6×10^{-8} *M* (d) 7.2×10^{-14} *M*

14. ■ Find the pH and pOH of solutions with the following [H+]. Classify each as acidic or basic.

(a) 1.0 *M* (b) 1.7×10^{-4} *M*
(c) 6.8×10^{-8} *M* (d) 9.3×10^{-11} *M*

15. Calculate [H+] and [OH−] in solutions with the following pH.

(a) 4.0 (b) 8.52 (c) 0.00 (d) 12.60

16. ■ Calculate [H+] and [OH−] in solutions with the following pH.

(a) 9.0 (b) 3.20 (c) −1.05 (d) 7.46

17. Complete the following table for solutions at 25°C.

	[H+]	[OH−]	pH	pOH	Acidic?
(a)	2.4×10^{-8}	______	______	______	______
(b)	______	1.9×10^{-2}	______	______	______
(c)	______	______	8.62	______	______
(d)	______	______	______	12.22	______

18. Complete the following table for solutions at 25°C.

	[H+]	[OH−]	pH	pOH	Basic?
(a)	______	______	______	9.32	______
(b)	______	______	11.95	______	______
(c)	______	6.8×10^{-9}	______	______	______
(d)	4.3×10^{-3}	______	______	______	______

19. Solution 1 has [H+] = 1.7×10^{-2}. Solution 2 has [H+] = 4.3×10^{-4}. Which solution is more acidic? Which has the higher pH?

20. Solution X has pH 11.7. Solution Y has [OH−] = 4.5×10^{-2}. Which solution is more basic? Which has the higher pOH?

21. Solution X has a pH of 4.35. Solution Y has [OH−] ten times as large as solution X. Solution Z has a pH 4.0 units higher than that of solution X.

(a) Calculate the ratio of [H+] in solutions X and Y and solutions X and Z.
(b) What is the pH of solutions Y and Z?
(c) Classify each solution as acidic, basic, or neutral.

22. Solution A has a pH of 12.32. Solution B has [H+] three times as large as that of solution A. Solution C has a pH half that of solution A.

(a) What is [H+] for all three solutions?
(b) What is the pH of solutions B and C?
(c) Classify each solution as acidic, basic, or neutral.

23. Unpolluted rain water has a pH of about 5.5. Acid rain has been shown to have a pH as low as 3.0. Calculate the [H+] ratio of acid rain to unpolluted rain.

■ in OWL Blue-numbered questions answered in Appendix 6 **WEB** Solution is available on companion website

24. Milk of Magnesia has a pH of 10.5.

(a) Calculate $[H^+]$.

(b) Calculate the ratio of the H^+ concentration of gastric juice, pH 1.5, to that of Milk of Magnesia.

25. ■ Find $[OH^-]$ and the pH of the following solutions.

(a) 0.25 g of $Ba(OH)_2$ dissolved in enough water to make 0.655 L of solution.

(b) A 3.00-L solution of KOH is prepared by diluting 300.0 mL of 0.149 *M* KOH with water. What is the molarity of the diluted solution? What is the effect of a tenfold dilution on the pH?

26. Find $[H^+]$ and the pH of the following solutions.

(a) 1.75 L of a 37.5% (by mass) solution ($d = 1.00$ g/mL) of HCl. What is the pH of 0.175 L of the same solution?

(b) A solution made up of 22 g of HBr dissolved in enough water to make 479 mL of solution. What is the pH if the same mass of HBr is dissolved in enough water to make 47.9 mL of solution?

27. Find $[OH^-]$, $[H^+]$, and the pH and pOH of the following solutions.

(a) 0.27 *M* $Sr(OH)_2$.

(b) a solution made by dissolving 13.6 g of KOH in enough water to make 2.50 L of solution.

28. ■ Find $[OH^-]$, $[H^+]$, and the pH and pOH of the following solutions.

(a) 45.0 mL of 0.0921 *M* $Ba(OH)_2$ diluted with enough water to make 350.0 mL of solution.

(b) A solution made by dissolving 4.68 g of NaOH in enough water to make 635 mL of solution.

29. What is the pH of a solution obtained by adding 5.00 g of HI to 295 mL of a 0.786 *M* solution of HNO_3? Assume that the HI addition does not change the volume of the resulting solution.

30. What is the pH of a solution obtained by adding 145 mL of 0.575 *M* HCl to 493 mL of a HNO_3 solution with a pH of 1.39? Assume that volumes are additive.

31. What is the pH of a solution obtained by adding 13.0 g of NaOH to 795 mL of a 0.200 *M* solution of $Sr(OH)_2$? Assume no volume change after NaOH is added.

32. What is the pH of a solution obtained by mixing 139 mL of KOH with a pH of 12.66 and 293 mL of $Ba(OH)_2$ with a pH of 11.79? Assume that volumes are additive.

Ionization Expressions, Weak Acids

33. Write the ionization equation and the K_a expression for each of the following acids.

(a) PH_4^+ (b) HS^- (c) $HBrO_2$

34. ■ Write the ionization equation and the K_a expression for each of the following acids.

(a) HSO_3^- (b) HPO_4^{2-} (c) HNO_2

35. Calculate K_a for the weak acids that have the following pK_a values.

(a) 3.9 (b) 10.12 (c) 13.07

36. Calculate pK_a for the weak acids that have the following K_a values.

(a) 1.8×10^{-4} (b) 6.8×10^{-8} (c) 4.9×10^{-11}

37. Consider these acids

Acid	A	B	C	D
pK_a	3.7	9.2	7.4	1.6

(a) Arrange the acids in order of decreasing acid strength from strongest to weakest.

(b) Which acid has the largest K_a value?

38. WEB Consider these acids

Acid	A	B	C	D
K_a	1.6×10^{-3}	9×10^{-4}	2×10^{-6}	3×10^{-4}

(a) Arrange the acids in order of increasing acid strength from weakest to strongest.

(b) Which acid has the smallest pK_a value?

39. Rank the following solutions in order of increasing $[H^+]$. (Use Table 13.2.)

0.1 *M* HNO_3, 0.1 *M* HNO_2, 0.1 *M* $HC_7H_5O_2$, 0.1 *M* HClO

40. Rank the following solutions in order of increasing $[H^+]$.

0.1 *M* HBr, 0.1 *M* HF, 0.1 *M* $HCHO_2$ 0.1 *M* HCN

41. Rank the solutions in Question 39 in order of increasing pH.

42. Rank the solutions in Question 40 in order of increasing pH.

Equilibrium Calculations, Weak Acids

43. ■ The pH of a 0.129 *M* solution of a weak acid, HB, is 2.34. What is K_a for the weak acid?

44. WEB The pH of a 2.642 *M* solution of a weak acid, HB, is 5.32. What is K_a for the weak acid?

45. Caproic acid, $HC_6H_{11}O_2$, is found in coconut oil and is used in making artificial flavors. A solution is made by dissolving 0.450 mol of caproic acid in enough water to make 2.0 L of solution. The solution has $[H^+] = 1.7 \times 10^{-3}$ *M*. What is K_a for caproic acid?

46. Para-aminobenzoic acid (PABA), $HC_7H_6NO_2$, is used in some sunscreen agents. A solution is made by dissolving 0.263 mol of PABA in enough water to make 750.0 mL of solution. The solution has $[H^+] = 2.6 \times 10^{-3}$ *M*. What is K_a for PABA?

47. Ascorbic acid, $HC_6H_7O_6$, also known as vitamin C, is a weak acid. It is an essential vitamin and an antioxidant. A solution of ascorbic acid is prepared by dissolving 2.00 g in enough water to make 100.0 mL of solution. The resulting solution has a pH of 2.54. What is K_a for ascorbic acid?

48. ■ Barbituric acid, $HC_4H_3N_2O_3$, is used to prepare barbiturates, a class of drugs used as sedatives. A 325-mL aqueous solution of barbituric acid has a pH of 2.34 and contains 9.00 g of the acid. What is K_a for barbituric acid?

49. When aluminum chloride dissolves in water, $Al(H_2O)_6^{3+}$ and Cl^- ions are obtained. Using the K_a in Table 13.2, calculate the pH of a 1.75 *M* solution of $AlCl_3$.

50. Using the K_a values listed in Table 13.2, calculate the pH of a 0.39 *M* solution of ammonium chloride.

51. Butyric acid, $HC_4H_7O_2$, is responsible for the odor of rancid butter and cheese. Its K_a is 1.51×10^{-5}. Calculate $[H^+]$ in solutions prepared by adding enough water to the following to make 1.30 L.

(a) 0.279 mol (b) 13.5 g

52. ■ Penicillin (MM = 356 g/mol), an antibiotic often used to treat bacterial infections, is a weak acid. Its K_a is 1.7×10^{-3}. Calculate $[H^+]$ in solutions prepared by adding enough water to the following to make 725 mL.

(a) 0.187 mol (b) 127 g

53. Uric acid, $HC_5H_3O_3N_4$, can accumulate in the joints. This accumulation causes severe pain and the condition is called *gout.* K_a for uric acid is 5.1×10^{-6}. For a 0.894 *M* solution of uric acid, calculate

(a) $[H^+]$ (b) $[OH^-]$

(c) pH (d) % ionization

■ in OWL Blue-numbered questions answered in Appendix 6 WEB Solution is available on companion website

54. Barbituric acid ($K_a = 1.1 \times 10^{-4}$) is used in the manufacture of some sedatives. For a 0.673 *M* solution of barbituric acid, calculate

(a) $[H^+]$ (b) $[OH^-]$
(c) pH (d) % ionization

55. Phenol, once known as carbolic acid, HC_6H_5O, is a weak acid. It was one of the first antiseptics used by Lister. Its K_a is 1.1×10^{-10}. A solution of phenol is prepared by dissolving 14.5 g of phenol in enough water to make 892 mL of solution. For this solution, calculate

(a) pH
(b) % ionization

56. Benzoic acid ($K_a = 6.6 \times 10^{-5}$) is present in many berries. Calculate the pH and % ionization of a 726-mL solution that contains 0.288 mol of benzoic acid.

Polyprotic Acids

Use the K_a values listed in Table 13.3 for polyprotic acids.

57. Write the overall chemical equation and calculate *K* for the complete ionization of oxalic acid, $H_2C_2O_4$.

58. Write the overall chemical equation and calculate *K* for the complete ionization of H_3PO_4.

59. Consider the diprotic acid H_2A. For the first dissociation of H_2A, $K_{a1} = 2.7 \times 10^{-4}$. For its second dissociation, $K_{a2} = 8.3 \times 10^{-7}$. What is the pH of a 0.20 *M* solution of H_2A? Estimate $[HA^-]$ and $[A^{2-}]$.

60. ■ Consider a 0.33 *M* solution of the diprotic acid H_2X.

$$H_2X \rightleftharpoons H^+(aq) + HX^-(aq) \qquad K_{a1} = 3.3 \times 10^{-4}$$
$$HX^- \rightleftharpoons H^+(aq) + X^{2-}(aq) \qquad K_{a2} = 9.7 \times 10^{-8}$$

Calculate the pH of the solution and estimate $[HX^-]$ and $[X^{2-}]$.

61. Phthalic acid, $H_2C_8H_4O_4$, is a diprotic acid. It is used to make phenolphthalein indicator. $K_{a1} = 0.0012$, and $K_{a2} = 3.9 \times 10^{-6}$. Calculate the pH of a 2.9 *M* solution of phthalic acid. Estimate $[HC_8H_4O_4^-]$ and $[C_8H_4O_4^{2-}]$.

62. Ascorbic acid, $H_2C_6H_6O_6$, also known as vitamin C, is present in many citrus fruits. It is a diprotic acid with the following K_a values: $K_{a1} = 7.9 \times 10^{-5}$; $K_{a2} = 1.6 \times 10^{-12}$. What is the pH of a 0.63 *M* solution of ascorbic acid? Estimate $[HC_6H_6O_6^-]$ and $[C_6H_6O_6^{2-}]$.

Ionization Expressions; Weak Bases

63. Write the ionization expression and the K_b expression for 0.1 *M* aqueous solutions of the following bases.

(a) F^- (b) HCO_3^- (c) CN^-

64. ■ Follow the instructions for Question 63 for the following bases.

(a) NH_3 (b) HS^- (c) $(CH_3)_3N$

65. Using the equilibrium constants in Table 13.2, rank the following 0.1 *M* aqueous solutions in order of increasing K_b

(a) NO_2^- (b) $H_2PO_4^-$ (c) CO_3^{2-}

66. Follow the instructions for Question 65 for the following bases.

(a) SO_3^{2-} (b) CHO_2^- (c) $C_2H_3O_2^-$

67. Using the equilibrium constants listed in Table 13.2, arrange the following 0.1 *M* aqueous solutions in order of increasing pH (from lowest to highest).

(a) $NaNO_2$ (b) HCl
(c) NaF (d) $Zn(H_2O)_3(OH)(NO_3)$

68. Using the equilibrium constants listed in Table 13.2, arrange the following 0.1 *M* aqueous solutions in order of decreasing pH (from highest to lowest).

(a) KOH (b) NaCN (c) HCO_3^- (d) $Ba(OH)_2$

Equilibrium Calculations; Weak Bases

69. ■ Find the value of K_b for the conjugate base of the following organic acids.

(a) picric acid used in the manufacture of explosives; $K_a = 0.16$
(b) trichloroacetic acid used in the treatment of warts; $K_a = 0.20$

70. Find the value of K_a for the conjugate acid of the following bases.

(a) pyridine, a pesticide; $K_b = 1.5 \times 10^{-9}$
(b) aniline, an important dye intermediate; $K_b = 3.8 \times 10^{-10}$

71. Determine $[OH^-]$, pOH and pH of a 0.28 *M* aqueous solution of Na_2CO_3.

72. Determine $[OH^-]$, pOH and pH of a 0.84 *M* aqueous solution of Na_2SO_3.

73. Codeine (Cod), a powerful and addictive painkiller, is a weak base.

(a) Write a reaction to show its basic nature in water. Represent the codeine molecule as Cod.
(b) The K_a for its conjugate acid is 1.2×10^{-8}. What is K_b for the reaction written in (a)?
(c) What is the pH of a 0.0020 *M* solution of codeine?

74. ■ Consider sodium acrylate, $NaC_3H_3O_2$. K_a for acrylic acid (its conjugate acid) is 5.5×10^{-5}.

(a) Write a balanced net ionic equation for the reaction that makes aqueous solutions of sodium acrylate basic.
(b) Calculate K_b for the reaction in (a).
(c) Find the pH of a solution prepared by dissolving 1.61 g of $NaC_3H_3O_2$ in enough water to make 835 mL of solution.

75. The pH of a household ammonia cleaning solution is 11.68. How many grams of ammonia are needed in a 1.25-L solution to give the same pH?

76. A solution of sodium cyanide (NaCN) has a pH of 12.10. How many grams of NaCN are in 425 mL of solution with the same pH?

Salt Solutions

77. Write formulas for two salts that

(a) contain Ni^{3+} and are acidic.
(b) contain Na^+ and are basic.
(c) contain ClO_4^- and are neutral.
(d) contain NH_4^+ and are acidic.

78. Write formulas for two salts that

(a) contain NH_4^+ and are basic.
(b) contain CO_3^{2-} and are basic.
(c) contain Br^- and are neutral.
(d) contain ClO_4^- and are acidic.

79. State whether 1 *M* solutions of the following salts in water are acidic, basic, or neutral.

(a) K_2CO_3 (b) NH_4F (c) LiH_2PO_4
(d) $NaNO_2$ (e) $Ba(ClO_4)_2$

80. ■ State whether 1 *M* solutions of the following salts in water would be acidic, basic, or neutral.

(a) $FeCl_3$ (b) BaI_2 (c) NH_4NO_2
(d) Na_2HPO_4 (e) K_3PO_4

81. Write net ionic equations to explain the acidity or basicity of the various salts listed in Question 79.

82. Write net ionic equations to explain the acidity or basicity of the various salts listed in Question 80.

83. ■ Arrange the following 0.1 *M* aqueous solutions in order of decreasing pH (highest to lowest).

$Ba(NO_3)_2$, HNO_3, NH_4NO_3, $Al(NO_3)_3$, NaF

■ in OWL Blue-numbered questions answered in Appendix 6 WEB Solution is available on companion website

84. Arrange the following 0.1 M aqueous solutions in order of increasing pH (lowest to highest).

$$KOH, \quad KF, \quad KCl, \quad ZnCl_2, \quad HCl$$

Unclassified

85. At 25°C, a 0.20 M solution of methylamine (CH_3NH_2) is 5.0% ionized. What is K_b for methylamine?

86. Using data in Table 13.2, classify solutions of the following salts as acidic, basic, or neutral.

(a) $NH_4C_2H_3O_2$ **(b)** $NH_4H_2PO_4$
(c) $Al(NO_2)_3$ **(d)** NH_4F

87. There are 324 mg of acetylsalicylic acid (MM = 180.15 g/mol) per aspirin tablet. If two tablets are dissolved in water to give two ounces ($\frac{1}{16}$ quart) of solution, estimate the pH. K_a of acetylsalicylic acid is 3.6×10^{-4}.

88. A student is asked to bubble enough ammonia gas through water to make 4.00 L of an aqueous ammonia solution with a pH of 11.55. What volume of ammonia gas at 25°C and 1.00 atm pressure is necessary?

89. Consider an acid HY (MM = 100 g/mol [3 significant figures]). What is the pH of a 33.0% by mass solution of HY (d = 1.10 g/mL)? The K_a of HY is 2.0×10^{-8}.

90. ■ A student prepares 455 mL of a KOH solution, but neglects to write down the mass of KOH added. His TA suggests that he take the pH of the solution. The pH is 13.33. How many grams of KOH were added?

91. Consider the process

$$H_2O \rightleftharpoons H^+(aq) + OH^-(aq) \qquad \Delta H° = 55.8 \text{ kJ}$$

(a) Will the pH of pure water at body temperature (37°C) be 7.0?
(b) If not, calculate the pH of pure water at 37°C.

92. Household bleach is prepared by dissolving chlorine in water.

$$Cl_2(g) + H_2O \rightleftharpoons H^+(aq) + Cl^-(aq) + HOCl(aq)$$

K_a for HOCl is 3.2×10^{-8}. How much chlorine must be dissolved in one liter of water so that the pH of the solution is 1.19?

93. A tablespoon of Milk of Magnesia, a common remedy for heartburn, contains 1.2 g of $Mg(OH)_2$. If the stomach can hold 2.0×10^2 mL, will a tablespoon of Milk of Magnesia neutralize an "acid stomach" with a pH of 1.5? Assume a tablespoon has volume 25 mL.

94. Consider a weak base, NaB (MM = 281 g/mol). An aqueous solution of NaB has a pH of 8.73 and an osmotic pressure of 55 mm Hg at 25°C. What is K_b for the weak base NaB?

95. Is a saline (NaCl) solution at 80°C acidic, basic, or neutral?

Conceptual Problems

96. Which of the following is/are true regarding a 0.10 M solution of a weak base, B^-?

(a) $[HB] = 0.10\ M$ **(b)** $[OH^-] \approx [HB]$
(c) $[B^-] > [HB]$ **(d)** $[H^+] = \dfrac{1.0 \times 10^{-14}}{0.10}$
(e) pH = 13.0

97. Which of the following is/are true about a 0.10 M solution of a strong acid, HY?

(a) $[Y^-] = 0.10\ M$ **(b)** $[HY] = 0.10\ M$
(c) $[H^+] = 0.10\ M$ **(d)** pH = 1.0
(e) $[H^+] + [Y^-] = 0.20\ M$

98. Consider the following six beakers. All have 100 mL of aqueous 0.1 M solutions of the following compounds:

beaker A has HI
beaker B has HNO_2
beaker C has NaOH
beaker D has $Ba(OH)_2$
beaker E has NH_4Cl
beaker F has $C_2H_5NH_2$

Answer the questions below, using **LT** (for *is less than*), **GT** (for *is greater than*), **EQ** (for *is equal to*), or **MI** (for *more information required*).

(a) The pH in beaker A ________ the pH in beaker B.
(b) The pH in beaker C ________ the pH in beaker D.
(c) The % ionization in beaker A ________ the % ionization in beaker C.
(d) The pH in beaker B ________ the pH in beaker E.
(e) The pH in beaker E ________ the pH in beaker F.
(f) The pH in beaker C ________ the pH in beaker F.

99. ■ Each box represents an acid solution at equilibrium. Squares represent H^+ ions. Circles represent anions. (Although the anions have different identities in each figure, they are all represented as circles.) Water molecules are not shown. Assume that all solutions have the same volume.

(a) Which figure represents the strongest acid?
(b) Which figure represents the acid with the smallest K_a?
(c) Which figure represents the acid with the lowest pH?

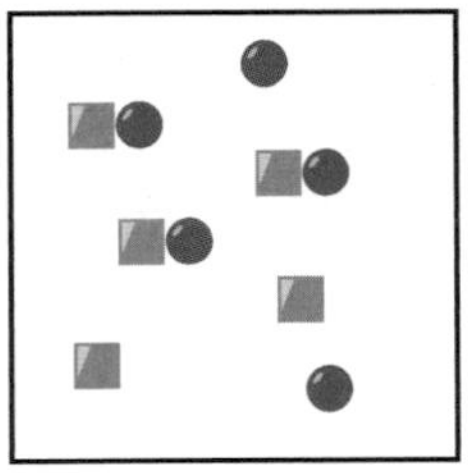
1

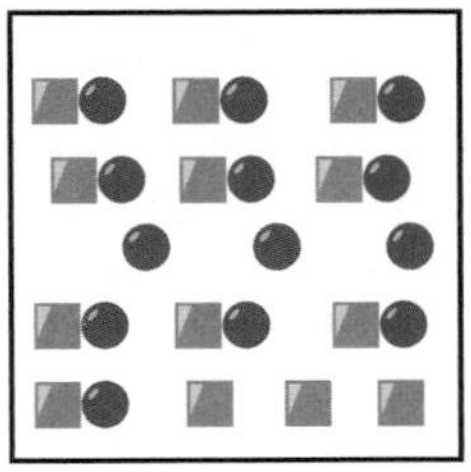
2

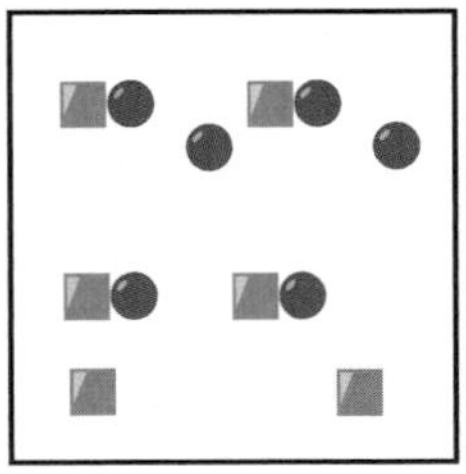
3

100. Each box represents an acid solution at equilibrium. Squares represent H^+ ions, and circles represent the anion. Water molecules are not shown. Which figure represents a strong acid? Which a weak acid?

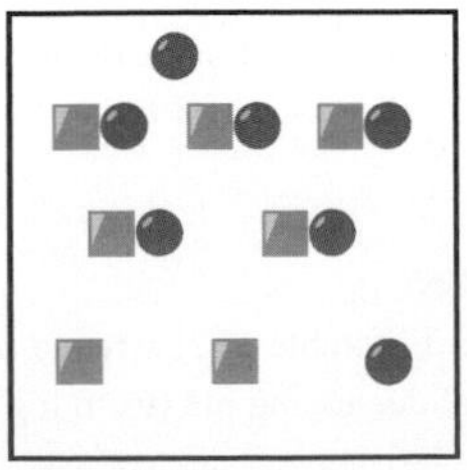
1

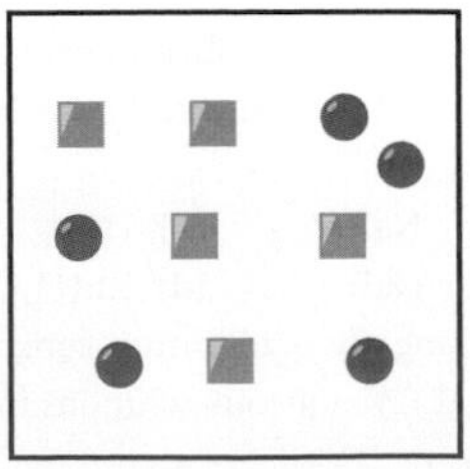
2

101. If □○ represents the weak acid HA (□ = H^+, ○ = A^-) in Figure a below, fill in Figure b with □○, □, and/or ○ to represent HA as being 10% ionized. (Water molecules are omitted.)

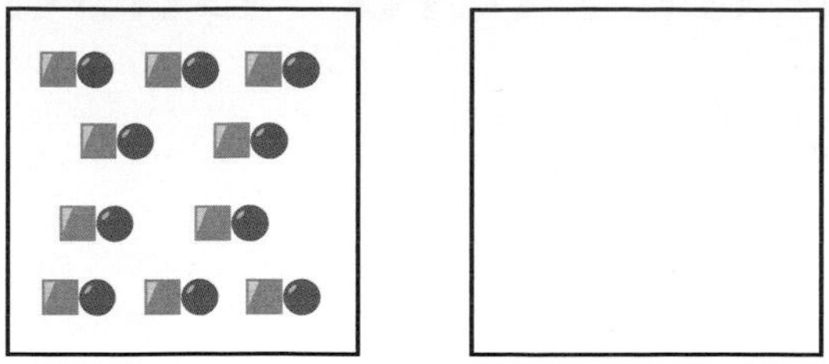

(a) (b)

102. You are asked to determine whether an unknown white solid is acidic or basic. You also need to say whether the acid or base is weak or strong. You are given the molar mass of the solid and told that it is soluble in water. Describe an experiment that you can perform to obtain the desired characteristics of the white solid.

Challenge Problems

103. ■ What is the pH of a 0.200 *M* solution of H_2SO_4? You may assume that the first ionization is complete. The second ionization constant is 0.010.

104. Using the Tables in Appendix 1, calculate ΔH for the reaction of the following.

(a) 1.00 L of 0.100 *M* NaOH with 1.00 L of 0.100 *M* HCl

(b) 1.00 L of 0.100 *M* NaOH with 1.00 L of 0.100 *M* HF, taking the heat of formation of HF(*aq*) to be −320.1 kJ/mol

105. What is the pH of a solution obtained by mixing 0.30 L of 0.233 *M* $Ba(OH)_2$ and 0.45 L of 0.12 *M* HCl? Assume that volumes are additive.

106. Show by calculation that when the concentration of a weak acid decreases by a factor of 10, its percent ionization increases by a factor of $10^{1/2}$.

107. What is the freezing point of vinegar, which is an aqueous solution of 5.00% acetic acid, $HC_2H_3O_2$, by mass (d = 1.006 g/cm^3)?

108. The solubility of $Ca(OH)_2$ at 25°C is 0.153 g/100 g H_2O. Assuming that the density of a saturated solution is 1.00 g/mL, calculate the maximum pH one can obtain when $Ca(OH)_2$ is dissolved in water.

109. Consider two weak acids, HA (MM = 138 g/mol) and HB (MM = 72.0 g/mol). A solution consisting of 11.0 g of HA in 745 mL has the same pH as a solution made up of 5.00 g of HB in 525 mL. Which of the two acids is stronger? Justify your answer by an appropriate calculation.

■ in OWL Blue-numbered questions answered in Appendix 6 **WEB** Solution is available on companion website

14 Equilibria in Acid–Base Solutions

The meeting of two personalities is like the contact of two chemical substances: if there is any reaction, both are transformed.

—Carl Jung
"Modern Man in Search of a Soul"

Chapter Outline

The rain falling on the people and the lake probably has a pH of about 5.5. Acid rain contaminated by SO_3 has a pH of about 3.0.

"Great Bridge: Sudden Rain at Atake (Ohashi, Atake no Yudaschi)" by Ando Hirishige/Photograph © 2007 Carnegie Museum of Art, Pittsburgh

In Chapter 13 we dealt with the equilibrium established when a single solute, either a weak acid or a weak base, is added to water. This chapter focuses on the equilibrium established when two different solutes are mixed in water solution. These solutes may be—

- ***a weak acid, HB, and its conjugate base, B^-.*** Solutions called *buffers* contain roughly equal amounts of these two species. The equilibria involved in buffer solutions are considered in Section 14.1.
- ***an acid and a base used in an acid-base titration.*** This type of reaction was discussed in Chapter 4. Section 14.3 examines the equilibria involved, the way pH changes during the titration, and the choice of indicator for the titration.

We will also consider the equilibrium involved when an acid-base indicator is used to estimate pH (Section 14.2). ■

Online homework for this chapter may be assigned in OWL

CENGAGENOW™

This icon introduces an opportunity for self-study and to explore interactive modules by signing in at **academic.cengage.com/now.**

14.1 BUFFERS

Any solution containing appreciable amounts of both a weak acid and its conjugate base—

- ***is highly resistant to changes in pH brought about by addition of strong acid or strong base.***
- ***has a pH close to the pK_a of the weak acid.***

CENGAGENOW™

Click Chemistry Interactive for a self-study module on **pH changes upon addition of HCl to water and a buffer solution.**

A solution showing these properties is called a **buffer,** because it cushions the "shock" (i.e., the drastic change in pH) that occurs when a strong acid or strong base is added to water.

To prepare a buffer, we can mix solutions of a weak acid HB and the sodium salt of that acid NaB, which consists of Na^+ and B^- ions. This mixture can react with either strong base

By definition, a buffer is any solution that resists a change in pH.

$$HB(aq) + OH^-(aq) \longrightarrow B^-(aq) + H_2O$$

or strong acid

$$B^-(aq) + H^+(aq) \longrightarrow HB(aq)$$

These reactions have very large equilibrium constants, as we will see in Section 14.3, and so go virtually to completion. As a result, the added H^+ or OH^- ions are consumed and do not directly affect the pH. This is the principle of buffer action, which explains why a buffered solution is much more resistant to a change in pH than one that is unbuffered (Figure 14.1, p. 384).

Buffers are widely used to maintain nearly constant pH in a variety of commercial products and laboratory procedures (Figure 14.2, p. 384). For these applications and others, it is essential to be able to determine—

- the pH of a buffer system made by mixing a weak acid with its conjugate base.
- the appropriate buffer system to maintain a desired pH.
- the (small) change in pH that occurs when a strong acid or base is added to a buffer.
- the capacity of a buffer to absorb H^+ or OH^- ions.

Determination of [H^+] in a Buffer System

CENGAGENOW™

Click Coached Problems for a self-study module on **pH of buffer solutions.**

The concentration of H^+ ion in a buffer can be calculated if you know the concentrations of the weak acid HB and its conjugate base B^-. These three quantities are related through the acid equilibrium constant of HB:

$$HB(aq) \rightleftharpoons H^+(aq) + B^-(aq) \qquad K_a = \frac{[H^+] \times [B^-]}{[HB]}$$

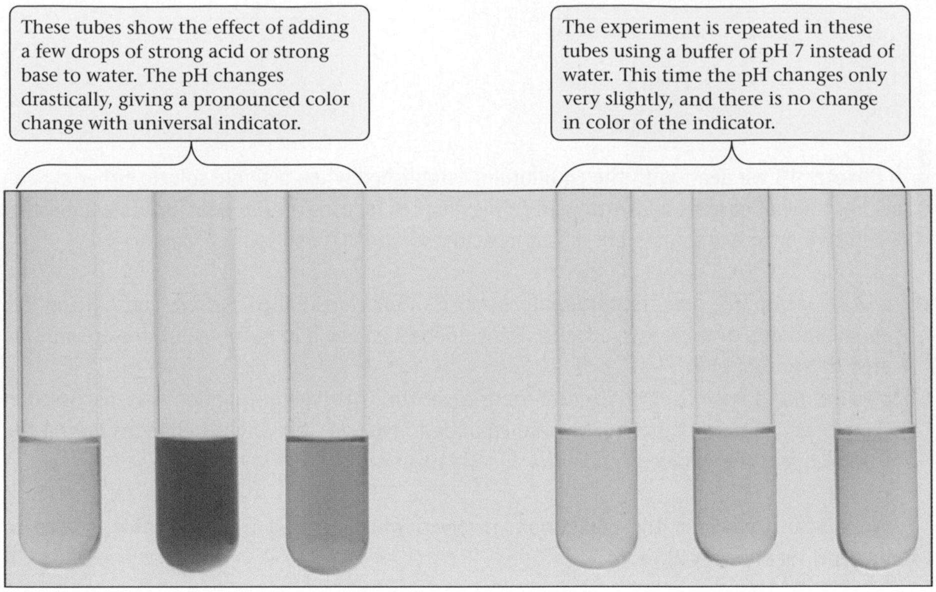

Figure 14.1
Comparison of pH changes in water and a buffer solution.

Solving for $[H^+]$,

$$[H^+] = K_a \times \frac{[HB]}{[B^-]} \quad \textbf{(14.1)}$$

By taking the logarithm of both sides of Equation 14.1 and multiplying through by -1, you can show (Problem 79) that, for any buffer system,

$$pH = pK_a + \log_{10} \frac{[B^-]}{[HB]}$$

This relation, known as the ***Henderson-Hasselbalch*** equation, is often used in biology and biochemistry to calculate the pH of buffers. Historically, it was Henderson who "discovered" Equation 14.1 in 1908. Hasselbalch put it in logarithmic form eight years later.

Equation 14.1 is a completely general equation, applicable to all buffer systems. The calculation of $[H^+]$—and hence pH—can be simplified if you keep two points in mind.

1. ***You can always assume that equilibrium is established without appreciably changing the original concentrations of either HB or B^-.*** That is,

B^- comes from adding a salt of the weak acid, such as NaB.

$$[HB] = [HB]_o$$
$$[B^-] = [B^-]_o$$

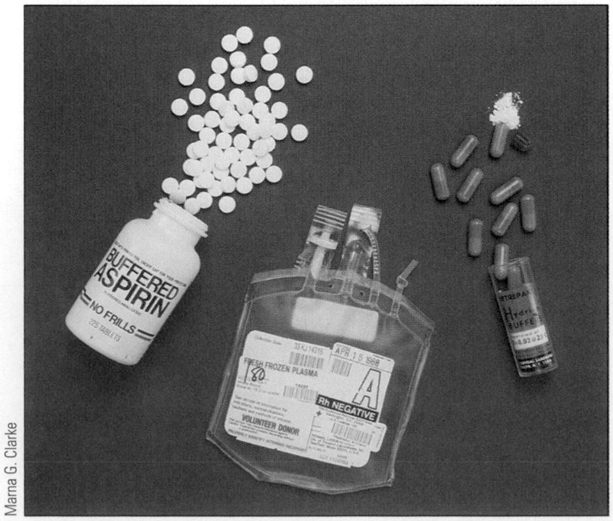

Figure 14.2
Some applications of buffers. Many products, including aspirin and blood plasma, are buffered. Buffer tablets are also available in the laboratory *(far right)* to make up a solution to a specified pH.

© Wally McNamee/CORBIS

An exhausted distance runner crouches in pain. Exertion beyond the point at which the body can clear lactic acid from the muscles causes the pain.

To explain why these relations hold, consider, for example, what happens when the weak acid HB is added to water:

$$HB(aq) \rightleftharpoons H^+(aq) + B^-(aq)$$

We saw in Chapter 13 that under these conditions, it is usually a good approximation to take $[HB] \approx [HB]_o$. The approximation is even more accurate when a considerable amount of B^- is added, as is the case with a buffer. By Le Châtelier's principle, the reverse reaction occurs, the ionization of HB is repressed, and $[HB] = [HB]_o$.

2. ***Because the two species HB and B^- are present in the same solution, the ratio of their concentrations is also their mole ratio.*** That is,

$$\frac{[HB]}{[B^-]} = \frac{\text{no. moles HB}/V}{\text{no. moles B}^-/V} = \frac{n_{HB}}{n_{B^-}}$$

where n = amount in moles and V = volume of solution. Hence Equation 14.1 can be rewritten as

$$[H^+] = K_a \times \frac{n_{HB}}{n_{B^-}} \qquad (14.2)$$

If you start with 0.20 mol HB and 0.10 mol B^-, $[H^+] = 2K_a$.

Frequently, Equation 14.2 is easier to work with than Equation 14.1.

Example 14.1 Graded

Lactic acid, $C_3H_6O_3$, is a weak organic acid present in both sour milk and buttermilk. It is also a product of carbohydrate metabolism and is found in the blood after vigorous muscular activity. A buffer is prepared by dissolving lactic acid, HLac ($K_a = 1.4 \times 10^{-4}$), and sodium lactate, $NaC_3H_5O_3$, NaLac. Calculate $[H^+]$ and the pH of the buffer if it is made of

*(a) 1.00 mol of sodium lactate and 1.00 mol of lactic acid in enough water to form 550.0 mL of solution.

**(b) 34.6 g of NaLac dissolved in 550.0 mL of a 1.20 M aqueous solution of HLac. (Assume no volume change after addition of NaLac.)

Strategy You are given K_a and enough information to determine n_{HLac} and n_{NaLac}. Because sodium lactate, like all ionic solids, is completely ionized in water, $n_{Lac^-} = n_{NaLac}$.

SOLUTION

(a)

$$[H^+] = K_a \times \frac{n_{HLac}}{n_{Lac^-}} = 1.4 \times 10^{-4} \times \frac{1.00}{1.00} = 1.4 \times 10^{-4}$$

$$pH = -\log_{10}(1.4 \times 10^{-4}) = 3.85$$

(b) You must first calculate n_{HLac} and n_{NaLac}.

$$n_{HLac} = 0.5500 \text{ L} \times \frac{1.20 \text{ mol HLac}}{1 \text{ L}} = 0.660 \text{ mol}$$

$$n_{NaLac} = n_{Lac^-} = 34.6 \text{ g NaLac} \times \frac{1 \text{ mol}}{112.06 \text{ g}} = 0.309 \text{ mol}$$

Now, substitute into Equation 14.2:

$$[H^+] = 1.4 \times 10^{-4} \times \frac{0.660}{0.309} = 3.0 \times 10^{-4}$$

$$pH = -\log_{10} (3.0 \times 10^{-4}) = 3.52$$

Reality Check When equal amounts of a weak acid and its conjugate base are present, the pH of the buffer is equal to pK_a.

Notice in Example 14.1(a) that the total volume of solution is irrelevant. All that is required to solve for $[H^+]$ is the number of moles of lactic acid and sodium lactate. The pH of the buffer is 3.85 whether the volume of solution is 550 mL, 1 L, or even 10 L. This explains why *diluting a buffer with water does not change the pH.*

Choosing a Buffer System

CENGAGENOW™
Click Coached Problems for a self-study module on **pH of buffer solutions**.

Suppose you want to make up a buffer in the laboratory with a specified pH (e.g., 4.0, 7.0, 10.0, . . .). Looking at the equation

$$[H^+] = K_a \times \frac{[HB]}{[B^-]} = K_a \times \frac{n_{HB}}{n_{B^-}}$$

it is evident that the pH of the buffer depends on two factors:

1. ***The acid equilibrium constant of the weak acid, K_a.*** The value of K_a has the greatest influence on buffer pH. Because HB and B^- are likely to be present in nearly equal amounts,

$$[H^+] \approx K_a \qquad pH \approx pK_a$$

Thus to make up a buffer with a pH close to 7, you should use a conjugate weak acid–weak base pair in which K_a of the weak acid is about 10^{-7}.

2. ***The ratio of the concentrations or amounts of HB and B^-.*** Small variations in pH can be achieved by adjusting this ratio. To obtain a slightly more acidic buffer, add more weak acid, HB; addition of more weak base, B^-, will make the buffer a bit more basic.

Example 14.2 Graded

Suppose you need to prepare a buffer with a pH of 9.00.

*(a) Which of the buffer systems in Table 14.1 would you choose?

**(b) What should be the ratio of the concentration of weak acid, HB, to its conjugate base, B^-?

***(c) What mass in grams of B^- should be added to 245 mL of 0.880 *M* HB to give a pH of 9.00?

SOLUTION

(a) Checking K_a values in Table 14.1, the clear choice is the NH_4^+–NH_3 system (pK_a NH_4^+ = 9.25).

(b) Note that HB is now NH_4^+, B is NH_3 and $[H^+] = 1.0 \times 10^{-9}$ since the required pH is 9.00. Substituting into Equation 14.2, we have

$$[H^+] = K_a \times \frac{[NH_4^+]}{[NH_3]}$$

and solving for the ratio $[NH_4^+]/[NH_3]$, we get

$$\frac{[NH_4^+]}{[NH_3]} = \frac{[H^+]}{K_a} = \frac{1.0 \times 10^{-9}}{5.6 \times 10^{-10}} = 1.8$$

(c) First, find the number of moles of NH_4^+:

$$n_{NH_4^+} = 0.245 \text{ L} \times \frac{0.880 \text{ mol } NH_4^+}{1 \text{ L}} = 0.216 \text{ mol}$$

Substitute again into Equation 14.2 and solve for n_{NH_3}:

$$n_{NH_3} = \frac{K_a}{[H^+]} \times n_{NH_4^+} = \frac{5.6 \times 10^{-10}}{1.0 \times 10^{-9}} \times 0.216 \text{ mol} = 0.12 \text{ mol}$$

$$\text{mass}_{NH_3} = 0.12 \text{ mol} \times 17.03 \text{ g/mol} = 2.0 \text{ g } NH_3$$

Table 14.1 Buffer Systems at Different pH Values

Desired pH	Weak Acid (Buffer System)	Weak Base (Buffer System)	K_a(Weak Acid)	pK_a
4	Lactic acid (HLac)	Lactate ion (Lac^-)	1.4×10^{-4}	3.85
5	Acetic acid ($HC_2H_3O_2$)	Acetate ion ($C_2H_3O_2^-$)	1.8×10^{-5}	4.74
6	Carbonic acid (H_2CO_3)	Hydrogen carbonate ion (HCO_3^-)	4.4×10^{-7}	6.36
7	Dihydrogen phosphate ion ($H_2PO_4^-$)	Hydrogen phosphate ion (HPO_4^{2-})	6.2×10^{-8}	7.21
8	Hypochlorous acid (HClO)	Hypochlorite ion (ClO^-)	2.8×10^{-8}	7.55
9	Ammonium ion (NH_4^+)	Ammonia (NH_3)	5.6×10^{-10}	9.25
10	Hydrogen carbonate ion (HCO_3^-)	Carbonate ion (CO_3^{2-})	4.7×10^{-11}	10.32

Most often, buffers are prepared, as implied in Example 14.2, by mixing a weak acid and its conjugate base. However, a somewhat different approach can be followed: partial neutralization of a weak acid or a weak base gives a buffer. To illustrate, suppose that 0.18 mol of HCl is added to 0.28 mol of NH_3. The following reaction occurs:

Note that complete neutralization would not produce a buffer; only NH_4^+ ions would be present.

$$H^+(aq) + NH_3(aq) \longrightarrow NH_4^+(aq)$$

The limiting reactant, H^+, is consumed. Hence we have

	n_{H^+}	n_{NH_3}	$n_{NH_4^+}$
original	0.18	0.28	0.00
change	−0.18	−0.18	+0.18
final	0.00	0.10	0.18

The solution formed contains appreciable amounts of both NH_4^+ and NH_3; it is a buffer. The ratio $[NH_4^+]/[NH_3]$ is 1.8, so, as we saw in Example 14.2, its pH is 9.00.

Example 14.3 Graded

The food industry uses the acetic acid/sodium acetate buffer to control the pH of food. Given the following mixtures of acetic acid, $HC_2H_3O_2$ (HAc), and sodium hydroxide, show by calculation which of the following solutions is a buffer.

*(a) 0.300 mol NaOH and 0.500 mol $HC_2H_3O_2$

**(b) 25.00 mL of 0.100 M NaOH and 35.00 mL of 0.125 M $HC_2H_3O_2$

***(c) 5.00 g of NaOH and 150.0 mL of 0.500 M $HC_2H_3O_2$

Strategy The reaction between NaOH (a strong base) and $HC_2H_3O_2$ is

$$OH^-(aq) + HC_2H_3O_2(aq) \longrightarrow C_2H_3O_2^-(aq) + H_2O$$

Make a table like the one above and determine the number of moles of acetic acid (HAc) and acetate ion (Ac^-) after the reaction is complete. Since the stoichiometric ratios are 1:1, the limiting reactant is the one with the smaller number of moles.

SOLUTION

(a)

	n_{OH^-}	n_{HAc}	n_{Ac^-}
original	0.300	0.500	0
change	−0.300	−0.300	+0.300
final	0	0.200	0.300

Since both a weak acid and its conjugate base are present, the solution is a buffer.

(b) Here, first calculate n_{OH^-} and n_{HAc}:

$$n_{OH^-} = n_{NaOH} = 0.02500 \times 0.100 = 2.50 \times 10^{-3}$$

$$n_{HAc} = 0.0350 \times 0.125 = 4.38 \times 10^{-3}$$

	n_{OH^-}	n_{HAc}	n_{Ac^-}
original	2.5×10^{-3}	4.38×10^{-3}	0
change	-2.5×10^{-3}	-2.5×10^{-3}	$+2.5 \times 10^{-3}$
final	0	1.9×10^{-3}	2.5×10^{-3}

The solution is a buffer.

(c)

$$n_{OH^-} = n_{NaOH} = 5.00\text{ g} \times \frac{1\text{ mol}}{40.0\text{ g}} = 0.125\text{ mol}$$

$$n_{HAc} = 0.150\text{ L} \times \frac{0.500\text{ mol HAc}}{1\text{ L}} = 0.0750\text{ mol}$$

	n_{OH^-}	n_{HAc}	n_{Ac^-}
original	0.125	0.0750	0
change	−0.0750	−0.0750	+0.0750
final	0.050	0	0.0750

The solution is not a buffer. It is made up of a strong base (OH^-) and a weak base (Ac^-).

Reality Check Note that in order to make a buffer from a strong base and a weak acid (or a strong acid and a weak base), the strong base (or strong acid) must be the limiting reactant. Putting it another way, you must have more moles of the weak-acid/weak-base component than the strong-base/strong-acid component.

Effect of Added H^+ or OH^- on Buffer Systems

CENGAGENOW™
Click Coached Problems for a self-study module on **buffer solutions: addition of reagents.**

The pH of a buffer does change slightly on addition of moderate amounts of a strong acid or strong base. Addition of H^+ ions converts an equal amount of weak base B^- to its conjugate acid HB:

$$H^+(aq) + B^-(aq) \longrightarrow HB(aq)$$

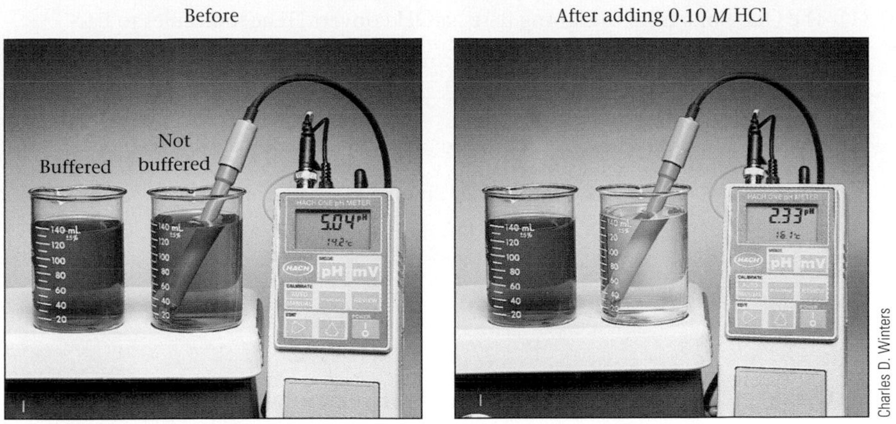

(a) The pH electrode is indicating the pH of water that contains a trace of acid (and bromphenol blue acid-base indicator). The solution at the left is a buffer solution with a pH of about 7. (It also contains bromphenol blue dye.)

(b) When 5 mL of 0.10 *M* HCl is added to each solution, the pH of the water drops several units, whereas the pH of the buffer stays constant as implied by the fact that the indicator color did not change.

By the same token, addition of OH^- ions converts an equal amount of weak acid to its conjugate base B^-:

$$HB(aq) + OH^-(aq) \longrightarrow B^-(aq) + H_2O$$

In either case, the ratio n_{HB}/n_{B^-} changes. This in turn changes the H^+ ion concentration and pH of the buffer. The effect ordinarily is small, as illustrated in Example 14.4.

A buffer "works" because it contains species (HB and B^-) that react with both H^+ and OH^-.

Example 14.4 Consider the buffer described in Example 14.1, where $n_{HLac} = n_{Lac^-} = 1.00$ mol (K_a HLac $= 1.4 \times 10^{-4}$). You will recall that in this buffer the pH is 3.85. Calculate the pH after addition of

(a) 0.08 mol of HCl (b) 0.08 mol of NaOH

Strategy First (1), write the chemical equation for the reaction that occurs when strong acid or base is added. Then (2), apply the principles of stoichiometry to find the numbers of moles of weak acid and weak base remaining after reaction. Finally (3), apply the relation $[H^+] = K_a \times n_{HB}/n_{B^-}$ to find $[H^+]$ and then the pH.

SOLUTION

To work this problem, you have to combine principles of stoichiometry and equilibrium.

(a) (1) The H^+ ions from the strong acid HCl convert Lac^- ions to HLac molecules:

$$H^+(aq) + Lac^-(aq) \longrightarrow HLac(aq)$$

(2) Because the reacting mole ratios are 1:1, the addition of 0.08 mol of H^+ produces 0.08 mol of HLac and consumes 0.08 mol of Lac^-. Originally there was 1.00 mol of both HLac and Lac^-, so

$$n_{HLac} = (1.00 + 0.08)\text{ mol} = 1.08\text{ mol}$$
$$n_{Lac^-} = (1.00 - 0.08)\text{ mol} = 0.92\text{ mol}$$

(3) $$[H^+] = 1.4 \times 10^{-4} \times \frac{n_{HLac}}{n_{Lac^-}} = 1.4 \times 10^{-4} \times \frac{1.08}{0.92} = 1.6 \times 10^{-4}$$
$$pH = -\log_{10}[H^+] = 3.80$$

(b) (1) The OH^- ions from the strong base NaOH convert HLac molecules to Lac^- ions:

$$HLac(aq) + OH^-(aq) \longrightarrow Lac^-(aq) + H_2O$$

(2) The reaction produces 0.08 mol of Lac^- and consumes 0.08 mol of HLac:

$$n_{HLac} = (1.00 - 0.08)\text{ mol} = 0.92\text{ mol}$$
$$n_{Lac^-} = (1.00 + 0.08)\text{ mol} = 1.08\text{ mol}$$

(3) $$[H^+] = 1.4 \times 10^{-4} \times \frac{n_{HLac}}{n_{Lac^-}} = 1.4 \times 10^{-4} \times \frac{0.92}{1.08} = 1.2 \times 10^{-4}$$

$$pH = -\log_{10}(1.2 \times 10^{-4}) = 3.92$$

Reality Check Notice that in both (a) and (b), the change in pH is quite small, less than 0.1 unit.

(a) $3.85 \longrightarrow 3.80$ (b) $3.85 \longrightarrow 3.92$

This is what is supposed to happen with buffer solutions. Addition of strong acid lowers the pH slightly; addition of strong base raises it slightly.

Example 14.4 shows, among other things, how effectively a buffer "soaks up" H^+ or OH^- ions. That can be important. Suppose you are carrying out a reaction whose rate is first-order in H^+. If the pH increases from 5 to 7, perhaps by the absorption of traces of ammonia from the air, the rate will decrease by a factor of 100. A reaction that should have been complete in three hours will still be going on when you come back ten days later. Small wonder that chemists frequently work with buffered solutions to avoid disasters of that type.

Buffer Capacity and Buffer Range

A buffer has a limited capacity to react with H^+ or OH^- ions without undergoing a drastic change in pH. To see why this is the case, consider Figure 14.3, which applies to the H_2CO_3–HCO_3^- buffer system ($K_a\ H_2CO_3 = 4 \times 10^{-7}$).

To interpret Figure 14.3, it is important to realize that the *capacity of a buffer to absorb added OH^- or H^+ ions is inversely related to the slope of the curve.* Notice that—

- at point A where

$$pH = pK_a\ H_2CO_3 = 6.4$$

the slope is very small and the buffer has its maximum capacity to absorb OH^- or H^+ ions without a drastic change in pH.

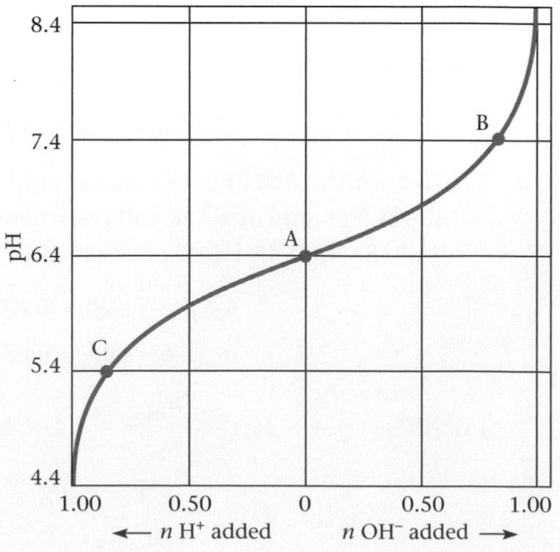

Figure 14.3
Variation of pH of an H_2CO_3–HCO_3^- buffer with addition of strong acid or base. Starting with one mole of both H_2CO_3 and HCO_3^- at point A, the curve to the left shows how pH decreases when H^+ is added. The curve to the right shows how pH increases as OH^- is added.

- at point B, where

$$pH = 7.4; \qquad [HCO_3^-] = 10 \times [H_2CO_3]$$

the slope is very large. So few H_2CO_3 molecules are left that the buffer has lost its capacity to absorb more OH^- ions.
- at point C, where

$$pH = 5.4; \qquad [H_2CO_3] = 10 \times [HCO_3^-]$$

the pH is dropping off precipitously. Very few HCO_3^- ions are left, so the buffer has lost its capacity to absorb added H^+ ions.

Blood is buffered at pH 7.4, in part by the H_2CO_3–HCO_3^- system. As you can see from Figure 14.3 and the above discussion, that puts us at point B on the curve. We conclude that blood has very little capacity to absorb OH^- ions (moving to the right of point B) but a large capacity to absorb H^+ ions (moving to the left of point B). This is indeed fortunate because life processes produce many more H^+ ions than OH^- ions.

The ***buffer range*** is the pH range over which the buffer is effective. It is related to the ratio of concentrations of the weak acid and its conjugate. The further the ratio is from 1, the less effective the buffering action. Ideally, the acid/base ratio should be between 0.1 and 10. Since $\log_{10} 10 = 1$ and $\log_{10} 0.1 = -1$, buffers are most useful within ± 1 pH unit of the weak acid's pK_a.

Example 14.5 Conceptual

Consider the buffer system shown in the box below. The symbol represents a mole of the weak acid; the symbol represents a mole of its conjugate base. The pH of the buffer is 6.0. What is K_a of the weak acid?

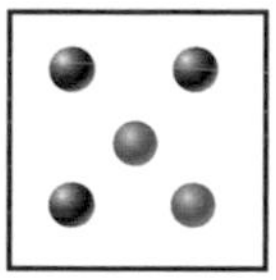

SOLUTION The fundamental equation for the K_a of a weak acid HB is

$$K_a = \frac{[H^+] \times [B^-]}{[HB]}$$

From the diagram, $[B^-]/[HB] = 2/3$

$$[H^+] = 1 \times 10^{-6}\,M$$

Hence

$$K_a = 1 \times 10^{-6} \times \tfrac{2}{3} = 7 \times 10^{-7}$$

14.2 ACID-BASE INDICATORS

As pointed out in Chapter 4, an *acid-base indicator* is useful in determining the **equivalence point** of an acid-base titration. This is the point at which reaction is complete; equivalent quantities of acid and base have reacted. If the indicator is chosen properly, the point at which it changes color (its **end point**) coincides with the equivalence point. To understand how and why an indicator changes color, we need to understand the equilibrium principle involved.

It's called an end point because that's when you stop the titration.

An acid-base indicator is derived from a weak acid HIn:

$$HIn(aq) \rightleftharpoons H^+(aq) + In^-(aq) \qquad K_a = \frac{[H^+] \times [In^-]}{[HIn]}$$

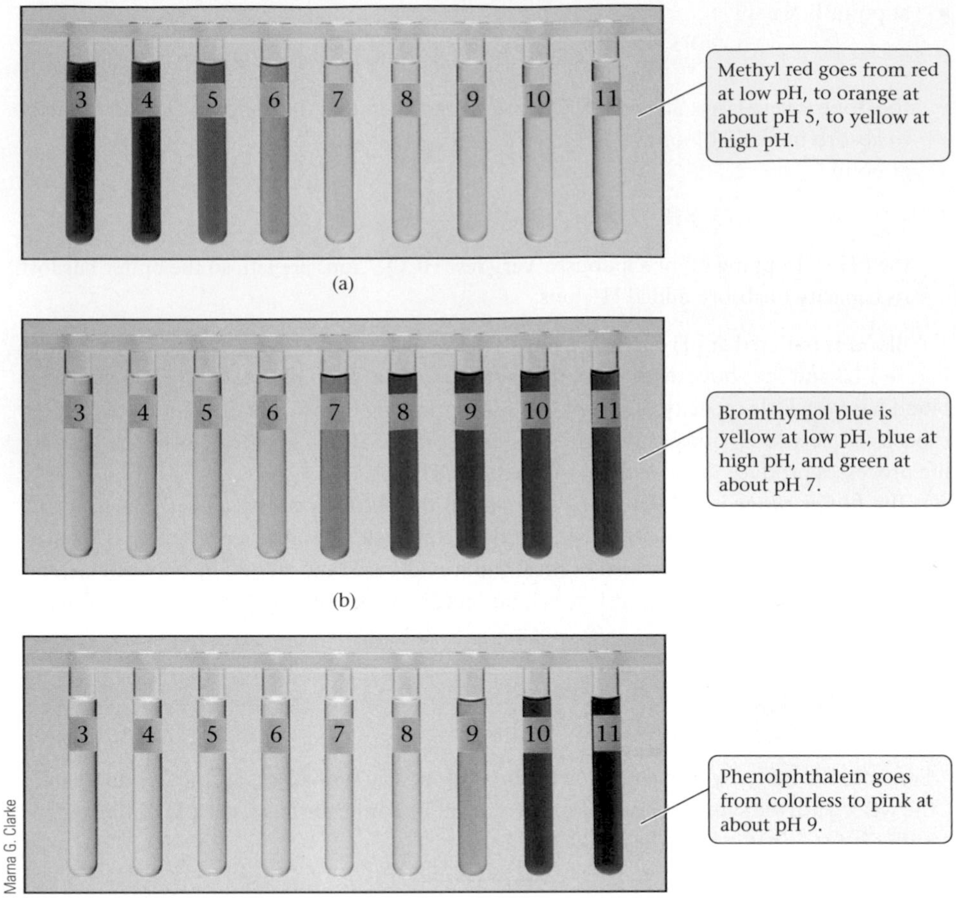

(c)

Figure 14.4
Acid-base indicators.

For litmus, HIn is red; In^- is blue.

where the weak acid HIn and its conjugate base In^- have different colors (Figure 14.4). The color that you see when a drop of indicator solution is added in an acid-base titration depends on the ratio

$$\frac{[\mathrm{HIn}]}{[\mathrm{In}^-]}$$

Three cases can be distinguished:

1. If $\frac{[\mathrm{HIn}]}{[\mathrm{In}^-]} \geq 10$
the principal species is HIn; you see the "acid" color, that of the HIn molecule.
2. If $\frac{[\mathrm{HIn}]}{[\mathrm{In}^-]} \leq 0.1$
the principal species is In^-; you see the "base" color, that of the In^- ion.
3. If $\frac{[\mathrm{HIn}]}{[\mathrm{In}^-]} \approx 1$
the color observed is intermediate between those of the two species, HIn and In^-.

The expression for the ionization of the indicator molecule, HIn,

$$K_a = \frac{[\mathrm{H}^+] \times [\mathrm{In}^-]}{[\mathrm{HIn}]}$$

Table 14.2 Colors and End Points of Indicators

	Color [HIn]	Color [In⁻]	K_a	pH at End Point
Methyl red	Red	Yellow	1×10^{-5}	5
Bromthymol blue	Yellow	Blue	1×10^{-7}	7
Phenolphthalein	Colorless	Pink	1×10^{-9}	9

Because only a drop or two of indicator is used, it does not affect the pH of the solution.

can be rearranged to give

$$\frac{[HIn]}{[In^-]} = \frac{[H^+]}{K_a} \qquad \textbf{(14.3)}$$

From this expression, it follows that the ratio $[HIn]/[In^-]$ and hence the color of an indicator depends on two factors.

1. ***$[H^+]$ or the pH of the solution.*** At high $[H^+]$ (low pH), you see the color of the HIn molecule; at low $[H^+]$ (high pH), the color of the In^- ion dominates.
2. ***K_a of the indicator.*** Because K_a varies from one indicator to another, different indicators change colors at different pHs. A color change occurs when

$$[H^+] \approx K_a \qquad pH \approx pK_a$$

Table 14.2 shows the characteristics of three indicators: methyl red, bromthymol blue, and phenolphthalein. These indicators change colors at pH 5, 7, and 9, respectively.

In practice it is usually possible to detect an indicator color change over a range of about two pH units. Consider, for example, what happens with bromthymol blue as the pH increases—

- below pH 6 (e.g., . . . 3, 4, 5) the color is pure yellow.
- between pH 6 and 7, the indicator starts to take on a greenish tinge; we might describe its color as yellow-green.
- at pH 7, the color is a 50 – 50 mixture of yellow and blue so it looks green.
- between pH 7 and 8, a blue color becomes visible.
- above pH 8 (or 9, 10, 11, . . .) the color is pure blue.

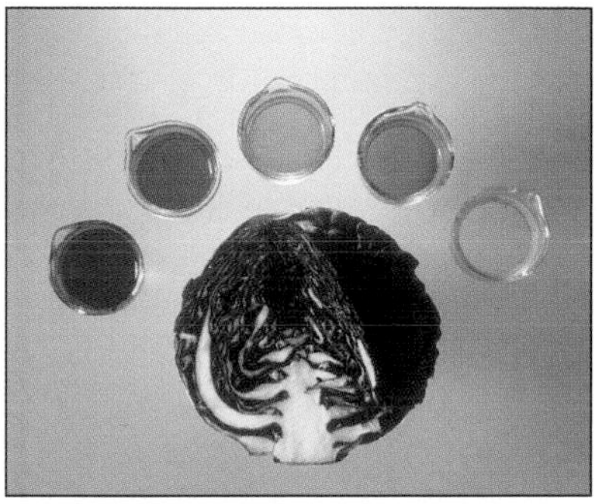
Charles Steele

Red cabbage juice, a natural acid-base indicator. The picture shows *(left to right)* its colors at pH 1, 4, 7, 10, and 13.

What is the color of phenolphthalein at pH 11? pH 7?

Example 14.6 Consider bromthymol blue ($K_a = 1 \times 10^{-7}$). At pH 6.5,

(a) calculate the ratio $[In^-]/[HIn]$.
(b) what is the color of the indicator at this point?

Strategy In (a), use the general relation:

$$K_a \text{ of HIn} = \frac{[H^+] \times [In^-]}{[HIn]}$$

to find the required ratio. In (b), use Table 14.2 to deduce the color of the indicator.

SOLUTION

(a) $[In^-]/[HIn] = K_a/[H^+]$
At pH 6.5, $[H^+] = 3 \times 10^{-7}$ *M*, so

$$[In^-]/[HIn] = (1 \times 10^{-7})/(3 \times 10^{-7}) = 1/3$$

(b) At pH 6.5, we are halfway between 7.0 (green) and the beginning of the yellow range at pH 6.0. The color is yellow-green.

14.3 ACID-BASE TITRATIONS

The discussion of acid-base titrations in Chapter 4 focused on stoichiometry. Here, the emphasis is on the equilibrium principles that apply to the acid-base reactions involved. It is convenient to distinguish between titrations involving—

- a strong acid (e.g., HCl) and a strong base (e.g., NaOH, $Ba(OH)_2$).
- a weak acid (e.g., $HC_2H_3O_2$) and a strong base (e.g., NaOH).
- a strong acid (e.g., HCl) and a weak base (e.g., NH_3).

Strong Acid–Strong Base

As pointed out in Chapter 13, strong acids ionize completely in water to form H_3O^+ ions; strong bases dissolve in water to form OH^- ions. The neutralization reaction that takes place when *any* strong acid reacts with *any* strong base can be represented by a net ionic equation of the Brønsted-Lowry type:

$$H_3O^+(aq) + OH^-(aq) \longrightarrow 2H_2O$$

or, more simply, substituting H^+ ions for H_3O^+ ions, as

$$H^+(aq) + OH^-(aq) \longrightarrow H_2O$$

The equation just written is the reverse of that for the ionization of water, so the equilibrium constant can be calculated by using the reciprocal rule (Chapter 12).

$$K = 1/K_W = 1/(1.0 \times 10^{-14}) = 1.0 \times 10^{14}$$

The enormous value of K means that for all practical purposes this reaction goes to completion, consuming the limiting reactant, H^+ or OH^-.

Consider now what happens when HCl, a typical strong acid, is titrated with NaOH. Figure 14.5 (p. 395) shows how the pH changes during the titration. Two features of this curve are of particular importance:

1. At the equivalence point, when all the HCl has been neutralized by NaOH, a solution of NaCl, a neutral salt, is present. The pH at the equivalence point is 7.
2. Near the equivalence point, the pH rises very rapidly. Indeed, the pH may increase by as much as six units (from 4 to 10) when half a drop, $\approx$ 0.02 mL, of NaOH is added (Example 14.7).

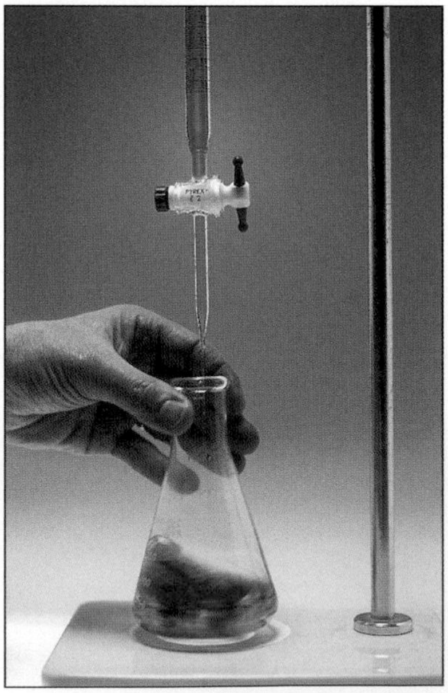
Charles D. Winters

Titrating a solution of HCl with NaOH using phenolphthalein as the indicator.

Example 14.7 When 50.00 mL of 1.000 M HCl is titrated with 0.7450 M NaOH, the pH increases.

(a) How many mL of NaOH are required to reach the equivalence point and a pH of 7.00?
(b) Find the pH when the volume of NaOH added is 0.02 mL less than the volume required to reach the equivalence point.
(c) Find the pH when the volume of NaOH added is 0.02 mL more than the volume required to reach the equivalence point.

Strategy Part (a) is essentially a stoichiometry problem of the type discussed in Chapter 4. For parts (b) and (c), start by calculating (1) the number of moles of OH^- added and then (2) the number of moles of H^+ or OH^- in excess. Finally, calculate (3) $[H^+]$ and pH. Remember to use the total volume of the solution at that point.

SOLUTION

(a) The reaction is $H^+(aq) + OH^-(aq) \longrightarrow H_2O$. The number of moles of H^+ in 50.00 mL of 1.000 M HCl is

$$n_{H^+} = 0.05000\text{ L} \times \frac{1.000\text{ mol H}^+}{1\text{ L}} = 0.05000\text{ mol H}^+$$

Since OH^- reacts in a 1:1 stoichiometric ratio with H^+, the number of moles of OH^- required is also 0.05000. The required volume is

$$V_{OH^-} = 0.05000 \text{ mol} \times \frac{1 \text{ L}}{0.7450 \text{ mol}} = 0.06711 \text{ L}$$

(b) The volume of OH^- in this part of the titration is 67.11 mL − 0.02 mL = 67.09 mL. Follow the steps outlined in the strategy:

(1) $n_{OH^-} = 0.06709 \text{ L} \times \dfrac{0.7450 \text{ mol } OH^-}{1 \text{ L}} = 0.04998 \text{ mol}$

(2) Because H^+ and OH^- react in a 1:1 mole ratio,

$$n_{H^+} \text{ reacted} = 0.04998 \text{ mol}$$

$$n_{H^+} \text{ excess} = 0.05000 \text{ mol} - 0.04998 \text{ mol} = 2 \times 10^{-5} \text{ mol}$$

(3) The total volume is

50.00 mL (from H^+) + 67.09 mL (from OH^-) = 117.09 mL = 0.11709 L.

Hence,

$$[H^+] = \frac{2 \times 10^{-5} \text{ mol}}{0.11709 \text{ L}} = 2 \times 10^{-4}\, M$$

$$pH = -\log_{10} [H^+] = 3.8$$

(c) The volume of OH^- for this part of the titration is 67.11 mL + 0.02 mL = 67.13 mL. We thus get

(1) $n_{OH^-} = 0.06713 \text{ L} \times \dfrac{0.7450 \text{ mol } OH^-}{1 \text{ L}} = 0.05001 \text{ mol}$

(2) n_{H^+} reacted = 0.05000 mol

n_{OH^-} excess = 0.05001 mol − 0.05000 mol = 1×10^{-5} mol

(3) $[OH^-] = \dfrac{1 \times 10^{-5}}{0.05000 + 0.06713} = 9 \times 10^{-5}\, M$

$$pOH = -\log_{10} [OH^-] = 4.0$$

$$pH = 14.00 - pOH = 10.0$$

We assume here that volumes are additive.

Reality Check Note that the pH changes from 3.8 at half a drop before the end point, to 7.0 at the end point, to 10.0 when half a drop is added after the end point. That is what is predicted by Figure 14.5.

In a strong acid–strong base titration, pH changes very rapidly near the end point.

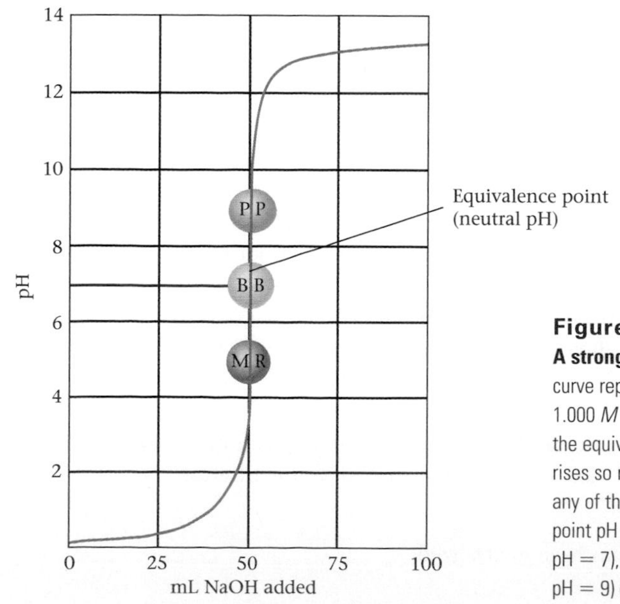

Figure 14.5
A strong acid–strong base titration. The curve represents the titration of 50.00 mL of 1.000 *M* HCl with 1.000 *M* NaOH. The solution at the equivalence point is neutral (pH = 7). The pH rises so rapidly near the equivalence point that any of the three indicators, methyl red (MR, end point pH = 5), bromthymol blue (BB, end point pH = 7), or phenolphthalein (PP, end point pH = 9) can be used.

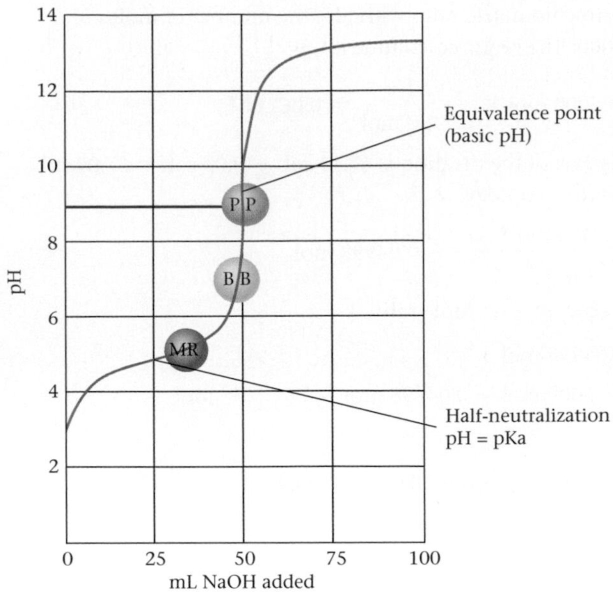

Figure 14.6
A weak acid–strong base titration. The curve represents the titration of 50.00 mL of 1.000 *M* acetic acid, $HC_2H_3O_2$, with 1.000 *M* NaOH. The solution at the equivalence point is basic (pH = 9.22). Phenolphthalein is a suitable indicator. Methyl red would change color much too early, when only about 33 mL of NaOH had been added. Bromthymol blue would change color slightly too quickly.

From Figure 14.5 and Example 14.7, we conclude that any indicator that changes color between pH 4 and 10 should be satisfactory for a strong acid–strong base titration. Bromthymol blue (BB: end point pH = 7) would work very well, but so would methyl red (MR: end point pH = 5) or phenolphthalein (PP: end point pH = 9).

Weak Acid–Strong Base

A typical weak acid–strong base titration is that of acetic acid with sodium hydroxide. The net ionic equation for the reaction is

$$HC_2H_3O_2(aq) + OH^-(aq) \longrightarrow C_2H_3O_2^-(aq) + H_2O$$

Notice that this reaction is the reverse of the reaction of the weak base $C_2H_3O_2^-$ (the acetate ion) with water (Chapter 13). It follows from the reciprocal rule that for this reaction,

For a titration to work, the reaction must go to completion, which requires $K > 10^4$ (approximately).

$$K = \frac{1}{(K_b\ C_2H_3O_2^-)} = \frac{1}{(5.6 \times 10^{-10})} = 1.8 \times 10^9$$

Here again, *K* is a very large number; the reaction of acetic acid with a strong base goes essentially to completion.

Figure 14.6 shows how the pH changes as fifty milliliters of one molar acetic acid is titrated with one molar sodium hydroxide. Notice that—

CENGAGENOW™
Click Coached Problems for a self-study module on **interpreting a pH-titration curve.**

- the pH starts off above 2; we are dealing with a weak acid, $HC_2H_3O_2$.
- there is a region, centered at the halfway point of the titration, where pH changes very slowly. The solution contains equal amounts of unreacted $HC_2H_3O_2$ and its conjugate base, $C_2H_3O_2^-$, formed by reaction with NaOH. As pointed out earlier, such a system acts as a buffer.
- at the equivalence point, there is a solution of sodium acetate, $NaC_2H_3O_2$. The acetate ion is a weak base, so the pH at the equivalence point must be greater than 7.

Example 14.8 50.00 mL of 1.000 *M* acetic acid, $HC_2H_3O_2$, is titrated with 0.8000 *M* NaOH. Find the pH of the solution at the following points in the titration:

(a) before any base is added
(b) when half the acetic acid has been neutralized
(c) at the equivalence point

Strategy In (a), before any base is added, we have a solution of 1.000 M $HC_2H_3O_2$ ($K_a = 1.8 \times 10^{-5}$). Its pH is calculated like that of any weak acid HB. Recall Example 13.7 (page 364), where we found that

$$[H^+]^2 \approx K_a \times [HB]_o$$

In (b), we are dealing with a buffer system; the pH is calculated as described in Section 14.1. In (c), we have a solution of a weak base, $C_2H_3O_2^-$ ($K_b = 5.6 \times 10^{-10}$). Recall Example 13.11 (page 369), where we found that for a weak base B^-,

$$[OH^-]^2 \approx K_b \times [B^-]_o$$

Remember that to find $[B^-]$, you must know n_{B^-}, which is equal to n_{HB}, and the total volume. You will therefore need to know the volume of NaOH required to reach the equivalence point.

SOLUTION

(a) $[H^+]^2 \approx K_a\ HC_2H_3O_2 \times [HC_2H_3O_2]_o = 1.8 \times 10^{-5} \times 1.000 = 1.8 \times 10^{-5}$

$[H^+] = (1.8 \times 10^{-5})^{1/2} = 4.2 \times 10^{-3}\ M;\qquad pH = 2.38$

(b) When half of the acetic acid has been neutralized, half of the $HC_2H_3O_2$ molecules have been converted to $C_2H_3O_2^-$, so

$$n_{HC_2H_3O_2} = n_{C_2H_3O_2^-}$$

This is referred to as "half-neutralization."

Under these conditions

$$[H^+] = K_a \text{ and } pH = pK_a = 4.74$$

(c) First find the volume of NaOH required to reach the equivalence point.

$$n_{HC_2H_3O_2} = n_{OH^-} = 5.000 \times 10^{-2}\ L \times \frac{1.000\ \text{mol}\ HC_2H_3O_2}{1\ L} = 5.000 \times 10^{-2}\ \text{mol}$$

$$V_{OH^-} = 5.000 \times 10^{-2}\ \text{mol} \times \frac{1\ L}{0.8000\ \text{mol}} = 0.0625\ L$$

Next find $[C_2H_3O_2^-]$ by taking $n_{C_2H_3O_2^-}$, which is equal to $n_{HC_2H_3O_2}$, and divide by the total volume (50.00 mL + 62.50 mL):

$$[C_2H_3O_2^-]_o = \frac{5.000 \times 10^{-2}\ \text{mol}}{0.1125\ L} = 0.4444\ M$$

Now,

$$[OH^-]^2 \approx K_b\ C_2H_3O_2^- \times [C_2H_3O_2^-]_o = (5.6 \times 10^{-10})\,(0.4444) = 2.5 \times 10^{-10}$$

$$[OH^-] = 1.6 \times 10^{-5}$$

$$pOH = -\log_{10} 1.6 \times 10^{-5} = 4.80$$

$$pH = 14.00 - pOH = 14.00 - 4.80 = 9.20$$

From Figure 14.6 and Example 14.8, it should be clear that the indicator used in this titration must change color at about pH 9. Phenolphthalein (end point pH = 9) is satisfactory. Methyl red (end point pH = 5) is not suitable. If we used methyl red, we would stop the titration much too early, when reaction is only about 65% complete. This situation is typical of *weak acid-strong base titrations*. For such a titration, we choose an indicator that *changes color above pH 7*.

If either the acid or base is weak, pH changes relatively slowly near the end point.

Strong Acid–Weak Base

The reaction between solutions of hydrochloric acid and ammonia can be represented by the Brønsted-Lowry equation:

$$H_3O^+(aq) + NH_3(aq) \longrightarrow NH_4^+(aq) + H_2O$$

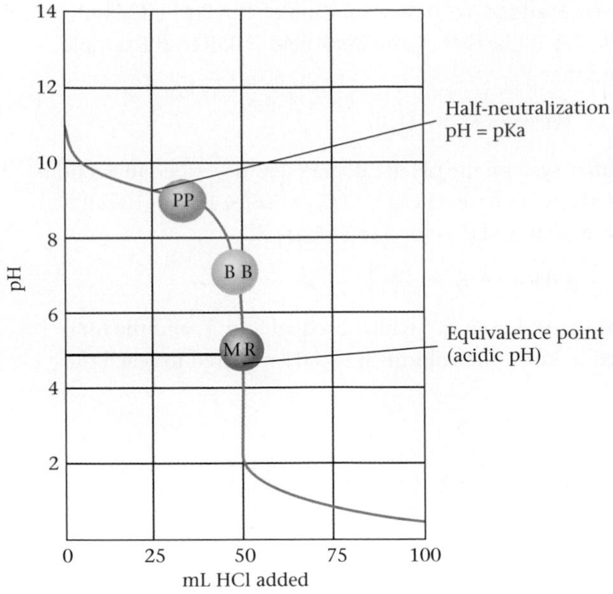

Figure 14.7
A strong acid–weak base titration. The curve represents the titration of 50.00 mL of 1.000 *M* ammonia, a weak base, with 1.000 *M* HCl. The solution at the equivalence point is acidic because of the NH_4^+ ion. Methyl red is a suitable indicator; phenolphthalein would change color much too early.

Again, we simplify the equation by replacing H_3O^+ with H^+:

$$H^+(aq) + NH_3(aq) \longrightarrow NH_4^+(aq)$$

To find the equilibrium constant, note that this equation is the reverse of that for the acid dissociation of the NH_4^+ ion. Hence

$$K = \frac{1}{K_a\ NH_4^+} = \frac{1}{5.6 \times 10^{-10}} = 1.8 \times 10^9$$

Because K is so large, the reaction goes virtually to completion.

Figure 14.7 shows how pH changes when fifty milliliters of one molar NH_3 is titrated with one molar HCl. In many ways, this curve is the inverse of that shown in Figure 14.6 for the weak acid–strong base case. In particular—

- the original pH is that of 1.000 *M* NH_3, a weak base ($K_b = 1.8 \times 10^{-5}$). As you would expect, it lies between 7 and 14:

$$[OH^-]^2 \approx K_b \times [NH_3]_o = (1.8 \times 10^{-5})(1.000)$$
$$[OH^-] = 4.2 \times 10^{-3}\ M;\ pOH = 2.38$$
$$pH = 14.00 - 2.38 = 11.62$$

- addition of 25 mL of HCl gives a buffer containing equal amounts of NH_3 and NH_4^+ ($K_a = 5.6 \times 10^{-10}$). Hence

As strong acid is added, the pH drops.

$$pH = pK_a \text{ of } NH_4^+ = 9.25$$

- at the equivalence point, there is a 0.5000 *M* solution of NH_4^+, a weak acid. As you would expect, the pH is on the acid side.

$$[H^+]^2 \approx 0.5000 \times 5.6 \times 10^{-10}$$
$$[H^+] = 1.7 \times 10^{-5}\ M$$
$$pH = 4.77$$

From Figure 14.7, it should be clear that the only suitable indicator listed is methyl red. The other two indicators would change color too early, before the equivalence point. In general, *for the titration of a weak base with a strong acid, the indicator should change color on the acid side of pH 7.*

Table 14.3 Characteristics of Acid-Base Titrations

Example	Equation	K	Species at Equivalence Point	pH at Equivalence Point	Indicator*
Strong Acid–Strong Base					
		$K = 1/K_w$			
NaOH–HCl	$H^+(aq) + OH^-(aq) \longrightarrow H_2O$	1.0×10^{14}	Na^+, Cl^-	7.00	MR, BB, PP
$Ba(OH)_2$–HNO_3	$H^+(aq) + OH^-(aq) \longrightarrow H_2O$	1.0×10^{14}	Ba^{2+}, NO_3^-	7.00	MR, BB, PP
Weak Acid–Strong Base					
		$K = 1/K_b$			
$HC_2H_3O_2$–NaOH	$HC_2H_3O_2(aq) + OH^-(aq) \longrightarrow C_2H_3O_2^-(aq) + H_2O$	1.8×10^9	Na^+, $C_2H_3O_2^-$	9.22†	PP
HF–KOH	$HF(aq) + OH^-(aq) \longrightarrow F^-(aq) + H_2O$	6.9×10^{10}	K^+, F^-	8.42†	PP
Strong Acid–Weak Base					
		$K = 1/K_a$			
NH_3–HCl	$NH_3(aq) + H^+(aq) \longrightarrow NH_4^+(aq)$	1.8×10^9	NH_4^+, Cl^-	4.78†	MR
ClO^-–HCl	$ClO^-(aq) + H^+(aq) \longrightarrow HClO(aq)$	3.6×10^7	HClO, Cl^-	3.93†	MR

*MR = methyl red (end point pH = 5); BB = bromthymol blue (end point pH = 7); PP = phenolphthalein (end point pH = 9).
†When 1 *M* acid is titrated with 1 *M* base.

Summary

Table 14.3 summarizes our discussion of acid-base titrations. Notice that for these three types of titrations—

- ***the equations (second column) written to describe the reactions are quite different.*** Strong acids and bases are represented by H^+ and OH^- ions, respectively; weak acids and weak bases are represented by their chemical formulas.
- ***the equilibrium constants (K) for all these reactions are very large, indicating that the reactions go essentially to completion.***
- ***the pH at the equivalence point is determined by what species are present.*** When only "spectator ions" are present, as in a strong acid–strong base titration, the pH at the equivalence point is 7. Basic anions (F^-, $C_2H_3O_2^-$), formed during a weak acid–strong base titration, make the pH at the equivalence point greater than 7. Conversely, acidic species (NH_4^+, HClO) formed during a strong acid–weak base titration make the pH at the equivalence point less than 7.

H^+ and OH^- ions are the reacting species in strong acids and strong bases, respectively.

Why do you suppose we ignore weak acid–weak base titrations?

Example 14.9

Consider the titration of formic acid, $HCHO_2$, with barium hydroxide.

(a) Write a balanced net ionic equation for the reaction.
(b) Calculate *K* for the reaction.
(c) Is the solution at the equivalence point acidic, basic, or neutral?
(d) What would be an appropriate indicator for the titration?

Strategy Once you realize that this is a weak acid–strong base titration, the problem unravels; follow the rules cited in Table 14.3.

SOLUTION

(a) $HCHO_2(aq) + OH^-(aq) \longrightarrow CHO_2^-(aq) + H_2O$
(b) $K = 1/(K_b\ CHO_2^-)$. From Table 13.2, page 361, $K_b\ CHO_2^- = 5.3 \times 10^{-11}$
$K = 1/(5.3 \times 10^{-11}) = 1.9 \times 10^{10}$
(c) At the equivalence point, we have a solution of $Ba(CHO_2)_2$, which is basic due to the CHO_2^- ion.
(d) phenolphthalein

CHEMISTRY Beyond the Classroom

Acid Rain

Natural rainfall has a pH of about 5.5. It is slightly acidic because of dissolved carbon dioxide, which reacts with water to form the weak acid H_2CO_3. In contrast, the average pH of rainfall in the eastern United States and southeastern Canada is about 4.4, corresponding to an H^+ ion concentration more than ten times the normal value. In an extreme case, rain with a pH of 1.5 was recorded in Wheeling, West Virginia (distilled vinegar has a pH of 2.4).

Acid rain results from the presence of two strong acids in polluted air: H_2SO_4 and HNO_3. Nitric acid comes largely from a three-step process. The first step involves the formation of NO from the elements by high-temperature combustion, as in an automobile engine. This is then oxidized to NO_2, which in turn undergoes the following reaction:

$$2NO_2(g) + H_2O \longrightarrow HNO_3(aq) + HNO_2(aq)$$

The principal source of sulfur dioxide, the precursor of sulfuric acid, is high-sulfur coal. Coal used in power plants can contain up to 4% sulfur, mostly in the form of minerals such as pyrite, FeS_2. Combustion forms sulfur dioxide:

$$4FeS_2(s) + 11\,O_2(g) \longrightarrow 2Fe_2O_3(s) + 8SO_2(g)$$

Sulfur dioxide formed by reactions such as this is converted to H_2SO_4 in the air by a two-step process:

$$(1)\ SO_2(g) + \tfrac{1}{2}O_2(g) \longrightarrow SO_3(g)$$

$$(2)\ SO_3(g) + H_2O \longrightarrow H_2SO_4(aq)$$

The sulfuric acid forms as tiny droplets high in the atmosphere. These may be carried by prevailing winds as far as 1500 km. The acid rain that falls in the Adirondacks of New York (where up to 40% of the lakes are acidic) comes from sulfur dioxide produced by power plants in Ohio and Illinois.

The effects of acid rain are particularly severe in areas where the bedrock is granite or other materials incapable of neutralizing H^+ ions. As the concentration of acid builds up in a lake, aquatic life, from algae to brook trout, dies. The end product is a crystal-clear, totally sterile lake.

Acid rain adversely affects trees as well (Figure A). It appears that the damage is largely due to the leaching of metal cations from the soil. In particular, H^+ ions in acid rain can react with insoluble aluminum compounds in the soil, bringing Al^{3+} ions into solution. The following reaction is typical:

$$Al(OH)_3(s) + 3H^+(aq) \longrightarrow Al^{3+}(aq) + 3H_2O$$

Al^{3+} ions in solution can have a direct toxic effect on the roots of trees. Perhaps more important, Al^{3+} can replace Ca^{2+}, an ion that is essential to the growth of all plants.

Strong acids in the atmosphere can also attack building materials such as limestone or marble (calcium carbonate):

$$CaCO_3(s) + 2H^+(aq) \longrightarrow Ca^{2+}(aq) + CO_2(g) + H_2O$$

The relatively soluble calcium compounds formed this way [$CaSO_4$, $Ca(NO_3)_2$] are gradually washed away (Figure B). This process is responsible for the deterioration of the Greek ruins on the Acropolis in Athens. These structures suffered more damage in the twentieth century than in the preceding 2000 years.

Sulfur dioxide emissions from power plants can be reduced by spraying a water solution of calcium hydroxide directly into the smokestack. This "scrubbing" operation brings about the reaction

$$Ca^{2+}(aq) + 2\,OH^-(aq) + SO_2(g) + \tfrac{1}{2}O_2(g) \longrightarrow CaSO_4(s) + H_2O$$

The good news is that processes such as this have reduced SO_2 emissions by 40% over the past 30 years. The bad news is that NO emissions have slowly but steadily increased.

Frederica Georgia/Photo Researchers, Inc.

Figure A
Trees damaged by acid rain in the Great Smoky Mountains.

Left, © NYC Parks Photo Archive/Fundamental Photographs NYC; right, © Kristen Brochmann/Fundamental Photographs

Figure B
Effect of acid rain on a marble statue of George Washington in New York City. The photograph on the left was taken in the 1930s; the one on the right was taken in the 1990s.

Chapter Highlights

Key Concepts

1. Calculate the pH of a buffer as originally prepared.
   (Example 14.1; Problems 9–14) ■ Questions and Problems assignable in OWL: 11, 13, 71
2. Choose a buffer to get a specified pH.
   (Example 14.2; Problems 23–26) ■ 23, 25
3. Determine whether a combination of a strong acid/base and its salt is a buffer.
   (Example 14.3; Problems 19–22) ■ 17, 19
4. Calculate the pH of a buffer after addition of H^+ or OH^- ions.
   (Example 14.4; Problems 29–36) ■ 29, 33
5. Determine the color of an indicator at a given pH.
   (Example 14.6; Problems 39–40) ■ 39
6. Calculate the pH during an acid-base titration.
   (Examples 14.7, 14.8; Problems 41–52) ■ 43, 45, 51, 61, 63, 69
7. Choose the proper indicator for an acid-base titration.
   (Example 14.9; Problems 37–38) ■ 37
8. Calculate K for an acid-base reaction.
   (Example 14.9; Problems 5–8) ■ 5

Select end of chapter Questions and Problems may be assigned in OWL and are cross-referenced in the Key Concepts list.

CENGAGENOW™

Sign in at **academic.cengage.com/now** to:

- Check your readiness for an exam by taking the Pre-Test and exploring the self-study modules recommended in your Personalized Study plan
- For quick review, download Go Chemistry mini-lecture flashcard modules (or purchase them at **www.ichapters.com**)

Key Equations

Buffer $$[H^+] = K_a \times \frac{[HB]}{[B^-]} = K_a \times \frac{n_{HB}}{n_{B^-}}$$ (Section 14.1)

Indicator $$\frac{[HIn]}{[In^-]} = \frac{[H^+]}{K_a}$$ (Section 14.2)

Key Terms

acid-base indicator	—capacity	equivalence point
buffer	end point	titration

Summary Problem

Consider nicotinic acid, $HC_6H_4NO_2$ (HNic, $K_a = 1.4 \times 10^{-5}$), and its conjugate base, $C_6H_4NO_2^-$ (Nic^-, $K_b = 7.1 \times 10^{-10}$).

(a) Write net ionic equations and calculate K for the reactions in aqueous solutions between the following:
  (1) HNic and $Ba(OH)_2$
  (2) Nic^- and HBr
  (3) HNic and NaF ($K_b = 1.4 \times 10^{-11}$)

(b) A buffer is prepared by dissolving 47.13 g of $NaC_6H_4NO_2$ (NaNic) in 1.25 L of a solution of 0.295 M $HC_6H_4NO_2$ (HNic).
  (1) Calculate the pH of the buffer.
  (2) Calculate the pH of the buffer after 0.100 mol HNO_3 is added.
  (3) Calculate the pH of the buffer after 5.00 g of NaOH is added.
  (4) Calculate the pH of the buffer after 95 mL of 5.00 M HCl is added. (Assume volumes to be additive.)
  (5) How many grams of NaOH must be added so that the resulting pH is 5.50?

(c) Forty mL of 0.575 M $HC_6H_4NO_2$ (HNic) is titrated with 0.335 M KOH.
  (1) What is the pH of the $HC_6H_4NO_2$ solution before titration?
  (2) How many milliliters of KOH are required to reach the equivalence point?
  (3) What is the pH of the solution halfway to neutralization?
  (4) What is the pH of the solution at the equivalence point?

Answers

(a) **(1)** $HC_6H_4NO_2(aq) + OH^-(aq) \rightleftharpoons H_2O + C_6H_4NO_2^-(aq)$ $K = 1.4 \times 10^9$
  (2) $C_6H_4NO_2^-(aq) + H^+(aq) \rightleftharpoons HC_6H_4NO_2\,(aq)$ $K = 7.1 \times 10^4$
  (3) $HC_6H_4NO_2(aq) + F^-(aq) \rightleftharpoons HF\,(aq) + C_6H_4NO_2^-(aq)$ $K = 0.020$

Summary Problem (cont'd)

(b) (1) 4.80
(2) 4.53
(3) 5.11
(4) 0.95
(5) 9.6 g

(c) (1) 2.55
(2) 68.7 mL
(3) 4.85
(4) 9.08

Questions and Problems

Blue-numbered questions have answers in Appendix 6 and fully-worked solutions in the *Student Solutions Manual.*

■ denotes questions assignable in OWL.

WEB indicates that the solution is available on this book's companion website.

Equilibrium constants required to solve these problems can be found in the tables in Chapter 13 or in Appendix 1.

Acid-Base Reactions

1. Write a net ionic equation for the reaction between aqueous solutions of
  (a) ammonia and hydrofluoric acid.
  (b) perchloric acid and rubidium hydroxide.
  (c) sodium sulfite and hydriodic acid.
  (d) nitric acid and calcium hydroxide.

2. ■ Write a net ionic equation for the reaction between aqueous solutions of
  (a) sodium acetate ($NaC_2H_3O_2$) and nitric acid.
  (b) hydrobromic acid and strontium hydroxide.
  (c) hypochlorous acid and sodium cyanide.
  (d) sodium hydroxide and nitrous acid.

3. Write a balanced net ionic equation for the reaction of each of the following aqueous solutions with H^+ ions.
  (a) sodium fluoride
  (b) barium hydroxide
  (c) potassium dihydrogen phosphate (KH_2PO_4)

4. **WEB** Write a balanced net ionic equation for the reaction of each of the following aqueous solutions with OH^- ions.
  (a) ammonium nitrate
  (b) sodium dihydrogen phosphate (NaH_2PO_4)
  (c) $Al(H_2O)_6^{3+}$

5. ■ Calculate *K* for the reactions in Question 1.

6. Calculate *K* for the reactions in Question 2.

7. Calculate *K* for the reactions in Question 3.

8. Calculate *K* for the reactions in Question 4.

Buffers

9. Calculate $[H^+]$ and pH in a solution in which lactic acid, $HC_3H_5O_3$, is 0.250 *M* and the lactate ion, $C_3H_5O_3^-$, is
  (a) 0.250 *M* **(b)** 0.125 *M*
  (c) 0.0800 *M* **(d)** 0.0500 *M*

10. Calculate $[OH^-]$ and pH in a solution in which dihydrogen phosphate ion, $H_2PO_4^-$, is 0.335 *M* and hydrogen phosphate ion, HPO_4^{2-}, is
  (a) 0.335 *M* **(b)** 0.100 *M*
  (c) 0.0750 *M* **(d)** 0.0300 *M*

11. ■ A buffer is prepared by dissolving 0.0250 mol of sodium nitrite, $NaNO_2$, in 250.0 mL of 0.0410 *M* nitrous acid, HNO_2. Assume no volume change after HNO_2 is dissolved. Calculate the pH of this buffer.

12. A buffer is prepared by dissolving 0.037 mol of potassium fluoride in 135 mL of 0.0237 *M* hydrofluoric acid. Assume no volume change after KF is dissolved. Calculate the pH of this buffer.

13. ■ A buffer solution is prepared by adding 15.00 g of sodium acetate ($NaC_2H_3O_2$) and 12.50 g of acetic acid to enough water to make 500 mL (three significant figures) of solution.
  (a) What is the pH of the buffer?
  (b) The buffer is diluted by adding enough water to make 1.50 L of solution. What is the pH of the diluted buffer?

14. A buffer solution is prepared by adding 5.50 g of ammonium chloride and 0.0188 mol of ammonia to enough water to make 155 mL of solution.
  (a) What is the pH of the buffer?
  (b) If enough water is added to double the volume, what is the pH of the solution?

15. ■ A solution with a pH of 8.73 is prepared by adding water to 0.614 mol of NaX to make 2.50 L of solution. What is the pH of the solution after 0.219 mol of HX is added?

16. An aqueous solution of 0.043 *M* weak acid, HX, has a pH of 3.92. What is the pH of the solution if 0.021 mol of KX is dissolved in one liter of the weak acid?

17. ■ Which of the following would form a buffer if added to 250.0 mL of 0.150 *M* SnF_2?
  (a) 0.100 mol of HCl **(b)** 0.060 mol of HCl
  (c) 0.040 mol of HCl **(d)** 0.040 mol of NaOH
  (e) 0.040 mol of HF

18. Which of the following would form a buffer if added to 650.0 mL of 0.40 *M* $Sr(OH)_2$?
  (a) 1.00 mol of HF **(b)** 0.75 mol of HF
  (c) 0.30 mol of HF **(d)** 0.30 mol of NaF
  (e) 0.30 mol of HCl

Explain your reasoning in each case.

19. ■ Calculate the pH of a solution prepared by mixing 2.50 g of hypobromous acid (HOBr) and 0.750 g of KOH in water. (K_a HOBr $= 2.5 \times 10^{-9}$).

20. Calculate the pH of a solution prepared by mixing 25.0 mL of pure pyridine, C_5H_5N ($d = 0.978$ g/mL), with 65.0 mL of 2.75 *M* HCl. K_b for pyridine is 1.5×10^{-9}.

21. Calculate the pH of a solution prepared by mixing 2.00 g of butyric acid ($HC_4H_7O_2$) with 0.50 g of NaOH in water (K_a butyric acid $= 1.5 \times 10^{-5}$).

22. Calculate the pH of a solution prepared by mixing 100.0 mL of 1.20 *M* ethanolamine, $C_2H_5ONH_2$, with 50.0 mL of 1.0 *M* HCl. K_a for $C_2H_5ONH_3^+$ is 3.6×10^{-10}.

23. ■ Consider the weak acids in Table 13.2. Which acid-base pair would be best for a buffer at a pH of
  (a) 3.0 **(b)** 6.5 **(c)** 12.0

■ in OWL Blue-numbered questions answered in Appendix 6 **WEB** Solution is available on companion website

24. Follow the instructions of Question 23 for a pH of
(a) 4.5 (b) 9.2 (c) 11.0

25. ■ A sodium hydrogen carbonate–sodium carbonate buffer is to be prepared with a pH of 9.40.
(a) What must the $[HCO_3^-]/[CO_3^{2-}]$ ratio be?
(b) How many moles of sodium hydrogen carbonate must be added to a liter of 0.225 M Na_2CO_3 to give this pH?
(c) How many grams of sodium carbonate must be added to 475 mL of 0.336 M $NaHCO_3$ to give this pH? (Assume no volume change.)
(d) What volume of 0.200 M $NaHCO_3$ must be added to 735 mL of a 0.139 M solution of Na_2CO_3 to give this pH? (Assume that volumes are additive.)

26. **WEB** To make a buffer with pH = 3.0 from $HCHO_2$ and CHO_2^-,
(a) what must the $[HCHO_2]/[CHO_2^-]$ ratio be?
(b) how many moles of $HCHO_2$ must be added to a liter of 0.139 M $NaCHO_2$ to give this pH?
(c) how many grams of $NaCHO_2$ must be added to 350.0 mL of 0.159 M $HCHO_2$ to give this pH?
(d) What volume of 0.236 M $HCHO_2$ must be added to 1.00 L of a 0.500 M solution of $NaCHO_2$ to give this pH? (Assume that volumes are additive.)

27. The buffer capacity indicates how much OH^- or H^+ ions a buffer can react with. What is the buffer capacity of the buffers in Problem 9?

28. The buffer capacity indicates how much OH^- or H^+ ions a buffer can react with. What is the buffer capacity of the buffers in Problem 10?

29. ■ A buffer is made up of 0.300 L each of 0.500 M KH_2PO_4 and 0.317 M K_2HPO_4. Assuming that volumes are additive, calculate
(a) the pH of the buffer.
(b) the pH of the buffer after the addition of 0.0500 mol of HCl to 0.600 L of buffer.
(c) the pH of the buffer after the addition of 0.0500 mol of NaOH to 0.600 L of buffer.

30. A buffer is made up of 355 mL each of 0.200 M $NaHCO_3$ and 0.134 M Na_2CO_3. Assuming that volumes are additive, calculate
(a) the pH of the buffer.
(b) the pH of the buffer after the addition of 0.0300 mol of HCl to 0.710 L of buffer.
(c) the pH of the buffer after the addition of 0.0300 mol of KOH to 0.710 L of buffer.

31. Enough water is added to the buffer in Question 29 to make the total volume 10.0 L. Calculate
(a) the pH of the buffer.
(b) the pH of the buffer after the addition of 0.0500 mol of HCl to 0.600 L of diluted buffer.
(c) the pH of the buffer after the addition of 0.0500 mol of NaOH to 0.600 L of diluted buffer.
(d) Compare your answers to Question 29(a)–(c) with your answers to (a)–(c) in this problem.
(e) Comment on the effect of dilution on the pH of a buffer and on its buffer capacity.

32. Enough water is added to the buffer in Question 30 to make the total volume 10.0 L. Calculate
(a) the pH of the buffer.
(b) the pH of the buffer after the addition of 0.0300 mol of HCl to 0.710 L of diluted buffer.
(c) the pH of the buffer after the addition of 0.0300 mol of NaOH to 0.710 L of diluted buffer.
(d) Compare your answers to Question 30(a)–(c) with your answers to (a)–(c) in this problem.
(e) Comment on the effect of dilution on the pH of a buffer and on its buffer capacity.

33. ■ A buffer is prepared in which the ratio $[H_2PO_4^-]/[HPO_4^{2-}]$ is 3.0.
(a) What is the pH of this buffer?
(b) Enough strong acid is added to convert 15% of HPO_4^{2-} to $H_2PO_4^-$. What is the pH of the resulting solution?
(c) Enough strong base is added to make the pH 7.00. What is the ratio of $[H_2PO_4^-]$ to $[HPO_4^{2-}]$ at this point?

34. A buffer is prepared using the propionic acid/propionate ($HC_3H_5O_2$/$C_3H_5O_2^-$) acid-base pair for which the ratio $[HC_3H_5O_2]/[C_3H_5O_2^-]$ is 4.50. K_a for propionic acid is 1.4×10^{-5}.
(a) What is the pH of this buffer?
(b) Enough strong base is added to convert 27% of $HC_3H_5O_2$ to $C_3H_5O_2^-$. What is the pH of the resulting solution?
(c) Strong base is added to increase the pH. What must the acid/base ratio be so that the pH increases by exactly one unit (e.g., from 2 to 3) from the answer in (a)?

35. Blood is buffered mainly by the HCO_3^-–H_2CO_3 buffer system. The normal pH of blood is 7.40.
(a) Calculate the $[H_2CO_3]/[HCO_3^-]$ ratio.
(b) What does the pH become if 15% of the HCO_3^- ions are converted to H_2CO_3?
(c) What does the pH become if 15% of the H_2CO_3 molecules are converted to HCO_3^- ions?

36. There is a buffer system ($H_2PO_4^-$–HPO_4^{2-}) in blood that helps keep the blood pH at about 7.40. (K_a $H_2PO_4^- = 6.2 \times 10^{-8}$).
(a) Calculate the $[H_2PO_4^-]/[HPO_4^{2-}]$ ratio at the normal pH of blood.
(b) What percentage of the HPO_4^{2-} ions are converted to $H_2PO_4^-$ when the pH goes down to 6.80?
(c) What percentage of $H_2PO_4^-$ ions are converted to HPO_4^{2-} when the pH goes up to 7.80?

Titrations and Indicators

37. ■ Given three acid-base indicators—methyl orange (end point at pH 4), bromthymol blue (end point at pH 7), and phenolphthalein (end point at pH 9)—which would you select for the following acid-base titrations?
(a) perchloric acid with an aqueous solution of ammonia
(b) nitrous acid with lithium hydroxide
(c) hydrobromic acid with strontium hydroxide
(d) sodium fluoride with nitric acid

38. Given the acid-base indicators in Question 37, select a suitable indicator for the following titrations:
(a) acetic acid with sodium hydroxide
(b) sulfurous acid with sodium hydroxide
(c) sulfuric acid with potassium hydroxide
(d) sodium acetate with hydrochloric acid

39. ■ Metacresol purple is an indicator that changes from yellow to purple at pH 8.2.
(a) What is K_a for this indicator?
(b) What is its pH range?
(c) What is the color of a solution with pH 9.0 and a few drops of metacresol purple?

40. Phenol red is an indicator with a pK_a of 7.4. It is yellow in acid solution and red in alkaline.
(a) What is its K_a? (b) What is its pH range?
(c) What would its color be at pH 7.4?

41. When 25.00 mL of HNO_3 are titrated with $Sr(OH)_2$, 58.4 mL of a 0.218 M solution are required.
(a) What is the pH of HNO_3 before titration?
(b) What is the pH at the equivalence point?
(c) Calculate $[NO_3^-]$ and $[Sr^{2+}]$ at the equivalence point. (Assume that volumes are additive.)

■ in OWL Blue-numbered questions answered in Appendix 6 **WEB** Solution is available on companion website

42. A solution of NaOH with pH 13.68 requires 35.00 mL of 0.128 *M* $HClO_4$ to reach the equivalence point.

(a) What is the volume of the NaOH solution?

(b) What is the pH at the equivalence point?

(c) Calculate $[Na^+]$ and $[ClO_4^-]$ at the equivalence point. (Assume that volumes are additive.)

43. ■ A solution consisting of 25.00 g NH_4Cl in 178 mL of water is titrated with 0.114 *M* KOH.

(a) How many mL of KOH are required to reach the equivalence point?

(b) Calculate $[Cl^-]$, $[K^+]$, $[NH_3]$, and $[OH^-]$ at the equivalence point. (Assume that volumes are additive.)

(c) What is the pH at the equivalence point?

44. **WEB** A 25.00-mL sample of formic acid, $HCHO_2$, is titrated with 39.74 mL of 0.117 *M* KOH.

(a) What is $[HCHO_2]$ before titration?

(b) Calculate $[HCHO_2]$, $[CHO_2^-]$, $[OH^-]$, and $[K^+]$ at the equivalence point. (Assume that volumes are additive.)

(c) What is the pH at the equivalence point?

45. ■ A 20.00-mL sample of 0.220 *M* triethylamine, $(CH_3CH_2)_3N$, is titrated with 0.544 *M* HCl.

$$(Kb(CH_3CH_2)_3N = 5.2 \times 10^{-4})$$

(a) Write a balanced net ionic equation for the titration.

(b) How many mL of HCl are required to reach the equivalence point?

(c) Calculate $[(CH_3CH_2)_3N]$, $[(CH_3CH_2)_3NH^+]$, $[H^+]$ and $[Cl^-]$ at the equivalence point. (Assume that volumes are additive.)

(d) What is the pH at the equivalence point?

46. Pyridine, C_5H_5N, has K_b of 1.7×10^{-9}. A 38.00-mL sample of pyridine requires 29.20 mL of 0.332 *M* HBr to reach the equivalence point.

(a) Write a balanced net ionic equation for the titration.

(b) How many grams of pyridine are in the sample?

(c) Calculate $[C_5H_5N]$, $[C_5H_5NH^+]$, $[H^+]$ and $[Br^-]$ at the equivalence point. (Assume that volumes are additive.)

(d) What is the pH at the equivalence point?

47. A 0.4000 *M* solution of nitric acid is used to titrate 50.00 mL of 0.237 *M* barium hydroxide. (Assume that volumes are additive.)

(a) Write a balanced net ionic equation for the reaction that takes place during titration.

(b) What are the species present at the equivalence point?

(c) What volume of nitric acid is required to reach the equivalence point?

(d) What is the pH of the solution before any HNO_3 is added?

(e) What is the pH of the solution halfway to the equivalence point?

(f) What is the pH of the solution at the equivalence point?

48. A 0.1375 *M* solution of potassium hydroxide is used to titrate 35.00 mL of 0.257 *M* hydrobromic acid. (Assume that volumes are additive.)

(a) Write a balanced net ionic equation for the reaction that takes place during titration.

(b) What are the species present at the equivalence point?

(c) What volume of potassium hydroxide is required to reach the equivalence point?

(d) What is the pH of the solution before any KOH is added?

(e) What is the pH of the solution halfway to the equivalence point?

(f) What is the pH of the solution at the equivalence point?

49. Consider the titration of butyric acid (HBut) with sodium hydroxide. In an experiment, 50.00 mL of 0.350 *M* butyric acid is titrated with 0.225 *M* NaOH. K_a HBut $= 1.5 \times 10^{-5}$.

(a) Write a balanced net ionic equation for the reaction that takes place during titration.

(b) What are the species present at the equivalence point?

(c) What volume of sodium hydroxide is required to reach the equivalence point?

(d) What is the pH of the solution before any NaOH is added?

(e) What is the pH of the solution halfway to the equivalence point?

(f) What is the pH of the solution at the equivalence point?

50. Morphine, $C_{17}H_{19}O_3N$, is a weak base ($K_b = 7.4 \times 10^{-7}$). Consider its titration with hydrochloric acid. In the titration, 50.0 mL of a 0.1500 *M* solution of morphine is titrated with 0.1045 *M* HCl.

(a) Write a balanced net ionic equation for the reaction that takes place during titration.

(b) What are the species present at the equivalence point?

(c) What volume of hydrochloric acid is required to reach the equivalence point?

(d) What is the pH of the solution before any HCl is added?

(e) What is the pH of the solution halfway to the equivalence point?

(f) What is the pH of the solution at the equivalence point?

51. ■ Consider a 10.0% (by mass) solution of hypochlorous acid. Assume the density of the solution to be 1.00 g/mL. A 30.0-mL sample of the solution is titrated with 0.419 *M* KOH. Calculate the pH of the solution

(a) before titration.

(b) halfway to the equivalence point.

(c) at the equivalence point.

52. At 25°C and 1.00 atm pressure, one liter of ammonia is bubbled into 725 mL of water. Assume that all the ammonia dissolves and the volume of the solution is the volume of the water. A 50.0-mL portion of the prepared solution is titrated with 0.2193 *M* HNO_3. Calculate the pH of the solution

(a) before titration.

(b) halfway to the equivalence point.

(c) at the equivalence point.

Unclassified

53. A student is given 250.0 g of sodium lactate, $NaC_3H_5O_3$, and a bottle of lactic acid marked "73.0% by mass $HC_3H_5O_3$, $d = 1.20$ g/mL." How many milliliters of 73.0% lactic acid should the student add to the sodium lactate to produce a buffer with a pH of 4.50?

54. Methylamine (CH_3NH_2) is a gas at room temperature and very soluble in water. An aqueous solution of methylamine has $K_b = 4.2 \times 10^{-4}$. How many liters of methylamine at 27°C and a pressure of 1.2 atm should be bubbled into 0.750 L of a solution that is 0.588 *M* in the methylammonium ion ($CH_3NH_3^+$) so that a buffer of pH 9.80 is obtained? Assume no volume changes after methylamine is bubbled into the solution and ignore the vapor pressure of water.

55. For an aqueous solution of acetic acid to be called "distilled white vinegar" it must contain 5.0% acetic acid by mass. A solution with a density of 1.05 g/mL has a pH of 2.95. Can the solution be called "distilled white vinegar"?

56. Consider an unknown base, RNH. One experiment titrates a 50.0-mL aqueous solution containing 2.500 g of the base. This titration requires 59.90 mL of 0.925 *M* HCl to reach the equivalence point. A second experiment uses an identical 50.0-mL solution of the unknown base that was used in the first experiment. To this solution is added 29.95 mL of 0.925 *M* HCl. The pH after the HCl addition is 10.77.

(a) What is the molar mass of the unknown base?

(b) What is K_b for the unknown base?

(c) What is K_a for RNH_2^+?

57. A painful arthritic condition known as gout is caused by an excess of uric acid HUric in the blood. An aqueous solution contains 4.00 g of uric acid. A 0.730 *M* solution of KOH is used for titration. After 12.00 mL of

■ in OWL Blue-numbered questions answered in Appendix 6 **WEB** Solution is available on companion website

KOH is added, the resulting solution has pH 4.12. The equivalence point is reached after a total of 32.62 mL of KOH is added.

$$\text{HUric}(aq) + \text{OH}^-(aq) \longrightarrow \text{Uric}^-(aq) + \text{H}_2\text{O}$$

(a) What is the molar mass of uric acid?
(b) What is its K_a?

58. ■ Water is accidentally added to 350.00 mL of a stock solution of 6.00 *M* HCl. A 75.00-mL sample of the diluted solution is titrated to pH 7.00 with 78.8 mL of 4.85 *M* NaOH. How much water was accidentally added? (Assume that volumes are additive.)

59. A solution of an unknown weak acid at 25°C has an osmotic pressure of 0.878 atm and a pH of 6.76. What is K_b for its conjugate base? (Assume that, in the equation for π [Chapter 10], $i \approx 1$.)

60. Consider an aqueous solution of HF. The molar heat of formation for aqueous HF is −320.1 kJ/mol.

(a) What is the pH of a 0.100 *M* solution of HF at 100°C?
(b) Compare with the pH of a 0.100 *M* solution of HF at 25°C.

Conceptual Problems

61. ■ Each symbol in the box below represents a mole of a component in one liter of a buffer solution; ○ represents the anion (X^-), □○ = the weak acid (HX), □ = H^+, and △ = OH^-. Water molecules and the few H^+ and OH^- from the dissociation of HX and X^- are not shown. The box contains 10 mol of a weak acid, □○, in a liter of solution. Show what happens upon

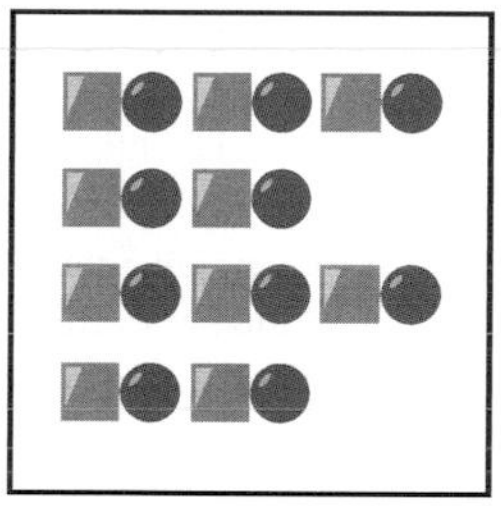

(a) the addition of 2 mol of OH^- (2 △).
(b) the addition of 5 mol of OH^- (5 △).
(c) the addition of 10 mol of OH^- (10 △).
(d) the addition of 12 mol of OH^- (12 △).

Which addition (a)–(d) represents neutralization halfway to the equivalence point?

62. Use the same symbols as in Question 61 (○ = anion, △ = OH^-) for the box below.

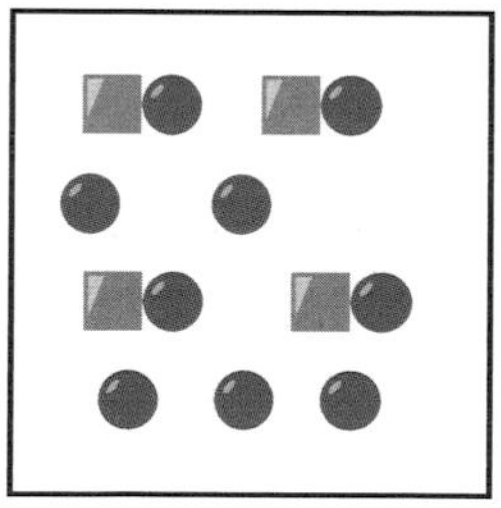

(a) Fill in a similar box (representing one liter of the same solution) after 2 mol of H^+ (2 □) have been added. Indicate whether the resulting solution is an acid, base, or buffer.
(b) Follow the directions of part (a) for the resulting solution after 2 mol of OH^- (2 △) have been added.
(c) Follow the directions of part (a) for the resulting solution after 5 mol of OH^- (5 △) have been added.

(*Hint:* Write the equation for the reaction before you draw the results.)

63. ■ The following is the titration curve for the titration of 50.00 mL of a 0.100 *M* acid with 0.100 *M* KOH.

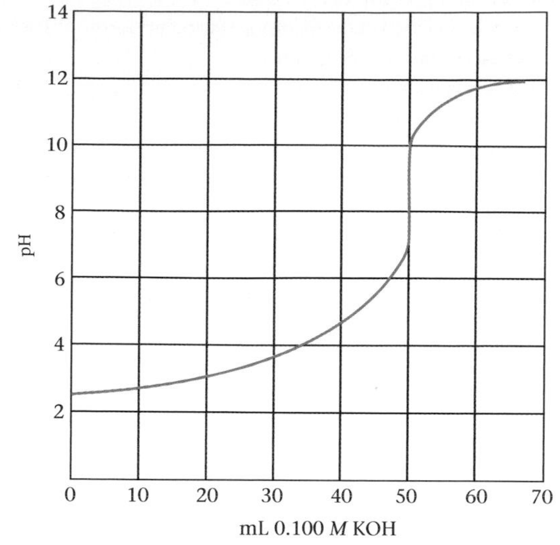

(a) Is the acid strong or weak?
(b) If the acid is weak, what is its K_a?
(c) Estimate the pH at the equivalence point.

64. Consider the following five beakers:

Beaker A has 0.100 mol HA and 0.100 mol NaA in 100 mL of solution.
Beaker B has 0.100 mol HA and 0.100 mol NaA in 200 mL of solution.
Beaker C has 0.100 mol HA, 0.100 mol NaA, and 0.0500 mol HCl in 100 mL of solution.
Beaker D has 0.100 mol HA, 0.100 mol NaA, and 0.100 mol NaOH in 100 mL of solution.
Beaker E has 0.100 mol HCl and 0.100 mol NaOH in 100 mL of solution.

Answer the questions below, using **LT** (for *is less than*), **GT** (for *is greater than*), **EQ** (for *is equal to*), or **MI** (for *more information required*).

(a) The pH in beaker A ________ the pH in beaker B.
(b) The pH in beaker A ________ the pH in beaker C.
(c) The pH in beaker D ________ the pH in beaker E.
(d) The pH in beaker A ________ the pH in beaker E.
(e) The pH in beaker A ________ the pH in beaker D.

65. Follow the directions of Question 64. Consider two beakers:

Beaker A has a weak acid ($K_a = 1 \times 10^{-5}$).
Beaker B has HCl.

The volume and molarity of each acid in the beaker are the same. Both acids are to be titrated with a 0.1 *M* solution of NaOH.

(a) Before titration starts (at zero time), the pH of the solution in Beaker A is ________ the pH of the solution in Beaker B.
(b) At half-neutralization (halfway to the equivalence point), the pH of the solution in Beaker A ________ the pH of the solution in Beaker B.
(c) When each solution has reached its equivalence point, the pH of the solution in Beaker A ________ the pH of the solution in Beaker B.
(d) At the equivalence point, the volume of NaOH used to titrate HCl in Beaker B ________ the volume of NaOH used to titrate the weak acid in Beaker A.

66. Explain why

(a) the pH decreases when lactic acid is added to a sodium lactate solution.
(b) the pH of 0.1 *M* NH_3 is less than 13.0.

(c) a buffer resists changes in pH caused by the addition of H^+ or OH^-.

(d) a solution with a low pH is not necessarily a strong acid solution.

67. Indicate whether each of the following statements is true or false. If the statement is false, restate it to make it true.

(a) The formate ion (CHO_2^-) concentration in 0.10 M $HCHO_2$ is the same as in 0.10 M $NaCHO_2$.

(b) A buffer can be destroyed by adding too much strong acid.

(c) A buffer can be made up by any combination of weak acid and weak base.

(d) Because K_a for HCO_3^- is 4.7×10^{-11}, K_b for HCO_3^- is 2.1×10^{-4}.

68. The solutions in three test tubes labeled A, B, and C all have the same pH. The test tubes are known to contain 1.0×10^{-3} M HCl, 6.0×10^{-3} M $HCHO_2$, and 4×10^{-2} M $C_6H_5NH_3^+$. Describe a procedure for identifying the solutions.

69. ■ Consider the following titration curves. The solution in the buret is 0.1 M. The solution in the beaker has a volume of 50.0 mL. Answer the following questions.

(a) Is the titrating agent (solution in the buret) an acid or a base?

(b) Which curve shows the titration of the weakest base?

(c) What is the K_a of the conjugate acid of the base titrated in curve B?

(d) What is the molarity of the solution in the beaker for curve C?

(e) What is the pH at the equivalence point for curve A?

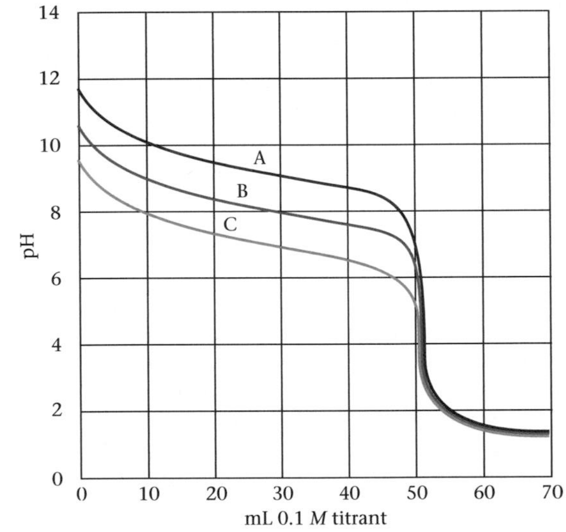

Challenge Problems

70. Consider the titration of HF ($K_a = 6.7 \times 10^{-4}$) with NaOH. What is the pH when a third of the acid has been neutralized?

71. ■ The species called *glacial acetic acid* is 98% acetic acid by mass (d = 1.0542 g/mL). What volume of glacial acetic acid must be added to 100.0 mL of 1.25 M NaOH to give a buffer with a pH of 4.20?

72. Four grams of a monoprotic weak acid are dissolved in water to make 250.0 mL of solution with a pH of 2.56. The solution is divided into two equal parts, A and B. Solution A is titrated with strong base to its equivalence point. Solution B is added to solution A after solution A is neutralized. The pH of the resulting solution is 4.26. What is the molar mass of the acid?

73. Explain why it is not possible to prepare a buffer with a pH of 6.50 by mixing NH_3 and NH_4Cl.

74. Fifty cm^3 of 1.000 M nitrous acid is titrated with 0.850 M NaOH. What is the pH of the solution

(a) before any NaOH is added?

(b) at half-neutralization?

(c) at the equivalence point?

(d) when 0.10 mL less than the volume of NaOH to reach the equivalence point is added?

(e) when 0.10 mL more than the volume of NaOH to reach the equivalence point is added?

(f) Use your data to construct a plot similar to that shown in Figure 14.6 (pH versus volume NaOH added).

75. In a titration of 50.00 mL of 1.00 M $HC_2H_3O_2$ with 1.00 M NaOH, a student used bromcresol green as an indicator ($K_a = 1.0 \times 10^{-5}$). About how many milliliters of NaOH would it take to reach the end point with this indicator? Is there a better indicator that she could have used for this titration?

76. What is the pH of a 0.1500 M H_2SO_4 solution if

(a) the ionization of HSO_4^- is ignored?

(b) the ionization of HSO_4^- is taken into account? (K_a for HSO_4^- is 1.1×10^{-2}.)

77. Two students were asked to determine the K_b of an unknown base. They were given a bottle with a solution in it. The bottle was labeled "aqueous solution of a monoprotic strong acid." They were also given a pH meter, a buret, and an appropriate indicator. They reported the following data:

volume of acid required for neutralization = 21.0 mL
pH after 7.00 mL of strong acid added = 8.95

Use the students' data to determine the K_b of the unknown base.

78. How many grams of NaOH must be added to 1.00 L of a buffer made from 0.150 M NH_3 and 10.0 g of NH_4Cl so that the pH increases by one unit (e.g., from 5 to 6)? K_a for NH_4^+ is 5.6×10^{-10}.

79. Starting with the relation

$$[H^+] = K_a \frac{[HB]}{[B^-]}$$

derive the Henderson-Hasselbalch equation

$$pH = pK_a + \log_{10} \frac{[B^-]}{[HB]}$$

■ in OWL Blue-numbered questions answered in Appendix 6 **WEB** Solution is available on companion website

15 Complex Ions

Chromium ions are sensitive to their
Chemical environment.
They make the ruby red.
The emerald green.
The ruby and emerald are similar.
You say red, I say green.

—Ann Rae Jonas
"The Causes of Color"

Chapter Outline

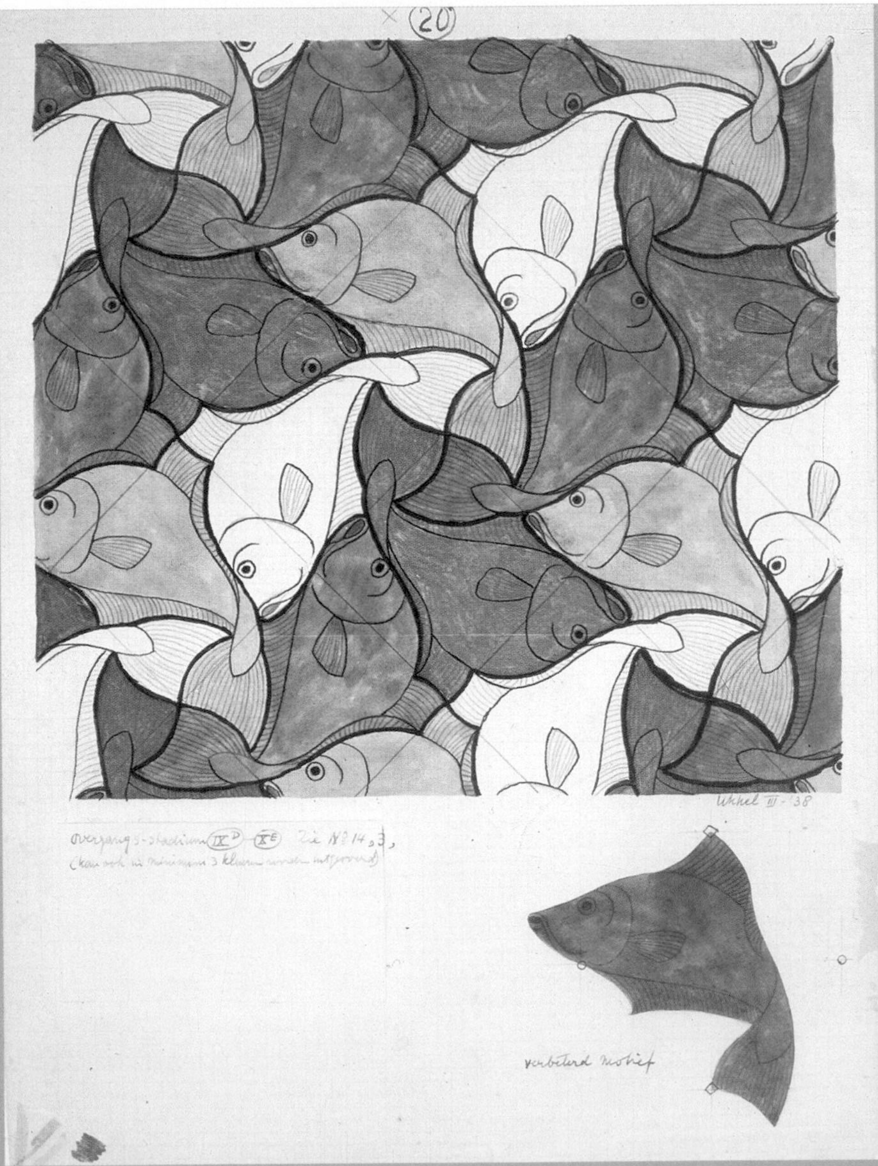

When a tetrahedron is reflected or rotated, a structure indistinguishable from the original is obtained. Chemists call the tetrahedron a *symmetric* structure. Escher, in his painting *Symmetry No. 20,* shows a translational repeating symmetry. He flips or moves his objects, creating a pattern.

In previous chapters we have referred from time to time to compounds of the transition metals. Many of these have relatively simple formulas such as $CuSO_4$, $CrCl_3$, and $Fe(NO_3)_3$. These compounds are ionic. The transition metal is present as a simple cation (Cu^{2+}, Cr^{3+}, Fe^{3+}). In that sense, they resemble the ionic compounds formed by the main-group metals, such as $CaSO_4$ and $Al(NO_3)_3$.

It has been known for more than a century, however, that transition metals also form a variety of ionic compounds with more complex formulas such as

$$[Cu(NH_3)_4]SO_4 \qquad [Cr(NH_3)_6]Cl_3 \qquad K_3[Fe(CN)_6]$$

In these so-called *coordination compounds*, the transition metal is present as a complex ion, enclosed within the brackets. In the three compounds listed above, the following complex ions are present:

$$Cu(NH_3)_4{}^{2+} \qquad Cr(NH_3)_6{}^{3+} \qquad Fe(CN)_6{}^{3-}$$

The charges of these complex ions are balanced by those of simple anions or cations (e.g., $SO_4{}^{2-}$, $3Cl^-$, $3K^+$).

This chapter is devoted to complex ions and the important role they play in inorganic chemistry. We consider in turn—

- the composition of complex ions* (Section 15.1).
- the geometry of complex ions (Section 15.2).
- the electronic structure of the central metal ion (or atom) in a complex (Section 15.3).
- the equilibrium constant for the formation of a complex ion (Section 15.4). ■

Online homework for this chapter may be assigned in OWL.

CENGAGENOW™
This icon introduces an opportunity for self-study and to explore interactive modules by signing in at **academic.cengage.com/now.**

Cu^{2+} is a simple cation; $Cu(NH_3)_4{}^{2+}$ is a complex ion.

15.1 COMPOSITION OF COMPLEX IONS

When ammonia is added to an aqueous solution of a copper(II) salt, a deep, almost opaque, blue color develops (Figure 15.1). This color is due to the formation of the $Cu(NH_3)_4{}^{2+}$ ion, in which four NH_3 molecules are bonded to a central Cu^{2+} ion. The formation of this species can be represented by the equation

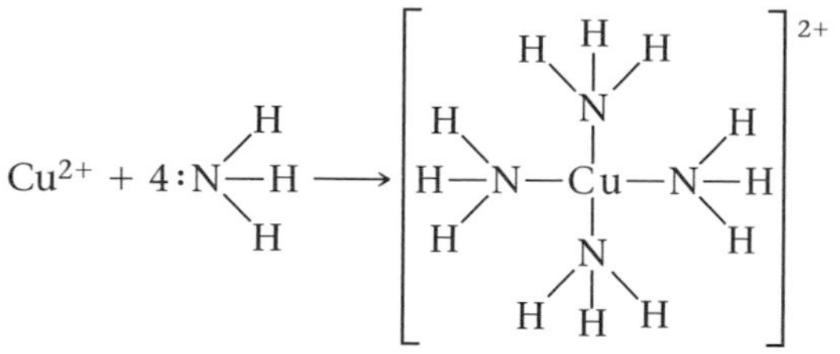

Charles D. Winters

Figure 15.1
Colors of copper complexes. When ammonia is added to 0.2 M Cu^{2+}, the $[Cu(NH_3)_4]^{2+}$ complex ion forms. The ammonia-containing ion is an intense deep blue, almost violet. The hydrated copper complex ion $[Cu(H_2O)_4]^{2+}$ is light blue.

The nitrogen atom of each NH_3 molecule contributes a pair of unshared electrons to form a covalent bond with the Cu^{2+} ion. This bond and others like it, where both electrons are contributed by the same atom, are referred to as *coordinate covalent bonds.*

The $Cu(NH_3)_4{}^{2+}$ ion is commonly referred to as a **complex ion,** a charged species in which a central metal cation is bonded to molecules and/or anions referred to collectively as **ligands.** The number of atoms bonded to the central metal cation is referred to as its **coordination number.** In the $Cu(NH_3)_4{}^{2+}$ complex ion—

- the central metal cation is Cu^{2+}.
- the ligands are NH_3 molecules.
- the coordination number is 4.

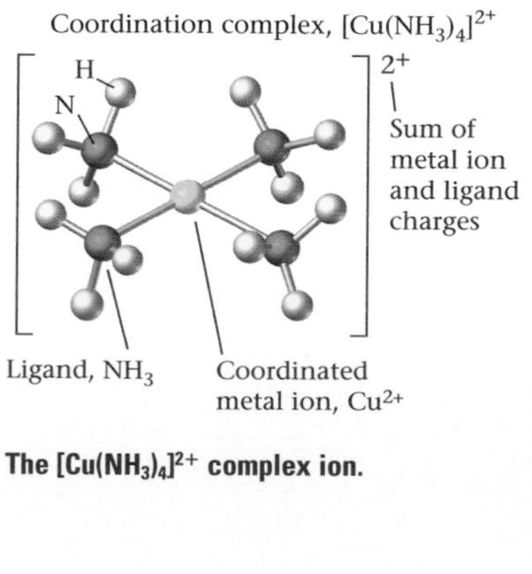

The $[Cu(NH_3)_4]^{2+}$ complex ion.

*The system used to name complex ions is described in Appendix 4.

Table 15.1 Complexes of Pt^{2+} with NH_3 and Cl^-

Complex	Oxid. No. of Pt	Ligands	Total Charge of Ligands	Charge of Complex
$Pt(NH_3)_4^{2+}$	+2	$4NH_3$	0	+2
$Pt(NH_3)_3Cl^+$	+2	$3NH_3$, $1Cl^-$	−1	+1
$Pt(NH_3)_2Cl_2$	+2	$2NH_3$, $2Cl^-$	−2	0
$Pt(NH_3)Cl_3^-$	+2	$1NH_3$, $3Cl^-$	−3	−1
$PtCl_4^{2-}$	+2	$4Cl^-$	−4	−2

Complex ions are commonly formed by transition metals, particularly those toward the right of a transition series ($_{24}Cr \rightarrow {}_{30}Zn$ in the first transition series). Nontransition metals, including Al, Sn, and Pb, form a more limited number of stable complex ions.

Cations of these metals invariably exist in aqueous solution as complex ions. Consider, for example, the zinc(II) cation. In a water solution of $Zn(NO_3)_2$, the $Zn(H_2O)_4^{2+}$ ion is present. Treatment with ammonia converts this to $Zn(NH_3)_4^{2+}$; addition of sodium hydroxide forms $Zn(OH)_4^{2-}$.

When a complex ion is formed from a simple cation, the electron pairs required for bond formation come solely from the ligands. Reactions such as these, in which one species donates an electron pair to another, are referred to as *Lewis acid-base reactions.* In particular—

The Lewis acid-base model is the most general of the three we have considered.

- a **Lewis base** is a species that donates a pair of electrons. Ligands such as the H_2O molecule, the NH_3 molecule, or the OH^- ion act as Lewis bases in complex ion formation.
- a **Lewis acid** is a species that accepts a pair of electrons. Cations such as Cu^{2+} and Zn^{2+} act as Lewis acids when they form complex ions. Thus we have

$$\underset{\text{Lewis acid}}{Cu^{2+}(aq)} + \underset{\text{Lewis base}}{4NH_3(aq)} \longrightarrow Cu(NH_3)_4^{2+}(aq)$$

$$\underset{\text{Lewis acid}}{Zn^{2+}(aq)} + \underset{\text{Lewis base}}{4OH^-(aq)} \longrightarrow Zn(OH)_4^{2-}(aq)$$

Notice that—

- species that act as Lewis bases (e.g., H_2O, NH_3, OH^-) are also Brønsted-Lowry bases in the sense that they can accept a proton.
- species that act as Lewis acids (e.g., Cu^{2+}, Zn^{2+}) need not be Brønsted-Lowry acids (proton donors). In that sense the Lewis model broadens the concept of an acid.

Charges of Complexes

The charge of a complex is readily determined by applying a simple principle:

$$\text{charge of complex} = \text{oxid. no. central metal} + \text{charges of ligands}$$

The application of this principle is shown in Table 15.1, where we list the formulas of several complexes formed by platinum(II), which shows a coordination number of 4. Notice that one of the species, $Pt(NH_3)_2Cl_2$, is a neutral complex rather than a complex ion; the charges of the two Cl^- ions just cancel that of the central Pt^{2+} ion.

Example 15.1 Consider the $Co(H_2O)_3Cl_3^-$ ion.

(a) What is the oxidation number of cobalt?

(b) What is the formula of the coordination compound containing this anion and the Na^+ cation? The Ca^{2+} cation?

Strategy To find the oxidation number, apply the relation

charge complex ion = oxid. no. central atom + charges of ligands

You know the charge of the complex and those of the ligands. To find the formulas of the coordination compounds, apply the principle of electrical neutrality.

SOLUTION

(a) H_2O molecules have zero charge; Cl^- ions have a charge of -1.

$$-1 = \text{oxid. no. Co} + 3(-1); \qquad \text{oxid. no. Co} = +2$$

(b) $Na[Co(H_2O)_3Cl_3]$ $\quad$ $Ca[Co(H_2O)_3Cl_3]_2$

The square brackets enclose the formula of the complex ion.

Ligands; Chelating Agents

In principle, any molecule or anion with an unshared pair of electrons can act as a Lewis base. In other words, it can donate a lone pair to a metal cation to form a coordinate covalent bond. In practice, a ligand usually contains an atom of one of the more electronegative elements (C, N, O, S, F, Cl, Br, I). Several hundred different ligands are known. Those most commonly encountered in general chemistry are NH_3 and H_2O molecules and CN^-, Cl^-, and OH^- ions.

Unshared pair = lone pair.

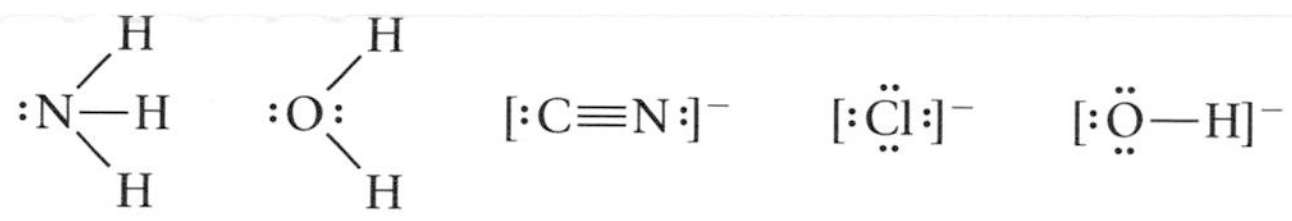

Some ligands have more than one atom with an unshared pair of electrons and hence can form more than one bond with a central metal atom. Ligands of this type are referred to as *chelating agents;* the complexes formed are referred to as **chelates** (from the Greek *chela,* crab's claw). Two of the most common chelating agents are the oxalate anion (abbreviated *ox*) and the ethylenediamine molecule (abbreviated *en*), whose Lewis structures are

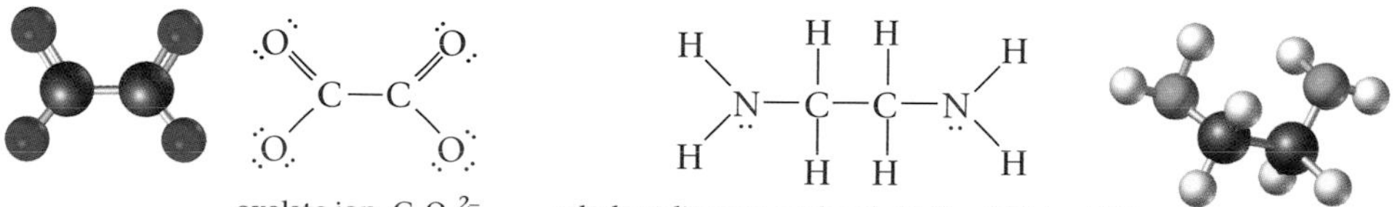

oxalate ion, $C_2O_4^{2-}$ $\quad$ ethylenediamine molecule $H_2N{-}(CH_2)_2{-}NH_2$

(The atoms that form bonds with the central metal are shown in color.)

Figure 15.2 (p. 412) shows the structure of the chelates formed by copper(II) with these ligands. Notice that in both of these complex ions, the coordination number of copper(II) is 4. The central cation is bonded to four atoms, two from each ligand.

For a ligand to act as a chelating agent, it must have at least two lone pairs of electrons. Moreover, these electron pairs must be far enough removed from one another to give a chelate ring with a stable geometry. In the chelates shown in Figure 15.2, the ring is five-membered, containing a Cu^{2+} ion and four nonmetal atoms. Most chelates contain five- or six-membered rings. Smaller or larger rings are less stable. For example, even though the hydrazine molecule

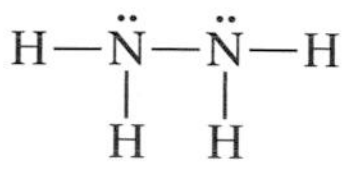

has two lone pairs, it does not form chelates. To do so, it would have to form a three-membered ring with 60° bond angles.

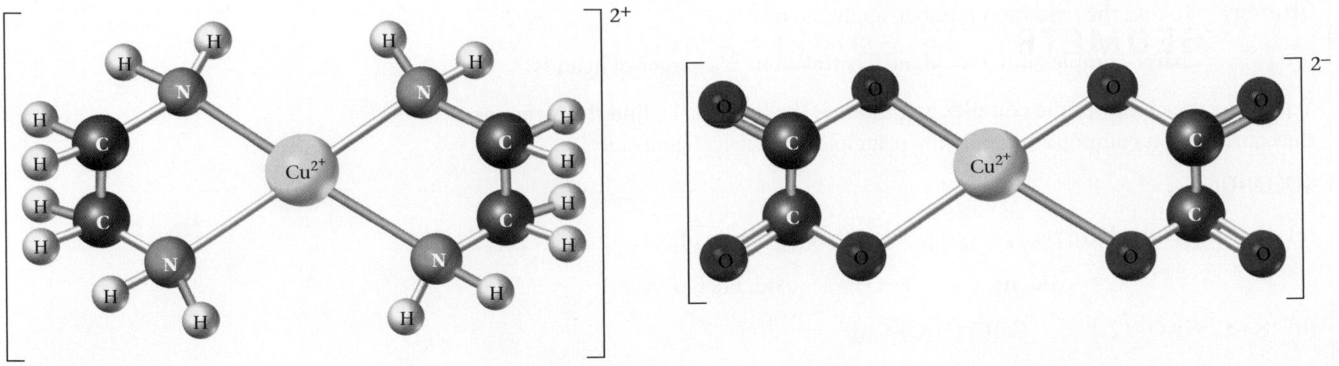

$Cu(en)_2^{2+}$ $Cu(C_2O_4)_2^{2-}$

Figure 15.2
Chelates formed by Cu^{2+} with the ethylenediamine molecules (*en*) and the oxalate ions ($C_2O_4^{2-}$).

Coordination Number

Odd coordination numbers are rare.

As shown in Table 15.2, the most common coordination number is 6. A coordination number of 4 is less common. A value of 2 is restricted largely to Cu^+, Ag^+, and Au^+.

A few cations show only one coordination number in their complexes. Thus Co^{3+} always shows a coordination number of 6, as in

$$Co(NH_3)_6^{3+} \qquad Co(NH_3)_4Cl_2^{+} \qquad Co(en)_3^{3+}$$

Other cations, such as Al^{3+} and Ni^{2+}, have variable coordination numbers, depending on the nature of the ligand.

Example 15.2 Write formulas (including charges) of all complex ions formed by cobalt(III) with the hydroxide ion and/or ethylenediamine (*en*) molecules as ligands.

Strategy As indicated in Table 15.2, the coordination number of Co^{3+} is 6. This means that Co^{3+} forms six bonds with ligands, *including two with each en molecule.* The complex ions can contain 0 to 3 *en* molecules. The *en* ligand is neutral, but the hydroxide ligand has a −1 charge, so the charge of each complex ion will vary depending on the number of hydroxide ligands.

SOLUTION There are four in all:

$$Co(OH)_6^{3-} \qquad Co(OH)_4(en)^{-} \qquad Co(OH)_2(en)_2^{+} \qquad Co(en)_3^{3+}$$

Reality Check Notice that moving from left to right, one *en* replaces two OH^- ions. This makes sense: an *en* molecule has two lone pairs that can bond to the metal; OH^- has only one.

Table 15.2 Coordination Number and Geometry of Complex Ions*

Metal Ion	Coordination Number	Geometry	Example
Ag^+, Au^+, Cu^+	2	Linear	$Ag(NH_3)_2^+$
Cu^{2+}, Ni^{2+}, **Pd^{2+}**, **Pt^{2+}**	4	Square planar	$Pt(NH_3)_4^{2+}$
Al^{3+}, Au^+, **Cd^{2+}**, Co^{2+}, Cu^+, Ni^{2+}, **Zn^{2+}**	4	Tetrahedral	$Zn(NH_3)_4^{2+}$
Al^{3+}, Co^{2+}, **Co^{3+}**, **Cr^{3+}**, Cu^{2+}, **Fe^{2+}**, **Fe^{3+}**, Ni^{2+}, **Pt^{4+}**	6	Octahedral	$Co(NH_3)_6^{3+}$

*Cations that commonly show only one coordination number are in bold type.

15.2 GEOMETRY OF COMPLEX IONS

The physical and chemical properties of complex ions and of the coordination compounds they form depend on the spatial orientation of ligands around the central metal atom. Here we consider the geometries associated with the coordination numbers 2, 4, and 6. With that background, we then examine the phenomenon of **geometric isomerism,** in which two or more complex ions have the same chemical formula but different properties because of their different geometries.

Coordination Number = 2

Complex ions in which the central metal forms only two bonds to ligands are *linear;* that is, the two bonds are directed at a 180° angle. The structures of $CuCl_2^-$, $Ag(NH_3)_2^+$, and $Au(CN)_2^-$ may be represented as

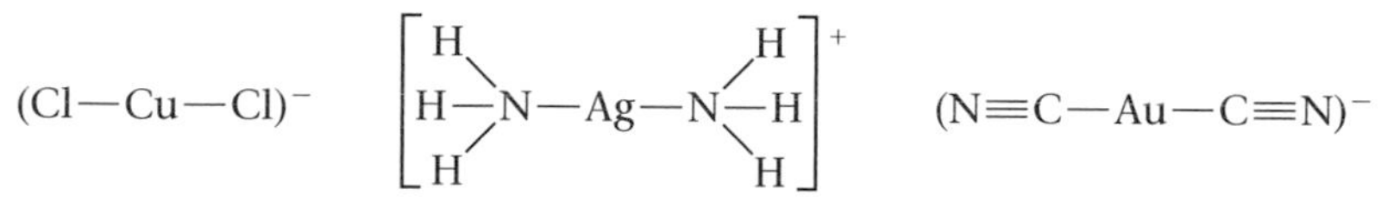

Coordination Number = 4

Four-coordinate metal complexes may have either of two different geometries (Figure 15.3). The four bonds from the central metal may be directed toward the corners of a regular *tetrahedron.* This is what we would expect from VSEPR model (recall Chapter 7). Two common **tetrahedral** complexes are $Zn(NH_3)_4^{2+}$ and $CoCl_4^{2-}$.

CENGAGENOW™
Click Coached Problems for a self-study module on the **geometry of transition metal complexes.**

Square planar complexes, in which the four bonds are directed toward the corners of a square, are more common. Certain complexes of copper(II) and nickel(II) show this geometry; it is characteristic of the complexes of Pd^{2+} and Pt^{2+}, including $Pt(NH_3)_4^{2+}$.

Coordination Number = 6

We saw in Chapter 7 that octahedral geometry is characteristic of many molecules (e.g., SF_6) in which a central atom is surrounded by six other atoms. (Remember, an *octa*hedron has eight sides, which is irrelevant here; it has *six* corners, which is important.) All complex ions

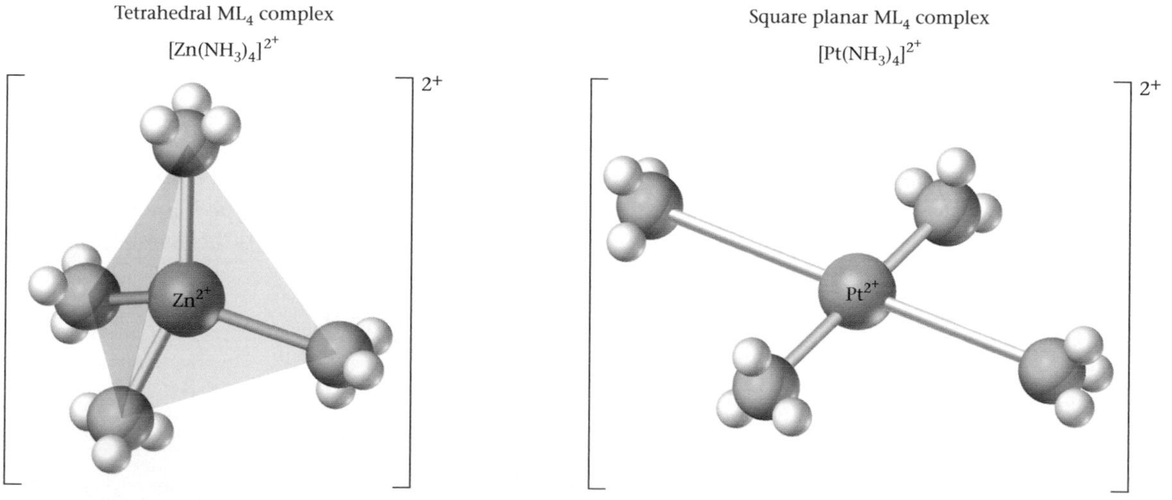

Figure 15.3
Geometry of four-coordinate complexes. Complexes in which the central metal has a coordination number of 4 may be tetrahedral or square planar.

Figure 15.4
An octahedral, six-coordinate complex. The drawing at the left shows six ligands (represented by spheres) at the corners of an octahedron with a metal atom at the center. A simpler way to represent an octahedral complex is shown at the right.

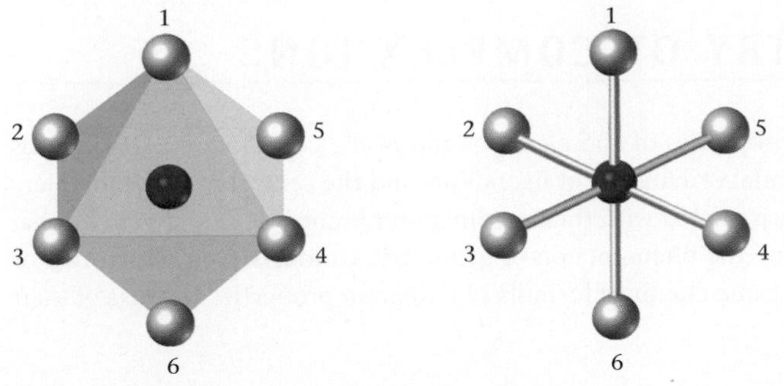

The structure is often shown simply as .

in which the coordination number is 6 are **octahedral.** The metal ion (or atom) is at the center of the *octahedron;* the six ligands are at the corners. This geometry is shown in Figure 15.4.

It is important to realize that—

- the six ligands can be considered equidistant from the central metal.
- an octahedral complex can be regarded as a derivative of a square planar complex. The two extra ligands are located above and below the square, on a line perpendicular to the square at its center.

Geometric Isomerism

CENGAGENOW™
Click Coached Problems for a self-study module on **geometric isomerism in transition metal complexes.**

Two or more species with different physical and chemical properties but the same formula are said to be **isomers** of one another. Complex ions can show many different kinds of isomerism, only one of which we will consider. *Geometric isomers* are ones that differ only in the spatial orientation of ligands around the central metal atom. Geometric isomerism is found in square planar and octahedral complexes. It cannot occur in tetrahedral complexes where all four positions are equivalent.

1. ***Square planar.*** There are two compounds with the formula $Pt(NH_3)_2Cl_2$, differing in water solubility, melting point, chemical behavior, and biological activity.* Their structures are

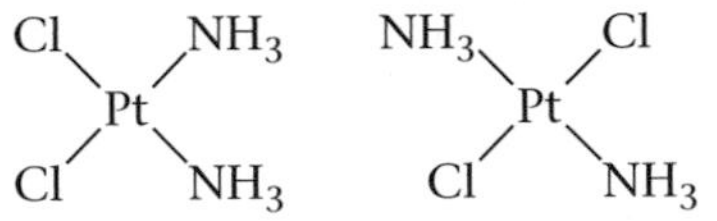

cis *trans*

cis = close together; *trans* = far apart.

The complex in which the two chloride ions are at adjacent corners of the square, as close to one another as possible, is called the ***cis*** isomer. It is made by reacting ammonia with the $PtCl_4^{2-}$ ion. In the ***trans*** isomer, made by reacting $Pt(NH_3)_4^{2+}$ with HCl, the two chloride ions are at opposite corners of the square, as far apart as possible.

Geometric isomerism can occur with any square complex of the type Mabcd, Ma_2bc, or Ma_2b_2, where M refers to the central metal and a, b, c, and d are different ligands. Conversely, geometric isomerism cannot occur with a square complex of the type Ma_4 or Ma_3b. Thus there are two different square complexes with the formula $Pt(NH_3)_2ClBr$ but only one with the formula $Pt(NH_3)_3Cl^+$.

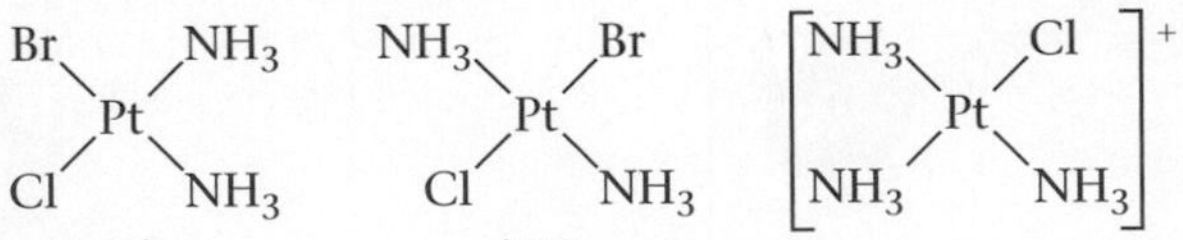

cis *trans*

*The *cis* isomer ("cisplatin") is an effective anticancer drug. This reflects the ability of the two Cl atoms to interact with the nitrogen atoms of DNA, a molecule responsible for cell reproduction. The *trans* isomer is ineffective in chemotherapy, presumably because the Cl atoms are too far apart to react with a DNA molecule.

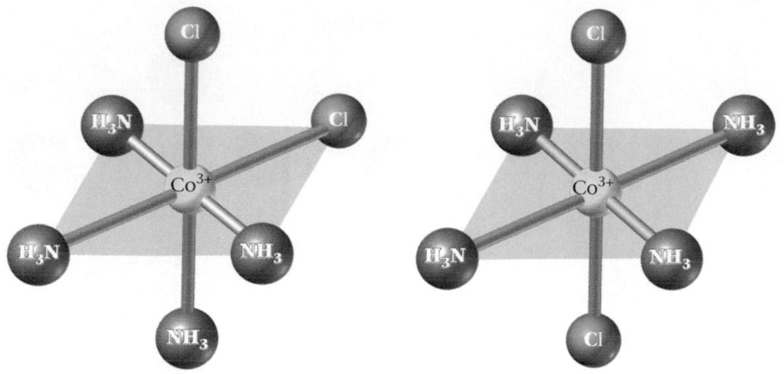

Figure 15.5
***Cis* and *trans* isomers of $Co(NH_3)_4Cl_2^+$.**

It doesn't matter where you start; the octahedron is symmetrical.

2. ***Octahedral.*** To understand how geometric isomerism can arise in octahedral complexes, refer back to Figure 15.4. Notice that for any given position of a ligand, four other positions are at the same distance from that ligand, and a fifth is at a greater distance.

Taking position 1 in Figure 15.4 as a point of reference, you can see that groups at 2, 3, 4, and 5 are equidistant from 1; 6 is farther away. In other words, positions 1 and 2, 1 and 3, 1 and 4, 1 and 5 are *cis* to one another; positions 1 and 6 are *trans.* Hence a complex ion like $Co(NH_3)_4Cl_2^+$ (Figure 15.5) can exist in two different isomeric forms. In the *cis* isomer, the two Cl^- ions are at adjacent corners of the octahedron, as close together as possible. In the *trans* isomer they are at opposite corners, as far away from one another as possible.

Example 15.3 How many geometric isomers are possible for the neutral complex $[Co(NH_3)_3Cl_3]$?

Strategy It's best to approach a problem of this type systematically. You might start (1) by putting two NH_3 molecules *trans* to one another and see how many different structures can be obtained by placing the third NH_3 molecule at different positions. Then (2) start over with two NH_3 molecules *cis* to one another, and follow the same procedure.

SOLUTION

(1) Starting with two NH_3 molecules *trans* to one another (Fig. 15.6a, p. 416), it clearly doesn't matter where you put the third NH_3 molecule. All the available vacancies are equivalent in the sense that they are *cis* to the two NH_3 molecules already in place. Choosing one of these positions arbitrarily for NH_3 gives the first isomer (Figure 15.6b); the Cl^- ions occupy the three remaining positions.

(2) Start again with the two NH_3 molecules *cis* to one another (Figure 15.6c). If you place the third NH_3 molecule at either of the other corners of the square, you will simply reproduce the first isomer. (Remember that the symmetry of a regular octahedron requires that the distance across the diagonal of the square be the same as that from "top" to "bottom.") The only way you can get a "new" isomer is to place the third NH_3 molecule above or below the square so that all three NH_3 molecules are *cis* to one another. Putting that molecule arbitrarily at the top gives the second isomer (Figure 15.6d). That's all there are.

Unless you're careful, you'll come up with too many isomers.

Geometric isomerism can also occur in chelated octahedral complexes (Figure 15.7, p. 416). Notice that an *ethylenediamine molecule,* here and indeed in all complexes, ***can only bridge cis positions.*** It is not long enough to connect to *trans* positions.

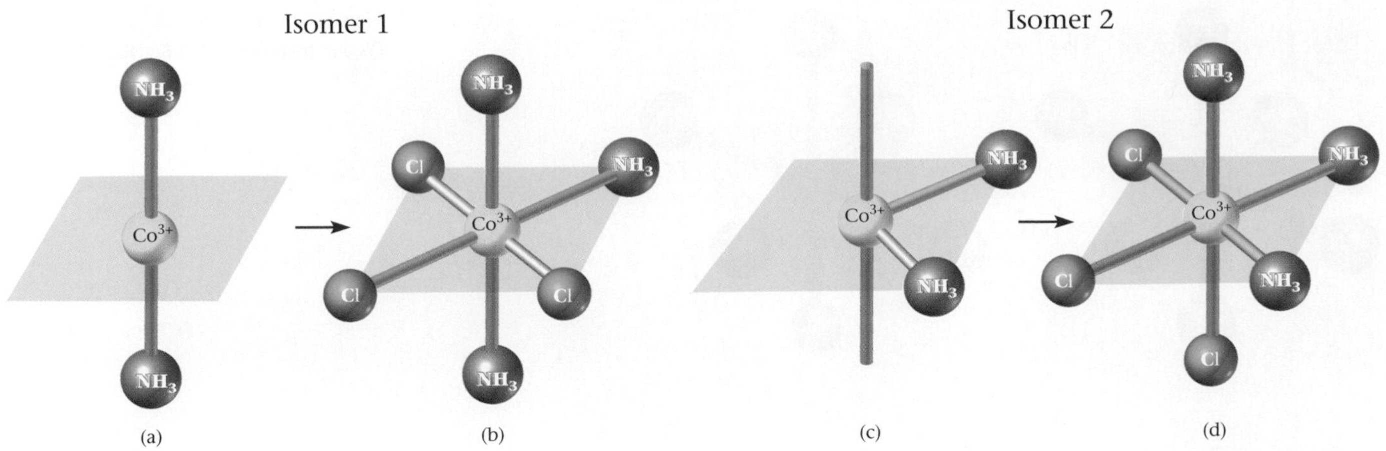

Figure 15.6
Isomers of $Co(NH_3)_3Cl_3$ (Example 15.3). You may be tempted to write down additional structures, but you will find that they are equivalent to one of the two isomers shown.

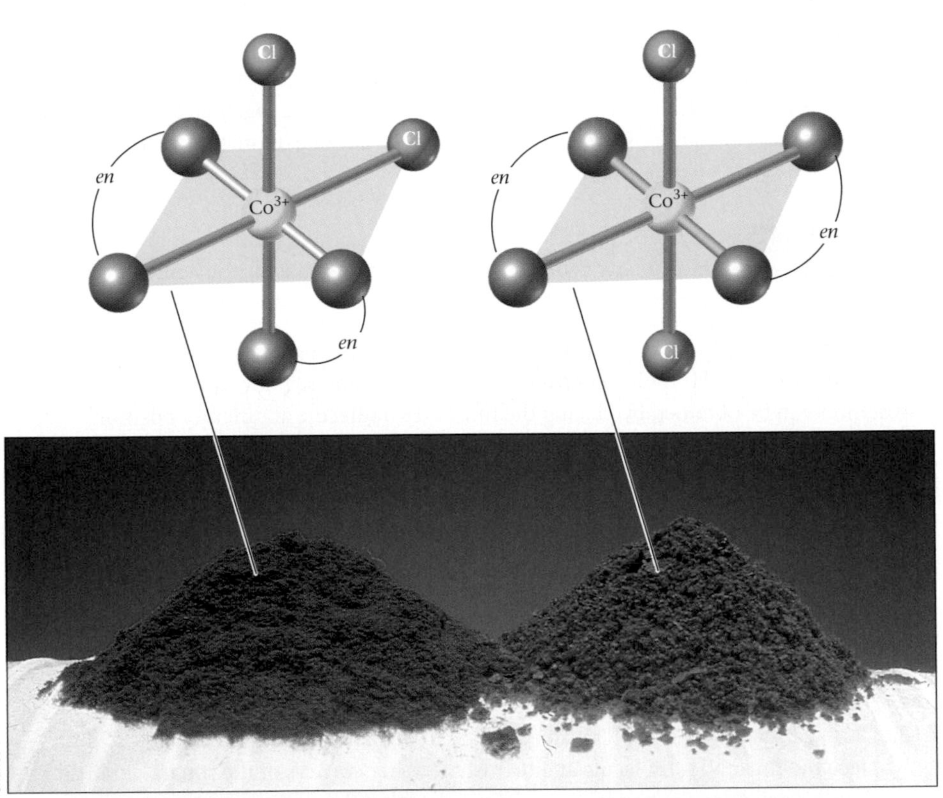

Charles D. Winters

Figure 15.7
***Cis* and *trans* isomers of $[Co(en)_2Cl_2]^+$.** The ethylenediamine molecule is represented by —*en*—. It forms two bonds per molecule. The *cis* isomer is reddish-purple and the *trans* is dark green.

15.3 ELECTRONIC STRUCTURE OF COMPLEX IONS

Until about 20 years ago, the *valence bond model* discussed in Chapter 7 was widely used to explain electronic structure and bonding in complex ions. It assumed that lone pairs of electrons were contributed by ligands to form covalent bonds with metal atoms. This model had two major deficiencies. It could not easily explain the magnetic properties of complex ions.

CHEMISTRY The Human Side

The basic ideas concerning the structure and geometry of complex ions presented in this chapter were developed by one of the most gifted individuals in the history of inorganic chemistry, Alfred Werner. His theory of coordination chemistry was published in 1893 when Werner was 26 years old. In his paper Werner made the revolutionary suggestion that metal ions such as Co^{3+} could show two different kinds of valences. For the compound $Co(NH_3)_6Cl_3$, Werner postulated a central Co^{3+} ion joined by "primary valences" (ionic bonds) to three Cl^- ions and by "secondary valences" (coordinate covalent bonds) to six NH_3 molecules. Moreover, he made the inspired guess that the six secondary valences were directed toward the corners of a regular octahedron.

Science Photo Library/Photo Researchers, Inc.

Alfred Werner
(1866–1919)

Werner spent the next 20 years obtaining experimental evidence to prove his theory. (At the University of Zürich, there remain several *thousand* samples of coordination compounds prepared by Werner and his students.) He was able to show, for example, that the electrical conductivities in water solution decreased in the order $[Co(NH_3)_6]Cl_3 >$ $[Co(NH_3)_5Cl]Cl_2 > [Co(NH_3)_4Cl_2]Cl$ in much the same way as with simple salts, for example, $ScCl_3 >$ $CaCl_2 > NaCl$. Another property he studied was isomerism. In 1907 he was able to isolate a second geometric isomer of $[Co(NH_3)_4Cl_2]Cl$, in complete accord with his theory. Six years later, Werner won the Nobel Prize in chemistry.

By all accounts, Werner was a superb lecturer. Sometimes as many as 300 students crowded into a hall with a capacity of 150 to hear him speak. So great was his reputation that students in theology and law came to hear him talk about chemistry. There was, however, a darker side to Werner that few students saw. A young woman badgered by Werner during an oral examination came to see him later to ask whether she had passed; he threw a chair at her. Werner died at 52 of hardening of the arteries, perhaps caused in part by his addiction to alcohol and strong black cigars.

More important, it offered no explanation of the most striking characteristic of coordination compounds: their color (Figure 15.8).

We will discuss the **crystal field model** here. It assumes that the bonding between metal ions and ligands is essentially ionic. More specifically, it considers the effect of approaching ligands upon the energies of electronic levels in transition metal cations. We will apply this model to octahedral complexes. Before doing so, it may be helpful to review the electronic structure of uncomplexed transition metal cations, originally covered in Chapter 6.

"Crystal field" isn't a very descriptive term, but it's part of the jargon.

Transition Metal Cations

In transition metal cations, 3d is lower in energy than 4s.

Recall (page 150) that in a simple transition metal cation—

- there are no outer s electrons. Electrons beyond the preceding noble gas are located in an inner d sublevel (3d for the first transition series).
- electrons are distributed among the five d orbitals in accordance with Hund's rule, giving the maximum number of unpaired electrons.

To illustrate these rules, consider the Fe^{2+} ion. Because the atomic number of iron is 26, this +2 ion must contain $26 - 2 = 24e^-$. Of these electrons, the first 18 have the argon structure; the remaining six are located in the 3d sublevel. The abbreviated electron configuration is

$$Fe^{2+} \qquad [Ar]3d^6$$

These six electrons are spread over all five orbitals; the orbital diagram is

$$\begin{array}{llc} & & 3d \\ Fe^{2+} & [Ar] & (\uparrow\downarrow)(\uparrow)(\uparrow)(\uparrow)(\uparrow) \end{array}$$

The Fe^{2+} ion is *paramagnetic,* with four unpaired electrons.

Marna G. Clarke

Figure 15.8
Brightly colored coordination compounds. Most coordination compounds are brilliantly colored, a property that can be explained by the crystal field model.

CENGAGENOW™
Click Coached Problems for a self-study module on **electronic structure in transition metal complexes.**

Example 15.4 For the Co^{3+} ion, derive the electron configuration, orbital diagram, and number of unpaired electrons.

Strategy First (1) find the total number of electrons (Z Co = 27). Then (2) find the electron configuration; the first 18 electrons form the argon core, and the remaining electrons enter the 3d sublevel. Finally (3) apply Hund's rule to obtain the orbital diagram.

SOLUTION

(1) no. of electrons = 27 − 3 = 24
(2) electron configuration [Ar] $3d^6$
(3) orbital diagram (beyond Ar) 3d (↑↓)(↑)(↑)(↑)(↑) 4 unpaired e^-

The shapes of the five d orbitals are shown in Figure 15.9. These orbitals are given the symbols

$$d_{z^2} \quad d_{x^2-y^2} \quad d_{xy} \quad d_{yz} \quad d_{xz}$$

In the uncomplexed transition metal cation, all of these orbitals have the same energy.

Octahedral Complexes

As six ligands approach a central metal ion to form an octahedral complex, they change the energies of electrons in the d orbitals. The effect (Figure 15.10, p. 419) is to split the five d orbitals into two groups of different energy.

1. A higher energy pair, the $d_{x^2-y^2}$ and d_{z^2} orbitals
2. A lower energy trio, the d_{xy}, d_{yz}, and d_{xz} orbitals

The difference in energy between the two groups is called the **crystal field splitting energy** and given the symbol Δ_o (the subscript "o" stands for "octahedral").

To see why this splitting occurs, consider what happens when six ligands (e.g., H_2O, CN^-, NH_3) approach a central metal cation along the x-, y-, and z-axes (Figure 15.9). The unshared electron pairs on these ligands repel the electrons in the d orbitals of the cation. The repulsion is greatest for the $d_{x^2-y^2}$ and d_{z^2} orbitals, which have their maximum electron density directly along the x-, y-, and z-axes, respectively. Electrons in the other three orbitals (d_{xy}, d_{yz}, d_{xz}) are less affected because their densities are concentrated between the axes rather than along them.

This gives the d_{xy}, d_{yz}, and d_{xz} orbitals a lower energy.

Depending on the magnitude of Δ_o, a cation may form either of two different kinds of complexes. This is illustrated for the Fe^{2+} ion in the two diagrams in Figure 15.11 (p. 419).

1. In the $Fe(CN)_6^{4-}$ ion shown at the left, Δ_o is so large that the six 3d electrons of the Fe^{2+} ion pair up in the lower energy orbitals. In this way, the Fe^{2+} ion achieves its most stable (lowest energy) electronic structure. The complex is diamagnetic, with no unpaired electrons.

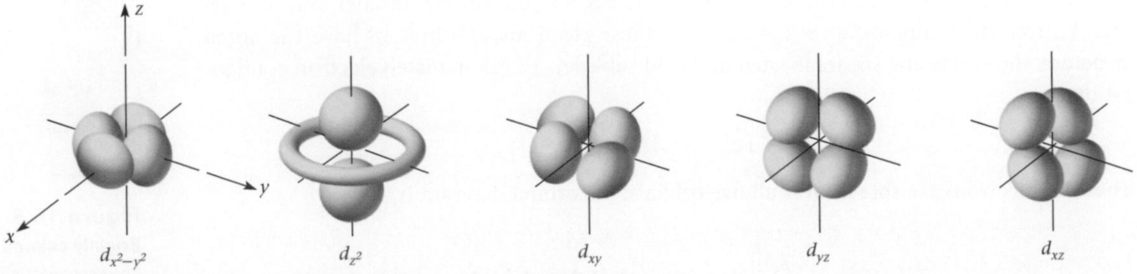

Figure 15.9
The five d orbitals and their relation to ligands on the x-, y-, and z-axes.

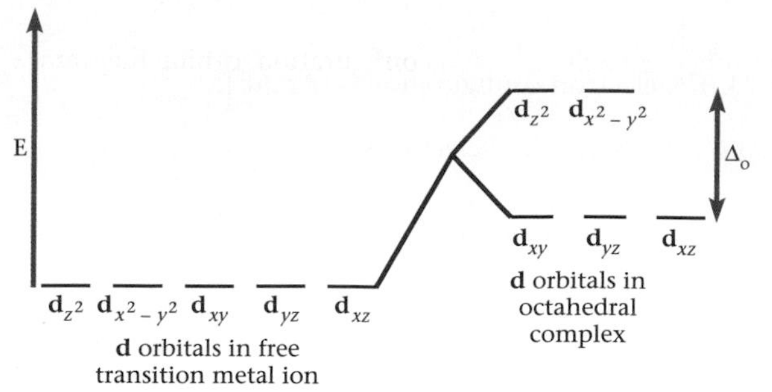

Figure 15.10
Change in the energy levels of d orbitals in complex formation. In a free transition metal ion, all five d orbitals have the same energy. When the ion forms an octahedral complex, two orbitals (d_{z^2}, $d_{x^2-y^2}$) have a higher energy than the other three (d_{xy}, d_{yz}, d_{xz}). The difference in energy between the two d orbital levels in the octahedral complex is known as the *crystal field splitting energy* and has the symbol Δ_o.

2. In the $Fe(H_2O)_6^{2+}$ ion shown at the right, Δ_o is relatively small, and the six 3d electrons of the Fe^{2+} ion spread out over all the orbitals as expected by Hund's rule. In other words, the electron distribution in the complex is the same as in the Fe^{2+} ion itself (where Δ_o is 0!). The $Fe(H_2O)_6^{2+}$ ion is paramagnetic, with four unpaired electrons.

When Δ_o is small, the electron distribution is the same as in the simple cation; if Δ_o is large, Hund's rule is not strictly followed.

More generally, it is possible to distinguish between—

- **low-spin complexes,** containing the minimum number of unpaired electrons, formed when Δ_o is large; electrons are concentrated in the lower energy orbitals.
- **high-spin complexes,** containing the maximum number of unpaired electrons, formed when Δ_o is small; electrons are spread out among the d orbitals, exactly as in the uncomplexed transition metal cation.

For a given cation—

- the high-spin complex always contains more unpaired electrons than the low-spin complex and so is more strongly paramagnetic.
- the value of Δ_o is determined by the nature of the ligand. So-called "strong-field" ligands (e.g., CN^-), which interact strongly with d-orbital electrons, produce a large Δ_o. Conversely, "weak-field" ligands (e.g., H_2O) interact weakly with d-orbital electrons, producing a small Δ_o.

Remember:
strong-field ligands → large Δ_o → low spin
weak-field ligands → small Δ_o → high spin

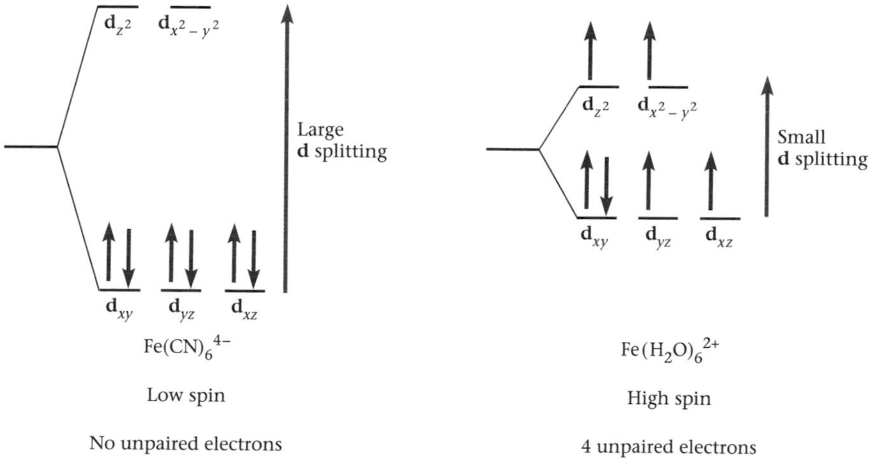

Figure 15.11
Electron distribution in low-spin and high-spin complexes of Fe^{2+}. Depending on the magnitude of Δ_o, either of two different complexes may be formed by Fe^{2+}.

Example 15.5 Derive the electron distribution of the Fe^{3+} ion in the low-spin and high-spin octahedral complexes.

Strategy First (1) find out how many 3d electrons there are in Fe^{3+}. Now (2) consider how those electrons will be distributed if Hund's rule is followed; that corresponds to the high-spin complex. Finally (3) sprinkle as many electrons as possible into the lower three orbitals; this is the low-spin complex.

SOLUTION

(1) no. of electrons = 26 − 3 = 23. The electron configuration is [Ar $3d^5$].

(2) (↑)(↑)
(↑)(↑)(↑) high spin ; 5 unpaired electrons

(3) (   )(   )
(↑↓)(↑↓)(↑) low spin ; 1 unpaired electron

This model of the electronic structure of complex ions explains why high-spin and low-spin complexes occur only with ions that have four to seven electrons (d^4, d^5, d^6, d^7). With three or fewer electrons, only one distribution is possible; the same is true with eight or more electrons.

3 electrons	8 electrons
( )( )	(↑)(↑)
(↑)(↑)(↑)	(↑↓)(↑↓)(↑↓)

Color

Most coordination compounds are brightly colored except for those of cations whose d sublevels are completely empty (such as Sc^{3+}) or completely filled (such as Zn^{2+}). These colors are readily explained, at least qualitatively, by the model we have just described. The energy difference between two sets of d orbitals in a complex is ordinarily equal to that of a photon in the visible region. Hence by absorbing visible light, an electron may be able to move from the lower energy set of d orbitals to the higher one. This removes some of the component wavelengths of white light, so that the light reflected or transmitted by the complex is colored. The relation between absorbed and transmitted light can be deduced from the color wheel shown in Figure 15.12. For example, a complex that absorbs blue-green light appears orange, and vice versa.

The color we see is what is left over after certain wavelengths are absorbed.

From the color (absorption spectrum) of a complex ion, it is sometimes possible to deduce the value of Δ_o, the crystal field splitting energy. The situation is particularly simple in $_{22}Ti^{3+}$, which contains only one 3d electron. Consider, for example, the $Ti(H_2O)_6^{3+}$ ion, which has an intense purple color. This ion absorbs at 510 nm, in the green region. The

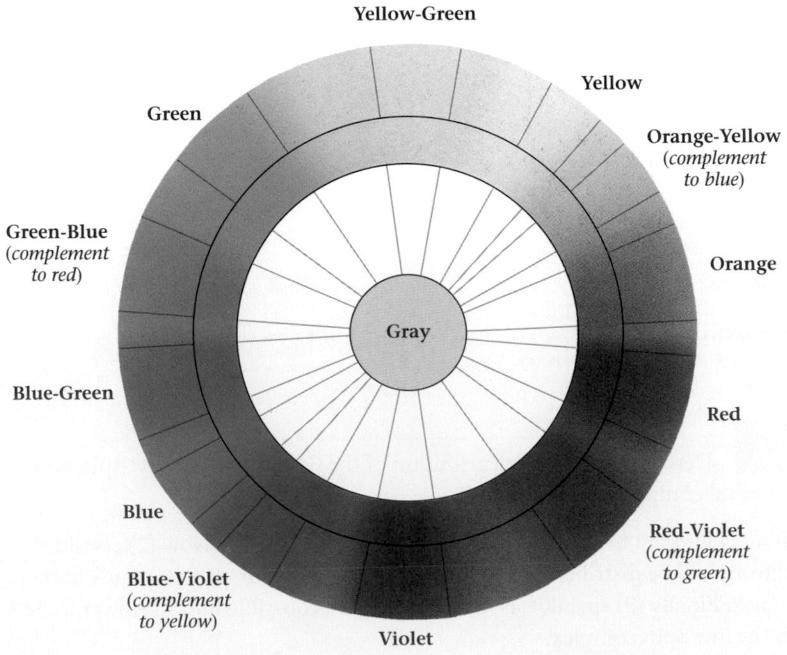

Figure 15.12
The color wheel. The color of a complex is complementary to (180° across from) the color of the light absorbed.

Charles D. Winters

Light absorption and color. The color of a solution is due to the color of the light *not* absorbed by the solution. Here a solution of Ni^{2+} ion in water absorbs red and blue light and so appears green.

purple (red-violet) color of a solution of $Ti(H_2O)_6{}^{3+}$ is what is left over when the green component is subtracted from the visible spectrum. Using the equation relating energy to wavelength (Chapter 6), it is possible to calculate the energy of a photon with a wavelength of 510 nm:

$$E = \frac{hc}{\lambda} = \frac{(6.626 \times 10^{-34}\ J \cdot s)(2.998 \times 10^{8}\ m/s)}{510 \times 10^{-9}\ m} = 3.90 \times 10^{-19}\ J$$

The energy in kilojoules per mole is

$$E = 3.90 \times 10^{-19}\ J \times \frac{1\ kJ}{10^3\ J} \times \frac{6.022 \times 10^{23}}{1\ mol} = 2.35 \times 10^2\ kJ/mol$$

This is the energy absorbed in raising the 3d electron from a lower to a higher orbital. In other words, in the $Ti(H_2O)_6{}^{3+}$ ion, the two sets of d orbitals are separated by this amount of energy. The splitting energy, Δ_o, is 235 kJ/mol.

The smaller the value of Δ_o, the longer the wavelength of the light absorbed. This effect is shown in Table 15.3 and Figure 15.13 (p. 422). When weak-field ligands such as NCS^-, H_2O, or Cl^- are substituted for NH_3, the light absorbed shifts to longer wavelengths (lower energies). On the basis of observations like this, ligands can be arranged in order of decreasing tendency to split the d orbitals. A short version of such a *spectrochemical series* is

$$CN^- > NO_2{}^- > en > NH_3 > NCS^- > H_2O > F^- > Cl^-$$

strong field — decreasing Δ_o → — weak field

This series is based on experiment, not theory.

Table 15.3 Colors of Complex Ions of Co^{3+}

Complex	Color Observed	Color Absorbed	Approximate Wavelength (nm) Absorbed
$Co(NH_3)_6{}^{3+}$	Yellow	Violet	430
$Co(NH_3)_5NCS^{2+}$	Orange	Blue-green	470
$Co(NH_3)_5H_2O^{3+}$	Red	Green-blue	500
$Co(NH_3)_5Cl^{2+}$	Purple	Yellow-green	530
trans-$Co(NH_3)_4Cl_2{}^+$	Green	Red	680

Ray Boyington/S. Ruven Smith

Figure 15.13
A spectrochemical series. The five cations listed in Table 15.3 vary in color from yellow $[Co(NH_3)_6]Cl_3$ to green [*trans*-$Co(NH_3)_4Cl_2$]Cl.

15.4 FORMATION CONSTANTS OF COMPLEX IONS

The equilibrium constant for the formation of a complex ion is called a **formation constant** (or stability constant) and given the symbol K_f. A typical example is

$$Cu^{2+}(aq) + 4NH_3(aq) \rightleftharpoons Cu(NH_3)_4^{2+}(aq) \qquad K_f = \frac{[Cu(NH_3)_4^{2+}]}{[Cu^{2+}] \times [NH_3]^4}$$

Table 15.4 lists formation constants of complex ions. In each case, K_f applies to the formation of the complex by a reaction of the type just cited. Notice that for most complex ions listed, K_f is a large number, 10^5 or greater. This means that equilibrium considerations strongly favor complex formation. Consider, for example, the system

$$Ag^+(aq) + 2NH_3(aq) \rightleftharpoons Ag(NH_3)_2^+(aq)$$

$$K_f = \frac{[Ag(NH_3)_2^+]}{[Ag^+] \times [NH_3]^2} = 1.7 \times 10^7$$

The large K_f value means that the forward reaction goes virtually to completion. Addition of ammonia to a solution of $AgNO_3$ will convert nearly all the Ag^+ ions to $Ag(NH_3)_2^+$ (see Example 15.6).

Table 15.4 Formation Constants of Complex Ions

Complex Ion	K_f	Complex Ion	K_f
$AgCl_2^-$	1.8×10^5	$CuCl_2^-$	1×10^5
$Ag(CN)_2^-$	2×10^{20}	$Cu(NH_3)_4^{2+}$	2×10^{12}
$Ag(NH_3)_2^+$	1.7×10^7	$FeSCN^{2+}$	9.2×10^2
$Ag(S_2O_3)_2^{3-}$	1×10^{13}	$Fe(CN)_6^{3-}$	4×10^{52}
$Al(OH)_4^-$	1×10^{33}	$Fe(CN)_6^{4-}$	4×10^{45}
$Cd(CN)_4^{2-}$	2×10^{18}	$Hg(CN)_4^{2-}$	2×10^{41}
$Cd(NH_3)_4^{2+}$	2.8×10^7	$Ni(NH_3)_6^{2+}$	9×10^8
$Cd(OH)_4^{2-}$	1.2×10^9	$PtCl_4^{2-}$	1×10^{16}
$Co(NH_3)_6^{2+}$	1×10^5	*trans*-$Pt(NH_3)_2Cl_2$	3×10^{28}
$Co(NH_3)_6^{3+}$	1×10^{23}	*cis*-$Pt(NH_3)_2Cl_2$	3×10^{29}
$Co(NH_3)_5Cl^{2+}$	2×10^{28}	$Zn(CN)_4^{2-}$	6×10^{16}
$Co(NH_3)_5NO_2^{2+}$	1×10^{24}	$Zn(NH_3)_4^{2+}$	3.6×10^8
		$Zn(OH)_4^{2-}$	3×10^{14}

Example 15.6 Graded

Consider the equilibrium

$$Ag^+(aq) + 2NH_3(aq) \rightleftharpoons Ag(NH_3)_2^+(aq) \qquad K_f = 1.7 \times 10^7$$

Calculate

* (a) the ratio $[Ag(NH_3)_2^+]/[Ag^+]$ in 0.10 M NH_3.

** (b) the concentration of NH_3 required to convert 99% of Ag^+ to $Ag(NH_3)_2^+$.

*** (c) the equilibrium constant for the reaction:

$$Ag(NH_3)_2^+(aq) + 2S_2O_3^{2-}(aq) \rightleftharpoons Ag(S_2O_3)_2^{3-}(aq) + 2NH_3(aq)$$

(Take K_f $Ag(S_2O_3)_2^{3-}$ to be 1×10^{13}.)

SOLUTION

(a) $K_f = 1.7 \times 10^7 = \dfrac{[Ag(NH_3)_2^+]}{[Ag^+] \times [NH_3]^2}$

$$\frac{[Ag(NH_3)_2^+]}{[Ag^+]} = K_f \times [NH_3]^2 = 1.7 \times 10^7(0.10)^2 = 1.7 \times 10^5$$

This means that in 0.10 M NH_3 there are 170,000 $Ag(NH_3)_2^+$ complex ions for every Ag^+ ion.

(b) $[Ag(NH_3)_2^+]/[Ag^+] = 99/1 = 99$

$$K_f = 1.7 \times 10^7 = \frac{[Ag(NH_3)_2^+]}{[Ag^+] \times [NH_3]^2} = \frac{99}{[NH_3]^2}$$

Solving, $[NH_3]^2 = \dfrac{99}{1.7 \times 10^7} = 6 \times 10^{-6}$

$$[NH_3] = 2 \times 10^{-3}\,M$$

(c) Applying the rule of multiple equilibria:

$$Ag^+(aq) + 2S_2O_3^{2-}(aq) \rightleftharpoons Ag(S_2O_3)_2^{3-}(aq) \qquad K_1 = 1 \times 10^{13}$$

$$Ag(NH_3)_2^+(aq) \rightleftharpoons Ag^+(aq) + 2NH_3(aq) \qquad K_2 = 1/(1.7 \times 10^7)$$

$$Ag(NH_3)_2^+(aq) + 2S_2O_3^{3-}(aq) \rightleftharpoons Ag(S_2O_3)_2^{3-}(aq) + 2NH_3(aq)$$

$$K = K_1K_2 = (1 \times 10^{13})\,(5.9 \times 10^{-8}) = 6 \times 10^5$$

From Example 15.6 we see that the reaction for the conversion of $Ag(NH_3)_2^+$ to $Ag(S_2O_3)_2^{3-}$ has a large equilibrium constant. Looking at it in a slightly different way, we can say that of these two complexes of Ag^+, the $Ag(S_2O_3)_2^{3-}$ ion is the more stable.

A similar situation applies to two complex ions of Co^{3+}:

$$Co(NH_3)_6^{3+}(aq) + Cl^-(aq) \rightleftharpoons Co(NH_3)_5Cl^{2+}(aq) + NH_3(aq)$$

$$K = \frac{K_f\, Co(NH_3)_5Cl^{2+}}{K_f\, Co(NH_3)_6^{3+}} = \frac{2 \times 10^{28}}{1 \times 10^{23}} = 2 \times 10^5$$

Addition of Cl^- ions to the yellow complex $Co(NH_3)_6^{3+}$ converts it to the more stable complex $Co(NH_3)_5Cl^{2+}$, which has an intense purple color (Table 15.3).

CHEMISTRY Beyond the Classroom

Chelates: Natural and Synthetic

Chelating agents, capable of bonding to metal atoms at more than one position, are abundant in nature. Certain species of soybeans synthesize and secrete organic chelating agents that extract iron from insoluble compounds in the soil, thereby making it available to the plant. Mosses and lichens growing on boulders use a similar process to obtain the metal ions they need for growth.

Many important natural products are chelates in which a central metal atom is bonded into a large organic molecule. In chlorophyll, the green coloring matter of plants, the central atom is magnesium; in the essential vitamin B_{12}, it is cobalt. The structure of heme, the pigment responsible for the red color of blood, is shown in Figure A. There is an Fe^{2+} ion at the center of the complex surrounded by four nitrogen atoms at the corners of a square. A fifth coordination position around the iron is occupied by an organic molecule globin, which in combination with heme, gives the protein referred to as hemoglobin.

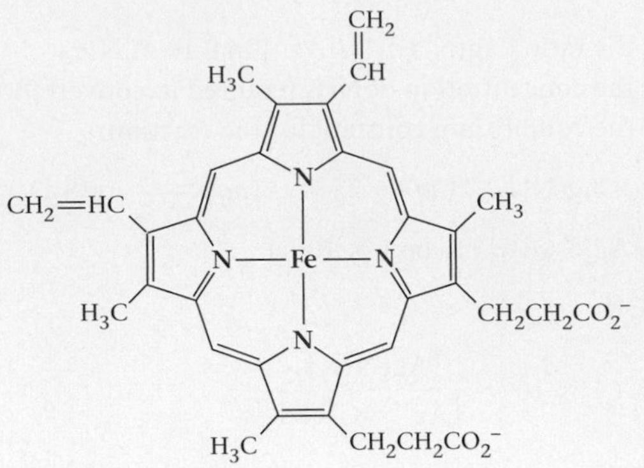

Figure A
Structure of heme. In the hemoglobin molecule, the Fe^{2+} ion is at the center of an octahedron, surrounded by four nitrogen atoms, a globin molecule, and a water molecule.

The sixth coordination position of Fe^{2+} in heme is occupied by a water molecule that can be replaced reversibly by oxygen to give a derivative known as oxyhemoglobin, which has the bright red color characteristic of arterial blood.

$$\text{hemoglobin} + O_2 \rightleftharpoons \text{oxyhemoglobin} + H_2O$$

The position of this equilibrium is sensitive to the pressure of oxygen. In the lungs, where the blood is saturated with air ($P_{O_2} = 0.2$ atm), the hemoglobin is almost completely converted to oxyhemoglobin. In the tissues, the partial pressure of oxygen drops, and the oxyhemoglobin breaks down to release O_2 essential for metabolism. In this way, hemoglobin acts as an oxygen carrier, absorbing oxygen in the lungs and liberating it to the tissues.

Unfortunately, hemoglobin forms a complex with carbon monoxide that is considerably more stable than oxyhemoglobin. The equilibrium constant for the reaction

$$\text{hemoglobin} \cdot O_2(aq) + CO(g) \rightleftharpoons \text{hemoglobin} \cdot CO(aq) + O_2(g)$$

is about 200 at body temperature. Consequently, the carbon monoxide complex is formed preferentially in the lungs even at CO concentrations as low as one part per thousand. When this happens, the flow of oxygen to the tissues is cut off, resulting eventually in muscular paralysis and death.

Many chelating agents have been synthesized in the laboratory to take advantage of their ability to tie up *(sequester)* metal cations. Perhaps the best known synthetic chelating agent is the ethylenediaminetetraacetate (EDTA) ion shown in Figure B. EDTA can bond at as many as six positions, thereby occupying all the octahedral sites surrounding a central metal cation.

EDTA forms 1 : 1 complexes with a large number of cations, including those of some of the main-group metals. The complex formed by calcium with EDTA is used to treat lead poisoning. When a solution containing the Ca-EDTA complex is given by injection, the calcium is displaced by lead. The more stable Pb-EDTA complex is eliminated in the urine. EDTA has also been used to remove radioactive isotopes of metals, notably plutonium, from body tissues.

You may have noticed Ca-EDTA on the list of ingredients of many prepared foods, ranging from beer to mayonnaise. EDTA acts as a scavenger to pick up traces of metal ions that catalyze the chemical reactions responsible for flavor deterioration, loss of color, or rancidity. Typically, Ca-EDTA is added at a level of 30 to 800 ppm.

Still another use of EDTA is in the field of art restoration. Figure C shows "before and after" photographs of Rodin's bronze sculpture "The Thinker." This stood in front of the Philadelphia Rodin Museum for about 60 years prior to its restoration in 1992. Over time the sculpture had picked up a thick coating of insoluble $CuSO_4 \cdot 3Cu(OH)_2(s)$. Application of a wet paste containing EDTA dissolved the coating by forming the soluble $Cu(EDTA)^{2-}$ complex.

$$CuSO_4 \cdot 3Cu(OH)_2(s) + 4EDTA^{4-}(aq) \longrightarrow 4Cu(EDTA)^{2-}(aq) + SO_4^{2-}(aq) + 6OH^-(aq)$$

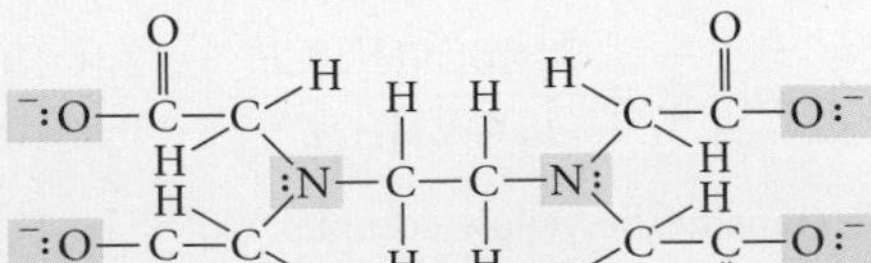

Figure B
Structure of the EDTA ion; the chelating atoms, six in all, have color screens.

Figure C
***The Thinker* by Rodin, before *(left)* and after *(right)*.**

Chapter Highlights

Key Concepts

1. Relate the composition of a complex ion to its charge, coordination number, and the oxidation number of the central metal.
   (Examples 15.1, 15.2; Problems 1–10) ■ Questions and Problems assignable in OWL: 2, 4, 6, 8, 12
2. Sketch the geometry of a complex ion and identify geometric isomers.
   (Example 15.3; Problems 17–24) ■ 21, 45
3. Give the electron configuration and/or orbital diagram of a transition metal cation.
   (Example 15.4; Problems 25–28) ■ 26, 28
4. Derive orbital diagrams for high-spin and low-spin complexes.
   (Example 15.5; Problems 29–36) ■ 29, 32, 33, 35, 37
5. Relate K_f for a complex ion to the ratio of concentrations of complex ion and metal cation.
   (Example 15.6; Problems 41–44) ■ 41, 43, 47, 49

Select end of chapter Questions and Problems may be assigned in OWL and are cross-referenced in the Key Concepts list.

CENGAGENOW™

Sign in at **academic.cengage.com/now** to:

- Check your readiness for an exam by taking the Pre-Test and exploring the self-study modules recommended in your Personalized Study plan
- For quick review, download Go Chemistry mini-lecture flashcard modules (or purchase them at **www.ichapters.com**)

Key Terms

chelate	formation constant	ligand
cis-	geometric isomerism	low-spin complex
complex ion	high-spin complex	octahedral
coordination number	isomer	square planar
crystal field model	Lewis acid	tetrahedral
—splitting energy	Lewis base	*trans-*

Summary Problem

Consider the complex ion $[Co(H_2O)_4(Cl)_2]^+$.

(a) Identify the ligands and their charges.
(b) What is the oxidation number of cobalt?
(c) Write the formula of the phosphate salt of the ion.
(d) Suppose that the metal is replaced by Pt(IV); write the formula of the complex ion.
(e) What is the coordination number of cobalt in the complex?
(f) Describe the geometry of the complex.
(g) How many different geometric isomers are possible?
(h) For this octahedral complex, how many d electrons are in cobalt?
(i) Water and chloride ions are ligands with weak crystal fields (small Δ_o).
 (1) Show the electron distribution for the d electrons in this complex.
 (2) Is this a high-spin complex?
 (3) Is the complex diamagnetic?
 (4) How many unpaired electrons are there?
(j) Write a net ionic equation to show the reaction between Co(III) ion, five ammonia ligands, and one chloride ligand to form the complex ion.
(k) Calculate the complex to metal ratio in a solution in which $[NH_3] = [Cl^-] = 0.20\ M$. What does your answer tell you about the stability of the complex at those concentrations?

Answers

(a) $H_2O = 0$; $Cl^- = -1$
(b) +3
(c) $[Co(H_2O)_4(Cl)_2]_3PO_4$
(d) $[Pt(H_2O)_4(Cl)_2]^{2+}$
(e) 6
(f) octahedral
(g) two
(h) 6
(i) (1) ↑ ↑
 ↑↓ ↑ ↑
 (2) yes
 (3) no
 (4) 4
(j) $Co^{3+}(aq) + 5NH_3(aq) + Cl^-(aq) \rightleftharpoons [Co(NH_3)_5Cl]^{2+}(aq)$
(k) 1×10^{24}; very stable

Questions and Problems

Blue-numbered questions have answers in Appendix 6 and fully-worked solutions in the *Student Solutions Manual.*

■ denotes questions assignable in OWL.

WEB indicates that the solution is available on this book's companion website.

Composition of Complex Ions and Coordination Compounds

1. Consider the complex ion $[Ni(H_2O)_2Cl_2(OH)_2]^{2-}$.
 (a) Identify the ligands and their charges.
 (b) What is the oxidation number of nickel?
 (c) What is the formula for the sodium salt of this ion?

2. ■ Consider the complex ion $[Co(en)_2(SCN)Cl]^+$.
 (a) Identify the ligands and their charges.
 (b) What is the oxidation number of cobalt?
 (c) What is the formula for the sulfide salt of this ion?

3. Chromium(III) forms many complexes, among them those with the following ligands. Give the formula and charge of each chromium complex ion described below.
 (a) two oxalate ions ($C_2O_4^{2-}$) and two water molecules
 (b) five ammonia molecules and one sulfate ion
 (c) one ethylenediamine molecule, two ammonia molecules, and two iodide ions

4. ■ **WEB** Platinum(II) forms many complexes, among them those with the following ligands. Give the formula and charge of each complex.
 (a) two ammonia molecules and one oxalate ion ($C_2O_4^{2-}$)
 (b) two ammonia molecules, one thiocyanate ion (SCN^-), and one bromide ion
 (c) one ethylenediamine molecule and two nitrite ions

5. What is the coordination number of the metal in the following complexes?
 (a) $[Mo(CNS)_2(en)_2]^+$ **(b)** $[Co(H_2O)(OH)_2Br]^-$
 (c) $[Ag(NH_3)_2]^+$ **(d)** $[PtCl_2(NO_2)_2]^{2-}$

6. ■ What is the coordination number of the metal in the following complexes?

(a) $[Mn(NH_3)_2(OH)_4]^{2+}$ (b) $[CuCl_4]^{3-}$
(c) $[Cr(H_2O)_2(ox)_2]^{2-}$ (d) $[Au(CN)_2]^{+}$

7. What is the oxidation number of the metal atom in the complex ions in Question 5?

8. ■ What is the oxidation number of the metal atom in the complex ions in Question 6?

9. Write the formula for the phosphate salt (if the complex ion is a cation) or the aluminum salt (if the complex ion is an anion) for the ions in Question 5.

10. Follow the directions for Question 9 for the complex ions in Question 6.

11. Refer to Table 15.2 to predict the formula of the complex formed by

(a) Ag^+ with H_2O (b) Pt^{2+} with H_2O
(c) Pd^{2+} with Br^- (d) Fe^{3+} with $C_2O_4^{2-}$

12. ■ Refer to Table 15.2 to predict the formula of the complex formed by

(a) Pt^{4+} with NH_3 (b) Ag^+ with CN^-
(c) Zn^{2+} with $C_2O_4^{2-}$ (d) Cd^{2+} with CN^-

13. What is the mass percent of nitrogen in the $Co(en)_3^{3+}$ complex ion?

14. ■ What is the mass percent of chromium in the chloride salt of $[Cr(H_2O)_5(OH)]^{2+}$?

15. There are four iron atoms in each hemoglobin molecule. The mass percent of iron in a hemoglobin molecule is 0.35%. Estimate the molar mass of hemoglobin.

16. Vitamin B_{12} is a coordination compound with cobalt as its central atom. It contains 4.4% cobalt by mass and has a molar mass of 1.3×10^3 g/mol. How many cobalt atoms are in a molecule of vitamin B_{12}?

Geometry of Complex Ions

17. Sketch the geometry of

(a) $[Zn(NH_3)_2Cl_2]$ (tetrahedral)
(b) *cis*-$[Co(H_2O)_4Cl_2]^+$
(c) *trans*-$[Pt(NH_3)_2Br_2]^{2+}$
(d) *trans*-$[Ni(ox)_2(OH)_2]^{3-}$
(e) $[Au(CN)Br]^+$

18. Sketch the geometry of

(a) $[Fe(H_2O)_2I_2]$ (tetrahedral)
(b) $[Ag(SCN)_2]^-$
(c) *cis*-$[Ni(OH)_2Cl_2]^-$
(d) *trans*-$[Cr(en)_2(NH_3)_2]^{3+}$
(e) *cis*-$[Co(ox)(H_2O)_2]^+$

19. The compound 1,2-diaminocyclohexane

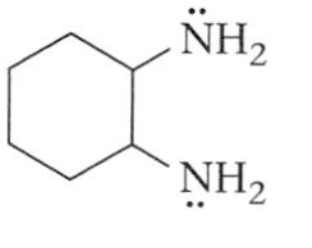

(abbreviated "dech") is a ligand in the promising anticancer complex *cis*-$Pd(H_2O)_2(dech)^{2+}$. Sketch the geometry of this complex.

20. The acetylacetonate ion ($acac^-$)

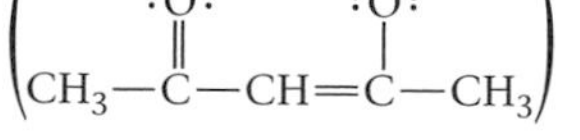

forms complexes with many metal ions. Sketch the geometry of $Fe(acac)_3$.

21. ■ Which of the following octahedral complexes show geometric isomerism? If geometric isomers are possible, draw their structures.

(a) $[Co(en)Cl_4]^-$
(b) $[Ni(C_2O_4)_2ClBr]^{4-}$
(c) $[Cd(NH_3)_2Cl_4]^{2-}$

22. WEB Follow the directions of Question 21 for the following.

(a) $[Cr(NH_3)_2(SCN)_4]^{2-}$
(b) $[Co(NH_3)_3(NO_2)_3]^-$
(c) $[Mn(H_2O)_2(NH_3)_3OH]^+$

23. Draw all the structural formulas for the octahedral complexes of Co^{3+} with only *ox* and/or NH_3 as ligands.

24. Draw all the structural formulas for the octahedral complexes of $[Ni(H_2O)_3(OH)_2Cl]$.

Electronic Structure of Metal Ions

25. Give the electronic configuration for

(a) Ti^{3+} (b) Cr^{2+} (c) Ru^{4+}
(d) Pd^{2+} (e) Mo^{3+}

26. ■ Give the electronic configuration for

(a) Fe^{3+} (b) V^{2+} (c) Zn^{2+}
(d) Cu^+ (e) Mn^{4+}

27. Write an abbreviated orbital diagram and determine the number of unpaired electrons in each species in Question 25.

28. ■ Write an abbreviated orbital diagram and determine the number of unpaired electrons in each species in Question 26.

Electron Distributions and Crystal Field Energy

29. ■ Give the electron distribution in low-spin and/or high-spin complexes of

(a) Ru^{4+} (b) Pt^{2+}

30. Follow the directions of Question 29 for

(a) Mo^{3+} (b) Pd^{4+}

31. For complexes of V^{3+}, only one distribution of electrons is possible. Explain.

32. ■ Explain why Mn^{3+} forms high-spin and low-spin octahedral complexes but Mn^{4+} does not.

33. ■ $[Cr(CN)_6]^{4-}$ is less paramagnetic than $[Cr(H_2O)_6]^{2+}$. Explain.

34. Why is $[Co(NH_3)_6]^{3+}$ diamagnetic while $[CoF_6]^{3-}$ is paramagnetic?

35. ■ Give the number of unpaired electrons in octahedral complexes with strong-field ligands for

(a) Rh^{3+} (b) Mn^{3+} (c) Ag^+
(d) Pt^{4+} (e) Au^{3+}

36. WEB For the species in Question 35, indicate the number of unpaired electrons with weak-field ligands.

37. ■ $Ti(NH_3)_6^{3+}$ has a d-orbital electron transition at 399 nm. Find Δ_o at this wavelength.

38. MnF_6^{2-} has a crystal field splitting energy, Δ_o, of 2.60×10^2 kJ/mol. What is the wavelength responsible for this energy?

39. The wavelength of maximum absorption of $Cu(NH_3)_4^{2+}$ is 580 nm (orange-yellow). What color is a solution of $Cu(NH_3)_4^{2+}$?

40. A solution of $Fe(CN)_6^{3-}$ appears red. Using Figure 15.12, estimate the wavelength of maximum absorption.

Formation Constants of Complex Ions

41. ■ At what concentration of ammonia is

(a) $[Cd^{2+}] = [Cd(NH_3)_4^{2+}]$?
(b) $[Co^{2+}] = [Co(NH_3)_6^{2+}]$?

42. At what concentration of cyanide ion is

(a) $[Cd^{2+}] = 10^{-8} \times [Cd(CN)_4^{2-}]$?
(b) $[Fe^{2+}] = 10^{-20} \times [Fe(CN)_6^{4-}]$?

43. ■ Consider the complex ion $[Ni(en)_3]^{2+}$. Its K_f is 2.1×10^{18}. At what concentration of *en* is 67% of the Ni^{2+} converted to $[Ni(en)_3]^{2+}$?

44. Consider the complex ion $[Cr(OH)_4]^-$. Its formation constant, K_f, is 8×10^{29}. At what pH will 85% of the Cr^{3+} be converted to $[Cr(OH)_4]^-$?

■ in OWL Blue-numbered questions answered in Appendix 6 WEB Solution is available on companion website

Unclassified

45. ■ A chemist synthesizes two coordination compounds. One compound decomposes at 280°C, the other at 240°C. Analysis of the compounds gives the same mass percent data: 52.6% Pt, 7.6% N, 1.63% H, and 38.2% Cl. Both compounds contain a +4 central ion.
   (a) What is the simplest formula of the compounds?
   (b) Draw structural formulas for the complexes present.

46. Analysis of a coordination compound gives the following results: 22.0% Co, 31.4% N, 6.78% H, and 39.8% Cl. One mole of the compound dissociates in water to form four moles of ions.
   (a) What is the simplest formula of the compound?
   (b) Write an equation for its dissociation in water.

47. ■ What are the concentrations of Cu^{2+}, NH_3, and $Cu(NH_3)_4^{2+}$ at equilibrium when 18.8 g of $Cu(NO_3)_2$ is added to 1.0 L of a 0.400 *M* solution of aqueous ammonia? Assume that the reaction goes to completion and forms $Cu(NH_3)_4^{2+}$.

48. Oxyhemoglobin is red, and hemoglobin is blue. Use Le Châtelier's principle to explain why venous blood is blue and arterial blood is bright red.

49. ■ For the system

$$\text{hemoglobin}\cdot O_2\,(aq) + CO(g) \rightleftharpoons \text{hemoglobin}\cdot CO(aq) + O_2(g)$$

$K = 2.0 \times 10^2$. What must be the ratio of P_{CO}/P_{O_2} if 12.0% of the hemoglobin in the bloodstream is converted to the CO complex?

50. Bipyridyl (Bipy) is a molecule commonly used as a bidentate ligand. When 0.17 mol of bipyridyl is dissolved in 2.4 L of a solution that contains 0.052 *M* Fe^{2+}, $[Fe(bipy)_3]^{2+}$ ($K_f = 1.6 \times 10^{17}$) is formed. What are the concentrations of all species when equilibrium is established?

Conceptual Problems

51. Explain why
   (a) oxalic acid removes rust stains.
   (b) there are no geometric isomers of tetrahedral complexes.
   (c) cations such as Co^{2+} act as Lewis acids.
   (d) $C_2O_4^{2-}$ is a chelating agent.
   (e) NH_3 can be a ligand but NH_4^+ is not.

52. ■ **WEB** Indicate whether each of the following is true or false. If the statement is false, correct it.
   (a) The coordination number of iron(III) in $Fe(NH_3)_4(en)^{3+}$ is 5.
   (b) $Ni(CN)_6^{4-}$ is expected to absorb at a longer wavelength than $Ni(NH_3)_6^{2+}$.
   (c) Complexes of Cr^{3+} are brightly colored, and those of Zn^{2+} are colorless.
   (d) Ions with seven or more d electrons cannot form both high- and low-spin octahedral complexes.

53. Consider three complexes of Ag^+ and their formation constants, K_f.

Complex Ion	K_f
$Ag(NH_3)_2^+$	1.6×10^7
$Ag(CN)_2^-$	5.6×10^{18}
$AgBr_2^-$	1.3×10^7

Which statements are true?
   (a) $Ag(NH_3)_2^+$ is more stable than $Ag(CN)_2^-$.
   (b) Adding a strong acid (HNO_3) to a solution that is 0.010 *M* in $Ag(NH_3)_2^+$ will tend to dissociate the complex ion into Ag^+ and NH_4^+.
   (c) Adding a strong acid (HNO_3) to a solution that is 0.010 *M* in $AgBr_2^-$ will tend to dissociate the complex ion into Ag^+ and Br^-.
   (d) To dissolve AgI, one can add either NaCN or HCN as a source of the cyanide-complexing ligand. Fewer moles of NaCN would be required.
   (e) Solution A is 0.10 *M* in Br^- and contains the complex ion $AgBr_2^-$. Solution B is 0.10 *M* in CN^- and contains the complex ion $Ag(CN)_2^-$. Solution B will have more particles of complex ion per particle of Ag^+ than solution A.

Challenge Problems

54. A child eats 10.0 g of paint containing 5.0% Pb. How many grams of the sodium salt of EDTA, $Na_4(EDTA)$, should he receive to bring the lead into solution as Pb · EDTA?

55. A certain coordination compound has the simplest formula $PtN_2H_6Cl_2$. It has a molar mass of about 600 g/mol and contains both a complex cation and a complex anion. What is its structure?

56. Two coordination compounds decompose at different temperatures but have the same mass percent analysis data: 20.25% Cu, 15.29% C, 7.07% H, 26.86% N, 10.23% S, and 20.39% O. Each contains Cu^{2+}.
   (a) Determine the simplest formula of the compounds.
   (b) Draw the structural formulas of the complex ion in each case.

57. In the $Ti(H_2O)_6^{3+}$ ion, the splitting between the d levels, Δ_o, is 55 kcal/mol. What is the color of this ion? Assume that the color results from a transition between upper and lower d levels.

■ in OWL Blue-numbered questions answered in Appendix 6 **WEB** Solution is available on companion website

16 Precipitation Equilibria

Surrounded by beakers, by strange coils,
By ovens and flasks with twisted necks,
The chemist, fathoming the whims of attractions,
Artfully imposes on them their precise meetings.

—Sully-Prudhomme
"The Naked World" (translated by William Dock)

Chapter Outline

This photograph by Ansel Adams was taken using film coated with water-insoluble silver bromide, AgBr.

In discussing precipitation reactions in Chapter 4, we assumed, in effect, that they went to completion. We must keep in mind, however, that precipitation reactions, like all reactions, reach a position of equilibrium. Putting it another way, even the most "insoluble" electrolyte dissolves to at least a slight extent, thereby establishing equilibrium with its ions in solution.

In this chapter, we consider two types of equilibria, both in water solution—

- that between a precipitate and its ions (Section 16.1), for example,

$$AgCl(s) \rightleftharpoons Ag^+(aq) + Cl^-(aq)$$

- that between a precipitate and a species used to dissolve it (Section 16.2), for example,

$$AgCl(s) + 2NH_3(aq) \rightleftharpoons Ag(NH_3)_2^+(aq) + Cl^-(aq)$$

Equilibria such as these have applications in fields as diverse as geology, medicine, and agriculture. In chemistry you are most likely to meet up with precipitation equilibria in the laboratory when you carry out experiments in qualitative analysis. ■

Online homework for this chapter may be assigned in OWL.

CENGAGENOW™
This icon introduces an opportunity for self-study and to explore interactive modules by signing in at **academic.cengage.com/now.**

16.1 PRECIPITATE FORMATION; SOLUBILITY PRODUCT CONSTANT (K_{sp})

As we saw in Chapter 4, a precipitate forms when a cation from one solution combines with an anion from another solution to form an insoluble ionic solid. We also considered how to predict whether such a reaction would occur and, if so, how to represent it by a net ionic equation.

Precipitation reactions, like all reactions, reach a position of equilibrium. Suppose, for example, solutions of $Sr(NO_3)_2$ and K_2CrO_4 are mixed. In this case, Sr^{2+} ions combine with CrO_4^{2-} ions to form a yellow precipitate of strontium chromate, $SrCrO_4$ (Figure 16.1). Very quickly, an equilibrium is established between the solid and the corresponding ions in solution:

$$SrCrO_4(s) \rightleftharpoons Sr^{2+}(aq) + CrO_4^{2-}(aq)$$

Charles D. Winters

Figure 16.1
Precipitation of strontium chromate. A solution prepared by mixing solutions of $Sr(NO_3)_2$ and K_2CrO_4 is in equilibrium with yellow $SrCrO_4(s)$. In such a solution $[Sr^{2+}] \times [CrO_4^{2-}] = 3.6 \times 10^{-5}$.

K_{sp} Expression

The equilibrium constant expression for the dissolving of $SrCrO_4$ can be written following the rules in Chapters 12 and 13. In particular, the solid does not appear in the expression; the concentration of each ion is raised to a power equal to its coefficient in the chemical equation.

$$K_{sp} = [Sr^{2+}] \times [CrO_4^{2-}]$$

Although the solid doesn't appear in K_{sp}, it must be present for equilibrium.

The symbol K_{sp} represents a particular type of equilibrium constant known as the **solubility product constant.** Like all equilibrium constants, K_{sp} has a fixed value for a given system at a particular temperature. At 25°C, K_{sp} for $SrCrO_4$ is about 3.6×10^{-5}; that is,

$$[Sr^{2+}] \times [CrO_4^{2-}] = 3.6 \times 10^{-5}$$

This relation says that the product of the two ion concentrations at equilibrium must be 3.6×10^{-5}, regardless of how equilibrium is established.

CENGAGENOW™
Click Coached Problems for a self-study module on **solubility product constant expressions.**

CENGAGENOW™

Click Coached Problems for a self-study module on **estimating salt solubility.**

Example 16.1 Write expressions for K_{sp} for

(a) Ag_2CrO_4 (b) $Ca_3(PO_4)_2$

Strategy Start by writing the chemical equation for the solution process (solid on the left, ions in solution on the right). Then write the expression for K_{sp}, noting that—

- solids do not appear.
- the concentration of each ion is raised to a power equal to its coefficient in the chemical equation.

SOLUTION

(a) $Ag_2CrO_4(s) \rightleftharpoons 2Ag^+(aq) + CrO_4^{2-}(aq)$

$K_{sp} = [Ag^+]^2 \times [CrO_4^{2-}]$

(b) $Ca_3(PO_4)_2(s) \rightleftharpoons 3Ca^{2+}(aq) + 2PO_4^{3-}(aq)$

$K_{sp} = [Ca^{2+}]^3 \times [PO_4^{3-}]^2$

K_{sp} and the Equilibrium Concentrations of Ions

The relation

$$K_{sp}\ SrCrO_4 = [Sr^{2+}] \times [CrO_4^{2-}] = 3.6 \times 10^{-5}$$

can be used to calculate the equilibrium concentration of one ion if you know that of the other. Suppose, for example, the concentration of CrO_4^{2-} in a certain solution in equilibrium with $SrCrO_4$ is known to be 2.0×10^{-3} *M*. It follows that

$$[Sr^{2+}] = \frac{K_{sp}\ SrCrO_4}{[CrO_4^{2-}]} = \frac{3.6 \times 10^{-5}}{2.0 \times 10^{-3}} = 1.8 \times 10^{-2}\ M$$

If in another case, $[Sr^{2+}] = 1.0 \times 10^{-4}$ *M*,

$$[CrO_4^{2-}] = \frac{K_{sp}\ SrCrO_4}{[Sr^{2+}]} = \frac{3.6 \times 10^{-5}}{1.0 \times 10^{-4}} = 3.6 \times 10^{-1}\ M$$

Example 16.2 illustrates the same kind of calculation for a different electrolyte; the math is a bit more difficult, but the principle is the same.

Example 16.2 Calcium phosphate, $Ca_3(PO_4)_2$, is a water-insoluble mineral, large quantities of which are used to make commercial fertilizers. Use the K_{sp} values for $Ca_3(PO_4)_2$ from Table 16.1 to answer the following questions.

(a) What is the concentration of Ca^{2+} in equilibrium with the solid if $[PO_4^{3-}] = 5 \times 10^{-5}$ *M*?

(b) How many moles of PO_4^{3-} are actually delivered when 275 mL of the solution described in (a) are sprayed onto a field?

Strategy The first step is to write down the K_{sp} expression:

$$Ca_3(PO_4)_2(s) \rightleftharpoons 3Ca^{2+}(aq) + 2PO_4^{3-}(aq)$$

$$K_{sp} = [Ca^{2+}]^3[PO_4^{3-}]^2 = 1 \times 10^{-33}$$

For (a), substitute the concentration.

SOLUTION

(a) $[Ca^{2+}]^3 = \frac{1 \times 10^{-33}}{[PO_4^{3-}]^2} = \frac{1 \times 10^{-33}}{(5 \times 10^{-5})^2} = 4 \times 10^{-25}$ $[Ca^{2+}] = 7 \times 10^{-9}$.

(To find the cube root of a number *y* on a scientific calculator, use the $\sqrt[x]{y}$ key, with $x = 3$. For graphics calculators, use the powers key ^ and raise *y* to the (1/3) power.)

(b) To find the moles of PO_4^{3-} in 275 mL of solution, remember that moles = $V \times M$. Then

$$\text{moles } PO_4^{3-} = \frac{5 \times 10^{-5} \text{ mol}}{1 \text{ L}} \times 0.275 \text{ L} = 1 \times 10^{-5} \text{ moles}$$

Reality Check To check the answer in (a), use the calculated concentration to determine K_{sp}:

$$[Ca^{2+}]^3 \times [PO_4^{3-}]^2 = (7 \times 10^{-9})^3(5 \times 10^{-5})^2 = 9 \times 10^{-34},$$

which is very close to the value listed in Table 16.1: 1×10^{-33}.

Table 16.1 Solubility Product Constants at 25°C

		K_{sp}			K_{sp}
Acetates	$AgC_2H_3O_2$	1.9×10^{-3}	Hydroxides	$Al(OH)_3$	2×10^{-31}
Bromides	$AgBr$	5×10^{-13}		$Ca(OH)_2$	4.0×10^{-6}
	Hg_2Br_2	6×10^{-23}		$Fe(OH)_2$	5×10^{-17}
	$PbBr_2$	6.6×10^{-6}		$Fe(OH)_3$	3×10^{-39}
Carbonates	Ag_2CO_3	8×10^{-12}		$Mg(OH)_2$	6×10^{-12}
	$BaCO_3$	2.6×10^{-9}		$Tl(OH)_3$	2×10^{-44}
	$CaCO_3$	4.9×10^{-9}		$Zn(OH)_2$	4×10^{-17}
	$MgCO_3$	6.8×10^{-6}	Iodides	AgI	1×10^{-16}
	$PbCO_3$	1×10^{-13}		Hg_2I_2	5×10^{-29}
	$SrCO_3$	5.6×10^{-10}		PbI_2	8.4×10^{-9}
Chlorides	$AgCl$	1.8×10^{-10}	Phosphates	Ag_3PO_4	1×10^{-16}
	Hg_2Cl_2	1×10^{-18}		$AlPO_4$	1×10^{-20}
	$PbCl_2$	1.7×10^{-5}		$Ca_3(PO_4)_2$	1×10^{-33}
Chromates	Ag_2CrO_4	1×10^{-12}		$Mg_3(PO_4)_2$	1×10^{-24}
	$BaCrO_4$	1.2×10^{-10}	Sulfates	$BaSO_4$	1.1×10^{-10}
	$PbCrO_4$	2×10^{-14}		$CaSO_4$	7.1×10^{-5}
	$SrCrO_4$	3.6×10^{-5}		$PbSO_4$	1.8×10^{-8}
Fluorides	BaF_2	1.8×10^{-7}		$SrSO_4$	3.4×10^{-7}
	CaF_2	1.5×10^{-10}			
	MgF_2	7×10^{-11}			
	PbF_2	7.1×10^{-7}			

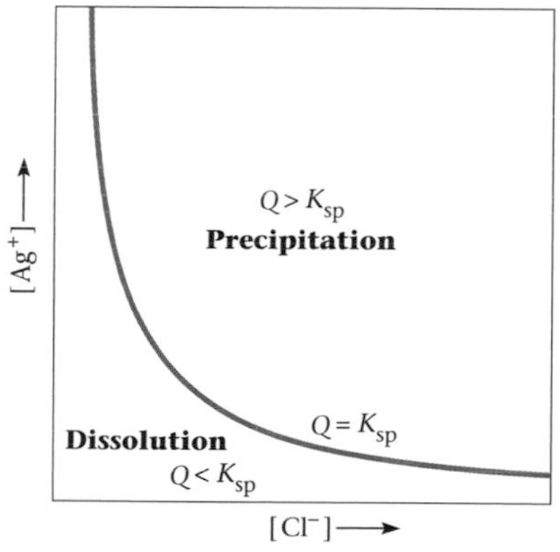

Figure 16.2
Equilibrium curve for silver chloride. Silver chloride (*s*) is in contact with Ag^+ and Cl^- ions in aqueous solution. The product *Q* of the concentration of ions $[Ag^+] \times [Cl^-]$ is equal to K_{sp} *(curved line)* when equilibrium exists. If $Q > K_{sp}$, AgCl(*s*) tends to precipitate out until equilibrium is reached. If $Q < K_{sp}$, additional solid dissolves.

K_{sp} and Precipitate Formation

K_{sp} values can be used to make predictions as to whether or not a precipitate will form when two solutions are mixed. To do this, we follow an approach very similar to that used in Chapter 12, to determine the direction in which a system will move to reach equilibrium. We work with a quantity Q, which has the same mathematical form as K_{sp}. The difference is that the concentrations that appear in Q are those that apply at a particular moment. Those that appear in K_{sp} are equilibrium concentrations. Putting it another way, the value of Q is expected to change as a precipitation reaction proceeds, approaching K_{sp} and eventually becoming equal to it.

Three cases can be distinguished (Figure 16.2):

1. If $Q > K_{sp}$, the solution contains a higher concentration of ions than it can hold at equilibrium. A ***precipitate forms,*** decreasing the concentrations until the ion product becomes equal to K_{sp} and equilibrium is established.
2. If $Q < K_{sp}$, the solution contains a lower concentration of ions than is required for equilibrium with the solid. The solution is unsaturated. ***No precipitate forms;*** equilibrium is not established.
3. If $Q = K_{sp}$, the solution is just saturated with ions and is at the point of precipitation.

K_{sp} is a constant; Q can have any value.

CENGAGENOW™
Click Coached Problems for a self-study module on **determining if a precipitation reaction will occur.**

Example 16.3 Graded

In the laboratory, strontium chromate ($K_{sp} = 3.6 \times 10^{-5}$) can be prepared by mixing solutions containing strontium ions and chromate ions, where the concentrations of these ions are high enough to form a precipitate. Decide whether a precipitate will form when

*(a) a solution has the following initial concentrations: $[Sr^{2+}] = 6.0 \times 10^{-3}\ M$, $[CrO_4^{2-}] = 3.0 \times 10^{-3}\ M$.

**(b) 275 mL of $6.0 \times 10^{-3}\ M\ Sr(NO_3)_2$ solution is mixed with 825 mL of 0.040 M K_2CrO_4.

***(c) 12.0 g of Na_2CrO_4 are added to 333 mL of $4.5 \times 10^{-3}\ M\ Sr(NO_3)_2$. Assume no volume change after Na_2CrO_4 is added.

SOLUTION

(a) Calculate Q and compare with K_{sp}.

$$Q = (6.0 \times 10^{-3})(3.0 \times 10^{-3}) = 1.8 \times 10^{-5} \qquad K_{sp} = 3.6 \times 10^{-5}$$

Since $Q < K_{sp}$, no precipitate forms.

(b) This is similar to (a), but with one new twist. You must first calculate the concentrations of Sr^{2+} and CrO_4^{2-} *after* mixing, taking the total volume into account. To do so, find the number of moles of each relevant ion and then divide by the total volume after mixing, 0.275 L + 0.825 L = 1.100 L.

$$n_{Sr^{2+}} = \frac{6.0 \times 10^{-3}\ \text{mol}}{1\ \text{L}} \times 0.275\ \text{L} = 1.65 \times 10^{-3}\ \text{mol}$$

$$[Sr^{2+}] = \frac{1.65 \times 10^{-3}\ \text{mol}}{1.100\ \text{L}} = 1.5 \times 10^{-3}\ M$$

$$n_{CrO_4^{2-}} = \frac{4.0 \times 10^{-2}\ \text{mol}}{1\ \text{L}} \times 0.825\ \text{L} = 3.3 \times 10^{-2}\ \text{mol}$$

$$[CrO_4^{2-}] = \frac{3.3 \times 10^{-2}\ \text{mol}}{1.100\ \text{L}} = 0.030\ M$$

$$Q = (1.5 \times 10^{-3})(3.0 \times 10^{-2}) = 4.5 \times 10^{-5} \qquad K_{sp} = 3.6 \times 10^{-5}$$

Since $Q > K_{sp}$, a precipitate forms (just barely!).

(c) Again, find the number of moles of each ion and solve for Q. Note that the source of CrO_4^{2-} is now given in grams.

$$n_{CrO_4^{2-}} = \frac{12.0\ \text{g}}{162\ \text{g/mol}} = 0.0741\ \text{mol}$$

$$[CrO_4^{2-}] = \frac{0.0741\ \text{mol}}{0.333\ \text{L}} = 0.222\ M \qquad [Sr^{2+}] = 4.5 \times 10^{-3}\ M$$

$$Q = (0.222)(4.5 \times 10^{-3}) = 1.0 \times 10^{-3} \qquad K_{sp} = 3.6 \times 10^{-5}$$

Again, since $Q > K_{sp}$, a precipitate forms.

K_{sp} and Water Solubility

The relationship between K_{sp} and s depends on the type of solid.

One way to establish equilibrium between a slightly soluble solid and its ions in solution is to stir the solid with water to form a saturated solution. As you might expect, the solubility of the solid, s, in moles per liter, is related to the solubility product constant, K_{sp}. In the case of barium sulfate dissolving in water we have

$$\underset{s}{BaSO_4(s)} \rightleftharpoons \underset{s}{Ba^{2+}(aq)} + \underset{s}{SO_4^{2-}(aq)}$$

The solubility of $BaSO_4$ is exactly equal to the equilibrium concentration of either Ba^{2+} or SO_4^{2-}. In other words,

$$[Ba^{2+}] = [SO_4^{2-}] = s$$

and

$$K_{sp}\ BaSO_4 = [Ba^{2+}] \times [SO_4^{2-}] = s^2$$

Solving,

$$s = (K_{sp})^{\frac{1}{2}} = (1.1 \times 10^{-10})^{\frac{1}{2}} = 1.0 \times 10^{-5}\ \text{mol/L}$$

This means that a saturated solution can be prepared by dissolving 2.3 mg of $BaSO_4$ in enough water to make 1.0 L of solution. Putting it another way, dissolving *less* than 2.3 mg results in an unsaturated solution. If more than 2.3 mg are added, an equilibrium is established between the solution containing $1.0 \times 10^{-5}\ M\ Ba^{2+}$ and SO_4^{2-} and the solid $BaSO_4$.

When an ionic solid consists of anions and cations of different charges, the relation between K_{sp} and s takes a different form, but the principle is the same (Example 16.4).

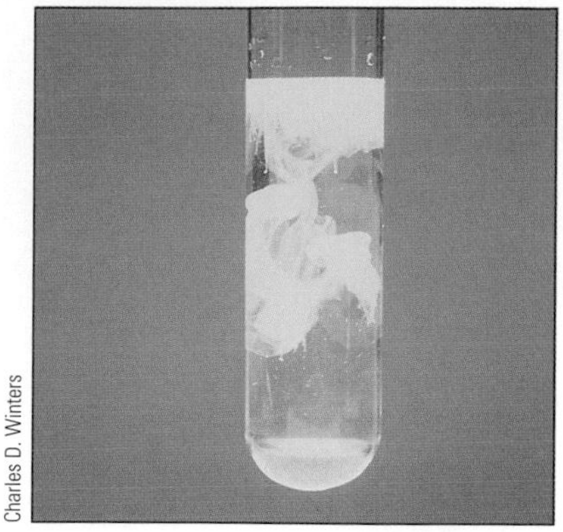

Charles D. Winters

Precipitation of barium sulfate from a mixture of barium chloride and sulfuric acid.

Example 16.4 Graded

Barium fluoride, BaF_2, is used in metallurgy as a welding and soldering agent. Its K_{sp} is 1.8×10^{-7}.

*(a) What is its solubility in moles/L?

**(b) What is its solubility in g/L?

***(c) How many grams of BaF_2 are required to prepare 298 mL of a saturated solution of BaF_2?

Strategy To relate s to K_{sp}, start by writing the equation for dissolving barium fluoride in water:

$$BaF_2(s) \rightleftharpoons Ba^{2+}(aq) + 2F^-(aq)$$

If s stands for the number of moles of BaF_2 that dissolve in one liter, then there will be s moles of Ba^{2+} ions (1 mole $BaF_2 \longrightarrow$ 1 mole Ba^{2+}) and $2s$ moles of F^- ions (1 mole $BaF_2 \longrightarrow$ 2 moles F^-). Substitute into the K_{sp} expression and solve for s. Remember the units for s are moles/L. You will have to do more calculations for (b) and (c).

SOLUTION

(a) $[Ba^{2+}] = s \quad [F^-] = 2s \quad K_{sp} = [Ba^{2+}]\,[F^-]^2 = (s)(2s)^2 = 4s^3$, which gives

$$s = \left(\frac{K_{sp}}{4}\right)^{1/3} = \left(\frac{1.8 \times 10^{-7}}{4}\right)^{1/3} = 3.6 \times 10^{-3}\ \text{mol/L}$$

(b) To find the solubility in g/L, use the molar mass of BaF_2, 175.3 g/mol:

$$\frac{3.6 \times 10^{-3}\ \text{mol}}{1\ \text{L}} \times \frac{175.3\ \text{g}}{1\ \text{mol}} = 0.63\ \text{g/L}$$

(c) To prepare a saturated solution, you must dissolve s moles in a liter of solution. Since only 298 mL are required, solve for the mass of BaF_2 for this volume using the solubility in g/L.

$$s = \frac{0.63\ \text{g}}{1\ \text{L}} \times 0.298\ \text{L} = 0.19\ \text{g}$$

Charles D. Winters

Sulfide minerals and K_{sp}. Sulfides are among the least soluble ionic compounds. Their K_{sp} values are often smaller than 10^{-25}. For this reason, many sulfides are found as minerals, for example *(clockwise from the left),* iron pyrite (FeS_2), yellow orpiment (As_2S_3), and black galena (PbS).

Frequently we find that the experimentally determined solubility of an ionic solid is larger than that predicted from K_{sp}. Consider, for example, $PbCl_2$, where the solubility calculated from the relation

$$4s^3 = K_{sp} = 1.7 \times 10^{-5}$$

is 0.016 mol/L. The measured solubility is considerably larger, 0.036 mol/L. The explanation for this is that some of the lead in $PbCl_2$ goes into solution in the form of species other than Pb^{2+}. In particular, we can detect the presence of the ions $Pb(OH)^+$ and $PbCl^+$.

The reverse of Example 16.4 involves finding K_{sp} of a compound given its solubility. The solubilities of many ionic compounds are determined experimentally and tabulated in chemical handbooks. Most solubility values are given in grams of solute dissolved in 100 grams of water. To obtain the molar solubility in moles/L, we have to assume that the density of the solution is equal to that of water. Then the number of grams of solute per 100 g water is equal to the number of grams of solute per 100 mL of solution. This assumption is valid because the mass of the compound in solution is small. To solve for K_{sp}, find the molar solubility of the solute and determine the concentration of its component ions. Substitute into the K_{sp} expression.

Example 16.5 Consider the pesticide magnesium arsenate ($Mg_3(AsO_4)_2$). Its solubility is determined experimentally to be 1.6×10^{-3} g/100 g H_2O. What is the K_{sp} for $Mg_3(AsO_4)_2$?

Strategy Assume the solubility to be 1.6×10^{-3} g/100 mL of solution. (The rationale for this assumption is discussed above.) Change 1.6×10^{-3} g/100 g of solution to moles $Mg_3(AsO_4)_2$/L. Relate $[Mg_3(AsO_4)_2]$ to $[Mg^{2+}]$ and $[AsO_4^{3-}]$. Substitute into the K_{sp} expression for $Mg_3(AsO_4)_2$.

SOLUTION Use the molar mass of $Mg_3(AsO_4)_2$ (350.7 g/mol) to calculate $[Mg_3(AsO_4)_2]$.

$$[Mg_3(AsO_4)_2] = \frac{1.6 \times 10^{-3}\ \text{g } Mg_3(AsO_4)_2}{0.100\ \text{L}} \times \frac{1\ \text{mol}}{350.7\ \text{g}} = 4.6 \times 10^{-5}\ M$$

When $Mg_3(AsO_4)_2$ dissolves, the following equilibrium is established between the solid and its ions.

$$Mg_3(AsO_4)_2(s) \rightleftharpoons 3Mg^{2+}(aq) + 2AsO_4^{3-}(aq)$$

Thus for every mole of solid dissolved, 3 moles of magnesium ion and 2 moles of arsenate ion are produced.

$$[Mg^{2+}] = 3[Mg_3(AsO_4)_2] = 3(4.6 \times 10^{-5}) = 1.4 \times 10^{-4}$$
$$[AsO_4^{3-}] = 2[Mg_3(AsO_4)_2] = 2(4.6 \times 10^{-5}) = 9.2 \times 10^{-5}$$

Substitute into the K_{sp} expression:

$$K_{sp} = [Mg^{2+}]^3 [AsO_4^{3-}]^2 = (1.4 \times 10^{-4})^3 (9.2 \times 10^{-5})^2 = 2.3 \times 10^{-20}$$

K_{sp} and the Common Ion Effect

How would you expect the solubility of barium sulfate in water

$$BaSO_4(s) \rightleftharpoons Ba^{2+}(aq) + SO_4^{2-}(aq)$$

A "common" ion comes from two sources such as $BaSO_4$ and Na_2SO_4.

to compare with that in a 0.10 *M* solution of Na_2SO_4, which contains the same *(common)* anion, SO_4^{2-}? A moment's reflection should convince you that the solubility in 0.10 *M* Na_2SO_4 must be *less* than that in pure water. Recall (page 435) that when $BaSO_4$ is dissolved in pure water, $[SO_4^{2-}]$ is 1.0×10^{-5} *M*. Increasing the concentration of SO_4^{2-} to 0.10 *M* should, by Le Châtelier's principle, drive the above equilibrium to the *left*, repressing the solubility of barium sulfate. This is, indeed, the case (Example 16.6).

Example 16.6 Taking K_{sp} of $BaSO_4$ to be 1.1×10^{-10}, estimate its solubility (moles per liter) in 0.10 *M* Na_2SO_4 solution.

Strategy Let s = solubility = no. of moles of $BaSO_4$ that dissolve per liter. Relate $[Ba^{2+}]$ and $[SO_4^{2-}]$ to s; notice that in this case *there are two different sources of* SO_4^{2-}. Substitute into the expression for K_{sp} and solve for s.

SOLUTION Every mole of $BaSO_4$ that dissolves forms 1 mol of Ba^{2+} and 1 mol of SO_4^{2-}. Because no Ba^{2+} was present originally, its concentration becomes s:

$$[Ba^{2+}] = s$$

The concentration of SO_4^{2-} was originally 0.10 *M*; it increases by s moles per liter. So

$$[SO_4^{2-}] = 0.10 + s$$

Setting up this reasoning in tabular form,

	$[Ba^{2+}]$	$[SO_4^{2-}]$
Original	0	0.10
Change	$+s$	$+s$
Equilibrium	s	$0.10 + s$

it follows that

$$K_{sp} = 1.1 \times 10^{-10} = [Ba^{2+}] \times [SO_4^{2-}] = s(0.10 + s)$$

This is a quadratic equation; as usual, we look for ways to avoid solving it by brute force. Note that because $BaSO_4$ is very insoluble, a reasonable approximation would seem to be

$$s + 0.10 \approx 0.10$$

With that assumption,

$$s(0.10) = 1.1 \times 10^{-10}; \qquad s = 1.1 \times 10^{-9}\ \text{mol/L}$$

The solubility is indeed much less than 0.10 *M*, so the approximation is justified.

Reality Check The solubility in 0.10 *M* Na_2SO_4 is much less than that in pure water ($1.1 \times 10^{-9} \ll 1.0 \times 10^{-5}$), which is exactly what we predicted.

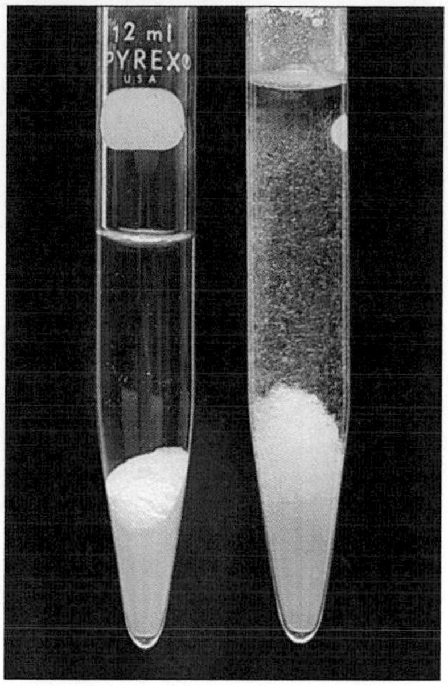

Charles D. Winters

Common ion effect. The tube at the left contains a saturated solution of silver acetate ($AgC_2H_3O_2$). Originally the tube at the right also contained a saturated solution of silver acetate. With the addition of a solution of silver nitrate ($AgNO_3$), the solubility equilibrium of the silver acetate is shifted by the common ion Ag^+ and additional silver acetate precipitates.

The effect illustrated in Example 16.6 is a general one. **An ionic solid is less soluble in a solution containing a common ion than it is in water** (Figure 16.3, p. 438).

CENGAGENOW™
Click Coached Problems for a self-study module on **the common ion effect.**

Selective Precipitation

One way to separate two cations in water solution is to add an anion that precipitates only one of the cations. This approach is known as *selective precipitation.* To see how it works, consider a simple case, a solution containing Mg^{2+} and Na^+ ions. Referring back to Table 16.1 (p. 433), you can see that Mg^{2+} forms a couple of insoluble compounds: $MgCO_3$ ($K_{sp} = 6.8 \times 10^{-6}$) and $Mg(OH)_2$ ($K_{sp} = 6 \times 10^{-12}$). In contrast, all of the common compounds of sodium are soluble, including the carbonate and hydroxide. It follows that you could readily separate Mg^{2+} from Na^+ by adding either CO_3^{2-} or OH^- ions to the solution. In either case, Mg^{2+} will precipitate while Na^+ remains in solution.

Now let us consider a somewhat more complex case. Suppose you have a solution containing Mg^{2+} and Ba^{2+}, both at 0.10 *M*, which you'd like to separate by adding CO_3^{2-} ions. From Table 16.1, it appears that $BaCO_3$ ($K_{sp} = 2.6 \times 10^{-9}$) is less soluble than $MgCO_3$ ($K_{sp} = 6.8 \times 10^{-6}$). Perhaps, by adding CO_3^{2-} ions carefully, you could precipitate Ba^{2+} selectively, leaving Mg^{2+} in solution.

The less soluble solid precipitates first; the more soluble solid stays in solution.

Figure 16.3
Sodium chloride and the common ion effect.

This is indeed the case. To precipitate $BaCO_3$, add enough CO_3^{2-} ions to make their concentration $2.6 \times 10^{-8}\ M$:

$$CO_3^{2-} = \frac{K_{sp}\ BaCO_3}{[Ba^{2+}]} = \frac{2.6 \times 10^{-9}}{0.10} = 2.6 \times 10^{-8}\ M$$

At this very low concentration of CO_3^{2-}, $MgCO_3$ does not precipitate:

$$Q = [Mg^{2+}] \times [CO_3^{2-}] = (0.10)(2.6 \times 10^{-8}) = 2.6 \times 10^{-9} < K_{sp}\ MgCO_3 = 6.8 \times 10^{-6}$$

To bring down $MgCO_3$, add more CO_3^{2-} until its concentration becomes $6.8 \times 10^{-5}\ M$:

$$[CO_3^{2-}] = \frac{K_{sp}\ MgCO_3}{[Mg^{2+}]} = \frac{6.8 \times 10^{-6}}{0.10} = 6.8 \times 10^{-5}\ M$$

At that point, virtually all of the Ba^{2+} ions have been precipitated:

$$[Ba^{2+}]\text{ remaining} = \frac{K_{sp}\ BaCO_3}{[CO_3^{2-}]} = \frac{2.6 \times 10^{-9}}{6.8 \times 10^{-5}} = 3.8 \times 10^{-5}\ M$$

$$\%\ Ba^{2+}\text{ remaining in solution} = \frac{3.8 \times 10^{-5}}{0.10} \times 100\% = 0.038\%$$

$$\%\ Ba^{2+}\text{ precipitated} = 100.000 - 0.038 = 99.962$$

In other words it is possible to precipitate essentially all of the Ba^{2+} ions before Mg^{2+} starts to precipitate.

Figure 16.4
Titration of Cl^- with Ag^+, using CrO_4^{2-} as an indicator. AgCl (cream color) comes down at first, then Ag_2CrO_4 (red) precipitates.

Example 16.7 A flask (Figure 16.4) contains a solution 0.10 *M* in Cl^- and 0.010 *M* in CrO_4^{2-}. When $AgNO_3$ is added,

(a) which anion, Cl^- or CrO_4^{2-}, precipitates first?
(b) what percentage of the first anion has been precipitated when the second anion starts to precipitate?

Strategy In (a), calculate $[Ag^+]$ required to precipitate AgCl and then Ag_2CrO_4. The anion that requires the lowest $[Ag^+]$ will precipitate first. In (b) find the concentration of the first anion still in solution when the second starts to precipitate. Then find the percentage of the first anion still in solution and finally the percentage of the anion that has precipitated. (Assume no volume change.)

SOLUTION

(a) For AgCl: $[Ag^+] = \frac{K_{sp}\ AgCl}{[Cl^-]} = \frac{1.8 \times 10^{-10}}{0.10} = 1.8 \times 10^{-9}\ M$

For Ag_2CrO_4: $[Ag^+]^2 = \frac{K_{sp}\ Ag_2CrO_4}{[CrO_4^{2-}]} = \frac{1 \times 10^{-12}}{0.010} = 1 \times 10^{-10}$

$[Ag^+] = (1 \times 10^{-10})^{\frac{1}{2}} = 1 \times 10^{-5}\ M$

Since Cl^- requires the lower $[Ag^+]$, it must precipitate first.

(b) When Ag_2CrO_4 starts to precipitate, $[Ag^+] = 1 \times 10^{-5}\ M$

$[Cl^-]_{remaining} = \frac{K_{sp}\ AgCl}{[Ag^+]} = \frac{1.8 \times 10^{-10}}{1 \times 10^{-5}} = 2 \times 10^{-5}\ M$

% Cl^- still in solution $= \frac{2 \times 10^{-5}}{0.10} \times 100\% = 0.02\%$

% Cl^- precipitated $= 100.00 - 0.02 = 99.98\%$

Reality Check Look at Figure 16.4. *White* AgCl does indeed come down first followed by *red* Ag_2CrO_4.

16.2 DISSOLVING PRECIPITATES

Many different methods can be used to bring water-insoluble ionic solids into solution. Most commonly, this is done by adding a reagent to react with either the anion or the cation. The two most useful reagents for this purpose are—

- a strong acid, H^+, used to react with basic anions.
- a complexing agent, most often NH_3 or OH^-, added to react with metal cations.

Strong Acid

CENGAGENOW™
Click Coached Problems for a self-study module on **solubility and pH.**

Water-insoluble metal hydroxides can be brought into solution with a strong acid such as HCl. The reaction with zinc hydroxide is typical:

$$Zn(OH)_2(s) + 2H^+(aq) \longrightarrow Zn^{2+}(aq) + 2H_2O$$

We can imagine that this reaction occurs in two (reversible) steps:

dissolving $Zn(OH)_2$ in water: $Zn(OH)_2(s) \rightleftharpoons Zn^{2+}(aq) + \cancel{2OH^-(aq)}$

neutralizing OH^- ions by H^+: $2H^+(aq) + \cancel{2OH^-(aq)} \rightleftharpoons 2H_2O$

$$Zn(OH)_2(s) + 2H^+(aq) \rightleftharpoons Zn^{2+}(aq) + 2H_2O$$

The equilibrium constant for the neutralization (Example 16.8) is so large that the overall reaction goes essentially to completion.

Example 16.8 Consider the following reaction:

$$Zn(OH)_2(s) + 2H^+(aq) \rightleftharpoons Zn^{2+}(aq) + 2H_2O$$

(a) Determine K for this system, applying the rule of multiple equilibria (page 327) to the two-step process referred to above.
(b) Using K, calculate the molar solubility, s, of $Zn(OH)_2$ in acid at pH 5.0.

Strategy Start by splitting the overall equation into two simpler equations, one for the dissolving of $Zn(OH)_2$ in water, the other for the neutralization of OH^- by H^+ ions. Find the equilibrium constants K_1 and K_2 for the two reactions. Then apply the relation $K = K_1 \times K_2$ to find the equilibrium constant for the overall reaction.

$BaSO_4$ cannot be dissolved by acid. Explain.

SOLUTION

(a) The first reaction is

$$Zn(OH)_2(s) \rightleftharpoons Zn^{2+}(aq) + 2OH^-(aq)$$

Hence $K_1 = K_{sp}\ Zn(OH)_2$. The second reaction,

$$2H^+(aq) + 2OH^-(aq) \rightleftharpoons 2H_2O$$

is the *reverse* of that for the ionization of water ($H_2O \rightleftharpoons H^+(aq) + OH^-(aq)$) with all the coefficients multiplied by *two.* Applying the reciprocal rule and the coefficient rule (Chapter 12) in succession, $K_2 = 1/K_W{}^2$.

Hence

$$K = K_1 \times K_2 = \frac{K_{sp}\ Zn(OH)_2}{K_w{}^2} = \frac{4 \times 10^{-17}}{(1 \times 10^{-14})^2} = 4 \times 10^{11}$$

The fact that the equilibrium constant is huge implies that $Zn(OH)_2$ is extremely soluble in strong acid.

(b) For the reaction $Zn(OH)_2(s) + 2H^+(aq) \rightleftharpoons Zn^{2+}(aq) + 2H_2O$:

$$K = \frac{[Zn^{2+}]}{[H^+]^2}$$

For every mole of $Zn(OH)_2$ that dissolves, a mole of Zn^{2+} is formed; in other words, $[Zn^{2+}] = s$. Hence

$$s = [H^+]^2 \times K$$

At pH 5.0,

$$[H^+] = 1 \times 10^{-5}\ M;$$

$$s = (1 \times 10^{-5})^2(4 \times 10^{11}) = 4 \times 10^1\ \text{mol/L}$$

Reality Check This extremely high concentration, 40 *M*, means that $Zn(OH)_2$ is completely soluble in acid at pH 5 (or any lower pH).

Strong acid can also be used to dissolve many water-insoluble salts in which the anion is a weak base. In particular, H^+ ions will dissolve—

- *virtually all carbonates* ($CO_3{}^{2-}$). The product is the weak acid H_2CO_3, which then decomposes into CO_2 and H_2O. The equation for the reaction of H^+ ions with $ZnCO_3$ is typical:

$$ZnCO_3(s) + 2H^+(aq) \longrightarrow Zn^{2+}(aq) + H_2CO_3(aq)$$

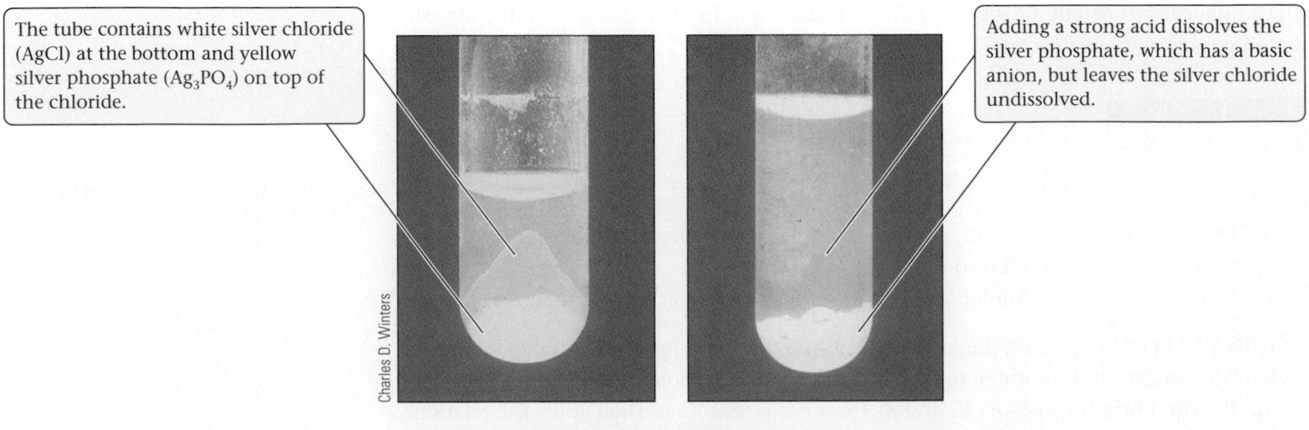

Dissolving a precipitate in acid.

- *many sulfides* (S^{2-}). The driving force behind this reaction is the formation of the weak acid H_2S, much of which evolves as a gas. The reaction in the case of zinc sulfide is

$$ZnS(s) + 2H^+(aq) \longrightarrow Zn^{2+}(aq) + H_2S(aq)$$

Example 16.9 Write balanced equations to explain why each of the following precipitates dissolves in strong acid.

(a) $Al(OH)_3$ (b) $CaCO_3$ (c) CoS

Strategy Compare the equations given above for dissolving $Zn(OH)_2$, $ZnCO_3$, and ZnS. In each case, the cation is brought into solution; the other product is H_2O, H_2CO_3, or H_2S.

SOLUTION

(a) $Al(OH)_3(s) + 3H^+(aq) \longrightarrow Al^{3+}(aq) + 3H_2O$
(b) $CaCO_3(s) + 2H^+(aq) \longrightarrow Ca^{2+}(aq) + H_2CO_3(aq)$
(c) $CoS(s) + 2H^+(aq) \longrightarrow Co^{2+}(aq) + H_2S(aq)$

Complex Formation

Ammonia and sodium hydroxide are commonly used to dissolve precipitates containing a cation that forms a stable complex with NH_3 or OH^- (Table 16.2). The reactions with zinc hydroxide are typical:

$$Zn(OH)_2(s) + 4NH_3(aq) \longrightarrow Zn(NH_3)_4^{2+}(aq) + 2\,OH^-(aq)$$
$$Zn(OH)_2(s) + 2OH^-(aq) \longrightarrow Zn(OH)_4^{2-}(aq)$$

CENGAGENOW™
Click Coached Problems for a self-study module on **solubility of metal ions and complex ion equilibria.**

The equilibrium constant for the solubility reaction is readily calculated. Consider, for example, the reaction by which zinc hydroxide dissolves in ammonia. Again, imagine that the reaction occurs in two steps:

$$Zn(OH)_2(s) \rightleftharpoons Zn^{2+}(aq) + 2OH^-(aq) \qquad K_{sp}\,Zn(OH)_2$$
$$Zn^{2+}(aq) + 4NH_3(aq) \rightleftharpoons Zn(NH_3)_4^{2+}(aq) \qquad K_f\,Zn(NH_3)_4^{2+}$$
$$Zn(OH)_2(s) + 4NH_3(aq) \rightleftharpoons Zn(NH_3)_4^{2+}(aq) + 2OH^-(aq)$$

$Mg(OH)_2$ cannot be dissolved by NH_3 or NaOH. Explain.

Applying the rule of multiple equilibria,

$$K = K_{sp}\,Zn(OH)_2 \times K_f\,Zn(NH_3)_4^{2+} = (4 \times 10^{-17})(3.6 \times 10^8) = 1 \times 10^{-8}$$

In general, for any reaction of this type

$$K = K_{sp} \times K_f$$

where K_{sp} is the solubility product constant of the solid and K_f is the formation constant of the complex.

Table 16.2 Complexes of Cations with NH_3 and OH^-

Cation	NH_3 Complex	OH^- Complex
Ag^+	$Ag(NH_3)_2^+$	—
Cu^{2+}	$Cu(NH_3)_4^{2+}$ (blue)	—
Cd^{2+}	$Cd(NH_3)_4^{2+}$	—
Sn^{4+}	—	$Sn(OH)_6^{2-}$
Sb^{3+}	—	$Sb(OH)_4^-$
Al^{3+}	—	$Al(OH)_4^-$
Ni^{2+}	$Ni(NH_3)_6^{2+}$ (blue)	—
Zn^{2+}	$Zn(NH_3)_4^{2+}$	$Zn(OH)_4^{2-}$

Dissolving a precipitate by complex formation. At the left, silver chloride (AgCl) is precipitated by adding a sodium chloride (NaCl) solution to a silver nitrate ($AgNO_3$) solution. At the right, as an ammonia solution is added, the AgCl precipitate is dissolving to form the complex ion $Ag(NH_3)_2^+$.

Example 16.10 Consider the reaction by which silver chloride dissolves in ammonia:

$$AgCl(s) + 2NH_3(aq) \rightleftharpoons Ag(NH_3)_2^+(aq) + Cl^-(aq)$$

(a) Taking K_{sp} AgCl $= 1.8 \times 10^{-10}$ and K_f $Ag(NH_3)_2^+ = 1.7 \times 10^7$, calculate K for this reaction.

(b) Calculate the number of moles of AgCl that dissolve in one liter of 6.0 M NH_3.

Strategy Apply the rule of multiple equilibria to find K. Then work with the expression for K to find the molar solubility of AgCl.

SOLUTION

(a) $K = K_{sp} \times K_f = (1.8 \times 10^{-10})(1.7 \times 10^7) = 3.1 \times 10^{-3}$

(b) $AgCl(s) + 2NH_3(aq) \rightleftharpoons Ag(NH_3)_2^+(aq) + Cl^-(aq)$

$$K = \frac{[Ag(NH_3)_2^+] \times [Cl^-]}{[NH_3]^2} = 3.1 \times 10^{-3}$$

For every mole of AgCl that dissolves, two moles of NH_3 are consumed; one mole of $Ag(NH_3)_2^+$ and one mole of Cl^- are formed. We can set up an equilibrium table

	$[NH_3]$	$[Ag(NH_3)_2^+]$	$[Cl^-]$
Original	6.0	0	0
Change	$-2x$	$+x$	$+x$
Equilibrium	$6.0 - 2x$	x	x

where x is the number of moles per liter that dissolves.

We then have the equation: $3.1 \times 10^{-3} = \dfrac{x^2}{(6.0 - 2x)^2}$

Taking the square root of both sides: $0.056 = \dfrac{x}{6.0 - 2x}$

Solving, $x = 0.30$

Example 16.11 Conceptual

Column A lists a series of ionic solids, all of which are insoluble in water. Match each of these compounds with the appropriate description(s) listed in Column B. Note that more than one description can fit a particular compound.

A	B
(a) $BaSO_4$	(e) $K_{sp} = s^2$
(b) AgCl	(f) $K_{sp} = 4s^3$
(c) $Zn(OH)_2$	(g) more soluble in water than in Na_2SO_4 solution
(d) $CaSO_4$	(h) soluble in strong acid
	(i) soluble in strong base
	(j) soluble in ammonia

SOLUTION

(a) matches with (e) and (g)
(b) matches with (e) and (j)
(c) matches with (f), (h), (i), (j)
(d) matches with (e) and (g)

CHEMISTRY Beyond the Classroom

Qualitative Analysis

In the laboratory you will most likely carry out one or more experiments involving the separation and identification of cations present in an "unknown" solution. A scheme of analysis for 21 different cations is shown in Table A. As you can see, the general approach is to take out each group (I, II, III, IV) in succession, using *selective precipitation.*

Group I consists of the only three common cations that form insoluble chlorides: Ag^+, Pb^{2+}, and Hg_2^{2+}. Addition of hydrochloric acid precipitates AgCl, $PbCl_2$, and Hg_2Cl_2. Cations in Groups II, III, and IV remain in solution, since their chlorides are soluble.

Group II consists of six different cations, all of which form very insoluble sulfides (Figure A). These compounds are precipitated selectively by adding hydrogen sulfide, a toxic, foul-smelling gas, at a pH of 0.5. At this rather high H^+ ion concentration, 0.3 *M*, the equilibrium

$$H_2S(aq) \rightleftharpoons 2H^+(aq) + S^{2-}(aq)$$

lies far to the left. The concentration of S^{2-} is extremely low, but sufficient to precipitate all the cations in this group, including Cu^{2+}

$$Cu^{2+}(aq) + H_2S(aq) \longrightarrow CuS(s) + 2H^+(aq) \qquad K = 1 \times 10^{16}$$

Hg_2^{2+} is a polyatomic cation; there is a covalent bond between the mercury atoms.

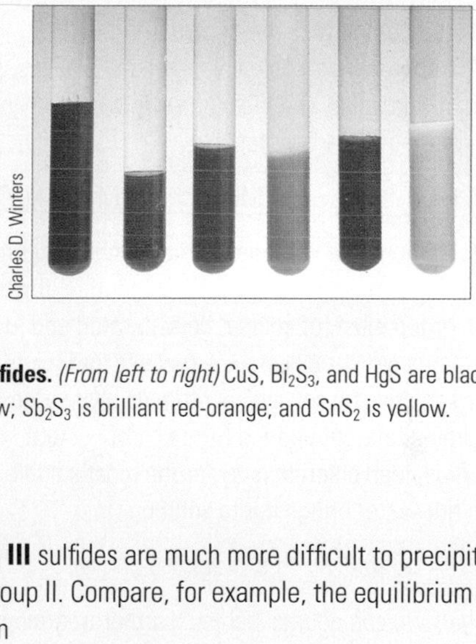

Figure A
Group II sulfides. *(From left to right)* CuS, Bi_2S_3, and HgS are black; CdS is orange-yellow; Sb_2S_3 is brilliant red-orange; and SnS_2 is yellow.

Group III sulfides are much more difficult to precipitate than those of Group II. Compare, for example, the equilibrium constant for the reaction

$$Mn^{2+}(aq) + H_2S(aq) \rightleftharpoons MnS(s) + 2H^+(aq) \qquad K = 2 \times 10^{-7}$$

with that given above for the precipitation of CuS. However, when the solution is made basic (pH = 9), the situation changes. The concentration of H^+ ion drops sharply and, as you would expect from Le Châtelier's principle, the reaction just cited becomes much more

Table A Cation Groups of Qualitative Analysis

Group	Cations	Precipitating Reagent/Conditions
I	Ag^+, Pb^{2+}, Hg_2^{2+}	6 *M* HCl
II	Cu^{2+}, Bi^{3+}, Hg^{2+}, Cd^{2+}, Sn^{4+}, Sb^{3+}	0.1 *M* H_2S at a pH of 0.5
III	Al^{3+}, Cr^{3+}, Co^{2+}, Fe^{2+}, Mn^{2+}, Ni^{2+}, Zn^{2+}	0.1 *M* H_2S at a pH of 9
IV	Ba^{2+}, Ca^{2+}, Mg^{2+}; Na^+, K^+	0.2 *M* $(NH_4)_2CO_3$ at a pH of 9.5. No precipitate with Na^+, K^+

(Continued)

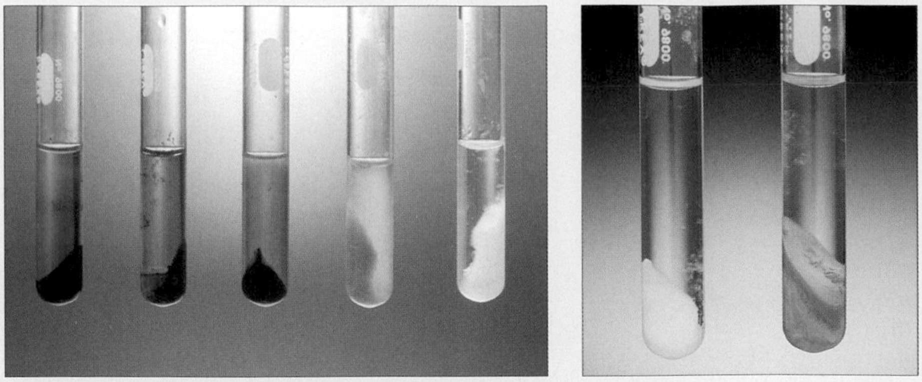

Charles D. Winters

Figure B

Group III sulfides and hydroxides. *(Left)* Five Group III cations precipitate as sulfides. These are NiS, CoS, and FeS (all of which are black), MnS (salmon), and ZnS (white). *(Right)* Two cations precipitate as hydroxides, $Al(OH)_3$ (white) and $Cr(OH)_3$ (gray-green).

spontaneous. Five of the Group III cations precipitate as sulfides. The other two come down as hydroxides, e.g.,

$$Al^{3+}(aq) + 3\,OH^-(aq) \longrightarrow Al(OH)_3(s)$$

The colors of these precipitates are shown in Figure B.

Group IV cations have soluble chlorides and sulfides, so they are still in solution at this point. The alkaline earth cations (Mg^{2+}, Ca^{2+}, Ba^{2+}) are precipitated as carbonates

$$M^{2+}(aq) + CO_3^{2-}(aq) \longrightarrow MCO_3(s) \qquad M = Mg, Ca, Ba$$

The alkali metal cations are identified by flame tests (Figure C).

Once the groups are separated from one another, the individual cations in each group must, of course, be separated and identified. This is where things get complicated. A process that might be referred to as "selective dissolving" is often involved. Consider, for example, the precipitate obtained in Group I: $PbCl_2$, AgCl, and Hg_2Cl_2. Of the three solids, lead chloride is by far the most soluble in water. Stirring it with hot water brings it into solution

$$PbCl_2(s) \longrightarrow Pb^{2+}(aq) + 2Cl^-(aq)$$

leaving the other two compounds behind. Further treatment with ammonia dissolves silver chloride

$$AgCl(s) + 2NH_3(aq) \longrightarrow Ag(NH_3)_2^+(aq) + Cl^-(aq)$$

but not Hg_2Cl_2.

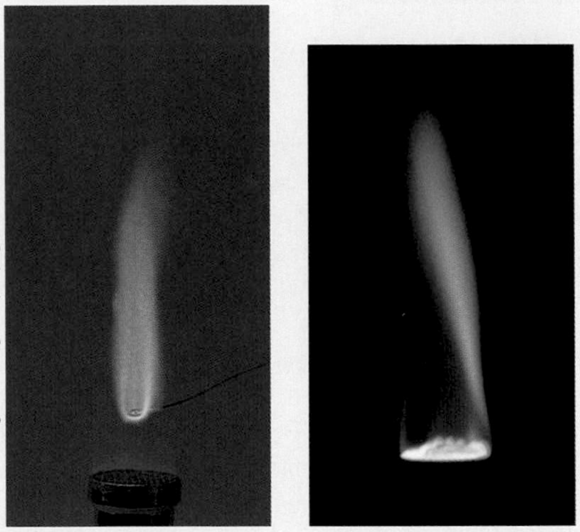

left, James Morgenthaler; *right,* Ray Boyington/S. Ruven Smith

Figure C

Flame tests for Na^+ (yellow) and K^+ (violet). A drop of solution is picked up on a platinum loop and immersed in the flame. The test for K^+ is best done with a filter that hides the strong Na^+ color.

Chapter Highlights

Key Concepts

1. Write the expression for K_{sp} for any ionic solid.
   (Example 16.1; Problems 1–4) ■ Questions and Problems assignable in OWL: 2, 4
2. Use the value of K_{sp} to
   ■ calculate the concentration of one ion, knowing that of the other.
   (Example 16.2; Problems 5–10) ■ 6, 8
   ■ determine whether a precipitate will form.
   (Example 16.3; Problems 13–16) ■ 12
   ■ calculate the water solubility of an ionic compound.
   (Example 16.4; Problems 17, 18, 23–28) ■ 18, 20, 26, 28
   ■ calculate the solubility in a solution containing a common ion.
   (Example 16.6; Problems 21, 22) ■ 22
   ■ determine which ion will precipitate first from a solution.
   (Example 16.7; Problems 31–36) ■ 32, 34
3. Calculate *K* for
   ■ dissolving a metal hydroxide in strong acid.
   (Example 16.8; Problem 44) ■ 44
   ■ dissolving a precipitate in a complexing agent.
   (Example 16.10; Problems 43, 45, 47, 48) ■ 49
4. Write balanced net ionic equations to explain why a precipitate dissolves in
   ■ strong acid.
   (Example 16.9; Problems 37, 38) ■ 38, 59
   ■ NH_3 or OH^-.
   (Example 16.11; Problems 39–42) ■ 40

Select end of chapter Questions and Problems may be assigned in OWL and are cross-referenced in the Key Concepts list.

CENGAGENOW™

Sign in at **academic.cengage.com/now** to:

- Check your readiness for an exam by taking the Pre-Test and exploring the self-study modules recommended in your Personalized Study plan
- For quick review, download Go Chemistry mini-lecture flashcard modules (or purchase them at **www.ichapters.com**)

Key Terms

common ion	selective precipitation
ion product, *Q*	solubility product constant, K_{sp}

Summary Problem

Consider lead(II) hydroxide. It can be formed when solutions of lead(II) nitrate and potassium hydroxide are mixed. Its K_{sp} at a certain temperature is 4.2×10^{-15}. Assume volumes are additive in all cases.

(a) Write the K_{sp} expression for lead(II) hydroxide.
(b) How many milligrams of KOH must be added to 295 mL of 0.00200 *M* $Pb(NO_3)_2$ to just start the precipitation of lead(II) hydroxide? Assume no volume change and ignore OH^- from water.
(c) Will a precipitate form if 15.00 mL of 0.0100 *M* KOH is added to 475 mL of 0.0075 *M* $Pb(NO_3)_2$?
(d) How many milligrams of lead(II) hydroxide are necessary to prepare 1.25 L of a saturated $Pb(OH)_2$ solution?
(e) What is the pH of a saturated solution of $Pb(OH)_2$?
(f) How many milligrams of $Pb(OH)_2$ can be added to 4.00 L of a 0.095 *M* KOH solution before precipitation starts? Assume no volume change.
(g) A 425-mL solution has 0.0200 mol Pb^{2+} and 0.0200 mol Fe^{2+} ions. Which will precipitate first when 0.0500 mol KOH is added? (K_{sp} of $Fe(OH)_2 = 5 \times 10^{-17}$)
(h) Write the equation for dissolving $Pb(OH)_2$ with a strong acid. Calculate *K* for this reaction.

Answers

(a) $K_{sp} = [Pb^{2+}][OH^-]^2$
(b) 0.024 mg
(c) yes
(d) 3.1 mg
(e) 9.30
(f) 4.5×10^{-7} mg
(g) $Fe(OH)_2$
(h) $Pb(OH)_2(s) + 2H^+(aq) \rightleftharpoons Pb^{2+}(aq) + 2H_2O \qquad K = 4.2 \times 10^{13}$

Questions and Problems

Blue-numbered questions have answers in Appendix 6 and fully-worked solutions in the *Student Solutions Manual.*

■ denotes questions assignable in OWL.

WEB indicates that the solution is available on this book's companion website.

Expression for K_{sp}

1. Write the equilibrium equation and the K_{sp} expression for each of the following.

(a) Co_2S_3 (b) $PbCl_2$
(c) $Zn_2P_2O_7$ (d) $Sc(OH)_3$

2. ■ Write the equilibrium equation and the K_{sp} expression for each of the following.

(a) $AgCl$ (b) $Al_2(CO_3)_3$
(c) MnS_2 (d) $Mg(OH)_2$

3. Write the equilibrium equations on which the following K_{sp} expressions are based.

(a) $[Hg_2^{2+}][Cl^-]^2$ (b) $[Pb^{2+}][CrO_4^{2-}]$
(c) $[Mn^{4+}][O^{2-}]^2$ (d) $[Al^{3+}]^2[S^{2-}]^3$

4. ■ Write the equilibrium equations on which the following K_{sp} expressions are based.

(a) $[Ca^{2+}][CO_3^{2-}]$ (b) $[Co^{3+}][OH^-]^3$
(c) $[Ag^+]^2[S^{2-}]$ (d) $[Pb^{2+}][Cl^-]^2$

K_{sp} and Precipitation

5. Given K_{sp} and the equilibrium concentration of one ion, calculate the equilibrium concentration of the other ion.

(a) cadmium(II) hydroxide: $K_{sp} = 2.5 \times 10^{-14}$; $[Cd^{2+}] = 1.5 \times 10^{-6}$ *M*
(b) copper(II) arsenate ($Cu_3(AsO_4)_2$): $K_{sp} = 7.6 \times 10^{-36}$; $[AsO_4^{3-}] = 2.4 \times 10^{-4}$ *M*
(c) zinc oxalate: $K_{sp} = 2.7 \times 10^{-8}$; $[C_2O_4^{2-}] = 8.8 \times 10^{-3}$ *M*

6. ■ Follow the directions for Question 5 for the following compounds:

(a) lithium phosphate: $K_{sp} = 3.2 \times 10^{-9}$; $[PO_4^{3-}] = 7.5 \times 10^{-4}$ *M*
(b) silver nitrite: $K_{sp} = 6.0 \times 10^{-4}$; $[Ag^+] = 0.025$ *M*
(c) tin(II) hydroxide: $K_{sp} = 1.4 \times 10^{-28}$; pH = 9.35

7. Calculate the concentration of each of the following ions in equilibrium with 0.019 *M* Br^-.

(a) Pb^{2+} (b) Hg_2^{2+} (c) Ag^+

8. ■ Calculate the concentration of each of the following ions in equilibrium with 0.0034 *M* Ba^{2+}.

(a) F^- (b) SO_4^{2-} (c) CrO_4^{2-}

9. Fill in the blanks in the following table.

Compound	[cation]	[anion]	K_{sp}
(a) $CoCO_3$	______	______	1×10^{-10}
(b) LaF_3	______	7×10^{-6}	2×10^{-19}
(c) $Ba_3(PO_4)_2$	4.2×10^{-8}	______	6×10^{-39}

10. **WEB** Fill in the blanks in the following table.

Compound	[cation]	[anion]	K_{sp}
(a) BaC_2O_4	______	______	1.6×10^{-6}
(b) $Cr(OH)_3$	2.7×10^{-8}	______	6.3×10^{-31}
(c) $Pb_3(PO_4)_2$	______	8×10^{-6}	1×10^{-54}

11. Barium nitrate is added to a solution of 0.025 *M* sodium fluoride.

(a) At what concentration of Ba^{2+} does a precipitate start to form?
(b) Enough barium nitrate is added to make $[Ba^{2+}] = 0.0045$ *M*. What percentage of the original fluoride ion has precipitated?

12. ■ Cadmium(II) chloride is added to a solution of potassium hydroxide with a pH of 9.62. (K_{sp} $Cd(OH)_2 = 2.5 \times 10^{-14}$)

(a) At what concentration of Cd^{2+} does a precipitate first start to form?
(b) Enough cadmium(II) chloride is added to make $[Cd^{2+}] = 0.0013$ *M*. What is the pH of the resulting solution?
(c) What percentage of the original hydroxide ion is left in solution?

13. Water from a well is found to contain 3.0 mg of calcium ion per liter. If 0.50 mg of sodium sulfate is added to one liter of the well water without changing its volume, will a precipitate form? What should $[SO_4^{2-}]$ be to just start precipitation?

14. Before lead in paint was discontinued, lead chromate was a common pigment in yellow paint. A 1.0-L solution is prepared by mixing 0.50 mg of lead nitrate with 0.020 mg of potassium chromate. Will a precipitate form? What should $[Pb^{2+}]$ be to just start precipitation?

15. A solution is prepared by mixing 13.00 mL of 0.0021 *M* aqueous $Hg_2(NO_3)_2$ with 25.0 mL of 0.015 *M* HCl. Assume that volumes are additive.

(a) Will precipitation occur?
(b) Calculate $[Hg_2^{2+}]$, $[Cl^-]$, and $[NO_3^-]$ after equilibrium is established.

16. A solution is prepared by mixing 35.00 mL of a 0.061 *M* solution of zinc nitrate with 20.0 mL of KOH with a pH of 9.00. Assume that volumes are additive.

(a) Will precipitation occur?
(b) Calculate $[Zn^{2+}]$, $[NO_3^-]$, $[K^+]$, and the pH after equilibrium is established.

K_{sp} and Solubility

17. Calculate the molar solubility of the following compounds.

(a) $PbCl_2$ (b) $Ca_3(PO_4)_2$ (c) Ag_2CO_3

18. ■ Calculate the molar solubility of the following compounds.

(a) MgF_2 (b) $Fe(OH)_3$ (c) $Mg_3(PO_4)_2$

19. Calculate the K_{sp} of the following compounds, given their molar solubilities.

(a) $ZnCO_3$, 1.21×10^{-5} *M*
(b) Ag_2SO_4, 0.014 *M*
(c) $Sr_3(PO_4)_2$, 2.5×10^{-7} *M*

20. ■ Calculate the K_{sp} of the following compounds, given their molar solubilities.

(a) AgCN, 7.73×10^{-9} *M*
(b) $Ni(OH)_2$, 5.16×10^{-6} *M*
(c) $Cu_3(PO_4)_2$, 1.67×10^{-8} *M*

21. Calculate the solubility (in grams per liter) of silver chloride in the following.

(a) pure water (b) 0.025 *M* $BaCl_2$ (c) 0.17 *M* $AgNO_3$

22. ■ Calculate the solubility (in grams per liter) of magnesium hydroxide in the following.

(a) pure water (b) 0.041 *M* $Ba(OH)_2$ (c) 0.0050 *M* $MgCl_2$

23. Lead azide, $Pb(N_3)_2$, is used as a detonator in car airbags. The impact of a collision causes $Pb(N_3)_2$ to be converted into an enormous amount of gas that fills the airbag. At 25°C, a saturated solution of lead azide is prepared by dissolving 25 mg in water to make 100.0 mL of solution. What is K_{sp} for lead azide?

24. A saturated solution of silver(I) sulfate at 25°C can be prepared by dissolving 1.2 g of silver(I) sulfate in water to make 250.0 mL of solution. What is K_{sp} for silver(I) sulfate?

25. One gram of $PbCl_2$ is dissolved in 1.0 L of hot water. When the solution is cooled to 25°C, will some of the $PbCl_2$ crystallize out? If so, how much?

26. ■ K_{sp} for silver acetate ($AgC_2H_3O_2$) at 80°C is estimated to be 2×10^{-2}. Ten grams of silver acetate are added to 1.0 L of water at 25°C.

(a) Will all the silver acetate dissolve at 25°C?
(b) If the solution (assume the volume to be 1.0 L) is heated to 80°C, will all the silver acetate dissolve?

27. Calculate the solubility (g/100 mL) of iron(II) hydroxide in buffered solutions with the following pH's.

(a) 4 (b) 7 (c) 10

28. ■ Calculate the solubility (g/100 mL) of magnesium hydroxide in buffered solutions with the following pH's:

(a) 4 (b) 7 (c) 9

29. At 25°C, 100.0 mL of a $Ba(OH)_2$ solution is prepared by dissolving $Ba(OH)_2$ in an alkaline solution. At equilibrium, the solution has 2.37 g of $Ba(OH)_2$ and a pH of 13.28. Estimate K_{sp} for $Ba(OH)_2$.

30. WEB At 25°C, 100.0 mL of a $Cr(OH)_2$ solution is prepared by dissolving $Cr(OH)_2$ in an alkaline solution. At equilibrium, the solution has 8.65 mg of $Cr(OH)_2$ and a pH of 8.50. Estimate K_{sp} for $Cr(OH)_2$.

Selective Precipitation

31. A solution is 0.035 *M* in Na_2SO_4 and 0.035 *M* in Na_2CrO_4. Solid $Pb(NO_3)_2$ is added without changing the volume of the solution.

(a) Which salt, $PbSO_4$ or $PbCrO_4$, will precipitate first?

(b) What is $[Pb^{2+}]$ when the salt in (a) first begins to precipitate?

32. ■ Solid lead nitrate is added to a solution that is 0.020 *M* in OH^- and SO_4^{2-}. Addition of the lead nitrate does not change the volume of the solution.

(a) Which compound, $PbSO_4$ or $Pb(OH)_2$ ($K_{sp} = 2.8 \times 10^{-16}$), will precipitate first?

(b) What is the pH of the solution when $PbSO_4$ first starts to precipitate?

33. A 65-mL solution of 0.40 *M* $Al(NO_3)_3$ is mixed with 125 mL of 0.17 *M* iron(II) nitrate. Solid sodium hydroxide is then added without a change in volume.

(a) Which will precipitate first, $Al(OH)_3$ or $Fe(OH)_2$?

(b) What is $[OH^-]$ when the first compound begins to precipitate?

34. ■ A solution is made up by adding 0.925 g of silver(I) nitrate and 6.25 g of magnesium nitrate to enough water to make 375 mL of solution. Solid sodium carbonate is added without changing the volume of the solution.

(a) Which salt, Ag_2CO_3 or $MgCO_3$, will precipitate first?

(b) What is the concentration of the carbonate ion when the first salt starts to precipitate?

35. A solution is made up by mixing 125 mL of 0.100 *M* $AuNO_3$ and 225 mL of 0.049 *M* $AgNO_3$. Twenty-five mL of a 0.0100 *M* solution of HCl is then added. K_{sp} of AuCl = 2.0×10^{-13}. When equilibrium is established, will there be—

- no precipitate?
- a precipitate of AuCl only?
- a precipitate of AgCl only?
- a precipitate of both AgCl and AuCl?

36. To a beaker with 500.0 mL of water are added 95 mg of $Ba(NO_3)_2$, 95 mg of $Ca(NO_3)_2$, and 100.0 mg of Na_2CO_3. After equilibrium is established, will there be—

- no precipitate?
- a precipitate of $BaCO_3$ only?
- a precipitate of $CaCO_3$ only?
- a precipitate of both $CaCO_3$ and $BaCO_3$?

Assume that the volume of the solution is still 500.0 mL after the addition of the salts.

Dissolving Precipitates

37. Write net ionic equations for the reaction of H^+ with

(a) Cu_2S (b) Hg_2Cl_2 (c) $SrCO_3$

(d) $Cu(NH_3)_4^{2+}$ (e) $Ca(OH)_2$

38. ■ Write net ionic equations for the reactions of each of the following with strong acid.

(a) $CaCO_3$ (b) NiS (c) $Al(OH)_3$

(d) $Sb(OH)_4^-$ (e) AgCl

39. Write a net ionic equation for the reaction with ammonia by which

(a) silver chloride dissolves.

(b) aluminum ion forms a precipitate.

(c) copper(II) forms a complex ion.

40. ■ WEB Write a net ionic equation for the reaction with ammonia by which

(a) $Cu(OH)_2$ dissolves. (b) Cd^{2+} forms a complex ion.

(c) Pb^{2+} forms a precipitate.

41. Write a net ionic equation for the reaction with OH^- by which

(a) Sb^{3+} forms a precipitate.

(b) antimony(III) hydroxide dissolves when more OH^- is added.

(c) Sb^{3+} forms a complex ion.

42. Write a net ionic equation for the reaction with OH^- by which

(a) Ni^{2+} forms a precipitate.

(b) Sn^{4+} forms a complex ion.

(c) $Al(OH)_3$ dissolves.

Solution Equilibria

43. Write an overall net ionic equation and calculate *K* for the reaction where CuCl ($K_{sp} = 1.9 \times 10^{-7}$) is dissolved by NaCN to form $[Cu(CN)_2]^-$ ($K_f = 1.0 \times 10^{16}$).

44. ■ Write an overall net ionic equation and calculate *K* for the reaction where $Co(OH)_2$ ($K_{sp} = 2 \times 10^{-16}$) is dissolved by HCl.

45. Consider the reaction

$$Zn(OH)_2(s) + 2CN^-(aq) \rightleftharpoons Zn(CN)_2(s) + 2OH^-(aq)$$

(a) Calculate *K* for the reaction. (K_{sp} $Zn(CN)_2 = 8.0 \times 10^{-12}$)

(b) Will $Zn(CN)_2$ precipitate if NaCN is added to a saturated $Zn(OH)_2$ solution?

46. Consider the reaction

$$AgCl(s) + I^-(aq) \rightleftharpoons AgI(s) + Cl^-(aq)$$

(a) Calculate *K* for the reaction.

(b) Will AgI precipitate if NaI is added to a saturated AgCl solution?

47. Aluminum hydroxide reacts with an excess of hydroxide ions to form the complex ion $Al(OH)_4^-$.

(a) Write an equation for this reaction.

(b) Calculate *K*.

(c) Determine the solubility of $Al(OH)_3$ (in mol/L) at pH 12.0.

48. Consider the reaction

$$Cu(OH)_2(s) + 4NH_3(aq) \rightleftharpoons Cu(NH_3)_4^{2+}(aq) + 2OH^-(aq)$$

(a) Calculate *K* given that for $Cu(OH)_2$ $K_{sp} = 2 \times 10^{-19}$ and for $Cu(NH_3)_4^{2+}$ $K_f = 2 \times 10^{12}$.

(b) Determine the solubility of $Cu(OH)_2$ (in mol/L) in 4.5 *M* NH_3.

49. ■ Calculate the molar solubility of gold(I) chloride ($K_{sp} = 2.0 \times 10^{-13}$) in 0.10 *M* NaCN. The complex ion formed is $[Au(CN)_2]^-$ with $K_f = 2 \times 10^{38}$. Ignore any other competing equilibrium systems.

50. When excess NaOH is added to $Zn(OH)_2$, the complex ion $Zn(OH)_4^{2-}$ is formed. Using Tables 15.4 and 16.1, determine the molar solubility of $Zn(OH)_2$ in 0.10 *M* NaOH. Compare with the molar solubility of $Zn(OH)_2$ in pure water.

51. For the reaction

$$CdC_2O_4(s) + 4NH_3(aq) \rightleftharpoons Cd(NH_3)_4^{2+}(aq) + C_2O_4^{2-}(aq)$$

(a) calculate *K*. (K_{sp} for CdC_2O_4 is 1.5×10^{-8}.)

(b) calculate $[NH_3]$ at equilibrium when 2.00 g of CdC_2O_4 is dissolved in 1.00 L of solution.

52. For the reaction

$$Fe(OH)_2(s) + 6CN^-(aq) \rightleftharpoons Fe(CN)_6^{4-}(aq) + 2OH^-(aq)$$

(a) calculate *K*.

(b) calculate $[CN^-]$ at equilibrium when 10.0 g of $Fe(OH)_2$ is dissolved in 1.00 L of solution.

Unclassified

53. Calcium ions in blood trigger clotting. To prevent that in donated blood, sodium oxalate, $Na_2C_2O_4$, is added to remove calcium ions according to the following equation.

$$C_2O_4^{2-}(aq) + Ca^{2+}(aq) \longrightarrow CaC_2O_4(s)$$

Blood contains about 0.10 mg Ca^{2+}/mL. If a 250.0-mL sample of donated blood is treated with an equal volume of 0.160 *M* $Na_2C_2O_4$, estimate $[Ca^{2+}]$ after precipitation. (K_{sp} $CaC_2O_4 = 4 \times 10^{-9}$)

54. A saturated solution of calcium chromate ($CaCrO_4$) freezes at $-0.10°C$. What is K_{sp} for $CaCrO_4$? Assume complete dissociation. The density of the solution is 1.0 g/mL.

55. A town adds 2.0 ppm of F^- ion to fluoridate its water supply (fluoridation of water reduces the incidence of dental caries). If the concentration of Ca^{2+} in the water is 3.5×10^{-4} *M*, will a precipitate of CaF_2 form when the water is fluoridated?

56. Predict what effect each of the following has on the position of the equilibrium

$$PbCl_2(s) \rightleftharpoons Pb^{2+}(aq) + 2Cl^-(aq) \qquad \Delta H = 23.4 \text{ kJ}$$

(a) addition of 1 *M* $Pb(NO_3)_2$ solution
(b) increase in temperature
(c) addition of Ag^+, forming AgCl
(d) addition of 1 *M* hydrochloric acid

57. When 25.0 mL of 0.500 *M* iron(II) sulfate is combined with 35.0 mL of 0.332 *M* barium hydroxide, two different precipitates are formed.
(a) Write a net ionic equation for the reaction that takes place.
(b) Estimate the mass of the precipitates formed.
(c) What are the equilibrium concentrations of the ions in solution?

58. Consider a 1.50-L aqueous solution of 3.75 *M* NH_3, where 17.5 g of NH_4Cl is dissolved. To this solution, 5.00 g of $MgCl_2$ is added.
(a) What is $[OH^-]$ before $MgCl_2$ is added?
(b) Will a precipitate form?
(c) What is $[Mg^{2+}]$ after equilibrium is established?

59. ■ Marble is almost pure $CaCO_3$. Acid rain has a devastating effect on marble statuary left outdoors. Assume that the reaction which occurs is

$$CaCO_3(s) + H^+(aq) \longrightarrow Ca^{2+}(aq) + HCO_3^-(aq)$$

Neglecting all other competing equilibria and using Tables 16.1 and 13.2, calculate
(a) *K* for the reaction.
(b) the molar solubility of $CaCO_3$ in pure water.
(c) the molar solubility of $CaCO_3$ in acid rainwater with a pH of 4.00.

60. Consider the following solubility data for calcium oxalate (CaC_2O_4):

$$K_{sp} \text{ at } 25°C = 4 \times 10^{-9}$$
$$K_{sp} \text{ at } 95°C = 1 \times 10^{-8}$$

Five hundred mL of a saturated solution is prepared at 95°C. How many milligrams of CaC_2O_4 will precipitate when the solution is cooled to 25°C? (Assume that supersaturation does not take place.)

Conceptual Questions

61. Shown below is a representation of the ionic solid MX, where M cations are represented by squares and X anions are represented by circles. Fill in the box after the arrow to represent what happens to the solid after it has been completely dissolved in water. For simplicity, do not represent the water molecules.

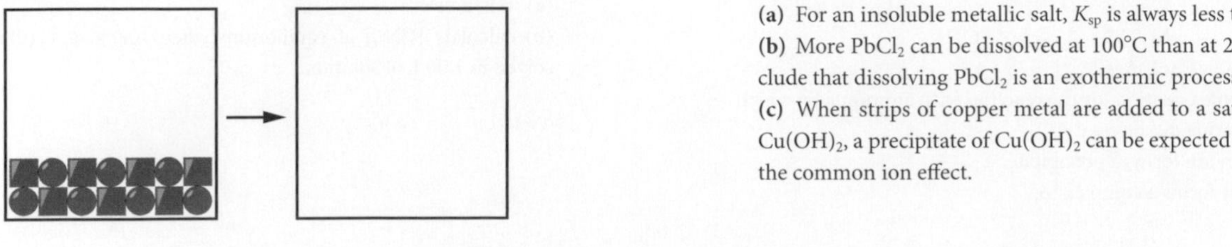

62. The box below represents one liter of a saturated solution of the species , where squares represent the cation and circles represent the anion. Water molecules, though present, are not shown.

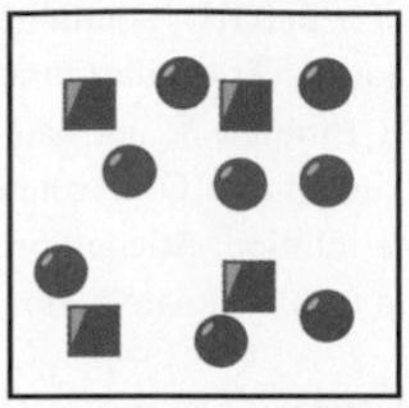

Complete the next three figures below by filling one-liter boxes to the right of the arrow, showing the state of the ions after water is added to form saturated solutions. The species represented to the left of the arrow is the solid form of the ions represented above. Do not show the water molecules.

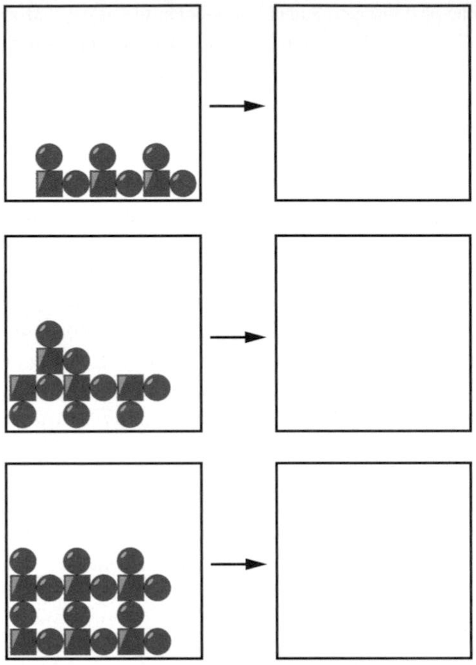

63. Using the same saturation data and species representation described in Question 62, complete the picture below.

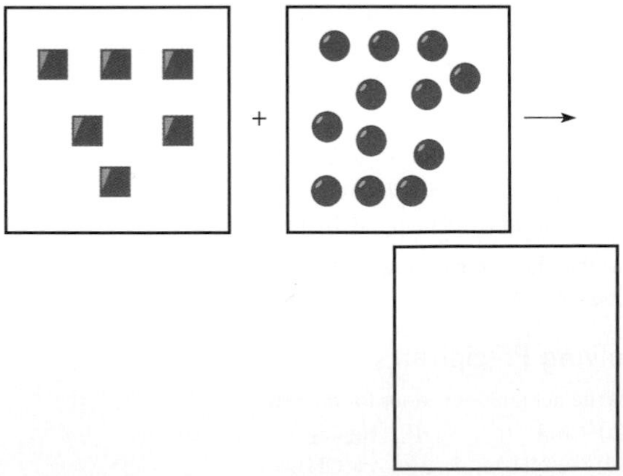

64. Which of the following statements are true?
(a) For an insoluble metallic salt, K_{sp} is always less than 1.
(b) More $PbCl_2$ can be dissolved at 100°C than at 25°C. One can conclude that dissolving $PbCl_2$ is an exothermic process.
(c) When strips of copper metal are added to a saturated solution of $Cu(OH)_2$, a precipitate of $Cu(OH)_2$ can be expected to form because of the common ion effect.

65. Consider the insoluble salts JQ, K_2R, L_2S_3, MT_2, and NU_3. They are formed from the metal ions J^+, K^+, L^{3+}, M^{2+}, and N^{3+} and the nonmetal ions Q^-, R^{2-}, S^{2-}, T^-, and U^-. All the salts have the same K_{sp}, 1×10^{-10}, at 25°C.

(a) Which salt has the highest molar solubility?

(b) Does the salt with the highest molar solubility have the highest solubility in g salt/100 g water?

(c) Can the solubility of each salt in g/100 g water be determined from the information given? If yes, calculate the solubility of each salt in g/100 g water. If no, why not?

66. A plot of the solubility of a certain compound (g/100 g H_2O) against temperature (°C) is a straight line with a positive slope. Is dissolving that compound an exothermic process?

67. ■ Consider the equilibrium curve for AgCl shown below. Which of the following statements about a solution at point A on the curve are true?

(a) The solution is saturated and at equilibrium.

(b) Addition of NaCl increases the concentration of Cl^- in solution.

(c) Addition of NaCl increases the concentration of Ag^+ in solution.

(d) Addition of Ag^+ results in the precipitation of AgCl.

(e) Addition of solid $NaNO_3$ to the solution without change in volume does not change $[Ag^+]$ or $[Cl^-]$.

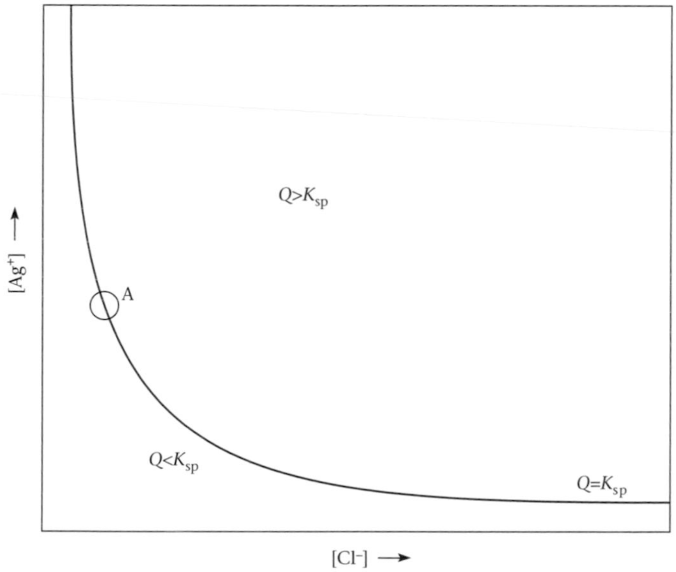

68. ■ Dissolving $CaCO_3$ is an endothermic reaction. The following five graphs represent an experiment done on $CaCO_3$. Match the experiment to the graph.

(a) HCl is added.

(b) The temperature is increased.

(c) $CaCl_2$ is added.

(d) NaCl is added.

(1)

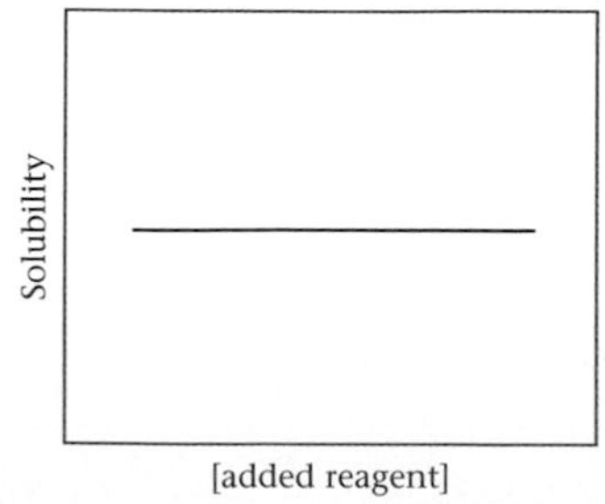

(2)

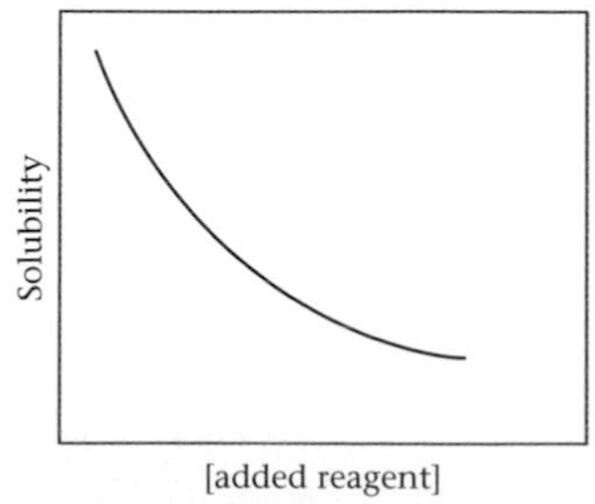

(3)

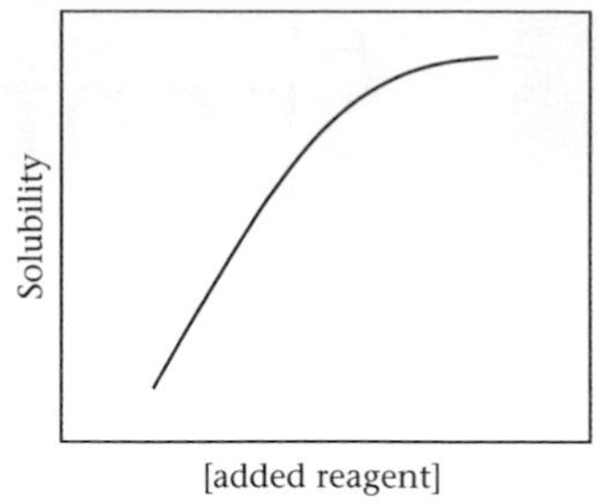

(4)

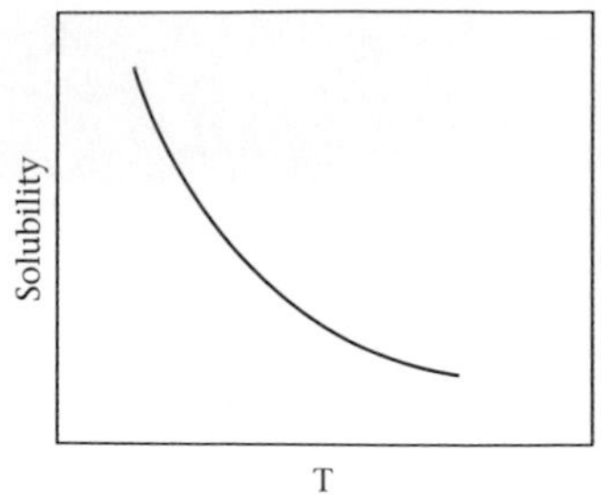

(5)

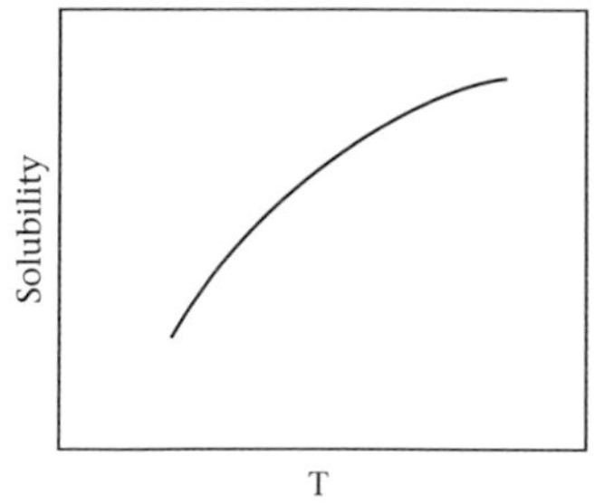

Challenge Problems

69. Ammonium chloride solutions are slightly acidic, so they are better solvents than water for insoluble hydroxides such as $Mg(OH)_2$. Find the solubility of $Mg(OH)_2$ in moles per liter in 0.2 *M* NH_4Cl and compare with the solubility in water. *Hint:* Find *K* for the reaction

$$Mg(OH)_2(s) + 2NH_4^+(aq) \longrightarrow Mg^{2+}(aq) + 2NH_3(aq) + 2H_2O$$

70. What is the solubility of CaF_2 in a buffer solution containing 0.30 *M* $HCHO_2$ and 0.20 *M* $NaCHO_2$? *Hint:* Consider the equation

$$CaF_2(s) + 2H^+(aq) \longrightarrow Ca^{2+}(aq) + 2HF(aq)$$

and solve the equilibrium problem.

71. What is the I^- concentration just as AgCl begins to precipitate when 1.0 *M* $AgNO_3$ is slowly added to a solution containing 0.020 *M* Cl^- and 0.020 *M* I^-?

72. The concentrations of various cations in seawater, in moles per liter, are

Ion	Na^+	Mg^{2+}	Ca^{2+}	Al^{3+}	Fe^{3+}
Molarity (*M*)	0.46	0.056	0.01	4×10^{-7}	2×10^{-7}

(a) At what $[OH^-]$ does $Mg(OH)_2$ start to precipitate?

(b) At this concentration, will any of the other ions precipitate?

(c) If enough OH^- is added to precipitate 50% of the Mg^{2+}, what percentage of each of the other ions will precipitate?

(d) Under the conditions in (c), what mass of precipitate will be obtained from one liter of seawater?

73. Consider the equilibrium

$$Zn(NH_3)_4^{2+}(aq) + 4OH^-(aq) \rightleftharpoons Zn(OH)_4^{2-}(aq) + 4NH_3(aq)$$

(a) Calculate *K* for this reaction.

(b) What is the ratio $[Zn(NH_3)_4^{2+}]/[Zn(OH)_4^{2-}]$ in a solution 1.0 *M* in NH_3?

74. Use the equilibrium constants in Appendix 1 to calculate *K* for the reaction

$$Ag(NH_3)_2^+(aq) + 2H^+(aq) + Cl^-(aq) \rightleftharpoons AgCl(s) + 2NH_4^+(aq)$$

■ in OWL Blue-numbered questions answered in Appendix 6 **WEB** Solution is available on companion website

17 Spontaneity of Reaction

I am a sleepless
Slowfaring eater,
Maker of rust and rot
In your bastioned fastenings,
I am the crumbler: tomorrow

—Carl Sandburg
"Under"

Chapter Outline

The ballerinas in Degas's painting *The Dancers* look like they have depleted their glucose by using it for energy to dance.

The goal of this chapter is to answer a basic question: Will a given reaction occur "by itself" at a particular temperature and pressure, without the exertion of any outside force? In that sense, is the reaction *spontaneous?* This is a critical question in just about every area of science and technology. A synthetic organic chemist looking for a source of acetylene, C_2H_2, would like to know whether this compound can be made by heating the elements together. A metallurgist trying to produce titanium metal from TiO_2 would like to know what reaction to use; would hydrogen, carbon, or aluminum be feasible reducing agents?

To develop a general criterion for spontaneity, we will apply the principles of *thermodynamics*, the science that deals with heat and energy effects. Three different thermodynamic functions are of value in analyzing spontaneity.

1. ΔH, the change in enthalpy (Chapter 8); a *negative* value of ΔH tends to make a reaction spontaneous.
2. ΔS, the change in entropy (Section 17.2); a *positive* value of ΔS tends to make a reaction spontaneous.
3. ΔG, the change in free energy (Sections 17.3, 17.4); a reaction at constant temperature and pressure will be *spontaneous* if ΔG is *negative*, no ifs, ands, or buts.

Besides serving as a general criterion for spontaneity, the free energy change can be used to—

- determine the effect of temperature, pressure, and concentration on reaction spontaneity (Section 17.5).
- calculate the equilibrium constant for a reaction (Section 17.6).
- determine whether coupled reactions will be spontaneous (Section 17.7). ■

Online homework for this chapter may be assigned in OWL.

CENGAGENOW™

This icon introduces an opportunity for self-study and to explore interactive modules by signing in at **academic.cengage.com/now.**

17.1 SPONTANEOUS PROCESSES

All of us are familiar with certain **spontaneous processes.** For example—

- an ice cube melts when added to a glass of water at room temperature

$$H_2O(s) \longrightarrow H_2O(l)$$

- a mixture of hydrogen and oxygen burns if ignited by a spark

$$2H_2(g) + O_2(g) \longrightarrow 2H_2O(l)$$

- an iron (steel) tool exposed to moist air rusts

$$2Fe(s) + \tfrac{3}{2}O_2(g) + 3H_2O(l) \longrightarrow 2Fe(OH)_3(s)$$

In other words, these three reactions are spontaneous at 25°C and 1 atm.

The word "spontaneous" does not imply anything about how rapidly a reaction occurs. Some spontaneous reactions, notably the rusting of iron, are quite slow. Often a reaction that is spontaneous does not occur without some sort of stimulus to get the reaction started. A mixture of hydrogen and oxygen shows no sign of reaction in the absence of a spark or match. Once started, though, a spontaneous reaction continues by itself without further input of energy from the outside.

A spark is OK, but a continuous input of energy isn't.

If a reaction is spontaneous under a given set of conditions, the reverse reaction must be nonspontaneous. For example, water does not spontaneously decompose to the elements by the reverse of the reaction referred to above.

$$2H_2O(l) \longrightarrow 2H_2(g) + O_2(g) \qquad \text{nonspontaneous}$$

However, it is often possible to bring about a nonspontaneous reaction by supplying energy in the form of work. Electrolysis can be used to decompose water to the elements. To do this, electrical energy must be furnished, perhaps from a storage battery.

Perhaps the simplest way to define spontaneity is to say that **a spontaneous process is one that moves the reaction system toward equilibrium.** A nonspontaneous process moves the system away from equilibrium.

The Energy Factor

Many spontaneous processes proceed with a decrease of energy. Boulders roll downhill, not uphill. A storage battery discharges when you leave your car's headlights on. Extrapolating to chemical reactions, one might guess that spontaneous reactions would be exothermic ($\Delta H < 0$). A century ago, P. M. Berthelot in Paris and Julius Thomsen in Copenhagen proposed this as a general principle, applicable to all reactions.

Instead it turns out that in almost all cases the reverse is true. Nearly all exothermic chemical reactions are spontaneous at 25°C and 1 atm. Consider, for example, the formation of water from the elements and the rusting of iron:

$$2H_2(g) + O_2(g) \longrightarrow 2H_2O(l) \qquad \Delta H = -571.6 \text{ kJ}$$

$$2Fe(s) + \tfrac{3}{2}O_2(g) + 3H_2O(l) \longrightarrow 2Fe(OH)_3(s) \qquad \Delta H = -788.6 \text{ kJ}$$

For both of these spontaneous reactions, ΔH is a negative quantity.

On the other hand, this simple rule fails for many familiar phase changes. An example of a spontaneous reaction that is not exothermic is the melting of ice. This takes place spontaneously at 1 atm above 0°C, even though it is endothermic:

$$H_2O(s) \longrightarrow H_2O(l) \qquad \Delta H = +6.0 \text{ kJ}$$

There is still another basic objection to using the sign of ΔH as a general criterion for spontaneity. Endothermic reactions that are nonspontaneous at room temperature often become spontaneous when the temperature is raised. Consider, for example, the decomposition of limestone:

$$CaCO_3(s) \longrightarrow CaO(s) + CO_2(g) \qquad \Delta H = +178.3 \text{ kJ}$$

At 25°C and 1 atm, this reaction does not occur. Witness the existence of the white cliffs of Dover and other limestone deposits over eons of time. However, if the temperature is raised to about 1100 K, limestone decomposes to give off carbon dioxide gas at 1 atm. In other words, this endothermic reaction becomes spontaneous at high temperatures. This is true despite the fact that ΔH remains about 178 kJ, nearly independent of temperature.

The Randomness Factor

Clearly, the direction of a spontaneous change is not always determined by the tendency for a system to go to a state of lower energy. There is another natural tendency that must be taken into account to predict the direction of spontaneity. ***Nature tends to move spontaneously from a state of lower probability to one of higher probability.*** Or, as G. N. Lewis put it,

> Each system which is left to its own will, over time, change toward a condition of maximum probability.

To illustrate what these statements mean, consider a pastime far removed from chemistry: tossing dice. If you've ever shot craps (and maybe even if you haven't), you know that when a pair of dice is thrown, a 7 is much more likely to come up than a 12. Figure 17.1 shows why this is the case. There are six different ways to throw a 7 and only one way to throw a 12. Over time, dice will come up 7 six times as often as 12. A 7 is a state of "high" probability; a 12 is a state of "low" probability.

Figure 17.1
Certain "states" are more probable than others. For example, when you toss a pair of dice, a 7 is much more likely to come up than a 12.

Now let's consider a process a bit closer to chemistry (Figure 17.2, p. 453). Two different gases, let us say H_2 and N_2, are originally contained in different glass bulbs, separated by a stopcock. When the stopcock is opened, the two different kinds of molecules distribute themselves evenly between the two bulbs. Eventually, half of the H_2 molecules will end up in

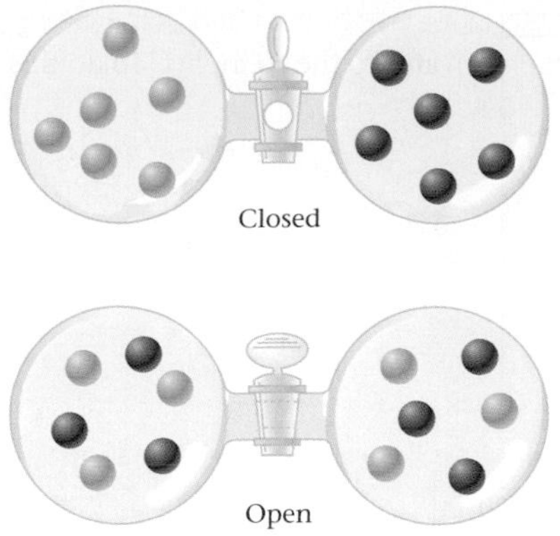

Figure 17.2
Spontaneous change. Different kinds of gas molecules mix spontaneously, going from a more ordered to a more random state.

the left bulb and half in the right; the same holds for the N_2 molecules. Each gas achieves its own most probable distribution, independent of the presence of the other gas.

We could explain the results of this experiment the way we did before; the final distribution is clearly much more probable than the initial distribution. There is, however, another useful way of looking at this process. The system has gone from a highly ordered state (all the H_2 molecules on the left, all the N_2 molecules on the right) to a more disordered, or random, state in which the molecules are distributed evenly between the two bulbs. The same situation holds when marbles rather than molecules are mixed (Figure 17.3). ***In general, nature tends to move spontaneously from more ordered to more random states.***

This statement is quite easy for parents or students to understand. Your room tends to get messy because an ordered room has few options for objects to be moved around (leaving socks on the floor is not an option for an orderly room). The comedian Bill Cosby insists that with an army of 80 two-year-olds he could take over any country in the world, because they have a remarkable ability for disorganization.

17.2 ENTROPY, *S*

Entropy is often described as a measure of disorder or randomness. While useful, these terms are subjective and should be used cautiously. It is better to think about entropic changes in terms of the change in the number of *microstates* of the system. Microstates are different ways in which molecules can be distributed. An increase in the number of possible microstates (i.e., disorder) results in an increase of entropy. Entropy treats the randomness factor quantitatively. Rudolf Clausius gave it the symbol *S* for no particular reason. In general, the more random the state, the larger the number of its possible microstates, the more probable the state, thus the greater its entropy.

CENGAGENOW™
Click Chemistry Interactive for the self-study module **trends in entropy.**

Entropy, like enthalpy (Chapter 8), is a state property. That is, the entropy depends only on the state of a system, not on its history. The entropy change is determined by the entropies of the final and initial states, not on the path followed from one state to another.

$$\Delta S = S_{\text{final}} - S_{\text{initial}}$$

Charles Steele

Figure 17.3
Probability. Some states are much more probable than others. If you shake red and black marbles with each other, the random distribution at the left is much more probable than the highly ordered distribution at the right.

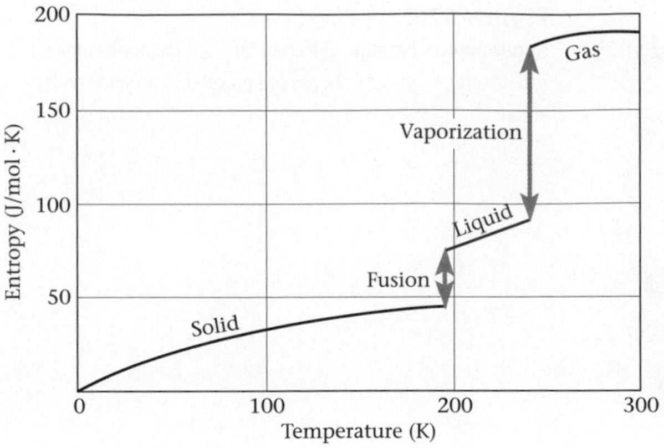

Figure 17.4
Molar entropy of ammonia as a function of temperature. Note the large increases in entropy upon fusion (melting) and vaporization.

Several factors influence the amount of entropy that a system has in a particular state. In general—

- ***a liquid has a higher entropy than the solid from which it is formed.*** In a solid the atoms or molecules are confined to fixed positions, so the number of microstates is small. In the liquid, these atoms or molecules can occupy many more positions as they move away from the lattice. Thus, the number of microstates increases and there are then many more ways to arrange the particles. The phase transition is from an "ordered" to a "disordered" system.
- ***a gas has a higher entropy than the liquid from which it is formed.*** When vaporization occurs, the particles acquire greater freedom to move about. They are distributed throughout the entire container instead of being restricted to a small volume. In vaporization, the number of microstates increases.
- ***increasing the temperature of a substance increases its entropy.*** Raising the temperature increases the kinetic energy of the molecules (or atoms or ions) and hence their freedom of motion. In the solid, the molecules vibrate with a greater amplitude at higher temperatures. In a liquid or a gas, they move about more rapidly.

One way or another, heating a substance increases its entropy.

These effects are shown in Figure 17.4, where the entropy of ammonia, NH_3, is plotted versus temperature. Note that the entropy of solid ammonia at 0 K is zero. This reflects the fact that molecules are completely ordered in the solid state at this temperature; there is no randomness whatsoever. More generally, the ***third law of thermodynamics*** tells us that ***a completely ordered pure crystalline solid has an entropy of zero at 0 K.***

We'll get to the second law shortly.

Notice from the figure that the effect of temperature on entropy is due almost entirely to phase changes. The slope of the curve is small in regions where only one phase is present. In contrast, there is a large jump in entropy when the solid melts and an even larger one when the liquid vaporizes. This behavior is typical of all substances; melting and vaporization are accompanied by relatively large increases in entropy.

What is the sign of ΔS for egg $\longrightarrow$ omelet?

Example 17.1 Conceptual

Predict whether ΔS is positive or negative for each of the following processes:

(a) taking dry ice from a freezer where its temperature is $-80°C$ and allowing it to warm to room temperature.
(b) dissolving bromine in hexane.
(c) condensing gaseous bromine to liquid bromine.

Strategy Consider the relative disorder of final and initial states; remember that entropy increases in the order solid < liquid < gas.

SOLUTION

(a) This process involves an increase in temperature and a phase change from solid to gas: $\Delta S > 0$.
(b) The solution is more random than the original liquids: $\Delta S > 0$.
(c) This is a phase change from gas to liquid, from disorder to order, $\Delta S < 0$.

Standard Molar Entropies

The entropy of a substance, unlike its enthalpy, can be evaluated directly. The details of how this is done are beyond the level of this text, but Figure 17.4 shows the results for one substance, ammonia. From such a plot you can read off the *standard molar entropy* at 1 atm pressure and any given temperature, most often 25°C. This quantity is given the symbol $S°$ and has the units of joules per mole per kelvin (J/mol·K). From Figure 17.4, it appears that

$$S° \ NH_3(g) \text{ at } 25°C \approx 192 \text{ J/mol·K}$$

Standard molar entropies of elements, compounds, and aqueous ions are listed in Table 17.1 (p. 456). Notice that—

- ***elements have nonzero standard entropies.*** This means that in calculating the standard entropy change for a reaction, $\Delta S°$, elements as well as compounds must be taken into account.
- ***standard molar entropies of pure substances*** (elements and compounds) ***are always positive quantities*** ($S° > 0$).
- ***aqueous ions may have negative S° values.*** This is a consequence of the arbitrary way in which ionic entropies are defined, taking

$$S° \ H^+(aq) = 0$$

The fluoride ion has a standard entropy 13.8 units less than that of H^+; hence $S° \ F^-(aq) = -13.8$ J/mol·K.

You will also notice that gases, as a group, have higher entropies than liquids or solids. Moreover, among substances of similar structure and physical state, entropy usually increases with molar mass. Compare, for example, the hydrocarbons

$$CH_4(g) \quad S° = 186.2 \text{ J/mol·K}$$
$$C_2H_6(g) \quad S° = 229.5 \text{ J/mol·K}$$
$$C_3H_8(g) \quad S° = 269.9 \text{ J/mol·K}$$

As the molecule becomes more complex, there are more ways for the atoms to move about with respect to one another, leading to a higher entropy.

Charles D. Winters

Decomposition of ammonium nitrate. The value of ΔS for this reaction,

$$NH_4NO_3(s) \longrightarrow N_2O(g) + 2H_2O(g)$$

is positive. That can be predicted because a solid decomposes to gases.

$\Delta S°$ for Reactions

Table 17.1 can be used to calculate the **standard entropy change,** $\Delta S°$, for reactions, using the relation

$$\Delta S° = \sum S°_{\text{products}} - \sum S°_{\text{reactants}} \qquad \textbf{(17.1)}$$

In taking these sums, the standard molar entropies are multiplied by the number of moles specified in the balanced chemical equation.

Table 17.1 Standard Entropies at 25°C (J/mol·K) of Elements and Compounds at 1 atm, Aqueous Ions at 1 *M*

Elements

$Ag(s)$	42.6	$Cl_2(g)$	223.0	$I_2(s)$	116.1	$O_2(g)$	205.0
$Al(s)$	28.3	$Cr(s)$	23.8	$K(s)$	64.2	$Pb(s)$	64.8
$Ba(s)$	62.8	$Cu(s)$	33.2	$Mg(s)$	32.7	$P_4(s)$	164.4
$Br_2(l)$	152.2	$F_2(g)$	202.7	$Mn(s)$	32.0	$S(s)$	31.8
$C(s)$	5.7	$Fe(s)$	27.3	$N_2(g)$	191.5	$Si(s)$	18.8
$Ca(s)$	41.4	$H_2(g)$	130.6	$Na(s)$	51.2	$Sn(s)$	51.6
$Cd(s)$	51.8	$Hg(l)$	76.0	$Ni(s)$	29.9	$Zn(s)$	41.6

Compounds

$AgBr(s)$	107.1	$CaCl_2(s)$	104.6	$H_2O(g)$	188.7	$NH_4NO_3(s)$	151.1
$AgCl(s)$	96.2	$CaCO_3(s)$	92.9	$H_2O(l)$	69.9	$NO(g)$	210.7
$AgI(s)$	115.5	$CaO(s)$	39.8	$H_2O_2(l)$	109.6	$NO_2(g)$	240.0
$AgNO_3(s)$	140.9	$Ca(OH)_2(s)$	83.4	$H_2S(g)$	205.7	$N_2O_4(g)$	304.2
$Ag_2O(s)$	121.3	$CaSO_4(s)$	106.7	$H_2SO_4(l)$	156.9	$NaCl(s)$	72.1
$Al_2O_3(s)$	50.9	$CdCl_2(s)$	115.3	$HgO(s)$	70.3	$NaF(s)$	51.5
$BaCl_2(s)$	123.7	$CdO(s)$	54.8	$KBr(s)$	95.9	$NaOH(s)$	64.5
$BaCO_3(s)$	112.1	$Cr_2O_3(s)$	81.2	$KCl(s)$	82.6	$NiO(s)$	38.0
$BaO(s)$	70.4	$CuO(s)$	42.6	$KClO_3(s)$	143.1	$PbBr_2(s)$	161.5
$BaSO_4(s)$	132.2	$Cu_2O(s)$	93.1	$KClO_4(s)$	151.0	$PbCl_2(s)$	136.0
$CCl_4(l)$	216.4	$CuS(s)$	66.5	$KNO_3(s)$	133.0	$PbO(s)$	66.5
$CHCl_3(l)$	201.7	$Cu_2S(s)$	120.9	$MgCl_2(s)$	89.6	$PbO_2(s)$	68.6
$CH_4(g)$	186.2	$CuSO_4(s)$	107.6	$MgCO_3(s)$	65.7	$PCl_3(g)$	311.7
$C_2H_2(g)$	200.8	$Fe(OH)_3(s)$	106.7	$MgO(s)$	26.9	$PCl_5(g)$	364.5
$C_2H_4(g)$	219.5	$Fe_2O_3(s)$	87.4	$Mg(OH)_2(s)$	63.2	$SiO_2(s)$	41.8
$C_2H_6(g)$	229.5	$Fe_3O_4(s)$	146.4	$MgSO_4(s)$	91.6	$SnO_2(s)$	52.3
$C_3H_8(g)$	269.9	$HBr(g)$	198.6	$MnO(s)$	59.7	$SO_2(g)$	248.1
$CH_3OH(l)$	126.8	$HCl(g)$	186.8	$MnO_2(s)$	53.0	$SO_3(g)$	256.7
$C_2H_5OH(l)$	160.7	$HF(g)$	173.7	$NH_3(g)$	192.3	$ZnI_2(s)$	161.1
$CO(g)$	197.6	$HI(g)$	206.5	$N_2H_4(l)$	121.2	$ZnO(s)$	43.6
$CO_2(g)$	213.6	$HNO_3(l)$	155.6	$NH_4Cl(s)$	94.6	$ZnS(s)$	57.7

Cations				Anions			
$Ag^+(aq)$	72.7	$Hg^{2+}(aq)$	−32.2	$Br^-(aq)$	82.4	$HPO_4^{2-}(aq)$	−33.5
$Al^{3+}(aq)$	−321.7	$K^+(aq)$	102.5	$CO_3^{2-}(aq)$	−56.9	$HSO_4^-(aq)$	131.8
$Ba^{2+}(aq)$	9.6	$Mg^{2+}(aq)$	−138.1	$Cl^-(aq)$	56.5	$I^-(aq)$	111.3
$Ca^{2+}(aq)$	−53.1	$Mn^{2+}(aq)$	−73.6	$ClO_3^-(aq)$	162.3	$MnO_4^-(aq)$	191.2
$Cd^{2+}(aq)$	−73.2	$Na^+(aq)$	59.0	$ClO_4^-(aq)$	182.0	$NO_2^-(aq)$	123.0
$Cu^+(aq)$	40.6	$NH_4^+(aq)$	113.4	$CrO_4^{2-}(aq)$	50.2	$NO_3^-(aq)$	146.4
$Cu^{2+}(aq)$	−99.6	$Ni^{2+}(aq)$	−128.9	$Cr_2O_7^{2-}(aq)$	261.9	$OH^-(aq)$	−10.8
$Fe^{2+}(aq)$	−137.7	$Pb^{2+}(aq)$	10.5	$F^-(aq)$	−13.8	$PO_4^{3-}(aq)$	−222
$Fe^{3+}(aq)$	−315.9	$Sn^{2+}(aq)$	−17.4	$HCO_3^-(aq)$	91.2	$S^{2-}(aq)$	−14.6
$H^+(aq)$	0.0	$Zn^{2+}(aq)$	−112.1	$H_2PO_4^-(aq)$	90.4	$SO_4^{2-}(aq)$	20.1

To show how this relation is used, consider the reaction

$$CaCO_3(s) \longrightarrow CaO(s) + CO_2(g)$$

$$\Delta S° = S°CaO(s) + S°CO_2(g) - S°CaCO_3(s)$$

The units of $S°$ are J/mol·K: Those of $\Delta S°$ are J/K. Why the difference?

$$\Delta S° = 1\ \text{mol}\left(39.8\ \frac{\text{J}}{\text{mol}\cdot\text{K}}\right) + 1\ \text{mol}\left(213.6\ \frac{\text{J}}{\text{mol}\cdot\text{K}}\right) - 1\ \text{mol}\left(92.9\ \frac{\text{J}}{\text{mol}\cdot\text{K}}\right)$$

$$= 39.8\ \text{J/K} + 213.6\ \text{J/K} - 92.9\ \text{J/K} = +160.5\ \text{J/K}$$

You will notice that $\Delta S°$ for the decomposition of calcium carbonate is a positive quantity. This is reasonable because the gas formed, CO_2, has a much higher molar entropy than either of the solids, CaO or $CaCO_3$. As a matter of fact, it is almost always found that ***a reaction that results in an increase in the number of moles of gas is accompanied by an increase***

in entropy. Conversely, if the number of moles of gas decreases, $\Delta S°$ is a negative quantity. Consider, for example, the reaction

$$2H_2(g) + O_2(g) \longrightarrow 2H_2O(l)$$

$$\Delta S° = 2S°\ H_2O(l) - 2S°\ H_2(g) - S°\ O_2(g)$$
$$= 139.8\ J/K - 261.2\ J/K - 205.0\ J/K = -326.4\ J/K$$

If there is no change to the number of moles of gas, ΔS is usually small.

Example 17.2 Calculate $\Delta S°$ for

(a) dissolving one mole of calcium hydroxide in water.
(b) the combustion of one gram of methane to form carbon dioxide and liquid water.

Strategy Start by writing a balanced chemical equation for the reaction involved. Then use Equation 17.1 in combination with Table 17.1 to calculate the difference in entropy between products and reactants. For (b) note that you are asked to calculate $\Delta S°$ for *one gram* of methane.

SOLUTION

(a) $Ca(OH)_2(s) \longrightarrow Ca^{2+}(aq) + 2\ OH^-(aq)$

$$\Delta S° = S°\ Ca^{2+}(aq) + 2S°\ OH^-(aq) - S°\ Ca(OH)_2(s)$$
$$= 1\ mol\left(\frac{-53.1\ J}{1\ mol \cdot K}\right) + 2\ mol\left(\frac{-10.8\ J}{1\ mol \cdot K}\right) - 1\ mol\left(\frac{+83.4\ J}{1\ mol \cdot K}\right) = -158.1\ J/K$$

(b) $CH_4(g) + 2O_2(g) \longrightarrow CO_2(g) + 2H_2O(l)$

$$\Delta S° = S°\ CO_2(g) + 2S°\ H_2O(l) - [S°\ CH_4(g) + 2S°\ O_2(g)]$$
$$= 1\ mol\left(\frac{+213.6\ J}{1\ mol \cdot K}\right) + 2\ mol\left(\frac{+69.9\ J}{1\ mol \cdot K}\right)$$
$$- \left[1\ mol\left(\frac{+186.2\ J}{1\ mol \cdot K}\right) + 2\ mol\left(\frac{205.0\ J}{1\ mol \cdot K}\right)\right]$$
$$= -242.8\ J/K \text{ for the combustion of one mole of } CH_4.$$

For the combustion of one gram:

$$\frac{-242.8\ J/K}{1\ mol\ CH_4} \times \frac{1\ mol}{16.04\ g} = -15.14\ J/K$$

Reality Check Notice that in (b), in which there is a decrease in the number of moles of gas, $\Delta S°$ is negative.

The Second Law of Thermodynamics

The relationship between entropy change and spontaneity can be expressed through a basic principle of nature known as the second law of thermodynamics. One way to state this law is to say that ***in a spontaneous process, there is a net increase in entropy, taking into account both system and surroundings.*** That is,

$$\Delta S_{universe} = (\Delta S_{system} + \Delta S_{surroundings}) > 0 \qquad \text{spontaneous process}$$

CENGAGENOW™
Click Coached Problems for a self-study module on **calculating ΔS for the universe.**

(Recall from Chapter 8 that the system is that portion of the universe on which attention is focused; the surroundings include everything else.)

In this sense, the universe is running down.

Notice that the second law refers to the total entropy change, involving both system and surroundings. For many spontaneous processes, the entropy change for the system is a *negative* quantity. Consider, for example, the rusting of iron, a spontaneous process:

$$2Fe(s) + \tfrac{3}{2}O_2(g) + 3H_2O(l) \longrightarrow 2Fe(OH)_3(s)$$

$\Delta S°$ for this system at 25°C and 1 atm can be calculated from a table of standard entropies; it is found to be −358.4 J/K. The negative sign of $\Delta S°$ is entirely consistent with the second law. All the law requires is that the entropy change of the surroundings be greater than 358.4 J/K, so that $\Delta S_{universe} > 0$.

In principle, the second law can be used to determine whether a reaction is spontaneous. To do that, however, requires calculating the entropy change for the surroundings, which is not easy. We follow a conceptually simpler approach (Section 17.3), which deals only with the thermodynamic properties of chemical *systems*.

17.3 FREE ENERGY, *G*

CENGAGENOW™
Click Coached Problems for a self-study module on **putting ΔH and ΔS together.**

As pointed out earlier, two thermodynamic quantities affect reaction spontaneity. One of these is the enthalpy, *H;* the other is the entropy, *S*. The problem is to put these two quantities together in such a way as to arrive at a single function whose sign will determine whether a reaction is spontaneous. This problem was first solved more than a century ago by J. Willard Gibbs, who introduced a new quantity, now called the **Gibbs free energy** and given the symbol *G*. Gibbs showed that for a reaction taking place at constant pressure and temperature, ΔG represents that portion of the total energy change that is available (i.e., "free") to do useful work. If, for example, ΔG for a reaction is −270 kJ, it is possible to obtain 270 kJ of useful work from the reaction. Conversely, if ΔG is +270 kJ, at least that much energy in the form of work must be supplied to make the reaction take place.

A spontaneous process is capable of producing useful work.

The basic definition of the Gibbs free energy is

$$G = H - TS$$

where *T* is the absolute (Kelvin) temperature. The free energy of a substance, like its enthalpy and entropy, is a state property; its value is determined only by the state of a system, not by how it got there. Putting it another way, ΔG for a reaction depends only on the nature of products and reactants and the conditions (temperature, pressure, and concentration). It does *not* depend on the path by which the reaction is carried out.

CENGAGENOW™
Click Coached Problems for a self-study module on **thermodynamics and spontaneity.**

The sign of the free energy change can be used to determine the spontaneity of a reaction carried out at constant temperature and pressure.

1. ***If ΔG is negative, the reaction is spontaneous.***
2. ***If ΔG is positive, the reaction will not take place spontaneously.*** Instead, the reverse reaction will be spontaneous.
3. ***If ΔG is 0, the system is at equilibrium;*** there is no tendency for reaction to occur in either direction.

A system has its minimum free energy at equilibrium.

Putting it another way, ΔG is a measure of the driving force of a reaction. ***Reactions, at constant pressure and temperature, go in such a direction as to decrease the free energy of the system.*** This means that the direction in which a reaction takes place is determined by the relative free energies of products and reactants. If the products at the specified conditions of temperature, pressure, and concentration have a lower free energy than the reactants ($G_{products} < G_{reactants}$), the forward reaction will occur (Figure 17.5). If the reverse is true

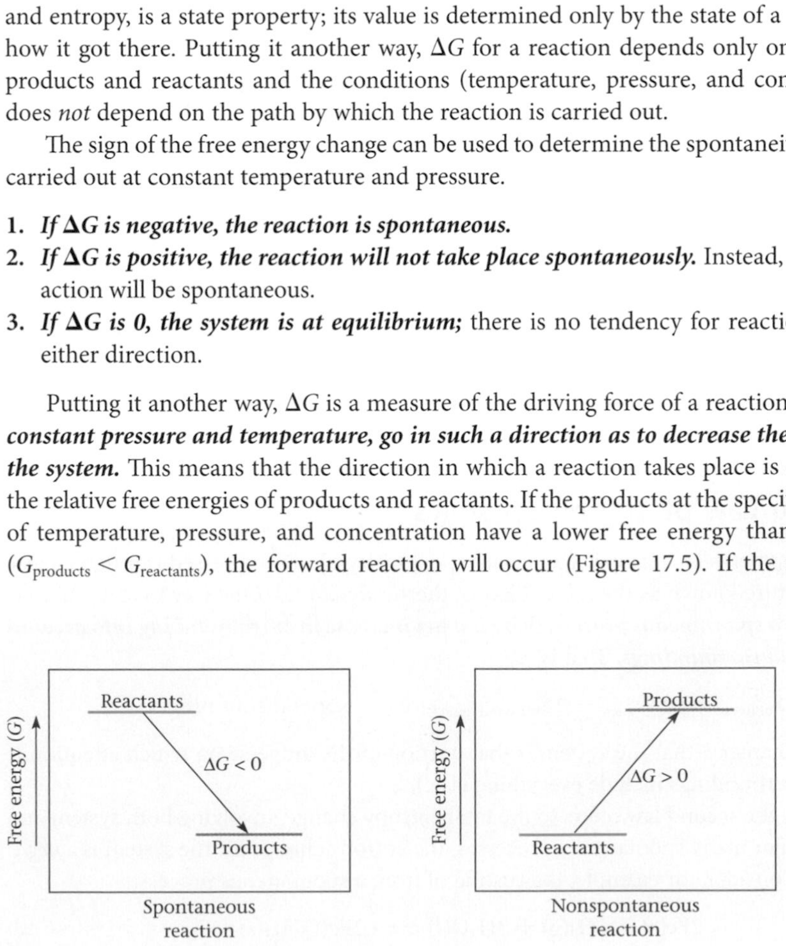

Figure 17.5
Sign of free energy and spontaneity. For a spontaneous reaction, the free energy of the products is less than that of the reactants: $\Delta G < 0$. For a nonspontaneous reaction, the reverse is true, $\Delta G > 0$.

CHEMISTRY The Human Side

Two theoreticians working in the latter half of the nineteenth century changed the very nature of chemistry by deriving the mathematical laws that govern the behavior of matter undergoing physical or chemical change. One of these was James Clerk Maxwell, whose contributions to kinetic theory were discussed in Chapter 5. The other was J. Willard Gibbs, Professor of Mathematical Physics at Yale from 1871 until his death in 1903.

J. Willard Gibbs (1839–1903)

In 1876 Gibbs published the first portion of a remarkable paper in the *Transactions of the Connecticut Academy of Sciences* titled, "On the Equilibrium of Heterogeneous Substances." When the paper was completed in 1878 (it was 323 pages long), the foundation was laid for the science of chemical thermodynamics. For the first time, the concept of free energy appeared. Included as well were the basic principles of chemical equilibrium (Chapter 12), phase equilibrium (Chapter 9), and the relations governing energy changes in electrical cells (Chapter 18).

If Gibbs had never published another paper, this single contribution would have placed him among the greatest theoreticians in the history of science. Generations of experimental scientists have established their reputations by demonstrating in the laboratory the validity of the relationships that Gibbs derived at his desk. Many of these relationships were rediscovered by others; an example is the Gibbs-Helmholtz equation developed in 1882 by Helmholtz, a prestigious German physiologist and physicist who was completely unaware of Gibbs's work.

J. Willard Gibbs is often cited as an example of the "prophet without honor in his own country." His colleagues in New Haven and elsewhere in the United States seem not to have realized the significance of his work until late in his life. During his first ten years as a professor at Yale he received no salary. In 1920, when he was first proposed for the Hall of Fame of Distinguished Americans at New York University, he received 9 votes out of a possible 100. Not until 1950 was he elected to that body. Even today the name of J. Willard Gibbs is generally unknown among educated Americans outside of those interested in the natural sciences.

They started paying him when he got an offer from Johns Hopkins.

Admittedly, Gibbs himself was largely responsible for the fact that for many years his work did not attract the attention it deserved. He made little effort to publicize it; the *Transactions of the Connecticut Academy of Sciences* was hardly the leading scientific journal of its day. Gibbs was one of those rare individuals who seem to have no inner need for recognition by contemporaries. His satisfaction came from solving a problem in his mind; having done so, he was ready to proceed to other problems. His papers are not easy to read; he seldom cites examples to illustrate his abstract reasoning. Frequently, the implications of the laws that he derives are left for the readers to grasp on their own. One of his colleagues at Yale confessed many years later that none of the members of the Connecticut Academy of Sciences understood his paper on thermodynamics; as he put it, "We knew Gibbs and took his contributions on faith."

($G_{\text{reactants}} < G_{\text{products}}$), the reverse reaction is spontaneous. Finally, if $G_{\text{products}} = G_{\text{reactants}}$, there is no driving force to make the reaction go in either direction.

Relation Among ΔG, ΔH, and ΔS

From the defining equation for free energy, it follows that at constant temperature

$$\Delta G = \Delta H - T\Delta S$$

where ΔG, ΔH, and ΔS are the changes in free energy, enthalpy, and entropy, respectively, for a reaction. This relation, known as the ***Gibbs-Helmholtz equation,*** is perhaps the most important equation in chemical thermodynamics. As you can see, two factors tend to make ΔG negative and hence lead to a spontaneous reaction:

1. ***A negative value of ΔH.*** Exothermic reactions ($\Delta H < 0$) tend to be spontaneous, inasmuch as they contribute to a negative value of ΔG. On the molecular level, this means that there will be a tendency to form "strong" bonds at the expense of "weak" ones.
2. ***A positive value of ΔS.*** If the entropy change is positive ($\Delta S > 0$), the term $-T\Delta S$ will make a negative contribution to ΔG. Hence there will be a tendency for a reaction to be spontaneous if the products are less ordered than the reactants.

In many physical changes, the entropy increase is the major driving force. This situation applies when two liquids with similar intermolecular forces, such as benzene (C_6H_6) and toluene (C_7H_8), are mixed. There is no change in enthalpy, but the entropy increases because the molecules of benzene and toluene are mixed randomly in solution.*

In certain reactions, ΔS is nearly zero, and ΔH is the only important component of the driving force for spontaneity. An example is the synthesis of hydrogen fluoride from the elements

$$\tfrac{1}{2}H_2(g) + \tfrac{1}{2}F_2(g) \longrightarrow HF(g)$$

For this reaction, ΔH is a large negative number, −271.1 kJ, showing that the bonds in HF are stronger than those in the H_2 and F_2 molecules. As you might expect for a gaseous reaction in which there is no change in the number of moles, ΔS is very small, about 0.0070 kJ/K. The free energy change, ΔG, at 1 atm is −273.2 kJ at 25°C, almost identical to ΔH. Even at very high temperatures, the difference between ΔG and ΔH is small, amounting to only about 14 kJ at 2000 K.

17.4 STANDARD FREE ENERGY CHANGE, $\Delta G°$

Although the Gibbs-Helmholtz equation is valid under all conditions we will apply it only under *standard conditions,* where—

"Standard conditions" has quite a different meaning from "STP."

- gases are at one atmosphere partial pressure.
- ions or molecules in solution are at one molar concentration.

In other words, we will use the equation in the form

$$\Delta G° = \Delta H° - T\Delta S° \qquad \textbf{(17.2)}$$

where $\Delta G°$ is the **standard free energy change** (1 atm, 1 *M*); $\Delta H°$ is the standard enthalpy change, which can be calculated from heats of formation, $\Delta H_f°$ (listed in Table 8.3, Chapter 8); and $\Delta S°$ is the standard entropy change (Table 17.1).

You will recall that the sign of ΔG can be correlated with the spontaneity of reaction. We can do the same thing with $\Delta G°$ provided we restrict our attention to standard conditions (1 atm, 1 *M*).

1. ***If $\Delta G°$ is negative, the reaction is spontaneous at standard conditions.*** For example, the following reaction is spontaneous at 25°C:

$$CaO(s) + CO_2(g, 1\ atm) \longrightarrow CaCO_3(s) \qquad \Delta G° \text{ at } 25°C = -130.4\ kJ$$

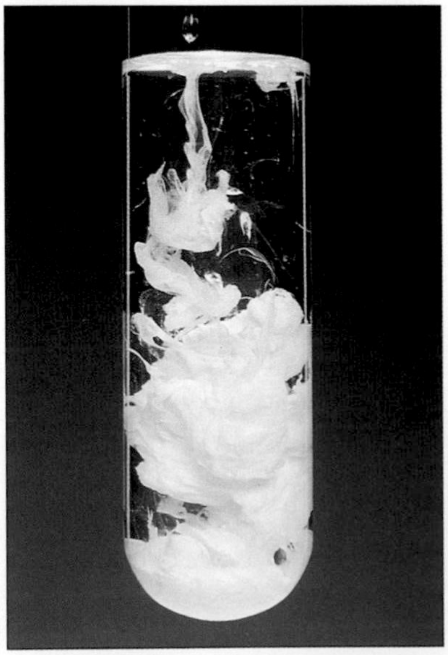

Charles D. Winters

Precipitation of silver chloride. A spontaneous reaction for which $\Delta G°$ is negative.

2. ***If $\Delta G°$ is positive, the reaction is nonspontaneous at standard conditions.*** The reaction

$$AgCl(s) \longrightarrow Ag^+(aq, 1\ M) + Cl^-(aq, 1\ M) \qquad \Delta G° \text{ at } 25°C = +55.7\ kJ$$

is nonspontaneous at 25°C. The reverse reaction is spontaneous; when solutions of $AgNO_3$ and HCl are mixed in such a way that $[Ag^+] = [Cl^-] = 1\ M$, silver chloride precipitates.

3. ***If $\Delta G°$ is 0, the system is at equilibrium at standard conditions;*** there is no tendency for the reaction to occur in either direction. An example is the vaporization of water at 100°C and 1 atm:

$$H_2O(l) \longrightarrow H_2O(g, 1\ atm) \qquad \Delta G° = 0$$

under these conditions (i.e., at the normal boiling point), the molar free energies of liquid and gaseous water are identical. Hence $\Delta G° = 0$ and the system is at equilibrium.

*The formation of a *water* solution is often accompanied by a *decrease* in entropy because hydrogen bonding or hydration effects lead to a highly ordered solution structure. Recall from Example 17.2 that when one mole of $Ca(OH)_2$ dissolves in water, $\Delta S° = -158.1$ J/K.

Calculation of $\Delta G°$ at 25°C; Free Energies of Formation

To illustrate the use of the Gibbs-Helmholtz equation

$$\Delta G° = \Delta H° - T\Delta S°$$

we apply it first to find $\Delta G°$ for a reaction at 25°C (Example 17.3). To do this, the units of $\Delta H°$ and $\Delta S°$ must be consistent. Using $\Delta H°$ in kilojoules, it is necessary to convert $\Delta S°$ from joules per kelvin to *kilojoules per kelvin.*

Example 17.3 Calcium sulfate, $CaSO_4$, is used as a drying agent and sold under the trade name Drierite. For the reaction

$$CaSO_4(s) \longrightarrow Ca^{2+}(aq) + SO_4^{2-}(aq),$$

calculate

(a) $\Delta H°$ (b) $\Delta S°$ (c) $\Delta G°$ at 25°C

Strategy $\Delta H°$ is calculated from Table 8.3, Chapter 8, using the relation

$$\Delta H° = \sum \Delta H°_{f\,products} - \sum \Delta H°_{f\,reactants}$$

$\Delta S°$ is obtained from Table 17.1 using the relation

$$\Delta S° = \sum S°_{products} - \sum S°_{reactants}$$

Convert $\Delta S°$ to kJ/K using the relation $1\ J = 10^{-3}\ kJ$. Finally, calculate $\Delta G°$ from the Gibbs-Helmholtz equation with $T = 298$ K.

SOLUTION

(a) $\Delta H° = \Delta H°_f\,Ca^{2+}(aq) + \Delta H°_f\,SO_4^{2-}(aq) - \Delta H°_f\,CaSO_4(s)$

$= -542.8\ kJ - 909.3\ kJ - (-1434.1\ kJ) = -18.0\ kJ$

(b) $\Delta S° = S°\ Ca^{2+}(aq) + S°\ SO_4^{2-}(aq) - S°\ CaSO_4(s)$

$= -53.1\ J/K + 20.1\ J/K - 106.7\ J/K = -139.7\ J/K$

$= -139.7\dfrac{J}{K} \times \dfrac{10^{-3}\ kJ}{1\ J} = -0.1397\dfrac{kJ}{K}$

This conversion is necessary to find $\Delta G°$ in kilojoules.

(c) $\Delta G° = \Delta H° - T\Delta S°$

$= -18.0\ kJ - 298\ K \times (-0.1397\ kJ/K) = +23.6\ kJ$

Reality Check $\Delta G°$ is positive, so this reaction at standard conditions

$$CaSO_4(s) \longrightarrow Ca^{2+}(aq, 1\ M) + SO_4^{2-}(aq, 1\ M)$$

should not be spontaneous. In other words, calcium sulfate should not dissolve in water to give a 1 *M* solution. This is indeed the case. The solubility of $CaSO_4$ at 25°C is considerably less than 1 mol/L.

The Gibbs-Helmholtz equation can be used to calculate the **standard free energy of formation** of a compound. This quantity, $\Delta G°_f$, is analogous to the enthalpy of formation, $\Delta H°_f$. It is defined as the free energy change per mole when a compound is formed from the elements in their stable states at 1 atm.

Tables of standard free energies of formation at 25°C of compounds and ions in solution are given in Appendix 1 (along with standard heats of formation and standard entropies). Notice that, for most compounds, $\Delta G°_f$ is a negative quantity, which means that the compound can be formed spontaneously from the elements. This is true for water:

$\Delta G°_f$ for an element, like $\Delta H°_f$, is zero.

$$H_2(g) + \tfrac{1}{2}O_2(g) \longrightarrow H_2O(l) \qquad \Delta G°_f\,H_2O(l) = -237.2\ kJ/mol$$

and, at least in principle, for methane:

$$C(s) + 2H_2(g) \longrightarrow CH_4(g) \qquad \Delta G_f^\circ CH_4(g) = -50.7 \text{ kJ/mol}$$

A few compounds, including acetylene, have positive free energies of formation ($\Delta G_f^\circ C_2H_2(g)$ $= +209.2$ kJ/mol). These compounds cannot be made from the elements at ordinary temperatures and pressures; indeed, they are potentially unstable with respect to the elements. In the case of acetylene, the reaction

$$C_2H_2(g) \longrightarrow 2C(s) + H_2(g) \qquad \Delta G^\circ \text{ at } 25°C = -209.2 \text{ kJ}$$

occurs with explosive violence unless special precautions are taken.

Values of ΔG_f° can be used to calculate free energy changes for reactions. The relationship is entirely analogous to that given for enthalpies in Chapter 8:

$$\Delta G^\circ_{\text{reaction}} = \sum \Delta G_f^\circ{}_{\text{products}} - \sum \Delta G_f^\circ{}_{\text{reactants}} \qquad \textbf{(17.3)}$$

To find ΔG° at temperatures other than 25°C, use the Gibbs-Helmholtz equation.

If you calculate ΔG° in this way, you should keep in mind an important limitation. ***$\Delta G^\circ_{\text{reaction}}$ is valid only at the temperature at which ΔG_f° data are tabulated, in this case 25°C.*** ΔG° varies considerably with temperature, so this approach is not even approximately valid at other temperatures.

Example 17.4 Using ΔG_f° values from Appendix 1, calculate the standard free energy change at 25°C for the reaction referred to in Example 17.3.

Strategy Use Equation 17.3.

SOLUTION

$$\Delta G^\circ = \Delta G_f^\circ Ca^{2+}(aq) + \Delta G_f^\circ SO_4{}^{2-}(aq) - \Delta G_f^\circ CaSO_4(s)$$
$$= -553.6 \text{ kJ} - 744.5 \text{ kJ} + 1321.8 \text{ kJ} = +23.7 \text{ kJ}$$

Reality Check Notice that the value of ΔG° at 25°C is essentially identical with that obtained in Example 17.3, which is reassuring.

Calculation of ΔG° at Other Temperatures

CENGAGENOW™
Click Coached Problems for a self-study module on **free energy: temperature, ΔS, and ΔH.**

To a good degree of approximation, the temperature variation of ΔH° and ΔS° can be neglected.* This means that to apply the Gibbs-Helmholtz equation

$$\Delta G^\circ = \Delta H^\circ - T\Delta S^\circ$$

at temperatures other than 25°C, you need only change the value of T. The quantities ΔH° and ΔS° can be calculated in the usual way from tables of standard enthalpies and entropies.

Example 17.5 Iron, a large component of steel, is obtained by reducing iron(III) oxide (present in hematite ore) with hydrogen in a blast furnace. Steam is a byproduct of the reaction. Calculate ΔS° at 230°C for the reduction of one mole of Fe_2O_3.

Strategy The first step is to write a balanced equation for the chemical reaction. Then calculate ΔH° using Table 8.3 (page 209) and ΔS° using Table 17.1 (page 456). Finally, use the Gibbs-Helmholtz equation to determine ΔG° at 230°C (3 sig. fig.)

*As far as the Gibbs-Helmholtz equation is concerned, there is another reason for ignoring the temperature dependence of ΔH and ΔS. These two quantities always change in the same direction as the temperature changes (i.e., if ΔH becomes more positive, so does ΔS). Hence the two effects tend to cancel each other.

SOLUTION

$$Fe_2O_3(s) + 3H_2(g) \longrightarrow 2Fe(s) + 3H_2O(g)$$

$$\Delta H° = 3\,\Delta H_f° H_2O(g) - \Delta H_f° Fe_2O_3(s) = -725.4\text{ kJ} + 824.2\text{ kJ} = +98.8\text{ kJ}$$

$$\Delta S° = 3S°\, H_2O(g) + 2S°\, Fe(s) - 3S°\, H_2(g) - S°\, Fe_2O_3(s)$$

$$= 566.1\text{ J/K} + 54.6\text{ J/K} - 391.8\text{ J/K} - 87.4\text{ J/K} = +141.5\text{ J/K} = +0.1415\text{ kJ/K}$$

The Gibbs-Helmholtz equation becomes

$$\Delta G° = +98.8\text{ kJ} - T(0.1415\text{ kJ/K})$$

$$= +98.8\text{ kJ} - 503\text{ K}(0.1415\text{ kJ/K}) = +27.6\text{ kJ}$$

From Example 17.5 and the preceding discussion, it should be clear that $\Delta G°$, unlike $\Delta H°$ and $\Delta S°$, is strongly dependent on temperature. This comes about, of course, because of the T in the Gibbs-Helmholtz equation:

$$\Delta G° = \Delta H° - T\Delta S°$$

Comparing this equation with that of a straight line,

$$y = b + mx$$

it is clear that a plot of $\Delta G°$ versus T should be linear, with a slope of $-\Delta S°$ and a y-intercept (at 0 K) of $\Delta H°$ (Figure 17.6).

17.5 EFFECT OF TEMPERATURE, PRESSURE, AND CONCENTRATION ON REACTION SPONTANEITY

A change in reaction conditions can, and often does, change the direction in which a reaction occurs spontaneously. The Gibbs-Helmholtz equation in the form

$$\Delta G° = \Delta H° - T\Delta S°$$

is readily applied to deduce the effect of temperature on reaction spontaneity. To consider the effect of pressure or concentration, we need an analogous expression for the dependence of ΔG on these factors.

Temperature

When the temperature of a reaction system is increased, the sign of $\Delta G°$, and hence the direction in which the reaction proceeds spontaneously, may or may not change. Whether it does or does not depends on the signs of $\Delta H°$ and $\Delta S°$. The four possible situations, deduced from the Gibbs-Helmholtz equation, are summarized in Table 17.2 (p. 464).

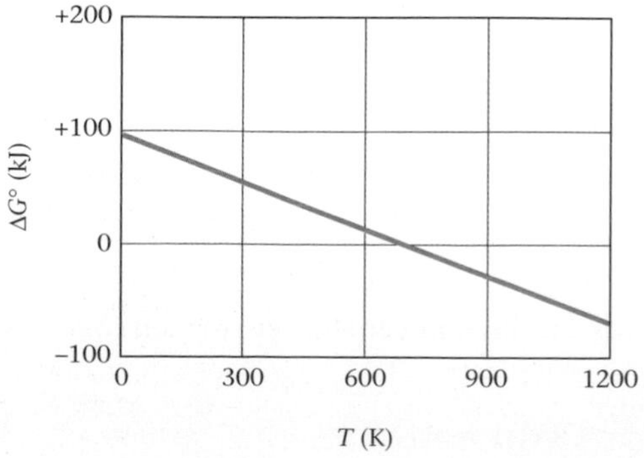

Figure 17.6
Variation of $\Delta G°$ with T. For the reaction:

$$Fe_2O_3(s) + 3H_2(g) \longrightarrow 2Fe(s) + 3H_2O(g)$$

$\Delta G°$ decreases from +98.8 kJ at 0 K (the value of $\Delta H°$), to +27.6 kJ at 503 K, 0.0 kJ at 698 K, and −71.0 kJ at 1200 K.

Table 17.2 Effect of Temperature on Reaction Spontaneity

	$\Delta H°$	$\Delta S°$	$\Delta G° = \Delta H° - T\Delta S°$	Remarks
I	−	+	Always −	Spontaneous at all *T*; reverse reaction always nonspontaneous
II	+	−	Always +	Nonspontaneous at all *T*; reverse reaction occurs
III	+	+	+ at low *T* − at high *T*	Nonspontaneous at low *T*; becomes spontaneous as *T* is raised
IV	−	−	− at low *T* + at high *T*	Spontaneous at low *T*; at high *T*, reverse reaction becomes spontaneous

If $\Delta H°$ and $\Delta S°$ have opposite signs (Table 17.2, I and II), it is impossible to reverse the direction of spontaneity by a change in temperature alone. The two terms $\Delta H°$ and $-T\Delta S°$ reinforce one another. Hence $\Delta G°$ has the same sign at all temperatures. Reactions of this type are rather uncommon. One such reaction is

$$Cu(s) + H_2O(g) \longrightarrow CuO(s) + H_2(g)$$

Here $\Delta H°$ is +84.5 kJ and $\Delta S°$ is −0.0487 kJ/K. Hence

$$\Delta G° = \Delta H° - T\Delta S°$$
$$= +84.5 \text{ kJ} + T(0.0487 \text{ kJ/K})$$

Copper metal doesn't react with water vapor, period.

Clearly $\Delta G°$ is positive at all temperatures. The reaction cannot take place spontaneously at 1 atm regardless of temperature.

It is more common to find that $\Delta H°$ and $\Delta S°$ have the same sign (Table 17.2, III and IV). When this happens, the enthalpy and entropy factors oppose each other. $\Delta G°$ changes sign as temperature increases, and the direction of spontaneity reverses. At low temperatures, $\Delta H°$ predominates, and the exothermic reaction, which may be either the forward or the reverse reaction, occurs. As the temperature rises, the quantity $T\Delta S°$ increases in magnitude and eventually exceeds $\Delta H°$. At high temperatures, the reaction that leads to an increase in entropy occurs. In most cases, 25°C is a "low" temperature, at least at a pressure of 1 atm. This explains why exothermic reactions are usually spontaneous at room temperature and atmospheric pressure.

An example of a reaction for which $\Delta H°$ and $\Delta S°$ have the same sign is the decomposition of calcium carbonate:

$$CaCO_3(s) \longrightarrow CaO(s) + CO_2(g)$$

Here $\Delta H° = +178.3$ kJ and $\Delta S° = +160.5$ J/K. Hence

$$\Delta G° = +178.3 \text{ kJ} - T(0.1605 \text{ kJ/K})$$

For this reaction at "low" temperatures, such as 298 K,

$$\Delta G° = +178.3 \text{ kJ} - 47.8 \text{ kJ} = +130.5 \text{ kJ}$$

the $\Delta H°$ term predominates, $\Delta G°$ is positive, and the reaction is nonspontaneous at 1 atm. Conversely, at "high" temperatures, such as 2000 K,

$$\Delta G° = +178.3 \text{ kJ} - 321.0 \text{ kJ} = -142.7 \text{ kJ}$$

CaO is made commercially by heating $CaCO_3$.

the $T\Delta S°$ term predominates, $\Delta G°$ is negative, and the reaction is spontaneous at 1 atm.

Example 17.6 At what temperature does $\Delta G°$ become zero for the reaction considered in Example 17.5?

$$Fe_2O_3(s) + 3H_2(g) \longrightarrow 2Fe(s) + 3H_2O(g)$$

Strategy This is another application of the Gibbs-Helmholtz equation. Setting $\Delta G° = 0$ gives $\Delta H° = T\Delta S°$; solving for T gives $T = \Delta H°/\Delta S°$. Since you know $\Delta H°$ and $\Delta S°$, T is readily calculated.

SOLUTION In Example 17.5, you found that

$$\Delta H° = 98.8 \text{ kJ} \qquad \Delta S° = 0.1415 \text{ kJ/K}$$

So,

$$T = \frac{\Delta H°}{\Delta S°} = \frac{98.8 \text{ kJ}}{0.1415 \text{ kJ/K}} = 698 \text{ K}$$

The development presented in Example 17.6 is an important one from a practical standpoint. It tells us the temperature at which the direction of spontaneity changes. In the reduction of Fe_2O_3 by hydrogen, this temperature is approximately 700 K. At lower temperatures, the reaction does not occur at standard conditions; recall from Example 17.5 that $\Delta G°$ at 500 K is +27.6 kJ. At temperatures above 700 K, $\Delta G°$ has a negative sign and the reaction

$$Fe_2O_3(s) + 3H_2(g) \longrightarrow 2Fe(s) + 3H_2O(g)$$

is spontaneous.

From a slightly different point of view, we can say that the equation $T = \Delta H°/\Delta S°$ allows us to calculate the temperature at which a chemical or physical change is at equilibrium at 1 atm pressure. Consider, for example, the vaporization of water:

$$H_2O(l) \longrightarrow H_2O(g)$$

where $\Delta H° = +40.7$ kJ, $\Delta S° = +0.109$ kJ/K. The temperature at which $\Delta G°$ is zero is

$$T = \frac{40.7}{0.109} \qquad T = 373 \quad K = 100°\text{C}$$

This is, of course, the normal boiling point of water (the temperature at which liquid water is at equilibrium with vapor at 1 atm).

Pressure and Concentration

P and *T* affect ΔG but not ΔH; *P* affects ΔS.

All of the free energy calculations to this point have involved the standard free energy change, $\Delta G°$. It is possible, however, to write a general relation for the free energy change, ΔG, valid under any conditions. This relation is a relatively simple one, but we will not attempt to derive it. It tells us that

If $Q < 1$, $\Delta G < \Delta G°$. Explain.

$$\Delta G = \Delta G° + RT \ln Q \qquad \textbf{(17.4)}$$

The quantity Q that appears in this equation is the "reaction quotient" referred to in Chapter 12. It has the same mathematical form as the equilibrium constant, K; the difference is that the terms that appear in Q are arbitrary, initial pressures or concentrations rather than equilibrium values.

To use this general expression for ΔG, you need to express T in degrees K, R in kilojoules per kelvin (8.31×10^{-3} kJ/K). As far as Q is concerned, the general rules are as follows:

- gases enter as their partial pressures in atmospheres.
- species in aqueous solution enter as their molar concentrations.
- pure liquids or solids do not appear; neither does the solvent in a dilute solution.

As an example, consider the reaction of zinc with strong acid:

$$Zn(s) + 2H^+(aq) \longrightarrow Zn^{2+}(aq) + H_2(g)$$

Here Equation 17.4 would take the following form:

$$\Delta G = \Delta G° + RT \ln \frac{[Zn^{2+}] \times P_{H_2}}{[H^+]^2}$$

Example 17.7 Graded

When zinc is dissolved in a strong acid, zinc ions and hydrogen gas are produced.

$$Zn(s) + 2H^+(aq) \longrightarrow Zn^{2+}(aq) + H_2(g)$$

At 25°C, calculate

*(a) $\Delta G°$.
**(b) ΔG when $P_{H_2} = 750$ mm Hg, $Zn^{2+} = 0.10\ M$, $[H^+] = 1.0 \times 10^{-4}\ M$.
***(c) the pH when $\Delta G = -100.0$ kJ, $P_{H_2} = 0.933$ atm, $[Zn^{2+}] = 0.220\ M$ and the mass of Zn is 155 g.

SOLUTION

(a) $\Delta G°$ at 25°C can be calculated from free energies of formation. Since $\Delta G_f°$ for H_2, Zn, and H^+ are all zero:

$$\Delta G° = \Delta G_f° Zn^{2+}(aq) = -147.1 \text{ kJ}$$

(b) Substitute into the above equation for ΔG. Note that the pressure of H_2 must be expressed in atmospheres.

$$\Delta G = -147.1 \text{ kJ} + (8.31 \times 10^{-3} \text{ kJ/K})(298 \text{ K}) \ln \frac{(0.10)(750/760)}{(1.0 \times 10^{-4})^2}$$
$$= -147.1 \text{ kJ} + 39.9 \text{ kJ} = -107.2 \text{ kJ}$$

(c) Substitute into the above equation for ΔG and solve for $[H^+]$, then for pH.

$$-100.0 \text{ kJ} = -147.1 \text{ kJ} + \left(\frac{8.31 \times 10^{-3} \text{ kJ}}{1 \text{ K}}\right)(298 \text{ K}) \ln\left[\frac{(0.220)(0.933)}{[H^+]^2}\right]$$

$$47.1 \text{ kJ} = \left(\frac{8.31 \times 10^{-3} \text{ kJ}}{1 \text{ K}}\right)(298 \text{ K}) \ln\left[\frac{0.205}{[H^+]^2}\right]$$

$$\ln\left[\frac{0.205}{[H^+]^2}\right] = 19.0 \qquad \frac{0.205}{[H^+]^2} = e^{19}$$

$$[H^+] = 3.39 \times 10^{-5}$$
$$pH = -\log_{10}(3.39 \times 10^{-5}) = 4.47$$

As Example 17.7 implies, changes in pressure and/or concentration can have a considerable effect on ΔG. Sometimes, when $\Delta G°$ is close to zero, changing the pressure from 1 atm to some other value can change the direction of spontaneity. Consider, for example, the reaction at 300°C:

$$NH_4Cl(s) \longrightarrow NH_3(g) + HCl(g) \qquad \Delta G° = +13.0 \text{ kJ}$$

The positive sign of $\Delta G°$ implies that ammonium chloride will not decompose at 300°C to give NH_3 and HCl, both at 1 atm pressure. However, notice what happens if $P_{NH_3} = P_{HCl} = 0.10$ atm, in which case $Q = (0.10)^2$:

$$\Delta G = \Delta G° + RT \ln(0.10)^2$$
$$= +13.0 \text{ kJ} + (8.31 \times 10^{-3})(573) \text{ kJ} \times \ln 0.010$$
$$= +13.0 \text{ kJ} - 21.9 \text{ kJ} = -8.9 \text{ kJ}$$

This means that NH_3 and HCl *can* be formed, each at 0.10 atm pressure, by heating ammonium chloride to 300°C.

Another example of how a change in concentration can change the direction of spontaneity involves the reaction

$$SrCrO_4(s) \longrightarrow Sr^{2+}(aq) + CrO_4^{2-}(aq) \qquad \Delta G° = +25.3 \text{ kJ at 25°C}$$

Because ΔG° is a positive quantity, $SrCrO_4$ does not dissolve spontaneously to form a 1 *M* solution at 25°C (Figure 17.7). Suppose, however, the concentrations of Sr^{2+} and CrO_4^{2-} are reduced to 0.0010 *M*:

$$\begin{aligned}\Delta G &= \Delta G^\circ + RT \ln [Sr^{2+}] \times [CrO_4^{2-}] \\ &= +25.3\text{ kJ} + (8.31 \times 10^{-3})(298)\text{ kJ} \times [\ln (1.0 \times 10^{-3})^2] \\ &= +25.3\text{ kJ} - 34.2\text{ kJ} = -8.9\text{ kJ}\end{aligned}$$

Strontium chromate should, and does, dissolve spontaneously to form a 0.0010 *M* water solution. As you might expect, its solubility at 25°C lies between 1 *M* and 0.0010 *M*, at about 0.0060 *M*.

$$\Delta G \text{ at } 0.0060\ M = +25.3\text{ kJ} + RT \ln (0.0060)^2 = 0$$

17.6 THE FREE ENERGY CHANGE AND THE EQUILIBRIUM CONSTANT

Throughout this chapter we have stressed the relation between the free energy change and reaction spontaneity. For a reaction to be spontaneous at standard conditions (1 atm, 1 *M*), ΔG° must be negative. Another indicator of reaction spontaneity is the equilibrium constant, *K*; if *K* is greater than 1, the reaction is spontaneous at standard conditions. As you might suppose, the two quantities ΔG° and *K* are related. The nature of that relationship is readily deduced by starting with the general equation

Remember, when $\Delta G = 0$, the system is at equilibrium.

$$\Delta G = \Delta G^\circ + RT \ln Q$$

Suppose now that reaction takes place until equilibrium is established, at which point $Q = K$ and $\Delta G = 0$.

$$0 = \Delta G^\circ + RT \ln K$$

or

$$\Delta G^\circ = -RT \ln K \qquad \textbf{(17.5)}$$

The equation just written is generally applicable to any system. The equilibrium constant may be the *K* referred to in our discussion of gaseous equilibrium (Chapter 12), or any of the solution equilibrium constants (K_w, K_a, K_b, K_{sp}, . . .) discussed in subsequent chapters. Notice that ΔG° is the *standard* free energy change (gases at *1 atm*, species in solution at 1 *M*). That is why, in the expression for *K*, gases enter as their partial pressures in *atmospheres* and ions or molecules in solution as their *molarities*.

Charles D. Winters

Figure 17.7
A saturated solution of strontium chromate. The solution of $SrCrO_4$ contains 0.006 mol/L of Sr^{2+} and CrO_4^{2-}. For the reaction at 25°C: $SrCrO_4(s) \rightleftharpoons Sr^{2+}(aq, 0.006\ M) + CrO_4^{2-}(aq, 0.006\ M)$, $\Delta G = 0$.

Example 17.8 Using ΔG_f° tables in Appendix 1, calculate the solubility product constant, K_{sp}, for $PbCl_2$ at 25°C.

Strategy Use free energies of formation to calculate ΔG° for the reaction

$$PbCl_2(s) \longrightarrow Pb^{2+}(aq) + 2Cl^-(aq)$$

Then use Equation 17.5 to calculate K_{sp}.

SOLUTION

$$\begin{aligned}\Delta G^\circ &= \Delta G_f^\circ Pb^{2+}(aq) + 2\,\Delta G_f^\circ Cl^-(aq) - \Delta G_f^\circ PbCl_2(s) \\ &= -24.4\text{ kJ} + 2(-131.2\text{ kJ}) + 314.1\text{ kJ} = +27.3\text{ kJ}\end{aligned}$$

$$\ln K_{sp} = \frac{-\Delta G^\circ}{RT} = \frac{-27.3\ \text{kJ}}{(8.31 \times 10^{-3}\ \text{kJ/K})(298\ \text{K})} = -11.0$$

$$K_{sp} = e^{-11.0} = 1.7 \times 10^{-5}$$

Reality Check This is the value listed in Chapter 16 for K_{sp} of $PbCl_2$.

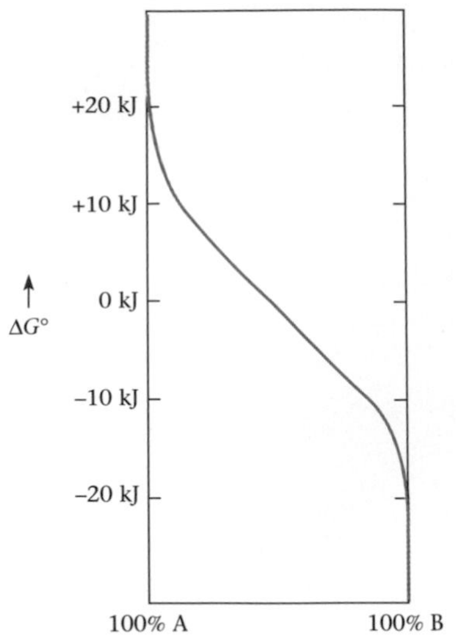

Figure 17.8
Dependence of extent of reaction on the value of $\Delta G°$ for the general system $A(g) \rightleftharpoons B(g)$.

The relationship $\Delta G° = -RT \ln K$ allows us to relate the standard free energy change to the extent of reaction. Consider, for example, the simple equilibrium system

$$A(g) \rightleftharpoons B(g)$$

at 25°C. Figure 17.8 shows how the extent of reaction varies with the value of $\Delta G°$ for this system. Notice that—

- if $\Delta G°$ is greater than about +20 kJ, the equilibrium constant is so small that virtually no A is converted to B. We would say that, for all practical purposes, the reaction does not occur.
- if $\Delta G°$ is less than about −20 kJ, the equilibrium constant is so large that virtually all of A is converted to B. In essence, the reaction goes to completion.
- only if $\Delta G°$ lies between +20 kJ and −20 kJ will the equilibrium mixture contain appreciable amounts of both A and B. In particular, if $\Delta G° = 0$, $K = 1$ and the equilibrium system contains equal amounts of A and B.

17.7 ADDITIVITY OF FREE ENERGY CHANGES; COUPLED REACTIONS

Free energy changes for reactions, like enthalpy or entropy changes, are additive. That is,

$$\text{if Reaction 3} = \text{Reaction 1} + \text{Reaction 2}$$
$$\text{then } \Delta G_3 = \Delta G_1 + \Delta G_2$$

This relation can be regarded as the free energy equivalent of Hess's law (Chapter 8). To illustrate its application, consider the synthesis of $CuCl_2$ from the elements

$$Cu(s) + \tfrac{1}{2}Cl_2(g) \longrightarrow CuCl(s) \qquad \Delta G° \text{ at } 25°C = -119.9\ \text{kJ}$$
$$CuCl(s) + \tfrac{1}{2}Cl_2(g) \longrightarrow CuCl_2(s) \qquad \Delta G° \text{ at } 25°C = -55.8\ \text{kJ}$$
$$Cu(s) + Cl_2(g) \longrightarrow CuCl_2(s)$$

For the overall reaction, $\Delta G°$ at 25°C = −119.9 kJ − 55.8 kJ = −175.7 kJ.

Because free energy changes are additive, it is often possible to bring about a nonspontaneous reaction by coupling it with a reaction for which $\Delta G°$ is a large negative number. As an example, consider the preparation of iron metal from hematite ore. The reaction

$$Fe_2O_3(s) \longrightarrow 2Fe(s) + \tfrac{3}{2}O_2(g) \qquad \Delta G° \text{ at } 25°C = +742.2\ \text{kJ}$$

is clearly nonspontaneous; even at temperatures as high as 2000°C, $\Delta G°$ is a positive quantity. Suppose, though, that this reaction is "coupled" with the spontaneous oxidation of carbon monoxide:

$$CO(g) + \tfrac{1}{2}O_2(g) \longrightarrow CO_2(g) \qquad \Delta G° \text{ at } 25°C = -257.2\ \text{kJ}$$

The overall reaction is spontaneous:

$$Fe_2O_3(s) \longrightarrow 2Fe(s) + \tfrac{3}{2}O_2(g)$$
$$3CO(g) + \tfrac{3}{2}O_2(g) \longrightarrow 3CO_2(g)$$
$$Fe_2O_3(s) + 3CO(g) \longrightarrow 2Fe(s) + 3CO_2(g)$$

For the coupled reaction at 25°C,

$$\Delta G° = +742.2\ \text{kJ} + 3(-257.2\ \text{kJ}) = -29.4\ \text{kJ}$$

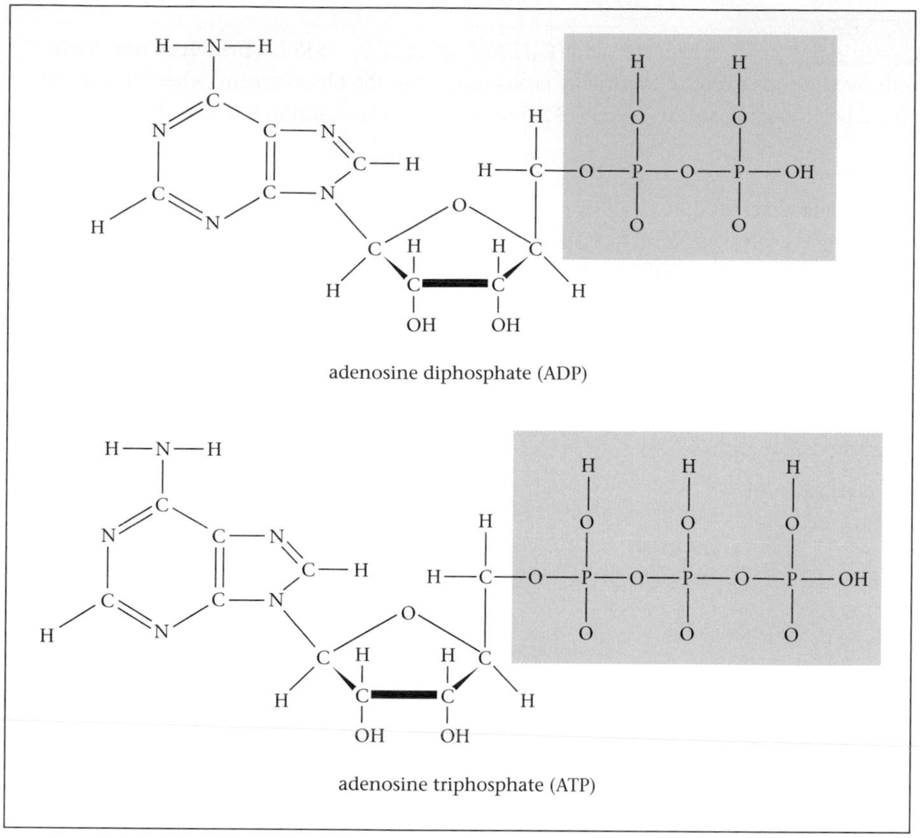

Figure 17.9
Structures of ADP and ATP.

The negative sign of $\Delta G°$ implies that although Fe_2O_3 does not spontaneously decompose, it can be converted to iron by reaction with carbon monoxide. This is in fact the reaction used in the blast furnace when iron ore consisting mainly of Fe_2O_3 is reduced to iron (Chapter 20).

Many industrial processes involve coupled reactions.

Coupled reactions are common in human metabolism. Spontaneous processes, such as the oxidation of glucose,

$$C_6H_{12}O_6(aq) + 6\,O_2(g) \longrightarrow 6CO_2(g) + 6H_2O \qquad \Delta G° = -2870 \text{ kJ at } 25°C$$

ordinarily do not serve directly as a source of energy. Instead these reactions are used to bring about a nonspontaneous reaction:

$$ADP(aq) + HPO_4^{2-}(aq) + 2H^+(aq) \longrightarrow ATP(aq) + H_2O \qquad \textbf{(17.6)}$$
$$\Delta G° = +31 \text{ kJ at } 25°C$$

ADP (adenosine diphosphate) and ATP (adenosine triphosphate) are complex organic molecules (Fig. 17.9) that, in essence, differ only by the presence of an extra phosphate group in ATP. In the coupled reaction with glucose, about 38 mol of ATP are synthesized for every mole of glucose consumed. This gives an overall free energy change for the coupled reaction of

$$-2870 \text{ kJ} + 38(+31 \text{ kJ}) \approx -1700 \text{ kJ}$$

In a very real sense, your body "stores" energy available from the metabolism of foods in the form of ATP. This molecule in turn supplies the energy required for all sorts of biochemical reactions taking place in the body. It does this by reverting to ADP, that is, by reversing reaction 17.6. The amount of ATP consumed is amazingly large; a competitive sprinter may hydrolyze as much as 500 g (about 1 lb) of ATP per minute.

Conversion of ATP to ADP gives you energy in a hurry.

Example 17.9 The lactic acid ($C_3H_6O_3(aq)$, $\Delta G_f^\circ = -559$ kJ) produced in muscle cells by vigorous exercise eventually is absorbed into the bloodstream, where it is metabolized back to glucose ($\Delta G_f^\circ = -919$ kJ) in the liver. The reaction is

$$2C_3H_6O_3(aq) \longrightarrow C_6H_{12}O_6(aq)$$

(a) Calculate ΔG° at 25°C for this reaction, using free energies of formation.
(b) If the hydrolysis of ATP to ADP is coupled with this reaction, how many moles of ATP must react to make the process spontaneous?

Strategy Use the relation

$$\Delta G^\circ = \sum \Delta G^\circ_{f\,products} - \sum \Delta G^\circ_{f\,reactants}$$

to find ΔG°. To solve part (b), note that 31 kJ of energy is produced per mole of ATP consumed (Equation 17.6).

SOLUTION

(a) $\Delta G^\circ = \Delta G_f^\circ C_6H_{12}O_6(aq) - 2\,\Delta G_f^\circ C_3H_6O_3(aq)$
$= -919\text{ kJ} + 2(559\text{ kJ}) = +199\text{ kJ}$

(b) $199\text{ kJ} \times \dfrac{1\text{ mol ATP}}{31\text{ kJ}} = 6.4\text{ mol ATP}$

CHEMISTRY Beyond the Classroom

Rubber Elasticity: An Entropic Phenomenon

Leslie Sperling, Lehigh University

Molecular Structure of Rubbery Materials

Along with such materials as plastics, adhesives, fibers, and coatings, rubber is polymeric in nature. Such materials consist of long chains, with molecular masses generally of the order of 50,000 to 500,000 g/mol. Common rubbery materials—often called elastomers—include automotive tires and rubber bands.

For a polymer to exhibit rubber elasticity, it must have two properties:

1. It must be *crosslinked* or *vulcanized.* Crosslinking is the chemical joining together of polymer chains, usually by sulfur bonds at random positions, to make a three-dimensional network (see Figure A).
2. It must be above its glass transition temperature, which means that the polymer chains have sufficient thermal energy to move freely. Many rubbery materials have glass transition temperatures around 200 K, below which they are glassy, like plastics.

Common rubbery materials consist of butadiene and styrene statistical copolymers, written poly(butadiene-*stat*-styrene). The butadiene polymer has the repeating structure ($—CH_2—CH{=}CH—CH_2^-$) while styrene has the repeating structure

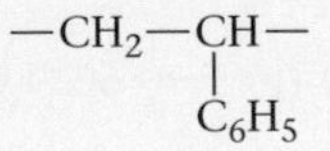

How Does Entropy Apply to Elastomeric Materials?

Entropy is a measure of disorder in materials. Relaxed polymer chains with a random conformation (shape in space), like cooked spaghetti or a box of fishing worms, have a high degree of entropy, which is favored by Mother Nature. If the chains are stretched out (stressed), the number of conformations the chains can have in space is limited, and the entropy is reduced (see Figure B). The ratio of final length to initial length is denoted α.

For materials such as rubber bands, the quantity α may be as large as five. At that point, the chains are substantially fully extended. Further stretching may break the rubber band, actually severing the polymer chains at the break point (a chemical reaction!).

There is an interesting demonstration experiment that you can do with a rubber band, preferably a large and/or thick one. Touch the unstretched rubber band to your lips. Then, stretch the rubber band rapidly and immediately, retouch it to your lips. The rubber band will be warmer. This motion creates a thermodynamic cycle in which the system goes through a series of different states and then returns to its original state. The cycle acts as a heat engine.

The major applications of rubbery materials today include automotive tires, rubber bands, tubing of various kinds, electric wire insulation, elastomeric urethane fibers for undergarments, and silicone rubber. Such types of polymers are important materials in our 21st-century world.

References

1. A. J. Etzel, S. J. Goldstein, H. J. Panabaker, D. G. Fradkin, and L. H. Sperling, *J. Chem. Ed.,* **63,** 731 (1986).
2. L. H. Sperling, *Introduction to Physical Polymer Science,* 4th Ed., Wiley, New York, 2006.

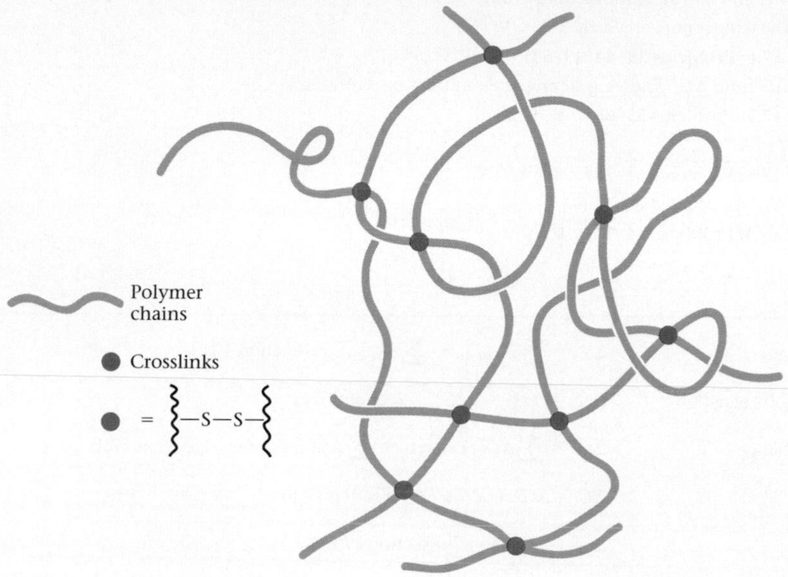

Figure A
Schematic of polymer chains randomly placed in space, with crosslinks also placed randomly, but frequently averaging every 5,000-10,000 g/mol along the chains.

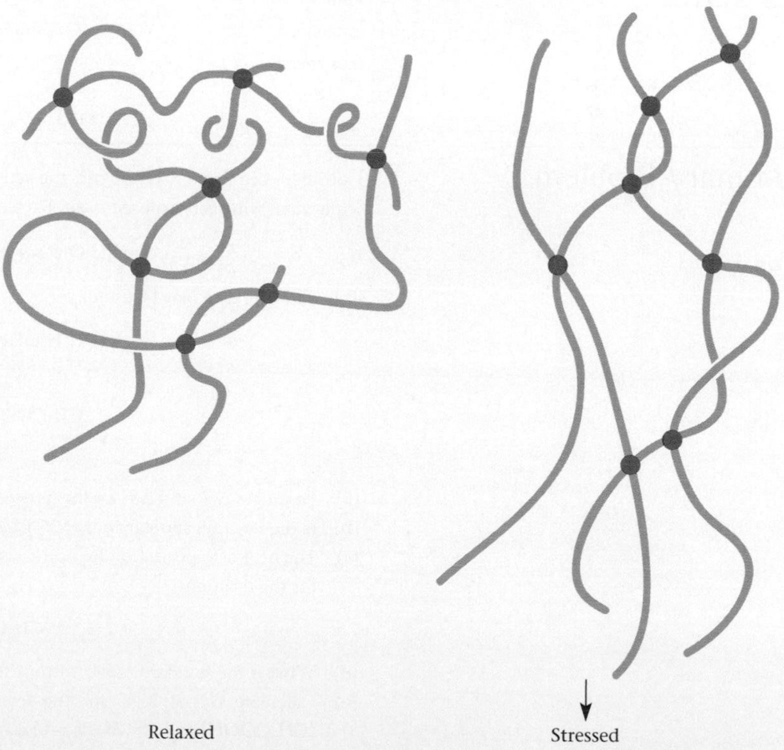

Figure B
Pulling down on the elastomer. The chains become oriented in the elongational direction, lowering the entropy of the system.

Chapter Highlights

Key Concepts

Select end of chapter Questions and Problems may be assigned in OWL and are cross-referenced in the Key Concepts list.

CENGAGENOW™

Sign in at **academic.cengage.com/now** to:

- Check your readiness for an exam by taking the Pre-Test and exploring the self-study modules recommended in your Personalized Study plan
- For quick review, download Go Chemistry mini-lecture flashcard modules (or purchase them at **www.ichapters.com**)

1. Deduce the sign of ΔS for a process from randomness considerations.
   (Example 17.1; Problems 7–14) ■ Questions and Problems assignable in OWL: 6, 8, 10, 16
2. Calculate $\Delta S°$ for a reaction, using Table 17.1.
   (Example 17.2; Problems 17–22) ■ 20
3. Calculate $\Delta G°$ at any temperature, knowing $\Delta H°$ and $\Delta S°$.
   (Examples 17.3, 17.5; Problems 23–26) ■ 24, 33, 36
4. Calculate $\Delta G°$ at 25°C from free energies of formation.
   (Examples 17.4, 17.7–17.9; Problems 27–32) ■ 29
5. Calculate the temperature at which $\Delta G° = 0$.
   (Example 17.6; Problems 39–44, 49–54) ■ 40, 42, 44
6. Calculate ΔG from $\Delta G°$, knowing all pressures and/or concentrations.
   (Example 17.7; Problems 55–60) ■ 55, 57
7. Relate $\Delta G°$ to K.
   (Example 17.8; Problems 61–70) ■ 65, 69, 83
8. Calculate $\Delta G°$ for coupled reactions.
   (Example 17.9; Problems 71–76) ■ 74

Key Equations

Entropy change	$\Delta S° = \sum S°_{\text{products}} - \sum S°_{\text{reactants}}$ (Section 17.2)
Gibbs-Helmholtz equation	$\Delta G° = \Delta H° - T\Delta S°$ (Section 17.4)
Free energy change	$\Delta G° = \sum \Delta G_f° \text{products} - \sum \Delta G_f° \text{reactants}$ (Section 17.4)
	$\Delta G = \Delta G° + RT \ln Q$ (Section 17.5)
	$\Delta G° = -RT \ln K$ (Section 17.6)

Key Terms

enthalpy, H
entropy, S
free energy, G
free energy of formation, $\Delta G_f°$
spontaneous process
standard entropy change, $\Delta S°$
standard free energy change, $\Delta G°$

Summary Problem

Consider acetic acid, CH_3COOH, the active ingredient in vinegar. It is also responsible for the sour taste of wine when wine gets exposed to air. Bacterial oxidation turns alcohol to acid.

$$C_2H_5OH(aq) + O_2(g) \longrightarrow CH_3COOH(aq) + H_2O(l)$$

The following data may be useful:

$C_2H_5OH(aq)$:	$\Delta H_f° = -288.3$ kJ/mol
	$S° = 148.5$ J/mol·K
$CH_3COOH(aq)$:	$\Delta H_f° = -485.8$ kJ/mol
	$S° = 178.7$ J/mol·K

(a) Calculate $\Delta H°$ and $\Delta S°$ for this process.
(b) Is the reaction spontaneous at 25°C? At 4°C?
(c) The heat of vaporization for acetic acid is 24.3 kJ/mol. Its normal boiling point is 118.5°C. Calculate $\Delta S°$ for the reaction

$$CH_3COOH(l) \longrightarrow CH_3COOH(g)$$

(d) What is the standard molar entropy for $CH_3COOH(g)$, taking $S°$ for $CH_3COOH(l)$ to be 159.8 J/mol·K?
(e) Calculate ΔG at 25°C for the formation of acetic acid from ethanol (see reaction above) when $[CH_3COOH] = 0.200\ M$, $P_{O_2} = 1.13$ atm, and $[C_2H_5OH] = 0.125\ M$.
(f) Calculate $\Delta G°$ for the ionization of acetic acid at 25°C ($K_a = 1.8 \times 10^{-5}$).

Answers

(a) $\Delta H^\circ = -483.3$ kJ; $\Delta S^\circ = -104.9$ J/K
(b) ΔG° (at 25°C) = -452.0 kJ; yes
ΔG° (at 4°C) = -454.2 kJ; yes
(c) 62.1 J/K
(d) 221.9 J/mol·K
(e) -451.1 kJ
(f) 27.1 kJ

Questions and Problems

Blue-numbered questions have answers in Appendix 6 and fully-worked solutions in the *Student Solutions Manual.*

■ denotes questions assignable in OWL.

WEB indicates that the solution is available on this book's companion website.

Spontaneous Processes

1. Which of the following processes are spontaneous?
   (a) building a sand castle
   (b) outlining your chemistry notes
   (c) wind scattering leaves in a pile
2. Which of the following processes are spontaneous?
   (a) a snowman melting in the sun
   (b) building a house of cards
   (c) sorting clothes in a laundry basket
3. Which of the following processes are spontaneous?
   (a) a ball rolling down a hill
   (b) a drop of ink dispersing in water
   (c) melting wax at 10°C
4. Which of the following processes are spontaneous?
   (a) cleaning up your desk
   (b) sugar dissolving in hot coffee
   (c) a bicycle going uphill
5. On the basis of your experience, predict which of the following reactions are spontaneous.
   (a) $Zn(s) + 2H^+(aq) \longrightarrow Zn^{2+}(aq) + H_2(g)$
   (b) $CaCO_3(s) + 2H_2O(l) \longrightarrow Ca(OH)_2(s) + H_2CO_3(aq)$
   (c) $CH_4(g) + O_2(g) \longrightarrow CO_2(g) + 2H_2O(g)$
   (d) $Ag^+(aq) + Cl^-(aq) \longrightarrow AgCl(s)$
6. ■ On the basis of your experience, predict which of the following reactions are spontaneous.
   (a) $CO_2(s) \longrightarrow CO_2(g)$ at 25°C
   (b) $NaCl(s) \longrightarrow NaCl(l)$ at 25°C
   (c) $2NaCl(s) \longrightarrow 2Na(s) + Cl_2(g)$
   (d) $CO_2(g) \longrightarrow C(s) + O_2(g)$

Entropy, ΔS°

7. In each of the following pairs, choose the substance with a lower entropy.
   (a) $H_2O(l)$ at 10°C, $H_2O(l)$ at 30°C
   (b) C (graphite), C (diamond)
   (c) $Cl_2(l)$, $Cl_2(g)$, both at room temperature
8. ■ **WEB** In each of the following pairs, choose the substance with a lower entropy.
   (a) One mole of $O_2(g)$ with 758 mm Hg pressure, one mole of $O_2(g)$ with 493 mm Hg pressure, both at room temperature
   (b) glucose (*s*), glucose (*aq*)
   (c) $Hg(l)$, $Hg(g)$, both at room temperature
9. Predict the sign of ΔS for the following.
   (a) ice cream melting
   (b) boiling water
   (c) dissolving instant coffee in hot water
   (d) sugar, $C_{12}H_{22}O_{11}$, decomposing to carbon and steam
10. ■ Predict the sign of ΔS for the following.
   (a) a lake freezing
   (b) precipitating lead chloride
   (c) a candle burning
   (d) weeding a garden
11. Predict the sign of ΔS° for each of the following reactions.
   (a) $2Na(s) + Cl_2(g) \longrightarrow 2NaCl(s)$
   (b) $2NO(g) + O_2(g) \longrightarrow 2NO_2(g)$
   (c) $C_2H_4(g) + 3O_2(g) \longrightarrow 2CO_2(g) + 3H_2O(l)$
   (d) $NH_4NO_3(s) + H_2O(l) \longrightarrow 2NH_3(g) + O_2(g)$
12. Predict the sign of ΔS° for each of the following reactions.
   (a) $CCl_4(l) + 5O_2(g) \longrightarrow CO_2(g) + 4ClO_2(g)$
   (b) $8H_2O(l) + S_8(s) \longrightarrow 8H_2S(g) + 4O_2(g)$
   (c) $Br_2(l) \longrightarrow Br_2(s)$
   (d) $2NH_3(g) \longrightarrow N_2(g) + 3H_2(g)$
13. Predict the sign of ΔS° for each of the following reactions.
   (a) $O_3(g) \longrightarrow O_2(g) + O(g)$
   (b) $PCl_3(g) + Cl_2(g) \longrightarrow PCl_5(g)$
   (c) $CuSO_4(s) + 5H_2O(l) \longrightarrow CuSO_4 \cdot 5H_2O(s)$
14. Predict the sign of ΔS° for each of the following reactions.
   (a) $H_2(g) + Ni^{2+}(aq) \longrightarrow 2H^+(aq) + Ni(s)$
   (b) $Cu(s) + 2H^+(aq) \longrightarrow H_2(g) + Cu^{2+}(aq)$
   (c) $N_2O_4(g) \longrightarrow 2NO_2(g)$
15. Predict the order of the following reactions in terms of increasing ΔS:
   (a) $NH_3(g) + HCl(g) \longrightarrow NH_4Cl(s)$
   (b) $H_2O(g) \longrightarrow H_2O(l)$
   (c) $2O_3(g) \longrightarrow 3O_2(g)$
   (d) $H_2(g) + F_2(g) \longrightarrow 2HF(g)$
16. ■ Predict the order of the following reactions in terms of increasing ΔS:
   (a) $N_2(g) + 3H_2(g) \longrightarrow 2NH_3(g)$
   (b) $2H_2(g) + O_2(g) \longrightarrow 2H_2O(l)$
   (c) $C(g) + O_2(g) \longrightarrow CO_2(s)$
   (d) $I_2(g) + Cl_2(g) \longrightarrow 2ICl(g)$

17. Use Table 17.1 to calculate $\Delta S°$ for each of the following reactions.
  (a) $CO(g) + 2H_2(g) \longrightarrow CH_3OH(l)$
  (b) $N_2(g) + O_2(g) \longrightarrow 2NO(g)$
  (c) $BaCO_3(s) \longrightarrow BaO(s) + CO_2(g)$
  (d) $2NaCl(s) + F_2(g) \longrightarrow 2NaF(s) + Cl_2(g)$
18. Use Table 17.1 to calculate $\Delta S°$ for each of the following reactions.
  (a) $4NH_3(g) + 7O_2(g) \longrightarrow 4NO_2(g) + 6H_2O(g)$
  (b) $2H_2O_2(l) + N_2H_4(l) \longrightarrow N_2(g) + 4H_2O(g)$
  (c) $C(s) + O_2(g) \longrightarrow CO_2(g)$
  (d) $CH_4(g) + 3Cl_2(g) \longrightarrow CHCl_3(l) + 3HCl(g)$
19. Use Table 17.1 to calculate $\Delta S°$ for each of the following reactions.
  (a) $2Cl^-(aq) + I_2(s) \longrightarrow Cl_2(g) + 2I^-(aq)$
  (b) $SO_4^{2-}(aq) + 4H^+(aq) + Cd(s) \longrightarrow Cd^{2+}(aq) + SO_2(g) + 2H_2O(l)$
  (c) $2Br^-(aq) + 2H_2O(l) \longrightarrow Br_2(l) + H_2(g) + 2OH^-(aq)$
20. ■ Use Table 17.1 to calculate $\Delta S°$ for each of the following reactions.
  (a) $5NO(g) + 3MnO_4^-(aq) + 4H^+(aq) \longrightarrow 5NO_3^-(aq) + 3Mn^{2+}(aq) + 2H_2O(l)$
  (b) $6Fe^{2+}(aq) + CrO_4^{2-}(aq) + 8H^+(aq) \longrightarrow Cr(s) + 6Fe^{3+}(aq) + 4H_2O(l)$
  (c) $C_2H_2(g) + \frac{5}{2}O_2(g) \longrightarrow 2CO_2(g) + H_2O(g)$
21. Use Table 17.1 to calculate $\Delta S°$ for each of the following reactions.
  (a) $2H_2S(s) + 3O_2(g) \longrightarrow 2H_2O(g) + 2SO_2(g)$
  (b) $Ag(s) + 2H^+(aq) + NO_3^-(aq) \longrightarrow Ag^+(aq) + H_2O(l) + NO_2(g)$
  (c) $SO_4^{2-}(aq) + 4H^+(aq) + Ni(s) \longrightarrow Ni^{2+}(aq) + SO_2(g) + 2H_2O(l)$
22. Use Table 17.1 to calculate $\Delta S°$ for each of the following reactions.
  (a) $2HNO_3(l) + 3H_2S(g) \longrightarrow 4H_2O(l) + 2NO(g) + 3S(s)$
  (b) $PCl_5(g) + 4H_2O(l) \longrightarrow 5Cl^-(aq) + H_2PO_4^-(aq) + 6H^+(aq)$
  (c) $MnO_4^-(aq) + 3Fe^{2+}(aq) + 4H^+(aq) \longrightarrow 3Fe^{3+}(aq) + MnO_2(s) + 2H_2O(l)$

$\Delta G°$ and the Gibbs-Helmholtz Equation

23. Calculate $\Delta G°$ at 45°C for reactions for which
  (a) $\Delta H° = -362$ kJ; $\Delta S° = 19.2$ J/K.
  (b) $\Delta H° = 745$ kJ; $\Delta S° = 113$ J/K
  (c) $\Delta H° = -22.5$ kJ; $\Delta S° = -0.0922$ kJ/K.
24. ■ Calculate $\Delta G°$ at 45°C for reactions for which
  (a) $\Delta H° = 293$ kJ; $\Delta S° = -695$ J/K.
  (b) $\Delta H° = -1137$ kJ; $\Delta S° = 0.496$ kJ/K.
  (c) $\Delta H° = -86.6$ kJ; $\Delta S° = -382$ J/K.
25. Calculate $\Delta G°$ at 355 K for each of the reactions in Question 17. State whether the reactions are spontaneous.
26. Calculate $\Delta G°$ at 415 K for each of the reactions in Question 18. State whether the reactions are spontaneous.
27. From the values for $\Delta G_f°$ given in Appendix 1, calculate $\Delta G°$ at 25°C for each of the reactions in Question 19.
28. Follow the directions of Problem 27 for each of the reactions in Question 20.
29. ■ Use standard entropies and heats of formation to calculate $\Delta G_f°$ at 25°C for
  (a) cadmium(II) chloride (*s*).
  (b) methyl alcohol, $CH_3OH(l)$.
  (c) copper(I) sulfide (*s*).
30. WEB Follow the directions of Question 29 for the following compounds.
  (a) ammonium nitrate (*s*)
  (b) chloroform, $CHCl_3(l)$
  (c) potassium chloride (*s*)
31. It has been proposed that wood alcohol, CH_3OH, a relatively inexpensive fuel to produce, be decomposed to produce methane. Methane is a natural gas commonly used for heating homes. Is the decomposition of wood alcohol to methane and oxygen thermodynamically feasible at 25°C and 1 atm?
32. A student warned his friends not to swim in a river close to an electric plant. He claimed that the ozone produced by the plant turned the river water to hydrogen peroxide, which would bleach hair. The reaction is

$$O_3(g) + H_2O(l) \longrightarrow H_2O_2(aq) + O_2(g)$$

Assuming that the river water is at 25°C and all species are at standard concentrations, show by calculation whether his claim is plausible. Take $\Delta G_f°$ $O_3(g)$ at 25°C to be +163.2 kJ/mol and $\Delta G_f°$ $H_2O_2(aq) = -134$ kJ/mol.
33. ■ Sodium carbonate, also called "washing soda," can be made by heating sodium hydrogen carbonate:

$$2NaHCO_3(s) \longrightarrow Na_2CO_3(s) + CO_2(g) + H_2O(l)$$
$$\Delta H° = +135.6 \text{ kJ}; \Delta G° = +34.6 \text{ kJ at } 25°C$$

  (a) Calculate $\Delta S°$ for this reaction. Is the sign reasonable?
  (b) Calculate $\Delta G°$ at 0 K; at 1000 K.
34. The reaction between magnesium metal and liquid water produces solid $Mg(OH)_2$ and hydrogen gas. Calculate $\Delta G°$ for the formation of one mole of $Mg(OH)_2$ at 25°C and at 15°C.
35. The alcohol in most liqueurs is ethanol, C_2H_5OH. It is produced by the fermentation of the glucose in fruit or grain.

$$C_6H_{12}O_6(aq) \longrightarrow 2C_2H_5OH(l) + 2CO_2(g)$$
$$\Delta H° = -82.4 \text{ kJ}; \Delta G° = -219.8 \text{ kJ at } 25°C$$

  (a) Calculate $\Delta S°$. Is the sign reasonable?
  (b) Calculate $S°$ for $C_6H_{12}O_6(aq)$.
  (c) Calculate $\Delta H_f°$ for $C_6H_{12}O_6(aq)$.
36. ■ Oxygen can be made in the laboratory by reacting sodium peroxide and water.

$$2Na_2O_2(s) + 2H_2O(l) \longrightarrow 4NaOH(s) + O_2(g)$$
$$\Delta H° = -109.0 \text{ kJ}; \Delta G° = -148.4 \text{ kJ at } 25°C$$

  (a) Calculate $\Delta S°$. Is the sign reasonable?
  (b) Calculate $S°$ for $Na_2O_2(s)$.
  (c) Calculate $\Delta H_f°$ for $Na_2O_2(s)$.
37. Phosgene, $COCl_2$, can be formed by the reaction of chloroform, $CHCl_3(l)$, with oxygen:

$$2CHCl_3(l) + O_2(g) \longrightarrow 2COCl_2(g) + 2HCl(g)$$
$$\Delta H° = -353.2 \text{ kJ}; \Delta G° = -452.4 \text{ kJ at } 25°C$$

  (a) Calculate $\Delta S°$ for the reaction. Is the sign reasonable?
  (b) Calculate $S°$ for phosgene.
  (c) Calculate $\Delta H_f°$ for phosgene.
38. When permanganate ions in aqueous solution react with cobalt metal in strong acid, the equation for the reaction that takes place is

$$2MnO_4^-(aq) + 16H^+(aq) + 5Co(s) \longrightarrow 2Mn^{2+}(aq) + 5Co^{2+}(aq) + 8H_2O(l)$$
$$\Delta H° = -2024.6 \text{ kJ}; \Delta G° \text{ at } 25°C = -1750.9 \text{ kJ}$$

  (a) Calculate $\Delta S°$ for the reaction at 25°C.
  (b) Calculate $S°$ for Co^{2+}, given $S°$ for Co is 30.04 J/mol·K.

Temperature Dependence of Spontaneity

39. Discuss the effect of temperature change on the spontaneity of the following reactions at 1 atm.
  (a) $2PbO(s) + 2SO_2(g) \longrightarrow 2PbS(s) + 3O_2(g)$

$$\Delta H° = +830.8 \text{ kJ}; \Delta S° = +168 \text{ J/K}$$

■ in OWL Blue-numbered questions answered in Appendix 6 WEB Solution is available on companion website

(b) $2As(s) + 3F_2(g) \longrightarrow 2AsF_3(l)$

$$\Delta H^\circ = -1643 \text{ kJ}; \Delta S^\circ = -0.316 \text{ kJ/K}$$

(c) $CO(g) \longrightarrow C(s) + \frac{1}{2}O_2(g)$

$$\Delta H^\circ = 110.5 \text{ kJ}; \Delta S^\circ = -89.4 \text{ J/K}$$

40. ■ Discuss the effect of temperature change on the spontaneity of the following reactions at 1 atm.

(a) $Al_2O_3(s) + 2Fe(s) \longrightarrow 2Al(s) + Fe_2O_3(s)$

$$\Delta H^\circ = +851.5 \text{ kJ}; \Delta S^\circ = +38.5 \text{ J/K}$$

(b) $N_2H_4(l) \longrightarrow N_2(g) + 2H_2(g)$

$$\Delta H^\circ = -50.6 \text{ kJ}; \Delta S^\circ = 0.3315 \text{ kJ/K}$$

(c) $SO_3(g) \longrightarrow SO_2(g) + \frac{1}{2}O_2(g)$

$$\Delta H^\circ = 98.9 \text{ kJ}; \Delta S^\circ = +0.0939 \text{ kJ/K}$$

41. At what temperature does ΔG° become zero for each of the reactions in Problem 39? Explain the significance of your answers.

42. ■ Over what temperature range are the reactions in Problem 40 spontaneous?

43. For the reaction

$$2Cl^-(aq) + Br_2(l) \longrightarrow Cl_2(g) + 2Br^-(aq)$$

calculate the temperature at which $\Delta G^\circ = 0$.

44. ■ For the reaction

$$SnO_2(s) + 2CO(g) \longrightarrow 2CO_2(g) + Sn(s)$$

calculate the temperature at which $\Delta G^\circ = 0$.

45. Earlier civilizations smelted iron from ore by heating it with charcoal from a wood fire:

$$2Fe_2O_3(s) + 3C(s) \longrightarrow 4Fe(s) + 3CO_2(g)$$

(a) Obtain an expression for ΔG° as a function of temperature. Prepare a table of ΔG° values at 100-K intervals between 100 K and 500 K.

(b) Calculate the lowest temperature at which the smelting could be carried out.

46. For the decomposition of Ag_2O,

$$2Ag_2O(s) \longrightarrow 4Ag(s) + O_2(g)$$

(a) Obtain an expression for ΔG° as a function of temperature. Prepare a table of ΔG° values at 100-K intervals between 100 K and 500 K.

(b) Calculate the temperature at which ΔG° becomes zero.

47. Two possible ways of producing iron from iron ore are

(a) $Fe_2O_3(s) + \frac{3}{2}C(s) \longrightarrow 2Fe(s) + \frac{3}{2}CO_2(g)$

(b) $Fe_2O_3(s) + 3H_2(g) \longrightarrow 2Fe(s) + 3H_2O(g)$

Which of these reactions proceeds spontaneously at the lower temperature?

48. It is desired to produce tin from its ore, cassiterite, SnO_2, at as low a temperature as possible. The ore could be

(a) decomposed by heating, producing tin and oxygen.

(b) heated with hydrogen gas, producing tin and water vapor.

(c) heated with carbon, producing tin and carbon dioxide.

Solely on the basis of thermodynamic principles, which method would you recommend? Show calculations.

49. Red phosphorus is formed by heating white phosphorus. Calculate the temperature at which the two forms are at equilibrium, given

white P: $\Delta H_f^\circ = 0.00 \text{ kJ/mol}; S^\circ = 41.09 \text{ J/mol·K}$

red P: $\Delta H_f^\circ = -17.6 \text{ kJ/mol}; S^\circ = 22.80 \text{ J/mol·K}$

50. Organ pipes in unheated churches develop "tin disease," in which white tin is converted to gray tin. Given

white Sn: $\Delta H_f^\circ = 0.00 \text{ kJ/mol}; S^\circ = 51.55 \text{ J/mol·K}$

gray Sn: $\Delta H_f^\circ = -2.09 \text{ kJ/mol}; S^\circ = 44.14 \text{ J/mol·K}$

calculate the equilibrium temperature for the transition.

51. Sulfur has about 20 different allotropes. The most common are rhombic sulfur (the stable form at 25°C and 1 atm) and monoclinic sulfur. They differ in their crystal structures. Given

S(*s*, monoclinic): $\Delta H_f^\circ = 0.30 \text{ kJ/mol}, S^\circ = 0.0326 \text{ kJ/mol·K}$

at what temperature are the two forms in equilibrium?

52. Pencil "lead" is almost pure graphite. Graphite is the stable elemental form of carbon at 25°C and 1 atm. Diamond is an allotrope of graphite. Given

diamond: $\Delta H_f^\circ = 1.9 \text{ kJ/mol}; S^\circ = 2.4 \text{ J/mol·K}$

at what temperature are the two forms in equilibrium at 1 atm?

$$C \text{ (graphite)} \rightleftharpoons C \text{ (diamond)}$$

53. Given the following data for sodium

$Na(s)$: $S^\circ = 51.2 \text{ J/mol·K}$

$Na(g)$: $S^\circ = 153.6 \text{ J/mol·K}$ $\quad \Delta H_f^\circ = 108.7 \text{ kJ/mol}$

estimate the temperature at which sodium sublimes at 1 atm.

$$Na(s) \rightleftharpoons Na(g)$$

54. Given the following data for bromine,

$Br_2(l)$: $S^\circ = 152.2 \text{ J/mol·K}$

$Br_2(g)$: $S^\circ = 245.4 \text{ J/mol·K}$ $\quad \Delta H_f^\circ = 30.91 \text{ kJ/mol}$

estimate the normal boiling point of bromine.

$$Br_2(l) \rightleftharpoons Br_2(g)$$

Effect of Concentration/Pressure on Spontaneity

55. ■ Show by calculation, using Appendix 1, whether dissolving lead(II) chloride

$$PbCl_2(s) \rightleftharpoons Pb^{2+}(aq) + 2Cl^-(aq)$$

is spontaneous at 25°C

(a) when $[Pb^{2+}] = 1.0\ M$; $[Cl^-] = 2.0\ M$.

(b) when $[Pb^{2+}] = 1.0 \times 10^{-5}$; $[Cl^-] = 2.0 \times 10^{-5}\ M$.

56. Show by calculation whether the reaction

$$HC_2H_3O_2(aq) \rightleftharpoons H^+(aq) + C_2H_3O_2^-(aq) \qquad \Delta G^\circ = +27.2 \text{ kJ}$$

is spontaneous at 25°C

(a) when $[H^+] = [C_2H_3O_2^-] = 0.85\ M$; $[HC_2H_3O_2] = 0.15\ M$.

(b) when $[H^+] = [C_2H_3O_2^-] = 2.0 \times 10^{-3}\ M$; $[HC_2H_3O_2] = 1.0\ M$.

57. ■ For the reaction

$$2H_2O(l) + 2Cl^-(aq) \longrightarrow H_2(g) + Cl_2(g) + 2OH^-(aq)$$

(a) calculate ΔG° at 25°C.

(b) calculate ΔG at 25°C when $P_{H_2} = P_{Cl_2} = 0.250$ atm, $[Cl^-] = 0.335\ M$, and the pH of the solution is 11.98.

58. For the reaction

$$O_2(g) + 4H^+(aq) + 4Fe^{2+}(aq) \longrightarrow 2H_2O(l) + 4Fe^{3+}(aq)$$

(a) calculate ΔG° at 25°C.

(b) calculate ΔG at 25°C when $[Fe^{2+}] = [Fe^{3+}] = 0.250\ M$, $P_{O_2} = 0.755$ atm, and the pH of the solution is 3.12.

■ in OWL Blue-numbered questions answered in Appendix 6 **WEB** Solution is available on companion website

59. Consider the reaction

$$2SO_2(g) + O_2(g) \longrightarrow 2SO_3(g)$$

(a) Calculate $\Delta G°$ at 25°C.
(b) If the partial pressures of SO_2 and SO_3 are kept at 0.400 atm, what partial pressure should O_2 have so that the reaction just becomes nonspontaneous (i.e., $\Delta G = +1.0$ kJ)?

60. Consider the reaction

$$AgCl(s) \longrightarrow Ag^+(aq) + Cl^-(aq)$$

(a) Calculate $\Delta G°$ at 25°C.
(b) What should the concentrations of Ag^+ and Cl^- be so that $\Delta G = -1.0$ kJ (just spontaneous)? Take $[Ag^+] = [Cl^-]$.
(c) The K_{sp} for AgCl is 1.8×10^{-10}. Is the answer to (b) reasonable? Explain.

Free Energy and Equilibrium

61. Consider the reaction

$$CO(g) + H_2O(g) \rightleftharpoons CO_2(g) + H_2(g)$$

Use the appropriate tables to calculate
(a) $\Delta G°$ at 552°C **(b)** K at 552°C

62. Consider the reaction

$$NH_4^+(aq) \rightleftharpoons H^+(aq) + NH_3(aq)$$

Use $\Delta G_f°$ for $NH_3(aq)$ at 25°C = −26.7 kJ/mol and the appropriate tables to calculate
(a) $\Delta G°$ at 25°C **(b)** K_a at 25°C

63. Consider the following reaction at 25°C:

$$Cl_2(g) \rightleftharpoons 2Cl(g) \qquad K = 1.0 \times 10^{-37}$$

(a) Calculate $\Delta G°$ for the reaction at 25°C.
(b) Calculate $\Delta G_f°$ for $Cl(g)$ at 25°C.

64. Consider the reaction

$$N_2O(g) + NO_2(g) \longrightarrow 3NO(g) \qquad K = 4.4 \times 10^{-19}$$

(a) Calculate $\Delta G°$ for the reaction at 25°C.
(b) Calculate $\Delta G_f°$ for N_2O at 25°C.

65. ■ For the reaction

$$CO(g) + 3H_2(g) \rightleftharpoons CH_4(g) + H_2O(g)$$

$K = 2.2 \times 10^{11}$ at 473 K and 4.6×10^{8} at 533 K. Calculate $\Delta G°$ at both temperatures.

66. **WEB** For the reaction

$$H_2(g) + I_2(g) \rightleftharpoons 2HI(g)$$

$K = 50.0$ at 721 K
(a) What is $\Delta G°$ at 721 K?
(b) What is K at 25°C? ($\Delta G_f°\ I_2(g) = +19.4$ kJ/mol)

67. Use the values for $\Delta G_f°$ in Appendix 1 to calculate K_{sp} for barium sulfate at 25°C. Compare with the value given in Chapter 16.

68. Given that $\Delta H_f°$ for $HF(aq)$ is −320.1 kJ/mol and $S°$ for $HF(aq)$ is 88.7 J/mol·K, find K_a for HF at 25°C.

69. ■ A 0.218 *M* solution of the weak acid HX has pH 4.57 at 25°C. What is $\Delta G°$ for the dissociation of the weak acid?

70. A 0.143 *M* solution of the weak base RNH_2 has pH 9.11 at 25°C. What is $\Delta G°$ for the dissociation of the weak base in water?

$$RNH_2(aq) + H_2O \rightleftharpoons RNH_3^+(aq) + OH^-(aq)$$

Additivity of Coupled Reactions

71. Given the following standard free energies at 25°C,

$$SO_2(g) + 3CO(g) \longrightarrow COS(g) + 2CO_2(g) \qquad \Delta G° = -246.5 \text{ kJ}$$
$$CO(g) + H_2O(g) \longrightarrow CO_2(g) + H_2(g) \qquad \Delta G° = -28.5 \text{ kJ}$$

find $\Delta G°$ at 25°C for the following reaction.

$$SO_2(g) + CO(g) + 2H_2(g) \longrightarrow COS(g) + 2H_2O(g)$$

72. Given the following standard free energies at 25°C,

$$N_2O_5(g) \longrightarrow 2NO(g) + \tfrac{3}{2}O_2(g) \qquad \Delta G° = -59.2 \text{ kJ}$$
$$NO(g) + \tfrac{1}{2}O_2(g) \longrightarrow NO_2(g) \qquad \Delta G° = -35.6 \text{ kJ}$$

calculate $\Delta G°$ at 25°C for the reaction

$$2NO_2(g) + \tfrac{1}{2}O_2(g) \longrightarrow N_2O_5(g)$$

73. Natural gas, which is mostly methane, CH_4, is a resource that the United States has in abundance. In principle, ethane can be obtained from methane by the reaction

$$2CH_4(g) \longrightarrow C_2H_6(g) + H_2(g)$$

(a) Calculate $\Delta G°$ at 25°C for the reaction. Comment on the feasibility of this reaction at 25°C.
(b) Couple the reaction above with the formation of steam from the elements:

$$H_2(g) + \tfrac{1}{2}O_2(g) \longrightarrow H_2O(g) \qquad \Delta G° = -228.6 \text{ kJ}$$

What is the equation for the overall reaction? Comment on the feasibility of the overall reaction.

74. ■ Theoretically, one can obtain zinc from an ore containing zinc sulfide, ZnS, by the reaction

$$ZnS(s) \longrightarrow Zn(s) + S(s)$$

(a) Show by calculation that this reaction is not feasible at 25°C.
(b) Show that by coupling the above reaction with the reaction

$$S(s) + O_2(g) \longrightarrow SO_2(g)$$

the overall reaction, in which Zn is obtained by roasting in oxygen, is feasible at 25°C.

75. How many moles of ATP must be converted to ADP by the reaction

$$ATP(aq) + H_2O \longrightarrow ADP(aq) + HPO_4^{2-}(aq) + 2H^+(aq) \qquad \Delta G° = -31 \text{ kJ}$$

to bring about a nonspontaneous biochemical reaction in which $\Delta G° = +372$ kJ?

76. Consider the following reactions at 25°C:

$$C_6H_{12}O_6(aq) + 6O_2(g) \longrightarrow 6CO_2(g) + 6H_2O \qquad \Delta G° = -2870 \text{ kJ}$$
$$ADP(aq) + HPO_4^{2-}(aq) + 2H^+(aq) \longrightarrow ATP(aq) + H_2O \qquad \Delta G° = 31 \text{ kJ}$$

Write an equation for a coupled reaction between glucose, $C_6H_{12}O_6$, and ADP in which $\Delta G° = -390$ kJ.

Unclassified

77. At 1200 K, an equilibrium mixture of CO and CO_2 gases contains 98.31 mol percent CO and some solid carbon. The total pressure of the mixture is 1.00 atm. For the system

$$CO_2(g) + C(s) \rightleftharpoons 2CO(g)$$

■ in OWL Blue-numbered questions answered in Appendix 6 **WEB** Solution is available on companion website

calculate

(a) P_{CO} and P_{CO_2} (b) K

(c) $\Delta G°$ at 1200 K

78. At 25°C, a 0.13 *M* solution of a weak acid, HB, has a pH of 3.71. What is $\Delta G°$ for

$$H^+(aq) + B^-(aq) \rightleftharpoons HB(aq)$$

79. A student is asked to prepare a 0.030 *M* aqueous solution of $PbCl_2$.

(a) Is this possible at 25°C? (*Hint:* Is dissolving 0.030 mol of $PbCl_2$ at 25°C possible?)

(b) If the student used water at 100°C, would this be possible?

80. Some bacteria use light energy to convert carbon dioxide and water to glucose and oxygen:

$$6CO_2(g) + 6H_2O(l) \longrightarrow C_6H_{12}O_6(aq) + 6O_2(g) \qquad \Delta G° = 2870 \text{ kJ at } 25°C$$

Other bacteria, those that do not have light available to them, couple the reaction

$$H_2S(g) + \tfrac{1}{2}O_2(g) \longrightarrow H_2O(l) + S(s)$$

to the glucose synthesis above. Coupling the two reactions, the overall reaction is

$$24H_2S(g) + 6CO_2(g) + 6O_2(g) \longrightarrow C_6H_{12}O_6(aq) + 18H_2O(l) + 24S(s)$$

Show that the reaction is spontaneous at 25°C.

81. It has been proposed that if ammonia, methane, and oxygen gas are combined at 25°C in their standard states, glycine, the simplest of all amino acids, can be formed.

$$2CH_4(g) + NH_3(g) + \tfrac{5}{2}O_2(g) \longrightarrow NH_2CH_2COOH(s) + 3H_2O(l)$$

Given $\Delta G_f°$ for glycine = −368.57 kJ/mol,

(a) will this reaction proceed spontaneously at 25°C?

(b) does the equilibrium constant favor the formation of products?

(c) do your calculations for (a) and (b) indicate that glycine is formed as soon as the three gases are combined?

82. Carbon monoxide poisoning results when carbon monoxide replaces oxygen bound to hemoglobin. The oxygenated form of hemoglobin, $Hb \cdot O_2$ carries O_2 to the lungs.

$$Hb \cdot O_2(aq) + CO(g) \rightleftharpoons Hb \cdot CO(aq) + O(g)$$

At 98.6°F (37°C), $\Delta G°$ for the reaction is about −14 kJ. What is the ratio of $[Hb \cdot O_2]$ to $[Hb \cdot CO]$ when the pressure of CO is the same as that of O_2?

83. ■ The formation constant for the following reaction at 25°C

$$Zn^{2+}(aq) + 4\,NH_3(aq) \rightleftharpoons Zn(NH_3)_4{}^{2+}(aq)$$

is 3.6×10^8.

(a) What is $\Delta G°$ at this temperature?

(b) If standard state concentrations of the reactants and products are combined, in which direction will the reaction proceed?

(c) What is ΔG when $[Zn(NH_3)_4{}^{2+}] = 0.010$ *M*, $[Zn^{2+}] = 0.0010$ *M* and $[NH_3] = 3.5 \times 10^{-4}$?

Conceptual Problems

84. ■ Determine whether each of the following statements is true or false. If false, modify it to make it true.

(a) An exothermic reaction is spontaneous.

(b) When $\Delta G°$ is positive, the reaction cannot occur under any conditions.

(c) $\Delta S°$ is positive for a reaction in which there is an increase in the number of moles.

(d) If $\Delta H°$ and $\Delta S°$ are both negative, $\Delta G°$ will be negative.

85. Which of the following quantities can be taken to be independent of temperature? Independent of pressure?

(a) ΔH for a reaction (b) ΔS for a reaction

(c) ΔG for a reaction (d) S for a substance

86. Fill in the blanks:

(a) $\Delta H°$ and $\Delta G°$ become equal at ________ K.

(b) $\Delta G°$ and ΔG are equal when Q = ________.

(c) $S°$ for steam is ________ than $S°$ for water.

87. Fill in the blanks:

(a) At equilibrium, ΔG is ________.

(b) For $C_6H_6(l) \rightleftharpoons C_6H_6(g)$, $\Delta H°$ is ________. (+, −, 0).

(c) When a pure solid melts, the temperature at which liquid and solid are in equilibrium and $\Delta G° = 0$ is called ________.

88. In your own words, explain why

(a) $\Delta S°$ is negative for a reaction in which the number of moles of gas decreases.

(b) we take $\Delta S°$ to be independent of *T*, even though entropy increases with *T*.

(c) a solid has lower entropy than its corresponding liquid.

89. Consider the following reaction with its thermodynamic data:

$$2A(g) + B_2(g) \longrightarrow 2AB(g) \qquad \Delta H° < 0;\ \Delta S° < 0;\ \Delta G° \text{ at } 60°C = +10 \text{ kJ}$$

Which statements about the reaction are true?

(a) When $\Delta G = 1$, the reaction is at equilibrium.

(b) When $Q = 1$, $\Delta G = \Delta G°$.

(c) At 75°C, the reaction is definitely nonspontaneous.

(d) At 100°C, the reaction has a positive entropy change.

(e) If A and B_2 are elements in their stable states, $S°$ for A and B_2 at 25°C is 0.

(f) K for the reaction at 60°C is less than 1.

90. Consider the graph below.

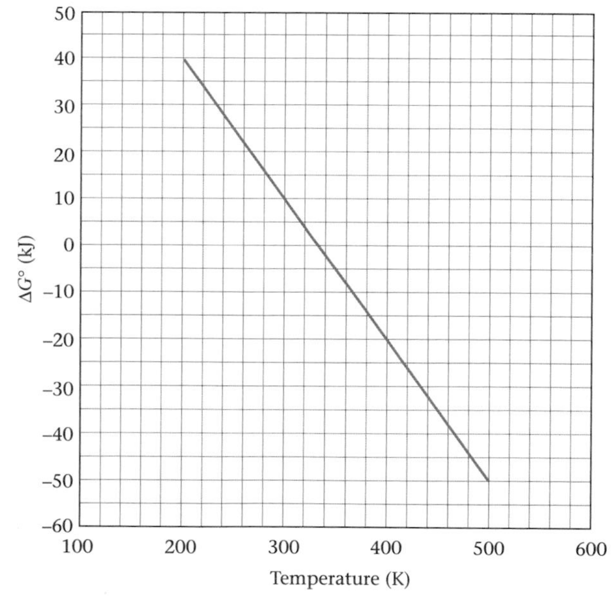

(a) Describe the relationship between the spontaneity of the process and temperature.

(b) Is the reaction exothermic?

(c) Is $\Delta S° > 0$?

(d) At what temperature is the reaction at standard conditions likely to be at equilibrium?

(e) What is *K* for the reaction at 27°C?

■ in OWL Blue-numbered questions answered in Appendix 6 **WEB** Solution is available on companion website

91. The relationship between $\Delta G°$ and T is linear. Draw the graph of a reaction with the properties described below. You need only label the point at which $\Delta G° = 0$.

- The reaction is exothermic.
- $\Delta n_g < 0$ (Δn_g = moles of gas products − moles of gas reactants).
- At 300 K, the system is at equilibrium and $K = 1$.

92. Answer the questions below by writing **LT** (for *is less than*), **GT** (for *is greater than*), **EQ** (for *is equal to*) or **MI** (for *more information required*) in the blanks.

The reaction given below takes place in a cylinder that feels warm to the touch after the reaction is complete.

$$A_2(g) + B_2(g) \longrightarrow 2AB(s)$$

(a) At all temperatures, $\Delta S°$ ________ 0.
(b) At all temperatures, $\Delta H°$ ________ 0.
(c) At all temperatures, $\Delta G°$ ________ 0.

Challenge Problems

93. The normal boiling point for ethyl alcohol is 78.4°C. $S°$ for $C_2H_5OH(g)$ is 282.7 J/mol·K. At what temperature is the vapor pressure of ethyl alcohol 357 mm Hg?

94. $\Delta H_f°$ for iodine gas is 62.4 kJ/mol, and $S°$ is 260.7 J/mol·K. Calculate the equilibrium partial pressures of $I_2(g)$, $H_2(g)$, and $HI(g)$ for the system

$$2HI(g) \rightleftharpoons H_2(g) + I_2(g)$$

at 500°C if the initial partial pressures are all 0.200 atm.

95. The heat of fusion of ice is 333 J/g. For the process

$$H_2O(s) \longrightarrow H_2O(l)$$

determine

(a) $\Delta H°$ (b) $\Delta G°$ at 0°C (c) $\Delta S°$
(d) $\Delta G°$ at −20°C (e) $\Delta G°$ at 20°C

96. The overall reaction that occurs when sugar is metabolized is

$$C_{12}H_{22}O_{11}(s) + 12\,O_2(g) \longrightarrow 12CO_2(g) + 11H_2O(l)$$

For this reaction, $\Delta H°$ is −5650 kJ and $\Delta G°$ is −5790 kJ at 25°C.

(a) If 25% of the free energy change is actually converted to useful work, how many kilojoules of work are obtained when one gram of sugar is metabolized at body temperature, 37°C?

(b) How many grams of sugar would a 120-lb woman have to eat to get the energy to climb the Jungfrau in the Alps, which is 4158 m high? ($w = 9.79 \times 10^{-3}\,mh$, where w = work in kilojoules, m is body mass in kilograms, and h is height in meters.)

97. Hydrogen has been suggested as the fuel of the future. One way to store it is to convert it to a compound that can be heated to release the hydrogen. One such compound is calcium hydride, CaH_2. This compound has a heat of formation of −186.2 kJ/mol and a standard entropy of 42.0 J/mol·K. What is the minimum temperature to which calcium hydride would have to be heated to produce hydrogen at one atmosphere pressure?

98. When a copper wire is exposed to air at room temperature, it becomes coated with a black oxide, CuO. If the wire is heated above a certain temperature, the black oxide is converted to a red oxide, Cu_2O. At a still higher temperature, the oxide coating disappears. Explain these observations in terms of the thermodynamics of the reactions

$$2CuO(s) \longrightarrow Cu_2O(s) + \tfrac{1}{2}O_2(g)$$

$$Cu_2O(s) \longrightarrow 2Cu(s) + \tfrac{1}{2}O_2(g)$$

and estimate the temperatures at which the changes occur.

99. K_a for acetic acid ($HC_2H_3O_2$) at 25°C is 1.754×10^{-5}. At 50°C, K_a is 1.633×10^{-5}. Assuming that $\Delta H°$ and $\Delta S°$ are not affected by a change in temperature, calculate $\Delta S°$ for the ionization of acetic acid.

100. Consider the reaction

$$2HI(g) \rightleftharpoons H_2(g) + I_2(g)$$

At 500°C, a flask initially has all three gases, each at a partial pressure of 0.200 atm. When equilibrium is established, the partial pressure of HI is determined to be 0.48 atm. What is $\Delta G°$ for the reaction at 500°C?

101. Consider the formation of ammonia from its elements:

$$N_2(g) + 3H_2(g) \longrightarrow 2NH_3(g)$$

At what temperature is $K = 1.00$? (*Hint:* Use the thermodynamic tables in the appendix.)

■ in OWL Blue-numbered questions answered in Appendix 6 **WEB** Solution is available on companion website

18 Electrochemistry

If by fire,
Of sooty coal th' empiric Alchymist
Can turn, or holds it possible to turn
Metals of drossiest Ore to Perfect Gold.

—John Milton
"Paradise Lost" (Book V, Lines 439–442)

Chapter Outline

Most "silver" pitchers like the one in the painting are not made of pure silver but rather silver-plated using an electrolytic cell.

"Still Life with Silver Jug" by Willem Kalf/Courtesy of Rijksmuseum, Netherlands

Electrochemistry is the study of the interconversion of electrical and chemical energy. This conversion takes place in an electrochemical cell that may be a(n)—

- **voltaic cell** (Section 18.1), in which a spontaneous reaction generates electrical energy.
- **electrolytic cell** (Section 18.5), in which electrical energy is used to bring about a nonspontaneous reaction.

All of the reactions considered in this chapter are of the oxidation-reduction type. You will recall from Chapter 4 that such a reaction can be split into two half-reactions. In one half-reaction, referred to as ***reduction,*** electrons are consumed; in the other, called ***oxidation,*** electrons are produced. There can be no net change in the number of electrons; the number of electrons consumed in reduction must be exactly equal to the number produced in the oxidation half-reaction.

In an electrochemical cell, these two half-reactions occur at two different **electrodes,** which most often consist of metal plates or wires. Reduction occurs at the **cathode;** a typical half-reaction might be

$$\text{cathode:} \quad Cu^{2+}(aq) + 2e^- \longrightarrow Cu(s)$$

Oxidation takes place at the **anode,** where a species such as zinc metal produces electrons:

$$\text{anode:} \quad Zn(s) \longrightarrow Zn^{2+}(aq) + 2e^-$$

It is always true that in an electrochemical cell, *anions* move to the *anode; cations* move to the *cathode.*

One of the most important characteristics of a cell is its *voltage,* which is a measure of reaction spontaneity. Cell voltages depend on the nature of the half-reactions occurring at the electrodes (Section 18.2) and on the concentrations of species involved (Section 18.4). From the voltage measured at standard concentrations, it is possible to calculate the standard free energy change and the equilibrium constant (Section 18.3) of the reaction involved.

The principles discussed in this chapter have a host of practical applications. Whenever you start your car, turn on your cell phone, or use a remote control for your television or other devices, you are making use of a voltaic cell. Many of our most important elements, including hydrogen and chlorine, are made in electrolytic cells. These applications, among others, are discussed in Section 18.6. ■

Online homework for this chapter may be assigned in OWL.

CENGAGENOW™
This icon introduces an opportunity for self-study and to explore interactive modules by signing in at **academic.cengage.com/now.**

Cathode = reduction; anode = oxidation. The consonants go together, as do the vowels.

18.1 VOLTAIC CELLS

In principle at least, any spontaneous redox reaction can serve as a source of energy in a **voltaic cell.** The cell must be designed in such a way that oxidation occurs at one electrode (anode) with reduction at the other electrode (cathode). The electrons produced at the anode must be transferred to the cathode, where they are consumed. To do this, the electrons move through an external circuit, where they do electrical work.

To understand how a voltaic cell operates, let us start with some simple cells that are readily made in the general chemistry laboratory.

The Zn-Cu^{2+} Cell

When a piece of zinc is added to a water solution containing Cu^{2+} ions, the following redox reaction takes place:

$$Zn(s) + Cu^{2+}(aq) \longrightarrow Zn^{2+}(aq) + Cu(s)$$

CENGAGENOW™
Click Chemistry Interactive for the self-study module **a voltaic electrochemical cell.**

Charles D. Winters

Figure 18.1
Zn-Cu^{2+} spontaneous redox reaction. The blue of the Cu^{2+} ion in solution fades *(from left to right)* as the ion is reduced to metallic Cu that deposits on the zinc strip in the solution.

The Zn electrode must not come in contact with Cu^{2+} ions. Why?

In this reaction, copper metal plates out on the surface of the zinc. The blue color of the aqueous Cu^{2+} ion fades as it is replaced by the colorless aqueous Zn^{2+} ion (Figure 18.1). Clearly, this redox reaction is spontaneous; it involves electron transfer from a Zn atom to a Cu^{2+} ion.

To design a voltaic cell using the Zn-Cu^{2+} reaction as a source of electrical energy, the electron transfer must occur indirectly; that is, the electrons given off by zinc atoms must be made to pass through an external electric circuit before they reduce Cu^{2+} ions to copper atoms. One way to do this is shown in Figure 18.2. The voltaic cell consists of two **half-cells**—

- a Zn anode dipping into a solution containing Zn^{2+} ions, shown in the beaker at the far right.
- a Cu cathode dipping into a solution containing Cu^{2+} ions (blue), shown in the beaker at the center of Figure 18.2.

The "external circuit" consists of a voltmeter with leads (red and black) to the anode and cathode.

Let us trace the flow of electric current through the cell.

1. At the zinc *anode* (connected to the red wire shown in Figure 18.2), electrons are produced by the oxidation half-reaction

$$Zn(s) \longrightarrow Zn^{2+}(aq) + 2e^-$$

This electrode, which "pumps" electrons into the external circuit, is ordinarily marked as the negative pole of the cell.

2. Electrons generated at the anode move through the external circuit (right to left in Figure 18.2) to the copper *cathode,* connected through the black wire to the voltmeter. At the cathode, the electrons are consumed, reducing Cu^{2+} ions present in the solution around the electrode:

$$Cu^{2+}(aq) + 2e^- \longrightarrow Cu(s)$$

The copper electrode, which "pulls" electrons from the external circuit, is considered to be the positive pole of the cell.

3. As the above half-reactions proceed, a surplus of positive ions (Zn^{2+}) tends to build up around the zinc electrode. The region around the copper electrode tends to become deficient in positive ions as Cu^{2+} ions are consumed. To maintain electrical neutrality, cations must move toward the copper cathode or, alternatively, anions must move toward the zinc anode. In practice, both migrations occur.

In the cell shown in Figure 18.2, movement of ions occurs through a **salt bridge** connecting the two beakers. The salt bridge shown is an inverted glass U-tube, plugged with glass wool at each end. The tube is filled with a solution of a salt that takes no part in the electrode

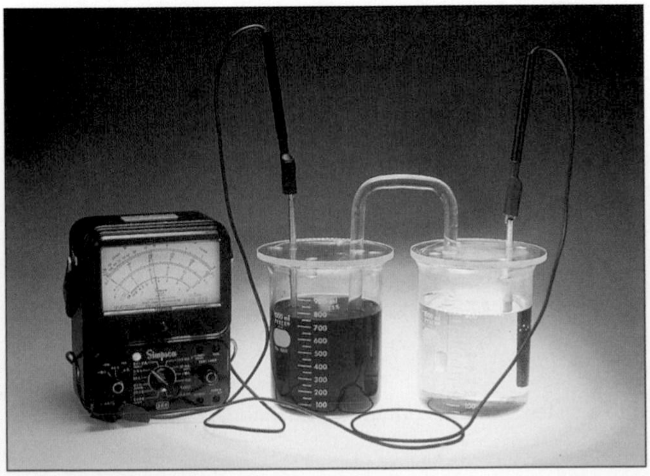

Charles D. Winters

Figure 18.2
A Zn-Cu^{2+} voltaic cell. In this voltaic cell, a voltmeter *(left)* is connected to a half-cell consisting of a Cu cathode in a solution of blue Cu^{2+} ions and a half-cell consisting of a Zn anode in a solution of colorless Zn^{2+} ions. The following spontaneous reaction takes place in this cell: $Zn(s) + Cu^{2+}(aq) \longrightarrow Zn^{2+}(aq) + Cu(s)$. The salt bridge allows ions to pass from one solution to the other to complete the circuit and prevents direct contact between Zn atoms and the Cu^{2+} ions.

reactions; potassium nitrate, KNO_3, is frequently used. As current is drawn from the cell, K^+ ions move from the salt bridge into the cathode half-cell. At the same time, NO_3^- ions move into the anode half-cell. In this way, electrical neutrality is maintained without Cu^{2+} ions coming in contact with the Zn electrode, which would short-circuit the cell.

The cell shown in Figure 18.2 is often abbreviated as

$$Zn \mid Zn^{2+} \parallel Cu^{2+} \mid Cu$$

In this notation—

Anode || cathode.

- the ***anode*** reaction ***(oxidation)*** is shown at the left. Zn atoms are oxidized to Zn^{2+} ions.
- the salt bridge (or other means of separating the half cells) is indicated by the symbol ||.
- the ***cathode*** reaction ***(reduction)*** is shown at the right. Cu^{2+} ions are reduced to Cu atoms.
- a single vertical line indicates a phase boundary, such as that between a solid electrode and an aqueous solution.

Notice that the anode half-reaction comes first in the cell notation, just as the letter *a* comes before *c*.

Other Salt Bridge Cells

Cells similar to that shown in Figure 18.2 can be set up for many different spontaneous redox reactions. Consider, for example, the reaction

$$Ni(s) + Cu^{2+}(aq) \longrightarrow Ni^{2+}(aq) + Cu(s)$$

This reaction, like that between Zn and Cu^{2+}, can serve as a source of electrical energy in a voltaic cell. The cell is similar to that shown in Figure 18.2 except that, in the anode compartment, a nickel electrode is surrounded by a solution of a nickel(II) salt, such as $NiCl_2$ or $NiSO_4$. The cell notation is $Ni \mid Ni^{2+} \parallel Cu^{2+} \mid Cu$.

Nichrome or graphite can also be used.

Another spontaneous redox reaction that can serve as a source of electrical energy is that between zinc metal and Co^{3+} ions:

$$Zn(s) + 2Co^{3+}(aq) \longrightarrow Zn^{2+}(aq) + 2Co^{2+}(aq)$$

A voltaic cell using this reaction is similar to the Zn-Cu^{2+} cell; the $Zn \mid Zn^{2+}$ half-cell and the salt bridge are the same. Because no metal is involved in the cathode half-reaction, an *inert* electrode that conducts an electric current is used. Frequently, the cathode is made of platinum (Figure 18.3, p. 484). In the cathode, Co^{3+} ions are provided by a solution of $Co(NO_3)_3$. The half-reactions occurring in the cell are

anode:	$Zn(s) \longrightarrow Zn^{2+}(aq) + 2e^-$	(oxidation)
cathode:	$Co^{3+}(aq) + e^- \longrightarrow Co^{2+}(aq)$	(reduction)

The cell notation is $Zn \mid Zn^{2+} \parallel Co^{3+}, Co^{2+} \mid Pt$. Note that a comma separates the half-cell components that are in the *same* phase. The symbol Pt is used to indicate the presence of an inert platinum electrode. A single vertical line separates Pt (a solid) from the components of the half-cell, which are in the liquid phase.

Example 18.1 When chlorine gas is bubbled through an aqueous solution of NaBr, chloride ions and liquid bromine are the products of the spontaneous reaction. For this cell,

(a) Draw a sketch of the cell, labeling the anode, the cathode, and the direction of electron flow.
(b) Write the half-reaction that takes place at the anode and at the cathode.
(c) Write a balanced equation for the cell reaction.
(d) Write an abbreviated notation for the cell.

Strategy Split the reaction into two half-reactions. Remember that oxidation occurs at the anode, reduction at the cathode. Anions move to the anode, cations to the cathode. Electrons are produced at the anode and transferred through the external circuit to the cathode, where they are consumed.

SOLUTION

(a) Figure 18.4 shows the cell with the appropriate labeled parts and the direction of electron flow indicated.

(b) cathode: $Cl_2(g) + 2e^- \longrightarrow 2Cl^-(aq)$ (reduction)
anode: $2Br^-(aq) \longrightarrow Br_2(l) + 2e^-$ (oxidation)

(c) $Cl_2(g) + 2Br^-(aq) \longrightarrow 2Cl^-(aq) + Br_2(l)$

(d) $Pt \mid Br_2, Br^- \parallel Cl^- \mid Cl_2 \mid Pt$

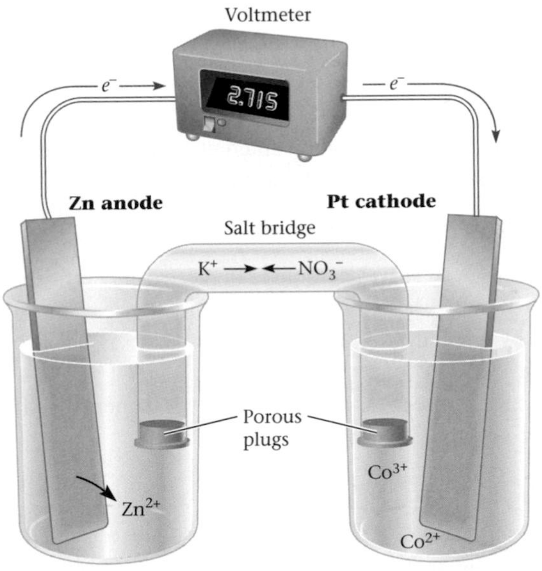

Figure 18.3
A Zn-Co^{3+} voltaic cell. A platinum electrode is immersed in a solution containing Co^{3+} and Co^{2+} ions. The spontaneous cell reaction is

$$Zn(s) + 2Co^{3+}(aq) \longrightarrow Zn^{2+}(aq) + 2Co^{2+}(aq)$$

The platinum electrode does not participate in the reaction. The zinc electrode does.

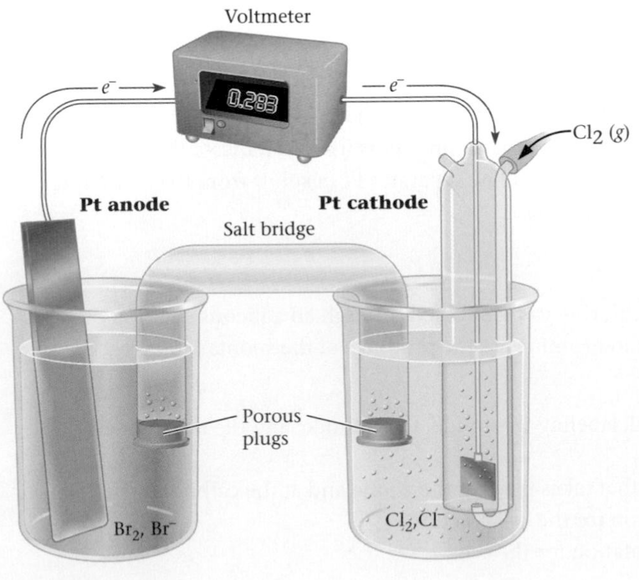

Figure 18.4
A Cl_2-Br_2 voltaic cell. In this cell the spontaneous cell reaction is

$$Cl_2(g) + 2Br^-(aq) \longrightarrow 2Cl^-(aq) + Br_2(l)$$

Both electrodes are platinum, with the anode at the left and the cathode at the right.

To summarize our discussion of the structure of voltaic cells, note that—

- *a voltaic cell consists of two half-cells.* They are joined by an external electric circuit through which electrons move and a salt bridge through which ions move.
- *each half-cell consists of an electrode dipping into a water solution.* If a metal participates in the cell reaction, either as a product or as a reactant, it is ordinarily used as the electrode; otherwise, an inert electrode such as platinum is used.
- *in one half-cell, oxidation occurs at the anode; in the other, reduction takes place at the cathode.* The overall cell reaction is the sum of the half-reactions taking place at the anode and cathode.

18.2 STANDARD VOLTAGES

The driving force behind the spontaneous reaction in a voltaic cell is measured by the cell voltage, which is an *intensive* property, independent of the number of electrons passing through the cell. Cell voltage depends on the nature of the redox reaction and the concentrations of the species involved; for the moment, we'll concentrate on the first of these factors.

The standard voltage for a given cell is that measured when the current flow is essentially zero, ***all ions and molecules in solution are at a concentration of 1 M, and all gases are at a pressure of 1 atm.*** To illustrate, consider the Zn-H^+ cell. Let us suppose that the half-cells are set up in such a way that the concentrations of Zn^{2+} and H^+ are both 1 *M* and the pressure of $H_2(g)$ is 1 atm. Under these conditions, the cell voltage at very low current flow is +0.762 V. This quantity is referred to as the **standard voltage** and is given the symbol $\boldsymbol{E°}$.

CENGAGENOW™ Click Coached Problems for a self-study module on **voltaic cell potentials.**

$$\mathrm{Zn}(s) + 2\mathrm{H}^+(aq, 1\,M) \longrightarrow \mathrm{Zn}^{2+}(aq, 1\,M) + \mathrm{H}_2(g, 1\text{ atm}) \qquad E° = +0.762\text{ V}$$

$E°_{red}$ and $E°_{ox}$

Any redox reaction can be split into two half-reactions, an oxidation and a reduction. It is possible to associate standard voltages $\boldsymbol{E°_{ox}}$ (standard oxidation voltage) and $\boldsymbol{E°_{red}}$ (standard reduction voltage) with the oxidation and reduction half-reactions. The standard voltage for the overall reaction, $E°$, is the sum of these two quantities

$$E° = E°_{red} + E°_{ox} \qquad \textbf{(18.1)}$$

To illustrate, consider the reaction between Zn and H^+ ions, for which the standard voltage is +0.762 V.

$$+0.762\text{ V} = E°_{red}(\mathrm{H}^+ \longrightarrow \mathrm{H}_2) + E°_{ox}(\mathrm{Zn} \longrightarrow \mathrm{Zn}^{2+})$$

There is no way to measure the standard voltage for a half-reaction; only $E°$ can be measured directly. To obtain values for $E°_{ox}$ and $E°_{red}$, the value zero is arbitrarily assigned to the standard voltage for reduction of H^+ ions to H_2 gas:

You need two half-cells to measure a voltage.

$$2\mathrm{H}^+(aq, 1\,M) + 2e^- \longrightarrow \mathrm{H}_2(g, 1\text{ atm}) \qquad E°_{red}(\mathrm{H}^+ \longrightarrow \mathrm{H}_2) = 0.000\text{ V}$$

Using this convention, it follows that the standard voltage for the oxidation of zinc must be +0.762 V; that is,

$$\mathrm{Zn}(s) \longrightarrow \mathrm{Zn}^{2+}(aq, 1\,M) + 2e^- \qquad E°_{ox}(\mathrm{Zn} \longrightarrow \mathrm{Zn}^{2+}) = +0.762\text{ V}$$

As soon as one half-reaction voltage is established, others can be calculated. For example, the standard voltage for the Zn-Cu^{2+} cell shown in Figure 18.2 is found to be +1.101 V. Knowing that $E°_{ox}$ for zinc is +0.762 V, it follows that

$$E°_{red}(\mathrm{Cu}^{2+} \longrightarrow \mathrm{Cu}) = E° - E°_{ox}(\mathrm{Zn} \longrightarrow \mathrm{Zn}^{2+})$$
$$= 1.101\text{ V} - 0.762\text{ V} = +0.339\text{ V}$$

Standard half-cell voltages are ordinarily obtained from a list of **standard potentials** such as those in Table 18.1 (page 487). The potentials listed are the standard voltages for reduction half-reactions, that is,

$$\text{standard potential} = E^\circ_{red}$$

For example, the standard potentials listed in the table for $Zn^{2+} \longrightarrow Zn$ and $Cu^{2+} \longrightarrow Cu$ are -0.762 V and $+0.339$ V, respectively; it follows that at 25°C

$$Zn^{2+}(aq, 1\,M) + 2e^- \longrightarrow Zn(s) \qquad E^\circ_{red} = -0.762\text{ V}$$
$$Cu^{2+}(aq, 1\,M) + 2e^- \longrightarrow Cu(s) \qquad E^\circ_{red} = +0.339\text{ V}$$

To obtain the standard voltage for an oxidation half-reaction, all you have to do is ***change the sign of the standard potential listed in Table 18.1.*** For example, knowing that

$$Zn^{2+}(aq) + 2e^- \longrightarrow Zn(s) \qquad E^\circ_{red} = -0.762\text{ V}$$

it follows that

$$Zn(s) \longrightarrow Zn^{2+}(aq) + 2e^- \qquad E^\circ_{ox} = +0.762\text{ V}$$

Standard potential = E°_{red}.

Again, we have

$$Cu^{2+}(aq) + 2e^- \longrightarrow Cu(s) \qquad E^\circ_{red} = +0.339\text{ V}$$

so,

$$Cu(s) \longrightarrow Cu^{2+}(aq) + 2e^- \qquad E^\circ_{ox} = -0.339\text{ V}$$

Another way to express this principle is to say that ***standard voltages for forward and reverse half-reactions are equal in magnitude but opposite in sign.***

Strength of Oxidizing and Reducing Agents

As pointed out in Chapter 4, an oxidizing agent is a species that can gain electrons; it is a reactant in a reduction half-reaction. Table 18.1 lists reduction half-reactions from left to right; it follows that ***oxidizing agents are located in the left column of the table.*** All of the species listed in that column (Li^+, . . . , F_2) are, in principle, oxidizing agents. A "strong" oxidizing agent is one that has a strong attraction for electrons and hence *can readily oxidize other species.* In contrast, a "weak" oxidizing agent does not gain electrons readily. It is capable of reacting only with those species that are very easily oxidized.

The strength of an oxidizing agent is directly related to the standard voltage for its reduction, E°_{red}. ***The more positive E°_{red} is, the stronger the oxidizing agent.*** Looking at Table 18.1, you can see that ***oxidizing strength increases moving down the left column.*** The Li^+ ion, at the top of that column, is a very weak oxidizing agent with a large negative reduction voltage ($E^\circ_{red} = -3.040$ V). In practice, cations of the Group 1 metals (Li^+, Na^+, K^+, . . .) and the Group 2 metals (Mg^{2+}, Ca^{2+}, . . .) never act as oxidizing agents in water solution.

Further down the left column of Table 18.1, the H^+ ion ($E^\circ_{red} = 0.000$ V) is a reasonably strong oxidizing agent. It is capable of oxidizing many metals, including magnesium and zinc:

$$Mg(s) + 2H^+(aq) \longrightarrow Mg^{2+}(aq) + H_2(g) \qquad E^\circ = +2.357\text{ V}$$
$$Zn(s) + 2H^+(aq) \longrightarrow Zn^{2+}(aq) + H_2(g) \qquad E^\circ = +0.762\text{ V}$$

The strongest oxidizing agents are those at the bottom of the left column. Species such as $Cr_2O_7^{2-}$ ($E^\circ_{red} = +1.33$ V) and Cl_2 ($E^\circ_{red} = +1.360$ V) are commonly used as oxidizing agents in the laboratory. The fluorine molecule, at the bottom of the left column, should be the strongest of all oxidizing agents. In practice, fluorine is seldom used as an oxidizing agent in water solution. The F_2 molecule takes electrons away from just about anything, including water, often with explosive violence.

The arguments we have just gone through can be applied, in reverse, to ***reducing agents, listed in the column to the right of Table 18.1*** (Li, . . . , F^-). In principle, at least, all of them can supply electrons to another species in a redox reaction. Their strength as reducing

Table 18.1 Standard Potentials in Water Solution at 25°C

Acidic Solution, $[H^+] = 1\ M$

Increasing strength of oxidizing agents (upward arrow)

Increasing strength of reducing agents (downward arrow)

		E°_{red} (V)
$Li^+(aq) + e^-$	$\longrightarrow Li(s)$	−3.040
$K^+(aq) + e^-$	$\longrightarrow K(s)$	−2.936
$Ba^{2+}(aq) + 2e^-$	$\longrightarrow Ba(s)$	−2.906
$Ca^{2+}(aq) + 2e^-$	$\longrightarrow Ca(s)$	−2.869
$Na^+(aq) + e^-$	$\longrightarrow Na(s)$	−2.714
$Mg^{2+}(aq) + 2e^-$	$\longrightarrow Mg(s)$	−2.357
$Al^{3+}(aq) + 3e^-$	$\longrightarrow Al(s)$	−1.68
$Mn^{2+}(aq) + 2e^-$	$\longrightarrow Mn(s)$	−1.182
$Zn^{2+}(aq) + 2e^-$	$\longrightarrow Zn(s)$	−0.762
$Cr^{3+}(aq) + 3e^-$	$\longrightarrow Cr(s)$	−0.744
$Fe^{2+}(aq) + 2e^-$	$\longrightarrow Fe(s)$	−0.409
$Cr^{3+}(aq) + e^-$	$\longrightarrow Cr^{2+}(aq)$	−0.408
$Cd^{2+}(aq) + 2e^-$	$\longrightarrow Cd(s)$	−0.402
$PbSO_4(s) + 2e^-$	$\longrightarrow Pb(s) + SO_4^{2-}(aq)$	−0.356
$Tl^+(aq) + e^-$	$\longrightarrow Tl(s)$	−0.336
$Co^{2+}(aq) + 2e^-$	$\longrightarrow Co(s)$	−0.282
$Ni^{2+}(aq) + 2e^-$	$\longrightarrow Ni(s)$	−0.236
$AgI(s) + e^-$	$\longrightarrow Ag(s) + I^-(aq)$	−0.152
$Sn^{2+}(aq) + 2e^-$	$\longrightarrow Sn(s)$	−0.141
$Pb^{2+}(aq) + 2e^-$	$\longrightarrow Pb(s)$	−0.127
$2H^+(aq) + 2e^-$	$\longrightarrow H_2(g)$	0.000
$AgBr(s) + e^-$	$\longrightarrow Ag(s) + Br^-(aq)$	0.073
$S(s) + 2H^+(aq) + 2e^-$	$\longrightarrow H_2S(aq)$	0.144
$Sn^{4+}(aq) + 2e^-$	$\longrightarrow Sn^{2+}(aq)$	0.154
$SO_4^{2-}(aq) + 4H^+(aq) + 2e^-$	$\longrightarrow SO_2(g) + 2H_2O$	0.155
$Cu^{2+}(aq) + e^-$	$\longrightarrow Cu^+(aq)$	0.161
$Cu^{2+}(aq) + 2e^-$	$\longrightarrow Cu(s)$	0.339
$Cu^+(aq) + e^-$	$\longrightarrow Cu(s)$	0.518
$I_2(s) + 2e^-$	$\longrightarrow 2I^-(aq)$	0.534
$Fe^{3+}(aq) + e^-$	$\longrightarrow Fe^{2+}(aq)$	0.769
$Hg_2^{2+}(aq) + 2e^-$	$\longrightarrow 2Hg(l)$	0.796
$Ag^+(aq) + e^-$	$\longrightarrow Ag(s)$	0.799
$2Hg^{2+}(aq) + 2e^-$	$\longrightarrow Hg_2^{2+}(aq)$	0.908
$NO_3^-(aq) + 4H^+(aq) + 3e^-$	$\longrightarrow NO(g) + 2H_2O$	0.964
$AuCl_4^-(aq) + 3e^-$	$\longrightarrow Au(s) + 4Cl^-(aq)$	1.001
$Br_2(l) + 2e^-$	$\longrightarrow 2Br^-(aq)$	1.077
$O_2(g) + 4H^+(aq) + 4e^-$	$\longrightarrow 2H_2O$	1.229
$MnO_2(s) + 4H^+(aq) + 2e^-$	$\longrightarrow Mn^{2+}(aq) + 2H_2O$	1.229
$Cr_2O_7^{2-}(aq) + 14H^+(aq) + 6e^-$	$\longrightarrow 2Cr^{3+}(aq) + 7H_2O$	1.33
$Cl_2(g) + 2e^-$	$\longrightarrow 2Cl^-(aq)$	1.360
$ClO_3^-(aq) + 6H^+(aq) + 5e^-$	$\longrightarrow \frac{1}{2}Cl_2(g) + 3H_2O$	1.458
$Au^{3+}(aq) + 3e^-$	$\longrightarrow Au(s)$	1.498
$MnO_4^-(aq) + 8H^+(aq) + 5e^-$	$\longrightarrow Mn^{2+}(aq) + 4H_2O$	1.512
$PbO_2(s) + SO_4^{2-}(aq) + 4H^+(aq) + 2e^-$	$\longrightarrow PbSO_4(s) + 2H_2O$	1.687
$H_2O_2(aq) + 2H^+(aq) + 2e^-$	$\longrightarrow 2H_2O$	1.763
$Co^{3+}(aq) + e^-$	$\longrightarrow Co^{2+}(aq)$	1.953
$F_2(g) + 2e^-$	$\longrightarrow 2F^-(aq)$	2.889

Basic Solution, $[OH^-] = 1\ M$

		E°_{red} (V)
$Fe(OH)_2(s) + 2e^-$	$\longrightarrow Fe(s) + 2OH^-(aq)$	−0.891
$2H_2O + 2e^-$	$\longrightarrow H_2(g) + 2OH^-(aq)$	−0.828
$Fe(OH)_3(s) + e^-$	$\longrightarrow Fe(OH)_2(s) + OH^-(aq)$	−0.547
$S(s) + 2e^-$	$\longrightarrow S^{2-}(aq)$	−0.445
$NO_3^-(aq) + 2H_2O + 3e^-$	$\longrightarrow NO(g) + 4OH^-(aq)$	−0.140
$NO_3^-(aq) + H_2O + 2e^-$	$\longrightarrow NO_2^-(aq) + 2OH^-(aq)$	0.004
$ClO_4^-(aq) + H_2O + 2e^-$	$\longrightarrow ClO_3^-(aq) + 2OH^-(aq)$	0.398
$O_2(g) + 2H_2O + 4e^-$	$\longrightarrow 4OH^-(aq)$	0.401
$ClO_3^-(aq) + 3H_2O + 6e^-$	$\longrightarrow Cl^-(aq) + 6OH^-(aq)$	0.614
$ClO^-(aq) + H_2O + 2e^-$	$\longrightarrow Cl^-(aq) + 2OH^-(aq)$	0.890

Lithium is the strongest reducing agent.

O = strongest oxidizing agent; R = strongest reducing agent.

Fluorine is the strongest oxidizing agent.

Lithium and fluorine are very dangerous materials to work with.

agents is directly related to their E°_{ox} values. ***The more positive E°_{ox} is, the stronger the reducing agent.*** Looking at the values, remembering that $E^\circ_{ox} = -E^\circ_{red}$,

$$Li(s) \longrightarrow Li^+(aq) + e^- \qquad E^\circ_{ox} = +3.040 \text{ V}$$
$$H_2(g) \longrightarrow 2H^+(aq) + 2e^- \qquad E^\circ_{ox} = 0.000 \text{ V}$$
$$2F^-(aq) \longrightarrow F_2(g) + 2e^- \qquad E^\circ_{ox} = -2.889 \text{ V}$$

It should be clear that ***reducing strength decreases moving down the table.*** Actually, the five metals at the top of the right column (Li, K, Ba, Ca, Na) cannot be used as reducing agents in water solution because they react directly with water, reducing it to hydrogen gas:

$$Li(s) + H_2O \longrightarrow Li^+(aq) + OH^-(aq) + \tfrac{1}{2}H_2(g)$$
$$Ba(s) + 2H_2O \longrightarrow Ba^{2+}(aq) + 2OH^-(aq) + H_2(g)$$

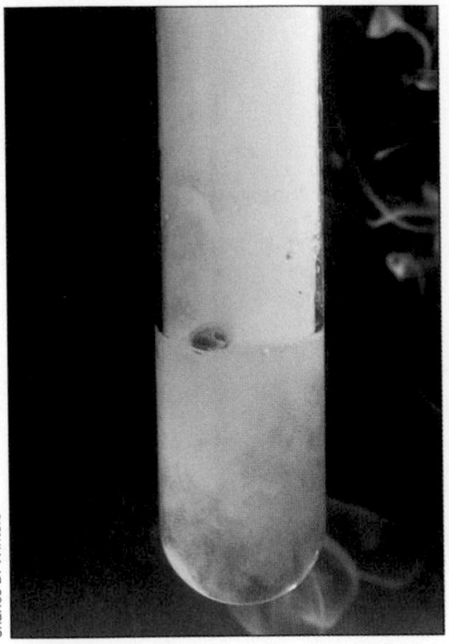

Charles D. Winters

Lithium as a reducing agent. Lithium, the strongest reducing agent listed in Table 18.1, is shown reacting with water. The heat of reaction is igniting the hydrogen produced.

Example 18.2 Conceptual

Consider the following species in acidic solution: MnO_4^-, I^-, NO_3^-, H_2S, and Fe^{2+}. Using Table 18.1,

(a) classify each of these as an oxidizing and/or reducing agent.
(b) arrange the oxidizing agents in order of increasing strength.
(c) do the same with the reducing agents.

Strategy Remember that oxidizing agents are located in the left column of Table 18.1, reducing agents in the right column. Large positive values of E°_{red} and E°_{ox} are associated with strong oxidizing and reducing agents, respectively.

SOLUTION

(a) Oxidizing agents:

$$Fe^{2+} (E^\circ_{red} = -0.409 \text{ V}),\ NO_3^- (E^\circ_{red} = +0.964 \text{ V}),\ MnO_4^- (E^\circ_{red} = +1.512 \text{ V})$$

Reducing agents:

$$Fe^{2+} (E^\circ_{ox} = -0.769 \text{ V}),\ I^- (E^\circ_{ox} = -0.534 \text{ V}),\ H_2S (E^\circ_{ox} = -0.144 \text{ V})$$

Note that Fe^{2+} can act either as an oxidizing agent, in which case it is reduced to Fe, or as a reducing agent, in which case it is oxidized to Fe^{3+}.

(b) Comparing values of E°_{red},

$$Fe^{2+} < NO_3^- < MnO_4^-$$

This ranking correlates with the positions of these species in the left column of Table 18.1; MnO_4^- is near the bottom, Fe^{2+} closest to the top.

(c) Comparing values of E°_{ox},

$$Fe^{2+} < I^- < H_2S$$

Calculation of E° from E°_{red} and E°_{ox}

As pointed out earlier, the standard voltage for a redox reaction is the sum of the standard voltages of the two half-reactions, reduction and oxidation; that is,

$$E^\circ = E^\circ_{red} + E^\circ_{ox}$$

This simple relation makes it possible, using Table 18.1, to calculate the standard voltages for more than 3000 different redox reactions.

Example 18.3 Graded

Consider the voltaic cell in which the reaction is

$$2Ag^+(aq) + Cd(s) \longrightarrow 2Ag(s) + Cd^{2+}(aq)$$

* (a) Use Table 18.1 to calculate $E°$ for the voltaic cell.

** (b) If the value zero is arbitrarily assigned to the standard voltage for the reduction of Ag^+ ions to Ag, what is $E°_{red}$ for the reduction of Cd^{2+} ions to Cd?

SOLUTION

(a) The oxidation number of silver drops from +1 (Ag^+) to zero (Ag), so the reduction half-reaction with its cell potential is

$$2Ag^+(aq) + 2e^- \longrightarrow 2Ag(s) \qquad E°_{red} = +0.799 \text{ V}$$

The oxidation number of cadmium increases from 0 (Cd) to +2 (Cd^{2+}), so the oxidation half-reaction is

$$Cd(s) \longrightarrow Cd^{2+}(aq) + 2e^- \qquad E°_{ox} = -E°_{red} = -(-0.402 \text{ V}) = 0.402 \text{ V}$$

We add the half-equations to obtain the overall reaction and add the half-reaction voltages to obtain the overall voltage:

$$2Ag^+(aq) + 2e^- \longrightarrow 2Ag(s) \qquad E°_{red} = +0.799 \text{ V}$$
$$Cd(s) \longrightarrow Cd^{2+}(aq) + 2e^- \qquad E°_{ox} = +0.402 \text{ V}$$
$$2Ag^+(aq) + Cd(s) \longrightarrow 2Ag(s) + Cd^{2+}(aq) \qquad E° = +1.201 \text{ V}$$

(b) Recall that $E° = E°_{ox} + E°_{red}$. If $E°_{red} = 0$ for the reduction of silver, then $E°_{ox}$ must satisfy

$$1.201 = 0 + E°_{ox} \qquad E°_{ox} = 1.201 \text{ V}$$

Since $E°_{red}$ for the reduction of Cd^{2+} is asked for, then $E°_{red} = -E°_{ox} = -1.201$ V.

Figure 18.5
Oxidation of Ni by Cu^{2+}. Nickel metal reacts spontaneously with Cu^{2+} ions, producing Cu metal and Ni^{2+} ions. Copper plates out on the surface of the nickel, and the blue color of Cu^{2+} is replaced by the green color of Ni^{2+}.

Two general points concerning cell voltages are illustrated by Example 18.3.

1. The calculated voltage, $E°$, is always a positive quantity for a reaction taking place in a voltaic cell.
2. The quantities $E°$, $E°_{ox}$, and $E°_{red}$ are independent of how the equation for the cell reaction is written. You *never* multiply the voltage by the coefficients of the balanced equation.

It would be nice if you could double the voltage by rewriting the equation, but you can't.

Spontaneity of Redox Reactions

Since you add to obtain $E°$ it makes no difference which you write first, $E°_{red}$ or $E°_{ox}$.

To determine whether a given redox reaction is spontaneous, apply a simple principle:

If the calculated voltage for a redox reaction is a positive quantity, the reaction will be spontaneous. If the calculated voltage is negative, the reaction is not spontaneous.

Ordinarily, this principle is applied at standard concentrations (1 atm for gases, 1 *M* for species in aqueous solution). Hence it is the sign of $E°$ that serves as the criterion for spontaneity. To show how this works, consider the problem of oxidizing nickel metal to Ni^{2+} ions. This cannot be accomplished by using 1 *M* Zn^{2+} ions:

$$Ni(s) + Zn^{2+}(aq, 1\,M) \longrightarrow Ni^{2+}(aq, 1\,M) + Zn(s)$$
$$E° = E°_{ox}\,Ni + E°_{red}\,Zn^{2+} = +0.236 \text{ V} - 0.762 \text{ V} = -0.526 \text{ V}$$

Sure enough, if you immerse a bar of nickel in a solution of 1 *M* $ZnSO_4$, nothing happens. Suppose, however, you add the nickel bar to a solution of 1 *M* $CuSO_4$ (Figure 18.5; left beaker). As time passes, the nickel is oxidized and the Cu^{2+} ions reduced (beaker at right of Figure 18.5) through the spontaneous redox reaction

$$Ni(s) + Cu^{2+}(aq, 1\ M) \longrightarrow Ni^{2+}(aq, 1\ M) + Cu(s)$$
$$E° = E°_{ox}\ Ni + E°_{red}\ Cu^{2+} = +0.236\ V + 0.339\ V = +0.575\ V$$

Example 18.4 Graded

Using standard potentials listed in Table 18.1, decide whether at standard concentrations

*(a) the reaction

$$2Fe^{3+}(aq) + 2I^-(aq) \longrightarrow 2Fe^{2+}(aq) + I_2(s)$$

will occur.

**(b) $Fe(s)$ will be oxidized to Fe^{2+} by treatment with hydrochloric acid.

***(c) a redox reaction will occur when the following species are mixed in acidic solution: Cl^-, Fe^{2+}, Cr^{2+}, I_2.

SOLUTION

(a) Breaking up the reaction into two half-reactions:

$$2Fe^{3+}(aq) + 2e^- \longrightarrow 2Fe^{2+}(aq) \qquad E°_{red} = +0.769\ V$$
$$2I^-(aq) \longrightarrow I_2(s) + 2e^- \qquad E°_{ox} = -0.534\ V$$
$$2Fe^{3+}(aq) + 2I^-(aq) \longrightarrow 2Fe^{2+}(aq) + I_2(s) \qquad E° = +0.235\ V$$

Since $E°$ is positive, we conclude that the reaction is spontaneous at standard concentrations.

(b) The oxidation half-reaction is

$$Fe(s) \longrightarrow Fe^{2+}(aq) + 2e^- \qquad E°_{ox} = +0.409\ V$$

Hydrochloric acid consists of H^+ and Cl^- ions. Of these two ions, only H^+ is listed in the left column of Table 18.1; the Cl^- ion cannot be reduced. The reduction half-reaction must be

$$2H^+(aq) + 2e^- \longrightarrow H_2(g) \qquad E°_{red} = 0.000\ V$$

Because the calculated voltage is positive,

$$E° = +0.409\ V + 0.000\ V = +0.409\ V$$

The following redox reaction, obtained by summing the half-reactions,

$$Fe(s) + 2H^+(aq) \longrightarrow Fe^{2+}(aq) + H_2(g)$$

should and does occur (Figure 18.6).

(c) The most straightforward way to solve this problem is to start by listing all the possible half-reactions of these species as given in Table 18.1. Then see if you can combine an $E°_{red}$ with an $E°_{ox}$ to give a positive $E°$.

Possible Reductions	Possible Oxidations
$Fe^{2+} \longrightarrow Fe$; $E°_{red} = -0.409\ V$	$Cl^- \longrightarrow Cl_2$; $E°_{ox} = -1.360\ V$
$I_2 \longrightarrow I^-$; $E°_{red} = +0.534\ V$	$Cr^{2+} \longrightarrow Cr^{3+}$; $E°_{ox} = +0.408\ V$
	$Fe^{2+} \longrightarrow Fe^{3+}$; $E°_{ox} = -0.769\ V$

The only combination that gives a positive $E°$ is the reaction of iodine with chromium(II):

$$I_2(s) + 2e^- \longrightarrow 2I^-(aq) \qquad E°_{red} = +0.534\ V$$
$$2Cr^{2+}(aq) \longrightarrow 2Cr^{3+}(aq) + 2e^- \qquad E°_{ox} = +0.408\ V$$
$$I_2(s) + 2Cr^{2+}(aq) \longrightarrow 2I^-(aq) + 2Cr^{3+}(aq) \qquad E° = +0.942\ V$$

Charles D. Winters

Figure 18.6
Oxidation of Fe by H^+. Finely divided iron in the form of steel wool reacts with hydrochloric acid to evolve hydrogen: $Fe(s) + 2H^+(aq) \longrightarrow Fe^{2+}(aq) + H_2(g)$. The hydrogen gas is creating foam as it is produced along the strands of the steel wool.

18.3 RELATIONS BETWEEN $E°$, $\Delta G°$, AND K

As pointed out previously, the value of the standard cell voltage, $E°$, is a measure of the spontaneity of a cell reaction. In Chapter 17, we showed that the standard free energy change, $\Delta G°$, is a general criterion for reaction spontaneity. As you might suppose, these two quantities have a simple relation to one another and to the equilibrium constant, K, for the cell reaction.

$E°$ and $\Delta G°$

It can be shown by a thermodynamic argument that we will not go through here that these two quantities are related by the equation

$$\Delta G° = -nFE° \qquad \textbf{(18.2)}$$

Spontaneous reaction: $E° > 0$, $\Delta G° < 0$, $K > 1$.

where—

- $\Delta G°$ is the standard free energy change (gases at 1 atm, species in solution at 1 M) for the reaction.
- $E°$ is the standard voltage for the cell reaction.
- n is the number of moles of electrons transferred in the reaction.
- F, called the **Faraday constant,** has the following value: 9.648×10^4 J/mol·V (J = joule, V = volt).

$F = 9.648 \times 10^4$ C/mol
$= 9.648 \times 10^4$ J/mol·V

Notice from this equation that $\Delta G°$ and $E°$ have opposite signs. This is reasonable; a spontaneous reaction is one for which $\Delta G°$ is *negative* but $E°$ is *positive.*

$E°$ and K

Redox reactions, like all reactions, eventually reach a state of equilibrium. It is possible to calculate the equilibrium constant for a redox reaction from the standard voltage. To do that, we start with the relation obtained in Chapter 17:

CENGAGENOW™
Click Coached Problems for a self-study module on **cell potential and the equilibrium constant.**

$$\Delta G° = -RT \ln K$$

We have just seen that $\Delta G° = -nFE°$. It follows that

$$RT \ln K = nFE°$$

or

$$E° = \frac{RT}{nF} \ln K$$

The quantity RT/F is readily evaluated at 25°C, the temperature at which standard potentials are tabulated.

$$\frac{RT}{F} = \frac{8.31 \text{ J/mol}\cdot\text{K} \times 298 \text{ K}}{9.648 \times 10^4 \text{ J/mol}\cdot\text{V}} = 0.0257 \text{ V}$$

Hence

$$E° = \frac{(0.0257 \text{ V})}{n} \ln K \qquad \text{(at 25°C)} \qquad \textbf{(18.3)}$$

Notice that if the standard voltage is positive, ln K is also positive, and K is greater than 1. Conversely, if the standard voltage is negative, ln K is also negative, and K is less than 1.

Example 18.5 For the reaction

$$3Ag(s) + NO_3^-(aq) + 4H^+(aq) \longrightarrow 3Ag^+(aq) + NO(g) + 2H_2O$$

use Table 18.1 to calculate, at 25°C,

(a) $\Delta G°$ (b) K

Strategy Split the redox equation into two half-equations (oxidation and reduction). This enables you to calculate both $E°$ and n. Then use Equations 18.2 and 18.3 to find $\Delta G°$ and K.

SOLUTION

(a) Ag is oxidized to Ag^+; NO_3^- is reduced to NO. The half-equations are

$$3Ag(s) \longrightarrow 3Ag^+(aq) + 3e^- \qquad E°_{ox} = -0.799\ V$$

Clearly, $n = 3$

$$NO_3^-(aq) + 4H^+(aq) + 3e^- \longrightarrow NO(g) + 2H_2O \qquad E°_{red} = +0.964\ V$$

$$E° = +0.165\ V$$

$$\Delta G° = -nFE = -3\ \text{mol} \times 9.648 \times 10^4 \frac{J}{\text{mol} \cdot V} \times 0.165\ V = -4.78 \times 10^4\ J = -47.8\ kJ$$

(b) $$\ln K = \frac{nE°}{(0.0257\ V)} = \frac{3(0.165)}{0.0257} = 19.3$$

$$K = e^{19.3} = 2.4 \times 10^8$$

Reality Check The answers to (a) and (b) are related through the equation $\Delta G° = -RT \ln K$. If you carry out the calculation, you will find that $\Delta G°$ and K are indeed consistent with one another.

Table 18.2 Relation Between $E°$, K, and $\Delta G°$ ($n = 2$)

$E°$ (V)	K	$\Delta G°$ (kJ)	$E°$ (V)	K	$\Delta G°$ (kJ)
+2.00	4×10^{67}	−400	−2.00	3×10^{-68}	+400
+1.00	6×10^{33}	−200	−1.00	2×10^{-34}	+200
+0.50	8×10^{16}	−100	−0.50	1×10^{-17}	+100
+0.25	3×10^{8}	−50	−0.25	4×10^{-9}	+50
+0.10	2×10^{3}	−20	−0.10	0.0004	+20
+0.05	50	−10	−0.05	0.02	+10
0.00	1	0			

The approach used in Example 18.5 to find the number of moles of electrons transferred, n, is generally useful. What you do is to break down the equation for the cell reaction into two half-equations, oxidation and reduction. The quantity n is the number of electrons appearing in either half-equation.

Table 18.2 lists values of K and $\Delta G°$ corresponding to various values of $E°$ with $n = 2$. Notice that—

- if $E°$ is greater than about +0.10 V, K is very large, and the reaction goes virtually to completion.
- if $E°$ is smaller than about −0.10 V, K is very small, so the reaction does not proceed to any appreciable extent.

Most redox reactions either go to completion or not at all.

Only if the standard voltage falls within a rather narrow range, say +0.10 to −0.10 V, will the value of K (and that of $\Delta G°$) be such that the reaction will produce an equilibrium mixture containing appreciable amounts of both reactants and products.

18.4 EFFECT OF CONCENTRATION ON VOLTAGE

CENGAGENOW™
Click Coached Problems for a self-study module on **voltaic cells under non-standard conditions.**

To this point, we have dealt only with "standard" voltages, that is, voltages when all gases are at 1 atm pressure and all species in aqueous solution are at a concentration of 1 M. When the concentration of a reactant or product changes, the voltage changes as well. Qualitatively, the direction in which the voltage shifts is readily predicted when you realize that cell voltage is directly related to reaction spontaneity.

1. Voltage will *increase* if the concentration of a reactant is increased or that of a product is decreased. Either of these changes increases the driving force behind the redox reaction, making it more spontaneous.
2. Voltage will *decrease* if the concentration of a reactant is decreased or that of a product is increased. Either of these changes makes the redox reaction less spontaneous.

When a voltaic cell operates, supplying electrical energy, the concentration of reactants decreases and that of the products increases. As time passes, the voltage drops steadily. Eventually it becomes zero, and we say that the cell is "dead." At that point, the redox reaction taking place within the cell is at equilibrium, and there is no driving force to produce a voltage.

That's what happens when you leave your car lights on, unless your car turns them off automatically.

Nernst Equation

To obtain a quantitative relation between cell voltage and concentration, it is convenient to start with the general expression for the free energy change discussed in Chapter 17:

$$\Delta G = \Delta G^\circ + RT \ln Q$$

where Q is the reaction quotient in which products appear in the numerator, reactants in the denominator. But $\Delta G^\circ = -nFE^\circ$ and $\Delta G = -nFE$, so we have

$$-nFE = -nFE^\circ + RT \ln Q$$

Solving for the cell voltage E,

$$E = E^\circ - \frac{RT}{nF} \ln Q$$

This relationship is known as the **Nernst equation,** after Walther Nernst (1864–1941), a brilliant and egocentric colleague of Arrhenius, who first proposed it in 1888. Recalling that, at 25°C, the quantity RT/F is 0.0257 V,

Nernst won the Nobel Prize in Chemistry in 1920.

$$E = E^\circ - \frac{(0.0257\ \text{V})}{n} \ln Q \qquad \textbf{(18.4)}$$

In this equation, E is the cell voltage, E° is the standard voltage, n is the number of moles of electrons exchanged in the reaction, and Q is the reaction quotient. Notice that—

- if $Q > 1$, which means that the concentrations of products are high relative to those of reactants, $\ln Q$ is positive and $E < E^\circ$.
- if $Q < 1$ (concentrations of products low relative to reactants), $\ln Q$ is negative and $E > E^\circ$.
- if $Q = 1$, as is the case under standard conditions, $\ln Q = 0$ and $E = E^\circ$.

Remember that gases enter Q as their partial pressures in atmospheres. Species in water solution enter as their molar concentrations. Pure liquids and solids do not appear in the expression for Q. For example,

$$a\text{A}(s) + b\text{B}(aq) \longrightarrow c\text{C}(aq) + d\text{D}(g) \qquad Q = \frac{[\text{C}]^c \times (P_\text{D})^d}{[\text{B}]^b}$$

Example 18.6 Graded

Consider a voltaic cell in which the following reaction occurs

$$O_2(g,\ 0.98\ \text{atm}) + 4H^+(aq,\ \text{pH} = 1.24) + 4Br^-(aq,\ 0.15\ M) \longrightarrow 2H_2O + 2Br_2(l)$$

*(a) Calculate E for the cell at 25°C.

**(b) When the voltaic cell is at 35°C, E is measured to be 0.039 V. What is E° at 35°C?

Strategy

(a) Find (1) Q, Then (2) n, (3) $E°$ and finally (4) substitute those values into the Nernst equation to find E.
(b) Use the same values for Q and n obtained in (a). Use the Nernst equation for any temperature T, *not* equation 18.4.

SOLUTION

(a) (1) $1.24 = -\log_{10}[H^+] \qquad [H^+] = 0.058\ M$

$$Q = \frac{1}{[H^+]^4\,(P_{O_2})\,[Br^-]^4} = \frac{1}{(0.058)^4(0.98)(0.15)^4}$$

(2) $= 1.8 \times 10^8$

To find n, break the reaction down into two half-reactions:

$$O_2(g) + 4H^+(aq) + 4e^- \longrightarrow 2H_2O$$
$$4Br^-(aq) \longrightarrow 4e^- + 2Br_2(l)$$

Clearly then, $n = 4$.

(3) $E° = E°_{red}\ O_2 + E°_{ox}\ Br^- = +1.229\ V - 1.077\ V = 0.152\ V$

(4) Substituting into the Nernst equation,

$$E = 0.152\ V - \frac{0.0257\ V}{4}\ln(1.8 \times 10^8) = 0.030\ V$$

(b) We solve for the standard voltage $E°$ by substituting into the equation

$$E = E° - \frac{RT}{nF}\ln Q$$

That gives

$$E° = 0.039\ V + \left[\frac{8.31\ J/mol \cdot K \times (273 + 35)\ K}{4 \times 9.648 \times 10^4\ J/mol \cdot V}\right]\ln(1.8 \times 10^8) = 0.165\ V$$

The Nernst equation can also be used to determine the effect of changes in concentration on the voltage of an individual half-cell, $E°_{red}$ or $E°_{ox}$. Consider, for example, the half-reaction

$$MnO_4^-(aq) + 8H^+(aq) + 5e^- \longrightarrow Mn^{2+}(aq) + 4H_2O \qquad E°_{red} = +1.512\ V$$

The Nernst equation takes the form

$$E_{red} = +1.512\ V - \frac{(0.0257\ V)}{5}\ln\frac{[Mn^{2+}]}{[MnO_4^-] \times [H^+]^8}$$

where E_{red} is the observed reduction voltage corresponding to any given concentrations of Mn^{2+}, MnO_4^-, and H^+.

Use of the Nernst Equation to Determine Ion Concentrations

In chemistry, the most important use of the Nernst equation lies in the experimental determination of the concentration of ions in solution. Suppose you measure the cell voltage E and know the concentration of all but one species in the two half-cells. It should then be possible to calculate the concentration of that species by using the Nernst equation (Example 18.7).

Example 18.7 Consider a voltaic cell at 25°C in which the reaction is

$$Zn(s) + 2H^+(aq) \longrightarrow Zn^{2+}(aq) + H_2(g)$$

It is found that the voltage is +0.560 V when $[Zn^{2+}] = 0.85\ M$ and $P_{H_2} = 0.988$ atm. What is the pH in the H_2-H half-cell?

Strategy This example is handled exactly like Example 18.6 except that you cannot obtain a numerical value for Q and in the last step you solve for $[H^+]$ instead of for E.

SOLUTION

(1) $$Q = \frac{[Zn^{2+}](P_{H_2})}{[H^+]^2} = \frac{(0.85)(0.988)}{[H^+]^2}$$

(2) $$n = 2 \quad \text{since } 2e^- \text{ are exchanged}$$

(3) $$E° = E°_{ox}\ Zn + E°_{red}\ H^+ = +0.762\ V$$

(4) Substituting into the Nernst equation, we have

$$E = E° - \frac{0.0257}{n} \ln Q$$

That gives

$$0.560\ V = +0.762\ V - \frac{0.0257}{2} \ln \frac{(0.85)(0.988)}{[H^+]^2}$$

$$\ln \frac{(0.84)}{[H^+]^2} = (0.762 - 0.560)\left(\frac{2}{0.0257}\right) = 15.7$$

$$\frac{0.84}{[H^+]^2} = 6.7 \times 10^6$$

$$[H^+] = 3.5 \times 10^{-4}$$

$$pH = 3.45$$

Reality Check E is less than $E°$ because the concentration of reactants, H^+ and Br^-, are less than 1 M.

As Example 18.7 implies, the $Zn|Zn^{2+}||H^+|H_2|Pt$ cell can be used to measure the concentration of H^+ or pH of a solution. Indeed, cells of this type are commonly used to measure pH; Figure 18.7 shows a schematic diagram of a cell used with a pH meter. The pH meter, referred to in Chapter 13, is actually a high-resistance voltmeter calibrated to read pH rather than voltage. The cell connected to the pH meter consists of two half-cells. One of these is a reference half-cell of known voltage. The other half-cell contains a solution of known pH separated by a thin, fragile *glass electrode* from a solution whose pH is to be determined. The voltage of this cell is a linear function of the pH of the solution in the beaker.

Specific ion electrodes, similar in design to the glass electrode, have been developed to analyze for a variety of cations and anions. One of the first to be used extensively was a fluoride ion electrode that is sensitive to F^- at concentrations as low as 0.1 part per million and hence is ideal for monitoring fluoridated water supplies. An electrode that is specific for Cl^- ions is used to diagnose cystic fibrosis. Attached directly to the skin, it detects the abnormally high concentrations of sodium chloride in sweat that are a characteristic symptom of this disorder. Diagnoses that used to require an hour or more can now be carried out in a few minutes; as a result, large numbers of children can be screened rapidly and routinely.

The general approach illustrated by Example 18.7 is widely used to determine equilibrium constants for solution reactions. The pH meter in particular can be used to determine acid or base equilibrium constants by measuring the pH of solutions containing known concentrations of weak acids or bases. Specific ion electrodes are readily adapted to the determination of solubility product constants. For example, a chloride ion electrode can be used to find $[Cl^-]$ in equilibrium with $AgCl(s)$ and a known $[Ag^+]$. From that information, K_{sp} of AgCl can be calculated.

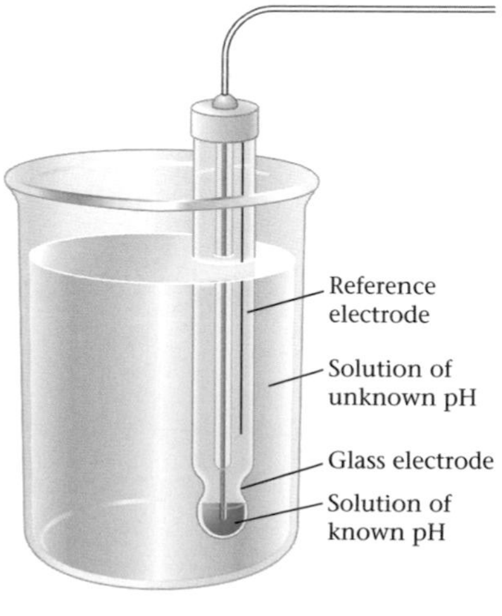

Figure 18.7
Electrode for a pH meter. The pH of a solution can be determined with the aid of a "glass electrode." The voltage between the glass electrode and the reference electrode is directly related to pH. The leads from the electrodes are connected to a pH meter.

18.5 ELECTROLYTIC CELLS

CENGAGENOW™
Click Coached Problems for a self-study module on **electrolytic cells.**

In an **electrolytic cell,** a nonspontaneous redox reaction is made to occur by pumping electrical energy into the system. A generalized diagram for such a cell is shown in Figure 18.8. The storage battery at the left provides a source of direct electric current. From the terminals of the battery, two wires lead to the electrolytic cell. This consists of two electrodes, A and C, dipping into a solution containing ions M^+ and X^-.

The battery acts as an electron pump, pushing electrons into the *cathode,* C, and removing them from the *anode,* A. To maintain electrical neutrality, some process within the cell must consume electrons at C and liberate them at A. This process is an oxidation-reduction reaction; when carried out in an electrolytic cell, it is called **electrolysis.** At the cathode, an ion or molecule undergoes reduction by accepting electrons. At the anode, electrons are produced by the oxidation of an ion or molecule.

Oxidation occurs at the anode, reduction at the cathode, in both voltaic and electrolytic cells.

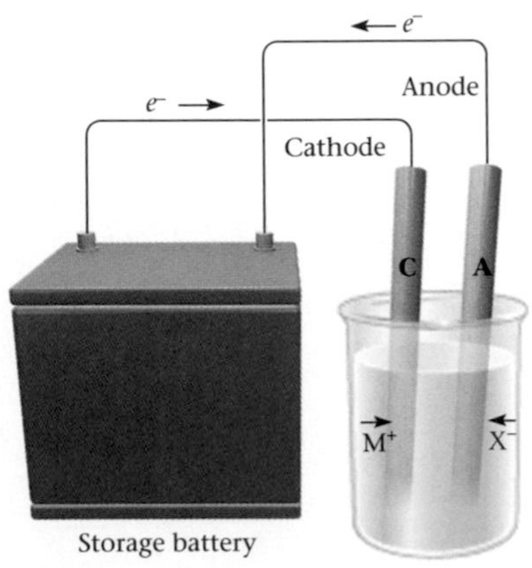

Figure 18.8
Diagram of an electrolytic cell. Electrons enter the cathode from an external source. Cations move to the cathode, where they are reduced, and anions move to the anode, where they are oxidized.

Quantitative Relationships

There is a simple relationship between the amount of electricity passed through an electrolytic cell and the amounts of substances produced by oxidation or reduction at the electrodes. From the balanced half-equations

$$Ag^+(aq) + e^- \longrightarrow Ag(s)$$
$$Cu^{2+}(aq) + 2e^- \longrightarrow Cu(s)$$
$$Au^{3+}(aq) + 3e^- \longrightarrow Au(s)$$

you can deduce that

$$1 \text{ mol of } e^- \longrightarrow 1 \text{ mol of Ag (107.9 g of Ag)}$$
$$2 \text{ mol of } e^- \longrightarrow 1 \text{ mol of Cu (63.55 g of Cu)}$$
$$3 \text{ mol of } e^- \longrightarrow 1 \text{ mol of Au (197.0 g of Au)}$$

Relations of this type, obtained from balanced half-equations, can be used in many practical calculations involving electrolytic cells. You will also need to become familiar with certain electrical units, including those of

quantity of electrical charge. The common unit here is the **coulomb, C.** The coulomb is related to the charge carried by a mole of electrons through the Faraday constant:

$$1 \text{ mol electrons} = 9.648 \times 10^4 \text{ C}$$

rate of current flow. Here the common unit is the **ampere, A.** When a current of one ampere passes through an electrical circuit, one coulomb passes a given point in the circuit in one second. That is,

$$1 \text{ A} = 1 \text{ C/s}$$

amount of electrical energy. This can be expressed in joules, J. When a charge of one coulomb (C) moves through a potential difference of one volt (V), it acquires an energy of one joule:

$$1 \text{ J} = 1 \text{ C}\cdot\text{V}$$

Table 18.3 Electrical Units

Quantity	Unit	Defining Relation	Conversion Factors
Charge	**coulomb (C)**	$1 \text{ C} = 1 \text{ A}\cdot\text{s} = 1 \text{ J/V}$	$1 \text{ mol } e^- = 9.648 \times 10^4 \text{ C}$
Current	**ampere (A)**	$1 \text{ A} = 1 \text{ C/s}$	
Potential	**volt (V)**	$1 \text{ V} = 1 \text{ J/C}$	
Power	watt (W)	$1 \text{ W} = 1 \text{ J/s}$	
Energy	joule (J)	$1 \text{ J} = 1 \text{ V}\cdot\text{C}$	$1 \text{ kWh} = 3.600 \times 10^6 \text{ J}$

Your electric bill deals with a different unit of electrical energy called the kilowatt hour (kWh). The joule and the kilowatt hour are related through a simple conversion factor:

$$1 \text{ kWh} = 3.600 \times 10^6 \text{ J} = 3.600 \times 10^3 \text{ kJ}$$

These relations and others are contained in Table 18.3.

Example 18.8 Chromium metal can be electroplated from an aqueous solution of potassium dichromate. The reduction half-reaction is

$$Cr_2O_7^{2-}(aq) + 14H^+(aq) + 12e^- \longrightarrow 2Cr(s) + 7H_2O$$

A current of 6.00 A and a voltage of 4.5 V are used in the electroplating.

(a) How many grams of chromium can be plated if the current is run for 48 minutes?
(b) How long will it take to completely convert 215 mL of 1.25 *M* $K_2Cr_2O_7$ to elemental chromium?
(c) How many kilowatt hours of electrical energy are required to plate 1.00 g of chromium?

SOLUTION

(a) Use a conversion-factor approach:

$$\text{ampere} \longrightarrow \text{coulomb} \longrightarrow \text{mol } e^- \longrightarrow \text{mol Cr} \longrightarrow \text{grams Cr}$$

Remember that 1A = 1 C/s.

$$6.00 \text{ A} \times \frac{1 \text{ C/s}}{1 \text{ A}} \times 48 \text{ min} \times \frac{60 \text{ s}}{1 \text{ min}} \times \frac{1 \text{ mol } e^-}{9.648 \times 10^4 \text{ C}} \times \frac{2 \text{ mol Cr}}{12 \text{ mol } e^-} \times \frac{52.00 \text{ g Cr}}{1 \text{ mol Cr}}$$

$$= 1.55 \text{ g}$$

(b) This time, we start by finding the number of moles of $Cr_2O_7^{2-}$.

$$n_{Cr_2O_7^{2-}} \longrightarrow n_{e^-} \longrightarrow \text{C} \longrightarrow \text{s}$$

$$0.215 \text{ L} \times \frac{1.25 \text{ mol } Cr_2O_7^{2-}}{1 \text{ L}} \times \frac{12 \text{ mol } e^-}{1 \text{ mol } Cr_2O_7^{2-}} \times \frac{9.648 \times 10^4 \text{ C}}{1 \text{ mol } e^-} \times \frac{1 \text{ A}}{1 \text{ C/s}} \times \frac{1}{6 \text{ A}}$$

$$= 5.19 \times 10^4 \text{ s} = 14.4 \text{ h}$$

(c) Here we start with the grams of chromium plated.

$$m_{Cr} \longrightarrow n_{Cr} \longrightarrow n_{e^-} \longrightarrow \text{C} \longrightarrow \text{energy(J)} \longrightarrow \text{energy(kWh)}$$

$$1.00 \text{ g Cr} \times \frac{1 \text{ mol Cr}}{52.00 \text{ g}} \times \frac{12 \text{ mol } e^-}{2 \text{ mol Cr}} \times \frac{9.648 \times 10^4 \text{ C}}{1 \text{ mol } e^-} \times \frac{1 \text{ J}}{1 \text{ C} \cdot \text{V}} \times 4.5 \text{ V} \times \frac{1 \text{ kWh}}{3.600 \times 10^6 \text{ J}}$$

$$= 0.014 \text{ kWh}$$

Reality Check Note that using an applied voltage of 4.5 V is irrelevant to parts (a) and (b).

Nobody is 100% efficient.

In working Example 18.8, we have in effect assumed that the electrolyses were 100% efficient in converting electrical energy into chemical energy. In practice, this is almost never the case. Some electrical energy is wasted in side reactions at the electrodes and in the form of heat. This means that the actual yield of products is less than the theoretical yield.

Figure 18.9
Electroplating. (a) Silver ions are reduced to metallic silver by electrolysis. The silver coats the spoon to be plated. (b) The Oscar statue is gold plated.

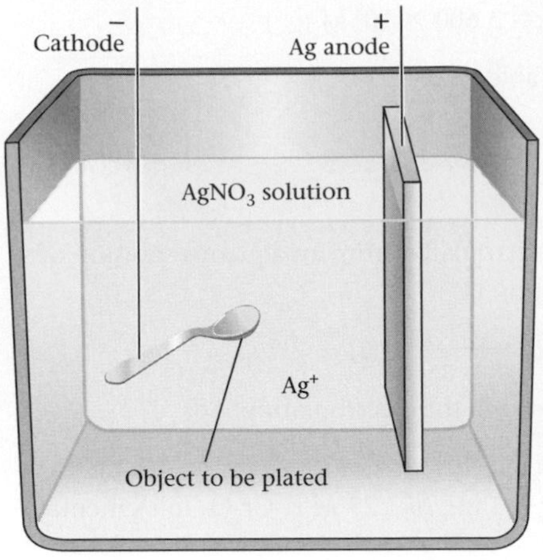

Cell Reactions (Water Solution)

As is always the case, a reduction half-reaction occurs at the cathode of an electrolytic cell. This half-reaction may be—

- *the reduction of a cation to the corresponding metal.* This commonly occurs with transition metal cations, which are relatively easy to reduce. Examples include

$$Ag^+(aq) + e^- \longrightarrow Ag(s) \qquad E^\circ_{red} = +0.799\ V$$
$$Cu^{2+}(aq) + 2e^- \longrightarrow Cu(s) \qquad E^\circ_{red} = +0.339\ V$$

  This type of half-reaction is characteristic of electroplating processes, in which a metal object serves as the cathode (Figure 18.9).

- *the reduction of a water molecule to hydrogen gas*

$$2H_2O + 2e^- \longrightarrow H_2(g) + 2OH^-(aq) \qquad E^\circ_{red} = -0.828\ V$$

  This half-reaction commonly occurs when the cation in solution is very difficult to reduce. For example, electrolysis of a solution containing K^+ ions ($E^\circ_{red} = -2.936$ V) or Na^+ ions ($E^\circ_{red} = -2.714$ V) yields hydrogen gas at the cathode (Table 18.4).

At the anode of an electrolytic cell, the half-reaction may be—

- *the oxidation of an anion to the corresponding nonmetal*

$$2I^-(aq) \longrightarrow I_2(s) + 2e^- \qquad E^\circ_{ox} = -0.534\ V$$

  Electrolysis of a water solution of KI gives a saturated solution of iodine at the anode (see photo at top of page 499).

- *the oxidation of a water molecule to oxygen gas*

$$2H_2O \longrightarrow O_2(g) + 4H^+(aq) + 4e^- \qquad E^\circ_{ox} = -1.229\ V$$

This half-reaction occurs when the anion cannot be oxidized. Examples include nitrate and sulfate anions, where the nonmetal present is already in its highest oxidation state (+5 for N, +6 for S).

Table 18.4 Electrolysis of Water Solutions

Solution	Cathode Product	Anode Product
$CuBr_2(aq)$	$Cu(s)$	$Br_2(l)$
$AgNO_3(aq)$	$Ag(s)$	$O_2(g)$
$KI(aq)$	$H_2(g)$	$I_2(s)$
$Na_2SO_4(aq)$	$H_2(g)$	$O_2(g)$

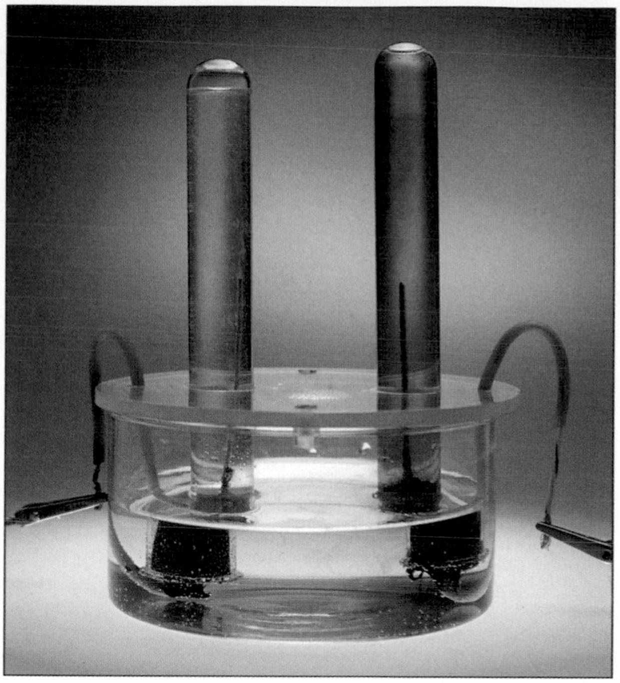

Charles D. Winters

Electrolysis of potassium iodide (KI) solution. The electrolysis of aqueous KI is similar to that of aqueous NaCl. The cathode reaction *(left)* is the reduction of water to $H_2(g)$ and OH^-, as shown by the pink color of phenolphthalein indicator in the water. The anode reaction *(right)* is the oxidation of $I^-(aq)$ to $I_2(aq)$, as shown by the brown color of the solution.

18.6 COMMERCIAL CELLS

To a chemist, electrochemical cells are of interest primarily for the information they yield concerning the spontaneity of redox reactions, the strengths of oxidizing and reducing agents, and the concentrations of trace species in solution. The viewpoint of an engineer is somewhat different; applications of electrolytic cells in electroplating and electrosynthesis are of particular importance. To the nonscientist, electrochemistry is important primarily because of commercial voltaic cells, which supply the electrical energy for instruments ranging in size from pacemakers to automobiles.

CENGAGENOW™
Click Chemistry Interactive for a self-study module on **batteries.**

Electrolysis of Aqueous NaCl

From a commercial standpoint, the most important electrolysis carried out in water solution is that of sodium chloride (Figure 18.10, p. 500). At the anode, Cl^- ions are oxidized to chlorine gas:

$$\text{anode:} \quad 2Cl^-(aq) \longrightarrow Cl_2(g) + 2e^-$$

At the cathode, the half-reaction involves H_2O molecules, which are easier to reduce ($E^\circ_{red} = -0.828$ V) than Na^+ ions ($E^\circ_{red} = -2.714$ V).

$$\text{cathode:} \quad 2H_2O + 2e^- \longrightarrow H_2(g) + 2OH^-(aq)$$

The overall cell reaction is obtained by summing the half-reactions:

$$2Cl^-(aq) + 2H_2O \longrightarrow Cl_2(g) + H_2(g) + 2OH^-(aq)$$

Chlorine gas bubbles out of solution at the anode. At the cathode, hydrogen gas is formed, and the solution around the electrode becomes strongly basic.

The products of this electrolysis have a variety of uses. Chlorine is used to purify drinking water; large quantities of it are consumed in making plastics such as polyvinyl chloride (PVC). Hydrogen, prepared in this and many other industrial processes, is used chiefly in the synthesis of ammonia (Chapter 12). Sodium hydroxide (lye), obtained on evaporation of the electrolyte, is used in processing pulp and paper, in the purification of aluminum ore, in the manufacture of glass and textiles, and for many other purposes.

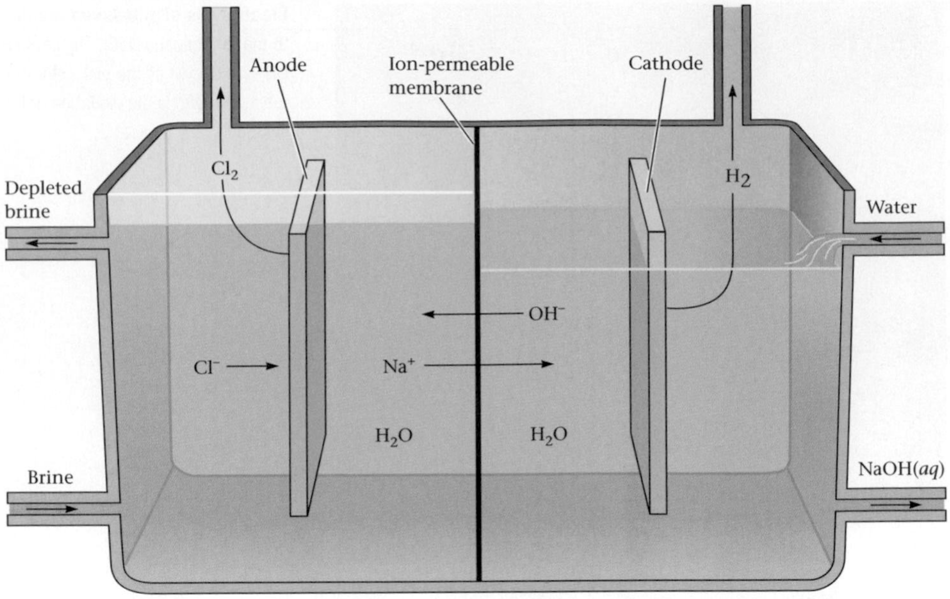

Figure 18.10
Electrolysis of aqueous NaCl (brine). The anode and cathode half-cells are separated by a membrane that is permeable to ions. Thus the flow of ions maintains charge balance. The products, NaOH(*aq*), Cl_2, and H_2, are all valuable industrial chemicals.

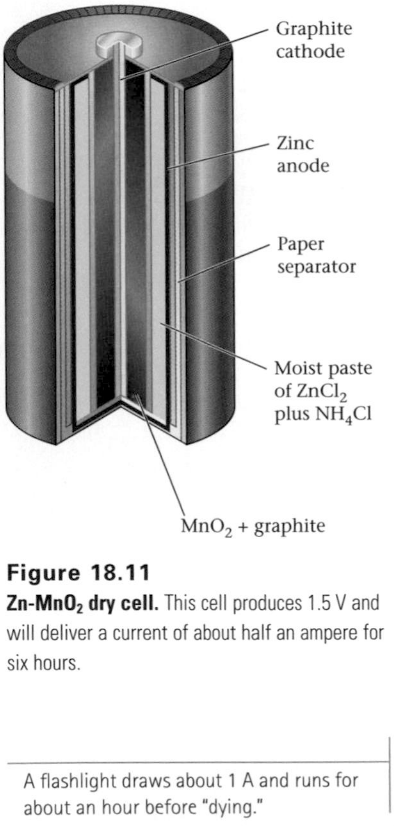

Figure 18.11
Zn-MnO₂ dry cell. This cell produces 1.5 V and will deliver a current of about half an ampere for six hours.

A flashlight draws about 1 A and runs for about an hour before "dying."

Primary (Nonrechargeable) Voltaic Cells

The construction of the ordinary dry cell (Leclanché cell) used in flashlights is shown in Figure 18.11. The zinc wall of the cell is the anode. The graphite rod through the center of the cell is the cathode. The space between the electrodes is filled with a moist paste. This contains MnO_2, $ZnCl_2$, and NH_4Cl. When the cell operates, the half-reaction at the anode is

$$Zn(s) \longrightarrow Zn^{2+}(aq) + 2e^-$$

At the cathode, manganese dioxide is reduced to species in which Mn is in the +3 oxidation state, such as Mn_2O_3:

$$2MnO_2(s) + 2NH_4^+(aq) + 2e^- \longrightarrow Mn_2O_3(s) + 2NH_3(aq) + H_2O$$

The overall reaction occurring in this voltaic cell is

$$Zn(s) + 2MnO_2(s) + 2NH_4^+(aq) \longrightarrow Zn^{2+}(aq) + Mn_2O_3(s) + 2NH_3(aq) + H_2O$$

If too large a current is drawn from a Leclanché cell, the ammonia forms a gaseous insulating layer around the carbon cathode. When this happens, the voltage drops sharply and then returns slowly to its normal value of 1.5 V. This problem can be avoided by using an alkaline dry cell, in which the paste between the electrodes contains KOH rather than NH_4Cl. In this case the overall cell reaction is simply

$$Zn(s) + 2MnO_2(s) \longrightarrow ZnO(s) + Mn_2O_3(s)$$

No gas is produced. The alkaline dry cell, although more expensive than the Leclanché cell, has a longer shelf life and provides more current.

Another important primary battery is the mercury cell. It usually comes in very small sizes and is used in hearing aids, watches, cameras, and some calculators. The anode of this cell is a zinc-mercury amalgam; the reacting species is zinc. The cathode is a plate made up of mercury(II) oxide, HgO. The electrolyte is a paste containing HgO and sodium or potassium hydroxide. The electrode reactions are

$$\text{anode:} \quad Zn(s) + 2OH^-(aq) \longrightarrow Zn(OH)_2(s) + 2e^-$$
$$\text{cathode:} \quad HgO(s) + H_2O + 2e^- \longrightarrow Hg(l) + 2OH^-(aq)$$
$$\overline{Zn(s) + HgO(s) + H_2O \longrightarrow Zn(OH)_2(s) + Hg(l)}$$

Notice that the overall reaction does not involve any ions in solution, so there are no concentration changes when current is drawn. As a result, the battery maintains a constant voltage of about 1.3 V throughout its life.

CHEMISTRY The Human Side

The laws of electrolysis were discovered by Michael Faraday, perhaps the most talented experimental scientist of the nineteenth century. Faraday lived his entire life in what is now greater London. The son of a blacksmith, he had no formal education beyond the rudiments of reading, writing, and arithmetic. Apprenticed to a bookbinder at the age of 13, Faraday educated himself by reading virtually every book that came into the shop. One that particularly impressed him was a textbook, *Conversations in Chemistry,* written by Mrs. Jane Marcet. Anxious to escape a life of drudgery as a tradesman, Faraday wrote to Sir Humphry Davy at the Royal Institution, requesting employment. Shortly afterward, a vacancy arose, and Faraday was hired as a laboratory assistant.

Oesper Collection in the History of Chemistry/University of Cincinnati

Michael Faraday
(1791–1867)

Davy quickly recognized Faraday's talents and as time passed allowed him to work more and more independently. In his years with Davy, Faraday published papers covering almost every field of chemistry. They included studies on the condensation of gases (he was the first to liquefy ammonia), the reaction of silver compounds with ammonia, and the isolation of several organic compounds, the most important of which was benzene. In 1825, Faraday began a series of lectures at the Royal Institution that were brilliantly successful. That same year he succeeded Davy as director of the laboratory. As Faraday's reputation grew, it was said that "Humphrey Davy's greatest discovery was Michael Faraday." Perhaps it was witticisms of this sort that led to an estrangement between master and protégé. Late in his life, Davy opposed Faraday's nomination as a Fellow of the Royal Society and is reputed to have cast the only vote against him.

To Michael Faraday, science was an obsession; one of his biographers described him as a "work maniac." An observer (Faraday had no students) said of him,

> *. . . if he had to cross the laboratory for anything, he did not walk, he ran; the quickness of his perception was equalled by the calm rapidity of his movements.*

In 1839, he suffered a nervous breakdown, the result of overwork. For much of the rest of his life, Faraday was in poor health. He gradually gave up more and more of his social engagements but continued to do research at the same pace as before.

Faraday developed the laws of electrolysis between 1831 and 1834. In mid-December of 1833, he began a quantitative study of the electrolysis of several metal cations, including Sn^{2+}, Pb^{2+}, and Zn^{2+}. Despite taking a whole day off for Christmas, he managed to complete these experiments, write up the results of three years' work, and get his paper published in the *Philosophic Transactions of the Royal Society* on January 9, 1834. In this paper, Faraday introduced the basic vocabulary of electrochemistry, using for the first time the terms "anode," "cathode," "ion," "electrolyte," and "electrolysis."

Storage (Rechargeable) Voltaic Cells

A storage cell, unlike an ordinary dry cell, can be recharged repeatedly. This can be accomplished because the products of the reaction are deposited directly on the electrodes. By passing a current through a storage cell, it is possible to reverse the electrode reactions and restore the cell to its original condition.

A 12-V storage battery can deliver 300 A for a minute or so.

The rechargeable 12-V lead storage battery used in automobiles consists of six voltaic cells of the type shown in Figure 18.12. A group of lead plates, the grids of which are filled

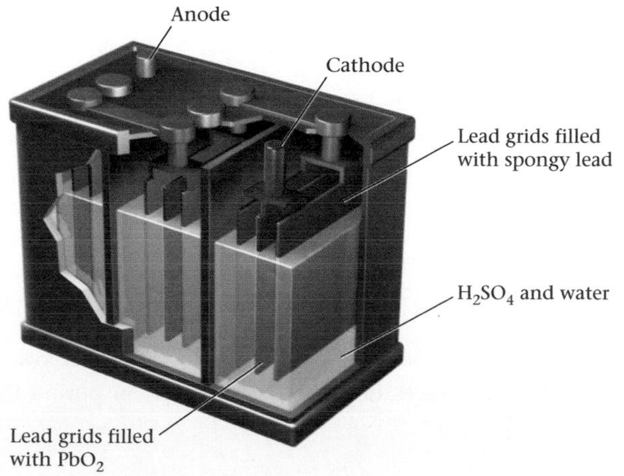

Figure 18.12
Lead storage battery. Three advantages of the lead storage battery are its ability to deliver large amounts of energy for a short time, the ease of recharging, and a nearly constant voltage from full charge to discharge. A disadvantage is its high mass-to-energy ratio.

A hydrogen-oxygen fuel cell used on U.S. space missions.

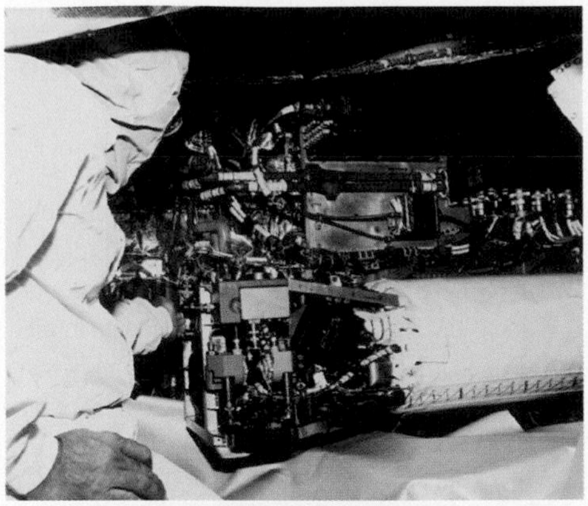

NASA

with spongy gray lead, forms the anode of the cell. The multiple cathode consists of another group of plates of similar design filled with lead(IV) oxide, PbO_2. These two sets of plates alternate through the cell. They are immersed in a water solution of sulfuric acid, H_2SO_4, which acts as the electrolyte.

When a lead storage battery is supplying current, the lead in the anode grids is oxidized to Pb^{2+} ions, which precipitate as $PbSO_4$. At the cathode, lead dioxide is reduced to Pb^{2+} ions, which also precipitate as $PbSO_4$.

$$\begin{array}{lr} \text{Anode:} & Pb(s) + HSO_4^-(aq) \longrightarrow PbSO_4(s) + H^+(aq) + 2e^- \\ \text{Cathode:} & PbO_2(s) + 3H^+(aq) + HSO_4^-(aq) + 2e^- \longrightarrow PbSO_4(s) + 2H_2O \\ \hline & Pb(s) + PbO_2(s) + 2H^+(aq) + 2HSO_4^-(aq) \longrightarrow 2PbSO_4(s) + 2H_2O \\ & \Delta G^\circ = -371.4 \text{ kJ } (25^\circ\text{C}) \end{array}$$

Deposits of lead sulfate slowly build up on the plates, partially covering and replacing the lead and lead dioxide.

To recharge a lead storage battery, a direct current is passed through it in the proper direction so as to reverse the above reaction. In an automobile, the energy required to carry out the recharging comes from the engine.

When the battery is charged, some water may be electrolyzed:

$$2H_2O \longrightarrow 2H_2(g) + O_2(g) \qquad \Delta G^\circ \text{ at } 25^\circ\text{C} = 474.4 \text{ kJ}$$

The hydrogen and oxygen produced create a safety hazard. Beyond that, they can cause Pb, PbO_2, and $PbSO_4$ to flake off the plates. In a modern "maintenance-free" battery, the lead plates are alloyed with small amounts of calcium, which inhibits the electrolysis reaction.

One of the advantages of the lead storage battery is that its voltage stays constant at 2 V per cell over a wide range of sulfuric acid concentrations. Only when the battery is nearly completely discharged does the voltage drop. It is also true that the cell voltage is virtually independent of temperature. You have trouble starting your car on a cold morning because the conductivity of the electrolyte drops off sharply with temperature; the voltage is still 2 V per cell at -40°C.

Fuel Cells

A fuel cell is a voltaic cell in which a fuel, usually hydrogen, is oxidized at the anode. At the cathode, oxygen is reduced. The reaction taking place in the alkaline fuel cells used in the space program since the 1960s is

$$\begin{array}{ll} \text{anode:} & 2H_2(g) + 4OH^-(aq) \longrightarrow 4H_2O + 4e^- \\ \text{cathode:} & O_2(g) + 2H_2O + 4e^- \longrightarrow 4OH^-(aq) \\ \hline & 2H_2(g) + O_2(g) \longrightarrow 2H_2O \qquad \Delta G^\circ \text{ at } 25^\circ\text{C} = -474.4 \text{ kJ} \end{array}$$

Using a platinum catalyst, this reaction can now be carried out at temperatures as low as 40°C. The hydrogen used must be very pure; traces of carbon monoxide can poison the catalyst.

Current research on fuel cells is directed toward the replacement of the internal combustion engine. To do this, hydrogen must be stored in the vehicle and replenished from time to time at "filling stations." Three kilograms of hydrogen should be enough to drive a small car 500 km (300 miles) between fill-ups.

The rationale for using a hydrogen fuel cell is that the cell reaction produces only water. In contrast, your car's engine produces small amounts of air pollutants such as NO and copious amounts of CO_2, which contributes to global warming. On the other hand, there are a couple of deterrents to the use of fuel cells, i.e.—

- the cost per kilojoule of energy is higher than with a gasoline- or diesel-powered engine.
- the storage of hydrogen in a vehicle is a serious problem. To carry three kilograms of hydrogen as a compressed gas at 200 atm (~3000 psi) requires a heavy tank with a volume of 200 L (50 gallons). Liquid hydrogen requires a smaller tank, but its extremely low critical temperature (−240°C) creates all sorts of problems. Another possibility is to convert hydrogen reversibly to a transition metal hydride (e.g., TiH_2). It's hard to say at this point how well that would work. All in all, it is almost certain that your next car will *not* use hydrogen as a fuel.

Fuel cells have been around for about 50 years.

CHEMISTRY Beyond the Classroom

Fuel Cells: The Next Step in Chemical- to Electrical-Energy Conversion?

Steven R. Shaw, Montana State University

Fuel cells have attracted considerable interest because of their potential for efficient conversion of the energy (ΔG) from a chemical reaction to electrical energy (ΔE). This efficiency is achieved by directly converting chemical energy to electricity. Conventional systems burn fuel in an engine and convert the resulting mechanical output to electrical power. Potential applications include stationary multi-megawatt power plants, battery replacements for personal electronics, and even fuel-cell-powered unmanned autonomous vehicles (UAVs).

The different types of fuel cells depend on the electrolytes used and the temperatures at which the electrolytes operate. One popular fuel cell that operates at low temperatures (80°C) used a polymer-electrolyte membrane, also known as a proton-exchange membrane (PEM). This membrane is made of a fluorinated polymer, like Teflon, that is highly conductive to electrons. It allows an energetically favorable reaction ($\Delta G < 0$) between the fuel gas and oxidant to be spatially confined, so that the electrons evolving from and consumed by the half-cell reactions can do work in an external circuit. Figure A shows a schematic of a hydrogen/oxygen fuel cell with a proton-exchange membrane.

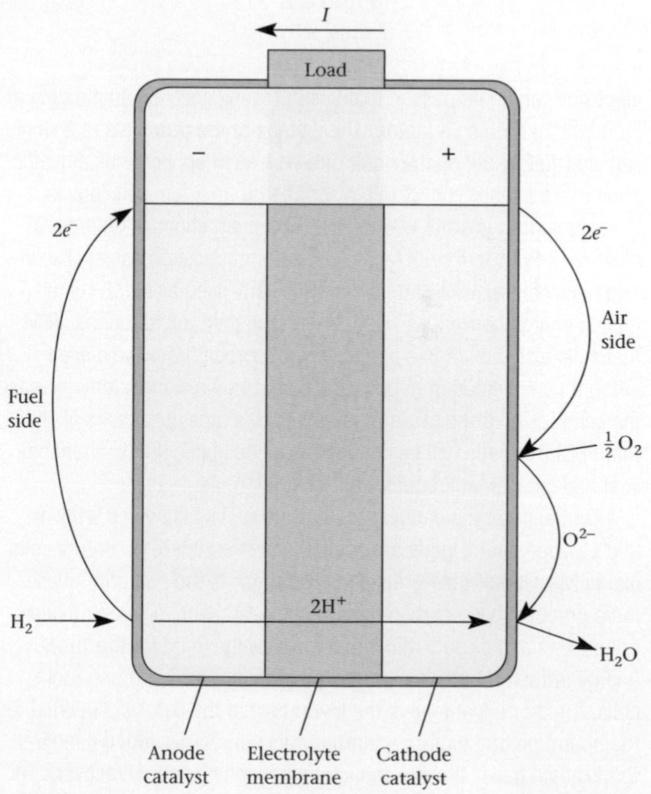

Figure A

The half-cell reactions supported by this structure are

$$H_2 \longrightarrow 2e^- + 2H^+$$

$$2H^+ + 2e^- + \tfrac{1}{2}O_2 \longrightarrow H_2O$$

Taken together, the overall reaction is simply the energetically favorable oxidation of hydrogen.

$$H_2(g) + \tfrac{1}{2}O_2(g) \longrightarrow H_2O$$

Unlike burning hydrogen in air, in a fuel cell the electrolyte partitions the overall reaction into half-cell reactions on either side of the cell. Hydrogen ions flow through the membrane, but since the electrolyte is nonconductive to electrons, it forces the electrons to flow through an external electrical circuit to complete the reaction. This flow of

(Continued)

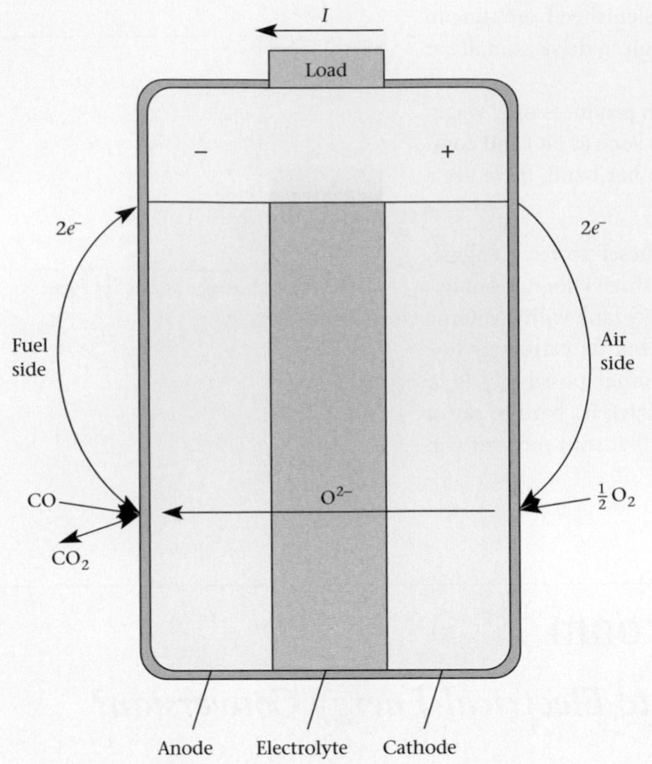

Figure B

electrons can be harnessed to do useful work, such as illuminating a light bulb or running a laptop. The voltage at the terminals of a single cell is rather small, on the order of a volt, so in applications a number of cells are usually connected in series to form a fuel cell "stack."

Although it is attractive to directly convert chemical energy to electricity, PEM fuel cells face significant practical obstacles. Expensive heavy metals like platinum are typically used as catalysts to reduce energy barriers associated with the half-cell reactions. PEM fuel cells also cannot use practical hydrocarbon fuels like diesel without complicated preprocessing steps. Those significantly increase the complexity of the overall system. At this time, it appears likely that PEM fuel cells will be confined to niche applications where high cost and special fuel requirements are tolerable.

On the other hand, high-temperature fuel cells, which work at 800°C, offer some significant advantages over low-temperature cells like PEMs. One of their principal advantages is the potential to use more practical hydrocarbon fuels such as methane, or even mixtures of gasoline and diesel. This feature avoids the need for the "new energy infrastructure" sometimes associated with hydrogen fuel cells. Another advantage is the lower cost of the catalysts needed for the operation of a high-temperature fuel cell. As an added benefit, the exhaust gases are hot enough for secondary energy recovery. For example, "waste heat" from a high-temperature fuel cell can supply energy needed to convert conventional hydrocarbon fuels into simpler components (like carbon monoxide and hydrogen) that work efficiently in the fuel cell. The exhaust of a high-temperature fuel cell can also

Figure C

be used to drive a conventional turbine and generator in what is called a combined cycle or hybrid system. Some high-temperature fuel-cell test installations use the exhaust to heat nearby buildings.

One leading prototype of a high-temperature fuel cell is the solid oxide fuel cell, or SOFC. The basic principle of the SOFC, like the PEM, is to use an electrolyte layer with high ionic conductivity but very small electronic conductivity. Figure B shows a schematic illustration of a SOFC fuel cell using carbon monoxide as fuel.

Unlike the PEM, the ionic conduction occurs for the oxygen ion instead of the hydrogen ion. SOFCs are made of ceramic materials like zirconium ($Z = 40$) stabilized by yttrium ($Z = 39$). High-temperature oxygen conductivity is achieved by creating oxygen vacancies in the lattice structure of the electrolyte material. The half-cell reactions in this case are

$$\tfrac{1}{2}O_2 + 2e^- \longrightarrow O^{2-}$$
$$O^{2-} + CO \longrightarrow CO_2 + 2e^-$$

Note that the overall reaction

$$\tfrac{1}{2}O_2(g) + CO(g) \longrightarrow CO_2(g)$$

is the oxidation of CO, but the fuel cell's materials partition the reaction so that the electrons flow through an external circuit and perform useful work.

Figure C shows an electron photomicrograph of a broken planar SOFC. The thick portion on the left is the porous anode structure. This is an anode-supported cell, meaning that in addition to collecting current and supporting the anode reaction, the anode layer stiffens the whole cell. The layer on the right is the cathode, and the interface between the two is the thin electrolyte. One of the challenges of this design is to ensure that the rates of expansion of the cathode and the anode match. If the anode expands faster than the cathode, the planar cell tends to curl like a potato chip when the temperature changes.

Note that fuel cells do not provide a new source of energy. They are designed to use conventional, currently available fuels. Their main advantage lies in the efficiency of their operation, which creates fewer byproducts to threaten the environment.

Chapter Highlights

Key Concepts

1. Draw a diagram for a voltaic cell, labeling electrodes and direction of current flow. **(Example 18.1; Problems 3–8)** ■ Questions and Problems assignable in OWL: 2, 6
2. Use standard potentials (Table 18.1) to—
   ■ compare the relative strengths of different oxidizing agents; different reducing agents. **(Example 18.2; Problems 9–18)** ■ 9, 10, 16, 18
   ■ calculate $E°$ and/or reaction spontaneity. **(Examples 18.3, 18.4; Problems 19–38)** ■ 20, 22, 26, 28, 32, 34
3. Relate $E°$ to $\Delta G°$ and K. **(Example 18.5; Problems 39–52)** ■ 41, 46, 48, 52
4. Use the Nernst equation to relate voltage to concentration. **(Examples 18.6, 18.7; Problems 53–66)** ■ 53
5. Relate mass of product to amount of electricity (coulombs) or amount of energy (joules) used in electrolysis reactions. **(Example 18.8; Problems 67–74)** ■ 67, 71, 72

Select end of chapter Questions and Problems may be assigned in OWL and are cross-referenced in the Key Concepts list.

CENGAGENOW™

Sign in at **academic.cengage.com/now** to:

- Check your readiness for an exam by taking the Pre-Test and exploring the self-study modules recommended in your Personalized Study plan
- For quick review, download Go Chemistry mini-lecture flashcard modules (or purchase them at **www.ichapters.com**)

Key Equations

Standard voltage $\quad E° = E°_{red} + E°_{ox}$ (Section 18.2)

$E°, \Delta G°, K$ $\quad E° = \dfrac{-\Delta G°}{nF} = \dfrac{RT \ln K}{nF} = \dfrac{0.0257\text{ V}}{n} \ln K$ (at 25°C) (Section 18.3)

Nernst equation $\quad E = E° - \dfrac{RT}{nF} \ln Q = E° - \dfrac{0.0257\text{ V}}{n} \ln Q$ (at 25°C) (Section 18.4)

Key Terms

ampere	electrode	salt bridge
anode	electrolysis	standard potential
cathode	electrolytic cell	standard voltage
coulomb	Faraday constant	volt
$E°, E°_{ox}, E°_{red}$	half-cell	voltaic cell

Summary Problem

A voltaic cell consists of two half-cells. One of the half-cells contains a platinum electrode surrounded by chromium(III) and dichromate ions. The other half-cell contains a platinum electrode surrounded by bromate ions and liquid bromine. Assume that the cell reaction, which produces a positive voltage, involves both chromium(III) and bromate ions. The cell is at 25°C. Information for the bromate reduction half reaction is as follows:

$$2BrO_3^-(aq) + 12H^+(aq) + 10e^- \longrightarrow Br_2(l) + 6H_2O \qquad E°_{red} = 1.478\text{ V}$$

(a) Write the anode half-reaction, the cathode half-reaction, and the overall equation for the cell.
(b) Write the cell description in abbreviated notation.
(c) Calculate $E°$ for the cell.
(d) For the redox reaction in (a), calculate K and $\Delta G°$.
(e) Calculate the voltage of the cell when all ionic species except H^+ are at 0.1500 M and the pH is at −0.301.

Summary Problem—cont'd

An electrolytic cell contains an aqueous solution of chromium(III) nitrate at 25°C. Assume that chromium plates out at one electrode and oxygen gas is evolved at the other electrode.

(f) Write the anode half-reaction, the cathode half-reaction, and the overall equation for the electrolysis.
(g) How many hours will it take to deposit 22.00 g of chromium metal, using a current of 5.4 A?
(h) A current of 3.75 A is passed through the cell for 45 minutes. Starting out with 1.25 L of 0.787 *M* $Cr(NO_3)_3$, what is $[Cr^{3+}]$ after electrolysis? What is the pH of the solution, neglecting the H^+ originally present? Assume 100% efficiency and no change in volume during electroysis.

Answers

(a) anode: $2Cr^{3+}(aq) + 7H_2O \longrightarrow Cr_2O_7^{2-}(aq) + 14H^+(aq) + 6e^-$
cathode: $2BrO_3^-(aq) + 12H^+(aq) + 10e^- \longrightarrow Br_2(l) + 6H_2O$
overall: $10Cr^{3+}(aq) + 6BrO_3^-(aq) + 17H_2O \longrightarrow 5Cr_2O_7^{2-}(aq) + 3Br_2(l) + 34H^+(aq)$
(b) $Pt \mid Cr^{3+}, Cr_2O_7^{2-} \parallel BrO_3^- \mid Br_2 \mid Pt$
(c) 0.15 V
(d) $K = 1 \times 10^{75}$; $\Delta G° = -4.3 \times 10^2$ kJ
(e) 0.110 V
(f) anode: $2H_2O \longrightarrow O_2(g) + 4H^+(aq) + 4e^-$
cathode: $Cr^{3+}(aq) + 3e^- \longrightarrow Cr(s)$
overall: $4Cr^{3+}(aq) + 6H_2O \longrightarrow 4Cr(s) + 3\,O_2(g) + 12H^+(aq)$
(g) 6.3 h
(h) 0.759 *M*; 1.09

Questions and Problems

Blue-numbered questions have answers in Appendix 6 and fully-worked solutions in the *Student Solutions Manual.*

■ denotes questions assignable in OWL.

WEB indicates that the solution is available on this book's companion website.

Voltaic Cells

1. Write a balanced chemical equation for the overall cell reaction represented as
(a) $Mg \mid Mg^{2+} \parallel Sc^{3+} \mid Sc$ **(b)** $Sn \mid Sn^{2+} \parallel Pb^{2+} \mid Pb$
(c) $Pt \mid Cl^- \mid Cl_2 \parallel NO_3^- \mid NO \mid Pt$

2. ■ Write a balanced chemical equation for the overall cell reaction represented as
(a) $Ag \mid Ag^+ \parallel Sn^{4+}, Sn^{2+} \mid Pt$ **(b)** $Al \mid Al^{3+} \parallel Cu^{2+} \mid Cu$
(c) $Pt \mid Fe^{2+}, Fe^{3+} \parallel MnO_4^-, Mn^{2+} \mid Pt$

3. Draw a diagram for a salt bridge cell for each of the following reactions. Label the anode and cathode, and indicate the direction of current flow throughout the circuit.
(a) $Zn(s) + Cd^{2+}(aq) \longrightarrow Zn^{2+}(aq) + Cd(s)$
(b) $2AuCl_4^-(aq) + 3Cu(s) \longrightarrow 2Au(s) + 8Cl^-(aq) + 3Cu^{2+}(aq)$
(c) $Fe(s) + Cu(OH)_2(s) \longrightarrow Cu(s) + Fe(OH)_2(s)$

4. **WEB** Follow the directions for Question 3 for the following reactions:
(a) $Sn(s) + 2Ag^+(aq) \longrightarrow Sn^{2+}(aq) + 2Ag(s)$
(b) $H_2(g) + Hg_2Cl_2(s) \longrightarrow 2H^+(aq) + 2Cl^-(aq) + 2Hg(l)$
(c) $Pb(s) + PbO_2(s) + 4H^+(aq) + 2SO_4^{2-}(aq) \longrightarrow 2PbSO_4(s) + 2H_2O$

5. Consider a salt bridge voltaic cell represented by the following reaction:

$$Fe(s) + 2Tl^+(aq) \longrightarrow Fe^{2+}(aq) + 2Tl(s)$$

Choose the best answer from the choices in each part below:
(a) What is the path of electron flow? Through the salt bridge, or through the external circuit?
(b) To which half-cell do the negative ions in the salt bridge move? The anode, or the cathode?
(c) Which metal is the electrode in the anode?

6. ■ Consider a salt bridge voltaic cell represented by the following reaction:

$$Ca(s) + 2H^+(aq) \longrightarrow Ca^{2+}(aq) + H_2(g)$$

(a) What is the direction of the electrons in the external circuit?
(b) What electrode can be used at the cathode?
(c) What is the reaction occurring at the anode?

7. Consider a salt bridge cell in which the anode is a manganese rod immersed in an aqueous solution of manganese(II) sulfate. The cathode is a chromium strip immersed in an aqueous solution of chromium(III) sulfate. Sketch a diagram of the cell, indicating the flow of the current throughout. Write the half-equations for the electrode reactions, the overall equation, and the abbreviated notation for the cell.

8. Follow the directions for Question 7 for a salt bridge cell in which the anode is a platinum rod immersed in an aqueous solution of sodium iodide containing solid iodine crystals. The cathode is another platinum rod immersed in an aqueous solution of sodium bromide with bromine liquid.

Strength of Oxidizing and Reducing Species

9. ■ Which species in each pair is the stronger oxidizing agent?
(a) NO_3^- or I_2 **(b)** $Fe(OH)_3$ or S **(c)** Mn^{2+} or MnO_2
(d) ClO_3^- in acidic solution or ClO_3^- in basic solution

10. ■ Which species in each pair is the stronger reducing agent?
(a) Cr or Cd **(b)** I^- or Br^- **(c)** OH^- or NO_2^-
(d) NO in acidic solution or NO in basic solution

11. Using Table 18.1, arrange the following reducing agents in order of increasing strength.

Br^- Zn Co $PbSO_4$ H_2S (acidic)

12. Using Table 18.1, arrange the following oxidizing agents in order of increasing strength.

Al^{3+} AgBr F_2 ClO_3^-(acidic) Ni^{2+}

13. Consider the following species.

Cr^{3+} Hg(*l*) H_2 (acidic) Sn^{2+} Br_2 (acidic)

Classify each species as oxidizing agent, reducing agent, or both. Arrange the oxidizing agents in order of increasing strength. Do the same for the reducing agents.

14. Follow the directions for Question 13 for the following species:

Cu^+ Zn Ni^{2+} Fe^{2+} H^+ (acidic)

15. For the following half-reactions, answer the questions below.

$$Ce^{4+}(aq) + e^- \longrightarrow Ce^{3+}(aq) \quad E° = +1.61 \text{ V}$$
$$Ag^+(aq) + e^- \longrightarrow Ag(s) \quad E° = +0.80 \text{ V}$$
$$Hg_2^{2+}(aq) + 2e^- \longrightarrow 2Hg(l) \quad E° = +0.80 \text{ V}$$
$$Sn^{2+}(aq) + 2e^- \longrightarrow Sn(s) \quad E° = -0.14 \text{ V}$$
$$Ni^{2+}(aq) + 2e^- \longrightarrow Ni(s) \quad E° = -0.24 \text{ V}$$
$$Al^{3+}(aq) + 3e^- \longrightarrow Al(s) \quad E° = -1.68 \text{ V}$$

(a) Which is the weakest oxidizing agent?
(b) Which is the strongest oxidizing agent?
(c) Which is the strongest reducing agent?
(d) Which is the weakest reducing agent?
(e) Will $Sn(s)$ reduce $Ag^+(aq)$ to $Ag(s)$?
(f) Will $Hg(l)$ reduce $Sn^{2+}(aq)$ to $Sn(s)$?
(g) Which ion(s) can be reduced by $Sn(s)$?
(h) Which metal(s) can be oxidized by $Ag^+(aq)$?

16. ■ WEB For the following half-reactions, answer the questions below.

$$Co^{3+}(aq) + e^- \longrightarrow Co^{2+}(aq) \quad E° = +1.953 \text{ V}$$
$$Fe^{3+}(aq) + e^- \longrightarrow Fe^{2+}(aq) \quad E° = +0.769 \text{ V}$$
$$I_2(aq) + 2e^- \longrightarrow 2I^-(aq) \quad E° = +0.534 \text{ V}$$
$$Pb^{2+}(aq) + 2e^- \longrightarrow Pb(s) \quad E° = -0.127 \text{ V}$$
$$Cd^{2+}(aq) + 2e^- \longrightarrow Cd(s) \quad E° = -0.402 \text{ V}$$
$$Mn^{2+}(aq) + 2e^- \longrightarrow Mn(s) \quad E° = -1.182 \text{ V}$$

(a) Which is the weakest reducing agent?
(b) Which is the strongest reducing agent?
(c) Which is the strongest oxidizing agent?
(d) Which is the weakest oxidizing agent?
(e) Will $Pb(s)$ reduce $Fe^{3+}(aq)$ to $Fe^{2+}(aq)$?
(f) Will $I^-(aq)$ reduce $Pb^{2+}(aq)$ to $Pb(s)$?
(g) Which ion(s) can be reduced by $Pb(s)$?
(h) Which if any metal(s) can be oxidized by $Fe^{3+}(aq)$?

17. Use Table 18.1 to select
(a) a reducing agent that converts Sn^{2+} to Sn but not Tl^+ to Tl.
(b) an oxidizing agent that converts Hg to Hg_2^{2+} but not Br^- to Br_2.
(c) a reducing agent that converts Sn^{4+} to Sn^{2+} but not Sn^{2+} to Sn.

18. ■ Use Table 18.1 to select
(a) an oxidizing agent in basic solution that converts ClO_3^- to ClO_4^- but not Cl^- to ClO_3^-.
(b) a reducing agent that converts Mg^{2+} to Mg but not Ba^{2+} to Ba.
(c) a reducing agent that converts Na^+ to Na but not Li^+ to Li.

Calculation of $E°$

19. Calculate $E°$ for the following voltaic cells:
(a) $MnO_2(s) + 4H^+(aq) + 2I^-(aq) \longrightarrow Mn^{2+}(aq) + 2H_2O + I_2(s)$
(b) $H_2(g) + 2\,OH^-(aq) + S(s) \longrightarrow 2H_2O + S^{2-}(aq)$
(c) an Ag-Ag^+ half-cell and an Au-$AuCl_4^-$ half-cell

20. ■ Calculate $E°$ for the following voltaic cells:
(a) $Pb(s) + 2Ag^+(aq) \longrightarrow Pb^{2+}(aq) + 2Ag(s)$
(b) $O_2(g) + 4Fe^{2+}(aq) + 4H^+(aq) \longrightarrow 2H_2O + 4Fe^{3+}(aq)$
(c) a Cd-Cd^{2+} half-cell and a Zn-Zn^{2+} half-cell

21. Using Table 18.1, calculate $E°$ for the reaction between
(a) iron and water to produce iron(II) hydroxide and hydrogen gas.
(b) iron and iron(III) ions to give iron(II) ions.
(c) iron(II) hydroxide and oxygen in basic solution.

22. ■ Using Table 18.1, calculate $E°$ for the reaction between
(a) chromium(II) ions and tin(IV) ions to produce chromium(III) ions and tin(II) ions.
(b) manganese(II) ions and hydrogen peroxide to produce solid manganese dioxide (MnO_2).

23. Calculate $E°$ for the following cells:
(a) $Mn \mid Mn^{2+} \| H^+ \mid H_2 \mid Pt$
(b) $Au \mid AuCl_4^- \| Co^{3+}, Co^{2+} \mid Pt$
(c) $Pt \mid S^{2-} \mid S \| NO_3^- \mid NO \mid Pt$ (basic medium)

24. Calculate $E°$ for the following cells:
(a) $Pb \mid PbSO_4 \| Pb^{2+} \mid Pb$
(b) $Pt \mid Cl_2 \mid ClO_3^- \| O_2 \mid H_2O \mid Pt$
(c) $Pt \mid OH^- \mid O_2 \| ClO_3^-, Cl^- \mid Pt$ (basic medium)

25. Suppose $E°_{red}$ for $Ag^+ \longrightarrow Ag$ were set equal to zero instead of that of $H^+ \longrightarrow H_2$. What would be
(a) $E°_{red}$ for $H^+ \longrightarrow H_2$?
(b) $E°_{ox}$ for $Ca \longrightarrow Ca^{2+}$?
(c) $E°$ for the cell in 23(c)? Compare your answer with that obtained in 23(c).

26. ■ Suppose $E°_{red}$ for $H^+ \longrightarrow H_2$ were taken to be 0.300 V instead of 0.000 V. What would be
(a) $E°_{ox}$ for $H_2 \longrightarrow H^+$?
(b) $E°_{red}$ for $Br_2 \longrightarrow Br^-$?
(c) $E°$ for the cell in 24(c)? Compare your answer with that obtained in 24(c).

Spontaneity and $E°$

27. Which of the following reactions is (are) spontaneous at standard conditions?
(a) $2NO_3^-(aq) + 8H^+(aq) + 6Cl^-(aq) \longrightarrow 2NO(g) + 4H_2O + 3Cl_2(g)$
(b) $O_2(g) + 4H^+(aq) + 4Cl^-(aq) \longrightarrow 2H_2O + 2Cl_2(g)$
(c) $3Fe(s) + 2AuCl_4^-(aq) \longrightarrow 2Au(s) + 8Cl^-(aq) + 3Fe^{2+}(aq)$

28. ■ Which of the following reactions is (are) spontaneous at standard conditions?
(a) $Zn(s) + 2Fe^{3+}(aq) \longrightarrow Zn^{2+}(aq) + 2Fe^{2+}(aq)$
(b) $Cu(s) + 2H^+(aq) \longrightarrow Cu^{2+}(aq) + H_2(g)$
(c) $2Br^-(aq) + I_2(s) \longrightarrow Br_2(l) + 2I^-(aq)$

29. Use the following half-equations to write three spontaneous reactions. Justify your answers by calculating $E°$ for the cells.
(1) $MnO_4^-(aq) + 8H^+(aq) + 5e^- \longrightarrow Mn^{2+}(aq) + 4H_2O \quad E° = +1.512 \text{ V}$
(2) $O_2(g) + 4H^+(aq) + 4e^- \longrightarrow 2H_2O \quad E° = +1.229 \text{ V}$
(3) $Co^{2+}(aq) + 2e^- \longrightarrow Co(s) \quad E° = -0.282 \text{ V}$

30. Follow the instructions of Question 29 for the following half-equations.
(1) $Cu^+(aq) + e^- \longrightarrow Cu(s) \quad E° = +0.518 \text{ V}$
(2) $H_2O_2(aq) + 2H^+(aq) + 2e^- \longrightarrow 2H_2O \quad E° = +1.963 \text{ V}$
(3) $MnO_2(s) + 4H^+(aq) + 2e^- \longrightarrow Mn^{2+}(aq) + 2H_2O \quad E° = 1.229 \text{ V}$

31. Use Table 18.1 to answer the following questions.
(a) Which cobalt ion, Co^{2+} or Co^{3+}, will oxidize Sn to Sn^{2+}?
(b) Will dichromate ions oxidize H_2O to H_2O_2 or to O_2?
(c) To obtain Mn^{2+} using Cl^- as a reducing agent, should you use MnO_2 or MnO_4^-?

■ in OWL Blue-numbered questions answered in Appendix 6 WEB Solution is available on companion website

32. ■ Use Table 18.1 to answer the following questions.

(a) Will chlorate ions in acidic solution oxidize Cl^- to Cl_2 or F^- to F_2?

(b) What is the product when Fe reduces Cr^{3+}? Cr or Cr^{2+}?

(c) Oxygen is reduced to water in acidic medium and to OH^- in basic medium. If ClO_3^- (oxidized to ClO_4^-) is the reducing agent, in which medium will oxygen be reduced spontaneously? (The standard reduction potential for ClO_4^- in acidic medium is 1.19 V.)

33. Write the equation for the reaction, if any, that occurs when each of the following experiments is performed under standard conditions.

(a) Crystals of iodine are added to an aqueous solution of potassium bromide.

(b) Liquid bromine is added to an aqueous solution of sodium chloride.

(c) A chromium wire is dipped into a solution of nickel(II) chloride.

34. ■ Write the equation for the reaction, if any, that occurs when each of the following experiments is performed under standard conditions.

(a) Sulfur is added to mercury.

(b) Manganese dioxide in acidic solution is added to liquid mercury.

(c) Aluminum metal is added to a solution of potassium ions.

35. Which of the following species will react with 1 M HNO_3?

(a) I^- (b) Fe (c) Ag (d) Pb

36. Which of the following species will be oxidized by 1 M HCl?

(a) Au (b) Mg (c) Cu (d) F^-

37. Use Table 18.1 to predict what reaction, if any, will occur when the following species are mixed in acidic solution at standard conditions.

(a) Cr, Ni^{2+}, Cl^- (b) F_2, Na^+, Br^- (c) SO_2, Fe^{3+}, NO_3^-

38. Use Table 18.1 to predict what reaction, if any, will occur if sulfur is added to acidic aqueous solutions of the following species at standard conditions.

(a) $MgBr_2$ (b) $Sn(NO_3)_2$ (c) $Cr(ClO_3)_2$

$E°$, $\Delta G°$, and K

39. Consider a cell reaction at 25°C where $n = 2$. Fill in the following table.

	$\Delta G°$	$E°$	K
(a)	19 kJ	______	______
(b)	______	0.035 V	______
(c)	______	______	0.095

40. Consider a cell reaction at 25°C where $n = 4$. Fill in the following table.

	$\Delta G°$	$E°$	K
(a)	______	______	1.6×10^{-3}
(b)	______	0.117 V	______
(c)	−5.8 kJ	______	______

41. ■ For a certain cell, $\Delta G° = 25.0$ kJ. Calculate $E°$ if n is

(a) 1 (b) 2 (c) 4

Comment on the effect that the number of electrons exchanged has on the voltage of a cell.

42. For a certain cell, $E° = 1.20$ V. Calculate $\Delta G°$ if n is

(a) 1 (b) 2 (c) 3

Comment on the effect that the number of electrons exchanged has on the spontaneity of a reaction.

43. Calculate $E°$, $\Delta G°$, and K at 25°C for the reaction

$$3Mn^{2+}(aq) + 2MnO_4^-(aq) + 2H_2O \longrightarrow 5MnO_2(s) + 4H^+(aq)$$

44. Calculate $E°$, $\Delta G°$, and K at 25°C for the reaction

$$3S^{2-}(aq) + 2NO_3^-(aq) + 4H_2O \longrightarrow 3S(s) + 2NO(g) + 8\,OH^-(aq)$$

45. Calculate $\Delta G°$ at 25°C for each of the reactions referred to in Question 19. Assume smallest whole-number coefficients.

46. ■ Calculate $\Delta G°$ at 25°C for each of the reactions referred to in Question 20. Assume smallest whole-number coefficients.

47. Calculate K at 25°C for each of the reactions referred to in Question 21. Assume smallest whole-number coefficients.

48. ■ Calculate K at 25°C for each of the reactions referred to in Question 22. Assume smallest whole-number coefficients.

49. Given the following standard reduction potentials

$$Ag^+(aq) + e^- \longrightarrow Ag(s) \qquad E° = 0.799\ V$$

$$Ag(CN)_2^- + e^- \longrightarrow Ag(s) + 2CN^-(aq) \qquad E° = -0.31\ V$$

find K_f for $Ag(CN)_2^-(aq)$ at 25°C.

50. Use Table 18.1 to find K_f for $AuCl_4^-(aq)$ at 25°C.

51. Given the following information:

$$Ag_2CrO_4(s) \rightleftharpoons 2Ag^+(aq) + CrO_4^{2-}(aq) \qquad K_{sp} = 1 \times 10^{-12}$$

$$Ag^+(aq) + e^- \longrightarrow Ag(s) \qquad E° = +0.799\ V$$

find the standard reduction potential at 25°C for the half-reaction

$$Ag_2CrO_4(s) + 2e^- \longrightarrow 2Ag(s) + CrO_4^{2-}(aq)$$

52. ■ What is $E°$ at 25°C for the following reaction?

$$Ba^{2+}(aq) + SO_4^{2-}(aq) \longrightarrow BaSO_4(s)$$

K_{sp} for $BaSO_4$ is 1.1×10^{-10}.

Nernst Equation

53. ■ Consider a voltaic cell at 25°C in which the following reaction takes place.

$$3H_2O_2(aq) + 6H^+(aq) + 2Au(s) \longrightarrow 2Au^{3+}(aq) + 6H_2O$$

(a) Calculate $E°$.

(b) Write the Nernst equation for the cell.

(c) Calculate E when $[Au^{3+}] = 0.250\ M$, $[H^+] = 1.25\ M$, $[H_2O_2] = 1.50\ M$.

54. Consider a voltaic cell at 25°C in which the following reaction takes place.

$$3O_2(g) + 4NO(g) + 2H_2O \longrightarrow 4NO_3^-(aq) + 4H^+(aq)$$

(a) Calculate $E°$.

(b) Write the Nernst equation for the cell.

(c) Calculate E under the following conditions: $[NO_3^-] = 0.750\ M$, $P_{NO} = 0.993$ atm, $P_{O_2} = 0.515$ atm, pH = 2.85.

55. Consider a voltaic cell in which the following reaction takes place.

$$2Fe^{2+}(aq) + H_2O_2(aq) + 2H^+(aq) \longrightarrow 2Fe^{3+}(aq) + 2H_2O$$

(a) Calculate $E°$.

(b) Write the Nernst equation for the cell.

(c) Calculate E under the following conditions: $[Fe^{2+}] = 0.00813\ M$, $[H_2O_2] = 0.914\ M$, $Fe^{3+} = 0.199\ M$, pH = 2.88.

56. Consider a voltaic cell in which the following reaction takes place.

$$2NO_3^-(aq) + 3H_2(g) \longrightarrow 2NO(g) + 2OH^-(aq) + 2H_2O$$

(a) Calculate $E°$.

(b) Write the Nernst equation for the cell.

■ in OWL Blue-numbered questions answered in Appendix 6 WEB Solution is available on companion website

(c) Calculate E under the following conditions: $[NO_3^-] = 0.0315\ M$, $P_{NO} = 0.922$ atm, $P_{H_2} = 0.437$ atm, pH = 11.50.

57. Calculate voltages of the following cells at 25°C and under the following conditions.

(a) $Fe \mid Fe^{2+}\ (0.010\ M) \parallel Cu^{2+}\ (0.10\ M) \mid Cu$

(b) $Pt \mid Sn^{2+}\ (0.10\ M), Sn^{4+}\ (0.010\ M) \parallel Co^{2+}\ (0.10\ M) \mid Co$

58. Calculate voltages of the following cells at 25°C and under the following conditions.

(a) $Zn \mid Zn^{2+}\ (0.50\ M) \parallel Cd^{2+}\ (0.020\ M) \mid Cd$

(b) $Cu \mid Cu^{2+}\ (0.0010\ M) \parallel H^+\ (0.010\ M) \mid H_2\ (1.00\ atm) \mid Pt$

59. Consider the reaction

$$2Cu^{2+}(aq) + Sn^{2+}(aq) \longrightarrow Sn^{4+}(aq) + 2Cu^+(aq)$$

At what concentration of Cu^{2+} is the voltage zero, if all other species are at 0.200 M?

60. Consider the reaction

$$S(s) + 2H^+(aq) + 2Ag(s) + 2Br^-(aq) \longrightarrow 2AgBr(s) + H_2S(aq)$$

At what pH is the voltage zero if all other species are at standard concentrations?

61. Complete the following cell notation.

$$Ag \mid Br^-\ (3.73\ M) \mid AgBr \parallel H^+\ (\quad) \mid H_2\ (1.0\ atm) \mid Pt \qquad E = -0.030\ V$$

62. Complete the following cell notation.

$$Zn \mid Zn^{2+}(1.00\ M) \parallel H^+\ (\quad) \mid H_2(1.0\ atm) \mid Pt \qquad E = +0.40\ V$$

63. Consider the reaction below at 25°C:

$$2MnO_4^-(aq) + 16H^+(aq) + 10Br^-(aq) \longrightarrow 2Mn^{2+}(aq) + 5Br_2(l) + 8H_2O$$

Use Table 18.1 to answer the following questions. Support your answers with calculations.

(a) Is the reaction spontaneous at standard conditions?

(b) Is the reaction spontaneous at a pH of 2.00 with all other ionic species at 0.100 M?

(c) Is the reaction spontaneous at a pH of 5.00 with all other ionic species at 0.100 M?

(d) At what pH is the reaction at equilibrium with all other ionic species at 0.100 M?

64. Consider the reaction below at 25°C:

$$3SO_4^{2-}(aq) + 12H^+(aq) + 2Cr(s) \longrightarrow 3SO_2(g) + 2Cr^{3+}(aq) + 6H_2O$$

Use Table 18.1 to answer the following questions. Support your answers with calculations.

(a) Is the reaction spontaneous at standard conditions?

(b) Is the reaction spontaneous at a pH of 3.00 with all other ionic species at 0.100 M and gases at 1.00 atm?

(c) Is the reaction spontaneous at a pH of 8.00 with all other ionic species at 0.100 M and gases at 1.00 atm?

(d) At what pH is the reaction at equilibrium with all other ionic species at 0.100 M and gases at 1.00 atm?

65. Consider a cell in which the reaction is

$$2Ag(s) + Cu^{2+}(aq) \longrightarrow 2Ag^+(aq) + Cu(s)$$

(a) Calculate $E°$ for this cell.

(b) Chloride ions are added to the $Ag \mid Ag^+$ half-cell to precipitate AgCl. The measured voltage is +0.060 V. Taking $[Cu^{2+}] = 1.0\ M$, calculate $[Ag^+]$.

(c) Taking $[Cl^-]$ in (b) to be 0.10 M, calculate K_{sp} of AgCl.

66. Consider a cell in which the reaction is

$$Pb(s) + 2H^+(aq) \longrightarrow Pb^{2+}(aq) + H_2(g)$$

(a) Calculate $E°$ for this cell.

(b) Chloride ions are added to the $Pb \mid Pb^{2+}$ half-cell to precipitate $PbCl_2$. The voltage is measured to be +0.210 V. Taking $[H^+] = 1.0\ M$ and $P_{H_2} = 1.0$ atm, calculate $[Pb^{2+}]$.

(c) Taking $[Cl^-]$ in (b) to be 0.10 M, calculate K_{sp} of $PbCl_2$.

Electrolytic Cells

67. ■ An electrolytic cell produces aluminum from Al_2O_3 at the rate of ten kilograms a day. Assuming a yield of 100%,

(a) how many moles of electrons must pass through the cell in one day?

(b) how many amperes are passing through the cell?

(c) how many moles of oxygen (O_2) are being produced simultaneously?

68. The electrolysis of an aqueous solution of NaCl has the overall equation

$$2H_2O + 2Cl^-(aq) \longrightarrow H_2(g) + Cl_2(g) + 2OH^-(aq)$$

During the electrolysis, 0.228 mol of electrons passes through the cell.

(a) How many electrons does this represent?

(b) How many coulombs does this represent?

(c) Assuming 100% yield, what masses of H_2 and Cl_2 are produced?

69. A solution containing a metal ion ($M^{3+}(aq)$) is electrolyzed by a current of 5.0 A. After 10.0 minutes, 1.19 g of the metal is plated out.

(a) How many coulombs are supplied by the battery?

(b) What is the metal? (Assume 100% efficiency.)

70. A solution containing a metal ion ($M^{2+}(aq)$) is electrolyzed by a current of 7.8 A. After 15.5 minutes, 2.39 g of the metal is plated out.

(a) How many coulombs are supplied by the battery?

(b) What is the metal? (Assume 100% efficiency.)

71. ■ A baby's spoon with an area of 6.25 cm^2 is plated with silver from $AgNO_3$ using a current of 2.00 A for two hours and 25 minutes.

(a) If the current efficiency is 82.0%, how many grams of silver are plated?

(b) What is the thickness of the silver plate formed ($d = 10.5\ g/cm^3$)?

72. ■ A metallurgist wants to goldplate a thin sheet with the following dimensions: 1.5 in × 8.5 in × 0.0012 in. The gold plating must be 0.0020 in thick.

(a) How many grams of gold ($d = 19.3\ g/cm^3$) are required?

(b) How long will it take to plate the sheet from AuCN using a current of 7.00 A? (Assume 100% efficiency.)

73. A lead storage battery delivers a current of 6.00 A for one hour and 22 minutes at a voltage of 12.0 V.

(a) How many grams of lead are converted to $PbSO_4$?

(b) How much electrical energy is produced in kilowatt hours?

74. **WEB** Calcium metal can be obtained by the direct electrolysis of molten $CaCl_2$, at a voltage of 3.2 V.

(a) How many joules of electrical energy are required to obtain 12.0 lb of calcium?

(b) What is the cost of the electrical energy obtained in (a) if electrical energy is sold at the rate of nine cents per kilowatt hour?

Unclassified

75. Given the following data:

$$PtCl_4^{2-}(aq) + 2e^- \longrightarrow Pt(s) + 4Cl^-(aq) \qquad E° = +0.73\ V$$
$$Pt^{2+}(aq) + 4Cl^-(aq) \longrightarrow PtCl_4^{2-}(aq) \qquad K_f = 1 \times 10^{16}$$

find $E°$ for the half-cell

$$Pt^{2+}(aq) + 2e^- \longrightarrow Pt(s)$$

■ in OWL Blue-numbered questions answered in Appendix 6 **WEB** Solution is available on companion website

76. In a nickel-cadmium battery (Nicad), cadmium is oxidized to $Cd(OH)_2$ at the anode, while Ni_2O_3 is reduced to $Ni(OH)_2$ at the cathode. A portable CD player uses 0.175 amp of current. How many grams of Cd and Ni_2O_3 are consumed when the CD player is used for an hour and a half?

77. Hydrogen gas is produced when water is electrolyzed.

$$2H_2O(g) \longrightarrow 2H_2(g) + O_2(g)$$

A balloonist wants to fill a balloon with hydrogen gas. How long must a current of 12.0 A be used in the electrolysis of water to fill the balloon to a volume of 10.00 L and a pressure of 0.924 atm at 22°C?

78. Consider the electrolysis of $CuCl_2$ to form Cu(*s*) and $Cl_2(g)$. Calculate the minimum voltage required to carry out this reaction at standard conditions. If a voltage of 1.50 V is actually used, how many kilojoules of electrical energy are consumed in producing 2.00 g of Cu?

79. An electrolysis experiment is performed to determine the value of the Faraday constant (number of coulombs per mole of electrons). In this experiment, 28.8 g of gold is plated out from a AuCN solution by running an electrolytic cell for two hours with a current of 2.00 A. What is the experimental value obtained for the Faraday constant?

80. An electrolytic cell consists of a 100.0-g strip of copper in 0.200 *M* $Cu(NO_3)_2$ and a 100.0-g strip of Cr in 0.200 *M* $Cr(NO_3)_3$. The overall reaction is:

$$3Cu(s) + 2Cr^{3+}(aq) \longrightarrow 3Cu^{2+}(aq) + 2Cr(s) \qquad E° = -1.083\text{ V}$$

An external battery provides 3 amperes for 70 minutes and 20 seconds with 100% efficiency. What is the mass of the copper strip after the battery has been disconnected?

81. After use, a nickel-cadmium (Nicad) battery has 0.129 g of $Cd(OH)_2$ deposited on the anode. The battery is inserted into a recharger, which supplies 0.175 A. How many hours does the Nicad battery need for recharging so that all the $Cd(OH)_2$ is converted back to Cd? Assume that the recharger is 100% efficient. (See Problem 76 for a description of the Nicad battery.)

82. Consider the following reaction carried out at 1000°C.

$$CO(g) + \tfrac{1}{2}O_2(g) \longrightarrow CO_2(g)$$

Assuming that all gases are at 1.00 atm, calculate the voltage produced at the given conditions. (Use Appendix 1 and assume that $\Delta H°$ and $\Delta S°$ do not change with an increase in temperature.)

83. Atomic masses can be determined by electrolysis. In one hour, a current of 0.600 A deposits 2.42 g of a certain metal, M, which is present in solution as M^+ ions. What is the atomic mass of the metal?

84. Consider the following reaction at 25°C.

$$O_2(g) + 4H^+(aq) + 4Br^-(aq) \longrightarrow 2H_2O + 2Br_2(l)$$

If $[H^+]$ is adjusted by adding a buffer that is 0.100 *M* in sodium acetate and 0.100 *M* in acetic acid, the pressure of oxygen gas is 1.00 atm, and the bromide concentration is 0.100 *M*, what is the calculated cell voltage? (K_a acetic acid = 1.8×10^{-5}.)

85. Given the standard reduction potential for $Zn(OH)_4^{2-}$:

$$Zn(OH)_4^{2-}(aq) + 2e^- \longrightarrow Zn(s) + 4OH^-(aq) \qquad E°_{red} = -1.19\text{ V}$$

Calculate the formation constant (K_f) for the reaction

$$Zn^{2+}(aq) + 4OH^-(aq) \rightleftharpoons Zn(OH)_4^{2-}(aq)$$

Conceptual Problems

86. Choose the figure below that best represents the results after the electrolysis of water. (Circles represent hydrogen atoms and squares represent oxygen atoms.)

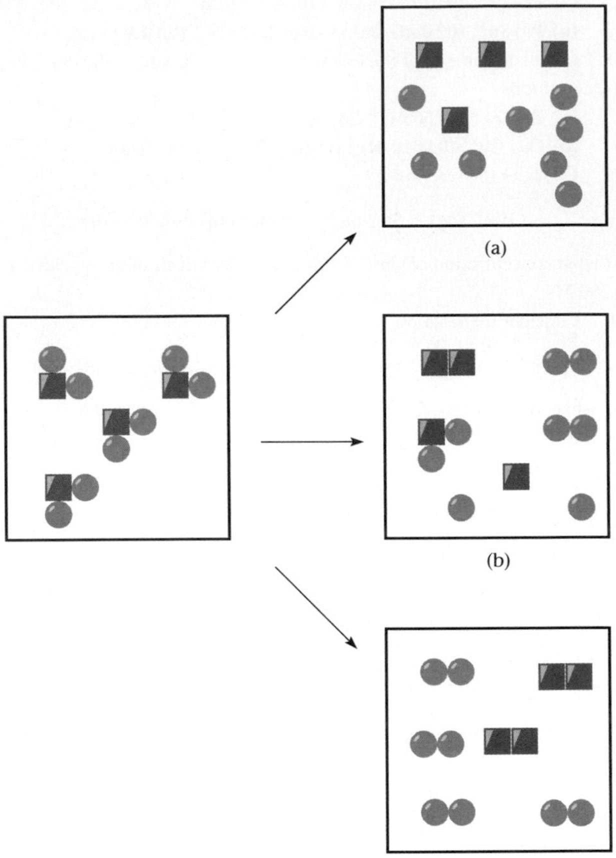

87. For the cell

$$Zn \mid Zn^{2+} \parallel Cu^{2+} \mid Cu$$

$E°$ is 1.10 V. A student prepared the same cell in the lab at standard conditions. Her experimental $E°$ was 1.0 V. A possible explanation for the difference is that

(a) a larger volume of Zn^{2+} than Cu^{2+} was used.
(b) the zinc electrode had twice the mass of the copper electrode.
(c) $[Zn^{2+}]$ was smaller than 1 *M*.
(d) $[Cu^{2+}]$ was smaller than 1 *M*.
(e) the copper electrode had twice the surface area of the zinc electrode.

88. Which of the changes below will increase the voltage of the following cell?

$$Co \mid Co^{2+}\ (0.010\ M) \parallel H^+\ (0.010\ M) \mid H_2\ (0.500\text{ atm}) \mid Pt$$

(a) Increase the volume of $CoCl_2$ solution from 100 mL to 300 mL.
(b) Increase $[H^+]$ from 0.010 *M* to 0.500 *M*.
(c) Increase the pressure of H_2 from 0.500 atm to 1 atm.
(d) Increase the mass of the Co electrode from 15 g to 25 g.
(e) Increase $[Co^{2+}]$ from 0.010 *M* to 0.500 *M*.

89. The standard potential for the reduction of AgSCN is 0.0895 V.

$$AgSCN(s) + e^- \longrightarrow Ag(s) + SCN^-(aq)$$

Find another electrode potential to use together with the above value and calculate K_{sp} for AgSCN.

90. Consider the following standard reduction potentials:

$$Tl^+(aq) + e^- \longrightarrow Tl(s) \qquad E^\circ_{red} = -0.34\ V$$
$$Tl^{3+}(aq) + 3e^- \longrightarrow Tl(s) \qquad E^\circ_{red} = 0.74\ V$$
$$Tl^{3+}(aq) + 2e^- \longrightarrow Tl^+(aq) \qquad E^\circ_{red} = 1.28\ V$$

and the following abbreviated cell notations:

(1) $Tl \mid Tl^+ \parallel Tl^{3+}, Tl^+ \mid Pt$
(2) $Tl \mid Tl^{3+} \parallel Tl^{3+}, Tl^+ \mid Pt$
(3) $Tl \mid Tl^+ \parallel Tl^{3+} \mid Tl$

(a) Write the overall equation for each cell.
(b) Calculate E° for each cell.
(c) Calculate ΔG° for each overall equation.
(d) Comment on whether ΔG° and/or E° are state properties. (*Hint:* A state property is path-independent.)

91. Use Table 18.1 to answer the following questions. Use **LT** (for *is less than*), **GT** (for *is greater than*), **EQ** (for *is equal to*), or **MI** (for *more information required*).

(a) For the half reaction

$$\tfrac{1}{2}Br_2(l) + e^- \longrightarrow Br^-(aq)$$

E°_{red} ________ 1.077 V.

(b) For the reaction

$$2Br^-(aq) + Co^{2+}(aq) \longrightarrow Br_2(l) + Co(s)$$

E° ________ 0.

(c) If the half reaction

$$Co^{2+}(aq) + 2e^- \longrightarrow Co(s)$$

is designated as the new standard where E°_{red} is 0.00, then E°_{red} for

$$2H^+(aq) + 2e^- \longrightarrow H_2(g)$$

is ________ 0.

(d) For the reaction

$$2Cr^{3+}(aq) + 3Co(s) \longrightarrow 2Cr(s) + 3Co^{2+}(aq)$$

the number of electrons exchanged is ________ 6.

(e) For the reaction described in (d), the number of coulombs that passes through the cell is ________ 9.648×10^4.

92. Consider three metals, X, Y, and Z, and their salts, XA, YA, and ZA. Three experiments take place with the following results:

- $X + \text{hot } H_2O \longrightarrow H_2 \text{ bubbles}$
- $X + YA \longrightarrow \text{no reaction}$
- $X + ZA \longrightarrow X \text{ discolored} + Z$

Rank metals X, Y, and Z, in order of decreasing strength as reducing agents.

Challenge Problems

93. An alloy made up of tin and copper is prepared by simultaneously electroplating the two metals from a solution containing $Sn(NO_3)_2$ and $Cu(NO_3)_2$. If 20.0% of the total current is used to plate tin, while 80.0% is used to plate copper, what is the percent composition of the alloy?

94. In a fully charged lead storage battery, the electrolyte consists of 38% sulfuric acid by mass. The solution has a density of 1.286 g/cm³. Calculate E for the cell. Assume all the H^+ ions come from the first dissociation of H_2SO_4, which is complete.

95. Consider a voltaic cell in which the following reaction occurs.

$$Zn(s) + Sn^{2+}(aq) \longrightarrow Zn^{2+}(aq) + Sn(s)$$

(a) Calculate E° for the cell.
(b) When the cell operates, what happens to the concentration of Zn^{2+}? The concentration of Sn^{2+}?
(c) When the cell voltage drops to zero, what is the ratio of the concentration of Zn^{2+} to that of Sn^{2+}?
(d) If the concentration of both cations is 1.0 *M* originally, what are the concentrations when the voltage drops to zero?

96. In biological systems, acetate ion is converted to ethyl alcohol in a two-step process:

$$CH_3COO^-(aq) + 3H^+(aq) + 2e^- \longrightarrow CH_3CHO(aq) + H_2O \qquad E^{\circ\prime} = -0.581\ V$$

$$CH_3CHO(aq) + 2H^+(aq) + 2e^- \longrightarrow C_2H_5OH(aq) \qquad E^{\circ\prime} = -0.197\ V$$

($E^{\circ\prime}$ is the standard reduction voltage at 25°C and pH of 7.00.)

(a) Calculate $\Delta G^{\circ\prime}$ for each step and for the overall conversion.
(b) Calculate $E^{\circ\prime}$ for the overall conversion.

97. Consider the cell

$$Pt \mid H_2 \mid H^+ \parallel H^+ \mid H_2 \mid Pt$$

In the anode half-cell, hydrogen gas at 1.0 atm is bubbled over a platinum electrode dipping into a solution that has a pH of 7.0. The other half-cell is identical to the first except that the solution around the platinum electrode has a pH of 0.0. What is the cell voltage?

98. A hydrogen-oxygen fuel cell operates on the reaction:

$$H_2(g) + \tfrac{1}{2}O_2(g) \longrightarrow H_2O(l)$$

If the cell is designed to produce 1.5 amp of current and if the hydrogen is contained in a 1.0-L tank at 200 atm pressure and 25°C, how long can the fuel cell operate before the hydrogen runs out? Assume that oxygen gas is in excess.

19 Nuclear Reactions

The universe passes along a way of cycles.
A process of matter dissolving in the stars,
Turned into radiation, passing through forms
Again to matter; again, perhaps, to birth.

—Muriel Rukeyser
sequence of poems of 1957 *"Time Hinder Not Me; His Arms Reach Here and There"*

Chapter Outline

These cave drawings, found in Chauvet Cave in France, have been authenticated by C-14 dating to 30,000–28,000 B.C. It is the oldest known artwork in the world.

Eurelios/French Ministry of Culture and Communication, Regional Direction for Cultural Affairs-Rhone-Alpes Region-Regional Department of Archaeology

The "ordinary chemical reactions" discussed to this point involve changes in the outer electronic structures of atoms or molecules. In contrast, nuclear reactions result from changes taking place within atomic nuclei. You will recall (Chapter 2) that atomic nuclei are represented by symbols such as

$$^{12}_{6}C \quad ^{14}_{6}C$$

The atomic number *Z* (number of protons in the nucleus) is shown as a left subscript. The mass number *A* (number of protons + number of neutrons in the nucleus) appears as a left superscript.

The reactions that we discuss in this chapter will be represented by **nuclear equations.** An equation of this type uses nuclear symbols such as those written above; in other respects it resembles an ordinary chemical equation. A nuclear equation must be balanced with respect to nuclear charge (atomic number) and nuclear mass (mass number). To see what that means, consider an equation that we will have a lot more to say about later in this chapter:

$$^{14}_{7}N + ^{1}_{0}n \longrightarrow ^{14}_{6}C + ^{1}_{1}H$$

The reactants are an N-14 nucleus and a neutron; the products are a C-14 nucleus and an H-1 nucleus. The atomic numbers add to 7 on both sides:

$$\text{reactants: } 7 + 0 = 7 \qquad \text{products} = 6 + 1 = 7$$

whereas the mass numbers add to 15:

$$\text{reactants: } 14 + 1 = 15 \qquad \text{products} = 14 + 1 = 15$$ ■

Online homework for this chapter may be assigned in OWL.

CENGAGENOW™
This icon introduces an opportunity for self-study and to explore interactive modules by signing in at **academic.cengage.com/now.**

Nuclear reactions usually involve the transmutation of elements.

19.1 RADIOACTIVITY

A radioactive nucleus spontaneously decomposes ("decays") with the evolution of energy. As pointed out in Chapter 2, a few such nuclei occur in nature, accounting for *natural radioactivity.* Many more can be made ("induced") in the laboratory by bombarding stable nuclei with high-energy particles.

Mode of Decay

Naturally occurring radioactive nuclei commonly decompose by—

- **alpha particle emission,** in which an ordinary helium nucleus, $^{4}_{2}He$, is given off. Uranium-238 behaves this way:

$$^{238}_{92}U \longrightarrow ^{4}_{2}He + ^{234}_{90}Th$$

  Notice that when alpha emission occurs, the atomic number decreases by two units; the mass number decreases by four units.
- **beta particle emission,** which produces an electron, given the symbol $^{0}_{-1}e$. An example of beta emission is

$$^{234}_{90}Th \longrightarrow ^{0}_{-1}e + ^{234}_{91}Pa$$

  Notice that the product nucleus, $^{234}_{91}Pa$, has the same mass number as the reactant, $^{234}_{90}Th$, but its atomic number is one unit larger. Putting it another way, beta emission converts a neutron to a proton. It occurs with nuclei that contain "too many neutrons" for stability.
- **gamma radiation emission,** which consists of high-energy photons. Because gamma emission changes neither the mass number nor the atomic number, it is ordinarily omitted in writing nuclear equations.

CENGAGENOW™
Click Coached Problems for a self-study module on **modes of radioactive decay.**

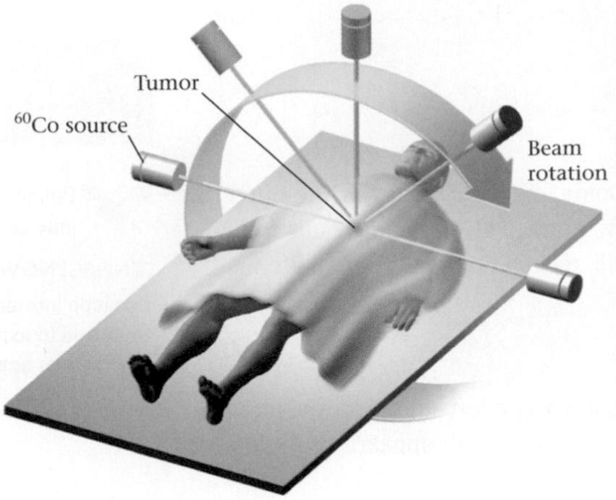

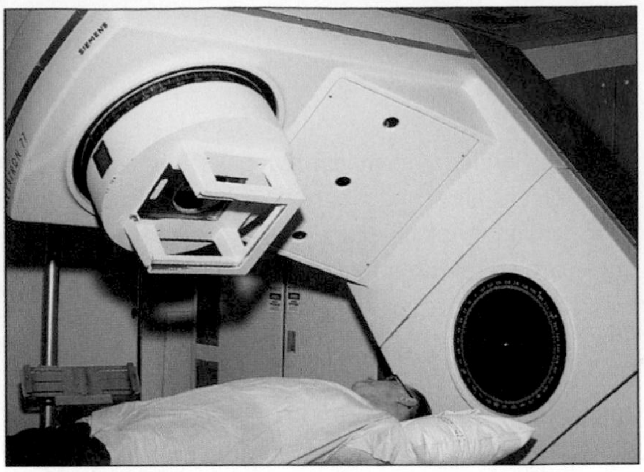

Cobalt-60 cancer therapy. Gamma rays from the rotating radiation source are concentrated at the location of the diseased tissue.

Radioactive nuclei produced "artificially" in the laboratory can show α-, β-, or γ-emission. They can also decompose by—

- **positron emission.** A **positron** is identical to an electron except that it has a charge of $+1$ rather than -1. A positron has the symbol ${}^{0}_{1}e$.

$$ {}^{40}_{19}\text{K} \longrightarrow {}^{0}_{1}e + {}^{40}_{18}\text{Ar} $$

Here, a proton in K-40 ($19\,p^+$, $21\,n$) is converted to a neutron in Ar-40 ($18\,p^+$, $22\,n$). Positron emission is characteristic of nuclei that have too many protons for stability.

- **K-electron capture,** in which an electron in the innermost energy level ($n = 1$) "falls" into the nucleus.

$$ {}^{82}_{37}\text{Rb} + {}^{0}_{-1}e \longrightarrow {}^{82}_{36}\text{Kr} $$

Notice that the result of K-electron capture is the same as positron emission; mass number remains unchanged, whereas atomic number decreases by one unit. Electron capture is more common with heavy nuclei, presumably because the $n = 1$ level is closer to the nucleus.

Promethium is by far the rarest of the "rare earths."

CENGAGENOW™
Click Coached Problems for a self-study module on **balancing nuclear reaction equations.**

Example 19.1 Promethium ($Z = 61$) is essentially nonexistent in nature; all of its isotopes are radioactive. Write balanced nuclear equations for the decomposition of

(a) Pm-142 by positron emission.
(b) Pm-147 by beta emission.
(c) Pm-150 by alpha emission.

Strategy Use the principle that atomic and mass numbers must balance to find the symbol of the product nucleus.

SOLUTION

(a) ${}^{142}_{61}\text{Pm} \longrightarrow {}^{0}_{1}e + {}^{142}_{60}\text{Nd}$
(b) ${}^{147}_{61}\text{Pm} \longrightarrow {}^{0}_{-1}e + {}^{147}_{62}\text{Sm}$
(c) ${}^{150}_{61}\text{Pm} \longrightarrow {}^{4}_{2}\text{He} + {}^{146}_{59}\text{Pr}$

Bombardment Reactions

More than 1500 radioactive isotopes have been prepared in the laboratory. The number of such isotopes per element ranges from 1 (hydrogen and boron) to 34 (indium). They are all prepared by bombardment reactions in which a stable nucleus is converted to one that is radioactive, which in turn decays to stable products. The bombarding particle may be—

- a *neutron,* usually of rather low energy, produced in a fission reactor (Section 19.4). A typical reaction of this type is

$$^{27}_{13}\text{Al} + ^{1}_{0}n \longrightarrow ^{28}_{13}\text{Al}$$

The product nucleus, Al-28, is radioactive, decaying by beta emission:

$$^{28}_{13}\text{Al} \longrightarrow ^{28}_{14}\text{Si} + ^{0}_{-1}e$$

- a *charged particle* (electron, positron, α-particle, . . .), which can be accelerated to very high velocities in electric and/or magnetic fields. In this way, the charged particle acquires enough energy to bring about a nuclear reaction, despite electrostatic repulsion with the components of the atom.

The first radioactive isotopes to be made in the laboratory were prepared in 1934 by Irene Curie and her husband, Frederic Joliot. They achieved this by bombarding certain stable isotopes with high-energy alpha particles. One reaction was

$$^{27}_{13}\text{Al} + ^{4}_{2}\text{He} \longrightarrow ^{30}_{15}\text{P} + ^{1}_{0}n$$

The product, phosphorus-30, is radioactive, decaying by positron emission:

$$^{30}_{15}\text{P} \longrightarrow ^{30}_{14}\text{Si} + ^{0}_{1}e$$

An interesting application of bombardment reactions is the preparation of the so-called transuranium elements. Beginning with neptunium (Np, $Z = 93$) in 1940, a series of elements with atomic numbers greater than that of uranium have been synthesized. Much of this work was done by a group at the University of California, Berkeley, under the direction of Glenn Seaborg (1912–1999) and later Albert Ghiorso (1915–). A Russian group at Dubna near Moscow, led by G. N. Flerov (1913–1999) made significant contributions. The heavy elements (197 through 212) were prepared in the late twentieth century by a German group at Darmstadt under the direction of Peter Armbruster (1931–). Most of the nuclei produced have half-lives of a few microseconds. Experiments reporting the formation of elements 113, 115, and 116 have been reported in peer-reviewed journals, but their identification is yet to be confirmed by IUPAC (International Union of Pure and Applied Chemists). Element 117 is unknown and there are no reports of its isolation.

In October 2006, a research team of scientists from the Lawrence Livermore National Laboratory in California, USA, and the Joint Institute of Nuclear Research in Dubna, Russia, reported the indirect detection of Uuo-294 (Element 118). It is reported to be produced by the following collisions.

$$^{249}_{98}\text{Cf} + ^{48}_{20}\text{Ca} \longrightarrow ^{294}_{118}\text{Uuo} + 3\,^{1}_{0}n$$

The decay products of Uuo-294, not the atoms themselves, were observed.

Some of the reactions used to prepare transuranium elements are listed in Table 19.1. Neutron bombardment is effective for the lower members of the series (elements 93 through

Table 19.1 Synthesis of Transuranium Elements

	Neutron Bombardment
Neptunium, plutonium	$^{238}_{92}\text{U} + ^{1}_{0}n \longrightarrow ^{239}_{93}\text{Np} + ^{0}_{-1}e$
	$^{239}_{93}\text{Np} \longrightarrow ^{239}_{94}\text{Pu} + ^{0}_{-1}e$
Americium	$^{239}_{94}\text{Pu} + 2\,^{1}_{0}n \longrightarrow ^{241}_{95}\text{Am} + ^{0}_{-1}e$
	Positive Ion Bombardment
Curium	$^{239}_{94}\text{Pu} + ^{4}_{2}\text{He} \longrightarrow ^{242}_{96}\text{Cm} + ^{1}_{0}n$
Californium	$^{242}_{96}\text{Cm} + ^{4}_{2}\text{He} \longrightarrow ^{245}_{98}\text{Cf} + ^{1}_{0}n$
Rutherfordium	$^{249}_{98}\text{Cf} + ^{12}_{6}\text{C} \longrightarrow ^{257}_{104}\text{Rf} + 4\,^{1}_{0}n$
Dubnium	$^{249}_{98}\text{Cf} + ^{15}_{7}\text{N} \longrightarrow ^{260}_{105}\text{Db} + 4\,^{1}_{0}n$
Seaborgium	$^{249}_{98}\text{Cf} + ^{18}_{8}\text{O} \longrightarrow ^{263}_{106}\text{Sg} + 4\,^{1}_{0}n$

The names of these elements reflect the names of their discoverers and other nuclear scientists.

95), but the yield of product decreases sharply with increasing atomic number. To form the heavier transuranium elements, it is necessary to bombard appropriate targets with high-energy positive ions. By using relatively heavy bombarding particles such as carbon-12, one can achieve a considerable increase in atomic number.

Applications

A large number of radioactive nuclei have been used both in industry and in many areas of basic and applied research. A few of these are discussed below.

Medicine

Radioactive isotopes are commonly used in cancer therapy, usually to eliminate any malignant cells left after surgery. Cobalt-60 is most often used; γ-rays from this source are focused at small areas where cancer is suspected. Certain types of cancer can be treated internally with radioactive isotopes. If a patient suffering from cancer of the thyroid drinks a solution of NaI containing radioactive iodide ions (^{131}I or ^{123}I), the iodine moves preferentially to the thyroid gland. There the radiation destroys malignant cells without affecting the rest of the body.

More commonly, radioactive nuclei are used for diagnosis (Table 19.2). Positron emission tomography (PET) is a technique used to study brain disorders. The patient is given a dose of glucose ($C_6H_{12}O_6$) containing a small amount of carbon-11, a positron emitter. The brain is then scanned to detect positron emission from the radioactive "labeled" glucose. In this way, differences in glucose uptake and metabolism in patients with normal and abnormal brains are established. For example, PET scans have determined that the brain of a schizophrenic metabolizes only about 20% as much glucose as that of most people.

Table 19.2 Diagnostic Uses of Radioactive Isotopes

Isotope	Use
$^{11}_{6}C$	Brain scan (PET); see text
$^{24}_{11}Na$	Circulatory disorders
$^{32}_{15}P$	Detection of eye tumors
$^{59}_{26}Fe$	Anemia
$^{67}_{31}Ga$	Scan for lung tumors, abscesses
$^{75}_{34}Se$	Pancreas scan
$^{99}_{43}Tc$	Imaging of brain, liver, kidneys, bone marrow
$^{133}_{54}Xe$	Lung imaging
$^{201}_{81}Tl$	Heart disorders

Chemistry

Radioactive nuclei are used extensively in chemical analysis. One technique of particular importance is *neutron activation analysis.* This procedure depends on the phenomenon of induced radioactivity. A sample is bombarded by neutrons, bringing about such reactions as

$$^{84}_{38}Sr + ^{1}_{0}n \longrightarrow ^{85}_{38}Sr$$

Ordinarily the element retains its chemical identity, but the isotope formed is radioactive, decaying by gamma emission. The magnitude of the energy change and hence the wavelength of the gamma ray vary from one element to another and so can serve for the qualitative analysis of the sample. The intensity of the radiation depends on the amount of the element present in the sample; this permits quantitative analysis of the sample. Neutron activation analysis can be used to analyze for 50 different elements in amounts as small as one picogram (10^{-12} g).

One application of neutron activation analysis is in the field of archaeology. By measuring the amount of strontium in the bones of prehistoric humans, it is possible to get some idea of their diet. Plants contain considerably more strontium than animals do, so a high strontium content suggests a largely vegetarian diet. Strontium analyses of bones taken from ancient farming communities consistently show a difference by sex; women have higher strontium levels than men. Apparently, in those days, women did most of the farming; men spent a lot of time away from home hunting and eating their kill.

Commercial Applications

Most smoke alarms (Figure 19.1, p. 517) use a radioactive species, typically americium-241. A tiny amount of this isotope is placed in a small ionization chamber; decay of Am-241 ionizes air molecules within the chamber. Under the influence of a potential applied by a battery, these ions move across the chamber, producing an electric current. If smoke particles get into the chamber, the flow of ions is impeded and the current drops. This is detected by electronic circuitry, and an alarm sounds. The alarm also goes off if the battery voltage drops, indicating that it needs to be replaced.

It also goes off when I use my fireplace (WLM).

Another potential application of radioactive species is in food preservation (Figure 19.2, p. 518). It is well known that gamma rays can kill insects, larvae, and parasites such as

CHEMISTRY The Human Side

The history of radiochemistry is in no small measure the story of two remarkable women, Marie and Irene Curie, and their husbands, Pierre Curie and Frederic Joliot. Marie Curie (1867–1934) was born Maria Sklodowska in Warsaw, Poland, then a part of the Russian empire. In 1891 she emigrated to Paris to study at the Sorbonne, where she met and married a French physicist, Pierre Curie (1859–1906). The Curies were associates of Henri Becquerel, the man who discovered that uranium salts are radioactive. They showed that thorium, like uranium, is radioactive and that the amount of radiation emitted is directly proportional to the amount of uranium or thorium in the sample.

Mütter Museum, Philadelphia College of Physicians

Marie and Pierre Curie with daughter Irene, at their home near Paris

In 1898, Marie and Pierre Curie isolated two new radioactive elements, which they named radium and polonium. To obtain a few milligrams of these elements, they started with several tons of pitchblende ore and carried out a long series of tedious separations. Their work was done in a poorly equipped, unheated shed where the temperature reached 6°C (43°F) in winter. Four years later, in 1902, Marie determined the atomic mass of radium to within 0.5%, working with a tiny sample.

In 1903, the Curies received the Nobel Prize in physics (with Becquerel) for the discovery of radioactivity. Three years later, Pierre Curie died at the age of 46, the victim of a tragic accident. He stepped from behind a carriage in a busy Paris street and was run down by a horse-driven truck. That same year, Marie became the first woman instructor at the Sorbonne. In 1911, she won the Nobel Prize in chemistry for the discovery of radium and polonium, thereby becoming the first person to win two Nobel Prizes.

When Europe exploded into war in 1914, scientists largely abandoned their studies to go to the front. Marie Curie, with her daughter Irene, then 17 years old, organized medical units equipped with X-ray machinery. These were used to locate foreign metallic objects in wounded soldiers. Many of the wounds were to the head; French soldiers came out of the trenches without head protection because their government had decided that helmets looked too German. In November of 1918, the Curies celebrated the end of World War I; France was victorious, and Marie's beloved Poland was free again.

In 1921, Irene Curie (1897–1956) began research at the Radium Institute. Five years later she married Frederic Joliot (1900–1958), a brilliant young physicist who was also an assistant at the Institute. In 1931, they began a research program in nuclear chemistry that led to several important discoveries and at least one near miss. The Joliot-Curies were the first to demonstrate induced radioactivity. They also discovered the positron, a particle that scientists had been seeking for many years. They narrowly missed finding another, more fundamental particle, the neutron. That honor went to James Chadwick in England. In 1935, Irene Curie and Frederic Joliot received the Nobel Prize in physics. The award came too late for Irene's mother, who had died of leukemia in 1934. Twenty-two years later, Irene Curie-Joliot died of the same disease. Both women acquired leukemia through prolonged exposure to radiation.

Chadwick, a student of Rutherford, discovered the neutron in 1932.

trichina that cause trichinosis in pork. Radiation can also inhibit sprouting of onions and potatoes. Perhaps most important from a commercial standpoint, it can extend the shelf lives of many foods for weeks or even months. Many chemicals used to preserve foods have later been shown to have adverse health effects, so irradiation is an attractive alternative. Finally, irradiation can destroy microorganisms such as *E. coli,* which explains its use in treating beef.

Marna G. Clarke

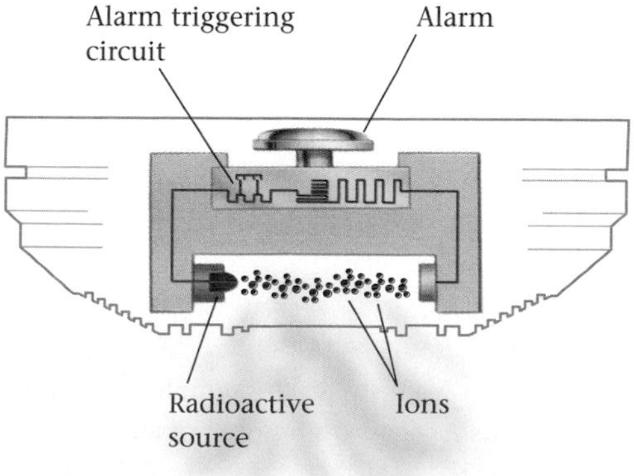

Figure 19.1
Smoke detector. Most smoke detectors use a tiny amount of a radioactive isotope to produce a current flow that drops off sharply in the presence of smoke particles, emitting an alarm in the process.

Figure 19.2
Food preservation. Strawberries irradiated with gamma rays from radioactive isotopes to keep them fresh.

Nordion International

19.2 RATE OF RADIOACTIVE DECAY

As pointed out in Chapter 11, radioactive decay is a first-order process. This means that the following equations, discussed on pages 294–295, apply:

k = rate constant = fraction of atoms decaying in unit time.

$$\text{rate} = kX$$

$$\ln\frac{X_0}{X} = kt$$

$$k = \frac{0.693}{t_{1/2}}$$

Courtesy of Beckman Industries

Figure 19.3
A liquid scintillation counter. This instrument is used to detect radiation and measure disintegrations per minute quickly and accurately.

where k is the first-order rate constant, $t_{1/2}$ is the half-life, X is the amount of radioactive species present at time t, and X_0 is the amount at $t = 0$.

Because of the way in which rate of decay is measured (Figure 19.3), it is often described by the **activity (A)** of the sample, which expresses the number of atoms decaying in unit time. The first equation above can be written

$$A = kN \qquad \textbf{(19.1)}$$

where A is the activity, k the first-order rate constant, and N the number of radioactive nuclei present.

Activity can be expressed in terms of the number of atoms decaying per second, or becquerels (Bq).

$$1\ \text{Bq} = 1\ \text{atom/s}$$

Alternatively, activity may be cited in disintegrations per minute or, perhaps most commonly, in **curies** (Ci)

$$1\ \text{Ci} = 3.700 \times 10^{10}\ \text{atom/s}$$

CENGAGENOW™
Click Coached Problems for a self-study module on **half-life and radiochemical dating.**

Example 19.2 Graded

The half-life of radium-226 is 1.60×10^3 y = 5.05×10^{10} s.

*(a) Calculate k in s^{-1}.
**(b) What is the activity in curies of a 1.00-g sample of Ra-226?
***(c) What is the mass in grams of a sample of Ra-226 that has an activity of 1.00×10^9 atoms/min?

SOLUTION

(a) $k = 0.693/(5.05 \times 10^{10}\ \text{s}) = 1.37 \times 10^{-11}/\text{s}$

(b) First find N for the 1.00-g sample, using the fact that one mole of radium (226 g) contains Avogadro's number of atoms.

$$N = 1.00\ \text{g} \times \frac{6.022 \times 10^{23}\ \text{atoms}}{226\ \text{g}} = 2.66 \times 10^{21}\ \text{atoms}$$

Now apply equation 19.1; $A = kN$:

$$A = (1.37 \times 10^{-11}/\text{s})(2.66 \times 10^{21}\ \text{atoms}) \times \frac{1\ \text{Ci}}{3.700 \times 10^{10}\ \text{atoms/s}} = 0.985\ \text{Ci}$$

(The curie was supposed to be the activity of a one-gram sample of radium, the element discovered by the Curies; it isn't quite.)

(c) Convert the activity to the number of atoms disintegrating per second to be consistent with the units of k.

$$A = 1.00 \times 10^9 \frac{\text{atoms}}{\text{min}} \times \frac{1\ \text{min}}{60\ \text{s}} = 1.67 \times 10^7\ \text{atoms/s}$$

$$N = A/k = \frac{1.67 \times 10^7\ \text{atoms/s}}{1.37 \times 10^{-11}/\text{s}} = 1.22 \times 10^{18}\ \text{atoms}$$

$$\text{mass Ra-226} = 1.22 \times 10^{18}\ \text{atoms} \times \frac{226\ \text{g}}{6.022 \times 10^{23}\ \text{atoms}} = 4.58 \times 10^{-4}\ \text{g}$$

Age of Organic Material

During the 1950s, Professor W. F. Libby (1908–1980) of the University of Chicago and others worked out a method for determining the age of organic material. It is based on the decay rate of carbon-14. The method can be applied to objects from a few hundred up to 50,000 years old. It has been used to determine the authenticity of canvases of Renaissance painters and to check the ages of relics left by prehistoric cave dwellers.

Carbon-14 is produced in the atmosphere by the interaction of neutrons from cosmic radiation with ordinary nitrogen atoms:

$$^{14}_{7}\text{N} + {}^{1}_{0}n \longrightarrow {}^{14}_{6}\text{C} + {}^{1}_{1}\text{H}$$

The carbon-14 formed by this nuclear reaction is eventually incorporated into the carbon dioxide of the air. A steady-state concentration, amounting to about one atom of carbon-14 for every 10^{12} atoms of carbon-12, is established in atmospheric CO_2. More specifically, the concentration of C-14 is such that a sample containing one gram of carbon has an activity of 15.3 atoms/min. A living plant, taking in carbon dioxide, has this same activity, as do plant-eating animals or human beings.

When a plant or animal dies, the intake of radioactive carbon stops. Consequently, the radioactive decay of carbon-14

$$^{14}_{6}\text{C} \longrightarrow {}^{14}_{7}\text{N} + {}^{0}_{-1}e \qquad t_{1/2} = 5730\ \text{y}$$

takes over, and the C-14 activity drops. The activity of a sample is directly proportional to the amount of C-14, so we can write:

$$\ln \frac{A_0}{A} = kt \qquad \textbf{(19.2)}$$

Since activity is directly proportional to amount, $X_0/X = A_0/A$.

where A_0 is the original activity, assumed to be 15.3 atoms/min, and A is the measured activity today; t is the age of the sample.

Example 19.3 A tiny piece of paper taken from the Dead Sea Scrolls, believed to date back to the first century A.D., was found to have an activity per gram of carbon of 12.1 atoms/min. Taking A_0 to be 15.3 atoms/min, estimate the age of the scrolls.

Strategy First (1), calculate the rate constant, knowing that the half-life is 5730 y. Then (2) find t, using the equation $\ln (A_0/A) = kt$.

SOLUTION

(1) $k = 0.693/5730\ \text{y} = 1.21 \times 10^{-4}/\text{y}$.

(2) $\ln \dfrac{15.3}{12.1} = 0.235 = 1.21 \times 10^{-4}/\text{y} \times t$

$$t = \frac{0.235}{1.21 \times 10^{-4}/\text{y}} = 1.94 \times 10^{3}\ \text{y}$$

Thus, the scrolls do date back to the first century A.D.

Santi Visali/The Image Bank

The Shroud of Turin. This piece of linen first appeared in about A.D. 1350. It bears a faint image (enhanced here) of a man who appears to have been crucified.

As you can imagine, it is not easy to determine accurately activities of the order of 10 atoms decaying per minute, about one "event" every six seconds. Elaborate precautions have to be taken to exclude background radiation. Moreover, relatively large samples must be used to increase the counting rate. Recently a technique has been developed whereby C-14 atoms can be counted very accurately in a specially designed mass spectrometer. This method was used to date the Shroud of Turin, using six samples with a total mass of about 0.1 g. Analysis by an international team of scientists in 1988 showed that the flax used to make the linen of which the Shroud is composed grew in the fourteenth century A.D. That means this remarkable burial garment could not have been used for the body of Christ.

19.3 MASS-ENERGY RELATIONS

The energy change accompanying a nuclear reaction can be calculated from the relation

$$\Delta E = c^2\, \Delta m$$

where

$$\Delta m = \text{change in mass} = \text{mass products} - \text{mass reactants}$$
$$\Delta E = \text{energy products} - \text{energy reactants}$$
$$c = \text{speed of light}$$

Such a reaction is exothermic; ΔH, like ΔE, is negative.

In a spontaneous nuclear reaction, the products weigh less than the reactants (Δm negative). In this case, the energy of the products is less than that of the reactants (ΔE negative) and energy is evolved to the surroundings.

In an "ordinary chemical reaction," Δm is immeasurably small. In a nuclear reaction, on the other hand, Δm is appreciable, amounting to 0.002% or more of the mass of reactants. The change in mass can readily be calculated from a table of nuclear masses (Table 19.3).

To obtain a more useful form of the equation $\Delta E = c^2\, \Delta m$, we substitute for c its value in meters per second.

$$c = 3.00 \times 10^{8}\ \text{m/s}$$

Thus $$\Delta E = 9.00 \times 10^{16}\ \frac{\text{m}^2}{\text{s}^2} \times \Delta m$$

But $$1\ \text{J} = 1\ \text{kg} \cdot \frac{\text{m}^2}{\text{s}^2}; \qquad 1\ \frac{\text{m}^2}{\text{s}^2} = 1\ \frac{\text{J}}{\text{kg}}$$

So $$\Delta E = 9.00 \times 10^{16}\ \frac{\text{J}}{\text{kg}} \times \Delta m$$

This equation can be used to calculate the energy change in *joules,* if you know Δm in *kilograms.* Ordinarily, Δm is expressed in *grams;* ΔE is calculated in *kilojoules.* The relationship between ΔE and Δm in these units can be found by using conversion factors:

$$\Delta E = 9.00 \times 10^{16}\ \frac{\text{J}}{\text{kg}} \times \frac{1\ \text{kg}}{10^3\ \text{g}} \times \frac{1\ \text{kJ}}{10^3\ \text{J}} \times \Delta m$$

$$\Delta E = 9.00 \times 10^{10}\ \frac{\text{kJ}}{\text{g}} \times \Delta m \qquad \textbf{(19.3)}$$

This is the most useful form of the mass-energy relation.

Table 19.3 Nuclear Masses on the ^{12}C Scale*

	At. No.	Mass No.	Mass (amu)		At. No.	Mass No.	Mass (amu)
e	0	0	0.00055				
n	0	1	1.00867	Br	35	79	78.8992
H	1	1	1.00728		35	81	80.8971
	1	2	2.01355		35	87	86.9028
	1	3	3.01550	Rb	37	89	88.8913
He	2	3	3.01493	Sr	38	90	89.8869
	2	4	4.00150	Mo	42	99	98.8846
Li	3	6	6.01348	Ru	44	106	105.8832
	3	7	7.01436	Ag	47	109	108.8790
Be	4	9	9.00999	Cd	48	109	108.8786
	4	10	10.01134		48	115	114.8791
B	5	10	10.01019	Sn	50	120	119.8748
	5	11	11.00656	Ce	58	144	143.8817
C	6	11	11.00814		58	146	145.8868
	6	12	11.99671	Pr	59	144	143.8809
	6	13	13.00006	Sm	62	152	151.8857
	6	14	13.99995	Eu	63	157	156.8908
O	8	16	15.99052	Er	68	168	167.8951
	8	17	16.99474	Hf	72	179	178.9065
	8	18	17.99477	W	74	186	185.9138
F	9	18	17.99601	Os	76	192	191.9197
	9	19	18.99346	Au	79	196	195.9231
Na	11	23	22.98373	Hg	80	196	195.9219
Mg	12	24	23.97845	Pb	82	206	205.9295
	12	25	24.97925		82	207	206.9309
	12	26	25.97600		82	208	207.9316
Al	13	26	25.97977	Po	84	210	209.9368
	13	27	26.97439		84	218	217.9628
	13	28	27.97477	Rn	86	222	221.9703
Si	14	28	27.96924	Ra	88	226	225.9771
S	16	32	31.96329	Th	90	230	229.9837
Cl	17	35	34.95952	Pa	91	234	233.9934
	17	37	36.95657	U	92	233	232.9890
Ar	18	40	39.95250		92	235	234.9934
K	19	39	38.95328		92	238	238.0003
	19	40	39.95358		92	239	239.0038
Ca	20	40	39.95162	Np	93	239	239.0019
Ti	22	48	47.93588	Pu	94	239	239.0006
Cr	24	52	51.92734		94	241	241.0051
Fe	26	56	55.92066	Am	95	241	241.0045
Co	27	59	58.91837	Cm	96	242	242.0061
Ni	28	59	58.91897	Bk	97	245	245.0129
Zn	30	64	63.91268	Cf	98	248	248.0186
	30	72	71.91128	Es	99	251	251.0255
Ge	32	76	75.90380	Fm	100	252	252.0278
As	33	79	78.90288		100	254	254.0331

*Note that these are *nuclear masses.* The masses of the corresponding atoms can be calculated by adding the masses of each extranuclear electron (0.000549). For example, for an *atom* of $^{4}_{2}He$ we have 4.00150 + 2(0.000549) = 4.00260. Similarly, for an atom of $^{12}_{6}C$, 11.99671 + 6(0.000549) = 12.00000.

Example 19.4 For the radioactive decay of radium, $^{226}_{88}Ra \longrightarrow {}^{222}_{86}Rn + {}^{4}_{2}He$, calculate ΔE in kilojoules when 10.2 g of radium decays.

Strategy (1) Using Table 19.3, calculate Δm when one mole of radium decays. Then (2) find Δm when 10.2 g of radium decays (1 mol Ra = 226.0 g Ra). Finally, (3) find ΔE using Equation 19.3.

Notice that the change in mass doesn't show up until you get to the third decimal place.

SOLUTION

(1) Using Table 19.3 for one mole of Ra-226,

$$\begin{aligned}\Delta m &= \text{mass 1 mol He-4} + \text{mass 1 mol Rn-222} - \text{mass 1 mol Ra-226}\\ &= 4.0015\text{ g} + 221.9703\text{ g} - 225.9771\text{ g}\\ &= -0.0053\text{ g/mol Ra}\end{aligned}$$

(2) When 10.2 g of radium decays,

$$\Delta m = \frac{-0.0053\text{ g}}{1\text{ mol Ra}} \times \frac{1\text{ mol Ra}}{226.0\text{ g Ra}} \times 10.2\text{ g Ra} = -2.4 \times 10^{-4}\text{ g}$$

(3) $\Delta E = 9.00 \times 10^{10}\frac{\text{kJ}}{\text{g}} \times (-2.4 \times 10^{-4}\text{ g}) = -2.2 \times 10^{7}\text{ kJ}$

Reality Check In ordinary chemical reactions, the energy change is of the order of 50 kJ/g or less. In this nuclear reaction, the energy change is much, much greater.

Nuclear Binding Energy

It is always true that ***a nucleus weighs less than the individual protons and neutrons of which it is composed.*** Consider, for example, the $^{6}_{3}\text{Li}$ nucleus, which contains three protons and three neutrons. According to Table 19.3, one mole of Li-6 nuclei weighs 6.01348 g. In contrast, the total mass of three moles of neutrons and three moles of protons is

$$3(1.00867\text{ g}) + 3(1.00728\text{ g}) = 6.04785\text{ g}$$

Clearly, one mole of Li-6 weighs *less* than the corresponding protons and neutrons. For the process

$$^{6}_{3}\text{Li} \longrightarrow 3\,^{1}_{1}\text{H} + 3\,^{1}_{0}n$$

$\Delta m = 6.04785\text{ g} - 6.01348\text{ g} = 0.03437\text{ g/mol Li}$.

The quantity just calculated is referred to as the *mass defect.* The corresponding energy difference is

$$\Delta E = 9.00 \times 10^{10}\frac{\text{kJ}}{\text{g}} \times 0.03437\frac{\text{g}}{\text{mol Li}} = 3.09 \times 10^{9}\frac{\text{kJ}}{\text{mol Li}}$$

This energy is referred to as the **binding energy.** It follows that 3.09×10^{9} kJ of energy would have to be absorbed to decompose one mole of Li-6 nuclei into protons and neutrons.

It takes a lot of energy to blow a nucleus apart.

$$^{6}_{3}\text{Li} \longrightarrow 3\,^{1}_{0}n + 3\,^{1}_{1}\text{H} \qquad \Delta E = 3.09 \times 10^{9}\frac{\text{kJ}}{\text{mol Li}}$$

By the same token, 3.09×10^{9} kJ of energy would be evolved when one mole of Li-6 is formed from protons and neutrons.

CENGAGENOW™

Click Coached Problems for a self-study module on **binding energy.**

Example 19.5 Calculate the binding energy of C-14, in kilojoules per mole.

Strategy Use Table 19.3 to find Δm for the decomposition of C-14 into neutrons and protons. Then calculate ΔE, using Equation 19.3.

SOLUTION The equation is $^{14}_{6}\text{C} \longrightarrow 6\,^{1}_{1}\text{H} + 8\,^{1}_{0}n$

$$\Delta m = 6(1.00728\text{ g}) + 8(1.00867\text{ g}) - 13.99995\text{ g} = 0.1131\text{ g per mol C-14}$$

$$\Delta E = 9.00 \times 10^{10}\frac{\text{kJ}}{\text{g}} \times 0.1131\frac{\text{g}}{\text{mol C-14}} = 1.02 \times 10^{10}\text{ kJ/mol C-14}$$

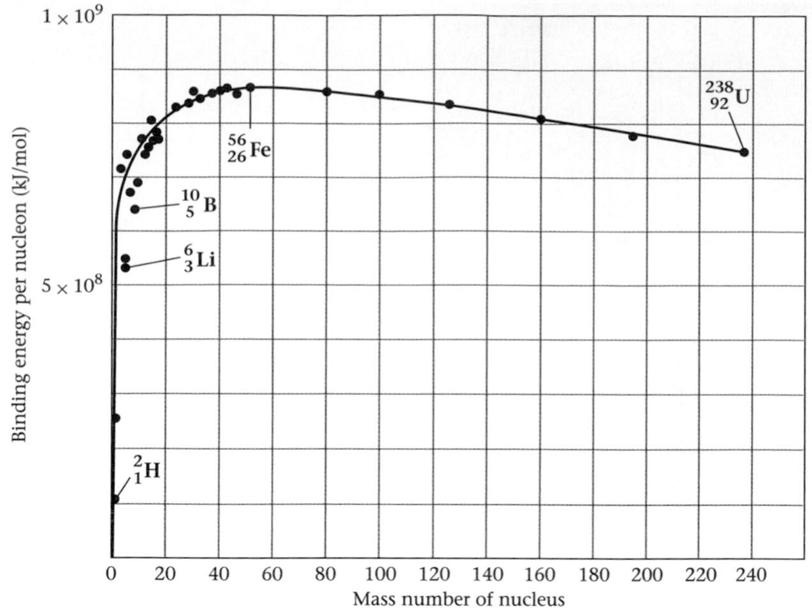

Figure 19.4
Binding energy per nucleon, a measure of nuclear stability. The binding energy has its maximum value for nuclei of intermediate mass, falling off for very heavy or very light nuclei. The form of this curve accounts for the fact that both fission and fusion give off large amounts of energy.

The binding energy of a nucleus is, in a sense, a measure of its stability. The greater the binding energy, the more difficult it would be to decompose the nucleus into protons and neutrons. As you might expect, the binding energy as calculated above increases steadily as the nucleus gets heavier, containing more protons and neutrons. A better measure of the relative stabilities of different nuclei is the ***binding energy per mole of nuclear particles (nucleons).*** This quantity is calculated by dividing the binding energy per mole of nuclei by the number of particles per nucleus. Thus

$$\text{Li-6:} \quad 3.09 \times 10^{9}\,\frac{\text{kJ}}{\text{mol Li-6}} \times \frac{1\text{ mol Li-6}}{6\text{ mol nucleons}} = 5.15 \times 10^{8}\,\frac{\text{kJ}}{\text{mol}}$$

$$\text{C-14:} \quad 1.02 \times 10^{10}\,\frac{\text{kJ}}{\text{mol}} \times \frac{1\text{ mol C-14}}{14\text{ mol nucleons}} = 7.29 \times 10^{8}\,\frac{\text{kJ}}{\text{mol}}$$

Figure 19.4 shows a plot of this quantity, binding energy/mole of nucleons, versus mass number. Notice that the curve has a broad maximum in the vicinity of mass numbers 50 to 80. Consider what would happen if a heavy nucleus such as $^{235}_{92}U$ were to split into smaller nuclei with mass numbers near the maximum. This process, referred to as **nuclear fission,** should result in an evolution of energy. The same result is obtained if very light nuclei such as $^{2}_{1}H$ combine with one another to form a heavier nucleus. Indeed, this process, called **nuclear fusion,** should evolve even more energy, because the binding energy per nucleon increases very sharply at the beginning of the curve.

Both very heavy and very light nuclei are relatively unstable; they decompose with the evolution of energy.

19.4 NUCLEAR FISSION

The process of nuclear fission was discovered more than half a century ago in 1938 by Lise Meitner (1878–1968) and Otto Hahn (1879–1968) in Germany. With the outbreak of World War II a year later, interest focused on the enormous amount of energy released in the process. At Los Alamos, in the mountains of New Mexico, a group of scientists led by J. Robert Oppenheimer (1904–1967) worked feverishly to produce the fission, or "atomic," bomb. Many of the members of this group were exiles from Nazi Germany. They were spurred on by the fear that Hitler would obtain the bomb first. Their work led to the explosion of the first atomic bomb in the New Mexico desert at 5:30 A.M. on July 16, 1945. Less than a month later (August 6, 1945), the world learned of this new weapon when another bomb was exploded

A nuclear fission explosion. Such a dramatic and destructive release of energy had never been seen before the development of the "atomic bomb" during World War II.

Courtesy of Library of Congress

over Hiroshima. This bomb killed 70,000 people and completely devastated an area of 10 square kilometers. Three days later, Nagasaki and its inhabitants met a similar fate. On August 14, Japan surrendered, and World War II was over.

The Fission Process ($^{235}_{92}U$)

Several isotopes of the heavy elements undergo fission if bombarded by neutrons of high enough energy. In practice, attention has centered on two particular isotopes, $^{235}_{92}U$ and $^{239}_{94}Pu$. Both of these can be split into fragments by relatively low-energy neutrons.

Our discussion concentrates on the uranium-235 isotope. It makes up only about 0.7% of naturally occurring uranium. The more abundant isotope, uranium-238, does not undergo fission. The first process used to separate these isotopes, and until recently the only one available, was that of gaseous effusion (Chapter 5). The volatile compound uranium hexafluoride, UF_6, which sublimes at 56°C, is used for this purpose.

When a uranium-235 atom undergoes fission, it splits into two unequal fragments and a number of neutrons and beta particles. The fission process is complicated by the fact that different uranium-235 atoms split up in many different ways. For example, while one atom of $^{235}_{92}U$ is splitting to give isotopes of rubidium (Z = 37) and cesium (Z = 55), another may break up to give isotopes of bromine (Z = 35) and lanthanum (Z = 57), while still another atom yields isotopes of zinc (Z = 30) and samarium (Z = 62):

$$^{1}_{0}n + ^{235}_{92}U \longrightarrow \begin{cases} ^{90}_{37}Rb + ^{144}_{55}Cs + 2\,^{1}_{0}n \\ ^{87}_{35}Br + ^{146}_{57}La + 3\,^{1}_{0}n \\ ^{72}_{30}Zn + ^{160}_{62}Sm + 4\,^{1}_{0}n \end{cases}$$

More than 200 isotopes of 35 different elements have been identified among the fission products of uranium-235.

The stable neutron-to-proton ratio near the middle of the periodic table, where the fission products are located, is considerably smaller (~1.2) than that of uranium-235 (1.6). Hence the immediate products of the fission process contain too many neutrons for stability;

they decompose by beta emission. In the case of rubidium-90, three steps are required to reach a stable nucleus:

$$^{90}_{37}\text{Rb} \longrightarrow ^{90}_{38}\text{Sr} + ^{0}_{-1}e \qquad t_{1/2} = 2.8 \text{ min}$$
$$^{90}_{38}\text{Sr} \longrightarrow ^{90}_{39}\text{Y} + ^{0}_{-1}e \qquad t_{1/2} = 29 \text{ y}$$
$$^{90}_{39}\text{Y} \longrightarrow ^{90}_{40}\text{Zr} + ^{0}_{-1}e \qquad t_{1/2} = 64 \text{ h}$$

The radiation hazard associated with fallout from nuclear weapons testing arises from radioactive isotopes such as these. One of the most dangerous is strontium-90. In the form of strontium carbonate, $SrCO_3$, it is incorporated into the bones of animals and human beings, where it remains for a lifetime.

Notice from the fission equations written above that two to four neutrons are produced by fission for every one consumed. Once a few atoms of uranium-235 split, the neutrons produced can bring about the fission of many more uranium-235 atoms. This creates the possibility of a *chain reaction*, whose rate increases exponentially with time. This is precisely what happens in the atomic bomb. The energy evolved in successive fissions escalates to give a tremendous explosion within a few seconds.

For nuclear fission to result in a chain reaction, the sample must be large enough so that most of the neutrons are captured internally. If the sample is too small, most of the neutrons escape, breaking the chain. The *critical mass* of uranium-235 required to maintain a chain reaction in a bomb appears to be about 1 to 10 kg. In the bomb dropped on Hiroshima, the critical mass was achieved by using a conventional explosive to fire one piece of uranium-235 into another.

The Hiroshima bomb was equivalent to 20,000 tons of TNT.

The evolution of energy in nuclear fission is directly related to the decrease in mass that takes place. About 80,000,000 kJ of energy is given off for every gram of $^{235}_{92}U$ that reacts. This is about 40 times as great as the energy change for simple nuclear reactions such as radioactive decay. The heat of combustion of coal is only about 30 kJ/g; the energy given off when TNT explodes is still smaller, about 2.8 kJ/g. Putting it another way, the fission of one gram of $^{235}_{92}U$ produces as much energy as the combustion of 2700 kg of coal or the explosion of 30 metric tons (3×10^4 kg) of TNT.

Nuclear Reactors

About 20% of the electrical energy produced in the United States comes from nuclear reactors using the fission of U-235. A so-called light water reactor (LWR) is shown schematically in Figure 19.5 (p. 526). The *fuel rods* are cylinders that contain fissionable material, uranium dioxide (UO_2) pellets, in a zirconium alloy tube. The uranium in these reactors is "enriched" so that it contains about 3% U-235, the fissionable isotope. The *control rods* are cylinders composed of substances, such as boron and cadmium, that absorb neutrons. Increased absorption of neutrons slows down the chain reaction. By varying the depth of the control rods within the fuel-rod assembly, the speed of the chain reaction can be controlled. Water at a pressure of 140 atm is passed through the reactor to absorb the heat given off by fission. The water, coming out of the reactor core at 320°C, circulates through a closed loop containing a heat exchanger that produces steam at 270°C. This steam is used to drive a turbogenerator that produces electrical energy.

In the light water reactor, the circulating water serves another purpose in addition to heat transfer. It acts to slow down, or *moderate,* the neutrons given off by fission. This is necessary if the chain reaction is to continue; fast neutrons are not readily absorbed by U-235. Reactors in Canada use "heavy water," D_2O, which has an important advantage over H_2O. Its moderating properties are such that naturally occurring uranium can be used as a fuel; enrichment in U-235 is not necessary.

In the 1970s it was generally supposed that nuclear fission would replace fossil fuels (oil, natural gas, coal) as an energy source. That hasn't happened. The most evident reasons are:

- *Nuclear accidents* at Three Mile Island, Pennsylvania, in 1979 and Chernobyl, Russia, in 1986 have had a devastating effect on public opinion in the United States and Europe. At Three Mile Island, only about 50 curies of radiation were released to the environment;

Figure 19.5
A pressurized water nuclear reactor. The control rods are made of a material such as cadmium or boron, which absorbs neutrons effectively. The fuel rods contain uranium oxide enriched in U-235.

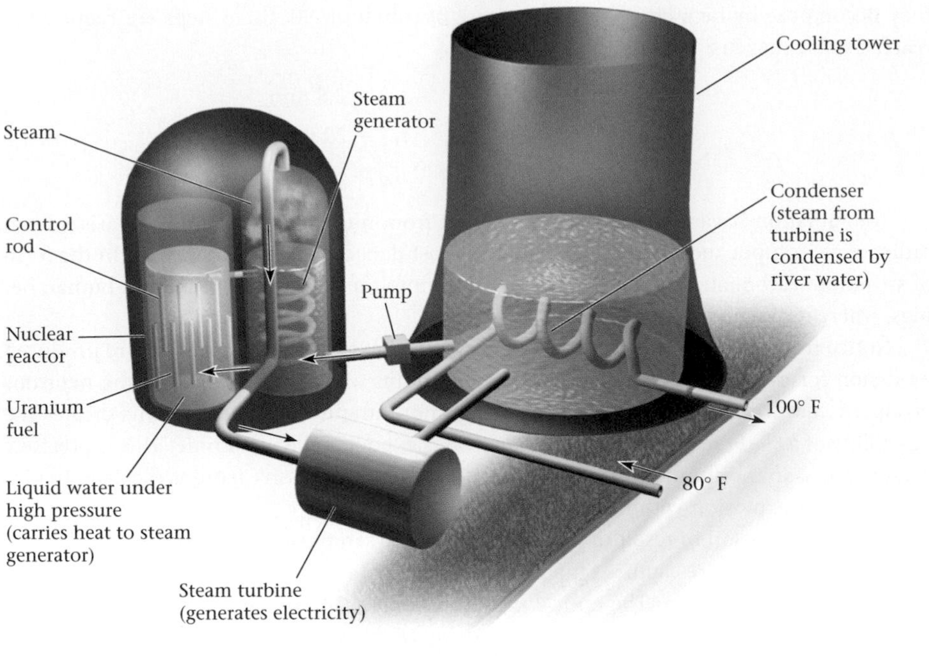

The worst nuclear accident occurred in 1951 in Russia when radioactive waste from Pu production was dumped into a lake.

there were no casualties. The explosion at Chernobyl was a very different story. About 100 million curies were released, leading to at least 31 fatalities. Moreover, 135,000 people had to be permanently evacuated from the Chernobyl area.

- *Disposal of radioactive wastes* from nuclear reactors has proved to be a serious political problem. The "NIMBY" syndrome (*n*ot *i*n *m*y *b*ack *y*ard) applies here.

In 1987, Congress designated Yucca Mountain, Nevada, 100 miles northwest of Las Vegas, as the site for burying some 70,000 metric tons of high-level nuclear waste. Over the years, some $6 billion has been spent on the project, which in 2002 was approved by the Bush administration and Congress. However, there is still no assurance that the facility will ever be licensed. Some 219 environmental groups and just about every elected official in Nevada are opposed to it and will fight it in the courts.

19.5 NUCLEAR FUSION

Recall (Figure 19.4) that very light nuclei, such as those of hydrogen, are unstable with respect to fusion into heavier isotopes. Indeed, the energy available from nuclear fusion is considerably greater than that given off in the fission of an equal mass of a heavy element (Example 19.6).

Example 19.6 Calculate ΔE, in kilojoules per gram of reactants, in

(a) a fusion reaction, ${}^{2}_{1}\text{H} + {}^{2}_{1}\text{H} \longrightarrow {}^{4}_{2}\text{He}$.
(b) a fission reaction, ${}^{235}_{92}\text{U} \longrightarrow {}^{90}_{38}\text{Sr} + {}^{144}_{58}\text{Ce} + {}^{1}_{0}n + 4\,{}^{0}_{-1}e$.

Strategy This problem is entirely analogous to Example 19.4. First, find Δm for the equation as written, and then find Δm for one gram of reactant. Finally, calculate ΔE: $\Delta E = 9.00 \times 10^{10}\ \text{kJ/g} \times \Delta m$.

SOLUTION

(a) (1) Using Table 19.3,

$$\Delta m = 4.00150\ \text{g} - 2(2.01355\ \text{g}) = -0.02560\ \text{g}$$

(2) The total mass of reactant, ${}^2_1H$, is 4.027 g:

$$\Delta m = \frac{-0.02560 \text{ g}}{4.027 \text{ g reactant}} = -6.357 \times 10^{-3} \text{ g/g reactant}$$

$$(3)\ \Delta E = 9.00 \times 10^{10} \frac{\text{kJ}}{\text{g}} \times \frac{(-6.357 \times 10^{-3} \text{ g})}{1 \text{ g reactant}} = \frac{-5.72 \times 10^{8} \text{ kJ}}{1 \text{ g reactant}}$$

(b) (1) $\Delta m = 89.8869 \text{ g} + 143.8817 \text{ g} + 1.0087 \text{ g} + 4(0.00055 \text{ g}) - 234.9934 \text{ g} = -0.2139 \text{ g}$

(2) The total mass of reactant, U-235, is 235.0 g:

$$\Delta m = \frac{-0.2139 \text{ g}}{235.0 \text{ g reactant}} = 9.102 \times 10^{-4} \text{ g/g reactant}$$

$$(3)\ \Delta E = 9.00 \times 10^{10} \frac{\text{kJ}}{\text{g}} \times \left(\frac{-9.102 \times 10^{-4} \text{ g}}{1 \text{ g reactant}}\right) = \frac{-8.19 \times 10^{7} \text{ kJ}}{1 \text{ g reactant}}$$

Reality Check Comparing the answers to (a) and (b), it appears that the fusion reaction produces about seven times as much energy per gram of reactant (57.2×10^7 versus 8.19×10^7 kJ) as does the fission reaction. This factor varies from about 3 to 10, depending on the particular reactions chosen to represent the fusion and fission processes.

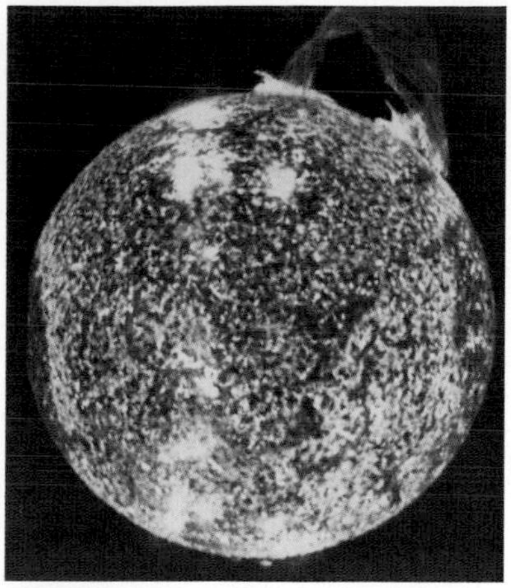
NASA

The Sun. Most of its energy is created by the fusion of hydrogen.

As an energy source, nuclear fusion possesses several additional advantages over nuclear fission. In particular, light isotopes suitable for fusion are far more abundant than the heavy isotopes required for fission. You can calculate, for example (Problem 73), that the fusion of only 2×10^{-9} % of the deuterium (${}^2_1H$) in seawater would meet the total annual energy requirements of the world.

Unfortunately, fusion processes, unlike neutron-induced fission, have very high activation energies. To overcome the electrostatic repulsion between two deuterium nuclei and cause them to react, they have to be accelerated to velocities of about 10^6 m/s, about 10,000 times greater than ordinary molecular velocities at room temperature. The corresponding temperature for fusion, as calculated from kinetic theory, is of the order of 10^{9}°C. In the hydrogen bomb, temperatures of this magnitude were achieved by using a fission reaction to trigger nuclear fusion. If fusion reactions are to be used to generate electricity, it will be necessary to develop equipment in which very high temperatures can be maintained long enough to allow fusion to occur and give off energy. In any conventional container, the reactant nuclei would quickly lose their high kinetic energies by collisions with the walls.

One fusion reaction currently under study is a two-step process involving deuterium and lithium as the basic starting materials:

$$\begin{array}{l} {}^2_1H + {}^3_1H \longrightarrow {}^4_2He + {}^1_0n \\ {}^6_3Li + {}^1_0n \longrightarrow {}^4_2He + {}^3_1H \\ \hline {}^2_1H + {}^6_3Li \longrightarrow 2\,{}^4_2He \end{array}$$

This process is attractive because it has a lower activation energy than other fusion reactions.

In April, 1997, the Tokomac fusion reactor at Princeton shut down when government funding was withdrawn.

One possible way to achieve nuclear fusion is to use magnetic fields to confine the reactant nuclei and prevent them from touching the walls of the container, where they would quickly slow down below the velocity required for fusion. Using 400-ton magnets, it is possible to sustain the reaction for a fraction of a second. To achieve a net evolution of energy, this time must be extended to about one second. A practical fusion reactor would have to produce 20 times as much energy as it consumes. Optimists predict that this goal may be reached in 50 years.

Figure 19.6
Laser fusion. (a) A mixture of deuterium and tritium is sealed inside the tiny capsule (1 mm in diameter) at the tip of the laser target. (b) Exposure of the capsule to the energy of a powerful laser beam produces a 0.5-picosecond burst of energy from the fusion of the deuterium and tritium.

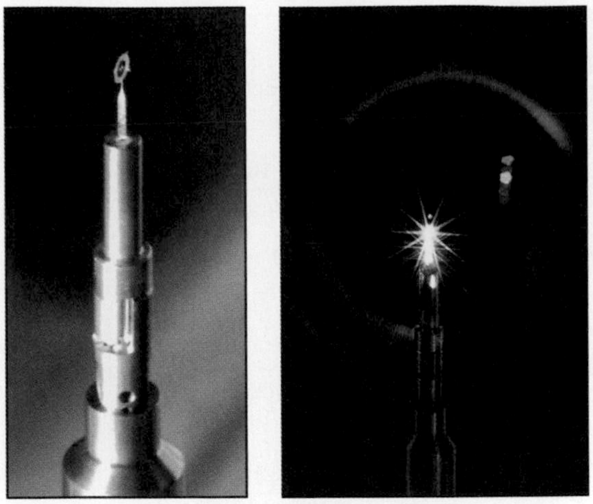

(a) (b)

a, Courtesy of the University of California, Lawrence Livermore National Laboratory, and the U.S. Department of Energy; b, Lawrence Livermore National Laboratory

Another approach to nuclear fusion is shown in Figure 19.6. Tiny glass pellets (about 0.1 mm in diameter) filled with frozen deuterium and tritium serve as a target. The pellets are illuminated by a powerful laser beam, which delivers 10^{12} kilowatts of power in one nanosecond (10^{-9} s). The reaction is the same as with magnetic confinement; unfortunately, at this point energy breakeven seems many years away.

CHEMISTRY Beyond the Classroom

Biological Effects of Radiation

The harmful effects of radiation result from its high energy, sufficient to form unstable free radicals (species containing unpaired electrons) such as

$$H\cdot \quad H{-}\ddot{\underset{\cdot\cdot}{O}}\cdot \quad :\ddot{\underset{\cdot\cdot}{O}}{-}\ddot{\underset{\cdot\cdot}{O}}\cdot$$

These free radicals can react with and in that sense destroy organic molecules essential to life.

The extent of damage from radiation depends mainly on two factors. These are the amount of radiation absorbed and the type of radiation. The former is commonly expressed in *rads* (*r*adiation *a*bsorbed *d*ose). A rad corresponds to the absorption of 10^{-2} J of energy per kilogram of tissue:

$$1 \text{ rad} = 10^{-2} \text{ J/kg}$$

The biological effect of radiation is expressed in *rems* (*r*adiation *e*quivalent for *m*an). The number of rems is found by multiplying the number of rads by a "damage" factor, *n*:

$$\text{no. of rems} = n(\text{no. of rads})$$

where *n* is 1 for gamma and beta radiation, 5 for low-energy neutrons, and 10 to 20 for high-energy neutrons and alpha particles. Table A lists some of the effects to be expected when a person is exposed to a single dose of radiation at various levels.

Table A Effect of Exposure to a Single Dose of Radiation

Dose (rems)	Probable Effect
0 to 25	No observable effect
25 to 50	Small decrease in white blood cell count
50 to 100	Lesions, marked decrease in white blood cells
100 to 200	Nausea, vomiting, loss of hair
200 to 500	Hemorrhaging, ulcers, possible death
500+	Fatal

The average exposure to radiation of people living in the United States is about 360 mrem (0.36 rem) per year. Notice (Figure A) that 82% of the radiation comes from natural sources; the greatest single source by far is radon (55%). The level of exposure to radon depends on location. In 1985 a man named Stanley Watras, who happened to work at a nuclear power plant, found that he was setting off the radiation monitors when he went to work in the morning. It turned out that the house he lived in had a radon level 2000 times the national average.

$^{222}_{86}Rn$, a radioactive isotope of radon, is a decay product of naturally occurring uranium-238. Because it is gaseous and chemically inert, radon seeps through cracks in concrete and masonry from the ground into houses. There its concentration builds up, particularly if the house is tightly insulated. Inhalation of radon-222 can cause health problems because its decay products, including Po-218 and Po-214, are intensely radioactive and readily absorbed in lung tissue. The Environmental Protection Agency (EPA) estimates that radon inhalation causes between 5,000 and 20,000 of the 130,000 deaths from lung cancer annually in the United States. The EPA recommends that special ventilation devices be used to remove radon from basements if tests show (Figure B) that the radiation level exceeds 4×10^{-12} Ci/L.

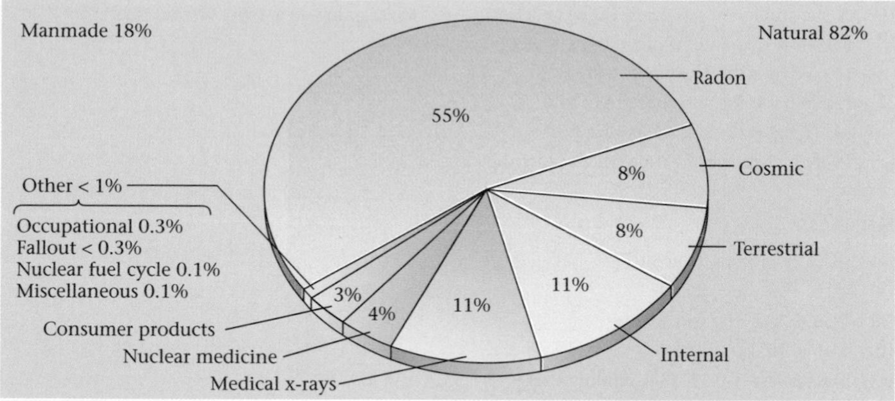

Figure A
Sources of average radiation exposure of the U.S. population.

Charles D. Winters

Figure B
A commercially available home-test kit for radon.

Chapter Highlights

Key Concepts

1. Write balanced nuclear equations.
   (Example 19.1; Problems 1–14) ■ Questions and Problems assignable in OWL: 1, 4, 6, 8, 12
2. Relate activity to rate constant and number of atoms.
   (Example 19.2; Problems 15–28) ■ 16, 19, 24, 27, 47, 53
3. Relate activity to age of objects.
   (Example 19.3; Problems 29–36) ■ 30, 33, 35, 60
4. Relate Δm to ΔE in a nuclear reaction.
   (Examples 19.4, 19.6; Problems 37, 38, 43–46) ■ 37
5. Calculate binding energies.
   (Example 19.5; Problems 39–42) ■ 40, 42

Select end of chapter Questions and Problems may be assigned in OWL and are cross-referenced in the Key Concepts list.

CENGAGENOW™

Sign in at **academic.cengage.com/now** to:

- Check your readiness for an exam by taking the Pre-Test and exploring the self-study modules recommended in your Personalized Study plan
- For quick review, download Go Chemistry mini-lecture flashcard modules (or purchase them at **www.ichapters.com**)

Key Equations

Rate of decay $\ln X_0/X = kt \qquad k = 0.693/t_{1/2} \qquad A = kN$ (Section 19.2)

Mass-energy $\Delta E = 9.00 \times 10^{10} \frac{\text{kJ}}{\text{g}} \times \Delta m$ (Section 19.3)

Key Terms

activity	curie (Ci)	nuclear equation
alpha particle	gamma radiation	nuclear fission
beta particle	half-life	nuclear fusion
binding energy	K-electron capture	positron

Summary Problem

Consider the isotopes of copper.

(a) Write the nuclear symbol for Cu-64, which is used medically to scan for brain tumors. How many protons are there in the nucleus? How many neutrons?

(b) Write the equation for the decomposition of Cu-64 by β-decay.

(c) When Cu-65 is bombarded by C-12, three neutrons and another particle are produced. Write the equation for this reaction.

(d) When Zn-63 (nuclear mass = 62.91674 amu) is bombarded with neutrons, Cu-63 (nuclear mass = 62.91367 amu) and a proton are produced. What is ΔE for this bombardment?

(e) What is the mass defect and binding energy of Cu-63?

(f) A one-milligram sample of Cu-64 (nuclear mass = 63.92 g) has an activity of 3.82×10^3 Ci.

(1) How many atoms are in the sample?
(2) What is the decay rate in atoms/s?
(3) What is the rate constant in min^{-1}?
(4) What is the half-life in minutes?

(g) What percentage of Cu-64 will decay in 4.00 h?

Answers

(a) $^{64}_{29}\text{Cu}$; 29 protons, 35 neutrons

(b) $^{64}_{29}\text{Cu} \longrightarrow {}^{0}_{-1}e + {}^{64}_{30}\text{Zn}$

(c) $^{65}_{29}\text{Cu} + {}^{12}_{6}\text{C} \longrightarrow {}^{74}_{35}\text{Br} + 3\,{}^{1}_{0}n$

(d) 4.01×10^8 kJ

(e) mass defect = 0.59223 g; binding energy = 5.33×10^{10} kJ

(f) (1) 9.421×10^{18} atoms
(2) decay rate = 1.41×10^{14} atom/s
(3) $k = 9.00 \times 10^{-4}\ \text{min}^{-1}$
(4) half-life = 7.70×10^2 min

(g) 19.4%

Questions and Problems

Blue-numbered questions have answers in Appendix 6 and fully-worked solutions in the *Student Solutions Manual.*

■ denotes questions assignable in OWL.

WEB indicates that the solution is available on this book's companion website.

Nuclear Equations

1. ■ Smoke detectors contain a small amount of americium-241. Its decay product is neptunium-237. Identify the emission from americium-241.

2. Lead-210 is used to prepare eyes for corneal transplants. Its decay product is bismuth-210. Identify the emission from lead-210.

3. Write balanced nuclear reactions for the following:
(a) Formation of Am-241 through β-emissions.
(b) Formation of Kr-81 by K-electron capture.
(c) Formation of Ra-223 by α-emission.

4. ■ **WEB** Write balanced nuclear equations for the following:
(a) Formation of Mn-52 by positron emission.
(b) Formation of Ac-228 by β-emission.
(c) Formation of Np-232 by α-decay.

5. Write balanced nuclear equations for
(a) the alpha emission resulting in the formation of Pa-233.
(b) the loss of a positron by Y-85.
(c) the fusion of two C-12 nuclei to give sodium-23 and another particle.
(d) the fission of Pu-239 to give tin-130, another nucleus, and an excess of two neutrons.

6. ■ Write balanced nuclear equations for
(a) the loss of an alpha particle by Th-230.
(b) the loss of a beta particle by lead-210.
(c) the fission of U-235 to give Ba-140, another nucleus, and an excess of two neutrons.
(d) the K-capture of Ar-37.

7. An isotope of rutherfordium, $^{257}_{104}\text{Rf}$, is formed by the bombardment of californium-249 by carbon-12. In the process, neutrons are emitted. The new isotope formed decays rapidly, emitting an alpha particle.
(a) How many neutrons are emitted for every Cf-249 bombarded?
(b) Write the nuclear symbol for the isotope formed by the decay of Rf-257.

8. ■ When bismuth-209 is bombarded with nickel-64, one neutron and a new isotope, X, is formed. The isotope then goes through a series of alpha particle emissions.
(a) Write the nuclear symbol for the isotope formed.
(b) Write the nuclear symbol for the isotope formed after the third alpha particle emission.

9. Consider the "new" isotope $^{282}_{115}\text{X}$. Compare the product nuclides after beta emission and positron emission.

10. Follow the directions for Question 9 but compare the product nuclides after K-capture and positron emission.

11. Write balanced nuclear equations for the bombardment of
(a) U-238 with a nucleus to produce Fm-249 and five neutrons.
(b) Al-26 with an alpha particle to produce P-30.
(c) Cu-63 with a nucleus producing Zn-63 and a neutron.
(d) Al-27 with deuterium ($^{2}_{1}\text{H}$) to produce an alpha particle and another nucleus.

12. ■ Write balanced nuclear equations for the bombardment of

(a) Fe-54 with an alpha particle to produce another nucleus and two protons.

(b) Mo-96 with deuterium (^2_1H) to produce a neutron and another nucleus.

(c) Ar-40 with an unknown particle to produce K-43 and a proton.

(d) a nucleus with a neutron to produce a proton and P-31.

13. Balance the following equations by filling in the blanks.

(a) $^{235}_{92}U + ^1_0n \longrightarrow ^{137}_{54}$_______ $+ 2\,^1_0n +$ _______

(b) $^{232}_{90}Th + ^{12}_{6}$_______ $\longrightarrow$ _______ $^1_0n + ^{240}_{96}Cm$

(c) $^4_2He + ^{96}_{42}Mo \longrightarrow ^{100}_{43}$_______ $+$ _______

(d) _______ $+ ^2_1H \longrightarrow ^{210}_{84}$_______ $+ ^1_0n$

14. Balance the following nuclear equations by filling in the blanks.

(a) Es-249 + neutron $\longrightarrow$ 2 neutrons + _______ + Gd-161

(b) _______ $\longrightarrow$ beta particle + Co-59

(c) $4\,^1_1H \longrightarrow$ _______ + 2 positrons

(d) Mg-24 + neutron $\longrightarrow$ proton + _______

Rate of Nuclear Decay

15. A source for gamma rays has an activity of 3175 Ci. How many disintegrations are there for this source per minute?

16. ■ How long (in hours) would it take to disintegrate 3.17×10^{17} atoms from a 12.0-mCi (millicuries) source?

17. A scintillation counter registers emitted radiation caused by the disintegration of nuclides. If each atom of nuclide emits one count, what is the activity of a sample that registers 3.00×10^4 disintegrations in five minutes?

18. A Geiger counter counts 0.070% of all particles emitted by a sample. What is the activity that registers 19.4×10^3 counts in one minute?

19. ■ Yttrium-87 has a rate constant of $2.6 \times 10^{-6}\ s^{-1}$. What is the activity of a 5.00-mg sample?

20. Krypton-87 has a rate constant of $1.5 \times 10^{-4}\ s^{-1}$. What is the activity of a 2.00-mg sample?

21. Iodine-131 is used to treat thyroid cancer. It decays by beta emission and has a half-life of 8.1 days.

(a) Write a balanced nuclear reaction for the decay of iodine-131.

(b) What is the activity (in Ci) of a 2.50-mg sample of the isotope?

22. Copper-64 is used to study tumors of the brain. It has a half-life of 12.8 hours. What is the activity (in Ci) of 1.50 mg of Cu-64?

23. Lead-210 has a half-life of 20.4 years. This isotope decays by beta particle emission. A counter registers 1.3×10^4 disintegrations in five minutes. How many grams of Pb-210 are there?

24. ■ Bromine-82 has a half-life of 36 hours. A sample containing Br-82 was found to have an activity of 1.2×10^5 disintegrations/min. How many grams of Br-82 were present in the sample? Assume that there were no other radioactive nuclides in the sample.

25. Fluorine-18 has a decay constant of $6.31 \times 10^{-3}\ min^{-1}$. How many counts will one get on a Geiger counter in one minute from 1.00 mg of fluorine-18? Assume the sensitivity of the counter is such that it intercepts 0.50% of the emitted radiation.

26. **WEB** Chlorine-36 decays by beta emission. It has a decay constant of $2.3 \times 10^{-6}\ y^{-1}$. How many β-particles are emitted in one minute from a 1.00-mg sample of Cl-36? How many curies does this represent?

27. ■ Cobalt-60 is used extensively in medicine as a source of γ-rays. Its half-life is 5.27 years.

(a) How long will it take a Co-60 source to decrease to 18% of its original activity?

(b) What percent of its activity remains after 29 months?

28. Phosphorus-32 is used in biochemical studies to follow the pathway taken by metabolites. Its half-life is 14.3 days. A vial containing 10.0 μg ($1\ \mu g = 1 \times 10^{-6}$ g) of P-32 is accidentally spilled into a sink.

(a) How long will it take P-32 in the drain to exhibit 68% of its original activity?

(b) How many atoms of P-32 remain in the sink after 755 days?

29. Carbon from a cypress beam obtained from the tomb of an ancient Egyptian king gave 9.2 disintegrations/minute of C-14 per gram of carbon. Carbon from living material gives 15.3 disintegrations/min of C-14 per gram of carbon. Carbon-14 has a half-life of 5730 years. How old is the beam?

30. ■ Sandals found in a cave were determined by carbon-14 dating to be 3.9×10^2 years old. Assuming that carbon from living material gives 15.3 disintegrations/min of C-14 per gram of carbon, what is the activity of the C-14 in the sandals in disintegrations/min/g of carbon? ($t_{1/2}$ of C-14 = 5730 years)

31. The remains of an ancient cave were unearthed. Analysis from charcoal in the cave gave 12.0 disintegrations/min/g of carbon. The half-life of C-14 is 5730 years. Analysis of a tree cut down when the cave was unearthed showed 15.3 disintegrations/min/g of carbon. How old are the remains in the cave?

32. A sample of a wooden artifact gives 5.0 disintegrations/min/g carbon. The half-life of carbon-14 is 5730 years, and the activity of C-14 in wood just cut down from a tree is 15.3 disintegrations/min/g carbon. How old is the wooden artifact?

33. ■ The radioactive isotope tritium, ^3_1H, is produced in nature in much the same way as $^{14}_{6}C$. Its half-life is 12.3 years. Estimate the ^3_1H ratio of the tritium of water in the area to the tritium in a bottle of wine claimed to be 25 years old.

34. Consider the information given about tritium in Problem 33. Estimate the age of a sample of Scotch whiskey that has a tritium content three-fifths that of the water in the area where the whiskey was produced.

35. ■ A rock from an archaeological dig was found to contain 0.255 g of Pb-206 per gram of U-238. Assume that the rock did not contain any Pb-206 at the time of its formation and that U-238 decayed only to Pb-206. How old is the rock? (For U-238, $t_{1/2} = 4.5 \times 10^9$ y.)

36. A meteor has a Pb-206:U-238 mass ratio of 0.813:1.00. Use the assumptions of Question 35 to estimate the age of the meteor.

Mass Changes

37. ■ Plutonium-239 is used as the energy source for heart pacemakers and space probes. It decays by alpha emission.

(a) Calculate Δm in grams when one mole of Pu-239 decays.

(b) How much energy (in kilojoules) is given off by the decay of 2.00 mg of Pu-239?

38. **WEB** Strontium-90 is a dangerous byproduct of atomic testing because it mimics the action of calcium in the body. It decays in two beta emissions to give zirconium-90 (Nuclear mass = 89.8824 g).

(a) Write a balanced nuclear reaction for the overall decay of Sr-90.

(b) Calculate Δm in grams when one mole of Sr-90 decays to Zr-90.

(c) How much energy (in kilojoules) is given off by the decay of 6.50 mg of Sr-90?

39. For beryllium-10, calculate

(a) the mass defect.

(b) the binding energy.

40. ■ For carbon-14, calculate

(a) the mass defect.

(b) the binding energy.

41. Which has the larger binding energy, fluorine-19 or oxygen-17?

42. ■ Which has the larger binding energy, Mg-26 or Al-26?

43. Consider the fusion of boron-10 with an alpha particle. The products of the fusion are carbon-13 and a proton.

(a) Write a nuclear reaction for this process.

(b) How much energy is released when 1.00 g of B-10 is fused with an α-particle?

■ in OWL Blue-numbered questions answered in Appendix 6 **WEB** Solution is available on companion website

44. Show by calculation which process produces more energy per gram of material reacting.

$$\text{fission of U-235:} \quad {}^{235}_{92}U + {}^{1}_{0}n \longrightarrow {}^{94}_{40}Zr + {}^{140}_{58}Ce + 6\,{}^{0}_{-1}e + 2\,{}^{1}_{0}n$$

$$\text{fusion of deuterium:} \quad {}^{2}_{1}H + {}^{2}_{1}H \longrightarrow {}^{3}_{1}H + {}^{1}_{1}H$$

Nuclear masses for Ce-140 and Zr-94 are 139.8734 and 93.8841, respectively.

45. Consider the fission reaction in which U-235 is bombarded by neutrons. The products of the bombardment are rubidium-89, cerium-144, beta particles, and more neutrons.

(a) Write a balanced nuclear equation for the bombardment.

(b) Calculate ΔE when one gram of U-235 undergoes fission.

(c) The detonation of TNT, an explosive, evolves 2.76 kJ/g. How many kilograms of TNT are required to produce the same amount of energy as one milligram of U-235?

46. The decomposition of ammonium nitrate, an explosive, evolves 37.0 kJ/mol. Use the reaction given in Problem 45 to calculate the mass of ammonium nitrate (in kilograms) required to produce the same amount of energy as that produced when one milligram of U-235 undergoes fission.

Unclassified

47. ■ How many disintegrations per second occur in a basement that is 40 × 40 × 10 feet if the radiation level from radon is the allowed 4×10^{-12} Ci/L?

48. Iodine-131 is used in the treatment of tumors in the thyroid gland. Its half-life is 8.1 days. Suppose that, due to a shipment delay, the I-131 in a hospital's pharmacy is 2.0 days old.

(a) What percentage of the I-131 has disintegrated?

(b) A patient is scheduled to receive 15.0 mg of I-131.

What dosage (in milligrams) should the hospital pharmacist recommend for this patient if the 2-day-old bottle of I-131 is used?

49. An explosion used five tons (1 ton = 2000 lb) of ammonium nitrate ($\Delta E = -37.0$ kJ/mol).

(a) How much energy was released by the explosion?

(b) How many grams of TNT ($\Delta E = -2.76$ kJ/g) are needed to release the energy calculated in (a)?

(c) How many grams of U-235 are needed to obtain the same amount of energy calculated in (a)? (See the equation in Problem 45.)

50. Smoke detectors contain small amounts of americium-241. Am-241 decays by emitting α-particles and has a decay constant of $1.51 \times 10^{-3}\ y^{-1}$. If a smoke detector gives off ten disintegrations per second, how many grams of Am-241 are present in the detector?

51. The amount of oxygen dissolved in a sample of water can be determined by using thallium metal containing a small amount of the isotope Tl-204. When excess thallium is added to oxygen-containing water, the following reaction occurs.

$$2Tl(s) + \tfrac{1}{2}O_2(g) + H_2O \longrightarrow 2Tl^+(aq) + 2OH^-(aq)$$

After reaction, the activity of a 25.0-mL water sample is 745 counts per minute (cpm), caused by the presence of Tl^+-204 ions. The activity of Tl-204 is 5.53×10^5 cpm per gram of thallium metal. Assuming that O_2 is the limiting reactant in the above equation, calculate its concentration in moles per liter.

52. A 35-mL sample of 0.050 M $AgNO_3$ is mixed with 35 mL of 0.050 M NaI labeled with I-131. The following reaction occurs.

$$Ag^+(aq) + I^-(aq) \longrightarrow AgI(s)$$

The filtrate is found to have an activity of 2.50×10^3 counts per minute per milliliter. The 0.050 M NaI solution had an activity of 1.25×10^{10} counts per minute per milliliter. Calculate K_{sp} for AgI.

53. ■ A 100.0-g sample of water containing tritium, ${}^{3}_{1}H$, emits 2.89×10^3 beta particles per second. Tritium has a half-life of 12.3 years. What percentage of all the hydrogen atoms in the water sample is tritium?

54. Use the half-life of tritium given in Problem 53 to calculate the activity in curies of 1.00 mL of ${}^{3}_{1}H_2$ at STP.

55. One of the causes of the explosion at Chernobyl may have been the reaction between zirconium, which coated the fuel rods, and steam.

$$Zr(s) + 2H_2O(g) \longrightarrow ZrO_2(s) + 2H_2(g)$$

If half a metric ton of zirconium reacted, what pressure was exerted by the hydrogen gas produced at 55°C in the containment chamber, which had a volume of 2.0×10^4 L?

56. To measure the volume of the blood in an animal's circulatory system, the following experiment was performed. A 5.0-mL sample of an aqueous solution containing 1.7×10^5 counts per minute (cpm) of tritium was injected into the bloodstream. After an adequate period of time to allow for the complete circulation of the tritium, a 5.0-mL sample of blood was withdrawn and found to have 1.3×10^3 cpm on the scintillation counter. Assuming that only a negligible amount of tritium has decayed during the experiment, what is the volume of the animal's circulatory system?

57. Consider the fission reaction

$${}^{1}_{0}n + {}^{235}_{92}U \longrightarrow {}^{89}_{37}Rb + {}^{144}_{58}Ce + 3\,{}^{0}_{-1}e + 3\,{}^{1}_{0}n$$

How many liters of octane, C_8H_{18}, the primary component of gasoline, must be burned to $CO_2(g)$ and $H_2O(g)$ to produce as much energy as the fission of one gram of U-235 fuel? Octane has a density of 0.703 g/mL; its heat of formation is −249.9 kJ/mol.

58. A chelate of Cr^{3+} and $C_2O_4^{2-}$ is made by a reaction that involves Na_2CrO_4 and oxalic acid, $H_2C_2O_4$, a reducing agent. The sodium chromate has an activity of 765 counts per minute per gram, from Cr-51. The oxalic acid has an activity of 512 counts per minute per gram. It is labeled with C-14. Because Cr-51 and C-14 emit different particles during decay, their activities can be counted independently. A sample of the chelate was found to have a Cr-51 count of 314 cpm and a C-14 count of 235 cpm. How many oxalate ions are bound to one Cr^{3+} ion?

59. Radium-226 decays by alpha emission to radon-222. Suppose that 25.0% of the energy given off by one gram of radium is converted to electrical energy. What is the minimum mass of lithium that would be needed for the voltaic cell $Li \mid Li^+ \parallel Cu^{2+} \mid Cu$, at standard conditions, to produce the same amount of electrical work ($\Delta G°$)?

60. ■ Polonium-210 decays to Pb-206 by alpha emission. Its half-life is 138 days. What volume of helium at 25°C and 1.20 atm would be obtained from a 25.00-g sample of Po-210 left to decay for 75 hours?

61. For how many years could all the energy needs of the world be supplied by the fission of U-235? Use the following assumptions:

The world has about 1.0×10^7 metric tons of uranium ore, which are about 0.75% U-235.

The energy consumption of the world is about 4.0×10^{15} kJ/y and does not change with time.

The fission of U-235 releases about 8.0×10^7 kJ/g of U-235.

62. When a positron and an electron collide, they annihilate each other and produce two gamma photons, which carry the same amount of energy. What is the wavelength (in nanometers) of these photons?

Conceptual Questions

63. Classify the following statements as true or false. If false, correct the statement to make it true.

(a) The mass number increases in beta emission.

(b) A radioactive species with a large rate constant, k, decays very slowly.

(c) Fusion gives off less energy per gram of fuel than fission.

■ in OWL Blue-numbered questions answered in Appendix 6 WEB Solution is available on companion website

64. Explain how
(a) alpha and beta radiation are separated by an electric field.
(b) radioactive C-11 can be used as a tracer to study brain disorders.
(c) a self-sustaining chain reaction occurs in nuclear fission.

65. Suppose the $^{14}C/^{12}C$ ratio in plants a thousand years ago was 10% higher than it is today. What effect, if any, would this have on the calculated age of an artifact found by the C-14 method to be a thousand years old?

66. The following data are obtained for a radioactive isotope. Plot the data and determine the half-life of the isotope.

Time (h)	0.00	0.50	1.00	1.50	2.00	2.50
Activity (disintegrations/h)	14,472	13,095	11,731	10,615	9,605	8,504

67. Fill in the following table:

Event	Change in Atomic Number	Change in Mass Number
α-decay	______	______
β-emission	______	______
positron emission	______	______
K-electron capture	______	______
γ-decay	______	______

68. The principle behind the home smoke detector is described on page 516. Americium-241 is present in such detectors. It has a decay constant of $1.51 \times 10^{-3}\ y^{-1}$. You are urged to check the battery in the detector at least once a year. You are, however, never encouraged to check how much Am-241 remains undecayed. Explain why.

69. The cleavage of ATP (adenosine triphosphate) to ADP (adenosine diphosphate) and H_3PO_4 may be written as follows:

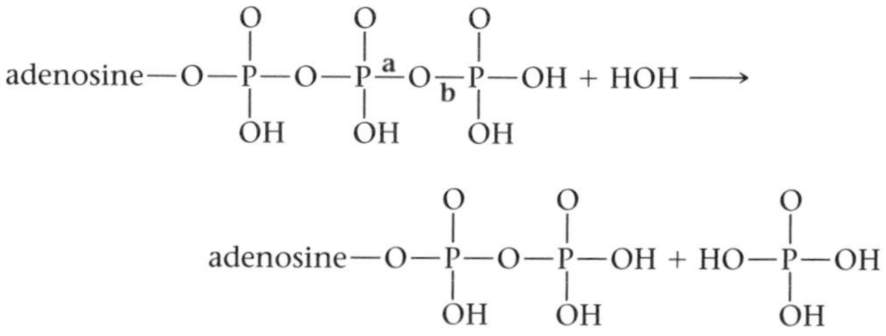

It is interesting to determine which bond (the P—O bond marked **a** or the O—P bond marked **b**) is cleaved by hydrolysis (reaction with water).
(a) Outline an experiment (using radioactivity) that can be used to determine where the cleavage results.
(b) Describe the results that would lead you to conclude that cleavage results at **a**.
(c) Describe the results that would lead you to conclude that cleavage results at **b**.
Results show that the cleavage occurs at **b**.

Challenge Problems

70. An activity of 20 picocuries (20×10^{-12} Ci) of radon-222 per liter of air in a house constitutes a health hazard to anyone living there. The half-life of radon-222 is 3.82 days. Calculate the concentration of radon in air (moles per liter) that corresponds to a 20-picocurie activity level.

71. Plutonium-239 decays by the reaction

$$^{239}_{94}Pu \longrightarrow ^{235}_{92}U + ^{4}_{2}He$$

Its rate constant is 5.5×10^{-11}/min. In a one-gram sample of Pu-239,
(a) how many grams decompose in 45 minutes?
(b) how much energy in kilojoules is given off in 45 minutes?
(c) what radiation dosage in rems (page 528) is received by a 75-kg man exposed to a gram of Pu-239 for 45 minutes?

72. It is possible to estimate the activation energy for fusion by calculating the energy required to bring two deuterons close enough to one another to form an alpha particle. This energy can be obtained by using Coulomb's law in the form $E = 8.99 \times 10^9\ q_1q_2/r$, where q_1 and q_2 are the charges of the deuterons (1.60×10^{-19} C), r is the radius of the He nucleus, about 2×10^{-15} m, and E is the energy in joules.
(a) Estimate E in joules per alpha particle.
(b) Using the equation $E = mv^2/2$, estimate the velocity (meters per second) each deuteron must have if a collision between the two of them is to supply the activation energy for fusion (m is the mass of the deuteron in kilograms).

73. Consider the reaction

$$2\,^{2}_{1}H \longrightarrow ^{4}_{2}He$$

(a) Calculate ΔE in kilojoules per gram of deuterium fused.
(b) How much energy is potentially available from the fusion of all the deuterium in seawater? The percentage of deuterium in water is about 0.0017%. The total mass of water in the oceans is 1.3×10^{24} g.
(c) What fraction of the deuterium in the oceans would have to be consumed to supply the annual energy requirements of the world (2.3×10^{17} kJ)?

74. Carbon-14 (C-14) with a half-life of 5730 years decays to nitrogen-14 (N-14). A sample of carbon dioxide containing carbon in the form of C-14 only is sealed in a vessel at 1.00-atmosphere pressure. Over time, the CO_2 becomes NO_2 through the radioactive decay process. The following equilibrium is established:

$$2NO_2(g) \rightleftharpoons N_2O_4(g)$$

If the equilibrium constant for the equation as written is 1×10^{-5}, what is the pressure of N_2O_4 after 20,000 years? Assume that the CO_2 does not participate in any chemical reactions.

75. ■ Uranium in water decays to form Zn^{2+} and Sm by fission. Uranium has a half-life of 7×10^8 years. The zinc ions complex with water and act as a weak acid according to the following equation:

$$Zn(H_2O)_4^{2+}(aq) \rightleftharpoons H^+(aq) + Zn(H_2O)_3(OH)^+(aq) \qquad K_a = 3.3 \times 10^{-10}$$

Assuming that this is the only radioactive decay of any significance and that neither Sm nor U acts as a weak acid, how many years will it take a 1.00 M solution of U to achieve a pH of 6.0?

76. To determine the K_{sp} value of Hg_2I_2, a solid sample is used, in which some of the iodine is present as radioactive I-131. The count rate of the sample is 5.0×10^{11} counts per minute per mole of I. An excess amount of $Hg_2I_2(s)$ is placed in some water, and the solid is allowed to come to equilibrium with its respective ions. A 150.0-mL sample of the saturated solution is withdrawn and the radioactivity measured at 33 counts per minute. From this information, calculate the K_{sp} value for Hg_2I_2.

■ in OWL Blue-numbered questions answered in Appendix 6 **WEB** Solution is available on companion website

20 Chemistry of the Metals

The fields of Nature long prepared and fallow
the silent cyclic chemistry
The slow and steady ages plodding, the unoccupied surface
ripening, the rich ores forming beneath;

—Walt Whitman
"Song of the Redwood Tree"

Chapter Outline

The metals Alexander Calder used to make *Mobile* were refined from ores using some of the processes discussed in this chapter.

CNAC/MNAM/Dist. Réunion des Musées Nationaux/Art Resource, NY

As you can see from the periodic table on the inside cover of this book, the overwhelming majority of elements, about 88%, are metals (shown in blue). In discussing the descriptive chemistry of the metals, we concentrate on—

- the ***main-group metals in Groups 1 and 2*** at the far left of the periodic table. These are commonly referred to as the *alkali metals* (Group 1) and *alkaline earth metals* (Group 2). The group names reflect the strongly basic nature of the oxides (K_2O, CaO, . . .) and hydroxides (KOH, $Ca(OH)_2$, . . .) of these elements.
- *the transition metals,* located in the center of the periodic table. There are three series of transition metals, each consisting of ten elements, located in the fourth, fifth, and sixth periods. We focus on a few of the more important transition metals (Figure 20.1), particularly those toward the right of the first series.

Section 20.1 deals with the processes by which these metals are obtained from their principal ores. Section 20.2 describes the reactions of the alkali and alkaline earth metals, particularly those with hydrogen, oxygen, and water. Section 20.3 considers the redox chemistry of the transition metals, their cations (e.g., Fe^{2+}, Fe^{3+}), and their oxoanions (e.g., CrO_4^{2-}). ■

Online homework for this chapter may be assigned in OWL.

CENGAGENOW™
This icon introduces an opportunity for self-study and to explore interactive modules by signing in at **academic.cengage.com/now.**

20.1 METALLURGY

The processes by which metals are extracted from their **ores** fall within the science of **metallurgy.** As you might expect, the chemical reactions involved depend on the type of ore (Figure 20.2, p. 536). We consider some typical processes used to obtain metals from chloride, oxide, sulfide, or "native" ores.

An ore is a natural source from which a metal can be extracted profitably.

Chloride Ores: Na from NaCl

Sodium metal is obtained by the electrolysis of molten sodium chloride (Figure 20.3, p. 537). The electrode reactions are quite simple:

$$\text{cathode:}\quad 2Na^+(l) + 2e^- \longrightarrow 2Na(l)$$
$$\text{anode:}\quad 2Cl^-(l) \longrightarrow Cl_2(g) + 2e^-$$
$$\overline{2NaCl(l) \longrightarrow 2Na(l) + Cl_2(g)}$$

$Na^+(l)$ and $Cl^-(l)$ are the ions present in molten NaCl.

The cell is operated at about 600°C to keep the electrolyte molten; calcium chloride is added to lower the melting point. About 14 kJ of electrical energy is required to produce one gram of sodium, which is drawn off as a liquid (mp of Na = 98°C). The chlorine gas produced at the anode is a valuable byproduct.

It's cheaper to electrolyze NaCl(*aq*), but you don't get sodium metal that way.

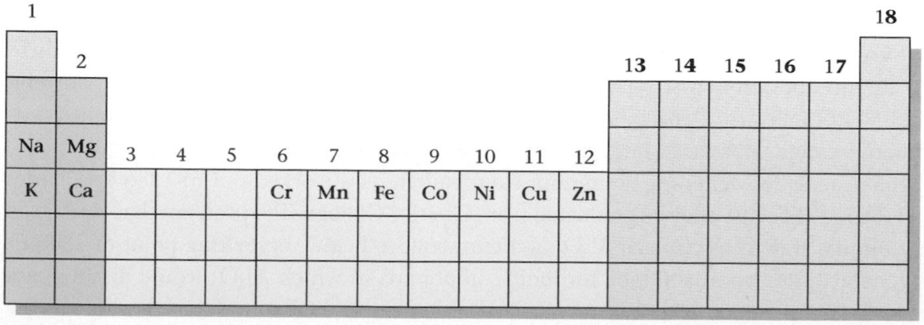

Figure 20.1
Metals and the periodic table. The periodic table groups discussed in this chapter are Groups 1 and 2, the alkali and alkaline earth metals (shaded in blue), and the transition metals (shaded in yellow). Symbols are shown for the more common metals.

Figure 20.2
Principal ores of the Group 1, Group 2, and transition metals.

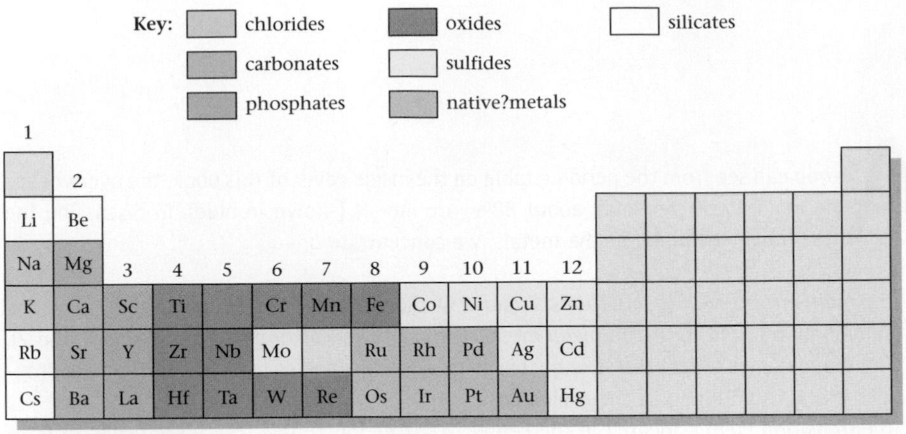

Example 20.1 Taking $\Delta H°$ and $\Delta S°$ for the reaction

$$2NaCl(l) \longrightarrow 2Na(l) + Cl_2(g)$$

to be +820 kJ and +0.180 kJ/K, respectively, calculate

(a) $\Delta G°$ at the electrolysis temperature, 600°C.
(b) the voltage required to carry out the electrolysis.

Strategy To find $\Delta G°$, apply the Gibbs-Helmholtz equation, $\Delta G° = \Delta H° - T\Delta S°$ (Chapter 17). To find $E°$, use the relation $\Delta G° = -nFE°$ (Chapter 18).

SOLUTION

(a) $\Delta G° = +820 \text{ kJ} - 873 \text{ K}(0.180 \text{ kJ/K}) = +663 \text{ kJ}$

(b) $E° = \dfrac{-\Delta G°}{nF} = \dfrac{-6.63 \times 10^5 \text{ J}}{(2 \text{ mol})(9.648 \times 10^4 \text{ J/mol} \cdot \text{V})} = -3.44 \text{ V}$

At least 3.44 V must be applied to carry out the electrolysis.

Reality Check Notice that the value of $\Delta G°$ calculated in (a), +663 kJ, is for two moles of Na, 45.98 g. The value of the free energy change per gram is

$$663 \text{ kJ}/45.98 \text{ g} = 14.4 \text{ kJ/g}$$

This is consistent with the statement in the text that "about 14 kJ of electrical energy is required to produce one gram of sodium. . . ."

Oxide Ores: Al from Al_2O_3, Fe from Fe_2O_3

Oxides of very reactive metals such as calcium or aluminum are reduced by electrolysis. In the case of aluminum, bauxite ore, Al_2O_3, is used.

$$2Al_2O_3(l) \longrightarrow 4Al(l) + 3\,O_2(g)$$

Cryolite, Na_3AlF_6, is added to Al_2O_3 to produce a mixture melting at about 1000°C. (A mixture of AlF_3, NaF, and CaF_2 may be substituted for cryolite.) The cell is heated electrically to keep the mixture molten so that ions can move through it, carrying the electric current. About 30 kJ of electrical energy is consumed per gram of aluminum formed. The high energy requirement explains in large part the value of recycling aluminum cans.

Chemistry majors can be very productive.

The process for obtaining aluminum from bauxite was worked out in 1886 by Charles Hall (1863–1914), just after he graduated from Oberlin College. The problem that Hall faced was to find a way to electrolyze Al_2O_3 at a temperature below its melting point of 2000°C. His general approach was to look for ionic compounds in which Al_2O_3 would dissolve at a reasonable temperature. After several unsuccessful attempts, Hall found that cryolite was the

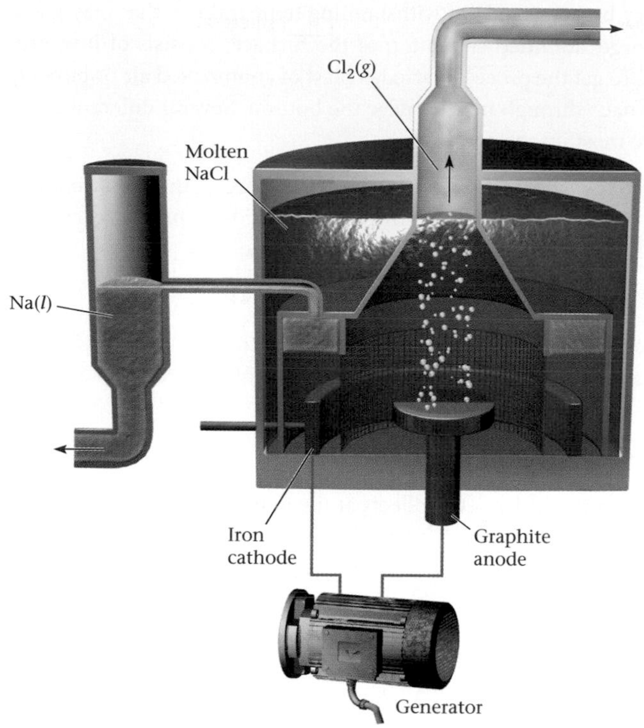

Figure 20.3
Electrolysis of molten sodium chloride. Calcium chloride ($CaCl_2$) is added to lower the melting point. The iron screen prevents sodium and chlorine from coming into contact with each other.

ideal "solvent." Curiously enough, the same electrolytic process was worked out by Paul Héroult (1863–1914) in France, also in 1886.

With less active metals, a chemical reducing agent can be used to reduce a metal cation to the element. The most common reducing agent in metallurgical processes is carbon, in the form of coke or, more exactly, carbon monoxide formed from the coke.

The most important metallurgical process involving carbon is the reduction of hematite ore, which consists largely of iron(III) oxide, Fe_2O_3, mixed with silicon dioxide, SiO_2. Reduction occurs in a blast furnace (Figure 20.4a) typically 30 m high and 10 m in diameter. The

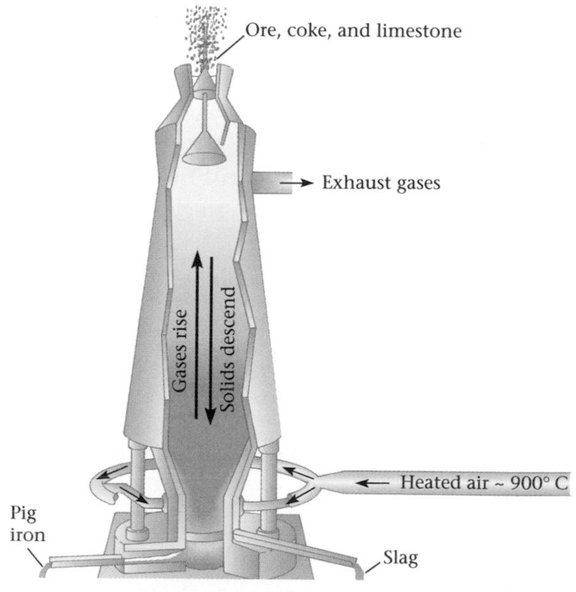

Figure 20.4
Iron and steel production. (a) A blast furnace for the production of pig iron. (b) A basic oxygen furnace, where the carbon content of pig iron is lowered by heating it with oxygen to form steel.

furnace is lined with refractory brick, capable of withstanding temperatures that may go as high as 1800°C. The solid charge, admitted at the top of the furnace, consists of iron ore, coke, and limestone ($CaCO_3$). To get the process started, a blast of compressed air or pure O_2 at 500°C is blown into the furnace through nozzles near the bottom. Several different reactions occur, of which three are most important:

1. ***Conversion of carbon to carbon monoxide.*** In the lower part of the furnace, coke burns to form carbon dioxide, CO_2. As the CO_2 rises through the solid mixture, it reacts further with the coke to form carbon monoxide, CO. The overall reaction is

$$2C(s) + O_2(g) \longrightarrow 2CO(g) \qquad \Delta H = -221 \text{ kJ}$$

The heat given off by this reaction maintains a high temperature within the furnace.

2. ***Reduction of Fe^{3+} ions to Fe.*** The carbon monoxide reacts with the iron(III) oxide in the ore:

$$Fe_2O_3(s) + 3CO(g) \longrightarrow 2Fe(l) + 3CO_2(g)$$

This is the key reaction; it produces molten iron.

Molten iron, formed at a temperature of 1600°C, collects at the bottom of the furnace. Four or five times a day, it is drawn off. The daily production of iron from a single blast furnace is about 1500 metric tons.

3. ***Formation of slag.*** The limestone added to the furnace decomposes at about 800°C:

$$CaCO_3(s) \longrightarrow CaO(s) + CO_2(g)$$

CENGAGENOW™
Click Coached Problems for a self-study module on **blast furnace production of iron.**

The calcium oxide formed reacts with impurities in the iron ore to form a glassy material called *slag.* The main reaction is with SiO_2 to form calcium silicate, $CaSiO_3$:

$$CaO(s) + SiO_2(s) \longrightarrow CaSiO_3(l)$$

The slag, which is less dense than molten iron, forms a layer on the surface of the metal. This makes it possible to draw off the slag through an opening in the furnace above that is used to remove the iron. The slag is used to make cement and as a base in road construction.

Where do you suppose the term "pig iron" came from?

The product that comes out of the blast furnace, called "pig iron," is highly impure. On the average, it contains about 4% carbon along with lesser amounts of silicon, manganese, and phosphorus. To make steel from pig iron, the carbon content must be lowered below 2%. Most of the steel produced in the world today is made by the basic oxygen process (Figure 20.4b). The "converter" is filled with a mixture of about 70% molten iron from the blast furnace, 25% scrap iron or steel, and 5% limestone. Pure oxygen under a pressure of about 10 atm is blown through the molten metal. The reaction

$$C(s) + O_2(g) \longrightarrow CO_2(g)$$

occurs rapidly; at the same time, impurities such as silicon are converted to oxides, which react with limestone to form a slag. When the carbon content drops to the desired level, the supply of oxygen is cut off. At this stage, the steel is ready to be poured. The whole process takes from 30 min to 1 h and yields about 200 metric tons of steel in a single "blow."

Example 20.2 Write balanced equations for the reduction of each of the following oxide ores by carbon monoxide:

Fe_3O_4 is really $FeO \cdot Fe_2O_3$.

(a) ZnO (b) MnO_2 (c) Fe_3O_4

Strategy In each case, the products are solid metal and $CO_2(g)$. The equations are most simply balanced by the process described in Chapter 3.

SOLUTION

(a) $ZnO(s) + CO(g) \longrightarrow Zn(s) + CO_2(g)$
(b) $MnO_2(s) + 2CO(g) \longrightarrow Mn(s) + 2CO_2(g)$
(c) $Fe_3O_4(s) + 4CO(g) \longrightarrow 3Fe(s) + 4CO_2(g)$

Sulfide Ores: Cu from Cu_2S

Sulfide ores, after preliminary treatment, most often undergo *roasting,* that is, heating with air or pure oxygen. With a relatively reactive transition metal such as zinc, the product is the oxide

$$2ZnS(s) + 3O_2(g) \longrightarrow 2ZnO(s) + 2SO_2(g)$$

which can then be reduced to the metal with carbon. With sulfides of less reactive metals such as copper or mercury, the free metal is formed directly on roasting. The reaction with cinnabar, the sulfide ore of mercury, is

$$HgS(s) + O_2(g) \longrightarrow Hg(g) + SO_2(g)$$

Because Cu can be produced by simple "roasting," it was one of the first metals known.

Among the several ores of copper, one of the most important is chalcocite, which contains copper(I) sulfide, Cu_2S, in highly impure form. Rocky material typically lowers the fraction of copper in the ore to 1% or less. The Cu_2S is concentrated by a process called *flotation* (Figure 20.5), which raises the fraction of copper to 20%–40%. The concentrated ore is then converted to the metal by blowing air through it at a high temperature, typically above 1000°C. (Pure O_2 is often used instead of air.) The overall reaction that occurs is a simple one:

$$Cu_2S(s) + O_2(g) \longrightarrow 2Cu(s) + SO_2(g)$$

The solid produced is called "blister copper." It has an irregular appearance due to air bubbles that enter the copper while it is still molten. Blister copper is impure, containing small amounts of several other metals.

Copper is purified by electrolysis. The anode, which may weigh as much as 300 kg, is made of blister copper. The electrolyte is 0.5 to 1.0 *M* $CuSO_4$, adjusted to a pH of about 0 with sulfuric acid. The cathode is a piece of pure copper, weighing perhaps 150 kg. The half-reactions are

$$\text{oxidation:} \quad Cu(s, \text{impure}) \longrightarrow Cu^{2+}(aq) + 2e^-$$

$$\text{reduction:} \quad Cu^{2+}(aq) + 2e^- \longrightarrow Cu(s, \text{pure})$$

The overall reaction, obtained by adding these two half-reactions, is

$$Cu(s, \text{impure}) \longrightarrow Cu(s, \text{pure})$$

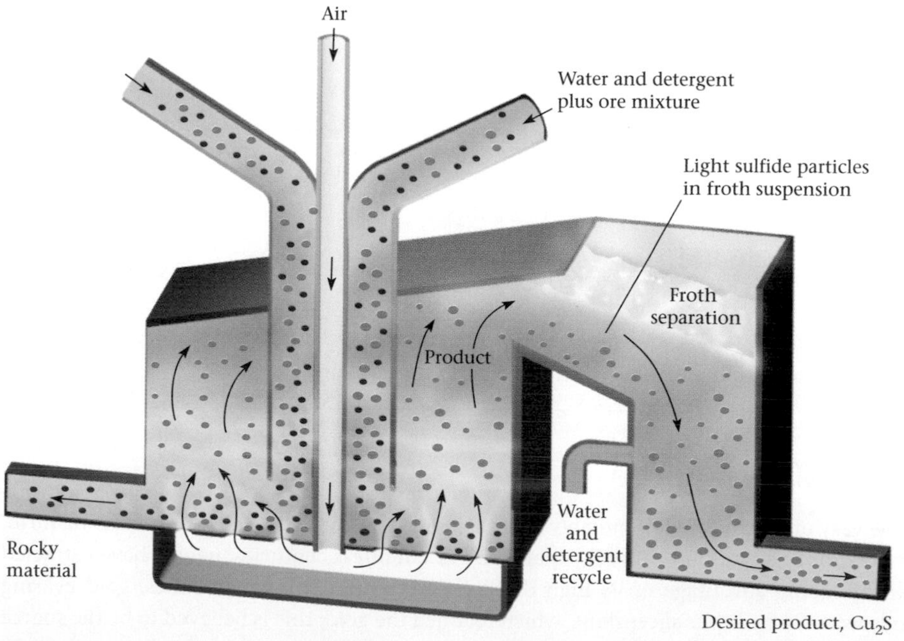

Figure 20.5
Flotation process for concentrating a sulfide ore. Low-grade sulfide ores, including Cu_2S, are often concentrated by flotation. The finely divided sulfide particles are trapped in soap bubbles; the rocky waste sinks to the bottom and is discarded.

An open-pit copper mine. This mine in Bingham Canyon, Utah, is 4 km in diameter and 0.8 km deep. It is the largest human-created hole on Earth.

Agricultural Stabilization and Conservation Service, USDA

Thus the net effect of electrolysis is to transfer copper metal from the impure blister copper used as one electrode to the pure copper sheet used as the other electrode. Electrolytic copper is 99.95% pure.

Example 20.3 A major ore of bismuth is bismuth(III) sulfide, Bi_2S_3. By roasting in air, it is converted to the corresponding oxide; sulfur dioxide is a byproduct. What volume of SO_2, at 25°C and 1.00 atm, is formed from one metric ton (10^6 g) of ore containing 1.25% Bi_2S_3?

Strategy First (1), write a balanced equation for the reaction, which is very similar to that for ZnS, except that Zn^{2+} is replaced by Bi^{3+}. (2) Using the balanced equation, calculate the number of moles of SO_2. Finally (3), use the ideal gas law to calculate the volume of SO_2.

SOLUTION

(1) The product is $Bi_2O_3(s)$; the equation is

$$2Bi_2S_3(s) + 9O_2(g) \longrightarrow 2Bi_2O_3(s) + 6SO_2(g)$$

$$(2)\ n_{SO_2} = 0.0125 \times 10^6 \text{ g } Bi_2S_3 \times \frac{1 \text{ mol } Bi_2S_3}{514.2 \text{ g } Bi_2S_3} \times \frac{6 \text{ mol } SO_2}{2 \text{ mol } Bi_2S_3} = 72.9 \text{ mol } SO_2$$

$$(3)\ V_{SO_2} = \frac{nRT}{P} = \frac{(72.9 \text{ mol})(0.0821 \text{ L}\cdot\text{atm/mol}\cdot\text{K})(298 \text{ K})}{1.00 \text{ atm}} = 1.78 \times 10^3 \text{ L}$$

Reality Check That is 1.78 cubic meters. The roasting of sulfide ores is a major source of the gaseous pollutant SO_2, which contributes to acid rain (Chapter 14).

Native Metals: Au

A few very unreactive metals, notably silver and gold, are found in nature in elemental form, mixed with large amounts of rocky material. For countless centuries, people have extracted gold by taking advantage of its high density (19.3 g/mL). In ancient times, gold-bearing sands were washed over sheepskins, which retained the gold; this is believed to be the source of the "Golden Fleece" of Greek mythology. The forty-niners in California obtained gold by

Table 20.1 Reactions of the Alkali and Alkaline Earth Metals

Reactant	Product	Comments
	Alkali Metals (M)	
$H_2(g)$	$MH(s)$	On heating in hydrogen gas
$X_2(g)$	$MX(s)$	X = F, Cl, Br, I
$N_2(g)$	$M_3N(s)$	Only Li reacts; product contains N^{3-} ion
$S(s)$	$M_2S(s)$	On heating
$O_2(g)$	$M_2O(s)$	Li; product is an oxide (O^{2-} ion)
	$M_2O_2(s)$	Na; product is a peroxide (O_2^{2-} ion)
	$MO_2(s)$	K, Rb, Cs; product is a superoxide (O_2^- ion)
$H_2O(l)$	$H_2(g)$, M^+, OH^-	Violent reaction with Na, K
	Alkaline Earth Metals (M)	
$H_2(g)$	$MH_2(s)$	All except Be; heating required
$X_2(g)$	$MX_2(s)$	Any halogen
$N_2(g)$	$M_3N_2(s)$	All except Be; heating required
$S(s)$	$MS(s)$	On heating
$O_2(g)$	$MO(s)$	All; product contains O^{2-} ion
	$MO_2(s)$	Ba; product contains O_2^{2-} ion
$H_2O(l)$	$H_2(g)$, M^{2+}, OH^-	Ca, Sr, Ba

swirling gold-bearing sands with water in a pan. Less dense impurities were washed away, leaving gold nuggets or flakes at the bottom of the pan.

Nowadays, the gold content of ores is much too low for these simple mechanical separation methods to be effective. Instead, the ore is treated with very dilute (0.01 *M*) sodium cyanide solution, through which air is blown. The following redox reaction takes place:

$$4Au(s) + 8CN^-(aq) + O_2(g) + 2H_2O \longrightarrow 4Au(CN)_2^-(aq) + 4OH^-(aq)$$

The oxidizing agent is O_2, which takes gold to the +1 state. The cyanide ion acts as a complexing ligand, forming the stable $Au(CN)_2^-$ ion. Metallic gold is recovered from solution by adding zinc; the gold in the complex ion is reduced to the metal.

$$Zn(s) + 2Au(CN)_2^-(aq) \longrightarrow Zn(CN)_4^{2-}(aq) + 2Au(s)$$

Tiffany & Co.

Modern gold jewelry. The gold was probably obtained by the cyanide process.

20.2 REACTIONS OF THE ALKALI AND ALKALINE EARTH METALS

The metals in Groups 1 and 2 are among the most reactive of all elements (Table 20.1). Their low ionization energies and high E°_{ox} values explain why they are so readily oxidized to cations, +1 cations for Group 1, +2 for Group 2. The alkali metals and the heavier alkaline earth metals (Ca, Sr, Ba) are commonly stored under dry mineral oil or kerosene to prevent them from reacting with oxygen or water vapor in the air. Magnesium is less reactive; it is commonly available in the form of ribbon or powder. Beryllium, as one would expect from its position in the periodic table, is the least metallic element in these two groups. It is also the least reactive toward water, oxygen, or other nonmetals.

Not under water!

Example 20.4

Write balanced equations for the reaction of

(a) sodium with hydrogen. (b) barium with oxygen.

Strategy The formulas of the products can be deduced from Table 20.1. Note that barium forms two products with oxygen, BaO and BaO_2.

SOLUTION

(a) $2Na(s) + H_2(g) \longrightarrow 2NaH(s)$
(b) $2Ba(s) + O_2(g) \longrightarrow 2BaO(s)$
$Ba(s) + O_2(g) \longrightarrow BaO_2(s)$

BaO_2 is barium peroxide.

Reaction with Hydrogen

Charles D. Winters

Reaction of calcium hydride (CaH_2) with water.

The compounds formed by the reaction of hydrogen with the alkali and alkaline earth metals contain H^- ions; for example, sodium hydride consists of Na^+ and H^- ions. These white crystalline solids are often referred to as saline hydrides because of their physical resemblance to NaCl. Chemically, they behave quite differently from sodium chloride; for example, they react with water to produce hydrogen gas. Typical reactions are

$$NaH(s) + H_2O(l) \longrightarrow H_2(g) + Na^+(aq) + OH^-(aq)$$
$$CaH_2(s) + 2H_2O(l) \longrightarrow 2H_2(g) + Ca^{2+}(aq) + 2\,OH^-(aq)$$

In this way, saline hydrides can serve as compact, portable sources of hydrogen gas for inflating life rafts and balloons.

Reaction with Water

The alkali metals react vigorously with water (Figure 20.6) to evolve hydrogen and form a water solution of the alkali hydroxide. The reaction of sodium is typical:

$$2Na(s) + 2H_2O(l) \longrightarrow 2Na^+(aq) + 2\,OH^-(aq) + H_2(g) \qquad \Delta H° = -368.6\text{ kJ}$$

The heat evolved in the reaction frequently causes the hydrogen to ignite.

Among the Group 2 metals, Ca, Sr, and Ba react with water in much the same way as the alkali metals. The reaction with calcium is

$$Ca(s) + 2H_2O(l) \longrightarrow Ca^{2+}(aq) + 2\,OH^-(aq) + H_2(g)$$

Beryllium does not react with water at all. Magnesium reacts very slowly with boiling water but reacts more readily with steam at high temperatures:

$$Mg(s) + H_2O(g) \longrightarrow MgO(s) + H_2(g)$$

This reaction, like that of sodium with water, produces enough heat to ignite the hydrogen. Firefighters who try to put out a magnesium fire by spraying water on it have discovered this reaction, often with tragic results. The best way to extinguish burning magnesium is to dump dry sand on it.

Marna G. Clarke

Figure 20.6
Reaction of sodium with water. When a *very small* piece of sodium is added to water, it reacts violently with the water. The OH^- ions formed in the reaction turn the acid-base indicator phenolphthalein from colorless to pink.

Reaction with Oxygen

Note from Table 20.1 that several different products are possible when an alkali or alkaline earth metal reacts with oxygen. The product may be a normal oxide (O^{2-} ion), a **peroxide** (O_2^{2-} ion), or **superoxide** (O_2^- ion).

The superoxide ion has an unpaired electron; KO_2 is paramagnetic.

$$[:\ddot{\underset{..}{O}}:]^{2-} \qquad [:\ddot{\underset{..}{O}}-\ddot{\underset{..}{O}}:]^{2-} \qquad [:\ddot{\underset{..}{O}}-\ddot{\underset{..}{O}}\cdot]^{-}$$

oxide ion — peroxide ion — superoxide ion

Lithium is the only Group 1 metal that forms the normal oxide in good yield by direct reaction with oxygen. The other Group 1 oxides (Na_2O, K_2O, Rb_2O, Cs_2O) must be prepared by other means. In contrast, the Group 2 metals usually react with oxygen to give the normal oxide. Beryllium and magnesium must be heated strongly to give BeO and MgO (Figure 20.7). Calcium and strontium react more readily to give CaO and SrO. Barium, the most reactive of the Group 2 metals, catches fire when exposed to moist air. The product is a mixture of the normal oxide BaO (Ba^{2+}, O^{2-} ions) and the peroxide BaO_2 (Ba^{2+}, O_2^{2-} ions). The higher the temperature, the greater the fraction of BaO in the mixture.

The oxides of these metals react with water to form hydroxides:

$$Li_2O(s) + H_2O(l) \longrightarrow 2LiOH(s)$$
$$CaO(s) + H_2O(l) \longrightarrow Ca(OH)_2(s)$$

The oxides of the Group 1 and Group 2 metals are sometimes referred to as "basic anhydrides" (bases without water) because of this reaction. The reaction with CaO is referred to as the "slaking" of lime; it gives off 65 kJ of heat per mole of $Ca(OH)_2$ formed. A similar reaction with MgO takes place slowly to form $Mg(OH)_2$, the antacid commonly referred to as "Milk of Magnesia."

When sodium burns in air, the principal product is yellowish sodium peroxide, Na_2O_2:

$$2Na(s) + O_2(g) \longrightarrow Na_2O_2(s)$$

Addition of sodium peroxide to water gives hydrogen peroxide, H_2O_2:

$$Na_2O_2(s) + 2H_2O(l) \longrightarrow 2Na^+(aq) + 2OH^-(aq) + H_2O_2(aq)$$

Through this reaction, sodium peroxide finds use as a bleaching agent in the pulp and paper industry.

The heavier alkali metals (K, Rb, Cs) form the superoxide when they burn in air. For example,

$$K(s) + O_2(g) \longrightarrow KO_2(s)$$

Potassium superoxide is used in self-contained breathing devices for firefighters and miners. It reacts with the moisture in exhaled air to generate oxygen:

$$4KO_2(s) + 2H_2O(g) \longrightarrow 3O_2(g) + 4KOH(s)$$

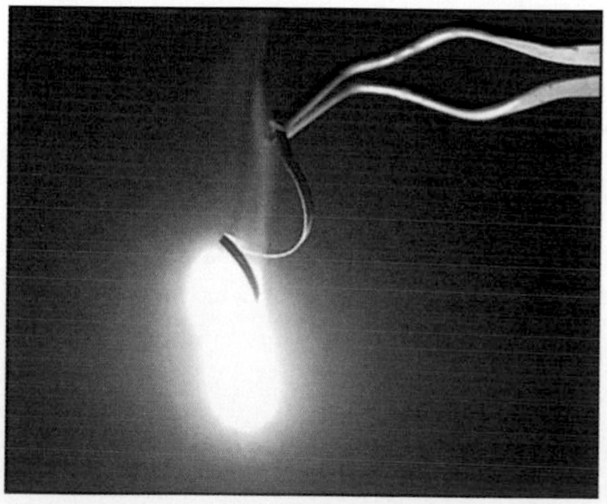

Charles D. Winters

Figure 20.7
Burning magnesium. A piece of magnesium ribbon bursts into flame when heated in the air; the product of the reaction is MgO(*s*).

The carbon dioxide in the exhaled air is removed by reaction with the KOH formed:

$$KOH(s) + CO_2(g) \longrightarrow KHCO_3(s)$$

A person using a mask charged with KO_2 can rebreathe the same air for an extended period of time. This allows that person to enter an area where there are poisonous gases or oxygen-deficient air.

Example 20.5 Consider the compounds strontium hydride, radium peroxide, and cesium superoxide.

(a) Give the formulas of these compounds.
(b) Write equations for the formation of these compounds from the elements.
(c) Write equations for the reactions of strontium hydride and radium peroxide with water.

Strategy The formulas can be deduced from the charges of the ions (Sr^{2+}, Ra^{2+}, Cs^+; H^-, O_2^{2-}, O_2^-). If you know the formulas, the equations are readily written. In part (c), note that—

- hydrides on reaction with water give $H_2(g)$ and a solution of the metal hydroxide.
- peroxides on reaction with water give $H_2O_2(aq)$ and a solution of the metal hydroxide.

SOLUTION

RaO_2 is a peroxide; CsO_2 is a superoxide. Explain.

(a) SrH_2, RaO_2, CsO_2
(b) $Sr(s) + H_2(g) \longrightarrow SrH_2(s)$
$Ra(s) + O_2(g) \longrightarrow RaO_2(s)$
$Cs(s) + O_2(g) \longrightarrow CsO_2(s)$
(c) $SrH_2(s) + 2H_2O(l) \longrightarrow 2H_2(g) + Sr^{2+}(aq) + 2OH^-(aq)$
$RaO_2(s) + 2H_2O(l) \longrightarrow H_2O_2(aq) + Ra^{2+}(aq) + 2OH^-(aq)$

20.3 REDOX CHEMISTRY OF THE TRANSITION METALS

The transition metals, unlike those in Groups 1 and 2, typically show several different oxidation numbers in their compounds. This tends to make their redox chemistry more complex (and more colorful). Only in the lower oxidation states (+1, +2, +3) are the transition metals present as cations (e.g., Ag^+, Zn^{2+}, Fe^{3+}). In higher oxidation states (+4 to +7) a transition metal is covalently bonded to a nonmetal atom, most often oxygen.

Table 20.2 Products of Reactions of the Transition Metals with Oxygen

Metal	Product
Cr	Cr_2O_3
Mn	Mn_3O_4
Fe	Fe_2O_3, Fe_3O_4
Co	Co_3O_4
Ni	NiO
Cu	Cu_2O, CuO
Zn	ZnO
Ag	—
Cd	CdO
Au	—
Hg	HgO

Reactions of the Transition Metals with Oxygen

Table 20.2 lists the formulas of the oxides formed when the more common transition metals react with oxygen. With one exception (Cu_2O), the transition metal is present as a +2 and/or a +3 ion. In Co_3O_4 and in other oxides of general formula M_3O_4, there are two different types of cations: +2 and +3. To be specific, there are twice as many +3 as +2 cations; we might show the composition of Co_3O_4 as

$$1Co^{2+} : 2Co^{3+} : 4O^{2-}$$

We should point out that many oxides of the transition metals beyond those listed in Table 20.2 can be prepared indirectly. For example, although silver does not react directly with oxygen, silver(I) oxide, Ag_2O, can be made by treating a solution of a silver salt with strong base.

$$2Ag^+(aq) + 2\,OH^-(aq) \longrightarrow Ag_2O(s) + H_2O$$

In another case, cobalt(II) oxide can be prepared by heating the carbonate in the absence of air.

$$CoCO_3(s) \longrightarrow CoO(s) + CO_2(g)$$

Many oxides of the transition metals can be *nonstoichiometric;* the atom ratios of the elements differ slightly from whole-number values. Stoichiometric nickel(II) oxide, in which the atom ratio is exactly 1:1 (i.e., $Ni_{1.00}O_{1.00}$), is a green, nonconducting solid. If this compound is heated to 1200°C in pure oxygen, it turns black and undergoes a change in composition to something close to $Ni_{0.97}O_{1.00}$. This nonstoichiometric solid was one of the early semiconductors; it has the structure shown in Figure 20.8. A few Ni^{2+} ions are missing from the crystal lattice; to maintain electrical neutrality, two Ni^{2+} ions are converted to Ni^{3+} ions for each missing Ni^{2+}.

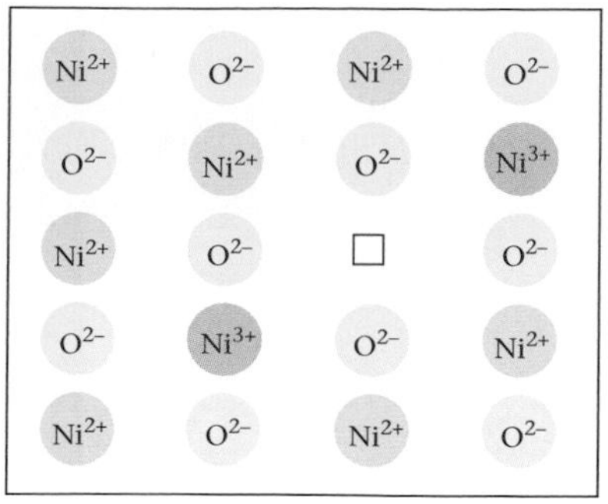

Figure 20.8
Nonstoichiometric nickel(II) oxide. For each missing Ni^{2+} ion, two others are converted to Ni^{3+} ions to maintain charge balance.

Nonstoichiometry is relatively common among "mixed" metal oxides, in which more than one metal is present. In 1986 it was discovered that certain compounds of this type showed the phenomenon of *superconductivity;* on cooling to about 100 K, their electrical resistance drops to zero (Figure 20.9). A typical formula here is $YBa_2Cu_3O_x$, where x varies from 6.5 to 7.2, depending on the method of preparation of the solid.

Reaction of Transition Metals with Acids

CENGAGENOW™
Click Coached Problems for a self-study module on **formulas and oxidation numbers in transition metal complexes.**

Any metal with a positive standard oxidation voltage, E°_{ox}, can be oxidized by the H^+ ions present in a 1 M solution of a strong acid. All the transition metals in the left column of Table 20.3 (p. 546) react spontaneously with dilute solutions of such strong acids as HCl, HBr, and H_2SO_4. The products are hydrogen gas and a cation of the transition metal. A typical reaction is that of nickel:

$$Ni(s) + 2H^+(aq) \longrightarrow Ni^{2+}(aq) + H_2(g)$$

The end result of this reaction is shown in Figure 20.10 (page 547). With metals that can form more than one cation, such as iron, the reaction product with H^+ in the absence of air is ordinarily the cation of lower charge, for example, Fe^{2+}:

$$Fe(s) + 2H^+(aq) \longrightarrow Fe^{2+}(aq) + H_2(g)$$

Metals with negative values of E°_{ox}, listed at the right of Table 20.3, are too inactive to react with hydrochloric acid. The H^+ ion is not a strong enough oxidizing agent to convert a metal such as copper ($E^\circ_{ox} = -0.339$ V) to a cation. However, copper can be oxidized

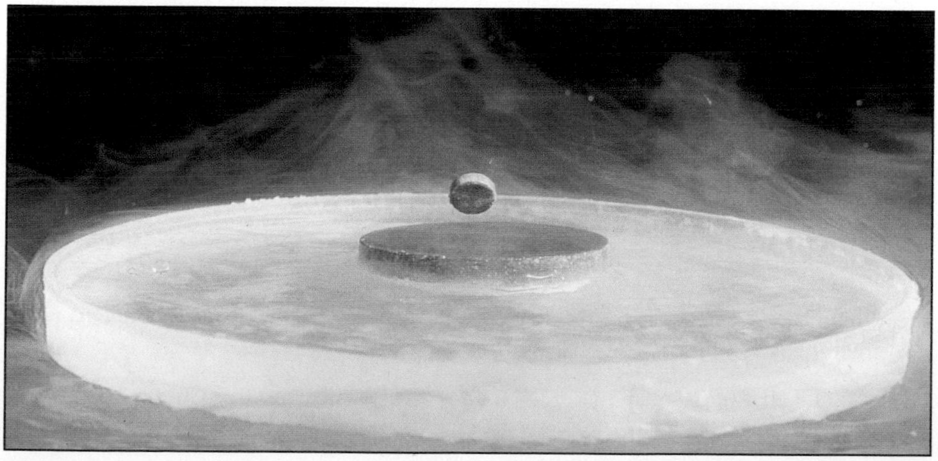

Courtesy of Edmund Scientific

Figure 20.9
A superconductor. A pellet of superconducting material, previously cooled to 77 K with liquid nitrogen, floats above a magnet.

Table 20.3 Ease of Oxidation of Transition Metals

Metal		Cation	E°_{ox} (V)	Metal		Cation	E°_{ox} (V)
Mn	⟶	Mn^{2+}	+1.182	Cu	⟶	Cu^{2+}	−0.339
Cr	⟶	Cr^{2+}	+0.912	Ag	⟶	Ag^{+}	−0.799
Zn	⟶	Zn^{2+}	+0.762	Hg	⟶	Hg^{2+}	−0.852
Fe	⟶	Fe^{2+}	+0.409	Au	⟶	Au^{3+}	−1.498
Cd	⟶	Cd^{2+}	+0.402				
Co	⟶	Co^{2+}	+0.282				
Ni	⟶	Ni^{2+}	+0.236				

by nitric acid. The oxidizing agent is the nitrate ion, NO_3^-, which may be reduced to NO_2 or NO:

$$3Cu(s) + 8H^+(aq) + 2NO_3^-(aq) \longrightarrow 3Cu^{2+}(aq) + 2NO(g) + 4H_2O$$
$$E^\circ = E^\circ_{ox}\ Cu + E^\circ_{red}\ NO_3^- = -0.339\ V + 0.964\ V = +0.625\ V$$

Example 20.6 Write balanced equations for the reactions, if any, at standard conditions of

(a) chromium with hydrochloric acid. (b) silver with nitric acid.

Strategy Use standard potentials to decide whether reaction will occur. Note that with HCl only the H^+ ion can be reduced (to H_2); in HNO_3, the NO_3^- ion can be reduced to NO ($E^\circ_{red} = +0.964$ V).

SOLUTION

(a)
$$Cr(s) \longrightarrow Cr^{2+}(aq) + 2e^- \qquad E^\circ_{ox} = +0.912\ V$$
$$2H^+(aq) + 2e^- \longrightarrow H_2(g) \qquad E^\circ_{red} = 0.000\ V$$

The reaction is

$$Cr(s) + 2H^+(aq) \longrightarrow Cr^{2+}(aq) + H_2(g) \qquad E^\circ = +0.912\ V$$

On exposure to air, Cr^{2+} is oxidized to Cr^{3+}.

If chromium metal is added to hydrochloric acid in the absence of air, it slowly reacts, forming blue Cr^{2+} and bubbles of hydrogen gas.

(b)
$$Ag(s) \longrightarrow Ag^+(aq) \qquad E^\circ_{ox} = -0.799\ V$$
$$NO_3^-(aq) \longrightarrow NO(g) \qquad E^\circ_{red} = +0.964\ V$$

Because E° is a positive quantity, +0.165 V, a redox reaction should occur. The balanced half-equations are

oxidation: $Ag(s) \longrightarrow Ag^+(aq) + e^-$

reduction: $NO_3^-(aq) + 4H^+(aq) + 3e^- \longrightarrow NO(g) + 2H_2O$

To obtain the final balanced equation, multiply the first half-equation by 3 and add to the second. The result is

$$3Ag(s) + NO_3^-(aq) + 4H^+(aq) \longrightarrow 3Ag^+(aq) + NO(g) + 2H_2O$$

"Aqua regia" = royal water.

Although gold is not oxidized by nitric acid, it can be brought into solution in *aqua regia*, a 3:1 mixture by volume of 12 *M* HCl and 16 *M* HNO_3:

$$Au(s) + 4H^+(aq) + 4Cl^-(aq) + NO_3^-(aq) \longrightarrow AuCl_4^-(aq) + NO(g) + 2H_2O$$

The nitrate ion of the nitric acid acts as the oxidizing agent. The function of the hydrochloric acid is to furnish Cl^- ions to form the very stable complex ion $AuCl_4^-$.

Figure 20.10
Oxidation of nickel. Nickel reacts slowly with hydrochloric acid to form $H_2(g)$ and Ni^{2+} ions in solution. Evaporation of the solution formed gives green crystals of $NiCl_2 \cdot 6H_2O$.

Equilibria Between Different Cations of a Transition Metal

Several transition metals form more than one cation. For example, chromium forms Cr^{2+} and Cr^{3+}; copper forms Cu^+ and Cu^{2+}. Table 20.4 lists values of E°_{red} for several such systems. Using the data in this table and in Table 18.1 (page 487), it is possible to decide on the relative stabilities of different transition metal cations in water solution.

Cations for which E°_{red} is a large, positive number are readily reduced and hence tend to be unstable in water solution. A case in point is the Mn^{3+} ion, which reacts spontaneously with water:

$$2Mn^{3+}(aq) + H_2O(l) \longrightarrow 2Mn^{2+}(aq) + \tfrac{1}{2}O_2(g) + 2H^+(aq)$$
$$E^\circ = E^\circ_{red}\ Mn^{3+} + E^\circ_{ox}\ H_2O = +1.559\ V - 1.229\ V = +0.330\ V$$

As a result of this reaction, Mn^{3+} cations are never found in water solution. Manganese(III) occurs only in insoluble oxides and hydroxides such as Mn_2O_3 and $MnO(OH)$.

Co^{3+} is also rare, except in complexes.

The cations in the center column of Table 20.4 (Cr^{2+}, Mn^{2+}, . . .) are in an intermediate oxidation state. They can be either oxidized to a cation of higher charge ($Cr^{2+} \longrightarrow Cr^{3+}$) or reduced to the metal ($Cr^{2+} \longrightarrow Cr$). With certain cations of this type, these two half-reactions occur simultaneously. Consider, for example, the Cu^+ ion. In water solution, copper(I) salts **disproportionate,** undergoing reduction (to copper metal) and oxidation (to Cu^{2+}) at the same time:

$$2Cu^+(aq) \longrightarrow Cu(s) + Cu^{2+}(aq); \qquad E^\circ = +0.518\ V - 0.161\ V = +0.357\ V$$

As a result, the only stable copper(I) species are insoluble compounds such as CuCN or complex ions such as $Cu(CN)_2^-$.

The Cu^+ ion is one of the few species in the center column of Table 20.4 that disproportionates in water, undergoing simultaneous reduction to the metal and oxidation to a cation of higher charge. However, cations of this type may be unstable for a quite different reason. Water ordinarily contains dissolved air; the O_2 in air may oxidize the cation. When a blue

Table 20.4 Ease of Reduction E°_{red} (V) of Transition Metal Cations

Chromium	Cr^{3+}	$\xrightarrow{-0.408\ V}$	Cr^{2+}	$\xrightarrow{-0.912\ V}$	Cr
Manganese	Mn^{3+}	$\xrightarrow{+1.559\ V}$	Mn^{2+}	$\xrightarrow{-1.182\ V}$	Mn
Iron	Fe^{3+}	$\xrightarrow{+0.769\ V}$	Fe^{2+}	$\xrightarrow{-0.409\ V}$	Fe
Cobalt	Co^{3+}	$\xrightarrow{+1.953\ V}$	Co^{2+}	$\xrightarrow{-0.282\ V}$	Co
Copper	Cu^{2+}	$\xrightarrow{+0.161\ V}$	Cu^+	$\xrightarrow{+0.518\ V}$	Cu
Gold	Au^{3+}	$\xrightarrow{+1.400\ V}$	Au^+	$\xrightarrow{+1.695\ V}$	Au
Mercury	Hg^{2+}	$\xrightarrow{+0.908\ V}$	Hg_2^{2+}	$\xrightarrow{+0.796\ V}$	Hg

The Hg_2^{2+} ion has the structure $(Hg{-}Hg)^{2+}$.

solution of chromium(II) salt is exposed to air, the color quickly changes to violet or green as the Cr^{3+} ion is formed by the reaction

$$2Cr^{2+}(aq) \longrightarrow 2Cr^{3+}(aq) + 2e^- \qquad E^\circ_{ox} = +0.408 \text{ V}$$
$$\tfrac{1}{2}O_2(g) + 2H^+(aq) + 2e^- \longrightarrow H_2O \qquad E^\circ_{red} = +1.229 \text{ V}$$
$$2Cr^{2+}(aq) + \tfrac{1}{2}O_2(g) + 2H^+(aq) \longrightarrow 2Cr^{3+}(aq) + H_2O \qquad E^\circ = +1.637 \text{ V}$$

As a result of this reaction, chromium(II) salts are difficult to prepare and even more difficult to store.

Solid Fe^{2+} salts are often contaminated with Fe^{3+}.

The Fe^{2+} ion ($E^\circ_{ox} = -0.769$ V) is much more stable toward oxidation than Cr^{2+}. However, iron(II) salts in water solution are slowly converted to iron(III) by dissolved oxygen. In acidic solution, the reaction is

$$2Fe^{2+}(aq) + \tfrac{1}{2}O_2(g) + 2H^+(aq) \longrightarrow 2Fe^{3+}(aq) + H_2O$$
$$E^\circ = E^\circ_{ox}\ Fe^{2+} + E^\circ_{red}\ O_2 = -0.769 \text{ V} + 1.229 \text{ V} = +0.460 \text{ V}$$

A similar reaction takes place in basic solution. Iron(II) hydroxide is pure white when first precipitated, but in the presence of air it turns first green and then brown as it is oxidized by O_2:

$$2Fe(OH)_2(s) + \tfrac{1}{2}O_2(g) + H_2O(l) \longrightarrow 2Fe(OH)_3(s)$$

Example 20.7 Using Table 20.4, find

(a) three different cations, in addition to Mn^{3+}, that react with H_2O to form $O_2(g)$ ($E^\circ_{ox}\ H_2O = -1.229$ V).
(b) another cation, in addition to Cu^+, that disproportionates in water.
(c) two other cations, in addition to Cr^{2+} and Fe^{2+}, that are oxidized by $O_2(g)$ dissolved in water ($E^\circ_{red}\ O_2 = +1.229$ V).

Strategy In each case, look for a reaction in which E° is a positive quantity. In (a), E°_{red} for the cation must exceed +1.229 V. In (b), $E^\circ_{red} + E^\circ_{ox}$ for the cation must be a positive quantity. In (c), the cation must have an E°_{ox} value no smaller than −1.229 V.

SOLUTION

(a) Co^{3+} ($E^\circ_{red} = +1.953$ V), Au^{3+} ($E^\circ_{red} = +1.400$ V) and Au^+ ($E^\circ_{red} = +1.695$ V)
(b) Au^+ ($E^\circ_{red} + E^\circ_{ox} = +1.695 \text{ V} - 1.400 \text{ V} = 0.295$ V)
(c) Cu^+ ($E^\circ_{ox} = -0.161$ V) and Hg_2^{2+} ($E^\circ_{ox} = -0.908$ V)

Reality Check All of these cations, at least in principle, are unstable in water solutions exposed to air.

Charles D. Winters

Figure 20.11
Oxidation states of chromium. The first two containers (green and violet) contain +3 chromium. The $[Cr(H_2O)_4Cl_2]^+$ ion is green; $[Cr(H_2O)_6]^{3+}$ is violet. The two bottles at the right contain +6 chromium; the CrO_4^{2-} ion is yellow, and the $Cr_2O_7^{2-}$ ion is red.

Oxoanions of the Transition Metals (CrO_4^{2-}, $Cr_2O_7^{2-}$, MnO_4^-)

Chromium in the +6 state forms two different oxoanions, the yellow chromate ion, CrO_4^{2-}, and the red dichromate ion, $Cr_2O_7^{2-}$ (Figure 20.11). The chromate ion is stable in basic or neutral solution; in acid, it is converted to the dichromate ion:

$$\underset{\text{yellow}}{2CrO_4^{2-}(aq)} + 2H^+(aq) \rightleftharpoons \underset{\text{red}}{Cr_2O_7^{2-}(aq)} + H_2O(l) \qquad K = 3 \times 10^{14}$$

The dichromate ion in acidic solution is a powerful oxidizing agent,

$$Cr_2O_7^{2-}(aq) + 14H^+(aq) + 6e^- \longrightarrow 2Cr^{3+}(aq) + 7H_2O(l) \qquad E^\circ_{red} = +1.33 \text{ V}$$

As you might expect from the half-equation for its reduction, the oxidizing strength of the dichromate ion decreases as the concentration of H^+ decreases (increasing pH).

Figure 20.12
Ammonium dichromate volcano.

The $Cr_2O_7^{2-}$ ion can act as an oxidizing agent in the solid state as well as in water solution. In particular, it can oxidize the NH_4^+ ion to molecular nitrogen. When a pile of ammonium dichromate is ignited, a spectacular reaction occurs (Figure 20.12).

$$\underset{\text{red}}{(NH_4)_2Cr_2O_7(s)} \longrightarrow N_2(g) + 4H_2O(g) + \underset{\text{green}}{Cr_2O_3(s)}$$

This makes a great lecture demonstration.

The ammonium dichromate resembles a tiny volcano as it burns, emitting hot gases, sparks, and a voluminous green dust of chromium(III) oxide.

Chromates and dichromates are gradually disappearing from chemistry teaching laboratories because of concern about their toxicity. Long-term exposure of industrial workers to dust containing chromates has, in a few cases, been implicated in lung cancer. More commonly, repeated contact with chromate salts leads to skin disorders; a few people are extremely allergic to CrO_4^{2-} and $Cr_2O_7^{2-}$ ions, breaking into a rash on first exposure.

The permanganate ion, MnO_4^-, has an intense purple color easily visible even in very dilute solution.* Crystals of solid potassium permanganate, $KMnO_4$, have a deep purple, almost black color. This compound is used to treat such diverse ailments as "athlete's foot" and rattlesnake bites. These applications depend on the fact that the MnO_4^- ion is a very powerful oxidizing agent. This is especially true in acidic solution, where MnO_4^- is reduced to Mn^{2+}:

$$MnO_4^-(aq) + 8H^+(aq) + 5e^- \longrightarrow Mn^{2+}(aq) + 4H_2O \qquad E^\circ_{red} = +1.512\text{ V}$$

In basic solution, MnO_4^- is reduced to MnO_2, with a considerably smaller value of E°_{red}:

$$MnO_4^-(aq) + 2H_2O + 3e^- \longrightarrow MnO_2(s) + 4OH^-(aq) \qquad E^\circ_{red} = +0.596\text{ V}$$

However, even in basic solution, MnO_4^- can oxidize water:

$$4MnO_4^-(aq) + 2H_2O \longrightarrow 4MnO_2(s) + 3O_2(g) + 4OH^-(aq)$$
$$E^\circ = E^\circ_{red}\,MnO_4^- + E^\circ_{ox}\,H_2O = +0.596\text{ V} - 0.401\text{ V} = +0.195\text{ V}$$

This reaction accounts for the fact that laboratory solutions of $KMnO_4$ slowly decompose, producing a brownish solid (MnO_2) and gas bubbles (O_2).

*The purple color of old bottles exposed to the sun for a long time is due to MnO_4^- ions. These are formed when ultraviolet light oxidizes manganese compounds in the glass.

CHEMISTRY Beyond the Classroom

Essential Metals in Nutrition

Four of the main-group cations are essential in human nutrition (Table A). Of these, the most important is Ca^{2+}. About 90% of the calcium in the body is found in bones and teeth, largely in the form of hydroxyapatite, $Ca(OH)_2 \cdot 3Ca_3(PO_4)_2$. Calcium ions in bones and teeth exchange readily with those in the blood; about 0.6 g of Ca^{2+} enters and leaves your bones every day. In a normal adult this exchange is in balance, but in elderly people, particularly women, there is sometimes a net loss of bone calcium, leading to the disease known as osteoporosis.

Although sodium is an essential metal, it has been statistically associated with hypertension. About 50% of people with high blood pressure (10% of the general population) are sensitive to high concentrations of Na^+ ions. For that reason, it is recommended that the daily consumption of Na^+ be limited to 2.4 g. The simplest way to cut back on Na^+ is to read the label carefully before buying processed foods, which account for about 75% of our sodium intake. For example, a single serving of packaged scalloped potatoes can contain as much as 0.5 g of Na^+ ion as opposed to only 0.006 g for a large baked potato.

Of the ten trace elements known to be essential to human nutrition, seven are transition metals. For the most part, transition metals in biochemical compounds are present as complex ions, chelated by organic ligands. You will recall (Chapter 15) that hemoglobin has such a structure with Fe^{2+} as the central ion of the complex. The Co^{3+} ion occupies a similar position in vitamin B_{12}, octahedrally coordinated to organic molecules somewhat similar to those in hemoglobin.

Charles D. Winters

Foods high in iron.

As you can judge from Table A, transition metal cations are frequently found in enzymes. The Zn^{2+} ion alone is known to be a component of at least 70 different enzymes. One of these, referred to as "alcohol dehydrogenase," is concentrated in the liver, where it acts to break down alcohols. Another zinc-containing enzyme is involved in the normal functioning of oil glands in the skin, which accounts for the use of Zn^{2+} compounds in the treatment of acne.

Although Zn^{2+} is essential to human nutrition, compounds of the two elements below zinc in the periodic table, Cd and Hg, are extremely toxic. This reflects the fact that Cd^{2+} and Hg^{2+}, in contrast to Zn^{2+}, form very stable complexes with ligands containing sulfur atoms. As a result, these two cations react with and thereby deactivate enzymes containing —SH groups.

Table A Essential Metal Ions

Major Species (Main-Group Cations)

Ion	Amount in Body	Daily Requirement	Function in Body	Rich Sources*
Na^+	63 g	~2 g	Principal cation *outside* cell fluid	Table salt, many processed and preserved foods
K^+	150 g	~2 g	Principal cation *within* cell fluid	Fruits, nuts, fish, instant coffee, wheat bran
Mg^{2+}	21 g	0.35 g	Activates enzymes for body processes	Chocolate, nuts, instant coffee, wheat bran
Ca^{2+}	1160 g	0.8 g	Bone and tooth formation	Milk, cheese, broccoli, canned salmon (with bones)

Trace Species (Transition Metal Cations)

Ion	Amount in Body	Daily Requirement	Function in Body	Rich Sources*
Fe^{2+}, Fe^{3+}	5000 mg	15 mg	Component of hemoglobin, myoglobin	Liver, meat, clams, spinach
Zn^{2+}	3000 mg	15 mg	Component of many enzymes, hormones	Oysters, crab, meat, nuts
Cu^{2+}, Cu^+	100 mg	2 mg	Iron metabolism, component of enzymes	Lobster, cherries, chocolate
Mn^{2+}	15 mg	3 mg	Metabolism of carbohydrates, lipids	Beet greens, nuts, blueberries
Mo(IV,V,VI)	10 mg	0.3 mg	Fe, N metabolism; component of enzymes	Legumes, ice cream
Cr^{3+}	5 mg	0.2 mg	Glucose metabolism; affects action of insulin	Corn, clams, nuts
Co^{2+}, Co^{3+}	1 mg	0.005 mg	Component of vitamin B_{12}	Liver, shellfish

*Other, more mundane, sources can be found in any nutrition textbook.

Chapter Highlights

Key Concepts

1. Calculate $\Delta G°$ from thermodynamic data.
   (Example 20.1; Problems 5, 6, 35) ■ Questions and Problems assignable in OWL: 5
2. Write balanced equations to represent—
   - metallurgical processes.
     (Examples 20.2, 20.3; Problems 1–4, 7, 8) ■ 2, 3, 8
   - reactions of Group 1 and Group 2 metals.
     (Examples 20.4, 20.5; Problems 13–16) ■ 13, 16, 41
   - redox reactions of transition metals.
     (Example 20.6; Problems 19–24) ■ 24, 43
3. Determine $E°$ and reaction spontaneity from standard potentials.
   (Example 20.7; Problems 25–28) ■ 28, 30

Select end of chapter Questions and Problems may be assigned in OWL and are cross-referenced in the Key Concepts list.

CENGAGENOW™

Sign in at **academic.cengage.com/now** to:

- Check your readiness for an exam by taking the Pre-Test and exploring the self-study modules recommended in your Personalized Study plan
- For quick review, download Go Chemistry mini-lecture flashcard modules (or purchase them at **www.ichapters.com**)

Key Terms

disproportionation
metallurgy
ore
peroxide
superoxide

Summary Problem

Consider the alkaline earth metal strontium and the transition metal manganese.

(a) Write a balanced equation for the reaction of strontium with oxygen; with water.
(b) Give the formulas of strontium hydride, strontium nitride, and strontium sulfide.
(c) Electrolysis of strontium chloride gives strontium metal and chlorine gas. What mass of the chloride must be electrolyzed to form one kilogram of strontium? One liter of $Cl_2(g)$ at STP?
(d) Give the formulas of three manganese compounds containing manganese in different oxidation states.
(e) Write a balanced equation for the reaction of manganese metal with hydrochloric acid; Mn^{3+} with water; Mn with O_2.
(f) Write a balanced equation for the reduction of the principal ore of manganese, pyrolusite, MnO_2, with CO.
(g) For the reaction

$$MnO(s) + H_2(g) \longrightarrow Mn(s) + H_2O(g),\ \Delta H° = +143\ kJ,\ \Delta S° = +0.0297\ kJ/K$$

would it be feasible to reduce MnO to the metal by heating with hydrogen?
(h) Given that $E°_{red}$ $Mn^{3+} \longrightarrow Mn^{2+} = +1.559$ V, $E°_{red}$ $Mn^{2+} \longrightarrow Mn = -1.182$ V, and $E°_{red}$ $O_2(g) \longrightarrow H_2O = +1.229$ V, show by calculation whether Mn^{2+} in water solution will disproportionate; whether it will be oxidized to Mn^{3+} by dissolved oxygen; whether it will be reduced by hydrogen gas to the metal.
(i) Given

$$MnO_4^-(aq) + 2H_2O + 3e^- \longrightarrow MnO_2(s) + 4OH^-(aq) \qquad E°_{red} = +0.59\ V$$

write a balanced equation for the reaction of MnO_4^- in basic solution with Fe^{2+} to form $Fe(OH)_3$. Calculate E_{red} for the MnO_4^- ion at pH 9.0, taking $[MnO_4^-] = 1$ M.

Answers

(a) $2Sr(s) + O_2(g) \longrightarrow 2SrO(s)$
$Sr(s) + 2H_2O \longrightarrow Sr^{2+}(aq) + 2OH^-(aq) + H_2(g)$
(b) SrH_2; Sr_3N_2; SrS
(c) 1.809 kg; 7.07 g
(d) $MnCl_2$, Mn_2O_3; $KMnO_4$
(e) $Mn(s) + 2H^+(aq) \longrightarrow Mn^{2+}(aq) + H_2(g)$
$2Mn^{3+}(aq) + H_2O \longrightarrow 2Mn^{2+}(aq) + \frac{1}{2}O_2(g) + 2H^+(aq)$
$3Mn(s) + 2O_2(g) \longrightarrow Mn_3O_4(s)$
(f) $MnO_2(s) + 2CO(g) \longrightarrow Mn(s) + 2CO_2(g)$
(g) no; $T_{calc} \approx 4800$ K
(h) no; in all cases, $E°$ is negative
(i) $MnO_4^-(aq) + 3Fe^{2+}(aq) + 5OH^-(aq) + 2H_2O \longrightarrow MnO_2(s) + 3Fe(OH)_3(s) \qquad E_{red} = +0.98$ V

Questions and Problems

Blue-numbered questions have answers in Appendix 6 and fully-worked solutions in the *Student Solutions Manual.*

■ denotes questions assignable in OWL.

WEB indicates that the solution is available on this book's companion website.

Metallurgy

1. Write a balanced equation to represent the electrolysis of molten sodium chloride. What volume of Cl_2 at STP is formed at the anode when 1.00 g of sodium is formed at the cathode?

2. ■ Write a balanced equation to represent the electrolysis of aluminum oxide. If 2.00 L of O_2 at 25°C and 751 mm Hg is formed at the anode, what mass of Al is formed at the cathode?

3. ■ Write a balanced equation to represent

(a) the roasting of nickel(II) sulfide to form nickel(II) oxide.

(b) the reduction of nickel(II) oxide by carbon monoxide.

4. Write a balanced equation to represent the roasting of copper(I) sulfide to form "blister copper."

5. ■ Show by calculation whether the reaction in Problem 3(b) is spontaneous at 25°C and 1 atm.

6. Calculate $\Delta G°$ at 200°C for the reaction in Problem 4.

7. Write a balanced equation for the reaction that occurs when

(a) finely divided gold is treated with $CN^-(aq)$ in the presence of $O_2(g)$.

(b) finely divided zinc metal is added to the solution formed in (a).

8. ■ Write a balanced equation for the reaction that occurs when

(a) iron(III) oxide is reduced with carbon monoxide.

(b) the excess carbon in pig iron is removed by the basic oxygen process.

9. How many cubic feet of air (assume 21% by volume of oxygen in air) at 25°C and 1.00 atm are required to react with coke to form the CO needed to convert one metric ton of hematite ore (92% Fe_2O_3) to iron?

10. **WEB** Zinc is produced by electrolytic refining. The electrolytic process, which is similar to that for copper, can be represented by the two half-reactions

$$Zn(\text{impure}, s) \longrightarrow Zn^{2+} + 2e^-$$

$$Zn^{2+} + 2e^- \longrightarrow Zn(\text{pure}, s)$$

For this process, a voltage of 3.0 V is used. How many kilowatt hours are needed to produce one metric ton of pure zinc?

11. When 2.876 g of a certain metal sulfide is roasted in air, 2.368 g of the metal oxide is formed. If the metal has an oxidation number of +2, what is its molar mass?

12. Chalcopyrite, $CuFeS_2$, is an important source of copper. A typical chalcopyrite ore contains about 0.75% Cu. What volume of sulfur dioxide at 25°C and 1.00 atm pressure is produced when one boxcar load (4.00×10^3 ft³) of chalcopyrite ore ($d = 2.6$ g/cm³) is roasted? Assume all the sulfur in the ore is converted to SO_2 and no other source of sulfur is present.

Reactions of Alkali Metals and Alkaline Earth Metals

13. ■ Give the formula and name of the compound formed by strontium with

(a) nitrogen (b) bromine

(c) water (d) oxygen

14. Give the formula and name of the compound formed by potassium with

(a) nitrogen (b) iodine (c) water

(d) hydrogen (e) sulfur

15. Write a balanced equation and give the names of the products for the reaction of

(a) magnesium with chlorine.

(b) barium peroxide with water.

(c) lithium with sulfur.

(d) sodium with water.

16. ■ **WEB** Write a balanced equation and give the names of the products for the reaction of

(a) sodium peroxide and water.

(b) calcium and oxygen.

(c) rubidium and oxygen.

(d) strontium hydride and water.

17. To inflate a life raft with hydrogen to a volume of 25.0 L at 25°C and 1.10 atm, what mass of calcium hydride must react with water?

18. ■ What mass of KO_2 is required to remove 90.0% of the CO_2 from a sample of 1.00 L of exhaled air (37°C, 1.00 atm) containing 5.00 mole percent CO_2?

Redox Chemistry of Transition Metals

19. Write a balanced equation to show

(a) the reaction of chromate ion with strong acid.

(b) the oxidation of water to oxygen gas by permanganate ion in basic solution.

(c) the reduction half-reaction of chromate ion to chromium(III) hydroxide in basic solution.

20. Write a balanced equation to show

(a) the formation of gas bubbles when cobalt reacts with hydrochloric acid.

(b) the reaction of copper with nitric acid.

(c) the reduction half-reaction of dichromate ion to Cr^{3+} in acid solution.

21. Write a balanced redox equation for the reaction of mercury with aqua regia, assuming the products include $HgCl_4^{2-}$ and $NO_2(g)$.

22. Write a balanced redox equation for the reaction of cadmium with aqua regia, assuming the products include $CdCl_4^{2-}$ and $NO(g)$.

23. Balance the following redox equations.

(a) $Cu(s) + NO_3^-(aq) \longrightarrow Cu^{2+}(aq) + NO_2(g)$ (acidic)

(b) $Cr(OH)_3(s) + ClO^-(aq) \longrightarrow CrO_4^{2-}(aq) + Cl^-(aq)$ (basic)

24. ■ **WEB** Balance the following redox equations.

(a) $Fe(s) + NO_3^-(aq) \longrightarrow Fe^{3+}(aq) + NO_2(g)$ (acidic)

(b) $Cr(OH)_3(s) + O_2(g) \longrightarrow CrO_4^{2-}(aq)$ (basic)

25. Show by calculation which of the following metals will react with hydrochloric acid (standard concentrations).

(a) Cd (b) Cr (c) Co

(d) Ag (e) Au

26. Show by calculation which of the metals in Problem 25 will react with nitric acid to form NO (standard concentrations).

27. Of the cations listed in Table 20.4, show by calculation which one (besides Cu^+) will disproportionate at standard conditions.

28. ■ Using Table 18.1 (Chapter 18) calculate $E°$ for

(a) $2Co^{3+}(aq) + H_2O \longrightarrow 2Co^{2+}(aq) + \frac{1}{2}O_2(g) + 2H^+(aq)$

(b) $2Cr^{2+}(aq) + I_2(s) \longrightarrow 2Cr^{3+}(aq) + 2I^-(aq)$

■ in OWL Blue-numbered questions answered in Appendix 6 **WEB** Solution is available on companion website

29. Using Table 20.4, calculate, for the disproportionation of Fe^{2+},
(a) the equilibrium constant, *K*.
(b) the concentration of Fe^{3+} in equilibrium with 0.10 *M* Fe^{2+}.

30. ■ Using Table 20.4, calculate, for the disproportionation of Au^+,
(a) *K*.
(b) the concentration of Au^+ in equilibrium with 0.10 *M* Au^{3+}.

Unclassified

31. A sample of sodium liberates 2.73 L of hydrogen at 752 mm Hg and 22°C when it is added to a large amount of water. How much sodium is used?

32. ■ A self-contained breathing apparatus contains 248 g of potassium superoxide. A firefighter exhales 116 L of air at 37°C and 748 mm Hg. The volume percent of water in exhaled air is 6.2. What mass of potassium superoxide is left after the water in the exhaled air reacts with it?

33. Taking K_{sp} $PbCl_2 = 1.7 \times 10^{-5}$ and assuming $[Cl^-] = 0.20$ *M*, calculate the concentration of Pb^{2+} at equilibrium.

34. ■ The equilibrium constant for the reaction

$$2CrO_4^{2-}(aq) + 2H^+(aq) \rightleftharpoons Cr_2O_7^{2-}(aq) + H_2O$$

is 3×10^{14}. What must the pH be so that the concentrations of chromate and dichromate ion are both 0.10 *M*?

35. Using data in Appendix 1, estimate the temperature at which Fe_2O_3 can be reduced to iron, using hydrogen gas as a reducing agent (assume $H_2O(g)$ is the other product).

36. A 0.500-g sample of zinc-copper alloy was treated with dilute hydrochloric acid. The hydrogen gas evolved was collected by water displacement at 27°C and a total pressure of 755 mm Hg. The volume of the water displaced by the gas is 105.7 mL. What is the percent composition, by mass, of the alloy? (Vapor pressure of H_2O at 27°C is 26.74 mm Hg.) Assume only the zinc reacts.

37. One type of stainless steel contains 22% nickel by mass. How much nickel sulfide ore, NiS, is required to produce one metric ton of stainless steel?

38. Silver is obtained in much the same manner as gold, using NaCN solution and O_2. Describe with appropriate equations the extraction of silver from argentite ore, Ag_2S. (The products are SO_2 and $Ag(CN)_2^-$, which is reduced with zinc.)

39. Iron(II) can be oxidized to iron(III) by permanganate ion in acidic solution. The permanganate ion is reduced to manganese(II) ion.
(a) Write the oxidation half-reaction, the reduction half-reaction, and the overall redox equation.
(b) Calculate $E°$ for the reaction.
(c) Calculate the percentage of Fe in an ore if a 0.3500-g sample is dissolved and the Fe^{2+} formed requires for titration 55.63 mL of a 0.0200 *M* solution of $KMnO_4$.

40. Of the cations listed in the center column of Table 20.4, which one is the
(a) strongest reducing agent?
(b) strongest oxidizing agent?
(c) weakest reducing agent?
(d) weakest oxidizing agent?

Challenge Problems

41. ■ A sample of 20.00 g of barium reacts with oxygen to form 22.38 g of a mixture of barium oxide and barium peroxide. Determine the composition of the mixture.

42. Rust, which you can take to be $Fe(OH)_3$, can be dissolved by treating it with oxalic acid. An acid-base reaction occurs, and a complex ion is formed.
(a) Write a balanced equation for the reaction.
(b) What volume of 0.10 *M* $H_2C_2O_4$ would be required to remove a rust stain weighing 1.0 g?

43. ■ A 0.500-g sample of steel is analyzed for manganese. The sample is dissolved in acid and the manganese is oxidized to permanganate ion. A measured excess of Fe^{2+} is added to reduce MnO_4^- to Mn^{2+}. The excess Fe^{2+} is determined by titration with $K_2Cr_2O_{27}$. If 75.00 mL of 0.125 *M* $FeSO_4$ is added and the excess requires 13.50 mL of 0.100 *M* $K_2Cr_2O_7$ to oxidize Fe^{2+}, calculate the percent by mass of Mn in the sample.

44. Calculate the temperature in °C at which the equilibrium constant (*K*) for the following reaction is 1.00.

$$MnO_2(s) \longrightarrow Mn(s) + O_2(g)$$

45. A solution of potassium dichromate is made basic with sodium hydroxide; the color changes from red to yellow. Addition of silver nitrate to the yellow solution gives a precipitate. This precipitate dissolves in concentrated ammonia but re-forms when nitric acid is added. Write balanced net ionic equations for all the reactions in this sequence.

■ in OWL Blue-numbered questions answered in Appendix 6 WEB Solution is available on companion website

21 Chemistry of the Nonmetals

For what can so fire us,
Enrapture, inspire us,
As Oxygen? What so delicious to quaff?
It is so stimulating,
And so titillating,
E'en grey-beards turn freshy, dance, caper, and laugh.

—John Shield
"Oxygen Gas"

Chapter Outline

The electrical charge that creates this bolt of lightning also changes some of the oxygen in the air to ozone.

Approximately 18 elements are classified as nonmetals; they lie above and to the right of the "stairway" that runs diagonally across the periodic table (Figure 21.1). As the word "nonmetal" implies, these elements do not show metallic properties; in the solid state they are brittle as opposed to ductile, insulators rather than conductors. Most of the nonmetals, particularly those in Groups **15** to **17** of the periodic table, are molecular in nature (e.g., N_2, O_2, F_2). The noble gases (Group **18**) consist of individual atoms attracted to each other by weak dispersion forces. Carbon in Group **14** has a network covalent structure.

As indicated in Figure 21.1, this chapter concentrates on the more common and/or more reactive nonmetals, namely—

- nitrogen and phosphorus in Group **15.**
- oxygen and sulfur in Group **16.**
- the halogens (F, Cl, Br, I) in Group **17.**

We will consider—

- the properties of these elements and methods of preparing them (Section 21.1).
- their hydrogen compounds (Section 21.2).
- their oxides (Section 21.3).
- their oxoacids and oxoanions (Section 21.4). ■

Online homework for this chapter may be assigned in OWL.

CENGAGENOW™
This icon introduces an opportunity for self-study and to explore interactive modules by signing in at **academic.cengage.com/now.**

21.1 THE ELEMENTS AND THEIR PREPARATION

Table 21.1 (p. 556) lists some of the properties of the eight nonmetals considered in this chapter. Notice that all of these elements are molecular; those of low molar mass (N_2, O_2, F_2, Cl_2) are gases at room temperature and atmospheric pressure (Figure 21.2, p. 556). Stronger dispersion forces cause the nonmetals of higher molar mass to be either liquids (Br_2) or solids (I_2, P_4, S_8).

Chemical Reactivity

Of the eight nonmetals listed in Table 21.1, ***nitrogen*** is by far the least reactive. Its inertness is due to the strength of the triple bond holding the N_2 molecule together (B.E. $N{\equiv}N$ = 941 kJ/mol). This same factor explains why virtually all chemical explosives are compounds of nitrogen (e.g., nitroglycerin, trinitrotoluene, ammonium nitrate,

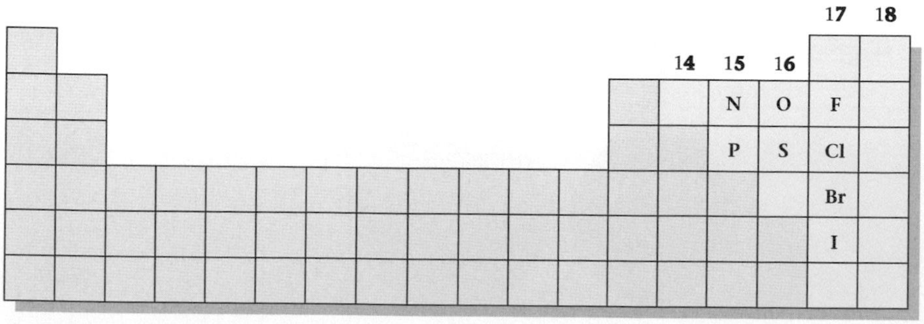

Figure 21.1
Nonmetals and the periodic table. The location of all nonmetals in the periodic table is shown in yellow. Symbols are given for the nonmetallic elements discussed in this chapter.

Table 21.1 Properties of Nonmetallic Elements

	Nitrogen	Phosphorus	Oxygen	Sulfur	Fluorine	Chlorine	Bromine	Iodine
Outer electron configuration	$2s^22p^3$	$3s^23p^3$	$2s^22p^4$	$3s^23p^4$	$2s^22p^5$	$3s^23p^5$	$4s^24p^5$	$5s^25p^5$
Molecular formula	N_2	P_4	O_2	S_8	F_2	Cl_2	Br_2	I_2
Molar mass (g/mol)	28	124	32	257	38	71	160	254
State (25°C, 1 atm)	gas	solid	gas	solid	gas	gas	liquid	solid
Melting point (°C)	−210	44	−218	119	−220	−101	−7	114
Boiling point (°C)	−196	280	−183	444	−188	−34	59	184
Bond enthalpy* (kJ/mol)	941	200	498	226	153	243	193	151
E°_{red}	—	—	—	—	+2.889 V	+1.360 V	+1.077 V	+0.534 V

*In the element (triple bond in N_2, double bond in O_2).

lead azide). These compounds detonate exothermically to form molecular nitrogen. The reactions with ammonium nitrate and lead azide are

$$2NH_4NO_3(s) \longrightarrow 4H_2O(l) + O_2(g) + 2N_2(g) \qquad \Delta H^\circ = -412 \text{ kJ}$$

$$Pb(N_3)_2(s) \longrightarrow Pb(s) + 3N_2(g) \qquad \Delta H^\circ = -476 \text{ kJ}$$

Fluorine is the most electronegative element.

Fluorine is the most reactive of all elements, in part because of the weakness of the F—F bond (B.E. F—F = 153 kJ/mol), but mostly because it is such a powerful oxidizing agent ($E^\circ_{red} = +2.889$ V). Fluorine combines with every element in the periodic table except He and Ne. With a few metals, it forms a surface film of metal fluoride, which adheres tightly enough to prevent further reaction. This is the case with nickel, where the product is NiF_2. Fluorine gas is ordinarily stored in containers made of a nickel alloy, such as stainless steel (Fe, Cr, Ni) or Monel (Ni, Cu). Fluorine also reacts with many compounds including water, which is oxidized to a mixture of O_2, O_3, H_2O_2, and OF_2.

A species disproportionates when it is oxidized and reduced at the same time.

Chlorine is somewhat less reactive than fluorine. Although it reacts with nearly all metals (Figure 21.3, p. 557), heating is often required. This reflects the relatively strong bond in the Cl_2 molecule (B.E. Cl—Cl = 243 kJ/mol). Chlorine disproportionates in water, forming Cl^- ions (oxid. no. Cl = −1) and HClO molecules (oxid. no. Cl = +1).

$$Cl_2(g) + H_2O \rightleftharpoons Cl^-(aq) + H^+(aq) + HClO(aq)$$

The hypochlorous acid, HClO, formed by this reaction is a powerful oxidizing agent ($E^\circ_{red} = +1.630$ V); it kills bacteria, apparently by destroying certain enzymes essential to their metabolism. The taste and odor that we associate with "chlorinated water" are actually due to compounds such as CH_3NHCl, produced by the action of hypochlorous acid on bacteria.

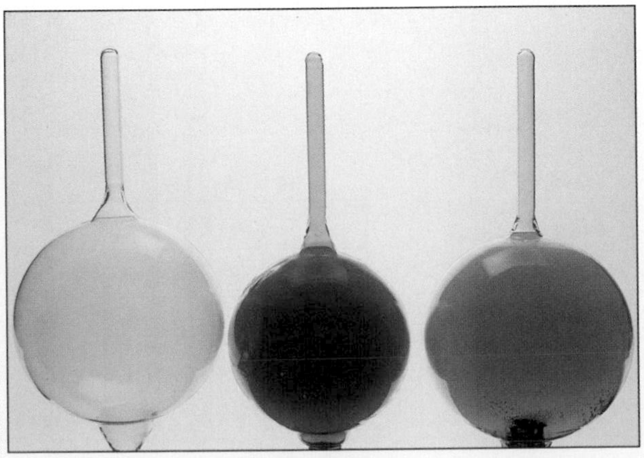

Figure 21.2
Chlorine (Cl_2), bromine (Br_2), and iodine (I_2). The bulbs contain *(left to right)* gaseous chlorine and the vapors in equilibrium with liquid bromine and solid iodine.

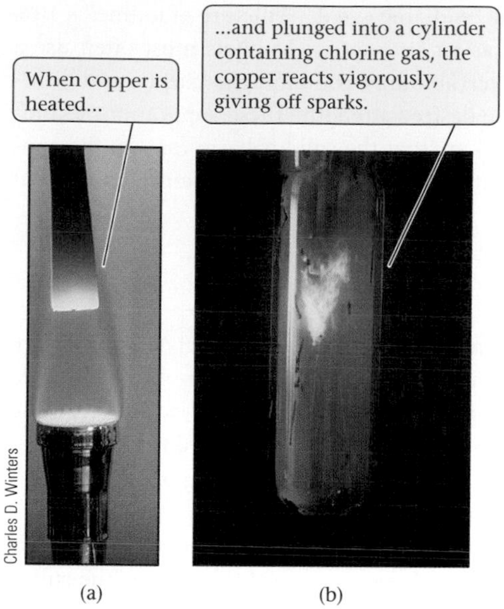

Figure 21.3
Reaction of chlorine with copper. The equation for the reaction is

$$Cu(s) + Cl_2(g) \longrightarrow CuCl_2(s)$$

Example 21.1 For the reaction $Cl_2(g) + H_2O \rightleftharpoons Cl^-(aq) + H^+(aq) + HClO(aq)$,

(a) write the expression for the equilibrium constant K.
(b) given that $K = 2.7 \times 10^{-5}$, calculate the concentration of HClO in equilibrium with $Cl_2(g)$ at 1.0 atm.

Strategy To answer (a), note that, in the expression for K, gases enter as their partial pressures in atmospheres, species in aqueous solution as their molarities; water does not appear, because it is the solvent. To answer (b), note that H^+ ions, Cl^- ions, and HClO molecules are formed in equimolar amounts.

SOLUTION

(a) $K = \dfrac{[HClO] \times [H^+] \times [Cl^-]}{P_{Cl_2}}$

(b) Let $x = [HClO]$. Since H^+, Cl^-, and HClO all have coefficients of 1 in the balanced equation, $[H^+] = [Cl^-] = [HClO] = x$. Substituting in the expression for K:

$$K = \frac{[HClO] \times [H^+] \times [Cl^-]}{P_{Cl_2}} \qquad 2.7 \times 10^{-5} = \frac{x^3}{1.0}$$

Solving

$$x = (2.7 \times 10^{-5})^{1/3} = 0.030\ M$$

Reality Check In other words, the concentration of hypochlorous acid in a solution formed by bubbling chlorine gas through water should be about 0.03 mol/L.

Chlorinated water. The oxidizing power of chlorine-containing chemicals keeps swimming pool water free of disease-causing microorganisms.

The oxidizing power of the halogens makes them hazardous to work with. Fluorine is the most dangerous, but it is very unlikely that you will ever come across it in a teaching laboratory. You are most likely to encounter chlorine as its saturated water solution, called "chlorine water." Remember that the pressure of chlorine gas over this solution (if it is freshly prepared) is 1 atm and that chlorine was used as a poison gas in World War I. Use small quantities of chlorine water and don't breathe the vapors. Bromine, although not as strong an oxidizing agent as chlorine, can cause severe burns if it comes in contact with your skin, particularly if it gets under your fingernails.

Of the four halogens, iodine is the weakest oxidizing agent. "Tincture of iodine," a 10% solution of I_2 in alcohol, is sometimes used as an antiseptic. Hospitals most often use a product called "povidone-iodine," a quite powerful iodine-containing antiseptic and disinfectant, which can be diluted with water to the desired strength. These applications of molecular iodine should not delude you into thinking that the solid is harmless. On the contrary, if $I_2(s)$ is allowed to remain in contact with your skin, it can cause painful burns that are slow to heal.

Occurrence and Preparation

Of the eight nonmetals considered here, three (nitrogen, oxygen, and sulfur) occur in nature in elemental form. *Nitrogen* and *oxygen* are obtained from air, where their mole fractions are 0.7808 and 0.2095, respectively. When liquid air at −200°C (73 K) is allowed to warm, the first substance that boils off is nitrogen (bp N_2 = 77 K). After most of the nitrogen has been removed, further warming gives oxygen (bp O_2 = 90 K). About 2×10^{10} kg of O_2 and lesser amounts of N_2 are produced annually in the United States from liquid air.

At the close of the Civil War in 1865, oil prospectors in Louisiana discovered (to their disgust) elemental *sulfur* in the caprock of vast salt domes up to 20 km^2 in area. The sulfur lies 60 to 600 m below the surface of the earth. The process used to mine sulfur is named after its inventor, Herman Frasch, an American chemical engineer (born in Germany). A diagram of the Frasch process is shown in Figure 21.4. The sulfur is heated to its melting point (119°C) by pumping superheated water at 165°C down one of three concentric pipes. Compressed air is used to bring the sulfur to the surface. The air and sulfur form a frothy mixture that rises through the middle pipe. On cooling, the sulfur solidifies, filling huge vats that may be 0.5 km long. The sulfur obtained in this way has a purity approaching 99.9%.

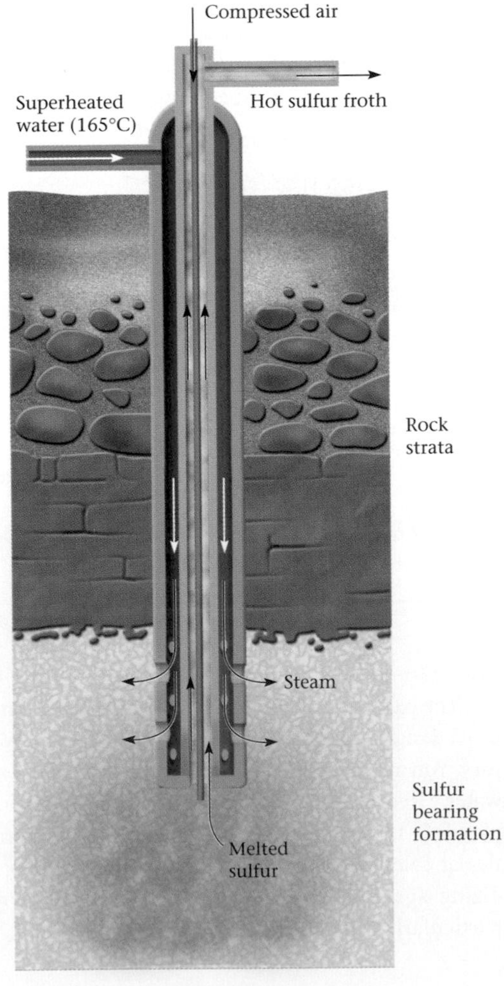

Figure 21.4
Frasch process for mining sulfur. Superheated water at 165°C is sent down through the outer pipe to form a pool of molten sulfur (mp = 119°C) at the base. Compressed air, pumped down the inner pipe, brings the sulfur to the surface. Sulfur deposits are often 100 m or more beneath the earth's surface, covered with quicksand and rock.

The *halogens* are far too reactive to occur in nature as the free elements. Instead, they are found as halide anions—

- F^- in the mineral calcium fluoride, CaF_2 (fluorite).
- Cl^- in huge underground deposits of sodium chloride, NaCl (rock salt), underlying parts of Oklahoma, Texas, and Kansas.
- $Br^-(aq)$ and $I^-(aq)$ in brine wells in Arkansas (conc. $Br^- = 0.05\ M$) and Michigan (conc. $I^- = 0.001\ M$), respectively.

Br_2 and I_2 can also be obtained from seawater.

The fluoride and chloride ions are very difficult to oxidize (E°_{ox} $F^- = -2.889$ V; E°_{ox} $Cl^- = -1.360$ V). Hence the elements fluorine and chlorine are ordinarily prepared by electrolytic oxidation, using a high voltage. As pointed out in Chapter 18, chlorine is prepared by the electrolysis of aqueous sodium chloride:

$$2Cl^-(aq) + 2H_2O \longrightarrow Cl_2(g) + H_2(g) + 2\,OH^-(aq)$$

The process used to prepare fluorine was developed by Henri Moissan in Paris more than a century ago; it won him one of the early (1906) Nobel Prizes in chemistry. The electrolyte is a mixture of HF and KF in a 2:1 mole ratio. At 100°C, fluorine is generated by the decomposition of hydrogen fluoride:

$$2HF(l) \longrightarrow H_2(g) + F_2(g)$$

Potassium fluoride furnishes the ions required to carry the electric current.

Bromide and iodide ions are easier to oxidize (E°_{ox} $Br^- = -1.077$ V; E°_{ox} $I^- = -0.534$ V), so bromine and iodine can be prepared by chemical oxidation. Commonly, the oxidizing agent is chlorine gas ($E^\circ_{red} = +1.360$ V):

$$Cl_2(g) + 2Br^-(aq) \longrightarrow 2Cl^-(aq) + Br_2(l)$$
$$Cl_2(g) + 2I^-(aq) \longrightarrow 2Cl^-(aq) + I_2(s)$$

21.2 HYDROGEN COMPOUNDS OF NONMETALS

Table 21.2 lists some of the more important hydrogen compounds of the nonmetals. (Those of carbon are discussed in Chapter 22.) The physical states listed are those observed at 25°C and 1 atm. The remainder of this section is devoted to a discussion of the chemical properties of the compounds shown in boldface in the table.

Ammonia, NH_3

Ammonia is one of the most important industrial chemicals; more than ten million tons of NH_3 are produced annually in the United States. You will recall (Chapter 12) that it is made by the Haber process

$$N_2(g) + 3H_2(g) \rightleftharpoons 2NH_3(g) \qquad 450°C,\ 200\text{–}600\ \text{atm, solid catalyst}$$

Table 21.2 Hydrogen Compounds of the Nonmetals

Group 15	Group 16	Group 17
Ammonia, $NH_3(g)$	Water, $H_2O(l)$	**Hydrogen fluoride, $HF(g)$**
Hydrazine, $N_2H_4(l)$	**Hydrogen peroxide, $H_2O_2(l)$**	
Hydrazoic acid, $HN_3(l)$		
Phosphine, $PH_3(g)$	**Hydrogen sulfide, $H_2S(g)$**	**Hydrogen chloride, $HCl(g)$**
Diphosphine, $P_2H_4(l)$		
		Hydrogen bromide, $HBr(g)$
		Hydrogen iodide, $HI(g)$

Ammonia has a sharp, irritating odor and is toxic at high concentrations.

Ammonia is used to make fertilizers and a host of different nitrogen compounds, notably nitric acid, HNO_3.

The NH_3 molecule acts as a *Brønsted-Lowry base* in water, accepting a proton from a water molecule:

$$NH_3(aq) + H_2O \rightleftharpoons NH_4^+(aq) + OH^-(aq) \qquad K_b = 1.8 \times 10^{-5}$$

Ammonia can also act as a *Lewis base* when it reacts with a metal cation to form a complex ion

The NH_3 molecule donates an electron pair to Ag^+.

$$2NH_3(aq) + Ag^+(aq) \longrightarrow Ag(NH_3)_2^+(aq)$$

or with an electron-deficient compound such as boron trifluoride:

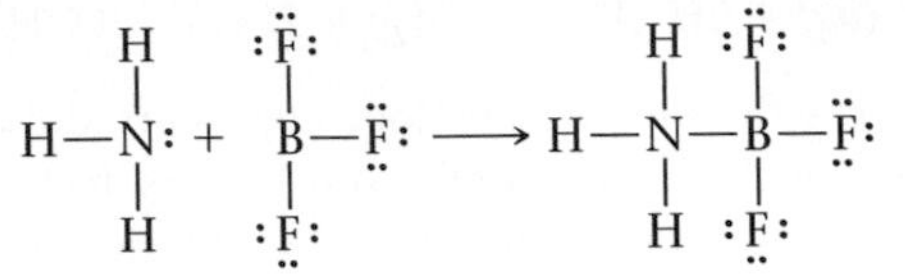

Lewis base Lewis acid

Ammonia is often used to precipitate insoluble metal hydroxides such as $Al(OH)_3$. The OH^- ions formed when ammonia reacts with water precipitate the cation from solution as the hydroxide. The overall equation for the reaction is

$$Al^{3+}(aq) + 3NH_3(aq) + 3H_2O \longrightarrow Al(OH)_3(s) + 3NH_4^+(aq)$$

Nitrogen cannot have an oxidation number lower than -3, which means that when NH_3 takes part in a redox reaction, it always acts as a *reducing agent.* Ammonia may be oxidized to elementary nitrogen or to a compound of nitrogen. An important redox reaction of ammonia is that with hypochlorite ion:

$$2NH_3(aq) + ClO^-(aq) \longrightarrow N_2H_4(aq) + Cl^-(aq) + H_2O$$

Hydrazine, N_2H_4, is made commercially by this process. Certain byproducts of this reaction, notably NH_2Cl and $NHCl_2$, are both toxic and explosive, so solutions of household bleach and ammonia should never be mixed with one another.

Hydrogen Sulfide, H_2S

In water solution, hydrogen sulfide acts as a *Brønsted-Lowry acid;* it can donate a proton to a water molecule:

$$H_2S(aq) + H_2O \rightleftharpoons HS^-(aq) + H_3O^+(aq) \qquad K_a = 1.0 \times 10^{-7}$$

Like ammonia, hydrogen sulfide can act as a precipitating agent toward metal cations. The reaction with Cd^{2+} is typical:

$$Cd^{2+}(aq) + H_2S(aq) \longrightarrow CdS(s) + 2H^+(aq)$$

Like ammonia, hydrogen sulfide (oxid. no. S = -2) can act only as a reducing agent when it takes part in redox reactions. Most often the H_2S is oxidized to elementary sulfur, as in the reaction

$$2H_2S(aq) + O_2(g) \longrightarrow 2S(s) + 2H_2O$$

The sulfur formed is often very finely dispersed, which explains why aqueous solutions of hydrogen sulfide in contact with air have a milky appearance.

If you've worked with H_2S in the laboratory, you won't soon forget its rotten-egg odor. In a sense, it's fortunate that hydrogen sulfide has such a distinctive odor. This gas is highly toxic, as poisonous as HCN. At a concentration of 10 parts per million, H_2S can cause headaches and nausea; at 100 ppm it can be fatal.

Example 21.2 When a solution containing Cu^{2+} is treated with hydrogen sulfide, a black precipitate forms. When another portion of the solution is treated with ammonia, a blue precipitate forms. This precipitate dissolves in excess ammonia to form a deep blue solution containing the $Cu(NH_3)_4^{2+}$ ion. Write balanced net ionic equations to explain these observations.

Strategy Before you can write the equations, you must identify the products. The black precipitate is CuS. The blue precipitate must be copper(II) hydroxide, $Cu(OH)_2$. The identity of the final product is given: $Cu(NH_3)_4^{2+}$. The equations are readily written if you know the formulas of the products.

SOLUTION

$$Cu^{2+}(aq) + H_2S(aq) \longrightarrow CuS(s) + 2H^+(aq)$$
$$Cu^{2+}(aq) + 2NH_3(aq) + 2H_2O \longrightarrow Cu(OH)_2(s) + 2NH_4^+(aq)$$
$$Cu(OH)_2(s) + 4NH_3(aq) \longrightarrow Cu(NH_3)_4^{2+}(aq) + 2OH^-(aq)$$

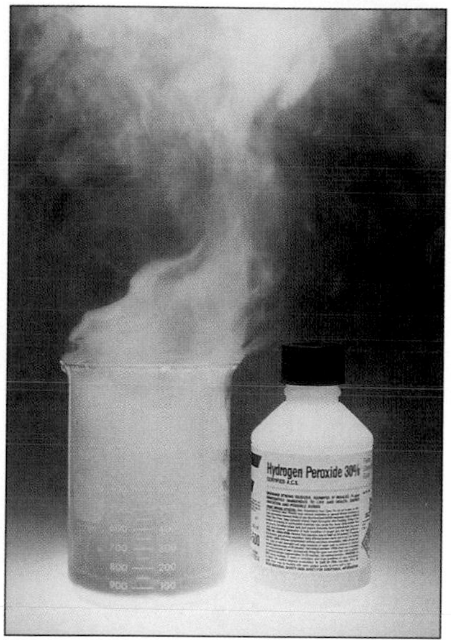

Charles D. Winters

Disproportionation of H_2O_2, catalyzed by MnO_2.

Hydrogen Peroxide

In hydrogen peroxide, oxygen has an oxidation number of −1, intermediate between the extremes for the element, 0 and −2. This means that H_2O_2 can act as either an oxidizing agent, in which case it is reduced to H_2O, or as a reducing agent, when it is oxidized to O_2. In practice, hydrogen peroxide is an extremely strong oxidizing agent:

$$H_2O_2(aq) + 2H^+(aq) + 2e^- \longrightarrow 2H_2O \qquad E^\circ_{red} = +1.763\text{ V}$$

but a very weak reducing agent:

$$H_2O_2(aq) \longrightarrow O_2(g) + 2H^+(aq) + 2e^- \qquad E^\circ_{ox} = -0.695\text{ V}$$

Hydrogen peroxide tends to decompose in water, which explains why its solutions soon lose their oxidizing power. The reaction involved is *disproportionation,* combining the two half-reactions referred to above:

$$\begin{array}{lr} H_2O_2(aq) + 2H^+(aq) + 2e^- \longrightarrow 2H_2O & E^\circ_{red} = +1.763\text{ V} \\ H_2O_2(aq) \longrightarrow O_2(g) + 2H^+(aq) + 2e^- & E^\circ_{ox} = -0.695\text{ V} \\ \hline 2H_2O_2(aq) \longrightarrow O_2(g) + 2H_2O & E^\circ = +1.068\text{ V} \end{array}$$

Half of the H_2O_2 molecules are reduced to H_2O; half are oxidized to O_2.

This reaction is catalyzed by a wide variety of materials, including I^- ions, MnO_2, metal surfaces (Pt, Ag), and even by traces of OH^- ions dissolved from glass.

You are most likely to come across hydrogen peroxide as its water solution. Solutions available in a drugstore for medicinal use contain 3% to 6% by mass of H_2O_2. Industrially, concentrations as high as 86% H_2O_2 are available. All water solutions of hydrogen peroxide contain stabilizers to prevent disproportionation from taking place during storage.

Example 21.3 Using Table 18.1 (page 487), decide whether hydrogen peroxide will react with (oxidize or reduce) the following ions in acid solution at standard concentrations.

(a) I^- (b) Sn^{2+} (c) Co^{2+}

Strategy For a redox reaction to occur spontaneously, either

$$E^\circ_{ox}\,X + E^\circ_{red}\,H_2O_2 > 0$$

or

$$E^\circ_{red}\,X + E^\circ_{ox}\,H_2O_2 > 0$$

where X is one of the ions listed and $E^\circ_{red}\,H_2O_2 = +1.763$ V; $E^\circ_{ox}\,H_2O_2 = -0.695$ V.

CENGAGENOW™
Click Chemistry Interactive for the self-study module **catalytic decomposition of H_2O_2.**

SOLUTION

(a) $E^\circ_{red}\ H_2O_2 + E^\circ_{ox}\ I^- = +1.763\ V - 0.534\ V = +1.229\ V$

Hydrogen peroxide oxidizes I^- ions to I_2.

(b) $E^\circ_{red}\ H_2O_2 + E^\circ_{ox}\ Sn^{2+} = +1.763\ V - 0.154\ V = +1.609\ V$
$E^\circ_{ox}\ H_2O_2 + E^\circ_{red}\ Sn^{2+} = -0.695\ V - 0.141\ V = -0.836\ V$

Hydrogen peroxide oxidizes Sn^{2+} to Sn^{4+}.

(c) Co^{2+} can be reduced to Co ($E^\circ_{red} = -0.282$ V) or oxidized to Co^{3+} ($E^\circ_{ox} = -1.953$ V). Neither gives a positive combination with H_2O_2; no reaction.

Hydrogen Fluoride and Hydrogen Chloride

The most common hydrogen halides are HF (U.S. production = 3×10^8 kg/yr) and HCl (3×10^9 kg/yr). They are most familiar as water solutions, referred to as hydrofluoric acid and hydrochloric acid, respectively. Recall (Chapter 13) that hydrofluoric acid is weak, incompletely dissociated in water, whereas HCl is a strong acid.

$$HF(aq) \rightleftharpoons H^+(aq) + F^-(aq) \qquad K_a = 6.9 \times 10^{-4}$$
$$HCl(aq) \longrightarrow H^+(aq) + Cl^-(aq) \qquad K_a \longrightarrow \infty$$

The difference in K_a values is due largely to the difference in bond strength. The H—F bond (bond enthalpy = 565 kJ/mol) is much stronger than the H—Cl bond (bond enthalpy = 431 kJ/mol).

Hydrofluoric and hydrochloric acids undergo very similar reactions with bases such as OH^- or CO_3^{2-} ions. The equations for these reactions look somewhat different because of the difference in acid strength. Thus for the reaction of hydrochloric acid with a solution of sodium hydroxide, the equation is simply

$$H^+(aq) + OH^-(aq) \longrightarrow H_2O$$

With hydrofluoric acid, the equation is

$$HF(aq) + OH^-(aq) \longrightarrow H_2O + F^-(aq)$$

Hydrochloric acid contains H^+ and Cl^- ions; hydrofluoric acid contains mostly HF molecules.

HF appears in this equation because hydrofluoric acid is weak, containing many more HF molecules than H^+ ions. Similarly, for the reaction of these two acids with a solution of sodium carbonate:

$$\text{hydrochloric acid:} \quad 2H^+(aq) + CO_3^{2-}(aq) \longrightarrow CO_2(g) + H_2O$$
$$\text{hydrofluoric acid:} \quad 2HF(aq) + CO_3^{2-}(aq) \longrightarrow CO_2(g) + H_2O + 2F^-(aq)$$

Concentrated hydrofluoric acid reacts with glass, which can be considered to be a mixture of SiO_2 and ionic silicates such as calcium silicate, $CaSiO_3$:

$$SiO_2(s) + 4HF(aq) \longrightarrow SiF_4(g) + 2H_2O$$
$$CaSiO_3(s) + 6HF(aq) \longrightarrow SiF_4(g) + CaF_2(s) + 3H_2O$$

How do you suppose HF(*aq*) was stored B.P. (before plastics)?

As you might guess, HF solutions are never stored in glass bottles; plastic is used instead. Hydrofluoric acid is sometimes used to etch glass. The glass object is first covered with a thin protective coating of wax or plastic. Then the coating is removed from the area to be etched and the glass is exposed to the HF solution. Thermometer stems and burets can be etched or light bulbs frosted in this way.

Hydrogen fluoride is a very unpleasant chemical to work with. If spilled on the skin, it removes Ca^{2+} ions from the tissues, forming insoluble CaF_2. A white patch forms that is agonizingly painful to the touch. To make matters worse, HF is a local anesthetic, so a person may be unaware of what is happening until it is too late.

Rest assured that you will never have occasion to use hydrofluoric acid in the general chemistry laboratory. Neither are you likely to come in contact with HBr or HI, both of which are relatively expensive. Hydrochloric acid, on the other hand, is a workhorse chemical of the teaching laboratory. It is commonly available as "dilute HCl" (6 *M*) or "concentrated HCl" (12 *M*). You will use it as a source of H^+ ions for such purposes as—

- dissolving insoluble carbonates or hydroxides.

$$Ag_2CO_3(s) + 2H^+(aq) \longrightarrow 2Ag^+(aq) + CO_2(g) + H_2O$$
$$Zn(OH)_2(s) + 2H^+(aq) \longrightarrow Zn^{2+}(aq) + 2H_2O$$

- converting a weak base such as NH_3 to its conjugate acid.

$$NH_3(aq) + H^+(aq) \longrightarrow NH_4^+(aq)$$

- generating $H_2(g)$ by reaction with a metal.

$$Zn(s) + 2H^+(aq) \longrightarrow Zn^{2+}(aq) + H_2(g)$$

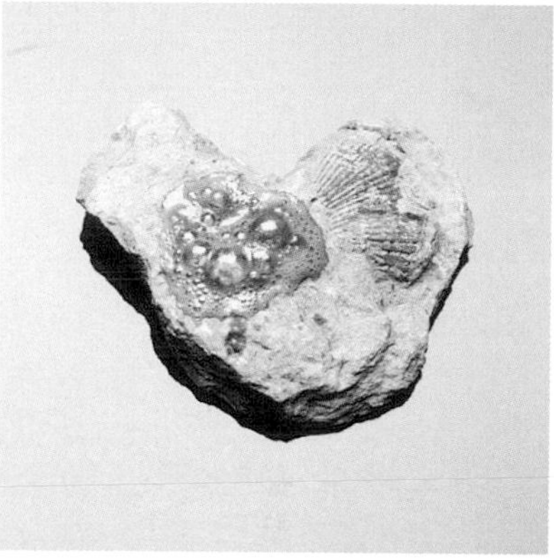

Charles D. Winters

A test for limestone. Geologists use a few drops of hydrochloric acid to identify limestone, which is calcium carbonate.

Example 21.4 Write balanced net ionic equations to explain why

(a) aluminum hydroxide dissolves in hydrochloric acid.
(b) carbon dioxide gas is evolved when calcium carbonate is treated with hydrochloric acid.
(c) carbon dioxide gas is evolved when calcium carbonate is treated with hydrofluoric acid.

Strategy In each case, decide on the nature of the products. You can reason by analogy with the equations cited in the text.

SOLUTION

(a) $Al(OH)_3(s) + 3H^+(aq) \longrightarrow Al^{3+}(aq) + 3H_2O$
(b) $CaCO_3(s) + 2H^+(aq) \longrightarrow Ca^{2+}(aq) + CO_2(g) + H_2O$
(c) $CaCO_3(s) + 2HF(aq) \longrightarrow Ca^{2+}(aq) + CO_2(g) + H_2O + 2F^-(aq)$

21.3 OXYGEN COMPOUNDS OF NONMETALS

Table 21.3 lists some of the more familiar nonmetal oxides. Curiously enough, only 5 of the 21 compounds shown are thermodynamically stable at 25°C and 1 atm (P_4O_{10}, P_4O_6, SO_3, SO_2, I_2O_5). The others, including all of the oxides of nitrogen and chlorine, have positive free energies of formation at 25°C and 1 atm. For example, ΔG_f° $NO_2(g) = +51.3$ kJ; $\Delta G_f^\circ ClO_2(g) = +120.6$ kJ. Kinetically, these compounds stay around long enough to have an extensive chemistry. Nitrogen dioxide, a reddish-brown gas, is a major factor in the formation of photochemical smog (Figure 21.5, p. 564). Chlorine dioxide, a yellow gas, is widely

Table 21.3 Nonmetal Oxides*

Group 15	Group 16	Group 17
$N_2O_5(s)$, $N_2O_4(g)$, $NO_2(g)$ **$N_2O_3(d)$, $NO(g)$, $N_2O(g)$**		$OF_2(g)$, $O_2F_2(g)$
$P_4O_{10}(s)$, $P_4O_6(s)$	**$SO_3(l)$, $SO_2(g)$**	$Cl_2O_7(l)$, $Cl_2O_6(l)$ $ClO_2(g)$, $Cl_2O(g)$ $BrO_2(d)$, $Br_2O(d)$ $I_2O_5(s)$, $I_4O_9(s)$, $I_2O_4(s)$

*The states listed are those observed at 25°C and 1 atm. Compounds that decompose below 25°C are listed as (*d*). Oxides shown in boldface are discussed in the text.

Figure 21.5
Smog over New York City. From a distance, you can clearly see the layer of smog containing reddish-brown nitrogen dioxide.

Peter Arnold/Peter Arnold, Inc.

used as an industrial bleach and water purifier, even though it tends to explode at partial pressures higher than 50 mm Hg.

Molecular Structures of Nonmetal Oxides

Dimerization occurs when two identical molecules combine.

The Lewis structures of the oxides of nitrogen are shown in Figure 21.6. Two of these species, NO and NO_2, are paramagnetic, with one unpaired electron. When nitrogen dioxide is cooled, it dimerizes; the unpaired electrons combine to form a single bond between the two nitrogen atoms:

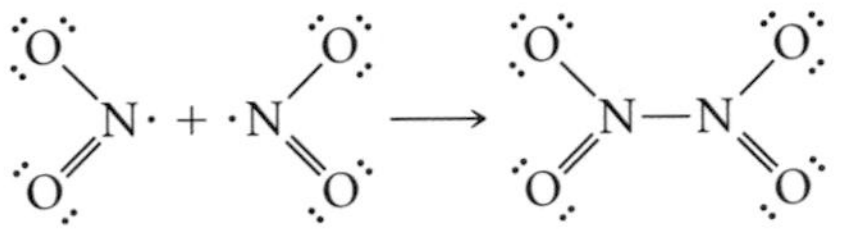

$$2NO_2(g) \rightleftharpoons N_2O_4(g)$$

A similar reaction occurs when an equimolar mixture of NO and NO_2 is cooled. Two odd electrons, one from each molecule, pair off to form an N—N bond:

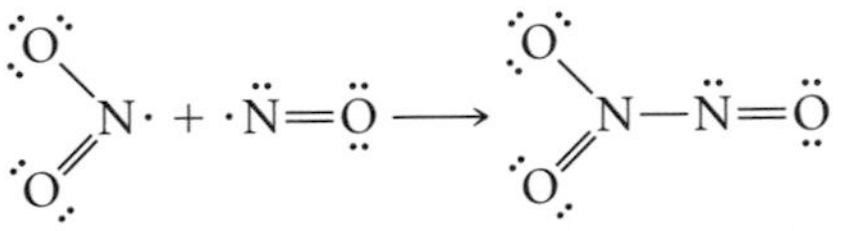

$$NO_2(g) + NO(g) \rightleftharpoons N_2O_3(g)$$

At −20°C, dinitrogen trioxide separates from the mixture as a blue liquid.

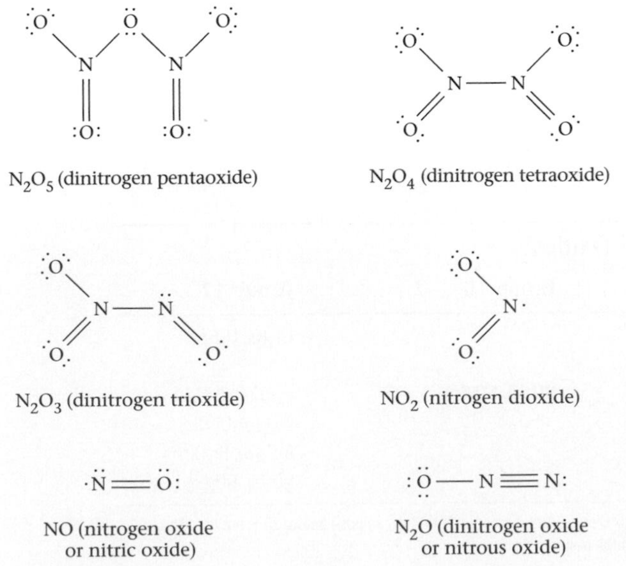

Figure 21.6
Lewis structures of the oxides of nitrogen. Many other resonance forms are possible.

CENGAGENOW™
Click Coached Problems for a self-study module on **structures of nitrogen oxides.**

Nitric oxide (NO) is a minor but villainous component of the atmosphere. It is involved in the formation of both smog (Chapter 11) and acid rain (Chapter 14). You may be surprised to learn that small amounts of NO are also produced in the human body, where it has a generally beneficial effect. In particular, it has the ability to dilate blood vessels, lowering blood pressure and reducing the likelihood of strokes or heart attacks. Beyond that, NO is effective in treating what television commercials refer to as "erectile dysfunction"; it increases blood flow to the penis.

Perhaps the best known oxide of nitrogen is N_2O, commonly called nitrous oxide or "laughing gas." Nitrous oxide is frequently used as an anesthetic, particularly in dentistry. It is also the propellant gas used in whipped cream containers; N_2O is nontoxic, virtually tasteless, and quite soluble in vegetable oils. The N_2O molecule, like all those in Figure 21.6, can be represented as a resonance hybrid.

Example 21.5 Consider the N_2O molecule shown in Figure 21.6.

(a) Draw another resonance form of N_2O.
(b) What is the bond angle in N_2O?
(c) Is the N_2O molecule polar or nonpolar?

Strategy Recall the discussion in Chapter 7, Sections 7.1 to 7.3, where the principles of resonance, molecular geometry, and polarity were considered.

SOLUTION

(a) $:\ddot{O}{=}N{=}\ddot{N}:$ or $:O{\equiv}N{-}\ddot{N}:$
(b) In any of the resonance forms, the central nitrogen atom, insofar as geometry is concerned, would behave as if it were surrounded by two electron pairs. The bond angle is 180°; the molecule is linear, like BeF_2.
(c) Polar (unsymmetrical).

CENGAGENOW™
Click Chemistry Interactive for a self-study module **carbon dioxide as a Lewis acid.**

The structures of SO_2 and SO_3 were referred to in Chapter 7. These molecules are often cited as examples of resonance; sulfur trioxide, for example, has three equivalent resonance structures:

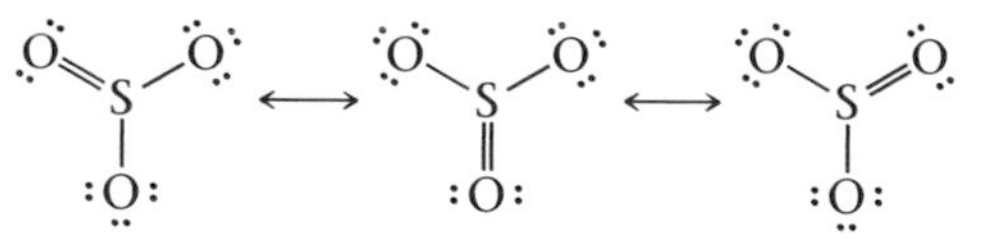

As you might expect, the SO_3 molecule is nonpolar, with 120° bond angles.

Of the two oxides of phosphorus, P_4O_6 and P_4O_{10}, the latter is the more stable; it is formed when white phosphorus burns in air:

$$P_4(s) + 5\,O_2(g) \longrightarrow P_4O_{10}(s)$$

In a limited supply of air, some P_4O_6 is formed.

Note from Figure 21.7 (p. 566) that in both oxides, as in P_4 itself, the four phosphorus atoms are at the corners of a tetrahedron. The P_4O_6 molecule can be visualized as derived from P_4 by inserting an oxygen atom between each pair of phosphorus atoms. In P_4O_{10}, an extra oxygen atom is bonded to each phosphorus.

Reactions of Nonmetal Oxides with Water

Many nonmetal oxides are acidic in the sense that they react with water to form acids. Looking at the reaction

$$SO_3(g) + H_2O(l) \longrightarrow H_2SO_4(l)$$

Figure 21.7
Ball-and-stick models of the oxides of phosphorus.

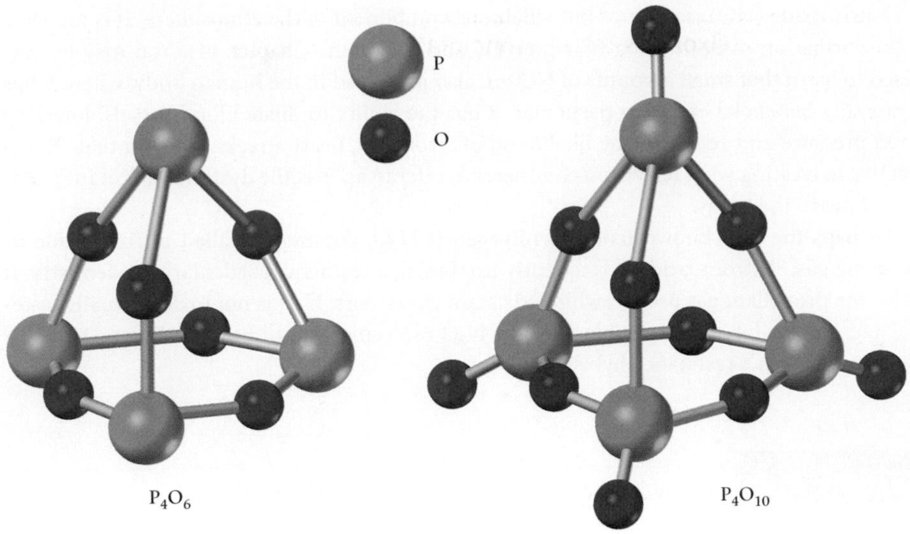

you can see that sulfur trioxide is an *acidic oxide.* Notice that in this reaction, the nonmetal does not change oxidation number; sulfur is in the +6 state in both SO_3 and H_2SO_4. Other acidic oxides include N_2O_5 and N_2O_3:

What is the acid derived from CO_2? Answer: H_2CO_3.

$$+5 \text{ nitrogen:} \quad N_2O_5(s) + H_2O(l) \longrightarrow 2HNO_3(l)$$
$$+3 \text{ nitrogen:} \quad N_2O_3(g) + H_2O(l) \longrightarrow 2HNO_2(aq)$$

The products are nitric acid, HNO_3, and an aqueous solution of nitrous acid, HNO_2.

One of the most important reactions of this type involves the +5 oxide of phosphorus, P_4O_{10}. Here the product is phosphoric acid, H_3PO_4:

$$P_4O_{10}(s) + 6H_2O(l) \longrightarrow 4H_3PO_4(s)$$

This reaction is used to prepare high-purity phosphoric acid and salts of that acid for use in food products. Phosphoric acid, H_3PO_4, is added in small amounts to soft drinks to give them a tart taste. It is present to the extent of about 0.05 mass percent in colas, 0.01 mass percent in root beers.

Charles D. Winters

Household products containing phosphoric acid or its salts.

Example 21.6 Give the formula of the oxide that reacts with water to form

(a) H_3PO_3 (b) $HClO$ (c) H_2SO_3

Strategy Referring to Table 21.3, find an oxide in which the central nonmetal atom has the same oxidation number as in the acid.

SOLUTION

(a) +3 P: H_3PO_3 and P_4O_6
(b) +1 Cl: $HClO$ and Cl_2O
(c) +4 S: H_2SO_3 and SO_2

21.4 OXOACIDS AND OXOANIONS

Table 21.4 lists some of the more important oxoacids of the nonmetals. In all these compounds, the ionizable hydrogen atoms are bonded to oxygen, not to the central nonmetal atom. Dissociation of one or more protons from the oxoacid gives the corresponding oxoanion (Figure 21.8, p. 567).

Table 21.4 Oxoacids of the Nonmetals

Group 15	Group 16	Group 17
HNO_3, HNO_2*		
H_3PO_4, H_3PO_3	H_2SO_4, H_2SO_3*	$HClO_4$, $HClO_3$*, $HClO_2$*, $HClO$*
		$HBrO_4$*, $HBrO_3$*, $HBrO$*
		HIO_4, H_5IO_6, HIO_3, HIO*

*These compounds cannot be isolated from water solution.

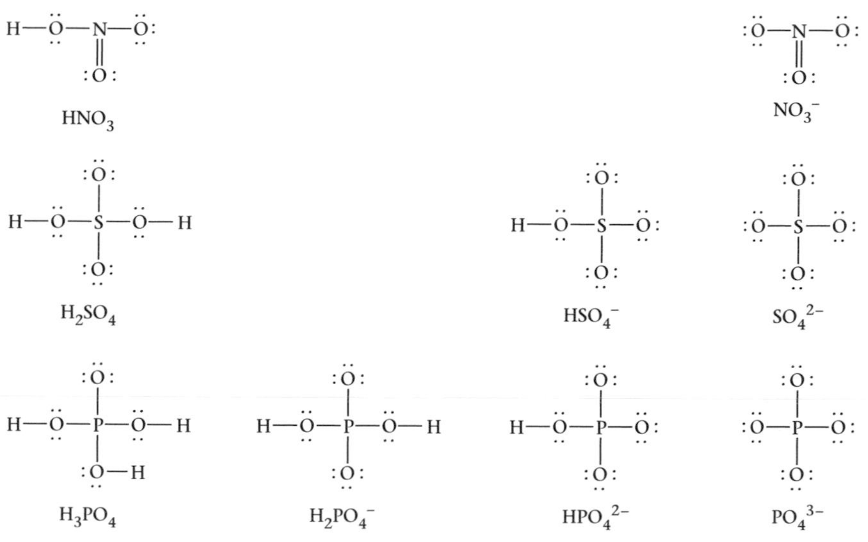

Figure 21.8
Lewis structures of the oxoacids HNO_3, H_2SO_4, H_3PO_4, and the oxoanions derived from them.

In this section we discuss the principles that allow you to predict the relative acid strengths of oxoacids such as those listed in Table 21.4. Then we consider their strengths as oxidizing and/or reducing agents. Finally, we take a closer look at the chemistry of three important oxoacids: HNO_3, H_2SO_4, and H_3PO_4.

Acid Strength

CENGAGENOW™
Click Coached Problems for a self-study module on **molecular structure and acid strength.**

The acid equilibrium constants of the oxoacids of the halogens are listed in Table 21.5. Notice that the value of K_a increases with—

- ***increasing oxidation number of the central atom*** ($HClO < HClO_2 < HClO_3 < HClO_4$)
- ***increasing electronegativity of the central atom*** ($HIO < HBrO < HClO$)

These trends are general ones, observed with other oxoacids of the nonmetals. Recall, for example, that nitric acid, HNO_3 (oxid. no. N = +5), is a strong acid, completely ionized in water. In contrast, nitrous acid, HNO_2 (oxid. no. N = +3), is a weak acid ($K_a = 6.0 \times 10^{-4}$). The electronegativity effect shows up with the strengths of the oxoacids of sulfur and selenium:

$$K_{a1}\ H_2SO_3 = 1.7 \times 10^{-2} \qquad K_{a1}\ H_2SeO_3 = 2.7 \times 10^{-3} \qquad (\text{E.N. S} = 2.6, \text{Se} = 2.5)$$

Table 21.5 Equilibrium Constants of Oxoacids of the Halogens

Oxid. State		K_a		K_a		K_a
+7	$HClO_4$	$\sim 10^7$	$HBrO_4$	$\sim 10^6$	HIO_4*	1.4×10^1
+5	$HClO_3$	$\sim 10^3$	$HBrO_3$	3.0	HIO_3	1.6×10^{-1}
+3	$HClO_2$	1.0×10^{-2}	—	—	—	—
+1	$HClO$	2.8×10^{-8}	$HBrO$	2.6×10^{-9}	HIO	2.4×10^{-11}

*Estimated; in water solution the stable species is H_5IO_6, whose first K_a value is 5×10^{-4}.

Trends in acid strength can be explained in terms of molecular structure. In an oxoacid molecule, the hydrogen atom that dissociates is bonded to oxygen, which in turn is bonded to a nonmetal atom, X. The ionization in water of an oxoacid H—O—X can be represented as

$$H{-}O{-}X(aq) \rightleftharpoons H^+(aq) + XO^-(aq)$$

For a proton, with its +1 charge, to separate from the molecule, the electron density around the oxygen should be as low as possible. This will weaken the O—H bond and favor ionization. The electron density around the oxygen atom is decreased when—

- ***X is a highly electronegative atom such as Cl.*** This draws electrons away from the oxygen atom and makes hypochlorous acid stronger than hypoiodous acid.
- ***Additional, strongly electronegative oxygen atoms are bonded to X.*** These tend to draw electrons away from the oxygen atom bonded to H. Thus we would predict that the ease of dissociation of a proton, and hence K_a, should increase in the following order, from left to right:

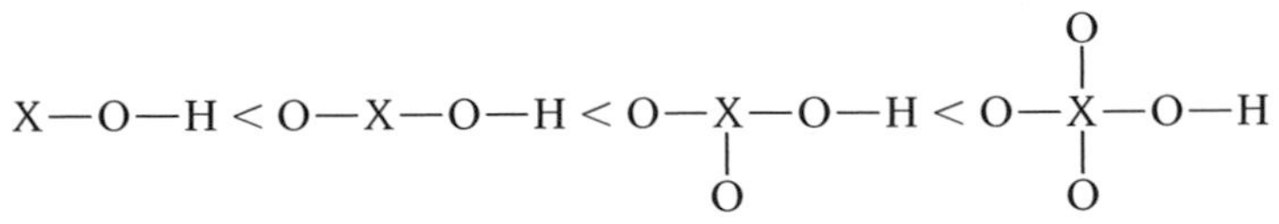

oxid. no. X = +1   +3   +5   +7

Example 21.7 Consider sulfurous acid, H_2SO_3.

(a) Show its Lewis structure and that of the HSO_3^- and SO_3^{2-} ions.
(b) How would its acid strength compare with that of H_2SO_4? H_2TeO_3?

Strategy The structure can be obtained by removing an oxygen atom from H_2SO_4 (Figure 21.8). Relative acid strengths can be predicted on the basis of the electronegativity and oxidation number of the central nonmetal atom, following the rules cited above.

SOLUTION

(a) 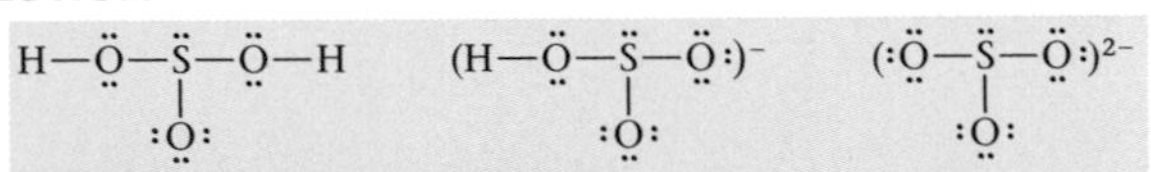

sulfurous acid   hydrogen sulfite ion   sulfite ion

(b) $H_2SO_3 < H_2SO_4$ (oxid. no. S = +4, +6)
$H_2SO_3 > H_2TeO_3$ (S more electronegative than Te)

Reality Check Both H_2SO_3 and H_2TeO_3 are weak acids; H_2SO_4 is a strong acid.

Oxidizing and Reducing Strength

Many of the reactions of oxoacids and oxoanions involve oxidation and reduction. There are certain general principles that apply, regardless of the particular species involved.

Many oxoanions are very powerful oxidizing agents.

1. ***A species in which a nonmetal is in its highest oxidation state can act only as an oxidizing agent, never as a reducing agent.*** Consider, for example, the ClO_4^- ion, in which chlorine is in its highest oxidation state, +7. In any redox reaction in which this ion takes part, chlorine must be reduced to a lower oxidation state. When that happens, the ClO_4^- ions act as an oxidizing agent, taking electrons away from something else. The same argument applies to—

- the SO_4^{2-} ion (highest oxid. no. S = +6).
- the NO_3^- ion (highest oxid. no. N = +5).

Note that, in general, *the highest oxidation number of a nonmetal is given by the second digit of its group number* (17 for Cl, 16 for S, 15 for N).

2. *A species in which a nonmetal is in an intermediate oxidation state can act as either an oxidizing agent or a reducing agent.* Consider, for example, the ClO_3^- ion (oxid. no. Cl = +5). It can be oxidized to the perchlorate ion, in which case ClO_3^- acts as a reducing agent:

$$ClO_3^-(aq) + H_2O \longrightarrow ClO_4^-(aq) + 2H^+(aq) + 2e^- \qquad E^\circ_{ox} = -1.226\text{ V}$$

Alternatively, the ClO_3^- ion can be reduced, perhaps to a Cl^- ion. When that occurs, ClO_3^- acts as an oxidizing agent:

$$ClO_3^-(aq) + 6H^+(aq) + 6e^- \longrightarrow Cl^-(aq) + 3H_2O \qquad E^\circ_{red} = +1.442\text{ V}$$

Notice that the ClO_3^- ion is a much stronger oxidizing agent ($E^\circ_{red} = +1.442$ V) than reducing agent ($E^\circ_{ox} = -1.226$ V). This is generally true of oxoanions and oxoacids in an intermediate oxidation state, at least in acidic solution. Compare, for example,

HClO	E°_{red} (to Cl_2) = +1.630 V; E°_{ox} (to $HClO_2$) = −1.157 V
HNO_2	E°_{red} (to NO) = +1.036 V; E°_{ox} (to NO_2) = −1.056 V

3. *Sometimes, with a species such as ClO_3^-, oxidation and reduction occur together, resulting in disproportionation:*

$$4ClO_3^-(aq) \longrightarrow 3ClO_4^-(aq) + Cl^-(aq) \qquad E^\circ = +0.216\text{ V}$$

In general, a ***species in an intermediate oxidation state is expected to disproportionate if the sum $E^\circ_{ox} + E^\circ_{red}$ is a positive number.***

4. *The oxidizing strength of an oxoacid or oxoanion is greatest at high [H⁺] (low pH). Conversely, its reducing strength is greatest at low [H⁺] (high pH).*

This principle has a simple explanation. Looking back at the half-equations written above, you can see that—

- when ClO_3^- acts as an oxidizing agent, the H^+ ion is a reactant, so increasing its concentration makes the process more spontaneous.
- when ClO_3^- acts as a reducing agent, the H^+ ion is a product; to make the process more spontaneous, $[H^+]$ should be lowered.

Example 21.8 Calculate E_{red} and E_{ox} for the ClO_3^- ion in neutral solution, at pH 7.00, assuming all other species are at standard concentration ($E^\circ_{red} = +1.442$ V; $E^\circ_{ox} = -1.226$ V). Will the ClO_3^- ion disproportionate at pH 7.00?

Strategy First (1) set up the Nernst equation for the reduction half-reaction and calculate E_{red}. Then (2) repeat the calculation for the oxidation half-reaction, finding E_{ox}. Finally (3), add $E_{red} + E_{ox}$; if the sum is positive, disproportionation should occur.

SOLUTION

(1) $ClO_3^-(aq) + 6H^+(aq) + 6e^- \longrightarrow Cl^-(aq) + 3H_2O$

$$E_{red} = +1.442\text{ V} - \frac{0.0257}{6}\ln\frac{1}{[H^+]^6}$$

$$= +1.442\text{ V} - \frac{0.0257}{6}\ln\frac{1}{(1.0\times10^{-7})^6}$$

$$= +1.442\text{ V} - \frac{0.0257}{6}(96.7) = +1.028\text{ V}$$

As expected, decreasing the concentration of H^+ makes the half-reaction less spontaneous and hence makes E_{red} less positive.

(2) $ClO_3^-(aq) + H_2O \longrightarrow ClO_4^-(aq) + 2H^+(aq) + 2e^-$

$$E_{ox} = -1.226\text{ V} - \frac{0.0257}{2}\ln\,[H^+]^2$$

$$= -1.226\text{ V} - \frac{0.0257}{2}\ln\,(1.0 \times 10^{-7})^2$$

$$= -1.226\text{ V} - \frac{0.0257}{2}(-32.2) = -0.812\text{ V}$$

(3) $E = +1.028\text{ V} - 0.812\text{ V} = +0.216\text{ V}$; disproportionation should occur.

Reality Check Notice that E is the same as $E°$, +0.216 V. You could have predicted that (and saved a lot of work!), because the overall equation for disproportionation

$$4ClO_3^-(aq) \longrightarrow 3ClO_4^-(aq) + Cl^-(aq)$$

does not involve H^+ or OH^- ions.

Nitric Acid, HNO_3

Commercially, nitric acid is made by a three-step process developed by the German physical chemist Wilhelm Ostwald (1853–1932). The starting material is ammonia, which is burned in an excess of air at 900°C, using a platinum-rhodium catalyst:

$$4NH_3(g) + 5O_2(g) \longrightarrow 4NO(g) + 6H_2O(g)$$

The gaseous mixture formed is cooled and mixed with more air to convert NO to NO_2:

$$2NO(g) + O_2(g) \longrightarrow 2NO_2(g)$$

Finally, nitrogen dioxide is bubbled through water to produce nitric acid:

$$3NO_2(g) + H_2O(l) \longrightarrow NO(g) + 2HNO_3(aq)$$

Nitric acid is a strong acid, completely ionized to H^+ and NO_3^- ions in dilute water solution:

$$HNO_3(aq) \longrightarrow H^+(aq) + NO_3^-(aq)$$

Charles D. Winters

Figure 21.9
A copper penny dissolving in nitric acid. Copper metal is comparatively inactive, but it reacts with concentrated nitric acid. The brown fumes are $NO_2(g)$, a reduction product of HNO_3. The copper is oxidized to Cu^{2+} ions, which impart their color to the solution. (The penny is an old one made of solid copper. Newer pennies have a coating of copper over a zinc core.)

Many of the reactions of nitric acid are those associated with all strong acids. For example, dilute (6 M) nitric acid can be used to dissolve aluminum hydroxide

$$Al(OH)_3(s) + 3H^+(aq) \longrightarrow Al^{3+}(aq) + 3H_2O$$

or to generate carbon dioxide gas from calcium carbonate:

$$CaCO_3(s) + 2H^+(aq) \longrightarrow Ca^{2+}(aq) + CO_2(g) + H_2O$$

Referring back to Example 21.4, you will find that these equations are identical with those written for the reactions of hydrochloric acid with $Al(OH)_3$ and $CaCO_3$. It is the H^+ ion that reacts in either case: Cl^- and NO_3^- ions take no part in the reactions and hence do not appear in the equation.

Concentrated (16 M) nitric acid is a strong oxidizing agent; the nitrate ion is reduced to nitrogen dioxide. This happens when 16 M HNO_3 reacts with copper metal (Figure 21.9):

$$Cu(s) + 4H^+(aq) + 2NO_3^-(aq) \longrightarrow Cu^{2+}(aq) + 2NO_2(g) + 2H_2O$$

You can always smell NO_2 over 16 M HNO_3.

Dilute nitric acid (6 M) gives a wide variety of reduction products, depending on the nature of the reducing agent. With inactive metals such as copper ($E°_{ox} = -0.339$ V), the major product is usually NO (oxid. no. N = +2):

$$3Cu(s) + 2NO_3^-(aq) + 8H^+(aq) \longrightarrow 3Cu^{2+}(aq) + 2NO(g) + 4H_2O$$

With very dilute acid and a strong reducing agent such as zinc ($E°_{ox} = +0.762$ V) reduction may go all the way to the NH_4^+ ion (oxid. no. N = −3):

$$4Zn(s) + NO_3^-(aq) + 10H^+(aq) \longrightarrow 4Zn^{2+}(aq) + NH_4^+(aq) + 3H_2O$$

As you would expect, the oxidizing strength of the NO_3^- ion drops off sharply as pH increases; the reduction voltage (to NO) is +0.964 V at pH 0, +0.412 V at pH 7, and −0.140 V at pH 14. The nitrate ion is a very weak oxidizing agent in basic solution.

Example 21.9 Write a balanced net ionic equation for the reaction of nitric acid with insoluble copper(II) sulfide; the products include Cu^{2+}, $S(s)$, and $NO_2(g)$.

Strategy Follow the general procedure for writing and balancing redox equations in Chapter 4 and reviewed in Chapter 18. Note that because nitric acid is strong, it should be represented as H^+ and NO_3^- ions.

SOLUTION

(1) The "skeleton" half-equations are

$$\text{oxidation:} \quad CuS(s) \longrightarrow S(s)$$
$$\text{reduction:} \quad NO_3^-(aq) \longrightarrow NO_2(g)$$

(2) The balanced half-equations are

$$\text{oxidation:} \quad CuS(s) \longrightarrow Cu^{2+}(aq) + S(s) + 2e^-$$
$$\text{reduction:} \quad NO_3^-(aq) + 2H^+(aq) + e^- \longrightarrow NO_2(g) + H_2O$$

(3) Multiplying the reduction half-equation by 2 and adding to the oxidation half-equation, you should obtain, after simplification,

$$CuS(s) + 2NO_3^-(aq) + 4H^+(aq) \longrightarrow Cu^{2+}(aq) + S(s) + 2NO_2(g) + 2H_2O$$

Concentrated nitric acid (16 *M*) is colorless when pure. In sunlight, it turns yellow (Figure 21.10) because it decomposes to $NO_2(g)$:

$$4HNO_3(aq) \longrightarrow 4NO_2(g) + 2H_2O + O_2(g)$$

The yellow color that appears on your skin if it comes in contact with nitric acid has quite a different explanation. Nitric acid reacts with proteins to give a yellow material called xanthoprotein.

Charles D. Winters

Figure 21.10
Nitric acid.

Sulfuric Acid, H_2SO_4

Sulfuric acid is made commercially by a three-step *contact process.* First, elemental sulfur is burned in air to form sulfur dioxide:

$$S(s) + O_2(g) \longrightarrow SO_2(g)$$

The sulfur dioxide is converted to sulfur trioxide by bringing it into contact with oxygen on the surface of a solid catalyst:

$$SO_2(g) + \tfrac{1}{2}O_2(g) \longrightarrow SO_3(g)$$

The catalyst used is divanadium pentoxide, V_2O_5, at a temperature of 450°C to 600°C. Sulfur trioxide is an acidic oxide that reacts with water to form sulfuric acid.

$$SO_3(g) + H_2O(l) \longrightarrow H_2SO_4(l)$$

Sulfuric acid is a strong acid, completely ionized to H^+ and HSO_4^- ions in dilute water solution. The HSO_4^- ion, in contrast, is only partially ionized.

$$H_2SO_4(aq) \longrightarrow H^+(aq) + HSO_4^-(aq) \qquad K_a \longrightarrow \infty$$
$$HSO_4^-(aq) \rightleftharpoons H^+(aq) + SO_4^{2-}(aq) \qquad K_a = 1.0 \times 10^{-2}$$

Most of the H^+ ions come from the first ionization; in 0.10 M H_2SO_4, $[H^+] = 0.11\ M$.

Sulfuric acid is a relatively weak oxidizing agent; most often it is reduced to sulfur dioxide:

$$SO_4^{2-}(aq) + 4H^+(aq) + 2e^- \longrightarrow SO_2(g) + 2H_2O \qquad E^\circ_{red} = +0.155\ V$$

This is the case when copper metal is oxidized by hot concentrated sulfuric acid:

$$Cu(s) + 4H^+(aq) + SO_4^{2-}(aq) \longrightarrow Cu^{2+}(aq) + 2H_2O + SO_2(g)$$

When dilute sulfuric acid (3 M) reacts with metals, it is ordinarily the H^+ ion rather than the SO_4^{2-} ion that is reduced. For example, zinc reacts with dilute sulfuric acid to form hydrogen gas:

$$Zn(s) + 2H^+(aq) \longrightarrow Zn^{2+}(aq) + H_2(g)$$

Concentrated sulfuric acid, in addition to being an acid and an oxidizing agent, is also a dehydrating agent. Small amounts of water can be removed from organic liquids such as gasoline by extraction with sulfuric acid. Sometimes it is even possible to remove the elements of water from a compound by treating it with 18 M H_2SO_4. This happens with table sugar, $C_{12}H_{22}O_{11}$; the product is a black char that is mostly carbon (Figure 21.11).

$$C_{12}H_{22}O_{11}(s) \longrightarrow 12C(s) + 11H_2O$$

Figure 21.11
Sugar plus sulfuric acid.

When concentrated sulfuric acid dissolves in water, a great deal of heat is given off, nearly 100 kJ per mole of H_2SO_4. Sometimes enough heat is evolved to bring the solution to the boiling point. To prevent this and to avoid splattering, the acid should be added slowly to water, with constant stirring. If it comes in contact with the skin, concentrated sulfuric acid can cause painful chemical burns. Never add water to concentrated H_2SO_4!

Phosphoric Acid, H_3PO_4

In water solution, +5 phosphorus can be present as—

- the H_3PO_4 molecule ($K_a = 7.1 \times 10^{-3}$), which is a (relatively strong) weak acid. A 0.10 *M* solution of H_3PO_4 has a pH of 1.6.
- the $H_2PO_4^-$ ion ($K_a = 6.2 \times 10^{-8}$; $K_b = 1.4 \times 10^{-12}$) is a (very) weak acid. A 0.10 *M* solution of NaH_2PO_4 has a pH of 4.
- the HPO_4^{2-} ion ($K_a = 4.5 \times 10^{-13}$; $K_b = 1.6 \times 10^{-7}$) is a (very) weak base. A 0.10 *M* solution of Na_2HPO_4 has a pH of 10.
- the PO_4^{3-} ion ($K_b = 2.2 \times 10^{-2}$) is a (relatively strong) weak base. A 0.10 *M* solution of Na_3PO_4 has a pH of 12.7.

Of the three compounds NaH_2PO_4, Na_2HPO_4, and Na_3PO_4, two are used as cleaning agents: NaH_2PO_4 in acid-type cleaners, Na_3PO_4 in strongly basic cleaners. The principal use of Na_2HPO_4 is in the manufacture of cheese; almost a century ago, J. L. Kraft discovered that this compound is an excellent emulsifying agent. To this day no one quite understands why this happens.

A great many "phosphates" are used in commercial fertilizers. Perhaps the most important of these is calcium dihydrogen phosphate, $Ca(H_2PO_4)_2$. In relatively pure form, this compound is known as "triple superphosphate of lime." A 1:2 mol mixture of $Ca(H_2PO_4)_2$ and gypsum, $CaSO_4 \cdot 2H_2O$, is commonly referred to as "superphosphate of lime."

CHEMISTRY Beyond the Classroom

Arsenic and Selenium

Arsenic and selenium, which fall directly below phosphorus and sulfur in the periodic table, are of interest for a variety of reasons. Arsenic is a true metalloid. A metallic form, called gray arsenic, has an electrical conductivity approaching that of lead. Another allotrope, yellow arsenic, is distinctly nonmetallic; it has the molecular formula As_4, analogous to white phosphorus, P_4. Selenium is properly classified as a nonmetal, although one of its allotropes has a somewhat metallic appearance and is a semiconductor. Another form of selenium has the molecular formula Se_8, analogous to sulfur.

The principal use of elemental arsenic is in its alloys with lead. Lead shot, formed by allowing drops of molten metal to fall through air, contains from 0.5% to 2.0% arsenic. Selenium has long been used as an additive in glassmaking. Particles of colloidally dispersed selenium give the ruby red color seen in traffic lights and stained glass windows (Figure A).

Physiological Properties

The "arsenic poison" referred to in true-crime dramas is actually the oxide of arsenic, As_2O_3, rather than the element itself. Less than 0.1 g of this white, slightly soluble powder can be fatal. The classic symptoms of acute arsenic poisoning involve various unpleasant gastrointestinal disturbances, severe abdominal pain, and burning of the mouth and throat.

In the modern forensic chemistry laboratory (Figure B) arsenic is detected by analysis of hair samples, where the element tends to concentrate in chronic arsenic poisoning. A single strand of hair is sufficient to establish the presence or absence of the element. The technique most commonly used is neutron activation analysis, described in Chapter 19. If the concentration found is greater than about 0.0003%, poisoning is indicated; normal arsenic levels are much lower than this.

David Michael Davies/FPG International

Figure A
Stained glass colors. Addition of a selenium compound produces red glass, and an addition of a cobalt compound produces blue glass.

(Continued)

This technique was applied in the early 1960s to a lock of hair taken from Napoleon Bonaparte (1769–1821) on St. Helena. Arsenic levels of up to 50 times normal suggested he may have been a victim of poisoning, perhaps on orders from the French royal family.

Arsenic is a known human carcinogen, found in drinking water in many parts of the world. The World Health Organization (WHO) has set the upper limit for arsenic in drinking water at ten parts per billion (10 ppb). The legal limit in the United States, set by the Environmental Protection Agency (EPA) is 50 ppb.

It has long been known that high concentrations of selenium are toxic. The cattle disease known picturesquely as "blind staggers" arises from grazing on grass growing in soil with a high selenium content. It is now known, however, that selenium is an essential element in human nutrition. A selenium-containing enzyme, glutathione peroxidase, in combination with vitamin E, destroys harmful free radicals in the body.

There is considerable evidence to suggest that selenium compounds are anticarcinogens. For one thing, tests with laboratory animals show that the incidence and size of malignant tumors are reduced when a solution containing Na_2SeO_3 is injected at the part per million level. Beyond that evidence, statistical studies show an inverse correlation between selenium levels in the soil and the incidence of certain types of cancer.

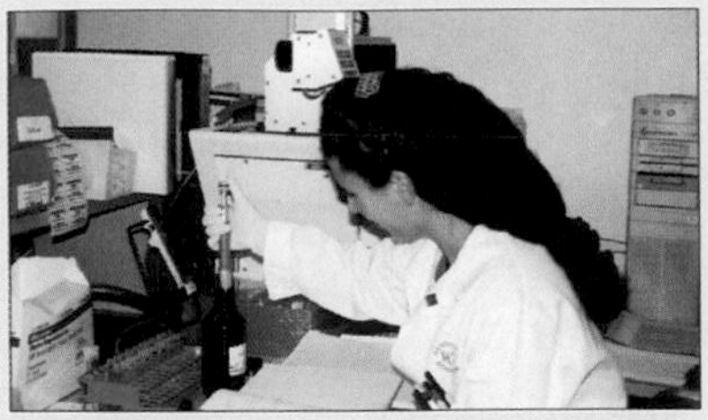
Photo courtesy of S. Ruven Smith

Figure B
A forensic toxicology laboratory. The young woman is working on a research project in the laboratory at Hartford Hospital.

Chapter Highlights

Key Concepts

Select end of chapter Questions and Problems may be assigned in OWL and are cross-referenced in the Key Concepts list.

CENGAGENOW™

Sign in at **academic.cengage.com/now** to:

- Check your readiness for an exam by taking the Pre-Test and exploring the self-study modules recommended in your Personalized Study plan
- For quick review, download Go Chemistry mini-lecture flashcard modules (or purchase them at **www.ichapters.com**)

1. Carry out equilibrium calculations for solution reactions.
   (Example 21.1; Problems 43–48) ■ Questions and Problems assignable in OWL: 44
2. Apply the Gibbs-Helmholtz equation.
   (Example 21.2; Problems 49–54) ■ 50, 54
3. Write balanced net ionic equations for solution reactions.
   (Examples 21.3, 21.5, 21.10; Problems 15–26) ■ 16, 18, 20, 24
4. Draw Lewis structures for compounds of the nonmetals.
   (Examples 21.6, 21.8; Problems 27–34) ■ 28, 31
5. Relate oxoacids to the corresponding oxides and compare their acid strengths.
   (Examples 21.7, 21.8; Problems 7, 8, 63) ■ 63
6. Carry out electrochemical calculations involving $E°$, the Nernst equation, and/or electrolysis.
   (Examples 21.4, 21.9; Problems 55–62) ■ 56

Summary Problem

Consider bromine, whose chemistry is quite similar to that of chlorine.

(a) Write equations for the reaction of bromine with I^- ions; for the reaction of Br_2 with water (disproportionation).
(b) Write equations for the preparation of bromine by the electrolysis of aqueous NaBr, by the reaction of chlorine with bromide ions in aqueous solution.
(c) Write equations for the reaction of hydrobromic acid with OH^- ions; with CO_3^{2-} ions; with ammonia.
(d) Consider the species Br^-, Br_2, BrO^-, BrO_4^-. In a redox reaction, which of these species can act only as an oxidizing agent? Only as a reducing agent? Which can act as either oxidizing or reducing agents?
(e) When aqueous sodium bromide is heated with a concentrated solution of sulfuric acid, the products include liquid bromine and sulfur dioxide. Write a balanced equation for the redox reaction involved.
(f) Write Lewis structures for the following species: Br^-, BrO^-, BrO_4^-. What is the bond angle in the BrO_4^- ion? For which of these ions is the conjugate acid the weakest?
(g) Give the formula for the acidic oxide of HBrO. Knowing that K_a of HBrO is 2.6×10^{-9}, calculate the ratio $[HBrO]/[BrO^-]$ at pH 10.00.
(h) For the reduction of HBrO to Br^-, what is the change in voltage when the pH increases by one unit?

Answers

(a) $Br_2(l) + 2I^-(aq) \longrightarrow 2Br^-(aq) + I_2(s)$
$Br_2(l) + H_2O \longrightarrow HBrO(aq) + H^+(aq) + Br^-(aq)$
(b) $2Br^-(aq) + 2H_2O \longrightarrow Br_2(l) + H_2(g) + 2OH^-(aq)$
$2Br^-(aq) + Cl_2(aq) \longrightarrow Br_2(l) + 2Cl^-(aq)$

(c) $H^+(aq) + OH^-(aq) \longrightarrow H_2O$; $2H^+(aq) + CO_3^{2-}(aq) \longrightarrow CO_2(g) + H_2O$
$H^+(aq) + NH_3(aq) \longrightarrow NH_4^+(aq)$

(d) BrO_4^-; Br^-; Br_2 or BrO^-

(e) $2Br^-(aq) + SO_4^{2-}(aq) + 4H^+(aq) \longrightarrow Br_2(l) + SO_2(g) + 2H_2O$

(f) 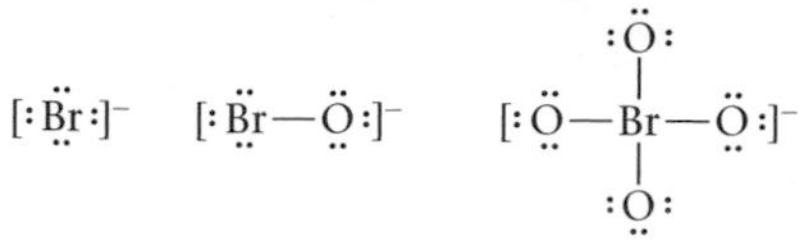 109.5°; BrO^-

(g) Br_2O; 0.038

(h) −0.0296 V

Questions and Problems

Blue-numbered questions have answers in Appendix 6 and fully-worked solutions in the *Student Solutions Manual.*

■ denotes questions assignable in OWL.

WEB indicates that the solution is available on this book's companion website.

Formulas, Equations, and Reactions

1. Name the following species.
(a) HIO_4 **(b)** BrO_2^- **(c)** HIO **(d)** $NaClO_3$

2. ■ Name the following compounds.
(a) $HBrO_3$ **(b)** KIO **(c)** $NaClO_2$ **(d)** $NaBrO_4$

3. Write the formula for each of the following compounds.
(a) chloric acid **(b)** periodic acid
(c) hypobromous acid **(d)** hydriodic acid

4. ■ Write the formula for each of the following compounds.
(a) potassium bromite **(b)** calcium bromide
(c) sodium periodate **(d)** magnesium hypochlorite

5. Write the formula of a compound of each of the following elements that *cannot* act as an oxidizing agent.
(a) N **(b)** S **(c)** Cl

6. Write the formula of an oxoanion of each of the following elements that *cannot* act as a reducing agent.
(a) N **(b)** S **(c)** Cl

7. Give the formula for the acidic oxide of
(a) HNO_3 **(b)** HNO_2 **(c)** H_2SO_4

8. Write the formula of the acid formed when each of these acidic oxides reacts with water.
(a) SO_2 **(b)** Cl_2O **(c)** P_4O_6

9. Write the formulas of the following compounds.
(a) ammonia **(b)** laughing gas
(c) hydrogen peroxide **(d)** sulfur trioxide

10. ■ Write the formula for the following compounds.
(a) sodium azide **(b)** sulfurous acid
(c) hydrazine **(d)** sodium dihydrogen phosphate

11. Write the formula of a compound of hydrogen with
(a) nitrogen, which is a gas at 25°C and 1 atm.
(b) phosphorus, which is a liquid at 25°C and 1 atm.
(c) oxygen, which contains an O—O bond.

12. Write the formula of a compound of hydrogen with
(a) sulfur.
(b) nitrogen, which is a liquid at 25°C and 1 atm.
(c) phosphorus, which is a poisonous gas at 25°C and 1 atm.

13. Give the formula of
(a) an anion in which S has an oxidation number of −2.
(b) two anions in which S has an oxidation number of +4.
(c) two different acids of sulfur.

14. Give the formula of a compound of nitrogen that is
(a) a weak base. **(b)** a strong acid.
(c) a weak acid. **(d)** capable of oxidizing copper.

15. Write a balanced net ionic equation for
(a) the electrolytic decomposition of hydrogen fluoride.
(b) the oxidation of iodide ion to iodine by hydrogen peroxide in acidic solution. Hydrogen peroxide is reduced to water.

16. ■ Write a balanced net ionic equation for
(a) the oxidation of iodide to iodine by sulfate ion in acidic solution. Sulfur dioxide gas is also produced.
(b) The preparation of iodine from an iodide salt and chlorine gas.

17. Write a balanced net ionic equation for the disproportionation reaction
(a) of iodine to give iodate and iodide ions in basic solution.
(b) of chlorine gas to chloride and perchlorate ions in basic solution.

18. ■ Write a balanced net ionic equation for the disproportionation reaction of
(a) hypochlorous acid to chlorine gas and chlorous acid in acidic solution.
(b) chlorate ion to perchlorate and chlorite ions.

19. Complete and balance the following equations. If no reaction occurs, write NR.
(a) $Cl_2(g) + I^-(aq) \longrightarrow$ **(b)** $F_2(g) + Br^-(aq) \longrightarrow$
(c) $I_2(s) + Cl^-(aq) \longrightarrow$ **(d)** $Br_2(l) + I^-(aq) \longrightarrow$

20. ■ **WEB** Complete and balance the following equations. If no reaction occurs, write NR.
(a) $Cl_2(g) + Br^-(aq) \longrightarrow$ **(b)** $I_2(s) + Cl^-(aq) \longrightarrow$
(c) $I_2(s) + Br^-(aq) \longrightarrow$ **(d)** $Br_2(l) + Cl^-(aq) \longrightarrow$

21. Write a balanced equation for the preparation of
(a) F_2 from HF **(b)** Br_2 from NaBr
(c) NH_4^+ from NH_3

22. Write a balanced equation for the preparation of
(a) N_2 from $Pb(N_3)_2$ **(b)** O_2 from O_3
(c) S from H_2S

23. Write a balanced equation for the reaction of ammonia with
(a) Cu^{2+} **(b)** H^+ **(c)** Al^{3+}

24. ■ Write a balanced equation for the reaction of hydrogen sulfide with
(a) Cd^{2+} **(b)** OH^- **(c)** $O_2(g)$

25. Write a balanced net ionic equation for the reaction of nitric acid with
(a) a solution of $Ca(OH)_2$.
(b) Ag(*s*); assume the nitrate ion is reduced to $NO_2(g)$
(c) Cd(*s*); assume the nitrate ion is reduced to $N_2(g)$.

26. Write a balanced net ionic equation for the reaction of sulfuric acid with
(a) $CaCO_3(s)$.
(b) a solution of NaOH.
(c) Cu; assume the SO_4^{2-} ion is reduced to SO_2.

Molecular Structure

27. Give the Lewis structure of
    (a) NO_2 (b) NO (c) SO_2 (d) SO_3
28. ■ Give the Lewis structure of
    (a) Cl_2O (b) N_2O (c) P_4 (d) N_2
29. Which of the molecules in Question 27 are polar?
30. Which of the molecules in Question 28 are polar?
31. ■ Give the Lewis structure of
    (a) HNO_3 (b) H_2SO_4 (c) H_3PO_4
32. **WEB** Give the Lewis structures of the conjugate bases of the species in Question 31.
33. Give the Lewis structure of
    (a) the strongest oxoacid of bromine.
    (b) a hydrogen compound of nitrogen in which there is an —N—N— bond.
    (c) an acid added to cola drinks.
34. Give the Lewis structure of
    (a) an oxide of nitrogen in the +5 state.
    (b) the strongest oxoacid of nitrogen.
    (c) a tetrahedral oxoanion of sulfur.

Stoichiometry

35. ■ The average concentration of bromine (as bromide) in seawater is 65 ppm. Calculate
    (a) the volume of seawater ($d = 64.0$ lb/ft^3) in cubic feet required to produce one kilogram of liquid bromine.
    (b) the volume of chlorine gas in liters, measured at 20°C and 762 mm Hg, required to react with this volume of sea water.
36. A 425-gal tank is filled with water containing 175 g of sodium iodide. How many liters of chlorine gas at 758 mm Hg and 25°C will be required to oxidize all the iodide to iodine?
37. Iodine can be prepared by allowing an aqueous solution of hydrogen iodide to react with manganese dioxide, MnO_2. The reaction is

$$2I^-(aq) + 4H^+(aq) + MnO_2(s) \longrightarrow Mn^{2+}(aq) + 2H_2O + I_2(s)$$

If an excess of hydrogen iodide is added to 0.200 g of MnO_2, how many grams of iodine are obtained, assuming 100% yield?

38. When a solution of hydrogen bromide is prepared, 1.283 L of HBr gas at 25°C and 0.974 atm is bubbled into 250.0 mL of water. Assuming all the HBr dissolves with no volume change, what is the molarity of the hydrobromic acid solution produced?
39. When ammonium nitrate explodes, nitrogen, steam, and oxygen gas are produced. If the explosion is carried out by heating one kilogram of ammonium nitrate sealed in a rigid bomb with a volume of one liter, what is the total pressure produced by the gases before the bomb ruptures? Assume that the reaction goes to completion and that the final temperature is 500°C. (3 significant figures)
40. ■ Sulfur dioxide can be removed from the smokestack emissions of power plants by reacting it with hydrogen sulfide, producing sulfur and water. What volume of hydrogen sulfide at 27°C and 755 mm Hg is required to remove the sulfur dioxide produced by a power plant that burns one metric ton of coal containing 5.0% sulfur by mass? How many grams of sulfur are produced by the reaction of H_2S with SO_2?
41. A 1.500-g sample containing sodium nitrate was heated to form $NaNO_2$ and O_2. The oxygen evolved was collected over water at 23°C and 752 mm Hg; its volume was 125.0 mL. Calculate the percentage of $NaNO_3$ in the sample. The vapor pressure of water at 23°C is 21.07 mm Hg.
42. ■ Chlorine can remove the foul smell of H_2S in water. The reaction is

$$H_2S(aq) + Cl_2(aq) \longrightarrow 2H^+(aq) + 2Cl^-(aq) + S(s)$$

If the contaminated water has 5.0 ppm hydrogen sulfide by mass, what volume of chlorine gas at STP is required to remove all the H_2S from 1.00×10^3 gallons of water ($d = 1.00$ g/mL)? What is the pH of the solution after treatment with chlorine?

Equilibria

43. The equilibrium constant at 25°C for the reaction

$$Br_2(l) + H_2O \rightleftharpoons H^+(aq) + Br^-(aq) + HBrO(aq)$$

is 1.2×10^{-9}. This is the system present in a bottle of "bromine water." Assuming that HBrO does not ionize appreciably, what is the pH of the bromine water?

44. ■ Calculate the pH and the equilibrium concentration of HClO in a 0.10 *M* solution of hypochlorous acid. K_a HClO $= 2.8 \times 10^{-8}$.
45. At equilibrium, a gas mixture has a partial pressure of 0.7324 atm for HBr and 2.80×10^{-3} atm for both hydrogen and bromine gases. What is *K* for the formation of two moles of HBr from H_2 and Br_2?
46. Given

$$HF(aq) \rightleftharpoons H^+(aq) + F^-(aq) \qquad K_a = 6.9 \times 10^{-4}$$

$$HF(aq) + F^-(aq) \rightleftharpoons HF_2^-(aq) \qquad K = 2.7$$

calculate *K* for the reaction

$$2HF(aq) \rightleftharpoons H^+(aq) + HF_2^-(aq)$$

47. What is the concentration of fluoride ion in a water solution saturated with BaF_2, $K_{sp} = 1.8 \times 10^{-7}$?
48. Calculate the solubility in grams per 100 mL of BaF_2 in a 0.10 *M* $BaCl_2$ solution.

Thermodynamics

49. Determine whether the following redox reaction is spontaneous at 25°C and 1 atm:

$$2KIO_3(s) + Cl_2(g) \longrightarrow 2KClO_3(s) + I_2(s)$$

Use data in Appendix 1 and the following information: ΔH_f° $KIO_3(s) = -501.4$ kJ/mol, S° $KIO_3(s) = 151.5$ J/mol·K. What is the lowest temperature at which the reaction is spontaneous?

50. ■ Follow the directions for Problem 49 for the reaction

$$2KBrO_3(s) + Cl_2(g) \longrightarrow 2KClO_3(s) + Br_2(l)$$

The following thermodynamic data may be useful:

$$\Delta H_f^\circ\ KBrO_3 = -360.2 \text{ kJ/mol}; S^\circ\ KBrO_3 = 149.2 \text{ J/mol·K}$$

51. Consider the equilibrium system

$$HF(aq) \rightleftharpoons H^+(aq) + F^-(aq)$$

Given ΔH_f° HF(*aq*) $= -320.1$ kJ/mol,

$$\Delta H_f^\circ F^-(aq) = -332.6 \text{ kJ/mol}; S^\circ\ F^-(aq) = -13.8 \text{ J/mol·K};$$

$$K_a\ HF = 6.9 \times 10^{-4} \text{ at } 25°C$$

calculate S° for HF(*aq*).

52. Applying the Tables in Appendix 1 to

$$4HCl(g) + O_2(g) \longrightarrow 2Cl_2(g) + 2H_2O(l)$$

determine
    (a) whether the reaction is spontaneous at 25°C and 1 atm.
    (b) *K* for the reaction at 25°C.

■ in OWL Blue-numbered questions answered in Appendix 6 **WEB** Solution is available on companion website

53. Consider the reaction

$$4NH_3(g) + 5O_2(g) \longrightarrow 4NO(g) + 6H_2O(g)$$

(a) Calculate ΔH° for this reaction. Is it exothermic or endothermic?
(b) Would you expect ΔS° to be positive or negative? Calculate ΔS°.
(c) Is the reaction spontaneous at 25°C and 1 atm?
(d) At what temperature, if any, is the reaction at equilibrium at 1 atm pressure?

54. ■ Data are given in Appendix 1 for white phosphorus, $P_4(s)$. $P_4(g)$ has the following thermodynamic values: $\Delta H_f^\circ = 58.9$ kJ/mol, $S^\circ = 280.0$ J/K·mol. What is the temperature at which white phosphorus sublimes at 1 atm pressure?

Electrochemistry

55. In the electrolysis of a KI solution, using 5.00 V, how much electrical energy in kilojoules is consumed when one mole of I_2 is formed?

56. ■ If an electrolytic cell producing fluorine uses a current of 7.00×10^3 A (at 10.0 V), how many grams of fluorine gas can be produced in two days (assuming that the cell operates continuously at 95% efficiency)?

57. Sodium hypochlorite is produced by the electrolysis of cold sodium chloride solution. How long must a cell operate to produce 1.500×10^3 L of 5.00% NaClO by mass if the cell current is 2.00×10^3 A? Assume that the density of the solution is 1.00 g/cm³.

58. Sodium perchlorate is produced by the electrolysis of sodium chlorate. If a current of 1.50×10^3 A passes through an electrolytic cell, how many kilograms of sodium perchlorate are produced in an eight-hour run?

59. Taking E°_{ox} $H_2O_2 = -0.695$ V, determine which of the following species will be reduced by hydrogen peroxide (use Table 18.1 to find E°_{red} values).

(a) $Cr_2O_7^{2-}$ (b) Fe^{2+} (c) I_2 (d) Br_2

60. Taking E°_{red} $H_2O_2 = +1.763$ V, determine which of the following species will be oxidized by hydrogen peroxide (use Table 18.1 to find E°_{ox} values).

(a) Co^{2+} (b) Cl^- (c) Fe^{2+} (d) Sn^{2+}

61. Consider the reduction of nitrate ion in acidic solution to nitrogen oxide ($E^\circ_{red} = 0.964$ V) by sulfur dioxide that is oxidized to sulfate ion ($E^\circ_{red} = 0.155$ V). Calculate the voltage of a cell involving this reaction in which all the gases have pressures of 1.00 atm, all the ionic species (except H^+) are at 0.100 *M*, and the pH is 4.30.

62. For the reaction in Problem 61 if gas pressures are at 1.00 atm and ionic species are at 0.100 *M* (except H^+), at what pH will the voltage be 1.000 V?

Unclassified

63. ■ Choose the strongest acid from each group.

(a) HClO, HBrO, HIO (b) HIO, HIO_3, HIO_4
(c) HIO, $HBrO_2$, $HBrO_4$

64. What intermolecular forces are present in the following?

(a) Cl_2 (b) HBr (c) HF
(d) $HClO_4$ (e) MgI_2

65. Write a balanced equation for the reaction of hydrofluoric acid with SiO_2. What volume of 2.0 *M* HF is required to react with one gram of silicon dioxide?

66. ■ State the oxidation number of N in

(a) NO_2^- (b) NO_2 (c) HNO_3 (d) NH_4^+

67. The density of sulfur vapor at one atmosphere pressure and 973 K is 0.8012 g/L. What is the molecular formula of the vapor?

68. Give the formula of a substance discussed in this chapter that is used

(a) to disinfect water. (b) in safety matches.
(c) to prepare hydrazine. (d) to etch glass.

69. Why does concentrated nitric acid often have a yellow color even though pure HNO_3 is colorless?

70. **WEB** Explain why

(a) acid strength increases as the oxidation number of the central nonmetal atom increases.
(b) nitrogen dioxide is paramagnetic.
(c) the oxidizing strength of an oxoanion is inversely related to pH.
(d) sugar turns black when treated with concentrated sulfuric acid.

Challenge Problems

71. Suppose you wish to calculate the mass of sulfuric acid that can be obtained from an underground deposit of sulfur 1.00 km² in area. What additional information do you need to make this calculation?

72. ■ The reaction

$$4HF(aq) + SiO_2(aq) \longrightarrow SiF_4(aq) + 2H_2O$$

can be used to release gold that is distributed in certain quartz (SiO_2) veins of hydrothermal origin. If the quartz contains 1.0×10^{-3}% Au by weight and the gold has a market value of \$425 per troy ounce, would the process be economically feasible if commercial HF (50% by weight, $d = 1.17$ g/cm³) costs 75¢ a liter? (1 troy ounce = 31.1 g.)

73. The amount of sodium hypochlorite in a bleach solution can be determined by using a given volume of bleach to oxidize excess iodide ion to iodine; ClO^- is reduced to Cl^-. The amount of iodine produced by the redox reaction is determined by titration with sodium thiosulfate, $Na_2S_2O_3$; I_2 is reduced to I^-. The sodium thiosulfate is oxidized to sodium tetrathionate, $Na_2S_4O_6$. In this analysis, potassium iodide was added in excess to 5.00 mL of bleach ($d = 1.00$ g/cm³). If 25.00 mL of 0.0700 *M* $Na_2S_2O_3$ was required to reduce all the iodine produced by the bleach back to iodide, what is the mass percent of NaClO in the bleach?

74. ■ What is the minimum amount of sodium azide, NaN_3, that can be added to an automobile airbag to give a volume of 20.0 L of $N_2(g)$ on inflation? Make any reasonable assumptions required to obtain an answer, but state what these assumptions are.

■ in OWL Blue-numbered questions answered in Appendix 6 **WEB** Solution is available on companion website

22 Organic Chemistry

What is life? It is the flash of a firefly in the night.
It is the breath of a buffalo in the wintertime.
It is the little shadow which runs across grass
And loses itself in the sunset.

—Dying words of Crowfoot (1890)

Chapter Outline

The wine in the goblet can be produced by the fermentation of glucose (present in all the fruits shown in the painting) to ethyl alcohol.

"Still Life with Fruit and a Wine Glass" by Severin Roesen/The Philadelphia Museum of Art/Art Resource, NY

Organic chemistry deals with the compounds of carbon, of which there are literally millions. More than 90% of all known compounds contain carbon atoms. There is a simple explanation for this remarkable fact. Carbon atoms bond to one another to a far greater extent than do atoms of any other element. Carbon atoms may link together to form chains or rings.

Online homework for this chapter may be assigned in OWL.

CENGAGENOW™

This icon introduces an opportunity for self-study and to explore interactive modules by signing in at **academic.cengage.com/now.**

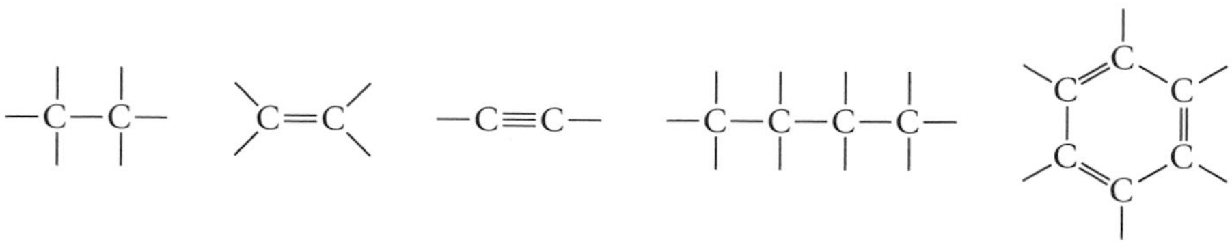

The bonds may be single (one electron pair), double (two electron pairs), or triple (three electron pairs).

There are a wide variety of different organic compounds that have quite different structures and properties. However, all these substances have certain features in common:

1. ***Organic compounds are ordinarily molecular rather than ionic.*** Most of the compounds we discuss consist of small, discrete molecules. Many of them are gases or liquids at room temperature.
2. ***Each carbon atom forms a total of four covalent bonds.*** This is illustrated by the structures written above. A particular carbon atom may form four single bonds, two single bonds and a double bond, two double bonds, or one single bond and a triple bond. One way or another, though, the bonds add up to four.
3. ***Carbon atoms may be bonded to each other or to other nonmetal atoms, most often hydrogen, a halogen, oxygen, or nitrogen.*** In most organic compounds—
   - a hydrogen or halogen atom (F, Cl, Br, I) forms one covalent bond, —H, —X
   - an oxygen atom forms two covalent bonds, —O— or =O
   - a nitrogen atom forms three covalent bonds, —N— (with a third bond below N), =N—, or ≡N

Carbon always follows the octet rule in stable compounds.

In this chapter, we consider—

- the simplest type of organic compound, called a **hydrocarbon,** which contains only two kinds of atoms, hydrogen and carbon. Hydrocarbons can be classified as alkanes (Section 22.1), alkenes and alkynes (Section 22.2), and aromatics (Section 22.3).
- organic compounds containing oxygen or nitrogen atoms in addition to carbon and hydrogen (Section 22.4).
- the phenomenon of isomerism, which is very common among organic compounds. This topic is introduced in Section 22.1 but discussed more generally in Section 22.5.
- different types of organic reactions (Section 22.6).

Throughout this chapter, we will represent molecules by *structural formulas,* which show all the bonds present. Thus we have

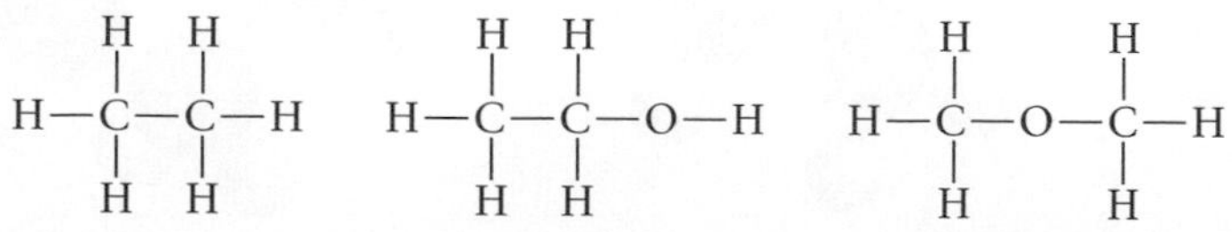

ethane ethanol dimethyl ether

To save space we often write condensed structural formulas such as

CH_3CH_3 $\quad$ CH_3CH_2OH or C_2H_5OH $\quad$ $CH_3{-}O{-}CH_3$ or $(CH_3)_2O$ ■

22.1 SATURATED HYDROCARBONS: ALKANES

One large and structurally simple class of hydrocarbons includes those substances in which all the carbon-carbon bonds are single bonds. These are called *saturated hydrocarbons,* or *alkanes.* In the alkanes the carbon atoms are bonded to each other in chains, which may be long or short, straight or branched.

The ratio of hydrogen to carbon atoms is a maximum in alkanes, hence the term "saturated" hydrocarbon. The general formula of an alkane containing n carbon atoms is

$$C_nH_{2n+2}$$

The simplest alkanes are those for which $n = 1$ (CH_4), $n = 2$ (C_2H_6), or $n = 3$ (C_3H_8):

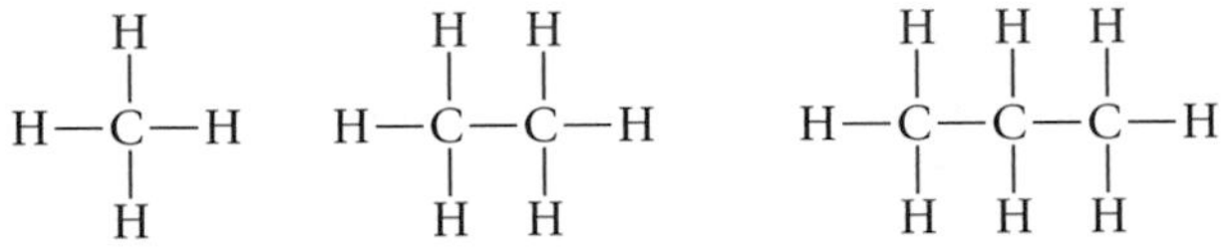

methane ethane propane

Around the carbon atoms in these molecules and indeed in any saturated hydrocarbon, there are four single bonds involving sp^3 hybrid orbitals. As would be expected from the VSEPR model, these bonds are directed toward the corners of a regular tetrahedron. The bond angles are approximately 109.5°, the tetrahedral angle. This means that in propane (C_3H_8) and in the higher alkanes, the carbon atoms are arranged in a "zigzag" pattern (Figure 22.1).

The outer surfaces of these molecules contain mainly H atoms.

Two different alkanes are known with the molecular formula C_4H_{10}. In one of these, called butane, the four carbon atoms are linked in a "straight (unbranched) chain." In the other, called 2-methylpropane, there is a "branched chain." The longest chain in the molecule contains three carbon atoms; there is a CH_3 branch from the central carbon atom. The geometries of these molecules are shown in Figure 22.2 (p. 581). The structures are

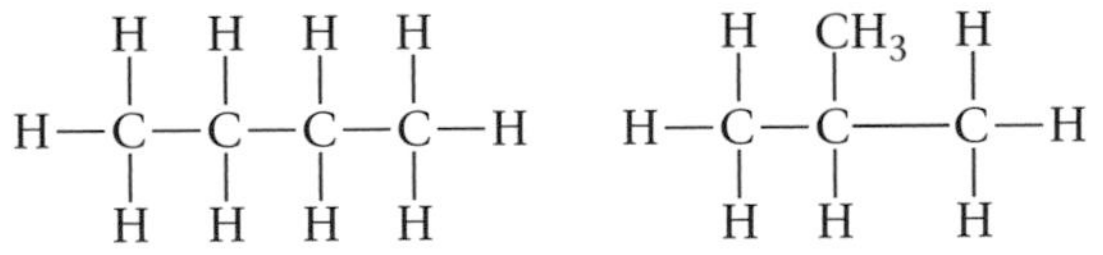

butane 2-methylpropane

Compounds having the same molecular formula but different molecular structures are called **structural isomers.** Butane and 2-methylpropane are referred to as structural isomers of C_4H_{10}. They are two distinct compounds with their own characteristic physical and chemical properties.

In structural isomers, the atoms are bonded in different patterns; the skeletons are different.

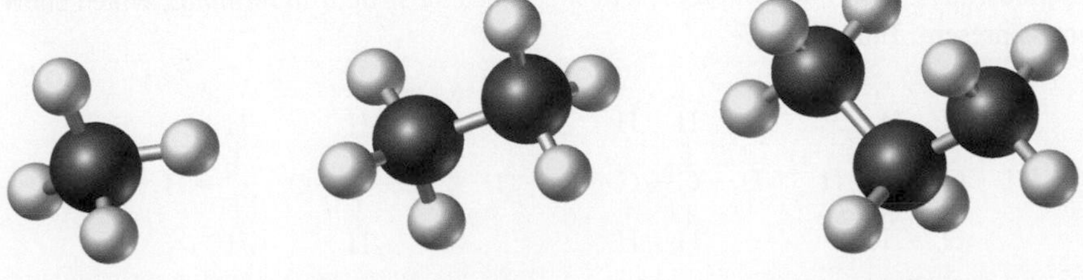

CH_4 methane $\quad$ CH_3CH_3 ethane $\quad$ $CH_3CH_2CH_3$ propane

Figure 22.1
The three simplest alkanes. The bond angles in methane, ethane, and propane are all close to 109.5°, the tetrahedral angle.

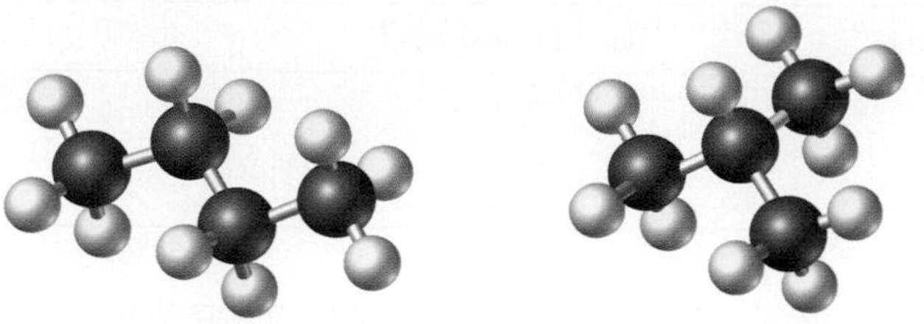

$CH_3CH_2CH_2CH_3$

butane

CH_3CHCH_3 (with CH_3 on the middle carbon)

2-methylpropane

Figure 22.2
Butane and 2-methylpropane, the isomers of C_4H_{10}.

Example 22.1

Draw structures for the isomers of C_5H_{12}.

Strategy Start with the straight-chain structure, stringing all five carbon atoms one after the other. Then work with structures containing four carbon atoms in a chain with one branch; find all the nonequivalent structures of this type. Continue this process using a three-carbon chain, which is the shortest one that can be drawn for C_5H_{12}.

SOLUTION For simplicity, we show only the carbon atoms; there is an H atom attached to each bond extending from a C atom.

five-C chain: 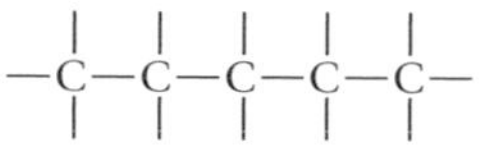 isomer (I)

four-C chain: 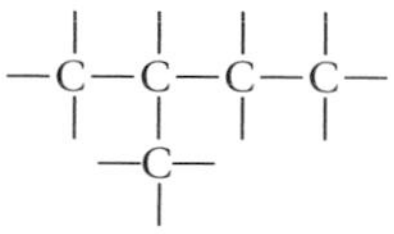 isomer (II)

three-C chain: 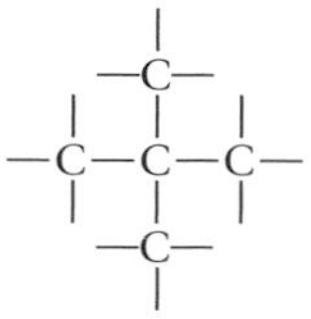 isomer (III)

Reality Check Working with only pencil and paper, you might be tempted to draw other structures, such as

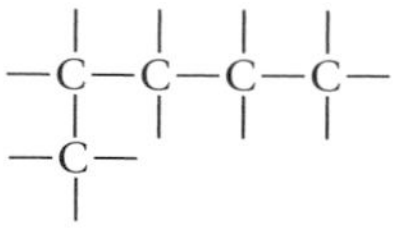

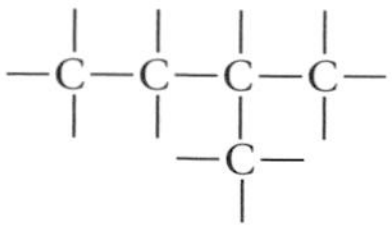

However, a few moments of reflection (or access to a molecular model kit) should convince you that these are in fact equivalent to structures written previously. In particular, the first one, like isomer I, has a five-carbon chain in which no carbon atom is attached to more than two other carbons. The second structure, like II, has a four-carbon chain with one carbon atom bonded to three other carbons. Structures I, II, and III represent the three possible isomers of C_5H_{12}; there are no others.

Remember, these molecules are three-dimensional.

If you want a really tedious job, try drawing the 366,319 structural isomers of $C_{20}H_{42}$.

Structural isomers have different properties. For example, the three isomers of C_5H_{12} listed in Example 22.1 boil at different temperatures.

Structure	Normal Boiling Point
I	36°C
II	28°C
III	10°C

In general, long "skinny" isomers like I tend to have higher boiling points than highly branched isomers like III. Dispersion forces become weaker as chain branching increases. This principle is used in the seasonal blending of gasoline. A greater percentage of more volatile, highly branched alkanes is included in winter, making combustion occur more readily at lower temperatures.

CENGAGENOW™

Click Coached Problems for a self-study module and a simulation on **naming alkanes.**

Nomenclature

As organic chemistry developed, it became apparent that some systematic way of naming compounds was needed. About 70 years ago, the International Union of Pure and Applied Chemistry (IUPAC) devised a system that could be used for all organic compounds. To illustrate this system, we will show how it works with alkanes.

For straight-chain alkanes such as

$$CH_3—CH_2—CH_3 \qquad CH_3—CH_2—CH_2—CH_3$$

propane   butane

the IUPAC name consists of a single word. These names, for up to eight carbon atoms, are listed in Table 22.1.

With alkanes containing a branched chain, such as

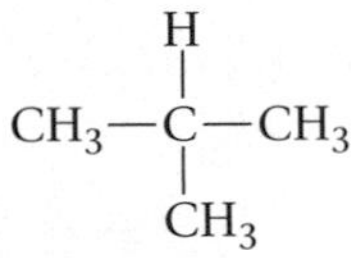

2-methylpropane

the name is more complex. A branched-chain alkane such as 2-methylpropane can be considered to be derived from a straight-chain alkane by replacing one or more hydrogen atoms by alkyl groups. The name consists of two parts—

- a **suffix** that identifies the parent straight-chain alkane. To find the suffix, count the number of carbon atoms in the longest continuous chain. For a three-carbon chain, the suffix is *propane;* for a four-carbon chain it is *butane,* and so on.
- a **prefix** that identifies the branching alkyl group (Table 22.1) and indicates by a number the carbon atom where branching occurs. In 2-methylpropane, referred to above, the methyl group is located at the second carbon from the end of the chain:

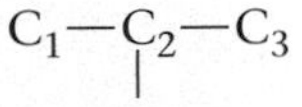

Table 22.1 Nomenclature of Alkanes

Straight-Chain Alkanes		Alkyl Groups	
Methane	CH_4	Methyl	$CH_3—$
Ethane	CH_3CH_3	Ethyl	$CH_3—CH_2—$
Propane	$CH_3CH_2CH_3$	Propyl	$CH_3—CH_2—CH_2—$
Butane	$CH_3(CH_2)_2CH_3$		
Pentane	$CH_3(CH_2)_3CH_3$	Isopropyl	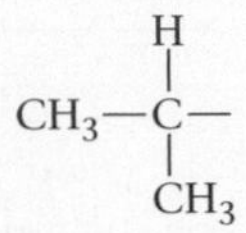
Hexane	$CH_3(CH_2)_4CH_3$		
Heptane	$CH_3(CH_2)_5CH_3$		
Octane	$CH_3(CH_2)_6CH_3$	Butyl	$CH_3—CH_2—CH_2—CH_2—$

Following this system, the IUPAC names of the isomers of pentane are

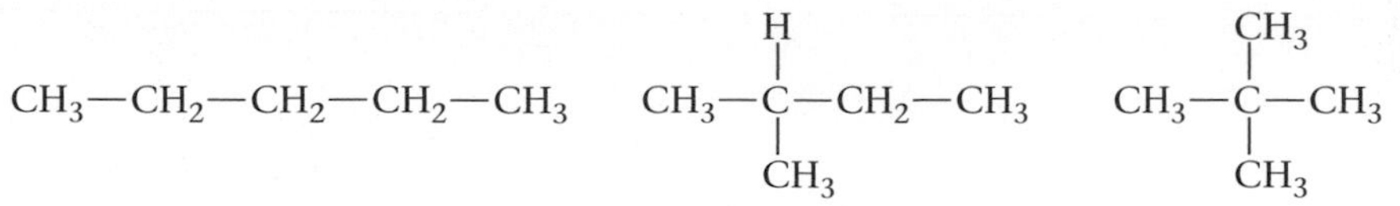

pentane — 2-methylbutane — 2,2-dimethylpropane

Notice that—

- if the same alkyl group is at two branches, the prefix *di-* is used (2,2-dimethylpropane). If there were three methyl branches, we would write trimethyl, and so on.
- the number in the name is made as small as possible. Thus, we write 2-methylbutane, numbering the chain from the left

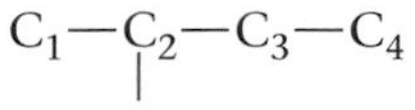

rather than from the right.

Example 22.2 Assign IUPAC names to the following:

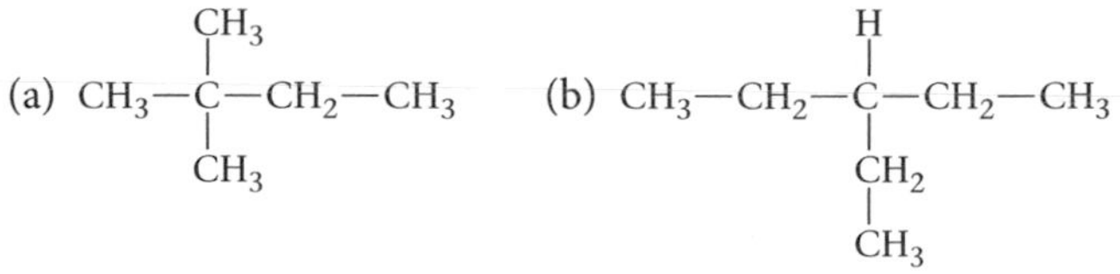

Strategy First, find the longest chain of carbon atoms. That tells you the suffix of the name, given in the far left column of Table 22.1. Then identify the prefix, or prefixes, by choosing the appropriate alkyl group from the right side of Table 22.1. Finally, number the carbon atoms as described above.

SOLUTION (a) The longest chain contains four carbon atoms (butane). There are two CH_3 (methyl) groups branching at the second carbon from the end of the chain (2). The correct name is

2,2-dimethylbutane

(b) The longest chain, however you count it, contains five carbon atoms. There is a $CH_3—CH_2$ branch at the number three carbon, whichever end of the chain you start from. The IUPAC name is

3-ethylpentane

Sources and Uses of Alkanes

Natural gas, transmitted around the United States and Canada by pipeline, consists largely of methane (80%–90%), with smaller amounts of C_2H_6, C_3H_8, and C_4H_{10}. Cylinders of "bottled gas," used with campstoves, barbecue grills, and the like, contain liquid propane (C_3H_8) and butane (C_4H_{10}) (Figure 22.3). The pressure remains constant as long as any liquid is present, then drops abruptly to zero, indicating that it's time for a recharge.

The higher alkanes are most often obtained from petroleum, a dark brown, viscous liquid dispersed through porous rock deposits. Distillation of petroleum gives a series of fractions of different boiling points (Figure 22.4, p. 584). The most important of these is gasoline; distillation of a liter of petroleum gives about 250 mL of "straight-run" gasoline. It is possible to double the yield of gasoline by converting higher- or lower-boiling fractions to hydrocarbons in the gasoline range (C_5 to C_{12}).

Figure 22.3
Bottled gas. These cylinders contain liquid propane (C_3H_8) and liquid butane (C_4H_{10}).

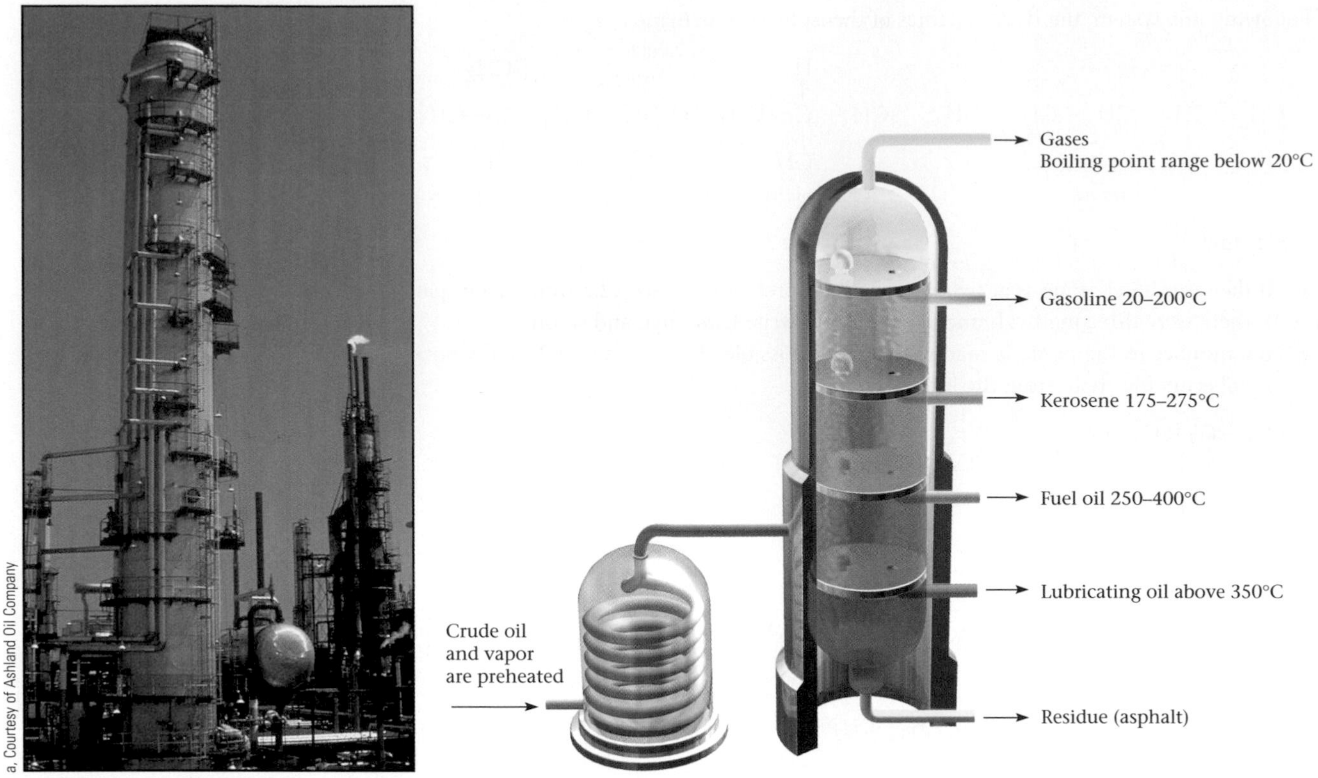

(a) (b)

Figure 22.4
Petroleum distillation. (a) A distillation tower at a petroleum refinery. (b) A diagram showing the boiling points of the petroleum fractions separated by distillation.

Gasoline-air mixtures tend to ignite prematurely, or "knock," rather than burn smoothly. The *octane number* of a gasoline is a measure of its resistance to knock. It is determined by comparing the knocking characteristics of a gasoline sample with those of isooctane (the common name of one of the isomers of octane) and heptane:

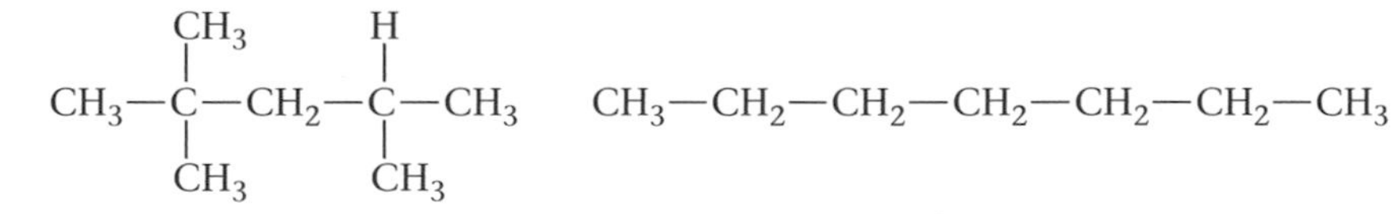

isooctane heptane

Isooctane, which is highly branched, burns smoothly with little knocking and is assigned an octane number of 100. Heptane, being unbranched, knocks badly. It is given an octane number of zero. Gasoline with the same knocking properties as a mixture of 90% isooctane and 10% heptane is rated as "90 octane."

To obtain premium gasoline of octane number above 80, it is necessary to use additives of one type or another. Until the mid-1970s, the principal antiknock agent was tetraethyllead, $(C_2H_5)_4Pb$. Its use was phased out because it poisons catalytic converters and contaminates the environment with lead compounds. To replace tetraethyllead, oxygen-containing organic compounds such as ethanol, C_2H_5OH, are added to gasoline to promote smooth, complete combustion.

Petroleum contains hydrocarbons other than the open-chain alkanes considered to this point. These include *cycloalkanes* in which 3 to 30 CH_2 groups are bonded into closed rings. The structures of the two most common hydrocarbons of this type are shown in Figure 22.5 (p. 585). Cyclopentane and cyclohexane, where the bond angles are close to the ideal tetrahedral angle of 109.5°, are stable liquids with boiling points of 49°C and 81°C, respectively.

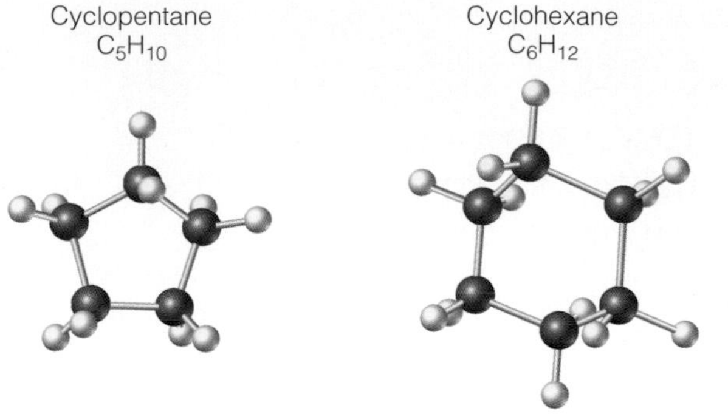

Figure 22.5
Cycloalkanes. Cyclopentane and cyclohexane, the two most common cycloalkanes.

Cycloalkanes, like alkanes, are saturated hydrocarbons containing only single bonds. Notice, though, that as a result of ring formation, each cycloalkane molecule contains two fewer hydrogen atoms than the corresponding alkane.

Number of C Atoms	3	4	5	6	*n*
Formula of alkane	C_3H_8	C_4H_{10}	C_5H_{12}	C_6H_{14}	C_nH_{2n+2}
Formula of cycloalkane	C_3H_6	C_4H_8	C_5H_{10}	C_6H_{12}	C_nH_{2n}

22.2 UNSATURATED HYDROCARBONS: ALKENES AND ALKYNES

In an *unsaturated hydrocarbon,* at least one of the carbon-carbon bonds in the molecule is a multiple bond. As a result, there are fewer hydrogen atoms in an unsaturated hydrocarbon than in a saturated one with the same number of carbons. We will consider two types of unsaturated hydrocarbons—

- **alkenes,** in which there is one carbon-carbon double bond in the molecule:

$$\rangle C{=}C \langle$$

  Replacing a single bond with a double bond eliminates two hydrogen atoms. Hence the general formula of an alkene is

$$C_nH_{2n}$$

  as compared with C_nH_{2n+2} for an alkane.
- **alkynes,** in which there is one carbon-carbon triple bond in the molecule:

$$—C{\equiv}C—$$

  Again, two hydrogen atoms are "lost" when a double bond is converted to a triple bond. Hence the general formula of an alkyne is

$$C_nH_{2n-2}$$

Example 22.3 What is the molecular formula of

(a) the alkane, alkene, and alkyne containing six carbon atoms?
(b) the alkane containing ten hydrogen atoms?

Strategy Apply the general formulas: C_nH_{2n+2} (alkane), C_nH_{2n} (alkene), C_nH_{2n-2} (alkyne).

SOLUTION

(a) In each case, $n = 6$. Hence

alkane:	C_6H_{14} $(2 \times 6 + 2 = 14 \text{ H atoms})$
alkene:	C_6H_{12} $(2 \times 6 = 12 \text{ H atoms})$
alkyne:	C_6H_{10} $(2 \times 6 - 2 = 10 \text{ H atoms})$

(Notice that cyclohexane also has the formula C_6H_{12}.)

(b) Here, $2n + 2 = 10$, so $n = (10 - 2)/2 = 4$; the formula is C_4H_{10}.

Alkenes

The simplest alkene is ethene, C_2H_4 (common name, ethylene). Its structural formula is

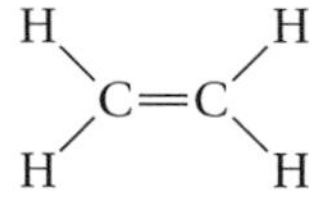
ethene

You may recall that we discussed the bonding in ethene in Chapter 7. The double bond in ethene and other alkenes consists of a sigma bond and a pi bond. The ethene molecule is planar. There is no rotation about the double bond, since that would require "breaking" the pi bond. The bond angle in ethene is 120°, corresponding to sp^2 hybridization about each carbon atom. The geometries of ethene and the next member of the alkene series, C_3H_6, are shown in Figure 22.6.

Ethene is produced in larger amounts than any other organic chemical, about 1.7×10^7 metric tons annually in the United States. It is made by heating ethane to about 700°C in the presence of a catalyst.

$$C_2H_6(g) \longrightarrow C_2H_4(g) + H_2(g)$$

Ethene is used to make a host of organic compounds; it is also the starting material for the preparation of polyethylene (Chapter 23). Since it is a plant hormone, ethene finds application in agriculture. It is used to ripen fruit that has been picked green to avoid spoilage in shipping. Exposure to ethene at very low concentrations produces the colors we associate with ripe bananas and oranges.

CENGAGENOW™
Click Coached Problems for a self-study module and a simulation on **naming alkenes.**

The names of alkenes are derived from those of the corresponding alkanes with the same number of carbon atoms per molecule. There are two modifications:

- the ending *-ane* is replaced by *-ene*.

$$\underset{\text{ethane}}{CH_3{-}CH_3} \qquad \underset{\text{ethene}}{CH_2{=}CH_2}$$

$H_2C{=}CH_2$ ethene — $CH_3CH{=}CH_2$ propene

Figure 22.6
The two simplest alkenes. Ethylene is planar, as is the —CH=CH₂ region of propene.

- where necessary, a number is used to designate the double-bonded carbon; the number is made as small as possible.

$$CH_2{=}CH{-}CH_2{-}CH_3 \qquad CH_3{-}CH{=}CH{-}CH_3$$

1-butene   2-butene

$$\underset{\displaystyle CH_3}{CH_2{=}\overset{}{C}}{-}CH_2{-}CH_3 \qquad CH_3{-}\underset{\displaystyle H_3C}{C}{=}\underset{\displaystyle H}{C}{-}CH_3$$

2-methyl-1-butene   2-methyl-2-butene

Example 22.4 Give the structural formula for the alkene with the IUPAC name 3-ethyl-2-pentene.

Strategy Here, in effect, you reverse the steps required in Example 22.2, this time converting a name to a structure. Start with a five-carbon skeleton, insert a double bond at the 2-position, and, finally, put an ethyl group at the 3-position.

SOLUTION The "skeleton" is

$$-C_1-C_2-C_3-C_4-C_5-$$

Putting the double bond between C_2 and C_3 and attaching the ethyl group to C_3,

$$-C-C{=}\underset{\displaystyle C_2H_5}{C}-C-C$$

Adding the missing hydrogen atoms gives the final structure:

$$CH_3{-}CH{=}\underset{\displaystyle C_2H_5}{C}{-}CH_2{-}CH_3 \qquad (C_7H_{14})$$

Alkynes

The IUPAC names of alkynes are derived from those of the corresponding alkenes by replacing the suffix *-ene* with *-yne*. Thus we have

$$H{-}C{\equiv}C{-}H \qquad H{-}C{\equiv}C{-}CH_3$$

ethyne   propyne

$$H{-}C{\equiv}C{-}CH_2{-}CH_3 \qquad CH_3{-}C{\equiv}C{-}CH_3$$

1-butyne   2-butyne

The most important alkyne by far is the first member of the series, commonly called acetylene. Recall from Chapter 7 that the C_2H_2 molecule is linear, with 180° bond angles. The triple bond consists of a sigma bond and two pi bonds; each carbon atom is sp-hybridized. The geometries of acetylene and the next member of the series, C_3H_4, are shown in Figure 22.7.

$HC{\equiv}CH$ acetylene $CH_3C{\equiv}CH$ methylacetylene

Figure 22.7
The two simplest alkynes. Both molecules contain four atoms in a straight line.

Charles D. Winters

Figure 22.8
Welding with an oxyacetylene torch.

Thermodynamically, acetylene is unstable with respect to decomposition to the elements:

$$C_2H_2(g) \longrightarrow 2C(s) + H_2(g) \qquad \Delta G° = -209.2 \text{ kJ at } 25°C$$

At high pressures, this reaction can occur explosively. For that reason, cylinders of acetylene do not contain the pure gas. Instead the cylinder is packed with an inert, porous material that holds a solution of acetylene gas in acetone.

You are probably most familiar with acetylene as a gaseous fuel used in welding and cutting metals (Figure 22.8). When mixed with pure oxygen in a torch, acetylene burns at temperatures above 2000°C. The heat comes from the reaction

$$C_2H_2(g) + \tfrac{5}{2}O_2(g) \longrightarrow 2CO_2(g) + H_2O(l) \qquad \Delta H = -1300 \text{ kJ}$$

The reaction gives off a brilliant white light, which served as a source of illumination in the headlights of early automobiles.

22.3 AROMATIC HYDROCARBONS AND THEIR DERIVATIVES

Aromatic hydrocarbons, sometimes referred to as *arenes,* can be considered to be derived from benzene, C_6H_6. Benzene is a transparent, volatile liquid (bp = 80°C) that was discovered by Michael Faraday in 1825. Its formula, C_6H_6, suggests a high degree of unsaturation, yet its properties are quite different from those of alkenes or alkynes.

As pointed out in Chapter 7, the atomic orbital (valence bond) model regards benzene as a resonance hybrid of the two structures

There are three pi bonds in the benzene molecule.

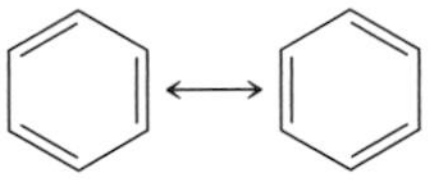

In these "line-angle" formulas it is understood that there is a carbon atom at each vertex of the hexagon; hydrogen atoms are not shown. This model is consistent with many of the properties of benzene. The molecule is a planar hexagon with bond angles of 120°. The hybridization of each carbon is sp^2. However, this structure is misleading in one respect. Chemically, benzene does not behave as if double bonds were present.

A more satisfactory model of the electron distribution in benzene, based on molecular orbital theory (Appendix 5), assumes that—

- each carbon atom forms three sigma bonds, one to a hydrogen atom and two to adjacent carbon atoms.
- the three electron pairs remaining are spread symmetrically over the entire molecule to form "delocalized" pi bonds.

This model is often represented by the structure

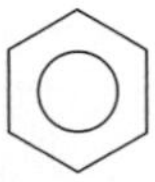

where it is understood that—

- a carbon atom is at each corner of the hexagon.
- an H atom is bonded to each carbon atom.
- the circle in the center of the molecule represents the six delocalized electrons.

At one time, benzene was widely used as a solvent, both commercially and in research and teaching laboratories. Its use for that purpose has largely been abandoned because of its toxicity. Chronic exposure to benzene vapor leads to various blood disorders and, in extreme cases, aplastic anemia and leukemia. It appears that the culprits are oxidation products of the aromatic ring, formed in an attempt to solubilize benzene and thus eliminate it from the body.

Benzene is a component of gasoline.

Derivatives of Benzene

CENGAGENOW™
Click Coached Problems for a self-study module on **naming derivatives of benzene.**

Among the more common monosubstituted benzenes are the following:

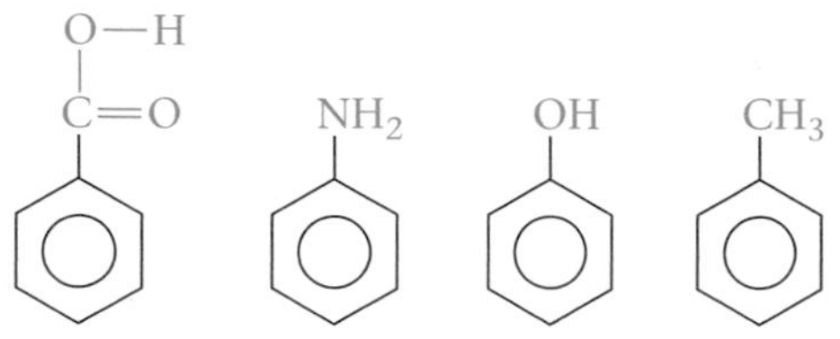

benzoic acid   aniline   phenol   toluene

Phenol was the first commercial antiseptic; its introduction into hospitals in the 1870s led to a dramatic decrease in deaths from postoperative infections. Its use for this purpose has long since been abandoned because phenol burns exposed tissue, but many modern antiseptics are phenol derivatives. Toluene has largely replaced benzene as a solvent because it is much less toxic. Oxidation of toluene in the body gives benzoic acid, which is readily eliminated and has none of the toxic properties of the oxidation products of benzene. Indeed, benzoic acid or its sodium salt (Na^+, $C_6H_5COO^-$ ions) is widely used as a preservative in foods and beverages, including fruit juices and soft drinks.

When there are two groups attached to the benzene ring, three isomers are possible. These are designated by the prefixes *ortho-*, *meta-*, and *para-*, often abbreviated as *o-*, *m-*, and *p-*.

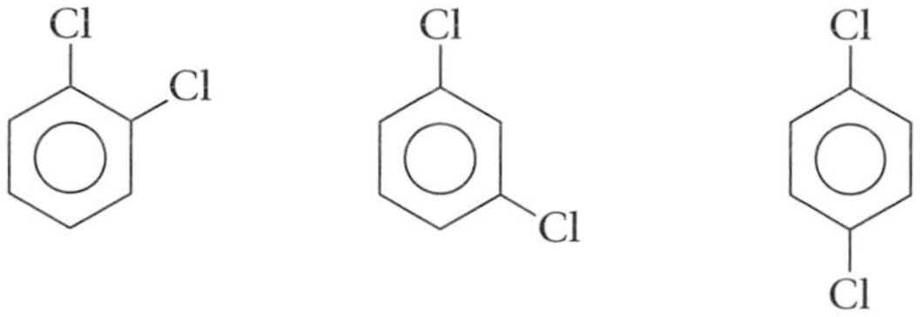

o-dichlorobenzene   *m*-dichlorobenzene   *p*-dichlorobenzene

Numbers can also be used; these three compounds may be referred to as 1,2-dichlorobenzene, 1,3-dichlorobenzene, and 1,4-dichlorobenzene, respectively. When three or more substituents are present, numbers become mandatory.

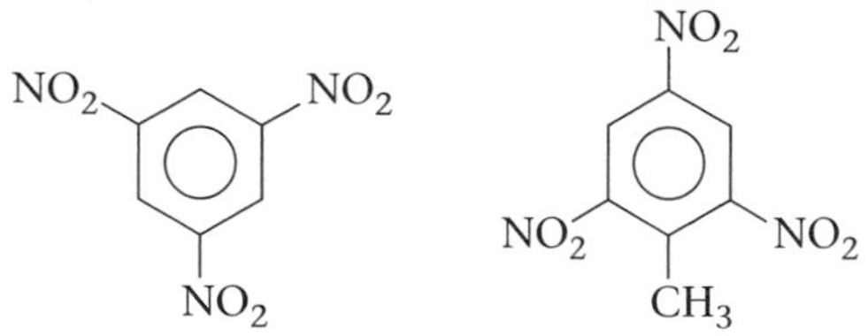

1,3,5-trinitrobenzene   2,4,6-trinitrotoluene (TNT)

In the structure at the right, it is understood that the CH_3 group of toluene is at position 1. Notice that the numbers used are as small as possible.

Example 22.5 Name the following compounds as derivatives of phenol.

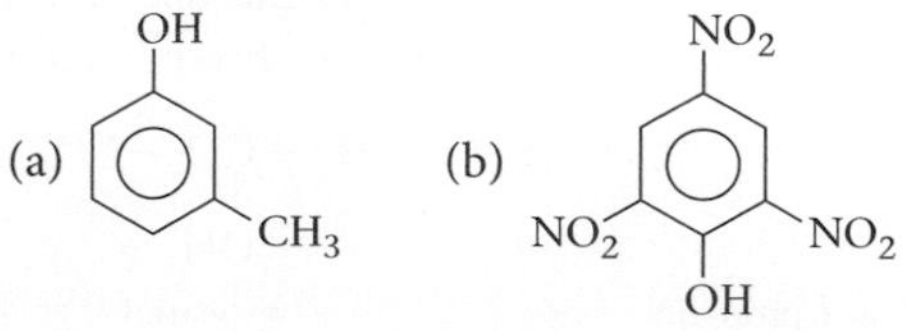

SOLUTION

(a) meta-methylphenol The common name of this compound is *meta*-cresol. It is one of the constituents of creosote, a black oily liquid used as a wood preservative and fungicide.

(b) 2,4,6-trinitrophenol The common name of this compound is picric acid, an explosive.

Condensed Ring Structures

In another type of aromatic hydrocarbon, two or more benzene rings are fused together. Naphthalene is the simplest compound of this type. Fusion of three benzene rings gives two different isomers, anthracene and phenanthrene.

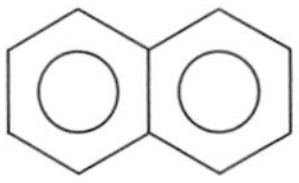

naphthalene
$C_{10}H_8$

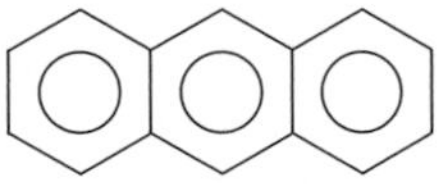

anthracene
$C_{14}H_{10}$

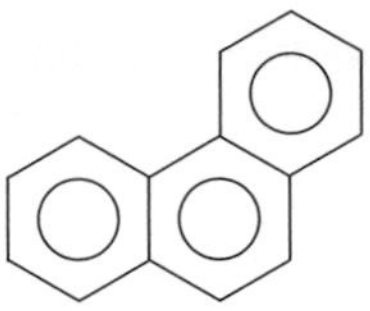

phenanthrene
$C_{14}H_{10}$

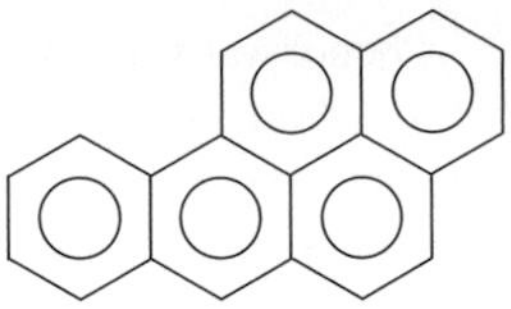

benzo[a]pyrene
$C_{20}H_{12}$

It is important to realize that in these structures no hydrogen atoms are bonded to the carbons at the juncture of two rings. The eight hydrogen atoms in naphthalene are located as shown below.

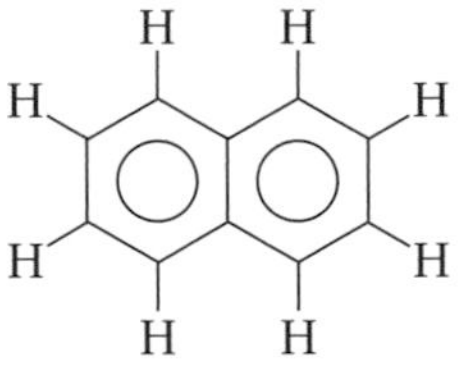

Certain compounds of this type are potent carcinogens. One of the most dangerous is benzo[a]pyrene, which has been detected in cigarette smoke. It is believed to be a cause of lung cancer, to which smokers are susceptible.

CENGAGENOW™
Click Coached Problems for a self-study module on **identifying functional groups.**

22.4 FUNCTIONAL GROUPS

Many organic molecules can be considered to be derived from hydrocarbons by substituting a **functional group** for a hydrogen atom. The functional group can be a nonmetal atom or small group of atoms that is bonded to carbon. Table 22.2 lists the types of functional groups commonly found in organic compounds.

Alcohols and Ethers

The general structural formula of an alcohol is

$$R—O—H$$

where R is an alkyl group. Alcohols are named by substituting the suffix *-ol* for the *-ane* suffix of the corresponding alkane. For the first four alcohols we have (common names shown in red):

CH_3OH	$CH_3—CH_2OH$	$CH_3—CH_2—CH_2OH$	$CH_3—CH(OH)—CH_3$
methanol (methyl alcohol)	ethanol (ethyl alcohol)	1-propanol (propyl alcohol)	2-propanol (isopropyl alcohol)

Table 22.2 Common Functional Groups

Group	Class	Example	Name*
$—OH$	Alcohols	C_2H_5OH	Ethanol (ethyl alcohol)
$—O—$	Ethers	$CH_3—O—CH_3$	Dimethyl ether
$—\overset{O}{\overset{\|}{C}}—H$	Aldehydes	$CH_3—\overset{O}{\overset{\|}{C}}—H$	Ethanal (acetaldehyde)
$—\overset{O}{\overset{\|}{C}}—$	Ketones	$CH_3—\overset{O}{\overset{\|}{C}}—CH_3$	Propanone (acetone)
$—\overset{O}{\overset{\|}{C}}—OH$	Carboxylic acids	$CH_3—\overset{O}{\overset{\|}{C}}—OH$	Ethanoic acid (acetic acid)
$—\overset{O}{\overset{\|}{C}}—O—$	Esters	$CH_3—\overset{O}{\overset{\|}{C}}—OCH_3$	Methyl acetate
$—\overset{\|}{N}—$	Amines	CH_3NH_2	Aminomethane (methylamine)

*Common names are shown in red.

Ethers have the general structure

$$R—O—R'$$

where the two alkyl groups can be the same (e.g., $R = R' = CH_3$) or different ($R = CH_3$; $R' = C_2H_5$). Ethers are ordinarily named by citing the two alkyl groups:

$$\underset{\text{dimethyl ether}}{CH_3—O—CH_3} \qquad \underset{\text{ethyl methyl ether}}{CH_3—O—C_2H_5}$$

Table 22.3 compares two physical properties, boiling point and water solubility, of alcohols, ethers, and alkanes of similar molar masses. Notice that—

- alcohols have boiling points much higher than those of alkanes of comparable molar mass. This reflects the fact that alcohol molecules, like H_2O, are strongly hydrogen-bonded to one another. Ethers cannot do this, since they do not contain OH groups, so they have boiling points much lower than those of comparable alcohols.
- alcohols and ethers of low molar mass are generally soluble in water. Ethers, like alcohols, can form hydrogen bonds with water, making use of the OH groups in the water molecule.

About 3×10^9 kg of methanol are produced annually in the United States from *synthesis gas,* a mixture of carbon monoxide and hydrogen:

$$CO(g) + 2H_2(g) \xrightarrow[250\text{ atm, }350°C]{ZnO,Cr_2O_3} CH_3OH(g)$$

Table 22.3 Physical Properties of Simple Alkanes, Alcohols, and Ethers

Name	Structure	Molar Mass	Boiling Point	Water Solubility
Propane	$CH_3CH_2CH_3$	44 g/mol	−42°C	Insoluble
Ethanol	CH_3CH_2OH	46 g/mol	78°C	Soluble
Dimethyl ether	CH_3OCH_3	46 g/mol	−23°C	Soluble
Butane	$CH_3CH_2CH_2CH_3$	58 g/mol	0°C	Insoluble
1-Propanol	$CH_3CH_2CH_2OH$	60 g/mol	97°C	Soluble
Ethyl methyl ether	$CH_3CH_2OCH_3$	60 g/mol	11°C	Soluble

Figure 22.9
Making wine. Wine *(far right)* is produced from the glucose in grape juice *(left)* by fermentation. The reaction is

$$C_6H_{12}O_6(aq) \longrightarrow 2C_2H_5OH(aq) + 2CO_2(g)$$

The purpose of the bubble chamber in the fermentation jug *(center)* is to allow the carbon dioxide to escape but prevent oxygen from entering and oxidizing ethyl alcohol to acetic acid.

Courtesy of Professor James M. Bobbitt, Twenty Mile Vineyard

Methanol is also formed as a byproduct when charcoal is made by heating wood in the absence of air. For this reason, it is sometimes called wood alcohol. Methanol is used in jet fuels and as a solvent, gasoline additive, and starting material for several industrial syntheses. It is a deadly poison; ingestion of as little as 25 mL can be fatal. The antidote in this case is a solution of sodium hydrogen carbonate, $NaHCO_3$.

Ethanol, the most common alcohol, can be made by the fermentation of sugar (Figure 22.9) or grain—hence its common name "grain alcohol." It is the active ingredient of alcoholic beverages, in which it is present at various concentrations (4%–8% in beer, 12%–15% in wine, and 40% or more in distilled spirits). The "proof" of an alcoholic beverage is twice the volume percentage of ethanol; an 86-proof bourbon whiskey contains 43% ethanol. The flavor of alcoholic beverages is due to impurities; ethanol itself is tasteless and colorless.

Industrial ethanol is made by the reaction of ethylene with water, using sulfuric acid as a catalyst.

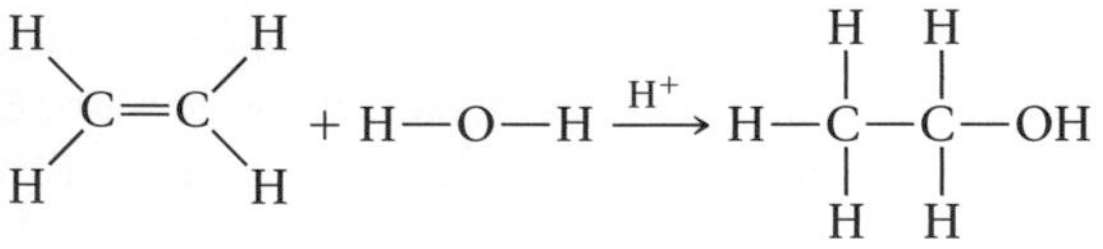

Frequently, ethanol that is not destined for human consumption is "denatured" by adding small quantities of methanol or benzene. This avoids the high federal tax on beverage alcohol; denatured alcohol is poisonous.

Certain alcohols contain two or more —OH groups per molecule. Perhaps the most familiar compounds of this type are ethylene glycol and glycerol:

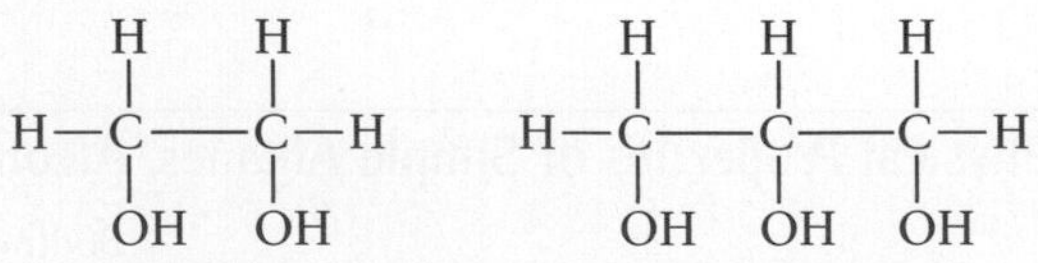

ethylene glycol glycerol

Ethylene glycol is widely used as an antifreeze. Glycerol is formed as a byproduct in making soaps. It is a viscous, sweet-tasting liquid, used in making drugs, antibiotics, plastics, and explosives (nitroglycerin).

"Laughing gas," N_2O, is often used by dentists.

The only ether that you are likely to encounter in the laboratory is diethyl ether, often referred to simply as "ether." It was first used as an anesthetic in the 1840s. Today we use other compounds for that purpose, for at least a couple of reasons. For one thing, ether vapor is highly flammable. For another, liquid ether, on standing in contact with air, tends to form compounds called hydroperoxides, which are potent explosives.

$$\underset{\text{diethyl ether}}{CH_3CH_2{-}O{-}CH_2CH_3(l)} + O_2(g) \longrightarrow \underset{\text{a hydroperoxide}}{CH_3CH_2{-}O{-}\underset{\displaystyle |\atop O{-}OH}{C}HCH_3}$$

Aldehydes and Ketones

All these compounds contain the *carbonyl group*

In a ketone, two hydrocarbon groups (alkyl or aromatic) are bonded to the central carbon atom, giving the general structure

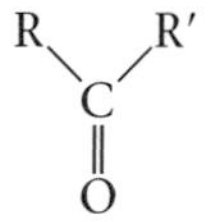

where (as with ethers) R and R′ can be the same or different. In the simplest ketone, commonly called *acetone,* R = R′ = CH_3. The structural formula of acetone is ordinarily written as

$$CH_3{-}\underset{\displaystyle \| \atop O}{C}{-}CH_3 \qquad \text{acetone (IUPAC name = propanone)}$$

with the understanding that the bond angle around the central carbon atom is approximately 120°.

In aldehydes, at least one of the two "groups" bonded to carbon must be a hydrogen atom:

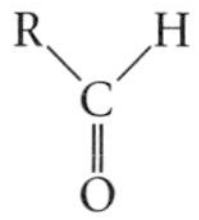

R can be any hydrocarbon group or, in the simplest case, *formaldehyde,* a second hydrogen atom:

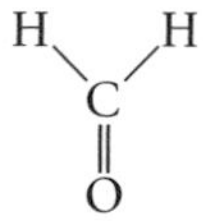

formaldehyde (IUPAC name = methanal)

Acetone (bp = 56°C) is completely water-soluble and dissolves a wide variety of organic compounds as well. Accordingly, it is one of the most important industrial solvents. You may be most familiar with it as the solvent in nail polish.

Normally, only small amounts of acetone are produced in the human body. Diabetics produce larger amounts, sometimes enough to give their breath a sweet odor.

Formaldehyde (bp = −21°C) is ordinarily found in the laboratory in the form of a concentrated water solution (37% HCHO) known as formalin. At one time it was widely used as a preservative for biological specimens. That application has declined now that formaldehyde has been shown to be carcinogenic. Industrially, it is still used as a component of adhesives used in making plywood and fiberboard.

Formaldehyde, as a gas or in water solution, has a distinctly unpleasant odor. Higher "aromatic" aldehydes such as those shown in Figure 22.10 (p. 594) are a lot more pleasant to deal with; they are used in flavorings and even perfumes.

Figure 22.10
"Aromatic" aldehydes. Benzaldehyde, vanillin, and cinnamaldehyde are aldehydes with pleasant aromas that are found in almonds, vanilla beans, and cinnamon, respectively.

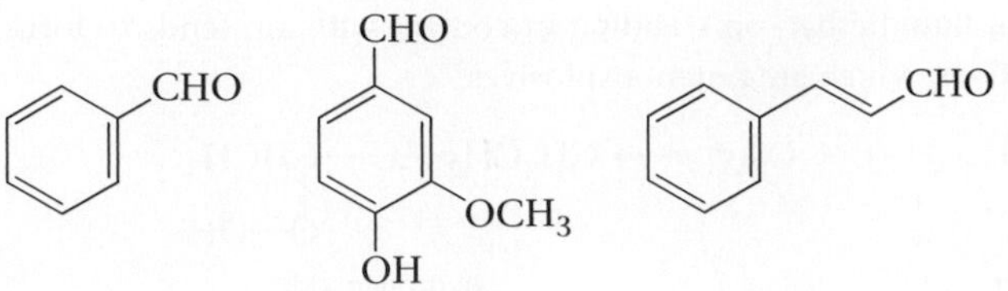

benzaldehyde (oil of almonds) | vanillin (vanilla bean) | cinnamaldehyde (oil of cinnamon)

Example 22.6 Classify each of the following as an alcohol, ether, aldehyde, or ketone.

(a) $CH_3—O—CH_2CH_2CH_3$ (b) 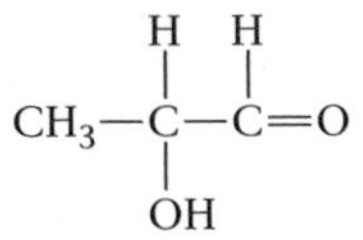

(c) 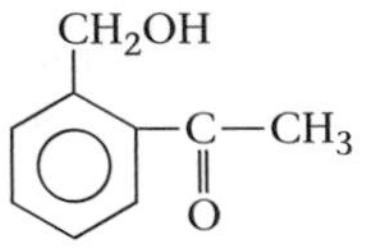

Strategy Locate the functional group present and use Table 22.2. Note that more than one functional group may be involved.

SOLUTION

(a) ether (b) alcohol, aldehyde (c) alcohol, ketone

Carboxylic Acids and Esters

The general structure of a carboxylic acid is

$$R—\underset{\underset{O}{\|}}{C}—OH$$

As usual, R is a hydrocarbon group or, in the simplest case, a hydrogen atom. The acidic hydrogen atom is the one bonded to oxygen. The IUPAC name of a carboxylic acid can be obtained by substituting the suffix "-oic acid" for the final "e" in the name of the corresponding alkane. In practice, such names are seldom used. For example, the first two members of the series are commonly referred to as formic acid and acetic acid.

$$H—\underset{\underset{O}{\|}}{C}—OH \qquad CH_3—\underset{\underset{O}{\|}}{C}—OH$$

methanoic acid (formic acid) | ethanoic acid (acetic acid)

According to legend, formic acid used to be made by distilling ants (Latin, *formica*). Acetic acid is the active ingredient of vinegar, responsible for its sour taste. "White" vinegar is made by adding pure acetic acid to water, forming a 5% solution. "Brown" or "apple cider" vinegar is made from apple juice; the ethyl alcohol formed by fermentation is oxidized to acetic acid.

Homemade wine often contains some vinegar.

The most impotant property of carboxylic acids is implied by their name: they act as weak acids in water solution.

$$RCOOH(aq) \rightleftharpoons H^+(aq) + RCOO^-(aq)$$

Carboxylic acids vary considerably in strength. Among the strongest is trichloroacetic acid ($K_a = 0.20$); a 0.10 M solution of $Cl_3C—COOH$ is about 73% ionized. Trichloroacetic acid is an ingredient of over-the-counter preparations used to treat canker sores and remove warts.

Treatment of a carboxylic acid with the strong base NaOH forms the sodium salt of the acid. With acetic acid, the acid-base reaction is

$$CH_3-\underset{\underset{\displaystyle O}{\|}}{C}-OH\,(aq) + OH^-(aq) \longrightarrow CH_3-\underset{\underset{\displaystyle O}{\|}}{C}-O^-(aq) + H_2O$$

Evaporation gives the salt sodium acetate, which contains Na^+ and CH_3COO^- ions. Many of the salts of carboxylic acids have important uses. Sodium and calcium propionate (Na^+ or Ca^{2+} ions, $CH_3CH_2COO^-$ ions) are added to bread, cake, and cheese to inhibit the growth of mold.

Soaps are sodium salts of long-chain carboxylic acids such as stearic acid:

$$\underset{\text{stearic acid}}{CH_3(CH_2)_{16}-\underset{\underset{\displaystyle O}{\|}}{C}-OH} \qquad \underset{\text{sodium stearate, a soap}}{Na^+,\ CH_3(CH_2)_{16}-\underset{\underset{\displaystyle O}{\|}}{C}-O^-}$$

The cleaning action of soap reflects the nature of the long-chain carboxylate anion. The long hydrocarbon group is a good solvent for greases and oils, and the ionic COO^- group gives water solubility.

The reaction between an alcohol and a carboxylic acid forms an **ester,** containing the functional group

$$-O-\underset{\underset{\displaystyle O}{\|}}{C}-$$

often abbreviated $-COO-$. The reaction between methyl alcohol and acetic acid is typical

$$\underset{\text{methyl alcohol}}{CH_3-OH} + \underset{\text{acetic acid}}{HO-\underset{\underset{\displaystyle O}{\|}}{C}-CH_3} \xrightarrow{H^+} \underset{\text{methyl acetate}}{CH_3-O-\underset{\underset{\displaystyle O}{\|}}{C}-CH_3} + H_2O$$

The common name of an ester consists of two words. The first word (methyl, ethyl, . . .) is derived from that of the alcohol; the second word (formate, acetate, . . .) is the name of the acid with the *-ic* suffix replaced by *-ate*. Thus ethyl formate (Table 22.4) is made from ethyl alcohol and formic acid:

$$\underset{\text{ethyl alcohol}}{CH_3CH_2OH} \qquad \underset{\text{formic acid}}{HCOOH}$$

Many esters have pleasant odors; they are commonly found in natural and synthetic fragrances.

Example 22.7 Show the structure of

(a) the three-carbon alcohol with an $-OH$ group at the end of the chain.
(b) the three-carbon carboxylic acid.
(c) the ester formed when these two compounds react.

Strategy To work (a) and (b), start by drawing the parent carbon chain. Put the functional group in the specified position; fill out the structural formula with hydrogen atoms. In (c), notice that an $-OH$ group comes from the acid, an H atom from the alcohol.

SOLUTION

(a) $CH_3CH_2CH_2-OH$ (b) $CH_3CH_2-\underset{\underset{\displaystyle O}{\|}}{C}-OH$

(c) $CH_3CH_2CH_2-O-\underset{\underset{\displaystyle O}{\|}}{C}-CH_2CH_3$

Table 22.4 Properties of Esters

Ester	Structure	Odor, Flavor
Ethyl formate	$CH_3CH_2{-}O{-}C({=}O){-}H$	Rum
Isobutyl formate	$(CH_3)_2CHCH_2{-}O{-}C({=}O){-}H$	Raspberry
Methyl butyrate	$CH_3{-}O{-}C({=}O){-}(CH_2)_2CH_3$	Apple
Ethyl butyrate	$CH_3CH_2{-}O{-}C({=}O){-}(CH_2)_2CH_3$	Pineapple
Isopentyl acetate	$(CH_3)_2CH(CH_2)_2{-}O{-}C({=}O){-}CH_3$	Banana
Octyl acetate	$CH_3(CH_2)_7{-}O{-}C({=}O){-}CH_3$	Orange
Pentyl propionate	$CH_3(CH_2)_4{-}O{-}C({=}O){-}CH_2CH_3$	Apricot

Amines

These compounds were discussed earlier (Chapter 13). Here we will concentrate on *primary* amines, in which two hydrogens are bonded to a nitrogen atom, giving as a general formula

$$R{-}NH_2$$

where R may be an alkyl or aromatic group:

CH_3NH_2

methylamine

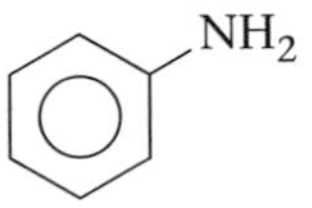

aniline

In Chapter 23, we'll look at the chemistry of amino acids, which contain both NH_2 and COOH groups.

Methylamine, the first member of the series,

- is a flammable gas at 25°C and 1 atm; its boiling point and critical temperature are −6°C and 157°C, respectively.
- has a somewhat unpleasant fishy smell. Other primary amines with more obnoxious odors include

$$H_2N{-}(CH_2)_4{-}NH_2 \qquad H_2N{-}(CH_2)_5{-}NH_2$$

putrescine — cadaverine

- is a weak base with a K_b (4×10^{-4}) about 20 times that of ammonia (1.8×10^{-5}) and a million times the value for aniline (4×10^{-10}).
- reacts essentially completely with strong acid:

$$CH_3NH_2(aq) + H^+(aq) \longrightarrow CH_3NH_3^+(aq)$$

but gives an equilibrium mixture with acetic acid:

$$CH_3NH_2(aq) + CH_3COOH(aq) \rightleftharpoons CH_3NH_3^+(aq) + CH_3COO^-(aq)$$

Example 22.8 Graded

Calculate equilibrium constants for the two acid-base reactions just cited.

$*$(a) $CH_3NH_2(aq) + H^+(aq) \longrightarrow CH_3NH_3^+(aq)$

$**$(b) $CH_3NH_2(aq) + CH_3COOH(aq) \rightleftharpoons CH_3NH_3^+(aq) + CH_3COO^-(aq)$

Strategy Use the following general relations:

(p. 370) $K_a = K_W/K_b$

(p. 327) reciprocal rule, $K'' = 1/K$

(p. 327) multiple equilibria, $K_3 = K_1 \times K_2$

Finally, use $K_b CH_3NH_2 = 4 \times 10^{-4}$; $K_a CH_3COOH = 1.8 \times 10^{-5}$

SOLUTION

(a) $CH_3NH_2(aq) + H^+(aq) \rightleftharpoons CH_3NH_3^+(aq); K''$

$$K'' = \frac{1}{K_a CH_3NH_3^+} = \frac{K_b CH_3NH_2}{K_W} = \frac{4 \times 10^{-4}}{1 \times 10^{-14}} = 4 \times 10^{10}$$

(b)

$$CH_3NH_2(aq) + H^+(aq) \rightleftharpoons CH_3NH_3^+(aq); K_1 = 4 \times 10^{10}$$

$$CH_3COOH(aq) \rightleftharpoons CH_3COO^-(aq) + H^+(aq); K_2 = 1.8 \times 10^{-5}$$

$$CH_3NH_2(aq) + CH_3COOH(aq) \rightleftharpoons CH_3COO^-(aq) + CH_3NH_3^+(aq)$$

$$K_3 = K_1 \times K_2 = 7 \times 10^5$$

Reality Check Notice that K for the second reaction is smaller than that for the first reaction. That is reasonable, since acetic acid is a weak acid ($K_a < 1$).

22.5 ISOMERISM IN ORGANIC COMPOUNDS

Isomers are distinctly different compounds, with different properties, that have the same molecular formula. In Section 22.1, we considered structural isomers of alkanes. You will recall that butane and 2-methylpropane have the same molecular formula, C_4H_{10}, but different structural formulas. In these, as in all structural isomers, the order in which the atoms are bonded to each other differs.

Structural isomerism is common among all types of organic compounds. For example, there are

1. Three structural isomers of the alkene C_4H_8:

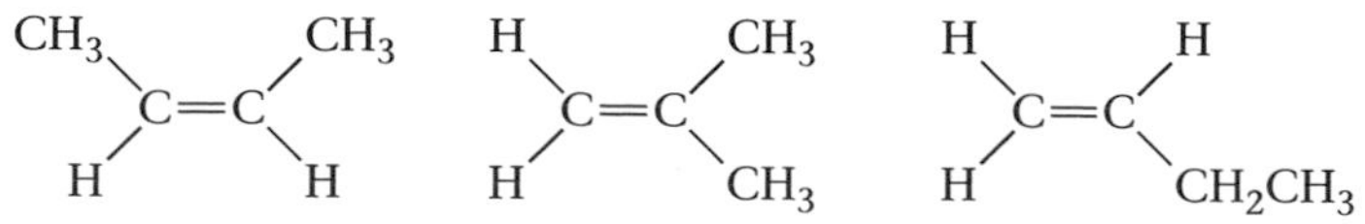

2. Three structural isomers with the molecular formula C_3H_8O. Two of these are alcohols; the third is an ether.

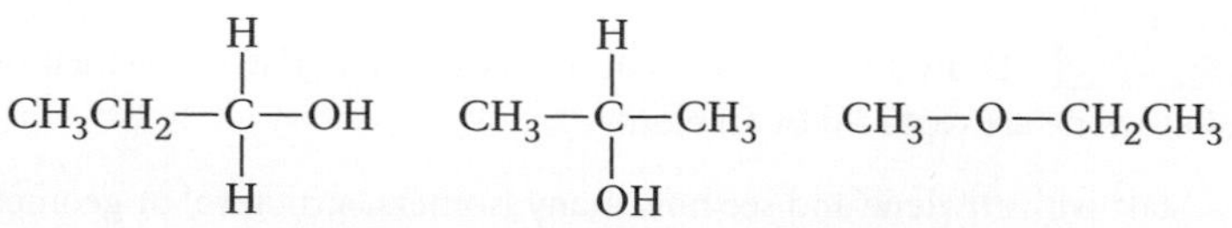

Example 22.9 Consider the molecule $C_3H_6Cl_2$, which is derived from propane, C_3H_8, by substituting two Cl atoms for H atoms. Draw the structural isomers of $C_3H_6Cl_2$.

Strategy All of these compounds have the same carbon skeleton, —C—C—C—. To find the isomers, notice that the two carbon atoms at the ends of the chain are equivalent. The carbon atom at the center of the chain is different because it is bonded to two carbon atoms rather than one.

SOLUTION There are four isomers. In one, both Cl atoms are bonded to a carbon atom at the end of the chain. In another, both Cl atoms are bonded to the central carbon atom:

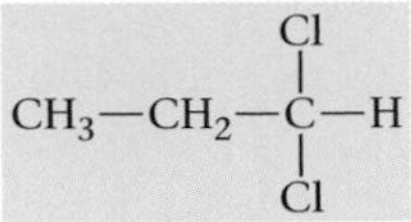

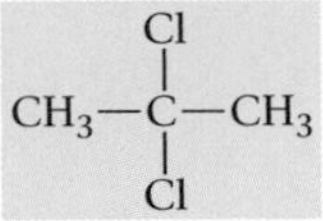

In the other two isomers, the Cl atoms are bonded to different carbons:

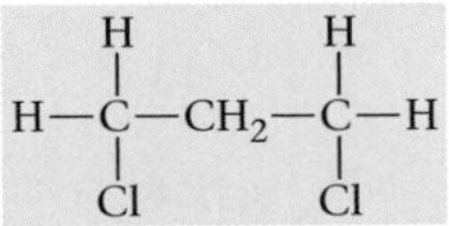

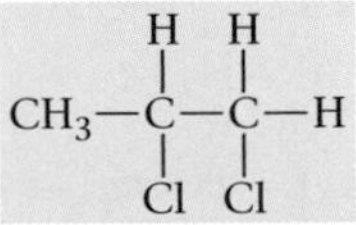

Geometric *(cis-trans)* Isomers

As we saw earlier, there are three structural isomers of the alkene C_4H_8. You may be surprised to learn that there are actually *four* different alkenes with this molecular formula. The "extra" compound arises because of a phenomenon called *geometric isomerism.* There are two different geometric isomers of the structure shown on the left, on page 597, under (1).

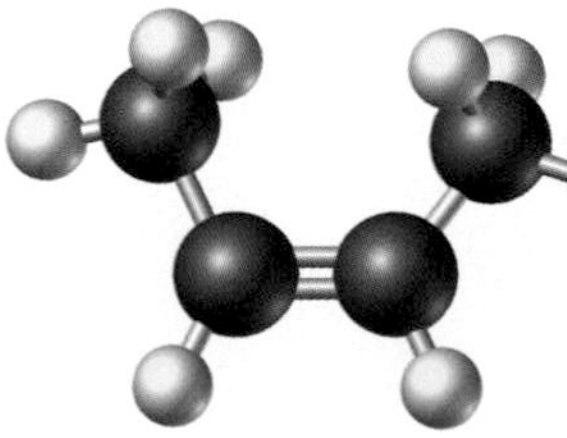

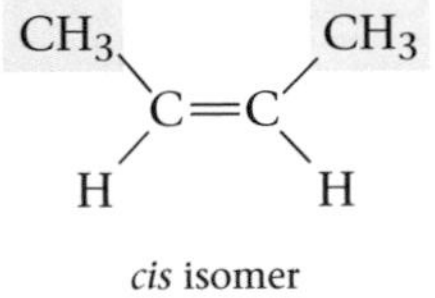

cis isomer
bp = 4°C

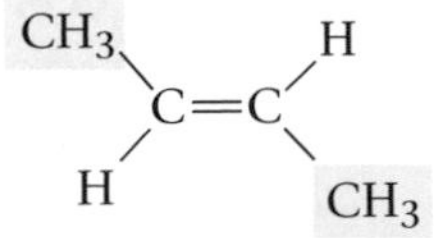

trans isomer
bp = 1°C

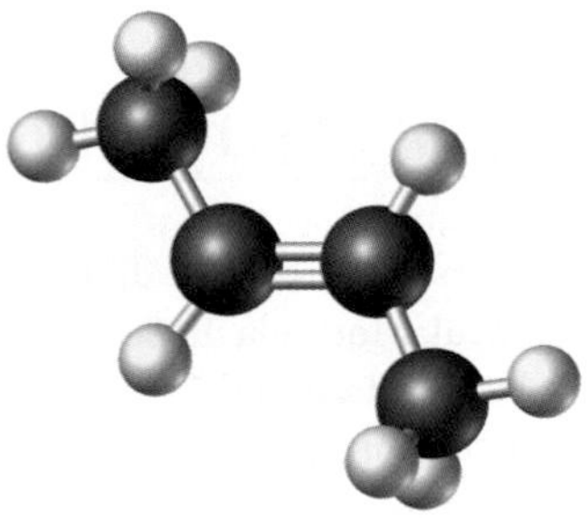

Name the compound

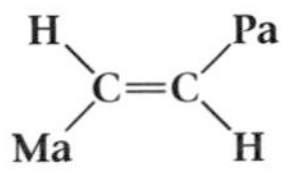

Answer: transparent.

In the *cis* isomer, the two CH_3 groups (or the two H atoms) are as close to one another as possible. In the *trans* isomer, the two identical groups are farther apart. The two forms exist because there is no free rotation about the carbon-to-carbon double bond. The situation is analogous to that with *cis-trans* isomers of square planar complexes (Chapter 15). In both cases, the difference in geometry is responsible for isomerism; the atoms are bonded to each other in the same way.

Geometric, or *cis-trans,* isomerism is common among alkenes. It occurs when both of the double-bonded carbon atoms are joined to two different atoms or groups. The other two structural isomers of C_4H_8 shown under (1) on page 597 do not show *cis-trans* isomerism. In both cases the carbon atom at the left is joined to two identical hydrogen atoms.

Example 22.10 Draw all the isomers of the molecule $C_2H_2Cl_2$ in which two of the H atoms of ethylene are replaced by Cl atoms.

Strategy Start with ethylene and see how many isomers, structural or geometric, you can make by substituting two chlorine atoms for hydrogen.

SOLUTION The isomers of $C_2H_2Cl_2$ are

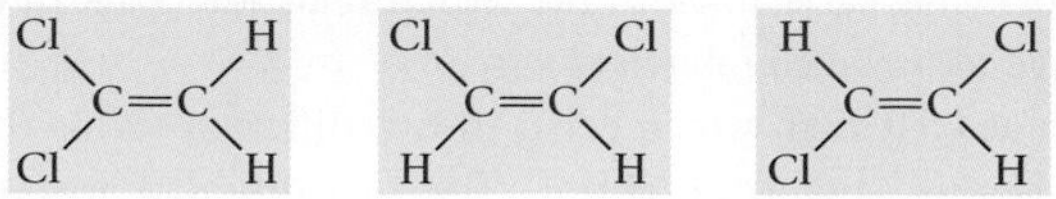

Reality Check Notice that the structural isomer shown on the left does not show *cis-trans* isomerism because two Cl atoms are bonded to the same carbon.

Cis and *trans* isomers differ from one another in their physical and, to a lesser extent, their chemical properties. They may also differ in their physiological behavior. For example, the compound *cis*-9-tricosene

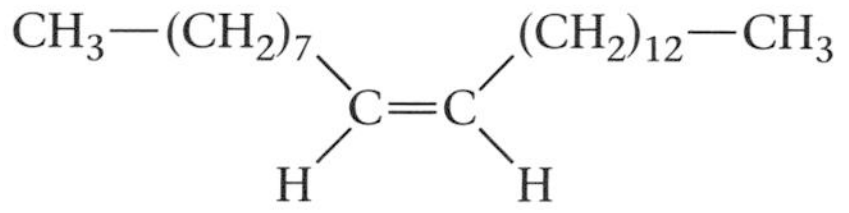

is a sex attractant secreted by the female housefly. The *trans* isomer is totally ineffective in this area.

Optical Isomers

Optical isomers arise when at least one carbon atom in a molecule is bonded to four different atoms or groups. Consider, for example, the methane derivative CHClBrI. As you can see from Figure 22.11, there are two different forms of this molecule, which are mirror images of one another. The mirror images are not superimposable; that is, you cannot place one molecule over the other so that identical groups are touching. In this sense, the two isomers resemble right- and left-hands (Figure 22.12).

There is another way to convince yourself that the two structures shown in Figure 22.11 are different isomers. Imagine that you are located directly above the hydrogen atom, looking

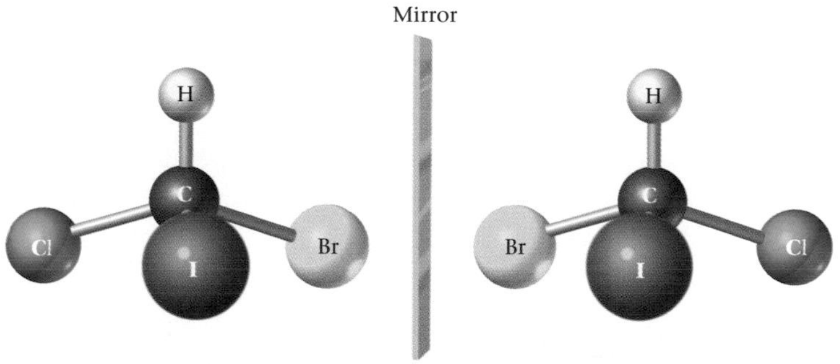

Figure 22.11
Optical isomers. These isomers of CHClBrI are mirror images of each other.

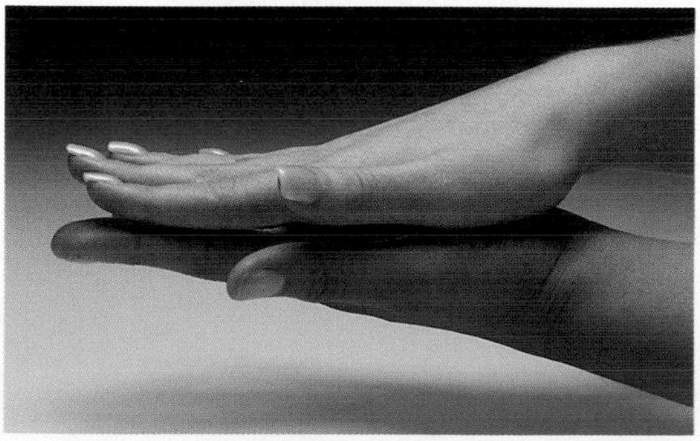

Charles D. Winters

Figure 22.12
Mirror images. The right hand cannot be superimposed on the left hand. They are mirror images of each other.

down at the rest of the molecule. In the structure at the left, the atoms Cl, Br, I, in that order, are arranged in a clockwise pattern. With the structure at the right, in order to move from Cl to Br to I, you have to move counterclockwise.

A molecule such as CHClBrI, which exists in two different forms that are not superimposable mirror images, is said to be **chiral.** The two different forms are referred to as **enantiomers,** or optical isomers. Any molecule in which four different groups are bonded to carbon will be chiral; the carbon atom serves as a **chiral center.** Molecules may contain more than one chiral center, in which case there can be more than two enantiomers.

CENGAGENOW™
Click Coached Problems for a self-study module on **identifying chiral carbon centers.**

Example 22.11 In the following structural formulas, locate each chiral carbon atom.

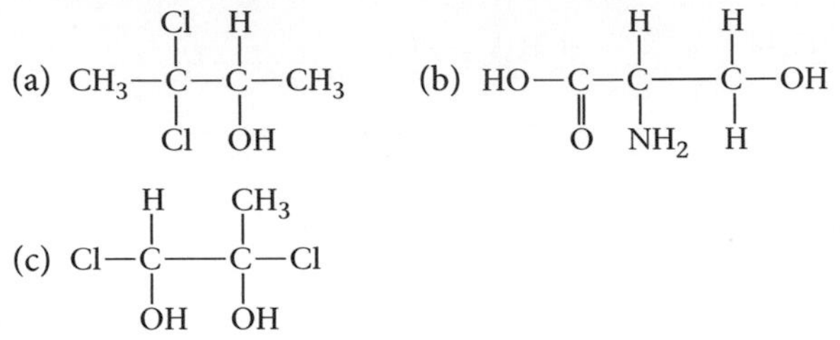

Strategy Look for carbon atoms that have four different atoms or groups attached.

SOLUTION In (a), the third carbon atom from the left is chiral; it is bonded to H, CH_3, OH, and CH_3—CCl_2. In (b), the second carbon atom is chiral. In (c), two of the three carbons are chiral. (C in CH_3 is not.)

The term "optical isomerism" comes from the effect that enantiomers have on plane-polarized light, such as that produced by a Polaroid lens (Figure 22.13). When this light is passed through a solution containing a single enantiomer, the plane is rotated from its original position. One isomer rotates it to the right (clockwise) and the other to the left (counterclockwise). If both isomers are present in equal amounts, we obtain what is known as a **racemic mixture.** In this case, the two rotations offset each other and there is no effect on plane-polarized light.

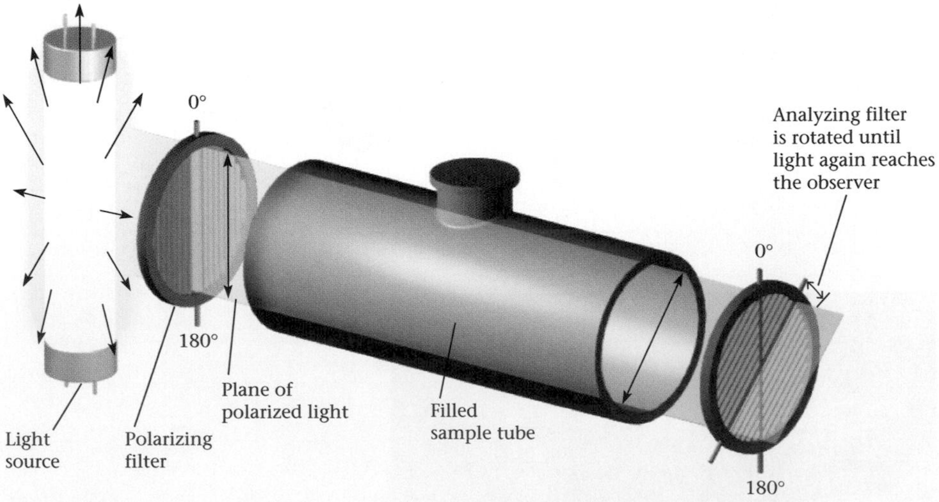

Figure 22.13
A polarimeter. The sample tube contains an optically active compound. The analyzing filter has been turned clockwise to restore the light field and measure the rotation caused by the sample.

Except for their effect on plane-polarized light, two enantiomers of a chiral compound have identical physical properties. For example, the two isomers of lactic acid shown below have the same melting point, 52°C, and density, 1.25 g/mL.

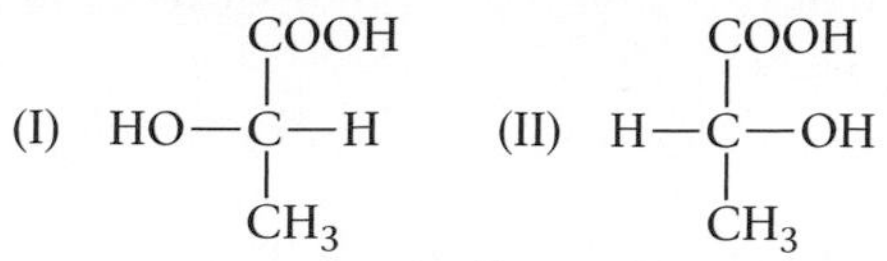

enantiomers of lactic acid

On the other hand, because enantiomers differ in their three-dimensional structure, they often interact with biochemical molecules in different ways. As a result, they may show quite different physiological properties. Consider, for example, amphetamine, often used illicitly as an "upper" or "pep pill." Amphetamine consists of two enantiomers:

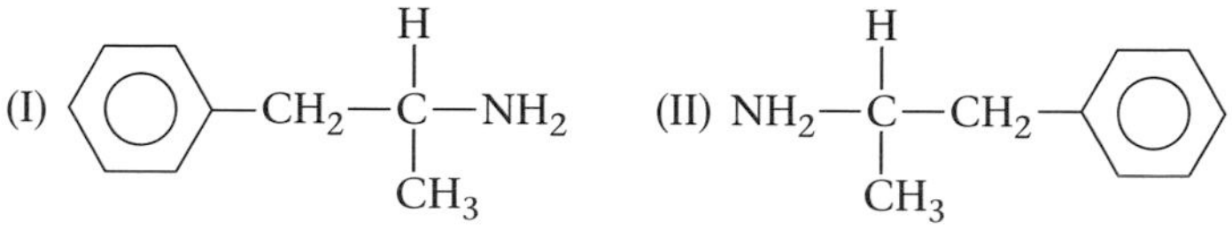

enantiomers of amphetamine

Enantiomer I, called Dexedrine, is by far the stronger stimulant. It is from two to four times as active as Benzedrine, the racemic mixture of the two isomers.

In the 1990s, a large number of so-called chiral drugs containing a single enantiomer came on the market. One of the first of these was naproxen (trade name Aleve).

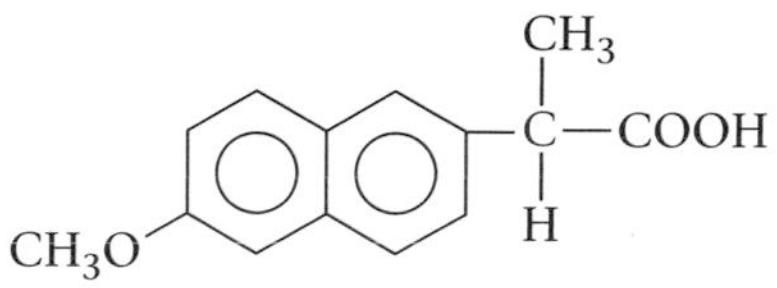

(chiral carbon shown in color)

The naproxen that you buy over the counter at your local pharmacy consists of a single enantiomer, which is an effective analgesic (pain killer). The other enantiomer is not a pain killer; even worse, it can cause liver damage.

Of the 100 best-selling drugs on the market today, about half consist of a single enantiomer. Chiral drugs are used to treat all kinds of illnesses, from arthritis to asthma, from heartburn to heart disease. In general, these drugs are prepared by either of two different methods. One possibility is to resolve a racemic mixture into its components. This was first done by Louis Pasteur more than 150 years ago. He used a magnifying glass and a pair of tweezers to separate crystals of enantiomers. Today resolution can be accomplished much more quickly by using modern separation techniques such as liquid chromatography (Chapter 1).

A different approach to making chiral drugs is *asymmetric synthesis.* An optically inactive precursor is converted to the drug by a reaction that uses a special catalyst, usually an enzyme (Chapter 11). If all goes well, the product is a single enantiomer with the desired physiological effect. In 2001, William S. Knowles, Ryogi Noyori, and K. Barry Sharpless won the Nobel Prize in chemistry for work in this area.

22.6 ORGANIC REACTIONS

The reactions that take place in organic chemistry differ in important ways from those discussed earlier in this text. In particular, the species taking part in organic reactions are most often molecules rather than ions. Again, most organic reactions take place between pure substances or in nonpolar solvents as opposed to water. Generally speaking, organic reactions occur more slowly than inorganic ones. In this section we will look at four general types of organic reactions known as addition, elimination, condensation, and substitution.

Ions tend to react fast.

CENGAGENOW™
Click Coached Problems for a self-study module on **addition reactions of alkenes.**

Double and triple bonds are much more reactive than single bonds.

Charles D. Winters

Figure 22.14
Test for an alkene. At the left is a solution of bromine in carbon tetrachloride. Addition of a few drops of an alkene causes the red color to disappear as the alkene reacts with the bromine.

The H_2SO_4 absorbs the H_2O and drives the reaction to the right.

Addition Reactions

In an addition reaction, a small molecule (e.g., H_2, Cl_2, HCl, H_2O) adds across a double or triple bond. A simple example is the addition of hydrogen gas to ethene in the presense of a nickel catalyst.

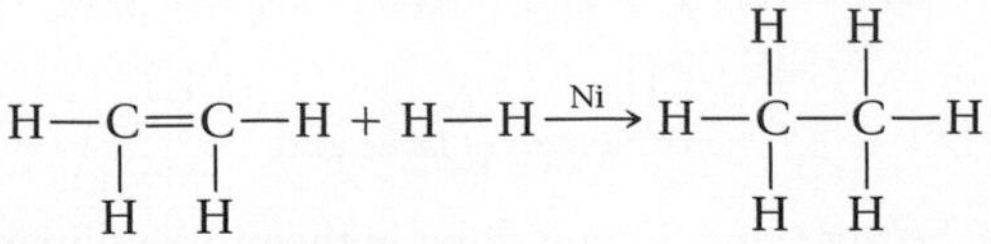

With ethyne (acetylene), one or two moles of H_2 may add, depending upon the catalyst and the conditions used.

Hydrogenation has found commercial application in the conversion of liquid to solid fats. Vegetable oils contain a relatively high proportion of double bonds. Treatment with hydrogen under pressure in the presence of a catalyst converts double bonds to single bonds and produces solids such as margarine.

As we saw earlier (Section 22.4), ethanol can be made from ethene by "adding" water in the presence of an acid catalyst. This process is referred to as *hydration:*

$$C_2H_4(g) + H_2O(l) \xrightarrow{H^+} C_2H_5OH(l)$$

Still another species that adds readily to ethene is elementary bromine (Figure 22.14):

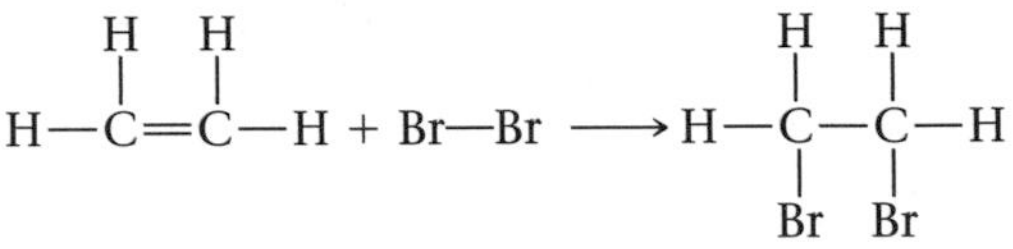

Elimination and Condensation Reactions

An elimination reaction is, in a sense, the reverse of an addition reaction. It involves the elimination of two groups from adjacent carbon atoms, converting a saturated molecule into one that is unsaturated. An example is the dehydration of ethanol, which occurs when it is heated with sulfuric acid:

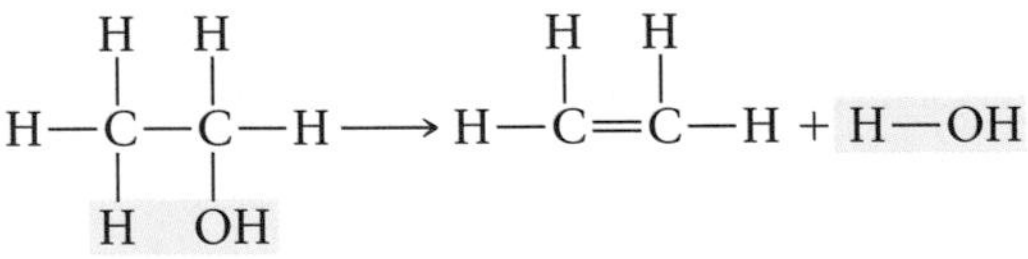

ethanol ethene

This is, of course, the reverse of the addition reaction by which ethanol is formed.

A somewhat similar reaction, referred to as condensation, occurs when two molecules combine by splitting out a small molecule such as H_2O. The molecules that combine may be the same or different:

$$\underset{\text{methanol}}{CH_3{-}OH} + \underset{\text{methanol}}{HO{-}CH_3} \longrightarrow \underset{\text{dimethyl ether}}{CH_3{-}O{-}CH_3} + H{-}OH$$

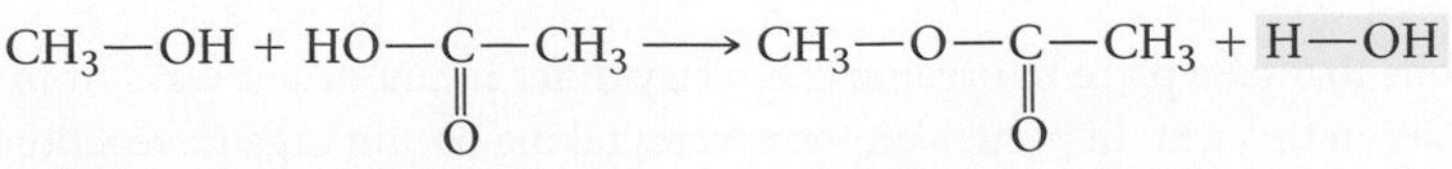

methanol acetic acid methyl acetate

The first reaction offers a general way of preparing ethers from alcohol. The second reaction is that of esterification, referred to earlier.

Substitution Reactions

A substitution reaction is one in which an atom or group of atoms in a molecule is replaced by a different atom or group. Substitution reactions are very common in organic chemistry. Examples include the following:

- chlorination of alkanes. When a mixture of methane and chlorine gases is exposed to light, the following reaction occurs:

$$CH_4(g) + Cl_2(g) \longrightarrow CH_3Cl(g) + HCl(g)$$

- A very similar reaction occurs with benzene:

$$C_6H_6(l) + Cl_2(g) \xrightarrow{FeCl_3} C_6H_5Cl(l) + HCl(g)$$

- the nitration of benzene:

$$C_6H_6(l) + HNO_3(l) \xrightarrow{H_2SO_4} C_6H_5NO_2(l) + H_2O(l)$$

In this case the nitro group, NO_2, substitutes for a hydrogen atom in the benzene ring.

- formation of an alcohol from an alkyl halide:

$$C_2H_5Br(l) + OH^-(aq) \longrightarrow C_2H_5OH(aq) + Br^-(aq)$$

Here a bromine atom is replaced by an —OH group.

Example 22.12 Classify each of the following as an addition, elimination, condensation, or substitution reaction.

(a) $C_2H_5OH(aq) + H^+(aq) + Br^-(aq) \longrightarrow C_2H_5Br(l) + H_2O$
(b) $C_6H_{12}(l) + Cl_2(g) \longrightarrow C_6H_{12}Cl_2(l)$
(c) $C_7H_8(l) + 2Cl_2(g) \longrightarrow C_7H_6Cl_2(l) + 2HCl(g)$
(d) $C_5H_{11}Cl(l) \longrightarrow C_5H_{10}(l) + HCl(g)$

SOLUTION

(a) substitution (Br for OH)   (b) addition (C_6H_{12} is an alkene)
(c) substitution (Cl for H)   (d) elimination (HCl lost)

CHEMISTRY Beyond the Classroom

Cholesterol

An organic compound that we hear a great deal about nowadays is cholesterol, whose structure is shown in Figure A. Your body contains about 140 g of cholesterol; it is synthesized in the liver at the rate of 2 to 3 g/day. Cholesterol is essential to life for two reasons. It is a major component of all cell membranes, and it serves as the starting material for the synthesis of sex hormones, adrenal hormones, bile acids, and vitamin D.

Cholesterol, which is water-insoluble, is transported through the blood in the form of soluble protein complexes known as lipoproteins. There are two types of complexes: low-density (LDL), which contain mostly cholesterol, and high-density (HDL), which contain relatively little cholesterol. Commonly, these complexes are referred to as "LDL cholesterol" and "HDL cholesterol," respectively.

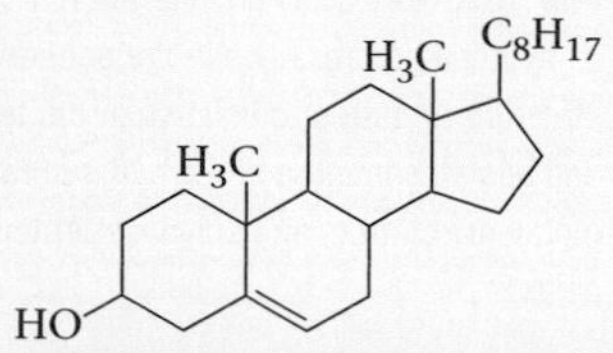

Figure A
Cholesterol.

(Continued)

LDL, or "bad," cholesterol builds up as a plaque-like deposit on the interior walls of arteries. This process used to be called hardening of the arteries; today it is referred to as *atherosclerosis*. It can lead to cardiovascular diseases, including strokes and heart attacks. In contrast, HDL or "good" cholesterol retards or even reduces arterial deposits.

The relative amounts of LDL and HDL cholesterol in your bloodstream depend, at least in part, on your diet. In particular, they depend on the total amount and the type of fat that you eat. Fats (triglycerides) are esters of glycerol with long-chain carboxylic acids. The general structure of a fat can be represented as

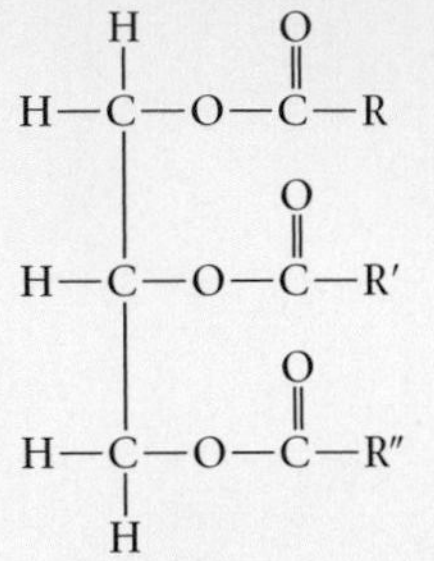

where R, R′, and R″, are hydrocarbon residues typically containing 13 to 21 carbon atoms. Depending on the nature of these residues, we can distinguish among—

- *saturated fats,* in which R, R′, and R″ contain no multiple bonds. These are "bad" in the sense that they lead to high levels of LDL relative to HDL cholesterol.
- *monounsaturated fats,* in which each residue contains one double bond. These are much better nutritionally unless, God forbid, the hydrogen atoms on opposite sides of the double bonds are trans to one another. So-called *trans* fats are bad news.
- *polyunsaturated fats,* in which the hydrocarbon residues contain more than one double bond, are good guys, particularly if a double bond is located on the third or sixth carbon atom from the —CH_3 end of the residue. These so-called omega fats are the best of all.

Figure B shows the composition of various fats (solids) and oils (liquids). Now you know why sunflower seeds are better for you than coconuts.

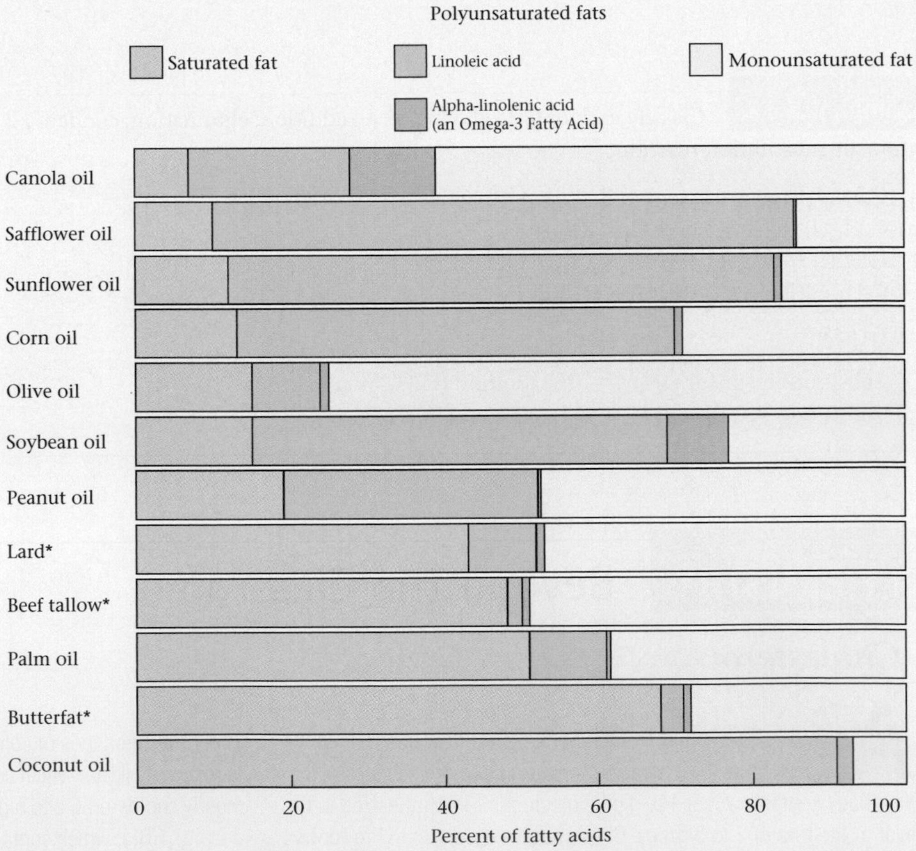

*Cholesterol Content (mg/Tbsp): Lard 12; Beef Tallow 14; Butterfat 33. No cholesterol in any vegetable-based oil.

Figure B
The composition of some common fats and oils. Fatty acids provide the R, R′, and R″ hydrocarbon residues in the general structure of a fat or oil shown in the text. Fats and oils all contain a mixture of saturated, monounsaturated, and polyunsaturated fatty acids.

Chapter Highlights

Key Concepts

1. Draw
   - structural isomers
     (Examples 22.1, 22.9; Problems 29–38) ■ Questions and Problems assignable in OWL: 30
   - geometric isomers
     (Example 22.10; Problems 39–42) ■ 42
   - optical isomers, containing chiral carbon atoms
     (Example 22.11; Problems 43–46) ■ 44, 46
2. Name
   - alkanes
     (Example 22.2; Problems 5–10) ■ 6, 8
   - unsaturated hydrocarbons
     (Example 22.4; Problems 11, 12) ■ 11, 12
   - aromatic compounds
     (Example 22.5; Problems 13, 14) ■ 14
3. Distinguish beteween alkanes, cycloalkanes, alkenes, and alkynes.
   (Example 22.3; Problems 1–4) ■ 2, 4
4. Distinguish between alcohols, ethers, aldehydes, ketones, carboxylic acids, esters, and amines.
   (Example 22.6; Problems 15–18) ■ 16, 18
5. Draw structural formulas for compounds containing the functional groups listed in Table 22.2.
   (Example 22.7; Problems 19–22) ■ 21
6. Determine equilibrium constants for the reaction of amines with strong or weak acids.
   (Example 22.8; Problems 27, 28) ■ 27
7. Classify an organic reaction as addition, elimination, condensation, or substitution.
   (Example 22.12; Problems 47–50) ■ 48

Select end of chapter Questions and Problems may be assigned in OWL and are cross-referenced in the Key Concepts list.

CENGAGENOW™

Sign in at **academic.cengage.com/now** to:

- Check your readiness for an exam by taking the Pre-Test and exploring the self-study modules recommended in your Personalized Study plan
- For quick review, download Go Chemistry mini-lecture flashcard modules (or purchase them at **www.ichapters.com**)

Key Terms

addition reaction
alcohol
aldehyde
alkane
alkene
alkyl group
alkyne
amine
aromatic hydrocarbon
carboxylic acid
chiral center
condensation reaction
cycloalkane
elimination reaction
enantiomer
ester
ether
functional group
geometric isomer
—*cis*
—*trans*
hydrocarbon
IUPAC name
ketone
meta
optical isomer
ortho
para
racemic mixture
structural isomer
substitution reaction

Summary Problem

Consider the alkyl halide that has the structure

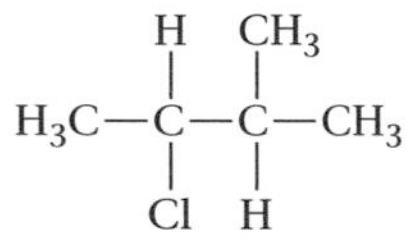

(a) Write the name of the alkyl halide and that of the alkane from which it is derived.

(b) Draw the structure of the compound formed when HCl is eliminated from the alkyl halide. Write its name and classify it as an alkane, alkene, or alkyne.

(c) Draw the structures and write the names of all the alkanes that are structurally isomeric to the alkane equivalent to (a).

(d) Write the names of all the alkenes that are structurally isomeric to (b).

(e) Does the alkyl halide exhibit optical isomerism? If so, how many chiral carbon atoms does it have?

(f) Take an isomer from (c) and add a functional group to make it
   (1) an aldehyde
   (2) a ketone
   (3) an amine
   (4) an ether
   (5) a carboxylic acid
   Write the structural formula of each species obtained.

(g) Draw the structure of the species formed when this alkyl halide undergoes substitution with an OH^- ion.

(h) Draw the condensed structural formula and write the name of the ester formed when 1-pentanol reacts with formic acid, HCOOH.

Answers

(a) 2-chloro-3-methylbutane; 2-methylbutane

(b) 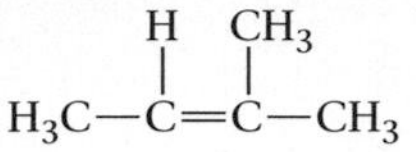 2-methyl-2-butene; alkene

(c) $CH_3CH_2CH_2CH_2CH_3$ pentane

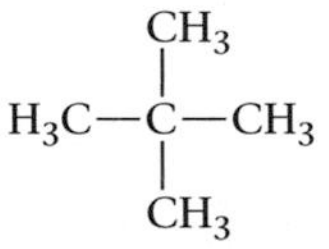 2,2-dimethylpropane

(d) 1-pentene; 2-methyl-1-butene; 3-methyl-1-butene; *cis*-2-pentene; *trans*-2-pentene

(e) yes; 1

(f) (1) 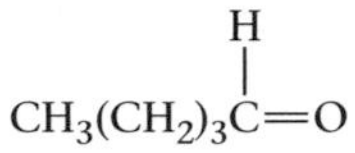

(2) 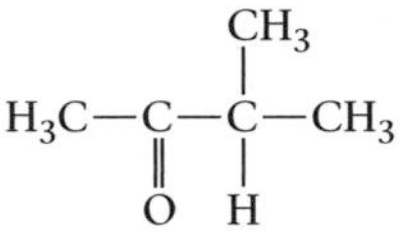

(3) 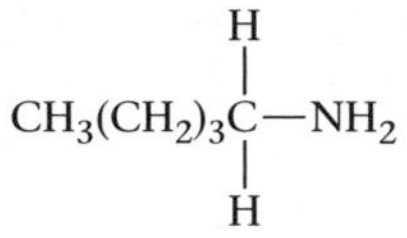

(4) 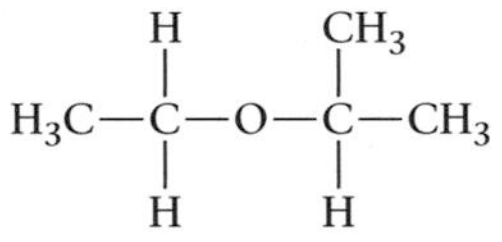

(5) 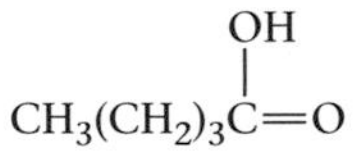

(g) 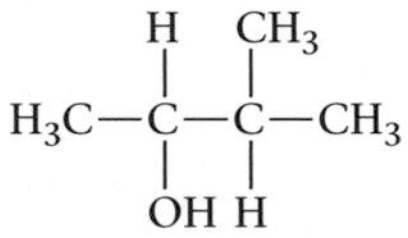

(h) pentyl formate

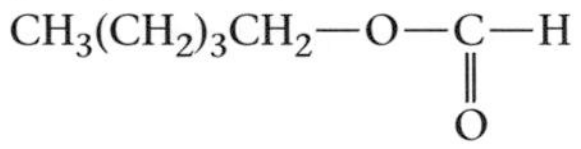

Questions and Problems

Blue-numbered questions have answers in Appendix 6 and fully-worked solutions in the *Student Solutions Manual*.

■ denotes questions assignable in OWL.

WEB indicates that the solution is available on this book's companion website.

Hydrocarbons

1. Classify each of the following hydrocarbons as alkanes, alkenes, or alkynes.
   (a) C_6H_{14} (b) C_3H_4 (c) C_9H_{18}

2. ■ Classify each of the following hydrocarbons as alkanes, alkenes, or alkynes.
   (a) $C_{12}H_{24}$ (b) C_7H_{12} (c) $C_{13}H_{28}$

3. Write the formula for
   (a) an alkene with two carbon atoms.
   (b) an alkane with 22 hydrogen atoms.
   (c) an alkyne with three carbon atoms.

4. ■ Write the formula for
   (a) an alkyne with 16 hydrogen atoms.
   (b) an alkene with 44 hydrogen atoms.
   (c) an alkane with ten carbon atoms.

5. Name the following alkanes.
   (a) 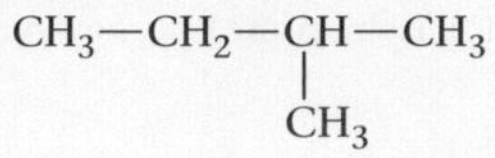

(b) 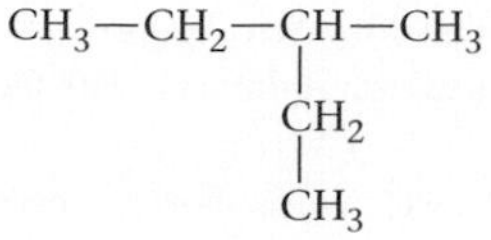

(c) 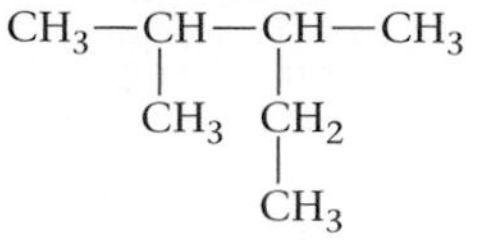

(d) 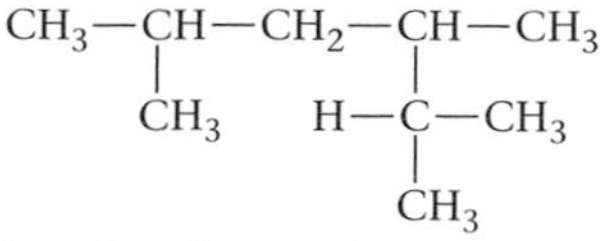

6\. ■ Name the following alkanes.

(a) 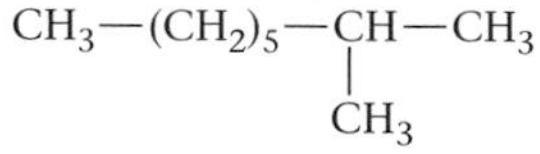

(b) $(CH_3)_4C$

(c) 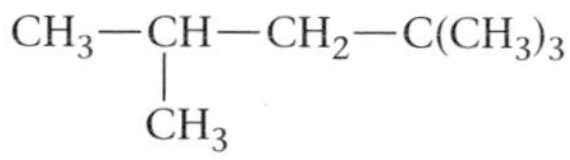

(d) 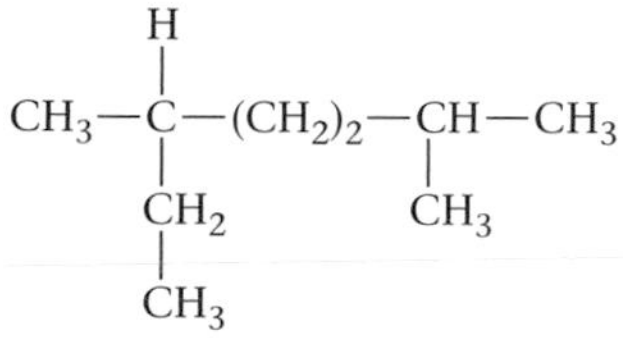

7\. Write structural formulas for the following alkanes.

(a) 3-ethylpentane (b) 2,2-dimethylbutane

(c) 2-methyl-3-ethylheptane (d) 2,3-dimethylpentane

8\. ■ Write structural formulas for the following alkanes.

(a) 2,2,4-trimethylpentane (b) 2,2-dimethylpropane

(c) 4-isopropyloctane (d) 2,3,4-trimethylheptane

9\. The following names are incorrect; draw a reasonable structure for the alkane and give the proper IUPAC name.

(a) 5-isopropyloctane (b) 2-ethylpropane

(c) 1,2-dimethylpropane

10\. Follow the directions of Problem 9 for the following names.

(a) 2, 2-dimethylbutane (b) 4-methylpentane

(c) 2-ethylpropane

11\. ■ Name the following alkenes.

(a) $CH_2{=}C{-}(CH_3)_2$

(b) $(CH_3)_2{-}C{=}C{-}(CH_3)_2$

(c) $CH_3{-}CH{=}CH{-}CH_2CH_3$

(d) 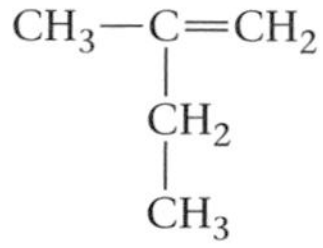

12\. ■ **WEB** Write structural formulas for the following alkynes.

(a) 2-pentyne (b) 4-methyl-2-pentyne

(c) 2-methyl-3-hexyne (d) 3,3-dimethyl-1-butyne

13\. Name the following compounds as derivatives of nitrobenzene.

(a) 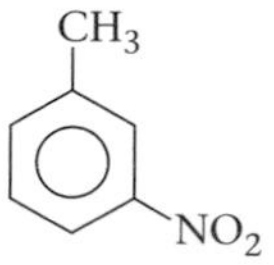

(b) 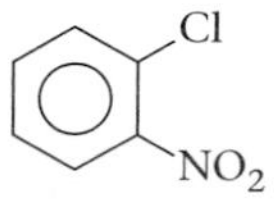

(c) 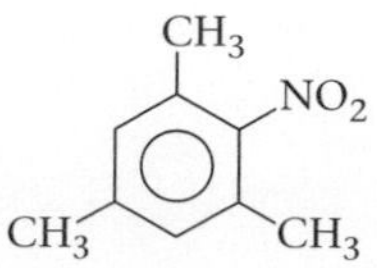

14\. ■ Name the following compounds as derivatives of toluene.

(a) 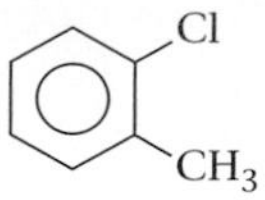

(b) 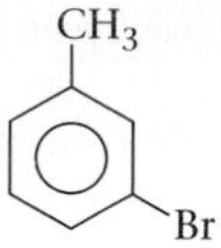

(c) 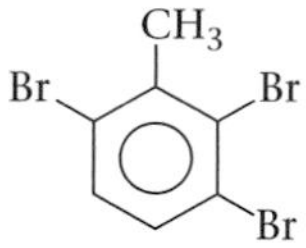

Functional Groups

15\. Classify each of the following as a carboxylic acid, ester, and/or alcohol.

(a) $HO{-}CH_2{-}CH_2{-}CH_2{-}OH$

(b) 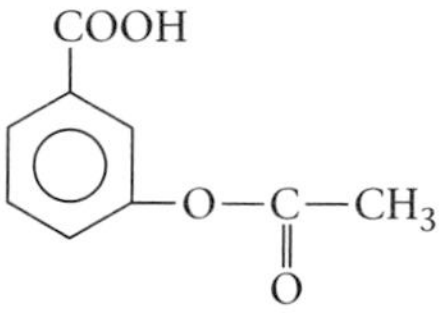

(c) 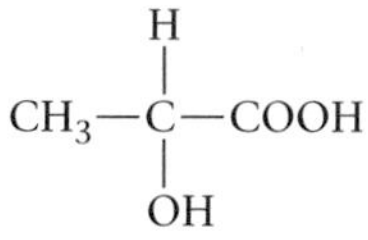

16\. ■ Classify each of the following as a carboxylic acid, ester, and/or alcohol.

(a) $CH_3{-}(CH_2)_3{-}OH$

(b) 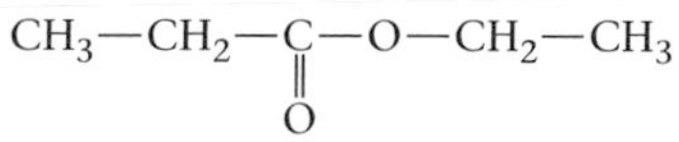

(c) 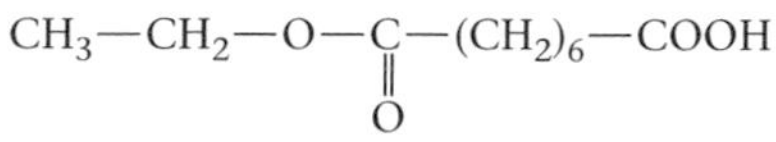

17\. In each of the following, name the functional group (i.e., ester, aldehyde, . . .).

(a) $CH_3{-}CH{=}CH{-}CH_2{-}OH$

(b) 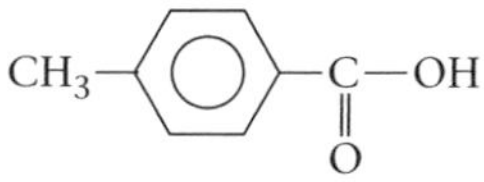

(c) 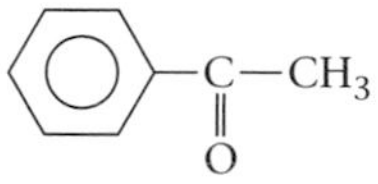

(d) 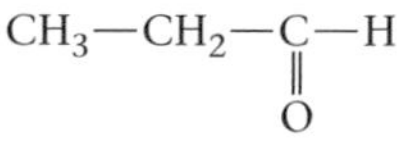

(e) 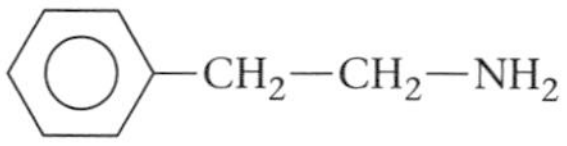

18\. ■ In each of the following, name the functional group (i.e., ester, aldehyde, . . .).

(a) $CH_2{=}CH{-}O{-}CH_3$

(b) 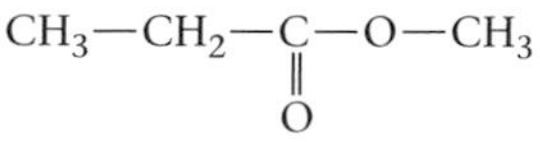

(c) $CH_3{-}CH_2{-}CH_2{-}NH_2$

(d) 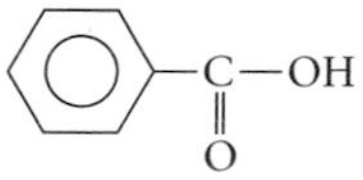

(e) 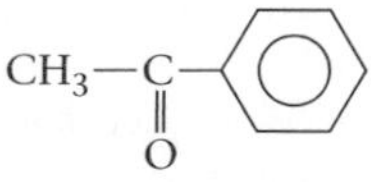

■ in OWL Blue-numbered questions answered in Appendix 6 **WEB** Solution is available on companion website

19. Give the structure of
(a) a four-carbon straight-chain alcohol with an —OH group not at the end of the chain.
(b) a five-carbon straight-chain carboxylic acid.
(c) the ester formed when these two compounds react.

20. Give the structure of
(a) a three-carbon alcohol with the —OH group on the center carbon.
(b) a four-carbon branched-chain carboxylic acid.
(c) the ester formed when these two compounds react.

21. ■ Write the structural formula of the ester formed by methyl alcohol with
(a) formic acid. (b) acetic acid.
(c) $CH_3—(CH_2)_6—COOH$.

22. Write the structural formulas of all the esters that can be formed by ethylene glycol with formic and acetic acids. (One or both of the —OH groups of ethylene glycol can react.)

23. Arrange these compounds in order of increasing boiling point. Values in °C are 0, 11, and 97.
(a) $CH_3CH_2CH_2OH$
(b) $CH_3CH_2—O—CH_3$
(c) $CH_3CH_2CH_2CH_3$

24. ■ Arrange these compounds in order of increasing boiling point.
(a) 1-butanol, butane, diethylether
(b) hexane, 1-hexanol, dipropylether

25. The K_b for ethylamine ($CH_3CH_2NH_2$) is 4.3×10^{-4}. What is the pH of a 0.250 *M* solution of ethylamine? Compare with the pH of a 0.250 *M* solution of ammonia ($K_b = 1.86 \times 10^{-5}$).

26. When aniline, $C_6H_5NH_2$ ($K_b = 7.4 \times 10^{-10}$), reacts with a strong acid, its conjugate acid, $C_6H_5NH_3^+$, is formed. Calculate the pH of a 0.100 *M* solution of $C_6H_5NH_3^+$ and compare it with the pH of acetic acid ($K_a = 1.86 \times 10^{-5}$).

27. ■ When ethylamine, a weak base ($K_b = 4.3 \times 10^{-4}$), reacts with formic acid, a weak acid ($K_a = 1.8 \times 10^{-4}$), the following reaction takes place:

$$CH_3CH_2NH_2(aq) + HCOOH(aq) \rightleftharpoons CH_3CH_2NH_3^+(aq) + HCOO^-(aq)$$

Calculate *K* for this reaction.

28. When the conjugate acid of aniline, $C_6H_5NH_3^+$, reacts with the acetate ion, the following reaction takes place:

$$C_6H_5NH_3^+(aq) + CH_3COO^-(aq) \rightleftharpoons C_6H_5NH_2(aq) + CH_3COOH(aq)$$

If K_a for $C_6H_5NH_3^+$ is 1.35×10^{-5} and K_a for CH_3COOH is 1.86×10^{-5}, what is *K* for the reaction?

Isomerism

29. Draw the structural isomers of the alkane C_6H_{14}.

30. ■ Draw the structural isomers of the alkene C_4H_8.

31. Draw the structural isomers of C_4H_9Cl in which one hydrogen atom of a C_4H_{10} molecule has been replaced by chlorine.

32. WEB Draw the structural isomers of $C_3H_6Cl_2$ in which two of the hydrogen atoms of C_3H_8 have been replaced by chlorine atoms.

33. There are three compounds with the formula C_6H_4ClBr in which two of the hydrogen atoms of the benzene molecule have been replaced by halogen atoms. Draw structures for these compounds.

34. There are three compounds with the formula $C_6H_3Cl_3$ in which three of the hydrogen atoms of the benzene molecule have been replaced by chlorine atoms. Draw structures for these compounds.

35. Write structures for all the structural isomers of double-bonded compounds with the molecular formula C_5H_{10}.

36. Write structures for all the structural isomers of compounds with the molecular formula C_4H_6ClBr in which Cl and Br are bonded to a double-bonded carbon.

37. Draw structures for all the alcohols with molecular formula $C_5H_{12}O$.

38. Draw structures for all the saturated carboxylic acids with four carbon atoms per molecule.

39. Of the compounds in Problem 35, which ones show geometric isomerism? Draw the *cis*- and *trans*- isomers.

40. Of the compounds in Problem 36, which ones show geometric isomerism? Draw the *cis*- and *trans*- isomers.

41. Maleic acid and fumaric acid are the *cis*- and *trans*- isomers, respectively, of $C_2H_2(COOH)_2$, a dicarboxylic acid. Draw and label their structures.

42. ■ For which of the following is geometric isomerism possible?
(a) $(CH_3)_2C{=}CCl_2$ (b) $CH_3ClC{=}CCH_3Cl$
(c) $CH_3BrC{=}CCH_3Cl$

43. Which of the following can show optical isomerism?
(a) 2-bromo-2-chlorobutane
(b) 2-methylpropane
(c) 2,2-dimethyl-1-butanol
(d) 2,2,4-trimethylpentane

44. ■ Which of the following compounds can show optical isomerism?
(a) dichloromethane
(b) 1,2-dichloroethane
(c) bromochlorofluoromethane
(d) 1-bromoethanol

45. Locate the chiral carbon(s), if any, in the following molecules.

(a) 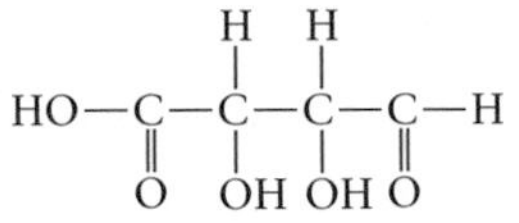

(b) 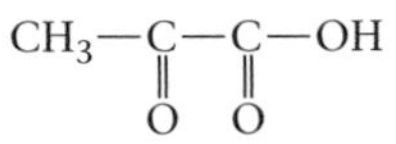

(c) 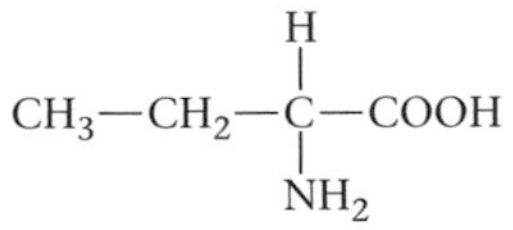

46. ■ WEB Locate the chiral carbon(s), if any, in the following molecules.

(a) 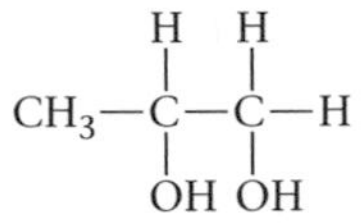

(b) 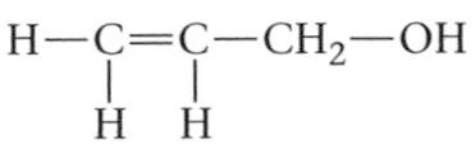

(c) 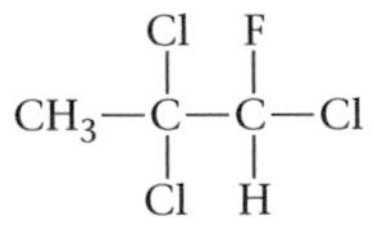

Types of Reactions

47. Classify the following reactions as addition, substitution, elimination, or condensation.
(a) $C_2H_2(g) + HBr(g) \rightarrow C_2H_3Br(l)$
(b) $C_6H_5OH(s) + HNO_3(l) \rightarrow C_6H_4(OH)(NO_2)(s) + H_2O(l)$
(c) $C_2H_5OH(aq) + HCOOH(aq) \rightarrow$
$C_2H_5—O—C(=O)—H(l) + H_2O(l)$

48. ■ Classify the following reactions according to the categories listed in Question 47.
(a) $PCl_3(g) + Cl_2(g) \rightarrow PCl_5(g)$
(b) $C_3H_7OH(l) \rightarrow C_3H_6(g) + H_2O(l)$
(c) $CH_3OH(l) + C_2H_5OH(l) \rightarrow CH_3—O—C_2H_5(l) + H_2O(l)$

49. Name the products formed when the following reagents add to 1-butene.
(a) H_2 (b) Br_2

■ in OWL Blue-numbered questions answered in Appendix 6 WEB Solution is available on companion website

50. ■ Name the products obtained when the following reagents add to 2-methyl-2-butene.

(a) Cl_2 (b) I_2

Unclassified

51. Which of the following are expected to show bond angles of 109.5°? 120°? 180°?

(a) $H_3C{-}CH_3$ (b) $H_3C{-}\overset{\displaystyle H}{\overset{|}{C}}{=}CH_2$

(c) $H_3C{-}C{\equiv}C{-}CH_3$

52. What does the "circle" represent in the structural formula of benzene?

53. Calculate $[H^+]$ and the pH of a 0.10 M solution of chloroacetic acid ($K_a = 1.5 \times 10^{-3}$).

54. Explain what is meant by the following.

(a) a saturated fat

(b) a soap

(c) the "proof" of an alcoholic beverage

(d) denatured alcohol

55. The general formula of an alkane is C_nH_{2n+2}. What is the general formula of an

(a) alkene? (b) alkyne?

(c) alcohol derived from an alkane?

56. Write a balanced net ionic equation for the reaction of

(a) $(CH_3)_2NH$ with hydrochloric acid.

(b) acetic acid with a solution of barium hydroxide.

(c) 2-chloropropane with a solution of sodium hydroxide.

Challenge Problems

57. The structure of cholesterol is given in the text. (See Figure A, p. 603) What is its molecular formula?

58. Draw structures for all the alcohols with molecular formula $C_6H_{14}O$.

59. What mass of propane must be burned to bring one quart of water in a saucepan at 25°C to the boiling point? Use data in Appendix 1 and elsewhere and make any reasonable assumptions.

60. Write an equation for the reaction of chloroacetic acid ($K_a = 1.5 \times 10^{-3}$) with trimethylamine ($K_b = 5.9 \times 10^{-5}$). Calculate the equilibrium constant for the reaction. If 0.10 M solutions of these two species are mixed, what will be their concentrations at equilibrium?

■ in OWL Blue-numbered questions answered in Appendix 6 **WEB** Solution is available on companion website

23 Organic Polymers, Natural and Synthetic

No single thing abides; but all things flow
Fragment to fragment clings—the things thus grow
Until we know and name them. By degrees
They melt, and are no more the things we know.

—Titus Lucretius Carus (92–52 B.C.)
"No Single Thing Abides"
(Translated by W. H. Mallock)

Chapter Outline

Dale Chihuly, Chihuly Bridge of Glass, Crystal Towers detail, 2002, Tacoma, Washington/Scott M. Leen

The glasslike sculpture is made of a polymer, which allows it to stand up to the outdoor weather. The repeating design, though random, recognizes the randomness and repetitiveness of the structure of polymers.

In previous chapters we have discussed the chemical and physical properties of many kinds of substances. For the most part, these materials were made up of either small molecules or simple ions. In this chapter, we will be concerned with an important class of compounds containing large molecules. We call these compounds polymers.

A polymer is made up of a large number of small molecular units, called *monomers*, combined together chemically. A typical polymer molecule contains a chain of monomers several thousand units long. The monomer units of which a given polymer is composed may be the same or different.

We start with synthetic organic polymers. Since about 1930, a variety of synthetic polymers have been made available by the chemical industry. The monomer units are joined together either by addition (Section 23.1) or by condensation (Section 23.2). They are used to make cups, plates, fabrics, automobile tires, and even artificial hearts.

The remainder of this chapter will deal with natural polymers. These are large molecules, produced by plants and animals, that carry out the many life-sustaining processes in a living cell. The cell membranes of plants and the woody structure of trees are composed in large part of cellulose, a polymeric carbohydrate. We will look at the structures of a variety of different carbohydrates in Section 23.3. Another class of natural polymers are the proteins. Section 23.4 deals with these polymeric materials that make up our tissues, bone, blood, and even hair. ■

Online homework for this chapter may be assigned in OWL.

CENGAGENOW™

This icon introduces an opportunity for self-study and to explore interactive modules by signing in at **academic.cengage.com/now.**

These polymers are usually called plastics.

23.1 SYNTHETIC ADDITION POLYMERS

When monomer units add directly to one another, the result is an addition polymer. Table 23.1 lists some of the more familiar synthetic addition polymers. You will notice that each of these is derived from a monomer containing a carbon-carbon double bond. Upon polymerization, the double bond is converted to a single bond:

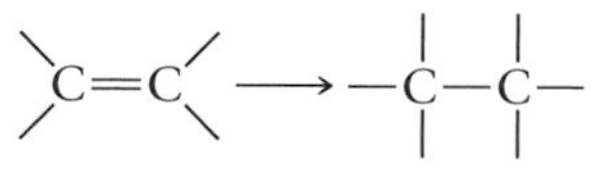

and successive monomer units add to one another.

Industrial chemists work more with polymers than with any other class of materials.

Polyethylene

Perhaps the most familiar addition polymer is *polyethylene*, a solid derived from the monomer ethylene. We might represent the polymerization process as

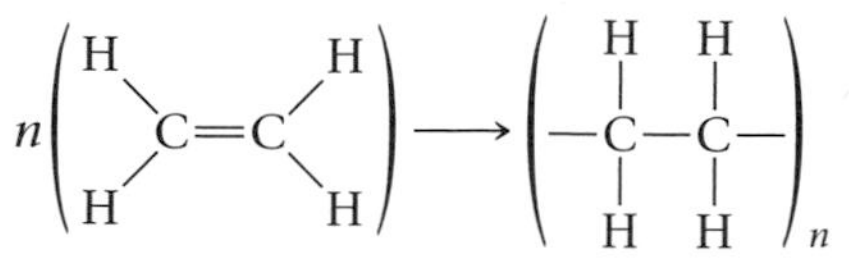

ethylene polyethylene

where n is a very large number, of the order of 2000.

Depending upon the conditions of polymerization, the product may be—

- ***branched*** polyethylene, which has a structure of the type

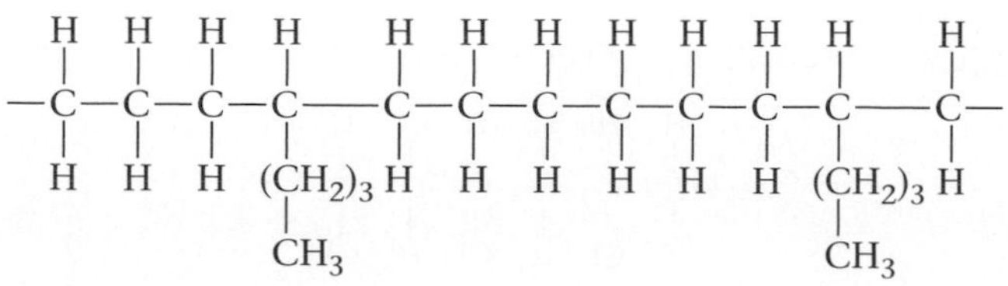

Table 23.1 Some Common Addition Polymers

Monomer	Name	Polymer	Uses
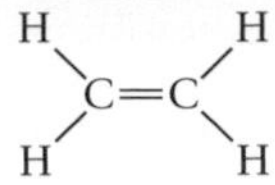	Ethylene	Polyethylene	Bags, coatings, toys
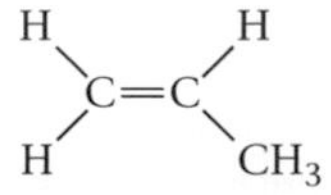	Propylene	Polypropylene	Beakers, milk cartons
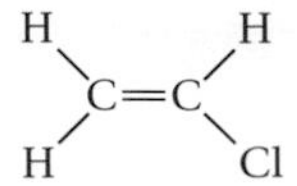	Vinyl chloride	Polyvinyl chloride (PVC)	Floor tile, raincoats, pipe, phonograph records
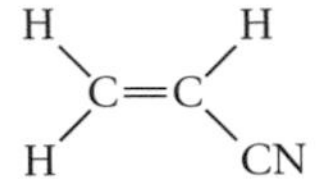	Acrylonitrile	Polyacrylonitrile (PAN)	Rugs; Orlon and Acrilan are copolymers with other monomers
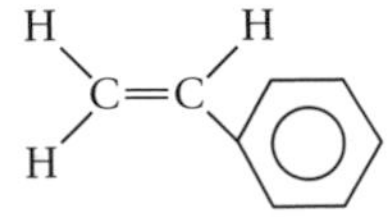	Styrene	Polystyrene	Cast articles using a transparent plastic
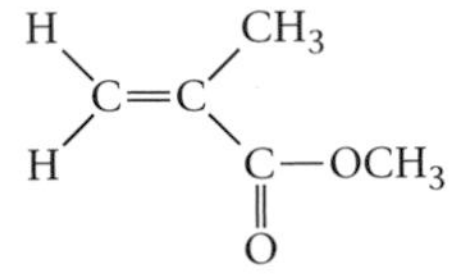	Methyl methacrylate	Plexiglas, Lucite, acrylic resins	High-quality transparent objects, latex paints
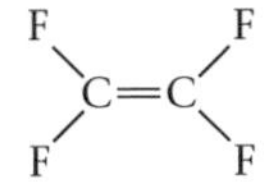	Tetrafluoroethylene	Teflon	Gaskets, insulation, bearings, pan coatings

Marna G. Clarke

Figure 23.1
Branched and linear polyethylene. The polyethylene bottle at the left is made of pliable, branched polyethylene. The one at the right is made of semirigid, linear polyethylene.

Here, neighboring chains are arranged in a somewhat random fashion, producing a soft, flexible solid (Figure 23.1). The plastic bags at the vegetable counters of supermarkets are made of this material.

- ***linear*** polyethylene, which consists almost entirely of unbranched chains:

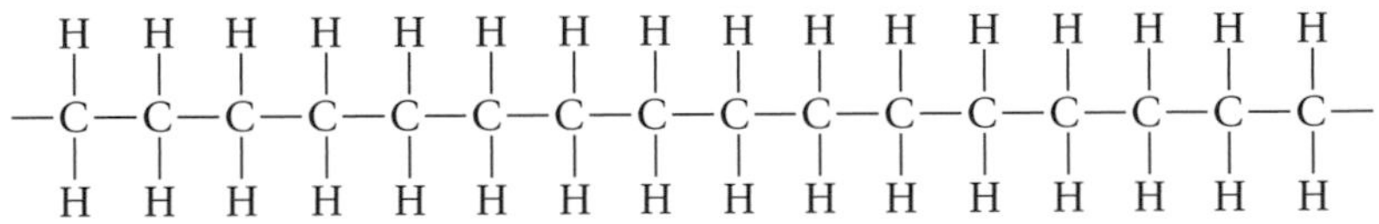

Neighboring chains in linear polyethylene line up nearly parallel to each other. This gives a polymer that approaches a crystalline material. It is used for bottles, toys, and other semirigid objects.

The two forms of polyethylene differ slightly in density. Linear polyethylene is referred to in the recycling business as *h*igh-*d*ensity *p*oly*e*thylene, represented by the symbol "HDPE #2" on the bottom of a plastic bottle. The corresponding symbol for branched polyethylene is "LDPE #4," indicating low-density polyethylene. (The smaller the number, the easier it is to recycle.)

Example 23.1 The addition polymer polyvinyl chloride (PVC) has the structure

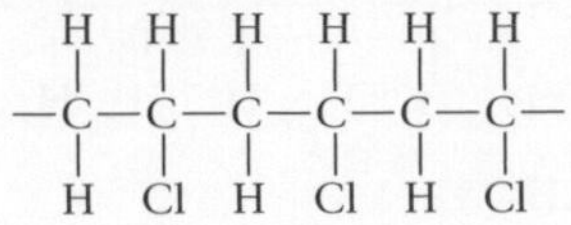

(a) Draw the structure of the monomer from which PVC is made.
(b) How many monomer units are in a PVC polymer that has a molar mass of 1.33×10^5 g/mol?

Strategy In (a), find the repeating unit from which the polymer chain is constructed. In (b), divide the molar mass of the polymer by that of the monomer.

SOLUTION

(a) 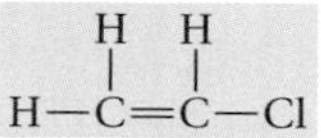

(b) MM of CH_2CHCl = 62.49 g/mol

no. of monomer units = $(1.33 \times 10^5)/62.49 = 2.13 \times 10^3$

Polyvinyl Chloride

Vinyl chloride, in contrast to ethylene, is an unsymmetrical molecule. We might refer to the CH_2 group in vinyl chloride as the "head" of the molecule and the CHCl group as the "tail":

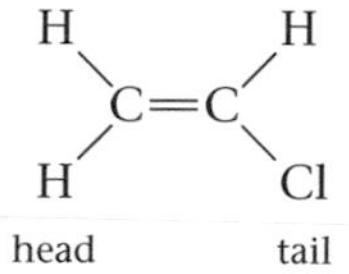

vinyl chloride

In principle at least, vinyl chloride molecules can add to one another in any of three ways to form:

1. A **head-to-tail** polymer, in which there is a Cl atom on every other C atom in the chain:

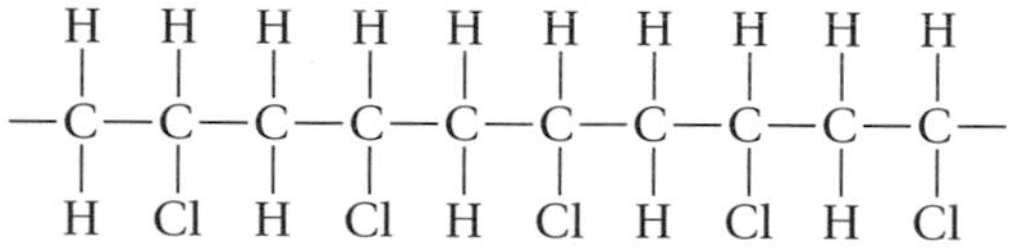

2. A **head-to-head, tail-to-tail** polymer, in which Cl atoms occur in pairs on adjacent carbon atoms in the chain:

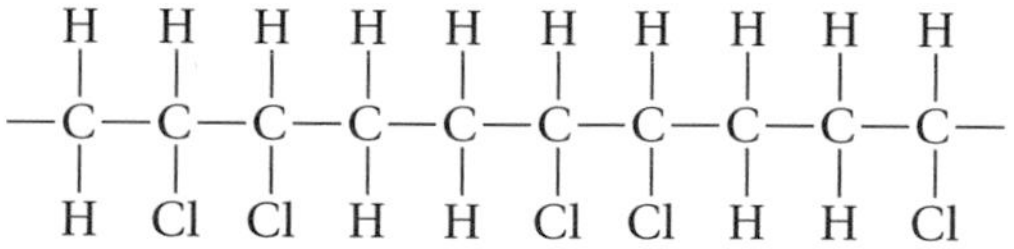

PVC is a stiff, rugged, cheap polymer.

3. A **random** polymer:

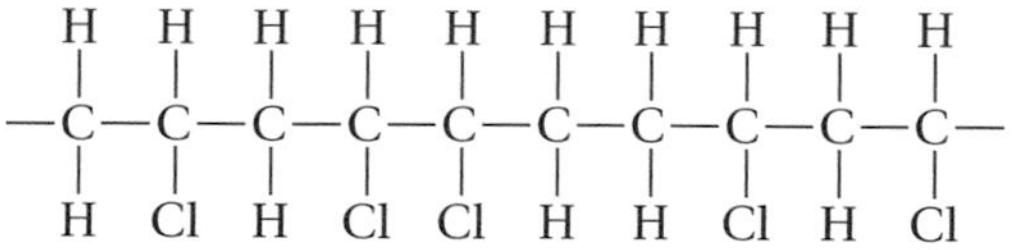

Similar arrangements are possible with polymers made from other unsymmetrical monomers (Example 23.2).

Example 23.2 Sketch a polymer derived from propene:

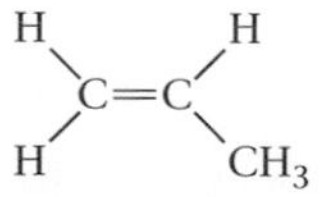

assuming it to be a

(a) head-to-tail polymer (b) head-to-head, tail-to-tail polymer.

SOLUTION

(a) 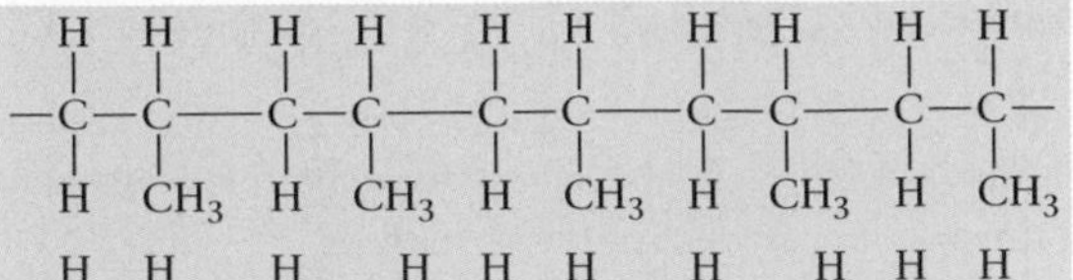

(b) 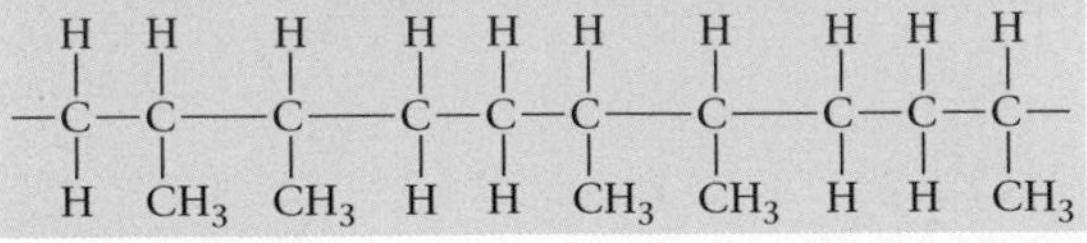

Figure 23.2
Teflon. The Teflon coating helps prevent food from sticking to this cookware.

Teflon

Teflon $(C_2F_2)_n$, where n is of the order of 10^4 to 10^5, is a versatile but expensive polymer ($10–20/kg). It is virtually impervious to chemical attack, even at high temperatures. Apparently the fluorine atoms form a protective shield around the central carbon chain:

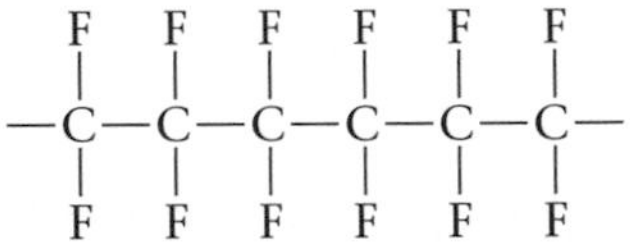

For much the same reason, Teflon is essentially invulnerable to attack by aqueous or organic solvents. Beyond that, Teflon is an excellent electrical insulator. Indeed, its largest industrial use is in that area.

You are probably most familiar with Teflon as a nonstick coating for kitchen utensils (Figure 23.2). The slippery surface of Teflon-coated fry pans and muffin tins results from Teflon's extremely low coefficient of friction.

23.2 SYNTHETIC CONDENSATION POLYMERS

As we pointed out in Chapter 22, a condensation reaction is one in which two molecules combine by splitting out a small molecule such as water. The reaction of an alcohol, ROH, or an amine, RNH_2, with a carboxylic acid R′COOH is a condensation:

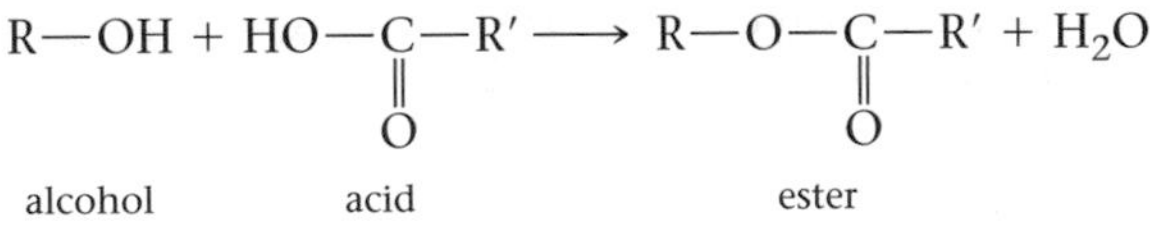

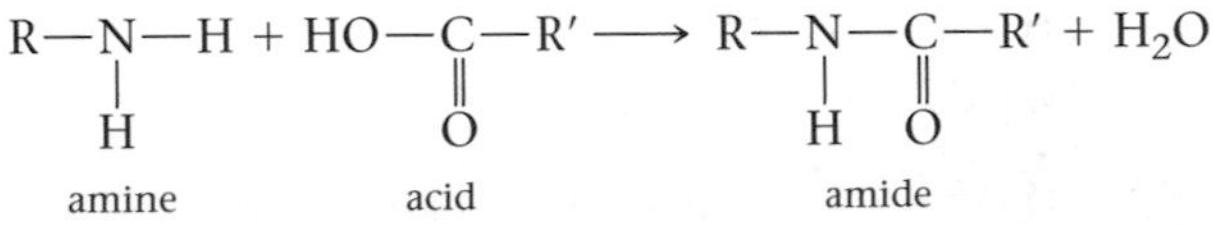

Condensation polymers are formed in a similar way; the molecule split out is most often water. In order to produce a condensation polymer, *the monomers involved must have functional groups at both ends of the molecule.* Most often these groups are

$$—NH_2 \qquad —OH \qquad —COOH$$

The products formed are referred to as polyesters and polyamides.

Polyesters

Consider what happens when an alcohol with two —OH groups, HO—R—OH, reacts with a dicarboxylic acid, HOOC—R′—COOH. In this case the ester formed still has a reactive group at both ends of the molecule.

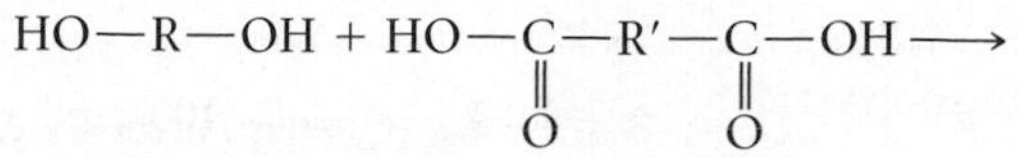

dihydroxy alcohol

dicarboxylic acid

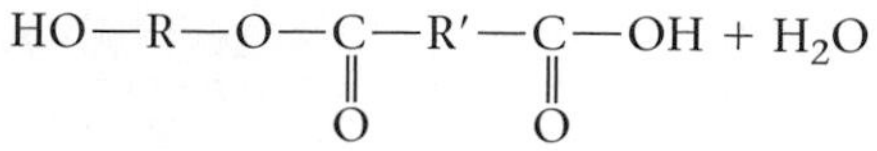

ester with active end groups

The COOH group at one end of the ester molecule can react with another alcohol molecule. The OH group at the other end can react with an acid molecule. This process can continue, leading eventually to a long-chain polymer containing 500 or more ester groups. The general structure of the polyester can be represented as

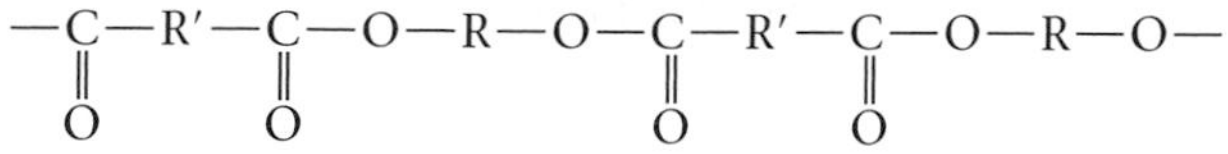

section of a polyester molecule

Perhaps the most important polyester is poly(ethylene terephthalate), commonly known as PET (or "PETE 1" on plastic beverage bottles). The annual production of PET in the United States is of the order of 10^8 kg (10^5 metric tons). Much of this is converted into fabric (trade name, Dacron) or magnetically coated film (Mylar).

The two monomers used to make PET are

$$HO{-}CH_2{-}CH_2{-}OH$$

ethylene glycol

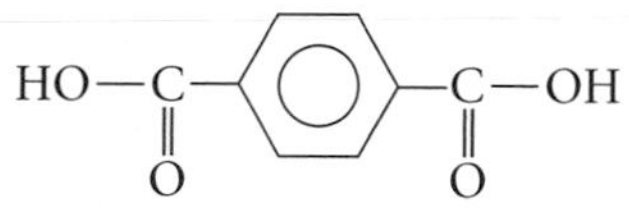

terephthalic acid

Example 23.3

(a) Write the structural formula of the ester formed when one molecule of ethylene glycol reacts with one molecule of terephthalic acid.
(b) Draw a section of the "PET" polymer.

SOLUTION

(a)

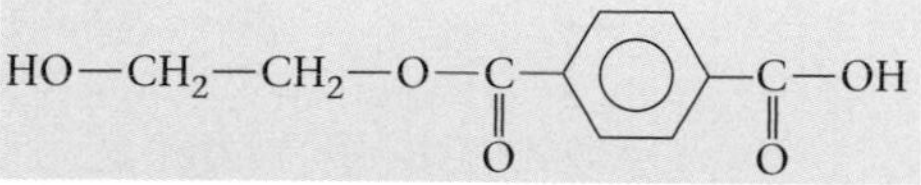

(b)

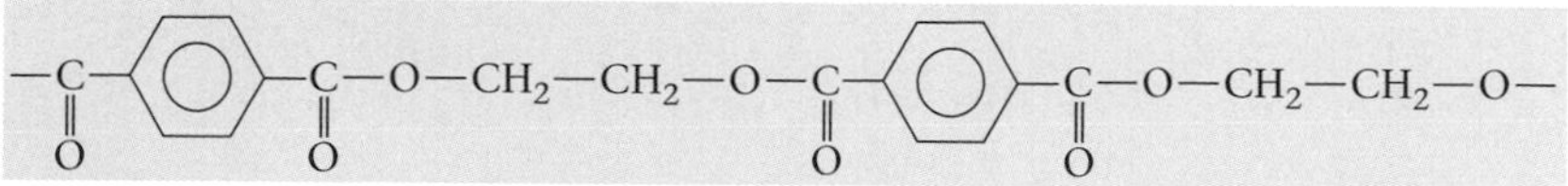

Polyamides

When a diamine (molecule containing two NH_2 groups) reacts with a dicarboxylic acid (two COOH groups), a **polyamide** is formed. This condensation polymerization is entirely analogous to that used to make polyesters. In this case, the NH_2 group of the diamine reacts with the COOH group of the dicarboxylic acid:

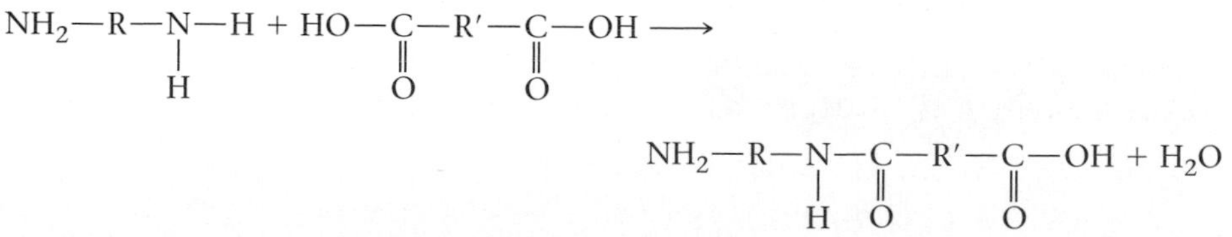

Condensation can continue to form a long-chain polymer.

Figure 23.3
Nylon. Nylon can be made by the reaction between hexamethylenediamine, $H_2N—(CH_2)_6—NH_2$, and adipic acid, $HOOC—(CH_2)_4—COOH$. It forms at the interface between the two reagents.

Example 23.4 Consider the following polyamide:

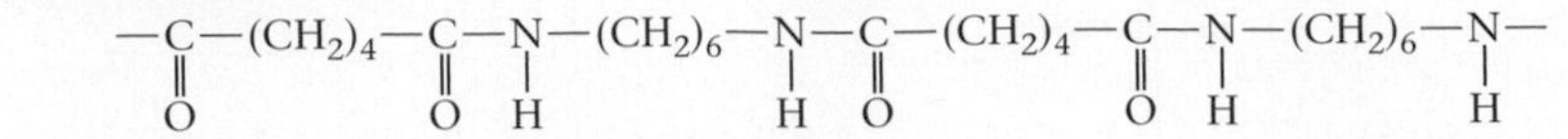

Give the structures of the two monomers, dicarboxylic acid and diamine, used to make this polymer.

Strategy Break the polymer into two fragments, each containing both monomers, and go on from there.

SOLUTION

Dicarboxylic acid: 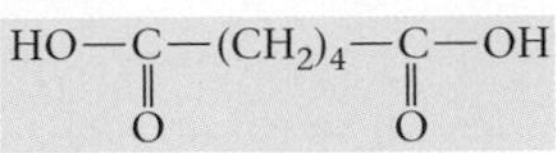

Diamine: 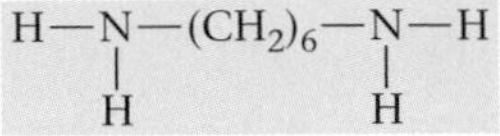

The polymer in Example 23.4 is "Nylon-66" (the numbers indicate the number of carbon atoms in the diamine and dicarboxylic acid molecules). This polymer was first made in 1935 by Wallace Carothers working at DuPont (Figure 23.3). Since then, other nylons, all polyamides, have been synthesized.

The elasticity of nylon fibers is due in part to hydrogen bonds between adjacent polymer chains. These hydrogen bonds join carbonyl oxygen atoms on one chain to NH groups on adjacent chains (Figure 23.4).

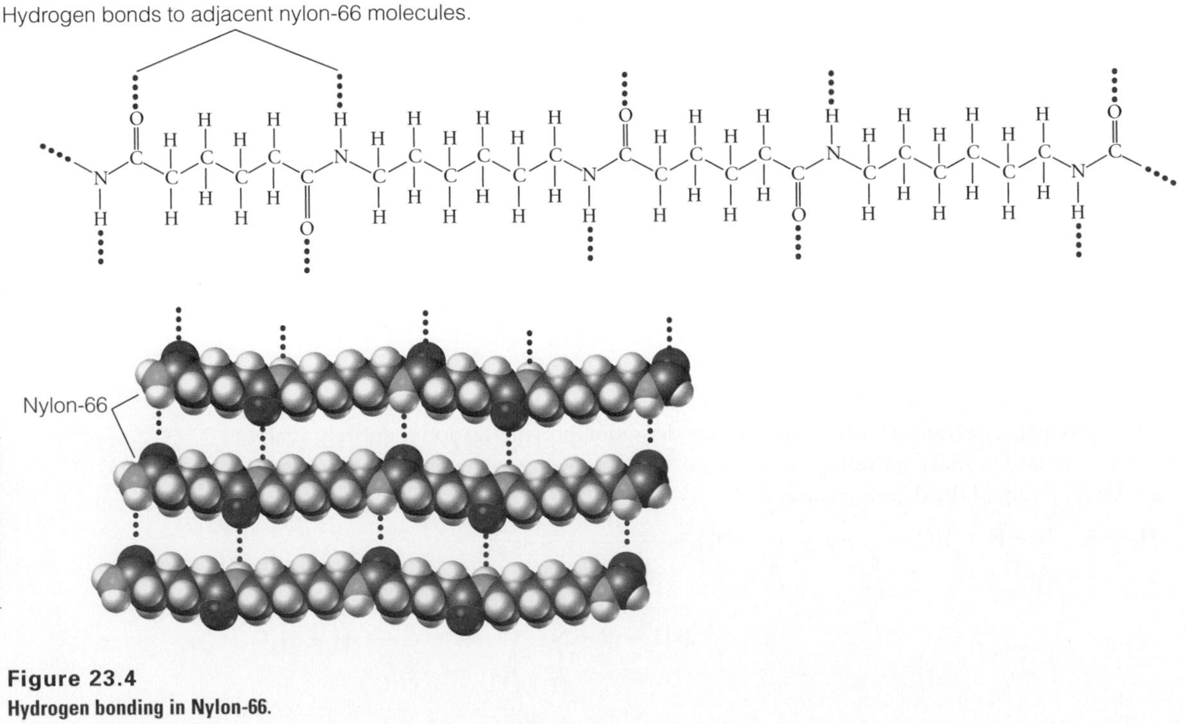

Figure 23.4
Hydrogen bonding in Nylon-66.

23.3 CARBOHYDRATES

Carbohydrates, which comprise one of the three basic classes of foodstuffs, contain carbon, hydrogen, and oxygen atoms. Their general formula, $C_n(H_2O)_m$, is the basis for their name. They can be classified as

1. *Monosaccharides,* which cannot be broken down chemically to simpler carbohydrates. The most familiar monosaccharides contain either six carbon atoms per molecule (glucose, fructose, galactose, . . .) or five (ribose, arabinose, . . .).
2. *Disaccharides,* which are dimers formed when two monosaccharide units combine with the elimination of H_2O. The monosaccharides may be the same (two glucose units in maltose) or different (a glucose and fructose unit in sucrose).
3. *Polysaccharides,* which are condensation polymers containing from several hundred to several thousand monosaccharide units. Cellulose and starch are the most common polysaccharides.

Glucose

By far the most important monosaccharide is glucose. As a pure solid, it has the "straight-chain" structure shown in the margin. In water solution, glucose exists primarily as six-membered ring molecules, shown below. The rings are not planar but have a three-dimensional "chair" form. The carbon atoms at each corner of the ring are not shown in the structure; they are represented by the numbers 1 to 5. The sixth atom in the ring is oxygen. There is a CH_2OH group bonded to carbon atom 5. There is an H atom bonded to each of the ring carbons; an OH group is bonded to carbon atoms 1 through 4. The heavy lines indicate the front of the ring, projected toward you.

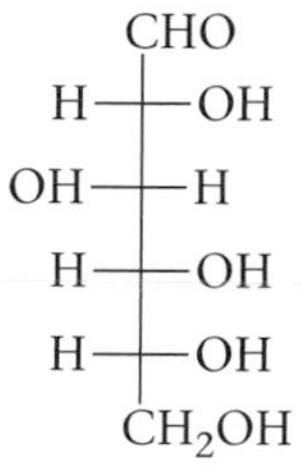

D-glucose

The bonds to the H and OH groups from the ring carbons are oriented either in the plane of the ring (*equatorial,* shown in blue) or perpendicular to it *(axial).* In β-glucose, all four OH groups are equatorial. This keeps these rather bulky groups out of each other's way. In α-glucose, the OH group on carbon atom 1 is axial; all the others are equatorial. In water solution, glucose exists as an equilibrium mixture, about 37% in the alpha form and 63% in the beta form; the straight-chain structure accounts for less than 0.1% of the dissolved glucose.

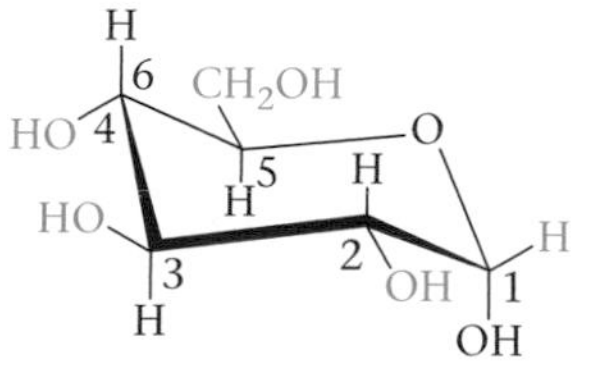

α-glucose

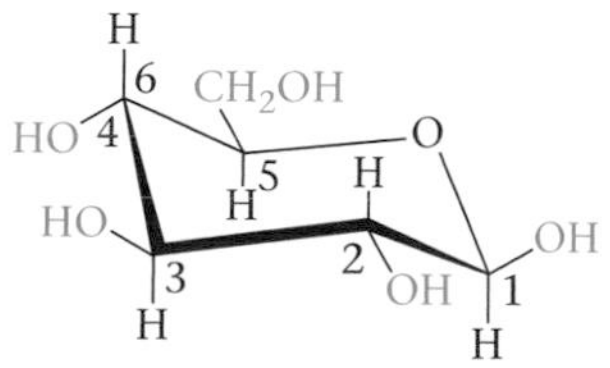

β-glucose

As you can see from their structures, α- and β-glucose have several chiral carbon atoms. Both isomers are optically active; they are *not* enantiomers (mirror images of one another) because they differ in configuration only at carbon atom 1. As it happens, both α- and β-glucose rotate the plane of polarized light to the right (clockwise).

Example 23.5

(a) What is the molecular formula of glucose?
(b) How many chiral carbon atoms are there in a molecule of α-glucose? β-glucose? The straight-chain isomer?

SOLUTION

(a) There are six carbon atoms per molecule. If you count carefully, you should find 12 hydrogen and 6 oxygen atoms in each structure shown. The molecular formula is

$C_6H_{12}O_6$, which corresponds to the general carbohydrate formula, $C_n(H_2O)_m$ with $n = m = 6$.

(b) α- and β-glucose both have five chiral carbon atoms (C_1–C_5), one more than the straight-chain structure (C_2–C_5).

Glucose is also called "blood sugar." It is absorbed readily into the bloodstream and is normally found there at concentrations ranging from 0.004 to 0.008 mol/L. If the concentration of glucose drops below 0.003 *M*, a condition called hypoglycemia is created, with symptoms ranging from nervousness to loss of consciousness. If the glucose level rises above 0.01 *M*, as can easily happen with diabetics, it is excreted in the urine.

Although glucose can exist as a simple sugar, it is most often found in nature in combined form, as a disaccharide or polysaccharide. Several glucose-containing disaccharides are known. We will consider two of these, maltose and sucrose.

Maltose and Sucrose

Maltose, a decomposition product of starch, is a dimer of two glucose molecules. These are combined head-to-tail; carbon atom 1 of one molecule is joined through an oxygen atom to carbon atom 4 of the second molecule. To form maltose, the two OH groups on these carbon atoms react, condensing out H_2O and leaving the O atom bridge.

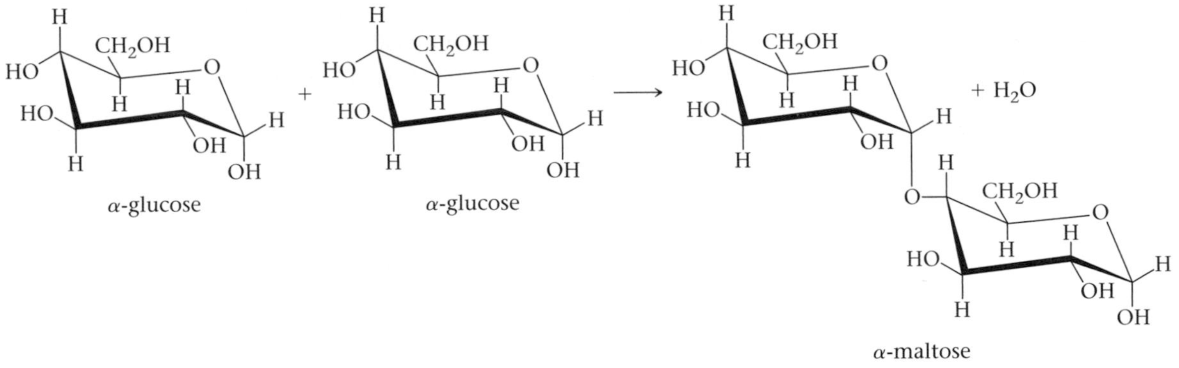

This reaction can be reversed either by using the enzyme maltase as a catalyst or by heating with acid. Two molecules of glucose are formed when this happens.

Sucrose, the compound we call "sugar," is the most common disaccharide. One of the monomer units in sucrose is α-glucose. The other is fructose, a monosaccharide found in honey and natural fruit juices.

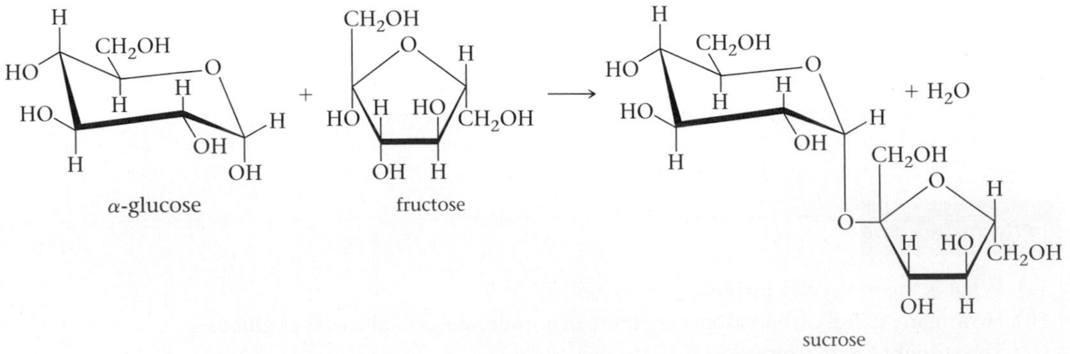

In the body, this reaction is reversed by the enzyme sucrase. This occurs in digestion, which makes glucose and fructose available for absorption into the blood. Honey bees also carry an enzyme that can hydrolyze sucrose. Honey consists mostly of a 1 : 1 mol mixture of glucose and fructose with a small amount of unreacted sucrose.

Example 23.6 Another common disaccharide is lactose, the sugar found in milk. Lactose is a dimer of glucose and galactose, a monosaccharide that is identical to glucose except that the positions of the H and OH groups at carbon atom 4 are switched.

(a) Draw the structure of β-galactose.

(b) Draw the structure of lactose, which is broken down by the enzyme lactase to give equimolar amounts of β-galactose and β-glucose. Linkage occurs between carbon atom 1 of galactose and 4 of glucose.

SOLUTION

(a) The structure of β-galactose is identical to that of β-glucose except at carbon atom 4. Showing equatorial groups in color,

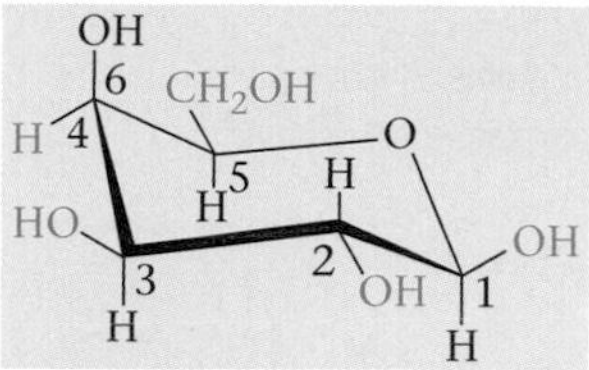

(b)

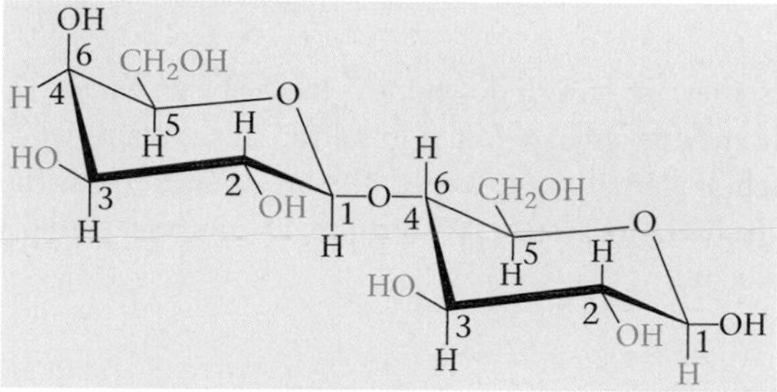

Table 23.2 gives the relative sweetness of the mono- and disaccharides considered here, along with sucrose substitutes.

Starch

Starch is a polysaccharide found in many plants, where it is stored in roots and seeds. It is particularly abundant in corn and potatoes, the major sources of commercial starch. Perhaps as much as 50% of our food energy comes from starch, mostly in the form of wheat products.

Starch is actually a mixture of two types of α-glucose polymers. One of these, called amylose, is insoluble in water and comprises about 20% of natural starch. It consists of long single chains of 1000 or more α-glucose units joined head-to-tail, (see Figure 23.5, p. 620). The other glucose polymer found in starch is amylopectin, which is soluble in water. The linkage between α-glucose units is the same as in amylose. However, amylopectin has a highly branched structure. Short chains of 20 to 25 glucose units are linked through oxygen atom bridges. The oxygen atom joins a number 1 carbon atom at the end of one chain to a number 6 carbon atom on an adjacent chain.

Starch and cellulose are both condensation polymers of glucose.

Table 23.2 Sweetness Relative to Sucrose

Lactose	0.16	Glucose	0.74	Aspartame (Equal)	180
Galactose	0.32	Sucrose	1.00	Saccharin (Sweet'N Low)	300
Maltose	0.33	Fructose	1.74	Sucralose (Splenda)	600

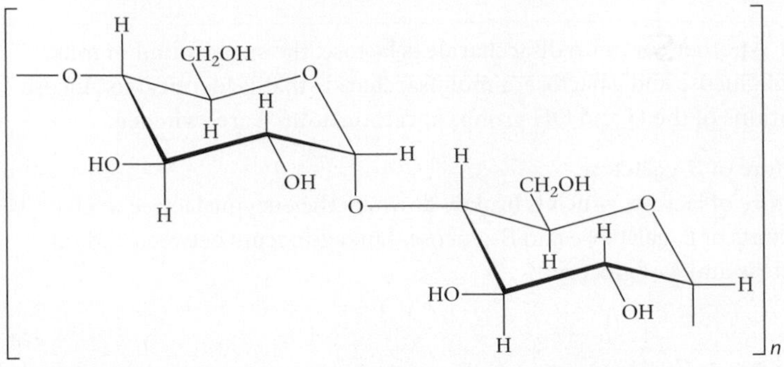

Figure 23.5
In starch, glucose molecules are joined head-to-tail through oxygen atoms. A thousand or more glucose molecules may be linked in this way, either in long single chains (amylose) or branched chains (amylopectin).

When you eat "starchy" foods, they are broken down into glucose by enzymes. The process starts in your mouth with the enzyme amylase found in saliva. This explains why, if you chew a piece of bread long enough, it starts to taste sweet. The breakdown of starch molecules continues in other parts of the digestive system. Within 1 to 4 hours after eating, all the starch in food is converted into glucose.

Cellulose

Cellulose contains long, unbranched chains of glucose units, about 10,000 per chain. It differs from starch in the way the glucose units are joined to each other. In starch, the oxygen bridge between the units is in the alpha position, as shown in Figure 23.5. In cellulose, it is in the beta position (Figure 23.6). Because humans lack the enzymes required to catalyze the hydrolysis of beta linkages, we cannot digest cellulose. The cellulose that we take in from fruits and vegetables remains undigested as "fiber." Ruminants, like cows and deer, and termites have bacteria in their intestines capable of breaking cellulose down into glucose.

The molecular structure of cellulose, unlike that of starch, allows for strong hydrogen bonding between polymer chains. This results in the formation of strong water-resistant fibers such as those found in cotton, which is 98% cellulose. Cotton actually has a tensile strength greater than that of steel. The major industrial source of cellulose is wood (~50% cellulose).

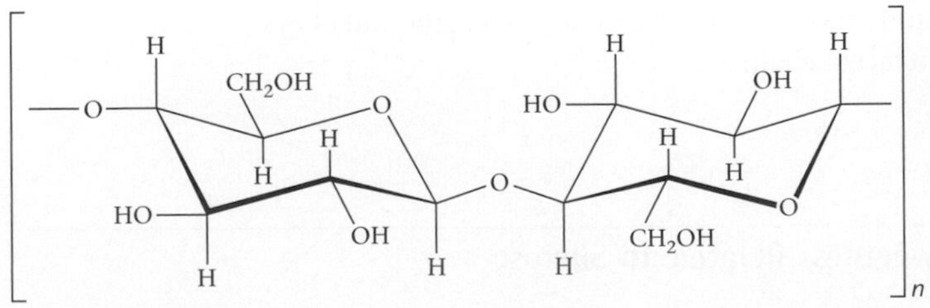

Figure 23.6
The bonding between glucose rings in cellulose is through oxygen bridges in the β position for each ring to the left of the bridge. This structure allows for ordered hydrogen bonding between chains and formation of long, strong fibers. Cotton and wood fiber have structures like this.

23.4 PROTEINS

The natural polymers known as proteins make up about 15% by mass of our bodies. They serve many functions. Fibrous proteins are the main components of hair, muscle, and skin. Other proteins found in body fluids transport oxygen, fats, and other substances needed for metabolism. Still others, such as insulin and vasopressin, are hormones. Enzymes, which catalyze reactions in the body, are chiefly protein.

Protein is an important component of most foods. Nearly everything we eat contains at least a small amount of protein. Lean meats and vegetables such as peas and beans are particularly rich in protein. In our digestive system, proteins are broken down into small molecules called *α-amino acids.* These molecules can then be reassembled in cells to form other proteins required by the body.

Proteins are condensation polymers of α-amino acids.

α-Amino Acids

The monomers from which proteins are derived have the general structure shown below. These compounds are called α-amino acids. They have an NH_2 group attached to the carbon atom (the α carbon) adjacent to a COOH group.

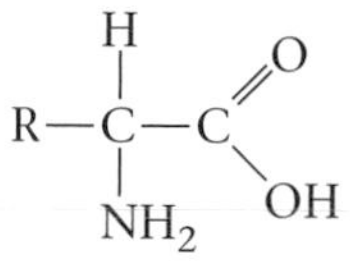

α-amino acid

The 20 α-amino acids shown in Table 23.3 (p. 622) are those most commonly found in natural proteins. They differ from one another in the nature of the R group attached to the alpha carbon. As you can see, R can be—

- a H atom (glycine).
- a simple hydrocarbon group (alanine, valine, . . .).
- a more complex group containing one or more atoms of oxygen (serine, aspartic acid, . . .), nitrogen (lysine, . . .), or sulfur (methionine, . . .).

Example 23.7 Consider the structures shown in Table 23.3.

(a) How many α-amino acids contain one and only one chiral carbon atom?
(b) How many contain one and only one $—NH_2$ group?

SOLUTION

(a) 17; the exceptions are glycine (0), isoleucine (2), and threonine (2).
(b) 17; the exceptions are proline (0), lysine (2), and glutamine (2).

In all the amino acids shown in Table 23.3 except glycine, the α-carbon is chiral. This means that these compounds are optically active. With alanine, for example, there should be two optical isomers:

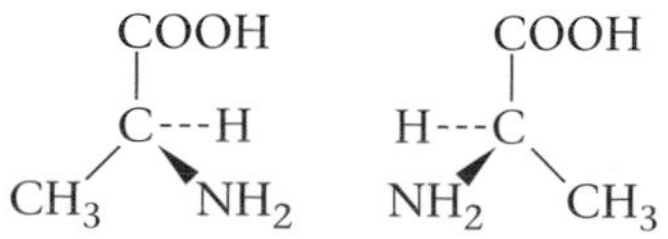

Of the 20 common amino acids, ten are "essential" in the sense that they are required by humans for protein construction and cannot be synthesized in the body. These are designated by an asterisk in Table 23.3. Clearly the proteins we eat should contain these essential amino acids. Beyond that, a "high-quality" protein contains the various amino acids in the

Table 23.3 The Common α-Amino Acids (names and abbreviations below structures)

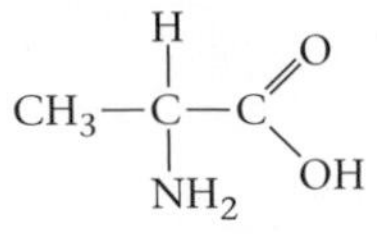
alanine Ala

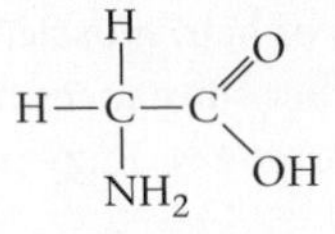
glycine Gly

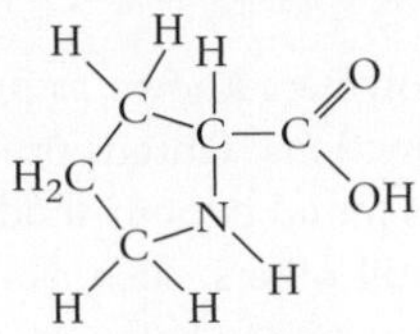
proline Pro

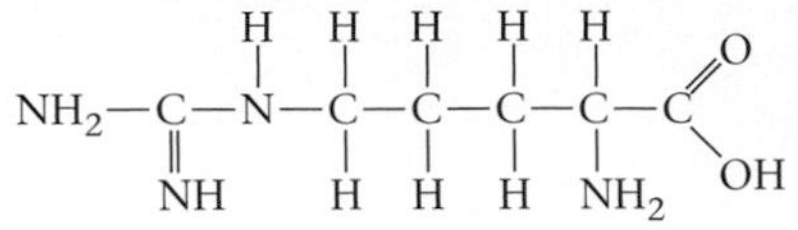
arginine* Arg

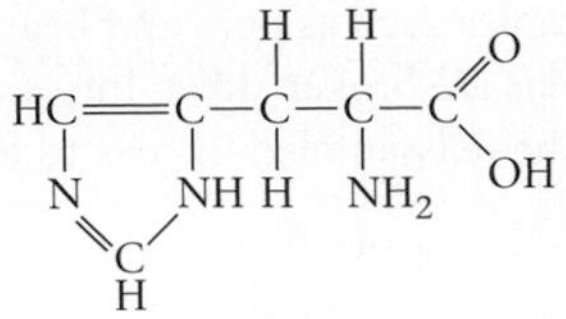
histidine* His

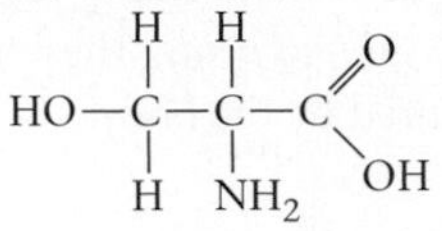
serine Ser

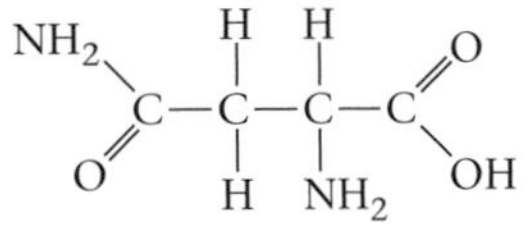
asparagine Asn

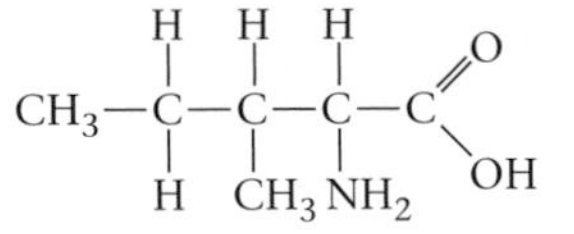
isoleucine* Ile

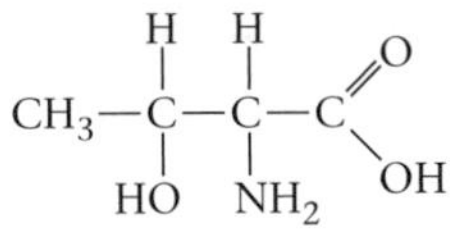
threonine* Thr

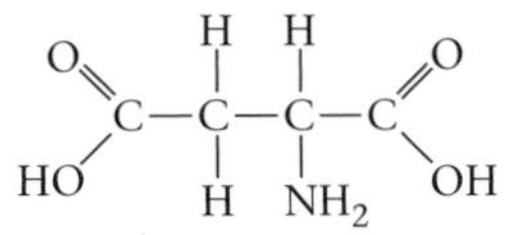
aspartic acid Asp

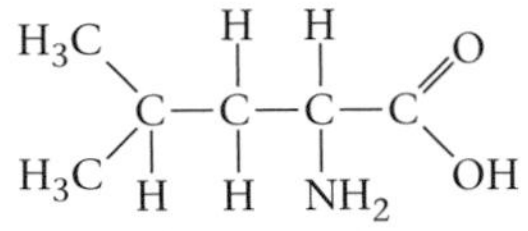
leucine* Leu

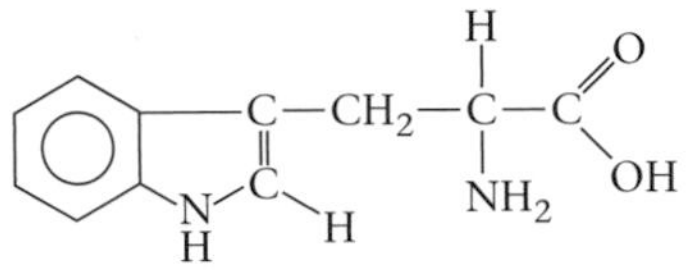
tryptophan* Trp

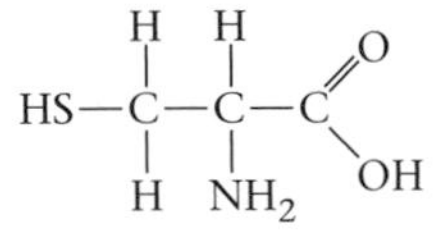
cysteine Cys

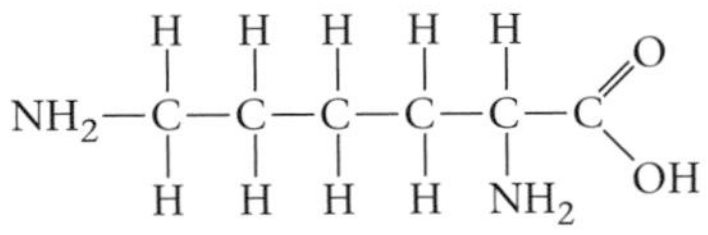
lysine* Lys

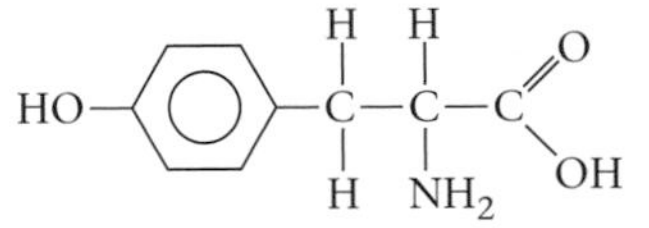
tyrosine Tyr

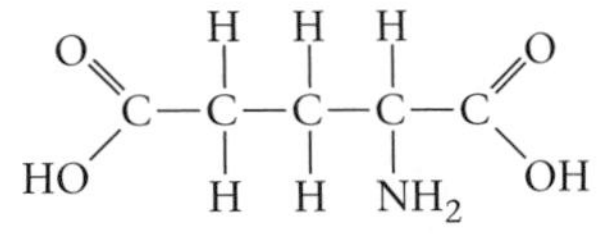
glutamic acid Glu

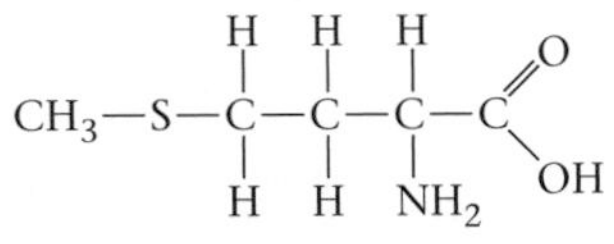
methionine* Met

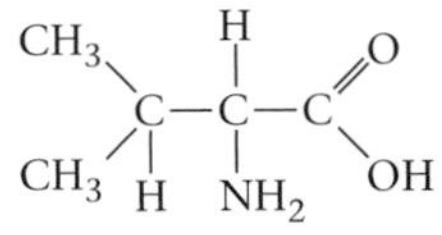
valine* Val

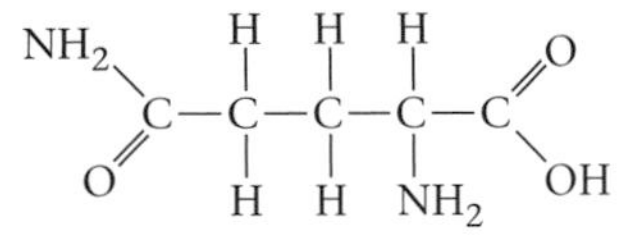
glutamine Gln

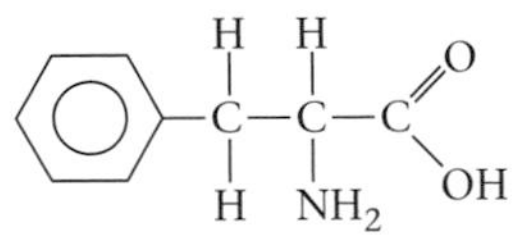
phenylalanine* Phe

*These are essential amino acids that cannot be synthesized by the body and therefore must be obtained from the diet.

CENGAGENOW™
Click Coached Problems for a self-study module on **naming amino acids.**

approximate ratio required by the body for protein synthesis. Generally speaking, animal proteins are of higher quality than plant proteins, with eggs at the head of the class. This is something to keep in mind if you're a vegetarian.

Acid-Base Properties of Amino Acids

You may recall from Example 22.8 (p. 597) that the reaction

$$CH_3COOH(aq) + CH_3NH_2(aq) \longrightarrow CH_3COO^-(aq) + CH_3NH_3^+(aq)$$

in which there is a proton transfer from a —COOH group to an $—NH_2$ group has a large equilibrium constant, 7×10^5. In other words, this reaction goes virtually to completion when solutions of acetic acid and methylamine are mixed.

A very similar reaction occurs with an amino acid; there is a proton transfer from the —COOH group to the —NH_2 group:

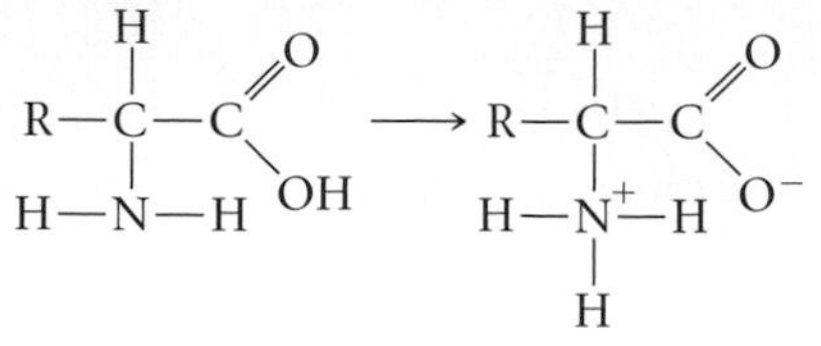

amino acid zwitterion

Here, too, the equilibrium constant is large and the reaction goes essentially to completion. Putting it another way, an amino acid does not exist in the form shown in Table 23.3, either in water solution or in the solid state. Instead it occurs as a **zwitterion,** which behaves like a polar molecule. Within it, there is a +1 charge on the nitrogen atom and a −1 charge at one of the oxygen atoms of the COOH group. Overall, the zwitterion has no net charge.

In water, zwitterions are stable only over a certain pH range. At low pH (high H^+ concentration), the COO^- group picks up a proton. The product, shown at the left below, has a +1 charge. At high pH (low H^+ concentration), the NH_3^+ group loses a proton. The species formed, shown at the right below, has a −1 charge.

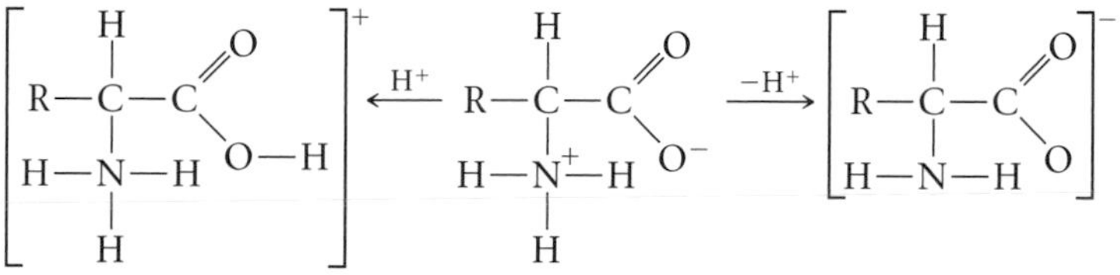

cation zwitterion anion

In a very real sense, a zwitterion is analogous to a species such as the HCO_3^- ion, which accepts a proton at low pH and donates a proton at high pH:

$$\underset{\text{low pH}}{H_2CO_3(aq)} \xleftarrow{H^+} HCO_3^-(aq) \xrightarrow{-H^+} \underset{\text{high pH}}{CO_3^{2-}(aq)}$$

Both the zwitterion and the HCO_3^- ion are amphiprotic, capable of acting as either a Brønsted acid or a Brønsted base.

To treat acid-base equilibria involving zwitterions, it is convenient to consider the cation stable at low pH to be a diprotic acid (analogous to H_2CO_3), which ionizes in two steps. Using the symbols C^+, Z, and A^- to stand for the cation, zwitterion, and anion, respectively, we have

CENGAGENOW™ Click Coached Problems for a self-study module on **zwitterions.**

$$C^+(aq) \rightleftharpoons H^+(aq) + Z(aq); \qquad K_{a1} = \frac{[H^+] \times [Z]}{[C^+]}$$

$$Z(aq) \rightleftharpoons H^+(aq) + A^-(aq); \qquad K_{a2} = \frac{[H^+] \times [A^-]}{[Z]}$$

For glycine,

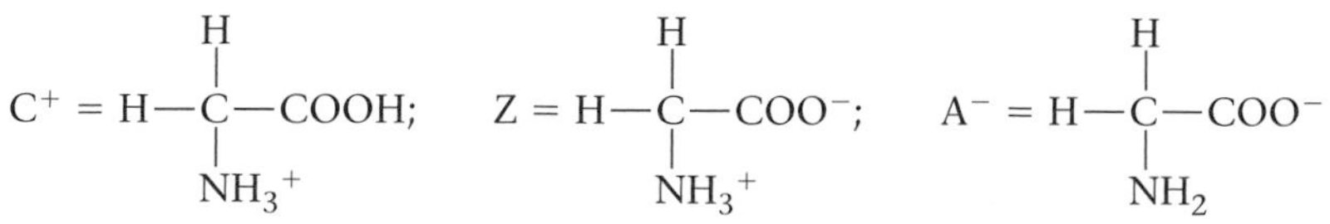

$$K_{a1} = 4.6 \times 10^{-3}; \qquad K_{a2} = 2.5 \times 10^{-10}$$

Example 23.8 Using these acid dissociation constants for glycine, calculate the ratios $[Z]/[C^+]$ and $[Z]/[A^-]$ at pH

(a) 2.00 (b) 6.00 (c) 10.00

Strategy Given the two general equations cited above with the appropriate equilibrium constants, we have

$$\frac{[Z]}{[C^+]} = \frac{K_{a1}}{[H^+]} = \frac{4.6 \times 10^{-3}}{[H^+]}; \qquad \frac{[Z]}{[A^-]} = \frac{[H^+]}{K_{a2}} = \frac{[H^+]}{2.5 \times 10^{-10}}$$

Using these relationships, we can readily calculate the required ratios at various pH's.

SOLUTION

(a) Here, the concentration of H^+ is 1.0×10^{-2} *M*, so we have

$$\frac{[Z]}{[C^+]} = \frac{4.6 \times 10^{-3}}{1.0 \times 10^{-2}} = 0.46;$$

$$\frac{[Z]}{[A^-]} = \frac{1.0 \times 10^{-2}}{2.5 \times 10^{-10}} = 4.0 \times 10^{7}$$

At this low pH, there is more cation than zwitterion, $[Z] < [C^+]$, and essentially no anion, $[Z] \gg [A^-]$.

(b)

$$\frac{[Z]}{[C^+]} = \frac{4.6 \times 10^{-3}}{1.0 \times 10^{-6}} = 4.6 \times 10^{3};$$

$$\frac{[Z]}{[A^-]} = \frac{1.0 \times 10^{-6}}{2.5 \times 10^{-10}} = 4.0 \times 10^{3}$$

If you dissolve glycine in water, you get mostly zwitterion.

At this intermediate pH, the zwitterion is the principal species present. Its concentration is much higher than that of either cation or anion.

(c)

$$\frac{[Z]}{[C^+]} = \frac{4.6 \times 10^{-3}}{1.0 \times 10^{-10}} = 4.6 \times 10^{7};$$

$$\frac{[Z]}{[A^-]} = \frac{1.0 \times 10^{-10}}{2.5 \times 10^{-10}} = 0.40$$

At this high pH, the anion is the principal species:

$$[C^+] \ll [Z] < [A^-]$$

From Example 23.8 or Figure 23.7, it is clear that the zwitterion of glycine is the principal species over a wide pH range, certainly from pH 3 to pH 9. The maximum concentration of zwitterion occurs at about pH 6; this is referred to as the *isoelectric point* of glycine. At this pH, glycine does not migrate in an electric field, since the zwitterion is a neutral species. At

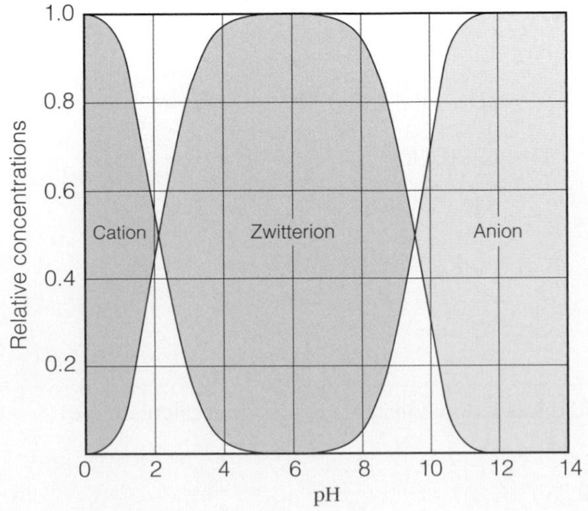

Figure 23.7
Relative concentrations of different glycine species as a function of pH. Between about pH 3 and 9, the zwitterion is the principal species; it has its maximum concentration at pH 6, the isoelectric point. Below pH 2, the cation dominates; above pH 10, the anion is the principal species.

low pH, the cation moves to the cathode; at high pH the anion migrates to the anode. In general, for an amino acid like glycine, where there is only one —COOH group and one $—NH_2$ group:

$$\text{pH at isoelectric point} = \frac{pK_{a1} + pK_{a2}}{2}$$

where K_{a1} and K_{a2} are the successive dissociation constants of the cation of the amino acid.

Polypeptides

As noted in Section 23.2, molecules containing NH_2 and COOH groups can undergo condensation polymerization. Amino acids contain both groups in the same molecule. Hence, two amino acid molecules can combine by the reaction of the COOH group in one molecule with the NH_2 group of the other molecule. If the acids involved are different, two different structural isomers are possible:

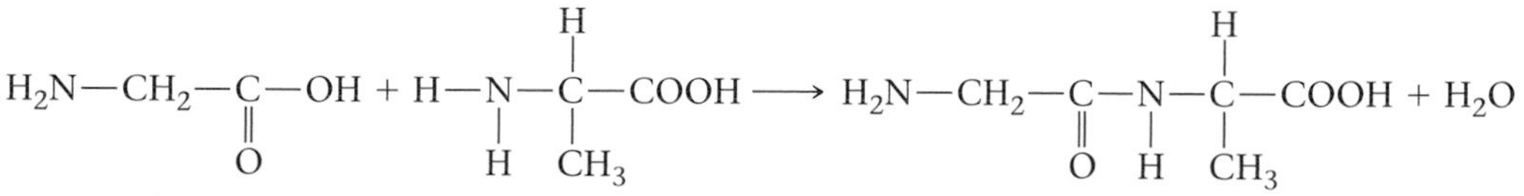

glycine alanine glycylalanine (Gly-Ala)

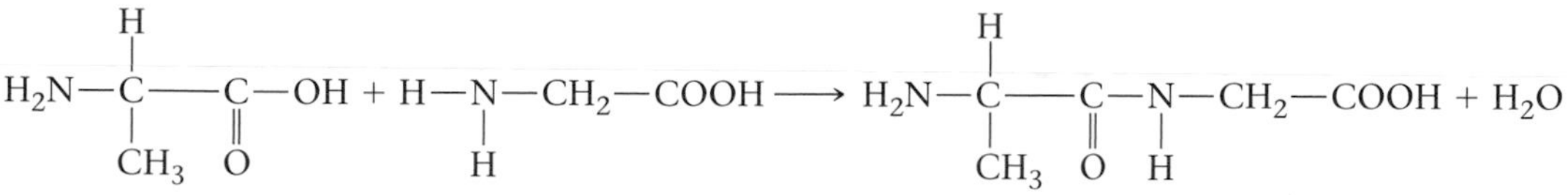

alanine glycine alanylglycine (Ala-Gly)

Each of these isomers is a dipeptide, formed from two amino acids by condensing out a water molecule and containing the group

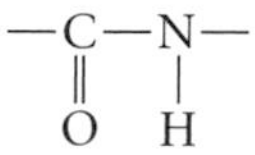

This linkage is similar to that in nylon.

commonly called a "peptide linkage." Dipeptides are named by writing first (far left) the amino acid that retains a free NH_2 group; the amino acid with a free COOH group is written last (far right).

Example 23.9 Draw the structural formula of glycylserine (Gly-Ser).

Strategy Write the condensation reaction that takes place between glycine and serine. To do this, start with the structural formulas of the two amino acids, glycine at the left, serine at the right. In each case, put the NH_2 group at the left, the COOH group at the right. Condense out a water molecule; what is left is the structural formula of Gly-Ser.

SOLUTION

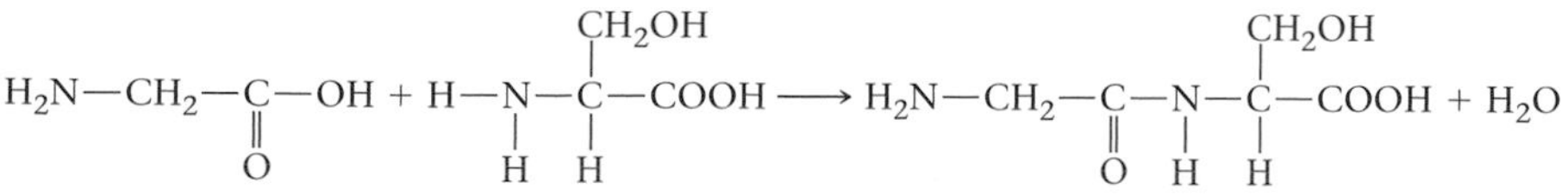

glycine serine glycylserine (Gly-Ser)

The dipeptide formed in Example 23.9 has a reactive group at both ends of the molecule (NH_2 at one end, COOH at the other). Hence it can combine further to give tripeptides (three amino acid units), tetrapeptides, . . . , and eventually long-chain polymers called polypeptides. Proteins are polypeptides containing a large number of amino acid units:

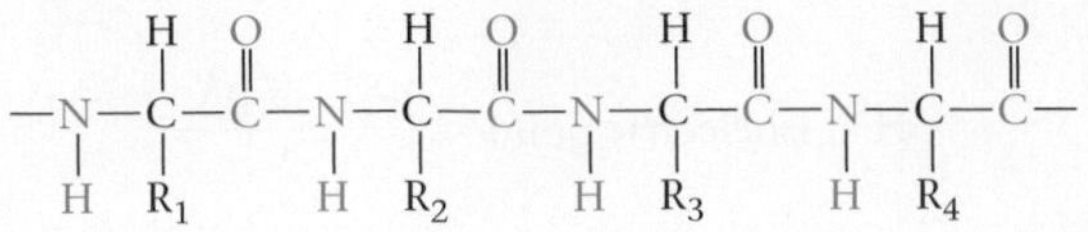

(peptide linkages in color).

Proteins differ from the other polymers we have discussed in that they may contain up to 20 different monomer units. This means that there are a huge number of possible proteins. Using the amino acids listed in Table 23.3, we could make

$20 \times 20 = 400$ different dipeptides.
$20 \times 20 \times 20 = 8000$ different tripeptides.
20^n polypeptides containing n monomer units.

For a relatively simple protein containing only 50 monomer units, we have

$20^{50} = 1 \times 10^{65}$ possibilities.

Proteins; Primary Structure

To determine the **primary structure** of a protein that may contain a hundred or more amino acid units, it is necessary to

The amino acid sequence in hemoglobin, with 574 units, is known.

1. identify the amino acids present.
2. determine the relative amounts of each amino acid.
3. establish the *sequence* of amino acid units in the protein.

Tasks (1) and (2) are relatively easy to accomplish. The sample is first heated with hydrochloric acid to break all of the "peptide linkages" (amide bonds) in the protein. The resulting solution is then passed through a chromatographic column (recall the discussion on pp. 5–6 in Chapter 1). This separates the different amino acids and allows you to determine their identities and concentrations.

Task (3) is more difficult. It uses a series of reagents each of which is capable of breaking only certain amide bonds. One of these reagents is the enzyme trypsin, which breaks only those bonds formed by the carboxyl groups in arginine and lysine. It would break the polypeptide

Ala-Gly-Ser-Lys-Gly-Leu-Arg-Met

into three fragments:

Ala-Gly-Ser-Lys; Gly-Leu-Arg; Met

Remember that, by convention, the NH_2 group of each amino acid is written at the left; the COOH group is at the right. Other reagents split the chain at different points. By correlating the results of different hydrolysis experiments, it is possible to deduce the primary structure of the protein (or polypeptide). Example 23.10 shows how this is done in a particularly simple case.

Example 23.10 A certain polypeptide is shown by acid hydrolysis to contain only three amino acids: serine(Ser), alanine(Ala), and methionine(Met) with mole fractions of $\frac{1}{2}$, $\frac{1}{4}$, and $\frac{1}{4}$, respectively. Enzymatic hydrolysis yields the following fragments: Ser-Ala; Ser-Met; Ala-Ser. Deduce the primary structure of the polypeptide.

Strategy It is helpful to align these fragments vertically in such a way that they overlap one another.

SOLUTION

Ser—Ala
  |
Ala—Ser
  |
Ser—Met

We conclude that this polypeptide contains four amino acid units in the following sequence:

Ser-Ala-Ser-Met

Since there are two serine units as compared to one alanine and one methionine, it follows that the mole fractions are $\frac{1}{2}$, $\frac{1}{4}$, and $\frac{1}{4}$ in that order.

In the body, proteins are built up by a series of reactions that in general produce a specific sequence of amino acids. Even tiny errors in this sequence may have serious effects. Among the genetic diseases known to be caused by improper sequencing are hemophilia, sickle cell anemia, and albinism. Sickle cell anemia is caused by the substitution of *one* valine unit for a glutamic acid unit in a chain containing 146 monomers.

Fortunately nature doesn't make too many mistakes.

Proteins; Secondary and Tertiary Structures

Protein chains (Figure 23.8) can align themselves so that certain patterns are repeated. These repeating patterns establish what we call the **secondary structure** of the protein. The nature of the pattern is determined in large part by hydrogen bonding. Oxygen atoms on C=O

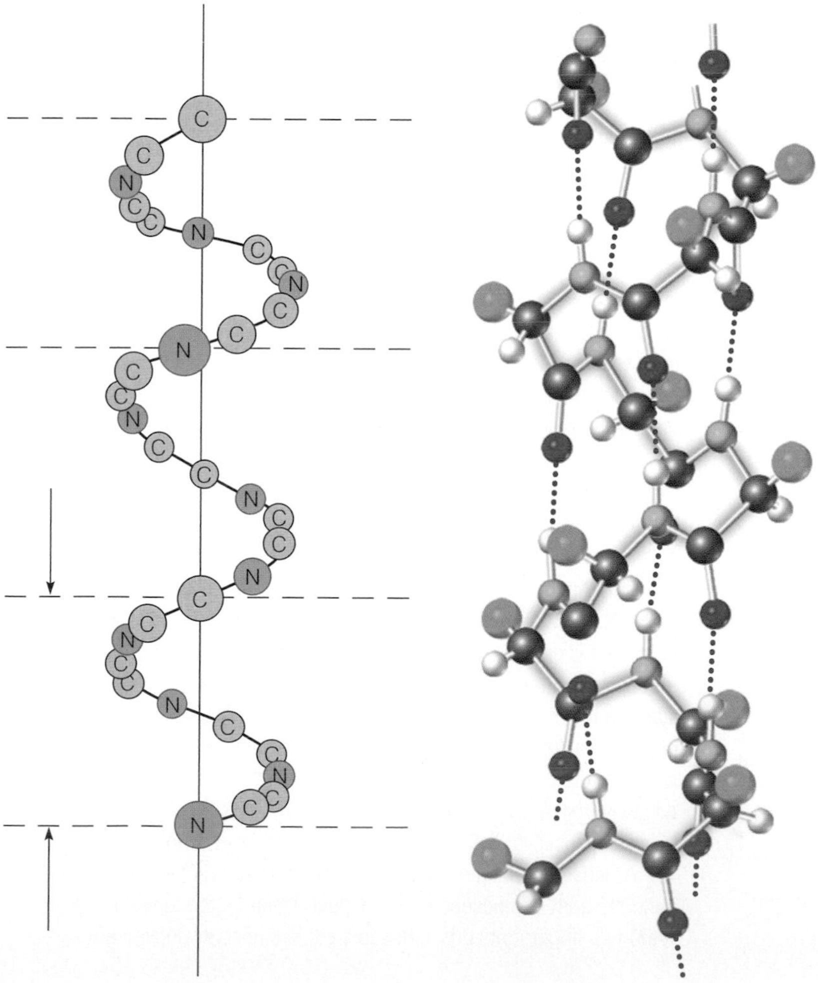

Figure 23.8
α-Helix structures of proteins. The main atom chain in the helix is shown schematically on the left. The sketch on the right more nearly represents the actual positions of atoms and shows where intrachain hydrogen bonding occurs. Wool and many other fibrous proteins have the α-helix structure.

This is a rather special kind of H bond.

groups can interact with H atoms in nearby N—H groups to form these bonds. This can occur within a single protein chain or between neighboring chains.

A common secondary structure is an α-helix, which maximizes hydrogen bonding between peptide linkages. At the left of Figure 23.8 (p. 627) is the outline of the protein chain forming the helix. The more complete structure is given at the right. This shows where the hydrogen bonds form between amino acid units in the protein chain. Notice that the bulky R groups are all on the outside of the helix, where they have the most room. The actual structure of the helix is nearly independent of the nature of the R groups. The dimensions of the helix correspond closely to those observed in such fibrous proteins as wool, hair, skin, feathers, and fingernails.

The three-dimensional conformation of a protein is called its **tertiary structure.** An α-helix can be either twisted, folded, or folded and twisted into a definite geometric pattern. These structures are stabilized by dispersion forces, hydrogen bonding, and other intermolecular forces.

Collagen, the principal fibrous protein in mammalian tissue, has a tertiary structure made up of twisted α-helices. Three polypeptide chains, each of which is a left-handed helix, are twisted into a right-handed super helix to form an extremely strong tertiary structure. It has remarkable tensile strength, which makes it important in the structure of bones, tendons, teeth, and cartilage.

CHEMISTRY Beyond the Classroom

DNA Fingerprinting

Within every living cell, there is an organic natural polymer called **d**eoxyribo**n**ucleic **a**cid or, more commonly, DNA. The DNA molecule is enormous; its molar mass is estimated to be of the order of 2×10^{10} g. The molecule takes the form of a narrow, tightly coiled band, which, if straightened out, would have a length of about 1 m.

Figure A (p. 629) shows the primary structure of the DNA molecule. Notice that—

- the backbone of the molecule consists of alternating units derived from phosphoric acid, H_3PO_4, and a 5-carbon sugar called deoxyribose.
- bonded to each sugar is a nitrogen base (amine). The base may be thymine (shown at the top in orange), adenine (red), guanine (green), or cytosine (blue). These are often abbreviated as the letters T, A, G, and C, respectively
- the structural unit of DNA, repeated over and over along the chain, is built from an H_3PO_4 molecule, a sugar molecule, and a nitrogen base, which may be any one of the four shown. Figure A shows four such structural units called *nucleotides;* an actual molecule of DNA would contain literally billions of such nucleotides.

The secondary structure of DNA is shown in Figure B. This "double helix" model was first proposed in 1953 by James Watson and Francis Crick, who used the x-ray crystallographic data of Rosalind Franklin and Maurice Wilkins. Beyond that, they were intrigued by the results of analyses that showed that in DNA the ratio of adenine to thymine molecules is almost exactly 1 : 1, as is the ratio of cytosine to guanine:

$$A/T = C/G = 1.00$$

This behavior is readily explained by the double helix; an A molecule in one strand is always hydrogen-bonded to a T molecule in the second strand. Similarly, a C molecule in one strand is situated properly to form a hydrogen bond with a G molecule in the other strand. In 1962, Watson, Crick, and Wilkins received the Nobel Prize in medicine (Franklin died in 1958).

The double helix model provides a simple explanation for cell division and reproduction. In the reproduction process, the two DNA chains unwind from each other. As this happens, a new matching chain of DNA is synthesized on each of the original ones, creating two double helices. Since the base pairs in each new double helix must match in the same way as in the original, the two new double helices must be identical to the original. Exact replication of genetic data is thereby accomplished, however complex that data may be.

The many millions of DNA molecules in the cells of your body are identical to each other. That is, the base sequence in all of these molecules is the same. In contrast, the base sequence of the DNA molecules in every other person in the world differs at least slightly from yours. In that sense, your "DNA fingerprint" is unique.

Alec Jeffryes, an English geneticist, discovered in the 1980s how to apply this principle to forensics. To do this, it is necessary to locate that portion of the DNA molecule in which the base sequence differs significantly from one individual to another. That part of the molecule is cut out by a "restrictive enzyme" in much the same way that trypsin splits a protein molecule into fragments. The DNA sample obtained in this way from a suspect can be compared with that derived from blood, hair, semen, saliva, and so on, found at the scene of a violent crime.

At least in principle, comparison of DNA fingerprints can determine the guilt or innocence of a suspect beyond a reasonable doubt. If the two fingerprints differ, the suspect is innocent. Conversely, if the fingerprints match perfectly, the odds that the suspect is guilty are about 80 billion to one.

In practice, the situation isn't quite that simple. DNA samples taken from a victim are almost certain to be contaminated with DNA from fungi or bacteria. Certain dyes can combine with restriction enzymes, causing them to cut in the wrong places. Finally, DNA may decay in a warm or moist environment.

A DNA fingerprint can be used for many purposes other than solving violent crimes. In particular, it can serve to identify deceased individuals. In June of 1998 the "Vietnam Unknown" buried in the Tomb of the Unknown Soldier at Arlington National Cemetery was identified by DNA technology. He was shown to be First Lieutenant Michael Blassie, shot down over Vietnam in May of 1972. DNA samples taken from his mother matched those obtained from his body. A month later Blassie, a native of St. Louis, Missouri, was reburied in a national cemetery located in that city.

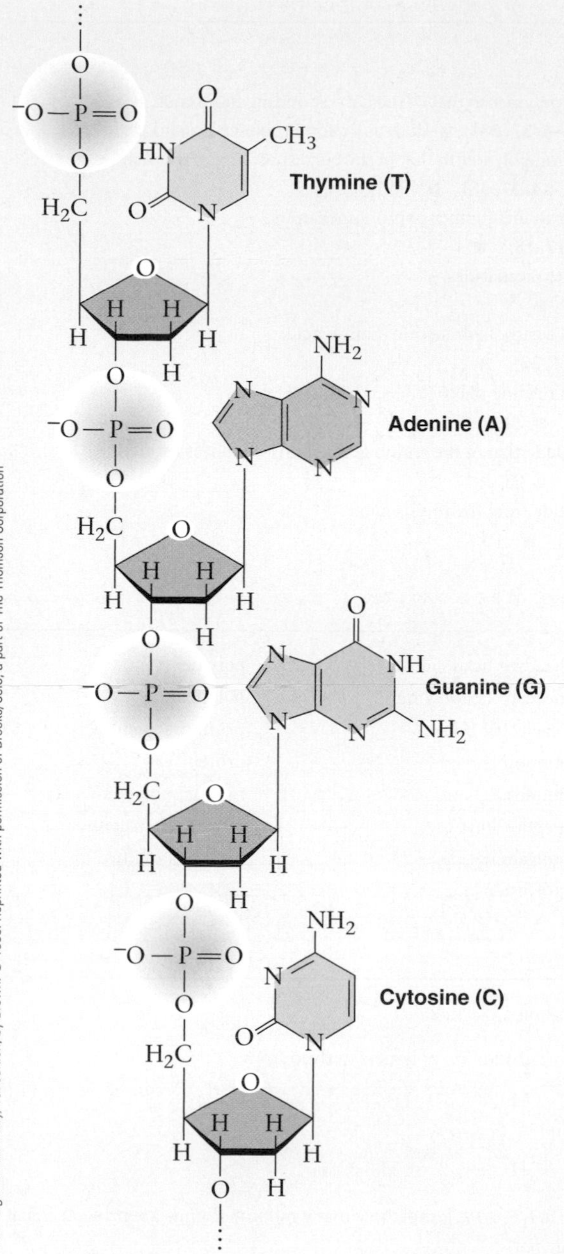

Figure A
A tetranucleotide section of a single-stranded DNA.

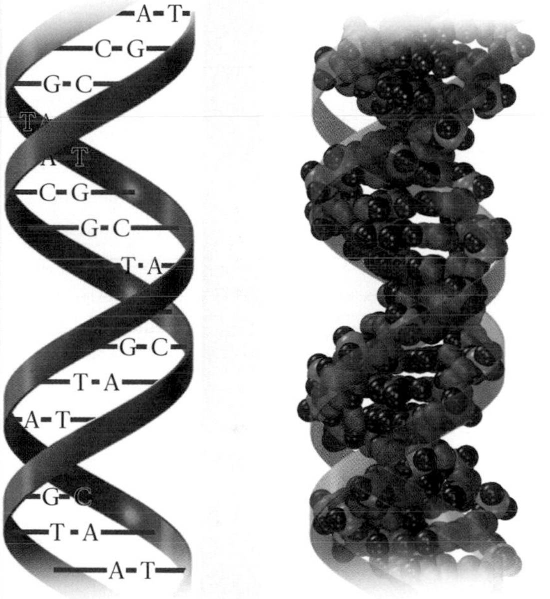

Figure B
The double-helical strand of a DNA molecule. The diagram at the left shows the hydrogen bonding between base pairs adenine-thymine and cystosine-guanine that hold the strands together.

Chapter Highlights

Key Concepts

Select end of chapter Questions and Problems may be assigned in OWL and are cross-referenced in the Key Concepts list.

CENGAGENOW™

Sign in at **academic.cengage.com/now** to:

- Check your readiness for an exam by taking the Pre-Test and exploring the self-study modules recommended in your Personalized Study plan
- For quick review, download Go Chemistry mini-lecture flashcard modules (or purchase them at **www.ichapters.com**)

1. Relate the structure of an addition polymer to that of the corresponding monomer.
   (Examples 23.1, 23.2; Problems 1–6, 37, 38) ■ Questions and Problems assignable in OWL: 1, 3, 6
2. Relate the structure of a condensation polymer to that of the corresponding monomer.
   (Examples 23.3, 23.4; Problems 9–14, 37, 38) ■ 10, 12
3. Relate the molar mass of a polymer to the number of monomer units.
   (Example 23.1; Problems 1, 2, 7, 17, 18) ■ 1, 17
4. Draw the structures of mono- and disaccharides.
   (Example 23.6; Problems 19, 20) ■ 19
5. Identify the chiral carbon atoms in a carbohydrate or α-amino acid.
   (Examples 23.5, 23.7; Problems 21, 22) ■ 21
6. Carry out equilibrium calculations relating pH to [Z], [C^+], and [A^-].
   (Example 23.8; Problems 29, 30) ■ 29, 30
7. Relate the structure of a polypeptide to that of the amino acids from which it is formed.
   (Example 23.9; Problems 23–26) ■ 23, 26
8. Deduce the structure of a polypeptide from hydrolysis data.
   (Example 23.10; Problems 31, 32) ■ 31

Key Terms

addition polymer
α-amino acid
axial
carbohydrate
condensation polymer
disaccharide
equatorial
functional group
head-to-head, tail-to-tail polymer
head-to-tail polymer
isoelectric point
monomer
monosaccharide
peptide linkage
polyamide
polyester
polymer
polypeptide
primary structure
protein
random polymer
secondary structure
tertiary structure
zwitterion

Summary Problem

All of these questions pertain to six-carbon molecules.

(a) Sketch the head-to-tail and tail-to-tail addition polymers derived from

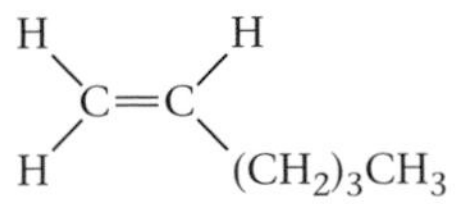

(b) If the molar mass of the polymer is 1.2×10^4 g/mol, how many monomer units are present? What is the mass percent of carbon in the polymer?

(c) Write the structure of the condensation polymer formed when a straight-chain, saturated, six-carbon dialcohol reacts with a straight-chain, saturated, six-carbon dicarboxylic acid.

(d) Write the structure of the disaccharide formed when α-glucose and β-glucose, both of formula $C_6H_{12}O_6$, combine to form an isomer of maltose.

(e) Draw the structures of the two polypeptides derived from the six-carbon amino acids lysine and leucine.

Answers

(a) 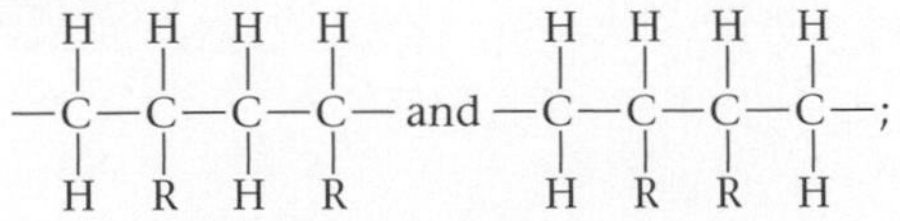

R = —$(CH_2)_3CH_3$

(b) 1.4×10^2; 85.6

(c) 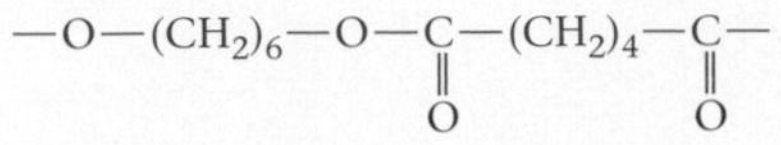

(d) See maltose structure (p. 618); invert OH and H on carbon atom at lower right.

(e) 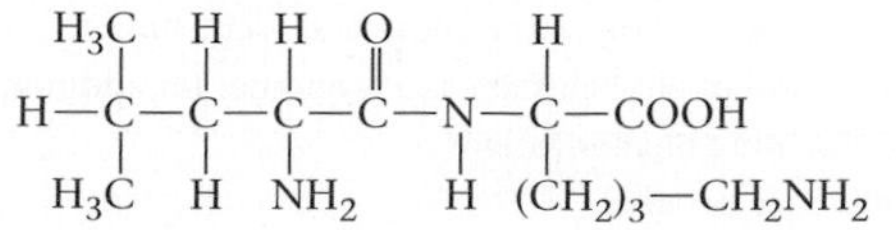 Leu-Lys

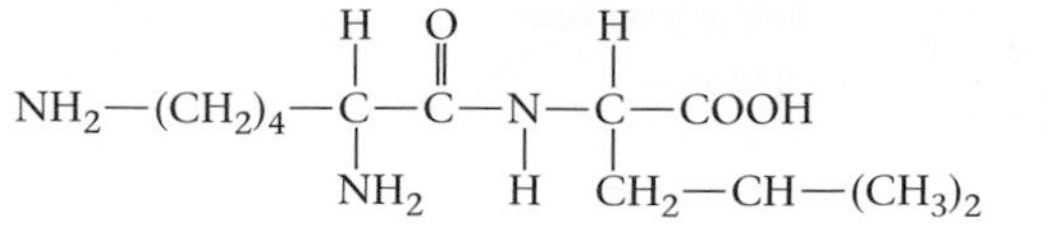 Lys-Leu

Questions and Problems

Blue-numbered questions have answers in Appendix 6 and fully-worked solutions in the *Student Solutions Manual.*

■ denotes questions assignable in OWL.

WEB indicates that the solution is available on this book's companion website.

Addition Polymers

1. ■ Consider a polymer made from tetrachloroethylene.
(a) Draw a portion of the polymer chain.
(b) What is the molar mass of the polymer if it contains 3.2×10^3 tetrachloroethylene molecules?
(c) What are the mass percents of C and Cl in the polymer?

2. Consider Teflon, the polymer made from tetrafluoroethylene.
(a) Draw a portion of the Teflon molecule.
(b) Calculate the molar mass of a Teflon molecule that contains 5.0×10^4 CF_2 units.
(c) What are the mass percents of C and F in Teflon?

3. ■ Sketch a portion of the acrylonitrile polymer (Table 23.1), assuming it is a
(a) head-to-tail polymer.
(b) head-to-head, tail-to-tail polymer.

4. **WEB** Styrene, 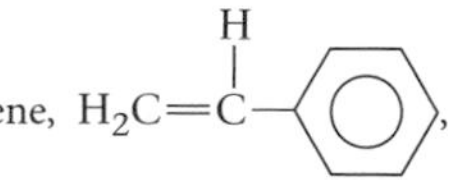, forms a head-to-tail addition polymer. Sketch a portion of a polystyrene molecule.

5. The polymer whose structure is shown below is made from two different monomers. Identify the monomers.

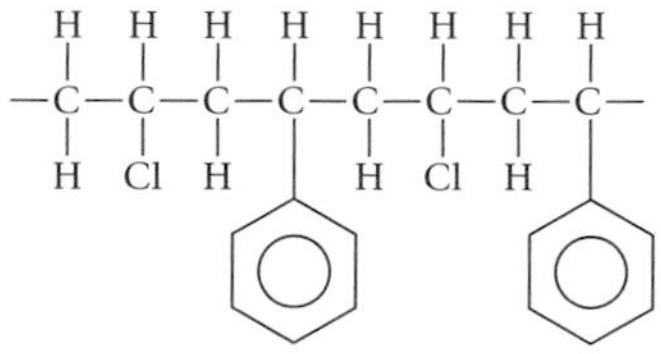

6. ■ Show the structure of the monomer used to make the following addition polymers.

(a) 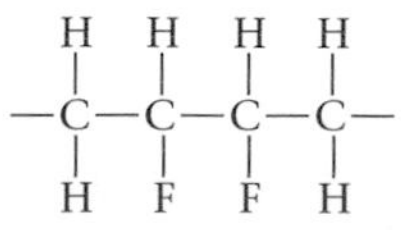 (b) 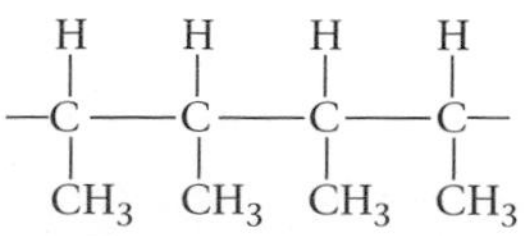

7. Consider the polymers referred to in Table 23.1. If each one contains the same number of monomer units, which one has the largest molar mass?

8. Of the polymers referred to in Table 23.1 which one contains the highest percentage by mass of carbon?

Condensation Polymers

9. A rather simple polymer can be made from ethylene glycol, $HO-CH_2-CH_2-OH$, and oxalic acid, 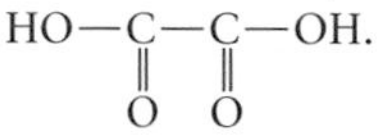.

Sketch a portion of the polymer chain obtained from these monomers.

10. ■ Lexan is a very rugged polyester in which the monomers can be taken to be carbonic acid, 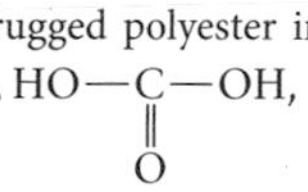,

and

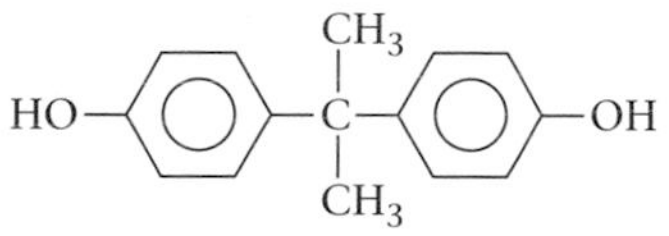

Sketch a section of the Lexan chain.

11. *Para*-aminobenzoic acid is an "essential vitamin" for many bacteria:

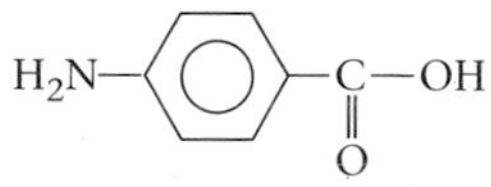

Sketch a portion of a polyamide polymer made from this monomer.

12. ■ Nylon-6 is made from a single monomer:

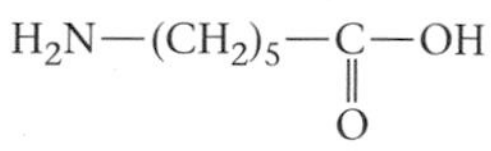

Sketch a section of the polymer chain in Nylon-6.

13. The following condensation polymer is made from a single monomer. Identify the monomer.

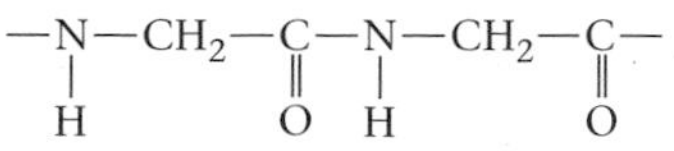

14. **WEB** Identify the monomers from which the following condensation polymers are made.

(a) 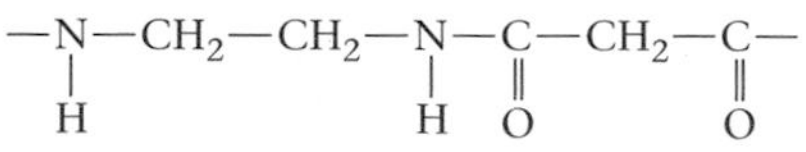

(b) 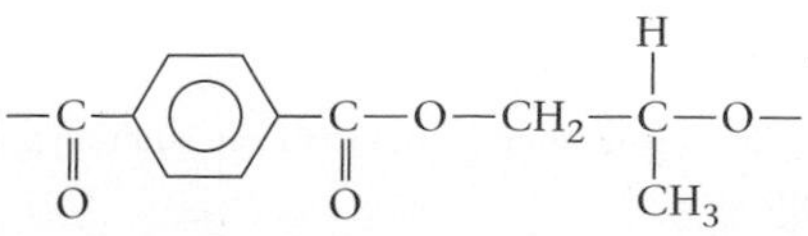

Carbohydrates

15. Write a chemical equation, using molecular formulas, for the reaction of sucrose with water to form glucose and fructose.

16. Write a chemical equation, using molecular formulas, for the reaction of maltose with water to form glucose.

17. ■ Cellulose consists of about 10,000 $C_6H_{10}O_5$ units linked together.
 (a) What are the mass percents of C, H, and O in cellulose?
 (b) What is the molar mass of cellulose?

18. Starch has the same empirical formula as cellulose and a molar mass of about 1.0×10^5 g/mol.
 (a) What are the mass percents of C, H, and O in starch?
 (b) How many $C_6H_{10}O_5$ units are linked together in a starch molecule?

19. ■ Mannose has the same molecular formula as glucose and the same geometry except at carbon-2, where the H and OH groups are interchanged. Draw the structures of α- and β-mannose.

20. Draw the structure of the disaccharide formed by two moles of α-mannose (see Question 19).

21. ■ How many chiral carbon atoms are there in α-glucose? in fructose?

22. How many chiral carbon atoms are there in sucrose? maltose?

Amino Acids and Proteins

23. ■ Give the structural formula of two different dipeptides formed between arginine and serine.

24. Give the structural formulas of two different dipeptides formed between leucine and lysine.

25. (a) How many tripeptides can be made from glycine, alanine, and leucine, using each amino acid only once per tripeptide?
 (b) Write the structural formulas of these tripeptides and name them in the shorthand abbreviation used for showing amino acid sequences.

26. ■ WEB A tripeptide contains valine, lysine, and phenylalanine residues.
 (a) How many tripeptides are possible from these amino acids?
 (b) Draw a structural formula for a possible form of the tripeptide and name it, using the shorthand form.

27. Consider the cysteine molecule shown in Table 23.3. Write structural formulas for
 (a) the zwitterion of cysteine.
 (b) the cation formed in acid.
 (c) the anion formed in base.

28. Follow the directions of Question 27 for serine.

29. ■ For alanine, $K_{a1} = 5.1 \times 10^{-3}$, $K_{a2} = 1.8 \times 10^{-10}$. Calculate the ratios $[Z]/[C^+]$ and $[Z]/[A^-]$ at pH
 (a) 2.00. (b) 6.00. (c) 10.50.
What is the principal species at each pH?

30. ■ Using the information given in Problem 29, calculate the pH
 (a) when $[Z] = [C^+]$.
 (b) when $[Z] = [A^-]$.
 (c) at the isoelectric point.

31. ■ On complete hydrolysis, a polypeptide gives two alanine, one leucine, one methionine, one phenylalanine, and one valine residue. Partial hydrolysis gives the following fragments: Ala-Phe, Leu-Met, Val-Ala, Phe-Leu. It is known that the first amino acid in the sequence is valine and the last one is methionine. What is the complete sequence of amino acids?

32. Suppose that, in the polypeptide referred to in Question 31, the first amino acid is alanine and the last one is also alanine. What is the complete sequence of amino acids?

Unclassified

33. Which of the following monomers could form an addition polymer? A condensation polymer?
 (a) C_2H_6 (b) C_2H_4
 (c) $HO—CH_2—CH_2—OH$ (d) $HO—CH_2—CH_3$

34. How would you explain to a young science student how to decide whether a given compound might be useful as a monomer for addition polymerization? Condensation polymerization?

35. Explain the difference between
 (a) a synthetic and natural polymer.
 (b) a polyester and polyamide.
 (c) α- and β-glucose.

36. Explain the difference between
 (a) linear and branched polyethylene.
 (b) glucose and fructose.
 (c) maltose and sucrose.

37. Draw the structures of the monomers that could be used to make the following polymers

(a) 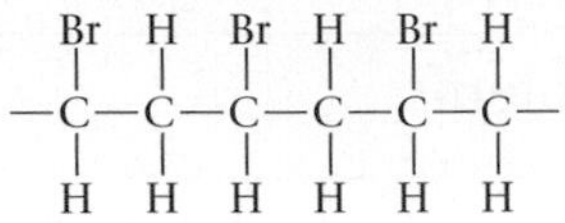

(b) 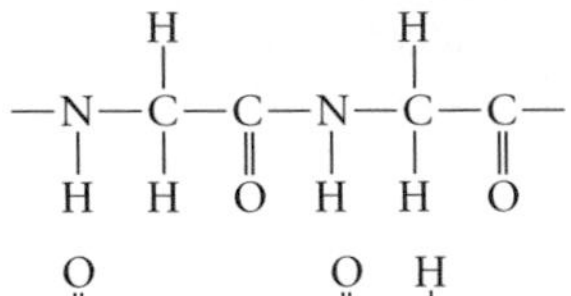

(c) 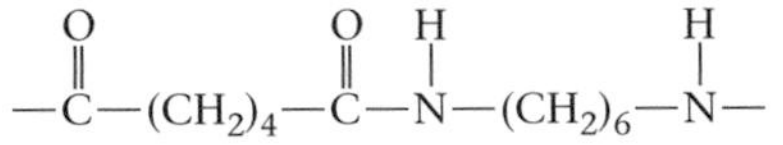

38. What monomers would be used to make the following polymers?

(a) 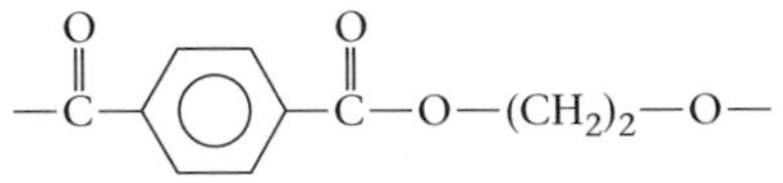

(b) 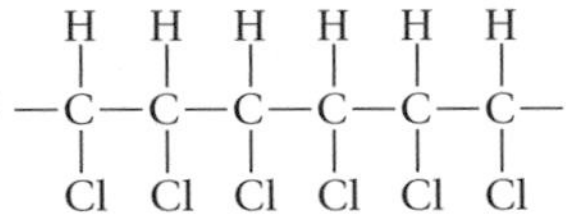

(c) 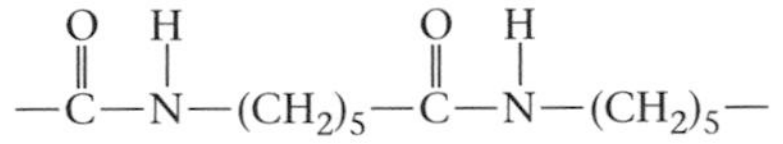

39. Sketch the tetrapeptide obtained from four molecules of the α-amino acid glycine.

40. Sketch a portion of a head-to-head, tail-to-tail, and a head-to-tail polymer made from acrylonitrile, $H_2C{=}CHCN$.

41. Using bond energies, estimate ΔH for the hydrolysis of maltose to glucose.

42. ■ Sketch the form in which leucine would exist in acid solution; in basic solution.

43. How many tripeptides could one make from glycine, valine, and lysine, using any number of each amino acid?

44. A 1.00-mg sample of a pure protein yielded on hydrolysis 0.0165 mg of leucine and 0.0248 mg of isoleucine. What is the minimum possible molar mass of the protein? (MM leucine = MM isoleucine = 131 g/mol)

45. Describe what is meant by
 (a) the primary structure of a protein.
 (b) the secondary structure of a protein.
 (c) the tertiary structure of a protein.

46. Glycolysis is the process by which glucose is metabolized to lactic acid according to the equation

$$C_6H_{12}O_6(aq) \longrightarrow 2C_3H_6O_3(aq)$$
$$\Delta G^\circ = -198 \text{ kJ at pH 7.0 and 25°C}$$

Glycolysis is the source of energy in human red blood cells. In these cells, the concentration of glucose is 5.0×10^{-3} *M*, while that of lactic acid is 2.9×10^{-3} *M*. Calculate ΔG for glycolysis in human blood cells under these conditions. Use the equation $\Delta G = \Delta G^\circ + RT \ln Q$, where Q is the concentration quotient, analogous to K.

■ in OWL Blue-numbered questions answered in Appendix 6 WEB Solution is available on companion website

47. ■ Plants synthesize carbohydrates from CO_2 and H_2O by the process of photosynthesis. For example,

$$6CO_2(g) + 6H_2O(l) \longrightarrow C_6H_{12}O_6(aq) + 6O_2(g)$$

$\Delta G° = 2.87 \times 10^3$ kJ at pH 7.0 and 25°C. What is K for the reaction at 25°C?

Challenge Problems

48. Glycerol, $C_3H_5(OH)_3$, and ortho-phthalic acid,

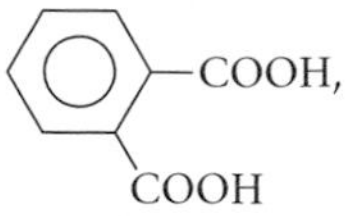

form a cross-linked polymer in which adjacent polymer chains are linked together; this polymer is used in floor coverings and dentures.

(a) Write the structural formula for a portion of the polymer chain.

(b) Use your answer in (a) to show how cross-linking can occur between the polymer chains to form a water-insoluble, network covalent solid.

49. Determine the mass percents of the elements in Nylon whose structure is shown in Example 23.4.

50. Using bond energies, estimate ΔH for protein formation, per mole of amino acid added to the chain. Does this value seem reasonable?

51. One of the earliest, and still one of the most important, polymers is the material known as Bakelite, which is a condensation polymer of phenol, C_6H_5OH, and formaldehyde, $H_2C{=}O$. Formaldehyde will react with phenol to produce the following compounds when the ratio is 1 : 1:

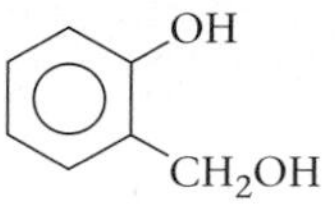

and

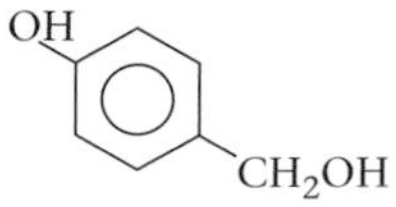

These species, which can be taken to be monomers, on being heated condense with each other and themselves, eliminating water (formed from the OH groups on CH_2OH and ring hydrogen atoms) and linking benzene rings by CH_2 groups. If the phenol:formaldehyde ratio is 1 : 1, a linear polymer forms. If the ratio is 1 : 2, two $H_2C{=}O$ molecules react with each ring, and the chains cross-link at every benzene ring, forming the infusible, insoluble, hard, brittle solid we know as Bakelite. Sketch the linear chain polymer and the cross-linked solid.

52. Aspartic acid acts as a triprotic acid with successive dissociation constants of 8.0×10^{-3}, 1.4×10^{-4}, and 1.5×10^{-10}. Depending upon pH, aspartic acid can exist in four different forms in water solution. Draw these forms and calculate the pH range over which each form is the principal species.

■ in OWL Blue-numbered questions answered in Appendix 6 **WEB** Solution is available on companion website

APPENDIX 1

Units, Constants, and Reference Data

SI UNITS

As pointed out in Chapter 1, most quantities are commonly expressed in a variety of different units. For example, temperature can be reported in °F, °C, or K. Volume is sometimes quoted in liters or cubic centimeters, at other times in quarts, cubic feet, and so on. In 1960, the General Conference of Weights and Measures attempted to end this proliferation of units. They recommended adopting a self-consistent set of units based on the metric system. In the so-called International System of Units (SI) each quantity is represented by a single unit or decimal multiple thereof, using the prefixes listed in Table 1.2 (page 7). For example, the fundamental SI unit of length is the meter; the length of an object can be expressed in meters, kilometers (1 km = 10^3 m), or nanometers (1 nm = 10^{-9} m), but *not* in inches, angstroms, or other non-SI units.

Table 1 lists the SI base and derived units for quantities commonly referred to in general chemistry. Perhaps the least familiar of these units to the beginning chemistry student are the ones used to represent force, pressure, and energy.

The *newton* is defined as the force required to impart an acceleration of one meter per second squared to a mass of one kilogram. Recall that Newton's second law can be stated as

$$\text{force} = \text{mass} \times \text{acceleration}$$

The *pascal* is defined as the pressure exerted by a force of one newton acting on an area of one square meter (recall that pressure = force/area).

The *joule* is defined as the work done when a force of one newton ($kg \cdot m/s^2$) acts through a distance of one meter (recall that work = force × distance).

Over the past 40 years, the International System of Units has met with a decidedly mixed reception, at least in the United States. On the one hand, scientists have adopted the joule as

Table 1 SI Units

Base Units			Derived Units		
Quantity	**Unit**	**Symbol**	**Quantity**	**Unit**	**Symbol**
length	meter	m	volume	cubic meter	m^3
mass	kilogram	kg	force	newton	N
time	second	s	pressure	pascal	Pa
temperature	kelvin	K	energy	joule	J
amount of substance	mole	mol	electric charge	coulomb	C
electric current	ampere	A	electric potential	volt	V

the base unit of energy, replacing the calorie. On the other hand, volumes are seldom if ever expressed in m^3. The cubic meter is simply too large a unit; the medium-sized test tube used in the general chemistry laboratory has a volume of about 0.00001 m^3. The density of water is commonly expressed as 1.00 g/cm^3, not as

$$\frac{1.00\ g}{cm^3} \times \frac{1\ kg}{10^3\ g} \times \frac{(10^2\ cm)^3}{1\ m^3} = 1.00 \times 10^3\ kg/m^3$$

(A cubic meter of water weighs about one metric ton!)

FUNDAMENTAL CONSTANTS

Acceleration of gravity (standard)	9.8066 m/s^2
Atomic mass unit (amu)	1.6605×10^{-24} g
Avogadro constant	6.0221×10^{23}/mol
Electronic charge	1.6022×10^{-19} C
Electronic mass	9.1094×10^{-28} g
Faraday constant	9.6485×10^{4} C/mol
Gas constant	0.082058 L·atm/mol·K
	8.3145 J/mol·K
Planck constant	6.6261×10^{-34} J·s
Rydberg constant	2.1799×10^{-18} J
Velocity of light	2.9979×10^{8} m/s
π	3.1416
e	2.7183
ln x	2.3026 $\log_{10}x$

VAPOR PRESSURE OF WATER (mm Hg)

T(°C)	vp	T(°C)	vp
0	4.58	35	42.2
5	6.54	40	55.3
10	9.21	45	71.9
12	10.52	50	92.5
14	11.99	55	118.0
16	13.63	60	149.4
17	14.53	65	187.5
18	15.48	70	233.7
19	16.48	80	355.1
20	17.54	90	525.8
21	18.65	92	567.0
22	19.83	94	610.9
23	21.07	96	657.6
24	22.38	98	707.3
25	23.76	100	760.0
26	25.21	102	815.9
27	26.74	104	875.1
28	28.35	106	937.9
29	30.04	108	1004.4
30	31.82	110	1074.6

THERMODYNAMIC DATA

	ΔH_f° (kJ/mol)	S° (kJ/K·mol)	ΔG_f° (kJ/mol) at 25°C
$Ag(s)$	0.0	+0.0426	0.0
$Ag^+(aq)$	+105.6	+0.0727	+77.1
$AgBr(s)$	−100.4	+0.1071	−96.9
$AgCl(s)$	−127.1	+0.0962	−109.8
$AgI(s)$	−61.8	+0.1155	−66.2
$AgNO_3(s)$	−124.4	+0.1409	−33.4
$Ag_2O(s)$	−31.0	+0.1213	−11.2
$Al(s)$	0.0	+0.0283	0.0
$Al^{3+}(aq)$	−531.0	−0.3217	−485.0
$Al_2O_3(s)$	−1675.7	+0.0509	−1582.3
$Ba(s)$	0.0	+0.0628	0.0
$Ba^{2+}(aq)$	−537.6	+0.0096	−560.8
$BaCl_2(s)$	−858.6	+0.1237	−810.4
$BaCO_3(s)$	−1216.3	+0.1121	−1137.6
$BaO(s)$	−553.5	+0.0704	−525.1
$BaSO_4(s)$	−1473.2	+0.1322	−1362.3
$Br_2(l)$	0.0	+0.1522	0.0
$Br^-(aq)$	−121.6	+0.0824	−104.0
$C(s)$	0.0	+0.0057	0.0
$CCl_4(l)$	−135.4	+0.2164	−65.3
$CHCl_3(l)$	−134.5	+0.2017	−73.7
$CH_4(g)$	−74.8	+0.1862	−50.7
$C_2H_2(g)$	+226.7	+0.2008	+209.2
$C_2H_4(g)$	+52.3	+0.2195	+68.1
$C_2H_6(g)$	−84.7	+0.2295	−32.9
$C_3H_8(g)$	−103.8	+0.2699	−23.5
$CH_3OH(l)$	−238.7	+0.1268	−166.3
$C_2H_5OH(l)$	−277.7	+0.1607	−174.9
$CO(g)$	−110.5	+0.1976	−137.2
$CO_2(g)$	−393.5	+0.2136	−394.4
$CO_3^{2-}(aq)$	−677.1	−0.0569	−527.8
$Ca(s)$	0.0	+0.0414	0.0
$Ca^{2+}(aq)$	−542.8	−0.0531	−553.6
$CaCl_2(s)$	−795.8	+0.1046	−748.1
$CaCO_3(s)$	−1206.9	+0.0929	−1128.8
$CaO(s)$	−635.1	+0.0398	−604.0
$Ca(OH)_2(s)$	−986.1	+0.0834	−898.5
$CaSO_4(s)$	−1434.1	+0.1067	−1321.8
$Cd(s)$	0.0	+0.0518	0.0
$Cd^{2+}(aq)$	−75.9	−0.0732	−77.6
$CdCl_2(s)$	−391.5	+0.1153	−344.0
$CdO(s)$	−258.2	+0.0548	−228.4
$Cl_2(g)$	0.0	+0.2230	0.0
$Cl^-(aq)$	−167.2	+0.0565	−131.2
$ClO_3^-(aq)$	−104.0	+0.1623	−8.0
$ClO_4^-(aq)$	−129.3	+0.1820	−8.5
$Cr(s)$	0.0	+0.0238	0.0
$CrO_4^{2-}(aq)$	−881.2	+0.0502	−727.8

	ΔH_f° (kJ/mol)	S° (kJ/K·mol)	ΔG_f° (kJ/mol) at 25°C
$Cr_2O_3(s)$	−1139.7	+0.0812	−1058.1
$Cr_2O_7^{2-}(aq)$	−1490.3	+0.2619	−1301.1
$Cu(s)$	0.0	+0.0332	0.0
$Cu^+(aq)$	+71.7	+0.0406	+50.0
$Cu^{2+}(aq)$	+64.8	−0.0996	+65.5
$CuO(s)$	−157.3	+0.0426	−129.7
$Cu_2O(s)$	−168.6	+0.0931	−146.0
$CuS(s)$	−53.1	+0.0665	−53.6
$Cu_2S(s)$	−79.5	+0.1209	−86.2
$CuSO_4(s)$	−771.4	+0.1076	−661.9
$F_2(g)$	0.0	+0.2027	0.0
$F^-(aq)$	−332.6	−0.0138	−278.8
$Fe(s)$	0.0	+0.0273	0.0
$Fe^{2+}(aq)$	−89.1	−0.1377	−78.9
$Fe^{3+}(aq)$	−48.5	−0.3159	−4.7
$Fe(OH)_3(s)$	−823.0	+0.1067	−696.6
$Fe_2O_3(s)$	−824.2	+0.0874	−742.2
$Fe_3O_4(s)$	−1118.4	+0.1464	−1015.5
$H_2(g)$	0.0	+0.1306	0.0
$H^+(aq)$	0.0	0.0000	0.0
$HBr(g)$	−36.4	+0.1986	−53.4
$HCl(g)$	−92.3	+0.1868	−95.3
$HCO_3^-(aq)$	−692.0	+0.0912	−586.8
$HF(g)$	−271.1	+0.1737	−273.2
$HI(g)$	+26.5	+0.2065	+1.7
$HNO_3(l)$	−174.1	+0.1556	−80.8
$H_2O(g)$	−241.8	+0.1887	−228.6
$H_2O(l)$	−285.8	+0.0699	−237.2
$H_2O_2(l)$	−187.8	+0.1096	−120.4
$H_2PO_4^-(aq)$	−1296.3	+0.0904	−1130.3
$HPO_4^{2-}(aq)$	−1292.1	−0.0335	−1089.2
$H_2S(g)$	−20.6	+0.2057	−33.6
$H_2SO_4(l)$	−814.0	+0.1569	−690.1
$HSO_4^-(aq)$	−887.3	+0.1318	−755.9
$Hg(l)$	0.0	+0.0760	0.0
$Hg^{2+}(aq)$	+171.1	−0.0322	+164.4
$HgO(s)$	−90.8	+0.0703	−58.6
$I_2(s)$	0.0	+0.1161	0.0
$I^-(aq)$	−55.2	+0.1113	−51.6
$K(s)$	0.0	+0.0642	0.0
$K^+(aq)$	−252.4	+0.1025	−283.3
$KBr(s)$	−393.8	+0.0959	−380.7
$KCl(s)$	−436.7	+0.0826	−409.1
$KClO_3(s)$	−397.7	+0.1431	−296.3
$KClO_4(s)$	−432.8	+0.1510	−303.2
$KNO_3(s)$	−494.6	+0.1330	−394.9
$Mg(s)$	0.0	+0.0327	0.0
$Mg^{2+}(aq)$	−466.8	−0.1381	−454.8

continued

	ΔH_f° (kJ/mol)	S° (kJ/K·mol)	ΔG_f° (kJ/mol) at 25°C		ΔH_f° (kJ/mol)	S° (kJ/K·mol)	ΔG_f° (kJ/mol) at 25°C
$MgCl_2(s)$	−641.3	+0.0896	−591.8	$NiO(s)$	−239.7	+0.0380	−211.7
$MgCO_3(s)$	−1095.8	+0.0657	−1012.1	$O_2(g)$	0.0	+0.2050	0.0
$MgO(s)$	−601.7	+0.0269	−569.4	$OH^-(aq)$	−230.0	−0.0108	−157.2
$Mg(OH)_2(s)$	−924.5	+0.0632	−833.6	$P_4(s)$	0.0	+0.1644	0.0
$MgSO_4(s)$	−1284.9	+0.0916	−1170.7	$PCl_3(g)$	−287.0	+0.3117	−267.8
$Mn(s)$	0.0	+0.0320	0.0	$PCl_5(g)$	−374.9	+0.3645	−305.0
$Mn^{2+}(aq)$	−220.8	−0.0736	−228.1	$PO_4^{3-}(aq)$	−1277.4	−0.222	−1018.7
$MnO(s)$	−385.2	+0.0597	−362.9	$Pb(s)$	0.0	+0.0648	0.0
$MnO_2(s)$	−520.0	+0.0530	−465.2	$Pb^{2+}(aq)$	−1.7	+0.0105	−24.4
$MnO_4^-(aq)$	−541.4	+0.1912	−447.2	$PbBr_2(s)$	−278.7	+0.1615	−261.9
$N_2(g)$	0.0	+0.1915	0.0	$PbCl_2(s)$	−359.4	+0.1360	−314.1
$NH_3(g)$	−46.1	+0.1923	−16.5	$PbO(s)$	−219.0	+0.0665	−188.9
$NH_4^+(aq)$	−132.5	+0.1134	−79.3	$PbO_2(s)$	−277.4	+0.0686	−217.4
$NH_4Cl(s)$	−314.4	+0.0946	−203.0	$S(s)$	0.0	+0.0318	0.0
$NH_4NO_3(s)$	−365.6	+0.1511	−184.0	$S^{2-}(aq)$	+33.1	−0.0146	+85.8
$N_2H_4(l)$	+50.6	+0.1212	+149.2	$SO_2(g)$	−296.8	+0.2481	−300.2
$NO(g)$	+90.2	+0.2107	+86.6	$SO_3(g)$	−395.7	+0.2567	−371.1
$NO_2(g)$	+33.2	+0.2400	+51.3	$SO_4^{2-}(aq)$	−909.3	+0.0201	−744.5
$NO_2^-(aq)$	−104.6	+0.1230	−32.2	$Si(s)$	0.0	+0.0188	0.0
$NO_3^-(aq)$	−205.0	+0.1464	−108.7	$SiO_2(s)$	−910.9	+0.0418	−856.7
$N_2O_4(g)$	+9.2	+0.3042	+97.9	$Sn(s)$	0.0	+0.0516	0.0
$Na(s)$	0.0	+0.0512	0.0	$Sn^{2+}(aq)$	−8.8	−0.0174	−27.2
$Na^+(aq)$	−240.1	+0.0590	−261.9	$SnO_2(s)$	−580.7	+0.0523	−519.6
$NaCl(s)$	−411.2	+0.0721	−384.2	$Zn(s)$	0.0	+0.0416	0.0
$NaF(s)$	−573.6	+0.0515	−543.5	$Zn^{2+}(aq)$	−153.9	−0.1121	−147.1
$NaOH(s)$	−425.6	+0.0645	−379.5	$ZnI_2(s)$	−208.0	+0.1611	−209.0
$Ni(s)$	0.0	+0.0299	0.0	$ZnO(s)$	−348.3	+0.0436	−318.3
$Ni^{2+}(aq)$	−54.0	−0.1289	−45.6	$ZnS(s)$	−206.0	+0.0577	−201.3

EQUILIBRIUM CONSTANTS OF WEAK ACIDS (K_a)

H_3AsO_4	5.7×10^{-3}	HNO_2	6.0×10^{-4}	$N_2H_5^+$	1.0×10^{-8}
$H_2AsO_4^-$	1.8×10^{-7}	H_3PO_4	7.1×10^{-3}	$Al(H_2O)_6^{3+}$	1.2×10^{-5}
$HAsO_4^{2-}$	2.5×10^{-12}	$H_2PO_4^-$	6.2×10^{-8}	$Ag(H_2O)_2^+$	1.2×10^{-12}
$HBrO$	2.6×10^{-9}	HPO_4^{2-}	4.5×10^{-13}	$Ca(H_2O)_6^{2+}$	2.2×10^{-13}
$HCHO_2$	1.9×10^{-4}	H_2S	1.0×10^{-7}	$Cd(H_2O)_4^{2+}$	4.0×10^{-10}
$HC_2H_3O_2$	1.8×10^{-5}	H_2SO_3	1.7×10^{-2}	$Fe(H_2O)_6^{3+}$	6.7×10^{-3}
HCN	5.8×10^{-10}	HSO_3^-	6.0×10^{-8}	$Fe(H_2O)_6^{2+}$	1.7×10^{-7}
H_2CO_3	4.4×10^{-7}	HSO_4^-	1.0×10^{-2}	$Mg(H_2O)_6^{2+}$	3.7×10^{-12}
HCO_3^-	4.7×10^{-11}	H_2Se	1.5×10^{-4}	$Mn(H_2O)_6^{2+}$	2.8×10^{-11}
$HClO_2$	1.0×10^{-2}	H_2SeO_3	2.7×10^{-3}	$Ni(H_2O)_6^{2+}$	2.2×10^{-10}
$HClO$	2.8×10^{-8}	$HSeO_3^-$	5.0×10^{-8}	$Pb(H_2O)_6^{2+}$	6.7×10^{-7}
HF	6.9×10^{-4}	$CH_3NH_3^+$	2.4×10^{-11}	$Sc(H_2O)_6^{3+}$	1.1×10^{-4}
HIO	2.4×10^{-11}	NH_4^+	5.6×10^{-10}	$Zn(H_2O)_4^{2+}$	3.3×10^{-10}
HN_3	2.4×10^{-5}				

EQUILIBRIUM CONSTANTS OF WEAK BASES (K_b)

AsO_4^{3-}	4.0×10^{-3}	N_3^-	4.2×10^{-10}	$HSeO_3^-$	3.7×10^{-12}
$HAsO_4^{2-}$	5.6×10^{-8}	NH_3	1.8×10^{-5}	$AlOH^{2+}$	8.3×10^{-10}
$H_2AsO_4^-$	1.8×10^{-12}	N_2H_4	1.0×10^{-6}	$AgOH$	8.3×10^{-3}
BrO^-	3.8×10^{-6}	NO_2^-	1.7×10^{-11}	$CaOH^+$	4.5×10^{-2}
CH_3NH_2	4.2×10^{-4}	PO_4^{3-}	2.2×10^{-2}	$CdOH^+$	2.5×10^{-5}
CHO_2^-	5.3×10^{-11}	HPO_4^{2-}	1.6×10^{-7}	$FeOH^{2+}$	1.5×10^{-12}
$C_2H_3O_2^-$	5.6×10^{-10}	$H_2PO_4^-$	1.4×10^{-12}	$FeOH^+$	5.9×10^{-8}
CN^-	1.7×10^{-5}	HS^-	1.0×10^{-7}	$MgOH^+$	2.7×10^{-3}
CO_3^{2-}	2.1×10^{-4}	SO_3^{2-}	1.7×10^{-7}	$MnOH^+$	3.6×10^{-4}
HCO_3^-	2.3×10^{-8}	HSO_3^-	5.9×10^{-13}	$NiOH^+$	4.5×10^{-5}
ClO_2^-	1.0×10^{-12}	SO_4^{2-}	1.0×10^{-12}	$PbOH^+$	1.5×10^{-8}
ClO^-	3.6×10^{-7}	HSe^-	6.7×10^{-11}	$ScOH^{2+}$	9.1×10^{-11}
F^-	1.4×10^{-11}	SeO_3^{2-}	2.0×10^{-7}	$ZnOH^+$	3.0×10^{-5}
IO^-	4.2×10^{-4}				

FORMATION CONSTANTS OF COMPLEX IONS (K_f)

$AgBr_2^-$	2×10^{7}	$Cu(CN)_2^-$	1×10^{24}	$PdBr_4^{2-}$	6×10^{13}
$AgCl_2^-$	1.8×10^{5}	$Cu(NH_3)_4^{2+}$	2×10^{12}	$PtBr_4^{2-}$	6×10^{17}
$Ag(CN)_2^-$	2×10^{20}	$FeSCN^{2+}$	9.2×10^{2}	$PtCl_4^{2-}$	1×10^{16}
AgI_2^-	5×10^{10}	$Fe(CN)_6^{3-}$	4×10^{52}	$Pt(CN)_4^{2-}$	1×10^{41}
$Ag(NH_3)_2^+$	1.7×10^{7}	$Fe(CN)_6^{4-}$	4×10^{45}	c-$Pt(NH_3)_2Cl_2$	3×10^{29}
$Al(OH)_4^-$	1×10^{33}	$HgBr_4^{2-}$	1×10^{21}	t-$Pt(NH_3)_2Cl_2$	3×10^{28}
$Cd(CN)_4^{2-}$	2×10^{18}	$HgCl_4^{2-}$	1×10^{15}	c-$Pt(NH_3)_2(H_2O)_2^{2+}$	4×10^{23}
CdI_4^{2-}	4.0×10^{5}	$Hg(CN)_4^{2-}$	2×10^{41}	c-$Pt(NH_3)_2I_2$	2×10^{33}
$Cd(NH_3)_4^{2+}$	2.8×10^{7}	HgI_4^{2-}	1×10^{30}	t-$Pt(NH_3)_2I_2$	5×10^{32}
$Cd(OH)_4^{2-}$	1.2×10^{9}	$Hg(NH_3)_4^{2+}$	2×10^{19}	c-$Pt(NH_3)_2(OH)_2$	1×10^{39}
$Co(NH_3)_6^{2+}$	1×10^{5}	$Ni(CN)_4^{2-}$	1×10^{30}	$Pt(NH_3)_4^{2+}$	2×10^{35}
$Co(NH_3)_6^{3+}$	1×10^{23}	$Ni(NH_3)_6^{2+}$	9×10^{8}	$Zn(CN)_4^{2-}$	6×10^{16}
$Co(NH_3)_5Cl^{2+}$	2×10^{28}	PbI_4^{2-}	1.7×10^{4}	$Zn(NH_3)_4^{2+}$	3.6×10^{8}
$Co(NH_3)_5NO_2^{2+}$	1×10^{24}	$Pb(OH)_3^-$	8×10^{13}	$Zn(OH)_4^{2-}$	3×10^{14}

SOLUBILITY PRODUCT CONSTANTS (K_{sp})

$AgBr$	5×10^{-13}	$Co(OH)_2$	2×10^{-16}	$NiCO_3$	1.4×10^{-7}
$AgC_2H_3O_2$	1.9×10^{-3}	$Co_3(PO_4)_2$	1×10^{-35}	$Ni_3(PO_4)_2$	1×10^{-32}
Ag_2CO_3	8×10^{-12}	$CuCl$	1.7×10^{-7}	NiS	1×10^{-21}
$AgCl$	1.8×10^{-10}	$CuBr$	6.3×10^{-9}	$PbBr_2$	6.6×10^{-6}
Ag_2CrO_4	1×10^{-12}	CuI	1.2×10^{-12}	$PbCO_3$	1×10^{-13}
AgI	1×10^{-16}	$Cu_3(PO_4)_2$	1×10^{-37}	$PbCl_2$	1.7×10^{-5}
Ag_3PO_4	1×10^{-16}	CuS	1×10^{-36}	$PbCrO_4$	2×10^{-14}
Ag_2S	1×10^{-49}	Cu_2S	1×10^{-48}	PbF_2	7.1×10^{-7}
$AgSCN$	1.0×10^{-12}	$FeCO_3$	3.1×10^{-11}	PbI_2	8.4×10^{-9}
AlF_3	1×10^{-18}	$Fe(OH)_2$	5×10^{-17}	$Pb(OH)_2$	1×10^{-20}
$Al(OH)_3$	2×10^{-31}	$Fe(OH)_3$	3×10^{-39}	PbS	1×10^{-28}
$AlPO_4$	1×10^{-20}	FeS	2×10^{-19}	$Pb(SCN)_2$	2.1×10^{-5}
$BaCO_3$	2.6×10^{-9}	GaF_3	2×10^{-16}	$PbSO_4$	1.8×10^{-8}
$BaCrO_4$	1.2×10^{-10}	$Ga(OH)_3$	1×10^{-35}	$Sc(OH)_3$	2×10^{-31}
BaF_2	1.8×10^{-7}	$GaPO_4$	1×10^{-21}	SnS	3×10^{-28}
$BaSO_4$	1.1×10^{-10}	Hg_2Br_2	6×10^{-23}	$SrCO_3$	5.6×10^{-10}
Bi_2S_3	1×10^{-99}	Hg_2Cl_2	1×10^{-18}	$SrCrO_4$	3.6×10^{-5}
$CaCO_3$	4.9×10^{-9}	Hg_2I_2	5×10^{-29}	SrF_2	4.3×10^{-9}
CaF_2	1.5×10^{-10}	HgS	1×10^{-52}	$SrSO_4$	3.4×10^{-7}
$Ca(OH)_2$	4.0×10^{-6}	Li_2CO_3	8.2×10^{-4}	$TlCl$	1.9×10^{-4}
$Ca_3(PO_4)_2$	1×10^{-33}	$MgCO_3$	6.8×10^{-6}	$TlBr$	3.7×10^{-6}
$CaSO_4$	7.1×10^{-5}	MgF_2	7×10^{-11}	TlI	5.6×10^{-8}
$CdCO_3$	6×10^{-12}	$Mg(OH)_2$	6×10^{-12}	$Tl(OH)_3$	2×10^{-44}
$Cd(OH)_2$	5×10^{-15}	$Mg_3(PO_4)_2$	1×10^{-24}	Tl_2S	1×10^{-20}
$Cd_3(PO_4)_2$	1×10^{-33}	$Mn(OH)_2$	2×10^{-13}	$ZnCO_3$	1.1×10^{-10}
CdS	1×10^{-29}	MnS	5×10^{-14}	$Zn(OH)_2$	4×10^{-17}

APPENDIX 2

Properties of the Elements

Element	At. No.	mp(°C)	bp(°C)	E.N.	Ion. Ener. (kJ/mol)	At. Rad. (nm)	Ion. Rad. (nm)
H	1	−259	−253	2.2	1312	0.037	(−1)0.208
He	2	−272	−269		2372	0.05	
Li	3	186	1326	1.0	520	0.152	(+1)0.060
Be	4	1283	2970	1.6	900	0.111	(+2)0.031
B	5	2300	2550	2.0	801	0.088	
C	6	3570	subl.	2.5	1086	0.077	
N	7	−210	−196	3.0	1402	0.070	
O	8	−218	−183	3.5	1314	0.066	(−2)0.140
F	9	−220	−188	4.0	1681	0.064	(−1)0.136
Ne	10	−249	−246		2081	0.070	
Na	11	98	889	0.9	496	0.186	(+1)0.095
Mg	12	650	1120	1.3	738	0.160	(+2)0.065
Al	13	660	2327	1.6	578	0.143	(+3)0.050
Si	14	1414	2355	1.9	786	0.117	
P	15	44	280	2.2	1012	0.110	
S	16	119	444	2.6	1000	0.104	(−2)0.184
Cl	17	−101	−34	3.2	1251	0.099	(−1)0.181
Ar	18	−189	−186		1520	0.094	
K	19	64	774	0.8	419	0.231	(+1)0.133
Ca	20	845	1420	1.0	590	0.197	(+2)0.099
Sc	21	1541	2831	1.4	631	0.160	(+3)0.081
Ti	22	1660	3287	1.5	658	0.146	
V	23	1890	3380	1.6	650	0.131	
Cr	24	1857	2672	1.6	653	0.125	(+3)0.064
Mn	25	1244	1962	1.5	717	0.129	(+2)0.080
Fe	26	1535	2750	1.8	759	0.126	(+2)0.075
Co	27	1495	2870	1.9	758	0.125	(+2)0.072
Ni	28	1453	2732	1.9	737	0.124	(+2)0.069
Cu	29	1083	2567	1.9	746	0.128	(+1)0.096
Zn	30	420	907	1.6	906	0.133	(+2)0.074
Ga	31	30	2403	1.6	579	0.122	(+3)0.062
Ge	32	937	2830	2.0	762	0.122	
As	33	814	subl.	2.2	944	0.121	
Se	34	217	685	2.5	941	0.117	(−2)0.198
Br	35	−7	59	3.0	1140	0.114	(−1)0.195
Kr	36	−157	−152	3.3	1351	0.109	
Rb	37	39	688	0.8	403	0.244	(+1)0.148
Sr	38	770	1380	0.9	550	0.215	(+2)0.113

continued

Element	At. No.	mp(°C)	bp(°C)	E.N.	Ion. Ener. (kJ/mol)	At. Rad. (nm)	Ion. Rad. (nm)
Y	39	1509	2930	1.2	616	0.180	(+3)0.093
Zr	40	1852	3580	1.4	660	0.157	
Nb	41	2468	5127	1.6	664	0.143	
Mo	42	2610	5560	1.8	685	0.136	
Tc	43	2200	4700	1.9	702	0.136	
Ru	44	2430	3700	2.2	711	0.133	
Rh	45	1966	3700	2.2	720	0.134	
Pd	46	1550	3170	2.2	805	0.138	
Ag	47	961	2210	1.9	731	0.144	(+1)0.126
Cd	48	321	767	1.7	868	0.149	(+2)0.097
In	49	157	2000	1.7	558	0.162	(+3)0.081
Sn	50	232	2270	1.9	709	0.140	
Sb	51	631	1380	2.0	832	0.141	
Te	52	450	990	2.1	869	0.137	(−2)0.221
I	53	114	184	2.7	1009	0.133	(−1)0.216
Xe	54	−112	−107	3.0	1170	0.130	
Cs	55	28	690	0.8	376	0.262	(+1)0.169
Ba	56	725	1640	0.9	503	0.217	(+2)0.135
La	57	920	3469	1.1	538	0.187	(+3)0.115
Ce	58	795	3468	1.1	528	0.182	(+3)0.101
Pr	59	935	3127	1.1	523	0.182	(+3)0.100
Nd	60	1024	3027	1.1	530	0.182	(+3)0.099
Pm	61	1027	2727	1.1	536	0.181	
Sm	62	1072	1900	1.1	543	0.180	
Eu	63	826	1439	1.1	547	0.204	(+2)0.097
Gd	64	1312	3000	1.1	592	0.179	(+3)0.096
Tb	65	1356	2800	1.1	564	0.177	(+3)0.095
Dy	66	1407	2600	1.1	572	0.177	(+3)0.094
Ho	67	1461	2600	1.1	581	0.176	(+3)0.093
Er	68	1497	2900	1.1	589	0.175	(+3)0.092
Tm	69	1356	2800	1.1	597	0.174	(+3)0.091
Yb	70	824	1427	1.1	603	0.193	(+3)0.089
Lu	71	1652	3327	1.1	524	0.174	(+3)0.089
Hf	72	2225	5200	1.3	654	0.157	
Ta	73	2980	5425	1.5	761	0.143	
W	74	3410	5930	1.7	770	0.137	
Re	75	3180	5885	1.9	760	0.137	
Os	76	2727	4100	2.2	840	0.134	
Ir	77	2448	4500	2.2	880	0.135	
Pt	78	1769	4530	2.2	870	0.138	
Au	79	1063	2966	2.4	890	0.144	(+1)0.137
Hg	80	−39	357	1.9	1007	0.155	(+2)0.110
Tl	81	304	1457	1.8	589	0.171	(+3)0.095
Pb	82	328	1750	1.9	716	0.175	
Bi	83	271	1560	1.9	703	0.146	
Po	84	254	962	2.0	812	0.165	
At	85	302	334	2.2			
Rn	86	−71	−62		1037	0.14	
Fr	87	27	677	0.7			
Ra	88	700	1140	0.9	509	0.220	
Ac	89	1050	3200	1.1	490	0.20	
Th	90	1750	4790	1.3	590	0.180	
Pa	91	1600	4200	1.4	570		
U	92	1132	3818	1.4	590	0.14	

APPENDIX 3

Exponents and Logarithms

The mathematics you will use in general chemistry is relatively simple. You will, however, be expected to—

- make calculations involving exponential numbers, such as 6.022×10^{23} or 1.6×10^{-10}.
- work with logarithms or inverse logarithms, particularly in problems involving pH:

$$pH = -\log_{10} (\text{conc. } H^+)$$

This appendix reviews each of these topics.

EXPONENTIAL NOTATION

Chemists deal frequently with very large or very small numbers. In one gram of the element carbon there are

$$50{,}140{,}000{,}000{,}000{,}000{,}000{,}000 \text{ atoms of carbon}$$

At the opposite extreme, the mass of a single atom is

$$0.00000000000000000000001994 \text{ g}$$

Numbers such as these are very awkward to work with. For example, neither of the numbers just written could be entered directly on a calculator. Operations involving very large or very small numbers can be simplified by using **exponential (scientific)** notation. To express a number in exponential notation, write it in the form

$$C \times 10^n$$

where C is a number between 1 and 10 (for example, 1, 2.62, 5.8) and n is a positive or negative integer such as 1, -1, -3. To find n, count the number of places that the decimal point must be moved to give the coefficient, C. If the decimal point must be moved to the *left*, n is a *positive* integer; if it must be moved to the *right*, n is a *negative* integer. Thus

$$26.23 = 2.623 \times 10^1 \quad \text{(decimal point moved 1 place to left)}$$
$$5609 = 5.609 \times 10^3 \quad \text{(decimal point moved 3 places to left)}$$
$$0.0918 = 9.18 \times 10^{-2} \quad \text{(decimal point moved 2 places to right)}$$

Multiplication and Division

A major advantage of exponential notation is that it simplifies the processes of multiplication and division. To *multiply, add exponents:*

$$10^1 \times 10^2 = 10^{1+2} = 10^3 \qquad 10^6 \times 10^{-4} = 10^{6+(-4)} = 10^2$$

To *divide, subtract* exponents:

$$10^3/10^2 = 10^{3-2} = 10^1 \qquad 10^{-3}/10^6 = 10^{-3-6} = 10^{-9}$$

It often happens that multiplication or division yields an answer that is not in standard exponential notation. For example,

$$(5.0 \times 10^4) \times (6.0 \times 10^3) = (5.0 \times 6.0) \times 10^4 \times 10^3 = 30 \times 10^7$$

The product is not in standard exponential notation because the coefficient, 30, does not lie between 1 and 10. To correct this situation, rewrite the coefficient as 3.0×10^1 and then add exponents:

$$30 \times 10^7 = (3.0 \times 10^1) \times 10^7 = 3.0 \times 10^8$$

In another case,

$$0.526 \times 10^3 = (5.26 \times 10^{-1}) \times 10^3 = 5.26 \times 10^2$$

Exponential Notation on the Calculator

On all scientific calculators it is possible to enter numbers in exponential notation. The method used depends on the brand of calculator. Most often, it involves using a key labeled EXP, EE, or EEX. Check your instruction manual for the procedure to be followed. To make sure you understand it, try entering the following numbers:

$$2.4 \times 10^6 \qquad 3.16 \times 10^{-8} \qquad 6.2 \times 10^{-16}$$

Multiplication, division, addition, and subtraction can be carried out directly on your calculator. Try the following exercises:

(a) $(6.0 \times 10^2) \times (4.2 \times 10^{-4}) = ?$

(b) $\dfrac{6.0 \times 10^2}{4.2 \times 10^{-4}} = ?$

(c) $3.6 \times 10^{-4} + 4 \times 10^{-5} = ?$

(d) $3.6 \times 10^{-4} - 4 \times 10^{-5} = ?$

The answers, expressed in exponential notation and following the rules of significant figures, are (a) 2.5×10^{-1} (b) 1.4×10^6 (c) 4.0×10^{-4} (d) 3.2×10^{-4}.

Exponential (or ordinary) numbers are readily raised to powers using a calculator. To square a number, use the x^2 key. For example,

$$(3 \times 10^4)^2 = 9 \times 10^8$$

For other powers, use the y^x key. To cube a number, y, enter that number, press the y^x key, enter 3, and read the answer. That way, you should find that

$$(2 \times 10^{-5})^3 = 8 \times 10^{-15}$$

Roots of exponentials are obtained in a similar way. To extract a square root, use the $\sqrt{x}$ key. For other roots, use the y^x key. To obtain a cube root, enter the number, press the y^x key, enter 1/3 (0.333333333) and read the answer:

$$(2.0 \times 10^{-5})^{1/3} = 2.7 \times 10^{-2}$$

(Many calculators have a $\sqrt[x]{y}$ key, in which case, enter $x = 3$ rather than 1/3.)

Try the following operations on your calculator.

$(3.12)^5 = ?$	answer: 2.96×10^2
$(3.12 \times 10^{-2})^5 = ?$	answer: 2.96×10^{-8}
$(3.12)^{1/5} = ?$	answer: 1.26
$(3.12 \times 10^{-2})^{1/5} = ?$	answer: 0.500

LOGARITHMS AND INVERSE LOGARITHMS

The logarithm of a number ***n*** to the base ***m*** is defined as the power to which ***m*** must be raised to give the number ***n***. Thus

$$\text{if } m^x = n, \text{ then } \log_m n = x$$

In other words, a *logarithm* is an *exponent,* which may be a whole number (e.g., 1, -1) but more often is not (e.g., 1.500, -0.301).

In general chemistry, you will encounter two kinds of logarithms.

1. *Common logarithms,* where the base is 10, ordinarily denoted as $\log_{10}$. If $10^x = n$, then $\log_{10} n = x$. Examples include the following:

$$\log_{10} 100 = 2.00 \qquad (10^2 = 100)$$
$$\log_{10} 1 = 0.000 \qquad (10^0 = 1)$$
$$\log_{10} 0.001 = -3.000 \qquad (10^{-3} = 0.001)$$

2. *Natural logarithms,* where the base is the quantity $e = 2.718\ldots$ Many of the equations used in general chemistry are expressed most simply in terms of natural logarithms, denoted as ln. If $e^x = n$, then $\ln n = x$.

$$\ln 100 = 4.606 \qquad (\text{i.e., } 100 = e^{4.606})$$
$$\ln 1 = 0 \qquad (\text{i.e., } 1 = e^0)$$
$$\ln 0.001 = -6.908 \qquad (\text{i.e., } 0.001 = e^{-6.908})$$

Notice that

(a) $\mathbf{\log_{10} 1 = \ln 1 = 0}$**.** The logarithm of 1 to any base is zero, because any number raised to the zero power is 1. That is

$$10^0 = e^0 = 2^0 = \cdots = n^0 = 1$$

(b) Numbers larger than 1 have a positive logarithm; numbers smaller than 1 have a negative logarithm. For example,

$$\log_{10} 100 = 2 \qquad \ln 100 = 4.606$$
$$\log_{10} 10 = 1 \qquad \ln 10 = 2.303$$
$$\log_{10} 0.1 = -1 \qquad \ln 0.1 = -2.303$$
$$\log_{10} 0.01 = -2 \qquad \ln 0.01 = -4.606$$

(c) The common and natural logarithms of a number are related by the expression

$$\mathbf{\ln n = 2.303 \log_{10} n}$$

That is, the natural logarithm of a number is 2.303 . . . times its base-10 logarithm.

(d) Finally, if $x \leq 0$, both $\log x$ and $\ln x$ are undefined.

An **inverse** logarithm (antilogarithm) is the number corresponding to a given logarithm. In general,

$$\text{if } m^x = n, \text{ then inverse } \log_m x = n$$

For example,

$$10^2 = 100 \qquad \text{inverse } \log_{10} 2 = 100$$
$$10^{-3} = 0.001 \qquad \text{inverse } \log_{10} (-3) = 0.001$$

In other words, the numbers whose base-10 logarithms are 2 and −3 are 100 and 0.001, respectively. The same reasoning applies to natural logarithms.

$$e^{4.606} = 100 \qquad \text{inverse } \ln 4.606 = 100$$
$$e^{-6.908} = 0.001 \qquad \text{inverse } \ln -6.908 = 0.001$$

The numbers whose natural logarithms are 4.606 and −6.908 are 100 and 0.001, respectively. Notice that if the inverse logarithm is positive, the corresponding number is larger than 1; if it is negative, the number is smaller than 1.

Finding Logarithms and Inverse Logarithms on a Calculator

To obtain a base-10 logarithm using a calculator, all you need to do is enter the number and press the LOG key. This way you should find that

$$\log_{10} 2.00 = 0.301\ldots$$
$$\log_{10} 0.526 = -0.279\ldots$$

Similarly, to find a natural logarithm, you enter the number and press the LN X key.

$$\ln 2.00 = 0.693\ldots$$
$$\ln 0.526 = -0.642\ldots$$

To find the logarithm of an exponential number, you enter the number in exponential form and take the logarithm in the usual way. This way you should find that

$$\log_{10} 2.00 \times 10^3 = 3.301\ldots \qquad \ln 2.00 \times 10^3 = 7.601\ldots$$
$$\log_{10} 5.3 \times 10^{-12} = -11.28\ldots \qquad \ln 5.3 \times 10^{-12} = -25.96\ldots$$

The base-10 logarithm of an exponential number can be found in a somewhat different way by applying the relation

$$\log_{10} (C \times 10^n) = n + \log_{10} C$$

Thus

$$\log_{10} 2.00 \times 10^3 = 3 + \log_{10} 2.00 = 3 + 0.301 = 3.301$$
$$\log_{10} 5.3 \times 10^{-12} = -12 + \log_{10} 5.3 = -12 + 0.72 = -11.28$$

The method used to find inverse logarithms depends on the type of calculator. On certain calculators, you enter the number and then press, in succession, the INV and either LOG or LN X keys. With other calculators, you press the 10^x or e^x key. Either way, you should find that

$$\text{inverse } \log_{10} 1.632 = 42.8\ldots \qquad \text{inverse } \ln 1.632 = 5.11\ldots$$
$$\text{inverse } \log_{10} - 8.82 = 1.5 \times 10^{-9} \qquad \text{inverse } \ln -8.82 = 1.5 \times 10^{-4}$$

Significant Figures in Logarithms and Inverse Logarithms

For base-10 logarithms, the rules governing significant figures are as follows:

1. ***In taking the logarithm of a number, retain after the decimal point in the log as many digits as there are significant figures in the number.*** (This part of the logarithm is often referred to as the *mantissa;* digits that precede the decimal point comprise the *characteristic* of the logarithm.) To illustrate this rule, consider the following:

$$\log_{10} 2.00 = 0.301 \qquad \log_{10} (2.00 \times 10^3) = 3.301$$
$$\log_{10} 2.0 = 0.30 \qquad \log_{10} (2.0 \times 10^1) = 1.30$$
$$\log_{10} 2 = 0.3 \qquad \log_{10} (2 \times 10^{-3}) = 0.3 - 3 = -2.7$$

2. ***In taking the inverse logarithm of a number, retain as many significant figures as there are after the decimal point in the number.*** Thus

$$\text{inverse } \log_{10} 0.301 = 2.00 \qquad \text{inverse } \log_{10} 3.301 = 2.00 \times 10^3$$
$$\text{inverse } \log_{10} 0.30 = 2.0 \qquad \text{inverse } \log_{10} 1.30 = 2.0 \times 10^1$$
$$\text{inverse } \log_{10} 0.3 = 2 \qquad \text{inverse } \log_{10} (-2.7) = 2 \times 10^{-3}$$

These rules take into account the fact that, as mentioned earlier,

$$\log_{10} (C \times 10^n) = n + \log_{10} C$$

The digits that appear before (to the left of) the decimal point specify the value of n, that is, the power of 10 involved in the expression. In that sense, they are not experimentally significant. In contrast, the digits that appear after (to the right of) the decimal point specify the value of the logarithm of C; the number of such digits reflects the uncertainty in C. Thus,

$$\log_{10} 209 = 2.320 \qquad \text{(3 sig. fig.)}$$
$$\log_{10} 209.0 = 2.3201 \qquad \text{(4 sig. fig.)}$$

The rules for significant figures involving natural logarithms and inverse logarithms are somewhat more complex than those for base-10 logs. However, for simplicity we will assume that the rules listed above apply here as well. Thus

$$\ln 209 = 5.342 \qquad \text{(3 sig. fig.)}$$
$$\ln 209.0 = 5.3423 \qquad \text{(4 sig. fig.)}$$

Operations Involving Logarithms

Because logarithms are exponents, the rules governing the use of exponents apply as well. The rules that follow are valid for all types of logarithms, regardless of the base. We illustrate the rules with natural logarithms; that is where you are most likely to use them in working with this text.

Multiplication: $\ln(xy) = \ln x + \ln y$

Example: $\ln(2.50 \times 1.25) = \ln 2.50 + \ln 1.25 = 0.916 + 0.223 = 1.139$

Division: $\ln(x/y) = \ln x - \ln y$

Example: $\ln(2.50/1.25) = 0.916 - 0.223 = 0.693$

Raising to a Power: $\ln(x^n) = n \ln x$

Example: $\ln(2.00)^4 = 4 \ln 2.00 = 4(0.693) = 2.772$

Extracting a Root: $\ln(x^{1/n}) = \frac{1}{n} \ln x$

Example: $\ln(2.00)^{1/3} = \frac{\ln 2.00}{3} = \frac{0.693}{3} = 0.231$

Taking a Reciprocal: $\ln(1/x) = -\ln x$

Example: $\ln(1/2.00) = -\ln 2.00 = -0.693$

APPENDIX 4

Nomenclature of Complex Ions

COMPLEX IONS (CHAPTER 15)

To name a complex ion, it is necessary to show—

- the number and identity of each ligand attached to the central metal ion.
- the identity and oxidation number of the central metal ion.
- whether the complex is a cation or an anion.

To accomplish this, a simple set of rules is followed.

1. The names of anionic ligands are obtained by substituting the suffix *-o* for the normal ending. Examples include

Cl^-	chlor*o*	SO_4^{2-}	sulfat*o*
OH^-	hydrox*o*	CO_3^{2-}	carbonat*o*

Ordinarily, the names of molecular ligands are unchanged. Two important exceptions are

H_2O	aqua	NH_3	ammine

2. The number of ligands of a particular type is ordinarily indicated by the Greek prefixes *di, tri, tetra, penta, hexa:*

$Cu(H_2O)_4^{2+}$	*tetra*aquacopper(II)
$Cr(NH_3)_6^{3+}$	*hexa*amminechromium(III)

If the name of the ligand is itself complex (e.g., ethylenediamine), the number of such ligands is indicated by the prefixes *bis, tris,* . . . The name of the ligand is enclosed in parentheses:

$Cr(en)_3^{3+}$	*tris*(ethylenediamine)chromium(III)

3. If more than one type of ligand is present, they are named in alphabetical order (without regard for prefixes):

$Cu(NH_3)_2(H_2O)_2^{2+}$	di*ammine*di*aqua*copper(II)
$Cr(NH_3)_5Cl^{2+}$	penta*ammine**chloro*chromium(III)

4. As you can deduce from the preceding examples, the oxidation number of the central metal ion is indicated by a Roman numeral written at the end of the name.

5. If the complex is an anion, the suffix *-ate* is inserted between the name of the metal and the oxidation number:

$Zn(OH)_4^{2-}$	tetrahydroxozinc*ate*(II)

Coordination compounds are named in much the same way as simple ionic compounds. The cation is named first, followed by the anion. Examples include

$[Cr(NH_3)_4Cl_2]NO_3$	tetraamminedichlorochromium(III) nitrate
$K_2[PtCl_6]$	potassium hexachloroplatinate(IV)
$[Co(NH_3)_2(en)_2]Br_3$	diamminebis(ethylenediamine)cobalt(III) bromide

APPENDIX 5

Molecular Orbitals

In Chapter 7, we used valence bond theory to explain bonding in molecules. It accounts, at least qualitatively, for the stability of the covalent bond in terms of the overlap of atomic orbitals. By invoking hybridization, valence bond theory can account for the molecular geometries predicted by electron-pair repulsion. Where Lewis structures are inadequate, as in SO_2, the concept of resonance allows us to explain the observed properties.

A major weakness of valence bond theory has been its inability to predict the magnetic properties of molecules. We mentioned this problem in Chapter 7 with regard to the O_2 molecule, which is paramagnetic, even though it has an even number (12) of valence electrons. The octet rule, or valence bond theory, would predict that all the electrons in O_2 should be paired, which would make it diamagnetic.

This discrepancy between experiment and theory (and many others) can be explained in terms of an alternative model of covalent bonding, the molecular orbital (MO) approach. Molecular orbital theory treats bonds in terms of orbitals characteristic of the molecule as a whole. To apply this approach, we carry out three basic operations.

1. The atomic orbitals of atoms are combined to give a new set of molecular orbitals characteristic of the molecule as a whole. *The number of molecular orbitals formed is equal to the number of atomic orbitals combined.* When two H atoms combine to form H_2, two s orbitals, one from each atom, yield two molecular orbitals. In another case, six p orbitals, three from each atom, give a total of six molecular orbitals.

2. The molecular orbitals are arranged in order of increasing energy. The relative energies of these orbitals are ordinarily deduced from experiment. Spectra and magnetic properties of molecules are used.

3. The *valence electrons* in a molecule are distributed among the available molecular orbitals. The process followed is much like that used with electrons in atoms. In particular, we find the following:

(a) *Each molecular orbital can hold a maximum of two electrons.* When an orbital is filled the two electrons have opposed spins, in accordance with the Pauli principle (Chapter 7).

(b) *Electrons go into the lowest energy molecular orbital available.* A higher orbital starts to fill only when each orbital below it has its quota of two electrons.

(c) *Hund's rule is obeyed.* When two orbitals of equal energy are available to two electrons, one electron goes into each, giving two half-filled orbitals.

DIATOMIC MOLECULES OF THE ELEMENTS

To illustrate molecular orbital theory, we apply it to the diatomic molecules of the elements in the first two periods of the periodic table.

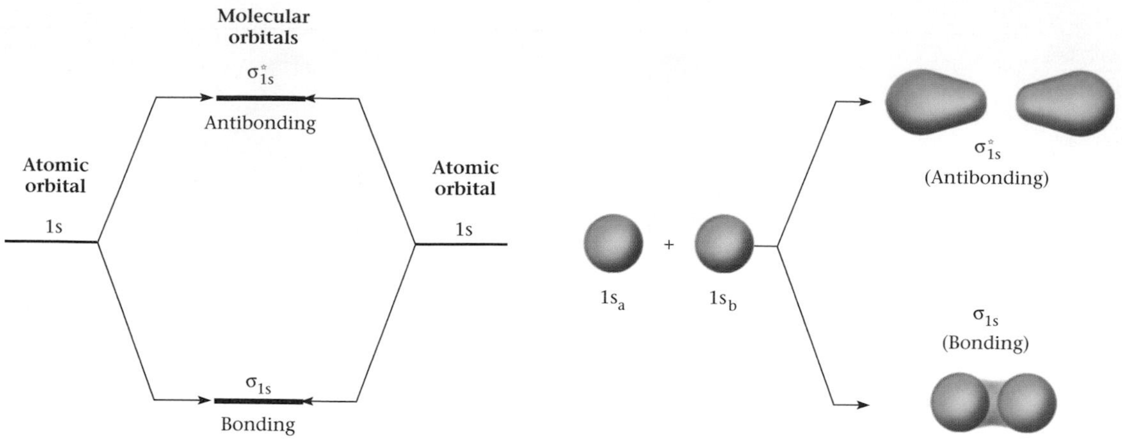

Figure 1
Molecular orbital formation. Two molecular orbitals are formed by combining two 1s atomic orbitals.

Hydrogen and Helium (Combination of 1s Orbitals)

Molecular orbital (MO) theory predicts that two 1s orbitals will combine to give two molecular orbitals. One of these has an energy lower than that of the atomic orbitals from which it is formed (Fig. 1). Placing electrons in this orbital gives a species that is more stable than the isolated atoms. For that reason the lower molecular orbital in Figure 1 is called a **bonding orbital.** The other molecular orbital has a higher energy than the corresponding atomic orbitals. Electrons entering it are in an unstable, higher energy state. It is referred to as an **antibonding orbital.**

The electron density in these molecular orbitals is shown at the right of Figure 1. Notice that the bonding orbital has a higher density between the nuclei. This accounts for its stability. In the antibonding orbital, the chance of finding the electron between the nuclei is very small. The electron density is concentrated at the far ends of the "molecule." This means that the nuclei are less shielded from each other than they are in the isolated atoms.

The electron density in both molecular orbitals is symmetrical about the axis between the two nuclei. This means that both of these are sigma orbitals. In MO notation, the 1s bonding orbital is designated as σ_{1s}. The antibonding orbital is given the symbol σ^*_{1s}. An asterisk designates an antibonding orbital.

In the H_2 molecule, there are two 1s electrons. They fill the σ_{1s} orbital, giving a single bond. In the He_2 molecule, there would be four electrons, two from each atom. These would fill the bonding and antibonding orbitals. As a result, the number of bonds (the *bond order*) in He_2 is zero. The general relation is

$$\text{no. of bonds} = \text{bond order} = \frac{\text{B} - \text{AB}}{2}$$

where B is the number of electrons in bonding orbitals and AB is the number of electrons in antibonding orbitals. In H_2, B = 2 and AB = 0, so we have one bond. In He_2, B = AB = 2, so the number of bonds is zero. The He_2 molecule should not and does not exist.

Second Period Elements (Combination of 2s and 2p Orbitals)

Among the diatomic molecules of the second period elements are three familiar ones, N_2, O_2, and F_2. The molecules Li_2, B_2, and C_2 are less common but have been observed and studied in the gas phase. In contrast, the molecules Be_2 and Ne_2 are either highly unstable or nonexistent. Let us see what molecular orbital theory predicts about the structure and stability of these molecules. We start by considering how the atomic orbitals containing the valence electrons (2s and 2p) are used to form molecular orbitals.

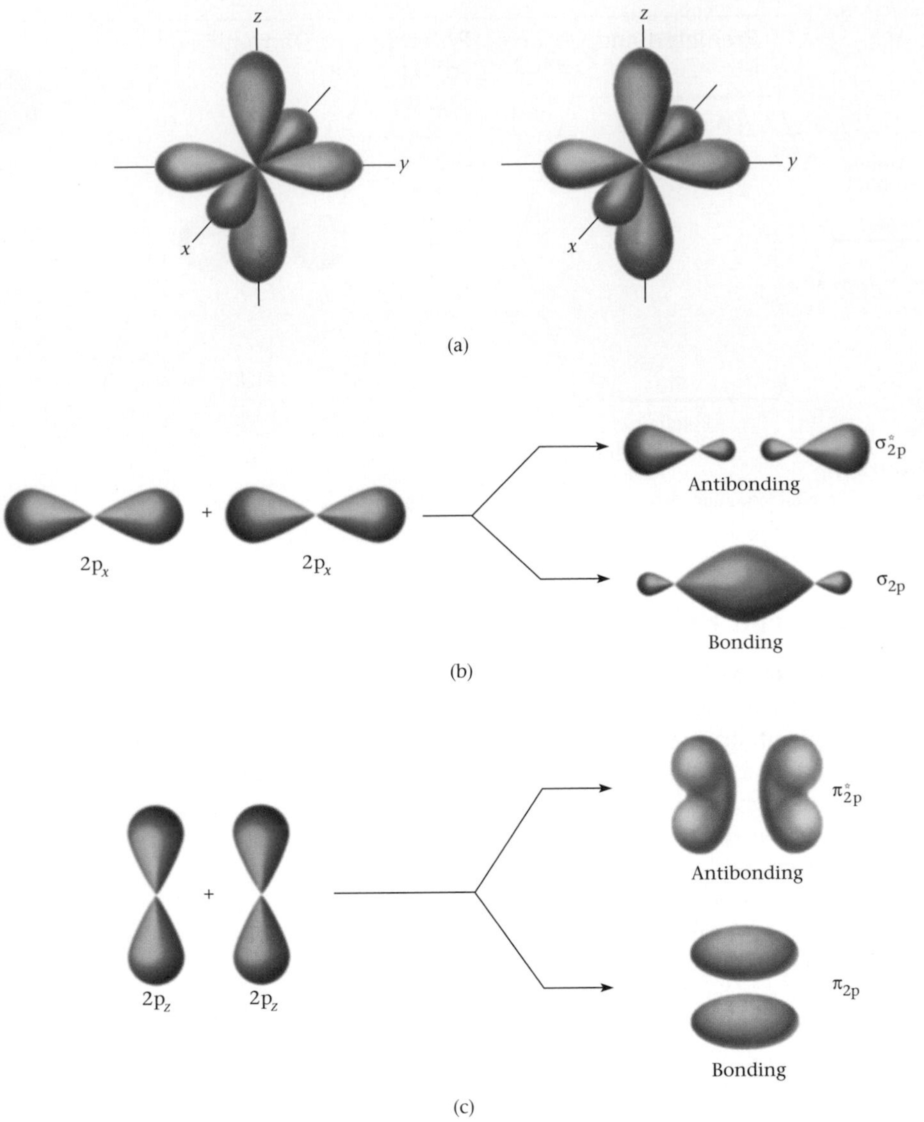

Figure 2
(See text below.) When p orbitals from two different atoms (a) overlap, there are two quite different possibilities. If they overlap head to head (b), two sigma molecular orbitals are produced. If, on the other hand, they overlap side to side (c), two pi molecular orbitals result.

Combining two 2s atomic orbitals, one from each atom, gives two molecular orbitals. These are very similar to the ones shown on page 651. They are designated as σ_{2s} (sigma, bonding, 2s) and σ^*_{2s} (sigma, antibonding, 2s).

Consider now what happens to the 2p orbitals. In an isolated atom, there are three such orbitals, oriented at right angles to each other. We call these atomic orbitals, p_x, p_y, and p_z (top of Figure 2). When two p_x atomic orbitals, one from each atom, overlap head-to-head, they form two sigma orbitals. These are a bonding orbital, σ_{2p}, and an antibonding orbital, σ^*_{2p}. The situation is quite different when the p_z orbitals overlap. Because they are oriented parallel to one another, they overlap side-to-side (Figure 2c). The two molecular orbitals formed in this case are pi orbitals; one is a bonding orbital, π_{2p}, the other a nonbonding orbital, π^*_{2p}. In an entirely similar way, the p_y orbitals of the two atoms interact to form another pair of pi molecular orbitals, π_{2p} and π^*_{2p} (these orbitals are not shown in Figure 2).

The relative energies of the molecular orbitals available for occupancy by the valence electrons of the second period elements are shown in Figure 3. This order applies at least through N_2.*

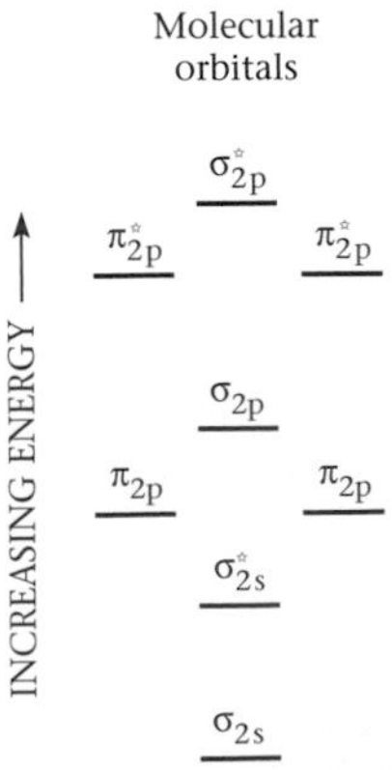

Figure 3
Relative energies, so far as filling order is concerned, for the molecular orbitals formed by combining 2s and 2p atomic orbitals.

To obtain the MO structure of the diatomic molecules of the elements in the second period, we fill the available molecular orbitals in order of increasing energy. The results are

*It appears that beyond N_2 the σ_{2p} orbital lies below the two π_{2p} orbitals. This does not affect the filling order, because in O_2 all of these orbitals are filled.

Table 1 Predicted and Observed Properties of Diatomic Molecules of Second Period Elements

	Occupancy of Orbitals							
	σ_{2s}	σ^*_{2s}	π_{2p}	π_{2p}	σ_{2p}	π^*_{2p}	π^*_{2p}	σ^*_{2p}
Li_2	(↑↓)	( )	( )	( )	( )	( )	( )	( )
Be_2	(↑↓)	(↑↓)	( )	( )	( )	( )	( )	( )
B_2	(↑↓)	(↑↓)	(↑)	(↑)	( )	( )	( )	( )
C_2	(↑↓)	(↑↓)	(↑↓)	(↑↓)	( )	( )	( )	( )
N_2	(↑↓)	(↑↓)	(↑↓)	(↑↓)	(↑↓)	( )	( )	( )
O_2	(↑↓)	(↑↓)	(↑↓)	(↑↓)	(↑↓)	(↑)	(↑)	( )
F_2	(↑↓)	(↑↓)	(↑↓)	(↑↓)	(↑↓)	(↑↓)	(↑↓)	( )
Ne_2	(↑↓)	(↑↓)	(↑↓)	(↑↓)	(↑↓)	(↑↓)	(↑↓)	(↑↓)

	Predicted Properties		Observed Properties	
	Number of Unpaired e^-	Bond Order	Number of Unpaired e^-	Bond Energy (kJ/mol)
Li_2	0	1	0	105
Be_2	0	0	0	Unstable
B_2	2	1	2	289
C_2	0	2	0	628
N_2	0	3	0	941
O_2	2	2	2	494
F_2	0	1	0	153
Ne_2	0	0	0	Nonexistent

shown in Table 1. Note the agreement between MO theory and the properties of these molecules. In particular, the number of unpaired electrons predicted agrees with experiment. There is also a general correlation between the predicted bond order:

$$\text{bond order} = \frac{\text{B} - \text{AB}}{2}$$

and the bond energy. We would expect a double bond (C_2 or O_2) to be stronger than a single bond (Li_2, B_2, and F_2). A triple bond, as in N_2, should be still stronger.

A major triumph of MO theory is its ability to explain the properties of O_2. It explains how the molecule can have a double bond and, at the same time, have two unpaired electrons.

Example Using MO theory, predict the electronic structure, bond order, and number of unpaired electrons in the peroxide ion, O_2^{2-}.

Strategy First, find the number of valence electrons. Then construct an orbital diagram, filling the available molecular orbitals (Figure 3) in order of increasing energy.

SOLUTION Recall that oxygen is in Group **16** of the periodic table.

$$\text{no. valence } e^- = 2(6) + 2 = 14$$

The orbital diagram is

	σ_{2s}	σ^*_{2s}	π_{2p}	π_{2p}	σ_{2p}	π^*_{2p}	π^*_{2p}	σ^*_{2p}
O_2^{2-}	(↑↓)	(↑↓)	(↑↓)	(↑↓)	(↑↓)	(↑↓)	(↑↓)	( )

There are eight electrons in bonding orbitals, six in antibonding orbitals.

$$\text{bond order} = \frac{8 - 6}{2} = 1$$

There are no unpaired electrons. These conclusions are in agreement with the Lewis structure of the peroxide ion: $(:\ddot{\underset{..}{O}}—\ddot{\underset{..}{O}}:)^{2-}$.

POLYATOMIC MOLECULES; DELOCALIZED π ELECTRONS

The bonding in molecules containing more than two atoms can also be described in terms of molecular orbitals. We will not attempt to do this; the energy level structure is considerably more complex than the one we considered. However, one point is worth mentioning. In polyatomic species, *a pi molecular orbital can be spread over the entire molecule* rather than being concentrated between two atoms.

This principle can be applied to species such as the nitrate ion, whose Lewis structure is:

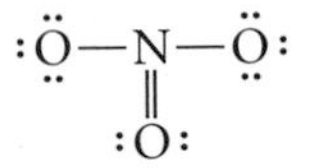

Valence bond theory (Chapter 7) explains the fact that the three N—O bonds are identical by invoking the idea of resonance, with three contributing structures. MO theory, on the other hand, considers that the skeleton of the nitrate ion is established by the three sigma bonds while the electron pair in the pi orbital is *delocalized*, shared by all of the atoms in the molecule. According to MO theory, a similar interpretation applies with all of the "resonance hybrids" described in Chapter 7, including SO_2, SO_3, and CO_3^{2-}.

Another species in which delocalized pi orbitals play an important role is benzene, C_6H_6. There are 30 valence electrons in the molecule, 24 of which are required to form the sigma bond framework:

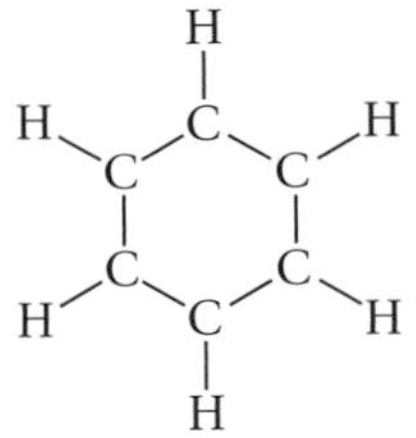

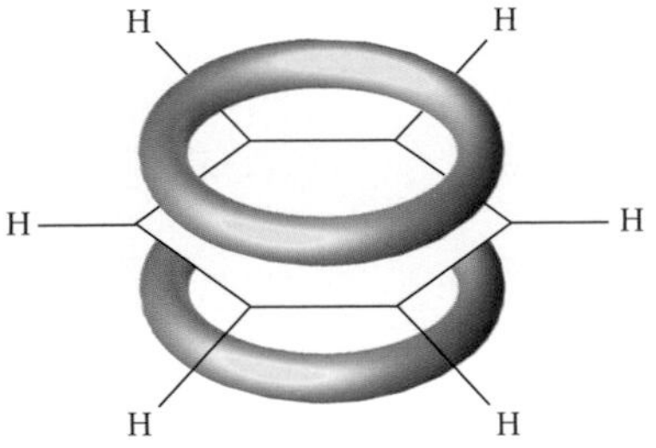

Figure 4

In benzene, three electron pairs are not localized on particular carbon atoms. Instead, they are spread out over two lobes of the shape shown, one above the plane of the benzene ring and the other below it.

The remaining six electrons are located in three π orbitals, which according to MO theory extend over the entire molecule. Figure 4 is one way of representing this structure; more commonly it is shown simply as

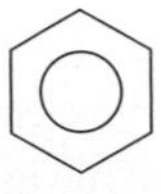

METALS; BAND THEORY

In Chapter 9, we considered a simple picture of metallic bonding, the electron–sea model. The molecular orbital approach leads to a refinement of this model known as *band theory*. Here, a crystal of a metal is considered to be one huge molecule. Valence electrons of the metal are fed into delocalized molecular orbitals, formed in the usual way from atomic orbitals. A huge number of these MOs are grouped into an energy band; the energy separation between adjacent MOs is extremely small.

For purposes of illustration, consider a lithium crystal weighing one gram, which contains roughly 10^{23} atoms. Each Li atom has a half-filled 2s atomic orbital (elect. conf. Li = $1s^22s^1$). When these atomic orbitals combine, they form an equal number, 10^{23}, of molecular orbitals. These orbitals are spread over an energy band covering about 100 kJ/mol. It follows that the spacing between adjacent MOs is of the order of

$$\frac{100\ \text{kJ/mol}}{10^{23}} = 10^{-21}\ \text{kJ/mol}$$

Because each lithium atom has one valence electron and each molecular orbital can hold two electrons, it follows that the lower half of the valence band (shown in color in Figure 5) is filled with electrons. The upper half of the band is empty. Electrons near the top of the filled MOs can readily jump to empty MOs only an infinitesimal distance above them. This is what happens when an electrical field is applied to the crystal; the movement of electrons through delocalized MOs accounts for the electrical conductivity of lithium metal.

The situation in beryllium metal is more complex. We might expect all of the 2s molecular orbitals to be filled because beryllium has the electron configuration $1s^22s^2$. However, in a crystal of beryllium, the 2p MO band overlaps the 2s (Figure 5). This means that, once again, there are vacant MOs that differ only infinitesimally in energy from filled MOs below them. This is indeed the basic requirement for electron conductivity; it is characteristic of all metals, including lithium and beryllium.

Materials in which there is a substantial difference in energy between occupied and vacant MOs are poor electron conductors. Diamond, where the gap between the filled valence band and the empty conduction band is 500 kJ/mol, is an insulator. Silicon and germanium, where the gaps are 100 kJ/mol and 60 kJ/mol respectively, are semiconductors.

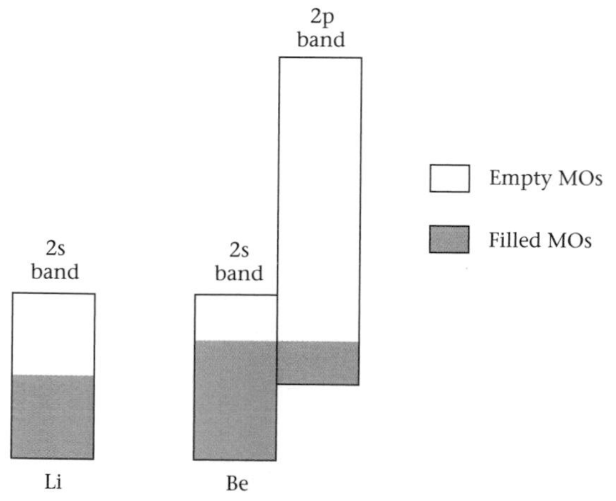

Figure 5
In both lithium and beryllium metal, there are vacant MOs only slightly higher in energy than filled MOs. This is the basic requirement for metallic conductivity.

APPENDIX 6

Answers to Even-Numbered and Challenge Questions & Problems

CHAPTER 1

2. **(a)** element **(b)** mixture **(c)** compound **(d)** mixture
4. **(a)** solution
(b) solution
(c) heterogeneous mixture
6. **(a)** chromatography
(b) distillation or chromatography
8. **(a)** Mn **(b)** Pb **(c)** Au **(d)** Ag
10. **(a)** chromium **(b)** calcium **(c)** iron **(d)** zinc
12. **(a)** meter stick **(b)** pipet or buret **(c)** thermometer
14. 177°C; 4.50×10^2 K
16. Gallium is still a solid
18. **(a)** 3 **(b)** 4 **(c)** 4 **(d)** 1 **(e)** 5
20. **(a)** 132.5 g **(b)** 298.69 cm
(c) 13 lb **(d)** 3.4×10^2 oz
22. **(a)** 4.0206×10^3 mL
(b) 1.006 g
(c) 1.001×10^2°C
24. c
26. 5 is exact; 4000 is ambiguous; 17 has two and 18.5 has three
28. **(a)** 0.5 **(b)** 401.4 **(c)** 0.2684 **(d)** 7.8
30. 23.6 cm^3
32. **(a)** less than **(b)** greater than **(c)** equal
34. **(a)** 6.743×10^4 Å **(b)** 2.655×10^{-4} in
(c) 4.190×10^{-9} mi
36. **(a)** 1.15078 mi **(b)** 1852 m **(c)** 25 mph
38. 1.2 minutes; 1.6 minutes
40. 1.85×10^{-3} g/mL
42. 3.97×10^{14} L
44. 393.8 mg
46. 1.07 g/mL
48. 1.6 g/mL
50. 5.10×10^2 m
52. 2.0×10^5 L
54. supersaturated; 5 g
56. **(a)** 62.3 g NH_4Br **(b)** 44.1 g H_2O **(c)** 2.6 g
58. **(a)** P **(b)** C **(c)** P **(d)** P
60. $\$2.0 \times 10^2$
62. 6.5×10^{-4} in
64. 8.2 g/mL
66. **(a)** Density is mass/unit volume; solubility can be expressed as mass/100 g solvent.
(b) A compound contains 2 or more elements in fixed percentages by mass.
(c) A solution is homogeneous (uniform composition).
68. Sugar increases density by adding mass without an appreciable change in volume.
70. 3
72. **(a)** A **(b)** ≈23° **(c)** no; (see answer to (a))
73. 320°F = 160°C
74. 1.2 km^2
75. 21.9 cm
76. 8.1×10^{-3} g Pb

CHAPTER 2

2. See page 27
4. **(a)** none **(b)** Conservation of mass **(c)** neither
6. Rutherford; see pages 26–27
8. 86 p^+, 134 n
10. **(a)** $^{54}_{26}Fe$; $^{56}_{26}Fe$
(b) They differ in the number of neutrons. Fe-54 has 28, while Fe-56 has 30.
12. **(a)** 34 **(b)** 41 **(c)** 34
14. **(a)** A is arsenic: 33 p^+, 42 n, 33 e^-
(b) L is vanadium: 23 p^+, 28 n, 23 e^-
(c) Z is xenon: 54 p^+, 77 n, 54 e^-
16. **(a)** $^{22}_{11}Na$ **(b)** $^{21}_{10}Ne$ **(c)** $^{23}_{11}Na$; yes
18. **(a)** manganese **(b)** sodium **(c)** arsenic
(d) sulfur **(e)** lead
20. **(a)** transition metal **(b)** main group metal
(c) metalloid **(d)** nonmetal
(e) main group, post-transition metal

22. (a) 5 (b) 3 (c) 2
24. (a) 1 (b) 7 (c) 4
26. (a) CH_3COOH, $C_2H_4O_2$ (b) CH_3Cl
28. (a) 360 p^+, 360 e^- (b) 13 p^+, 14 e^-
(c) 22 p^+, 22 e^- (d) 7 p^+, 10 e^-
30.

Nuclear symbol	Charge	Number of protons	Number of neutrons	Number of electrons
$^{79}_{35}Br$	0	35	44	35
$^{14}_{7}N^{3-}$	−3	7	7	10
$^{75}_{33}As^{5+}$	+5	33	42	28
$^{90}_{40}Zr^{4+}$	+4	40	50	36

32. c
34. (a) H_2O (b) NH_3 (c) N_2H_4 (d) SF_6 (e) PCl_5
36. (a) carbon monoxide (b) silicon carbide
(c) xenon hexafluoride (d) tetraphosphorus decaoxide
(e) acetylene
38. (a) BaI_2, Ba_3N_2 (b) FeO, Fe_2O_3
40. (a) $Co(C_2H_3O_2)_2$ (b) BaO (c) Al_2S_3
(d) $KMnO_4$ (e) $NaHCO_3$
42. (a) scandium(III) chloride (b) strontium hydroxide
(c) potassium permanganate (d) rubidium sulfide
(e) sodium carbonate
44. (a) HCl (*aq*) (b) $NaNO_2$ (c) $Cr_2(SO_3)_3$
(d) $KClO_3$ (e) $Fe(BrO_4)_3$
46. $Na_2Cr_2O_7$, bromine triiodide, $Cu(ClO)_2$, disulfur dichloride, K_3N
48. (a) Sn; tin (b) V; vanadium
(c) Cs; cesium (d) Sb; antimony
50. (a) C_2H_7N (b) $C_2H_5NH_2$
52. (a) usually true (b) always true (c) usually true
54. a
56. only #4.
58.

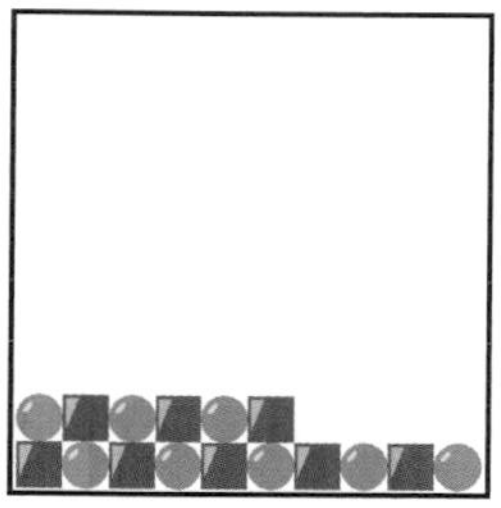

60. $^{126}_{52}Te^{2-}$
62. (a) K, Sr (b) O, F, Ar, S
(c) S, K, Sr (d) S
(e) S, F or S, O, or O, F (f) Sr, S or K, F
(g) Sr, F (h) K, S or K, O
(i) Ar (j) O, F, Ar
63. c
64. (a) Ratio of C in ethane to C in ethylene/g H is 3 : 2.
(b) CH_3, CH_2; C_2H_6, C_2H_4
65. 3.71 g/cm^3; lots of space between atoms
66. 1.4963×10^{-23} g
67. (a) 2.5×10^{24} molecules (b) 2.3×10^{-20}
(c) $\approx 2.8 \times 10^2$ molecules

CHAPTER 3

2. $a < d < b < c$
4. Si-28
6. d
8. 16.00 amu
10. 64.94 amu; $^{65}_{29}Cu$
12. K-39: 91%; K-40: 3%
14. (a) two—HCl-35 and HCl-37 (b) 36 and 38
(c)

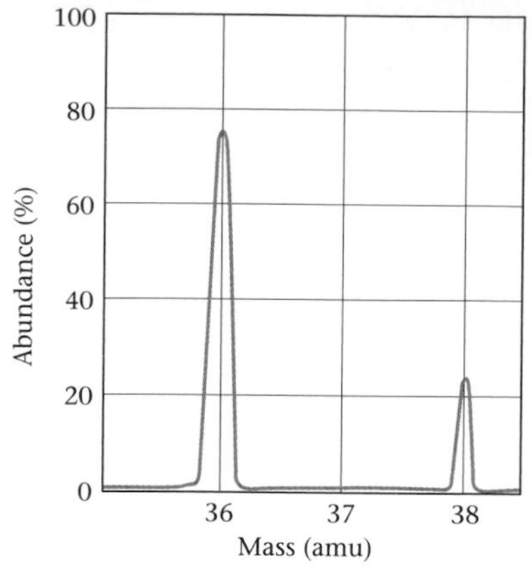

16. (a) 5.93×10^{17} g
(b) 7.65×10^{-22} mol
18. (a) 6×10^{13} atoms (b) 9×10^{-11} mol
20. (a) 78 p^+ (b) 4.697×10^{25} p^+ (c) 2.408×10^{23} p^+
22. (a) 1275 neutrons (b) 7.68×10^{24} (c) 3.4×10^{14}
24. 8.92×10^{23} atoms
26. (a) 69.72 g/mol
(b) 145.16 g/mol
(c) 242.22 g/mol
28. (a) 0.2895 mol
(b) 6.582×10^{-4} mol
(c) 0.00733 mol
30. (a) 844 g (b) 4.12×10^3 g (c) 3.84×10^3 g
32.

	Number of Grams	Number of Moles	Number of Molecules	Number of O Atoms
(a)	0.1364 g	7.100×10^{-4} mol	4.276×10^{20} molec.	2.993×10^{21} atoms
(b)	239.8 g	1.248 mol	7.515×10^{23} molec.	5.261×10^{24} atoms
(c)	13.8 g	7.17×10^{-2} mol	4.32×10^{22} molec.	3.02×10^{23} atoms
(d)	0.00253 g	1.32×10^{-5} mol	7.93×10^{18} molec.	5.55×10^{19} atoms

34. 30.93% Al; 45.86% O; 2.889% H; 20.32% Cl
36. 5.48 g
38. 40.0%
40. 38.40% C; 1.50% H; 52.3% Cl; 7.80% O
42. R is sulfur; MM of RO_2: 64.06 g/mol
44. Ni_2S_3; nickel(III) sulfide
46. (a) $C_7H_5O_3SN$ (b) $C_6H_{10}S_2O$ (c) $Na_2S_2O_3$
48. $C_8H_8O_3$
50. $C_{17}H_{20}N_4O_6$
52. Simplest formula: CH_4N Molecular formula: $C_2H_8N_2$
54. 51.18%; 3.825 g
56. (a) $2H_2S(g) + SO_2(g) \longrightarrow 3S(s) + 2H_2O(g)$
(b) $2CH_4(g) + 2NH_3(g) + 3O_2(g) \longrightarrow 2HCN(g) + 6H_2O(g)$
(c) $Fe_2O_3(s) + 3H_2(g) \longrightarrow 2Fe(l) + 3H_2O(g)$
58. (a) $2Al(s) + 3S(s) \longrightarrow Al_2S_3(s)$
(b) $2Al(s) + 3Br_2(l) \longrightarrow 2AlBr_3(s)$
(c) $2Al(s) + N_2(g) \longrightarrow 2AlN(s)$
(d) $4Al(s) + 3O_2(g) \longrightarrow 2Al_2O_3(s)$
(e) $2Al(s) + 3O_2(g) \longrightarrow Al_2(O_2)_3(s)$
60. (a) $2F_2(g) + H_2O(l) \longrightarrow OF_2(g) + 2HF(g)$
(b) $7O_2(g) + 4NH_3(g) \longrightarrow 4NO_2(g) + 6H_2O(l)$
(c) $Au_2S_3(s) + 3H_2(g) \longrightarrow 2Au(s) + 3H_2S(g)$
(d) $2NaHCO_3(s) \longrightarrow Na_2CO_3(s) + H_2O(l) + CO_2(g)$
(e) $SO_2(g) + 4HF(l) \longrightarrow SF_4(g) + 2H_2O(l)$

62. (a) 0.9742 mol (b) 0.595 mol
(c) 2.980 mol (d) 6.656 mol

64. (a) 882.2 g (b) 16.7 g
(c) 2.368 g (d) 38.60 g

66. (a) $SiO_2(s) + 2C(s) \longrightarrow Si(s) + 2CO(g)$
(b) 0.4528 mol
(c) 89.72 g

68. (a) 98.4 g (b) 76 L

70. 28 g KO_2

72. (a) $3MO_2(s) + 4NH_3(g) \longrightarrow 3M(s) + 6H_2O(l) + 2N_2(g)$
(b) M is lead; MM: 207.2 g/mol

74. (a) $2Al(s) + 3S(s) \longrightarrow Al_2S_3(s)$
(b) Al (c) 0.590 mol (d) 0.48 mol

76. 9.4×10^2 g

78. (a) $3Al(s) + 3NH_4ClO_4(s) \longrightarrow Al_2O_3(s) + AlCl_3(s) + 3NO(g) + 6H_2O(g)$
(b) 2.70 g Al_2O_3 (c) 57.8% (d) 4.86 g

80. 2.76×10^3 g; 526 mL

82. (a)

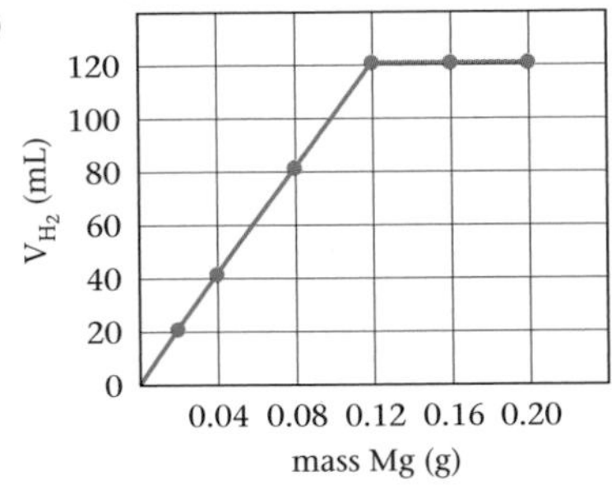

(b) Mg (c) Mg
(d) acid (e) 4
(f) 122 mL; 11 mL

84. 9.64×10^3 cm^3

86. 123 g

88. 6.0220×10^{23}/mol

90. $2AB_3 + 3C \longrightarrow 3CB_2 + 2A$

92.

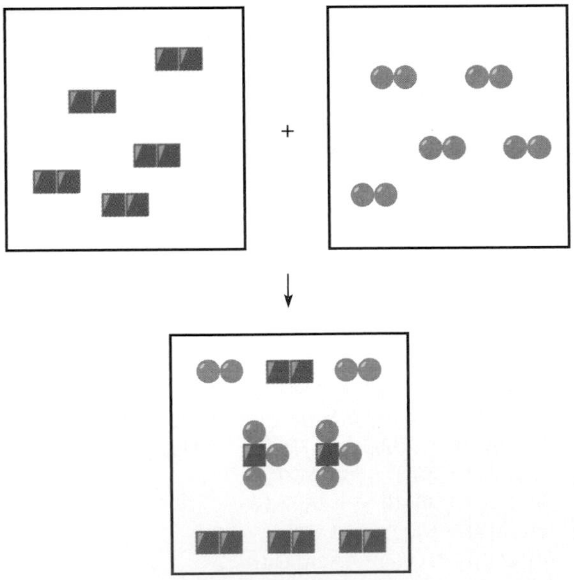

94. (a) false—theoretical yield is 4.0 mol
(b) false—theoretical yield is 2.9×10^2 g
(c) true
(d) false—need only to know the amount of limiting reactant
(e) true
(f) false—total mass of reactants equal to total mass of products
(g) false—2 mol HF consumed/mol CCl_4 used
(h) true

96. 12.5 g

98. (a) False (b) False (c) True (d) False
(e) False (f) False (g) True (h) False

99. 893 g/mol

100. 6.01×10^{23} atoms

101. 3.657 g CaO; 2.972 g Ca_3N_2

102. 46.9 g BaO; 75.6 g SO_2

103. 34.7%

104. (a) V_2O_3; V_2O_5 (b) 2.271 g

105. 28%

CHAPTER 4

2. 0.14 M

4. (a) $[Sc^{3+}] = 0.0538\ M$; $[I^-] = 0.161\ M$
(b) $[Na^+] = 0.432\ M$; $[CO_3^{2-}] = 0.216\ M$
(c) $[Mg^{2+}] = 0.261\ M$; $[PO_4^{3-}] = 0.174\ M$
(d) $[K^+] = 0.486\ M$; $[O^{2-}] = 0.243\ M$

6. (a) Dissolve 2.50×10^2 g of $Ni(NO_3)_2$ in 2.00 L of solution
(b) Dissolve 184 g of $CuCl_2$ in 2.00 L of solution
(c) Dissolve 241 g of $C_6H_8O_6$ in 2.00 L of solution

8. (a) 0.0205 mol (b) 1.78 L
(c) 152 g (d) 0.180 M

10. 0.295 M

12. (a) $BaCl_2$; soluble (b) $Mg(OH)_2(s)$; insoluble
(c) $Cr_2(CO_3)_3$; insoluble (d) K_3PO_4; soluble

14. (a) sodium phosphate (b) sodium carbonate
(c) sodium hydroxide

16. (a) $Ca^{2+}(aq) + CO_3^{2-}(aq) \longrightarrow CaCO_3(s)$
(b) $Ba^{2+}(aq) + SO_4^{2-}(aq) + Fe^{3+}(aq) + 3\,OH^-(aq) \longrightarrow BaSO_4(s) + Fe(OH)_3(s)$

18. (a) no reaction
(b) $Mn^{2+}(aq) + 2OH^-(aq) \longrightarrow Mn(OH)_2(s)$
(c) $Ag^+(aq) + Cl^-(aq) \longrightarrow AgCl(s)$
(d) $Co^{2+}(aq) + 2OH^-(aq) \longrightarrow Co(OH)_2(s)$;
$Ba^{2+}(aq) + SO_4^{2-}(aq) \longrightarrow BaSO_4(s)$
(e) no reaction

20. (a) $3Ba^{2+}(aq) + 2PO_4^{3-}(aq) \longrightarrow Ba_3(PO_4)_2(s)$
(b) $Zn^{2+}(aq) + 2OH^-(aq) \longrightarrow Zn(OH)_2(s)$
(c) no reaction
(d) $Co^{3+}(aq) + PO_4^{3-}(aq) \longrightarrow CoPO_4(s)$

22. (a) 51.80 mL (b) 362.5 mL (c) 108 mL

24. (a) $2Al^{3+}(aq) + 3CO_3^{2-}(aq) \longrightarrow Al_2(CO_3)_3(s)$
(b) 0.108 M (c) 0.379 g

26. (a) $Al^{3+}(aq) + 3OH^-(aq) \longrightarrow Al(OH)_3(s)$
(b) 0.553 g
(c) 0.043 M

28. (a) weak acid (b) weak base
(c) strong base (d) strong acid

30. (a) H_2SO_3 (b) $HClO_2$
(c) H^+ (d) H^+
(e) $HCHO_2$

32. (a) C_8H_6NH (b) OH^-
(c) NH_3 (d) OH^-

34. (a) $HC_2H_3O_2(aq) + OH^-(aq) \longrightarrow H_2O + C_2H_3O_2^-(aq)$
(b) $(C_2H_5)_2NH(aq) + H^+(aq) \longrightarrow (C_2H_5)_2NH_2^+(aq)$
(c) $HCN(aq) + OH^-(aq) \longrightarrow H_2O + CN^-(aq)$

36. **(a)** $H^+(aq) + C_5H_5N(aq) \longrightarrow C_5H_5NH^+(aq)$
(b) $H^+(aq) + OH^-(aq) \longrightarrow H_2O$
(c) correct
(d) $NH_3(aq) + H^+(aq) \longrightarrow NH_4^+(aq)$
(e) correct

38. 0.0121 L

40. **(a)** 8.14 mL
(b) 282 mL
(c) 84.4 mL

42. 1.80×10^2 g/mol

44. 5.630%; Yes

46. 73.9%

48. one

50. **(a)** CH_4: C = −4; H = +1
(b) H_2SO_3: O = −2; H = +1; S = +4
(c) Na_2O: O = −2; Na = +1
(d) $H_2PO_4^-$: O = −2; H = +1; P = +5

52. **(a)** H = +1, I = +5, O = −2
(b) Na = +1, Mn = +7, O = −2
(c) Sn = + 4, O = −2
(d) N = +3, O = −2, F = −1
(e) Na = +1, O = $-\frac{1}{2}$

54. **(a)** reduction **(b)** reduction
(c) oxidation **(d)** oxidation

56. **(a)** $ClO^-(aq) + 2e^- + H_2O \longrightarrow Cl^-(aq) + 2OH^-(aq)$; reduction
(b) $NO_3^-(aq) + 3e^- + 4H^+(aq) \longrightarrow NO(g) + 2H_2O$; reduction
(c) $2Ni^{2+}(aq) + 6OH^-(aq) \longrightarrow Ni_2O_3(s) + 2e^- + 3H_2O$; oxidation
(d) $Mn^{2+}(aq) + 2H_2O \longrightarrow MnO_2(s) + 2e^- + 4H^+(aq)$; oxidation

58. **(a)** $TiO_2(s) + 4H^+(aq) + e^- \longrightarrow Ti^{3+}(aq) + 2H_2O$
(b) $Zn^{2+}(aq) + 2e^- \longrightarrow Zn(s)$
(c) $2NH_4^+(aq) + 8OH^-(aq) \longrightarrow N_2(g) + 8H_2O + 6e^-$
(d) $CH_3OH(aq) + 2OH^-(aq) \longrightarrow CH_2O(aq) + 2e^- + 2H_2O$

60. **(a)** reduction: $H_2O_2(aq) + e^- \longrightarrow H_2O$; H_2O_2—reduced, oxidizing agent
oxidation: $Ni^{2+}(aq) \longrightarrow Ni^{3+}(aq) + e^-$; Ni^{2+}—oxidized, reducing agent
(b) reduction: $Cr_2O_7^{2-}(aq) + 3e^- \longrightarrow Cr^{3+}(aq)$; $Cr_2O_7^{2-}$—reduced, oxidizing agent
oxidation: $Sn^{2+}(aq) \longrightarrow Sn^{4+}(aq) + 2e^-$; Sn^{2+}—oxidized, reducing agent

62. **(a)** $2Ni^{2+}(aq) + H_2O_2(aq) \longrightarrow 2Ni^{3+}(aq) + 2OH^-(aq)$
(b) $Cr_2O_7^{2-}(aq) + 3Sn^{2+}(aq) + 7H_2O \longrightarrow$
$2Cr^{3+}(aq) + 14OH^-(aq) + 3Sn^{4+}(aq)$

64. **(a)** $P_4(s) + 12Cl^-(aq) + 12H^+(aq) \longrightarrow 4PH_3(g) + 6Cl_2(g)$
(b) $2MnO_4^-(aq) + 6H^+(aq) + 5NO_2^-(aq) \longrightarrow$
$2Mn^{2+}(aq) + 3H_2O + 5NO_3^-(aq)$
(c) $3HBrO_3(aq) + 2Bi(s) \longrightarrow 3HBrO_2(aq) + Bi_2O_3(s)$
(d) $2CrO_4^{2-}(aq) + 3SO_3^{2-}(aq) + 10H^+(aq) \longrightarrow$
$2Cr^{3+}(aq) + 3SO_4^{2-}(aq) + 5H_2O$

66. **(a)** $2Ni(OH)_2(s) + N_2H_4(aq) \longrightarrow 2Ni(s) + N_2(g) + 4H_2O$
(b) $3Fe(OH)_3(s) + Cr^{3+}(aq) + 5OH^-(aq) \longrightarrow$
$3Fe(OH)_2(s) + CrO_4^{2-}(aq) + 4H_2O$
(c) $2MnO_4^-(aq) + 3BrO_3^-(aq) + H_2O \longrightarrow$
$2MnO_2(s) + 3BrO_4^-(aq) + 2OH^-(aq)$
(d) $2H_2O_2(aq) + IO_4^-(aq) \longrightarrow 2O_2(g) + IO_2^-(aq) + 2H_2O$

68. **(a)** $2NO(g) + 5H_2(g) \longrightarrow 2NH_3(g) + 2H_2O(g)$
(b) $H_2O_2(aq) + 2ClO^-(aq) + 2H^+(aq) \longrightarrow O_2(g) + Cl_2(g) + 2H_2O$
(c) $Zn(s) + 2VO^{2+}(aq) + 4H^+(aq) \longrightarrow$
$Zn^{2+}(aq) + 2V^{3+}(aq) + 2H_2O$

70. **(a)** $I_2(aq) + 2S_2O_3^{2-}(aq) \longrightarrow 2I^-(aq) + S_4O_6^{2-}(aq)$
(b) 0.807 L

72. **(a)** $2H^+(aq) + NO_3^-(aq) + Ag(s) \longrightarrow Ag^+(aq) + NO_2(g) + H_2O$
(b) 27.5 g

74. 0.0834 *M*; 2.65 g

76. yes

78. 0.379%

80. **(a)** $Au(s) + 4Cl^-(aq) + NO_3^-(aq) + 4H^+(aq) \longrightarrow$
$AuCl_4^-(aq) + NO(g) + 2H_2O$
(b) 4HCl : $1HNO_3$
(c) 7.9 mL HNO_3; 42 mL HCl

82. **(a)** SA/WB
(b) WA/SB
(c) PPT
(d) PPT
(e) NR

84. **(a)** (1) **(b)** (3) **(c)** (2)

86. **(a)** weak **(b)** non
(c) strong **(d)** weak

88. $X^+ < W^+ < Z^+ < Y^+$

90. **(a)** F **(b)** T **(c)** F **(d)** F **(e)** T

91. 0.794 g CaC_2O_4; yes

92. 0.29 L

93. 1.09 g Cu; 3.09 g Ag

94. 0.0980 *M* Fe^{2+}; 0.0364 *M* Fe^{3+}

95. oxalic acid

96. 5.27 g

CHAPTER 5

2. $V = 2.5 \times 10^3$L; $n_{He} = 2.14 \times 10^4$ mol; $T = 298$ K

4.

1215 mm Hg	1.600 atm	161.9 kPa	1.619 bar
543 mm Hg	0.714 atm	72.3 kPa	0.723 bar
1.07×10^3 mm Hg	1.41 atm	143 kPa	1.43 bar
678 mm Hg	0.892 atm	90.4 kPa	0.904 bar

6. 75°C

8. **(a)** −44°C
(b) −197°C

10. 31.5 psi (gauge pressure); 46.2 psi (actual pressure)

12. 827 mm Hg; yes

14. 0.76 mol

16. 0.20 atm

18. 734.1 g

20.

Pressure	Volume	Temperature	Moles	Grams
22.7 atm	1.75 L	19°C	1.66 mol	96.5 g
0.895 atm	6.16 L	6°C	0.241 mol	14.0 g
433 mm Hg	92.4 mL	1.62 K	0.395 mol	23.0 g
1.74 bar	8.66 L	98°F	0.584 mol	33.9 g

22. **(a)** 1.19 g/L
(b) 2.10 g/L
(c) 1.90 g/L

24. 1.29 g/L at sea level; 0.358 g/L on Mt. Everest

26. **(a)** 98.8 g/mol
(b) $COCl_2$

28. **(a)** 28.6 g/mol
(b) density exhaled air = 1.12 g/L; density ordinary air = 1.13 g/L

30. sulfur hexafluoride

32. 248 L

34. **(a)** $2H_2S(g) + O_2(g) \longrightarrow 2H_2O(g) + 2SO_2(g)$
(b) 13.6 L

36. **(a)** $NH_4NO_3(s) \longrightarrow N_2O(g) + 2H_2O(g)$
(b) 2.7 L

38. 2.83 L

40. **(a)** $2NH_4NO_3(s) \longrightarrow 2N_2(g) + O_2(g) + 4H_2O(g)$
(b) 76.1 atm
42. 3.04 atm; HCl
44. CH_4: 1.06 atm
C_2H_6: 0.11 atm
C_3H_8: 0.030 atm
46. 8.49 L
48. 2.20 atm
50. **(a)** $5N_2(g) + 6H_2O(g) \longrightarrow 4NH_3(g) + 6NO(g)$
(b) 1.81 atm
(c) $P_{NH_3} = 0.724$ atm; $P_{NO} = 1.09$ atm
52. **(a)** 724 mm Hg **(b)** 3.20×10^{-4}
(c) 9.73×10^{-3} **(d)** 346 mm Hg
(e) 1094 mm Hg
54. **(a)** $Xe < CH_2F_2 < F_2 < CH_4$ **(b)** $CH_4 < F_2 < CH_2F_2 < Xe$
56. 3.74 times faster
58. **(a)** yes **(b)** 100.1 g/mol
60. 15.8 s
62. **(a)** 217 m/s
(b) 2.70×10^2 m/s
64. **(a)** more
(b) less
66. **(a)** 84 g/L
(b) 65.5 g/L
(c) ≈ 340 atm
68. 4 m
70. **(a)** 1.000
(b) 0.5535
(c) 1.000
(d) 1.000
72. **(a)** 0.00454
(b) 0.038 g
74. C = 32.0%; H = 6.72%; N = 18.7%; O = 42.6%; $C_2H_5NO_2$
76. **(a)** T **(b)** F **(c)** F **(d)** T **(e)** T
78. **(a)** The two sketches look identical.
(b) The pressure reads lower at the lower temperature.
80. **(a)** $P_B = P_A$ **(b)** $P_B = \frac{1}{2} P_A$
82. **(a)** A **(b)** B **(c)** B
84. **(a)** bulb C **(b)** 1.00 atm **(c)** 4.50 atm
(d) 3.50 atm; 4.50 atm; same total pressure

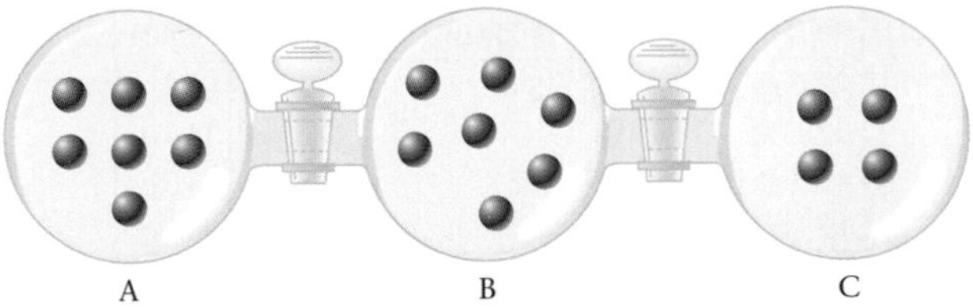

(e) 3.00 atm; 4.50 atm; same total pressure

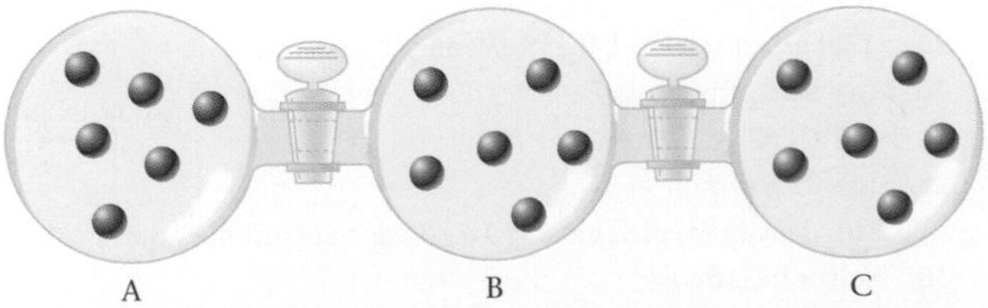

86. Ideal gas pressures: at 40°C = 25.0 mm Hg; at 70°C = 27.3 mm Hg; at 100°C = 29.7 mm Hg
Vapor pressures: at 40°C = 55.3 mm Hg; at 70°C = 233.7 mm Hg; at 100°C = 760 mm Hg
Vapor pressure implies the presence of some liquid together with the vapor. As *T* increases, more liquid becomes gas, increasing *n* and thus *P*.
87. 5.74 g/mol; at $T = 15$°C, He and H_2 are in outer space. Ar is present in Earth's atmosphere.
88. 3.0 ft from NH_3 end
89. 0.0456 L-atm/mol-°R
90. 78.7%
91. 6.62 m
92. 0.897 atm
93. $\frac{V_A}{V} = \frac{n_A}{n}$; but $\frac{n_A}{n} \neq \frac{\text{mass}_A}{\text{mass}_{TOT}}$

CHAPTER 6

2. **(a)** 0.750 m
(b) 2.65×10^{-25} J
(c) 1.60×10^{-4} kJ/mol
4. **(a)** infrared **(b)** $2.001 \times 10^{14}\ s^{-1}$ **(c)** 1.326×10^{-19} J
6. **(a)** 127 nm **(b)** ultraviolet
8. 3.8×10^{22} photons
10. **(a)** 102.5 nm **(b)** ultraviolet **(c)** yes
12.

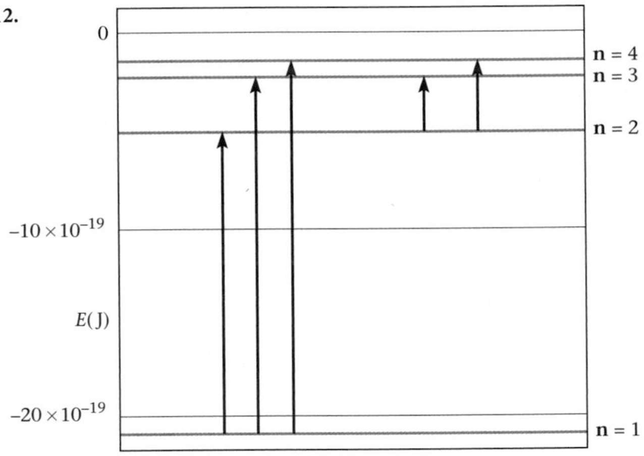

14. **(a)** 4.050×10^3 nm **(b)** infrared
16. 1.875×10^3 nm
18. **(a)** −1, 0, 1 **(b)** −3, −2, −1, 0, 1, 2, 3
(c) $\ell = 0$; $\mathbf{m}_\ell = 0$ $\ell = 1$; $\mathbf{m}_\ell = -1, 0, 1$ $\ell = 2$; $\mathbf{m}_\ell = -2, -1, 0, 1, 2$
20. **(a)** 3s **(b)** 4d **(c)** 4f **(d)** 2s
22. **(a)** p **(b)** s **(c)** d
24. **(a)** 9 **(b)** 3 **(c)** 7 **(d)** 5
26. **(a)** 2 **(b)** 2 **(c)** 10
28. **(b)** No 1p sublevel **(d)** $\mathbf{m}_\ell$ cannot exceed 1
(e) $\mathbf{m}_\ell = 0$
30. **(a)** $1s^2\ 2s^2\ 2p^1$
(b) $1s^2\ 2s^2\ 2p^6\ 3s^2\ 3p^6\ 4s^2\ 3d^{10}\ 4p^6\ 5s^2\ 4d^{10}\ 5p^6\ 6s^2$
(c) $1s^2\ 2s^2$
(d) $1s^2\ 2s^2\ 2p^6\ 3s^2\ 3p^6\ 4s^2\ 3d^{10}\ 4p^6\ 5s^2\ 4d^{10}\ 5p^6\ 6s^2\ 4f^{14}\ 5d^{10}\ 6p^3$
(e) $1s^2\ 2s^2\ 2p^6\ 3s^2\ 3p^6\ 4s^2\ 3d^{10}\ 4p^5$
32. **(a)** $[_{54}Xe]\ 6s^2\ 4f^{14}\ 5d^6$ **(b)** $[_{10}Ne]\ 3s^2$
(c) $[_{18}Ar]\ 4s^2\ 3d^{10}\ 4p^2$ **(d)** $[_{18}Ar]\ 4s^2\ 3d^3$
(e) $[_{54}Xe]\ 6s^2\ 4f^{14}\ 5d^{10}\ 6p^5$
34. **(a)** Yb **(b)** Sn **(c)** Zr **(d)** I
36. **(a)** 6/12 **(b)** 12/25 **(c)** 18/42
38. **(a)** excited **(b)** ground **(c)** excited
(d) impossible **(e)** impossible

40.

	1s	2s	2p	3s	3p	4s	3d
(a)	(↑↓)	(↑↓)	(↑↓)(↑↓)(↑↓)	(↑)			
(b)	(↑↓)	(↑↓)	(↑↓)(↑)(↑)				
(c)	(↑↓)	(↑↓)	(↑↓)(↑↓)(↑↓)	(↑↓)	(↑↓)(↑↓)(↑↓)	(↑↓)	(↑↓)(↑↓)(↑)(↑)(↑)
(d)	(↑↓)	(↑↓)	(↑↓)(↑↓)(↑↓)	(↑↓)	(↑↓)(↑↓)(↑)		

42. **(a)** Mg **(b)** P **(c)** O

44. **(a)** Sn, Sb, Te **(b)** K, Rb, Cs, Fr **(c)** Ge, As, Sb, Te **(d)** none

46. **(a)** 0 **(b)** 5 **(c)** 0

48. **(a)** Ca **(b)** K, Ga **(c)** none **(d)** none

50. **(a)** S: $1s^2\,2s^2\,2p^6\,3s^2\,3p^4$ S^{2-}: $1s^2\,2s^2\,2p^6\,3s^2\,3p^6$
(b) Al: $1s^2\,2s^2\,2p^6\,3s^2\,3p^1$ Al^{3+}: $1s^2\,2s^2\,2p^6$
(c) V: $1s^2\,2s^2\,2p^6\,3s^2\,3p^6\,4s^2\,3d^3$ V^{4+}: $1s^2\,2s^2\,2p^6\,3s^2\,3p^6\,3d^1$
(d) Cu^+: $1s^2\,2s^2\,2p^6\,3s^2\,3p^6\,3d^{10}$ Cu^{2+}: $1s^2\,2s^2\,2p^6\,3s^2\,3p^6\,3d^9$

52. **(a)** 0 **(b)** 0 **(c)** 0 **(d)** 0

54. **(a)** S < Si < Na
(b) Na < Si < S
(c) S > Si > Na

56. **(a)** K **(b)** Cl **(c)** Cl

58. **(a)** N **(b)** Ba^{2+} **(c)** Se **(d)** Co^{3+}

60. **(a)** Kr < K < Rb < Cs **(b)** Ar < Si < Al < Cs

62. **(a)** green
(b) 247 kJ/mol at 485 nm; 234 kJ/mol at 512 nm
(c) $1s^2\,2s^2\,2p^6\,3s^2\,3p^5$:

1s	2s	2p	3s	3p
(↑↓)	(↑↓)	(↑↓)(↑↓)(↑↓)	(↑↓)	(↑↓)(↑↓)(↑)

64. **(a)** Cl—chlorine
(b) theoretically: Pb—lead; actually: Sn—tin
(c) Mn—manganese **(d)** Li—lithium
(e) Kr—krypton

66. **(a)** (2) and (4) **(b)** (1) and (3) **(c)** (1)
(d) (2) **(e)** (1)

68. **(a)** Li: $[_2He]\,2s^1$ **(b)** Ra: $[_{86}Rn]\,7s^2$
(c) Sc: $[_{18}Ar]\,4s^2\,3d^1$ **(d)** Sb: $[_{36}Kr]\,5s^2\,4d^{10}\,5p^3$
(e) Ca: $[_{18}Ar]\,4s^2$

70. **(a)** See pages 138–139
(b) See page 134, Figure 6.1
(c) See page 143, Figure 6.7

72. **(a)** [illegible] **(b)** false; inversely proportional to n^2
(c) false; as soon as 4p is full

74. **(a)** True
(b) True
(c) False; absorbed

76. +2954 kJ

77. $\Delta E = 2.180 \times 10^{-18}\left(\frac{1}{4} - \frac{1}{n^2}\right)$

$$\lambda = \frac{hc}{\Delta E} = \frac{(6.626 \times 10^{-34})(2.998 \times 10^{8}) \times 10^{9}}{2.180 \times 10^{-18}\left(\frac{1}{4} - \frac{1}{n^2}\right)}$$

$$= \frac{91.12}{\left(\frac{1}{4} - \frac{1}{n^2}\right)} = \frac{364.5\,n^2}{n^2 - 4}$$

78. $1s^4\,1p^4$

79. **(a)** s sublevel: $m_\ell = 0 = 3\,e^-$; p sublevel: $m_\ell = -1, 0, 1 = 9\,e^-$; d sublevel: $m_\ell = -2, -1, 0, 1, 2 = 15\,e^-$
(b) $n = 3$, $\ell = 0, 1, 2$; total electrons = 27
(c) $1s^3\,2s^3\,2p^2$ $1s^3\,2s^3\,2p^9\,3s^2$

80. **(a)** 3.42×10^{-19} J
(b) 581 nm

CHAPTER 7

2. **(a)** 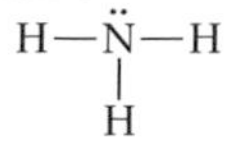 **(b)** :F—Kr—F:
(c) $(:N{\equiv}O:)^+$ **(d)** $(:O—Br—O:)^-$

4. **(a)** 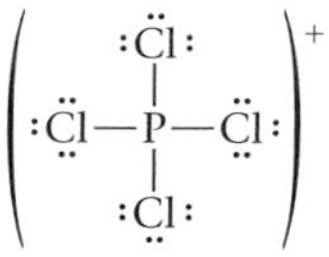 **(b)** $(:F—Br—F:)^+$
(c) $(:I—I—I:)^-$ **(d)** 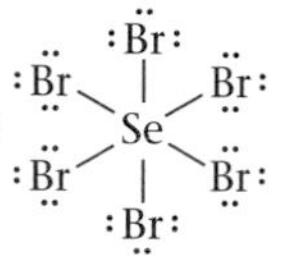

6. **(a)** $(:C{\equiv}C:)^{2-}$ **(b)** :F—N=O:
(c) 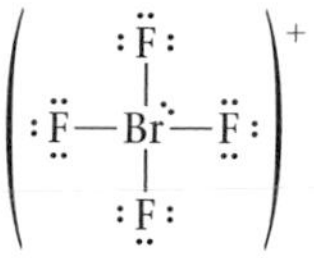 **(d)** 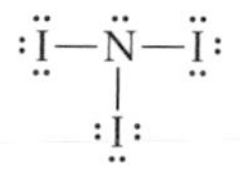

8. $(H—C{\equiv}O:)^+$

10. **(a)** 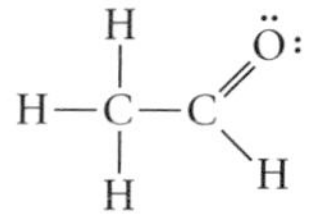 **(b)** 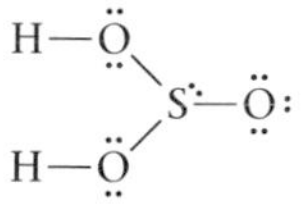
(c) 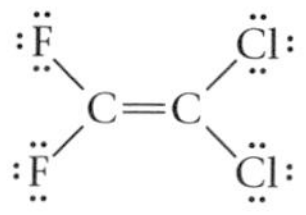

12. 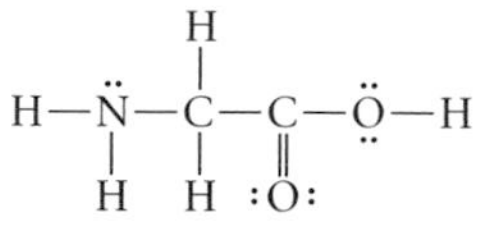

14. 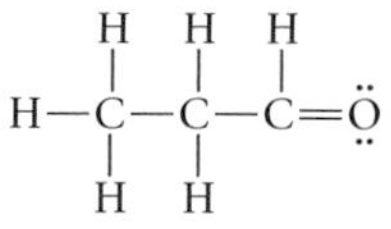 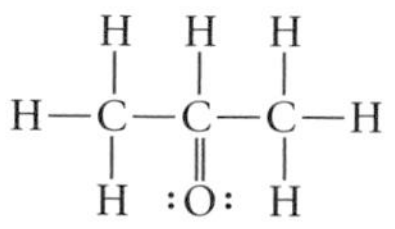

16. **(a)** HCl **(b)** Cl_2 **(c)** CO **(d)** CCl_4

18. **(a)** 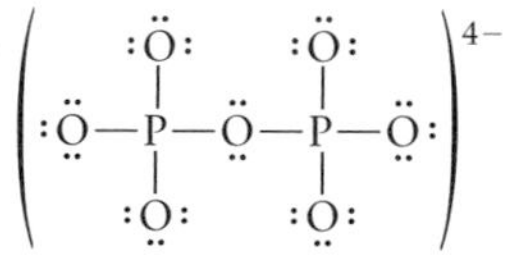 **(b)** H—O—Br:
(c) 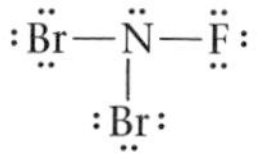 **(d)** 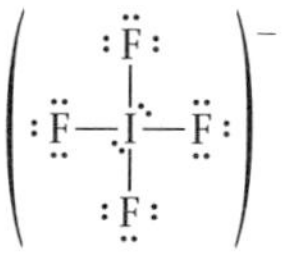

20. **(a)** H—Be—H **(b)** $(:\dot{C}{=}O:)^-$
(c) $(:O—S—O:)^-$ **(d)** 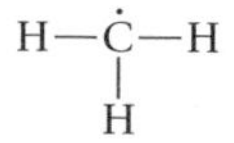

22. (a) 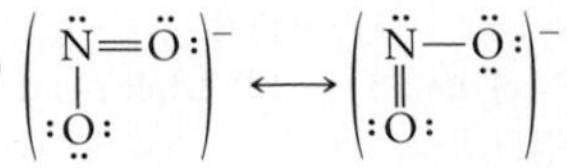

(b) :N≡N—Ö: ⟷ :N̈—N≡O: ⟷ :N=N=Ö:

(c) 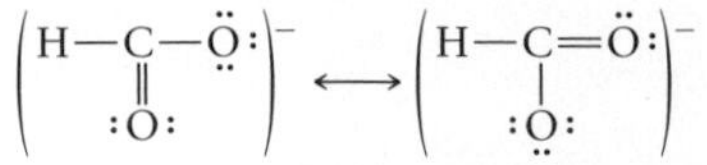

24. (a) 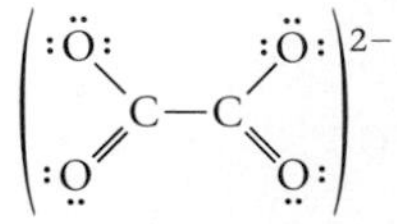

(b) 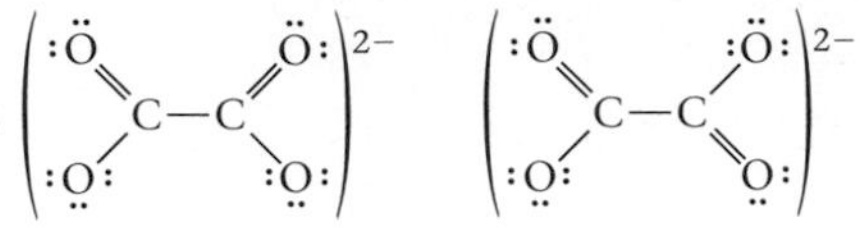 and

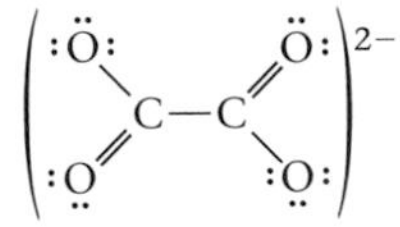

(c) No. Different skeleton.

26.

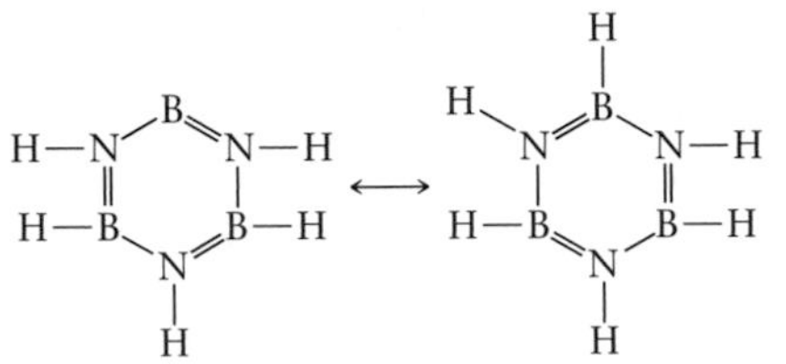

28. (a) −1 (b) 0 (c) 0
30. Structure I
32. (a) bent (b) linear
(c) see-saw (d) trigonal bipyramid
34. (a) linear (b) bent
(c) tetrahedron (d) bent
36. (a) linear (b) octahedron
(c) trigonal pyramid (d) bent
38. (a) 180° (b) 120°
(c) 120° around N, 109.5° around O at left
(d) 109.5° around C at left, 120° around other C
40. (a)

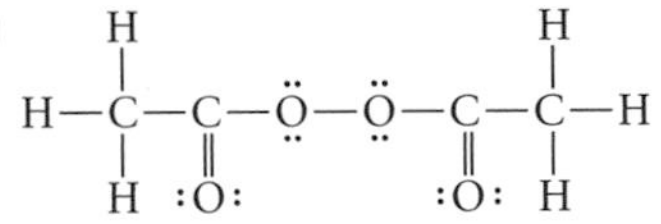

(b) around CH_3-109.5°, around C—O-120°; around O—O-109.5°
42. 1 = 120°; 2 = 109°; 3 = 120°
44. a and c
46. a, b, d
48. First structure is polar; dipoles do not cancel.
50. (a) sp^2 (b) sp
(c) sp^3d (d) sp^3d
52. (a) sp (b) sp^2
(c) sp^3 (d) sp^2
54. (a) sp^3d (b) sp^3d^2
(c) sp^3 (d) sp^3
56. (a) 6 e^- pairs; sp^3d^2 (b) 6 e^- pairs; sp^3d^2
(c) 5 e^- pairs; sp^3d
58. All B atoms and N atoms are sp^2.
60. (a) sp^3 (b) sp^2 (c) sp (d) sp^2
62. (a) sp^3 (b) sp^3 (c) sp^3
64. 12 σ, 3 π
66. (a) 4 σ (b) 3 σ, 1 π (c) 2 σ, 2 π (d) 4 σ, 1 π
68.

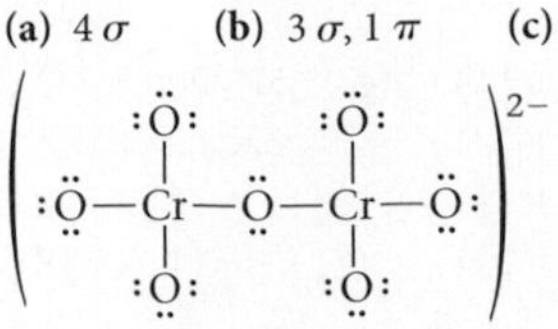

70.

AX_2E_2	2	2	bent	sp^3	polar
AX_3	3	0	trigonal planar	sp^2	nonpolar
AX_4E_2	4	2	square planar	sp^3d^2	nonpolar
AX_5	5	0	trigonal bipyramid	sp^3d	nonpolar

72. (a) C (b) N
74. PH_3 and H_2S—unshared pairs on central atom
76. $SnCl_2$ and SO_2; unshared pairs occupy more space
78. $x = 3$; T-shaped; polar; sp^3d; 90°, 180°; 3 σ bonds
79. 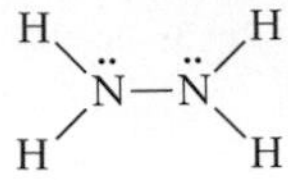 bent; 109.5°; polar
80. 6; octahedron; sp^3d^2
81. (a) 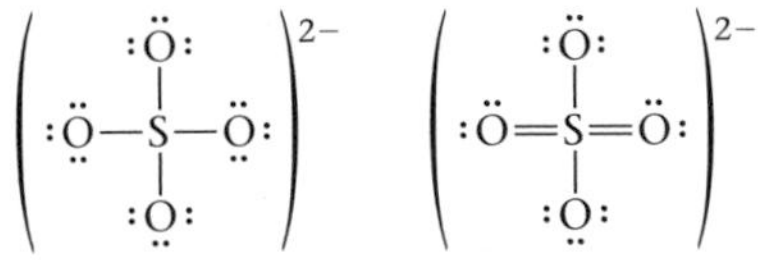

(b) tetrahedral for both (c) sp^3; sp^3
(d) 1st structure: O = −1; S = 2
2nd structure: S = 0; O = −1; O = −1, O = 0

82. (a) 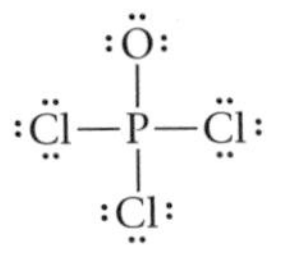 Formal charges: P = +1; Cl = 0; O = −1

(b) 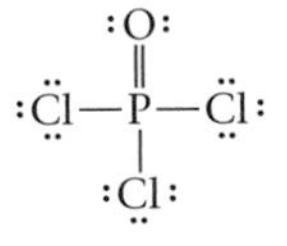 Formal charges: P = 0; Cl = 0; O = 0

CHAPTER 8

2. 2.06°C
4. 0.385 J/g-°C
6. 7.28 J
8. (a) no (b) −27.6 kJ
(c) 3.6°C (d) $t_i = 86.0°F$ $t_f = 38.5°F$
10. 1.3×10^2 mL
12. 27.3°C
14. (a) 168 kJ (b) −168 kJ (c) -3.49×10^3 kJ
16. 1.12×10^4 J/°C
18. 22.1°C
20. 8.1×10^2 mg
22. (a) $CaO(s) + 3C(s) \longrightarrow CO(g) + CaC_2(s)$ $\Delta H = 464.8$ kJ
(b) endothermic
(c)

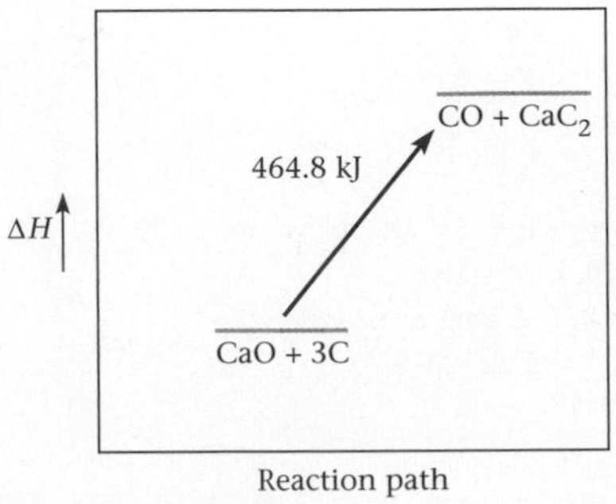

(d) 7.25 kJ (e) 1.550 g

24. (a) 466.8 kJ (b) 233.2 kJ

26. (a) $2C_3H_5(NO_3)_3(l) \longrightarrow 3N_2(g) + 6CO_2(g) + 5H_2O(g) + \frac{1}{2}O_2(g)$; $\Delta H = -2.84 \times 10^3$ kJ
(b) −911 kJ

28. 0.0367 g

30. freezing 100.0 g benzene

32. −48.9 kJ

34. (a) $SiO_2(s) + 2Mg(s) + 2Cl_2(g) + 2C(s) \longrightarrow Si(s) + 2MgCl_2(s) + 2CO(g)$
(b) −592.7 kJ (c) yes

36. +11.3 kJ

38. (a) $2C(s) + H_2(g) \longrightarrow C_2H_2(g)$ $\Delta H° = 226.7$ kJ
(b) $\frac{1}{2}N_2(g) + O_2(g) \longrightarrow NO_2(g)$ $\Delta H° = 33.2$ kJ
(c) $Pb(s) + Br_2(l) \longrightarrow PbBr_2(s)$ $\Delta H° = -278.7$ kJ
(d) $P(s) + \frac{5}{2}Cl_2(g) \longrightarrow PCl_5(s)$ $\Delta H° = -374.9$ kJ

40. (a) −157.3 kJ (b) −26.85 kJ

42. 9.38 kJ evolved

44. (a) −153.9 kJ (b) −1036.0 kJ (c) −714.8 kJ

46. (a) −125.7 kJ (b) 163.9 kJ

48. (a) $CaCO_3(s) + 2NH_3(g) \longrightarrow CaCN_2(s) + 3H_2O(l)$ $\Delta H° = 90.1$ kJ
(b) −351.6 kJ/mol

50. (a) $4C_3H_5(NO_3)_3(l) \longrightarrow 12CO_2(g) + 10H_2O(l) + 6N_2(g) + O_2(g)$ $\Delta H° = -2.29 \times 10^4$ kJ
(b) 3.830×10^3 kJ/mol

52. −3.36 kJ

54. 1.20×10^2 L · atm

56. (a) −18 J (b) +64 J

58. 596 J; work done by the surroundings

60. (a) 40.7 kJ (b) 3.1 kJ (c) −37.6 kJ

62. (a) −1299.5 kJ (b) −1295.7 kJ

64. 1.00 BTU/lb-°F

66. 29 minutes

68. -8.451×10^4 kJ

70. $\Delta E = -885$ kJ; $\Delta H = -890$ kJ

72. 0.793

74. 83.9°C

76. (a) $Hg(s) \longrightarrow Hg(l)$ $\Delta H° = 2.33$ kJ
(b) $Br_2(l) \longrightarrow Br_2(g)$ $\Delta H° = 29.6$ kJ
(c) $C_6H_6(l) \longrightarrow C_6H_6(g)$ $\Delta H° = -9.84$ kJ
(d) $Hg(g) \longrightarrow Hg(l)$ $\Delta H° = -59.4$ kJ
(e) $C_{10}H_8(s) \longrightarrow C_{10}H_8(g)$ $\Delta H° = 62.6$ kJ

78. Piston goes down.

80. $c_A > c_B$

82. (a) True (b) False (c) False (d) False

84. 2.1×10^{28} photons

85. (a) 1.69×10^5 J (b) 505 g

86. 22%

87. (a) −851.5 kJ (b) 6.6×10^3°C (c) yes

88. 76.0%

89. 7.5 g

CHAPTER 9

2. (a) 50°C: 297 mm Hg; 60°C: 307 mm Hg
(b) 297 mm Hg > 269 mm Hg 307 mm Hg < 389 mm Hg
(c) 269 mm Hg at 50°C 307 mm Hg at 60°C

4. (a) 6.26 mg (b) 0.15 mm Hg (c) 0.466 mm Hg

6. (a) 2.4 mg (b) 2.6 mg (c) 0.40 mm Hg; yes

8. (a) 38 kJ (b) 2.6×10^2 mm Hg

10. 97°C

12. 17°C

14. 29 kJ/mol

16. (a) liquid + vapor (b) vapor (c) liquid

18. (a) vapor (b) liquid (c) liquid (d) triple point
(e) normal boiling point (f) freezing (g) no (h) yes

20. (a) solid (b) liquid (c) liquid

22. (a)

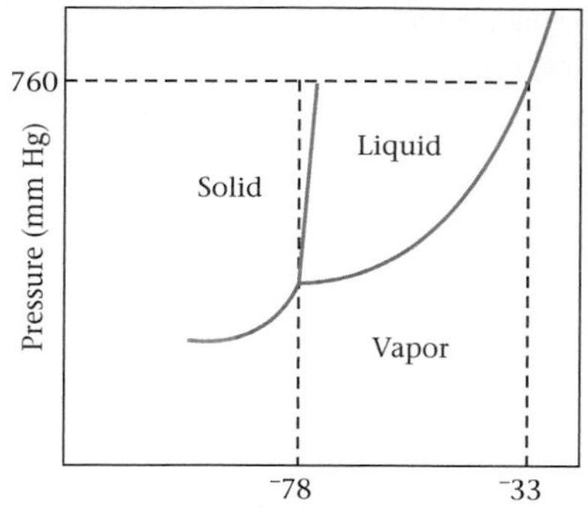

(b) ≈40 atm

24. (a) See figure below.

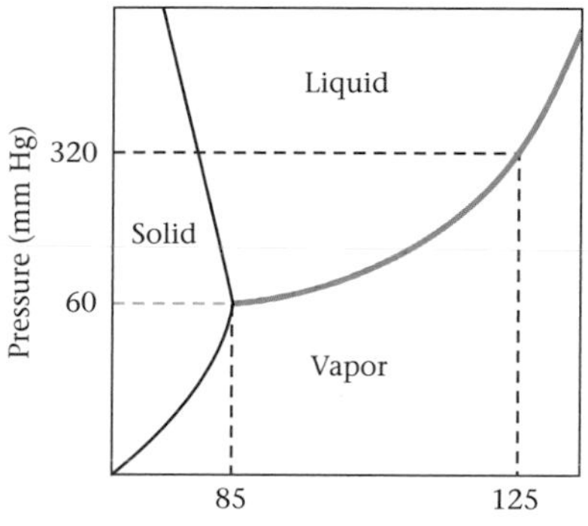

(b) 145°C (c) vapor condenses to liquid

26. He < Ne < Ar < Xe

28. All have dispersion forces; a and d have dipole forces.

30. b, c

32. (a) NaBr is ionic (b) hydrogen bonding
(c) hydrogen bonding (d) larger dispersion forces

34. c, d

36. (a) CCl_4—is a molecule (b) CH_3F—no hydrogen bonding
(c) SO_2—no hydrogen bonding
(d) N_2—has smaller dispersion forces

38. (a) H-bonds (b) dispersion forces
(c) dispersion and dipole forces (d) dispersion forces

40. (a) molecular or possibly metallic (b) ionic
(c) metallic

42. (a) metallic, network covalent
(b) network covalent, metallic (c) metallic

44. (a) metallic (b) molecular (c) network covalent
(d) ionic (e) molecular

46. (a) NO (b) CaO (c) SiO_2 (d) O_2

48. (a) C atoms (b) Si and C atoms
(c) ions (d) C_2H_2 molecules

50. face-centered

52. 0.131 nm

54. (a) 0.698 nm (b) 0.987 nm

56. (a) 0.700 nm (b) 0.404 nm

58. 1 Cs^+, 1 Cl^-

60. (a) 14.8 cm^3 (b) 1.5×10^{10} cm^3 (c) 9.39 cm^3
(d) $Hg(l)$: 63.4%; $Hg(g)$: 6.3×10^{-8}%

62. (a) 52% (b) 74% (c) 68%

64. 0.0436 atm

66. (a) F (b) T (c) F (d) T
68. (a) GT (b) MI (c) LT (d) EQ (e) MI
70. (a) I (b) G (c) L/G
72. (a) The covalent bond is the force within molecules; hydrogen bonds are forces between molecules.
(b) Normal boiling point is the temperature where vapor pressure is 760 mm Hg. Boiling point is the temperature where vapor pressure is pressure above the liquid.
(c) Triple point is the point where all three phases are in equilibrium. Critical point is the last point at which liquid and vapor can be at equilibrium.
(d) The vapor pressure curve is part of a phase diagram.
(e) Increasing temperature increases the vapor pressure.
74. (a) A (b) A (c) ≈34°C
(d) gas (e) ≈200 mm Hg
75. 6.65×10^3 kJ
76. 6.05×10^{23} atoms/mol
77. (a) liquid and vapor (b) 26.7 mm Hg (c) 3.4 atm
78. 41%
79. 80 atm; 0.60°C; see *Scientific American*, February 2000
80. $\frac{r_{cation}}{r_{anion}} = 0.414$
81. $P_{C_3H_8}$ is the vapor pressure of propane, which decreases exponentially with T. P_{N_2} is gas pressure, which decreases linearly with T.

CHAPTER 10

2. (a) 41.2% (b) 58.8% (c) 0.357
4. 0.15 *M*
6. 1.21×10^{-9} mol
8. (a) 38.76 g (b) 617 mL (c) 0.02860 *M*
10.

	Molality	Mass Percent Solvent	Ppm Solute	Mole Fraction Solvent
(a)	2.577	86.58	1.342×10^5	0.9556
(b)	20.4	45.0	5.50×10^5	0.731
(c)	0.07977	99.5232	4768	0.9986
(d)	12.6	57.0	4.30×10^5	0.815

12. (a) Dissolve 128 g $Ba(OH)_2$ in 1.00 L of solution.
(b) Dilute 125 mL to 1.00 L of solution.
14. (a) 109.3 g
(b) K_2S: 0.4953 *M*; K^+: 0.9906 *M*; S^{2-}: 0.4953 *M*
16. (a) 15.73 *M* (b) 1.31 *M*
18.

	Density (g/mL)	Molarity	Molality	Mass Percent of Solute
(a)	1.06	0.886	0.939	11.0
(b)	1.15	2.27	2.66	26.0
(c)	1.23	2.71	3.11	29.1

20. 0.54 *m*
22. (a) hexane (b) CBr_4 (c) C_6H_6 (d) I_2
(All are nonpolar molecules like CCl_4.)
24. (a) CH_3OH; hydrogen bonding
(b) KI; ionic
(c) LiCl; ionic
(d) NH_3; hydrogen bonding
26. (a) −44.5 kJ (b) no
28. (a) 1.3×10^{-6} mol/L-mm Hg
(b) 9.1×10^{-4} *M*
(c) 0.91 g
30. (a) 0.0022 g (b) 0.0019 g (c) 14%
32. −11°C
34. (a) 468 mm Hg
(b) 554 mm Hg
(c) 6.30×10^2 mm Hg
36. Dissolve 89 g in 1.00 L of solution.
38. 2.46 mm Hg
40. (a) 14 g; 0.95 g (b) 14.1 g; 0.96 g
42. (a) 15 *m* (b) 2.1×10^2 mL ethylene glycol
44. 9.08°C/*m*
46. 1.41×10^4 g/mol
48. 403 g/mol
50. $C_6H_4N_2O_4$
52. 6.50×10^4 g/mol
54. freezing: $Fe(NO_3)_3 < Ba(OH)_2 < CaCr_2O_7 < C_2H_5OH$
boiling: $C_2H_5OH < CaCr_2O_7 < Ba(OH)_2 < Fe(NO_3)_3$
56. 18.3 atm
58. (a) 2.0 (b) (ii)
60. Li
62. (a) 2.002 *M* (b) 2.17 *m* (c) 196 atm (d) −16.1°C
64. (a) 3.6°C/*m* (b) $i = 3$
66. (a) 5.5×10^{-7} mol/L (b) 0.12
68. 0.32 *M*
70. 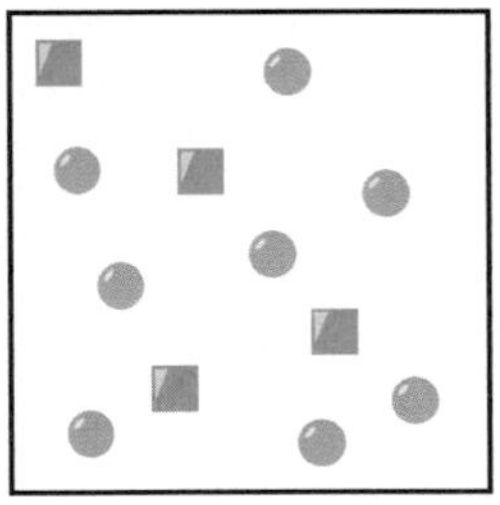
4 *M* Ca^{2+}; 8 *M* Cl^-
72. (a) solution 2 (b) same (c) solution 2
(d) same (e) solution 1
74. HF molecules
76. b
78. (a) not if solubility is very low
(b) can increase if solubility process is exothermic
(c) in general, they are not equal; difference increases with concentration
(d) $i = 3$ vs. $i = 2$, so freezing point lowering is about 3/2 as great
(e) $i = 2$ for NaCl, so osmotic pressure is about twice as great
80. (a) Check electrical conductivity.
(b) Solubility of gas decreases with increasing temperature.
(c) Number of moles of water is large so X_{solute} is small.
(d) Colligative property; the presence of a solute decreases vapor pressure.
82. 1.1 g/mL
83. Add 1.03×10^3 g of water.
84. $m = \frac{n \text{ solute}}{\text{kg solvent}}$; in 1 L of solution n solute $= M$

$$\text{kg solvent} = \frac{\text{mass solution (g)} - \text{mass solute (g)}}{1000}$$
$$= \frac{(1000 \times d) - M(\text{MM})}{1000} = d - \frac{M(\text{MM})}{1000}$$
$$m = \frac{M}{d - \frac{M(\text{MM})}{1000}}$$

In dilute solution, $m \rightarrow M/d$; and for water, $d = 1.00$ g/mL
85. 48%
86. 0.0018 g/cm³—intoxicated

87. (a) 2.08 M
(b) 1.872 mol
(c) 47.4 L

88. $V_{gas} = \dfrac{n_{gas} \times RT}{P_{gas}}$; $n_{gas} = k \times P_{gas}$; $V_{gas} = kRT$
V_{gas} depends only on temperature.

CHAPTER 11

2. (a) rate $= \dfrac{-\Delta[N_2O_4]}{\Delta t}$ (b) rate $= \dfrac{\Delta[N_2]}{3\Delta t}$

4. (a)

Time (min)	0	10	20	30	40	50
Moles AB_2	0.384	0.276	0.217	0.140	0.098	0.071

(b) 2.92×10^{-3} mol/min
(c) 1.73×10^{-3} mol/min

6. (a) 0.039 mol/L · s (b) 0.065 mol/L · s
(c) 0.078 mol/L · s

8. (a) $N_2(g) + 3H_2(g) \longrightarrow 2NH_3(g)$
(b) rate $= \dfrac{\Delta[NH_3]}{2\Delta t}$ (c) 0.0186 mol/L · min

10. (a)

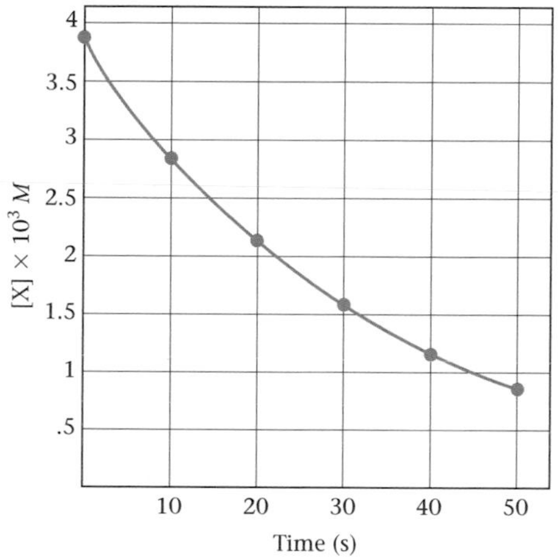

(b) 3.7×10^{-5} mol/L · s (c) 4.8×10^{-5} mol/L · s
(d) instantaneous rate < average rate

12. (a) 2, 1, 3 (b) 1, 0, 1 (c) 2, 2, 4 (d) 0, 0, 0

14. (a) $L^2/mol^2 \cdot s$ (b) s^{-1} (c) $L^3/mol^3 \cdot s$
(d) mol/L · s

16. (a) 0 (b) rate $= k[Y]^0$ (c) $k = 0.045\ M/h$

18. (a) 0.0756 mol/L · h (b) 0.300 M (c) 0.143 M
(d) 8.12×10^{-3} L/mol · h

20. (a) rate = 2.5×10^{-4} mol/L · min
(b) 2.5×10^{-4} mol/L · min
(c) any concentration

22. (a) 0.016 L/mol · s (b) 0.13 M (c) 1.4 M

24. (a) 1 (b) rate $= k[Y]$ (c) 1.44 min^{-1}

26. (a) 1st order in BF_3, 1st order in NH_3, 2nd order overall
(b) rate $= k[BF_3][NH_3]$
(c) 3.41 L/mol · s
(d) 0.566 mol/L · s

28. (a) 1 for I_2, 1 for $(C_2H_5)_2(NH)_2$, 2 overall
(b) rate $= k[I_2][(C_2H_5)_2(NH)_2]$
(c) 2.88×10^{-3} L/mol · h (d) 0.347 M

30. (a) 1st order in CH_3COCH_3, 1st order in H^+, 0 order in I_2
(b) rate $= k[CH_3COCH_3][H^+]$
(c) 2.6×10^{-5} L/mol · s
(d) 6.8×10^{-5} mol/L · s

32. (a) rate $= k[Cr(H_2O)_6^{3+}][SCN^-]$ (b) 0.43 L/mol · min
(c) 2.2×10^{-6} mol/L · min

34. plot of 1/[NOBr] vs t is linear; 2nd order

36. (a) linear plot obtained for ln[HOF] vs t
(b) 1.00 min^{-1}
(c) 2.80 min
(d) 0.0500 mol/L · min

38. (a) $2.03 \times 10^{-3}\ min^{-1}$ (b) 342 min (c) 0.0450 M

40. (a) 0.758 g (b) 3.22 months (c) 4.9 months

42. (a) $4.17 \times 10^{-4}\ s^{-1}$ (b) 6.34×10^{-3} mol/L · h
(c) 52 min (d) 42%

44. 112 g

46. 16 days

48. 15 hours

50. (a) 3.0 mg/min (b) 47 min (c) 3.0 mg/min
(d) 3.0 mg/min

52. (a) 10.0 min (b) 1.2 h

54. (a) 0.68 L/mol · h (b) 15 h (c) 2.2 h
(d) 0.48 mol/L · h

56. 2.9 L/mol · min

58. 17%

60. $E_a = 2.2 \times 10^2$ kJ/mol

62.

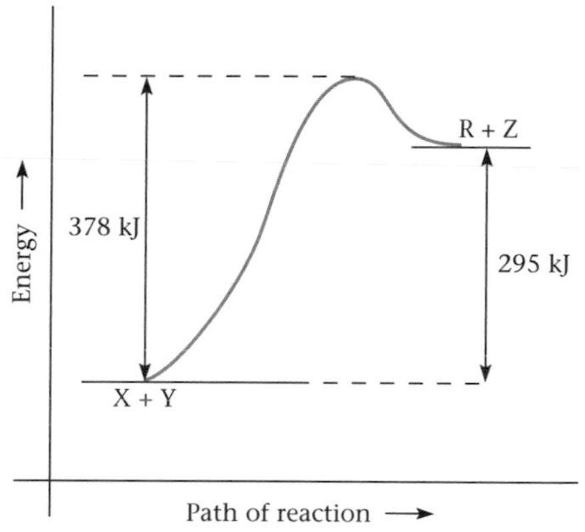

64. 68%

66. (a) At 25°C: 148 chirps/min; at 35°C: 220 chirps/min
(b) 3.0×10^1 kJ (c) 49%

68. (a) 8.61×10^{-4} L/mol · h (b) 775°C

70. 86 kJ/mol

72.

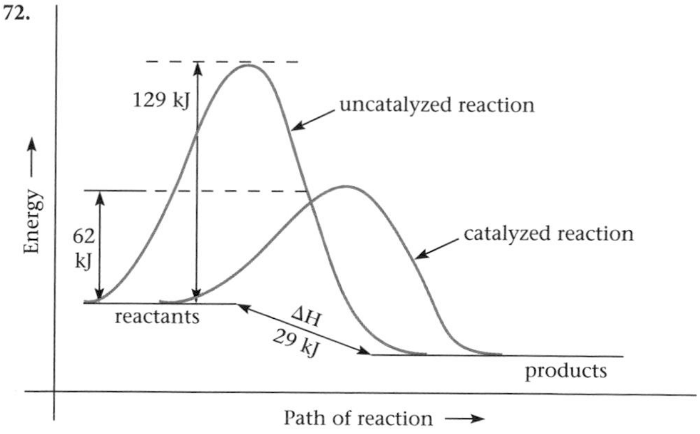

74. 357 kJ

76. (a) rate $= k \times [NO] \times [O_3]$
(b) rate $= k \times [NO_2]^2$
(c) rate $= k \times [K] \times [HCl]$

78. yes

80. (1) rate $= k \times [NO_3] \times [NO]$; $k_2 \times [NO_3] = k_1 \times [NO] \times [O_2]$

$$\text{rate} = \frac{kk_1}{k_2} \times [NO]^2 \times [O_2]$$

(2) rate $= k \times [N_2O_2] \times [O_2]$ $k_2 \times [N_2O_2] = k_1 \times [NO]^2$

$$\text{rate} = \frac{kk_1}{k_2} \times [NO]^2 \times [O_2]$$

82. 0.0966 mol/L · s

84. ≈ 20

86. 7×10^{17} years; very unlikely

88. $\ln\left(\frac{k_2}{k_1}\right) = \frac{1}{RT}(E_{a_{uncat}} - E_{a_{cat}})$

90. zero order ($t_{1/2}$ is directly related to original concentration)

92. 1 represents the decrease of [X] with time
2 represents the increase of [Z] with time
3 represents the increase of [Y] with time

94. (a) A (b) C (c) A

96. (a) rate $= k[A]^2[B]$
(b) rate $= 36k$
(c) add nine circles to the vessel

98. Expt. 1: rate = 0.05 mol/L · min
Expt. 2: k = 0.5/min; rate = 0.1 mol/L · min; E_a = 32 kJ
Expt. 3: rate = 0.1 mol/L · min; E_a cannot be determined
Expt. 4: rate = 0.06 mol/L · min; E_a = 32 kJ

99. (a) 174 kJ (b) 46 L/mol · s (c) 1.8 mol/L · s

100. 12 min

101. $\frac{-d[A]}{a\,dt} = k[A]; \frac{-d[A]}{[A]} = k\,a\,dt; \ln\frac{[A_o]}{[A]} = a\,k\,t$

102. rate $= k[A]^2[B][C]$

103. (a) $\frac{-d[A]}{dt} = k[A]^2; \frac{-d[A]}{[A]^2} = k\,dt; \frac{1}{[A]} - \frac{1}{[A_o]} = k\,t$

(b) $\frac{-d[A]}{dt} = k[A]^3; \frac{-d[A]}{[A]^3} = k\,dt; \frac{1}{2[A]^2} - \frac{1}{2[A_o]^2} = k\,t;$

$\frac{1}{[A]^2} - \frac{1}{[A_o]^2} = 2\,k\,t$

104. 0.90 g; 54 mg no more than three times a day

CHAPTER 12

2. (a) $\approx$75 s (b) greater than; equal to

4.

Time (min)	0	1	2	3	4	5	6
P_A (atm)	1.000	0.778	0.580	0.415	0.355	0.325	0.325
P_B (atm)	0.400	0.326	0.260	0.205	0.185	0.175	0.175
P_C (atm)	0.000	0.148	0.280	0.390	0.430	0.450	0.450

6. (a) $K = \frac{(P_{CO})(P_{H_2})^3}{P_{CH_4}}$ (b) $K = \frac{(P_{NO})^4(P_{H_2O})^6}{(P_{NH_3})^4(P_{O_2})^5}$

(c) $K = P_{CO_2}$ (d) $K = \frac{1}{(P_{NH_3})(P_{HCl})}$

8. (a) $\frac{P_{Ni(CO)_4}}{(P_{CO})^4}$ (b) $\frac{[H^+] \times [F^-]}{[HF]}$

(c) $\frac{[Cl^-]^2}{(P_{Cl_2}) \times [Br^-]^2}$

10. (a) $C_3H_6O(l) \rightleftharpoons C_3H_6O(g)$ $K = P_{C_3H_6O}$
(b) $7H_2(g) + 2NO_2(g) \rightleftharpoons 2NH_3(g) + 4H_2O(g)$

$$K = \frac{(P_{NH_3})^2(P_{H_2O})^4}{(P_{H_2})^7(P_{NO_2})^2}$$

(c) $H_2S(g) + Pb^{2+}(aq) \rightleftharpoons PbS(s) + 2H^+(aq)$

$$K = \frac{[H^+]^2}{(P_{H_2S})[Pb^{2+}]}$$

12. (a) $2H_2O(g) + 2SO_2(g) \rightleftharpoons 2H_2S(g) + 3O_2(g)$
(b) $IF(g) \rightleftharpoons \frac{1}{2}F_2(g) + \frac{1}{2}I_2(g)$
(c) $Cl_2(g) + 2Br^-(aq) \rightleftharpoons 2Cl^-(aq) + Br_2(l)$
(d) $2NO_3^-(aq) + 8H^+(aq) + 3Cu(s) \rightleftharpoons$
$2NO(g) + 3Cu^{2+}(aq) + 4H_2O(g)$

14. (a) $K_1 = \frac{(P_{SO_2})^2(P_{O_2})}{(P_{SO_3})^2}$ (b) $K_2 = \frac{(P_{SO_2})(P_{O_2})^{1/2}}{(P_{SO_3})}$

(c) $K_2 = (K_1)^{1/2}$

16. (a) 0.87 (b) 1.3

18. 3.1×10^{15}

20. 9×10^{15}

22. 0.838

24. (a) $CH_4(g) + 2H_2S(g) \rightleftharpoons CS_2(g) + 4H_2(g)$ (b) 334

26. 3.39

28. (a) Q = 34; no (b) to the left

30. (a) $\longrightarrow$ (b) $\longrightarrow$ (c) $\longrightarrow$

32. $\longrightarrow$

34. 2.3 atm

36. 0.25 atm

38. P_{NO} = 0.42 atm; P_{NO_2} = 0.32 atm

40. $P_{N_2} = P_{O_2}$ = 0.417 atm; $P_{SO_2} = P_{NO}$ = 0.067 atm

42. (a) $P_{NO} = P_{SO_3}$ = 2.25 atm; P_{NO_2} = 0.25 atm
(b) P = 5.00 atm before and after; true only if $\Delta n_g = 0$

44. (a) 0.928 atm (b) 6.1 g

46. $P_{H_2} = P_{I_2}$ = 0.021 atm

48. (a) increases (b) increases (c) remains the same

50. (a) (1) increase (2) increase (3) no effect (4) increase (5) increase
(b) none; (5) will decrease it

52. (a) $\longleftarrow$ (b) $\longrightarrow$ (c) no change

54. (a) 0.067 (b) P_{H_2} = 6.0 atm; P_{H_2S} = 0.40 atm
(c) P_{H_2} = 6.6 atm; P_{H_2S} = 0.4 atm

56. (a) 0.18
(b) P_{CO} = 1.02 atm; P_{Br_2} = 0.52 atm; P_{COBr_2} = 0.10 atm

58. 0.132

60. −59 kJ

62. (a) $P_{S(CH_2CH_2Cl)_2}$ = 0.168 atm; P_{SCl_2} = 1.07 atm; $P_{C_2H_4}$ = 2.51 atm
(b) 0.0249

64. 5.40 g

66. $K_{700°C}$ = 2.0 $K_{600°C}$ = 0.06

68. (a) $3A(g) \rightleftharpoons 2B(g)$
(b) no; pressures still changing at 250 s

70. b

72. Will decrease and then level off sooner at a somewhat higher level

74. Endothermic; more product at a higher temperature

76. Balanced equation; temperature

77. 27

78. $K = \frac{(P_C)^c(P_D)^d}{(P_A)^a(P_B)^b} = \frac{([C]RT)^c([D]RT)^d}{([A]RT)^a([B]RT)^b} = \frac{[C]^c[D]^d}{[A]^a[B]^b}(RT)^{(c+d)-(a+b)}$

$\Delta n_g = (c + d) - (a + b); K = K_c(RT)^{\Delta n_g}$

79. P_{N_2} = 0.33 atm; P_{H_2} = 0.99 atm; P_{NH_3} = 0.34 atm

80. 0.0442

81. 0.52 atm

82. 1.1

83. 25; 0.65 atm

84. (a) 0.22 atm (b) 0.4 g

CHAPTER 13

2. (a) Brønsted-Lowry acid: H_2O, HCN
Brønsted-Lowry base: CN^-, OH^-
acid-base pairs: H_2O, OH^-; HCN, CN^-

(b) Brønsted-Lowry acid: H_3O^+, H_2CO_3
Brønsted-Lowry base: HCO_3^-, H_2O
acid-base pairs: H_3O^+, H_2O; H_2CO_3, HCO_3^-
(c) Brønsted-Lowry acid: $HC_2H_3O_2$, H_2S
Brønsted-Lowry base: HS^-, $C_2H_3O_2^-$
acid-base pairs: $HC_2H_3O_2$, $C_2H_3O_2^-$; H_2S, HS^-

4. as acid: HSO_3^-, NH_4^+ as base: CHO_2^-, HSO_3^-

6. (a) CO_3^{2-} (b) $Cu(OH)_4^{2-}$ (c) NO_2^-
(d) $(CH_3)_2NH$ (e) HSO_3^-

8. as acid: $HCO_3^-(aq) + H_2O \rightleftharpoons H_3O^+ + CO_3^{2-}(aq)$
as base: $HCO_3^-(aq) + H_2O \rightleftharpoons H_2CO_3(aq) + OH^-(aq)$

10. (a) $Zn(H_2O)_3OH^+(aq) + H_2O \rightleftharpoons Zn(H_2O)_2(OH)_2(aq) + H_3O^+(aq)$
(b) $HSO_4^-(aq) + H_2O \rightleftharpoons SO_4^{2-}(aq) + H_3O^+(aq)$
(c) $HNO_2(aq) + H_2O \rightleftharpoons NO_2^-(aq) + H_3O^+(aq)$
(d) $Fe(H_2O)_6^{2+}(aq) + H_2O \rightleftharpoons Fe(H_2O)_5OH^+(aq) + H_3O^+(aq)$
(e) $HC_2H_3O_2(aq) + H_2O \rightleftharpoons C_2H_3O_2^-(aq) + H_3O^+(aq)$
(f) $H_2PO_4^-(aq) + H_2O \rightleftharpoons HPO_4^{2-}(aq) + H_3O^+(aq)$

12. (a) $(CH_3)_3N(aq) + H_2O \rightleftharpoons (CH_3)_3NH^+(aq) + OH^-(aq)$
(b) $PO_4^{3-}(aq) + H_2O \rightleftharpoons HPO_4^{2-}(aq) + OH^-(aq)$
(c) $HPO_4^{2-}(aq) + H_2O \rightleftharpoons H_2PO_4^-(aq) + OH^-(aq)$
(d) $H_2PO_4^-(aq) + H_2O \rightleftharpoons H_3PO_4(aq) + OH^-(aq)$
(e) $HS^-(aq) + H_2O \rightleftharpoons H_2S(aq) + OH^-(aq)$
(f) $C_2H_5NH_2(aq) + H_2O \rightleftharpoons C_2H_5NH_3^+(aq) + OH^-(aq)$

14. (a) pH = 0.00; pOH = 14.00; acidic
(b) pH = 3.77; pOH = 10.23; acidic
(c) pH = 7.17; pOH = 6.83; basic
(d) pH = 10.03; pOH = 3.97; basic

16.

	$[H^+]$	$[OH^-]$		$[H^+]$	$[OH^-]$
(a)	1×10^{-9}	1×10^{-5}	(b)	6.3×10^{-4}	1.6×10^{-11}
(c)	11.2	8.9×10^{-16}	(d)	3.5×10^{-8}	2.9×10^{-7}

18.

	$[H^+]$	$[OH^-]$	pH	pOH	Basic?
(a)	2.1×10^{-5}	4.8×10^{-10}	4.68	9.32	no
(b)	1.1×10^{-12}	8.9×10^{-3}	11.95	2.05	yes
(c)	1.5×10^{-6}	6.8×10^{-9}	5.83	8.17	no
(d)	4.3×10^{-3}	2.3×10^{-12}	2.37	11.63	no

20. (Y) more basic; (X) has a higher pOH

22. (a) A: 4.8×10^{-13} *M* B: 1.4×10^{-12} *M* C: 6.9×10^{-7} *M*
(b) B: 11.85 C: 6.16
(c) A is basic, B is basic, C is acidic

24. (a) 3.2×10^{-11} (b) $1 \times 10^9:1$

26. (a) $[H^+] = 10.3$ *M*; pH = −1.01; pH of 0.175 L is the same.
(b) $[H^+] = 0.57$ *M*; pH = 0.24; pH of 47.9 mL solution = −0.76

28. (a) $[OH^-] = 0.0237$ *M*; $[H^+] = 4.2 \times 10^{-13}$ *M*; pH = 12.37; pOH = 1.63
(b) $[OH^-] = 0.184$ *M*; $[H^+] = 5.4 \times 10^{-14}$ *M*; pH = 13.26; pOH = 0.74

30. 0.792

32. 12.28

34. (a) $HSO_3^-(aq) \rightleftharpoons H^+(aq) + SO_3^{2-}(aq)$ $\quad K_a = \dfrac{[H^+][SO_3^{2-}]}{[HSO_3^-]}$
(b) $HPO_4^{2-}(aq) \rightleftharpoons H^+(aq) + PO_4^{3-}(aq)$ $\quad K_a = \dfrac{[H^+][PO_4^{3-}]}{[HPO_4^{2-}]}$
(c) $HNO_2(aq) \rightleftharpoons NO_2^-(aq) + H^+(aq)$ $\quad K_a = \dfrac{[H^+][NO_2^-]}{[HNO_2]}$

36. (a) 3.74 (b) 7.17 (c) 10.31

38. (a) C < D < B < A (b) A

40. $HCN < HCHO_2 < HF < HBr$

42. $HBr < HF < HCHO_2 < HCN$

44. 8.7×10^{-12}

46. 1.9×10^{-5}

48. 1.0×10^{-4}

50. 4.83

52. (a) 2.0×10^{-2} (b) 2.8×10^{-2}

54. (a) 0.0086 *M* (b) 1.2×10^{-12} *M*
(c) 2.07 (d) 1.3%

56. 2.29; 1.3%

58. $H_3PO_4(aq) \rightleftharpoons 3H^+(aq) + PO_4^{3-}(aq)$ $\quad K = 2.0 \times 10^{-22}$

60. pH = 2.00; $[HX^-] = 1.0 \times 10^{-2}$ *M*; $[X^{2-}] = 9.7 \times 10^{-8}$ *M*

62. pH = 2.15; $[HC_6H_6O_6^-] = 7.1 \times 10^{-3}$ *M*,
$[C_6H_6O_6^{2-}] = 1.6 \times 10^{-12}$ *M*

64. (a) $NH_3(aq) + H_2O \rightleftharpoons NH_4^+(aq) + OH^-(aq)$
$$K_b = \frac{[NH_4^+][OH^-]}{[NH_3]}$$
(b) $HS^-(aq) + H_2O \rightleftharpoons H_2S(aq) + OH^-(aq)$
$$K_b = \frac{[H_2S][OH^-]}{[HS^-]}$$
(c) $(CH_3)_3N(aq) + H_2O \rightleftharpoons (CH_3)_3NH^+(aq) + OH^-(aq)$
$$K_b = \frac{[(CH_3)_3NH^+][OH^-]}{[(CH_3)_3N]}$$

66. $CHO_2^- < C_2H_3O_2^- < SO_3^{2-}$

68. $Ba(OH)_2 > KOH > NaCN > NaHCO_3$

70. (a) 6.7×10^{-6} (b) 2.6×10^{-5}

72. $[OH^-] = 3.8 \times 10^{-4}$ *M*; pOH = 3.42; pH = 10.58

74. (a) $C_2H_3O_2^-(aq) + H_2O \rightleftharpoons HC_2H_3O_2(aq) + OH^-(aq)$
(b) 1.8×10^{-10} (c) 8.28

76. 2.1×10^2 g

78. (a) $(NH_4)_2SO_3$, NH_4CN (b) Na_2CO_3, K_2CO_3
(c) NaBr, KBr (d) $Fe(ClO_4)_3$, NH_4ClO_4

80. (a) acidic (b) neutral (c) acidic (d) basic
(e) basic

82. (a) $Fe(H_2O)_6^{3+}(aq) + H_2O \rightleftharpoons [Fe(H_2O)_5OH]^{2+}(aq) + H_3O^+$
(b) BaI_2 is neutral
(c) $NH_4^+(aq) + H_2O \rightleftharpoons NH_3(aq) + H_3O^+$ $\quad K_a = 5.6 \times 10^{-10}$
$NO_2^-(aq) + H_2O \rightleftharpoons OH^-(aq) + HNO_2$ $\quad K_b = 1.7 \times 10^{-11}$
(d) $HPO_4^{2-} + H_2O \rightleftharpoons PO_4^{3-} + H_3O^+$ $\quad K_a = 4.5 \times 10^{-13}$
$HPO_4^{2-} + H_2O \rightleftharpoons H_2PO_4^- + OH^-(aq)$ $\quad K_b = 1.6 \times 10^{-7}$
(e) $PO_4^{3-} + H_2O \rightleftharpoons HPO_4^{2-} + OH^-(aq)$

84. $HCl < ZnCl_2 < KCl < KF < KOH$

86. (a) neutral (b) acidic
(c) acidic (d) acidic

88. 68 L

90. 5.5 g

92. 4.6 g

94. 9.8×10^{-9}

96. b, c

98. (a) LT (b) LT (c) EQ
(d) MI (e) LT (f) GT

100. (1) weak acid; (2) strong acid

102. Dissolve 0.10 mol in water, measure pH. If pH > 7, solid is basic; pH < 13.0, it is a weak base. If pH < 7, solid is acidic; if pH > 1.0, it is a weak acid.

103. 1.59

104. (a) −5.58 kJ (b) −6.83 kJ

105. 13.06

106. % ionization $= \frac{[H^+]}{[HA]_o} \times 100$; $[H^+]^2 \approx K_a \times [HA]_o$;

$[H^+] \approx K_a^{1/2} \times [HA]_o^{1/2}$;

% ionization $= \frac{K_a^{1/2}}{[HA]_o^{1/2}} \times 100$;

% ionization is inversely proportional to $[HA]_o^{1/2}$

107. −1.64°C

108. 12.62

109. HA

CHAPTER 14

2. **(a)** $H^+(aq) + C_2H_3O_2^-(aq) \longrightarrow HC_2H_3O_2(aq)$
(b) $H^+(aq) + OH^-(aq) \longrightarrow H_2O$
(c) $HOCl(aq) + CN^-(aq) \longrightarrow HCN(aq) + OCl^-(aq)$
(d) $HNO_2(aq) + OH^-(aq) \longrightarrow NO_2^-(aq) + H_2O$

4. **(a)** $NH_4^+(aq) + OH^-(aq) \rightleftharpoons NH_3(aq) + H_2O$
(b) $H_2PO_4^-(aq) + OH^-(aq) \rightleftharpoons HPO_4^{2-}(aq) + H_2O$
(c) $Al(H_2O)_6^{3+}(aq) + OH^-(aq) \rightleftharpoons [Al(H_2O)_5OH]^{2+}(aq) + H_2O$

6. **(a)** 5.6×10^4 **(b)** 1.0×10^{14} **(c)** 48
(d) 6.0×10^{10}

8. **(a)** 5.6×10^4 **(b)** 6.2×10^6 **(c)** 1.2×10^9

10. **(a)** 7.21; 1.6×10^{-7} **(b)** 6.68; 4.8×10^{-8}
(c) 6.55; 3.6×10^{-8} **(d)** 6.16; 1.4×10^{-8}

12. 4.22

14. **(a)** 8.51 **(b)** pH remains the same.

16. 6.17

18. (a) and (b)

20. 5.04

22. 9.59

24. **(a)** $HC_2H_3O_2/C_2H_3O_2^-$ **(b)** HCN/CN^-
(c) HCO_3^-/CO_3^{2-}

26. **(a)** 5 **(b)** 0.7 mol **(c)** 0.7 g **(d)** 1×10^1 L

28. Theoretically, one liter of buffer can absorb
(a) 0.335 mol base; 0.335 mol acid
(b) 0.335 mol base; 0.100 mol acid
(c) 0.335 mol base; 0.0750 mol acid
(d) 0.335 mol base; 0.0300 mol acid

30. **(a)** 10.15 **(b)** 9.57 **(c)** 10.60

32. **(a)** 10.15 **(b)** 1.43 **(c)** 12.55
(d) There are large fluctuations in pH when base and acid are added.
(e) Buffer capacity is diminished by dilution.

34. **(a)** 4.20 **(b)** 4.68 **(c)** 0.45:1

36. **(a)** 0.64 **(b)** 54% **(c)** 47%

38. **(a)** phenolphthalein **(b)** phenolphthalein
(c) all three indicators **(d)** methyl orange

40. **(a)** 4×10^{-8} **(b)** 6.4 − 8.4 **(c)** orange

42. **(a)** 9.4 mL **(b)** 7.00 **(c)** $[ClO_4^-] = [Na^+] = 0.101\ M$

44. **(a)** 0.186 *M*
(b) $[HCHO_2] = [OH^-] \approx 2.0 \times 10^{-6}\ M$; $[CHO_2^-] = [K^+] = 0.0718\ M$
(c) 8.30

46. **(a)** $C_5H_5N(aq) + H^+(aq) \rightleftharpoons C_5H_5NH^+(aq)$
(b) 0.767 g
(c) $[H^+] = [C_5H_5N] = 9.2 \times 10^{-4}\ M$; $[Br^-] = [C_5H_5NH^+] = 0.144\ M$
(d) 3.04

48. **(a)** $H^+(aq) + OH^-(aq) \rightleftharpoons H_2O$ **(b)** K^+, Br^-
(c) 65.4 mL **(d)** 0.590 **(e)** 1.177 **(f)** 7.00

50. **(a)** $C_{17}H_{19}O_3N(aq) + H^+(aq) \rightleftharpoons C_{17}H_{19}O_3NH^+(aq)$
(b) $C_{17}H_{19}O_3NH^+, Cl^-$, **(c)** 71.8 mL **(d)** 10.52
(e) 7.87 **(f)** 4.54

52. **(a)** 11.00 **(b)** 9.25 **(c)** 5.30

54. 1.4 L

56. **(a)** 45.1 g/mol **(b)** 5.9×10^{-4} **(c)** 1.7×10^{-11}

58. 62 mL

60. **(a)** 2.30 **(b)** 2.10

62. **(a)**

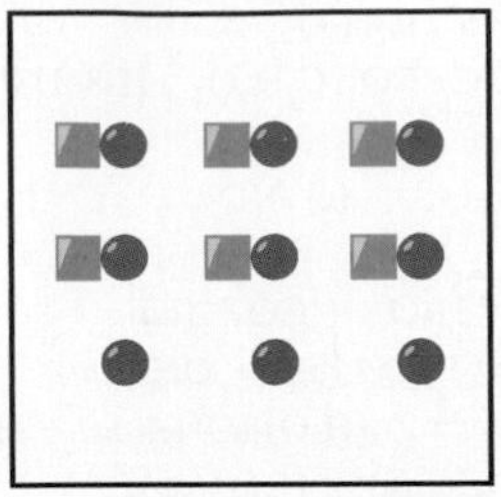

buffer

(b)

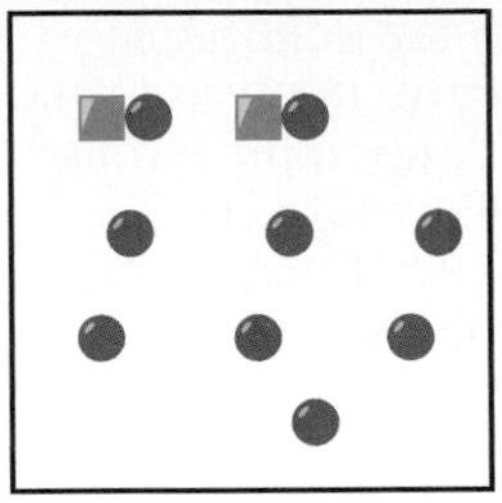

buffer

(c)

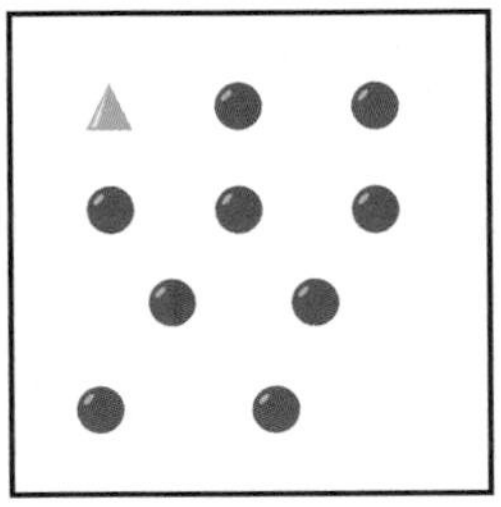

base

64. **(a)** EQ **(b)** GT **(c)** GT **(d)** MI **(e)** LT

66. **(a)** basic solution becomes a buffer with pH ≈ 4
(b) weak base; not completely ionized
(c) contains two species; one can react with H^+ ions, the other with OH^- ions
(d) could be a concentrated weak acid

68. Measure freezing point of solution:
1 L HCl has 2.0×10^{-3} mol particles (H^+, Cl^- ions)
1 L $HCHO_2$ has $\approx 6.0 \times 10^{-3}$ mol particles ($HCHO_2$ molecules)
1 L $C_6H_5NH_3^+$ has $\approx 8.0 \times 10^{-2}$ mol particles ($C_6H_5NH_3^+$, Cl^- ions)
Or one could measure the pH at the equivalence point after titration with a strong base.
$HCl < HCHO_2 < C_6H_5NH_3^+$

70. 2.87

71. 33 mL

72. 1.1×10^2 g/mol

73. $\frac{[NH_4^+]}{[NH_3]} = 5.7 \times 10^2$

74. **(a)** 1.61 **(b)** 3.22 **(c)** 8.44 **(d)** 5.92 **(e)** 10.89

75. ≈30 mL; phenolphthalein

76. **(a)** 0.8239 **(b)** 0.80

77. 4.6×10^{-6}

78. 6.0 g

79. $-\log[H^+] = -\log K_a - \log\left(\frac{[HB]}{[B^-]}\right)$;

$$pH = pK_a - \log\frac{[HB]}{[B^-]} = pK_a + \log\frac{[B^-]}{[HB]}$$

CHAPTER 15

2. **(a)** Ethylenediamine molecule, SCN^- ion, Cl^- ion
(b) +3 **(c)** $[Co(en)_2(SCN)Cl]_2S$

4. **(a)** $Pt(NH_3)_2(C_2O_4)$ **(b)** $Pt(NH_3)_2(SCN)Br$
(c) $Pt(en)(NO_2)_2$

6. **(a)** 6 **(b)** 4 **(c)** 6 **(d)** 2

8. **(a)** +6 **(b)** +1
(c) +2 **(d)** +3

10. **(a)** $[Mn(NH_3)_2(OH)_4]_3(PO_4)_2$
(b) $Al[CuCl_4]$
(c) $Al_2[Cr(H_2O)_2(ox)_2]_3$
(d) $[Au(CN)_2]_3PO_4$

12. **(a)** $Pt(NH_3)_6{}^{4+}$ **(b)** $Ag(CN)_2{}^-$
(c) $Zn(C_2O_4)_2{}^{2-}$ **(d)** $Cd(CN)_4{}^{2-}$

14. 22.61%

16. one

18. **(a)**

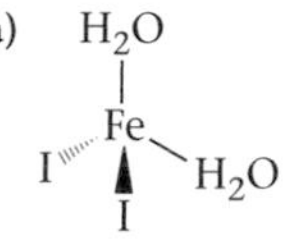

(b) $[CNS\text{-}Ag\text{-}SCN]^-$

(c)

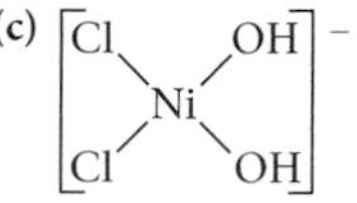

(d)

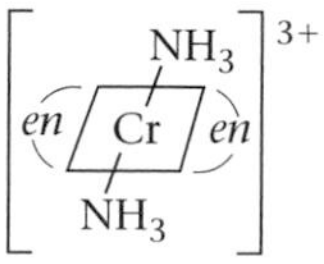

(e)

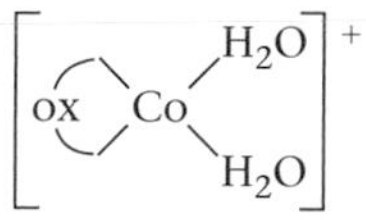

20.

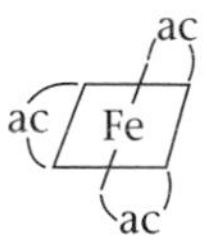

22. **(a)**

(b)

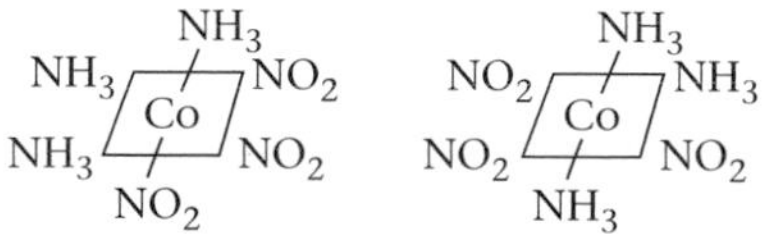

(c)

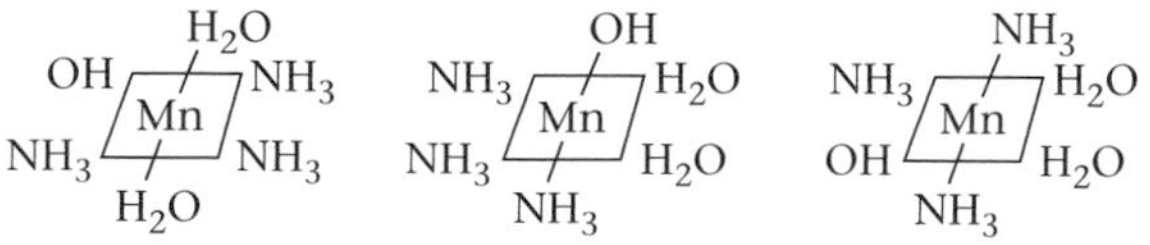

24.

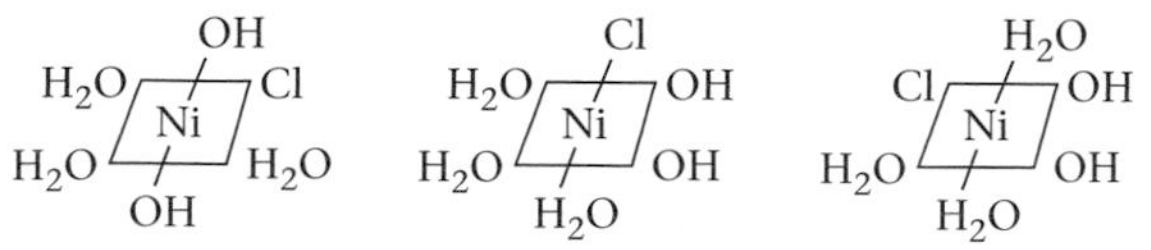

26. **(a)** $1s^22s^22p^63s^23p^63d^5$ **(b)** $1s^22s^22p^63s^23p^63d^3$
(c) $1s^22s^22p^63s^23p^63d^{10}$ **(d)** same as (c)
(e) same as **(b)**

	3d	unpaired e^-
28. **(a)**	(↑)(↑)(↑)(↑)(↑)	5
(b)	(↑)(↑)(↑)( )( )	3
(c)	(↑↓)(↑↓)(↑↓)(↑↓)(↑↓)	0
(d)	same as (c)	
(e)	same as (b)	

30. **(a)** high spin

__ __
↑ ↑ ↑

(b) high spin low spin

↑ ↑ — __ __
↑↓ ↑ ↑ — ↑↓ ↑↓ ↑↓

32. Mn^{3+} contains four 3d electrons, so can form
( )( ) (↑)( )
(↑↓)(↑)(↑) (↑)(↑)(↑)
low spin high spin
Mn^{4+}, with only three 3d electrons, cannot do this.

34. NH_3 has a large Δ_o; low spin; no unpaired electrons.
F^- has a small Δ_o; high spin; unpaired electrons present.

36. **(a)** 4 **(b)** 4 **(c)** 0 **(d)** 4 **(e)** 2

38. 4.60×10^2 nm

40. ≈ 500 nm; green

42. **(a)** $3 \times 10^{-3}\,M$ **(b)** $5 \times 10^{-5}\,M$

44. 6.7

46. **(a)** $CoN_6H_{18}Cl_3$
(b) $Co(NH_3)_6Cl_3(s) \rightleftharpoons Co(NH_3)_6{}^{3+}(aq) + 3Cl^-(aq)$

48. Lungs saturated with oxygen so the shift is to oxyhemoglobin formation. Tissues low in oxygen, so in venal blood, the shift is to hemoglobin formation.

50. $[Fe^{2+}] = 0.028\,M$; $[Fe(bipy)_3]^{2+} = 0.024\,M$; $[bipy] \approx 0$

52. **(a)** 6, not 5 **(b)** shorter, not longer
(c) true **(d)** eight, not seven

54. 0.92 g

55. $[Pt(NH_3)_4]\,[PtCl_4]$ or $[Pt(NH_3)_3Cl]\,[Pt(NH_3)Cl_3]$

56. **(a)** $CuC_4H_{22}N_6SO_4$
(b)

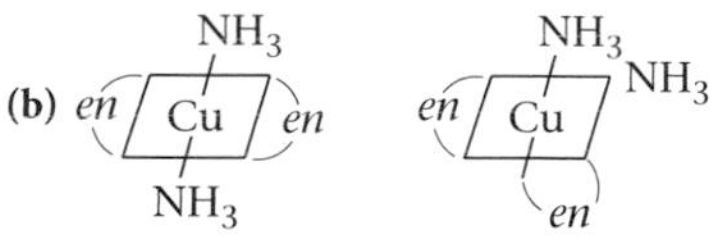

57. red-violet

CHAPTER 16

2. **(a)** $AgCl(s) \rightleftharpoons Ag^+(aq) + Cl^-(aq)$ $K_{sp} = [Ag^+] \times [Cl^-]$
(b) $Al_2(CO_3)_3 \rightleftharpoons 2Al^{3+}(aq) + 3CO_3{}^{2-}(aq)$
$K_{sp} = [Al^{3+}]^2 \times [CO_3{}^{2-}]^3$
(c) $MnS_2(s) \rightleftharpoons Mn^{4+}(aq) + 2S^{2-}(aq)$ $K_{sp} = [Mn^{4+}] \times [S^{2-}]^2$
(d) $Mg(OH)_2(s) \rightleftharpoons Mg^{2+}(aq) + 2OH^-(aq)$
$K_{sp} = [Mg^{2+}] \times [OH^-]^2$

4. **(a)** $CaCO_3(s) \rightleftharpoons Ca^{2+}(aq) + CO_3{}^{2-}(aq)$
(b) $Co(OH)_3(s) \rightleftharpoons Co^{3+}(aq) + 3OH^-(aq)$
(c) $Ag_2S(s) \rightleftharpoons 2Ag^+(aq) + S^{2-}(aq)$
(d) $PbCl_2(s) \rightleftharpoons Pb^{2+}(aq) + 2Cl^-(aq)$

6. **(a)** $[Li^+] = 0.016\,M$ **(b)** $[NO_2{}^-] = 0.024\,M$
(c) $[Sn^{2+}] = 2.9 \times 10^{-19}\,M$

8. **(a)** $7.3 \times 10^{-3}\,M$ **(b)** $3.2 \times 10^{-8}\,M$ **(c)** $3.5 \times 10^{-8}\,M$

10. **(a)** $[Ba^{2+}] = [C_2O_4{}^{2-}] = 1.3 \times 10^{-3}\,M$
(b) $[OH^-] = 2.9 \times 10^{-8}\,M$
(c) $[Pb^{2+}] = 2 \times 10^{-15}\,M$

12. **(a)** $[Cd^{2+}] = 1.4 \times 10^{-5}\,M$
(b) 8.64
(c) 1.0×10^1%

14. yes; $2 \times 10^{-7}\,M$

16. **(a)** yes
(b) $[Zn^{2+}] = 0.039\,M$; $[NO_3{}^-] = 0.078\,M$; $[K^+] = 3.6 \times 10^{-6}\,M$; pH = 6.5

18. **(a)** $3 \times 10^{-4}\,M$ **(b)** $1 \times 10^{-10}\,M$ **(c)** $6 \times 10^{-6}\,M$

20. **(a)** 5.98×10^{-17} **(b)** 5.50×10^{-16} **(c)** 1.40×10^{-37}

22. (a) 6×10^{-3} g/L (b) 5×10^{-8} g/L (c) 1×10^{-3} g/L
24. 1.5×10^{-5}
26. (a) no (b) yes
28. (a) 3×10^{9} g/100 mL (b) 3×10^{3} g/100 mL (c) 0.3 g/100 mL
30. 9×10^{-15}
32. (a) $Pb(OH)_2$ (b) 9.26
34. (a) Ag_2CO_3 (b) 4×10^{-8} *M*
36. Both $BaCO_3$ and $CaCO_3$ will precipitate.
38. (a) $CaCO_3(s) + 2H^+(aq) \longrightarrow Ca^{2+}(aq) + H_2CO_3(aq)$
(b) $NiS(s) + 2H^+(aq) \longrightarrow Ni^{2+}(aq) + H_2S(aq)$
(c) $Al(OH)_3(s) + 3H^+(aq) \longrightarrow Al^{3+}(aq) + 3H_2O$
(d) $Sb(OH)_4^-(aq) + 4H^+(aq) \longrightarrow Sb^{3+}(aq) + 4H_2O$
(e) no reaction
40. (a) $Cu(OH)_2(s) + 4NH_3(aq) \longrightarrow Cu(NH_3)_4^{2+}(aq) + 2OH^-(aq)$
(b) $Cd^{2+}(aq) + 4NH_3(aq) \longrightarrow Cd(NH_3)_4^{2+}(aq)$
(c) $Pb^{2+}(aq) + 2NH_3(aq) + 2H_2O \longrightarrow Pb(OH)_2(s) + 2NH_4^+(aq)$
42. (a) $Ni^{2+}(aq) + 2OH^-(aq) \longrightarrow Ni(OH)_2(s)$
(b) $Sn^{4+}(aq) + 6OH^-(aq) \longrightarrow Sn(OH)_6^{2-}(aq)$
(c) $Al(OH)_3(s) + OH^-(aq) \longrightarrow Al(OH)_4^-(aq)$
44. $Co(OH)_2(s) + 2H^+(aq) \rightleftharpoons Co^{2+}(aq) + 2H_2O$; $K = 2 \times 10^{12}$
46. (a) 2×10^{6} (b) yes
48. (a) 4×10^{-7} (b) 0.03 mol/L
50. 1×10^{-4} *M* in 0.10 *M* NaOH; 2×10^{-6} *M* in pure water
52. (a) 2×10^{29} (b) 5×10^{-6} *M*
54. 7.2×10^{-4}
56. (a) $\longleftarrow$ (b) $\longrightarrow$ (c) $\longrightarrow$ (d) $\longleftarrow$
58. (a) 3.1×10^{-4} *M* (b) yes (c) 6×10^{-5} *M*
60. ≈ 2 mg
62.

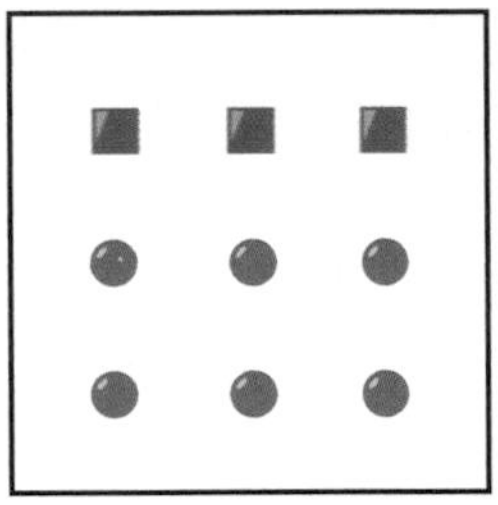

(1)

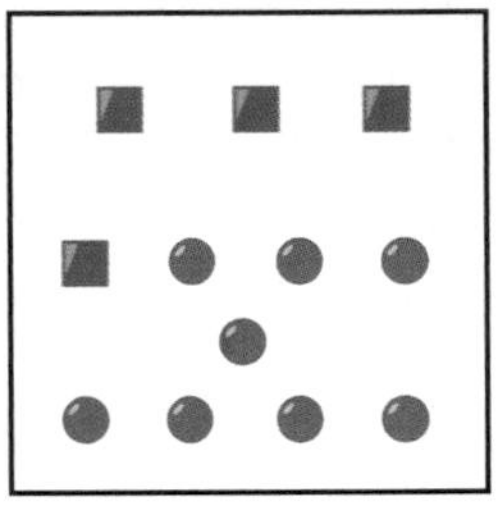

(2)

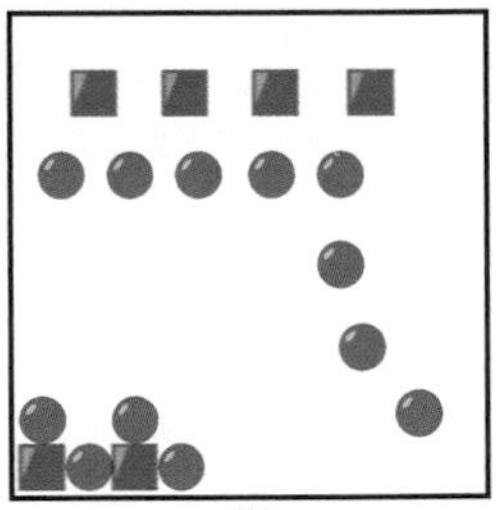

(3)

64. a
66. No—increasing temperature favors an endothermic process.
68. (a) (3) (b) (5) (c) (2) (d) (1)
69. in water: 1×10^{-4} mol/L in NH_4Cl: 0.06 mol/L
70. 1.9×10^{-4} mol/L
71. 1×10^{-8} *M*
72. (a) 1×10^{-5} *M* (b) $Al(OH)_3$, $Fe(OH)_3$
(c) virtually all (d) 1.6 g
73. (a) 8×10^{5} (b) 4×10^{3}
74. 1.0×10^{21}

CHAPTER 17

2. a
4. b
6. a
8. (a) $O_2(g)$ with 758 mm Hg pressure
(b) glucose(*s*)
(c) Hg(*l*)
10. (a) − (b) − (c) + (d) −
12. (a) can't say (b) + (c) − (d) +
14. (a) − (b) + (c) +
16. (c) < (b) < (a) < (d)
18. (a) −112.0 J/K (b) 605.9 J/K
(c) 2.9 J/K (d) −93.1 J/K
20. (a) −976.1 J/K (b) −816.0 J/K (c) −97.4 J/K
22. (a) −0.1319 kJ/K (b) −0.2712 kJ/K
(c) −0.5330 kJ/K
24. (a) +514 kJ (b) −1295 kJ (c) 34.9 kJ
26. (a) −1087.1 kJ; spontaneous
(b) −894 kJ; spontaneous
(c) −394.7 kJ; spontaneous
(d) −298.0 kJ; spontaneous
28. (a) −793.6 kJ (b) 224.2 kJ (c) −1226.6 kJ
30. (a) −184.1 kJ/mol (b) −73.8 kJ/mol
(c) −409.0 kJ/mol
32. $\Delta G° = -6.0 \times 10^{1}$ kJ; plausible
34. at 25°C: −359.2 kJ; at 15°C: −359.0 kJ
36. (a) 0.132 kJ/K; yes (b) 0.0956 kJ/mol · K
(c) −510.9 kJ/mol
38. (a) −0.918 kJ/K (b) −0.159 kJ/mol · K
40. (a) *T*-dependent; spontaneous at high *T*
(b) *T*-independent; spontaneous at any *T*
(c) *T*-dependent; spontaneous at high *T*
42. (a) spontaneous above 2.2×10^{4} K
(b) *T*-independent; spontaneous at any *T*
(c) spontaneous above 1.05×10^{3} K
44. 197°C
46. (a) $\Delta G° = 62.0 - 0.1328\,T$
(b) 467 K
48. b
50. 282 K
52. not at equilibrium at any temperature when $P = 1$ atm
54. 59°C
56. (a) $\Delta G = 31.1$ kJ; not spontaneous
(b) $\Delta G = -3.6$ kJ; spontaneous
58. (a) −177.6 kJ (b) −105.8 kJ
60. (a) 55.7 kJ (b) 1.08×10^{-5} *M* (c) yes—close to K_{sp}
62. (a) 52.6 kJ (b) 6×10^{-10}
64. (a) 105 kJ (b) 104 kJ/mol
66. (a) −23.4 kJ (b) 6.4×10^{2}
68. 6.9×10^{-4}
70. 51 kJ
72. 130.4 kJ
74. (a) $\Delta G° = 201.3$ kJ (nonspontaneous)
(b) $\Delta G° = -98.9$ kJ
76. $C_6H_{12}O_6(s) + 6O_2(g) + 80ADP + 80HPO_4^{2-}(aq) + 160H^+(aq) \longrightarrow 80ATP + 86H_2O + 6CO_2(g)$
78. −37.3 kJ
80. ΔG for overall reaction is −2016 kJ
82. 4.4×10^{-3}

84. **(a)** False— . . . is often spontaneous
(b) False— . . . under standard conditions
(c) False— . . . moles of gas
(d) False—If $\Delta H° < 0$, and $\Delta S° > 0$, . . .

86. **(a)** 0 K **(b)** 1 **(c)** larger

88. **(a)** Entropy decreases because $S°_{gas} > S°_{solid}$ or $S°_{liq}$
(b) $\Delta S°$ is the difference between entropy of products and reactants.
(c) A solid has fewer options for placement of particles, i.e., more orderly.

90. **(a)** reaction becomes more spontaneous at high T
(b) no ($\Delta H° > 0$)
(c) yes ($\Delta G°$ becomes more spontaneous at high T)
(d) $\approx$ 320 K
(e) $\approx 2 \times 10^{-2}$

92. **(a)** LT **(b)** LT **(c)** MI

93. 61°C

94. $P_{H_2} = P_{I_2} = 0.07$ atm $P_{HI} = 0.46$ atm

95. **(a)** 6.00 kJ **(b)** 0 **(c)** 0.0220 kJ/K
(d) 0.43 kJ **(e)** −0.45 kJ

96. **(a)** 4.2 kJ **(b)** $\approx 5.2 \times 10^2$ g

97. 1430 K

98. (1) $\Delta G° = 146 - 0.1104\,T$; becomes spontaneous above 1050°C
(2) $\Delta G° = 168.6 - 0.0758\,T$; becomes spontaneous above 1950°C

99. −0.010 kJ/mol·K

100. 26.7 kJ

101. 464 K

CHAPTER 18

2. **(a)** $2Ag(s) + Sn^{4+}(aq) \longrightarrow 2Ag^+(aq) + Sn^{2+}(aq)$
(b) $2Al(s) + 3Cu^{2+}(aq) \longrightarrow 3Cu(s) + 2Al^{3+}(aq)$
(c) $5Fe^{2+}(aq) + MnO_4^-(aq) + 8H^+(aq) \longrightarrow Mn^{2+}(aq) + 5Fe^{3+}(aq) + 4H_2O$

4. **(a)** Sn anode, Ag cathode; e^- move from Sn to Ag. Anions move to Sn and cations to Ag.
(b) Pt both anode and cathode. Anode has H_2 gas and H^+; cathode has chloride ions, Hg and Hg_2Cl_2. e^- move from anode to cathode. Anions move to the anode; cations move to the cathode.
(c) Pb anode and PbO_2 cathode. e^- move from Pb to PbO_2. Anions move to Pb; cations to PbO_2.

6. **(a)** anode to cathode
(b) platinum, graphite, or any nonreacting conductor
(c) $Ca(s) \longrightarrow Ca^{2+}(aq) + 2e^-$

8. anode: $2I^-(aq) \longrightarrow I_2(s) + 2e^-$ cathode: $Br_2(l) + 2e^- \longrightarrow 2Br^-(aq)$
overall: $Br_2(l) + 2I^-(aq) \longrightarrow 2\,Br^-(aq) + I_2(s)$
cell notation: $Pt \mid I^- \mid I_2 \parallel Br_2 \mid Br^- \mid Pt$

10. **(a)** Cr **(b)** I^- **(c)** NO_2^- **(d)** NO (basic)

12. $Al^{3+} < Ni^{2+} < AgBr < ClO_3^- < F_2$

14. oxidizing agents: $Fe^{2+} < Ni^{2+} < H^+ < Cu^+$
reducing agents: $Fe^{2+} < Cu^+ < Zn$
both: Fe^{2+}, Cu^+

16. **(a)** Co^{2+} **(b)** Mn **(c)** Co^{3+} **(d)** Mn^{2+}
(e) yes **(f)** no **(g)** Co^{3+}, Fe^{3+} **(h)** Cd, Pb, Mn

18. **(a)** O_2 **(b)** Na, Ca **(c)** Ca, Ba, K

20. **(a)** 0.926 V **(b)** 0.460 V **(c)** 0.360 V

22. **(a)** 0.562 V **(b)** 0.534 V

24. **(a)** 0.229 V **(b)** −0.229 V **(c)** 0.213 V

26. **(a)** −0.300 V **(b)** +1.377 V **(c)** +0.213 V; same

28. Reaction (a)

30. $H_2O_2(aq) + Mn^{2+}(aq) \longrightarrow MnO_2(s) + 2H^+(aq)$ $E° = 0.734$ V
$H_2O_2(aq) + 2H^+(aq) + 2Cu(s) \longrightarrow 2Cu^+(aq) + 2H_2O$ $E° = 1.445$ V
$MnO_2(s) + 4H^+(aq) + 2Cu(s) \longrightarrow 2Cu^+(aq) + Mn^{2+}(aq) + 2H_2O$ $E° = 0.711$ V

32. **(a)** Cl^- **(b)** Cr^{2+} **(c)** both mediums will work

34. **(a)** no reaction
(b) $MnO_2(s) + 4H^+(aq) + 2Hg(l) \longrightarrow Mn^{2+}(aq) + 2H_2O + Hg_2^{2+}(aq)$
$E° = +0.433$ V
(c) no reaction

36. b

38. **(a)** no reaction
(b) no reaction
(c) $2Cr^{2+}(aq) + S(s) + 2H^+(aq) \longrightarrow 2Cr^{3+}(aq) + H_2S(aq)$

40.

	$\Delta G°$	$E°$	K
(a)	+15.9 kJ	−0.041 V	1.6×10^{-3}
(b)	−45.2 kJ	+0.117 V	8.1×10^7
(c)	−5.8 kJ	+0.015 V	10

42. **(a)** −116 kJ **(b)** −232 kJ **(c)** −347 kJ
There is no effect on spontaneity, since the sign of $\Delta G°$ does not change, nor does the position of equilibrium.

44. $E° = 0.305$ V $\Delta G° = -177$ kJ $K = 1 \times 10^{31}$

46. **(a)** −179 kJ **(b)** −178 kJ **(c)** −69.5 kJ

48. **(a)** 1×10^{19} **(b)** 1×10^{18}

50. 1.57×10^{25}

52. 0.29 V

54. **(a)** 0.265 V **(b)** $E = 0.265 - \frac{0.0257}{12}\ln\frac{[NO_3^-]^4[H^+]^4}{(P_{NO})^4(P_{O_2})^3}$
(c) 0.319 V

56. **(a)** 0.688 V **(b)** $E = 0.688 - \frac{0.0257}{6}\ln\frac{(P_{NO})^2[OH^-]^2}{[NO_3^-]^2(P_{H_2})^3}$
(c) 0.698 V

58. **(a)** 0.319 V **(b)** −0.369 V

60. 1.20

62. $[H^+] = 8 \times 10^{-7}\,M$

64. **(a)** $E° = 0.899$ V; yes **(b)** $E = 0.534$ V; yes
(c) $E = -0.058$ V; no **(d)** 7.50

66. **(a)** 0.127 V **(b)** $1.6 \times 10^{-3}\,M$ **(c)** 1.6×10^{-5}

68. **(a)** 1.37×10^{23} **(b)** $2.20 \times 10^4\,M$
(c) 0.230 g H_2; 8.08 g Cl_2

70. **(a)** 7.3×10^3 C **(b)** Cu

72. **(a)** 16 g **(b)** 19 min

74. **(a)** 8.4×10^7 J **(b)** \$2.1

76. 0.550 g Cd; 0.810 g Ni_2O_3

78. 9.11 kJ

80. 96 g

82. 0.896 V

84. −0.188 V

86. c

88. b

90. **(a)** (1) $2Tl(s) + Tl^{3+}(aq) \longrightarrow 3Tl^+(aq)$
(2) $2Tl(s) + Tl^{3+}(aq) \longrightarrow 3Tl^+(aq)$
(3) $2Tl(s) + Tl^{3+}(aq) \longrightarrow 3Tl^+(aq)$
(b) (1) 1.62 V (2) 0.54 V (3) 1.08 V
(c) (1) −313 kJ (2) −313 kJ (3) −313 kJ
(d) $\Delta G°$ is a state property; $E°$ is not.

92. Y > X > Z
93. ≈31.8% Sn and 68.2% Cu
94. 2.007 V
95. (a) 0.621 V (b) increases; decreases (c) 1×10^{21}
(d) $[Zn^{2+}] = 2.0\ M$; $[Sn^{2+}] = 2 \times 10^{-21}\ M$
96. (a) 1.12×10^5 J; 0.38×10^5 J; 1.50×10^5 J
(b) −0.389 V
97. 0.414 V
98. 12 days

CHAPTER 19

2. beta-emission
4. (a) ${}^{52}_{26}Fe \longrightarrow {}^{52}_{25}Mn + {}^{0}_{1}e$
(b) ${}^{228}_{88}Ra \longrightarrow {}^{228}_{89}Ac + {}^{0}_{-1}e$
(c) ${}^{236}_{95}Am \longrightarrow {}^{232}_{93}Np + {}^{4}_{2}He$
6. (a) ${}^{230}_{90}Th \longrightarrow {}^{4}_{2}He + {}^{226}_{88}Ra$
(b) ${}^{210}_{82}Pb \longrightarrow {}^{0}_{-1}e + {}^{210}_{83}Bi$
(c) ${}^{235}_{92}U + {}^{1}_{0}n \longrightarrow {}^{140}_{56}Ba + 3{}^{1}_{0}n + {}^{93}_{36}Kr$
(d) ${}^{37}_{18}Ar + {}^{0}_{-1}e \longrightarrow {}^{37}_{17}Cl$
8. (a) ${}^{272}_{111}Rg$
(b) ${}^{260}_{105}Db$
10. The product (${}^{282}_{114}Z$) is the same.
12. (a) ${}^{54}_{26}Fe + {}^{4}_{2}He \longrightarrow 2{}^{1}_{1}H + {}^{56}_{26}Fe$
(b) ${}^{96}_{42}Mo + {}^{2}_{1}H \longrightarrow {}^{1}_{0}n + {}^{97}_{43}Tc$
(c) ${}^{40}_{18}Ar + {}^{4}_{2}He \longrightarrow {}^{43}_{19}K + {}^{1}_{1}H$
(d) ${}^{31}_{16}S + {}^{1}_{0}n \longrightarrow {}^{1}_{1}H + {}^{31}_{15}P$
14. (a) ${}^{87}_{35}Br$ (b) ${}^{59}_{26}Fe$ (c) ${}^{4}_{2}He$ (d) ${}^{24}_{11}Na$
16. 1.98×10^5 h
18. 1.25×10^{-5} Ci
20. 5.6×10^4 Ci
22. 5.72×10^3 Ci
24. 5.1×10^{-14} g
26. 7.3×10^7 β-particles/minute; 3.3×10^{-5} Ci
28. (a) 7.94 days (b) 22 atoms
30. 14.6
32. 9.2×10^3 yr
34. 9.07 yr
36. 4.3×10^9 yr
38. (a) ${}^{90}_{38}Sr \longrightarrow 2{}^{0}_{-1}e + {}^{90}_{40}Zr$
(b) −0.0034 g
(c) 2.2×10^4 kJ
40. (a) 0.11309 g/mol (b) 1.02×10^{10} kJ/mol
42. Mg-26
44. fusion
46. 167 kg
48. (a) 16% (b) 18 mg
50. 8.4×10^{-11} g
52. 1.0×10^{-16}
54. 2.60 Ci
56. 6.5×10^2 mL
58. $2C_2O_4^{2-}/Cr^{3+}$
60. 38 mL
62. 2.42×10^{-3} nm
64. (a) Alpha rays (He nuclei) attracted to negative pole; beta rays (electrons) attracted to positive pole.
(b) Can follow path of C-11 in organic compounds in brain, using radiation counter.
(c) Neutrons produced can continue fission reaction.
66. $t_{1/2} = 3.3$ hours
68. 99.8% remains after one year. Decay is slow.
70. 5.8×10^{-19} mol/L
71. (a) 2.5×10^{-9} g (b) 5.5×10^{-3} kJ (c) 73 rems
72. (a) 1×10^{-13} J (b) 6×10^6 m/s
73. (a) -5.72×10^8 kJ/g (b) -1.3×10^{28} kJ
(c) 1.8×10^{-11}
74. 8.3×10^{-6} atm
75. 3×10^6 yr
76. 4.3×10^{-29}

CHAPTER 20

2. $2Al_2O_3(l) \longrightarrow 4Al(l) + 3O_2(g)$; 2.91 g
4. $Cu_2S(s) + O_2(g) \longrightarrow 2Cu(s) + SO_2(g)$
6. −211.9 kJ
8. (a) $Fe_2O_3(s) + 3CO(g) \longrightarrow 2Fe(l) + 3CO_2(g)$
(b) $C(s) + O_2(g) \longrightarrow CO_2(g)$
10. 2.5×10^3 kWh
12. 1.7×10^6 L
14. (a) potassium nitride, K_3N
(b) potassium iodide, KI
(c) potassium hydroxide, KOH
(d) potassium hydride, KH
(e) potassium sulfide, K_2S
16. (a) $Na_2O_2(s) + 2H_2O \longrightarrow 2Na^+(aq) + 2OH^-(aq) + H_2O_2(aq)$
sodium and hydroxide ions, hydrogen peroxide
(b) $2Ca(s) + O_2(g) \longrightarrow 2CaO(s)$; calcium oxide
(c) $Rb(s) + O_2(g) \longrightarrow RbO_2(s)$; rubidium superoxide
(d) $SrH_2(s) + 2H_2O \longrightarrow Sr^{2+}(aq) + 2OH^-(aq) + 2H_2(g)$
strontium and hydroxide ions, hydrogen gas
18. 0.126 g
20. (a) $Co(s) + 2H^+(aq) \longrightarrow Co^{2+}(aq) + H_2(g)$
(b) $3Cu(s) + 2NO_3^-(aq) + 8H^+(aq) \longrightarrow 3Cu^{2+}(aq) + 2NO(g) + 4H_2O$
(c) $Cr_2O_7^{2-}(aq) + 6e^- + 14H^+(aq) \longrightarrow 2Cr^{3+}(aq) + 7H_2O$
22. $3Cd(s) + 12Cl^-(aq) + 2NO_3^-(aq) + 8H^+(aq) \longrightarrow 3CdCl_4^{2-}(aq) + 2NO(g) + 4H_2O$
24. (a) $Fe(s) + 3NO_3^-(aq) + 6H^+(aq) \longrightarrow Fe^{3+}(aq) + 3NO_2(g) + 3H_2O$
(b) $4Cr(OH)_3(s) + 3O_2(g) + 8OH^-(aq) \longrightarrow 4CrO_4^{2-}(aq) + 10H_2O$
26. (a) Cd ($E° = 1.366$ V) (b) Cr ($E° = 1.708$ V)
(c) Co ($E° = 1.246$ V) (d) Ag ($E° = 0.165$ V)
28. (a) 0.724 V (b) 0.942 V
30. (a) 9×10^9 (b) $2 \times 10^{-4}\ M$
32. 208 g
34. 6.7
36. 53.8% Zn, 46.2% Cu
38. $2Ag_2S(s) + 8CN^-(aq) + 3O_2(g) + 2H_2O \longrightarrow 4Ag(CN)_2^-(aq) + 2SO_2(g) + 4OH^-(aq)$
$2Ag(CN)_2^-(aq) + Zn(s) \longrightarrow Zn(CN)_4^{2-}(aq) + 2Ag(s)$
40. (a) Cr^{2+} (b) Au^+ (c) Co^{2+} (d) Mn^{2+}
41. 2% BaO_2
42. (a) $Fe(OH)_3(s) + 3H_2C_2O_4(aq) \longrightarrow Fe(C_2O_4)_3^{3-}(aq) + 3H_2O + 3H^+(aq)$
(b) 0.28 L
43. 2.80%
44. 2.83×10^3 K

45. $Cr_2O_7^{2-}(aq) + 2OH^-(aq) \longrightarrow 2CrO_4^{2-}(aq) + H_2O$
$2Ag^+(aq) + CrO_4^{2-}(aq) \longrightarrow Ag_2CrO_4(s)$
$Ag_2CrO_4(s) + 4NH_3(aq) \longrightarrow 2Ag(NH_3)_2^+(aq) + CrO_4^{2-}(aq)$
$2Ag(NH_3)_2^+(aq) + 4H^+(aq) + CrO_4^{2-}(aq) \longrightarrow Ag_2CrO_4(s) + 4NH_4^+(aq)$

CHAPTER 21

2. (a) bromic acid (b) potassium hypoiodite (c) sodium chlorite (d) sodium perbromate
4. (a) $KBrO_2$ (b) $CaBr_2$ (c) $NaIO_4$ (d) $Mg(ClO)_2$
6. (a) NO_3^- (b) SO_4^{2-} (c) ClO_4^-
8. (a) H_2SO_3 (b) HClO (c) H_3PO_3
10. (a) NaN_3 (b) H_2SO_3 (c) N_2H_4 (d) NaH_2PO_4
12. (a) H_2S (b) N_2H_4 (c) PH_3
14. (a) NH_3, N_2H_4 (b) HNO_3 (c) HNO_2 (d) HNO_3
16. (a) $2I^-(aq) + SO_4^{2-}(aq) + 4H^+(aq) \longrightarrow I_2(s) + SO_2(g) + 2H_2O$
(b) $2I^-(aq) + Cl_2(g) \longrightarrow I_2(s) + 2Cl^-(aq)$
18. (a) $3HClO(aq) \longrightarrow Cl_2(g) + HClO_2(g) + H_2O$
(b) $2ClO_3^-(aq) \longrightarrow ClO_4^-(aq) + ClO_2^-(aq)$
20. (a) $Cl_2(g) + 2Br^-(aq) \longrightarrow 2Cl^-(aq) + Br_2(l)$
(b) NR (c) NR (d) NR
22. (a) $Pb(N_3)_2(s) \longrightarrow 3N_2(g) + Pb(s)$
(b) $2O_3(g) \longrightarrow 3O_2(g)$
(c) $2H_2S(g) + O_2(g) \longrightarrow 2S(s) + 2H_2O$
24. (a) $Cd^{2+}(aq) + H_2S(aq) \longrightarrow CdS(s) + 2H^+(aq)$
(b) $H_2S(aq) + OH^-(aq) \longrightarrow H_2O + HS^-(aq)$
(c) $2H_2S(aq) + O_2(g) \longrightarrow 2H_2O + 2S(s)$
26. (a) $2H^+(aq) + CaCO_3(s) \longrightarrow CO_2(g) + H_2O + Ca^{2+}(aq)$
(b) $H^+(aq) + OH^-(aq) \longrightarrow H_2O$
(c) $Cu(s) + 4H^+(aq) + SO_4^{2-}(aq) \longrightarrow Cu^{2+}(aq) + 2H_2O + SO_2(g)$
28. 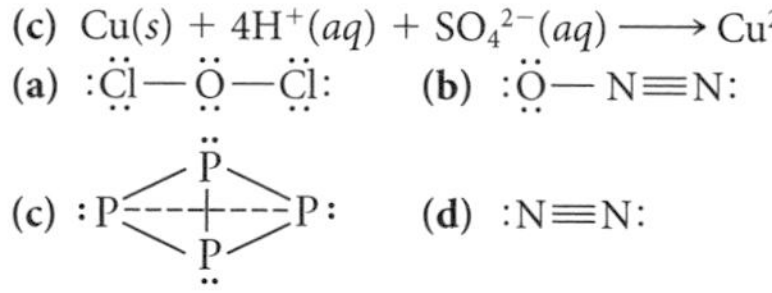

30. a and b

32. 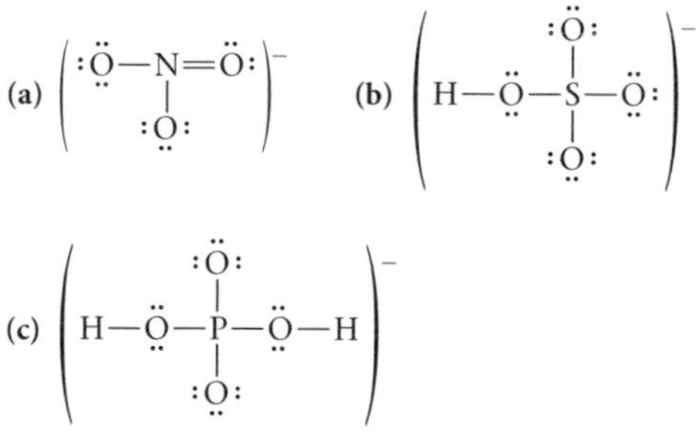

34. 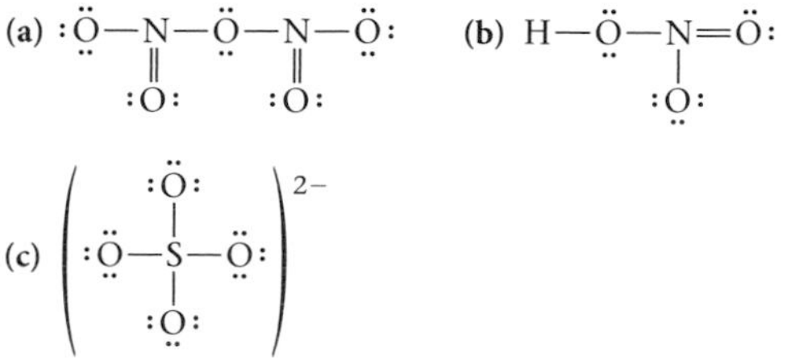

36. 14.3 L
38. 0.204 *M*
40. 7.7×10^4 L; 1.5×10^5 g
42. 12 L; 3.53
44. 4.28, 0.10 *M*
46. 1.9×10^{-3}
48. 0.012 g/100 mL
50. yes; 0 K
52. (a) yes (b) 2×10^{16}
54. 510 K
56. 2.26×10^5 g
58. 27.4 kg
60. b, c, d
62. 4.6
64. (a) dispersion (b) dispersion, dipole (c) dispersion, H—bonds (d) dispersion, H—bonds (e) no intermolecular forces; not a molecule
66. (a) +3 (b) +4 (c) +5 (d) −3
68. (a) HClO (b) S, $KClO_3$ (c) NH_3, NaClO (d) HF
70. (a) See text pages 568–569. (b) has an unpaired electron (c) H^+ is a reactant. (d) C is a product.
71. density of sulfur; depth of deposit, purity of S
72. no
73. 1.30%
74. Assume reaction is: $NaN_3(s) \longrightarrow Na(s) + \frac{3}{2}N_2(g)$
Assume 25°C, 1 atm pressure; mass of NaN_3 is 35 g

CHAPTER 22

2. (a) alkene (b) alkyne (c) alkane
4. (a) C_9H_{16} (b) $C_{22}H_{44}$ (c) $C_{10}H_{22}$
6. (a) 2-methyloctane (b) 2,2-dimethylpropane (c) 2,2,4-trimethylpentane (d) 2,5-dimethylheptane
8. 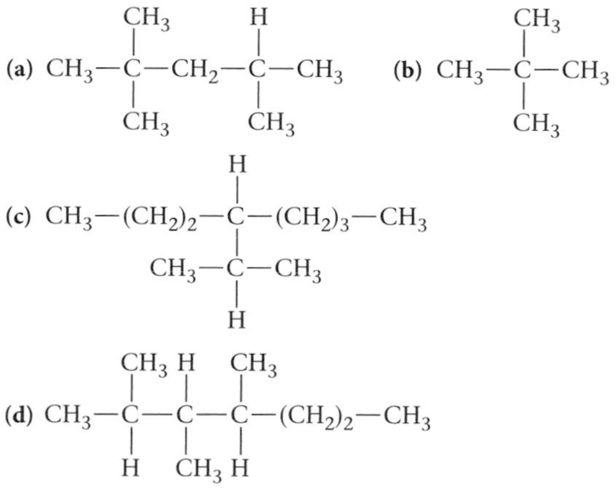

10. 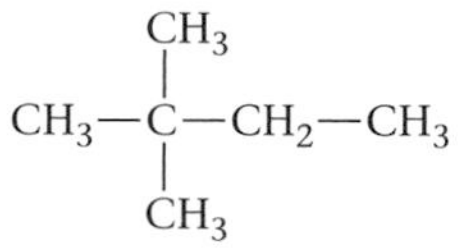
2,2-dimethylbutane
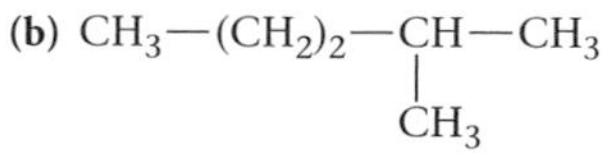
2-methylpentane
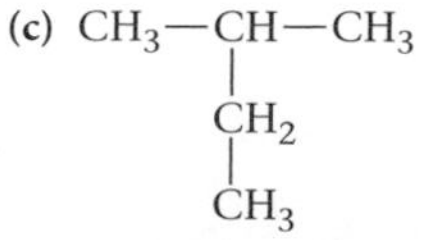
2-methylbutane

12. **(a)** $CH_3—C{\equiv}C—CH_2—CH_3$

(b) 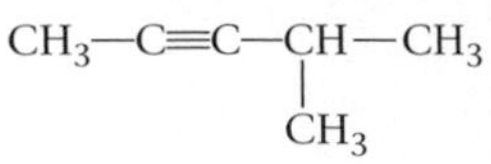

(c) 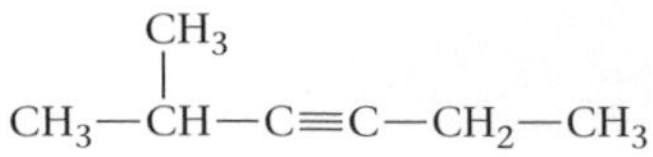

(d) 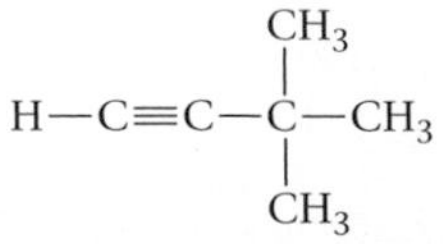

14. **(a)** *o*-chlorotoluene **(b)** *m*-bromotoluene
(c) 1,2,5-tribromotoluene

16. **(a)** alcohol **(b)** ester **(c)** ester, acid

18. **(a)** ether **(b)** ester **(c)** amine
(d) carboxylic acid **(e)** ketone

20. **(a)** 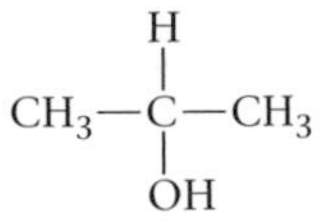 **(b)** 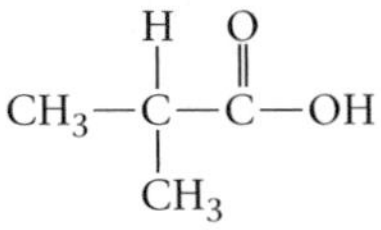

(c) 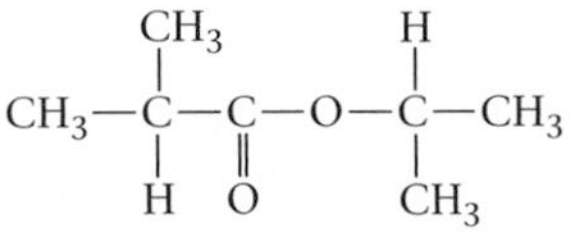

22.

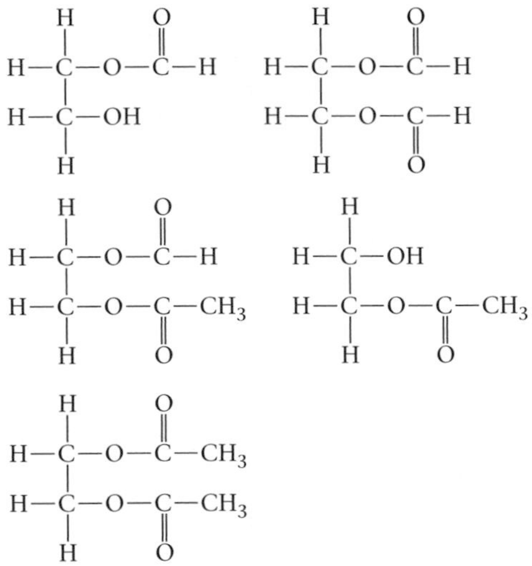

24. **(a)** butane < diethylether < 1-butanol
(b) hexane < dipropylether < 1-hexanol

26. pH of $C_6H_5NH_3^+ = 2.93$; pH of $CH_3COOH = 2.86$; pH's are comparable.

28. 0.73

30.

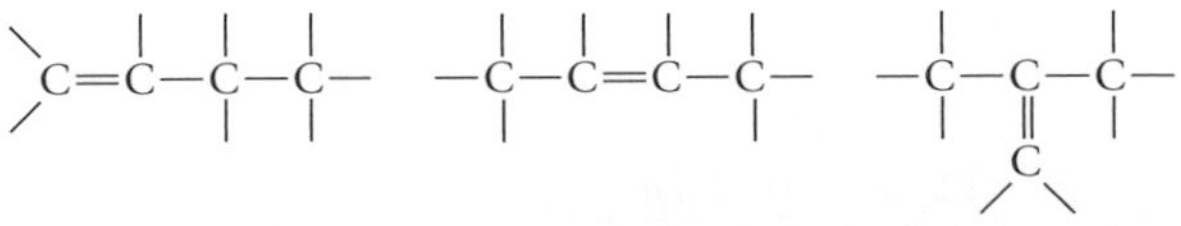

32.

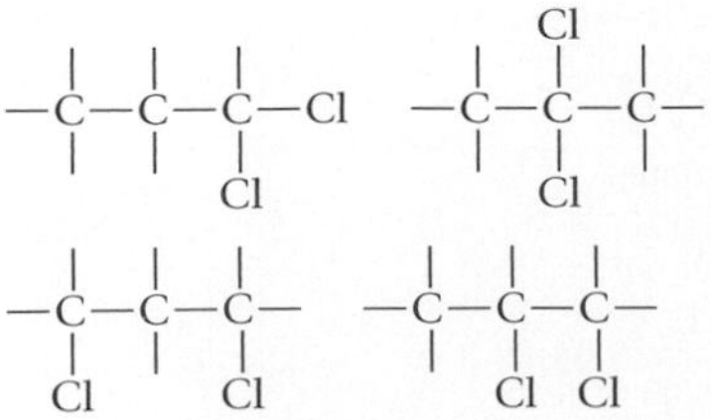

34.

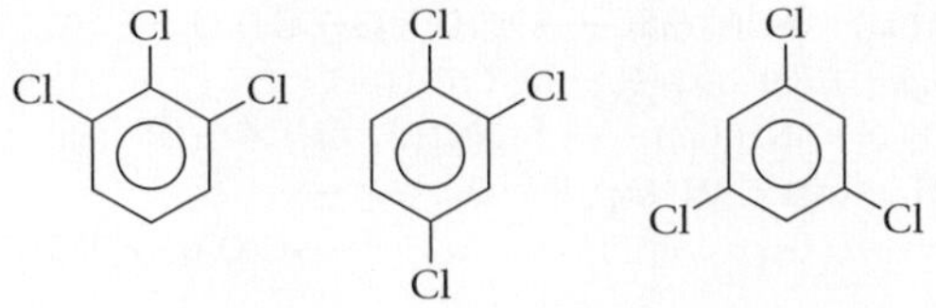

36.

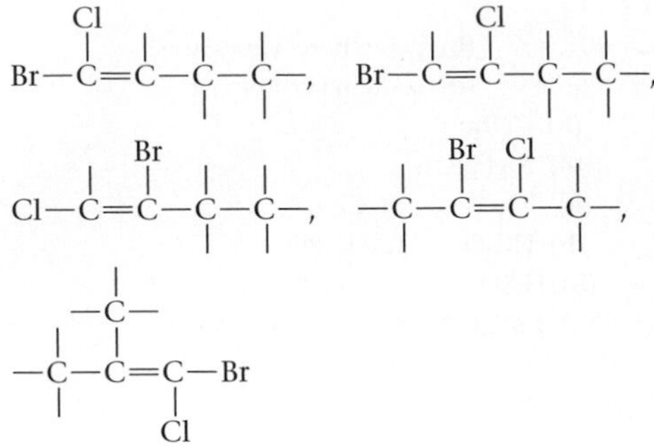

38.

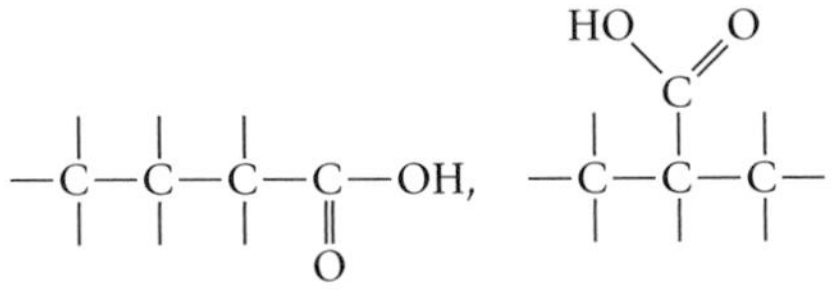

40. All of the compounds in Problem 36 show *cis-trans* isomerism except

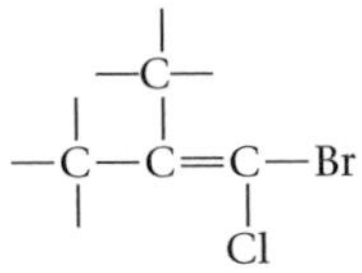

where there are two $—CH_3$ groups attached to the same carbon.

42. b, c

44. c and d

46. **(a)** —center carbon **(b)** none
(c) —carbon atom at right

48. **(a)** addition **(b)** elimination **(c)** condensation

50. **(a)** 2,3-dichloro-2-methylbutane
(b) 2,3-diodo-2-methylbutane

52. Three pairs of electrons spread around the ring

54. **(a)** no multiple bonds
(b) sodium salt of a long-chain carboxylic acid
(c) twice the volume of alcohol present
(d) ethanol with additives (mainly methanol) that make it unpalatable, sometimes even poisonous

56. **(a)** $(CH_3)_2NH(aq) + H^+(aq) \longrightarrow (CH_3)_2NH_2^+(aq)$
(b) $CH_3COOH(aq) + OH^-(aq) \longrightarrow CH_3COO^-(aq) + H_2O$
(c) 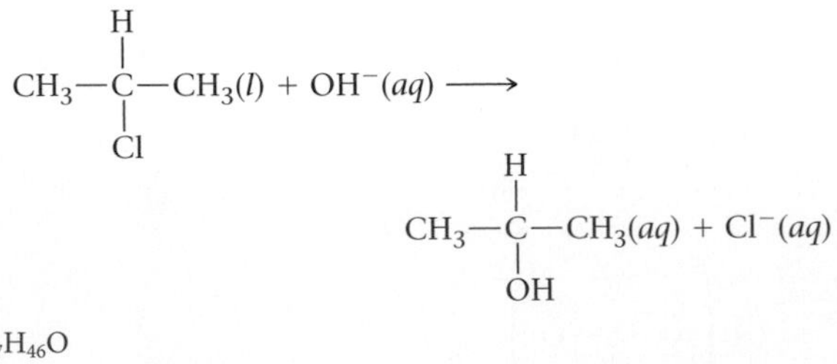

57. $C_{27}H_{46}O$

58. 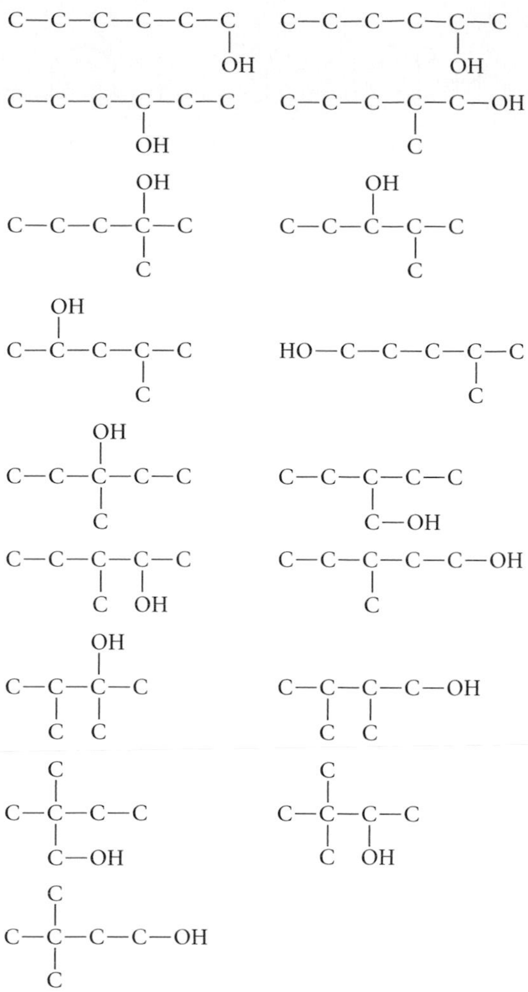

59. Approximately 6 g (Assume $H_2O(l)$ is a product; neglect heat capacity of pan.)

60. $ClCH_2COOH(aq) + (CH_3)_3N(aq) \longrightarrow ClCH_2COO^-(aq) + (CH_3)_3NH^+(aq)$

$K = 8.8 \times 10^6$; $3.4 \times 10^{-5}\ M$

CHAPTER 23

2. (a) 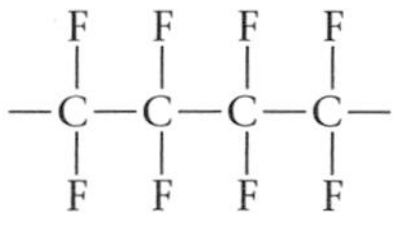

(b) 2.5×10^6 g/mol

(c) 24.02% C, 75.98% F

4. 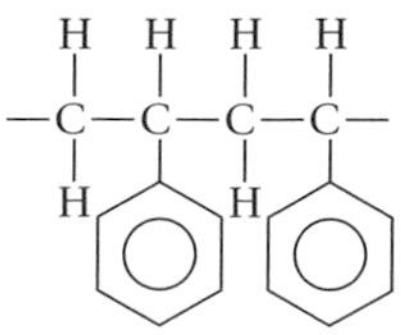

6. (a) $H_2C{=}CHF$

(b) 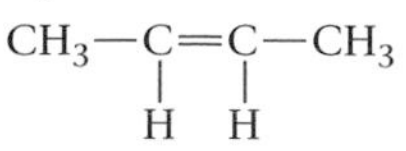

8. Polystyrene

10. 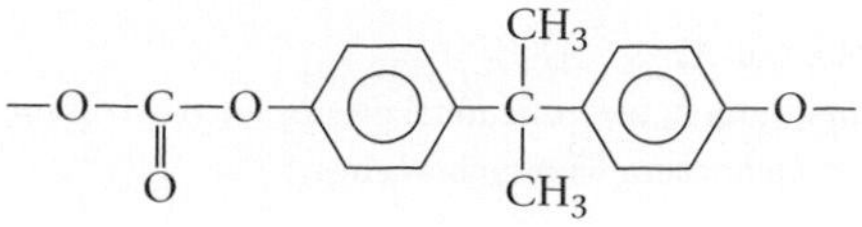

12. 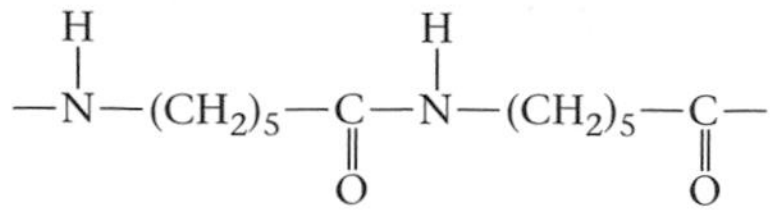

14. (a) $H_2N{-}CH_2{-}CH_2{-}NH_2$ and $HOOC{-}CH_2{-}COOH$

(b) 

16. $C_{12}H_{22}O_{11}(aq) + H_2O \longrightarrow 2C_6H_{12}O_6(aq)$

18. (a) 44.44% C, 6.22% H, 49.34% O (b) 6.2×10^2

20. 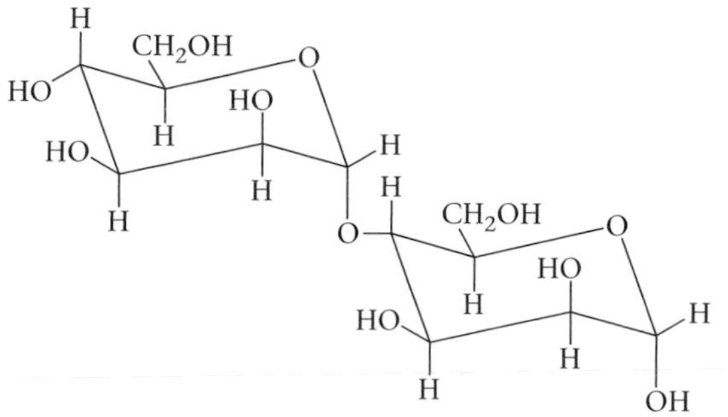

22. 9; 10

24. Leu-Lys:

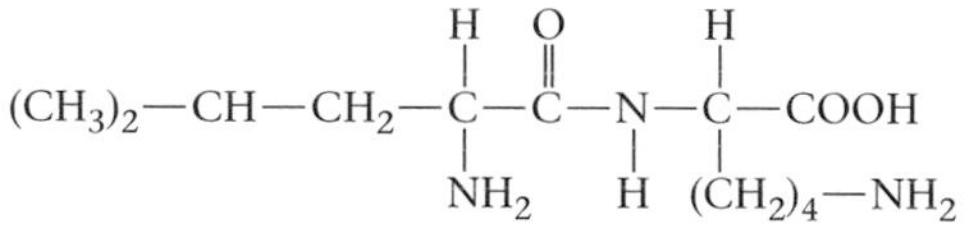

Lys-Leu:

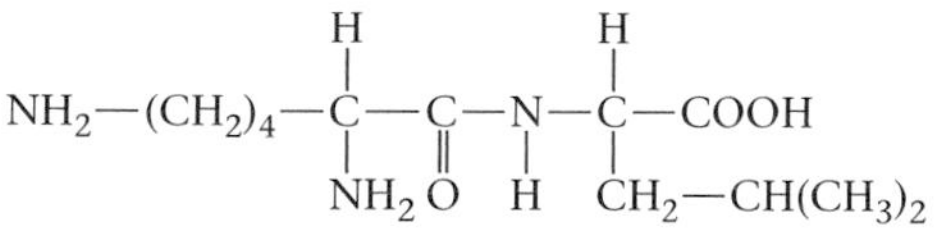

26. (a) 6

(b) 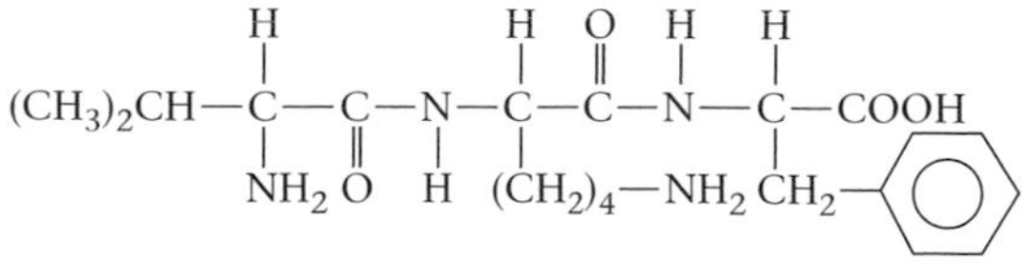

Val-Lys-Phe

28.

(a) 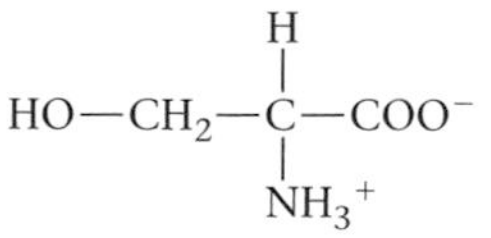

(b) 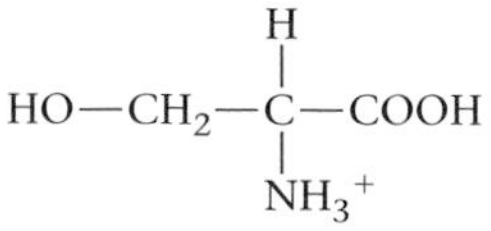

(c) 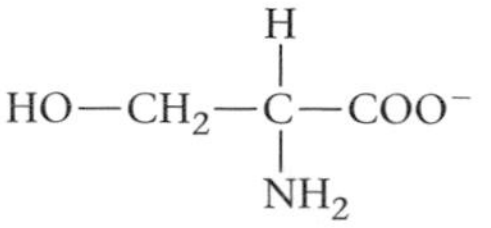

30. (a) 2.29 (b) 9.74 (c) 6.0

32. Ala-Phe-Leu-Met-Val-Ala

34. Double bond for addition; two functional groups for condensation

36. **(a)** Linear has straight chain with no branches.
 (b) See p. 618
 (c) See p. 618

38. **(a)** 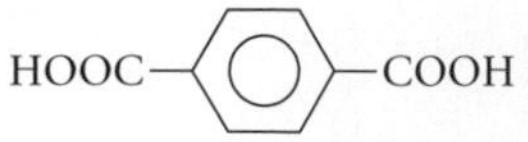 and HO—$(CH_2)_2$—OH

 (b) ClHC=CHCl **(c)** H_2N—$(CH_2)_5$—COOH

40. Head to head: 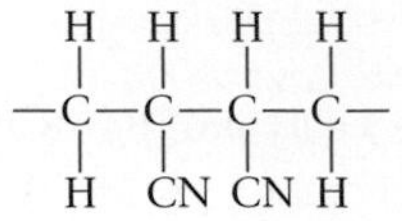

 Head to tail: 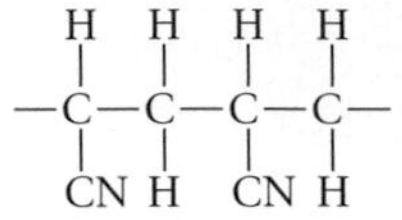

42. 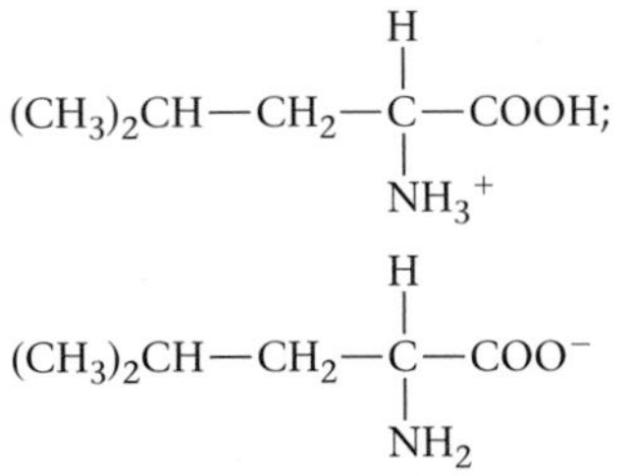

44. 1.59×10^4 g/mol

46. −214 kJ

48. **(a)** 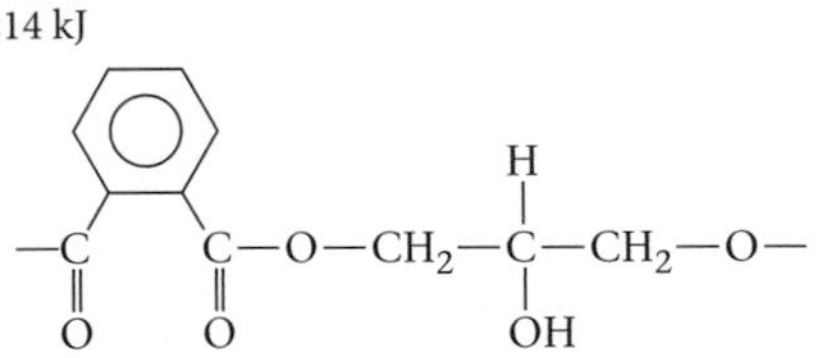

 (b) Orthophthalic acid condenses with OH groups in two adjacent chains.

49. 63.68% C, 9.80% H, 14.14% O, 12.38% N

50. −17 kJ

51. linear: 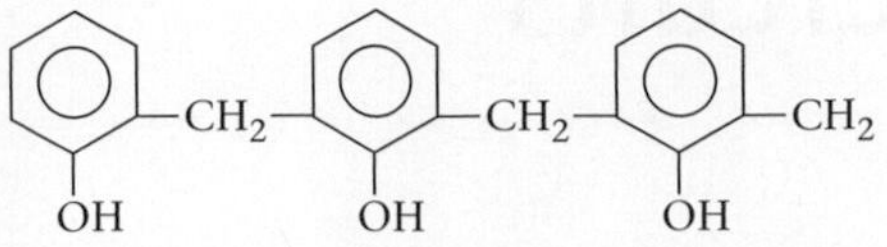

 crossed-linked: 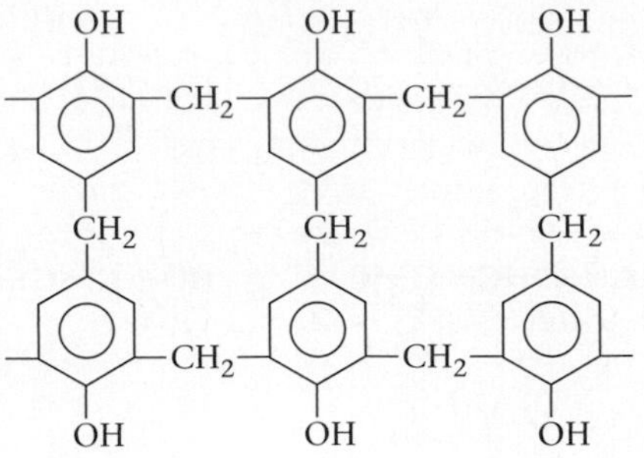

52. 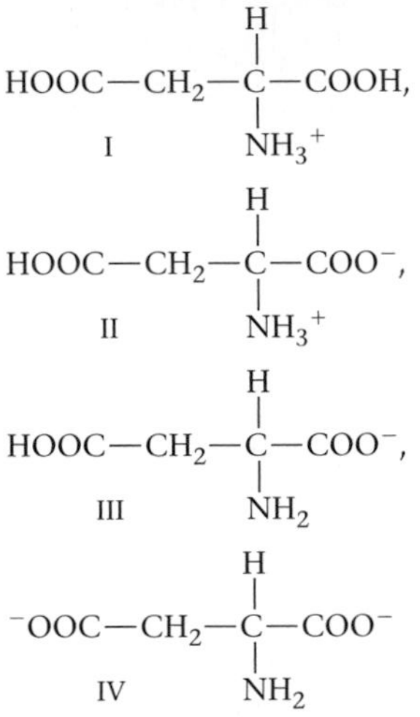

I, pH < 2.10; II, pH 2.10–3.85; III, pH 3.85–9.82; IV, pH > 9.82

Credits

These pages constitute an extension of the copyright page. We have made every effort to trace the ownership of all copyrighted material and to secure permission from copyright holders. In the event of any question arising as to the use of any material, we will be pleased to make the necessary corrections in future printings. Thanks are due to the following authors, publishers, and agents for permission to use the material indicated.

Frontmatter

Unnumbered Figures, pages vii, viii, xi, xii, xiii, and xv: Charles D. Winters. **Unnumbered Figure, p. ix:** S. Ruven Smith. **Unnumbered Figure, p. x:** George Semple. **Unnumbered Figure, p. xiv:** NASA. **Cartoon on p. xvii:** *Close to Home* © 1999 John McPherson. Reprinted with permission of Universal Press Syndicate. All rights reserved.

Chapter 1

Opening Figure: "The Alchemist" by William F. Douglas/© Victoria & Albert Museum, London/Art Resource, NY. **Figure 1.2 (a):** Charles D. Winters. **Figure 1.2 (b):** Charles D. Winters. **Figure 1.3 (a):** Charles D. Winters. **Figure 1.3 (b):** Charles D. Winters. **Figure 1.3 (c):** Charles D. Winters. **Figure 1.4:** Charles D. Winters. **Figure 1.5 (left):** Charles D. Winters. **Figure 1.5 (right):** Charles D. Winters. **Figure 1.8:** Charles D. Winters. **Figure 1.9:** Charles D. Winters. **Figure 1.11:** Marna G. Clarke. **Unnumbered Figure, p. 13 (top):** Photo by J. Antonio Nespral. **Unnumbered Figure, p. 13 (bottom):** Charles D. Winters. **Unnumbered Figure, The Human Side Box, p. 14:** Science Photo Library/Custom Medical Stock Photo. **Unnumbered Figure, p. 15:** Charles D. Winters. **Figure 1.13:** Marna G. Clarke. **Figure 1.14:** Charles D. Winters. **Figure A, Beyond the Classroom Box:** Erika Barahona Ede © FMGB Guggenheim Bilbao Museo.

Chapter 2

Opening Figure: Redrawn from Lepsius, *Metals in Egyptian Inscriptions,* 1860. **Opener poetry on p. 24:** "The Naming of Cats" from *Old Possum's Book of Practical Cats,* copyright 1939 by T. S. Eliot and renewed 1967 by Esme Valerie Eliot, reprinted by permission of Harcourt, Inc. and Faber and Faber Ltd. **Figure. 2.2:** AIP Emilio Segre Visual Archives, Bainbridge Collections. **Unnumbered Figure, The Human Side Box, p. 27:** The Edgar Fahs Smith Memorial Collection in the History of Chemistry, Department of Special Collections, Van Pelt-Dietrich Library, University of Pennsylvania. **Figure A, The Human Side Box, p. 27:** Marna G. Clarke. **Unnumbered Figure, p. 29:** Charles D. Winters. **Unnumbered Figure, p. 32:** Charles D. Winters. **Unnumbered Figure, p. 33, part (a):** Charles D. Winters. **Unnumbered Figure, p. 33, part (b):** Charles D. Winters. **Unnumbered Figure, p. 33, part (c):** Charles D. Winters. **Unnumbered Figure, p. 36:** Charles D. Winters. **Figure 2.12 (a):** Marna G. Clarke. **Figure 2.12 (b):** Marna G. Clarke. **Figure 2.12 (c):** Marna G. Clarke. **Unnumbered Figure, p. 38:** Charles D. Winters. **Unnumbered Figure, p. 41:** Charles D. Winters. **Unnumbered Figure, Beyond the Classroom Box, p. 43:** Charles D. Winters.

Chapter 3

Opening Figure: "The Money-Lender (Banker) and His Wife" by Quentin Metsys/© Erich Lessing/Art Resource, NY. **Figure 3.3:** Charles D. Winters. **Unnumbered Figure, p. 55:** Charles D. Winters **Unnumbered Figure, p. 57:** Jo Edkins, 2007. Used with permission. **Unnumbered Figure, p. 59:** Charles D. Winters. **Figure 3.4:** NASA. **Unnumbered Figure, p. 61:** Photo courtesy of Martin Walker. **Unnumbered Figure, p. 62:** © Thomson Learning/George Semple. **Figure 3.5 (left):** Charles D. Winters. **Figure 3.5 (middle):** Charles D. Winters. **Figure 3.5 (right):** Charles D. Winters. **Unnumbered Figure, p. 65:** Charles D. Winters. **Figure A, Beyond the Classroom Box:** Marna G. Clarke. **Figure C, Beyond the Classroom Box:** John Pinkston and Laura Stern/U.S. Geological Survey/Science News 11/9/96.

Chapter 4

Opening Figure: "Amphora with Four Men Holding Various Objects" by Kleophrades painter/Araldo de Luca/CORBIS. **Figure 4.1 (left):** Marna G. Clarke. **Figure 4.1 (middle):** Marna G. Clarke. **Figure 4.1 (right):** Marna G. Clarke. **Unnumbered Figure, p. 76:** Charles D. Winters. **Figure 4.4:** Charles D. Winters. **Figure 4.5:** Charles D. Winters. **Unnumbered Figure, p. 80:** Charles D. Winters. **Figure 4.6:** Charles D. Winters. **Unnumbered Figure, p. 81:** Charles D. Winters. **Figure 4.7 (a):** Charles D. Winters. **Figure 4.7 (b):** Charles D. Winters. **Figure 4.7 (c):** Charles D. Winters. **Unnumbered Figure, The Human Side Box, p. 86:** Photo provided courtesy of the Nobel Foundation. **Figure 4.8:** Charles D. Winters. **Unnumbered Figure, p. 87:** Charles D. Winters. **Figure 4.9 (a):** Charles D. Winters. **Figure 4.9 (b):** Charles D. Winters. **Figure 4.9 (c):** Charles D. Winters. **Figure A, Beyond the Classroom Box:** Photos provided courtesy of Mateusz Zuchowski.

Chapter 5

Opening Figure: © Historical Picture Archive/Corbis. Photographer Philip de Bay. **Opener poetry on p. 102:** "Innate Helium" from *The Poetry of Robert Frost,* edited by Edward Connery Lathem. Copyright 1947, 1969 by Henry Holt and Company. Copyright 1975 by Lesley Frost Ballantine. Reprinted by permission of Henry Holt and Company, LLC. **Unnumbered Figure, p. 106, part (a):** Charles D. Winters. **Unnumbered Figure, p. 106, part (b):** Charles D. Winters. **Unnumbered Figure, p. 106, part (c):** Charles D. Winters. **Unnumbered Figure, p. 106, part (d):** Charles D. Winters. **Unnumbered Figure, p. 107:** Charles D. Winters. **Unnumbered Figure, p. 111, part (a):** Charles D. Winters. **Unnumbered Figure, p. 111, part (b):** Ken M. Johns/Photo Researchers, Inc. **Figure 5.5:** Charles D. Winters. **Unnumbered Figure, The Human Side Box, p. 113:** Biblioteca civica centrale di Torino. Sezione Manoscritti e rari. **Figure 5.6 (a):** Marna G. Clarke. **Figure 5.6 (b):** Marna G. Clarke. **Figure 5.8 (left):** Marna G. Clarke. **Figure 5.8 (right):** Marna G. Clarke. **Figure A, Beyond the Classroom Box:** © Despotovic Dusko/Corbis Sygma.

Chapter 6

Opening Figure: "Grazing Sheep and Rainbow," 1989 by Wright, Liz (Contemporary Artist) © Private Collection/The Bridgeman Art Library. **Unnumbered Figure, p. 133:** Paul Silverman/ Fundamental Photographs NYC. **Unnumbered Figure, p. 135:** Charles D. Winters. **Unnumbered Figure, The Human Side Box, p. 147:** Lawrence Berkeley National Laboratory. **Unnumbered Figure, p. 151, part (a):** Charles D. Winters. **Unnumbered Figure, p. 151, part (b):** Charles D. Winters. **Figure B, Beyond the Classroom Box:** © Harry A. Frank. Used with permission.

Chapter 7

Opening Figure: "Almost Hex." © Arthur Silverman, 2007. **Unnumbered Figure, p. 168:** Charles D. Winters. **Unnumbered Figure, p. 172:** Charles D. Winters. **Figure 7.3:** S. Ruven Smith. **Unnumbered Figure, The Human Side Box, p. 174:** Dr. Glenn Seaborg, University of California, Lawrence Berkeley Laboratories. **Figure 7.4 (a):** Charles D. Winters. **Figure 7.4 (b):** Charles D. Winters. **Figure 7.4 (c):** Charles D. Winters. **Figure 7.4 (d):** Charles D. Winters. **Figure 7.4 (e):** Charles D. Winters. **Figure A, Beyond the Classroom Box:** Argonne National Laboratory.

Chapter 8

Opening Figure: "Young Girl with a Candle" by Godfried Schalcken/© Scala/Art Resource, NY. **Unnumbered Figure, p. 199 (left):** Charles D. Winters. **Unnumbered Figure, p. 199 (right):** Jeff J. Daly/Fundamental Photographs NYC. **Unnumbered Figure, p. 200:** Charles D. Winters. **Unnumbered Figure, p. 203 (top):** Charles D. Winters. **Unnumbered Figure, p. 203 (bottom):** Charles D. Winters. **Figure 8.5 (left):** Marna G. Clarke. **Figure 8.5 (middle):** Marna G. Clarke. **Figure 8.5 (right):** Marna G. Clarke. **Unnumbered Figure, p. 208:** Charles D. Winters. **Figure 8.7 (left):** Charles D. Winters. **Figure 8.7 (middle):** Charles D. Winters. **Figure 8.7 (right):** Charles D. Winters. **Figure 8.8:** Charles D. Winters. **Unnumbered Figure, p. 215, part (a):** Dennis Bradbury Photos. **Unnumbered Figure, p. 215, part (b):** Dennis Bradbury Photos.

Chapter 9

Opening Figure: "Ice Flows on the Seine" by Claude Monet/Erich Lessing/Art Resource, NY. **Figure 9.1:** Richard Megna/ Fundamental Photographs NYC. **Unnumbered Figure, p. 227:** Charles D. Winters. **Figure 9.3:** Charles D. Winters. **Figure 9.4 (a):** Marna G. Clarke. **Figure 9.4 (b):** Marna G. Clarke. **Figure 9.4 (c):** Marna G. Clarke. **Figure 9.6:** Charles D. Winters. **Unnumbered Figure, p. 235:** Charles D. Winters. **Unnumbered Figure, p. 244, part (a):** Charles D. Winters. **Unnumbered Figure, p. 244, part (b):** Marna G. Clarke. **Unnumbered Figure, p. 244, part (c):** Charles D. Winters. **Unnumbered Figure, The Human Side Box, p. 248:** Bettmann/Corbis. **Figure A, Beyond the Classroom Box, part (b):** George Semple. **Figure B, Beyond the Classroom Box:** Charles D. Winters. **Figure C, Beyond the Classroom Box, p. 251 (top):** © Gregory G. Dimijian/Photo Researchers, Inc. **Figure C, Beyond the Classroom Box, p. 251 (bottom):** © Kip Peticolas/ Fundamental Photographs NYC.

Chapter 10

Opening Figure: "Sugaring Off" by Grandma Moses/© Copyright Grandma Moses Properties Co. Edward Owen/Art Resource, NY. **Opener poetry on p. 258:** "Metamorphosis" from *Honey and Salt*, copyright © 1963 by Carl Sandburg and renewed 1991 by Margaret Sandburg, Helga Sandburg Crile and Janet Sandburg. **Figure 10.1 (a):** Marna G. Clarke. **Figure 10.1 (b):** Marna G. Clarke. **Figure 10.1 (c):** Marna G. Clarke. **Figure 10.2:** Marna G. Clarke. **Unnumbered Figure, p. 263:** Charles D. Winters. **Unnumbered Figure, p. 264:** Charles D. Winters. **Unnumbered Figure, p. 266, part (a):** Taxi/Getty Images. **Unnumbered Figure, p. 266, part (b):** Peter Arnold, Inc. **Unnumbered Figure, p. 267:** Charles D. Winters. **Figure 10.11:** Marna G. Clarke. **Unnumbered Figure, p. 275:** Charles D. Winters. **Figure A, Beyond the Classroom Box:** From Masterton photo collection.

Chapter 11

Opening Figure: "The Persistence of Memory" by Salvador Dali/ Digital Image © The Museum of Modern Art/Licensed by SCALA/ Art Resource, NY. **Opener poetry on p. 284:** Excerpt from Roald Hoffmann, "Men and Molecules," 1984. Reprinted by permission of the author. **Unnumbered Figure, p. 286, part (a):** Charles D. Winters. **Unnumbered Figure, p. 286, part (b):** Charles D. Winters. **Unnumbered Figure, p. 286, part (c):** Charles D. Winters. **Unnumbered Figure, p. 288, part (a):** Charles D. Winters. **Unnumbered Figure, p. 288, part (b):** Charles D. Winters. **Unnumbered Figure, p. 291, part (a) (left):** Charles D. Winters. **Unnumbered Figure, p. 291, part (a) (right):** Charles D. Winters. **Unnumbered Figure, p. 291, part (b) (left):** Charles D. Winters. **Unnumbered Figure, p. 291, part (b) (right):** Charles D. Winters. **Unnumbered Figure, The Human Side Box, p. 301:** AIP Emilio Segre Visual Archives. **Unnumbered Figure, p. 302, part (a):** Charles D. Winters. **Unnumbered Figure, p. 302, part (b):** Charles D. Winters. **Figure 11.13:** Charles D. Winters. **Figure A, Beyond the Classroom Box:** Courtesy of NOAA.

Chapter 12

Opening Figure: "Unstable Equilibrium" by Paul Klee/Paul Klee, Schwankendes Gleichgewicht, 1922, 159, Unstable equilibrium, watercolour and pencil on paper on cardboard, 31,4 × 15,7/15,2 cm, Zentrum Paul Klee, Bern. Reprinted by permission of Zentrum Paul Klee and Artist Rights Society, Inc. **Figure 12.1 (a):** Marna G. Clarke. **Figure 12.1 (b):** Marna G. Clarke. **Figure 12.1 (c):** Marna G. Clarke. **Unnumbered Figure, p. 330:** Charles D. Winters. **Figure 12.4:** Marna G. Clarke. **Figure A, Beyond the Classroom Box:** Oesper Collection in the History of Chemistry/University of Cincinnati.

Chapter 13

Opening Figure: Réunion des Musées Nationaux/Art Resource, NY. **Unnumbered Figure, p. 356:** Art Brewer/Tony Stone Images. **Figure 13.4:** Charles D. Winters. **Figure 13.5:** Charles D. Winters. **Figure 13.6 (left):** Michael Dalton/Fundamental Photographs NYC. **Figure 13.6 (right):** Michael Dalton/Fundamental Photographs NYC. **Unnumbered Figure, p. 362:** Charles D. Winters. **Unnumbered Figure, p. 365:** Charles D. Winters. **Unnumbered Figure, p. 369:** Charles D. Winters. **Unnumbered Figure, p. 371:** Charles D. Winters. **Unnumbered Figure, p. 372:** Charles D. Winters. **Figure 13.9:** Charles D. Winters. **Figure A, Beyond the Classroom:** Scott Camazine/Photo Researchers, Inc.

Chapter 14

Opening Figure: "Great Bridge: Sudden Rain at Atake (Ohashi, Atake no Yudaschi)" by Ando Hirishige/Photograph © 2007 Carnegie Museum of Art, Pittsburgh. **Figure 14.1:** Marna G.

Clarke. **Figure 14.2:** Marna G. Clarke. **Unnumbered Figure, p. 385:** © Wally McNamee/CORBIS. **Unnumbered Figure, p. 389, part (a):** Charles D. Winters. **Unnumbered Figure, p. 389, part (b):** Charles D. Winters. **Figure 14.4 (a):** Marna G. Clarke. **Figure 14.4 (b):** Marna G. Clarke. **Figure 14.4 (c):** Marna G. Clarke. **Unnumbered Figure, p. 393:** Charles Steele. **Unnumbered Figure, p. 394:** Charles D. Winters. **Figure A, Beyond the Classroom Box:** Frederica Georgia/Photo Researchers, Inc. **Figure B, Beyond the Classroom Box (left):** © NYC Parks Photo Archive/Fundamental Photographs NYC. **Figure B, Beyond the Classroom Box (right):** © Kristen Brochmann/Fundamental Photographs.

Chapter 15

Opening Figure: © 2002 Cordon Art B.V.-Baarn-Holland. All rights reserved. **Opener poetry on p. 408:** Excerpt from Ann Rae Jonas, "The Causes of Color," in Bonnie Bilyeu Gordon, Songs from Unsung Worlds: Science in Poetry (Boston/Basel/Stuttgart: Birkhäuser, 1985). With kind permission of Springer Science and Business Media. **Figure 15.1:** Charles D. Winters. **Figure 15.7:** Charles D. Winters. **Unnumbered Figure, The Human Side Box, p. 417:** Science Photo Library/Photo Researchers, Inc. **Figure 15.8:** Marna G. Clarke. **Unnumbered Figure, p. 421:** Charles D. Winters. **Figure 15.13:** Ray Boyington/S. Ruven Smith. **Figure C, Beyond the Classroom Box (left):** "The Thinker," 1880, Auguste Rodin. The Rodin Museum, Philadelphia, Gift of Jules E. Mastbaum, 1929. Photography by Joe Mikuliak. **Figure C, Beyond the Classroom Box (right):** "The Thinker," 1880, Auguste Rodin. The Rodin Museum, Philadelphia, Gift of Jules E. Mastbaum, 1929. Photography by Joe Mikuliak.

Chapter 16

Opening Figure: "Sand Dunes in California" (© Ansel Adams Publishing Rights Trust/CORBIS). **Figure 16.1:** Charles D. Winters. **Unnumbered Figure, p. 435 (top):** Charles D. Winters. **Unnumbered Figure, p. 435 (bottom):** Charles D. Winters. **Unnumbered Figure, p. 437:** Charles D. Winters. **Figure 16.3 (a):** Marna G. Clarke. **Figure 16.3 (b):** Marna G. Clarke. **Figure 16.4 (top):** Charles D. Winters. **Figure 16.4 (bottom):** Charles D. Winters. **Unnumbered Figure, p. 440:** Charles D. Winters. **Unnumbered Figure, p. 442 (left):** Charles D. Winters. **Unnumbered Figure, p. 442 (right):** Charles D. Winters. **Figure A, Beyond the Classroom Box:** Charles D. Winters. **Figure B, Beyond the Classroom Box (left):** Charles D. Winters. **Figure B, Beyond the Classroom Box (right):** Charles D. Winters. **Figure C, Beyond the Classroom Box (left):** James Morgenthaler. **Figure C, Beyond the Classroom Box (right):** Ray Boyington/S. Ruven Smith.

Chapter 17

Opening Figure: © Geoffrey Clements/Corbis. **Opener poetry on p. 450:** Excerpt from "Under" in *Chicago Poems* by Carl Sandburg, copyright 1916 by Holt, Rinehart and Winston and renewed 1944 by Carl Sandburg, reprinted by permission of Harcourt, Inc. **Figure 17.3:** Charles Steele. **Unnumbered Figure, p. 455:** Charles D. Winters. **Unnumbered Figure, The Human Side Box, p. 459:** Bundy Library, AIP/Emilio Segre Visual Archives. **Unnumbered Figure, p. 460:** Charles D. Winters. **Figure 17.7:** Charles D. Winters.

Chapter 18

Opening Figure: "Still Life with Silver Jug" by Willem Kalf/Courtesy of Rijksmuseum, Netherlands. **Figure 18.1:** Charles D. Winters. **Figure 18.2:** Charles D. Winters. **Unnumbered Figure, p. 488:** Charles D. Winters. **Figure 18.5:** Marna G. Clarke. **Figure 18.6:** Charles D. Winters. **Figure 18.9 (b):** AP Photo/Alan Diaz. **Unnumbered Figure, p. 499:** Charles D. Winters. **Unnumbered Figure, The Human Side Box, p. 501:** Oesper Collection in the History of Chemistry/University of Cincinnati. **Unnumbered Figure, p. 502:** NASA. **Figure C, Beyond the Classroom Box:** © Steven Shaw, 2007.

Chapter 19

Opening Figure: Eurelios/French Ministry of Culture and Communication, Regional Direction for Cultural Affairs-Rhone-Alpes-Region-Regional Department of Archaeology. **Opener poetry on p. 512:** Reprinted by permission of International Creative Management, Inc. Copyright © 1957 by Muriel Rukeyser; from The Collected Poems of Muriel Rukeyser, University of Pittsburgh Press 2005. **Unnumbered Figure, The Human Side Box, p. 517:** Mütter Museum, Philadelphia College of Physicians. **Figure 19.1 (left):** Marna G. Clarke. **Figure 19.2:** Nordion International. **Figure 19.3:** Courtesy of Beckman Industries. **Unnumbered Figure, p. 520:** Santi Visali/The Image Bank. **Unnumbered Figure, p. 524:** Courtesy of Library of Congress. **Unnumbered Figure, p. 527:** NASA. **Figure 19.6 (a):** Courtesy of the University of California, Lawrence Livermore National Laboratory, and the U.S. Department of Energy. **Figure 19.6 (b):** Lawrence Livermore National Laboratory. **Figure B, Beyond the Classroom Box:** Charles D. Winters.

Chapter 20

Opening Figure: CNAC/MNAM/Dist. Réunion des Musées Nationaux/Art Resource, NY. **Figure 20.4 (b):** Courtesy of Bethlehem Steel Corporation. **Unnumbered Figure, p. 540:** Agricultural Stabilization and Conservation Service, USDA. **Unnumbered Figure, p. 541:** Tiffany & Co. **Unnumbered Figure, p. 542:** Charles D. Winters. **Figure 20.6 (left):** Marna G. Clarke. **Figure 20.6 (right):** Marna G. Clarke. **Figure 20.7:** Charles D. Winters. **Figure 20.9:** Courtesy of Edmund Scientific. **Figure 20.10 (left):** Charles D. Winters. **Figure 20.10 (right):** Charles D. Winters. **Figure 20.11:** Charles D. Winters. **Figure 20.12 (left):** Charles D. Winters. **Figure 20.12 (middle):** Charles D. Winters. **Figure 20.12 (right):** Charles D. Winters. **Unnumbered Figure, Beyond the Classroom, p. 550:** Charles D. Winters.

Chapter 21

Opening Figure: "Mountain Landscape with Lightning" by Francisque Millet/© National Gallery Collection by kind permission of the Trustees of the National Gallery, London/CORBIS. **Figure 21.2:** Marna G. Clarke. **Figure 21.3 (a):** Charles D. Winters. **Figure 21.3 (b):** Charles D. Winters. **Unnumbered Figure, p. 557:** VCG/FPG International. **Unnumbered Figure, p. 561:** Charles D. Winters. **Unnumbered Figure, p. 563:** Charles D. Winters. **Figure 21.5:** Peter Arnold/Peter Arnold, Inc. **Unnumbered Figure, p. 566:** Charles D. Winters. **Figure 21.9:** Charles D. Winters. **Figure 21.10 (left):** Charles D. Winters. **Figure 21.10 (middle):** Charles D. Winters. **Figure 21.10 (right):** Charles D. Winters. **Figure 21.11 (left):** Charles D. Winters. **Figure 21.11 (middle):** Charles D. Winters. **Figure 21.11 (right):** Charles D. Winters. **Figure A, Beyond the Classroom Box:** David Michael

Davies/FPG International. **Figure B, Beyond the Classroom Box:** Photo courtesy of S. Ruven Smith.

Chapter 22

Opening Figure: "Still Life with Fruit and a Wine Glass" by Severin Roesen/The Philadelphia Museum of Art/Art Resource, NY. **Figure 22.3:** © Steven Lunetta Photography, 2007. **Figure 22.4 (a):** Courtesy of Ashland Oil Company. **Figure 22.8:** Charles D. Winters. **Figure 22.9:** Courtesy of Professor James M. Bobbitt, Twenty Mile Vineyard. **Figure 22.12:** Charles D. Winters. **Figure 22.14:** Charles D. Winters.

Chapter 23

Opening Figure: Dale Chihuly, Chihuly Bridge of Glass, Crystal Towers detail, 2002, Tacoma, Washington/Scott M. Leen. **Figure 23.1:** Marna G. Clarke. **Figure 23.2:** Charles D. Winters. **Figure 23.3:** Charles D. Winters.

Index

Note: **Boldface** terms are defined in the context used in the text; *italic* locators indicate figures; t indicates a table; q indicates an end-of-chapter question.

B

D

I

M

N

O

W

X

Y

Z

Conversion Factors

Electrical Units	1 C	=	1 A · s
	1 V	=	1 J/C
	1 W	=	1 J/s
	1 mol e^-	=	9.648×10^4 C
Energy	1 cal	=	4.184 J
	1 L · atm	=	0.103 kJ
	1 kWh	=	3.600×10^6 J
	1 BTU	=	1.055×10^3 J
Length	1 nm	=	10^{-9} m = 10Å
	1 in	=	2.54 cm
	1 m	=	39.37 in
	1 mile	=	1.609 km
Mass	1 metric ton	=	10^3 kg
	1 lb	=	453.6 g
Pressure	1 atm	=	760 mm Hg = 14.70 lb/in^2
	1 atm	=	1.01325×10^5 Pa = 1.01325 bar
	1 torr	=	1 mm Hg
Volume	1 m^3	=	10^3 L
	1 cm^3	=	1 mL
	1 ft^3	=	28.32 L
	1 L	=	1.057 qt